Handbook of **Public Administration**

Handbook of **Public Administration**

Edited by
B. Guy Peters & Jon Pierre

SAGE Publications
London • Thousand Oaks • New Delhi

SAGE Publications Ltd
6 Bonhill Street
London EC2A 4PU

SAGE Publications Inc.
2455 Teller Road
Thousand Oaks, California 91320

Sage Publications India Pvt. Ltd.
B-42 Panchsheel Enclave
Post Box 4109
New Delhi 110-017 India

British Library Cataloguing in Publication data
A catalogue record for this book is available from the British Library

ISBN 0 7619 7224 2

Library of Congress Control Number 2002 109398

Typeset by C&M Digitals Pvt Ltd.
Printed in Great Britain by The Cromwell Press Ltd, Trowbridge, Wiltshire

Contents

List of Contributors

Attila Ágh is Professor of Public Administration, Budapest University of Economics and Public Administration, Hungary

James Warner Björkman is Professor of Public Policy and Administration, Institute of Social Studies, The Hague, The Netherlands, and Professor of Administration and Development, Leiden University, The Netherlands

Marleen Brans is Lecturer in Public Management Institute, Catholic University of Leuven, Belgium

Gary C. Bryner is Director of the Natural Resources Law Center, School of Law, University of Colorado at Denver, USA

John M. Bryson is Professor of Planning and Public Affairs, Hubert H. Humphrey Institute of Public Affairs, University of Minnesota, USA

Jørgen Grønnegaard Christensen is Professor of Public Administration, Department of Political Science, University of Aarhus, Denmark

Tom Christensen is Professor of Public Administration and Organization Theory, Department of Political Science, University of Oslo, Norway

Paul Craig is Professor in English Law, Department of Law, University of Oxford, UK

Linda deLeon is Associate Professor, Graduate School of Public Affairs, University of Colorado, Denver, USA

Dionyssis G. Dimitrakopoulos is Lecturer in Politics, School of Politics and Sociology, Birkbeck College, University of London, UK

Gavin Drewry is Professor of Public Administration and Director of the Centre for Political Studies, Department of Social and Political Science, Royal Holloway University of London, UK

O.P. Dwivedi is University Professor Emeritus in Political Science, University of Guelph, Canada

Morten Egeberg is a Professor at the Department of Political Science and Director of the ARENA Program, University of Oslo, Norway

David Feldman is the Legal Adviser to the Joint Committee on Human Rights in the UK Parliament

Robert Gregory is Associate Professor of Public Policy and Administration, School of Government, Victoria University of Wellington, New Zealand

Mark Hallerberg is Assistant Professor of Political Science, Department of Political Science, University of Pittsburgh, USA

John Halligan is Professor of Public Administration, School of Management and Policy, University of Canberra, Australia

Thomas H. Hammond is Professor, Department of Political Science, Michigan State University, USA

Carolyn J. Heinrich is Assistant Professor of Public Policy, Department of Public Policy, University of North Carolina, USA

Rita M. Hilton is Senior Economist in the Office of the Vice-President for Environmentally and Socially Sustainable Development, The World Bank

Karen M. Hult is Professor, Department of Political Science, Virginia Polytechnic Institute and State University, USA

Goran Hyden is Distinguished Professor, Department of Political Science, University of Florida, USA

Patricia W. Ingraham is Distinguished Professor of Public Administration, The Maxwell School of Citizenship and Public Affairs, Syracuse University, USA

Philip G. Joyce is Associate Professor of Public Administration, School of Business and Public Management, The George Washington University, USA

Michael Katula is a doctoral candidate, School of Public and Environmental Affairs, Indiana University, Bloomington, USA

Kevin P. Kearns is Associate Professor, Graduate School of Public and International Affairs, University of Pittsburgh, USA

Jack H. Knott is Professor of Public Policy and Director of the Institute of Government and Public Affairs (IGPA), University of Illinois, USA

Leonard Kok is Deputy Permanent Secretary at the Ministry of Justice, The Hague, Netherlands

Pierre Lascoumes is Director of Scientific Research at CEVIPOF (CNRS and IEP Paris) and Associate Professor of Sociology and Politics, Institut d'Etudes Politiques, Paris, France

Patrick Le Galès is CNRS Senior Research Fellow at CEVIPOF and Associate Professor of Sociology and Politics, Institut d'Etudes Politiques, Paris, France

Martin Lodge is Lecturer in Political Science and Public Policy, Department of Government, London School of Economics and Political Science, UK

Elke Loffler is Senior Research Associate, School of Strategy and International Business, Bristol Business School, UK

Larry S. Luton is Professor of Public Administration, Graduate Program of Public Administration, Eastern Washington University, USA

Laurence E. Lynn, Jr is George Bush Chair and Professor of Public Affairs, George Bush School of Government and Public Service, Texas A&M University, USA

Helen Margetts is Professor of Political Science and Director of the School of Public Policy, University College London, UK

Peter J. May is Professor of Political Science, Center for American Politics and Public Policy, University of Washington, Seattle, USA

Marcia K. Meyers is Associate Professor, School of Social Work, University of Washington, Seattle, USA

John L. Mikesell is Professor of Public Finance and Policy Analysis, School of Public and Environmental Affairs, Indiana University, Bloomington, USA

Nicole de Montricher is Research Scholar at CERSA (CNRS and Paris 2) and Associate Professor of Comparative Administration, University of Paris 2, France

Jorge Nef is Professor, Department of Rural Extension Studies, University of Guelph, Canada

Dele Olowu is Convenor, Public Policy and Administration, Institute of Social Studies, The Hague, The Netherlands

Laurence J. O'Toole, Jr is Golembiewski Professor and Head, Department of Public Administration and Policy, School of Public and International Affairs, University of Georgia, USA

Edward C. Page is the Sidney and Beatrice Webb Professor of Public Policy, London School of Economics and Political Science, UK

Martin Painter is Professor, Discipline of Government and International Relations, City University of Hong Kong, Hong Kong

Argyris G. Passas is Assistant Professor, Department of Law, Panteion University of Social and Political Science, Athens, Greece

James L. Perry is Chancellor's Professor and Associate Dean for the Indianapolis Programs, School of Public and Environmental Affairs, Indiana University, USA

B. Guy Peters is Professor, Department of Political Science, University of Pittsburgh, Pennsylvania, USA

Jon Pierre is Professor, Department of Political Science, University of Gothenburg, Sweden

Jos C.N. Raadschelders is Professor of Public Administration and Henry Bellmon Chair of Public Service, Department of Political Science, University of Oklahoma, USA

Beryl A. Radin is Professor, School of Public Affairs, University of Baltimore, USA

Hal G. Rainey is the Alumni Foundation Distinguished Professor, School of Public and International Affairs, University of Georgia, USA

Bo Rothstein is August Röhss Professor of Political Science, Department of Political Science, Goteborg University, Sweden

Luc Rouban is Director of Scientific Research at CEVIPOF (CNRS and IEP Paris) and Institut d'Etudes Politiques, Paris, France

Fabio Rugge is Professor of Administrative History, Department of Political Science, University of Pavia, Italy

Sally Coleman Seldon is Associate Professor of Management, School of Business and Economics at Lynchburg College, USA

Andy Smith is a Research Fellow, Fondation nationale des sciences politiques, CERVL research centre, Sciences-Po Bordeaux, France

Steven Rathgeb Smith is Associate Professor, Daniel J. Evans School of Public Affairs, University of Washington, Seattle, USA

Jean-Claude Thoenig is Senior Research Fellow, Groupe d'Analyse des Politiques Publiques, CNRS and Ecole Normale Superieure de Cachan, Paris, and Professor of Sociology, INSEAD, France

Paul G. Thomas is Duff Roblin Professor of Government, St John's College, University of Manitoba, Canada

James R. Thompson is Assistant Professor of Public Administration, College of Planning and Public Affairs, University of Illinois, Chicago, USA

Theo A.J. Toonen is Professor of Public Administration, Leiden University, The Netherlands

Frans K.M. van Nispen is Associate Professor of Public Administration, Faculty of Social Sciences, Erasmus University of Rotterdam, The Netherlands

A.J.G. Verheijen is Senior Public Sector Management Specialist, Poverty Reduction and Economic Management Network, The World Bank, Washington, DC

Susan Vorsanger is Lecturer, School of Social Work, Columbia University, New York, USA

Søren C. Winter is Research Professor, Danish National Institute of Social Research, Copenhagen, Denmark

Lois R. Wise is Professor of Policy and Administration, School of Public and Environmental Affairs, Indiana University, Bloomington, USA

Hellmut Wollmann is Emeritus Professor of Public Administration, Institute of Social Sciences, Humboldt University, Germany

Jacques Ziller is Professor of Comparative Public Law, Department of Law, European University Institute, Florence, Italy

Preface

The publication of this volume reflects the culmination of a great deal of effort by a large number of people. The work of the authors and the section editors is obvious, but much of the work although less apparent is no less important. As editors we would like to express our gratitude to a number of individuals who were important in helping us to complete the project and to produce a book which we believe will make a major contribution to both the academic study and the practice of public administration.

The first person we should thank is Lucy Robinson at Sage. We had not thought of undertaking the project ourselves, but when Lucy proposed the Handbook we were sufficiently audacious, or foolhardy, to accept that challenge. After we began the process Lucy and her colleagues, including but not limited to Vanessa Harwood and David Mainwaring, have been a delight to work with. They have been generous with useful professional advice, yet allowed us the freedom to develop the project in the way we thought best. They were also patient and supportive when some parts of the manuscript were not ready as soon as they might be. We look forward to a long publishing relationship with this team at Sage. We also want to thank the members of our Editorial Advisory Board:

Professor Geert Bouackaert, Catholic University of Leuven, Belgium
Professor Hans-Ulrich Derlien, University of Bamberg, Germany
Professor H. George Frederickson, University of Indiana, USA
Professor John Halligan, University of Canberra, Australia
Professor Christopher Hood, All Souls College, University of Oxford, United Kingdom
Professor Jose Luis Mendez, El Colegio de Mexico, Mexico
Professor Akira Nakamura, Meiji University, Japan
Professor Donald Savoie, University of Moncton, Canada

This group of distinguished scholars assisted us with the design of the project, with the selection of the section editors and authors, and with the assessment of the chapters when submitted. We are indebted to them for their time and efforts.

Sheryn Peters and Monika Pierre responded to our enthusiasm for this project with a mixture of amusement and concern. They represent what makes it all worthwhile, whether they take us birdwatching or put us in a boat and head up the coast.

We should also thank the staff at the Gold Wing lounge at the Frankfurt International Airport for providing refuge and time to reflect on public administration and related issues.

Finally, somewhat unusually, we want to thank each other. This has been a cooperative and collaborative effort, and each of us has been able to pick up the slack at times when the other has been overwhelmed by other tasks, or family commitments, or life in general. This has been an academic partnership that continues to work well, and further continues to be a great deal of fun. We hope the readers will gain as much enjoyment in absorbing this product as we have had in creating it.

BGP   JP

Introduction:
The Role of Public Administration in Governing

B. Guy Peters and Jon Pierre

Enter the bureaucrat, the true leader of the Republic.

(Senator Palpadine, *Star Wars*, *Episode 1*)

This Handbook represents an attempt to address the major issues in, and perspectives on, public administration. The Handbook is an international treatment of this subject, with scholars drawn from a wide range of countries and intellectual traditions. Further, although the large majority of the participants in the project are academics, the attempt has been made also to confront issues of practice, and the relevance of academic research to the day-to-day problems of making government programs perform as they are designed to. Public administration is an area of substantial academic activity, but it is also the focus of important practical work, and public servants have a wealth of experience that is important for understanding public administration. No single volume could hope to cover in any comprehensive manner the full range of concerns about public administration, but we have, we believe, illuminated the crucial issues and also provided a starting point for those readers who wish to pursue this field of inquiry and practice more thoroughly.

WHY ADMINISTRATION MATTERS

The most important premise of this Handbook is that public administration matters. There is a tendency among the public, and even among scholars of the public sector, to equate politics and government with dramatic events such as elections, or with the visible conflicts between politicians that shape major policy developments. Those activities are indeed important for governing, but there is a massive amount of activity involved in translating laws and decrees made by politicians into action, and in delivering public programs to citizens. That work is often less visible, but is crucial for making things happen in government. Legislatures and political executives may pass all the laws they wish, but unless those laws are administered effectively by the public bureaucracy, little or nothing will actually happen. The bureaucracy[1] is often the favorite target for newspaper leader writers and for politicians, but without administrators little would happen in government.

Public administrators comprise the bulk of government employment and activity. In the United Kingdom the central government in London has 650 members of the House of Commons, a few hundred members of the House of Lords, a few hundred political appointees in the executive departments, a few thousand judges, but several hundred thousand public administrators. In addition, there are several hundred thousand public employees in local authorities and the devolved governments of Scotland and Wales. The majority of the employees of government are not the paper-pushers one usually associates with public administration but rather are responsible for delivering public services to the public. Many public administrators in central governments are responsible for providing services, but on average local and provincial public servants are even more so.

The principal activity of public administration is implementing laws, but there are also a range of other important activities carried on in these public organizations. One is that bureaucracies make policy, and in essence make law. The laws passed by legislatures are often general, and require elaboration by administrators (Kerwin, 1999; Page, 2000). The secondary legislation prepared by the bureaucracy not only makes the meaning of the laws clearer but it permits the application of the expertise of the career administrators to policy. This style of making policy may raise questions of democratic accountability, but it almost certainly also makes the policies being implemented more technically appropriate for the circumstances, as well as making them more flexible. Although even less visible than their rule-making activities, bureaucracies also are important adjudicators.

In addition to writing secondary legislation, administrators also influence policy by advising the politicians formally responsible for making law. Political leaders may have numerous talents but most politicians do not have extensive expert knowledge about the policies for which they are responsible. Therefore, they require assistance in writing laws and setting policy. The senior public bureaucracy has traditionally had a major role in providing their ministers with the needed advice and information (see Plowden, 1984). That role for public administration is, however, under attack as politicians become more distrustful of bureaucrats and want advice from their own politically committed advisors (Peters and Pierre, 2001). In addition, the reforms of the public sector that have been implemented over the past several decades have stressed the role of the senior public administrator as a manager rather than as a policy advisor, and that has altered the career incentives of senior public managers.

We said above that the work of public administration may be less visible than that of other aspects of government, yet at the same time it is the major point of contact between citizens and the State. The average citizen will encounter the postal clerk, the tax collector and the policeman much more frequently than their elected representatives. This contact between state and society has two important consequences for government. One is that the implementation of laws by the lowest echelons of the public service defines what the laws actually mean for citizens. The laws of a country are what is implemented, and lower echelon employees – policemen, social workers, teachers, etc. – often have substantial discretion over how implementation occurs and who actually gets what from government.

The second impact of the lower echelons of government is that these face-to-face interactions often define what government is for citizens. How am I treated by government? Is government fair, efficient and humane or is it the arbitrary and bureaucratic (in the pejorative sense of the term) structure that it is often alleged to be? The bureaucracy is therefore important in creating an image of government in the popular mind. The good news is that evidence about these interactions tends to be rather positive. Citizens in a number of countries report that most of their interactions with government are positive. The bad news, however, is that many of those same citizens still have a generally negative view of government and of the bureaucracy.

PUBLIC ADMINISTRATION AND THE SURROUNDING SOCIETY

Throughout this Handbook, contributors are maintaining the perspective of the public administration as embedded in the surrounding society. While this might appear to be a rather obvious point of departure, the approach emphasizes something often forgotten; that the public administration is an explication of the collective interest and that its legitimacy to a significant extent hinges on its ability to play a part in the pursuit of those interests. Much of the recent debate on new public management and market-based models of public service delivery, just to give an example, has tended to portray the public bureaucracy as a generic structure. Ironically, however, introducing market-based solutions in public service production has significant effects on the relationship between the public administration and the surrounding society, as we will argue below.

Furthermore, emphasizing the embedded nature of the public administration helps us understand the rationale for creating links between civil society and the public administration, or more generally, links with the state. The governance perspective on the public bureaucracy highlights those links because they are elements of a broader strategy for service production and delivery that is open to a range of means of generating service. By including societal actors in service delivery the bureaucracy enhances its capacity to act and to 'do more for less', as the Gore Report put it.

Finally, the society-centered perspective on the public administration portrays the public bureaucracy as a potential target for group political pressure. The public administration controls vast resources, and operates frequently at an increasing distance from elected officials, and is also a major source of regulation. All this contributes to making it attractive to a wide variety of societal groups, ranging from trade unions and employers' association to local environmental protection groups and neighborhood organizations. An understanding of the exchanges between the public bureaucracy and its external environment is critical to an analysis of the bureaucracy in a wider sense.

Politics, administration and society

In order to understand how the public bureaucracy relates to society, we need to generate a broader picture of public–private exchanges in society. The triangular relationships between politics, administration and society are, needless to say, manifold and complex. Starting with the politics–administration linkage, most observers of public policy and administration today agree that this is a false dichotomy. The argument coming out of the classic debate between Friedrich and Finer – 'Policies are implemented when they are formulated and formulated when they are implemented' – seems to be a more accurate representation of the current understanding of the politics–administration relationship. If anything, this statement has gained additional currency since the 1940s along with recent administrative reform and structural changes in the public sector. Reforms aiming at empowering lower-level public sector employees and the greater discretion exercised at that organizational level is but one example of recent changes that support Friedrich's argument (Peters, 2001; Peters and Pierre, 2000).

Thus, politics and administration should be thought of different elements of the same process of formulating and implementing policy. But politics and administration differ in terms of how they relate to society; while both are critical components of democratic governance, 'politics' in the present context is a matter of representation and accountability whereas 'administration' refers to policy implementation and the exercise of political power and law. Citizens, organized interests, private businesses and other societal actors interact with both politics and administration albeit for different reasons. Put in a larger perspective, then, we are interested in the nature of the interface between state and society. Leaving aside the input that is channeled primarily through political parties, we now need to look more closely at the linkage between the public bureaucracy and society.

While historically speaking the public administration's main task has been to implement and communicate political decisions to society, one of the key changes that has occurred over the past decade or so has been the increasing opportunities for citizens to have a more direct input into the public bureaucracy. The experiments with *maison services publiques* in France, the concept of *Bürgernähe* in German administrative reform during the 1990s, the emphasis on (even) more transparency in the Scandinavian countries, and the search for different ways to customer-attune public services in the United States all testify to an almost global tendency to reduce the distance (both physical and intellectual) between the bureaucracy and the individual citizen. This pattern, in turn, is evidence of a strong felt need to strengthen the legitimacy of public sector institutions. With some exaggeration it could be argued that while previously that legitimacy was derived from the public and legal nature of the public administration, legitimacy is currently to an increasing extent contingent on the bureaucracy's ability to deliver customer-attuned services swiftly and accurately.

Perhaps the most powerful and comprehensive strategy of bridging the distance between citizens and the public service is found in the various consumer-choice-based models of public service production. The overall purpose here is not so much to bring citizens (now referred to as consumers) physically closer to service producers but rather to empower consumers through market choice. By exercising such choice, consumers can receive public services more attuned to their preferences that would otherwise have been possible. Furthermore, consumer choice sends a signal to the public sector about the preferences of its consumers, which in aggregated form can inform resource allocation. Described in a slightly different way, this model of consumer choice thus provides society with an input on decisions made in the public bureaucracy with the important difference that the input is not funneled through political parties but is rather an instant communication from the individual to the bureaucracy.

Civil society

The role of civil society in the context of public administration takes on many different forms. Perhaps the most conspicuous arrangement of involvement of civil society is the long-established system of so-called laymen boards (*lekmannastyrelser*) in Swedish agencies. But civil society plays many different roles in different national contexts. In much of continental Europe, for example, civil society plays an important part in delivering public – or quasi-public – services. Much of this cooperation between the public administration and civil society takes place at the local level.

The growing interest in governance during the 1990s highlighted these forms of cooperation between the state and civil society. The governance perspective draws on broad strategies of resource mobilization across the public–private border. This is a pattern which has for long been established in the 'corporatist' democracies in Western Europe. As well as the mobilization of resources a focus on civil society also has a democratic element, with the relationship with groups providing a source of ideas, legitimation and feedback for government from its society. There are real dangers of these ties limiting the autonomy of government, but they can be the means of making administration less remote from the citizens.

Closing the gap: emerging models of administration – citizen exchange

Much of the administrative reform that has been conducted during the past ten to fifteen years has been implemented against the backdrop of a weakened legitimacy for the public bureaucracy, and, indeed, for the public sector as a whole. The 1980s in particular was the heyday in the belief of the market as an instrument of resource allocation, leaving little support for public institutions. Additionally, the neoliberal elected leaders emerging during that decade – primarily Reagan, Thatcher and Mulroney – made a strong critique of the public sector and its employees part of their political *Leitmotif* (Hood, 1998; Savoie, 1994). As a result, public sector budgets were drastically cut back. Reaffirming the legitimacy for the public sector, it seemed, could only be accomplished by proving that the public sector could deliver services in a fashion not too different from that of private organizations, that is, in close contact between organization and client with a purpose to provide services adapted to the particular needs and expectations of the individual client. Put slightly differently, the strategy seems to have been that the future legitimacy of public sector institutions should rest less on traditional values like universality, equality and legal security but more on performance and service delivery.

Much of the administrative reform we witnessed during the late 1980s and 1990s was characterized by these objectives. If we look more closely at the points of contact between citizens and the public sector, they can be summarized in two general trends. First of all, there was a clear emphasis on transparency and accessibility. Structural changes in the public bureaucracy aimed at enhancing exchange between individuals and the public sector. Across Western Europe, governments embarked on a decentralization project, partly to bring political and administrative decisions closer to the citizens. In addition, many public service functions were devolved further, and thus closer to the clients.

The other general trend in administrative reform manifested itself in an effort to make exchanges between citizens and the public bureaucracy easier. Obviously, structural changes like decentralization were necessary, albeit not sufficient, for this type of reform. Here, the general idea was to develop less formal and more accessible means of exchange between clients and the public sector employees. So-called one-stop shops were introduced in several countries, frequently on an experimental basis. More recently, we have seen a wide variety of channels into the public sector available to the citizens via the Internet. It is quite likely that we have only seen the beginning of 'e-government'.

Together, these structural and procedural changes have significantly altered the relationships between the public bureaucracy and its clients. There is today a much stronger emphasis on proximity – if not physical, at least technological – between the public sector and clients. More importantly, perhaps, the tenor of these exchanges has tended to change towards a less formal and more service-oriented communication.

The changing role of public administration

Some aspects of contemporary public administration would appear similar to someone working in government decades earlier, while other aspects have been undergoing fundamental transformation. While the changes are numerous, there are two that deserve highlighting. The first, as alluded to previously, is the increasing emphasis on the role of the public administrator as a manager, and the need to apply the managerial tools familiar in the private sector. This drive toward generic management has almost certainly enhanced the efficiency and perhaps the effectiveness of the public sector, but its critics argue that it has also undervalued the peculiarly public nature of management in government, and the need to think about public sector values other than sheer economic efficiency (Stein, 2002).

A second major change in public administration has been the increasing linkage of state and society in the delivery of public services. Government is no longer an autonomous actor in implementing its policies[2] but often depends upon the private sector and/or the third sector to accomplish its ends. This linkage of state and society may enhance the effectiveness and the legitimacy of government but it also presents government with problems of accountability and control. Blending state and society means that public administrators must become more adept at bargaining and governing through instruments such as contracts, rather than depending upon direct authority to achieve the ends of government.

Finally, the bureaucracy is now less centralized and less hierarchical than ever in its recent history. The degree of centralization of the bureaucracy and of government policy has varied by country, but in almost all there is less power now vested in the center than in the past. Just as working with civil society may require a different set of skills than governing alone, so too will working more closely with subnational governments, or with quasi autonomous organizations that are nominally connected to ministerial authority but which may be designed to act more on their own.

A strong bureaucracy in a weak state?

Bert Rockman has observed that 'If one distinguishes between outlays on the one hand and personnel and organizational structure on the other, it may be that the future holds a sizeable public sector, but one that will have less government' (Rockman, 1998: 38). If the new public management reform paradigm continues to dominate the orientation of administrative reform we may soon find ourselves with a hollow administrative structure processing huge transfers but with service provision increasingly conducted under the auspices of market actors, Rockman argues. We have already discussed the changing channels of exchange between the public bureaucracy and its external environment as well as the overarching objectives of the administrative reform that has been conducted during the late 1980s and 1990s.

Rockman is probably too optimistic (or perhaps pessimistic) about the extent to which administrative reform can shrink public employment and the public bureaucracy. We argued earlier that much of our contacts with the state is not with elected representatives but with front staff of the public bureaucracy like police officers, tax collectors, nurses or social workers. There may be some decrease in the number of such personnel but these functions cannot be automated. Instead, the cutbacks in public employment have been conducted either by transferring entire functions from the state to the market, for example railway, telecommunications, and postal services. The public sector remains a fairly labor-intensive sector, not least because of the nature of the services it delivers.

What is at stake here is the relationship between strength and external orientation. Not least in an historical perspective, the notion of a 'strong bureaucracy' frequently invoked an image of a self-serving and self-referential bureaucracy. A more contemporary definition of a strong bureaucracy is one which swiftly can deliver a wide variety of public services, adapted to the needs of the individual. Furthermore, a strong bureaucracy is characterized by the rule of law. The law-governed nature of the public administration is a safeguard against clientalism, corruption and favoritism. Arguably, there is a potential contradiction between the service-delivery aspect and the law-governed nature of the bureaucracy. The point here is that a public bureaucracy will most likely never be able to compete with private-sector companies in terms of flexibility and service but, as we will argue later in this chapter, that is hardly surprising given that public administration was designed primarily according to other objectives.

The strength of the public administration is nearly always a mirror-image of the strength of the state. Internal strength is critical to the public bureaucracy's ability to fulfill its role in society regardless of the degree to which the state encroaches society. Also, a strong public bureaucracy is critical to sustain core democratic values like equality, legal security and equal treatment. For these reasons, a strong bureaucracy in a weak state need not be an arrangement that cannot be sustained in the longer term.

MANAGING IN THE PUBLIC SECTOR

We dealt above with one crucial aspect of public administration – its link with society and the political system. We now shift our attention more to the internal dynamics of these organizations (or aggregations of organization), and especially with their management. The reform of public administration over the past several decades has concentrated on the managerial aspects of government, attempting to make government more efficient, effective and economical. These three Es have driven a massive change in the public sector, much of it focusing on the role of the market as an exemplar for good management.

Goodbye to hierarchies?

Much of the administrative reform that has been implemented has been a series of attacks against the hierarchical structure of the public administration. Hierarchies, the dominant argument goes, are rigid and slow, unable to change, inefficient and fail to draw on the professional expertise inside the organization. Furthermore, hierarchical structures are said to be unable to relate effectively to clients and cannot provide customer-attuned services to the public. How valid is this critique, what alternatives are there to hierarchies, and what values and norms are associated with this type of organization? addressing these questions – and the future hierarchies in the public administration more in general – we first need to discuss the strengths of hierarchies, given the expectation placed on the public bureaucracy. From that perspective, we can proceed to discuss the extent to which the preferred role of the public administration has changed and how these developments impact on the organizational structure of the bureaucracy.

In most countries, the public bureaucracy found its organizational form at a time when the primary role of these organizations was the implementation of law. Public service production of the scale we know it today did not exist; it is to a very large extent a feature of the latter half of the twentieth century. Hierarchy thus early on became the preferred organizational model as it is an efficient instrument for the implementation of law, a process where values such as uniformity, accountability and predictability are essential. The initial growth of the public sector service production did not significantly challenge the hierarchical structure of the public bureaucracy. These services were rather uniform in character with little or no flexibility or 'customer-attuning', to quote a contemporary concept. Given the limited and one-way exchange between the public bureaucracy and its clients, hierarchies could prevail. Instead, it was the massive attack on the public sector during the 1980s and 1990s which presented a major threat to the hierarchical structures in the public sector. Hierarchies could not sustain the accumulated challenges from within in the form of drastic budget cutbacks and from clients expecting a higher degree of flexibility. Thus, structure in and of itself became an issue in the administrative reform of the 1990s (Peters, 2001); if the hierarchical nature of public organizations was replaced by some form of flat and flexible organization which accorded greater autonomy to the front-line staff many of the problems of lacking legitimacy and inefficiency would be resolved, critics argued.

It would be incorrect to argue that the critique concerning the inertia and rigidity in the public bureaucracy is without justification. In some ways, however, that is not the issue. Public organizations were never designed to maximize on efficiency, flexibility and customer friendliness but rather to ensure a uniform and unbiased implementation of the law. Thus, to some extent the critique during the past couple of decades has employed an irrelevant yardstick for its assessment of public organizations. Moreover, this critique sees only one side of the modern bureaucracy – the service-producing side – and disregards the other side, the exercise and implementation of law. That having been said, it is clear that some relaxation of hierarchy and structure has become

critical to the public sector and, indeed, such organizational change is already taking place in most countries.

Does this mean the farewell to hierarchies? As we have pointed out in a different context, hierarchies have more to offer as instruments of governance than is often recognized (Pierre and Peters, 2000). Ironically, some of the problems frequently associated with more flexible and market-like public organizations, such as accountability and a poor responsiveness to the political echelons of government, are often argued to be among the stronger aspects of the hierarchical model. The challenge in the longer term for the architects of government therefore is to design organizations that combine the efficiency and service capacity of decentralized organizations with the uniform and legalistic nature of hierarchical organizations.

Is marketization the answer?

The same arguments that denigrate the role of hierarchies emphasize the importance of markets as an alternative to more traditional forms of organization and management in the public sector. The assumption is that if government were to use the principles of the market, both in the design of individual programs and in the internal management of government programs, then government will do its job much better. Advocates of the market argue that adopting market principles will make government more efficient, and could reduce the costs of public sector programs to taxpayers.

Although the market has become a popular exemplar for reforming the public sector there are also a number of critics of the market. Perhaps most fundamentally the public sector should not have efficiency as its fundamental value, but rather should be concerned with effectiveness and accountability. Relatedly, market mechanisms may reduce the accountability of public programs by emphasizing internal management rather than relationships with the remainder of the political system. Finally, much of what the public sector does is not amenable to market provision, or they might never have been put into government in the first place, and hence attempting to apply market principles may be mildly absurd. Although an unthinking acceptance of the market is not likely to produce all the benefits promised, there are certainly things to be gained by using some of these techniques. As with so many things in the public sector, the real trick may be in finding the balance between different approaches.

The less politics the better?

There are several circumstances suggesting that the involvement of elected officials in administration is not conducive to maximum performance of the administrative system. The most important argument against too much involvement by politicians in public sector management is that it means not taking management very seriously, or at least not as seriously as electoral considerations. Running large-scale operations, public or private, requires managerial skills and there is nothing in elected office that in and of itself guarantees that the person elected holds those skills. Indeed, the careers of most elected officials rarely involve managing an organization of any significant size. Part of the mantra of administrative reform in the past several decades has been to 'let the managers manage' and that has been in part a claim for a stronger role for public administrators in the governing process.

Clarifying what separates the roles of elected officials and organizational managers in public administration is important (Peters, 1987; Peters and Pierre, 2001). Career officials are expected to provide continuity, expertise and loyalty. Elected officials are expected to provide legitimacy, political judgment, and policy guidance. Bureaucrats are sometimes accused of attempting to monopolize policymaking through their expertise, and their control of the procedures of government, while politicians are accused of micro-management and attempting to politicize the day-to-day management of organizations and personnel. Certainly public administration cannot ignore their nominal political 'masters' but they must also be sure to maintain their own rightful position in governing.

APPROACHES TO PUBLIC ADMINISTRATION

We have already pointed out that public administration stands at the intersection of theory and practice. Within this field of study there have from time to time been heated debates over the relative weights that should be assigned to those two ways of approaching the field. The practitioners have seen academics as hopelessly wound up in theoretical debates that had little or nothing to do with actually making a program run successfully. Academics, on the other hand, have seen practitioners as hopelessly mired in 'manhole counting' and incapable of seeing the larger issues that affect their practice.

As well as standing at the interaction of theory and practice, public administration also stands at the intersection of a number of academic disciplines, as well as having a distinctive literature of its own. Leaving aside for the time being the literature that can be labeled 'purely' public administration, political science, economics, sociology, psychology, law, management, and philosophy, and probably others, have had some influence on the study of public administration. Political science has probably had the longest relationship with public administration, given the importance of the bureaucracy for governing and the fundamental concern in democratic countries about means of holding the bureaucracy accountable to elected officials. That having been said, however, law has been the foundation of public administration in much of continental Europe. More recently, economics and management science have come to play a dominant role in thinking about public administration, as reforms of the public sector have tended to rely upon procedures found in the private sector.

While theory and practice, and an array of academic disciplines contend for control over the study of public administration, the fundamental point that should be emphasized is that all of these perspectives bring something with them that helps to illuminate administration in the public sector. Political science has emphasized the role of public administration as a component of the process of governing, and has, along with law, also emphasized the importance of enforcing the accountability of the bureaucracy, while philosophy has emphasized the need for an ethical framework for public administrators. Economics has pointed to the role of public administration in taxing and spending decisions, as well as providing a theoretical frame through which to understand bureaucracy (Niskanen, 1971; Breton, 1996). Sociology has brought a long tradition of organizational theory, as well as a concern for the linkage of state and society (Rothstein, 1996). Administrative reforms of the past several decades have placed a substantial emphasis on the similarities of public and private management and there has been a good deal of borrowing from business management to transform government.

WHAT'S SO SPECIAL ABOUT THE PUBLIC SECTOR?

The reader will have noticed by this time that he or she has opened a rather large book containing thousands of words. What about public administration merits this attention, especially when most citizens appear as happy to avoid their own bureaucracy? And could both this attention have been lavished on more general questions of management, not just on administration in the public sector? What indeed is so special about this area of inquiry and, perhaps more importantly, what is so special about this area of human activity?

To some extent the answers to those far from simple questions should be evident from the material already discussed in this introduction. Most fundamentally, public administration is central to the process of governing society, no matter what form that governance may take. Without their public administration legislatures could make all the laws they wished but unless they were extraordinarily lucky, and the population was extraordinarily cooperative, nothing would actually happen.[3] In Bagehot's terminology, the public bureaucracy is much of the effective part of government, and it is crucial for providing the services that the public expect from their governments.

The absence of public administration is an extremely unlikely occurrence, and the more relevant question is what happens for governing when public administration is not effective, or efficient, or ethical. The various forms of failure of administration each has its own negative consequences for government and society. Almost certainly an unethical and parasitic administration is the worst form of failure, especially in a government that aspires to be democratic and legitimate (see Chapman, 2000). Honesty and accountability are crucial for building a government that is respected by the public, and may even be central to building an efficient and effective government. A government that is perceived as equitable and fair builds trust which in turn can make government more effective.

Losses of effectiveness are also important as governments increasingly are being judged by their capacity to deliver, and the contemporary emphasis on performance management provides quantitative indications of how well governments are doing their jobs (Bouckaert and Pollitt, 2003). Despite all the emphasis in the New Public Management, efficiency may be the least important value for the public sector, especially in the eyes of the public. They may mind much more that services are delivered, and that they are delivered in an accountable and humane manner, than they care about the cost per unit of service delivered. This does not mean that public administrators should not care about efficiency, but only that this is not necessarily the dominant value that it has been made to be.

ORGANIZATION OF THE HANDBOOK

The remainder of the Handbook is organized in fourteen sections, each having been shaped and edited by a Section Editor. Those editors have each added an Introduction to their section, discussing its contents and relating it to general themes that run throughout the volume. These fourteen sections represent the principal dimensions of the literature within public administration, attempting to cover both traditional themes as well as more contemporary managerialist approaches to administration.

NOTES

1   Bureaucracy is often a word of opprobrium, but we are using it here in a more neutral manner, meaning the formal administrative structures in the public sector.
2   The degree of autonomy enjoyed by the public bureaucracy in traditional patterns of governing is often exaggerated, but there has been a marked shift in the involvement of the private sector.
3   A conservative American politician once commented that he should like it if Congress were placed on a cruise ship and had to put all its laws into bottles to float back to land. Only the laws in those bottles that were found would go into effect. Without public administration, governing might be a good deal like that.

REFERENCES

Bouckaert, G. and Pollitt, C. (2003) *Public Management Reform: A Comparative Analysis*, 2nd edn. Oxford: Oxford University Press.
Breton, A. (1996) *Competitive Government: An Economic Theory of Politics and Public Finance*. Cambridge: Cambridge University Press.
Chapman, R.A. (2000) *Ethics in the Public Service for the New Millennium*. Aldershot: Ashgate.
Hood, C. (1998) *The Art of the State: Culture, Rhetoric and Public Management*. Oxford: Oxford University Press.
Kerwin, C. (1999) *Rulemaking*. Washington, DC: CQ Press.
Niskanen, W. (1971) *Bureaucracy and Representative Government*. Chicago: Aldine/Atherton.
Page, E.C. (2000) *Government by the Numbers*. Oxford: Hart.
Peters, B.G. (1987) 'Politicians and Bureaucrats in the Politics of Policy-making', in J.-E. Lane, (ed.), *Bureaucracy and Public Choice*. London: Sage.
Peters, B.G. (2001) *The Future of Governing*, 2nd edn. Lawrence: University Press of Kansas.
Peters, B.G. and Pierre, J. (2000) 'Citizens Versus the New Public Manager: The Problem of Mutual Empowerment', *Administration and Society*, 32: 9–28.

Peters, B.G. and Pierre, J. (2001) *Politicians, Bureaucrats and Administrative Reform*. London: Routledge.

Pierre, J. and Peters, B.G. (2000) *Governance, Politics and the State*. Basingstoke: Palgrave.

Plowden, W. (1984) *Ministers and Mandarins*. London: Royal Institute of Public Administration.

Rockman, B.A. (1998) 'The Changing Role of the State', in B.G. Peters and D.J. Savoie (eds), *Taking Stock: Assessing Public Sector Reforms*. Montreal and Kingston: McGill-Queen's University Press. pp. 20–44.

Rothstein, B. (1996) *The Social Democratic State: The Swedish Model and the Bureaucratic Problems of Social Reform*. Pittsburgh: University of Pittsburgh Press.

Savoie, D.J. (1994) *Reagan, Thatcher, Mulroney: In Search of A New Bureaucracy*. Pittsburgh: University of Pittsburgh Press.

Stein, J.G. (2002) *The Cult of Efficiency*. Toronto: Ananasi Press.

Section 1

PUBLIC MANAGEMENT: OLD AND NEW

Introduction

Hal G. Rainey

In the past two decades, in nations around the world, the topic of *public management* has taken on an increased significance in the theory and practice of public administration. One might wonder what this development is all about, since public management and public administration sound synonymous. Just what it is all about is what this first section of the book is largely about.

For people in public administration as scholars and as practicing managers and professionals, this new interest in public management – or renewed interest, as we shall see – has major implications. Scholars note that this worldwide movement involves increased emphasis on certain patterns and reforms in the management of government agencies and programs. One major implication involves the widespread perception that government needs to give more attention to achieving effective management, often through the adoption of management procedures or arrangements resembling those of business firms. Kettl (2000), for example, observes that the international movement towards 'public management', including variants of it called 'new public management', involves a number of common themes in many nations. These include increasing the productivity of government activities, using economic market or market-like strategies, enhancing attention to citizens as service recipients, decentralizing

responsibilities to local governments and to front-line managers, and sharpening accountability for results by focusing more on outputs and outcomes than on processes and structures.

In addition to these developments in reform and practice, academics have pondered the implications of a public management emphasis for research and intellectual development. Some scholars in public administration employed the public management rubric in expressing their conviction that their field needs a richer base of theory and empirical research on management skills, responsibilities and procedures akin to that available in the academic fields of business management and organizational analysis (for example, Perry and Kraemer, 1983). They pointed to the need for more research on how people in management positions in government can carry out their responsibilities and effectively operate their agencies and programs. In related fields such as political science and public policy studies, the prevailing assumption appeared to be that management matters do not matter much – that managerial activities by middle- and upper-level 'bureaucrats' in government simply do not play a significant role in the political system and public policy processes. Still other academics in prestigious schools of public affairs at leading universities also sought to develop the topic of public management, and expressed less concern with the field of public administration than with developing a body of knowledge to support high-level executive leadership in government (Lynn, 1996).

The chapters in this section elaborate and respond to this movement in several ways. Laurence Lynn's chapter provides a rich description of the evolution of the topic of public management and of major current issues in its continuing development. He describes how the major public administration scholars early in the twentieth century concerned themselves with the role of 'management' in the field, often emphasizing its importance in relation to other foci, such as the legal context of administration. He describes how scholars have differentiated between administration and management, and between management in the public and private sectors. This leads him to consider several perspectives on public management: as a *structure of governance*, a 'formalization of managerial discretion intended to enable government to effect the will of the people', as a *craft* or set of skills applied by public managers and as an *institution* embodying legitimate values and constitutional constraints to which public managers adhere. Lynn also analyzes recent developments, such as a tendency for some scholars to so heavily emphasize the craft perspective that they lose sight of the others. Ultimately, he argues that the main challenge involves maintaining appropriate emphasis on all three of these perspectives simultaneously.

Carolyn Heinrich then describes and assesses developments in one of the major trends in public management around the world, an increasing emphasis on performance measurement for public organizations and programs. Here again, as she describes, this topic has a classic character, with experts and scholars attending to it in a variety of ways for a very long time. Heinrich provides a historical overview of many of the conceptions and systems of performance measurement that have emerged and evolved since the nineteenth century. In addition, however, she points to new developments in the recent upsurge of emphasis on performance measurement, such as its increasing scope, sophistication and visibility, as well as certain common themes across nations such as an increase in formal reporting requirements involving comparisons of performance measures to pre-established performance goals and standards. Heinrich goes on to discuss major current issues in performance measurement such as the challenges involved in specifying and measuring goals, due to such factors as the conflicting values and priorities for many public programs and agencies, and the multiple actors and levels involved in them. With emphasis on the need to provide public managers with information about how their decisions and actions affect performance, she also discusses prospects for addressing such challenges and provides numerous examples of recent models and methods of performance measurement.

As we come to John Bryson's chapter, Lynn has told us that one major reason for increasing interest in public management arises from concern with enhancing the skills and practices that public managers can use proactively to increase program and agency performance, and to contribute effectively to governance. Heinrich has added valuable description and analysis of one of the most important challenges in the pursuit of performance – its conception and measurement. Another of the most important challenges concerns formulation of purposes and of plans for pursuing them, through strategic planning and management. As Bryson tells us, these priorities are 'becoming a way of life for public organizations around the globe'. Bryson, whose book *Strategic Planning for Public and Nonprofit Organizations* is almost certainly the most widely used and cited book on the topic, provides a highly authoritative description and analysis of strategic planning and management, of strategic management systems and models, and of current trends in thought and practice of the topic, such as increasing pursuit of speed, inclusion of diverse interests and groups, and systems thinking.

Obviously, the analysis of public management and its relation to public administration derives its value not from the parsing of these two rubrics, but from the more fundamental issues involved. As these chapters show, these issues include the institutional and structural context of public management, and the roles, responsibilities, skills and practices it involves. These three authoritative chapters provide description, conceptualization and analysis of clear value to those who think, research and write about public administration, as well as to those charged with carrying out in practice its vital responsibilities.

REFERENCES

Kettl, Donald F. (2000) *The Global Public Management Revolution: A Report on the Transformation of Governance.* Washington, DC: Brookings Institution.

Lynn, Laurence E., Jr (1996) *Public Management as Art, Science, and Profession.* Chatham, NJ: Chatham House.

Perry, James L. and Kraemer, Kenneth L. (eds) (1983) *Public Management: Public and Private Perspectives.* Palo Alto, CA: Mayfield.

1

Public Management

Laurence E. Lynn, Jr

[H]e liked to organize, to contend, to administer; he could make people work his will, believe in him, march before him and justify him. This was the art, as they said, of managing ...

(Henry James, *The Portrait of a Lady*)

[P]ublic management ... is a world of settled institutions designed to allow imperfect people to use flawed procedures to cope with insoluble problems.

James Q. Wilson (*Bureaucracy: What Government Agencies Do and Why They Do It*)

Public management is the subject of a rapidly growing literature that is international in scope and multifarious in content.[1] The common sense of public management is relatively straightforward. Good public managers, whatever their particular positions or responsibilities, are men and women with the temperament and skills to organize, motivate and direct the actions of others in and out of government toward the creation and achievement of goals that warrant the use of public authority. Few public laws and policies are self-executing, and, in their formulation, all might benefit from managerial insight and experience. Under virtually any political philosophy or regime, then, the achievement of good government requires the responsible and competent use of public authority by a government's managers.

Common sense obscures issues that have been at the heart of public management from its inception as a field of study and practice, however. What if the goals to be achieved and their possible costs and consequences are unclear or in conflict? What if public managers are given insufficient authority, resources and tools to organize, motivate and monitor the efforts needed to accomplish those purposes for which they are responsible? How does effective management compare in importance to good policy design, rational organization, adequate resources, effective monitoring and the approbation of affected publics? What is effective managerial practice and how does it vary across the many contexts in which public management is practiced? How might effective public management be enabled by legislators, executives and judicial authorities, and how might particular managerial reforms or strategies affect governmental performance?

The objective of public management scholarship is to provide theoretical and empirical foundations for addressing both the above questions and the myriad specific questions that arise in organizing and carrying out managerial responsibilities in government departments, bureaux and offices: means–ends rationality; the role of political-legal constraints; appropriate levels of discretion and resources; *ex ante* versus *ex post* controls over administration; accountability to the public; criteria for evaluating administration; and administrative reform. The purpose of this chapter is to provide an overview of the field that is concerned with these issues.

It will be useful at the outset to introduce distinctions that are fundamental to the perspective of this chapter. Public administration's classic American literature understood management to be the responsible and lawful exercise of discretion by public administrators. In this view, public management is a *structure* of governance (Scott, 1998), that is, a constitutionally appropriate formalization of managerial discretion intended to enable government to effect the will of the people. In contrast, recent literature has tended to view public management as a *craft*, that is, as skilled practice by individuals performing managerial roles. To the extent that public managers practice their craft responsibly, that is, that they respect constitutional restraints and routinely evince values that are widely held to be legitimate and appropriate (rather than narrowly partisan or self regarding), then public management becomes even more: an *institution* of constitutional governance (Weimer, 1995). Public management as an institution observes 'rules of practice', that is, *de facto* restraints on or guides to behavior, that ensure their legitimacy within a constitutional, or *de jure*, regime. Properly understood, then, public management is structure, craft and institution: 'management', 'manager' and 'responsible practice'.

In the initial sections of this chapter, two issues that define the scope of public management as a field of scholarship and practice are discussed: the relationship between 'public administration' and 'public management' and the similarities and differences between 'public management' and 'private management'. With these discussions as background, public management as structure, as craft and as institution are explored in detail in the following three sections. There follows in the penultimate section a consideration of public management as it relates to the concept of governance, a discussion which brings into focus the enduring challenges of public management in theory and practice. Summary observations conclude the chapter.

MANAGEMENT AND ADMINISTRATION

When we talk of 'public management' or of 'public administration', are we talking of the same subject or of different subjects? Arguments to the effect that management and administration are fundamentally different have a long history in American literature, although the distinction often seems arbitrary.[2] Many such arguments relegate management to subordinate, specialized or even stigmatized status with the result that the structural and institutional aspects of public management that are vital to understanding its significance to constitutional governance are overlooked.

Numerous early commentaries either view the two terms as synonymous or regard management as the more general concept.[3] In public administration's first textbook, published in 1926, Leonard D. White, rebuking the notion that public law is the proper foundation of public administration, argued that 'The study of administration should start from the base of management rather than the foundation of law' (White, 1926: vii).[4] According to Henri Fayol (1930), 'It is important not to confuse *administration* with *management*. To manage ... is to conduct [an organization] toward the best possible use of all the resources at its disposal ... [i.e.,] to ensure the smooth working of the ... essential functions. Administration is only one of these functions' (quoted in Wren, 1979: 232). In Roscoe C. Martin's view, by 1940, 'administration was equated with management', although, he noted, there was comparatively little talk about the 'nature of the craft' (Martin, 1965: 8). Paul Van Riper (1990), in assaying mid- to late-nineteenth century antecedents to Woodrow Wilson's 1887, says: 'Note ... that the words *administration* and *management* have been treated here as synonymous' (p. 8). Dwight Waldo observed, 'Perhaps as much as any other one thing, the "management" movement has molded the outlook of those to whom public administration is an independent inquiry or definable discipline' (Waldo, 1984: 12).

Yet many public administration scholars have held that, of the two concepts, administration is original and primary, public management is novel and subordinate or specialized. 'Public management as a special focus of modern public administration is new,' say Perry and Kraemer (1983), a view echoed by Rainey (1990: 157): 'In the past two decades, the topic of public management has come forcefully onto the agenda of those interested in governmental administration,' perhaps, he suggests, because of the growing unpopularity of government. In their *Public Management: The Essential Readings*, Ott, Hyde and Shafritz (1991) argue that 'Public management is a major segment of the broader field of public administration ... Public management focuses on public administration as a profession and on the public manager as a practitioner of that profession' (p. 1).

Such viewpoints seem to represent a reaction to the opportunistic appropriation of the term public management in the 1970s and 1980s by the newly formed graduate schools of public policy at Harvard University, the University of California, Princeton University and elsewhere.[5] According to Joel Fleishman, the policy schools' focus on public management originated with Mark Moore's efforts to 'refocus political and organizational analysis into prescriptive subject matter, with a point of view that is decidedly strategic' (1990: 743). Donald Stokes observed that '[S]trategic political thinking sets off the public manager who is able to *move* an agency from one who plays a custodial role ... [T]he strategic manager sees the small openings presented by the agency's routine to induce change toward an identified goal, step-by-step. ...' (1986: 55). By 1984, Moore summarized the emerging state of the public management art:

> Our conception of 'public management' adds responsibility for goal setting and political management to the traditional responsibilities of public administration. ... Our conception of public management adds some quintessential executive functions such as setting purpose, maintaining credibility with overseers, marshaling authority and resources, and positioning one's organization in a given political environment as central components of a public manager's job. (Moore, 1984: 2, 3)

In Moore's view, the gist of public management is 'conceiving and implementing public policies that realize the potential of a given political and institutional setting' (1984: 3), potential he later termed 'public value' (Moore, 1995). Thus Moore's view was new, that is, a departure from traditional conceptions of administration, in that it appeared to disavow interest in the settings for public management and to emphasize its behavioral and psychological aspects.

The newer behavioral approach to public management has tended to become more action-oriented and prescriptive. As such it says both more and less about public management than traditional conceptions. Briefly, the older view is that public management is the responsible exercise of administrative discretion. The newer conception adds to this what Roscoe Martin called 'the craft perspective', that is, a concern for decisions, actions and outcomes, and for the political skill needed to perform effectively in specific managerial roles. However, by emphasizing the strategic political role of public managers *within given political and institutional settings*, the newer conception is concerned more with the immediate, pragmatic concerns of managers at executive levels of governmental organizations. As Robert Behn has put it, 'any emphasis on the perspective of practicing public managers will have a short run focus' (Behn, 1991). A lower priority is placed on the manager's role in developing institutional capacity and in adhering to durable democratic values – that is, to public management as an institution – and on management at middle and lower levels of administration.

Precision concerning the distinction between administration and management is of more than antiquarian interest.[6] Because the concept of public management as the responsible exercise of discretion is at least implied by the intellectual development of public administration as a field,

public administration's literature is also a literature of public management. Together, the older and more recent, craft-oriented literatures provide foundations for the structural, craft and institutional aspects of the subject. These three aspects, because they emphasize that practice must conform to constitutional structures and values, supply an analytic framework for evaluating particular public management reform proposals and developments, whether they be those of the Brownlow Report, the New Public Administration, the Blacksburg Manifesto, the US Government Performance and Results Act, the Clinton Administration's National Performance Review, or the New Public Management. Of all such proposals, we wish to understand their structural, craft and institutional implications in order to determine whether they befit constitutional requirements.

One particular argument for distinguishing between administration and management deserves further scrutiny, however. 'Those who define public administration in managerial terms,' argues David Rosenbloom, 'tend to minimize the distinctions between public and private administration' (1998: 16). The term administration, in this view, conveys respect for the constitutional and political foundations of governance in a way that the term management does not.

PUBLIC AND PRIVATE MANAGEMENT

How alike or unalike are managing in the public and private sectors? Can and should government be more business-like? Is management generic? To the extent that public and private management involve similar temperaments, skills and techniques, then the extensive body of ideas and practices relating to corporate success can be applied to the problems of public management, and the public sector can in principle draw on the large pool of private sector managers to meet its own managerial needs. To the extent that, from structural or craft perspectives, they are different, then the public sector must have access to sources of knowledge, techniques and skills suited to its unique character.

This issue was addressed with authority at the dawn of public administration as a profession. Frank J. Goodnow argued in 1893, '[i]n transacting its business [the government's] object is not usually the acquisition of gain but the furtherance of the welfare of the community. This is the great distinction between public and private business' ([1893]1902: 10). At a more subtle level, Goodnow argued that 'the grant to the administration of ... enormous discretionary powers' means that '[t]here has ... been a continuous attempt on the part of the people to control the discretion of the administration in the exercise of the sovereign powers of the state' ([1893]1902: 10, 11). In 1926, Leonard D. White added the consideration that the principle of consistency – today, we say equity – governs public administration to an extent not observed in business administration (White, 1926; cf. Stamp, 1923).

The basic elements of the argument that public and private management are fundamentally unalike in all important respects are: (1) that the public interest differs from private interests, (2) that public officials, because they exercise the sovereign power of the state, are necessarily accountable to democratic values rather than to any particular group or material interest, and (3) that the constitution requires equal treatment of persons and rules out the kind of selectivity that is essential to sustaining profitability. Moreover, the extent of the differences between the two sectors has been well documented empirically (Rainey, 1997).

Some will argue nonetheless that an enumeration of such differences is misleading because it obscures important similarities. 'All organizations are public,' argues Barry Bozeman (1987), by which he means that all organizations, whether governmental, for-profit, or nonprofit, are affected to at least some degree by political authority. Thus, he argues, '[p]ublic managers can be found in most every type of organization' because public managers are not limited to government employees but encompass 'persons who manage publicness' (p. 146) in any sector. However, one might also argue the converse, that all organizations are 'private' to the extent that they are responsible for tasks that are performed by experts who are governed by professional or technocratic authority rather than by stakeholder interests. These tasks were first recognized by Goodnow (1900: 85) as 'the semi-scientific, quasi-judicial, and quasi-business or commercial' functions of administration, although as Don Price later warned, 'the expert may come to believe that his science justifies exceeding his authority' (1959: 492), a pervasive danger in all organizations requiring specialized expertise.

The distinction between public and private management, then, is arguably definitive from structural, craft and institutional perspectives. The two sectors are constituted to serve different kinds of societal interests, and distinctive kinds of skills and values are appropriate to serving these different interests. The distinctions may be blurred or absent, however, when analyzing particular managerial responsibilities, functions and tasks in particular organizations. The implication of this argument is that lesson drawing and knowledge transfer across sectors is likely to be useful and should never be rejected on ideological grounds.

PUBLIC MANAGEMENT AS STRUCTURE

As already noted, the earliest conception of public management was as a structure of governance, that is, a formal means for constraining and overseeing the exercise of state authority by public managers. From a structural perspective, public management involves two interrelated elements: lawful delegation of authority and external control over the exercise of delegated authority. The design of arrangements that balance these elements constitutes the paradigmatic problem of public management viewed as a structure of governance (Bertelli and Lynn, 2001).

Overcoming the reluctance of legislatures and courts to delegate authority to unelected bureaucrats constituted the first challenge to establishing public management as a structure of governance. As early as 1893, Goodnow asserted that 'A large discretion must be given to the administrative authorities to adapt many general rules of law to the wants of the people' ([1893] 1902: 28). He noted further that 'while the main duty of the executive is to execute the will of the legislature as expressed in statutes, ... there is a realm of action in which the executive authority possesses large discretion, and that it looks for its authority not to the legislature but to the constitution' ([1893]1902: 33). John Dickinson asked (1927: 156), 'if ... we ... imply that the main purpose [of administrative agencies] ... is to adjudicate according to rules, will we not have abandoned the characteristic and special advantage of a system of administrative justice, which consists in a union of legislative, executive, and judicial functions in the same body to secure promptness of action, and the freedom to arrive at decisions based on policy?'

Discretion must be controlled, however, and thus a second challenge arose: ensuring adequate legislative, judicial and public oversight of public management. As legal scholar Ernest Freund put it, '[i]ncreased administrative powers call for increased safeguards against their abuses, and as long as there is the possibility of official error, partiality or excess of zeal, the protection of private right is as important an object as the effectuation of some governmental policy' (quoted by White, 1926). Leonard D. White explored the problem of 'control of the administration' at length in his 1926 textbook. 'The problem,' he argued, 'has gradually developed into that of finding means to ensure that the acts of administrative officers shall be consistent not only with the law but equally with the purposes and temper of the mass of citizens' (1926: 419). In Paul Appleby's later view, '[p]erhaps there is no single problem in public administration of moment equal to the reconciliation of the increasing dependence upon experts with an enduring democratic reality' (1952: 145).

Delegation and oversight by legislatures and deference to administrators by courts are now accepted features of constitutional governance. Striking the right balance between capacity and control remains a controversial aspect of public management, however, and failure to do so often defeats efforts to achieve public management reform. As Kettl has expressed it (1997), tensions continue to exist between 'making managers manage', that is, imposing substantial *ex ante* and *ex post* controls over managerial discretion, and 'letting managers manage', that is, holding public managers accountable for their performance rather than for their compliance with formal rules and procedures. These two strategies, Kettl notes, 'require culture shifts in opposite directions' (1997, p. 449), a reality not always fully appreciated by advocates of public management reform.

PUBLIC MANAGEMENT AS CRAFT

In recent decades, increasing emphasis has been placed on public management as a craft practiced by specific individuals in specific managerial roles. An intellectual development of seminal importance to this movement was the appearance in 1938 of Chester Barnard's *The Functions of the Executive* (1968), which laid the groundwork for new perspectives, including that of Herbert Simon, on managerial responsibility. As Frederick Mosher interpreted him, Barnard 'defined administrative responsibility as primarily a moral question or, more specifically, as the resolution of competing and conflicting codes, legal, technical, personal, professional, and organizational, in the reaching of individual decisions' (Mosher, 1968: 210).

Barnard clearly influenced John Millett, whose 1954 book, *Management in the Public Service*, constitutes an early example of the craft perspective:

> The challenge to any administrator is to overcome obstacles, to understand and master problems, to use imagination and insight in devising new goals of public service. No able administrator can be content to be simply a good caretaker. He seeks rather to review the ends of organized effort and to advance the goals of administrative endeavor toward better public service. (1954: 401)

Millett goes on in a manner prefiguring later ideas from the policy schools:

> In a democratic society this questing is not guided solely by the administrator's own personal sense of desirable social ends. The administrator must convince others as well. He must work with interest groups, with legislators, with chief executives, and with the personnel of his own agency to convince them all that a particular line of policy or program is desirable. (p. 401)

The newer literature within the craft perspective is based, by and large, on the careful study and analysis of particular cases of managerial experience.[7] As Graham Allison noted in a seminal article, 'The effort to develop public management as a field of knowledge should start from problems faced by practicing public managers' (Allison, 1979: 38). The focus of such study is on what managers did or should do in specific settings. A more critical view saw this enterprise as representing an 'ongoing effort to create a new "myth" for public management … by emphasizing a political and activist orientation – heroes and entrepreneurs became the stock and trade of its case studies' *at the expense of institutions* (Dobel, 1992: 147). Among the numerous examples of this perspective, Heymann's *The Politics of Public Management* (1987), Reich's *Public Management in a Democratic Society* (1990), Behn's *Leadership Counts* (1991) and Moore's *Creating Public Value* (1995) are representative.

Anxious to inspire public officials with the conviction that 'management counts' and with an entrepreneurial, proactive spirit, the craft literature emanating from the public policy schools turned heavily to prescription (Lynn, 1996). The best of this literature – for example, Light's *Sustaining Innovation* (1998) and Bardach's *Getting Agencies to Work Together* (1998) – represents a thoughtful appreciation of the existential challenges of public management and an attempt to deduce best practices from closely observed successful stories. Other contributions – such as Cohen and Eimicke's *The New Effective*

Public Manager (1995) and Haass's *The Bureaucratic Entrepreneur* (1999) – are explicitly didactic and feature numerous prescriptions and principles based on the experiences and reflections of effective practitioners.

Within this genre, many craft-oriented public management scholars have assumed away the structural elements of public management, concerning themselves with the temperamental and psychological aspects of management. This approach leads to a highly reductive view of public management that hearkens back to an earlier preoccupation with leadership traits and managerial personalities. Thus, successful managers are characterized as enterprising or entrepreneurial, disposed to take risks, purposeful, imaginative and intuitive, and inclined to act. Others emphasize simple, generic processes – establishing and reiterating clear goals, managing by walking around – or adhering to unexceptionable principles – develop and focus on a narrow agenda, look for opportunities to act and the like. Says Behn: 'Most management concepts are simple, and, to have any impact these simple management ideas must be expressible in some pithy phrase' (1988: 651). After citing five unexceptionable principles for achieving influence as a manager, Haass asserts: 'Being effective is that simple – and that complicated' (1994: 230).

The oversimplifications of its proponents should not discredit the importance of craft as an element of public management, however, at least in principle. Beyond structural considerations are the behavioral and intellectual challenges that any good manager must take into account. There are, as well, what Barnard called the 'non-logical' aspects that give rise to timely reactions, intuitive insights and, ultimately, good judgment. From a craft perspective, some public managers are better than others. Though there has been relatively little rigorous empirical research on managerial contributions to governmental performance (Lynn et al., 2001), it is reasonable to assume that public management will be only as effective as public managers are masters of their craft.

PUBLIC MANAGEMENT AS INSTITUTION

How, and on behalf of what values, should public managers practice their craft? The answer to this question bears directly on the issue, discussed above, of the feasibility of 'letting managers manage' and the consequences of doing so for constitutional governance.

The appropriateness of intrinsic or self-control by public managers has been a recurring issue since the Friedrich–Finer debate of 1940 (Finer, 1940; Friedrich, 1940). Against Finer's view that public managers should be subject to minute legislative control, Friedrich countered that the best means for ensuring that management is responsive to the polity is the professionalism of the manager. More substantively, Rohr has argued that '[a]dministrators should use their discretionary power in order to maintain the constitutional balance of powers in support of individual rights' (1986: 181). Denhardt has urged that public managers commit themselves to 'values that relate to the concept of freedom, justice, and the public interest' (1993: 20). Wamsley insists that 'the only possible source of governing impetuses that might keep our complex political system from either a dangerous concentration of power on the one hand, or impotence or self-destruction, on the other, is a public administration with the necessary professionalism, dedication, self-esteem, and legitimacy to act as the constitutional center of gravity' (1990: 26). In asserting that public managers 'must resist, thwart, or refuse to implement policy that runs counter to the founding documents or to American regime values', George Frederickson comes tantalizingly close to enunciating a doctrine of administrative nullification (Frederickson, 1997: 229).

The notion that public management should be a self-regulated institution evokes the concept of responsibility, another paradigmatic value in traditional public administration. Woodrow Wilson observed that '[t]here is no danger in power, if only it be not irresponsible' (1887: 213). Morstein Marx argued, '[t]he heart of administrative responsibility is a unified conception of duty, molded by ideological and professional precepts' (1940: 251). To Frederick Mosher, '[r]esponsibility may well be the most important word in all the vocabulary of administration, public and private' (1968: 7), adding later that responsibility 'would seem to me to be the first requisite of a democratic state' (1992: 201).

How should responsible public management be defined? Rohr, Denhardt, Wamsley and others tend to define it in terms of adherence to a liberal political philosophy. Mosher (1968) distinguished between objective responsibility, or answerability for one's actions, a structural perspective, and subjective responsibility, which is akin to identification, loyalty and conscience, a craft perspective. More specifically, Bertelli and Lynn (2001) identify in the classic literature of public administration four distinct and demonstrable qualities – accountability, judgment, balance and rationality – which, they argue, constitute a *precept of managerial responsibility* that, when observed in managerial practice, justifies judicial deference when agencies are defendants in litigation and qualifies as a general norm of responsibility. The logic of this precept is as follows.

Accountability has been defined in general terms as 'those methods, procedures, and forces that determine what values will be reflected in administrative decision' (Simon et al., 1950: 513). Accountability is complicated in the United States by the fact that all three branches of government compete for control of public management. Despite this competition, 'no one [branch], nor all three jointly, provide the [public manager] with the totality of the value premises that enter into his [*sic*] decision' (p. 539). The responsible public manager is not, however, a free agent empowered to act on the basis of whim or ideology: '[m]anagement guided by [the value of responsible performance] abhors the idea of arbitrary authority present in its own wisdom and recognizes the reality of external direction and constraint' (Millett, 1954: 403).

After all external direction is taken into account, however, public managers still 'have considerable freedom to decide matters on the basis of their own ethical promptings' (Simon et al., 1950: 539). Thus no combination of mechanisms for enforcing administrative responsibility can extinguish the element of *judgment* from public management. What kind of managerial judgment fulfills a precept of managerial responsibility? Schuyler B. Wallace argued that, apart from 'the primary purpose of Congress in establishing the unit', good judgment makes 'reference to some ideal purpose more comprehensive than that of Congress' (1941: 89). The notion of idealism is an unacceptably open-ended standard for judgment, however, because it appears to authorize the public manager to enact political philosophies that may not reflect the will of the polity. More precision is needed.

Because public managers are necessarily accountable to numerous stakeholders in their political environments, one characteristic of good judgement is *balance*. Public managers, argues Morstein Marx, should 'give careful thought to the legislative balance of power, the enunciated or anticipated preferences of the chief executive, and the probabilities of public reactions. Ideally, political and administrative thinking should blend into a joint process' (1959: 102). The act of striking a balance is termed 'adjustive activity' by Emmette Redford: 'In the concept of administration as adjustive activity, [public management] is an extension of the political process of adjustment among interests' (1969: 188). Thus public managers must strike a balance among competing interests, political philosophies and interpretations of fact. The real agenda of public management, say Ott, Hyde and Shafritz, is 'balancing political, economic, and social concerns for equity, justice, and fairness, as well as integrating perspectives for bettering "the public good" in complex, highly diverse, competitive, and inequitable environments' (1991: xvi).

A second characteristic of good judgment is *rationality*. Marshall Dimock conceptualized managerial discretion as 'the liberty to decide between alternatives' (1936: 46). To be responsible, judgment concerning the merits of alternative strategies or actions, whether devised by the public manager or by other stakeholders, should aspire to be logical or rational as well as politically balanced. A rational action is one for which the relationship between the goals and the means for achieving them in the mind of the manager corresponds to the relationship between goals and means for achieving them in reality (or as might be confirmed by independent analysis) (Aron, 1998: 121). To be responsible, the public manager must seek out and master arguments and evidence concerning the relationships between means and ends. Inescapable, however, is what Nicholas Rescher termed 'the predicament of reason', or 'the irresolvable tension between the demands of rationality and its practical possibilities' (Rescher, 1998: 169). The fact that the public managers cannot anticipate or calculate all consequences following from their actions, however, does not vitiate the argument for intentional rationality in management decisions.

The institutional perspective on public management might be summarized as follows: the structures of the administrative state constitute an appropriate framework for achieving balance between a jurisdiction's need for administrative capacity to pursue public purposes and citizen control of that capacity (Lynn, 2001). When managerial craft practiced within this framework is guided by a sense of responsibility, public management becomes a primary institution for preserving the balance between the state's capacity to effect the public interest and the citizen's power to hold office holders accountable. The issue was perhaps best stated by Goodnow:

> [D]etailed legislation and judicial control over its execution are not sufficient to produce harmony between the governmental body, which expresses the will of the state, and the governmental authority, which executes that will. ... The executive officers may or may not

enforce the law as it was intended by the legislature. Judicial officers, in exercising control over such executive officers, may or may not take the same view of the law as did the legislature. No provision is thus made in the governmental organization for securing harmony between the expression and the execution of the will of the state. The people, the ultimate sovereign in a popular government, must ... have a control over the officers who execute their will, as well as over those who express it. (1900: 97–8)

As early as 1900, then, the contemporary problem of balancing the competing values of democratic institutions, including the institution of public management, was clearly in view.

PUBLIC MANAGEMENT AND GOVERNANCE

Public management performs its institutional role when public managers conform to lawful constraints, manage responsibly within them, and respond creatively to opportunities for policy making and structural reform. But public management is not the only institution that preserves balance in a constitutional regime. The capacity to effect the public interest, as Goodnow foresaw, does not reside solely in the executive agencies of government, nor does the maintenance of control reside solely with legislatures and courts. Capacity and control, and the balance between them, depend upon the actions of executives, legislatures, judicial institutions and citizens acting in their many capacities. A term for this complex reality is 'governance'. From a public management perspective, governance may usefully be defined as regimes of laws, rules, judicial decisions and administrative practices that constrain, prescribe and enable the exercise of public authority on behalf of the public interest (Lynn et al., 2001).[8]

The broader issue for any self-governing jurisdiction, then, is distributing power among lawful organizations and institutions so as to establish a governance regime that ensures a satisfactory balance among competing interests and values. Achieving that balancing is the stuff of partisan politics and, as such, is infused with group interests (Pollitt and Bouckaert, 2000). The task of political actors, argues Terry Moe, is 'to find and institute a governance structure that can protect ... public organizations from control by opponents' (Moe, 1995: 125). However, as Moe has put it, '[a] bureaucracy that is structurally unsuited for effective action is precisely the kind of bureaucracy that interest groups and politicians

routinely and deliberately create' (1995: 328). As James Q. Wilson notes, referring to America's constitutional separation of powers, '[t]he governments of the United States were not designed to be efficient or powerful, but to be tolerable and malleable' (Wilson, 1989: 376). Therein lies the continuing challenge to public management as an institution. As a result of regime restraints and the politics they authorize, the public manager may have to deal with inadequate resources, unreasonable or unrealistic workload or reporting requirements, inconsistent guidance, or missions defined so as to be virtually unachievable.

While the consequences for public management of the way governance is organized are ultimately relevant to virtually every regulation, policy and program, these consequences are discussed most explicitly during debates over administrative reform proposals intended to improve the performance of government as a whole. In the United States beginning in the early 1990s, reforms provoking a discourse on governance have included the enactment of the Government Performance and Results Act and the Clinton administration's efforts to implement the National Performance Review. Internationally, these issues have arisen under the rubric of the New Public Management in its many national expressions. To the extent that they are actually implemented, which is often in doubt, these kinds of reforms, intended variously to increase the use of performance measurement in resource allocation, to empower public employees to engage in continuous improvement in public programs and operations, and to mobilize the theoretical advantages of markets to induce greater efficiency, all have major implications for public management as an institution (Pollitt, 2000).

Such implications may remain inadequately defined, however, both because they are obscured by partisan claims during the debate over the reform proposals and because widely accepted standards for evaluating such claims are for the most part lacking. Greater clarity concerning the nature of public management as structure, craft and institution, a purpose of this chapter, might, as suggested earlier, prove helpful in facilitating such evaluations. For example, traditional conceptions of public management discussed throughout this chapter incorporate far more respect for the difficulties of harmonizing law, politics, citizens and democratic values than do customer-oriented managerialism or populist-oriented civic philosophies that, in promoting employee, community and citizen empowerment, ignore the inevitability of the kind of factionalism and partisanship fully foreseen by the authors of *The Federalist*. Many managerial reforms barely acknowledge or actually denigrate the constitutional role of legislatures, courts and elected executives and the need to anticipate political competition. Proposed reforms of governance which do not exhibit respect for a nation's basic institutions should be regarded with profound suspicion.

CONCLUSION

Notwithstanding the vagaries of politics, public management as an institution and public managers as individuals must attempt to do the best they can under difficult, if not impossible circumstances, even when that means doing little more than 'muddling through' or 'coping' (Lindblom, 1959; Wilson, 1989). Doing the best that they can is unquestionably a matter of craft, which can benefit from training and practice based on the study and analysis of particular cases. It is also, and maybe even primarily, a matter of institutionalized, and internalized, values, of public managers being self-consciously guided by a precept of managerial responsibility. Though the particular character of structure, craft and institution varies across organizations, levels of government and countries with different legal and political traditions, a strong argument can be made for the general relevance of these concepts to effective public management and to successful administrative reform.

In the final analysis, public management is also a matter of common sense. Governments authorize imperfect people to use flawed procedures to cope with insoluble problems. The results of their efforts are remarkably effective given the exigencies of their roles. Responsible public management is indispensable to sound governance.

NOTES

1   As defined in this chapter, public management varies across countries with different legal and political traditions. Public management literature offering a comparative perspective includes Peters (1996), Kickert (1997), Kettl (2000), Pollitt and Bouckaert (2000) and Christensen and Lægreid (2001). For a survey and analysis of various definitions of public management from a European perspective, see Pollitt and Bouckaert (2000: pp. 8–16).
2   The *Oxford English Dictionary* provides no basis for distinguishing between 'administration' and 'management'. The definition of each refers to the other.

3   Barry Karl (1987) notes that '[f]or American reformers, the term "administration" served to focus a kind of pragmatic attention on the governing process. The term became part of en elite reform vocabulary' (p. 27).
4   'The study of administration from the point of view of management', White said, 'began with the bureaus of municipal research and was first systematically formulated in the 1920s' (White, 1926: viii). An accurate understanding of public administration's intellectual history requires the disentangling of those influences originating in problems of municipal administration, fertile ground for applications of an apolitical 'scientific management', and those originating in problems of national administration, where issues concerning legislative delegation, judicial deference and managerial accountability were more prominent.
5   As argued in Lynn (1996), public administration scholars would have been justified in claiming that their field had 'owned' the subject of public management for decades. As evidence, in addition to the citations in the text, the journal of the International City Management Association took the title *Public Management* in 1927. In 1940 a volume edited by Fritz Morstein Marx was titled *Public Management in the New Democracy* (Morstein Marx, 1940). John Millett's 1954 book *Managing in the Public Service* hits a strikingly contemporary note (Millett, 1954). A 1955 'classic' in public administration is Catheryn Seckler-Hudson's 'Basic Concepts in the Study of Public Management' (Shafritz and Hyde, 1992).
6   It is of particular interest in the United States because the combination of the constitutional separation of powers and common law tradition establishes the power of precedent which, in the case of public management, is to be found in its traditional literature.
7   A more extensive review of this literature is in Lynn (1996: 55–88).
8   According to Pollitt and Bouckaert (2000), the terms 'steering', 'guidance' and 'managerialism' are preferred to 'governance' outside the United States (for an exception, see van Heffen, Kickert and Thomassen 2000). The complex interrelationships associated with such terms have also been described by Pollitt and Bouckaert and others in terms of an input/output model.

REFERENCES

Allison, Graham T., Jr (1979) 'Public and Private Management: Are They Fundamentally Alike in All Unimportant Respects?', *Proceedings for the Public Management Research Conference*, 19–20 November. Washington, DC: Office of Personnel Management. pp. 27–38.

Appleby, Paul (1952) *Morality and Administration in Democratic Government*. New York: Greenwood Press.

Aron, Raymond (1998) *Main Currents in Sociological Thought*, Vol. 2. New Brunswick, NJ: Transaction Books.

Bardach, Eugene (1998) *Getting Agencies to Work Together: The Practice and Theory of Managerial Craftsmanship*. Washington, DC: Brookings Institution.

Barnard, Chester I. (1968) *The Functions of the Executive*. Cambridge, MA: Harvard University Press.

Behn, Robert D. (1988) 'Managing by Groping Along', *Journal of Policy Analysis and Management*, 8 (3): 643–63.

Behn, Robert D. (1991) *Leadership Counts: Lessons for Public Managers from the Massachusetts Welfare, Training, and Employment Program*. Cambridge, MA: Harvard University Press.

Bertelli, Anthony M. and Lynn, Laurence E., Jr (2001) 'A Precept of Managerial Responsibility: Securing Collective Justice in Institutional Reform Litigation', *Fordham Urban Law Journal*, 29 (1): 317–86.

Bozeman, Barry (1987) *All Organizations are Public: Bridging Public and Private Organization Theories*. San Francisco, CA: Jossey–Bass.

Christensen, Tom and Lægreid, Per (2001) *New Public Management: The Transformation of Ideas and Practice*. Aldershot: Ashgate.

Cohen, Steven and Eimicke, William (1995) *The New Effective Public Manager: Achieving Success in a Changing Government*. San Francisco, CA: Jossey–Bass.

Denhardt, Robert B. (1993) *The Pursuit of Significance: Strategies for Managerial Success in Public Organizations*. Belmont, CA: Wadsworth.

Dickinson, John (1927) *Administrative Justice and the Supremacy of Law in the United States*. Cambridge, MA: Harvard University Press.

Dimock, Marshall E. (1936) 'The Role of Discretion in Modern Administration', in John M. Gaus, Leonard D. White and Marshall E. Dimock, *The Frontiers of Public Administration*. Chicago, IL: University of Chicago Press. pp. 45–65.

Dobel, J. Patrick (1992) Review of *Impossible Jobs in Public Management*. *Journal of Policy Analysis and Management*, 11 (1): 144–47.

Fayol, Henri (1930) *Industrial and General Administration*, translated by J.A. Coubrough. Geneva: International Management Institute.

Finer, Herman (1940) 'Administrative Responsibility in Democratic Government', *Public Administration Review*, 1 (4): 335–50.

Fleishman, Joe L. (1990) 'A New Framework for Integration: Policy Analysis and Public Management', *American Behavioral Scientist*, 33 (6): 733–54.

Frederickson, H. George (1997) *The Spirit of Public Administration*. San Francisco: CA: Jossey–Bass.

Friedrich, Carl Joachim (1940) 'Public Policy and the Nature of Administrative Responsibility', in *Public Policy: A Yearbook of the Graduate School of Public Administration, Harvard University, 1940*, edited by C.J. Friedrich and Edward S. Mason. Cambridge, MA: Harvard University Press. pp. 3–24.

Goodnow, Frank J. ([1893]1902) *Comparative Administrative Law: An Analysis of the Administrative Systems National and Local, of the United States, England, France, and Germany*. New York: G.P. Putnam's Sons.

Goodnow, Frank J. (1900) *Politics and Administration*. New York: Macmillan.

Haass, Richard N. (1994) *The Power to Persuade: How to Be Effective in Government, the Public Sector, or Any Unruly Organization*. New York: Houghton Mifflin.

Haass, Richard N. (1999) *The Bureaucratic Entrepreneur: How to Be Effective in Any Unruly Organization*. Washington, DC: Brookings Institution.

Heymann, Philip B. (1987) *The Politics of Public Management*. New Haven, CT: Yale University Press.

Karl, Barry D. (1987) 'The American Bureaucrat: A History of a Sheep in Wolves' Clothing', *Public Administration Review*, 47: 26–34.

Kettl, Donald F. (1997) 'The Global Revolution in Public Management: Driving Themes, Missing Links', *Journal of Policy Analysis and Management*, 16 (3): 446–62.

Kettl, Donald F. (2000) *The Global Public Management Revolution: A Report on the Transformation of Governance*. Washington, DC: Brookings Institution.

Kickert, Walter J.M. (ed.) (1997) *Public Management and Administrative Reform in Western Europe*. Cheltenham: Edward Elgar.

Light, Paul C. (1998) *Sustaining Innovation: Creating Nonprofit and Government Organizations that Innovate Naturally*. San Francisco, CA: Jossey–Bass.

Lindblom, Charles E. (1959) 'The Science of Muddling Through', *Public Administration Review*, 19 (1): 79–88.

Lynn, Laurence E., Jr (1996) *Public Management as Art, Science, and Profession*. Chatham, NJ: Chatham House.

Lynn, Laurence E., Jr (2001) 'The Myth of the Bureaucratic Paradigm: What Traditional Public Administration Really Stood For', *Public Administration Review*, 61 (2): 144–60.

Lynn, Laurence E., Jr, Heinrich, Carolyn J. and Hill, Carolyn J. (2001) *Improving Governance: A New Logic for Empirical Research*. Washington, DC: Georgetown University Press.

Martin, Roscoe C. (1965) 'Paul H. Appleby and His Administrative World', in Roscoe C. Martin, (ed.), *Public Administration and Democracy: Essays in Honor of Paul H. Appleby*. Syracuse, NY: Syracuse University Press.

Millett, John D. (1954) *Management in the Public Service*. New York: McGraw–Hill.

Moe, Terry M. (1995) 'The Politics of Structural Choice: Toward a Theory of Public Bureaucracy', in Oliver E. Williamson (ed.), *Organization Theory: From Chester Barnard to the Present and Beyond*, expanded edn. New York: Oxford University Press, pp. 116–53.

Moore, Mark H. (1984) 'A Conception of Public Management', in *Teaching Public Management*, 1–12 Boston, MA: Public Policy and Management Program for Case and Course Development, Boston University.

Moore, Mark H. (1995) *Creating Public Value: Strategic Management in Government*. Cambridge, MA: Harvard University Press.

Morstein Marx, Fritz (1940) *Public Management in the New Democracy*. New York: Harper & Brothers.

Morstein Marx, Fritz (ed.) (1959) 'The Social Function of Public Administration', in *Elements of Public*

Administration. Englewood Cliffs, NJ: Prentice–Hall. pp. 89–109.

Mosher, Frederick C. (1968) *Democracy and the Public Service*. New York: Oxford University Press.

Mosher, Frederick C. (1992) 'Public Administration Old and New: A Letter from Frederick C. Mosher', *Journal of Public Administration Research and Theory*, 2 (2): 199–202.

Ott, J. Steven, Hyde, Alkbert C. and Shafritz, Jay M. (eds) (1991) *Public Management: The Essential Readings*. Chicago, IL: Nelson Hall.

Perry, James L. and Kraemer, Kenneth L. (1983) *Public Management: Public and Private Perspectives*. Palo Alto, CA: Mayfield.

Peters, B. Guy (1996) *The Future of Governing: Four Emerging Models*. Lawrence, KS: University Press of Kansas.

Pollitt, Christopher (2000) 'Is the Emperor in His Underwear? An Analysis of the Impacts of Public Management Reform', *Public Management*, 2 (2): 181–99.

Pollitt, Christopher and Bouckaert, Geert (2000) *Public Management Reform: A Comparative Perspective*. Oxford: Oxford University Press.

Price, Don K. (1959) 'The Judicial Test', in Fritz Morstein Marx (ed.), *Elements of Public Administration*. Englewood Cliffs, NJ: Prentice–Hall. pp. 475–99.

Rainey, Hal G. (1990) 'Public Management: Recent Developments and Current Prospects', in Naomi B. Lynn and Aaron Wildavsky (eds), *Public Administration: The State of the Discipline*. Chatham, NJ: Chatham House. pp. 157–84.

Rainey, Hal G. (1997) *Understanding and Managing Public Organizations*, 2nd edn. San Francisco, CA: Jossey–Bass.

Redford, Emmette S. (1969) *Democracy in the Administrative State*. New York: Oxford University Press.

Reich, Robert B. (1990) *Public Management in a Democratic Society*. Englewood Cliffs, NJ: Prentice–Hall.

Rescher, Nicholas (1998) *Complexity: A Philosophical Overview*. New Brunswick, NJ: Transaction Books.

Rohr, John A. (1986) *To Run a Constitution*. Lawrence, KS: University Press of Kansas.

Rosenbloom, David H. (1998) *Understanding Management, Politics, and Law in the Public Sector*. New York: McGraw–Hill.

Scott, W. Richard (1998) *Organizations: Rational, Natural, and Open Systems*, 4th edn. Upper Saddle River, NJ: Prentice–Hall.

Shafritz, Jay M. and Albert C. Hyde (eds) (1992) *Classics of Public Administration*. Pacific Grove, CA: Brooks/Cole.

Simon, Herbert A., Smithburg, Donald W. and Thompson, Victor A. (1950) *Public Administration*. New York: Knopf.

Stamp, Josiah C. (1923) 'The Contrast Between the Administration of Business and Public Affairs', *Journal of Public Administration*, 1: 158–71.

Stokes, Donald E. (1986) 'Political and Organizational Analysis in the Policy Curriculum', *Journal of Policy Analysis and Management*, 6 (1): 45–55.

van Heffen, Oscar, Kickert, Walter J.M. and Thomassen, Jacques J.A. (2000) *Governance in Modern Society: Effects, Change and Formation of Government Institutions*. Dordrecht, NL: Kluwer Academic Publishers.

Van Riper, Paul P. (1990) 'Administrative Thought in the 1880s', in Paul P. Van Riper (ed.), *The Wilson Influence on Public Administration: From Theory to Practice*. Washington, DC: American Society for Public Administration. pp. 7–16.

Waldo, Dwight (1984) *The Administrative State*, 2nd edn. New York: Holmes and Meier.

Wallace, Schuyler C. (1941) *Federal Departmentalization: A Critique of Theories of Organization*. New York: Columbia University Press.

Wamsley, Gary L. (1990) 'The Agency Perspective: Public Administrators as Agential Leaders', in Gary L. Wamsley et al. (eds), *Refounding Public Administration*. Newbury Park, CA: Sage.

Weimer, David L. (1995) 'Institutional design: an overview', in David L. Weimer (ed.), *Institutional Design*. Boston, MA: Kluwer Academic Publishers.

White, Leonard D. (1926) *Introduction to the Study of Public Administration*', New York: Macmillan.

Wilson, James Q. (1989) *Bureaucracy: What Government Agencies Do and Why They Do It*. New York: Basic Books.

Wilson, Woodrow (1887) 'The Study of Administration', *Political Science Quarterly*, 1 (2): 197–222.

Wren, Daniel (1979) *The Evolution of Management Thought*, 2nd edn. New York: Wiley.

2

Measuring Public Sector Performance and Effectiveness

Carolyn J. Heinrich

In *Beyond Machiavelli: Policy Analysis Comes of Age*, Beryl Radin (2000a: 168) observes: 'If there is a single theme that characterizes the public sector in the 1990s, it is the demand for performance. A mantra has emerged in this decade, heard at all levels of government, that calls for documentation of performance and explicit outcomes of government action.' Responding to increasing demands for performance documentation, governments in the United States, Canada, Western Europe, New Zealand, Australia and in countries in Asia, Africa and Latin America have made performance measurement a core component of public management reforms (Behn, 2001; Kettl and DiIulio, 1995; Pollitt and Bouckaert, 2000). While the broad objectives of these reforms to promote more 'effective, efficient, and responsive government' are the same as those of reforms introduced more than a century ago, what is new are the increasing scope, sophistication and external visibility of performance measurement activities, impelled by legislative requirements aimed at holding governments accountable for *outcomes* (Gore, 1993: xxiii; Pollitt and Bouckaert, 2000). The ramifications of reform initiatives that mandate formal, outcomes-based performance measurement in public programs are being debated by public management scholars and practitioners, with discourse extending from the 'New Public Management' (NPM) reforms to local level performance contracts that aim to 'use market forces to hold the public sector accountable' (Kaboolian, 1998: 191; Lægreid, 2000; Radin, 2000b).

Accountability – to legislative bodies, taxpayers and program stakeholders – is a primary goal of public sector performance measurement. In *The International Encyclopedia of Public Policy and Administration*, Romzek and Dubnick (1998: 6) define accountability as 'a relationship in which an individual or agency is held to answer for performance that involves some delegation of authority to act'. By this definition, accountability compels some measure or appraisal of performance, particularly of those individuals and agencies with the authority to act on behalf of the public. A historical review of public sector performance measurement shows that the majority of initiatives have focused on holding agencies or executive administrators accountable for financial performance or efficiency. Behn (2001) describes 'accountability for finances' as a 'rules, procedures and standards' form of accountability. The NPM and other recent reform initiatives, which ostensibly differ from earlier approaches in their promotion of a 'customer service' focus, 'market-driven management', and accountability for 'results', are also still concerned with 'saving money' and 'productive and allocational efficiencies' (or a government that 'costs less') (Kaboolian, 1998; Pollitt and Bouckaert, 2000; Terry, 1998).

If, however, the legacy of public management reform is likely to be a 'stronger emphasis on performance-motivated administration' that advances the art of public management, as Lynn (1998: 232) suggests, then public sector performance measurement has to involve more than accounting for finances and 'answering for performance'. As John Kamensky (1993: 395) exhorts, 'there have been enough paperwork exercises in government'. We need to develop measures that will inform and be used by public managers, not only 'accountability holders' such as legislators and oversight agencies, to guide them in improving service quality and results. This begs the question: What information is most useful for public managers striving to improve government performance? For example, under the US Government Performance and Results Act (GPRA) or the United Kingdom's Next Steps, how do public managers use the information from annual program performance reports that compare measured performance with performance goals? Simply knowing that they have achieved or failed to achieve target objectives or standards is not likely to aid public managers in understanding *why* performance is at the level it is or *how* managers can effect change. As Hatry (1999: 6) observes: 'A major purpose of performance measurement is to raise questions' it seldom, if ever, provides answers by itself as to what should be done.'

The types of questions public managers can answer depend critically on the types of performance information that are collected. Kamensky (1993) and Hatry (1999), for example, distinguish among categories of performance information that include: (1) input information (for example, resources and staff); (2) process information (such as workload and job complexity); (3) efficiency information (such as productivity and unit costs); (4) outputs (products and services delivered); (5) outcomes (in relation to intermediate or end goals), including quality assessment; and (6) impact information. In an ideal performance measurement system, the full range of information – from inputs to outcomes or impacts – would be used by public managers in a logical flow, linking performance monitoring (of ongoing processes, efficiency and outputs) to performance evaluation (of program outcomes and/or impacts) to performance management; that is, using performance information to guide program planning and improve future performance (Osborne et al., 1995).

Supported by public management reforms and aided by advances in information technology, some performance measurement activities are progressing toward this ideal, providing public managers with more information about how and the extent to which programs are contributing to outcomes or impacts (Abramson and Kamensky, 2001). This chapter focuses largely on these 'state-of-the-art' performance measurement approaches, although a broader range of performance measurement activities and processes are also discussed. In the following section,

an interdisciplinary review of public sector performance measurement approaches is presented, integrated with a discussion of literatures on performance measurement and management/ organizational effectiveness. The 'state of the art' is described next, including challenges and prospects for improving performance measurement systems and increasing their usefulness to public managers at all levels of government. The concluding section summarizes major points and discusses the prospects for continuing advances in public sector performance measurement.

A CHRONOLOGICAL REVIEW OF LITERATURES AND SYSTEMS OF PERFORMANCE MEASUREMENT

An interdisciplinary review of historical and contemporary conceptions of performance measurement highlights the diversity in disciplinary perspectives and approaches to this subject. Human resource management scholars, for example, trace the origins of performance measurement to the development of employee rating forms based on psychological traits by industrial psychologists in the 1800s (Scott et al., 1941). The US Federal Civil Service has used these types of performance ratings, narrowly focused on individual performance, since at least the late 1800s (Murphy and Cleveland, 1995).

A more generic view of public sector performance measurement, also originating in the late 1800s, can be traced to scholars and experts who called for the government to become more rational and efficient like the private sector. This perspective emerged early in the writings of Woodrow Wilson (1887), who proposed a new 'scientific' or more 'business-like' approach to administration, and was later elaborated by members of the 'scientific management' movement in the early 1900s. Scientific management promoted the careful analysis of workers' tasks and work arrangements, with the objective of maximizing efficiency by 'planning [work] procedures according to a technical logic, setting standards, and exercising controls to ensure conformity with standards' (Taylor, 1911; Thompson, 1967: 5). The 1910 Taft Commission on Economy and Efficiency, one of the first of a series of major US commissions aimed at improving the executive management and performance of government, was significantly influenced by scientific management ideas. Shades of the rational and technical logic of scientific management are also evident in recent performance measurement initiatives such as GPRA, Next Steps and Taiwan's Research, Development and Evaluation Commission, which require agencies to develop strategic plans for achieving specific, quantitatively measurable goals and annual performance reports that compare actual performance with performance goals or standards.

By the 1930s, scholars of 'administrative management', such as Gulick and Urwick (1937), were shifting public discussion from the micro-level design of efficient work tasks and procedures to the structure of large administrative systems. The writings of administrative management influenced major government reform proposals, including the report by the 1936–7 Brownlow Committee on Administrative Management. Like scientific management, these reforms centered on improving government efficiency, yet the Brownlow Committee report also made a point to distinguish administrative management from scientific management, declaring the 'administrative efficiency is not merely a matter of paper clips, time clocks, and standardized economies of motion … [but] must be built into the structure of government just as it is built into a piece of machinery' (1937: 16). The structural reforms proposed by the committee called for the delegation of power within hierarchical structures to managers with 'administrative expertise'. As Feldman and Khademian (2000: 152) observe, 'that expertise would be exercised within rules, regulations, and administrative structures established by political overseers and top managers'. Performance measurement activities of the administrative management era primarily involved auditing of inputs and outputs and fiscal accountability at department – or higher – organization levels where control was centralized and administrative decisions were checked (Rosenbloom, 1986).

At the same time, the organization theorist Chester Barnard (1938), in a watershed work that diverged from the administrative management perspective, was urging greater attention to the integral role of incentives in organizations (for example, money, status, power, autonomy) and the 'social character' of cooperative systems. Barnard suggested that individuals' social interactions and awareness of their relative positions in a 'hierarchy of rewards' would be more influential motivators of performance than clear channels of hierarchical authority and rule-based processes for producing outputs (Pfeffer, 1990).

Into the 1940s and following the Second World War, however, Barnard's ideas about the importance of social relations and incentives in formal organizations were still having little appreciable influence on government performance

management. Instead, ongoing concerns about the size and efficiency of government led to two more major commissions – the First (1947–49) and Second (1953–55) Hoover Commissions – to 'promote economy, efficiency, and improved service in the transaction of the public business …' (Hoover Commission Report, 1949: xiii). The Commissions' reviews of the organizational structure and performance of the US executive branch reflected former President Hoover's beliefs, adhering to some principles of scientific management, that 'management research technicians' should advise policy and executive agency decisions (Moe, 1982). The series of management reforms that followed included the 1960s Planning, Programming, Budgeting System (PPBS), which featured a 'systems analysis' approach to central planning, objective analysis of programs *based on research and evaluation*, and multi-year plans and budgets. Central governments in other countries such as The Netherlands (with its Government Accounts Act of 1976) readily adopted the PPBS or performance budgeting approach and continue performance budgeting activities in some form today.

Also gaining recognition at this time, the Management by Objectives (MBO) approach, advanced by Drucker (1954) and later adopted by the Nixon administration, departed from administrative and scientific management approaches by prodding performance measurement systems to involve both organization- and individual-level performance measures. The MBO approach, still in use in many public and private organizations, aimed to link *organizational* planning for financial, technical and strategic performance goals with *employee* actions and objectives through their input in participatory processes, feedback from management and financial rewards allocated on the basis of measured organizational progress. Unlike the top-down, rules-based focus of administrative management, which social-psychologists had criticized by for its 'mechanical view' of individuals, MBO sought to coordinate objectives at top and lower organizational levels and to give explicit consideration to employees' understanding of goals and rewards for improving performance (Campbell et al., 1970).

Still, while attractive to government reformers at first, the limitations of PPBS, MBO and similar systems such as Zero-Base Budgeting (ZBB) that required managers to narrowly define and measure progress toward financial, technical and strategic performance goals became more evident over time. Thompson (1967: 4–6) described these types of performance measurement systems as 'closed-system' strategies. In a closed or rational model system, there are a relatively small number of variables for managers to control, and they can reliably predict their relationships. Goals and production tasks are known, organizational objectives are verifiable, resources are available and employees are responsive to incentives (that is, self-interest dominates) (Simon, 1957). As a result, they are more likely to be effective when managers are able to achieve clarity, consensus and consistency about organizational goals such as economic performance or efficiency in service delivery. MBO-type approaches to performance measurement are more commonly used today by local governments, where budgetary accountability and service efficiency are focal public priorities (Rivenbark, 2001).

As dissatisfaction with these rational model approaches to performance evaluation was growing, organization and management theories were evolving toward more open, adaptive system models that assumed, instead of closure, 'that a system contains more variables than we can comprehend at one time, or that some variables are subject to influences we cannot control or predict' (Thompson, 1967: 6). Thompson (1967) cited the study of 'informal organization' as an example of an open-system approach, and referring to Barnard's (1938) work, described variables such as cliques, social controls based on informal norms and status that influence the performance and 'survival' of organizations. These open-system and contingency theories – that relate organizational structures and functioning to their contexts or environments – broadened the array of variables viewed as important in managing organizational performance and measuring the contributions of public managers to organization outcomes.

Perhaps the most prominent example of a more open, adaptive system approach to performance analysis that emerged at this time was W. Edwards Deming's Total Quality Management (TQM) system. Deming (1986) challenged the 'narrow, simple-minded' focus of rational 'management by the numbers, management by MBO' approaches on bottom-line cost and efficiency targets and urged managers to instead strive for and measure *quality* (Kelly, 1998: 202; Walton, 1986). Quality-focused (TQM) systems feature long-term commitment by top managers to continuous quality improvement, full involvement by employees at all organizational levels and a shared 'vision' of quality, a customer orientation and the 'systematic collection and analysis of data' that are expected to indicate where potential for quality improvement lies (Halachmi, 1995: 266). Acknowledging the challenges of assessing quality, that is, the higher level of knowledge and information that is required to evaluate and manage performance in terms of quality and the importance of factors outside the control of employees, Deming strongly advocated the use of statistical analysis to understand the causal influence of systemic and situational/environmental factors on performance.

The influence of TQM ideas and their focus on quality or results, in conjunction with the decline of systems more narrowly aimed at increasing outputs and efficiency such as PPBS, were accelerating the advance of public sector performance measurement toward outcomes-based measurement systems. In the early 1980s, for example, under the Reagan administration's New Federalism, the US Job Training Partnership Act (JTPA) introduced a performance measurement system that has been described as a 'pioneer' of outcomes-based performance management (Barnow, 2000).[1] The JTPA performance measurement system was distinct in its focus on program outcomes (for example, job placements and trainee earnings) rather than outputs (the number of persons trained), the use of budgetary incentives for managers based on *outcomes* and the linking of performance measures across federal, state and local governments. It also incorporated the use of regression models with performance data to statistically adjust performance standards for local population characteristics and economic conditions.

Another example of a public sector performance management system that was working to infuse quality management principles and moving toward a focus on results, or 'value for money' (VFM), was the United Kingdom's Financial Management Initiative (FMI) of 1983. As Osborne et al. (1995: 20) explain, VFM was assessed by measuring 'economy, efficiency and effectiveness', but with 'an explicit concern with organizational structures and processes likely to lead to the 'three Es'; of 'management' as opposed to 'administration' as the task of senior staff in the public sector; and of decentralization, especially of budget holding, as an integral dimension of organizational design'. Both Reagan's and Thatcher's initiatives incorporated at least three of the four public management reform principles that were emerging in the 'reinventing government' and NPM reforms of the 1990s: (1) measure results, (2) put the customer in the driver's seat, (3) introduce a market orientation and (4) decentralize (Gore, 1993).

This light probing of the history of performance measurement and public management reforms shows the progression of public sector performance measurement away from a more rational or technical focus on work procedures and process efficiency and a top-down, hierarchical approach to accountability for organization inputs and outputs, and toward more participatory, multi-level systems that consider a broader range of factors affecting performance while maintaining an explicit focus on the outcomes or results of programs. Barbara Romzek (1998) has more generally described these emerging approaches to performance measurement as systems of *professional* accountability. Professional accountability, as Romzek (1998: 204) explains, defers to the discretion of managers 'as they work within broad parameters, rather than on close scrutiny to ensure compliance with detailed rules and organizational directives'. The broad parameters in public sector performance measurement systems of the twenty-first century are outcomes, and a central challenge for public managers is to effectively use the different types of information obtained through performance measurement activities to better understand the link between their own actions and these more broadly defined organizational goals and outcomes.

THE STATE OF THE ART IN PERFORMANCE MEASUREMENT: CHALLENGES AND PROSPECTS

As the introduction and preceding review suggest, there are some important commonalities across local and national boundaries among evolving public sector performance measurement systems. The more prominent features include:

1 performance measures focused on quality, outcomes or results;
2 formal report requirements for comparing actual performance with performance goals or standards;
3 multiple levels of performance accountability in decentralized programs; and
4 market-oriented provisions such as financial/ budgetary incentives for performance, as in the JTPA program, and plans to use performance information to promote continuous improvement and increased citizen ('customer') satisfaction.

It is also clear, however, that public managers are still struggling with how to make the 'state-of-the-art' systems work.

Challenges

One challenge public managers confront in broadening performance measures beyond more straightforward, bottom-line targets (such as efficiency) to a focus on outcomes are problems in reaching a consensus – at all levels of organization and management – on clearly defined, verifiable public objectives. In a review of agency performance plans, the US Government Accounting Office (US GAO, 1999: 6) stated that 'mission fragmentation and program overlap are widespread across the federal government'. Sometimes the multiplicity or fragmentation of goals are inherent in originating legislation, making it more difficult for public managers to get staff and stakeholders to think about how their diverse activities are related to a common outcome. The JTPA legislation, for example, stated that programs should serve 'those who can benefit from, and are most in need of' employment and training services. Heckman and Smith (1995) established empirically the tradeoff between these equity and efficiency goals in JTPA programs, showing that targeting those most in need (the bottom 20 per cent of the skill distribution) significantly lowered the value-added gains from program participation.

Behn (2001) contends that public managers can 'jump this hoop' and avoid goal conflicts by choosing vague, uncontroversial, inconsequential, or easily attainable goals (effectively repudiating the requirement). In Lindblom's (1959: 576) classic work on 'the science of muddling through', he notes that 'much of organization theory argues the virtues of common values and agreed organizational objectives', but when administrators cannot agree on values or objectives, the preservation of a diversity of views and fragmented decision making, where some parts of the organization provide a check on others, is an acceptable strategy for managing complex policies and problems.

Agencies' choices for performance objectives have important implications, however, for the complex task of determining quantitative measures of performance goals. If objectives are broadly or vaguely defined, or if multiple goals are in conflict, it will be more challenging to specify accurate and informative measures. For example, the US Department of Veterans' Affairs Veterans Health Administration defined its goal to 'improve the health status of veterans' and identified performance measures of cost reductions per patient and the number of patients served to evaluate progress (US GAO, 1999: 23). The disparities between this health quality goal and the input/efficiency performance measures used are glaring. Alternatively, Anne Khademian (1995) concluded in her study of the US Federal Deposit Insurance Corporation (FDIC) that a clear mandate about organizational objectives, that is, the solvency of the Bank Insurance Fund, and an explicit measure of organizational performance toward that objective, were important motivators and guides for agency professionals and managers who facilitated key changes to lead the agency out of crisis.

In the case of the FDIC, the measure of the Bank Insurance Fund's solvency was directly related to the central organizational goal of protecting the health of banks; as Khademian (1995: 19) explains, 'to the extent that failures can be prevented through effective examination and supervision, the fund will remain sound'. In their discussion of performance outcome measures, Gormley and Weimer (1999: 9) point out that 'direct measures of outcomes require no relational theories as they are operationalizations of conceptualized values'. As measures become more distant from outcomes, associated through hypothesized relationships and proxy or scalar variables (for example, test scores for school performance, mortality rates for health care services), verification becomes more complex and the degree of uncertainty in performance analysis increases.

An additional challenge for public managers is that performance requirements may contribute to what Bouckaert (1993: 403) describes as the 'time-shortening disease', which 'makes the organization focus on the short instead of on the intermediate or long run'. Agency executives report that it is especially difficult to translate their long-term missions or strategic goals into annual performance goals and to predict the level of results that might be achieved over a shorter term (US GAO, 1997a; Cabinet Office, 1998). John Ahearne, a former high-ranking official in the energy field, described GPRA's performance requirements as disastrous for the US Department of Energy's nuclear waste clean-up programs, as they can shift managers' attention to short-term goals that will likely impede progress toward longer-term clean-up and environmental health objectives (decades into the future).

If shorter-term performance objectives and their measures are strongly correlated with longer-term program goals and impacts, public managers might avoid this dilemma. Research on public programs suggests, however, that one is likely to err in assuming a positive correlation between short-term measures and long-term organizational performance. In their studies of federal job training programs, Heckman and

Smith (1995) and Barnow (2000) showed that short-term performance measures of participants' employment rates and earnings levels following program discharge were at best weakly (and sometimes negatively) related to longer-term employment and earnings impacts estimated using experimental data. Burghardt and Schochet (2001) of the US National Job Corps Study compared impact estimates from an experimental study of education and earnings outcomes across Job Corps centers rated as high-, medium- and low-performers by the Job Corps performance measurement system and found that the Job Corps performance measurement system failed to distinguish between more and less effective centers. In addition, studies of school effectiveness have found that some teachers respond to performance requirements based on student test scores by 'teaching to the test', with likely negative implications for students' longer-term educational success (Gormely and Weimer, 1999; Koretz, 1999).

At least one US GAO report (1997b) has suggested supplementing performance data with impact evaluation studies to obtain a more precise understanding of program effects and to verify (or disprove) relationships between short-term measures and long-term goals. The National JTPA and Job Corps Studies are examples of these types of evaluations. A primary advantage of experimental impact evaluations is their potential to identify causal linkages and the 'unique contribution' that an organization makes to outcomes (Hatry, 1999; Bloom et al., 2001). A disadvantage is that multi-site experiments are frequently costly and potentially disruptive to program operations. While they are unlikely to generate the timely, regular feedback that public managers require to produce performance reports and make adjustments (in budget allocations, service strategies, management practices etc.) to improve performance, they do provide an important check on the performance measurement systems routinely used (as in the case of the Job Corps program.)

A final issue or challenge embedded in this discussion is the level of accountability and analysis in performance measurement systems. In organization science and public administration literatures, a conventional view distinguishes 'top-down' and 'bottom-up' approaches to performance accountability. The government of New Zealand, for example, only holds officials at the top (policy making) level accountable for program outcomes, exempting public managers and personnel in operating departments from performance requirements (Hatry, 1999). Bottom-up approaches, alternatively, focus on performance management activities originating at a lower level that have emergent properties at higher levels. TQM, for example, has been described as a bottom-up approach to improving organizational performance, where individual TQM training, work behaviors and social interactions combine at a lower level and emerge over time to influence organizational outcomes. The fact is, however, that in a majority of organizations, performance analysis is likely occurring at more than one level of organization. As DeNisi (2000: 121) explains, performance measurement is 'both a multi-level and a cross-level phenomenon'; either explicitly (as in the JTPA performance measurement system) or informally, public managers at multiple levels of organization measure performance, and activities and responses at one level are likely to have effects at other levels. Bouckaert (1993: 38) describes this as a 'top-down and bottom-up interaction'. He argues that the more the bottom and middle management are involved in performance measurement activities, the greater their commitment to them.

The challenge for public managers and researchers is to ascertain and understand the effects, multi-level and cross-level, planned and unintended, occurring in performance measurement systems. In studies of the implementation of GPRA, for example, Radin (2000a) and Mintzberg (1996) conclude that rather than freeing public managers to focus on results, the performance requirements have increased administrative constraints, elevated conflict among multiple levels of program management, and engendered distrust between agencies and legislators about gaming of measures. In their study of the JTPA program, Courty and Marschke (1997) showed empirically how some local program managers chose to 'game' the federal performance standards in order to increase their agencies' measured performance in ways independent of actual performance. Given the limited or indirect influence that public managers commonly have on organizational outcomes and the difficulties of separating out effects of multiple layers of policy and management, managers' desire to manipulate performance measures in ways that will improve their *measured* but *not actual* performance is understandable, if not acceptable.

Prospects

A central theme of this chapter is that rather than simply documenting performance outcomes, public sector performance measurement activities

and research should help public managers to understand how their own policy and management decisions are linked to outcomes and the systemic and situational factors that might constrain or intervene in these relationships to affect performance. Along these lines, Laurence E. Lynn, Jr (1998: 236), deliberating the 'legacy' of the New Public Management, urged a 'theory-based research agenda' that addresses questions about how and to what extent institutions, leadership and management influence government performance or 'the creation of effective, accountable democratic states'. Rainey and Steinbauer (1999) reviewed the literature on government effectiveness and also called for a more theoretical approach to research on government performance, in particular, theories linking the organization, management, resources and external stakeholders of agencies to their effectiveness. As Bouckaert (1993) implores, 'performance measures have to contribute to the maintenance or to the development of the organization itself'. The theoretical 'building blocks' for this undertaking exist; the corresponding challenge is to integrate the intellectual contributions of multiple disciplines in an analytical framework that will produce, on an ongoing basis, useful information and insights for public managers.

Context, process and level of analysis

A major concern about performance accountability, public managers profess, is that their responsibility is not commensurate with their authority (Mintzberg, 1996). As Lynn, Heinrich and Hill (2001) note, public policies and programs are being administered through increasingly complex, decentralized governance structures, including networks, collaborations and partnerships among public, nonprofit and for-profit organizations. In accounting for performance across 'diverse and dispersed' administrative entities and service units, many of which may operate in varying social, political, and fiscal contexts, public managers need to achieve a tenable balance between demands for analytical rigor and accuracy in performance measurement and political and practical limitations on what is feasible to measure in complex governing systems. Furthermore, if results are publicized and agencies are rewarded or penalized for performance, then performance standards have to take into account the ability of agencies or managers to effect change and contribute to improved outcomes or program value-added.

One strategy promoted in some public management reform circles is to adopt a narrower focus on a single, relatively straightforward measure of performance such as a scalar measure of client/citizen satisfaction. Described as 'bottom-up accountability', holding governments accountable to citizens (voters) is seen as 'replicating the virtues of the marketplace' (Gormley and Weimer, 1999: 198). This approach assumes that public managers can ignore context and levels and also assumes that citizens are sufficiently informed to provide reliable feedback. Research on the determinants of citizens' attitudes and their evaluations of public activities and services, however, shows 'considerable ambivalence and volatility in their preferences' and 'inconsistent evaluations of services and taxes', reflecting their own conflicting attitudes, values and perspectives (Beck et al., 1990: 71–2). Thus, public managers are not likely to get a clear picture of whether or not government performance is improving simply by tracking citizen satisfaction ratings.

At another extreme, scholars might collaborate with public managers to construct and apply multidisciplinary, theory-based models of organizational performance that fully account for all potential interrelationships within and between organizations, employee and client/citizen characteristics, and intervening political and environmental factors. For example, sociologists and social-psychologists identify contextual factors such as organizational complexity, coordination, climate, culture and values, competition among or within functional units, and individual member characteristics, cognitive and social behaviors that affect performance (Marcoulides and Heck, 1993; Murphy and Cleveland, 1995). Political scientists highlight the influence of legislative mandates and coalitions, bureaucratic discretion and control, political ideology and values, and other dynamics of political processes. Economists focus on the role of information asymmetries, transaction costs, monetary incentives and competition, among other variables affecting public sector performance management (Dixit, 1999). In formulating a model to evaluate performance, including a broad range of variables at multiple levels of government organization or structure, one would confront many obvious conceptual and methodological challenges.

In view of these formidable challenges, public administration/management scholars, along with public managers, have been striving to elucidate a constructive 'middle ground' for public sector performance measurement. While there is no singular strategy or archetype that all public managers might adapt and use, there are a number of well-articulated theoretical and analytical models that executive administrators might draw upon in developing more effective systems for measuring and managing government performance. The differing capabilities and needs for collecting and analyzing performance data among government agencies performing different functions at different levels of government also has implications for the strategy or approach to performance measurement they might use. The models discussed below explicitly consider context, process, levels of analysis and the data available to public managers in measuring performance and evaluating the relationship of management to outcomes.

Models for public sector performance measurement and their application

Hatry (1999) presents a 'logical model' of 'relevant factors' in a performance measurement system – one that links inputs, activities, outputs and outcomes – and describes the relationships among these different types of performance information. His very simple model does not formally identify the influence of context or environmental factors nor the relationships among performance measures across different levels of government or analysis. However, he calls for public managers to obtain 'explanatory information' along with their performance data – from qualitative assessments by program personnel to in-depth program evaluations that produce statistically reliable information – to interpret the data and identify problems and possible management or organizational responses.

In their 'revised rationalist model of performance assessment' that acknowledges the 'bounded rationality' of public managers, political interests and other contextual and catalytic influences, Osborne et al. (1995) incorporate the same basic elements as Hatry's model but develop a more complex, formal model or framework for understanding the role and influence of Hatry's 'explanatory' factors. Like Hatry's model, their framework depicts the types and purposes of different performance monitoring/ measurement activities and performance indicators and data required for measures.[2] They also identify different levels and frequency of monitoring/measurement in public programs and combine the different types of performance information with three *levels* of measurement – the project/team level, program level and strategic (local or national senior management) level – to construct a multidimensional 'matrix-framework' for assessing performance that recognizes different types of monitoring/ measurement will occur at different levels. In applying their model in a study of the British Social Programme of the Rural Development Commission, they recounted the dearth of information for all types of monitoring and measures and the challenges of integrating performance assessment practices at multiple levels into a 'holistic framework of performance management' (Osborne et al., 1995: 30). The main strength of their model for public managers lies in its use for conceptually organizing and planning a system of performance data collection.

In an approach that moves closer toward program evaluation in explaining performance, Mead (forthcoming) describes 'performance analysis' as a strategy that aims 'to relate the practices of programs to measures of performance'. The performance studies he sets forth as exemplars involve statistical modeling to associate program features with performance outcomes, while controlling for demographics, economic conditions and other contextual factors. Mead urges researchers to use field interviews with program administrators to gain an in-depth understanding of how programs operate and to guide the development of hypotheses for statistical analysis. Public managers who possess this information would need to develop operational definitions and measures of administrative practices, organizational capacity and other program-level variables that could be monitored and used in statistical analysis. In Mead's generally conceptualized statistical model for evaluating performance, the dependent variable is a program-level performance indicator. His approach is probably best regarded, as he describes it, as a quantitative *process* research methodology applied at a specific level of analysis.[3]

Mead's approach to statistically modeling the processes and practices of programs and their relationship to performance measures is taken a step further in a multi-level, organizing framework for performance analysis advanced by Lynn, Heinrich and Hill (2001). Their framework delineates a hierarchy of relationships (across multiple levels of government) among: legislative and political choice (that is, responsibilities for implementing public law), governance structures, management strategies, core technologies and organizational functions, outcomes and client/ citizen assessments. Heinrich and Lynn (2000) describe a number of applications of this framework – in studies of public school performance, welfare and job-training program outcomes, and health care services outcomes – that use a multilevel statistical modeling strategy to identify causal relationships within and across

hierarchical levels of government and in a broader environmental context, while recognizing the potential influence of unmeasured factors on performance analysis findings. Bloom, Hill and Riccio (2001), for example, recently completed a multi-level re-analysis of data from the multi-site Job Opportunities and Basic Skills (JOBS) evaluation. In analyzing the effects of program management, services, economic environment and client characteristics on the earnings of welfare-to-work clients across local offices, they found that *management choices and practices* related to goals, client–staff interfaces and service strategies had substantive, statistically significant effects on client outcomes and impacts.

Some public managers and scholars interested in following a more advanced analytical and statistical approach to performance analysis might be constrained by the data requirements and costs associated with data collection and analysis. The best data typically available to public managers for ongoing performance analyses are administrative data that are regularly and consistently collected in support of an organization's functions. Administrative data commonly include detailed information about clients of public programs, their progression through program services and outcomes, and the marginal costs of collecting data across multiple programs, sites or fiscal years are generally low. Goerge (1999) notes that nearly every Federal and state program in the United States now has a database for administrative and performance management.

Recent studies that compare the use of experimental data (for estimating program impacts) with regularly collected administrative data on program operations and outcomes generate encouraging findings for public managers about the potential for using administrative data in performance management (Hill, 2001; Heinrich, 2002). Hill and Heinrich both find that relying on administrative data to generate information about *how* to improve program performance is not likely to misdirect managers away from program impact goals, although particular estimates of the magnitude of outcomes may differ from those of the size of impacts. If governments with administrative data systems are able to incorporate data fields that describe management policies and processes across sites or local service locations, public managers might more effectively use administrative and performance data to understand the effects of different policies and approaches to managing and delivering government services.

The analytical models highlighted here, and their applications in measuring and managing public sector performance, are clearly moving toward more in-depth investigations of how outcomes are produced. As Hatry (1999: 8) explains, 'performance measurement can be considered a field of program evaluation', where program evaluations 'not only examine a program's outcomes but also identify the *whys*, including the extent to which the program actually caused the outcomes'. As the time and costs involved in these performance measurement/ evaluation approaches continue to decline with advances in information technology, their recognition as viable strategies for improving the quality and usefulness of performance information available to public managers (and the resulting performance outcomes) is likely to grow.

CONCLUSION

Distinct from the 1990s public sector theme calling for documentation of explicit government outcomes, this chapter elaborates another theme, calling for performance *management* that goes beyond documentation of outcomes. It advocates the collection and use of performance information that will aid public managers in understanding *how* their decisions and actions are linked to outcomes, and what environmental or contextual factors might limit or increase their effectiveness as managers.

The historical review of performance measurement and organizational effectiveness literatures showed that scholars and managers have long recognized the influence of a range of organizational, individual-level and contextual factors on organizational performance. Until recently, the analytical challenges of separating out the role and effects of policy and management from other factors were beyond the technical capabilities of performance analysis. With advances in data collection and storage, theory and statistical modeling, and computing capacity, we have an obligation to increase our understanding of the contributions public managers *can* make to organizational performance and what realistic expectations for results are, given the context and environment in which they operate.

The examples of models for performance measurement described in this chapter suggest an ambitious path for future research and performance measurement activities, while also recognizing that the differing functions, levels, capabilities, resources and objectives of government organizations will influence the strategy or approach to performance measurement they use.

Where resources for performance are fewer, initial goals for using performance data may have to be modest, following an approach like that outlined by Hatry (1999). In North Carolina, for example, local governments cooperate in data collection activities that allow for the production of comparative measures of service efficiency and fiscal performance. Local government officials then participate in dialogues that encourage the sharing and discussion of information about 'explanatory factors' – management practices, service processes and local environment and population characteristics – to help them to understand differences or disparities in observed performance. While there is no formal modeling of relationships between possible explanatory variables and performance measures, the project has established a support structure for the types of discussions that may continue to advance the use of performance data across sites and in a broader management context. As Rivenbark (2001: v) comments, 'The cities and counties that participate in the North Carolina project do not endure the challenges of data collection, cleaning, and reporting simply to produce a report. They participate with the belief that performance measurement and benchmarking are the catalysts to service or process improvement.'

The importance of work that has been done in the 1990s, in the context of public management reforms, to advance the use of government administrative data and to link these data across programs or to other databases with economic/ environmental/contextual data (for example, local labor market information data) should not be underestimated. A recent University of California data study, involving twenty-six US states and nine social service program areas, identified over 100 examples where administrative databases had been linked across programs or levels to facilitate multi-site and/or multi-level analyses of program dynamics and performance (UC Data, 1999). In their discussion of organizational 'report cards,' Gormley and Weimer (1999) describe a number of other examples of national, state and local government organizations that collect data regularly and 'transform' them into information that can be interpreted by external audiences and used to assess and improve performance.

At the same time, this chapter also addressed some of the continuing challenges and tradeoffs in performance measurement between: comprehensive or broadly defined goals and precision of measures; short-term, measurable objectives and long-term program goals; and more simple, direct approaches to documenting and understanding performance outcomes versus more complex statistical strategies for performance analysis that aim to identify performance drivers or the causal influences of systemic and environmental factors on performance. Public managers and scholars will have to decide how to continue balancing these tradeoffs, guided by the performance management questions they are addressing, the data available to them and their capacity for analyzing data. In the face of these challenges and complexities, we, as a public, also need to acknowledge that some quantitative performance measures will be indicators at best and not highly accurate or informative measures of a program's value or effectiveness. Our 'demands for performance' documentation should focus more on what public managers can learn about *how* to improve performance and less on the precise measurement of performance levels or 'bottom-line' outcomes.

NOTES

1 Because of the comparatively long tenure of outcomes-based standards in the JTPA program and its distinctively advanced use of statistical analysis in determining performance ratings, I draw additional examples from the JTPA performance standards experience throughout this chapter.

2 Among the types of performance monitoring and measures, Osborne et al. include: 'context monitoring' (e.g., of changing socioeconomic and institutional factors); three types of input/process assessment ('strategy', 'progress' and 'activity' monitoring); 'impact' measures, both quantitative and qualitative, that evaluate performance 'against the highest level objectives and targets'; and 'catalytic monitoring' of influences or impacts on the wider service delivery system, other agencies or people (Osborne et al., 1995: 27).

3 Mead applies his 'performance analysis' approach in a study of welfare reform outcomes in Wisconsin.

REFERENCES

Abramson, Mark A. and Kamensky, John M. (2001) *Managing for Results 2002*. Lanham, MA: Rowman & Littlefield.

Barnard, Chester (1938) *Functions of the Executive*. Cambridge, MA: Harvard University Press.

Barnow, Burt S. (2000) 'Exploring the Relationship between Performance Management and Program Impact: a Case Study of the Job Training Partnership Act', *Journal of Policy Analysis and Management*, 19 (1): 118–41.

Beck, Paul A., Rainey, Hal G. and Traut, Carol (1990) 'Disadvantage, Disaffection, and Race as Divergent Bases for Citizen Fiscal Policy Preferences', *Journal of Politics*, 52 (1): 71–93.

Behn, Robert D. (2001) *Rethinking Democratic Accountability*. Washington, DC: Brookings Institution.

Bloom, Howard S., Hill, Carolyn J. and Riccio, James (2001) 'Modeling the Performance of Welfare-to-Work Programs: The Effects of Program Management and Services, Economic Environment, and Client Characteristics', Manpower Demonstration Research Corporation Working Papers on Research Methodology.

Bouckaert, Geert (1993) 'Measurement and Meaningful Management', *Public Productivity and Management Review*, 17 (1): 31–43.

Burghardt, John and Schochet, Peter Z. (2001) 'National Job Corps Study: Impacts by Center Characteristics'. Mathematica Policy Research Document No. PR01-45.

Cabinet Office (1998) *Next Steps Report 1998*. London: Cabinet Office.

Campbell, J.P., Dunnette, M., Lawler, E. and Weick, K. (1970) *Managerial Behavior, Performance and Effectiveness*. New York: McGraw–Hill.

Courty, Pascal and Marschke, Gerald R. (forthcoming) 'An Empirical Investigation of Gaming Responses to Performance Incentives', *Journal of Labor Economics*, 22 (1).

Deming, W. Edwards (1986) *Out of the Crisis*. Cambridge, MA: MIT Institute for Advanced Engineering Study.

DeNisi, Angelo S. (2000) 'Performance Appraisal and Performance Management', in Katherine J. Klein and Steve W.J. Kozlowski (eds), *Multilevel Theory, Research, and Methods in Organizations: Foundations, Extensions and New Directions*. San Francisco: Jossey–Bass.

Dixit, Avinash (1999) 'Incentives and Organizations in the Public Sector: An Interpretive Review'. Paper presented at the National Academy of Sciences Conference, Devising Incentives to Promote Human Capital, Irvine, CA.

Drucker, Peter F. (1954) *The Practice of Management*. New York: Harper.

Feldman, Martha S. and Khademian, Anne M. (2000) 'Managing for Inclusion: Balancing Control and Participation', *International Public Management Journal*, 3: 149–67.

Goerge, Robert M. (1999) 'The Use of Administrative Data for Implementation Research'. Working paper, Chapin Hall Center for Children, Chicago.

Gore, Al (1993) *Creating a Government that Works Better and Costs Less*. New York: Penguin Books.

Gormley, William T. and Weimer, David L. (1999) *Organizational Report Cards*. Cambridge, MA: Harvard University Press.

Gulick, Luther and Urwick, L. (1937) *Papers on the Science of Administration*. New York: Institute of Public Administration, Columbia University.

Halachmi, Arie (1995) 'Is TQM Ready for the Public Sector?', in Arie Halachmi and Geert Bouckaert (eds), *Public Productivity Through Quality and Strategic Management*. Amsterdam: IOS Press.

Hatry, Harry P. (1999) *Performance Measurement: Getting Results*. Washington, DC: Urban Institute Press.

Heckman, James J. and Smith, Jeffrey A. (1995) 'The Performance of Performance Standards: The Effects of

JTPA Performance Standards on Efficiency, Equity and Participant Outcomes', University of Chicago, Department of Economics.

Heinrich, Carolyn J. (2002) 'Outcomes-based Performance Management in the Public Sector: Implications for Government Accountability and Effectiveness', *Public Administration Review*, 62 (6): 712–25.

Heinrich, Carolyn J. and Lynn, Laurence E., Jr (eds) (2000) *Governance and Performance: New Perspectives*. Washington, DC: Georgetown University Press.

Hill, Carolyn J. (2001) 'Impacts, Outcomes, and Management in Welfare-to-Work Programs'. PhD dissertation, University of Chicago.

Hoover Commission (1949) The Hoover Commission Report. New York: McGraw–Hill.

Kaboolian, Linda (1998) 'The New Public Management: Challenging the Boundaries of the Management vs. Administration Debate', *Public Administration Review*, 58 (3): 189–93.

Kamensky, John M. (1993) 'Program Performance Measures: Designing a System to Manage for Results', *Public Productivity and Management Review*, 16 (4): 395–402.

Kelly, Rita Mae (1998) 'An Inclusive Democratic Polity, Representative Bureaucracies, and the New Public Management', *Public Administration Review*, 58 (3): 201–8.

Kettl, Donald F. and DiIulio, John J. (eds) (1995) *Inside the Reinvention Machine*. Washington, DC: Brookings Institution.

Khademian, Anne M. (1995) 'Reinventing a Government Corporation: Professional Priorities and a Clear Bottom Line', *Public Administration Review*, 55 (1): 17–28.

Koretz, Daniel (1999) 'Foggy Lenses: Limitations in the Use of Achievement Tests as Measures of Educators' Productivity'. Paper presented at the National Academy of Sciences Conference, Devising Incentives to Promote Human Capital, Irvine, CA.

Lægreid, Per (2000) 'Top Civil Servants Under Contract', *Public Administration Review*, 78 (4): 879–96.

Lindblom, Charles (1959) 'The Science of Muddling Through', *Public Administration Review*, 19 (1): 79–88.

Lynn, Laurence E., Jr (1998) 'The New Public Management: How to Transform a Theme into a Legacy', *Public Administration Review*, 58 (3): 231–8.

Lynn, Laurence E., Jr, Heinrich, Carolyn J. and Hill, Carolyn J. (2001) *Improving Governance: A New Logic for Research*. Washington, DC: Georgetown University Press.

Marcoulides, George A. and Heck, Ronald H. (1993) 'Organizational Culture and Performance: Proposing and Testing a Model', *Organization Science*, 4 (2): 209–25.

Mead, Lawrence M. (forthcoming) 'Performance Analysis', in Mary Clare Lennon and Thomas Corbett (eds), *Implementation Analysis: An Evaluation Approach Whose Time Has Come*. Washington, DC: Urban Institute Press.

Mintzberg, Henry (1996) 'Managing Government, Governing Management', *Harvard Business Review*, 74 (May/June): 75–83.

Moe, Ronald C. (1982) 'A New Hoover Commission: A Timely Idea or Misdirected Nostalgia?', *Public Administration Review*, 42 (3): 270–7.

Murphy, Kevin R. and Cleveland, Jeanette N. (1995) *Understanding Performance Appraisal: Social, Organizational, and Goal-Based Perspectives*. Thousand Oaks, CA: Sage.

Osborne, Stephen P., Boviard, Tony, Martin, Steve, Tricker, Mike and Waterston, Piers (1995) 'Performance Management and Accountability in Complex Programmes', *Financial Accountability and Management*, 11 (1): 19–37.

Pfeffer, Jeffrey (1990) 'Incentives in Organizations: The Importance of Social Relations', in Oliver E. Williamson (ed.), *Organization Theory: From Chester Barnard to the Present and Beyond*. New York: Oxford University Press. pp. 72–97.

Pollitt, Christopher and Bouckaert, Geert (2000) *Public Management Reform: A Comparative Analysis*. Oxford: Oxford University Press.

President's Committee on Administrative Management (1937) 'Administrative Management in the Government of the United States', Senate document 8, 75th Congress, 1st session. Washington, DC: United States Government Printing Office.

Radin, Beryl A. (2000a) *Beyond Machiavelli: Policy Analysis Comes of Age*. Washington, DC: Georgetown University Press.

Radin, Beryl A. (2000b) 'The Government Performance and Results Act and the Tradition of Federal Management Reform: Square Pegs in Round Holes?', *Journal of Public Administration Research and Theory*, 10 (1): 11–35.

Rainey, Hal G. and Steinbauer, Paula (1999) 'Galloping Elephants: Developing Elements of a Theory of Effective Government Organizations', *Journal of Public Administration Research and Theory*, 9 (1): 1–32.

Rivenbark, William C. (ed.) (2001) *A Guide to the North Carolina Local Government Performance Measurement Project*. Chapel Hill, NC: Institute of Government, University of North Carolina at Chapel Hill.

Romzek, Barbara S. (1998) 'Where the Buck Stops: Accountability in Reformed Public Organizations', in Patricia W. Ingraham, James R. Thompson and Ronald P. Sanders (eds), *Transforming Government: Lessons from the Reinvention Labs*. San Francisco: Jossey–Bass.

Romzek, Barbara S. and Dubnick, Melvin J. (1998) 'Accountability', in Jay M. Shafritz (ed.), *The International Encyclopedia of Public Policy and Administration*. Boulder, CO: Westview Press.

Rosenbloom, David H. (1986) *Public Administration: Understanding Management, Politics, and Law in the Public Sector*. New York: Random House.

Scott, W.D., Clothier, R.C. and Spriegel, W.R. (1941) *Personnel Management*. New York: McGraw–Hill.

Simon, Herbert A. (1957) *Administrative Behavior*. New York: Macmillan.

Taylor, Frederick Winslow (1911) *The Principles of Scientific Management*. New York: Harper & Brothers.

Terry, Larry D. (1998) 'Administrative Leadership, Neo-Managerialism, and the Public Management

Movement', *Public Administration Review*, 58 (3): 194–200.

Thompson, James D. (1967) *Organizations in Action*. New York: McGraw–Hill.

UC Data (1999) 'An Inventory of Research Uses of Administrative Data in Social Services Programs in the United States 1998'. Report by University of California at Berkeley to the Northwestern University/University of Chicago Joint Center for Poverty Research.

US Government Accounting Office (1999) 'Managing for Results: Opportunities for Continued Improvements in Agencies' Performance Plans', GAO/AIMD-99-215.

US Government Accounting Office (1997a) 'Managing for Results: Prospects for Effective Implementation of the Government Performance and Results Act', GAO/AIMD-97-113.

US Government Accounting Office (1997b) 'Managing for Results: Analytical Challenges in Measuring Performance', GAO/AIMD-97-138.

Walton, Mary (1986) *The Deming Management Method*. New York: Pedigree Books.

Wilson, Woodrow (1887) 'The Study of Administration', *Political Science Quarterly*, 2 (2): 197–222.

3

Strategic Planning and Management

John M. Bryson

Strategic planning and management are increasingly becoming a way of life for public organizations across the globe. As a result, strategic planning and management are being relied upon to deal with the three tasks of coming up with important ideas worth implementing, forging the coalition needed to adopt and to implement the changes and implementing the changes in a timely fashion. In the process, planning and implementation and strategic and operational concerns are becoming fused.

The chapter is in five parts. The first part presents the basic elements of strategic planning, including its attention to the environment, stakeholders, mission, mandates, strategic issues and strategies. Strategic planning is the basic building block of strategic management, which is described in the second part. The basic approaches to institutionalizing strategic management strategic planning systems are presented next in a section on strategic planning systems. In the fourth section current trends in strategic planning and management are discussed. Finally, a number of conclusions are presented.

STRATEGIC PLANNING[1]

Strategic planning may be defined as 'a disciplined effort to produce fundamental decisions and actions that shape and guide what an organization (or other entity) is, what it does, and why it does it' (Bryson, 1995: 4–5). While many authors have suggested generic strategic planning processes (for example, Nutt and Backoff, 1992; Bryson, 1995; Eden and Ackermann, 1998), this definition implies that strategic planning is not a *single* thing, but is instead a *set* of concepts, procedures and tools that must be tailored carefully to situations if desirable outcomes are to be achieved (Bryson and Roering, 1996; Christensen, 1999; Mintzberg et al., 1998). Poister and Streib (1999), in a review summarizing the field of strategic planning and management, assert that strategic planning:

- Is concerned with identifying and responding to the most fundamental issues facing an organization
- Addresses the subjective question of purpose and the often competing values that influence mission and strategies
- Emphasizes the importance of external trends and forces as they are likely to affect the organization and its mission
- Attempts to be politically realistic by taking into account the concerns and preferences of internal, and especially external, stakeholders
- Relies heavily on the active involvement of senior level managers, and sometimes elected officials, assisted by staff support where needed
- Requires the candid confrontation of critical issues by key participants in order to build commitment to plans
- Is action-oriented and stresses the importance of developing plans for implementing strategies, and
- Focuses on implementing decisions now in order to position the organization favorably for the future.

Strategic planning for organizations has developed primarily in the private sector. This history has been amply documented by others (Eden and Ackermann, 1998). In the past twenty years, however, public and nonprofit use of strategic planning has skyrocketed. This experience, and a growing body of literature, have indicated that strategic planning approaches either developed in the private sector, or else strongly influenced by them, can help public organizations, as well as communities or other entities, deal in effective ways with their dramatically changing environments.

In the United States, for example, a substantial majority of municipal and state governments, and an overwhelming majority of federal agencies and nonprofit organizations, make use of strategic planning. Strategic planning has been applied principally to public and nonprofit organizations, but applications to communities have increased substantially as well (Poister and Streib, 1994; Berman and West, 1998). Other nations – and particularly OECD countries – also make use to varying degrees of strategic planning concepts, procedures and tools for public and nonprofit organizations and communities (for example, Osborne and Plastrik, 1997; Faludi and Salet, 2000).

When done well, strategic planning offers a number of benefits. Advocates usually point to four main potential benefits. The first is the *promotion of strategic thought and action*. The second is *improved decision making*, while the third is *enhanced organizational responsiveness and improved performance*. Finally, strategic planning can *directly benefit the organization's people* by helping them better perform their roles, meet their responsibilities and enhance teamwork and expertise. There is no guarantee, however, that these benefits will be achieved. For one thing, strategic planning is simply a set of concepts, procedures and tools that must be applied wisely to specific situations. For another, even when they are applied wisely, there is no guarantee of success.

Beyond that, strategic planning is not always advisable, particularly for an organization facing an immediate crisis (although every crisis should be managed strategically), or when the organization lacks the skills, resources, or commitment by key decision makers to produce a good plan. Such situations embody what may be called 'the paradox of strategic planning': it is most needed where it is least likely to work, and least needed where it is most likely to work (Bryson and Roering, 1988).

It is important to highlight what strategic planning is *not*. Strategic planning is not a substitute for *strategic thinking and acting*. It may help people do that, but used unwisely may hinder strategic thinking and acting. Strategic planning is not a substitute for *leadership*. At least some key actors must be committed to the process or it is bound to fail. Said differently, strategic planning is best seen as a leadership tool, where leadership is broadly conceived to include more than top positional leaders. Strategic planning also is not a substitute for an organizational or community *strategy*. Strategies have numerous sources, both planned and unplanned. Strategic planning is likely to result in a statement of organizational or community *intentions*, but what is *realized* in practice will be some combination of what is intended with what emerges along the way (Mintzberg et al., 1998). Finally, strategic planning is not synonymous with what is called *comprehensive planning* for communities in the US, or has been called *structure planning* in Europe. There may be little difference if the agency doing the comprehensive or structure planning is tied directly to governmental decision makers. However, in practice, there may be three significant differences (Bryson, 2000).

First, the plans often are prepared to meet legal requirements and must be formulated according to a legally prescribed process with legally prescribed content. As legal instruments, these plans have an important influence. On the other hand, the plans' typical rigidity can conflict with the political process with which public officials must cope. Strategic plans therefore can provide a bridge from legally required and relatively rigid policy statements to actual decisions and operations.

Second, comprehensive or structure plans usually are limited to less than a government's full agenda of roles and responsibilities. For that reason, they are of less use to key decision makers than strategic planning, which can embrace all of a government's actual and potential roles before deciding why, where, when and how to act.

Third, as Kaufman and Jacobs (1987) argue, strategic planning on behalf of a community is more action-oriented, more broadly participatory, more emphatic about the need to understand the community's strengths and weaknesses as well as the opportunities and threats it faces, and more attentive to intercommunity competitive behavior. Strategic planning thus typically is more comprehensive than comprehensive planning or structure planning, while at the same time producing a more limited action focus.

STRATEGIC MANAGEMENT

Strategic *planning* also is typically distinguished from strategic *management*. Strategic planning is the cornerstone of strategic management, but the latter is a far more encompassing process, 'concerned with managing an organization in a strategic manner on a continuing basis' (Poister and Streib, 1999: 310). Strategic management links strategic planning and implementation by adding ongoing attention to budgeting, to performance measurement, management and evaluation, and to feedback relationships among these elements.

Poster and Streib (1999) present a framework for thinking about strategic management as a process. The framework incorporates seven elements: values, mission, and vision; strategic planning; results-oriented budgeting; performance management; strategic measurement; assessment of the internal and external environment; and feedback relationships among these elements. These elements will be discussed briefly in turn.

Values, mission and vision are seen as a central organizing force for strategic management efforts. If consensus can be achieved on these elements among key stakeholders, the creation and operation of a strategic management system will be far easier than it would be otherwise. If consensus is not possible, then the system no doubt will be looser and less integrated. In fact, because consensus on values, mission and vision is difficult to achieve in many – perhaps most – circumstances, tightly integrated strategic management systems are not particularly common, and probably should not be pursued in most situations.

Strategic planning can be used to help organizations articulate their values, mission and visions and to develop strategic initiatives to realize them in practice. The initiatives must be resourced properly if they are to be implemented effectively. Results-oriented budgeting is one answer to this challenge and is rapidly gaining currency throughout the world. Such an approach begins with the organization's strategic agenda, specifies expected outputs or outcomes for each strategy, program, project, or activity, and then links funding to these elements. This sort of budgeting process can be used to garner adequate resources for specific strategic initiatives and to provide incentives to organizational members and other stakeholders to support the strategic agenda.

Performance management involves strategies and mechanisms for assigning responsibility for strategic initiatives to specific units and individuals and holding them accountable for results. For example, management by objectives (MBO) systems are widely used for this purpose. Balanced Scorecard (BSC) approaches are gaining attention globally as another method for translating values, mission and vision into measurable and manageable organizational performance. BSC approaches try to 'balance' attention to financial outcomes with attention to outcomes focused on stakeholders' or customers' concerns, crucial internal process, and the learning and growth of the organization and its employees (Kaplan and Norton, 1992, 1993; Kaplan, 1998; Poister and Streib, 1999).

Strategic measurement involves the identification and tracking of valid measures of the organization's performance as it attempts to achieve its strategic objectives. Attending to these measures helps chart progress and success, assess whether budget allocations are appropriate and figure out what to do next. Unfortunately, development of valid and politically supported measures can be very difficult for public organizations and often represents an Achilles heel for strategic management systems (Ammons, 1995; Innes, 1996, 1998).

These various elements must be pursued in a context of ongoing internal and external monitoring, assessment and engagement with key stakeholders or they are unlikely to result in wise or politically realistic information, decisions and actions. Adequate feedback across the various system elements is needed for effective learning, adaptation and leadership to occur.

The job certainly is not easy and success is hardly guaranteed. Nonetheless, in the United States and many OECD countries, in particular, powerful forces are prompting public organizations to try, if not to fully embrace, strategic management approaches. These forces include growing demands for public accountability, increased legislative oversight, fiscal conservatism, and professional attention to leadership, improved performance and customer service. The idea of 'managing for results' is a rallying point for public management scholars and practitioners. As Poister and Streib (1999: 323) assert;

[In] public agencies of any size and complexity, it is impossible to manage for results without a well-developed capacity for strategic management. Indeed, on a macro level, strategic management, with its emphasis on developing and implementing a strategic agenda, is synonymous with managing for results ... While treatment of more specific tools, such as strategic planning, performance measurement, quality improvement, work process reengineering, and results-based budgeting, has been more prevalent in the public administration literature, strategic management is the central integrative process which gives the organization a sense of direction and assures a concerted effort to achieve strategic goals and objectives.

Although the implementation of strategic management has its difficulties, the success of this innovation in the United States, in particular, is a marked improvement over previous related efforts (for example, Planning, Programming, and Budgeting Systems, and Zero-Based Budgeting). Clearly, there appears to be something quite different about the current situation. Perhaps it is the cumulative experience of prior reform efforts that has led to greater understanding of how to pursue results-oriented management. Perhaps it is an embrace of the rhetoric of business, the language of customer service and the ideas of Total Quality Management, along with politicians' and professionals' pursuit of downsizing, reengineering and reinvention (Fesler and Kettl, 1996: 68–87). Perhaps it is the rise of a 'results-oriented' discourse, as in Osborne and Gaebler's best-selling *Reinventing Government* (1992), Vice President Al Gore's *The Gore Report on Reinventing Government* (1993), Moore's *Creating Public Value* (1995), or Osborne and Plastrik's *Banishing Bureaucracy* (1997). Perhaps it is the rise of a new cadre of political leaders and professional managers who feel free to challenge old shibboleths and homilies about the way things are now and always will be. Whatever the causes, managing for results and public strategic management appear to be embedded in US public administration practice in a way they have not before.

STRATEGIC MANAGEMENT SYSTEMS[2]

Experience suggests that it is relatively easy to get a small group of people – say, five to a few hundred – through a strategic planning process. What is more difficult is to embed strategic thought and action throughout an organization, interorganizational network, or community (that is, small and large cities, counties, regions, or states). Strategic management systems are one means of inducing and linking strategic thinking and acting throughout an organization or other entity. The systems are meant to *promote* strategic thought and action in appropriate places at appropriate times, and to *control* or *guide* the way strategies are implemented.

Because organizational strategies typically remain fairly stable for long periods of time and then change rather abruptly (Mintzberg, 1994), these systems are usually more focused on strategy implementation than on strategy formulation. The systems are thus mostly organizational mechanisms or arrangements for strategically managing the implementation of agreed-upon strategies. Said somewhat differently, these systems are themselves a kind of organizational (or interorganizational, or community) strategy for implementing policies and plans.

At the same time, the systems do usually embody procedures and occasions for routinely reassessing strategies. It is during the reassessment process that new strategies tend to be 'found' or 'formulated'. These strategies typically are present in nascent or emergent form already in the organization. The strategy reassessment process simply raises them to prominence in an incremental, or otherwise non-disruptive, fashion. The 'new' strategies that these systems produce are thus mainly variations on existing themes, rather than new themes. The really big changes, when they occur, usually are either induced from outside via new mandates, new leadership, or drastic environmental changes, or else represent the cumulative minor organizational adjustments to persistent environmental pressures – changes in degree – that lead to changes in kind (Bryson and Crosby, 1992; Mintzberg, 1994; Bryson, 1995).

While it is often important to create and maintain a strategic management system, it is also important to guard against the tendency such systems have of driving out wise strategic thought and action – precisely those phenomena that strategic planning and management (at their best) promote. An important guideline therefore should be that whenever any strategic management system (or strategic planning process) threatens to drive out wise strategic thought and action, efforts should be made to change the system (or process) and get back to promoting effective strategic thought and action.

There appear to be five main types of strategic management systems in the United States and other OECD countries, although every strategic management system that I have seen appears to be a hybrid of the five types. The 'types' therefore refer to dominant tendencies. The types are: the layered or stacked units of management model, strategic issues management models, contract models, portfolio management models and goal or 'benchmark' models. Each will be discussed briefly in turn.

The purpose of *the layered or stacked units of management model* is to effectively link inside and outside environments through development and implementation of an integrated set of strategies across levels and functions of the organization (Boschken, 1988; Poister and Streib, 1999). Often the model is applied through public application of the classic, private – sector, corporate-style 'goals down – plans up' two-cycle strategic planning process. In the first cycle, there is a 'bottom up' development of strategic plans within a framework of goals, objectives and other guidance established at the top, followed by review and reconciliation at each succeeding level. In the second cycle, operating plans are developed to implement the strategic plans. In each cycle efforts are made to explicitly, logically and persuasively relate levels, functions and inside and outside environments. The process is repeated each year within the general framework established by the organization's grand or umbrella strategies. Every three to five years these overarching strategies are reviewed and modified based on experience, changing conditions and the emergence of new strategies that were not necessarily planned in advance. In the United States, the Government Performance and Results Act of 1993 (Public Law 103–62) has been an ambitious attempt to establish a sort of layered or stacked units of management system for each Federal agency and for the Executive Branch as a whole.

It is precisely this sort of system that is most prone to driving out strategic thought and action. That occurs when the system is underpinned by a belief that the future actually can be predicted accurately, is too detached from the messiness of operational reality and is characterized by excessive centralization of power and formality (Roberts, 1993; Mintzberg, 1994; Roberts and Wargo, 1994). Such systems are very likely to be blind-sided by events that cannot be predicted and wreak havoc on existing strategies and plans. The systems therefore must be used with extreme caution, since they can take on a life of their own, promote incremental change when major change is needed and serve only the interests of the leaders, managers and planners who wish to resist – not promote – major change.

Strategic issues management systems are the most common form of institutionalized strategic management system in public organizations. These systems do not attempt to integrate strategies across levels and functions to the extent that layered or stacked units of management approaches do. The reason is that most of the issues are on different time frames, involve different constituencies and politics, and do not need to be considered in the light of all other issues. As a result, issues are not managed comprehensively as a set, but instead are dealt with one by one within an overarching framework of organizational mission and strategic goals or objectives. While each issue is managed relatively separately, it is of course necessary to make sure choices in one issue area do not cause trouble in other issue areas.

While many public organizations have several task forces in operation at any one time, fewer go

the next step to design and use a strategic issues management system. They do not establish an overall framework of organizational mission, goals or policy objectives, systematically seek out issues to address, or make sure their various issues-management activities add up to increased organizational effectiveness. Organizational leaders and managers thus should consider establishing a strategic issues management system, keeping in mind that the resulting centralization of certain key decisions at the top is likely to draw the attention and resistance of those who do not want to see power concentrated in that way or who dislike the resulting decisions.

The *contract model* is becoming an increasingly popular approach to institutionalizing strategic planning and management (Osborne and Plastrik, 1997). It is the basic model for organizing the National Health Service in the United Kingdom, where area boards assess health needs for their geographic area and then contract with various providers for the delivery of desired services. The contract model also is employed for much of the planning and delivery of many publicly financed services in the United States via either public or nonprofit service providers. And the model is used to institutionalize strategic planning and management in US school districts utilizing site-based management.

In this model, there is a 'center' that establishes strategic objectives for the jurisdiction or organization as a whole, negotiates contracts with individual units of management, monitors performance and ensures the integrity of the system. The contract between the center and a unit outlines the unit's expected performance, indicates the resources it will receive from the center, lists other support the unit can expect from the center and describes a review and re-negotiation sequence. Within the framework and legal strictures of the contract, general managers of individual units and their staffs are free to do whatever they think is necessary or desirable to ensure adequate performance. The approach allows both the center and the individual units to focus on what is important for them; both are empowered to do their jobs better. In such a system, there would be a strategic plan for the center and one for each of the units. Key system concerns will include the content and approach embodied in the center's plan, the center's difficulties in acquiring adequate information and the difficulties the center may have in exercising control and ensuring accountability when using a large number of contractors (Milward et al., 1993; Osborne and Plastrik, 1997).

In the *portfolio approach* entities of various sorts (programs, projects, products, services, or providers) are arrayed against dimensions that have some strategic importance. The dimensions usually consist of the attractiveness or desirability of the entity (from high to low) and the capability of the organization or community to deliver what is needed. Portfolio methods are quite flexible, in that any dimensions of interest may be arrayed against one another and entities mapped on to the resulting matrix. Portfolio methods also can be used at sub-organizational and supra-organizational levels as well to assess options against strategically important factors (Bryson and Roering, 1987; Nutt and Backoff, 1992). Unfortunately, few public and nonprofit organizations or communities use formal portfolio models, even though many probably use portfolio methods informally. The problem, of course, with use of formal models is that they create comparisons that may be troubling for politically powerful actors.

Goal or benchmark models also are much 'looser' than the layered or stacked units of management models and are generally applied at the community, regional, or state levels (Broom, 1995). They are designed to gain reasonable agreement on overarching goals or indicators (benchmarks) toward which relatively independent groups, units, or organizations might then direct their energies. Consensual agreement on goals and indicators thus provides a weak surrogate for the corporate control exercised in layered models. Nonetheless, when agreement can be reached and support for implementation can be generated, the models can work reasonably well. Besides, in the fragmented, shared-power environments in which most public problems are embedded, the approach may be the only viable approach. For example, most community strategic plans are implemented via goal or benchmark models. Large numbers of leaders and citizens typically are involved in the process of goal-setting and strategy development. Then action plans outline what each organization might do to help implement the strategies and achieve the goals on a voluntary basis.

While there are five general types of strategic management systems, any actual system is likely to be a hybrid of all five types. For example, in the British National Health Service, the main model for each area is the *contract model*. But strategic issues that cut across the area are handled via a *strategic issues management* approach. And there typically is also an attempt to develop participative approaches (at least involving the major providers) to develop overall *goals or benchmarks* for each area. Each hospital relies primarily on a *layered or stacked units of management* model, but also would use

explicit or implicit *portfolio* methods as well. The question is simply which type dominates at which level.

Each type of system has characteristic strengths and weaknesses. They each represent a different kind of organizational (or interorganizational, or community) strategy for implementing other strategies that are already agreed upon, at least in broad outline. It is also important to remember that each system embodies a set of arrangements that empowers particular actors, makes particular kinds of issues more likely to arise than others, and particular strategies more likely to be pushed than others. Whenever the environment around the system changes to the extent that the system no longer produces effective strategies, the system itself is unlikely to be able to change enough on its own. Instead, the big changes must be forced from the outside in some way, but also find favor in significant ways inside, or the changes are unlikely to occur without significant and damaging dislocations and distress.

CURRENT TRENDS

A variety of trends are apparent that involve the use of public strategic planning and management. The first is that there is an increased emphasis on organizational and community effectiveness worldwide. People understand that their organizations and communities must be effective if important public purposes and the common good are to be advanced. Three trends are apparent as part of this effort, and they involve exploring ways to increase *inclusivity*, the *speed* of the process and *systems thinking*. In other words, many people know that the participation of a variety of different kinds of stakeholders is important, and so is achieving a clearer understanding of the system to be improved and how to improve it. It is also apparent, however, that involving more stakeholders and achieving a better understanding of the system can take a great deal of time, so there is also an emphasis on figuring out how to speed up the process. The final trend involves increasing use of strategic planning and management to help on all three fronts, by fusing planning and implementation, and by attending to strategic and operational concerns simultaneously. As a result, the number of concepts, procedures and tools that comprise strategic planning and management is increasing because work in a variety of areas is being incorporated into the theory and practice of the field (see Figure 3.1).

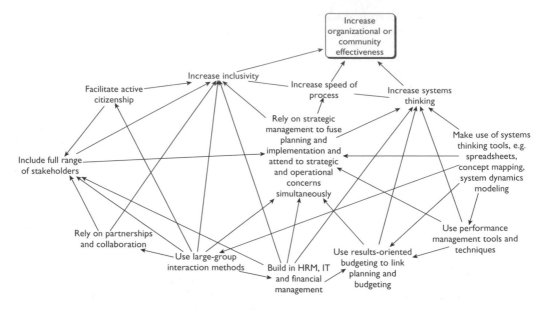

Figure 3.1   *Current trends in strategic planning and management*

The emphasis on *inclusivity* comes from two sources: the need for information and the need for participation (Thomas, 1993). Information is needed from a variety of sources in order to properly inform action. Participation is needed from key stakeholders in order to build understanding and commitment to collective action. Participation also is an important key to fostering active citizenship, which is of growing interest and emphasis. The renewed emphasis on citizenship comes from several sources: a reaction to the often inappropriate emphasis on 'customers' in public management (Denhardt and Denhardt, 2000), a recognition of the importance of social capital to the achievement of broad public purposes (Putnam, 2000), and a desire to reclaim the full meaning of democracy (Boyte and Kari, 1996).

First and foremost, increasing inclusivity means finding ways to include the full range of stakeholders. When a multi-organization or multi-unit response is required, this means an increased reliance on the use of partnerships and collaboration (Winer and Ray, 1994; Huxham and Vangen, 2000). The explosive growth of interest in, and use of, large-group interaction methods – such as Future Search (Weisbord and Janoff, 1995), Open Space Technology (Owen, 1997), and Real Time Strategic Planning (Jacobs, 1994) – also reflects the need to find ways to incorporate large numbers of diverse individuals into the process (Bryson and Anderson,

2000). Finally, building in attention to HRM, IT and financial management is seen as vital in order to develop viable and self-sustaining 'enterprise schemes' or 'business plans' for government organizations (Pfeffer, 1998; Bryson et al., 2000). In the past, when funding typically was more secure, strategic plans usually were prepared without much consideration for their HRM, IT and financial management implications; or else separate plans for each function were prepared without adequate attention to the organization's core business. Now it is important that strategic plans reflect the organization or collaborative as an integrated, self-sustaining enterprise. The enterprise schemes or business plans thus become or may be viewed as *dynamic* strategic plans.

The emphasis on *systems thinking* also comes from a number of sources. First, people are increasingly framing their situations in systems terms, and typically at levels that transcend individual organizations (Schon, 1971). For example, the challenges of elementary and secondary education are being framed in ways that include parents, employers, social services, public health and safety interests, and whole communities. Education generally is seen as an economic development issue, and not just as a matter of personal growth and development. In addition, there is now widespread awareness of the basic elements of the systems view of the world, including attending to the environment, inputs, throughputs, outputs and feedback. This awareness facilitates the process of talking in systems terms and increases the expectation that such discourse will occur. And finally, there is awareness that without decent systems thinking there is high likelihood that the problem will be conceptualized at the wrong level, the wrong problem will be solved, or else the problem will be made worse (Senge, 1990).

Systems thinking is made easier by the increased availability of systems thinking tools, perhaps the most common of which is spread-sheet software (such as Microsoft Excel) loaded onto computers. Electronic spreadsheets make it possible to develop models of important aspects of systems to understand how they behave in the present and to explore 'what if' scenarios for the future. Beyond that, the use of concept mapping techniques is growing in popularity, including, for example, mind mapping (Buzan, 1996) and oval mapping (Eden and Ackermann, 1998). Finally, system dynamics modeling is increas-ingly widely used (Sterman, 2000). This metho-dology allows for the creation of very complex quantitative models that can be manipulated to explore the effects over time of numerous policy interventions.

Systems thinking is also assisted by building attention to HRM, IT and financial management, using results-oriented budgeting to link planning and budgeting and relying on the range of per-formance management tools and techniques. The need to accommodate these conceptual pieces of the puzzle is broadly recognized and the development of systems thinking tools and large-group interaction methods now makes it easier to do. While still relatively uncommon, the practice of linking sophisticated systems thinking tools with inclusive participation methods is on the rise.

As noted, the final trend involves *increasing use of strategic planning and management* to help increase *inclusivity*, the *speed* of the process and *systems thinking* by fusing planning and implementation and attending to strategic and operational concerns simultaneously. As a result, strategic planning and management are coming to embrace the entire management process in a way they have not in the past, and the number of concepts, procedures and tools that comprise the field of strategic planning and management is increasing (Lynn, 1987, 1996; Barzelay, 2001).

One of the really big challenges these days is figuring out how to be inclusive *and* incorporate systems thinking *and* be quick. Some years ago, Cleveland (1993) described the first part of the challenge as figuring out how to get everyone in on the act and still get some action. The second part of the challenge is figuring out what to do

when systems thinking matters. The third part of the challenge is how to do both before it is too late. In other words, strategic planning and man-agement must deal with the three tasks of com-ing up with ideas worth implementing, forging the coalition needed to adopt and to implement the changes, and implementing them in a timely fashion. Inclusion can speed things up when it shortens the time for consultation and re-work. Systems thinking also can speed things up when it leads to prompt and good problem formulation and solution development and to the identifica-tion of which stakeholders need to be involved and how. But performing the three tasks well places a real premium on having adequate management talent and analysis skill on tap, and adequate institutional designs and relation-ships available or in the offing. Identifying or developing models of the talents, skills, designs and relationships to make strategic planning and management work well in the new circumstances should be high on the academic and practice agendas.

CONCLUSIONS

First, it should be clear that strategic planning and management represent a range of approaches that vary in their applicability to the public sector and in the conditions that govern their successful use. Second, while any generic approach may be a useful guide to thought and action, it will have to be applied with care in a given situation, as is true of any planning and management process (Christensen, 1999). Because every strategic planning and manage-ment process should be tailored to fit specific situations, every process in practice will be a hybrid. Third, public sector strategic planning and management are well on the way to becoming part of the standard repertoire of public leaders, managers and planners. Because of the often dramatic changes these people and their organi-zations confront, we can hypothesize that the most effective leaders, managers and planners are now, and will be increasingly in the future, the ones who are best at *strategic* planning and management.

Fourth, the field of public strategic planning and management is expanding in response to a variety of pressures. As noted in the introduc-tion, people understand that their organizations and communities must be effective if important public purposes and the common good are to be advanced. Increased effectiveness implies a need for increased inclusivity, speed and systems thinking. Unfortunately, there can be a significant trade-off between inclusivity and systems thinking on the one hand and speed on the other. Thus finding ways to enrich and improve strategic planning and management so that gains are made against all three desires simultaneously is and should be an important part of the research and practice agenda.

Along the way, strategic planning and management are incorporating concepts, tools and techniques from a variety of cognate fields. Both the theory and practice are changing to the point that the entire management process is embraced in a way it has not in the past. As a result, planning and implementation and strategic and operational concerns are increasingly fused.

Finally, research must explore a number of theoretical and empirical issues in order to advance the knowledge and practice of public sector strategic planning and management. In particular, strategic planning and management processes that are responsive to different situations must be developed and tested. These processes should: specify key situational factors governing their use; provide specific advice on how to formulate and implement strategies in different situations; be explicitly political; indicate how to deal with plural, ambiguous or conflicting goals or objectives; link content, process, tools and techniques; indicate how collaboration as well as competition is to be handled; and specify roles for those involved in the process. Other topics in need of attention include: the nature of strategic leadership; ways to promote and institutionalize strategic planning across organizational levels, functions that bridge organizational boundaries and intra- and interorganizational networks; and the ways in which HRM, IT and financial management concepts and technologies can help or hinder the process. Finally, work is needed on how strategic planning and management ought to be pursued in order to strengthen *democratic* institutions, citizenship, responsiveness and accountability. Progress has been made on all of these fronts, but more work clearly is necessary if we are to understand better when and how to use strategic planning and management.

NOTES

1 The discussion in this section draws on Bryson (2002).
2 This section of the paper is adapted from Bryson (1995: 193–200; 1996; 2000). In the first two references I referred to strategic management systems as strategic *planning* systems, but here have chosen to use what is probably the more accurate label.

REFERENCES

Ammons, David N. (ed.) (1995) *Accountability for Performance*. Washington, DC: International City/County Management Association.

Barzelay, Michael (2001) *The New Public Management, Improving Research and Policy Dialogue*. Berkeley, CA: University of California Press.

Berman, Evan M. and West, Jonathan P. (1998) 'Productivity Enhancement Efforts in Public and Nonprofit Organizations', *Public Productivity and Management Review*, 22 (2): 207–19.

Boschken, H.L. (1988) *Strategic Design and Organizational Change*. London: University of Alabama Press.

Boyte, Harry C. and Kari, Nancy N. (1996) *Building America: The Democratic Promise of Public Work*. Philadelphia: Temple University Press.

Broom, C.A. (1995) 'Performance-Based Government Models: Building a Track Record', *Public Budgeting and Finance*, 15 (4): 3–17.

Bryson, John M. (1995) *Strategic Planning for Public and Nonprofit Organizations*, rev. edn. San Francisco, CA: Jossey–Bass.

Bryson, John M. (1996) 'Attore Pubblico e Pianificazione Strategica', in Fausto Curti and Maria Cristina Gibelli (eds), *Pianificazione Strategica e Gestione Della Sviluppo Urbano*. Alinea Editrice, pp. 55–81.

Bryson, John M. (2000) 'Strategic Planning and Management for Public and Nonprofit Organizations and Communities in the United States', in A. Faludi and W. Salet (eds), *The Revival of Spatial Strategic Planning in Europe*. Amsterdam: Royal Netherlands Academy of Science, pp. 205–17.

Bryson, John M. (2002) 'Strategic Planning for Public and Nonprofit Purposes', in *International Encyclopedia of the Behavioral and Social Sciences*. Oxford: Elsevier.

Bryson, John M. and Anderson, Sharon R. (2000) 'Applying Large-Group Interaction Methods to the Planning and Implementation of Major Change Efforts', *Public Administration Review*, 60 (2): 143–62.

Bryson, John M. and Crosby, Barbara C. (1992) *Leadership for the Common Good*. San Francisco, CA: Jossey–Bass.

Bryson, John M. Gibbons, Michael and Shaye, Gary (2000) 'Enterprise Schemes for Nonprofit Survival, Growth, and Mission Accomplishment', *Nonprofit Management and Leadership*, 11 (3): 271–88.

Bryson, J.M. and Roering, W.D. (1987) 'Applying Private Sector Strategic Planning in the Public Sector', *Journal of the American Planning Association*, 53: 9–22.

Bryson, John M. and Roering, William D. (1988) 'Initiation of Strategic Planning by Governments', *Public Administration Review*, 48: 995–1004.

Bryson, John M. and Roering, William D. (1996) 'Strategic Planning Options for the Public Sector', in James L. Perry (ed.), *Handbook of Public Administration*, 2nd edn. San Francisco, CA: Jossey–Bass.

Buzan, Tony (1996) *The Mind Map Book*. London: BBC Books.

Cleveland, H. (1993) *Birth of a New World: An Open Moment for International Leadership.* San Francisco, CA: Jossey–Bass.

Christensen, Karen (1999) *Cities and Complexity.* Thousand Oaks, CA: Sage.

Denhardt, Robert and Denhardt, Janet Vinzant (2000) 'The New Public Service: Serving Rather than Steering', *Public Administration Review*, 60 (6): 549–59.

Eden, Colin and Ackermann, Fran (1998) *Making Strategy: The Journey of Strategic Management.* Newbury Park, CA: Sage.

Faludi, A. and Salet, W. (eds) (2000) *The Revival of Spatial Strategic Planning in Europe.* Amsterdam: Royal Netherlands Academy of Science.

Fesler, James W. and Kettl, Donald F. (1996) *The Politics of the Administrative Process.* Chatham, NJ: Chatham House.

Gore, A. (1993) *The Gore Report on Reinventing Government.* New York: Times Books.

Huxham, C. and Vangen, S. (2000) 'Leadership in the Shaping and Implementation of Collaboration Agendas: How Things Happen in a (Not Quite) Joined-Up World', *Academy of Management Journal,* 43 (6): 1159–75.

Innes, Judith E. (1996) 'Planning through Consensus Building: A New View of the Comprehensive Planning Ideal', *Journal of the American Planning Association,* 62 (4): 460–72.

Innes, Judith E. (1998) 'Information in Communicative Planning', *Journal of the American Planning Association,* 64 (1): 52–64.

Jacobs, Robert W. (1994) *Real-Time Strategic Planning.* San Francisco, CA: Berritt-Koehler.

Kaplan, Robert S. (1998) *City of Charlotte (A).* Cambridge, MA: Harvard Business School, Case No. N9-199–036.

Kaplan, R.S. and Norton, D.P. (1992) 'The Balanced Scorecard: Measures that Drive Performance', *Harvard Business Review,* 70 (1): 71–9.

Kaplan, R.S. and Norton, D.P. (1993) 'Putting the Balanced Scorecard to Work', *Harvard Business Review,* 70 (1): 71–9.

Kaufman, Jerome and Jacobs, Harvey (1987) *Journal of the American Planning Association*, 53: 23–33.

Lynn, Laurence E., Jr (1987) *Managing Public Policy.* Boston, MA: Little, Brown.

Lynn, Laurence. E., Jr (1996) *Public Management as Art, Science, and Profession.* Chatham, NJ: Chatham House.

Milward, B., Provan, K. and Else, B. (1993) 'What Does the "Hollow State" Look Like?', in B. Bozeman (ed.), *Public Management, the State of the Art.* San Francisco, CA: Jossey–Bass.

Mintzberg, H. (1994) *The Rise and Fall of Strategic Planning.* New York: Free Press.

Mintzberg, H., Ahlstrand, B. and Lampel, J. (1998) *Strategy Safari.* New York: Free Press.

Moore, Mark H. (1995) *Creating Public Value: Strategic Management in Government.* Cambridge, MA: Harvard University Press.

Nutt, Paul and Backoff, Robert (1992) *Strategic Management of Public and Third Sector Organizations.* San Francisco, CA: Jossey–Bass.

Osborne, David and Gaebler, T. (1992) *Reinventing Government.* Reading, MA: Addison–Wesley.

Osborne, David and Plastrik, Peter (1997) *Banishing Bureaucracy: The Five Strategies for Reinventing Government.* Reading, MA: Addison–Wesley.

Owen, Harrison (1997) *Open Space Technology: A User's Guide,* 2nd edn. San Francisco, CA: Berritt–Koehler.

Pfeffer, Jeffrey (1998) *The Human Equation: Building Profits by Putting People First.* Cambridge, MA: Harvard Business School Press.

Poister, Theodore H. and Streib, Gregory (1994) 'Municipal Management Tools from 1976 to 1993: An Overview and Update', *Public Productivity and Management Review*, 18 (2): 115–25.

Poister, Theodore H. and Streib, Gregory (1999) 'Strategic Management in the Public Sector: Concepts, Models, and Processes', *Public Productivity and Management Review,* 22: 308–25.

Putnam, Robert (2000) *Bowling Alone.* New York: Simon and Schuster.

Roberts, N. (1993) 'Limitations of Strategic Action in Bureaus', in B. Bozeman (ed.), *Public Management, the State of the Art.* San Francisco, CA: Jossey–Bass.

Roberts, N. and Wargo, L. (1994) 'The Dilemma of Planning in Large Scale Public Organizations: The Case of the United States Navy', *Journal of Public Administration Research and Theory*, 4: 469–91.

Schon, D. (1971) *Beyond the Stable State.* New York: Norton.

Senge, P. (1990) *The Fifth Discipline: The Art and Practice of the Learning Organization.* New York: Doubleday.

Sterman, J. (2000) *Business Dynamics: Systems Thinking and Modeling for a Complex World.* Homewood, IL: Irwin.

Thomas, J.C. (1993) 'Public Involvement and Governmental Effectiveness: A Decision-Making Model for Public Managers', *Administration and Society*, 24 (4): 444–69.

Weisbord, Marvin R. and Janoff, Sandra (1995) *Future Search: An Action Guide to Finding Common Ground in Organizations and Communities.* San Francisco, CA: Berrett –Koehler.

Winer, M. and Ray, K. (1994) *Collaboration Handbook.* St Paul, MN: Amherst H. Wilder Foundation.

HUMAN RESOURCE MANAGEMENT

Introduction

Patricia W. Ingraham

BACKGROUND

In many nations, human resource management – personnel or civil service in the old terminology – has changed profoundly in the past decade. From a theoretical perspective, the management of public employees and the institutions of the public service have moved from being treated as atheoretical and mechanistic add-ons to the machinery of government to new identities as powerful institutions in their own right, from bland personnel systems to highly valued human capital management endeavors, and from neutral bureaucracies to primary targets of policy change and reform.

Structure has changed and continues to change as well. The rigid, centralized, rule-bound structures commonly associated with traditional civil service systems, have morphed in highly reformed nations into more decentralized, flexible systems, which place greater emphasis on management and leadership than on process and procedure. Many of the more dramatic reforms in traditionally centralized systems were driven by concerns for improved performance and accountability. Others emerged from simple economics: public employees are often the single greatest expense in a ministry or department's budget and cutting their numbers and benefits is a

clear and direct attack on cost. Whether under the flag of reinvention, new public management, or budget cutting, human resource management reforms have altered roles, numbers, structures, expectations and rewards of national civil service systems.

The patterns of these changes, however, are difficult to describe tidily. This is clearly demonstrated by the chapters in this section. Discretionary reforms – those granting greater flexibilities to managers and public entities – most often occur in Western industrial nations and Westminster democracies. Other nations in the world – those in Eastern Europe, for example – struggle to create new structures and institutions to replace the crumbling remains of Communist years. In these cases, the new structures often look remarkably like old bureaucracies. Other nations – those in Latin and South America, for example – reflect a variation on this pattern, arguing that centralized institutions must become a part of the political culture before decentralization can occur. Flexibility and discretion can be created to combat structural dysfunction, reformers from this perspective note, but structure and stability are necessary antecedents to the reforms blossoming in more developed nations. Corruption and patronage in its many forms are reasons commonly cited by those who advocate the creation of traditional civil service structures as the first step toward reform.

THEORETICAL PERSPECTIVES FOR ANALYSIS

For much of the past century, Western civil service systems were viewed as technical appendages to the institutions of government, rather than as institutions in their own right (Bekke et al., 1997). Legal historians would take issue with the statement, but, generally, it is true. Increasingly, however, it is clear that the succinct separation provided by differences in politics and administration – while real – masked enormous complexity.

MODELS FOR COMPARISON

Despite the complexity and disparity of reform efforts, several patterns or models for managing and leading the human capital of government can be identified across the world. The first, not surprisingly, is the traditional civil service model: a closed hierarchical system designed to be neutral and to exclude inappropriate political influence, to admit based on testing and expertise, and to reward and dismiss based on merit. It is now commonly noted that protection and process are hallmarks of the traditional model, and that performance is, at best, an afterthought and therein lie future reform seeds (Ingraham, 1995; Bekke et al., 1997; Pollitt and Bouckaert, 2000). The promise the model delivers is one of efficiency and order; the reality has been somewhat different, often reflecting bureaucratic pathologies, stagnation and resistance to change.

A variation on the civil service model, but one that does not reject the structures per se, can be termed the strategic human resources model (Kettl et al., 1996). Underpinning this model is the recognition that civil service systems and constraints frequently inhibit governments and their employees from responding to new challenges, but also keep governments from utilizing and rewarding public employees in the most effective way.

Alternative compensation structures, variations on traditional classification structures and some decentralization of authority from a central office to individual agencies are generally included in strategic HR reforms. It is important to note, however, that many of these reforms proceed from the assumption that traditional structures can be altered incrementally at the edges to achieve new objectives. It is not unusual, therefore, to find more strategic human resource management objectives being pursued from within the old structures. The United States is a leading example of this approach.

The third, and most recent, general model now being advocated for public employees is termed the human capital model (Walker, 2000). Based, to some extent, on the perception (real in some cases) that governments need to compete for employees in what is fundamentally a 'War for Talent', the human capital model urges that human resources be viewed as critical strategic resources to be developed, not as sunk costs to the organization (McKinsey, 1998). This perspective has become more widespread as governments encountered more and more difficulty in recruiting and retaining qualified employees (OECD Public Management Service, 2001). The human capital model is notable in that it places human resource management at the very center of agency strategic direction and management, not as a technical activity removed from daily management, as does the traditional civil service model.

COMMON CHALLENGES

These general models emerged and persevered as leaders and managers in government faced a set of challenges quite different from those civil service systems were created to address. One of the most important of these was the need to move from pact to performance; that is, from protection of employees and guarantees of security to an emphasis on performance that placed the burden on the employee, not on the government employer. Pay for performance, performance contracts and downsizing were common responses here. Michael Katula and James Perry provide broad insight into the theory and practice of performance management and pay for performance. So commonplace as to be nearly inherent in reform discussions, pay for performance is a policy tool whose popularity has not been diminished by very modest success. Katula and Perry detail the experiences with pay for performance as an incentive in public systems, but also explore other potential alternatives.

New examinations of the role of public sector unions and collective bargaining are also common reform themes. The 'partnerships' that evolved from reinventing government are one manifestation. James Thompson's excellent chapter provides a rare and very useful summary of the current state of collective bargaining arrangements across the world, detailing the differences among those nations whose political and institutional history allowed consensualist patterns of cooperation between public unions and the leaders and managers of government, and those nations with a fundamentally confrontational labor/management relationship. He asks, 'What is the current practice and future outlook of collective bargaining and unions?' He examines the potential and the experience with collaboration versus confrontation and explores the potential for the partnership model so favored by reinvention efforts. Finally, he queries if a reconfiguration of the relationship is necessary or likely.

A second new challenge involved the need to rethink the nature of the public workforce. A permanent stable workforce, eligible for full benefits and compensated and utilized in traditional civil service ways, does not fit the needs of many governments today. Smaller, more flexible core workforces, seasonal or temporary workers, contract employees and even permanent employees who do not view government as their long-term career choice both shape and are shaped by governments' emerging analysis of workforce needs. This new workforce context has also led to significant challenging of the 'government as model employer' idea. The emerging idea is that government must restructure and redesign many human resource functions so that it can be a competitive employer. Sally Coleman Selden's chapter discusses general patterns and trends in recruiting and retaining a highly qualified

and able public service. What are current trends in recruitment, retention and in performance management in nations that have addressed these issues? Selden finds more flexible recruiting tools, a heightened sense of the need to be an effective recruiter, increased use of both recruitment and retention bonuses, a new focus on workforce planning, and a growing awareness of – if not complete adherence to – principles of performance management.

An additional challenge underpins all of those just described. As governments subcontract or outsource many of their activities – including core functions, in some cases – they increasingly manage a 'shadow' or 'hollow' workforce (Milward and Provan, 1999). Contract employees are not technically government employees, but responsibility and accountability for the jobs they do often remains with the employees who monitor the contracts – the contract managers of government. Many core human resource management functions are among those on the frequently contracted list: management of retirement benefits is one example. Training provision is also a very frequent contract activity. Managing contractors, particularly when they are providing services that shape the nature and skills of government employees, is an increasingly critical activity. The struggles to balance accountability with the reality of authority and control is manifested to some extent in the recent attention focused on the roles and responsibilities of public leaders. Senior executive corps, performance contracts, new recruiting patterns and new definitions of how leaders should 'look' are thoughtfully described and critiqued by John Halligan, in a chapter that is an important update to emerging views of public leadership. Halligan explores the nature and characters of several national leadership cadres, identifies and examines models of leadership development and asks the extent to which these models contain fundamental components of learning for effective leadership, such as the capacity to change.

Finally, Jørgen Grønnegaard Christensen explores leadership – political and administrative – in another way, examining comparative executive pay through a variety of theoretical lenses. In a far-reaching analysis, he concludes that neither pure market nor pure political explanations suffice to explain variations in executive pay. Neither are there simple categories for the variation. Instead, Christensen finds persistent cross-national differences in countries otherwise alike and inconsistent developments in countries that are otherwise similar. Concluding that theoretical explanations fall far short of explaining such diversity, he also notes that 'paying for good governance' is a constant policy challenge for all nations, no matter their level of political or economic development.

No brief explanation of the complexities of managing modern public services could cover the subject adequately. In combination, however, the chapters in this section provide both overviews and incisive analysis of broad issues, relevant comparisons and lessons learned thus far.

REFERENCES

Bekke, Hans, Perry, James and Toonen, Theo (1997) *Civil Service Reform in Comparative Perspective*. Bloomington, IN: Indiana University Press.

Ingraham, Patricia W. (1995) *The Foundation of Merit: Public Service in American Democracy*. Baltimore, MD: Johns Hopkins University Press.

Kettl, Donald F., Ingraham, Patricia W. Sanders, Ronald P. and Horner, Constance (1996) *Civil Service Reform: Building a Government That Works*. Washington, DC: Brookings Institution.

McKinsey Group (1998) 'The War for Talent', *The McKinsey Quarterly*, 3: 44–57.

Milward, H. Brinton and Provan, Keith (1999) 'How Networks are Governed'. Paper Delivered at the Fifth National Public Management Conference, Texas A&M University, December.

OECD Public Management Service (2001) *Report of the Committee on Public Workforce Issues*. Paris: OECD.

Pollitt, Christopher and Bouckaert, Geert (2000) *Public Management Reform: A Comparative Analysis*. Oxford: Oxford University Press.

Walker, David O. (2000) *Creating Human Capital Value for Government*. Washington, DC: Pricewaterhousecoopers.

4

Comparative Performance Pay

Michael Katula and James L. Perry

During the past two decades, governments around the world have sought to reform their public sectors. As the result of both political and fiscal pressures, the emphasis of successive waves of reform has been on making government more efficient and more effective. The public sector has often looked to the private sector for ideas in this effort. One of the more visible products of this exchange is the New Public Management (NPM), which emphasizes the role of private sector management techniques in the public sector (Flynn, 1990).

Although governments have experimented with NPM in many different areas, one of its most prominent applications has been in the area of civil service reform. Civil services around the world came under scrutiny, especially in the 1980s, for being bloated (in Western Europe, especially Scandinavia), for wage bills that were perceived as too large (in developing nations) and for being unresponsive (United States). One of the solutions that NPM offered to reform civil services was the introduction of performance pay schemes. In this chapter we provide an introduction to comparative performance pay. We present five propositions to summarize the existing literature about performance pay.

When performance pay plans are put into practice they typically involve a process that can be simplistically represented by the following model:

Goal setting → Performance → Appraisal of performance → Reward decision[1]

Performance pay plans are essentially instruments that are used to tie worker or work unit motivation, effort and performance to compensation.

Pay-for-performance schemes are grounded in expectancy theory (Milkovich and Wigdor, 1991;

OECD, 1993). Expectancy theory postulates that levels of effort and performance are linked with levels of compensation (Vroom, 1964; Lawler, 1973). Rational choice is integral to the theory (Lawler, 2000). In short, a manager can achieve the desired level of effort and performance from an employee through formulating a worthy reward, usually monetary in nature. Individual decision makers will evaluate the worth of that reward and gauge their effort accordingly. Assuming that individual employees are rational decision makers, the trick for management is to offer rewards that will lead to the desired level of output by workers.

Theories of goal setting also come into play in the conceptualization of performance pay plans. Goal setting theory states that employee performance is likely to improve when employees believe that the goals are attainable (Locke, 1968; Locke and Latham, 1990). Again, this theory considers the individual to be rational. Employees are able to discern between goals that are attainable and those that are beyond accomplishment at a given level of effort. Although the expectancy and goal setting theoretical foundations of performance pay are elegant and straightforward, the practice of implementing actual plans has proven more complicated. We will discuss these problems at greater length in later sections of this chapter. We first discuss different types of performance pay.

TYPES OF PERFORMANCE PAY PLANS

Pay-for-performance schemes can take several forms. These forms are perhaps best examined in

		Level of performance	
		Individual	Group
Contribution to base Salary	Added to base	(a) Merit plans	(d) Small group incentives
	Not added to base	(b) Piece rates Commissions Bonuses	(c) Profit sharing Gainsharing Bonuses

the two-by-two matrix established by Milkovich and Wigdor (1991). We have reproduced their matrix in Figure 4.1 as a frame for the following discussion.

Milkovich and Wigdor categorize the elements of the matrix based on individual versus group level of performance and whether or not the incentive compensation is added to an employee's base salary. The individual or group nature of the plan is important. Performance pay that links individuals rather than groups to work-related goals may be viewed by employees as being easier to accomplish when goals and appraisals are considered to be fair (Milkovich and Wigdor, 1991). In such plans, at least at the theoretical level, perceived or actual collective action dilemmas become less of a problem for individual employees. The way plans are tied to base salary may also have serious repercussions for performance. Lawler (2000) states that plans utilizing bonuses may have a more positive motivational effect on employees, as the reward granting process becomes flexible over time. When pay is tacked on base salaries, the implication is that employees may have less to strive for in terms of gaining rewards. We introduce the various plans below, noting that some of our discussion comes from literature that primarily analyzes the private sector.

Cell (a): Merit plans

Merit plans, which tie individual base salaries to pay, are perhaps the most common type of public sector pay-for-performance plan in practice today and have been widely used within the United States. The beginning of the merit pay movement in the public sector can be traced to the Civil Service Reform Act of 1978 (CSRA), which marked a significant change in the way that public sector employees were paid. The CSRA attempted to make public employees

more accountable and also to move away from the previous system of virtually automatic step pay increases (Perry, 1992).

Cell (b): Piece rates, commissions and bonuses

In piece rate systems compensation is determined based upon the amount of output that an employee generates (Mitchell et al., 1990). Discussions of piece rate systems begin with Frederick Taylor (1911) and the scientific management movement. Taylor observed both the way that workers performed their tasks and how they were compensated, which often involved perverse incentive structures. In his fieldwork, Taylor discovered that workers who were compensated under piece rate plans were often more productive than their counterparts. However, piece rate systems often engender problems between labor and management and have become less popular in the post Second World War era (Risher and Fay, 1997). As Miller points out (1992), the trust and credible commitment necessary for a successful piece rate system are often difficult to achieve.

Cell (c): Profit sharing, gainsharing and bonuses

Profit sharing and gainsharing plans are similar in several ways. For example, both types of plans tie pay to group-level performance. In addition, both gainsharing and profit sharing plans work by redistributing earnings. Profit sharing plans begin by establishing a level of earnings for a particular time frame. Profits that exceed this base level are redistributed to eligible employees within the organization (Lawler, 2000).

Gainsharing allows employees to benefit from a redistribution of profits resulting from improved performance. In gainsharing plans, baseline measures are established to determine the actual gains in productivity. If an increase is made, the leftover profits are divided between the organization and the employees. A prominent gainsharing plan was implemented at McClelland Air Force Base in California. Employees involved in 'Pacer Share' received gainshares for ten of the twenty-one quarters of the project. The reward level from Pacer Share was $1,924 per employee (http://www.opm.gov/demos/demo-fact. htm).[2]

Gainsharing plans have distinct advantages and disadvantages. For example, since there is no guaranteed payout under a gainsharing plan, employees who are looking to minimize uncertainty in their pay are not attracted to gainsharing. On the other hand, if gainsharing plans have been successful in a particular organization, then employees who are not necessarily risk averse may be drawn to the plan. As one of the leading scholars of pay-for-performance plans notes, gainsharing plans in the private sector have survived for decades in certain companies, and seem to work best in stable work situations where performance evaluation takes place in small to medium-sized groups (Lawler, 2000).

Cell (d): Small group incentives

While numerous examples of gainsharing or profit sharing plans for small groups of employees can be found, small group incentive plans that add rewards to an employee's base pay are rare. Organizations that utilize group-based performance evaluation are perhaps more likely to favor compensation that does not become a permanent part of the employee's pay. This can lead to horizontal pay discrepancies and mistrust between management and employees within the organization.

PROPOSITIONS

Although performance pay plans have been utilized in the public sector for decades, there have been relatively few attempts by scholars to sum up the state of research in this subfield of public management. The rest of this chapter represents an attempt to offer some general and preliminary observations on performance pay plans both in the United States and abroad. We hope that the following propositions will act both as guideposts for further discussions of

performance pay plans in the public sector and as platforms for deeper inquiry into the subject.

Proposition 1: Performance pay plans are commonplace in the West and are gaining legitimacy across the globe

While the debate over results continues, performance pay plans have become a fact in the public sectors of Western industrial democracies. Many examples of such plans exist at various vertical and horizontal levels of government in the OECD countries. For example, a 1993 OECD study details nineteen performance pay plans in nine countries ranging from state-level to senior civil servants in the national government. Although the degree to which the plans are used varies heavily within some of these countries (Elliott et al., 1999), and correlates with the degree of centralization of particular countries' pay determination plans, there is no doubt that performance pay plans are viewed as a useful tool in motivating public sector employees in the West.

While performance pay plans are common in the OECD states, they are less common in other parts of the world. Singapore, for example, does offer bonuses to civil servants, but these are based on the performance of the national economy (Chew, 1997). Civil servants on the super scale in Singapore are eligible for merit bonuses based on their performance during the previous year (Chew, 1997). However, neither of these activities can really be considered a performance pay plan in the NPM tradition. There is some evidence of attempts to implement performance pay plans in other countries as well. China has an appraisal system in its civil service but assessing individual employees has proven difficult and has led to the uniform disbursement problem (Mukherjee and Manning, 2000). The Hong Kong government also considered a performance pay system, but ultimately decided against implementation despite inadequacies in current incentive structures (Perry and Frederickson, 1999).

Other areas of the developing world have been troubled by more fundamental reform challenges, such as bloating of the public sector, redundancy in public sector employment and wage bills that consume too much government revenue (Lindauer, 1994). In many of these countries, incentives are not monetary in nature. Instead, rewards or entitlements come in the form of services or perquisites, such as free or subsidized lodging (Colclough, 1997). In many developing countries, then, injecting more money into the public sector for performance pay plans is simply not an option.

Proposition II: There is no clear and emergent pattern to predict the rise or use of performance pay plans

One of the unresolved issues within the literature on performance pay concerns patterns of adoption and implementation, and can be summed up by the following two questions. First, are there variables that predict performance pay adoption and can help us to distinguish between adopters and non-adopters? Second, what do we know about reasons for variation in the types of performance pay plans that are adopted?

These are broad questions. Even when we apply them to the larger category of NPM reforms, of which performance pay is just a subset, answers are still elusive (Hood, 1996). While patterns and predictive constellations of variables may exist to explain the adoption of performance pay schemes, scholars have yet to uncover them. While we declare that no pattern is evident, we also review attempts to identify the crucial variables.

One of the more interesting analyses of performance pay adoption in the OECD countries comes from Dell'Aringa and Lanfranchi (1999), who array the degree of the use of performance pay in thirteen countries alongside several other descriptive categories.[4] It is noteworthy that within the four countries that make 'strong use of' performance pay, Australia, the United States, Canada and the United Kingdom, the authors also find that the countries have 'no link' (US, Canada, UK) or only 'some link' (Australia) between cost of living and pay; the countries have 'no use of' (US, Canada, UK) or only 'some use of' (Australia) allowances as a proportion of total pay; and all four countries make 'strong use of' comparability principles. Dell'Aringa and Lanfranchi conclude that the degree of centralization has much to do with the presence of performance pay schemes. The decentralized, flexible systems of Australia, Canada, the United States and the United Kingdom tend also to include performance pay systems, whereas the centralized systems of France, Germany and Italy exhibit little or no use of performance pay. The OECD (1993) also echoes Dell'Aringa and Lanfranchi's findings on centralization. While the authors make an important contribution to the literature, it is important to note that their study unveils correlation, not a causal relationship.

Perhaps no general pattern exists at all. Or perhaps one exists that is not based in the logical adoption of performance pay, but rather in a sort of follower's behavior. Institutional theory provides some support for this notion. Meyer and Rowan (1977) write that myths explain organizational similarity, and that institutionalization of a set of rules within an organization is an attempt to attain legitimacy, to enhance resources and to enhance survival prospects. DiMaggio and Powell (1982) also stressed the fact that there are three reasons that can lead organizations to become similar to one another. First, organizations can be coerced from above to make changes to their form. Second, organizations can decide to mimic the form of another organization that is perceived as successful. Third, in some cases, professional norms can lead managers to reshape organizations in a pattern that leads to high levels of similarity between organizations.

Both sets of authors leave students of performance pay systems with much to consider. As we noted earlier, the simplicity of the theoretical underpinning of performance pay systems is very attractive to managers and policy makers. However, the ideas offered by Meyer and Rowan (1977) and DiMaggio and Powell (1982) indicate that the adoption of performance pay plans may have as much to do with the way ideas spread across organizations as with the attractiveness of the rational underpinnings of expectancy theory.

A logical extension of this line of thought on performance pay systems suggests that the adoption and implementation question may not have a neat answer at all. As Ingraham (1993) notes, the implementation of performance pay schemes is often the result of a policy diffusion process that takes place without consultation. Instead, Ingraham notes that the popularity of performance pay systems in the private sector has led to large-scale diffusion in the public sectors of the OECD countries. In short, while higher degrees of pay decentralization may allow governments more leeway in experimenting with performance pay, there are still no plainly identifiable macro-level variables that predict when performance pay schemes will be adopted or implemented.

What about the predictability of different types of performance pay schemes? As Milkovich and Wigdor (1991) point out, policy makers and managers have a variety of choices when deciding which performance pay plan to adopt. Within the OECD countries, most performance pay plans consist of individual merit increments and bonuses (OECD, 1993, 1997). While there is little direct evidence to suggest why these two types of performance pay are the most popular, some conjecture is possible. For example, from an employee's standpoint, pay goals based on individual achievement may be considered easier to attain than those tied to group performance (Milkovich and Wigdor, 1991). This may be the case because plans based on individual achievement may avoid potential collective action problems that so often complicate work in small groups. In turn, from a managerial standpoint, bonuses may be popular because they represent a one-time payout that employees have to earn from year to year. Certain types of performance pay schemes, such as piece rate work or commissions, may simply fit better in private sector settings than they do in the public sector.

It is difficult to understand the exact reasons for the relative lack of creativity in performance pay plans. However, the most convincing reason again may have to do with diffusion. As Ingraham suggests (1993), performance pay schemes are quite often diffused both domestically and cross-nationally with seemingly little attention paid to the appropriateness of the plan.

Proposition III: The performance pay plan must fit into the various contexts into which it is introduced

One of the primary tasks of a manager seeking to adopt a performance pay plan is to design a plan that fits into the organizational situation (Perry, 1995). There are at least two ways to examine the issue of fit. The first is intraorganizational in nature. Perry (1995) discusses a number of potential problems, such as issues of structure and process that managers face when implementing performance pay within their organizations. For example, if employees perform tasks whose results are inherently difficult to measure, the implementing manager should avoid performance pay plans based on quantitative measurement of individuals. In short, it is necessary to keep the nature of the task and the nature of the evaluation system similar.

The nature of the game is also important. Some performance pay plans are either zero-sum in nature (Perry, 1995) or entail thresholds for the number of employees who can be rewarded (OECD, 1993). Rules of this nature are often necessary for budget control or when top management expects evaluations to be inflated. However, many organizations will have large numbers of high performers, and the performance pay plan must be able to cope with this reality. Funding shortages in performance pay systems can often lead employees to adopt a cynical attitude about the connection between performance and pay, in which case the organization may be better off

without any sort of merit plan at all. In our own research at a facility of the United States Navy, one of the most common concerns voiced regarding the performance pay plan is that there is not enough money available to reward all the high performers. The OECD (1993) also notes that achieving the correct intraorganizational fit often involves cycles of experimentation and policy adjustment. Thus, any adoption of a performance pay plan should be considered a work in progress in the short run, if not permanently.

As Ingraham (1993) notes, the diffusion of performance pay schemes has proceeded in many cases without consultation and without a level of empirical support that would indicate the appropriateness of the plan. The seemingly haphazard diffusion has taken place across states within the United States and also cross-nationally. This leads us to concerns about extra-organizational fit. Performance pay plans must fit appropriately not only into the organization's cultural context, but also into the national context in which they are being adopted.

Issues of national fit are often resolved on their own. Morgan (1996) has written about the relationship between the type of state and the possibility of reforming the civil service. Intervening macro-level variables often determine, *ex ante*, which plans will succeed. For example, a simple lack of funds in developing countries often precludes the adoption of a performance pay system, although perhaps not a merit system based on non-monetary rewards. Furthermore, as several of the contributors to Elliott, Lucifora and Meurs (1999) note, the degree of centralization of the pay determination process dictates where decisions regarding merit plans can be made.

Regardless of whether the country is in the OECD or is developing, the first question that should be asked during the performance pay implementation process concerns the nature and needs of the organization. Ingraham has phrased this concern most eloquently in stating: 'Ask what public organizations *need*, not what private organizations do' (Ingraham, 1993: 354). When managers consider the local circumstances affecting the potential of performance pay plans they are more likely to design one that fits into the given organizational context.

Proposition IV: Measurement problems will continue to be a problem in designing and implementing performance pay plans

One of the most difficult tasks facing managers, whether in the public or private sectors, is measuring performance. This is primarily because the data necessary to rank employee performance in a precise manner are not available (Lawler, 2000). Furthermore, is it possible to devise objective performance measures? The tasks that public sector employees perform vary greatly both within and across agencies, and public sector organizations often perform tasks that do not have a tangible result that can be measured. Indeed, the measurement problem has engaged public managers for decades (Perry, 1986, 1992) and is not likely to disappear in the near future.

Perry (1986) notes one of the underlying logical flaws of merit pay systems. Performance is often defined as the sum of the employee's activities on the job. However, organizations are complex webs of social interaction that inherently tie one employee's performance to the actions of many others. Thus, Perry asserts, there is an element of uncertainty in every manager's job that cannot be accounted for in a fixed contract. Furthermore, Perry identifies the problem of vertical information asymmetries and incomplete monitoring that are mentioned by other authors in a theoretical sense (Miller, 1992) and a practical one (Griener et al., 1981; O'Toole and Churchill, 1982). Perry also notes that employees may have incentives to devote more attention to personal performance goals at the expense of larger organizational ones. All three of these potential problems deal with the fact that in organizational hierarchies information often becomes difficult to attain, making an accurate rating system difficult to implement.

Milkovich and Wigdor (1991) also identify several measurement problems with performance pay plans, centering on the different ways that evaluators can inappropriately rate employee contribution. In short, the problems the authors discuss entail overrating, underrating, or inconsistent rating error. Overrating senior managers has been reported in Canada, the United States and Australia (OECD, 1993).

One of the problems that Milkovich and Wigdor (1991) consider is one they term 'restriction in range', when all employees receive ratings in the same range. This observation merits some discussion. As we mentioned earlier, performance pay systems are usually the result of a reform effort. In many cases, the previous pay regime neither motivated employees nor compensated them effectively. In our own field research, we observed the adoption and implementation of a performance pay system at a field activity of the United States Navy. The system that pre-dated the reforms suffered from the restriction in range problem identified by Milkovich and Wigdor. Employees were almost uniformly awarded the same rating during each evaluation period, a mark that allowed them to receive a small raise in pay, but not one that would drive the employees to work considerably harder. The uniform marks were not guaranteed by the system itself, but had become a norm instituted by managers. Very few, if any, employees received a negative evaluation that would have led to no increase in pay. Due to this norm of range restriction, the old system contained significant measurement error.

The implementation of the new performance pay system evoked some ill will toward management at the facility. The same reviews that employees took for granted some months earlier were no longer guaranteed to them. In short, the employees missed the restriction in range feature of the old system because it offered them a way to eliminate uncertainty in their evaluations. Although the new system offered the possibility of greater rewards, it also removed the restriction in range feature of the old system. Although this innovation was a step forward for management, some employees now feared they would be inappropriately rated.

One of the lessons we have learned from this and other research (Perry, 1995), and one that we believe can be generalized, involves the inevitability of measurement problems. There are three primary factors at work that will keep the designers of performance pay plans busy for years to come. First, managers will constantly be challenged to design and improve systems that seek to measure tasks that often have intangible or even invisible results. Second, designers will need to write rules to guard against the tendency for systems to slip toward a comfortable but restricted pay range for all employees. Third, employees will remain averse to performance pay plans that involve inherent uncertainty, so designers and managers will need to engage in strong leadership and effective communication to inform and motivate their employees.

Proposition V: Despite some failures, performance pay plans represent an effective tool for the public sector

In lieu of conclusions, we would like to close with a note about the effectiveness of performance pay in the public sector. Much of this chapter has been devoted to both the theoretical and practical shortcomings of performance pay plans. Despite the negative evidence, we believe that when adopted under the proper conditions, performance pay can help lead public organizations toward greater effectiveness in achieving their goals. We offer three broad suggestions to help in this matter.

For performance pay plans to be effective, the implementation of the plans must follow the logic dictated by theory. We return briefly to our simple model:

Goal setting → Performance → Appraisal of performance → Reward decision

Expectancy theory tells us that rational employees will understand the linkage expressed in the model – positive results in performance and appraisal will lead to rewards. Indeed, we have witnessed this behavior in field settings. Therefore, public managers must be certain that improved performance leads to positive appraisals and yields pecuniary rewards. If this practical application of the theory does not take place employees are likely to quickly lose faith in the logic behind performance pay, their management and possibly the organization in which they work.

Although data are limited, there are examples of both effective and ineffective performance pay plans within the OECD countries. The OECD (1993) reports that 61 per cent of the employees covered by the US Navy's China Lake demonstration project believed there was a connection between pay and performance. Other significant findings have emerged from public sector performance pay projects. Schay (1997) states that federal government employee satisfaction with pay was much higher for those covered under the Pacer Share and Navy demonstration projects than for their colleagues in traditional pay plans.[5] There have also been failures. The OECD (1993) notes that public managers in Australia and Canada exhibited little confidence that pay was connected to performance, although both of these countries used quota systems that restricted the amount of rewards that could be distributed. Therefore, the negative results in these projects could have more to do with the rules attached to the operation of the performance pay plans and less to do with the logic of performance pay.

Information is a precious resource in performance pay plans. In addition to the crucial role that information plays in performance appraisals, which we mentioned earlier in the chapter, information also allows all actors in the performance pay plan to take advantage of the plan. Furthermore, when information about payouts and other aspects of the operation of performance pay plans is thoroughly disseminated by management it has the potential to preemptively counter mistrust by employees.

Ingraham (1993) supports the first of these points with her observations on performance pay in the Netherlands. Ingraham notes that managers covered under the plan needed more direction from a central authority, and that there was a wide variation concerning 'awareness of the system and its intent' across managers working in the same ministry. Not surprisingly, the plan did not work well. We have also found in our own fieldwork that making sure that employees are not only aware of the performance pay plan but also understand its workings can assuage employee apprehension about switching compensation systems. It is critical for employees to understand the institutions that govern their pay at work. Information must not only be disseminated heavily at the beginning of the performance pay plan but also throughout the life of the project.

In complex organizations trust can be crucial to attaining organizational goals, and it must come by example from leadership (Miller, 1992). If leaders demonstrate that they are aware of employee concerns and can be trusted to address them, a norm of trust may arise within the organization. Therefore, strong leadership may be the most critical element in implementing effective performance pay plans. If employees do not trust management to conduct accurate appraisals, to secure enough money for all high performers, or to change the performance pay plan if it falters, then the likelihood of establishing an effective pay system is very low. Management can address these issues by making sure that enough money is available to satisfy all high performers (Milkovich and Wigdor, 1991), by allowing employees a voice in creating the plan (Perry, 1995), and by soliciting feedback from employees regarding the plan while it is in effect.

When leadership fails to convince employees that the performance pay plan is fair, accusations follow fairly quickly. We have observed this in our own fieldwork, where we have heard employees negatively characterize performance pay plans as tools of management, used to satisfy a particular group within the organization over another. We have also heard employees misidentify some of the most basic rules of the performance pay plan as much as two years after its inception. Top management is not solely responsible for these complaints. After all, employees have a duty to understand the environment of their workplace. However, preemptive moves by leadership can improve the situation.

There is no doubt that performance pay plans will remain oft-used tools within the public sector for years to come. The pressure for greater effectiveness in government may be as old as government itself, and performance pay plans provide public managers with the opportunity to instill greater accountability and also a more generous rewards system into their organizations. However, performance pay plans will only experience widespread adoption when a large enough number of success stories allows us to understand the intricacies of implementation. This accumulation of data and knowledge could represent a tipping point that would help institutionalize the concept of performance pay in the public sector.

NOTES

1   See OECD (1993) for a more complete model.
2   The overall results of the plan, however, were mixed. Pacer Share was implemented in February 1988 and expired in February 1993.
3   Given the available data, our discussion here draws upon only OECD.
4   France, Germany, Italy, Spain, Finland, Ireland, Denmark, Netherlands, Sweden, Australia, US, Canada, UK.
5   Schay (1997) also notes other benefits achieved at the performance pay sites.

REFERENCES

Chew, D. (1997) 'Economic Restructuring and Flexible Civil Service Pay in Singapore', in C. Colclough (ed.), *Public-Sector Pay and Adjustment: Lessons from Five Countries*. New York: Routledge.

Colclough, C. (1997) 'Economic Stagnation and Earnings Decline in Zambia, 1975–91', in C. Colclough (ed.), *Public Sector Pay and Adjustment: Lessons from Five Countries*. New York: Routledge.

Dell'Aringa, C. and Lanfranchi, N. (1999) 'Pay Determination in the Public Service: An International Comparison', in R. Elliot, C. Lucifora and D. Meurs (eds), *Public Sector Pay Determination in the European Union*. New York: St Martin's Press.

DiMaggio, P. and Powell, W. (1982) *The Iron Cage Revisited: Institutional Isomorphism and Collective Rationality in Organizational Fields*. New Haven, CT: Institution for Social and Policy Studies, Yale University.

Elliot, R., Lucifora, C. and Meurs, D. (1999) 'Public Sector Pay Determination in the European Union: Issues and Outcomes', in R. Elliot, C. Lucifora and D. Meurs (eds), *Public Sector Pay Determination in the European Union*. New York: St Martin's Press.

Flynn, N. (1990) *Public Sector Management*. London: Harvester Wheatsheaf.

Griener, J., Hatry, H., Koss, M., Millar, A. and Woodward, J. (1981) *Productivity and Motivation*. Washington, DC: Urban Institute Press.

Hood, C. (1996) 'Exploring Variations in Public Management Reform of the 1980s', in A. Bekke, J. Perry and T. Toonen (eds), *Civil Service Systems in Comparative Perspective*. Bloomington, IN: Indiana University Press.

Ingraham, P. (1993) 'Of Pigs in Pokes and Policy Diffusion: Another Look at Pay-For-Performance', *Public Administration Review*, 53 (July/August): 348–56.

Lawler, E. (1973) *Motivation in Work Organizations*. Monterey, CA: Brooks/Cole.

Lawler, E. (2000) *Rewarding Excellence: Pay Strategies for the New Economy*. San Francisco: Jossey–Bass.

Lindauer, D. (1994) 'Government Pay and Employment Policies and Economic Performance', in D. Lindauer and B. Nunberg (eds), *Rehabilitating Government: Pay and Employment Reform in Africa*. Washington, DC: World Bank.

Locke, E. (1968) 'Toward a Theory of Task Motivation and Incentives', *Organizational Behavior and Human Performance*, 3: 157–89.

Locke, E. and Latham, G. (1990) *Toward a Theory of Goal Setting and Task Performance*. Upper Saddle River, NJ: Prentice–Hall.

Meyer, J. and Rowan, B. (1977) 'Institutionalized Organizations: Formal Structures as Myth and Ceremony', *American Journal of Sociology*, 83: 340–63.

Milkovich, G.T. and Wigdor, A.K. (eds), (1991) *Pay for Performance: Evaluating Performance Appraisal and Merit Pay*. Washington, DC: National Academy Press.

Miller, G. (1992) *Managerial Dilemmas: The Political Economy of Hierarchy*. New York: Cambridge University Press.

Mitchell, D., Lewin, D. and Lawler, E. (1990) 'Alternative Pay Systems, Firm Performance, and Productivity', in A. Blinder (ed.), *Paying for Productivity: A Look at the Evidence*. Washington, DC: Brookings Institution.

Morgan, P. (1996) 'Analyzing Fields of Change: Civil Service Systems in Developing Countries', in A. Bekke, J. Perry and T. Toonen (eds), *Civil Service Systems in Comparative Perspective*. Bloomington, IN: Indiana University Press.

Mukherjee, R. and Manning, N. (2000) 'Administrative and Civil Service Reform: Rewards and Incentives' (*www1.worldbank.org/publicsector/civilservice/agency .htm#incentives*).

O'Toole, D. and Churchill, J. (1982) 'Implementing Pay-for-Performance: Initial Experiences', *Review of Public Personnel Administration*, 2 (Summer): 13–28.

OECD (1993) *Private Pay for Public Work: Performance-Related Pay for Public Sector Managers*. Paris: OECD.

OECD (1997) *In Search of Results: Performance Management Practices*. Paris: OECD.

Perry, J. (1986) 'Merit Pay in the Public Sector: The Case for a Failure of Theory', *Review of Public Personnel Administration*, 7 (1): 57–69.

Perry, J. (1992) 'The Merit Pay Reforms', in P. Ingraham and D. Rosenbloom (eds), *The Promise and Paradox of Civil Service Reform*. Pittsburgh, PA: University of Pittsburgh Press.

Perry, J. (1995) 'Compensation, Merit Pay, and Motivation', in S. Hays and R. Kearney (eds), *Public Personnel Administration: Problems and Prospects*, 3rd edn. Englewood Cliffs, NJ: Prentice–Hall.

Perry, J. and Frederickson, D. (1999) 'Civil Service Reform in Hong Kong: Lessons from US Experience', *Public Administration and Policy*, 8 (2): 57–70.

Risher, H. and Fay, C. (1997) 'Rethinking Government Compensation Programs', in H. Risher and C. Fay (eds), *New Strategies for Public Pay: Rethinking Government Compensation Programs*. San Francisco: Jossey–Bass.

Schay, B. (1997) 'Paying for Performance: Lessons Learned in Fifteen Years of Federal Demonstration Projects', in H. Risher and C. Fay (eds), *New Strategies for Public Pay: Rethinking Government Compensation Programs*. San Francisco: Jossey–Bass.

Taylor, F. (1911) *The Principles of Scientific Management*. New York: Harper and Row.

Vroom, V.H. (1964) *Work and Motivation*. New York: Wiley.

5

Innovations and Global Trends in Human Resource Management Practices

Sally Coleman Selden

For more than a decade, public sector entities have been making substantial changes in how they manage their human resources (HR). As the barriers to communication have broken down through telecommunication, information and partnerships, the field has witnessed a globalization of human resource management (HRM) practices. Reforms, driven by political, administrative and technical reasons, have transformed some public human resource management systems from regulatory and reactive into strategic and proactive. While public sector reforms have been called by many different labels – including reinvention, reengineering, privatization and organizational learning – the challenge has been similar. How do public sector human resource practices and policies change to improve the current and future operations of government?

Many countries, states and local governments have decentralized their human resource practices to provide managers with more latitude and responsibility, have adopted innovations to improve the efficiency and quality of HR services and have reconceptualized dramatically the role of human resource management (OECD, 2001a; Selden et al., 2001). Despite the litany of changes observed worldwide, there are no absolute solutions to the challenges facing different governments. Reformers tend to identify approaches that best fit their national or local contexts, as well as their reform objectives. While the general purpose of reform may be similar – citizens and policy makers want public sector workforces that meet citizen needs better and more efficiently – the specific needs of individual governments vary. Some governments may be motivated to change in order to democratize

their administration while others want to reduce costs (World Bank, 2001a). A recent OECD report captures the phenomena of reform best (2001a: 2): 'The public's needs are rapidly changing as societies become more diverse, complex and fragmented. Technological advances and more knowledgeable citizenry create new opportunities and expectations. The pace of change is faster than ever.' In short, the synergy of reform is contingent upon a government's ability to align the changing demands of its environment with innovative human resource management practices in a manner that best addresses its particular, and perhaps unique, needs (World Bank, 2001c).

The objectives of this chapter are threefold: to describe the environmental demands influencing human resource management globally; to describe trends and innovations in the areas of recruitment, compensation and performance management globally; and to describe models of reform and reform strategies that governments have employed, with particular emphasis on changes that have occurred within the United States.

THE GLOBAL ENVIRONMENT: TRENDS IN EMPLOYMENT DEMOGRAPHICS AND LABOR MARKETS

Today public sector organizations worldwide are struggling to recruit and retain qualified workers (Ingraham et al., 2000; PUMA/HRM, 2000e). Three primary factors – downsizing, a tight labor market and an aging workforce – contribute to these trends. Because of the amount of downsizing that occurred in the 1990s in countries such as Finland, Luxembourg, Sweden, the United Kingdom, Australia, Italy, Sweden, Hungary, Austria and Korea, the number of public sector employees in many OECD countries fell drastically in the mid-1990s (PUMA/HRM, 2000e). Shortly therefore, labor market conditions changed causing many countries, such as France, Germany, Austria, Norway and Sweden, to compete with private sector firms to recruit employees (OECD, 2000). In recent years, France, for example, has lost many senior public civil servants to the private sector, in part because of the higher salaries offered (PUMA/HRM, 2000c). Globally, governments are facing critical skills shortages, particularly in highly technical areas (Ingraham et al., 2000; PUMA/HRM, 2000a).

In the Netherlands, where the economy is flourishing, the labor supply is limited and those not employed are able to be selective because of the many jobs available (PUMA/HRM, 2000a). The Netherlands, like other countries, is facing labor shortages because of its aging workforce. The number of persons leaving the labor market exceeds the number of younger individuals joining it. A recent report indicates that for 'three out of every four employees working in the general government sector labour market tensions are expected to be severe by 2004' (PUMA/HRM, 2000a: 6). These positions include police, military, fire, librarians, lawyers, social workers, economists, accountants, engineers, architects, computer-scientists and environmental and agricultural specialists. In Finland, approximately 42 per cent of the public workforce are expected to retire within the next ten years (PUMA/HRM, 2000d). As a result of these trends, one of the primary concerns of governments is how to 'increase and maintain their competitiveness as an employer' (OECD, 2001a: 1).

TRENDS AND INNOVATIONS IN HUMAN RESOURCE MANAGEMENT PRACTICES

Recruiting and retaining public sector workers

The recruitment process, arguably, is one of the most critical human resource functions because it supplies persons with specific knowledge skills, and abilities needed to perform public services. Currently, governments are competing for skilled labor in an economy with a low unemployment rate and changing notions about work and organizational commitment. Each year, governments must fill hundreds of positions. Just as private sector firms recruit aggressively for the best-qualified and most competent workers, so must public sector organizations as well. The Netherlands, for example, cited recruiting qualified staff as a significant challenge (OECD, 2000). A recent report notes (PUMA/HRM 2000d: 2) that 'lower wages, the loss of prestige and mundane job duties have caused many young graduates as well as senior civil servants to choose a career in private sector over public service …, [particularly in] Korea, Netherlands, Norway, the United States and Sweden.' In an effort to counter the falling interest in public service careers, a number of governments, such as Canada, the Netherlands and Portugal, are targeting college campuses to recruit new talent (PUMA/HRM, 2000d).

Until recently, the state of Minnesota, like other governments, acknowledged that its recruiting and hiring system had been untouched since it was adopted in 1939:

> As I tell people it is not that what they did was wrong at the time. It was appropriate at the time. However, today in a very competitive marketplace, where you have to compete with places for a limited labor pool, you must have a recruitment process that is fast and based on merit. (Minnesota Survey Response, 1998)

Realizing this shortcoming, some human resource managers have targeted recruiting and developing human capital as an important part of their job. For example, Colorado's HR department's mission reads as follows:

> Our mission is to enable state agencies to accomplish their missions by developing systems to attract, develop, motivate, and retain the best and brightest employees, and to provide expertise, leadership and consultation in human resource management while protecting state assets.

The United Kingdom, France and Sweden centralized policies and procedures that standardize the recruitment process, even if the point of recruitment occurs locally, rather than centrally. North Carolina, for example, established a statewide recruitment network. Recruiters from agencies and universities work in partnership with the Office of State Personnel to identify the state's recruitment needs, to design a statewide recruitment plan, to promote the state as the employer of choice, and to maximize existing resources. In Phoenix, the HR department coordinates the recruiting process by forming a partnership between the operating department and the HR department. HR analysts are assigned to individual departments to improve service and foster better working relationships around recruiting. Other places, such as Germany, Denmark and Norway, operate highly decentralized recruitment systems. The recruiting process in the city of Austin is decentralized to allow departments to establish recruitment plans that address their departments' specific hiring needs.

Confronted by the dilemmas posed by increasing competition for skilled labor, large numbers of open positions and growing job turnover rates – particularly in hard to hire occupations – some governments streamlined hiring practices, turned to technological innovations to improve the selection process, and adopted public relations strategies to address their image.

The past five years represents a period of significant change in the procedural requirements governing hiring. Several states, such as Iowa, Delaware and Maryland, passed legislation to eliminate the 'Rule of X' (three, seven, ten, etc.) or to expand the number of names or scores on a certified list. To keep that list fresh, Idaho and Missouri reduced the length of time a register of eligible candidates is valid. Indiana decentralized hiring authority for entire occupational categories to agencies. Iowa, Indiana and Kansas eliminated testing. Wisconsin repealed its residency requirement, repealed all restrictions on out-of-state recruiting, and eliminated the restrictions on the number of qualified candidates that can be interviewed. The Connecticut legislature passed an act that required all examinations to become pass/fail. Ohio and Wisconsin accommodate walk-in testing so that individuals can file an application and take the appropriate test at the same time. Some countries, such as Switzerland and Japan, adopted laws and policies that make it easier for personnel to move back and forth between public and private sector employment.

Technological advances are also transforming government's ability to recruit. Currently, all states in the United States post jobs openings on-line, and forty-five states offer applications on-line. South Carolina's website generates more than a million 'hits' a month. Twenty-three states currently have technology that accepts state government applications on-line. Florida's Web-based application system allows applicants to input and store their state employment application and apply for as many vacancies as they choose. The Tennessee Employment Application Monitoring System (TEAMS) allows applicants to conduct job searches, submit applications and take employment examinations on-line. Job applicants receive their examination score that day. Nineteen states operate on-line resumé banks and twelve states use virtual job fairs. Maryland's approach to recruiting includes using its own website, as well as commercial recruitment sites. In addition to these technological advances, fifteen states provide job information at kiosks located throughout the state. The state of Arizona's system scans in resumés and files them in a central database that is used to match applicants' skills with skill-sets required by particular jobs.

A new strategy adopted by some governments is to launch image campaigns to demonstrate the positive attributes of public sector work. Finland, the Netherlands, the UK and New Zealand have initiated public relations campaigns to attract younger residents to civil service and to renew the calling of public service (PUMA/HRM, 2000d). France's civil service noticed that its image improved significantly after assisting residents address the damage caused by a severe storm in 1999. Maryland state government launched a television campaign to highlight the valuable jobs state employees hold. Indiana's Brand campaign promotes positive aspects of working for the state through print ads, radio ads, television ads, brochures, websites and video. Phoenix uses theme-oriented advertisements to entice prospective employees. For example, the HR department worked with the police department to identify traits and attitudes, such as a 'sense of community', of successful employees in the position, and used those attributes to attract similarly motivated individuals. To attract and retain quality candidates in Canada, a leadership group publishes a magazine, *A Day in the Life of the Public Service of Canada*, which features stories of individual public servants – their commitment and satisfaction with public service (PUMA, 2001).

Financial incentives

In order to be more competitive employers, a number of governments altered their compensation systems to become more competitive and to reward performance (PUMA/HRM, 2000b). However, a clear answer to the question of how to reward good performance has not yet emerged. In search of the answers, governments have adopted several different strategies including performance-based compensation structures, skill and competency pay and market-based pay rates (PUMA/HRM, 2000b; Selden et al., 2001).

Iceland, Switzerland and the UK implemented a flexible pay structure to reward performance (PUMA/HRM, 2000d). While the most common remuneration program in state governments in the United States continues to be an annual step increase to an employee's salary, many states now also rely on some form of pay-for-performance to allocate salary increases based on performance. In 2000, the Government Performance Project (GPP) witnessed a jump from 1998 in the use of individual and group performance bonuses. In 2000, about 64 per cent of states allowed for individual performance bonuses and 38 per cent used group bonuses. Those figures were 14.3 per cent and 2 per cent, respectively, in 1998 (Selden et al., 2001). Japan revised its seniority system so that promotions and pay are related to ability and performance (PUMA, 1997). While the trend is toward performance-based salaries in industrial countries, this is not true in developing countries (World Bank, 2001e). While performance-based rewards are not typical in developing countries, a few examples exist. Singapore and China give employees an annual bonus. In Thailand, 15 per cent of government officials within each grade are awarded an extra pay increment for exceptional performance.

In the past few years, more governments granted skill- and competency-based pay (Ingraham and Selden, 2001). Skill-based pay was introduced in Ireland in the mid-1990s (European Foundation, 2001). The state of Indiana, for example, allows agencies to customize their compensation strategy by selecting the appropriate strategies ranging from competency-based pay, to skill-based pay, to gainsharing, to pay-for-performance. An analysis of Indiana's Department of Financial Institution's workforce revealed that the majority of financial examiners were leaving between the four-and seven-year service mark. At this point, examiners had attained a highly technical skill set because the state had sent individuals to advanced and expensive training. The agency's investment was not paying off. As a result, the department structured a variable competency pay program to target employees at the four- to seven-year mark, hoping to improve retention.

A third strategy adopted by governments, such as Germany, Austria and Korea, is setting wages based on market rates (PUMA/HRM, 2000d). Within the United States, the trend in states is to adjust salaries to be more competitive with market wages, to provide more flexibility in starting salaries and to allow for signing bonuses. Florida conducts annual pay studies to determine where class salaries are in association with the labor market. Idaho routinely shifts the pay

schedule to address market wages. Missouri has a long-term plan to move state employee salaries to the identified market rates of pay to improve recruitment and retention. Oregon developed a market pricing system for selected management benchmark jobs. Kentucky allows agencies to negotiate starting salaries; Virginia offers more flexibility in starting salaries depending on education, training and experience (up to 15 per cent above prior salary). Some public sector employers, such as Belgium and Hungary, decreased the gap between public and private sector pay rates.

Performance management

The common approach to performance appraisals is to have supervisors evaluate the performance of their employees and then tell them what the rating is. Currently, the trend is toward adopting performance management systems that are results-oriented, participative and developmental (World Bank, 2001b). For example, Malta reviews employees four times a year based on a work plan developed between employees and their supervisors. A part of this process involves developing a training plan to support the developmental needs of the individual employee. Some governments, such as Korea, are moving toward 360-degree appraisals that require multiple sources of input into an employee's evaluation (PUMA/HRM, 2000d).

Recent innovations include developing performance management systems that support a performance-driven culture. A performance management system requires that employees and managers jointly prioritize and determine goals and objectives, establishes how employees or teams contribute to the organization's goals, identifies strengths and weaknesses of an individual's performance and recognizes and rewards high performance. The first step is for top-level executives to articulate an agency's mission and goals. Then, managers and program directors work from this directive to determine strategic and measurable objectives for their unit. From these objectives, managers and employees collaborate to establish team and individual performance objectives.

This approach assumes that by aligning individual and team objectives with agency goals, employees at all levels will have greater ownership of the agency's goals. The agency benefits because employees should be more results-driven. Employees benefit because they feel a greater sense of accomplishment by achieving meaningful objectives and by having the potential to be rewarded based on their performance. Several states, such as Maryland, New Jersey, Colorado, Georgia, Louisiana and Delaware, have explicitly attempted to link employee performance to agency goals.

The City of Austin's Success Strategy Performance Review (SSPR) is a complex and integrative performance management system. It consists of three phases, incorporating collaborative performance planning, ongoing feedback and coaching and performance evaluation throughout the year. Using a performance standards approach, the evaluation is customized to each job title. The evaluation sessions are conducted in concert with the city's business planning cycle to ensure that employees and their supervisors develop achievable performance objectives based on the department's business goals. Progress toward these objectives is expected to be discussed throughout the year as part of the continuous performance management system. In addition, departmental directors are accountable for SSPR program results.

In Denmark, some public sector employees, particularly at the senior level, undergo an annual evaluation of performance against goals stipulated in the employment contract. Similarly, in New Zealand, chief executives sign a performance agreement upon which they are assessed annually.

Colorado's Peak Performance system revamps the state's performance appraisal system and links it to a compensation plan. The performance evaluation component links individual objectives to state business objectives and strategies, and the compensation plan directly ties pay to an employee's performance. Agencies are required to develop a plan for adopting performance management rules and procedures tailored to their unique business needs, while supporting the overall goals and strategies of the state's leaders. The performance management system requires supervisors to create a written performance plan for each employee at the beginning of a rating period, prepare a written evaluation, and then review that evaluation. Evaluation systems adopted must translate into three ratings: needs improvement, fully competent and peak performer. Within those parameters, agencies are free to develop any system that works for them. Monetary awards will then be based on two items: whether the employee is at or above the job rate for the occupational group and the employee's performance level. Employees below the job rate are eligible for base and/or non-base building awards. Employees at or above job rate are eligible for non-base building awards that must be re-earned annually.

Ireland adopted a performance management system to monitor and evaluate performance at all levels. The system develops performance plans based on role profiles (establish primary focus of the job), the required job competencies and related training and development (PUMA, 2001).

Many of the new approaches to performance evaluation require that employees and managers collaborate on setting performance expectations that are directly linked to agency goals. Managers are encouraged to track performance and provide regular feedback and some governments even require more than one formal evaluation each year. Some systems are designed to allow other stakeholders, such as customers and subordinates, to rate employee performance. The key to the success of performance management is providing employees opportunities to develop, through training or mentoring, in areas in which they show weakness. Finally, employees should be rewarded financially for their contribution to the agency's success. Governments vary in terms of the formula used for rewarding high performance. For example, in Georgia, performance increases are comprised of two components. For employees who meet, exceed or far exceed their performance expectations, they receive a market adjustment, to increase competitiveness with the outside job market, and a variable award, based on the level of performance.

THE CREATION AND EVOLUTION OF PUBLIC HUMAN RESOURCE MANAGEMENT – MERIT – SYSTEMS

Traditionally, merit systems have typed as either 'career' or 'position-based' systems. Career-based systems are founded on bringing individuals into the system at the entry level, and building their career within government. Position-based systems, on the other hand, are more focused on selecting the best candidate, whether internal or external, for the position, allowing for greater lateral entry to the system. Examples of closed career systems include Belgium, France and Japan, who make appointments through promotion only from within the civil service (World Bank, 2001d). In some countries there is a trend toward blending the two systems. For example, in Spain civil servants are often recruited through entry-level civil service exams but then further scrutinized to ensure that they meet the needs of a particular position (World Bank, 2001d). The United States, on the other hand, operates a position-based system that allows more open access to the jobs in the federal government.

In addition, public sector employees have traditionally enjoyed greater protection from dismissal than those in the private sector. There is an emerging movement away from this approach, as seen in the abolishment of the civil service system in Georgia. Senior officials in Australia, Canada, France, Ireland, Switzerland, Turkey and the United Kingdom can have their appointments terminated at the will of the government.

Some countries are beginning to utilize both open- and fixed-term employment contracts, especially for senior positions (World Bank, 2001d). In a survey of twenty-one countries, ten indicated that they had provisions for employment contracts for senior public servants (PUMA/HRM, 2000b). In New Zealand, for example, all chief executives and senior managers are employed on a contractual basis – typically fixed-term contracts for chief executives and open-term contracts for senior managers (PUMA/HRM, 2000b). Approximately 23 per cent of the senior managers are employed on contracts fixed for a maximum of five years (PUMA/HRM, 2000b). Most of the heads of government agencies in Sweden are appointed on six-year fixed-term contracts (PUMA/HRM, 2000b). In Switzerland a public law contract exists between employer and employee; the contract may be open-ended and terminated by either party (PUMA, 2001). Recently, a European Union directive stipulated that fixed-term employees should receive equal treatment to permanent staff (Sinclair, 2001). As discussed below, looking at the changes in HRM practices across international governments, and federal, state and local government within the United States, no single approach to contemporary merit system reform emerges.

Global human resource reform

Most proposals for reforming public human resource management systems fit into five broad categories:

1   those that create a civil service system that promises open recruitment, selection based on qualifications and a separation of politics and administration (for example, Albania, Estonia, Hungary and Poland);
2   those that modernize existing systems, such as making it easier to enter public service, ensuring that compensation is competitive in the marketplace, and providing training that develops skills needed to manage in the future (for example, Canada, Denmark, Norway and Italy);
3   those that propose to create flexibilities within the existing civil service system to improve a manager's ability to manage that typically include reducing personnel regulations, reducing classification titles and creating incentives for high performance – without abandoning core merit principles (for example, Iceland, Switzerland and the state of Virginia);
4   those that decentralize and devolve HR-related authority to agencies and managers (such as Australia, Italy and the state of South Carolina);
5   those that abolish civil service (such as the state of Georgia).

Regardless of the approach taken, governments seek to improve how they work by adopting innovative techniques and technologies.

Civil service reform in the United States[1]

The notion of civil service with a uniform system of employment, recruitment, classification and compensation in the United States is giving way to a more flexible and varied structure. The emerging strategy is to decentralize or share authority for personnel functions between central and line agencies and managers (Ingraham and Selden, 2001; Selden et al., 2001). The patterns of reform range on a continuum from the traditional, centralized civil service system of Rhode Island and New York to the largely decentralized human resource management system of Texas and North Dakota (Ingraham and Selden, 2001). The middle of the continuum is represented by the increasing number of states that have moved from either strongly centralized or decentralized systems toward one reflecting shared responsibility between a central agency or authority, agencies and managers. These patterns create different foundations for change and reform, but also suggest different paths for further changing.

Traditional centralized systems

When many civil service systems were created in the United States there was a strong belief that rigidly centralized systems were the only way to exclude undue partisan influence and pressure on public employment systems. Many of the components of the personnel systems that grew from this conviction had an interactive influence with centralization to create a hierarchical structure increasingly bounded by laws, rules and regulations. Graded authority structures and public compensation systems, for example, reinforced principles of centralization and hierarchy. In their favor, centralized, hierarchical structures promoted standardization, stability and predictability. They did not, however, create or support the discretion and flexibilities that many public organizations and their leaders now find critical to longer-term effectiveness.

One indicator of centralized hierarchy is central control of recruiting, testing and hiring. The state's classification system and total number of classifications is important here, because it reflects not only complexity of the hiring system and the extent to which it is flexible and responsive to changing employment demands, but the extent to which standardization has yielded to some tailoring to individual agency needs and employment climates. New Jersey represents an extreme example of centralization, as the state controls the classification system for its municipalities.

Even though some reform to this rigid model has occurred in those states that adopted it originally, many states continue to retain remarkable classification complexities. In 2000, New York has 4,000 classification titles for about 158,000 state employees (down from an earlier high of about 7,000). Pennsylvania, a strong advocate of the centralized model, has 89,000 employees and 2,838 classification titles. Despite some decentralization, Minnesota retains 2,152 classification titles for its 33,773 employees. By contrast, South Carolina works with 452 classification titles for its nearly 72,000 employees. Interestingly, the states that have decentralized the most authority have created a classification system similar to those that grew out of a traditional system. In two years, the number of classification titles in Florida and Georgia increased by 84.65 per cent and 56.22 per cent, respectively.

Another indicator of strongly centralized systems is the continued reliance on central control of testing and on a narrow definition of 'testing'; that is, a written examination for a narrow skill or technical knowledge set, offered in a limited number of places at set periods of time. These narrow and rigid tests conform to the needs of the complicated classification systems described above. Several states, such as Indiana, Kansas, Montana, North Carolina and South Dakota, have eliminated testing. Traditional classification systems are also linked to equally narrow and rigid compensation guidelines and procedures in the traditional centralized model. The practice of small, annual and within-grade step

increases for salary increments is a common mark of the traditional system, for example. States such as Alaska, Nevada and New Hampshire rely primarily on annual, step increases. The interlocking complexity and rigidity of these components of the personnel system is often exacerbated in traditional system states by labor/management agreements, which create additional limits and constraints on hiring, promotion, discipline and compensation.

Decentralized systems

At the other end of the continuum – and essentially standing alone there – is Texas. Texas does not have a central personnel agency. Job classification is a central function but falls within the purview of the State Auditor's office, which reports to the legislature. Although many herald the flexibility accorded agencies in such a setting, many managers report that it is difficult to obtain statewide information for comparative or evaluative purposes. Central workforce planning is difficult, if not impossible (Barrett et al., 2000).

Although there was limited adoption of the completely decentralized model, several of its elements continue to be attractive. First, the model offers a system that is responsive to the different needs of different agencies, and that allows agencies and managers the flexibility they need to adapt to changing circumstances. Second, the model provides clearer accountability for personnel and for hiring and firing. Central personnel authorities diffuse accountability by interceding in the relationship between agency, manager and employee. A decentralized system links responsibility and accountability more tightly in that regard. Finally, proponents of decentralization argue that, because a decentralized personnel system is more flexible and managers have more discretion, human resources will be better utilized and better matched to real agency needs.

However, as the findings presented earlier suggest, states are also discovering that decentralization has several downsides for human resource management. First, in a strongly decentralized system, it is difficult to monitor and assess personnel activities and needs. No central information gathering or evaluation is in place. Planning on a statewide basis is severely restricted, and incentives for better coordination are limited. Further, managing human resources in a decentralized system may place talent and skill demands on managers that they do not have. In the 1998 GPP survey, for example, many states noted that 'managing' decentralization was an extremely difficult task.

Shared responsibility systems

For all of the reasons noted above, many states have created human resource management systems that balance or share responsibility and authority between the central personnel agency and the other agencies of government. Within this 'middle ground' there can be wide variation in the extent to which authority is formally delegated away from the center, or to which it is shared in more informal and narrow arrangements. Such sharing allows continued consideration of broad governmental concerns such as equity, but combines them with the HR customization necessary to better agency performance.

Research based on the Government Performance Project suggests that the movement in the field is not toward either decentralization or centralization but rather toward shared responsibility (in terms of implementation of systems designed centrally). In other words, strategic responsibilities and design and the continued protection of broad governmental values have a central focus; mission-specific strategies and implementation have an agency focus. Responsibility for the integrity of the system is shared.

South Carolina provides one example of this model: within the state's broad HR framework, agencies are given substantial flexibility in creating reward and recognition programs and are given broad discretion in designing disciplinary policies. Indiana has applied the central strategy/agency choice model to compensation. Actual hiring decisions are delegated to agencies and managers in twenty-six states. Georgia represents a state that is learning the lessons of extreme decentralization and is moving toward balancing decentralization with central guidance. For example, Georgia recently passed legislation requiring agencies to conduct human resource planning, using a framework developed centrally. In addition, it acknowledges that decentralizing classification authority to the agencies resulted in a surge of classification titles, many of which are redundant across agencies. The state is currently contemplating how to address this problem.

Utah delegates personnel functions through a signed contract between the Department of Human Resource Management (DHRM) and the individual agency. The agreement stipulates that the personnel function must be 'conducted in accordance with applicable state code, DHRM rules, standards, policies, and procedures'. Although responsibility is delegated, the DHRM provides support to the contract agencies through training, manuals and technical assistance. North Carolina's central personnel office put together a division solely dedicated to program evaluation. The state sends a team into an agency to examine the entire human resources program, including compliance with statutes and federal civil rights laws.

Role and mission of central personnel departments in the United States

As personnel functions are becoming increasingly decentralized, diffused and shared, human resource management departments are assuming a consultative role to support and provide advice to their clients (Selden et al., 2001). The state of Indiana commented on its 1998 GPP survey that

> as agencies fulfill more of these functions, they need more guidance and assistance in how to do it. Many of our agencies – we have 100 or more agencies – are so small that they don't have a human resource professional doing their personnel work. It may be a secretary to the director, or it may be the director so these people are not technical experts and they need a lot of hands on guidance – more so now that they are doing it themselves rather than us doing it.

This statement illustrates an important ramification of decentralization. Agencies and their managers are expected to carry out functions that they do not necessarily have the skills, experience or training to perform. Several personnel offices acknowledged that it took time for them to adjust to a different role under the new structural arrangement. For example, Ohio observed that even after decentralizing, 'we would audit an agency, making sure that every "i" was dotted and "t" crossed, and produce a 60-page report.' In effect, the personnel office was taking back all the responsibility that it had delegated. As a result, the personnel office revamped its regulatory audit process that emphasized a 'just say no' attitude to a more analytic process aimed at improving agency practices. Often a shift in personnel responsibilities is preceded or accompanied by a change in the mission of the personnel department.

The preoccupation with policing the merit system has given way to a broader human resources focus in the public sector. Mission statements echo much of the language of reform. Terms such as flexibility, streamlining, business, cost-effective, partnerships and customers are used in many government HR mission statements. For example, Idaho's mission is

> To provide world-class Human Resource management services designed to: help state employees compete and thrive in this century; provide a high-tech, fast paced,

customer-oriented, and career-based environment to attract, retain, and maximize a talented state workforce and keep Idaho state government a competitive employer in today's market.

New Mexico's mission

is to be the leader in state government in providing a flexible system of personnel administration and stream-lined service that meets the evolving needs of our customers in a timely and accountable manner utilizing the latest available technology in a cost-effective manner, while protecting the interest of the public.

These statements suggest that a paradigm shift is occurring. States are replacing the bureaucratic paradigm that once dominated the culture of personnel departments (consisting of bureaucracy, control and hierarchy) with paradigms that emphasize service, front line workers, excellence, competence, results and being an employer of choice. Prior to the recent wave of reforms, civil service structures and responsibilities were nearly universal in the United States (Tolbert and Zucker, 1983). Whether or not 'new' models of civil service will become similarly institutionalized or widely accepted as both appropriate and necessary remains to be seen.

CONCLUSION

A one-size-fits-all model of HRM reform is not an appropriate strategy for any government. Rather, reform must be strategic. However, only through identifying its own needs and demands will government be able to formulate a strategic approach to reform. Governments should carefully consider the pros and cons of different HRM strategies based upon the theories underlying them, as well as the experiences and lessons learned by other governments throughout the world. For example, one means of making government employment more attractive is to emphasize the benefits of working in the public sector. Some governments, such as Poland, Norway and New Zealand, adopted shorter workweeks, offered flexi time and operated childcare facilities to attract and retain workers (PUMA/HRM, 2000d). The impact of these practices could inform a larger community about the potential benefits or costs.

What do the findings suggest about the direction of public human resource management systems? The public personnel system of the future will need to couple managerial and system flexibilities and modernization with issues of system fit or congruence. As personnel responsibilities are increasingly shared between a central office and agencies, the role of the central HRM office will evolve in order to meet the needs of its partners, clients and customers. Central offices will focus less on 'micro' issues of human resources, such as reclassification and testing, and more on 'macro' issues, such as workforce planning, change management, employee development and training, and leadership development. The most significant contribution of the HRM office, however, remains the pivotal role it plays in helping agencies compete for, hire and develop a highly skilled labor force.

NOTE

1 Some of this material is adopted from a book chapter by Patricia W. Ingraham and Sally Coleman Selden (2001) in Carolyn Ban and Norma Riccucci's *Public Personnel Management*. New York: Longman Press.

REFERENCES

Barrett, Katherine, Greene, Richard with Marian, Michelle (2001) Grading the States. *Governing Magazine*, February 2001. Available online: *http://governing.com/gpp/gplintro.htm*

European Foundation (2001) Variable Pay in Europe. Internet 6 July 2001. Available: *www.eiro.eurfound.ie/2001/04/study/TN0104201S.html*

Ingraham, Patricia W. and Selden, Sally Coleman (2001) 'Human Resource Management and Capacity in the States', in Carolyn Ban and Norma Riccucci (eds), *Issues in Human Resource Management,* 3rd edn. New York: Longman Press. pp. 210–24.

Ingraham, Patricia W., Selden, Sally Coleman and Moynihan, Donald P. (2000) 'People and Performance: Challenges for the Future Public Service – the Report from the Wye River Conference'. *Public Administration Review*, 60: 54–60.

Minnesota Survey Response (1998) *Minnesota Survey Response for the Government Performance Project.*

OECD (2000) Summary Record of the Expert Meetings on Human Resources Management, 25–26 January 2000. Internet 29 June 2001. Available: *http://www.olis.oecd.org/olis/2000doc.nsf/LinkTo/PUMA-HRM (2000)12*

OECD (2001a) Government of the Future, OECD Public Management Policy Brief No. 9, June 2001. Internet 29 June 2001. Available: *http://www.oecd.org//puma/pubs/Govt_FutureE.pdf*

OECD (2001b) Human Resources Management: Key Issues. Internet 29 June 2001. Available: *http://www.oecd.org/puma/hrm/issues.htm*

PUMA/HRM (1997) The Setting: Changing the Scope, Role, and Structure of Government. Internet 6 July

2001. Available: *http://www.oecd.org/puma/gvnance/ minister/session1.htm*

PUMA (2001) Country Web Pages. Internet 7 July 2001. Available: *http://www.oecd.org//puma/sigmaweb*

PUMA/HRM (2000a) Emerging Issues – In Search of Employees: The Case of the Dutch Public Service. HRM Working Party Meeting Paris 3–4 July. Internet 29 June 2001. Available: *http://www.olis.oecd.org/olis/ 2000doc.nsf/LinkTo/PUMA-HRM(2000)9*

PUMA/HRM (2000b) Managing the Senior Public Service: A Survey of OECD. HRM Working Party Meeting Paris 3–4 July. Internet 29 June 2001. Available: *http://www.olis.oecd.org/olis/2000doc.nsf/ LinkTo/sps9*

PUMA/HRM (2000c) Recent Developments in the Field of Professionalism and Ethics in the Public Administration: The Case of France. HRM Working Party Meeting Paris 3–4 July. Internet 29 June 2001. Available: *http://www.olis.oecd.org/olis/2000doc.nsf/ LinkTo/PUMA-HRM(2000)8*

PUMA/HRM (2000d) Recent Developments and Future Challenges in Human Resource Management in OECD Member Countries: Background Paper by the Secretariat. HRM Working Party Meeting Paris 3–4 July. Internet 29 June 2001. Available: *http://www.olis.oecd. org/olis/2000doc.nsf/LinkTo/PUMA-HRM (2000)6*

PUMA/HRM (2000e) Summary of the PSPE Data Analysis and Future Directions for HRM Data Collection. Internet 29 June 2001. Available: *http://www.olis.oecd.org/olis/ 2000doc.nsf/LinkTo/PUMA-HRM(2000)7*

Selden, Sally Coleman, Ingraham, Patricia Wallace and Jacobson, Willow (2001) 'Human Resource Practices in State Governments: Findings from a National Survey', *Public Administration Review*, 61 (5): 598–607.

Sinclair, Diane (2001) 'EU Directive Set to Change Face of Fixed-Term Employment Contracts', *People Management*, 7: 12.

World Bank (2001a) Engaging Support for Reform. Internet 18 June 2001. Available: *http://www1.world- bank.org/publicsector/civilservice/engaging.htm*

World Bank (2001b) Individual Performance and Management. Internet 18 June 2001. Available: *http://www1.worldbank.org/publicsector/civilservice/in dividual.htm*

World Bank (2001c) Public Officials and Their Institutional Environment: An Analytical Model for Assessing the Impact of Institutional Change on Public Sector Performance. *World Bank Policy Research Working Paper No. 2427*. Internet 18 June 2001. Available: *http://www1.worldbank.org/publicsector/ civilservice/posconceptual.htm*

World Bank (2001d) Recruitment and Promotion. Internet 18 June 2001. Available: *http://www1.worldbank.org/ publicsector/civilservice/recruitment.htm*

World Bank (2001e) Rewards and Incentives. Internet 18 June 2001. Available: *http://www1.worldbank.org/ publicsector/civilservice/agency.htm*

6

Pay and Perquisites for Government Executives

Jørgen Grønnegaard Christensen

On first consideration it seems a trivial question to ask what government pays its executives and how it does it. The simple answer is that they are paid according to their value on the labor market. The caveat to this interpretation is equally simple. Deviations from the market pattern would be expected only if somebody could exploit his or her political power to contrive a better deal. This chapter shows that both the market and the political power interpretations are far from the reality of how the rewards are set for political and administrative executives in government. It also shows that in the real world it is hard to separate the two types of government executives, even if it may seem odd that the settling of the salaries of master and servant are as closely related as is often the case in government.

The discussion only covers central government executives. There are very few analyses of pay awarded to executives in subnational government. One hypothesis might be that salaries of local and regional government executives are set according to principles that are in each country related to the principles governing executive pay in central government. But the fact is that there are no analyses that can confirm or refute this hypothesis and also that data that could be used for this purpose are not easily available.

The market interpretation relies on the assumption that to attract able persons to a government career, be it in administration or politics, the government has to pay a price that is competitive with what the private sector pays its executives, allowing for differences in tenure and pension rights. The political power interpretation relies on a similar premise. It presumes executive pay in government to be set by the

incumbents who have both the motive and the opportunity to serve themselves. Much speaks for either interpretation. According to the former it is hard to imagine a long-term insulation of the public sector from the general labor market, including the market for managerial and leadership talent. It is equally hard to abstract from the fact that in the end it is a political decision how and how much the holders of governmental office should be rewarded for their services and that with this power they do not have to respond to the constraints of the market.

Both extremes overlook important aspects of political and administrative life. First, in modern government elaborate civil service regulations are in place. They establish internal labor markets for the public sector, and even for particular sub-sectors of government (Wise, 1996). As a result, any competitive exchange with the private labor market, and especially the corporate part, is limited and probably operates only at the margins where young people have to choose their lifetime careers and senior executives ponder the prospect for entering into a second career in a sector hitherto foreign to them. Second, modern government is very often democratic government. The precise form may vary, but classical political theorists puzzled with the issue of how to provide the holders of political and administrative office with proper rewards and incentives. Tocqueville expected democratic competition (and behind it popular envy) to place strict constraints on politicians when they had to determine their own salaries. The implication was a strong trend towards an egalitarian pay system that compressed the governmental pay scale and guaranteed that people in high public office didn't distance themselves too far from the people they ruled (Tocqueville, 1835/ 1963: 130–4). The Tocquevillian hypothesis thus clearly contradicts the rent-seeking behavior inherent in the political power interpretation, but to Tocqueville the risk was that only people of mediocre talent or people so well-off that they did not have to concern themselves with their actual pay would be attracted to public service.

Third, modern government is highly specialized, and for the political decision makers, citizens and private business it serves and regulates the issue is how to ensure that it will operate in a reliable, consistent, professionally competent and equitable manner. This was the concern of a much later classic theorist, Max Weber. His answer was to combine democracy and the rule of law with a professional civil service organized along bureaucratic lines. His ideal type civil servant was recruited on the basis of merit, and a career system with lifelong tenure and a deferred pension at the end of service provided sufficient incentives for civil servants to concentrate on their official duties as specified by general legal rules and their place in the hierarchy. But like Tocqueville, Weber was not overly optimistic about the prospects that his model would succeed. Therefore, the challenge was to create a set of institutions that as far as possible could keep in check bureaucrats bent on usurping political power and a new class of professional politicians making a living off, rather than living for, politics (Weber, 1919/1988).

The classic theories point to the complexity and tensions involved when the rewards for political and administrative executives are to be settled, but hardly lead to precise predictions as to how much and how government executives are paid. Nor is there much assistance to be gained from modern theories. They are often quite as broad as their classical ancestors. One of these theories is Horn's transaction cost theory of public administration. Here he forcefully argues that to cope with the problems of commitment inherent in democratic policy making politicians are inclined to set up a tenured and merit-based civil service that provides its members with prospects of promotion and pension (Horn, 1995). Even Horn's elaborate theory does not lead to any precise predictions of the reward schemes to be expected for administrative executives, not to speak of their political superiors. The situation is no better if we alternatively take recourse to cultural theories that focus on ensuring an appropriate fit between salaries and other rewards in differing organizational and social contexts. The problem with both theories is that they cope much better with the complexities of the real world if the analyst's task can be restricted to providing an ex post rationalization of patterns that have been found to converge or diverge (Hood, 1994: 67).

PATTERNS TO BE EXPLAINED

Even a scant look at the real world of executive pay in government suffices to convince us that we are faced with a complex, but fascinating topic. Table 6.1 shows some of the issues involved in a cross-national comparison of the patterns of executive pay in government. The basic distinction concerns the structure of executive rewards: they may consist solely, or to a very great extent, of a taxable salary, the level of which is in principle open to the public. Or they may to some, or even a considerable, extent consist of perquisites to the holders of executive office. Such perquisites can consist of cash and be taxable. However, they can also be more substantial (cars, accommodation, traveling, *per diems*) or immaterial (social status and public esteem derived from the executive position) rewards. Finally, perquisites may be deferred, thus securing future compensation for relative hardships endured while holding public office. The more important such perquisites are the less transparent the system of rewards is. More importantly, the more weight assigned to such perquisites, the less clear the incentives connected with a particular job or career.

One level of analysis involves only comparative statistics. The primary focus is on differences between countries. It reveals considerable differences between countries and political and administrative systems, differences that are not in any way directly related to the wealth of the countries. This generalization holds not only for the countries of the OECD but also the emerging economies of South East Asia (Hood and Lambert, 1994: 34–7; Hood and Askim, 2003). The pattern is even more variegated when pay relativities are included. As Table 6.1 shows, determining the pay relativities requires a series of comparisons, and it is difficult to speak of a consistent pattern of countries falling within distinct categories. Certainly, there are countries where egalitarian modesty dominates and where pay differentials are compressed, whether the standard is relativities within the elite, within the administrative hierarchy or between the executive elite and the general public. Norway is the prime instance, but the other Nordic countries share many of its traits (Lægreid, 1994). At the other end Hong Kong and Singapore, for

Table 6.1   *Analyzing the structure of rewards for government executives*

Level of analysis	Rewards	
	Pay	Perquisites
Cross-national comparisons	Level	As percentage of direct pay
	Pay relativities	As option for second career outside government
	Political vs. administrative executives	
	Executives vs. MPs	
	Intra-hierarchical differentials	
	Executive pay vs. general population	
Over-time comparisons	Real term changes in purchasing power	Expansion/restriction of perquisites
	Erosion/improvement in pay relativities	

instance, display a uniform pattern of exquisite pay to members of the executive elite, disregarding the standard of comparison.

When the comparison is extended to a larger number of countries it becomes evident that they are not easily categorized into country families that share certain constitutional, institutional or cultural traits. The numbers rather reveal patterns that are specific to each country. Some empirical examples are illuminating. It is quite nearly a general pattern that the pay to political and administrative executives – explicitly and implicitly – is mutually strongly related, and that their pay is related to the pay members of parliament receive. But there are conspicuous deviations. So both the members of the New Zealand and Swiss parliaments are poorly paid compared to administrative executives, but when it comes to political executives New Zealand cabinet ministers share the humble lot of their country's MPs. Their Swiss colleagues, however, are comparatively well off as are the country's senior civil servants (Gregory, 2003; Klöti, 1994). The implication is that New Zealand and Switzerland resemble Asian countries like Hong Kong, Japan, Singapore and South Korea rather than the Western countries with which they share cultural and political traits that are otherwise deemed to be important.

The presumption behind the direct pay governmental executives receive is that it is open. The salaries are decided according to well-specified and well-known procedures, and information on them is available through public accounts and official statistics. Similar transparency is hardly connected with the perquisites that governmental executives to varying extents receive. The more important such perquisites ('perks'), the more opaque becomes the systems of rewards for people in high public office. As this happens sleaze and, at the extreme, the risk of corruption

become problems that may negatively affect citizens' trust in government (Ridley and Doig, 1995). For the same reason it is difficult to determine their value in exact, preferably monetary, terms. It is to some extent possible to identify the kind of perquisites allowed, accepted or at least operative in different systems and whether members of the political and administrative are eligible for them. Table 6.2 tries to bring a minimum of order to a phenomenon that by definition constitutes the submerged part of the iceberg (Hood and Peters, 1994, 2003).

First, Table 6.2 reveals an almost universal pattern, showing that especially political executives and, to a lesser extent, top civil servants receive different sorts of allowances. Mostly they are of minor importance and clearly linked to job-related activities. This is the case with allowances for representation and provision of free government cars. The most conspicuous exception is that in a few systems like China and the EU, allowances of this kind apply also to family members and that, in the Chinese case, they are for life. The implication is that perks of this kind make up a large share of the Chinese elite's income, and further that these invisible allowances make the rewards for the country's governmental executives highly inequitable when compared to other countries.

Second, especially top civil servants receive monetary add-ons. Different models are used, for instance the practice of a thirteenth month's salary in the German and Swiss civil services, and the confidential practice of handing over closed envelopes to French civil servants who merit a cash benefit; the discretionary one-off payments in the Danish civil service law have a very similar status. Civil servants serving ex officio on particular boards and commissions may even continue to hold such posts and the ensuing honoraria upon retirement.

Table 6.2 *Prevalent types of perquisites for government executives*

	In office	Life time and/or extended to family	Deferred
Cash allowances and services			
Political executives	Free, chauffeur driven cars; tax free allowances for representation; prevalent in most countries	Common in e.g. China and in the EU	
Top civil servants	Varying, but smaller	Common in e.g. China and in the EU	
Add-ons			
Political executives	Political executives who hold a parliamentary seat keep their salary or allowance in this capacity; non-MPs receive a compensation that neutralizes the absence of this source of income		
Top civil servants	Bonus, e.g. confidential envelopes handed over to French civil servants and pay for a 13th month to German and Swiss civil servants	Side-business allowed to continue after retirement reimbursed through honorarium	
Accumulation			
Political executives	French 'cumul des mandats' allowing national politicians, including ministers, to serve in elected offices at the subnational level; in other countries ministers and other political executives are by law obliged to give up other tasks and jobs, be they in private business or government while in office	Pension schemes set up according to different principles; in the traditional Danish system a minister earned a life-long pension that increased with the accumulated length of service and that came to payment at retirement, regardless of age	Directorships on boards in government corporations, state-owned enterprises or private and semi-private corporations; exchange of executive staff between the federal administration in Washington and Washington law firms and the US corporate community
Top civil servants	Accumulation of perks for civil servants serving on boards etc. as government representatives, e.g. in Danish civil service; Honoraria for side jobs for Danish judges	Civil service pensions regulated according to seniority in office in traditional Western civil service systems; retaining pay at move to 'Ruhestand' for German top civil servants	'Descent from heaven' for Japanese top civil servants moving to directorships in private business; French 'pantouflage' for civil servants moving from administrative positions to managerial positions in state or private business; in-and-outers political appointees in the US federal administration

Third, a more important source of rewards is connected with the possibility of accumulating offices. While some countries set strict limitations on this for members of government (for example, Germany, the Nordic countries and the EU Commission), 'cumul des mandats' is part of the French political tradition, providing national politicians not only with an extra source of income, but also a separate platform for their political career. Top civil servants, as was once the case in Danish central government, may have similar opportunities to accumulate side tasks to which they are appointed by the government, sometimes leaving it to others to pay for their services. Pension schemes have a similar function in a lifetime perspective, although their value depends entirely on the principles regulating their calculation. Finally, in many countries life does not necessarily come to a halt when a career in government ends. In France as well as Japan and South Korea, a fairly low salary government career paves the way to a later, much more lucrative career in business. In other countries this opportunity is less well integrated into the civil service career system, but former ministers and retired top civil servants have a chance to pursue a second career in the borderland between the public and the private sector (Christensen and Pallesen, forthcoming).

In this discussion the rewards of administrative and political executives have been treated in parallel. As noted in the introduction, one reason is that they are often connected. From a classic perspective, derived from either Weber's theory of bureaucracy or Wilson's politics–administration dichotomy, these executive roles are different and should not be blurred. In a comparative perspective, however, it becomes clear that they are, in fact, often difficult to distinguish. Part of the problem lies in an ambiguous conceptualization that is exploited by politicians and bureaucrats alike to institute various ploys against each other (Peters, 1978). But another reason is that empirically the careers of political and administrative executives often converge. This happens when appointments to positions in the administration are made on political grounds, thereby departing from the principles of the merit civil service. The political appointees that staff the higher echelons of American federal bureaucracy fall within this category, as do the directors-general in charge of the independent agencies of Swedish central government (Pierre, forthcoming). In other European countries like Austria and Belgium a long tradition of coalition government has led to elaborate procedures for selecting and allocating political appointees to leading positions in the administration (Brans, 1994; Liegl and Müller, 1999). The other side of the issue is the bureaucratization of politics found in some countries. In democratic France one road to a political career has traditionally been elite training as a civil servant, followed by a career that over time merged into politics (Rouban, 1998). In other, more autocratic countries a similar pattern is evident in that technocrats are indistinguishable from higher civil servants occupying the highest posts in government.

Cross-national comparison of the pay policies has not exactly revealed a consistent pattern. Pay levels, pay relativities and the use of perquisites show so much variation that national idiosyncrasies must be said to prevail. On the surface this is different for changes over time. The Hood and Peters study, covering a number of Western European countries and the USA, revealed a general trend towards erosion of pay to people serving in high public office. This applied not only to political and administrative executives; especially members of parliament seemed to suffer a gradual, but constant erosion of their monetary rewards. As the erosion proceeded the reward systems also became more egalitarian and showed more compressed pay relativities within the governmental hierarchy, combined with a narrowing of income differentials between governmental executives and the general public. A side effect has been a deepening of differences in pay and perquisites earned by business and government executives. But even this pattern is not without exceptions, as demonstrated by the Swiss and, to some extent, the German cases, where members of the elite in comparative terms have been able to uphold their very high earnings, if yet another exception is allowed for Swiss parliamentarians (Derlien, 1994; Klöti, 1994). Further, the trend towards erosion is not confirmed when the scope of comparison is expanded to include, for example, South East Asia and the Antipodes. Here emerging economies like China, Hong Kong, Singapore and South Korea have not experienced a trend corresponding to the one found in several Western countries. Nor has this been the case for industrialized and democratic countries like Australia, Japan and New Zealand (Hood and Askim, 2003).

For those Western countries that have experienced a gradual erosion of pay to government executives this raises two questions. The first is whether the trend towards erosion of executive pay has been accompanied by substituting salaried rewards with increased perquisites. No systematic data allows a general answer to this question, but there are sufficient examples to demonstrate that no such logic seems to be at play. First, German politicians, who have otherwise been comparatively well off, as well as their American colleagues, have experienced difficulties in maintaining their perquisites at a level that kept up with the costs of living. Corporatist Denmark has always had plenty of posts for civil servants on boards and commissions. This is still the case, but where such side-activities in the past carried an honorarium, consecutive rounds of perk clearance (*bensanering*) have led to their total eradication. As a consequence civil servants serving on such bodies in their official capacity either receive no financial reward or they must turn it over to their government employer. But for both civil servants and political executives such posts represent a kind of deferred perquisites to be enjoyed upon retirement.

The second question is whether the trend towards erosion is inescapable. This might seem to be the conclusion to which the postwar trend observed in several Western countries points. But once more the real world surprises us, as since the early 1990s there are indications that both political and administrative executives are regaining some of the terrain lost over the preceding decades. This applies when their pay is measured in terms of purchasing power and relative to other groups within or outside government.

ACCOUNTING FOR EXTREME DIVERSITIES

Pay policy for the public sector sounds like a fairly well-defined policy field. This is even more so when, as here, the focus is narrowed down to the setting of pay and perquisites for government executives. The advantage should be that much of the ambiguity so often at play when it comes to conducting comparative public policy analysis is here under control. Still, the descriptive pattern that has been unraveled is one of extreme diversity. This diversity is in fact so extreme that it seems questionable whether it is prudent to speak of a consistent pattern of observations. Any viable theoretical account therefore has, apparently, to cope with

1 persistent cross-national differences among countries otherwise alike in economic, institutional, and political terms; and
2 inconsistent developments in countries otherwise alike in all relevant respects.

This situation does not exactly make it easy to follow the standard prescription for analytical parsimony through the reliance on one, simple theoretical account. Table 6.3 presents in a simplified form the complex analytical issues involved. It specifies for each the causal logic, the empirical predictions derived from it and the inconsistent observations that would lead either to falsification or preempt severe modification. The dismal conclusion is that none of the theories survives an encounter with the real world (Hood and Peters, 1995).

Public choice theory offers the most parsimonious way to account for the setting of salaries and perquisites for people serving in high public office. Starting from the assumption of individuals rationally pursuing their own interests, it is reasonable to expect that those holding the actual positions of public power will also see to their own material welfare. This goes for their income in absolute terms and relative position compared to other groups within and outside the public sector. The problem is that most, although not all, government executives in Western countries have had difficulty in upholding their former income in real terms, and further, they have experienced an increasing degree of wage compression within the government hierarchy. There is even doubt as to whether people in positions of power actually pursue a policy of increasing their own salary, as witnessed by the politics of setting salaries and allowances for members of parliament.

The obvious caveat to the pure public choice interpretation is that it does not consider the institutional constraints within which people in high public office operate. One analytic approach follows Alexis de Tocqueville's theory of democratic institutionalism. Its causal logic is closely related to public choice rationalism, but its predictions run counter to it. Instead of striving to improve their personal lots, politicians engage themselves in a competition that over time causes their salaries to spiral down. What is more, if they seek compensation through more or less hidden perquisites they set into motion a devious game that undermines public trust in political office, making it unattractive to people of quality and unaffordable to people without considerable private means. The theory is supported by the trend observed in several Western countries for which we have data. The fact that in these countries the elite has not been able to keep perquisites out of the political debate lends further support to the Tocquevillian interpretation. After all, it is also notable that this development is particular to democratic countries. For countries with more autocratic or technocratic regimes the situation is very different, as witness South East Asian countries like Hong Kong and Singapore, and in the EU where the principles of democratic governance are at best highly circumscribed. It does not even undermine the theory that members of representative assemblies in these countries have not got their share of the spoils derived from high public office.

Still, the theory runs into severe difficulties because in a number of Western countries (Australia, Germany, New Zealand and Switzerland), as well as democratic Japan, members of the executive elite in government have successfully defended their positions in absolute and relative terms. Thus, even if empirically this kind of macro-institutional theory has a lot of good points, it is unable to stand alone.

Table 6.3   *Theoretical accounts for patterns of pay and perquisites*

Theory	Causal logic	Predicted pattern	Inconsistent pattern
Public choice	Individual maximization of pay and perquisites among governmental executives	Increasing rewards and increasingly inequitable rewards to governmental executives	Erosion Increasing equity
Macro-institutional theory – Tocquevillian theory of democracy	Democratic competition provides efficient constraint on income maximizing politicians	Erosion of pay and perquisites in democracies Over time Compared to autocratic regimes	Constant or improving patterns of pay and perquisites in absolute and relative terms in democratic regimes
Rational choice institutionalism	Government executives are individual utility maximizers who operate within institutional constraints beyond their control	Specific predictions depend on the detailed institutional architecture such as Pay and perquisites settled within a universal bargaining system for the labor market: Tocquevillian pattern Pay and perquisites determined through automatic procedure not coupled to bargaining in the labor market or to current political bargaining: Government executives keep or improve their absolute and relative position To the extent possible, government executives will evade institutional constraints by opting for less visible perquisites	The approach generally has difficulty in accounting for changes such as Government executives uphold or improve position in spite of integration into egalitarian institutions Government executives experience erosion in spite of automatic procedures that keep the setting of their pay and perquisites out of labor market or parliamentary politics Erosion of perquisites
Historical institutionalism	Past policy choices persist as they bring about increasing returns to present incumbents	Long-term continuity in past and present pay policies	Radical change and policy reversals breaking with e.g. long-term trend towards erosion of executive pay
Cultural theory	Policy choices are framed by the dominant cultural context that defines the values that can legitimate them	Specific predictions depend on the prevalent set of values such as Egalitarianism Hierarchism The theory predicts a change in policy if the prevalent set of values is replaced by an alternative set of values	Change in dominant cultural values not followed by changes in policy

A logical extension is to turn to modern rational choice institutionalism. It shares the actor assumptions of public choice theory with the focus on institutional mechanisms found in Tocqueville's theory of democracy. Further, in spite of its rather narrow focus on an institutionally constrained game, in which elected members of parliament engage, it can easily be expanded to include other strata within the governing elite. The problem is that the gains in realism come at a price. It is impossible from these assumptions

to derive any specific predictions as to how and at what level rewards for the executive elite will be set. Any ex ante propositions as to this require a quite detailed specification of the architecture of the system in question. Still, this analytic strategy is not without promise, as it might be a way to account for variation among countries that are otherwise alike in democratic terms.

Table 6.3 mentions two such specifications. One prescribes pay and perquisites to be set within a universal bargaining system applied to the entire public sector and may be closely connected to the general labor market. The implication is that the salaries of the governing elite are linked to those of public employees in the lower echelons, and the ensuing prediction is gradual erosion similar to the Tocquevillian pattern described above, but expanded to cover also the executive elites, be they political or bureaucratic. This by and large corresponds to what is found in some Western countries, for instance the Nordic ones. The other institutional setup stylized in Table 6.3 presupposes that pay and perquisites are to be determined through a semi-automatic procedure that is neither coupled to labor market bargaining, nor to current political bargaining in parliament. As a result the settling of salaries for the executive elite is highly depoliticized, a fact that protects them against Tocquevillian erosion. Again this interpretation finds support in the experience of democratic countries like Australia and New Zealand. The same goes for Switzerland, where the executive over time has upheld high salaries protected against inflation through cost of living indexation.

In other countries that experienced high levels of inflation during the 1970s, an important part of the stabilization programs enacted in the early 1980s was the modification and eventual suspension of automatic cost of living indexation. The policy of economic reconstruction involved considerable political costs, but in order to keep them under control the reforms were designed in a way that emphasized equity between high- and low-level wage earners. The Danish case is illustrative in this respect. The gradual modification of cost of living indexation was designed in a way that hit higher civil servants harder than the general wage earner. Due to the rigidity of the traditional civil service system executives and members of the higher civil service are particularly vulnerable to modifications of automatic regulatory mechanisms, and, for a long period, could not have recourse to political action in order to compensate for their loss. This interaction between economic and political factors can explain why government executives in the Western countries fared so differently from the 1970s up through the 1980s.

This type of rational choice institutionalism basically argues for a strong trend towards stability, and that changes, if they take place at all, will be incremental in relation to the status quo. In this respect it is similar to the different versions of historical institutionalism. They all argue that strong path dependencies prevail in public policy. In some cases the causal logic is clearly institutional, with its focus on the transaction costs created by the institutions in place; in other cases the logic approaches sociological

reasoning, emphasizing norms and values shared over time; in yet another version economic logic is translated into politics through the argument that policies already in place will, as time goes by, engender increasing political returns to the coalition behind them (Pierson, 2000). The problem with historical explanations of this kind is their lack of a precise causal logic and the scarcity of generalized empirical insights they produce. Their analytical strength lies in their argument that the historical dimension in public policy should not be forgotten, while their Achilles' heel is their inherent concentration on unique historical cases and events and their inability to account for radical change and policy reversals (Peters, 1999). Despite such criticisms, history is certainly at play, as both policies and institutions prove to be sticky in any of the countries for which evidence has been available on executive pay and perquisites.

The problem shared by several of the theories reviewed above is that they either predict a gradual, but unidirectional erosion of rewards to the executive elite or a basic stability in the prevailing pattern. The reality is, however, that change, whether it is radical change or incremental changes that over a few years accumulate to a policy reversal, can be observed in some countries that seemed to follow either a Tocquevillian path or a leveling-down path characteristic of countries where rewards to the governing elite are settled together with other public service salaries. In countries like Denmark, Sweden and Britain top civil servants have gained ground vis-à-vis other groups in the public sector. It might be argued that this is the result of market forces at play, because in the long run only such improvements would enable government to attract able persons – a hypothesis whose validity was questioned in the introduction to this chapter. Empirically, the problem with it is that this trend has also been observed in Australia and New Zealand, countries that did not experience the material degradation of the higher civil service during the 1970s and 1980s. Another problem is that cabinet ministers, who in some countries had difficulty in keeping up with other groups (due to Tocquevillian erosion), have recovered in a country like Denmark, but this has certainly not been the case in, for example, New Zealand (Christensen and Gregory, 2001, forthcoming).

Cultural theory has been brought in to reconcile such reversals of policy. The logic is that policy choices are embedded in a dominant cultural context that defines the values invoked to legitimate specific decisions and choices. They not only define what is appropriate in a particular social or organizational situation, they may also frame actor preferences. As a theory its deficiencies are similar to those found in rational choice institutionalism because in its general form it points nowhere. To derive any predictions from it, it is essential to specify the cultural context within which the analysis is set, for example, an egalitarian or a hierarchical one. As such specifications are by their very nature deemed to be quite vague it might seem difficult to travel far along this road. Yet, logically this is one way in which it would be possible to account for non-trivial change and policy reversals.

In his book *The Art of the State*, Christopher Hood (1999) has shown how thinking about governmental organization and public management is heavily dependent on particular modes of reasoning about human motivation and human action in organizational and social contexts. During a period starting in the 1990s the public sector in the Western world has experienced a change in basic reasoning concerning its organization and operation. This change is usually referred to as New Public Management (NPM) thinking. Although in no way constituting a coherent program, the NPM movement emphasizes the importance of management and leadership over formal structure and of economic incentives operating at the individual level over roles and rules. In addition, it tends to replace the ideal of a Weberian bureaucracy with that of corporate governance. Some countries have been highly resistant not only to the rhetoric but also the design prescriptions contained in the program. This appears to be the case in both Germany and Norway (Derlien, 1996; Lægreid, 2001; Olsen, 1996). In other countries the ideas seem to have gained more ground. Most Western countries have always organized some of their government activities in state-owned enterprises or government corporations. To the conventional way of thinking about the management of such enterprises, the director received a salary and a pension similar to that of a high ranking civil servant. With the reforms enacted in accordance with the NPM model these countries have displayed a strong preference for the corporatization of government activities. In addition, it has also turned out that *pari passu* with this transformation of the public sector the point of reference used for setting the salaries and contractual conditions for members of corporate management has been changed to correspond to those presumably applied in the private business sector.

A similar transformation has taken place within the civil service proper in some countries. This happened when the traditional ideas of civil service tenure, set salary scales and deferred pensions were replaced by the ideas of fixed term appointments and individual contracts for leading civil servants. In some countries this form of contractualism applies to agency directors and other top civil servants formally operating at arm's length from the political executive; other countries have applied a more extreme version of the model, for instance Sweden has extended performance pay to judges, while in the New Zealand model permanent secretaries have become chief executives working on contract with their departmental ministers (Boston et al., 1996; Gregory, 2001; Sjölund, 1989).

PAYING FOR GOOD GOVERNANCE

One of the most distinctive traits of merit bureaucracy is its separation of administrative office from the private property of its incumbents. Civil servants are not only recruited on the basis of their professional merits; they also carry out their job without eyeing their personal interests. This is in contrast to the practice of patrimonial and patronage forms of public administration. In the former, public authority was closely linked to feudal structures of property rights, while in the latter the selection of people for public office was linked to one party's conquest of political power at the expense of its political competitors.

The rationale behind Weberian bureaucracy rests on the interaction between the superior quality of civil servants solely recruited on their merits and the blend of economic incentives and norms that are integral to this form of administration. One presumption therefore is that the combination of lifelong tenure, a fixed salary and inalienable pension rights shields public bureaucracies and their civil servants from undue political pressure and also against corruption. Even a cursory inspection of the indexes that are compiled on a regular basis reveals a relatively low level of corruption in countries that have basically organized their public administration in accordance with the principles of merit bureaucracy, while it is on average much higher in countries where political patronage is still important and political interference into even routine administrative dealings is a daily practice. Hence the emphasis that the World Bank and academic analysts place on the enactment of civil service reforms in emerging economies as well as developing countries is very well founded indeed (Geddes, 1994; Lindauer and Nunberg, 1994; Nunberg, 1995; World Bank, 1997).

In bureaucratic theory the focus is on the selection, promotion and rewards for civil servants rather than the level of these rewards. The implicit logic is that it is the certainty of future income rather than short-term economic gains that provides the incentives (and the courage) to behave as befits a civil servant. A further corollary is that their pay should be calculated according to formulas that are general, and in addition that formal pay that is taxable and open to public scrutiny, rather than invisible perquisites, should form the core of their rewards.

The conventional logic raises intriguing policy issues. One is whether it is wise to virtually leave the level of rewards paid to civil servants and members of the political executive out of the discussion. This issue that complements and to some extent challenges the conventional civil service logic is in no way unfounded. Above, it was repeatedly noted how Tocqueville expressed concern for the ability of democracies to recruit sufficiently able persons to governing positions because in a democracy it was politically unsustainable to pay them a competitive salary in the long run. The same long-term concern can be raised for the civil service if the politics of settling their salaries lead to a gradual and continuous erosion of their pay.

A related policy issue addressed by the World Bank is whether low pay to incumbents of executive office can be an independent source of corruption. The argument is that low levels of pay create a strong impulse to seek additional income, and as people in executive office command much demanded authority to get things moving, corrupt dealings with business people are a potential independent source of income. Yet, empirically it is far from clear whether low levels of income are in fact connected with corrupt practices, and if so, whether this happens among both executives and street-level bureaucrats.

Another policy issue arises when advocates of NPM reforms invoke the insights of principal–agent theory to note that the incentives of a merit civil service with tenure are poorly engineered. Their argument is that such a system tends to create managers and civil servants who pay little attention to costs and efficiency, and who are in addition not very responsive to the concerns of their clients because their implicit employment contracts do not contain proper incentives at the level of the individual civil servant. Their solution is to replace tenure with fixed term appointments based on individual contracts between the political executive and professional managers. When advocating contractual reforms, they refer to the practices of corporate governance whose comparative supremacy is claimed to be due to the very incentives tenured civil service fails to provide.

This diagnosis and the prescription that accompanies it has, as also noted above, to some extent been implemented in some, though far from all, OECD countries. Seeking to determine whether this form of contractualism is sound policy advice gives rise to a series of new and serious issues. First, has it been verified empirically that fixed term appointments combined with an element of performance pay improve managerial performance? Second, to what extent can performance contracts be engineered such that incentives are not twisted in a direction that is at odds with the 'sine ira ac studio' commitment of the merit civil service? Third, is it, after all, possible to devise a contractual structure in which the incentives of administrative agents and political principals are aligned and which is robust to short-term opportunism on either side? Fourth, does the model of the firm provide the kind of empirical support that the advocates of reform so vehemently invoke? And fifth, is it at all politically sustainable to enact and implement reforms that rely on a high degree of individual differentiation in a democratic setting?

THE CONTINGENCIES OF PAY POLICIES

The discussion of patterns of pay and perquisites for government executives revealed a motley pattern of practices. It is unsurprising that given such circumstances it is impossible to boil down the observations to a simple and consistent set of descriptive generalizations. It is equally unsurprising, but nevertheless disappointing, that although a set of sometimes sophisticated analytical tools is at hand, it is equally difficult to account for the variation in a way that allows for consistent predictions, not to mention clear policy recommendations.

Still, having reviewed the literature, certain non-trivial conclusions seem justified. First, it is a fairly well-established fact that general market economics and specific labor market forces only play a minor role in the setting of rewards for political and administrative executives. This mainly political issue is usually dealt with through political procedures and bargaining. But it is worth noticing that economic constraints may be important for the political bargaining that determines the pay of government executives. Second, even if economic forces don't explain the empirical observations, individuals' rational pursuit of material and immaterial rewards cannot be dismissed as valid motivators of individual and collective choices. Constraints on executives are so tight that there are severe limits to how far they can move to maximize their own rewards. Third, these constraints hardly point in a specific direction. One distinction is that between the macro- and micro-institutional setup. In a macro perspective there seems to be a marked difference with regard to the outcomes of either democratic competition or autocratic seclusion. In micro-institutional perspective, however, much seems to depend on whether executive pay and perquisites are set according to semi-automatic procedures or integrated into a general bargaining round, politically connecting the regulation of elite rewards to those of public employees at the bottom of the hierarchy. Fourth, these strategic games are embedded in a wider social and cultural context. This will over long periods make it politically costly and illegitimate to institute a new policy, but when a change in cultural or ideological context comes about, which has actually happened in this field, the changed context provides new points of reference to be strategically exploited by groups who have considered themselves to be disadvantaged by past pay policies. Finally, when it comes to the policy lessons to be drawn, two conclusions seem justified. One is negative in as far as there is no clear evidence for linking executive pay clearly to either macro-economic performance at the societal level or micro-performance at the organizational or policy sector level. The other is positive in that it is far too early to discard tenured merit bureaucracy as unsustainable. For one thing the experience from the Western democracies seems to be that its adaptive capacity is much higher than certain theories will have it. For another thing, it also seems that the creation of a merit bureaucracy is one of the pre-conditions for better governance in third world and emerging democracies and economies.

REFERENCES

Boston, Jonathan et al. (1996) *Public Management: The New Zealand Model.* Auckland: Oxford University Press.

Brans, Marleen (1994) 'Belgium: Public Office and Private Awards', in Christopher Hood and B. Guy Peters (eds), *Rewards at the Top. A Comparative Study of High Public Office.* London: Sage.

Christensen, Jørgen Grønnegaard and Gregory, Robert (2001) 'Public Personnel Policies and Personnel Administration'. Contribution to the Comparative Personnel Study.

Christensen, Jørgen Grønnegaard and Gregory, Robert (forthcoming) 'Similar Ends, Differing Means: Contractualism and Civil Service Reform in Denmark and New Zealand', *Governance.*

Christensen, Jørgen Grønnegaard and Pallesen, Thomas (forthcoming) 'The Political Benefits of Corporatization and Privatization', *Journal of Public Policy,*

Derlien, Hans-Ulrich (1994) 'Germany: The Structure and Dynamics of the Reward System for Bureaucratic and Political Elites', in Christopher Hood and B. Guy Peters (eds), *Rewards at the Top. A Comparative Study of High Office.* London: Sage.

Derlien, Hans-Ulrich (1996) 'Germany: The Intelligence of Bureaucracy in a Decentralized Polity', in Johan P. Olsen and B. Guy Peters (eds), *Lessons from Experience.* Oslo: Scandinavian University Press.

Geddes, Barbara (1994) *Politician's Dilemma: Building State Capacity in Latin America.* Berkeley, CA: University of California Press.

Gregory, Robert (2001) 'Transforming Governmental Culture: A Sceptical View of New Public Management', in Tom Christensen and Per Lægreid (eds), *New Public Management. The Transformation of Ideas and Practice.* Aldershot: Ashgate.

Gregory, Robert (2003) 'New Zealand – The End of Egalitarianism', in Christopher Hood and B. Guy Peters (eds), *Reward for High Public Office: Asian and Pacific Rim States.* London: Routledge.

Hood, Christopher (1994) 'The UK', in Christopher Hood and B. Guy Peters (eds), *Rewards at the Top. A Comparative Study of High Public Office.* London: Sage.

Hood, Christopher (1999) *The Art of the State.* Oxford: Clarendon Press.

Hood, Christopher and Lambert, Sonia (1994) 'Mountain Tops or Iceberg Tips? Some Comparative Data on RHPOs', in Christopher Hood and B. Guy Peters (eds), *Rewards at the Top. A Comparative Study of High Office.* London: Sage.

Hood, Christopher and Peters, B. Guy (eds) (1994) *Rewards at the Top. A Comparative Study of High Public Office.* London: Sage.

Hood, Christopher and Peters, B. Guy (1995) 'Erosion and Variety in Pay for High Public Office', *Governance,* 8: 171–94.

Hood, Christopher and Peters, B. Guy (eds) (2003) *Reward for High Public Office: Asian and Pacific Rim States.* London: Routledge.

Hood, Christopher and Askim, Jostein (2003) 'Alike at the Summit?', in Christopher Hood and B. Guy Peter (eds), *Reward for High Public Office: Asian and Pacific Rim States.* London: Routledge.

Horn, Murray J. (1995) *The Political Economy of Public Administration.* New York: Cambridge University Press.

Klöti, Ulrich (1994) 'Switzerland: Serving the State and Maximizing Income', in Christopher Hood and B. Guy Peters (eds), *Rewards at the Top. A Comparative Study of High Office.* London: Sage.

Liegl, Barbara and Müller, Wolfgang C. (1999) 'Senior Officials in Austria', in Edward C. Page and Vincent Wright (eds), *Bureaucratic Élites in Western European States.* Oxford: Oxford University Press.

Lindauer, David and Nunberg, Barbara (eds) (1994). *Rehabilitating Government: Pay and Employment Reform in Africa.* Washington, DC: World Bank.

Lægreid, Per (1994) 'Norway' in Christopher Hood and B. Guy Peters (eds), *Rewards at the Top. A Comparative Study of High Office*. London: Sage.

Nunberg, Barbara (1995) *Managing the Civil Service. Reform Lessons from Advanced Industrialized Countries*. Washington, DC: World Bank.

Olsen, Johan P. (1996) 'Norway: Slow Learner – or Another Triumph of the Tortoise?', in Johan P. Olsen and B. Guy Peters (eds), *Lessons from Experience*. Oslo: Scandinavian University Press.

Peters, B. Guy (1978) *The Politics of Bureaucracy*. London: Longman.

Peters, B. Guy (1999) *Institutional Theory in Political Science*. London: Pinter.

Pierre, Jon (forthcoming) 'Politicization of the Swedish Civil Service: A Necessary Evil – or Just Evil?' Contribution to the Comparative Politicization Project.

Pierson, Paul (2000) 'Increasing Returns, Path Dependence, and the Study of Politics', *American Political Science Review*, 94: 251–67.

Ridley, F.F. and Doig, Alan (eds) (1995) *Sleaze: Politicians, Private Interests and Public Reaction*. Oxford: Oxford University Press.

Rouban, Luc (1998) *La Fin des technocrates?* Paris: Presses de Science Po.

Sjölund, Maivor (1989) *Statens lönepolitik, 1966–1988*. Stockholm: Allmänna Förlaget.

Tocqueville, Alexis de (1835/1963) *De la Démocratie en Amérique*. Paris: Union Générale d'Éditions.

Weber, Max (1919/1988) *Politik als Beruf*, in *Gesammelte Politische Schriften*. Tübingen: J.C.B. Mohr.

Wise, Lois Recascino (1996) 'Internal Labor Markets', in Hans A.G.M. Bekke et al. (eds), *Civil Service Systems in Comparative Perspective*. Bloomington, IN: Indiana University Press.

World Bank (1997) *The State in a Changing World*. Washington DC: World Bank.

7

Labor–Management Relations and Partnerships: Were They Reinvented?

James R. Thompson

Workers, managers, politicians and the public have important stakes in the outcomes of public sector labor relations processes. At issue for workers are pay levels and working conditions, for managers, workforce quality and the degree of authority wielded at the workplace, and for politicians, the support or opposition of an important constituency as well as the fiscal consequences of pay decisions. At issue for the public are jobs, tax rates related to decisions about public pay, and service quality as impacted by employee ability and motivation.

In the postwar years in many Western countries accommodation was reached among these parties on an approach to labor–management relations which tended to advantage both politicians and workers. Politicians retained the authority to unilaterally set terms and conditions of employment while workers gained the right to organize and were granted high levels of job security with adequate if not liberal levels of remuneration. Managers and the general public fared less well; mid- and upper-level managers generally wielded limited influence over the pay and working conditions of their subordinates and quality of service was rarely accorded high priority.

Specific features of labor–management relations and pay determination practices associated with this model included:

- Statute-based job selection, promotion and pay criteria
- Centralized wage negotiations
- Wage agreements covering whole governments or entire sectors of government
- Retention by governments of the right to unilaterally impose settlements where

agreements with employee representatives were not forthcoming
- Limited managerial flexibility on pay matters
- Internal equity as a primary criterion for pay setting
- Pay progression based on seniority.

This equation began to change in the 1970s and 1980s. Politicians in many nations were caught in a squeeze between rising costs associated with expanded social programs and a decline in revenues due to economic recession. Globalizing influences jeopardized industrial competitiveness in many countries, posing threats of job loss and economic dislocation. Publics became increasingly amenable to proposals to enhance competitiveness by reducing the size and the cost of the state administrative apparatus. There were simultaneous pressures for improved service from public organizations as a result of enhancements made to product quality in the private sector.

The consequences of these broad secular shifts for public sector labor relations were direct; if costs were to be reduced, efficiency enhanced and service improved, changes in work practices were required. Consistent with the 'economistic' logic which underlay these trends, politicians and senior civil servants looked to the private sector for new models of management. One set of private-sector-based prescriptions that gained particular currency has been identified as the New Public Management. The New Public Management (NPM) and its associated prescriptions provide a framework for this discussion of recent developments in labor–management relations in selected OECD member countries.

One element of NPM, the privatization of state enterprises, has provided a relatively quick means of reducing the number of public employees and of subjecting service delivery practices to market pressures. The degree to which governments resorted to privatization was a function of several factors, including the extent of economic and fiscal difficulties experienced, the availability of state-run functions suitable for privatization and the degree to which ideological disposition of the ruling coalition favored private rather than public means of service delivery. Where these factors converged, as in the United Kingdom under Prime Minister Thatcher, extensive privatization ensued.[1]

Transferring functions wholesale to the private sector is a relatively blunt instrument of reform. It often engenders vehement opposition from public employees and their representatives and is not generally suitable for 'core' government services such as tax administration, the provision of justice and the protection of social welfare. Governments have hence resorted to a variety of devices to achieve higher productivity and improved service within the core government sector. Devices associated with the NPM model include:[2]

- 'Hands-on professional management'
- Explicit standards and measures of performance
- Greater emphasis on output controls
- Shift to disaggregation of units in the public sector
- Shift to greater competition in public sector
- Stress on private-sector styles of management practice
- Stress on greater discipline and parsimony in resource use. (Hood, 1991)

Although there is no direct reference to human resource (HR) management and/or labor–management relations (LMR) practices in this list, the HR and LMR consequences of NPM doctrine are apparent.

- 'Hands-on professional management' implies at least a partial shift in control over human resource management processes and procedures from politicians to managers.
- The 'disaggregation' of administrative units implies a disaggregation of the civil service and the development of personnel systems 'tailored' to agency mission.
- A 'shift to greater competition' and 'greater discipline and parsimony in resource use' imply the privatization of public services, a reduction in the size of the public sector workforce and the containment of public sector wage increases.

- The 'stress on private-sector styles of management practice' is associated with 'greater flexibility in hiring and rewards'.

In this analysis, the NPM model is used to analyze recent trends in labor–management practices and to ascertain the breadth and extent of movement away from traditional management approaches. The reform movement itself is another focus of the study. Of interest is the extent to which NPM-type reforms have been adopted and therefore to which administrative practices generally have 'converged' on a new model. Finally, the NPM framework allows an exploration of the limits of reform. Whether and to what extent a private sector-oriented approach to labor–management relations can 'take' in the public sector provides a means for examining the general viability of this type of reform.

Several sets of questions will be addressed. First, what have been the trends in labor–management relations over the past fifteen years in selected OECD member countries? Second, is there evidence of movement away from traditional, 'closed' civil service models to more open 'market' models which incorporate contracting out, disaggregated structures and higher levels of discretion for management? Third, to the extent there has been such movement, how broad has it been and does it support the 'convergence' hypothesis? Finally, an examination of how labor–management processes have evolved can provide important insight into a key question that underlies the entire NPM dynamic: to what extent is substantive decentralization possible in systems in which hierarchical accountability is the dominant organizing principle.

CROSS-NATIONAL TRENDS IN LABOR–MANAGEMENT RELATIONS

Changes in public management practices across governments in the past two decades have been attributed to a number of factors. One of the most widely cited explanations of the NPM phenomenon and of the generally high level of 'ferment' in public management practices generally is that of economic globalization and the competitive pressures that have been released as a consequence of globalization. One manifestation of this dynamic has been the Maastricht Treaty, pursuant to which European countries committed themselves to reducing operating deficits and overall debt loads for purposes of adopting a common currency. Keller (1999: 58) comments that, 'the convergence criteria for European

Monetary Union created enormous pressure not only to stabilize public employment levels, but to decrease gradually the number of public employees, especially at the local/municipal level, and to introduce public sector reform plans'. Other factors contributing to pressures to curtail the size of, and improve the performance of the state sector have included public dissatisfaction with government, the ascension to power of the 'New Right' in several countries, and a perception of poor performance in the critical education and health sectors (Bach, 1999; Barlow et al., 1996; Farnham and Horton, 2000).

The ensuing reforms have resulted in a 'deprivileging' of public sector workers. Common interventions have included making some portion of worker pay contingent on performance, providing managers with more discretion over working conditions, disaggregating pay systems to allow pay for different occupations to fluctuate with the market and increased use of a 'contingent' workforce. This trend forced unions in many places to assume a defensive posture, particularly where and when rightist governments have prevailed, as in the United Kingdom in the early and mid-1990s, Australia in the mid- and late 1990s and New Zealand in the mid-1990s.[3] As the following review of NPM 'exemplars', 'laggards' and 'in-betweens' reveals, however, there was substantial variation in the extent to which these practices were adopted.[4]

New Public Management exemplars

The United Kingdom, New Zealand and Sweden are generally regarded as leading examples of the New Public Management (NPM) in practice (Hood, 1996; Naschold, 1996). All have made radical changes in governance practices consistent with NPM precepts over the past fifteen years. In each instance, the changes have had major implications for the character and operations of the public workforce. All three countries have taken a two-pronged approach to reform; reducing the size of the public sector through the privatization of state enterprises and restructuring the core public sector to provide more operational flexibility at the agency level.

New Zealand

Key milestones in the evolution of the New Zealand public service were the State-Owned Enterprises Act of 1986 and the State Sector Act

of 1988. Under the State-Owned Enterprises Act, a number of commercial, state 'trading' organizations such as the Airways Corporation of New Zealand, the Coal Corporation of New Zealand and the Electricity Corporation of New Zealand, were made autonomous state-owned enterprises and required to operate on a for-profit basis. Some state-owned 'enterprises' such as the PostBank and the Telecom Corporation were subsequently transferred to private ownership.[5] In part as a result of these changes, public service staffing levels fell from 66,000 in 1983 to 34,500 in 1994 (Boston et al., 1996).

Pursuant to the State Sector Act of 1988, service delivery units within the core public sector were given semi-autonomous status as 'executive agencies'. Although the intention was to give the chief executive of each agency a high level of discretion in management matters for purposes of improving efficiency and service, the negotiation of employment conditions initially remained under the tight control of the State Services Commission. According to Boston et al. (1996: 230), 'the government wanted to ensure that inexperienced negotiators did not jeopardize its fiscal stance'. In 1991, the State Services Commission (SSC) delegated negotiating authority to the heads of the executive agencies but the authority had to be exercised in consultation with the SSC and could be withdrawn by the SSC. Further, bargaining outcomes had to be fiscally neutral (Boston et al., 1996).

Despite the changes wrought by the State Sector Act, the Labor government (1983–90) retained many features of the traditional labor-relations system. Unions retained exclusive rights to bargain for public sector employees and agency shop provisions with compulsory union membership could be included in employment contracts. In 1991, however, the new National government enacted the Employment Contracts Act (ECA) which removed the special privileges enjoyed by the unions. The ECA was actively opposed by the labor movement. Pursuant to the ECA, agency shop provisions were prohibited and there was a shift from collective to individual employment contracts. The bargaining power of the public employees was significantly reduced by the legislation: the New Zealand State Services Commission identifies a 6 per cent decline in real wages for members of the New Zealand Public Service between 1992 and 1997 (New Zealand State Services Commission, 1998). The Employment Relations Act passed by the new Labor Government in 2000 restored some of the collective bargaining rights that had been withdrawn with ECA.

Sweden

As a proportion of gross domestic product, the public sector in Sweden has historically been one of the largest in the world. In 1990, government employees constituted 31.7 per cent of the total workforce (Wilks, 1996). Facing fiscal difficulties in the early 1990s, the government took various steps both to reduce the size of the public sector and to reform administrative practices in ways that could enhance efficiency and effectiveness. Between 1990 and 1996, thirteen agencies became public companies contributing to a reduction of about 18 per cent in the number of public employees.[6]

Although Sweden has long had a set of semi-autonomous service delivery agencies, pay determination processes remained highly centralized until 1989. An agreement was reached between the National Agency for Government Employers (AgV)[7] and the major public sector trade unions to abolish the uniform system of pay grades and replace it with 'a system of individual and differentiated pay of the type that had long applied to salaried employees in the private sector' (Andersson and Schager, 1999: 247).

Pursuant to a 'frame agreement' negotiated between the three top public sector trade unions and AgV, each agency or area of government is now allocated a pay fund from which pay increases for employees are distributed. Wage increases received by the employees in each agency are then settled through local negotiations. Centralized influence over the process remains both in setting the amount of the pay fund (which effectively establishes limits on pay increases) and in stipulations for minimum pay increase guarantees. According to Roness (2001: 181), even though the unions were 'skeptical towards specific proposals for structural devolution ... they have been more concerned with securing jobs and working conditions for their members within the new form of association than with actively opposing the conversions'. Pay rates for public workers are generally set according to the prevailing wages for those in similar occupations in the private sector. Each agency has the option of introducing a pay-for-performance system.

United Kingdom

As in both New Zealand and Sweden, the reforms in the United Kingdom featured a two-pronged strategy, first to reduce the size of the public sector through the privatization of state enterprises, and second, to restructure the core public sector to provide more operational flexibility at the agency level. In the UK, approximately 800,000 employees were transferred from the public to the private sector as a consequence of the privatization of various state enterprises (Pollitt and Bouckaert, 2000). The total public sector workforce declined by approximately 30 per cent between 1981 and 1997 (Winchester and Bach, 1995).

The key structural reform was the decentralization of management authority to semi-autonomous service delivery units called 'Next Steps' agencies. As in New Zealand and Sweden, the intent was to induce greater efficiency and higher levels of performance by providing line managers with greater discretion over operational matters. Also as in New Zealand and Sweden, central government units relinquished control over pay determination gradually and continued to perform an important oversight and monitoring role.

Although the Next Steps program was initiated in 1988, the Minister for the Civil Service was not authorized to delegate the authority to set pay and working conditions until passage of the Civil Service Act of 1992 and the Conservative Government did not terminate service-wide bargaining until 1996 (Fredman, 1999; Winchester and Bach, 1995). Since that time, the delegations of authority have been extensive, including 'the prescription of terms and conditions of employment of home civil servants in so far as they relate to the classification of staff, remuneration, allowances, expenses, holidays, hours of work and attendance, part time and other working arrangements, performance and promotion, retirement age and redundancy, and redeployment of staff within and between departments' (Fredman, 1999: 56). The intent, consistent with 'strategic human resource management' precepts, was to allow each agency to tailor its human resource policies to its 'business needs'. Despite the delegations, there was an implicit tension between the delegation of control for managerial purposes and retention of budget control centrally. Agreements reached between agencies and unions have to remain within 'running cost' limitations and have to be approved by the Treasury.[8]

Associated with the change was an expansion in the use of performance-related pay, although this has subsequently been subject to reconsideration under the Labour government. Corby and White (1999: 18), state that 'by 1997 virtually all civil servants had at least an element of their pay determined by some form of individual performance review'. Horton (2000), however, reports that under the Labour government agencies are being given the option to abandon performance-related pay schemes.

New Public Management laggards

Bach and Della Rocca (2000) identify France, Germany and Spain as adherents of a 'traditional' approach to public administration. That the New Public Management has had only a limited impact in these countries is attributable to a variety of factors, including corporatist modes of governance and legally based approaches to administration.

France

Additional factors identified by Clark (1998) that account for the relatively low level of NPM penetration in France are:

- The tradition of a strong state and state direction of the economy ('*dirigisme*')
- The high social and political status of the civil service and particularly the elite grands corps
- A tradition of administrative centralization as evident in the prefectoral system.[9]

Consistent with these elements of the French administrative tradition, pay setting is highly centralized. Negotiations with the seven major public employee unions for employees in the central government, local government and hospitals are conducted centrally. A common pay grid applies to employees in all three sectors. Although there is a legal requirement to negotiate, the government retains the authority to impose a settlement unilaterally if an agreement is not reached. With the exception of certain categories such as the police, public employees have the right to strike.

Although pay scales are set centrally and pay progression proceeds according to seniority, a system of allowances and bonuses allows some flexibility in adjusting for market conditions. Allowances and bonuses comprise, on average, approximately 20 per cent of pay and vary widely by profession (OECD, 1997). According to Burnham (2000: 110), 'Pay progression is still dominated by incremental progression up the scales according to years of service ... Most allowances and bonuses are independent of performance or the particular demands of a post.'

Despite a generally centralized and rigid set of administrative practices, there have been intermittent attempts to modernize conditions in ways that are consistent with NPM precepts. In 1991, state corporations providing postal and telecommunications services were privatized, resulting in a reduction of public sector employment of approximately 440,000 (Guillotin and Meurs, 1999). There is also provision under French law for employee participation in the determination of some working conditions through a process of 'concertation' (Bazex, 1987).

Clark (1998) and Flynn and Strehl (1996) describe a series of attempts at administrative modernization. For example, in the late 1980s Prime Minister Rocard launched a modernization campaign, one element of which was to 'renovate' internal working relationships by devolving management authority from central ministries to territorial field services through a system of 207 'Centres de Responsabilités' ('responsibility centers' or CDRs) (Clark, 1998; Postif, 1997). Similar to the 'contractualization' of intradepartmental relationships that is now the norm in the UK, New Zealand and Sweden, CDR chief executives were to 'negotiate a set of objectives and targets with their parent department, and engage in a dialog about the budget required to deliver those targets' (Flynn and Strehl, 1996: 113). This was extended by a 1995 circular intended to transform the ministries into holding companies 'limited to the functions of policy setting, resource allocation, monitoring and evaluation' (Clark, 1998: 107). Citing Fialaire (1993), however, Flynn and Strehl (1996: 118) state that, 'the implementation of the accountability centres has not produced the management freedoms which were expected when they were established', and that, 'there is, in practice, still a great deal of a priori budgetary control by the Ministry of Finance which has been reluctant to move towards global running cost budgets because such a change would challenge the power of that ministry'.

Among the opponents of decentralization have been the *grands corps* (top civil servants) and the public employee unions. According to Burnham (2000), unions favor the centralized pay setting process which serves as 'their main source of power' and hence are a 'significant cause of inflexibility in human resource management'.

Germany

Keller (1999) attributes Germany's low-NPM status to the limited federal role in service provision, a high incidence of representation by civil servants in parliament and the highly centralized structure of collective bargaining. Bach and Della Rocca (2000: 93) observe that, 'the existence of elaborate rights of co-determination has diluted moves to develop a managerial culture', and Naschold and Arnkil (1997: 285) comment that Germany belongs in a group of countries which have 'rejected results steering ... and the selective reduction in the scope of state activity by means of competitive instruments and privatization programs'.

Pay setting continues to be centralized and uniformity of employment conditions prevails for both the civil service (*Beamte*) and non-civil service public employees (*Angestellte* – nonmanual; *Arbeiter* – manual). Although civil servants are prohibited from bargaining, other public employees, who comprise approximately 60 per cent of the total public workforce, can bargain over pay and working conditions. The unions representing public sector employees bargain jointly on behalf of employees at the federal, state (*Länder*) and local levels. In general, members of the *Beamte* receive the same pay increase negotiated by the *Angestellte* and *Arbeiter* (OECD, 1993). As in France, special allowances provide some flexibility in pay determination. Keller (1999: 63), citing Tondorf (1995), comments that, 'this system has been criticized as being highly inflexible because of its purely collective and uniform character, its independence from individual performance on the job and its high degree of job security'.

Despite the predominance of 'administrative rule steering' (Naschold, 1996), however, the influence of NPM ideas is apparent in Germany. Certain natural monopolies such as the postal service and railways have been privatized and, as a result of the Civil Service Reform Law of 1997, 'more weight is given to the idea of performance and merit in the law governing the civil service' (OECD, 1997: 55). Labor relations in the public sector as in the private sector features the 'co-determination' of working conditions by staff councils in conjunction with employers. With co-determination, staff councils elected by employees have 'statutory rights of co-determination covering a wide range of powers, from an effective veto to full informational rights in social and personnel affairs (e.g. hiring, promotion, transfers), but not economic matters' (Keller, 1999: 75).

Reform activities consistent with NPM ideas have been under way at the *Länder* and local levels. The Tilburg model being adopted by some German municipalities includes 'specialized departments' analogous to the New Zealand and United Kingdom-type executive agencies (Klages and Loffler, 1996). In some locations 'workplace-related forms of participation' have led to a 'diminished role for unions' as representatives of workers (Keller, 1999). There has also been a substantial increase in the number of part-time workers in the public sector (Keller, 1999).

Spain

Public administration in Spain has a legalistic orientation with 'considerable emphasis on regulation and codification of the law to ensure uniformity in the handling of cases' and with lawyers filling many of the top positions in the civil service (Parrado, 1996: 260). Similar to France, Spain has a system of administrative 'corps' which dominate the central government and which have presented an obstacle to administrative modernization. Both the general corps, consisting of public employees performing administrative and management duties, and the special corps, such as economists, accountants, diplomats and professors, largely control processes of recruitment and selection for the Spanish civil service (Parrado, 1996).

Non-civil service public employees, who make up approximately 50 per cent of the workforce of the central government, enjoy full bargaining rights, equivalent to those of private sector employees. In contrast, the bargaining rights of civil servants are governed by a specific law. The law allows for trade union representation and for a process of negotiation but, as in France, the openness of the negotiations is constrained by provisions allowing the government to unilaterally set employment terms in case of an impasse (Jódar et al., 1999).

Bargaining occurs at two levels. A general joint council addresses general employment conditions for all central government civil servants; separate bargaining addresses employment conditions for individual sectors such as education, the health service, the Post Office and the courts. With the exception of certain groups such as the military and the police, civil servants are allowed to strike.

As with the 'allowances' used in France, a system of 'supplements' allows some pay flexibility. Included are a 'specific' supplement, 'designed to compensate for particular positions requiring special dedication, responsibility, or ability', a seniority supplement and a productivity supplement (Albert et al., 1999: 234).

According to Parrado (1996), an administrative modernization effort launched in the late 1980s has had little effect. Included in the initiative were a number of NPM elements, including the provision of a high degree of autonomy in the management of human and budgetary resources to a set of 'autonomous organizations'. The managers in charge of these units were to identify 'predetermined objectives and deploy appropriate resources to achieve them, without detailed control by central units over the allocation of money and personnel' (p. 268). However, according to Parrado (p. 268), this philosophy 'has been strongly opposed by horizontal departments, especially the Ministry of Economy and Finance, which resisted a loss of power'.

New Public Management 'in betweens'

Levels of reform activity in Australia, Italy and the United States have been higher than in France, Germany or Spain but the results have been less radical than those achieved in New Zealand, Sweden or the United Kingdom.

Australia

The evolution of the Australian public service over the past ten years, including its labor–management relations elements, reflects considerable NPM influence. First, there have been 'very significant reductions in government employment' (Fairbrother and MacDonald, 1999: 351) as a result of the privatization of state-owned enterprises, including Aussat, the Commonwealth Bank, Qantas Airlines and Australian National Railways. Although no use has been made of semi-autonomous service delivery agencies, Australia has been able to decentralize pay setting authority to management through a variety of mechanisms.

During the period that the Labor Party controlled the government (1983–1992), there was extensive consultation and negotiation over pay and other conditions of federal government employees. The Coalition Government that took power in 1996, however, sought to move from collective to individual contracts and hence to consign unions to the representation of individual employees (O'Brien and Fairbrother, 2000).

Provisions of the Public Service Bill of 1997 were implemented administratively by the Coalition Government subsequent to the failure of passage in the Senate. Consistent with that legislation, authority over personnel and pay matters have been substantially devolved to departments. Fairbrother and MacDonald (1999: 352) comment, 'The Public Service Bill envisaged that "employment powers (will) rest predominantly with Secretaries (or Chief Executives) and

that the primary employment relationship (will be) between the employer and employee at the agency level" (Australian Public Service and Merit Protection Commission, 1999: 14) … Under the new system, only general concepts of engagement, promotion and transfer will be retained within the APS [Australian Public Service] employment framework and the duties of employees and their work location will be determined by Departmental Secretaries.'

Despite the changes, however, central staff units have continued to play an important role in pay setting. The Department of Workplace Relations and Small Business (DWRSB) has been given a 'watchdog' role to ensure high degrees of procedural uniformity across all federal government employment; any agency-level agreements must receive approval from DWRSB and agreements must comply with policy parameters on funding, classification, performance management etc.

Italy

Wage determination in Italy has traditionally been both fragmented and centralized. Separate bargaining was conducted for eight separate sectors, including the central administration, national enterprises, local administrations, 'parastatal bodies' and the National Health Service. Bargaining between the unions and the state took place centrally and the pay guidelines that resulted afforded little flexibility at lower levels. Pursuant to Act 93 of 1983, all agreements were subject to review by the Council of Ministers for compatibility with budget limitations (Treu, 1987).

In 1993, reforms were instituted as part of the effort to comply with the guidelines for entry into the European Monetary Union. With legislative decree No. 29 of 1993, labor relations practices in the public sector were made to conform with those in the private sector. A new agency (ARAN)[10] was created to bargain on behalf of public employers, at both the national and local levels. According to Bordogna, Dell'Aringa and Della Rocca (1999: 115), 'the determination of wages and salaries, which in the past was often subject to intervention on the part of the parliament or the administrative courts, is now almost entirely given to the exclusive competence of collective negotiations'. The basic pay for different grades is fixed by national collective agreements for each sector with provision for expanded managerial autonomy at the local level, including the authority to 'award small lump-sum bonuses on the basis of individual performance' (Bach and Della Rocca, 2000: 89).

Consistent with NPM precepts, the 1993 reform 'defines the responsibility of public sector management as directed towards achieving measurable results in terms of efficiency and effectiveness, rather than just towards assuring the formal legitimacy of administrative acts ...' (Bordogna et al., 1999: 115). Bach and Della Rocca (2000: 93), however, caution that 'the attempts to "empower" management have been constrained by the continuation of an all encompassing framework of administrative and legal regulations with rules defining personnel policies such as recruitment and promotions'.

United States

In the United States President Clinton's National Performance Review incorporated some NPM-type reforms but the effect on the public service has been limited. The federal government generally does not negotiate with unions over pay, leaving unions with a limited representational role.[11] President Clinton sought to provide the unions with a more substantive role with Executive Order 12871 of 1993 on labor–management partnerships. The executive order, consistent with the emphasis placed by NPR on employee empowerment, created a National Partnership Council consisting of the heads of the major federal employee unions and senior, executive branch management officials. Among the charges given the council were to work with the president and vice president in executive branch reform, to oversee the creation of partnership councils within the major federal departments and agencies, and to recommend statutory changes to facilitate better workplace relations.

An attempt at reforming the civil service system in 1994–5 fell foul of Republican antipathy toward allowing the unions more of a presence in the workplace (Thompson, 2001). However, a provision included in Executive Order 12871 would have accomplished that end without congressional involvement. Specifically, the executive order directed agency heads to 'negotiate over the subjects set forth in 5 U.S.C. 7106(b) (1), and instruct subordinate officials to do the same'. Section 7106(b) (1) sets forth issues over which management is permitted but not required to bargain.[12] This provision was widely ignored by the agencies until late in the Clinton administration when the employee unions put on a major push to have it implemented. The issue came to a head in 1999 when the unions attempted to get the courts to direct agencies to bargain over these matters. The courts decreed that the executive order could only be enforced by the president through his authority to appoint and remove agency heads and, in general, Clinton was unwilling to take such steps in the face of management and agency resistance (Friel, 1999).

An evaluation of the partnership program commissioned by the Office of Personnel Management in 2001 found some success indicators; 55 per cent of management and union representatives surveyed agreed that their councils were an important decision making body.[13] Survey results showed that partnerships had resulted in improved labor–management communications, and improved labor relations. However, relatively few participants perceived that partnership had resulted in any significant cost savings or avoidance or improved productivity (Masters, 2001).

Vice President Gore attempted to emulate Britain's 'Next Steps' program by recommending the designation of selected service delivery units as 'performance-based organizations' (PBOs). Similar to the executive agencies in Britain and New Zealand, the heads of these units were to be provided with additional management flexibilities and were to be held accountable for achieving specific performance objectives. Paybanding, which would allow pay to be tied more directly to individual performance, was one such flexibility. Of the twelve such agencies proposed for PBO status by the administration however, Congress approved only two and neither was granted paybanding authority (Thompson, 2001).

TRENDS IN LABOR–MANAGEMENT RELATIONS IN OECD COUNTRIES

The management practices associated with the New Public Management became widespread as a direct consequence of economic globalization and the competitive pressures released thereby. Proponents of economic liberalization determined that management practices in the public sector were an important determinant of economic performance and that the market logic driving the need for competitiveness should be applied to public bureaucracies. A hallmark of the forthcoming reforms was flexibility. Traditional instruments of public sector reform were slow and blunt and not well suited to a dynamic economic environment. The competitive dynamic demanded more nimble systems and approaches. This in turn implied privatization and a decentralization of authority to subordinate levels of the bureaucracy. Results rather than rules were to serve as a means of accountability.

Management practices relating to labor relations and pay setting were among those affected. Table 7.1 lists the implications of the NPM/market logic for various key dimensions of labor–management relations. Consistent with the decentralizing dynamic integral to NPM, agencies were to be provided with greater discretion in managing resources, including pay and hence the ability to tailor their pay systems to agency requirements. The quest for performance requires that agencies be competitive in the external market for individuals with skill sets required to achieve high levels of performance and that pay rules allow individual traits and attributes to be considered in hiring and promotion. The economistic logic that underlies NPM further mandates that managers be given the authority to use pay as a basis for rewarding and sanctioning workers. Allowing variation in pay across agencies in turn implies that the rules be set locally, that managers be given broad negotiating authority and that employment be contractual rather than statutory with expanded use of a 'contingent' workforce.

Table 7.1 shows the extent of adoption of these alternative, labor relations/pay determination practices during the period 1985–2000. As shown, the movement has been fairly extensive, particularly among the NPM exemplars. NPM ideas have gained currency even among the laggards, as discussed above with regard to the 'Centres de Responsabilités' in France, the Tilburg model in Germany and attempts at bureaucratic modernization in Spain, although the degree of actual change was dampened during implementation in each instance.

The pervasiveness of the adoption or at least exploration of NPM-type practices lends support to the convergence hypothesis. However, while it is possible to identify when new techniques have been formally adopted, it is much more problematic to detect the extent to which the various interventions have taken hold. Subtle aspects of implementation often undermine the purported intent of the reform programs. In the United States, for example, the pay of federal employees is ostensibly linked to performance; 'step' increases for bargaining unit employees in most departments are contingent on a satisfactory performance appraisal. However, only a very small proportion of employees receive less than a satisfactory performance appraisal, making the step increase virtually automatic. Similarly, performance-related pay programs have been put in place in Italy but, according to

Ruffini (2000), are ineffective because of a low level of funding.

That reality sometimes belies appearance is not uncharacteristic of administrative reform generally. Also at work, however, is a fundamental conflict between the hierarchical exigencies of governance structures and the decentralized, flexible, market-based logic that underlies NPM. The tension is particularly apparent with regard to pay determination processes for which the requirement to maintain tight control over expenditures directly conflicts with the NPM-based prescription for decentralized negotiations over pay and working conditions. In general, the necessity to maintain budgetary control has prevailed over considerations of improved bureaucratic performance.

Even the NPM 'exemplars' maintain tight central control over the budget. In the UK for example, Winchester and Bach (1995: 30) report that,

> the government has invoked the model of the multidivisional company. The center ('head office') makes most of the strategic decisions and monitors the financial performance and service standards of separate organizational units whose senior managers are responsible for operational efficiency.

Consistent with this model, 'trade union negotiators and senior managers … report that the Treasury still exerts a strong influence on their agreements'. White (1999: 85) confirms that 'freedom to establish new pay systems is subject to strict central government controls, under which all changes must be cleared by the Treasury. Even pay offers must be cleared before negotiation with the unions commences.'

In Australia, which under the Coalition government of the late 1990s has moved aggressively to implement NPM-type reforms, Fairbrother and MacDonald (1999: 352) report that,

> despite the Howard government's professed ambitions to create a more decentralized (if not deregulated) approach to industrial relations in the public sector, the Department of Workplace Relations and Small Business has been given the important 'watchdog' role to ensure high degrees of procedural, if not substantive, uniformity across all federal government employment. Certified Agreements must receive both 'first stage' (i.e. proposal stage) and 'second stage' (i.e. preendorsement stage) approval by the Department before they can go to be voted on by the union membership and/or the staff. To be approved, they must comply with at least twelve policy parameters that include funding, classification structures, performance management and relationship to awards, other agreements and legislation.

Table 7.1 *Changes in labor–management relations and pay determination practices in selected OECD member countries, 1985–2000*

	NPM 'exemplars'			NPM 'In-betweens'			NPM 'laggards'		
	NZ	SW	UK	AS	IT	US	FR	GR	SP
Pay determination									
Pay negotiation: centralized > decentralized	xx	xx	xx	x	x				
Pay rules across agencies: uniform > variable	xx	xx	xx	x	x	x			x
Basis of pay determination: internal > external equity	xx	xx	x	x					
Unit of pay: collective > individual	xx	x	x	x					x
Pay progression: seniority > performance	x	x	x	x	x			x	
Employment system									
Workforce: permanent/career > flexible/contingent	x	x	x	x	x	x	x	xx	
Legal basis of employment: statutory > contractual	x	x			x				
Partnership									
Determination of outcomes: unilateral > mutual		x			x			x[1]	
Scope of bargaining: narrow > broad		x				x	x	xx[1]	x

NZ, New Zealand; SW, Sweden; UK, United Kingdom; AS, Australia; IT, Italy; US, United States; FR, France; GR, Germany; SP, Spain.

xx, Major emphasis/change; x, minor emphasis/change.

[1]*Angestellte* and *Arbeiter* (non-civil service workers) only.

Partnership and workplace organization

The apparent conflict between the requirement to maintain central control for purposes of accountability and the decentralizing mandate implicit in NPM raises fundamental questions about the long-term viability of the NPM model. Naschold (1996) associates traditional approaches to governance with 'rule steering' and the NPM model with 'results steering'. He comments (p. 99), 'the precarious balance between the two poles of results and rule steering cannot be seen as stable, however. Experience with modernization processes in the OECD countries has convincingly shown that ... MbR [management by results] systems tend to be reabsorbed by the pressure of rule steering and to degenerate into formalistic bureaucratic paperwork if they cannot be pushed beyond a given threshold level by means of political mobilization.' Similarly Massey (1997: 6) observes that attempting to marry the old and new paradigms is 'unlikely to succeed due to each approach "involving an underlying logic which, if taken to its limits, will tend to destroy all the others"' (Hood, 1995).

A key question then becomes whether a variant of NPM can be identified which accommodates both accountability and performance needs. For Naschold (1996), a key relates to the extent to which NPM incorporates changes in 'work organization' in ways that develop employee capacity and improve the quality of work life. The underlying ideas derive from programs such as Total Quality Management, which endorse concepts of worker involvement and worker empowerment. Supporters of these ideas rely on the 'humanistic' thesis that by addressing the social and psychological needs of employees a higher level of 'commitment' to organizational objectives can be achieved (Abrahamson, 1997; Walton, 1980).

The data suggest that, with few exceptions (Sweden), the reform experiences of most countries have not been driven by humanistic concerns. Nor, in general, have rank and file workers been beneficiaries of the changes. Horton (2000: 230) reports that in the UK, 'There is evidence of high levels of dissatisfaction and stress, whilst low morale appears to be at an all-time high in some public services, especially the NHS and education.' According to the Industrial Relations Review and Report (1993: 5), 'All the civil service unions and the CCSU have resisted the break-up of national pay agreements, the decentralization of pay bargaining, and the delegation of other conditions of service. In particular, therefore, they opposed the introduction and extension of pay delegation.' Winchester and

Bach (1995: 41) report that 'the balance of power between trade unions and employers has shifted decisively in favour of the latter' in the six European countries they studied. Naschold (1996: 55) reports as a finding from a study of compulsory competitive tendering in the UK that 'in the vast majority of cases additional fringe benefits above and beyond basic wages were cut, working conditions deteriorated and jobs were lost'. Naschold (p. 59) also cites a finding by Walsh (1993) that 'in the vast majority of cases the main source of the productivity gains induced by [the modernization program in the UK] was cuts in staffing levels, cuts in wage levels, and a deterioration in working conditions'.

In the United States, techniques for organizational and personnel development such as teaming, employee involvement, partnership, job enlargement and process redesign were an official part of the National Performance Review. Doeringer et al. (1996: 184), however, identify 'inherent contradictions between management prerogative and employee voice' due to the 'long-term systemic problems' of 'grafting greater employee voice onto a merit model that was grounded in management prerogative'.

Fairbrother and MacDonald (1999: 353) identify initiatives by the Labor governments of the 1980s in Australia to promote industrial democracy and employee participation but state that, 'By the mid-1990's these experiments had largely ended, partly because of the competing demands between compelling participation experiments and the promotion of enterprise bargaining'.

Of eleven OECD countries, Naschold (1996) identifies 'work organization' as an element of the reform program in only four: Denmark, Sweden, Norway and the Netherlands. According to Naschold (1996: 34), both the United Kingdom and New Zealand feature 'neo-Taylorist' structures 'and low human resource quality levels'. Importantly, he contends that the 'decoupling' of managerial reform with changes in the labor process 'serves to perpetuate traditional forms of bureaucratic division of labour ... or leads to a neo-taylorism of managerial mass production within the framework of private sector market models'. Naschold (p. 62) argues that, 'One of the most important tasks for public sector modernization will therefore lie in the codevelopment of the managerial and labour process'.

The implications of Naschold's (1996) analysis is that in the absence of a more fundamental realignment, even NPM exemplars like New Zealand and the United Kingdom are likely to regress to 'rule steering' as a basis for administrative practice with the reform model likely to be sustained only in Sweden of the countries reviewed here. Problematic, from the perspective of NPM advocates, is that Sweden's success appears attributable to somewhat idiosyncratic historical and cultural elements, including a corporatist, consensual approach to governance to which its small size and demographic homogeneity are conducive.

CONCLUSION

This study reveals that with regard to labor relations practices, NPM prescriptions have gained a high degree of currency. Particularly notable in this regard are the decentralization of authority over pay determination to the agency level, the linking of pay to performance, an expanded use of a contingent workforce and reference to external rather than internal benchmarks for pay setting purposes. Even in the NPM 'laggards' where the contextual factors have inhibited implementation, NPM approaches to governance are in evidence.

This outcome appears largely attributable to the dominance of an economistic logic pursuant to which economic productivity and prosperity assume preeminent performance. The institutional disaggregation implicit in this logic has undermined collectivist institutions like the civil service while disadvantaging lower-status groups including rank-and-file government workers for whom these institutions provided a degree of protection. The extension of the economistic logic poses a challenge to the authority of the state itself, however, a challenge that has been met to date in many places by compromising the substance of some of the reforms.

The long-range challenge for reformers will be to identify a model that can accommodate the dual but conflicting needs for performance and accountability. If, as Naschold suggests, aspects of 'work organization' are central to the problem, labor–management relations will take on increasing importance in reform strategies.

NOTES

1 The term 'privatization' is defined here as transfer to private ownership as opposed to the contracting out of a function to the private sector.

2 The list provided is that of Hood (1991). Massey's (1997) list includes the following:

   1 The reduction of bureaucratic rules and hierarchies.
   2 Budget transparency and to identify the costs of inputs and outputs.

3 The use of a network of contracts rather than fiduciary relationships.
4 To disaggregate organizations and their functions, introducing purchaser/provider distinctions.
5 To increase provider competition.
6 To increase consumer power through enhanced scope for exit and redress.

3 Although the reform strategies of leftist governments in these same countries included similar elements, ways were generally found of mitigating the adverse impact on unions and their members.

4 Hood (1996) categorizes a number of countries as high, medium, or low 'NPM emphasis'. In general, his categorization tracks that utilized here with the exception of Australia, which he considers 'high' NPM emphasis but which is categorized here as an 'in-between', and France, which Hood categorizes as 'medium NPM emphasis' but which is considered here to be a 'laggard'.

5 Boston et al. (1996) provide a comprehensive list of public sector 'trading' enterprises that changed status between 1987 and 1995.

6 According to the OECD Public Management Service (2000), total public employment in Sweden declined from 1,275,000 in 1990 to 1,044,000 in 1995.

7 AgV stands for Arbetsgivarverket.

8 Key groups of public employees, including medical staff in the National Health Service, continue to have their pay set through national pay review bodies which recommend pay increases to the government and which are normally accepted. Thus, there are important differences between the civil service, for which pay determination has been decentralized, the National Health Service which remains centralized, and the local service for which there is a national framework with local flexibility (White, 1999).

9 A prefect serves as the central government's representative in each department and 'exercises powers of supervision or prior approval over the decisions of locally-elected politicians' (Clark, 1998: 99).

10 ARAN stands for Agenzia per la rappresentanza sindacale nel pubblico impiego.

11 The Postal Service, with over 800,000 employees, is an important exception. Pursuant to the Postal Service Reorganization Act of 1970, the Postal Service does negotiate over wages with its employees.

12 Section 7106(b)(1) states, 'Nothing in this section shall preclude any agency and any labor organization from negotiating:

   (1) at the election of the agency, on the numbers, types, and grades of employees or positions assigned to any organizational subdivision, work project, or tour of duty, or on the technology, methods, and means of performing work;
   (2) procedures which management officials of the agency will observe in exercising any authority under this section; or
   (3) appropriate arrangements for employees adversely affected by the exercise of any authority under this section by such management officials.'

13 A total of 651 partnership council participants at fifty-four sites in eight agencies were surveyed (Masters, 2001).

REFERENCES

Abrahamson, E. (1997) 'The emergence and prevalence of employee management rhetorics: the effects of long waves, labor unions, and turnover, 1987 to 1992', *Academy of Management Journal*, 40: 491–533.

Albert, C., Jimeno, J. and Moreno, G. (1999) 'Pay determination in the Spanish public sector,' in R. Elliott, C. Lucifora and D. Meurs (eds), *Public Sector Pay Determination in the European Union*. New York: St Martin's Press.

Andersson, P. and Schager, N. (1999) 'The reform of pay determination in the Swedish public sector', in R. Elliott, C. Lucifora, and D. Meurs (eds), *Public Sector Pay Determination in the European Union*. New York: St Martin's Press.

Australian Public Service and Merit Protection Commission (1999) 'Agreement Making'. www. psmpc.gov.au/publications98/apsreformsummary.pdf, 16/7/99.

Bach, S. (1999) 'Europe: changing public service employment relations', in S. Bach, L. Bordogna, G. Della Rocca and D. Winchester (eds), *Public Service Employment Relations in Europe: Transformation, Modernization, or Inertia?* Routledge: London.

Bach, S. and Della Rocca, G. (2000) 'The management strategies of public service employers in Europe', *Industrial Relations Journal*, 31 (2): 82–96.

Barlow, J., Farnham, D., Horton, S. and Ridley, F. (1996) Comparing public managers, in D. Farnham, S. Horton, J. Barlow and A. Hondeghem, *New Public Managers in Europe: Public Servants in Transition*. London: Macmillan Business.

Bazex, M. (1987) 'Labour relations in the public service in France', in T. Treu et al. (eds), *Public Service Labour Relations: Recent Trends and Future Prospects: A Comparative Survey of Seven Industrialised Market Economy Countries*. Geneva: International Labour Office.

Bordogna, L., Dell'Aringa, C. and Della Rocca, G. (1999) 'Italy: a case of coordinated decentralization', in S. Bach, L. Bordogna, G. Della Rocca and D. Winchester, *Public Service Employment Relations in Europe: Transformation, Modernization, or Inertia?* London: Routledge.

Boston, J., Martin, J. Pallot, J. and Walsh, P. (1996) *Public Management: The New Zealand Model*. Auckland: Oxford University Press.

Burnham, J. (2000) 'Human resource flexibilities in France', in D. Farnham and S. Horton (eds), *Human Resource Flexibilities in the Public Services: International Perspectives*. London: Macmillan.

Clark, D. (1998) 'The modernization of the French civil service: crisis, change and continuity', *Public Administration*, 76: 97–115.

Corby, S. and White, G. (1999) 'From the New Right to New Labour', in S. Corby and G. White, *Employee Relations in the Public Services: Themes and Issues*. London: Routledge.

Doeringer, P., Watson, A., Kaboolian, L. and Watson, M. (1996) 'Beyond the merit model: new directions at the federal workplace?' in D. Belman, M. Gunderson and D. Hyatt (eds), *Public Sector Employment in a Time of Transition*. Madison, WI: Industrial Relations Research Association.

Fairbrother, P. and MacDonald, D. (1999) 'The role of the state and Australian public sector industrial relations: depoliticisation and direct intervention', *New Zealand Journal of Industrial Relations*, 24 (3): 343–63.

Farnham, D. and Horton, S. (2000) 'The flexibility debate', in D. Farnham and S. Horton (eds), *Human Resource Flexibilities in the Public Services: International Perspectives*. London: Macmillan.

Farnham, D., Horton, S., Barlow, J. and Hondeghem, A. (1996), *New Public Managers in Europe: Public Servants in Transition*. London: Macmillan Business.

Fialaire, J. (1993) 'Les stratégies de la mise en œuvre des centers de responsibilité', *Politiques et Management Public*, 11 (2).

Flynn, N. and Strehl, F. (1996) 'France', in N. Flynn and F. Strehl (eds), *Public Sector Management in Europe*. London: Prentice-Hall.

Fredman, S. (1999) 'The legal context: public or private?', in S. Corby and G. White (eds), *Employee Relations in the Public Services: Themes and Issues*. London: Routledge.

Friel, B. (1999) 'Daily Briefing: Court rules managers can't be legally forced to bargain', www.govexec.com. 30 June 1999.

Guillotin, Y. and Meurs, D. (1999) 'Wage heterogeneity in the French public sector: some first insights', in R. Elliott, C. Lucifora and D. Meurs (eds), *Public Sector Pay Determination in the European Union*. New York: St Martin's Press.

Hood, C. (1991) 'A public management for all seasons?', *Public Administration*, 69: 3–19.

Hood, C. (1995) 'Contemporary public management: a new global paradigm?', *Public Policy and Administration*, 10: 104–17.

Hood, C. (1996) 'Exploring variations in public management reform of the 1980s', in H. Bekke, J. Perry and T. Toonen (eds), *Civil Service Systems in Comparative Perspective*. Bloomington, IN: Indiana University Press.

Horton, S. (2000) 'Human resources flexibilities in UK public services', in D. Farnham and S. Horton (eds), *Human Resource Flexibilities in the Public Services: International Perspectives*. London: Macmillan.

Industrial Relations Review and Report (1993) 'Agenda for delegation in the civil service', *Industrial Relations Review and Report*, 549: 4–11.

Jódar, P., Jordana, J. and Alós, R. (1999) 'Public service employment relations since the transition to democracy', in S. Bach, L. Bordogna, G. Della Rocca and D. Winchester (eds), *Public Service Employment Relations in Europe: Transformation, Modernization, or Inertia?* London: Routledge.

Keller, B. (1999) 'Germany: negotiated change, modernization and the challenge of unification', in S. Bach, L. Bordogna, G. Della Rocca and D. Winchester (eds), *Public Service Employment Relations in Europe: Transformation, Modernization, or Inertia?* London: Routledge.

Klages, H. and Loffler, E. (1996) 'Germany', in N. Flynn and F. Strehl (eds), *Public Sector Management in Europe.* London: Prentice-Hall.

Massey, A. (1997) 'In search of the state', in A. Massey (ed.), *Globalization and Marketization of Government Services: Comparing Contemporary Public Sector Developments.* New York: St Martin's Press.

Masters, M. (2001) 'A Final Report to the National Partnership Council on Evaluating Progress and Improvements in Agencies Organizational Performance Resulting from Labor Management Partnerships'. Copy provided by author.

Naschold, F. (1996) *New Frontiers in Public Sector Management: Trends and Issues in State and Local Government in Europe.* Berlin: Walter de Gruyter.

Naschold, F. and Arnkil, R. (1997) 'Modernization of the labour market organization: Scandinavian and Anglo-Saxon experiences in an international benchmarking perspective', in J. Dolvik and A. Steen (eds), *Making Solidarity Work? The Norwegian Labour Market Model in Transition.* Oslo and Stockholm: Scandinavian University Press.

New Zealand State Services Commission (1998) *Assessment of the State of the New Zealand Public Service.* Occasional Paper No. 1.

O'Brien, J. and Fairbrother, P. (2000) 'A changing public sector: developments at the Commonwealth level'. *Australian Journal of Public Administration,* 59 (4): 59–66.

Organisation for Economic Co-operation and Development (1993) *Pay Flexibility in the Public Sector.* Public Management Studies. Paris: OECD.

Organisation for Economic Co-operation and Development (1995) *Trends in Public Sector Pay in OECD Countries.* Paris: OECD.

Organisation for Economic Co-operation and Development (1997) *Trends in Public Sector Pay in OECD Countries.* Paris: OECD.

Organisation for Economic Co-operation and Development (2000) *Summary of the PSPE Data Analysis and Future Direction for HRM Data Collection.* Paris: OECD.

Parrado, S. (1996) 'Spain', in D. Farnham, S. Horton, J. Barlow and A. Hondeghem (eds), *New Public Managers in Europe: Public Servants in Transition.* London: Macmillan.

Pollitt, C. and Bouckaert, G. (2000) *Public Management Reform: A Comparative Analysis.* Oxford: Oxford University Press.

Postif, T. (1997) 'Public sector reform in France', in J. Lane (ed.), *Public Sector Reform: Rationale, Trends and Problems.* London: Sage.

Roness, P. (2001) 'Transforming state employees unions', in T. Christensen and P. Laegreid (eds), *New Public Management: The Transformation of Ideas and Practice.* Aldershot: Ashgate.

Ruffini, R. (2000) 'Employment flexibilities and the New People Management in Italy', in D. Farnham and S. Horton (eds), *Human Resource Flexibilities in the Public Services: International Perspectives.* London: Macmillan.

Thompson, J. (2001) 'The Civil Service under Clinton: the institutional consequences of disaggregation', *Review of Public Personnel Administration,* 21: 87–113.

Tondorf, K. (1995) *Leistungszulage als Reforminstrument? Neue Lohnpolitik zwischen Sparzwang and Modernisierung.* Berlin.

Treu, T. (1987) 'Labour relations in the public service in Italy', in T. Treu et al. (eds), *Public Service Labour Relations: Recent Trends and Future Prospects: A Comparative Survey of Seven Industrialised Market Economy Countries.* Geneva: International Labour Office.

Walsh, K. (1993) Contracting Out and Compulsory Competitive Tendering. Berlin: WZB.

Walton, R. (1980) 'Establishing and maintaining high commitment work systems', in J. Kimberly, R. Miles and Associates (eds), *The Organizational Life Cycle: Issues in the Creation, Transformation, and Decline of Organizations.* San Francisco: Jossey–Bass.

White, G. (1999) 'The remuneration of public servants: fair pay or new pay?', in S. Corby and G. White (eds), *Employee Relations in the Public Services: Themes and Issues.* London: Routledge.

Wilks, S. (1996) 'Sweden', in N. Flynn and F. Strehl (eds), *Public Sector Management in Europe.* London: Prentice-Hall.

Winchester, D. and Bach, S. (1995) 'The state: the public sector', in P. Edwards (ed.), *Industrial Relations: Theory and Practice in Britain.* Oxford: Blackwell Business.

8

Leadership and the Senior Service from a Comparative Perspective

John Halligan

The leadership of the senior service has been subject to substantial change that reflects the era of public sector reform, environmental trends and new thinking about how civil service systems should operate. The environment that was once relatively stable for public organizations has become more competitive, public–private differences have narrowed and the constraints and rules that once dictated much of the character of public organizations have less importance, with the notable exception of those reflecting democratic governance. Senior services are becoming more open, managerial and generalist and placing greater emphasis on leadership development.

Nevertheless, there continue to be wide variations within senior services and between country systems. The nature of the senior service and the significance of leadership development vary with administrative traditions, societal factors, institutions and level of reform. Two patterns can be discerned for some purposes: the first, of senior services that are being modernized but within state traditions, and which may be relatively closed and somewhat impervious to extensive change; and the second, of services that are more receptive to change, including management and new leadership concepts, and are more open.

The newer concepts of leadership are not universally accepted and applied in similar ways. Leadership frameworks have been developed and tested in a number of countries, and several have established a senior executive corps. For other countries senior services remain more in alignment with their administrative traditions.

A number of leadership issues remain salient, reflecting the special character of public organizations, challenges of new leadership demands, the results (often inconclusive) of management experiments and the unresolved tensions between neutral and responsive competence. This chapter reviews these dimensions of the changing approaches to leadership and the senior service within a comparative perspective that recognizes different patterns and the role of institutional factors.

SENIOR SERVICES

Defining the senior service

The senior service comprises heads of departments, bureaus and agencies within the core civil service (variously known as departmental or permanent secretaries, chief executives, director-generals etc.) and other senior officials as designated within the central government of each country. The 'higher' components of Anglo-American civil services have ranged from 0.13 per cent to 2.1 per cent, with 1 per cent being suggested as an ideal size (Hede, 1991: 505).

It is important to recognize both the wide variations between country systems and within senior services. A senior service may comprise a range of generalists and specialists for policy, management, delivery, regulation and technical work. Mainstream public servants may co-exist with private sector technocrats and political operatives. Senior officials may have well-defined responsibilities (say policy advice) or combine several elements including political and administrative/management roles. Professional specialization and defined corps within the civil service contribute to the complexity. The senior service in France is 'a heterogeneous category whose members share neither the same careers nor the same prestige nor the same professional culture' (Rouban, 1999: 65).

The civil service may be more differentiated with functions associated with specialized organizations that have distinctive cultures. Almost 80 per cent of British civil servants are in some form of agency. Significant differences are reported between British civil servants and agency chief executives, the former being less disposed to change but more willing to be pragmatic (that is, bending rules to achieve results), while the latter value control more where it concerns future-oriented activity (Dawson, 2001: 265; Mellon, 2000). There is also considerable variability in the dividing line between middle and senior management, and some systems seem decapitated compared to others in so far as one or more layers of the most senior positions are assigned to political appointments that may not derive from the civil service.

For all these reasons, and the complexity of unreformed governmental systems, it is often difficult either to define explicitly the senior service or to characterize it in simple terms. The question has also been posed as to whether there was a US higher civil service in the sense of other systems, and that images derived from several systems could be observed as well as 'loose groupings of people where the lines of policy, politics, and administration merge in a jumble of bodies' (Heclo, 1984: 8–9). The identification of the senior service may be facilitated in reformed systems (where classification systems have been simplified and organizational rationalization has occurred), or where a defined senior service, such as a 'senior executive service' (SES), exists (although in one reformed system, New Zealand, most senior appointments were made outside the SES).

Patterns of senior service

Two patterns of senior service can be identified: those that have been modernized within state traditions, and which may continue to be relatively closed and less responsive to major change; and systems that have been receptive to management change and leadership concepts, and have become increasingly open. Support for the two patterns might be sought from the tendency to analyse dimensions of senior services in terms of opposing perspectives: centralized and decentralized approaches to leadership development (OECD, 2001), merit versus patronage in recruitment (Peters, 2001), position versus career recruitment (OECD, 1997), dichotomized characteristics of heads of departments and ministries (Rhodes and Weller, 2001), and the two broad conceptions of 'public authority' (based on a distinctive service with rights and privileges) and 'service provision' (based on comparability with the private sector) (Page and Wright, 1999). However, these features of senior services do not necessarily coincide, and the exceptions indicate greater complexity.

The standard distinction between *Rechtsstaat* (or rule of law) and public interest systems continues to provide the basis for the two patterns. The differentiation is grounded in distinctive administrative cultures and associated structures, with the legal regulation of administration, judicial review and stronger state traditions of the European systems dominating the first, and the greater flexibilities of the Westminster model and the predisposition to private management of Anglo-Saxon countries underlying the second pattern. There are a number of variations on the two patterns, with a number of the smaller European states exhibiting features of both, perhaps forming a third category. There is also the Korean and Japanese mix of elitism and legalism, and until recently, closed career systems (Kim, 2002; Pierre, 1995; Pollitt and Bouckaert, 2000).

Comparing and managing senior services

The important questions about the senior service centre on its constitution and the provision for the systemic handling of the higher service. The relationship between the conception and the organization of the civil service influences the roles (and potential) of the senior service. Three elements that particularly shape and control the capacity for leadership are the relationship between politicians and bureaucrats, the definition of the senior management role, and the organization of the service.

In terms of relations between politicians and the senior service, three approaches to comparison can be noted. A policy role approach seeks to locate responsibilities focusing on politicians and bureaucrats but also on the relative importance of other actors internal and external to government (Aberbach et al., 1981; Peters and Pierre, 2001). A focus on political control yields three distinctive options: the neutral senior service (the British model), 'commanding heights' approach (through control of the most senior appointments and/or through political advisers) and politicization of the service through party membership (Page and Wright, 1999). A career approach produces a spectrum of possibilities ranging from blended careers (France) to separate careers (Anglo countries), with other systems falling between the two. Under the truncated hierarchy (for example, the United States), the career official is unable to rise to the highest positions in an agency (Peters, 1988).

Specific comparisons of the organization of senior services can be made in terms of several dimensions. First is whether there is a career service or not and the approach to recruitment is closed or open. Recruitment systems can be divided into the career and position systems (OECD, 1997: 5). A standard traditional system was distinguished by boundaries and career differentiation and distinctiveness. Many systems have opened up positions to external recruitment and have modified (even minimized) the differentiation between public and private sectors. Sweden, for example, does not maintain a career service and agencies appoint staff to positions that are publicly advertised. In contrast, the career services of some systems have been closed in the past with controlled (and often limited) entry from the outside.

Second is the level of commitment to public management, and in particular performance. This may entail reliance on different types of contract and performance incentives and appraisal. It has become standard practice to use individual performance agreements for the senior service.

Third, is the location of responsibility for the management of the senior service: is it centralized, decentralized or shared? Related questions are the level and mode of integration (including the use or not of a special corps, discussed later), and the relative importance of structure, culture and ethos, and elite recruitment. Several roles are relevant including recruitment, training, system maintenance and preservation and enhancement of civil service values. The roles may be divided among one or more central agencies, and between the centre and line agencies. Rule making for the senior service might be expected to be a responsibility of the centre, but agencies may have considerable discretion (OECD, 1997).

Most OECD countries have no central agency involvement in the recruitment of the senior service (OECD, 1997: 18–20). Several of the exceptions have an operational SES. Senior recruitment is otherwise decentralized, although standard procedures may exist, and where there is no explicit senior management system, senior

officials may nevertheless be subject to special terms and conditions of employment. Central training institutes are relied on in systems that are otherwise fairly decentralized (such as Germany: OECD, 2001).

Central agencies play a range of systemic roles. The role of the Senior Public Service office in the Netherlands is to seek greater integration through the senior service, including the development of interdepartmental links and service-wide initiatives (Korsmit and Velders, 1997). An extreme case is the New Zealand State Services Commission, which relinquished responsibility for cultivating the senior service once staffing had been devolved to chief executives of line agencies, but recently reassessed this position (State Services Commission, 2001).

The final question is oversight of the senior service and promotion of the core values of public service (Ingraham, 1998: 177). Institutional leadership can be provided in the form of either a central agency with systemic responsibilities and/or a specified head of the civil service. The inculcation of values might best be achieved through recruitment, training or role models.

CHANGING CONCEPTIONS OF LEADERSHIP

The scope of our interest here is both with changing conceptions and approaches, and with the nature of leaders and leadership qua members of the senior service (which is picked up in the next section). Executive leadership (Campbell and Wyszomirski, 1991) is beyond this focus on the senior service, but relations between appointed and elected leaders are highly relevant (for example, Peters and Pierre, 2001).

Traditional academic questions about leadership fall into two important categories for our purposes here. First, there is the question of what shapes organizational leadership. The familiar option is that it derives from the attributes of unusual individuals in top positions, but another (either an alternative or complementary) position, is that leadership is a product of an organizational context (for example, the 'density of administrative competence': James March quoted in Doig and Hargrove, 1987: 3). The second question is how significant is leadership? The responses range from positions that leadership is either unimportant (Kaufman, 1981) or change is determined environmentally, to arguments that individual leadership does register an impact

(Doig and Hargrove, 1987; Sanders, 1998), but it may be subtle (for example, Rayner in Britain: Theakston, 1999). A more inclusive approach is to see leadership (adapting Rockman, 1991: 37), as interrelated with and dependent upon situational factors, administrative culture, institutional forms and the agenda of political leaders.

Questions about the nature of and potential for leadership in a civil service are not settled. One strongly argued case is that civil service leadership remains different from that of business because of constitutional and political contexts (do they not *serve* political leaders?), and that even the most senior civil servants cannot be rated as leaders in terms of the business management literature because they are managers or clerks (Performance and Innovation Unit, 2001; Theakston, 1999). Yet some management studies focus on corporate change across public and private sectors and the types of leader that are associated with different tasks (for example, Stace and Dunphy, 2001).

There has been movement in conceptions and analysis of civil service leadership. Specific leaders rather than leadership were inclined to be the focus. Leaders were the outstanding individuals who were recognized as having made a significant contribution to public service. Newer analyses have taken the form of comparative biography and the linking of case studies of leadership to institutional development and performance (Chapman, 1984; Theakston, 1999, 2000), whether of 'entrepreneurs' who display 'uncommon rationality' (Doig and Hargrove, 1987) or to the attributes of effective leadership (Riccucci, 2000).[1]

A resurgence of interest in leadership development has been reported, with the main impetus being the changing environment, which is seen to require a new type of leadership (OECD, 2001: 13–15). Several propositions about leadership have become increasingly accepted. First is the recognition that leadership now matters. This largely reflects a substantial shift from traditional administration dominated by the tasks of policy advice to political leaders and process implementation, to acceptance of leadership defined increasingly in management terms and often within a broader governance environment. This includes leaders being expected to manage down through handling and empowering staff more effectively (for example, the importance of human relations in the EU: Maor, 2000).

Second, there is better understanding that there are different types of leadership, and that this is a situational question. Recognition of distinctive leadership styles is contingent upon different organizational contexts and demands.

Leadership styles may be defined in terms of the scale of change (incremental to transformational), style of change (ranging from consultative to directive) and commitment to the civil service (for example, conservator and guardian) (Stace and Dunphy, 2001; Theakston, 1999).

Third is the more radical position, which reflects the movement from leadership conceived in terms of mandarins' attributes to that of acquired skills, which suggests that everyone can become a leader. One expression of this is the assumption of the former head of the British civil service that leaders can be nurtured and the skills can be learned (Wilson, 2000). Accordingly, leadership becomes less exclusive and more inclusive. A related aspect is that leadership applies at several levels. According to OECD, requiring leadership 'at all levels is revolutionary in its potential impact, and is an important driver of the move to redefine public sector leadership' (2001: 15). Leading within public organizations has acquired new dimensions and now extends to a range of staff with resource management responsibilities.

New processes have been adopted for leading change and focusing complex organizations. An example is the application of Kotter's injunction to assemble a group – a 'Guiding Coalition' with sufficient power to lead change – to Australia's large multi-purpose delivery agency Centrelink, where a corporate board of sixty SES officers regularly meets to discuss strategic issues and decide on management directions (Kotter and Cohen, 2002; Vardon, 2000).

CHANGING SENIOR SERVICES

The changing environment and government responses internationally have been well documented (for example, Ingraham et al., 1999; Pollitt and Bouckaert, 2000). The drivers of change can be categorized in several ways. The exogenous impacts of global economic and technological change mean that civil services have to respond more rapidly. As the rate of change increases so it is argued leadership becomes more important, and responsibility for change has to be broadened organizationally.

The reputation of the civil service has been under greater scrutiny reflecting *inter alia* declining support for key public and private institutions in many countries, loss of trust in government, and particularly of politicians, and the questioning that arises where a system has been under constant pressure to reform. It has also been recognized by OECD (2001) that a number of the long-established elite civil services have experienced a loss in popular legitimacy.

Related to this has been the intensifying of pressures on government with greater policy complexity and increasing public expectations for services. Two results are that these pressures are translated into demands for the civil service to deliver, and politicians turn to other levers where officials are perceived to be inadequate.

While the drivers are common to many countries, the variations in responses reflect obstacles to change (for example, unions, structures and constitutions) and preferences derived from administrative culture and traditions (OECD, 2001; Pollitt and Bouckaert, 2000).

Several broad trends both define the directions in which some services are moving and provide the boundaries for others. Senior services are becoming more open, relying more on generalists, expanding their management roles and under particular circumstances cultivating leadership development (OECD, 1997, 2001). There has also been a tendency towards greater organizational specialization (for example, in production and policy advice to ministers) and stronger political direction. However, while the impact of New Public Management may be substantial within a country's public sector, this is often not the case at the senior service level of central government of countries where there is a strong public authority conception of the state (Page and Wright, 1999: 275).

Roles

The roles of the senior service have evolved over time, but the rate of change has accelerated and responsibilities now differ from those performed under traditional public administration. There is greater consciousness of the tasks of leading in systems operating within management cultures (for example, leaders are controlling and applying rules less, and motivating and supporting people more: Strand, 1993). The infusion of private sector values and techniques means business planning, being entrepreneurial and even the application of corporate governance principles. Managing externally is now routinely conceived of in terms of customers, clients and stakeholders. These relationships feature contract management and increasingly extend to alliances and partnerships within broader governance arrangements.

The policy role of the senior public service has experienced progressive attrition from the traditional position. The rise of managerialism in the 1980s was a reaction against both the emphasis on policy work and the lack of management skills. At the same time, a tendency has been for the political executive to rely increasingly on alternative sources of advice and on their private office staff as conduits for extra-government proposals. As the policy capacity of the ministerial office has been strengthened, the public servant's role has contracted.

With contestable advice, there are more competitors than before: the senior service may no longer be the government's sole source of advice, although it remains the key advisory voice for the public interest. The policy advisory role may be lost to the civil service, shared with the political executive or diffused across a range of internal and external actors that are competing for attention.

The senior civil servant's role, then, has been transformed over time in a number of ways. In Germany, for example, the decline in opportunities to initiate and champion policies has produced gradual changes in 'the profile of the effective senior official from an agenda setter and policy initiator to a political highly sensitive policy coordinator' (Goetz, 1999: 149). Roles now emphasized are more likely to be those of broker, coordinator and fine-tuning of other's policy contributions, with 'political craft' also featuring (Barberis, 1998; Campbell and Halligan, 1992; Goetz, 1999: 149; Ingraham, 1998).

The implications of these changing roles, new relationships and the associated features of careers and profession have important long-term implications for senior services that are discussed later. Here we can note that the US position, where officials have long been largely confined to the roles of manager or technician (but not adviser with direct access to the political executive, and who may engage in 'bureaucratic corner-fighting'), begins to look more familiar to other systems (Rockman, 1995).

Leadership characteristics

Most members of the senior service continue to be recruited from within the civil service in OECD countries (and the majority from the same agency), but several draw more on external recruitment (more like 25 per cent compared to less than 10 per cent) (OECD, 1997: Tables 6 and 8).

The age of senior public servants has declined in some countries, but remains stable in others. Seniority continues to be important in a number of countries, particularly in continental Europe. Turnover and tenure were similarly variable. Lawyers continue to predominate overall in continental countries (OECD, 1997; Page and Wright, 1999; Peters, 2001).

There have been significant increases in the proportion of women in senior positions, but the proportion remains below 20 per cent for the majority of OECD countries (with exceptions such as Denmark, France, New Zealand, Norway and Portugal) (OECD, 1997; OECD, 2001: 28). The contrasts are most striking with heads of ministries and departments, where some countries (such as Australia) have negligible numbers.

The careers of departmental secretaries have been tracked for the past thirty years, with differences being strongest between European and Antipodean countries. The latter recruit them younger, for shorter terms and dispatch them earlier. Of the European countries, France differed from Denmark and the Netherlands in significant respects (Rhodes and Weller, 2001: 232).

While subject to change in some services, the elite corps has been substantially preserved. In Britain, for example, they have remained fairly constant in terms of collective characteristics (including Oxbridge backgrounds), although more diversity is apparent. They continue to be minister–oriented even if they are now managerially inclined (Barberis, 1998). The overwhelming dominance of one university in both Japan and Korea in the education of the upper echelons of their civil services is possibly unequalled by other OECD countries (Kim and Kim, 1997: 176–8).

The different patterns are indicated by the striking contrasts that exist in the perceptions of higher civil servants: the French regard themselves still as intellectuals rather than managers, while the British secretary is now more inclined to being 'a Manager than a Mandarin' (Dargie and Locke, 1998: 179; Rouban, 1999: 66).

Leadership development

Leadership development is being given more attention in rapidly changing environments, but its significance still depends on state traditions, societal factors, institutional structures and the extent of reform. Many countries have long maintained arrangements for recruiting and cultivating a senior elite. Leadership development is more important where society is diversified, government is decentralized, public administration is less traditional and where comprehensive reform has succeeded incremental change (OECD, 2000: 2).

Two generalized approaches are apparent: either highly centralized or decentralized (OECD, 2001: 19–20). The centralized approach involves high intervention to identify and cultivate potential at an early stage through processes of selection, training and career management. This approach is best exemplified by the French Ecole Nationale d'Administration (ENA), but is also apparent in Japan and Korea. The decentralized approach is identified with market-driven principles. The so-called 'purest form' of this approach, New Zealand, has however been reviewing its position, as discussed below.[2]

In practice, programs contain centralized and decentralized elements (Maor, 2000). Approaches include the use of comprehensive strategies (for example, Norway), institutions for leadership development (for example, Sweden and the United States), targeting high flyers in the fast stream from the beginning of their careers (Singapore and the United Kingdom), and some form of senior executive service. New leadership frameworks have been developed and tested in a number of countries (with some emphasis now on core competencies) (Bhatta, 2001; Dawson, 2001; OECD, 2001; PSMPC, 2001).

Senior executive service

A senior executive corps has been another means for developing leadership, although it is designed to serve other purposes as well. Such systems are focused with a few exceptions on Anglo-American countries, and may either be termed the senior executive service (SES) or go under another name.

The first group of senior executive services were created in Australia, New Zealand and the United States in the late 1970s and 1980s (as well as some states in the two federal systems). Canada's 'management category' also qualifies, although somewhat differently conceived (Hede, 1991). In these systems the heads of agencies have not been members of the SES, in the US case because they are political positions.

The SES originated with the United States in 1978 as a scheme to develop executive management, accountability and competences reflecting private sector incentives and practices. The standard concepts that have become identified with an SES date from then: the generalist elite with an emphasis on performance, capacity for redeployment, appraisal and merit pay. For a variety of reasons, some deriving from the US context, the scheme did not achieve the objectives for mobility, remuneration and becoming a corps of generalist managers operating within a performance culture. The SES was successful politically in that it aided responsiveness. Despite concerns about the fate of the civil service ethos, there is evidence of commitment to core public service values (Aberbach and Rockman, 2000: 95; Ingraham and Moynihan, 2000: 109; Ingraham et al., 1999).

Two contrasting experiences are the Australian and that of New Zealand, the first relatively positive, the second negative. A central component of the Australian reform program was a reformulation of the senior public service as the SES in 1984. Following the existing schemes in the United States and the state of Victoria, the basic principles were the concept of a service-wide executive group that was internally mobile and increasingly invigorated by the recruitment of persons externally, more emphasis on the development of managerial skills and more flexibility for department heads in allocating staff resources (Halligan, 1992; Renfrow et al., 1998). The long-term results of the SES have been reasonably successful (compared to other schemes), with some mobility, steady infusions of outsiders, a degree of corporate identity and regular use of performance appraisal and (more problematically) performance pay.

A senior executive service was also created in New Zealand, with appointments on contracts of up to five years. The SES was meant to produce a unified set of career professionals, but this objective was not realized under this contractual model and highly decentralized system. The SES never developed an ethos and inclusive membership, the problem deriving from the salary ceiling, which meant that in order to attract qualified staff from outside the outsiders had to be employed outside the SES. Established in 1988 as the OECD system that was most based on contract appointments, the SES was pronounced a failure by 1992, and moribund by 2000 (Bhatta, 2001; Scott, 2001). It has since been terminated and is being replaced by a scheme that involves greater central influence over executive development.

The second-generation experiments with the concept of a senior corps, in the United Kingdom (Senior Civil Service) and the Netherlands (Senior Public Service), moved in this direction in the mid-1990s. Both emphasized mobility and interdepartmental cooperation as well as other standard SES considerations (for example, expanding management skills). The Dutch model – open, job-oriented and decentralized – moved towards an integrated service with the creation of a Senior Public Service in 1995 for the top three scales. The rationale included the growing policy complexity and internationalization (Korsmit and Velders, 1997). The advantages of such a

system include the integration of 'a loose collection' of officials into a leadership team that shares values and visions for the future of government (OECD, 2001: 27).

LEADERSHIP ISSUES

The long-term impact of trends on the character of public organizations has implications for autonomy, the handling of values and guidance of the senior service, the capacity to approximate business organizations through the new management experiments, and the implications of changing roles. There is a more intense range of challenges involved in leading in competitive environments where governance conditions prevail, alternative providers exist and the arrangements are contestable and diffuse.

One set of questions centres on the performance of public officials under different operating environments, such as the legalistic bureaucracy and the managerialized system. It is possible that the increasing emphasis on outcomes will produce insights about comparative performance, at least within the latter category as management systems become more sophisticated. The results are inconclusive about the efficacy of management approaches to public officials who are operating under contracts and conflicting incentives. There has been high investment in performance management systems based on performance agreements in Anglo-American systems (for example, on Canada see United States General Accounting Office, 2002), but lack of analysis of their efficacy. There are mixed reports about how to measure and reward performance (Ingraham, 1998), and there is the paradox of performance pay: while not overly successful, it remains popular (Lægreid, 2001).

Secondly, the results of experiments with new leadership approaches are unclear. Several schemes have been implemented following extensive testing of competencies and there is high commitment to leadership at several levels, but without independent evaluation there continues to be some uncertainty about how well these ideas have transferred to the public sector. This leads to the third point, which is that the demands of political responsiveness have meant the scope for leadership is contracting and changing. Where such demands are intense, the potential for leadership may be limited. Relations with politicians are notable for a range of broadly similar experiences: the senior service had become more vulnerable (for example, Australia), under mounting pressure from political advisers (for example, the UK), politicized (for example, France and Germany) or more generally subject to short-term responsiveness. This relationship has become more ambiguous, and may require that 'communication and facilitation replace uni-dimensional direction and leadership' (Ingraham, 1998: 181; Halligan, 2001; Heclo, 2000: 229; Pierre and Peters, 2001; Rouban, 1999: 66).

The importance of these trends and issues raises the question about the character of senior services in the long term. The rebalancing of relationships during recent decades was a reaction by political executives to a period in which senior officials were seen as too independent and influential. But is the redistribution of power part of a cyclical process and is it irreversible? Where the result is excessive political influence, a new imbalance may result, and greater ambiguity in the mediation of relationships.

In this regard, another possibility is suggested by Belgium's attempt at reversing historic patterns. The country has traditionally relied on ministerial cabinets, and been characterized by high political penetration of the administrative system and a marginalized role for the civil service in policy formulation. It recently instituted policy boards at the interface between the minister and department in order to strengthen civil servants' role in producing advice (Brans, 2002).

In a number of contexts, debate has occurred about whether trends mean the loss of fundamental elements that define the senior service. With changes to core relationships, the professional standing of the senior service, conceptions of ministerial responsibility and good governance, the survivability of models is threatened (see Campbell and Wilson, 1995 on the Whitehall model). The durability of administrative traditions appears to ensure adherence to core values where there is the prospect of system adaptation.

Debate also continues about different views of the role of the senior service and the importance of state traditions (for example, ranging from guardians of the public interest to political instruments). Fundamental is the conception of what leadership should be and how it relates to the broader conception of the senior service (Denhardt, 1993; Hunt and O'Toole, 1998). Of concern in countries such as the United States has been the lack of institutional leadership that seeks to infuse organizations with value and a sense of the worthiness beyond day-to-day operations. The lament about the lack of a voice to champion higher civil service values has echoes in other systems (Heclo, 2000: 227–8). In these

days of responsive servants, the role of the head of the civil service, where such a position exists, may be preoccupied with serving the government's short-term interests rather than the tasks of transmitting and protecting the values of the civil service, and providing a role model (Theakston, 1999).

But perhaps civil service systems have come full circle. A British study on *Strengthening Leadership* (Performance Innovation Unit, 2001) adopts a balanced approach to the nature of the civil service, while arguing for the generic features of public sector leadership that arise from an operating environment distinguished by political leaders, accountability, public ethos and cooperation in service delivery.[3] OECD countries report that there is a missing element between the public interest and public service cultures: 'A common complaint is lack of dedication to the underlying values of public service and the interests of the citizens served.' Enhancing public sector leadership is advanced as the means for promoting institutional change in the public interest, and involves espousing fundamental values depicted as 'public spiritedness' (OECD, 2000: 7, 12).

CONCLUSION

The senior service provides the front line at which major issues have to be confronted, and the key mechanism for the transmission of change and direction in the administrative apparatus. The constitution of the service assumes a spectrum of forms, but two broad patterns assist with explaining basic variations between systems. Despite these differences, systems are exploring the middle ground where senior services are more managerial and open, leadership is being reviewed and greater balance is sought between central guidance and decentralized implementation.

Senior servants have experienced changes to their status and roles. The special rights and privileges of a separate and distinctive service, and elite status, have become less common. The incorporation of principles from external influences, such as business management, has promoted similarities (and convergence) between the public and private sectors. At the same time, the combination of decentralization, internal differentiation and outsourcing has often diminished the public service ethos and identity.

Those operating at the interface with the political executive have been subjected to heightened demands for performance from political leaders under pressure from resource constraints and expanding public expectations. The managing of ambiguity has become a skill of senior executives operating within political-administrative arrangements that proclaim allegiance to neutrality and professionalism while not sufficiently supporting these principles in practice.

The interest in leadership reflects management thinking and the need to more effectively deliver change and performance in the public sector. The changing conceptions and approaches to leadership development within senior services have reinforced variations among systems according to their commitment, although the common environments and imperatives have been recognized. The reorientation of leadership has moved the emphasis from an inward focus to the external task of managing inter-sector boundaries, such as relationships with business and communities.

There is a renewed interest in core values that define the publicness of services, and of expectations for trust and greater inclusiveness and the role of leaders in promoting them. But it remains unclear whether this will lead to greater senior service identity, distinctiveness and professionalism, for its standing remains contingent on a range of factors, in particular, the stance of politicians ultimately determining whether such aspirations can be realized. The golden age of mandarins and civil service elites is unlikely to be revisited in this era of governance and performance.

NOTES

1 There continue to be important differences between the academic and practitioner formulations which are more interested in how to cultivate and manage senior officials (e.g. Dawson, 2001; OECD 2001; PSMPC, 2001).

2 But note that New Zealand has been operating one of the most rigorous and systematic performance assessment programs for agency heads, the main function of the central personnel agency, the State Services Commission.

3 Compare an earlier survey of Australian public servants (Korac-Kakabadse and Korac-Kakabadse, 1998) that drew unfavourable contrasts with the private sector (despite unresolved methodological issues about comparability), and which was used by the government as a lever for further change.

REFERENCES

Aberbach, Joel D. and Rockman, Bert A. (2000) 'Senior Executives in a Changing Political Environment', in James P. Pfiffner and Douglas A. Brook (eds), *The*

Future of Merit: Twenty Years after the Civil Service Reform Act. Washington, DC: Woodrow Wilson Centre Press. pp. 81–99.

Aberbach, Joel D., Putnam, Robert D. and Rockman, Bert A. (1981) *Bureaucrats and Politicians in Western Democracies.* Cambridge, MA: Harvard University Press.

Barberis, Peter (1998) 'The Changing Role of Senior Civil Servants Since 1979', in Michael Hunt and Barry J. O'Toole (eds), *Reform, Ethics and Leadership in the Public Service*: A Festschrift in Honour of Richard A. Chapman. Aldershot: Ashgate.

Bhatta, Gambhir (2001) 'A Cross-Jurisdictional Scan of Practices in Senior Public Services: Implications for New Zealand'. Working Paper No. 13, State Services Commission, Wellington.

Brans, Marlene (2002) 'Abolishing Ministerial Cabinets for Re-inventing Them? Comparative Observations on Professional Advice and Political Control'. Paper for 63 Annual Conference of American Society for Public Administration, Phoenix, Arizona, 23–26 March.

Campbell, Colin and Halligan, John (1992) *Political Leadership in an Age of Constraint: The Australian Experience.* Pittsburgh: University of Pittsburgh Press.

Campbell, Colin and Wilson, Graham K. (1995) *The End of Whitehall: Death of a Paradigm?* Oxford and Cambridge, MA: Blackwell.

Campbell, Colin and Wyszomirski, Margaret Jane (eds) (1991) *Executive Leadership in Anglo-American Systems.* Pittsburgh: University of Pittsburgh Press.

Chapman, Richard (1984) *Leadership in the British Civil Service.* London: Croom Helm.

Dargie, Charlotte and Locke, Rachel (1998) 'The British Senior Civil Service', in Edward C. Page and Vincent Wright (eds), *Bureaucratic Elites in West European States.* Oxford: Oxford University Press. pp. 179–204.

Dawson, Malcolm (2001) 'Leadership in the 21st Century in the UK Civil Service', *International Review of Administrative Sciences*, 67 (2): 263–71.

Denhardt, Robert B. (1993) *The Pursuit of Significance: Strategies for Managerial Success in Public Organizations.* Belmont, CA: Wadsworth Publishing.

Doig, Jameson W. and Hargrove, Erwin C. (1987) '"Leadership" and Political Analysis', in Jameson W. Doig and Erwin C. Hargrove (eds), *Leadership and Innovation: Entrepreneurs in Government.* Baltimore, MD and London: Johns Hopkins University Press.

Goetz, Klaus H. (1999) 'Senior Officials in the German Federal Administration: Institutional Change and Position Differentiation', in Edward C. Page and Vincent Wright (eds), *Bureaucratic Elites in West European States.* Oxford: Oxford University Press. pp. 146–77.

Halligan, John (1992) 'A Comparative Lesson: The Senior Executive Service in Australia', in Patricia W. Ingraham and David H. Rosenbloom (eds), *The Promise and Paradox of Bureaucratic Reform.* Pittsburgh: University of Pittsburgh Press.

Halligan, John (2001) 'Politicians, Bureaucrats and Public Sector Reform in Australia and New Zealand', in B. Guy Peters and Jon Pierre (eds), *Politicians,*

Bureaucrats and Administrative Reform. London: Routledge.

Heclo, Hugh (1984) 'In Search of a Role: America's Higher Civil Service', in Ezra N. Suleiman (ed.), *Bureaucrats and Policy Making: A Comparative Overview*. New York: Holmes and Meier. pp. 8–34.

Heclo, Hugh (2000) 'The Future of Merit', in James P. Pfiffner and Douglas A. Brook (eds), *The Future of Merit: Twenty Years after the Civil Service Reform Act*. Washington, DC: Woodrow Wilson Centre Press. pp. 226–37.

Hede, Andrew (1991) 'Trends in the Higher Civil Services of Anglo-American Systems', *Governance*, 4 (4): 489–510.

Hunt, Michael and J. O'Toole, Barry (eds) (1998) *Reform, Ethics and Leadership in the Public Service*: A *Festschrift in Honour of Richard A. Chapman*. Aldershot: Ashgate.

Ingraham, Patricia W. (1998) 'Making Public Policy: The Changing Role of the Higher Civil Service', in B. Guy Peters and Donald J. Savoie (eds), *Taking Stock: Assessing Public Sector Reforms*. Montreal and Kingston: McGill–Queen's University Press. pp. 164–86.

Ingraham, Patricia W. and Moynihan, Donald P. (2000) 'Evolving Dimensions of Performance from the CSRA Onward', in James P. Pfiffner and Douglas A. Brook (eds), *The Future of Merit: Twenty Years after the Civil Service Reform Act*. Washington, DC: Woodrow Wilson Centre Press. pp. 103–26.

Ingraham, Patricia W., Murlis, Helen and Peters, B. Guy (1999) *The State of the Higher Civil Service after Reform: Britain, Canada and the United States*. Paris: OECD.

Kaufman, Herbert (1981) *The Administrative Behavior of Federal Bureau Chiefs*. Washington, DC: Brookings Institution.

Kim, Bun Woong and Kim, Pan Suk (1997) *Korean Public Administration: Managing the Uneven Development*. Elizabeth, NJ and Seoul: Hollym.

Kim, Pan S. (2002) 'Civil Service Reform in Japan and Korea: Toward Competitiveness and Competency', *International Review of Administrative Sciences*, 68 (3): 389–403.

Korac-Kakabadse, Andrew and Korac-Kakabadse, Nada (1998) *Leadership in Government: Study of the Australian Public Service*. Aldershot: Ashgate.

Korsmit, J.C. and Velders, B. (1997) 'Action Plan for the Development of a Senior Public Service in the Netherlands'. Dutch Ministry of the Interior Senior Public Service, The Hague, The Netherlands. Paper presented at the Civil Service Systems in Comparative Perspective Conference 5–8 April 1997, Indiana University.

Kotter, John P. and Cohen, Dan S. (2002) *The Heart of Change*. Boston, MA: Harvard Business School Press.

Lægreid, Per (2001) 'Transforming Top Civil Servant Systems', in Tom Christensen and Per Lægreid (eds), *New Public Management: The Transformation of Ideas and Practice*. Aldershot: Ashgate.

Maor, Moshe (2000) 'A Comparative Perspective on Executive Development: Trends in 11 European Countries', *Public Administration*, 78 (1): 135–52.

Mellon, Elizabeth (2000) 'Executive Agency Chief Executives: Their Leadership Values', in Kevin Theakston (ed.), *Bureaucrats and Leadership*. Basingstoke: Macmillan. pp. 200–21.

Organization for Economic Co-operation and Development (1997) *Managing the Senior Public Service: A Survey of OECD Countries*. Paris: OECD.

Organization for Economic Co-operation and Development (2000) 'Developing Public Service Leaders for the Future'. Background Paper by the Secretariat, HRM Working Party Meeting, Paris, 3–4 July.

Organization for Economic Co-operation and Development (2001) *Public Sector Leadership for the 21st Century*. Paris: OECD.

Page, Edward C. and Wright, Vincent (1999) 'Conclusion: Senior Officials in Western Europe', in Edward C. Page and Vincent Wright (eds), *Bureaucratic Elites in West European States*. Oxford: Oxford University Press. pp. 266–79.

Performance and Innovation Unit (2001) *Strengthening Leadership in the Public Sector: A Research Study by the PIU*. Cabinet Office, London.

Peters, B. Guy (1988) 'The Machinery of Government: Concepts and Issues', in Colin Campbell and B. Guy Peters, *Organizing Governance and Governing Organizations*. Pittsburgh: University of Pittsburgh Press. pp. 19–53.

Peters, B. Guy (2001) *The Politics of Bureaucracy*, 5th edn. London and New York: Routledge.

Peters, B. Guy and Pierre, Jon (eds) (2001) *Politicians, Bureaucrats and Administrative Reform*. London: Routledge.

Pierre, Jon (1995) 'Comparative Public Administration: the State of the Art', in J. Pierre (ed.), *Bureaucracy in the Modern State: An Introduction to Comparative Public Administration*. Aldershot: Edward Elgar.

Pollitt, Christopher and Bouckaert, Geert (2000) *Public Management Reform: A Comparative Analysis*. Oxford: Oxford University Press.

PSMPC/Public Service and Merit Protection Commission (2001) Leadership Project: Information on the Senior Executive Leadership Capability Framework, Canberra. http://www.psmpc.gov.au/leadership

Renfrow, P., Hede, A. and Lamond, D. (1998) 'A Comparative Analysis of Senior Executive Services in Australia', *Public Productivity and Management Review*, June, pp. 369–85.

Rhodes, R.A.W. and Weller, Patrick (2001) 'Conclusion: "Antipodean Exceptionalism, European Traditionalism"', in R.A.W. Rhodes and Patrick Weller (eds), *The Changing World of Top Officials: Mandarins or Valets?* Buckingham and Philadelphia: Open University Press. pp. 228–55.

Rockman, Bert (1991) 'The Leadership Question: Is There an Answer?', in Colin Campbell and Margaret Jane Wyszomirski (eds), *Executive Leadership in Anglo-American Systems*. Pittsburgh: University of Pittsburgh Press. pp. 35–56.

Rockman, Bert A. (1995) 'The Federal Executive: Equilibrium and Change', in Bryan D. Jones (ed.), *The*

New American Politics: Reflections on Political Change and the Clinton Administration. Boulder, CO: Westview Press.

Riccucci, Norma M. (2000) 'Excellence in Administrative Leadership: an Examination of Six US Federal Execucrats', in Kevin Theakston (ed.), *Bureaucrats and Leadership.* Basingstoke: Macmillan. pp. 17–38.

Rouban, Luc (1999) 'The Senior Civil Service in France', in Edward C. Page and Vincent Wright (eds), *Bureaucratic Elites in West European States.* Oxford: Oxford University Press. pp. 65–89.

Sanders, Ronald P. (1998) 'Heroes of the Revolution: Characteristics and Strategies of Reinvention Leaders', in Patricia W. Ingraham, James R. Thompson and Ronald P. Sanders (eds*), Transforming Government: Lessons from the Reinvention Laboratories.* San Francisco: Jossey–Bass. pp. 29–57.

Scott, Graham (2001) *Public Management in New Zealand: Lessons and Challenges.* Wellington: Business Roundtable.

Stace, Doug and Dunphy, Dexter (2001) *Beyond the Boundaries: Leading and Re-creating the Successful Enterprise*, 2nd edn. Sydney: McGraw–Hill.

State Services Commission (2001) *Annual Report for Year Ended 30 June 2001.* Wellington: SSC.

Strand, Torodd (1993) 'Bureaucrats and Other Managers: Roles in Transition', in Kjell A. Eliassen and Jan Kooiman (eds), *Managing Public Organizations: Lessons from Contemporary European Experience.* London: Sage. pp.157–73.

Theakston, Kevin (1999) *Leadership in Whitehall.* London: Macmillan.

Theakston, Kevin (2000) *Bureaucrats and Leadership.* Basingstoke: Macmillan.

United States General Accounting Office (2002) *Results-Oriented Cultures: Insights for U.S. Agencies from Other Countries' Performance Management Initiatives*, Washington, DC: GAO.

Vardon, Sue (2000) Centrelink: 'A Three-stage Evolution', in Gwynneth Singleton (ed.), *The Howard Government: Australian Commonwealth Administration 1996–1998.* Sydney: University of New South Wales Press.

Wilson, Sir Richard (2000) 'A New Civil Service'. FDA/Shareholder Conference, 11 April.

Section 3

ORGANIZATION THEORY AND PUBLIC ADMINISTRATION

Introduction

Tom Christensen

The systematic development of organization theory has traditionally been associated with studies of private organizations, particularly business firms. Studies of public administration, on the other hand, for a long time had no explicit basis in organization theory, even though some pioneering work was done (Scott, 1998). These studies show clearly that there is a close connection between the practice of public administration and the development of organization theory; in other words, aspects of organization theory have been deployed in the running of public administrations, which in turn has yielded new theoretical insights. Over the past few decades an organization theory more specifically geared to studies of public administration has developed (Scott, 1995). This is not a homogeneous field but embraces a number of different theories expounded both separately and in combination. Moreover, it has grown much more complex over time. Having started out with rather simple ideas about 'economic man', 'administrative man' and 'social or cultural man', it has evolved into a complicated pattern of institutional theories in which the original ideas have been further developed and combined in various ways with new ideas.

The introduction to this section provides a brief overview of four main types of public administration organization theory, covered by the four chapters, and reflects on some of the broader questions associated with this field of study. After discussing the different driving forces behind decision making behaviour – whether individual or organizational/institutional – in public administration, a brief historical outline of the development of the organization theory of public administration is given. The comparative aspect of this type of organization theory is discussed, looking into the dynamic relationship between organization theory perspectives and structural and cultural features of various groups of countries. Finally, and related to the third point, the development of organization theory under New Public Management is briefly discussed.

HOW TO DEFINE THE ORGANIZATION THEORY OF PUBLIC ADMINISTRATION?

In a wide and complex body of literature it is not easy to isolate the organization theory of public administration from other kinds of organization theory. One approach is to ask what we want to explain, that is, what are the *dependent variables*? The simplest answer is that we are interested in public decision making behaviour, that is, the authoritative allocation of responsibility and resources between actors and levels in the political–administrative system. This answer signals that we see the public administration as an integral part of the political–administrative system and that we will therefore also focus on the dynamic relationship between political and administrative actors in a democratic context (March and Olsen, 1989). This is an important distinction from theories that have primarily evolved in the context of private organizations.

A focus on decision making behaviour may involve studies that aim to produce a theory of political–administrative systems and study their internal life. Such investigations might look at how administrative policies change the internal structure of the civil service – changing such things as the formal structure, recruitment policies and the rights and participation of employees (Egeberg, 1994). Conversely, one might be interested in how different kinds of internal organization result in certain types of public policies, aimed at influencing the environment. A further, rather seldom explored option is to use political science-oriented organization theory and related studies to analyse the societal effects and impact of these decisions and policies. One reason why such studies are rather rare is that they overlap with other research traditions in the fields of sociology, economics, psychology and anthropology.

A further focus might be to analyse the driving forces behind decision making using the main perspectives of organization theory, in other words, to ask which *independent variables* can be used to explain features of decision making processes and their effects. It is possible to divide these explanatory variables into four categories of theories or perspectives – hence the four chapters in this section. The first chapter, by Morten Egeberg, reviews the tradition of theories and research connected to the seminal work of people like Gulick, March and Simon. This tradition primarily focuses on the importance of formal, normative organizational structures for decision making and on the formal organization of units and roles and includes elements from social

psychology (March and Simon, 1958; Simon, 1945). Decision makers, whether individuals or organizational units, have problems of capacity and with coping with large quantities of information and varieties of premises. Public organizations, therefore, have to be designed or organized in ways that modify these problems. Actors have to select certain decision making premises and reach 'satisfactory' decisions based on 'bounded rationality'. A decision-making structure of this kind channels attitudes and attention in certain directions, thereby also creating special roles and patterns of contact. One challenge of creating a public administration built on a combination of different principles of specialization is that of coordinating units and roles and balancing their varied decision making behaviour (Gulick, 1937).

Within this 'formal structure matters' mode of thinking, there are a number of different strands, two of which we will mention here. We use Dahl and Lindblom's (1953) concepts of political–administrative control and 'rational calculation' to define them. The hierarchical version holds that the leaders of a public administration are homogeneous and have tight control over decision making processes, and that their organizational or means–end thinking is relatively unambiguous, that is, they know what to do and exercise full control over the means to do it (March and Olsen, 1976). Another version assumes a heterogeneous leadership and actors and different kinds of means–end thinking, resulting in negotiations and compromises. This is what March and Olsen (1983) labelled 'Realpolitik' and Allison (1971) called 'governmental or bureaucratic politics'.

The second perspective on what influences decision making behaviour, covered by Jack Knott and Thomas Hammond's chapter in this section, is what can broadly be labelled formal theories. This type of theory is generally based on the premise of rational individual or group actors seeking to advance their own interests through utility-maximizing behaviour. Strictly speaking, this theory is not confined to organization theory, but it has developed in certain ways that allow it to be partly included here. Some formalized models in this theoretical tradition try to explain decisions by rational actors who have more complex decision-making strategies, based partly on institutional factors and formal constraints. Theorists who come under this label are, for example, interested in how formal rules and procedures inside political-administrative bodies shape rational decision making behaviour, how markets and hierarchies can be blended and how the environment can be made negotiable to modify insecurity (Coase, 1937; Hammond, 1996; Williamson, 1975).

A third branch of organization theory, covered mainly in Jean-Claude Thoenig's chapter, is the cultural–institutional perspective, which is closely associated with Selznick's work (1949, 1957). According to this perspective, public organizations gradually develop into institutions, infusing and adding values to the formal framework. This process of institutionalization and adaptation gradually produces certain informal norms and values that go further in explaining decision making behaviour than formal norms. Public administrative bodies develop different and unique cultures, characters or 'souls' through this process. This theory combines different types of institutional theories (Peters, 1999): theories of historical institutionalism (Steinmo et al., 1992), which emphasize historical roots and path dependency, sociological theories of institutionalism, like those represented by Selznick, and theories of normative institutionalism, like March and Olsen's (1989) theory of appropriateness, where public institutions are seen in a broader normative democratic context as integrating, shaping and developing actors on a collective basis.

The fourth type of organization theory, presented primarily in Karen Hult's chapter but also in Thoenig's, revolves around the belief that the environment drives decision making behaviour. Public administration and its actors can, of course, influence their environment as well, but here the focus is on the environment influencing the public administration. This type of theory can be divided into two parts. One is primarily concerned with the 'technical environment' and how the internal organization of the public administration – its structure, function, roles and resource allocation – is dependent on relevant actors in the environment and their demands and organization. Typical theories here are contingency theories and resource-dependency theories (Lawrence and Lorsch, 1967; Pfeffer and Salancik, 1978). The other main type focuses on the 'institutional

environment' and stresses that a complex political-administrative system creates a demand for some simple 'rules of thumb' (Meyer and Rowan, 1977; Powell and DiMaggio, 1991). These are defined on a macro level through the creation of myths, that is, ideas based on some kind of social-constructivist tradition. It is assumed that certain organizational models, budget or planning systems, types of knowledge etc., are 'appropriate' for public administrations (March, 1994). A structure of dominance is created for these ideas, often supported by public authority centres or professional groups 'certifying' them, and public organizations have to adapt to them, at least on the surface. Brunsson (1989) emphasizes that the two types of environment and their demands have to be in balance, often in different ways in different organizations, something that strengthens the legitimacy of the public administration. Public leaders have to act, take decisions and deliver services, but they can also gain from 'double-talk', that is, talking as if they intend to act, even if they have no intention of doing so and no idea of what to do if they run into problems of implementation.

The distinctions between the different types of organization theory implied by the structure of this section of course offer no clear-cut categorization of the different theories, but that is not the purpose here. Theories may combine elements of bounded rationality, culture and myths, like the broad institutional theory of March and Olsen (1989, 1995); they may mix elements of structure and culture with internal and environmental factors, like Selznick (1957) does; or else myth theories may be combined with structural elements, as Brunsson (1989) does.

Another distinction between the theories outlined here is the level on which they focus. The theory of bounded rationality, for instance, often focuses on the micro level and on individual decision makers, while the formal framework in which these actors operate is the organizational or sub-organizational level. Social choice theories have some of the same focus, while cultural theories combine theoretical ideas at the organizational level with elements from the task environment. Environmental theories of a technical nature share the focus on task environment with central cultural theories, while myth theories often focus on phenomena at a macro or organizational field level but relate these to effects and implications on an organizational level.

The theories presented also vary in how they believe public administrative units become established and change. Bounded rationality and social choice theories both perceive such processes as the result of the intentions of certain actors, such as political and administrative leaders, and as such as 'revolutionary' processes that are the result of design and strategy. However, they differ concerning the importance of self-interest and the formal structure that shapes intentions and actions. Cultural theories see change processes as the gradual and incremental evolution of public units, while the theories of both the technical and institutional environment have typical elements of determinism, that is to say public administrations have to adjust to their environment and do not have much leeway. It is also worth pointing out that cultural theories, at least of the Selznick type, mainly emphasize uniqueness, variety and divergence in public administration, while myth theories and certain other environmental theories, like population ecology, often stress isomorphism and convergence, that public administrative units are becoming more similar (Scott, 1998).

THE DEVELOPMENT OF THEORIES AND THE VARIETY OF TRADITIONS

It is always difficult to describe the development of theory, in this case organization theory for the study of public administration, because theories very seldom appear in neat categories in specific periods. Instead they overlap, sometimes run parallel, disappear, are revived in new versions and so on. Therefore, typologies will always need to bend reality to some extent and post-rationalize. In our case it is also a problem that a strand of theory may develop in one period as a more general theory but be more specifically related to studies of public administration at a later stage. With all this in mind, this section offers a chronology of the four types of theory mentioned.

Early studies of public administration, or political-administrative systems in general, were often oriented towards the judicial-constitutional framework, in other words, to the more formal aspects of such systems (Peters, 1999). However, it was not until Gulick (1937) advanced his theory, based on Weber and Fayol, about the effects of principles of specialization and co-ordination in public administration that public administration was associated with any particular organization theory. The breakthrough, in the form of the theory of bounded rationality, came in 1945, with Simon's *Administrative Behaviour*, but was also developed by March and Simon (1958) and Cyert and March (1963). What was distinctive about this development was that it combined organization or decision making theory with political science or political theory. According to March (1997), this tradition was later lost or partly disappeared in the United States, but it has survived in parts of Europe, particularly in Scandinavia (Christensen and Lægreid, 1998).

Scott (1995) sees the roots of institutional theory in the economics of the late nineteenth and early twentieth centuries, in Germany and the United States, and concludes that this theoretical tradition, which questions the simplistic assumptions of a model of economic man by adding the social context of economic processes, had more in common with later sociological and anthropological theories of institutions than with the new institutional economics. With the emergence of the theory of new institutionalism in economics in the late 1930s, many of the traditional institutional factors were disregarded. The empirical focus was also primarily the firm and the market. When formal theories started to be applied to studies of public institutions from the 1970s onwards, seeing them as governance or rules systems, this implied both a theoretical and an empirical extension of new institutionalism in economics and related theories. They did not, however, discard the main premises of the theory regarding the factors driving actors or similarities between the public and private sectors. Studies of public administration using this approach began during the 1990s (Peters, 1999).

Selznick (1949, 1957) developed his cultural–institutional theory in organizational sociology parallel to the main works on bounded rationality. His work was historically rooted in the theoretical developments of the 1920s and 1930s and specifically connected to the Human Relations School and Barnard's (1938) work but also to contemporary theoretical developments, like Parsons' (Scott, 1998). He embraced the tradition of looking at formal organizations as social systems with complex goals and social needs besides instrumental goals and of stressing the importance of informal norms and integrative features. His work was revived in the 1980s and 1990s, both in organizational sociology and in political science theory, by people like Scott (1995; Scott et al., 2000) and March and Olsen (1989).

Even though influential theorists, like Goffman, and Berger and Luckman, published interesting work in the social–constructivist tradition in the 1960s, it was not until 1977 that Meyer and Rowan (1977), in a pioneering article, formulated a systematic myth theory in organization theory. During the 1980s and 1990s this strand of theory, often labelled the 'new institutionalism', was developed further by many scholars (Powell and DiMaggio, 1991; Scott, 1995) and became more specifically connected to studies of public administration (Brunsson, 1989).

Another, more challenging and perhaps speculative way of looking at the development of the organization theory of public administration is to relate it to the characteristics of the political–administrative structure and cultural traditions in different countries. This can only be done by grouping the political–administrative systems in different countries into some broad categories and indicating possible connections. At the one extreme, the political–administrative system in the United States is characterized by extreme structural and cultural fragmentation and complexity, by a small public sector, by a cultural tradition that caters more to the private sector, efficiency and individual rationality and by greater hostility and mistrust towards politicians and civil servants than elsewhere (Christensen and Peters, 1999). This seems to be reflected in the very complex body of organization theory for public administration generated in the United States, which ignores grand theories of the state and tends instead to emphasize theories like formal theories, which portray strategic actors operating in their own interests in a fragmented system with few integrative features. The emergence of myth theory in the United States can also be seen as a reflection of the fragmented nature of the system, that is, there is a need for symbols capable of integrating the system.

The development of organization theory in the United States is, of course, not without collective features, which we find both in theories on organizational rationality and in cultural–institutional theory, but these features are relatively weaker than in, say, the Anglo-Saxon countries that are generally considered to belong to the same type of tradition.

At the other extreme are the features of the political–administrative systems in Scandinavia. These are countries that are much more homogeneous structurally and culturally, attend much more to collective norms and values and less to individual rationality and efficiency, and place greater emphasis on integrating societal groups in public decision making, even though some of these features are slowly beginning to change. These characteristics seem to be reflected in the historically strong position of theories on organizational rationality and cultural–institutional theories. A specifically Scandinavian version of institutional theory has emerged over the past two decades that is characterized by a blend of culture and myth theory (Forsell, 2001). Some Continental European countries have much in common with Scandinavia concerning the structure and culture of the political–administrative system, with strong and centralized states and an emphasis on collectivity. This is also reflected in the way their theory of the public administration has developed. As Thoenig points out in his chapter, France was rather early in developing a cultural–integrative tradition in organization theory (Crozier, 1964). Unlike the United States, neither Scandinavia nor Continental Europe have a particularly strong tradition of formal theorists working in the field of public administration.

INCREASED COMPLEXITY IN THEORIES AND PUBLIC ADMINISTRATION?

Organization theories of public administration seem in some ways to have grown more complex, both concerning the number of theories developed, the internal differentiation of each theory and the growing number of combinations of different theories. This may reflect the increasing complexity of political–administrative systems and decision making processes. Civil service systems are more specialized than before, both horizontally and vertically. New and hybrid structures have developed both inside the public apparatus and in its links with the private and societal sectors. Traditional political–administrative cultures have been partly transformed and new norms and values have appeared, blending or melding with the old ones. Public decision making processes currently involve actors with more ambiguous mandates, involve more and different types of actors and there are more connections over time between levels and institutions. Moreover, decisions are more often appealed or changed in the implementation phase, either because of changing conditions or because actors would like to change the content of policies. All this may lead to a more differentiated set of theories that one can combine to understand the workings of public administration.

Another, rather different way of looking at the development of both the theory and practice of public administration is to take New Public Management as a point of departure. NPM has spread all over the world, albeit more in the form of ideas than in practice in some countries, but it is still widely influential. Boston et al. (1996) stress in their book about NPM in New Zealand that there is a close connection between the theories of reform and the actual implementation of reform measures, that is to say the reforms are theory-driven to a large extent. The theories behind NPM in New Zealand and other Anglo-American countries are primarily different versions of formal theories. They stress simplicity much more than complexity, concerning theoretical preconditions, the structure of the political–administrative system, role differentiation between politicians and administrative leaders and the unambiguous chain-of-command and they attach importance to clear goals and means, efficiency and rationality. An interesting question is whether the simplification of theory also leads to the simplification of practice in the political–administrative system or whether it actually generates more complexity (Christensen and Lægreid, 2001).

The example of NPM illustrates how organization theory can lead more directly to certain ways of organizing the public administration. What the coming chapters should ideally do is to cover how the different theories have been applied in studies of political–administrative systems more generally and public administration specifically. It is beyond our reach to give a comprehensive overview of such studies, so the different chapters instead give representative examples of empirical studies within each theoretical tradition.

REFERENCES

Allison, G.T. (1971) *Essence of Decision. Explaining the Cuban Missile Crisis*. Boston, MA: Little, Brown.

Barnard, C.I. (1938) *The Functions of the Executive*. Cambridge, MA: Harvard University Press.

Boston, J., Martin, J. Pallot, J. and Walsh, P. (1996) *Public Management: The New Zealand Model*. Auckland: Oxford University Press.

Brunsson, N. (1989) *The Organization of Hypocrisy. Talk, Decisions and Actions in Organizations*. Chichester: Wiley.

Christensen, T. and Lægreid, P. (1998) 'Public Administration in a Democratic Context – A Review of Norwegian Research', in N. Brunsson and J.P. Olsen (eds), *Organizing Organizations*. Bergen: Fagbokforlaget.

Christensen, T. and Lægreid, P. (2001) *New Public Management. The Transformation of Ideas and Practice*. Aldershot: Ashgate.

Christensen, T. and Peters, B. Guy (1999) *Structure, Culture and Governance. A Comparison of Norway and the United States*. Lanham, MA: Rowman & Littlefield.

Coase, R. (1937) 'The Nature of the Firm', *Economica*, 4 (November): 386–405.

Crozier, M. (1964) *The Bureaucratic Phenomenon*. Chicago: University of Chicago Press.

Cyert, R.M. and March, J.G. (1963) *A Behavioral Theory of the Firm*. Englewood Cliffs, NJ: Prentice–Hall.

Dahl, R.A. and Lindblom, C. (1953) *Politics, Economics and Welfare*. New York: Harper and Row.

Egeberg, M. (1994) 'Bridging the Gap between Theory and Practice: The Case of Administrative Policy', *Governance*, 7: 83–98.

Forsell, A. (2001) 'Reform Theory Meets New Public Management', in T. Christensen and P. Lægreid (eds), *New Public Management: Transforming Ideas and Practice*. Aldershot: Ashgate.

Gulick, L. (1937) 'Notes on the Theory on Organizations. With Special Reference to Government', in L. Gulick and L. Urwin (eds), *Papers on the Science of Administration*. New York: A.M. Kelley.

Hammond, T.H. (1996) 'Formal Theory and the Institutions of Governance', *Governance*, 9 (2): 107–85.

Lawrence, P.R. and Lorsch, J.W. (1967) *Organization and Environment: Managing Differentiation and Integration*. Boston, MA: Graduate School of Business Administration, Harvard University.

March, J.G. (1994) *A Primer on Decision Making*. New York: Free Press.

March, J.G. (1997) 'Administrative Practice, Organization Theory, and Political Philosophy: Ruminations and

Reflections of John M. Gaus', *PS Political Science*, 30 (3): 689–98.

March, J.G. and Olsen, J.P. (1976) *Ambiguity and Choice in Organizations*. Bergen: Scandinavia University Press.

March, J.G. and Olsen, J.P. (1983) 'Organizing Political Life: What Administrative Reorganization Tells Us About Government', *American Political Science Review*, 77 (2): 281–97.

March, J.G. and Olsen, J.P. (1989) *Rediscovering Institutions: The Organizational Basis of Politics*. New York: Free Press.

March, J.G. and Olsen, J.P. (1995) *Democratic Governance*. New York: Free Press.

March, J.G. and Simon, H.A. (1958) *Organizations*. New York: Wiley.

Meyer, J.W. and Rowan, B. (1977) 'Institutionalized Organizations: Formal Structure as Myth and Ceremony.' *American Journal of Sociology*, 83 (September): 340–63.

Peters, B. Guy (1999) *Institutional Theory in Political Science. The 'New Institutionalism'*. London: Pinter.

Pfeffer, J. and Salancik, G.R. (1978) *The External Control of Organizations*. New York: Harper and Row.

Powell, W.W. and DiMaggio, P.J. (eds) (1991) *The New Institutionalism in Organizational Analysis*. Chicago: University of Chicago Press.

Scott, W.R. (1995) *Institutions and Organizations*. Thousand Oaks, CA: Sage.

Scott, W.R. (1998) *Organizations. Rational, Natural, and Open Systems*. Upper Saddle River, NJ: Prentice–Hall.

Scott, W.R., Ruef, M., Mendel, P.J. and Caronna, C.A. (2000) *Institutional Change and Health Care Organizations. From Professional Dominance to Managed Care*. Chicago: University of Chicago Press.

Selznick, P. (1949) *TVA and the Grass Roots*. Berkeley, CA: University of California Press.

Selznick, P. (1957) *Leadership in Administration*. New York: Harper and Row.

Steinmo, S., Thelen, K. and Longstreth, F. (1992) *Structuring Politics: Historical Institutionalism in Comparative Analysis*. Cambridge: Cambridge University Press.

Simon, H.A. (1945) *Administrative Behavior*. New York: Macmillan.

Williamson, O.E. (1975) *Markets and Hierarchies: Analysis and Antitrust Implications*. New York: Free Press.

9

How Bureaucratic Structure Matters: An Organizational Perspective

Morten Egeberg

The purpose of this chapter is to analyse the relationship between bureaucratic structure and actual decision behaviour within a governmental apparatus. Thus, the chapter does not deal with the role of the executive in the overall political system. Rather, it focuses on how the organizational structure of a government bureaucracy might, in a sense, intervene in the policy process and, eventually, shape its outputs. The relationship is a crucial one. The extent to which organizations or institutions impact on individual actors' interests and preferences is a theme that attracts enduring scholarly interest and debate. At the same time, the topic is of great concern to practitioners too, who want to know more exactly how organizational design and redesign could affect agenda setting, co-ordination, choices and implementation in their respective ministries or government agencies. Nevertheless, a previous review of relevant literature revealed that our theme has clearly not attained the scholarly attention it deserves (Egeberg, 1999). It seems to be much easier to find studies on bureaucratic structures, on how such structures have come about and on administrative behaviour itself than on the *relationship* between structure and actual decisions (cf., for instance, Derlien, 1992; Farazmand, 1994; Hesse, 1995; Page, 1995; Bekke et al., 1996; Nelson, 1996; Peters and Wright, 1996; Farazmand, 1997).

This chapter's theoretical approach draws heavily on the notion of 'bounded rationality' (March and Simon, 1958; Simon, 1965). There are strict limits to the mind's cognitive and computational capacities. Not everything can be attended to simultaneously. We act in an extremely information-rich environment; however, before information can be used by an individual it must proceed through the bottleneck of attention which means that only one facet of a multi-faceted matter is considered before a decision is reached (Simon, 1985: 302). Thus, since policy makers base their choices on highly simplified models of the world, it becomes crucial to understand the selection mechanisms and filters that are at work. An organizational perspective highlights the role of a decision maker's *organizational* context in this respect by paying attention to an organization's structure, demography, locus and degree of institutionalization (cf. the next section below).

Theorists seem to agree that organizations and institutions might affect individual actors' strategies, or how they want to achieve their goals. They disagree, however, on how interests and goals themselves are shaped and reshaped. While rational choice institutionalists consider preference formation as exogenous to their models, other institutionalists argue that interests are indeed endogenously forged (March and Olsen, 1996; Peters, 1999). From an organizational perspective, as argued in the next section, organizations and institutions are capable of endowing individual actors with goals and interests, provided that certain organizational features are in place. What decision makers know and believe is also partly determined by their organizational position (Simon, 1999: 113). Since preference and identity formation are vital aspects of political life, the study of politics and administration cannot rely extensively on approaches that do not accommodate these phenomena into their models.

In the next section I will present what I see as the key variables of an organizational perspective. Although the empirical part of this chapter will focus on the impact of bureaucratic (organizational) *structure*, I find it useful to present the other key variables as well, since this provides us with a more solid background for interpreting the observations referred to.

ORGANIZATIONAL KEY VARIABLES

Organizational structure

An organizational structure is a normative structure composed of rules and roles specifying, more or less clearly, who is expected to do what, and how (Scott, 1981). Thus, the structure broadly defines the interests and goals that are to be pursued, and the considerations and alternatives that should be treated as relevant. The 'relevance criteria' embedded in role expectations guide search processes, and bias information exposure. Thus, normative structures forge information networks for the development of agendas, alternatives and learning. Since a decision maker is unable to attend to everything at the same time, and to consider all possible alternatives and their consequences (cf. 'bounded rationality'), it seems to be a perfect match between her/his need for simplification on the one hand and the selection and filter that organization provides on the other (Simon, 1965; Augier and March, 2001). The structure can therefore never be neutral, it always represents a mobilization of bias in preparation for action (Schattschneider, 1975: 30).

What reasons then do we have to expect that people will comply with organizational norms from the moment they enter an organization? First, they may feel a moral obligation to do so. Modern cultures, emphasizing impersonal relationships and 'rationalized' codes of conduct in organizational life, assist individuals at separating their private interests from those that should be catered for in their capacity as employees or representatives. Second, they may find compliance to be in accordance with their self-interest. Organizations are incentive systems that inform members at lower levels of their potential career prospects, thus inducing them to adopt autonomously to role expectations and codes of conduct. And managers may apply rewards and

punishments in order to achieve obedience. Third, and finally, social control and 'peer review' by colleagues are supposed to make deviant behaviour less likely. Thus, these mechanisms do not imply that organizational members give up their private interests from the moment they enter an organization. However, personal policy preferences are, due to compensation, put aside and are thus supposed to be of minor importance in explaining *organizational* behaviour. Even if the mechanisms fail, it could be argued that participants would be unable to define and operationalize their genuine private interests in any meaningful and coherent way in most issue areas. One obvious exception to this could, however, be decision processes that might impact more directly on their career prospects, for example, reorganization processes.

I now turn to various dimensions of organizational structure. The *size*, the sheer number of roles that are to be filled, may indicate its capacity to initiate policies, develop alternatives, or to implement final decisions. *Horizontal specialization* expresses how different issues and policy areas, for example transport and environmental protection, are supposed to be linked together or de-coupled from each other. Those areas that are encompassed by the same organizational unit are more likely to be co-ordinated than those that belong to different units (Gulick, 1937). However, in a hierarchy (that is, a horizontally *and vertically specialized* organization), separation of issues at lower levels only means that co-ordination responsibility is moved up to higher echelons. According to Gulick (1937), there are four fundamental ways in which tasks may be distributed horizontally among units, namely in relation to *territory, purpose (sector), function (process)* or *clientele served*. If, for example, an organization is internally specialized according to the geographical area served, it is expected to induce spatial perspectives and encourage policy makers to pay attention primarily to particular territorial concerns and need for 'intra-local' policy coherence. In this case, the structure reflects the territorial composition of the system and focuses attention along territorial lines of cleavage. Organizations based on a purpose principle, on the other hand, are supposed to foster sectoral horizons among decision makers and policy standardization across territorial units.

The structure may express whether *co-ordination* is supposed to be *hierarchical* or *collegial*. 'Collegiality' usually means that decisions have to be reached through arguing, bargaining or voting rather than through command. Most government organizations are basically hierarchical in their set-up. However, collegial bodies in the form of committees, task forces, project groups etc. increasingly seem to complement hierarchical structures. Thus, since organizational units are in this way woven together more densely than before, horizontally as well as vertically, a kind of network administration seems to emerge (Kickert, 1997; Bogason and Toonen, 1998; Rhodes, 2000). Committees usually engage people only on a part-time basis, though. Most participants remain primarily attached to another organization. Still it is reason to believe that also committee members are affected to some extent by being exposed to new agendas, alternatives and actors. We would expect the impact to be less profound, however, than in organizations to which persons have a primary affiliation. Finally, an organizational structure may be more *ambiguous* or *loosely coupled* than other structures, thus facilitating innovative behaviour, flexible responses and extensive policy dynamics (Landau, 1969; March and Olsen, 1976; Hood, 1999). Enduring tensions and unresolvable conflicts may also be dealt with more intelligently through ambiguous designs (Olsen, 1997).

Organizational demography

According to Pfeffer (1982: 277) demography refers to the composition, in terms of basic attributes such as age, sex, ethnicity, education and length of service of the social entity under study. Such factors are supposed to impact on decision behaviour, although the strength of potential effects has to depend on characteristics of the organizational structure, for example how 'demanding' it is (Meier and Nigro, 1976; Lægreid and Olsen, 1984). Even more, a wide variety of socialization experiences are not relevant to policy disputes and thus are unlikely to reveal a representational linkage (Selden, 1997: 65). One may say that the demographic perspective emphasizes the effects that flows of personnel (where people come from, their present and future careers) might have on their decision behaviour. Whereas the effects of organizational structure are thought to occur without any socialization of personnel, the impacts of demographic factors are closely related to *socialization*. Socialization usually means that values, norms and role expectations have become internalized in individuals. New recruits arrive 'pre-packed' with images and attitudes acquired over the years in particular social, geographical and educational settings. With increasing length of service in a particular organization, they may, however, become resocialized. Socialized organizational

members *identify themselves strongly* with a particular organization, and are supposed to advocate its interests 'automatically' in the sense that these interests are taken for granted and legitimate without further consideration. Arguably, the extent to which an organization has to rely on external control mechanisms (incentives and sanctions) depends on the extent to which decision makers have become socialized within that same organization.

Considered as individual attributes, only length of service can, in a strict sense, qualify as a real *organizational* factor among the demographic variables mentioned. However, this becomes different if we instead deal with *proportions* of a given organizational population that come from, for example, different regions or professions. Clusters, or 'enclaves', seem to make it more likely that particular group interests might be pursued (Selden, 1997).

Organizational locus

The physical dimension of organizational life has not been emphasized very much in the literature (Goodsell, 1977; Pfeffer, 1982: 260–71). However, most organizations are located in particular places and buildings. First, features of location and physical space segregate personal lives and their associated role conceptions and identities from organizational roles and identities. Second, overlapping organizational structures that are separated in space (and then often time) provide cues for evoking different roles and identities, while concentration in space (and then often time) makes it more probable that role perceptions and identities are carried over from one unit into another (March, 1994: 70–3). Third, physical distance within and between government buildings seems to affect contact patterns and co-ordination behaviour (Egeberg, 1994). In short, organizational locus, like organizational structure, creates boundaries that focus decision makers' attention and assist them in coping with a complex reality. Processes involving considerable uncertainty, unpredictability and surprise require information exchange via face-to-face contacts and group conversation. Thus, such processes are in a sense highly locus-dependent (Jönsson et al., 2000: 186).

Institutionalization

From an organizational point of view, and within this tradition of organizational research, all institutions are organizations, but not all organizations are institutions. Institutionalization is a dimension of organizations that adds important characteristics. Thus, the present tendency to classify all kinds of rules, regimes and organizations as institutional phenomena has given us a poorer concept of institution. According to Selznick (1957), institutionalization necessarily takes time. It means that organizations are growing increasingly complex by *adding informal norms and practices*. This increased complexity stems from the organization's continuous interaction with its environments (for example, information exchange, recruitment), and provides it with a broader repertoire for handling major challenges. These informal norms and role expectations are *impersonal* in the sense that they exist independently of the concrete individuals who happen to be in the organization at different points in time.

To become a real institution, however, Selznick (1957: 17–22) argued that the 'grown-up' and complex organization also had to be *infused with value* beyond the technical requirements of the task at hand. By this he meant that an organization acquires a self, a distinctive identity, involving the taking on of values, ways of acting and believing that are deemed important for their own sake. For the individuals who participate directly in it, an organization may acquire much institutional value, yet in the eyes of the larger community the organization may be readily expendable. Thus, arguably, from a *political* perspective, organizations become *real* institutions as they come to symbolize the *community's* aspirations, *its* sense of identity. Real institutions embody *societal* values, and strive to impose those same values on society. Institutionalization could mean that not only particular organizational structures and informal norms become infused with value and meaning, but also a particular demographic composition of the organization, for example as regards professional groups, and also the place and building associated with the organization (Goodsell, 1988). Thus, it is probably no coincidence that revolting groups often occupy the presidential palace or the parliamentary building. Such action may be interpreted primarily as symbolic action; it does not aim at making political decisions in the first place.

A broad context of 'understood' meanings may represent a considerable aid to communication in institutions. It may create energy that increases performance and co-ordination, and be of special importance in times of crisis or threat (Selznick, 1957: 18; Brunsson and Olsen, 1993: 5). Thus, compared to an organization, an institution probably does not have to rely on external control mechanisms (rewards and punishments)

to the same extent. Another implication of institutionalization deals with the possibilities for deliberate reform and reorganization: 'An organization that does take on this symbolic meaning has some claim on the community to avoid liquidation or transformation on purely technical or economic grounds' (Selznick, 1957: 19). The inherent robustness of institutions now seems widely acknowledged in the literature. Changes that accord with the institutional identity are supposed to be carried out as a matter of routine. However, sudden big changes which violate this identity are rare, and when they do occur they are assumed to be the result of serious performance crises (March and Olsen, 1989; Brunsson and Olsen, 1993: 5–6). An alternative interpretation is that identity-challenging reforms are indeed implemented, but only in a highly history-, path-dependent and distorted way (Christensen and Lægreid, 2001). Since institutions are more complex than organizations, changing the organizational structure of an institution cannot, however, be expected to have the same degree of impact on actual decision behaviour as changing the structure of an organization.

METHODOLOGICAL NOTE

The empirical studies that I draw on are mainly confined to research on central government bureaucracies at the national level and how their structures affect *substantive* policy making. 'Substantive policy making' is the kind of policy making most bureaucrats are supposed to engage in most of the time. On the other hand, policy making dealing with aspects of the administrative apparatus itself – its structure, personnel composition, physical structure and location – is called 'administrative policy making'.

Which criteria have been used then for selecting the relevant empirical studies? First, a study, to merit inclusion, has to focus explicitly on the relationship between organizational structure and the actual decision behaviour of officials, although it does not have to concentrate *solely* on this independent variable. Second, the study's sources of data and the method applied for analysing the data should be clearly stated by the author(s). Third, the relationships that are observed should be meaningful and understandable from a theoretical point of view, that is, they should be possible to subsume under one theoretical dimension or another. Government reports on reform evaluation most often fail to meet these criteria. So do some of the works of social scientists. We could ourselves be more conscious of the extent to which statements of an empirical nature are really based on systematic research, or are more loosely founded, or are merely meant to be assumptions. In order to substantiate postulates empirically, scholars too often seem to refer to the works of other researchers without separating clearly between research that is 'really' empirical in its character, and, on the other hand, works that are primarily of a theoretical or 'impressionistic' nature.

Research on the relationship between organizational structure and actual decision behaviour seems to have taken place *against the mainstream* of contemporary scholarly work in the field. Volumes and single articles aimed at reviewing the state of the art of public administration research do not have much to say, if anything, about the relationship focused on in this chapter (cf. for instance Derlien, 1992; Farazmand, 1994; Hesse, 1995; Page, 1995; Bekke et al., 1996; Nelson, 1996; Peters and Wright, 1996; Farazmand, 1997). Hood and Dunsire (1981) concluded their 'bureaumetrics approach' book by saying that investigating this relationship was the important *next* step to be taken. Fourteen years later, their compatriots Martin J. Smith et al. (1995: 50), in their review of research on the British central government, ascertained that many of the scholars seem content to describe the structural changes and problems with implementation rather than dealing with the questions of how these changes affect the internal politics of the departments and the policy process. Thomas Hammond (1990) argues that one reason for this lack of systematic empirical research on the relationship between bureaucratic structure and actual decision behaviour may be found in Herbert Simon's massive criticism of the so-called classical school of administrative theory. Thus, the widespread feeling that Simon had definitely won the duel in the 1940s may have contributed to the lack of studies on the formal structure and its implications (cf. also Augier and March, 2001). Another reason may be the behaviouralist turn in the social sciences in general in this period.

EMPIRICAL EVIDENCE

The impact of size (structural capacity)

The fact that most officials most of the time seem to comply fairly well with formal role expectations is fundamental for all further reasoning about effects of structural designs (Egeberg, 1999). It implies that various concerns and interests can be guaranteed at least some systematic and continuous attention and support in the policy process provided they are embedded in organizational units. Thus, to what extent different interests will be taken care of will partly depend on the structural *capacity* (that is, the number of positions) that can be mobilized behind various considerations.

Cross-national comparisons of environmental policy formation and implementation assign some weight to structural capacity: countries considered as 'leaders' in this policy field tend to have built up separate environmental ministries and agencies (Underdal, 1996; Weale et al., 1996). Intra-national comparisons show, however, that other variables must have been more important. Variance in institutional capacity cannot explain the changes that occurred in German, British and Norwegian policies over time (Underdal, 1996).

A study of road and rail infrastructure planning in Norway revealed how varying organizational capacity really created policy outputs that were not intended by the government. To solve the unemployment problem in 1991–92, additional grants were transferred to the Ministry of Transport from other ministries. However, because of much larger planning capacity in the road sector than in the rail sector, most of the extra funds ended up in the road agency. The road directorate was able to realize the potential political gains stemming from increased government efforts to fight joblessness in a shorter period of time, but on this occasion it was not the intention of the cabinet to give priority to road infrastructure investments (Egeberg, 1995).

The impact of horizontal specialization

In theory, structural designs are expected to 'route' information exchange, co-ordination processes and conflict resolution. Thus, how we draw organizational boundaries is supposed to determine which problems and solutions policy makers become aware of, and at which level in a hierarchy various concerns are considered simultaneously, or are allowed to be sheltered from other interests. But do organizational boundaries really matter? Let us first take a look at aspects of *horizontal* specialization.

Studies reveal that contact patterns and exchange of information to a large degree reflect the organizational structure of the administrative apparatus. The flow of information diminishes across organizational boundaries (Lægreid and

Olsen, 1984; Larsson, 1986; Gerding and Sevenhuijsen, 1987; Petterson, 1989). Lægreid (1988) found that actual contact patterns neatly reflected the formal chart, even in bureaucracies with small potential for socialization and disciplining through promotions. Extensive use of e-mail in the 1990s does not seem to have changed this close relationship between structure and behaviour (Christensen and Egeberg, 1997). Scharpf (1977), in his study of the German Federal Ministry of Transport, found that 'objective' needs for co-ordination across divisions were recognized by the ministerial bureaucracy itself and reflected in the actual patterns of information exchange and participation between lower level organizational units. Further empirical analyses showed, however, that the existing division structure caused serious information deficits and conflicts over substantive policy as well as over jurisdiction. Data indicated that perceived deficits in information supply were four times as likely to occur in interactions across divisions than within divisions; that conflicts over policy substance were more than twice as frequent in inter-divisional interaction; and that conflicts over jurisdiction had a 50 per cent higher probability of occurring in interactions between divisions than within divisions (1977: 62). Scharpf concluded that organizational boundaries may not prevent interaction, but they seem to create semi-permeable walls which impede the flow of information (on the demand side as well as on the supply side) and which reduce the capacity for conflict resolution in the case of substantive and jurisdictional conflict.

The drawing of organizational boundaries *between* as well as within ministries tends to bias the allocation of attention and the formation of preferences and identities (Allison, 1971; Rhodes and Dunleavy, 1995). Broad interministerial interaction is typical for officials affiliated with units like the prime minister's office or the ministry of finance (Campbell and Szablowski, 1979). In general, officials' contacts across organizational units have a strong, positive relationship with their participation in working groups and task forces (Stigen, 1991), and with their ranks (Lægreid and Olsen, 1984; Jablin, 1987; Christensen and Egeberg, 1997).

Strictly speaking, the synchronous research designs of most of the studies dealt with so far make it rather problematic to infer anything about a cause–effect relationship between structure and policy. Fortunately, however, we also find studies in which behaviour has been observed *subsequent to* a reorganization. If behavioural changes can be traced under this circumstance, it is more likely that a cause–effect relationship really exists.

Splitting divisions in a hierarchy means in theory to move processes of co-ordination and conflict resolution upward in the organization, thus making it more likely that higher level leadership gets involved. Mergers, on the other hand, are supposed to push such processes downward, thus relieving higher levels of some of their work load (but as a result less insight will be available at the top in this particular issue area). Results from a study of ministerial reorganizations seem to give some support to these expectations. Egeberg (1994) observed that officials affiliated with divisions that had been split experienced less conflict, whereas those in merged divisions tended to experience more conflict. In the first case, conflicts did not disappear; they became 'externalized', that is, they moved upward, whereas in the second case conflicts were 'internalised', that is, pushed downward. A study of bureaucratic mergers by Hult (1987) supports these findings. She also discovered that departmental mergers had an impact on the relations with client groups. As more concerns and interests had to be taken care of by the merged unit, external networks became more differentiated, and established 'iron triangles' were softened up.

Mortensen (1993) studied the effects of a transport ministry reorganization where the main principle of specialization had been changed. The previous structure was process-specialized so that the ministry comprised of divisions for budgetary matters, planning and judicial affairs. The new organization was arranged according to the purpose principle so that each mode of transport and communication got its 'own' division. Focusing on the air transport unit, he observed how a new sectoral orientation emerged and replaced the previous inter-sectoral 'budgetary perspective', or the 'integrated infrastructure planning perspective'. This change occurred without decoupling officials from their previous tasks; those working on air transport affairs in the old structure became in charge of the same matters in the new unit. The new arrangement also eased the access of the ministry's subordinated agencies to ministerial policy making processes. Previously an agency had to approach ministerial decision making through different divisions in the ministry, depending on the issue discussed. After the reorganization an agency could deal with its 'own' division in the ministry. The study by Hult (1987) indicates that this kind of segmented power structure, emerging from purpose- or sector-based bureaucracies, can be partly neutralized by returning to a process-based structure.

While central governments in unitary as well as federal states usually specialize their administration according to purpose (sector) or process (function), the British government has inserted a couple of territorially oriented ministries (for example, the Scottish and Welsh Offices) among its sector and functional ministries. It seems to have been a widespread assumption that this arrangement has allowed the development of coherent policies, even of an interventionist kind in the Thatcher years, for the respective regions (Griffiths, 1999). As a result of his own case studies of education and housing policies in Wales, however, Griffiths (1999: 803) concludes that, with few significant exceptions, uniformity with, and not divergence from, the overall British practice is most striking. The seemingly moderate effects of the 'territorial ministries' may be due to the fact that the sector and function principles are still dominating the organizational set-up of the British executive.

Central governments may be represented at the regional level by sectorally specialized units reflecting the ministry structure, or by integrated government offices (like the 'prefects') reflecting instead the territorial composition of the system. By setting up Government Offices for the Regions (GORs) in the UK, the reformers aimed at improving the co-ordination between the regional offices of Whitehall departments and to meet the demand for a single point of contact, thus counteracting the compartmentalized traditions of the civil service. Research shows that GORs in fact led to greater co-ordination in the regions and became important mechanisms for developing 'holistic governance' (Mawson and Spencer, 1997; Rhodes, 2000).

A quite parallel study confirms these results. Bonesvoll (1997) studied a reorganization in which a (purpose-based) sector administration at the regional level was transferred to a geographically arranged 'prefect'-like institution. In this case, the regional parts of the Norwegian agricultural administration became, in principle, subordinated to the 'prefects' instead of to the Ministry of Agriculture. As could be expected, a formal restructuring of a highly institutionalized bureaucracy, in which administrative units were transferred intact, did not revolutionize decision-making processes. However, rather significant changes *were* observed: after the reorganization, officials reported that new patterns of interaction occurred, connecting them more tightly to other sector administrations already incorporated in the portfolios of the 'prefects'. More weight was assigned to regional concerns and coherence, and less importance was attached to national standardization efforts.

The impact of vertical specialization

The *internal* vertical specialization of ministries does matter. Officials' level of position is positively correlated with contact with the political leadership, emphasis put on political signals, as well as with the amount of horizontal interaction (Aberbach et al., 1981; Christensen, 1991; Aberbach and Rockman, 2000). Senior officials identify themselves with larger parts of central government than those at lower echelons, who tend to perceive of themselves more as section or division representatives (Egeberg and Sætren, 1999). This pattern is not without significance: those with few horizontal contacts and who identify themselves with lower level units are supposed to consider only a narrow range of problems, solutions and consequences, while those who conceive of themselves as parts of more over-arching entities and have extensive lateral relations are likely to address broader agendas, competing demands and system-wide concerns.

Central government bureaucracies can also be specialized vertically into separate institutions at the national level, for example a ministerial (cabinet level) department and a central (subordinated) agency (*external* vertical specialization). So-called 'agencification' is an increasing phenomenon in many countries (Kickert and Beck Jørgensen, 1995). Where such vertical specialization exists, studies indicate that many of the same kinds of tasks are performed at either administrative level; for example, the subordinated agencies engage in policy making by setting goals, preparing budgets, legislation and guidelines, recruiting senior officials and shaping administrative structures (Christensen, 1982; Jacobsson, 1984; Greer, 1994). Policy choices are, however, not unaffected by the organizational context in which they are made. Officials in central agencies, in contrast to their colleagues in cabinet level departments, exercise their discretion comparatively insulated from ongoing political processes at the cabinet level (Wood and Waterman, 1991; Greer, 1994). They have relatively little contact with the political leadership of the ministry, with other ministerial departments than their 'own', and with parliament. When they exercise discretion, they attach most importance to professional and expert considerations, and somewhat less importance to user and client interests. To assign weight to signals from the political leadership of the ministry is their third priority only. However, their relative autonomy from the ministerial department implies that they have fewer opportunities to influence decision makers at that level.

In ministerial departments, on the other hand, top priority is given to signals from the minister and, also, to professional concerns. Considerably less attention is paid to signals from user and client groups (Christensen, 1982; Beck Jørgensen, 1991; Christensen and Egeberg, 1997).

The study by Egeberg (1995) of transport infrastructure planning processes shows that even if a sectoral orientation may be traced in the way the Transport Ministry's divisions behaved, it would be wrong to describe them as mere spokesmen for their respective agencies. The divisions were, at the same time, organizations in their own right. Their perspectives deviated on several occasions from those of the agencies. The rail transport division, for example, found it impossible to approve a rather expansive investments proposal from the railway company. And the road transport division informed the minister that further investments in new roads probably would show decreasing economic utility since most gains had already been realized. Such somewhat divergent and critical views taken by the ministerial divisions make sense when we take into account *their* structural position: as units in the same ministry they were, after all, both subordinated to the same administrative and political leadership. As units in a ministry they were also related to co-ordination ministries, like the Ministry of Finance. These conditions provided the officials in the ministerial divisions with a broader view than that of their counterparts in the subordinated agencies.

In general, vertical specialization seems to diminish the potential for political steering and control. Studies indicate that this loss of political direction can be partly compensated for by creating an organizational unit in the ministerial department that *duplicates* parts of the work being done in the agency (Jacobsson, 1984). More drastic, integrating an agency into the ministry, or transforming an agency into a ministerial department ('vertical *de*specialization'), has been shown to enhance the political grip of a policy sector (Hult, 1987; Desveaux, 1995).

Subordinated and 'independent' agencies sometimes have collegial structures attached to their leadership. Such executive and advisory boards may have representatives from interest groups (clients, users, affected parties, public employees), representatives from political parties and independent experts. Executive boards at the top of agencies seem to balance and reconcile several interests and concerns simultaneously. They are arenas not only for political steering from above, but also for the articulation of affected group interests and expert appraisals.

The existence of such a board blurs political signals on their way down through the administrative apparatus, thus providing more autonomy to the agency (Egeberg, 1994). A study of a reorganization of the state/central health administration in Kansas that included the removal of the agency's own executive board shows that the agency lost its protection from political processes, which the board had previously ensured (Maynard-Moody et al., 1986).

In the era of the so-called 'New Public Management' the external vertical specialization process has been pushed further ahead in the sense that numerous commercial agencies also have become corporatized in a lot of countries (Wright, 1994). Thus, in order to increase efficiency and competitiveness several public services have been organized 'outside' government. One main lesson that can be drawn across countries seems to be that devolution entails a decrease in political steering capacity and authority, and that less attention is given to political considerations in the 'decoupled' enterprises (Boston et al., 1996; Pollitt and Bouckaert, 2000; Christensen and Lægreid, 2001; Zuna, 2001). However, as is the case for administrative agencies, the ability to steer public companies politically depends heavily on the extent to which organizational resources are available at the ministerial level (Christensen and Lægreid, 2001).

CONCLUSION

How the executive branch of government is organized is only one of numerous factors to be considered to explain and understand public policy outputs. The purpose of this chapter has not been to assess the relative importance of different explanations, but rather to identify theoretical components that assign weight to bureaucratic structure, and to systematize empirical findings that shed light on how administrative structure might intervene in the substantive policy processes of central government. Until now, most students of public administration seem to have focused on behaviour and attitudes without relating them explicitly to the organizational structure. They also have concentrated on structural descriptions, and on processes preceding organizational changes. From a scholarly as well as from a practical viewpoint, it is, however, more important to learn about the behavioural and policy consequences of various designs. Dimensions of organizational structure, like size, horizontal and vertical specialization and 'collegialization' are all sufficiently definable theoretically as well as operationally, and are all, at the same time, sufficiently abstract to allow empirical observations to be transferred and aggregated across different contexts.

The dependent variable, substantive policy making, needs more development in the future. 'Procedural considerations', like importance attached to political loyalty or professional autonomy in this kind of policy making, make sense. The same may be said about substantive concerns that can be derived from the principles of specialization, and about information exchange, actual co-ordination and conflict resolution that can be linked to different ways of structuring hierarchies. It is possible that the traditional categorization of the policy process into different stages, like formation and implementation, should be revisited. Since the implementation process often takes as its point of departure an already established policy programme, or a law or regulation, it follows that less leeway is left for the bureaucratic structure to make a substantial difference in this phase than in the policy formation stage. Concerning study designs, synchronous studies of the relationship between organizational structure and policy making within one context should be increasingly supplemented by observations made across time, and also across space.

NOTE

I am grateful to Tom Christensen, Johan P. Olsen and Christopher Pollitt for their valuable comments on this chapter.

REFERENCES

Aberbach, J.D. and Rockman, B.A. (2000) *In the Web of Politics. Three Decades of the US Federal Executive.* Washington, DC: Brookings Institution.

Aberbach, J.D., Putnam, R.D. and Rockman, B.A. (1981) *Bureaucrats and Politicians in Western Democracies.* Cambridge, MA: Harvard University Press.

Allison, G.T. (1971) *Essence of Decision.* Boston, MA: Little, Brown.

Augier, M. and March, J.G. (2001) 'Remembering Herbert A. Simon (1916–2001)', *Public Administration Review*, 61: 396–402.

Beck Jørgensen, T. (1991) 'Moderne myndigheder. Generel profil af danske direktorater, styrelser og statslige institutioner'. Working Paper. Copenhagen: Department of Political Science.

Bekke, H.A.G.M., Perry, J.L. and Toonen, T.A.J. (eds) (1996) *Civil Service Systems in Comparative Perspective.* Bloomington, IN: Indiana University Press.

Bogason, P. and Toonen, T.A.J. (1998) 'Introduction: networks in public administration', *Public Administration*, 76: 205–27.

Bonesvoll, B. (1997) Fra sektor- til områdeorganisering: Effekter av reorganiseringen av fylkeslandbrukskontorene inn under fylkesmannsembetene. Thesis. Oslo: Department of Political Science.

Boston, J., Martin, J., Pallot, J. and Walsh, P. (1996) *Public Management. The New Zealand Model.* Auckland: Oxford University Press.

Brunsson, N. and Olsen, J.P. (1993) *The Reforming Organization.* London: Routledge.

Campbell, C. and Szablowski, G.J. (1979) *The Super-Bureaucrats: Structure and Behavior in Central Agencies.* Toronto: Macmillan of Canada.

Christensen, J.G. (1982) 'Den administrative ledelsesfunktion i centraladministrationen', *Nordisk Administrativt Tidsskrift*, 63: 317–47.

Christensen, T. (1991) 'Bureaucratic roles: political loyalty and professional autonomy', *Scandinavian Political Studies*, 14: 303–20.

Christensen, T. and Egeberg, M. (1997) 'Sentraladministrasjonen – en oversikt over trekk ved departement og direktorat', in T. Christensen and M. Egeberg (eds), *Forvaltningskunnskap*. Oslo: Tano.

Christensen, T. and Lægreid, P. (2001) 'New public management – undermining political control?', in T. Christensen and P. Lægreid (eds), *New Public Management. The Transformation of Ideas and Practice.* Aldershot: Ashgate.

Derlien, H.-U. (1992) 'Observations on the state of comparative administration research in Europe – rather comparable than comparative', *Governance*, 5: 279–311.

Desveaux, J.-A. (1995) *Designing Bureaucracies. Institutional Capacity and Large-Scale Problem Solving.* Stanford, CA: Stanford University Press.

Egeberg, M. (1994) 'Bridging the gap between theory and practice: the case of administrative policy', *Governance*, 7: 83–98.

Egeberg, M. (1995) 'The policy–administration dichotomy revisited: the case of transport infrastructure planning in Norway', *International Review of Administrative Sciences*, 61: 565–76.

Egeberg, M. (1999) 'The impact of bureaucratic structure on policy making', *Public Administration*, 77: 155–70.

Egeberg, M. and Sætren, H. (1999) 'Identities in complex organizations: a study of ministerial bureaucrats', in M. Egeberg and P. Lægreid (eds), *Organizing Political Institutions. Essays for Johan P. Olsen.* Oslo: Scandinavian University Press.

Farazmand, A. (ed.) (1994) *Handbook of Bureaucracy.* New York: Marcel Dekker.

Farazmand, A. (1997) *Modern Systems of Government. Exploring the Role of Bureaucrats and Politicians.* Thousand Oaks, CA: Sage.

Gerding, G. and Sevenhuijsen, R.F. (1987) 'Public managers in the middle', in J. Kooiman and K.A. Eliassen (eds), *Managing Public Organizations.* London: Sage.

Goodsell, C.T. (1977) 'Bureaucratic manipulation of physical symbols: an empirical study', *American Journal of Political Science*, 21: 79–91.

Goodsell, C.T. (1988) *The Social Meaning of Civic Space. Studying Political Authority through Architecture.* Lawrence, KS: University Press of Kansas.

Greer, P. (1994) *Transforming Central Government. The Next Steps Initiative.* Buckingham: Open University Press.

Griffiths, D. (1999) 'The Welsh Office and Welsh autonomy', *Public Administration*, 77: 793–807.

Gulick, L. (1937) 'Notes on the theory of organization. With special reference to government', in L. Gulick and L. Urwick (eds), *Papers on the Science of Administration.* New York: Institute of Public Administration, Columbia University.

Hammond, T.H. (1990) 'In defence of Luther Gulick's "Notes on the theory of organization"', *Public Administration*, 68: 143–73.

Hesse, J.J. (1995) 'Comparative public administration: the state of the art', in J.J. Hesse and T.A.J. Toonen (eds), *The European Yearbook of Comparative Government and Public Administration.* Baden-Baden: Nomos.

Hood, C. (1999) 'The garbage can model of organization: Describing a condition or a prescriptive design principle?', in M. Egeberg and P. Lægreid (eds), *Organizing Political Institutions. Essays for Johan P. Olsen.* Oslo: Scandinavian University Press.

Hood, C. and Dunsire, A. (1981) *Bureaumetrics.* London: Gower.

Hult, K.M. (1987) *Agency Merger and Bureaucratic Redesign.* Pittsburgh: University of Pittsburgh Press.

Jablin, F.M. (1987) 'Formal organization structure' in F.M. Jablin, L. Putnam, K. Roberts and L. Porter (eds), *Handbook of Organizational Communication. An Interdisciplinary Perspective.* Newbury Park, CA: Sage.

Jacobsson, B. (1984) *Hur styrs forvaltningen?* Lund: Studentlitteratur.

Jönsson, C., Tägil, S. and Törnqvist, G. (2000) *Organizing European Space.* London: Sage.

Kickert, W.J.M. (1997) 'Public governance in the Netherlands: an alternative to Anglo-American "managerialism"', *Public Administration*, 75: 731–52.

Kickert, W.J.M. and Beck Jørgensen, T. (1995) 'Introduction: managerial reform trends in Western Europe', *International Review of Administrative Sciences*, 61: 499–510.

Landau, M. (1969) 'Redundancy, rationality, and the problem of duplication and overlap', *Public Administration Review*, 29: 346–58.

Larsson, T. (1986) *Regeringen och dess kansli.* Lund: Studentlitteratur.

Lægreid, P. (1988) *Oljebyråkratiet. Om statsadministrasjonen i en oljealder.* Oslo: Tano.

Lægreid, P. and Olsen, J.P. (1984) 'Top civil servants in Norway: key players – on different teams?', in E.N. Suleiman (ed.), *Bureaucrats and Policy-Making.* New York: Holmes and Meier.

March, J.G. (1994) *A Primer on Decision Making. How Decisions Happen.* New York: Free Press.

March, J.G. and Olsen, J.P. (1976) *Ambiguity and Choice in Organizations.* Bergen: Scandinavian University Press.

March, J.G. and Olsen, J.P. (1989) *Rediscovering Institutions. The Organizational Basis of Politics.* New York: Free Press.

March, J.G. and Olsen, J.P. (1996) 'Institutional perspectives on political institutions', *Governance,* 9: 247–64.

March, J.G. and Simon, H.A. (1958) *Organizations.* New York: John Wiley.

Mawson, J. and Spencer, K. (1997) 'The Government Offices for the English regions: towards regional governance?', *Policy and Politics*, 25: 71–84.

Maynard-Moody, S., Stull, D.D. and Mitchell, J. (1986) 'Reorganization as status drama: building, maintaining, and displacing dominant subcultures', *Public Administration Review*, 46: 301–10.

Meier, K.J. and Nigro, L.G. (1976) 'Representative bureaucracy and policy preferences: a study in the attitudes of federal executives', *Public Administration Review*, 36: 458–69.

Mortensen, R. (1993) 'Formell struktur et styringsverktøy? En case studie av en reorganisering i Samferdselsdepartementet'. Thesis. Oslo: Department of Political Science.

Nelson, B.J. (1996) 'Public policy and administration: an overview', in R.E. Goodin and H.-D. Klingemann (eds), *A New Handbook of Political Science.* Oxford: Oxford University Press.

Olsen, J.P. (1997) 'Institutional design in democratic contexts', *Journal of Political Philosophy*, 5: 203–29.

Page, E.C. (1995) 'Comparative public administration in Britain', *Public Administration*, 73: 123–41.

Peters, B.G. (1999) *Institutional Theory in Political Science. The 'New Institutionalism'.* London: Continuum.

Peters, B.G. and Wright, V. (1996) 'Public policy and administration, old and new', in R.E. Goodin and H.-D. Klingemann (eds), *A New Handbook of Political Science.* Oxford: Oxford University Press.

Petterson, O. (1989) *Maktens netverk.* Stockholm: Carlssons.

Pfeffer, J. (1982). *Organizations and Organization Theory.* Boston, MA: Pitman.

Pollitt, C. and Bouckaert, G. (2000) *Public Management Reform. A Comparative Analysis.* Oxford: Oxford University Press.

Rhodes, R.A.W. (2000) 'The governance narrative: key findings and lessons from the ESRC's Whitehall programme', *Public Administration*, 78: 345–63.

Rhodes, R.A.W. and Dunleavy, P. (eds) (1995) *Prime Minister, Cabinet and Core Executive.* Houndmills: Macmillan Press.

Scharpf, F. (1977) 'Does organization matter? Task structure and interaction in the ministerial bureaucracy', in E. Burack and A. Negandhi (eds), *Organization Design.* Kent State University Press.

Schattschneider, E.E. (1975) *The Semisovereign People.* Hinsdale: Dryden Press.

Scott, W.R. (1981) *Organizations: Rational, Natural, and Open Systems.* Englewood Cliffs, NJ: Prentice–Hall.

Selden, S.C. (1997) *The Promise of Representative Bureaucracy. Diversity and Responsiveness in a Government Agency.* Armonk, NY: M.E. Sharpe.

Selznick, P. (1957) *Leadership in Administration. A Sociological Interpretation*. Berkeley, CA: University of California Press.

Simon, H.A. (1965) *Administrative Behavior. A Study of Decision-Making Processes in Administration Organization*. New York: Free Press.

Simon, H.A. (1985) 'Human nature in politics: the dialogue of psychology and political science', *American Political Science Review*, 79: 293–304.

Simon, H.A. (1999) 'The potlatch between economics and political science', in J.E. Alt, M. Levi and E. Ostrom (eds), *Competition and Cooperation. Conversations with Nobelists about Economics and Political Science*. New York: Russell Sage Foundation.

Smith, M.J., Marsh, D. and Richards, D. (1995) 'Central government departments and the policy process', in R.A.W. Rhodes and P. Dunleavy (eds), *Prime Minister, Cabinet and Core Executive*. Houndmills: Macmillan.

Stigen, I. (1991) 'Avbyråkratisering og modifisert forhandling? Om bruk av prosjektorganisasjon i norsk sentraladministrasjon', *Norsk Statsvitenskapelig Tidsskrift*, 7: 173–91.

Underdal, A. (1996) 'Comparative analysis: accounting for variance in actor behavior', in K. Hanf (ed.), *The Domestic Basis of International Environmental Agreements: Modelling National/International Linkages*. Final Report to the European Commission.

Weale, A., Pridham, G., Williams, A. and Porter, M. (1996) 'Environmental administration in six European states: secular convergence or national distinctiveness?', *Public Administration*, 74: 255–74.

Wood, B.D. and Waterman, R.W. (1991) 'The dynamics of political control of the bureaucracy', *American Political Science Review*, 85: 801–28.

Wright, V. (1994) 'Reshaping the state: the implications for public administration', *West European Politics*, 17: 102–37.

Zuna, H.R. (2001) 'The effects of corporatisation on political control', in T. Christensen and P. Lægreid (eds), *New Public Management. The Transformation of Ideas and Practice*. Aldershot: Ashgate.

10

Institutional Theories and Public Institutions: Traditions and Appropriateness

Jean-Claude Thoenig

OLD INSTITUTIONALISM: A PRE-SCIENTIFIC PERSPECTIVE

More than a dozen schools of thought deal with public institutions (Peters, 1998). The present chapter presents in detail four of such streams: historical institutionalism, sociological institutionalism, new institutionalism and local order institutionalism. Each develops a set of theoretical interpretations which are empirically grounded. Together, they also cover major facets of what institutionalization processes are. Political and administrative machineries experience path dependencies. They are embedded in societal environments. They function like specific social systems. They produce social norms and cognitive references.

Up to the late 1960s, rather formal–legal approaches had been dominating the discipline: *public administration theory* in the United States, *administrative science* in European countries influenced by Roman law. Despite a few exceptions (Langrod, 1966; Chevallier, 1986), these approaches share some common characteristics. They are referred to as 'old institutionalism' (March and Olsen, 1984).

Public administration as a specific domain is defined by the concrete political bodies and administrative structures which are governing public affairs; constitutions, organigrams and procedures provide the conceptual glue which generates its unity and its limits. Institutions are taken for granted, as given phenomena. They are neither an issue for knowledge nor a problem for action. For this very descriptive genre, formal designs provide the raw material for a scientific approach.

Avoiding empirical observation, being quite sensitive to rationalization principles, old institutionalism discusses official structures by reference to normative debates around the applicability of principles or axioms derived from theory and philosophy of law. Clear-cut boundaries separate polity from society (which leaves sociology outside the field of public administration) and politics from administration (which implies that bureaucracy is linked to some form of consensual rationality). The public sector is considered as a homogeneous and coherent actor. It relies upon a tightly coupled set of specific entities (ministries, agencies etc.). It is subordinated to the will of its leaders. It is able to define a general interest criterion. Legal authority and political legitimacy provide the backbone of governance.

Institutional excellence could and should be achieved. Three sources are considered as influential: the separation between discretionary choice made by elected officials and conformistic implementation delivered by appointed agents (Wilson, 1887), the instrumental superiority of the pure bureaucratic form (Weber, 1978), administrative principles such as specialization, centralization, proceduralization or unity of command (Fayol, 1916). Institutions are defined and classified according to some basic components such as their morphology (Darbel and Schnapper, 1972) or their degree of development (Riggs, 1971).

Public institutions constitute a kind of iconography of order (Orren and Skowronek, 1994). They function as crucial determinants of a polity's essential character, history and future development. They also provide stability. Old institutionalism shares one common perspective with the behavioral mainstream which was dominant during the 1950s and 1960s in political science. Voters, lobbyists and political entrepreneurs are supposed to accept rules that are immutable, and forms of state leadership that are legitimate. Institutions are defined as being in a state of equilibrium, unless crises or disruptive periods occur and induce rapid and visible adaptations. Institutions *per se* do not generate change in an endogenous way. Interactions between societal evolution and administrative reform are not covered by old institutionalism.

PUBLIC INSTITUTIONS IN CHANGING SOCIETIES: NEW AGENDAS

The 1970s and the early 1980s coincide in social sciences with growing dissatisfaction about behavioralism and structuro-functionalism. Public administration as a field opens up to disciplines such as history, economics or sociology of organizations. The (re)discovery of institutions as independent variables or as explicit causes reflects a general trend.

Some failures of the welfare state, such as increasing costs, corporatism, urban revolts or technocratic arrogance, generate growing debates. The capacity of state and local governments to manage society policies becomes increasingly questioned in terms of efficiency and social justice by all kinds of social movements as well as by neoliberal and communitarian ideologies.

Bringing public institutions back in, social sciences set up new agendas. What roles do institutions play in providing social and economic outcomes to markets, polities and societies? Do welfare states produce and allocate goods and services in an efficient and effective way?

A rather loose set of new schools of thought emerges. Two of them play a pioneering role in underlining the impacts of society upon public institutions: historical institutionalism and sociological institutionalism.

Historical institutionalism

Historical institutionalism as a theoretical stream was born in the early 1980s (Hall, 1986) and labeled as such later on (Steinmo et al., 1992). This perspective defines public administration as part of political life. It criticizes the idea that the state functions as a single and hands-off agent. The essence of politics is made out of competition processes for scarce resources between rival groups and interests. The state does not act as a neutral agent elaborating consensual compromises. It looks like a complex set of differentiated institutions, as underlined by neomarxist (Katzenstein, 1978; Evans, 1985), neocorporatist (Anderson, 1979) or pluralist scholars (Dupuy and Thoenig, 1985). The UK Treasury is fragmented into several policy communities, each of them gathering public servants and private associations who share convergent views or are involved in common problem handling (Heclo and Wildavsky, 1974).

Why are resources and power allocated in an unequal way by the public sector? Why do old issues and solutions based upon routines influence in such a massive way the present agenda? The hypothesis tested by historical institutionalism is that the current outcomes of public policies do not reflect the mere preferences or interests of the current strongest competitors. They are rather channeled by the existing and past institutional arrangements in which competition takes place. Policy choices made in the past shape choices made today. Political and administrative organizations, conventions and procedures regulating the relationships between economic actors and the state are *path-dependent*. Modes of conflict–cooperation and the structure of outcomes are persistently identical throughout time.

Radical changes in public administration are a hopeless endeavour in such contexts. Existing institutions structure the design and the content of the decisions themselves. Future action is the reflection of experience. Such a perspective explains, for instance, how and why trade unions carry such divergent views of the world, as is the case in the United States and in Great Britain. Different institutional contexts between countries, characterized by the real power of the judiciary, model divergent preferences and interpretations of action by the labor movement organizations (Hattam, 1993).

Comparative approaches are favoured between different countries, combining in-depth study and longitudinal research. They bring political conflict and social dissensus back in, studying a variety of settings in which collective action implies interactions between the public sector and society at large.

Some public agencies have more influence than others. They also use loosely coupled procedures which may contradict or conflict. The public sector is structured around asymmetric power relationships. Other institutions such as trade unions, economic associations of employers or of farmers may also generate public order and political legitimacy (Rose and Davies, 1994). Certain groups or coalitions consistently win while others consistently lose.

Public institutions influence administrative and socio-political players in two ways. They offer some degree of predictability about the issues discussed; they also define models of behaviors and sets of protocols which are rather stereotyped and ready for immediate use. Public agencies provide moral and cognitive frameworks which allow their own members as well as third parties to make sense of events and to act in specific circumstances. They supply information. They also shape the identity, the image of self and the preferences of administrative behaviors.

Institutional designs do not reflect intentionality. Criteria used when public policies and organizations were initially designed rapidly vanish. Political stakes and coalition games take over and determine outcomes. A model of punctuated equilibrium posits that institutions simply respond to changes in the power balance within society (Krasner, 1984). The pressures for change are external to them.

While old institutionalism postulates that institutions shape policies and politics, historical or longitudinal approaches underline the fact that politics and policies shape institutions. Public institutions are taken for granted and provide the infrastructure for collective action. Acquiring the status of social conventions, they are never questioned. As social constructs, they resist any incremental change or any reform made by one single actor (Graftstein, 1992).

Sociological institutionalism

Another approach which has rather strongly influenced public administration as a body of grounded knowledge focuses upon institutional environment-oriented perspectives. It criticizes the validity of the distinction usually made between rationality – bureaucracy provides a consensual or ideal ends–means linkage which is valid *hic et nunc* – and culture – social practices are determined by norms and values which reflect societal attributes and which vary from one country to another.

Such a perspective goes back to Philip Selznick's pioneering study of the Tennessee Valley Authority (Selznick, 1948, 1949). It defines a public organization as a community in and of itself, and not as a collectivity deliberately constructed in order to achieve specific goals.

As field observation suggests, incongruities exist between the declared ends and those that the agency actually achieves or seeks to achieve. It pursues self-support and self-maintenance goals, as well as productive ends. It turns into a polymorphous system whose struggle to survive induces it to neglect or to distort its goals. Organizations are not passive instruments, they possess a life of their own and even become active entrepreneurs. People who participate do not act solely in accordance with the roles assigned to them.

Public management is not defined as the art of designing formalized structures aimed at regulating performance and coordinating behaviors. Basically, it deals with the way participants are influenced, transformed and completed by informal structures. What happens at the bottom of the hierarchy, in grass roots units in charge of implementing national policies, matters a lot, in some cases even more than what happens at the top level.

An agency must cope with the constraints and pressures applied by the outside social context in which it operates. Therefore it develops its own organization character. Institutionalization is a concept that defines the process through which the members of an agency acquire values that go beyond the technical requirements of organizational tasks. No organization is completely free of such a process: 'To institutionalize is to infuse with value beyond the technical requirements of the task at hand' (Selznick, 1957: 17). It takes place by selective recruiting of personnel, by establishing strong ties or alliances with outside groups through processes such as cooptation etc.

Thick institutionalization is achieved when some rules or procedures are sanctified, when some units or members of the public agency become semi-autonomous centers of power and develop their own vested interests, when administrative rituals, symbols and ideologies exist. Expectations, behaviors, beliefs are channeled and stabilized. Moral communities get set up. A public institution develops in a gradual manner, without any explicit design forces behind it. It becomes valued by some of its members and by outside vested interests for the special place it holds in the larger social system.

The Selznick perspective was surprisingly neglected for many years. Research attention was mainly allocated to the topic of business firms, much less to public administrations. The influence of institutional environments nevertheless experienced a revival with the birth of sociological institutionalism in the late 1970s in the United States (Meyer and Scott, 1983). This latter approach borrows from Selznick but adds novelty and breadth.

It studies the process of institutionalization as a set of socially legitimized activities which, in the long run, come to characterize certain aspects of social life (Scott, 1995). While Selznick emphasized political processes such as group conflict and intentional cooptation of external constituencies, the new generation downplays their importance. But it underlines the importance of other constraints, such as conformity and legitimacy imperatives. It also locates irrationality in the formal structure itself, not only in informal interactions such as influence patterns. Institutionalization is a process of a cognitive nature (Powell and DiMaggio, 1991).

The focus is less on such and such single organization with its specific context relegated to the background, and more on population of organizations defined as a consequence of this context. Institutional sociologists do not only identify mere pressures exerted locally on the organization, they also study what they define as organizational fields (DiMaggio, 1983). Such fields are formed by bodies ranging from public institutions (hospitals, aging centers etc.) to professional activities (doctors, teachers etc.). The field in which a public system is embedded is examined as a whole, as an activity making rules, supervising or surveying. It defines an institutional context within which each single organization plots its courses of action: sets of public art museums (DiMaggio, 1983), city administrations (Tolbert and Zucker, 1983), private and public elementary schools, or health care programs (Scott and Meyer, 1994). Organizational reality is theoretically framed as a symbolic construction. Cultural messages are transmitted by specific sets. Institutionalized myths offer explanatory significance. Formal structure is also myth and ceremony (Meyer and Rowan, 1977).

Compared to historical institutionalism, the sociological perspective defines what institutional means in a very macro way. Beside formal rules and procedures, it includes symbols, moral models and cognitive schemes. Institutions providing the frames of meaning which guide human action are similar to cultural systems. They influence the conduct of public administrators not only by stating what they have to do when where and how, but also by shaping the imagination of the actors about alternatives and solutions in new contexts. Society or culture as a whole shapes the acts and non-acts, the structures and the values of the public sector. To some extent action operates without specific actors.

Why do so many organizations, whether public or private, adopt formal structures, procedures and symbols which are so identical? Within a few years, most cities in a given country drop patronage systems and refer to modern human resource methods in order to run their public agencies. The ministries in charge of education in most countries around the world adopt rather identical formal structures and modes of functioning. Diffusion processes are characterized by institutional isomorphic change (DiMaggio and Powell, 1983). Innovation is adopted because it provides conformism. Mechanisms are at work such as coercive isomorphism – change results from pressures exerted by political influence or by outside organizations considered as legitimate – mimetic isomorphism – uncertainty and ambiguity about goals or technology increases the adoption of imitation conducts – and normative isomorphism – the existence across different organizations of individuals belonging to the same profession or having followed the same educational processes accelerates similarities of various kinds. Existing organizations provide references and models for the new ones. Designing institutions that are radically different from the existing ones becomes an illusion in a world that constrains autonomy of choice and limits action-oriented imagination.

Under what conditions do public organizations imitate each others and prefer not to be innovative? In the short term, pressures toward isomorphism are strong. Reinforcing their political legitimacy or improving the social image of their members is a major reason why public organizations conform. Values that are recognized by their environment drive transformation much more than instrumental rationalities increasing their efficiency or effectiveness. In the long term, more diversity or competition between alternative organizational models is possible. Isomorphic pressures become weaker within a given institutional framework (Kondra and Hinings, 1998).

The concept of archetype is used to operationalize organizational transformation. Archetype refers to a configuration of structures and systems of organizing with a common orientation or underlying interpretative scheme. Evolutionary change occurs slowly and gradually, as a fine-tuning process within the parameters of an existing archetype (Greenwood and Hinings, 1996). Organizational transformation or revolutionary change happens swiftly and affects all the parts of the organization simultaneously. It is associated with interactions between exogenous dynamics (institutional contexts) and endogenous dynamics of interests, values and power dependencies. Pressures for change are precipitated under two conditions. Inside, group dissatisfaction with accommodation of interests within the existing template for organizing are coupled with a value commitment. Outside the public agency, exogenous dynamics exist which also push for an alternative template. Situations are also identified in which deinstitutionalization processes occur (Oliver, 1992). Some practices get eroded or are facing discontinuity or rejection over time.

INSTITUTIONS AS DETERMINANTS OF POLITICAL LIFE: A NORMATIVE THEORY

'New institutionalism' as an explicit school of thought finds its origins in a paper published by two political scientists (March and Olsen, 1984). It claims that public administration as a domain should be action-oriented and actionable. A deliberately normative or governance-oriented perspective should mobilize scholars. What are the foundations of government in contemporary societies? Is it possible to fight bureaucracy and at the same time to develop democracy in a voluntary way? Public institutions should be considered as key factors.

Government is in the business of forming its environments, not adapting to it. Public administration is driven by societal visions and political projects. Therefore organizations that handle public affairs should be 'conceptualized as institutions rather than as instruments' (Brunsson and Olsen, 1997: 20). They generate and implement prescriptions that define how the game has to be played: who is legitimate to participate, what are the acceptable agendas, which sanctions to apply in case of deviations as well as the process by which changes should occur. The way people think, interpret facts, act and cope with conflicts are influenced and simplified by public administration. Democratic governance implies a good understanding of the properties of political institutions, of their construction processes and of their real modes of functioning. Academics should observe empirically two aspects. Do public administration reforms match societal needs? Do they also help found democratic participation?

New institutionalism considers as dangerous and inefficient the very idea that it is possible to reform and control public organizations. Social science research has to make explicit the less than convincing axioms or hypotheses that current fashions such as New Public Management and existing theories such as rational choice carry about organizations and institutions.

Contextualism, for instance, stipulates that politics is a component of society which is the mere product of factors such as social classes, culture or demography: in no case is it considered as a cause of such factors. Reductionism postulates that political phenomena are mere consequences of individual behaviors: the functioning of a public agency is explainable by the behavior model of the single bureaucrat. Economic utilitarianism implies that conducts of individuals are basically driven by their own selfish interest: nobody is in charge of the collective interest. Functionalist approaches adopt darwinian views: historical evolution selects the organizational forms that fit the environmental requirements and kills those that do not. An instrumental perspective claims that the core role political life fulfills is to allocate scarce resources and that it is therefore legitimate to rationalize the criteria of choice governments and budgets use.

The founding fathers of new institutionalism suggest alternative ideas or hypotheses to such perspectives. New institutionalism questions how far organized action is manageable and to what degree some public order is achievable in pluralistic societies. Public institutions may experience a large degree of autonomy and follow a logic of their own, independently of outside influences or requirements. The historical process happens to select organizational forms which are not always efficient. Symbols, myths and rituals have more impact upon political and administrative events than immediate, narrow and selfish economic or power interests.

The logic of consequentiality is an illusion. Action in organizations is not to any great extent instrumentally oriented. In fact, absolute or pure rationality is impossible to enact. Only bounded rationality is available. Public administrators make decisions according to some criterion of satisficing which expresses a compromise they make between the content of the problem they address and the level of uncertainty they face at the time they face it.

In order to understand how policy making really functions inside organizations, three fundamental dimensions or aspects should be considered: the actual goals the various units pursue, the way information, opportunities and support are built and elaborated, and the choice or decisions processes. Observation suggests that four main mechanisms can occur: conflict avoidance, uncertainty reduction, problem solving as solution seeking initiator, organizational learning through former experience and rules of attention allocation.

In fact public organizations function like political arenas. Power issues and power games model their functioning and their policies. Collective goals do not necessarily exist that would provide common references subsuming individual goals or particularistic preferences. Therefore institutional devices are needed in order to channel opportunistic behaviors and ensure some collective stability.

Two basic socialization mechanisms make behaviors predictable; they channel the potential risk factor individuals represent – organizational routines and institutions. Actors select their conducts according to a logic of appropriateness or conformism (March and Olsen, 1989). The implication is that routines or legacies from the past are powerful sources of integration, and create risk-adverse conditions for collective action. So also are cognitive patterns and values which are diffused through institutionalization processes. Action mobilizes cultural elements; actors fulfill identities by following rules that they imagine as appropriate to the situations. The new institutionalists suggest a theory of learning in ambiguous environments. It provides a framework that predicts and explains how individuals and organizations try to reach some degree of understanding and some form of intelligence of the contexts they face (March and Olsen, 1975), how they allocate their attention to a particular subject at a given time and how information is collected and exploited (March and Olsen, 1976).

The platform designed by March and Olson gave birth in 1988 to a research consortium involving American and Scandinavian scholars. More than thirty field studies were conducted on public sector organizations, especially in Sweden and Norway (Christensen and Lægreid, 1998b). Reforms of various kinds were observed, such as introducing corporate strategic planning in the relationships between the national government and state agencies, running a public rail company in a decentralized way and with a strong market orientation, introducing a three-year budgeting methodology into national government administration and setting up active and participative county councils (Brunsson and Olsen, 1997). A new generation of social scientists retained interest in phenomena such as national administrative reform policy (Christensen and Lægreid, 1998a), complex public building projects (Sahlin-Andersson, 1998), decentralization policies in municipalities (Czarniawska and Jørges, 1998), constitutive reforms of the European Union (Blichner and Sangolt, 1998), municipal

accounting reforms (Bergeværn et al., 1998) or central government officials (Egeberg and Sætren, 1999).

As evidence shows, any comprehensive approach to organizational change fails. Governments are unable to reconstruct public institutions from scratch. Politicians are acting short-term, not long-term. Actual administrative reforms look more like processes of organized attention (Lægreid and Roness, 1999). Time, energy and attention are scarce resources for governmental leaders. Politicians influence reform policies in an indirect way, maneuvering the scene by steering the actors' role through procedure more than substance, using various degrees of hierarchy, specialization and random control.

Public management is the consequence of human activities, not the result of applied techniques. Contrary to what most New Public Management supporters advocate, leaders are not in full control, organizations are not passive, policy choices are not consensual. Actual administrative reforms, whether successful or not, are characterized by a low degree of simplicity and clarity. Normativity, which should bring order into chaotic reality, is somewhat lacking. No one-sidedness is manifest which would allow a single set of values to be accepted as legitimate. Many promises are made about the future, but the instant production of results is irrelevant. Intentions are ambiguous. Public administration organizations cannot be controlled and changed through pure thought. It is easy to initiate administrative reforms, but few are completed (Brunsson and Olsen, 1993). Reformers are prisoners of walls that are mental.

Reforms generate more reforms and less changes. They become routines. Organizational forgetfulness allows acceleration of reforms and helps people accept them. Top-down reforms should be avoided because their relationship with change outcomes is problematic. They paradoxically contribute to stability and prevent change from occurring.

While actual organizational changes are not generated by planned or comprehensive reform, observation suggests that they are abundant. Public administrations as such are not innovation-adverse. They may follow a sequence of transformations which reflect outside factors such as labor market dynamics or inside initiatives informally taken by low-ranking units. Real big changes when they happen take place without much prior thought and discussion. It is also easier to generate them when reforms are undertaken in non-controversial areas. In controversial contexts, attempts at reform make for stability. Hotly debated issues are not subjected to any great change.

Normative institutionalism suggests two main prescriptions for public administration changes to occur: first, there should be a match between rules, identities and situations – successful reforms are culturally sensitive; second, context matters because contexts are diverse – so-called good practices are questionable.

INSTITUTIONS AS CO-CONSTRUCTED LOCAL ORDERS: A CHALLENGE

While institutional theories have become a leading school of thought in the Anglo-Saxon countries, their influence is less visible in continental Europe. In countries such as France, Germany or Italy, scepticism developed quite early about rationalization techniques applied to government. Another reason is that a recognized tradition of social science research existed well before the 1980s. When Anglo-Saxon political scientists were still challenging behavioralism and rational choice, European sociologists had already got rid of macro theories such as marxist sociology of the state (Mény and Thoenig, 1989). The idea that public institutions may have a thickness of their own inside societies and polities was common sense quite early. Such is the case with the French tradition of *sociologie des organisations*. It considers institutional phenomena as both independent and dependent variables (Thoenig, 1987b).

Michel Crozier made pioneering studies of several public agencies (Crozier, 1963). Bureaucracies are modeled by societal factors such as the education system, national culture patterns or social stratification. Public servants trained in exclusive schools such as the ENA and Ecole Polytechnique control the public agenda of a whole country (Suleiman, 1978). Institutions and institutionalization allow *bourgeois* classes to stabilize their cultural and social domination (Bourdieu, 1989).

Public institutions shape societies and polities. Criteria of efficiency and effectiveness applied to urban development and housing policies are institutional outcomes of intra-administrative practices and values (Thoenig, 1987a). The cognitive content defining general interest is socially constructed by small groups of public agents.

Organizational change processes are used as heuristic entry points. While Anglo-Saxon intellectuals were debating about the marketization and the economization of public choices, French social scientists had questioned the idea that the central state could manage the whole polity, integrate society and guide the economy with the help of rational tools such as economic planning, social indicators or Planning, Programming, Budgeting Systems (PPBS) (Crozier et al., 1974). Redesigning formal structures remains a cosmetic game, given the vicious circles of change in which ministers and bureaucrats are caught.

Cooptation mechanisms are widely diffused across the public sector. Both groups are linked by asymmetric interdependence relationships. Norms circulate and get shared between state agents and civil society leaders. Mutual socialization occurs. State prefects think and act like advocates of the interests of their respective territory. Mayors behave as brokers between the state and their constituents. Local agencies of the national ministries – 95 per cent of the two and a half million state servants are located in field agencies across the country – are strongly embedded in subnational communities. They get legitimacy from their environment, especially from local elected politicians. It becomes a resource they use to increase their autonomy in the relationship with their respective headquarters located in Paris (Grémion, 1976).

Cooptation processes give structure to informal and stable relation patterns which link state agencies to specific environments such as local political and economic leaders (Crozier and Thoenig, 1976). A politico-administrative system, which is very different from the hierarchical model and which ignores formal division of power between national and local authorities, structures public governance all across France. The machinery of the central state looks like a fragmented organizational fabric in which various subparts cooperate less than each of them cooperates with its local environment leaders. Complex cross-regulation practices develop between partners who otherwise perceive each other as antagonistic. They give birth and legitimacy to implicit rules of exchange and to stable interest coalitions. Tacit arrangements are set during the implementation stage of national policies. Rigid rules decided in Paris are balanced by flexible arrangements negotiated locally (Dupuy and Thoenig, 1985). A secondary norm of implementation, of which the content varies according to time and space and which is perceived as legitimate, prevails over a rule of formal conformism and of equality of treatment. State agencies generate exceptions which become local norms; they reinforce differentiation of outcomes. Local polities and politics are shaped in two ways.

Bureaucratic ways of doing things model the cognitions and the expectations of social groups.

Traffic violations, for instance, are considered as normal, especially by truck drivers, as far as they are widely tolerated by the police and by the courts. Such massive fraud generates costs which are externalized and paid by third parties, such as private car drivers and Social Security (Ocqueteau and Thoenig, 1997).

Easy access to state agencies allocates relevant resources to specific social categories who benefit from them. For instance, a local politician may use her/his networks inside the state machineries in favour of her/his constituency. Parties unable to get such access pay the full cost or become marginalized. Such is the case for low income families living in suburbs of large cities: they experience political alienation and are distanced from civic concerns (Peyrefitte, 1976).

The French perspective also treats public institutions as one partner among many who intervene in handling public affairs. Freight transportation (Dupuy and Thoenig, 1979) and agricultural affairs (Jobert and Müller, 1988) have offered pioneering examples. Studying how governmental agendas are set up, how decisions are elaborated and how they are implemented, they suggest that for each policy a specific system of organized action exists which has a logic of its own. Even when some Paris ministry or some regional authority may play a hegemonic role, its acts and non-acts remain dependent on the presence of other public agencies, firms or voluntary associations. The fight against water pollution is regulated by national laws and managed by a state agency, but its outcome is also the consequence of the initiatives taken by industrial sites or of the attention given to it by groups of citizens. Public affairs are not governed in an autarchic way by public institutions. They are institutionally and functionally embedded within macro as well as micro social fabrics.

Public administrations have experienced dramatic changes since the 1960s (Duran and Thoenig, 1996). The central state agencies no longer play a dominant role, governing national as well as local public affairs through the allocation of subsidies and the elaboration of technical rules. A different political and administrative system emerges. There is massive decentralization in favor of regional and local authorities. New private, associative or public players, such as the European Commission, get a role in policy making. Public issues coincide less and less with the way subnational territories are subdivided and administrative jurisdictions defined. Collective problems are of a horizontal nature and are addressed with uncertain solutions.

Cross-regulation gives poor results when the challenge is to identify the nature of collective problems and to set public agendas. State agencies adopt another political integration approach: constitutive policies. New institutional frameworks coordinate the views and mindsets of multiple partners, make them speak a common language and share a common perception about what to do, how, when and for whom. Facing a polity that is fragmented, active and non-consensual, a weakened state discovers institutionalization and institutional design.

A rather rigorous analytical framework characterizes the French academic approach. Fieldwork and in-depth interviews generate thick empirical evidence. Interdependence phenomena are interpreted as results of strategic behaviors of actors operating in power settings (Crozier and Friedberg, 1980). Social regulation – how different actors set up normative arrangements and make their respective logics of action compatible – and systemic implications of such social co-constructions, are studied. Understanding the inner functioning of public agencies is a key point in order to study their societal impacts (Thoenig, 1987b). Scholars belonging to this tradition question the ability of neo-institutionalism to deliver convincing evidence (Friedberg, 1998).

Discourses are not reliable indicators of behaviors. Public agents may carry some norms or cognitions, but they may not use them in relational settings and in decision making processes. Institutions remain beliefs without acts.

While the new institutionalism perspective favours a vision of democratic order in which responsibility is a consequence of the institution of the individual, citizens are free, equal and discipline-oriented agents, and governance is enlightened and rule-constrained (Olsen, 1998), their continental colleagues are more pessimistic. They adopt a vision of politics which is rather cynical or machiavellian. Public institutions are political devices. The essence of politics is power. Do-gooders are a scarce resource. Individuals behave in an opportunistic way.

French sociologists interpret public institutions as systems of action in which what the actors do matters. As specific social arrangements, they are fragile constructs because they are the non-intended outcomes of permanent collective tinkering. Discontinuities in time characterize the essence of public administration and of societal order. Many institutional theories identify some macro logics shaping social regimes. They underestimate meso variations. Public organizations should be considered as local social orders, as meso or intermediary social configurations, which are neither passive nor intentional, but are constantly reconstructed in terms of social norms and of membership. Government is of a more collective nature:

public institutions have no monopoly on public problems. Public affairs are co-constructed.

American institutionalists, for instance, emphasize the intrinsic homogeneity of education institutions, in part because they negate the importance of actors. Either formally or in terms of discourses, schools look alike within the same country or even across different countries. European scholars suggest that, below the surface, schools may differ quite markedly in terms of their real mode of functioning. Local orders exist which create heterogeneities in space. In a nation-state such as France, whose founding values incorporate the ideals of unity and equality and where enforcement is handled in a centralized-authoritarian manner, public institutions are not alike. At least four different types of functioning exist across state agencies: inward-oriented bureaucracies, environment-sensitive institutions, outward-driven organizations and interorganizational systems (Thoenig, 1996).

Another school has developed in Germany under the influence of Renate Mayntz, a sociologist of organizations who has written a comprehensive book on public administration (Mayntz, 1978). After having led a study on policy implementation (Mayntz, 1980), she and Fritz Scharpf have set up a perspective called actor-centered institutionalism (Mayntz and Scharpf, 1995). Institutional factors are not as such direct causes of public practices and norms. They provide negotiation arenas and interaction resources between corporative actors, whether public or private. Various action and actor constellations exist in real life which handle collective issues; numerous studies on the European Union and Germany underline this (Mayntz et al., 1988).

CONCLUSION

Empirically grounded theories consider public institutions through three different lenses: as pillars of political order, as outcomes of societal values, or as self constructed social systems. Public administration as a discipline faces a massive challenge. Change processes such as globalization and issues such as economic development suggest that governmental organizations are also vehicles for social and political identities, not only passive technocratic machineries. Reconciling performance requirements with social consensus, production of social norms with democratic pluralism, remain in unstable and fragmented worlds two perspectives that institutional theorists have still to explore.

REFERENCES AND FURTHER READING

Anderson, C. (1979) 'Political design and the representation of interests', in P. Schmitter and G. Lehmbruch (eds), *Trends towards Corporatist Intermediation.* Beverly Hills, CA: Sage. pp. 145–73.

Bergeværn, L.E., Mellomvik, F. and Olson, O. (1998) 'Institutionalization of municipal accounting – a comparative study between Sweden and Norway', in N. Brunsson and J.P. Olsen (eds), *Organizing Organizations.* Bergen: Fagbokforlaget. pp. 279–302.

Blichner, L.C. and Sangolt, L. (1998) 'The concept of subsidiarity and the debate on European cooperation: pitfalls and possibilities', in N. Brunsson and J.P. Olsen (eds), *Organizing Organizations.* Bergen: Fagbokforlaget. pp. 107–32.

Bourdieu, P. (1989) *La Noblesse d'état.* Paris: Editions de Minuit.

Brunsson, N. (1999) 'Standardization as organization', in M. Egeberg and P. Lægreid (eds), *Organizing Political Institutions.* Oslo: Scandinavian University Press. pp. 107–28.

Brunsson, N. and Olsen, J.P. (1997) *The Reforming Organization.* Bergen: Fagbokforlaget.

Brunsson, N. and Olsen, J.P. (eds) (1993) *Organizing Organizations.* Bergen: Fagbokforlaget.

Chevallier, J. (1986) *Science administrative.* Paris: Presses Universitaires de France.

Christensen, Tom and Lægreid, Per (1998a) 'Administrative reform policy: the case of Norway', *International Review of Administrative Sciences,* 64 (4): 457–75.

Christensen, T. and Lægreid, P. (1998b) 'Public administration in a democratic context – a review of Norwegian research', in N. Brunsson and J.P. Olsen (eds), *Organizing Organizations.* Bergen: Fagbokforlaget. pp. 147–70.

Christensen, T. and Rovik, K.A. (1999) 'The ambiguity of appropriateness', in M. Egeberg and P. Lægreid (eds), *Organizing Political Institutions.* Oslo: Scandinavian University Press. pp. 159–80.

Crozier, M. (1963) *The Bureaucratic Phenomenon.* Chicago: University of Chicago Press.

Crozier, M. and Friedberg, E. (1980) *The Actor and the System.* Chicago: University of Chicago Press.

Crozier, M. and Thoenig, J.C. (1976) 'The regulation of complex organized systems', *Administrative Science Quarterly,* 2 (4): 547–70.

Crozier, M., Friedberg, E., Gremion, C., Gremion, P., Thoenig, J.C. and Worms, J.P. (1974) *Où va l'administration française?* Paris: Editions d'Organisation.

Czarniawska, B. and Jørges, B. (1998) 'Winds of organizational change: how ideas translate into objects and actions', in N. Brunsson and J.P. Olsen (eds), *Organizing Organizations.* Bergen: Fagbokforlaget. pp. 197–236.

Darbel, A. and Schnapper, D. (1972) *Le Système administratif.* Paris: Mouton.

DiMaggio, P.J. (1991) 'Constructing an organizational field as a professional project: U.S. art museums', in Walter W. Powell and Paul J. DiMaggio (eds), *The New*

Institutionalism in Organizational Analysis. Chicago: University of Chicago Press. pp. 267–92.

DiMaggio, P.J. and Powell, W.W. (1983) 'The iron-cage revisited: institutional isomorphism and collective rationality in organizational fields', *American Sociological Review*, 38 (2): 147–60.

Dupuy, F. and Thoenig, J.C. (1979) 'Public transportation policymaking in France as an implementation problem', *Policy Science*, 12 (1): 1–18.

Dupuy, F. and Thoenig, J.C. (1985) *L'Administration en miettes*. Paris: Le Seuil.

Duran, P. and Thoenig, J.C. (1996) 'L'état et la gestion publique territoriale', *Revue Française de Science Politique*, 46 (4): 580–623.

Egeberg, M. (1998) 'The policy–administration dichotomy revisited', in N. Brunsson and J.P. Olsen (eds), *Organizing Organizations*. Bergen: Fagbokforlaget. pp. 133–46.

Egeberg, M. and Lægreid, P. (eds) (1999) *Organizing Political Institutions*. Oslo: Scandinavian University Press.

Egeberg, M. and Sætren, H. (1999) 'Identities in complex organizations: a study of ministerial bureaucrats', in M. Egeberg and P. Lægreid (eds), *Organizing Political Institutions*. Oslo: Scandinavian University Press. pp. 93–108.

Evans, P.B., Rueschemeyer, D. and Skocpol, T. (eds) (1985) *Bringing the State Back In*. New York: Cambridge University Press.

Fayol, H. (1916) *General and Industrial Management*. London: Pitman.

Friedberg, E. (1998) 'Néo-institutionnalisme et ordres locaux', *Revue Française de Science Politique*, 48 (3–4): 507–14.

Graftstein, R. (1992) *Institutional Realism: Social and Political Constraints on Rational Actors*. New Haven, CT: Yale University Press.

Greenwood, R. and Hinings, C.R. (1996) 'Understanding radical organisational change: bringing together the old and the new institutionalism', *Academy of Management Journal*, 21 (4): 1022–54.

Grémion, P. (1976) *Le Pouvoir périphérique: bureaucratie et notables dans le système politique français*. Paris: Le Seuil.

Hall, P.A. (1986) *Governing the Economy: The Politics of State Intervention in Britain and France*. New York: Oxford University Press.

Hattam, V.C. (1993) *Labor Visions and State Power: The Origins of Business Unionism in the United States*. Princeton, NJ: Princeton University Press.

Heclo, H. and Wildavsky, A. (1974) *The Private Governement of Public Money: Community and Policy Inside British Politics*. London: Macmillan.

Jobert, B. and Müller, P. (1988) *L'Etat en action*, Paris: Presses Universitaires de France.

Katzenstein, P. (ed.) (1978) *Between Power and Plenty: Foreign Economic Policies of Advanced Industrial States*, Madison, WI: University of Wisconsin Press.

Kondra, A.Z. and Hinings, C.R. (1998) 'Organizational diversity and change in institutional theory', *Organization Studies*, 19 (5): 743–67.

Krasner, S.D. (1984) 'Approaches to the state: alternative conceptions and historical dynamics', *Comparative Politics*, 16 (2): 223–46.

Lægreid, P. and Roness, P.G. (1999) 'Administrative reform as organized attention', in M. Egeberg and P. Lægreid (eds), *Organizing Political Institutions*. Oslo: Scandinavian University Press. pp. 301–29.

Langrod, Georges (ed.) (1966) *Traité de science administrative*. Paris: Mouton.

March, J.G. and Olsen, J.P. (1975) 'The uncertainty of the past: organizational learning under ambiguity', *European Journal of Political Research*, 3: 147–71.

March, J.G. and Olsen, J.P. (1976) *Ambiguity and Choice in Organizations*. Bergen: Universitetsforlaget.

March, J.G. and Olsen, J.P. (1983) 'Organizing political life: what administrative reorganization tells us about governement', *American Political Science Review*, 77 (2): 281–97.

March, J.G. and Olsen, J.P. (1984) 'The New Institutionalism: organizational factors in political life', *American Political Science Review*, 78 (5): 734–49.

March, J.G. and Olsen, J.P. (1989) *Rediscovering Institutions: The Organizational Basis of Politics*. New York: Free Press.

Mayntz, R. (1978) *Soziologie der Oeffentlichen Verwaltung*. Heidelberg: C.F. Müller.

Mayntz, R. (ed.) (1980) *Implementation politischer Programme*. Königstein: Athenäum.

Mayntz, R. and Scharpf, F.W. (1995) 'Der Ansatz des akteurzentrierten Institutionalismus', in R. Mayntz and F.W. Scharpf (eds), *Gesellschaftliche Selbstregelung and Politische Steuerung*. Frankfurt a.M.: Campus. pp. 39–72.

Mayntz, R., Rosewitz, B., Schimank, U. and Stichweh, R. (1988) *Differenzierung und Verselbständigung. Zur Entwicklung gesellschqfltlicher Teilsysteme*. New York: Campus.

Mény, Y. and Thoenig, J.C. (1989) *Les Politiques publiques*. Paris: Presses Universitaires de France.

Meyer, J.W. and Rowan, B. (1977) 'Institutionalized organizations: formal structure as myth and ceremony', *American Journal of Sociology*, 83 (2): 340–63.

Meyer, J.W. and Scott, W.R. (1983) *Organizational Environments: Rituals and Rationality*. London: Sage.

Ocqueteau, F. and Thoenig, J.C. (1997) 'Mouvements sociaux et action publique: le transport routier de marchandises', *Sociologie du Travail*, 4: 397–424.

Oliver, C. (1992) 'The antecedents of deinstitutionalization', *Organization Studies*, 13 (4): 563–88.

Olsen, J.P. (1998) 'Institutional design in democratic contexts', in N. Brunsson and J.P. Olsen (eds), *Organizing Organizations*. Bergen: Fagbokforlaget. pp. 319–49.

Orren, K. and Skowronek, S. (1994) 'Beyond the iconography of order: notes for a 'New Institutionalism', in L.C. Dodd and C. Jillson (eds), *The Dynamics of American Politics*. Boulder, CO: Westview Press.

Peters, B.G. (1998) *Comparative Politics: Theory and Methods*. Basingstoke: Macmillan.

Peters, B.G. (1999) 'Institutional theory and administrative reform', in M. Egeberg and P. Lægreid (eds),

Organizing Political Institutions. Oslo: Scandinavian University Press. pp. 331–55.

Peyrefitte, A. (ed.) (1976) *Décentraliser les responsabilités. Pourquoi? Comment?* Paris: La Documentation française.

Powell, W.W. and DiMaggio, P.J. (eds) (1991) *The New Institutionalism in Organizational Analysis*. Chicago: University of Chicago Press.

Riggs, F. (ed.) (1971) *Frontiers of Development Administration*. Durham, NC: Duke University Press.

Rose, R. and Davies, P. (1994) *Inheritance in Public Policy*. New Haven, CT: Yale University Press.

Sahlin-Andersson, K. (1998) 'The social construction of projects. A case study of organizing of an extraordinary building project – the Stockholm Globe Arena', in N. Brunsson and J.P. Olsen (eds), *Organizing Organizations*. Bergen: Fagbokforlaget, pp. 89–106.

Scott, W.R. (1995) *Institutions and Organizations*. London: Sage.

Scott, W.R. and Meyer, J.W. (1994) 'Environmental linkages and organizational complexity. Public and private schools', in W.R. Scott, J.W. Meyer and associates, *Institutional Environments and Organizations. Structural Complexity and Individualism*. Thousand Oaks, CA: Sage. pp. 137–59.

Scott, W.R., Meyer, J.W. and associates (1994) *Institutional Environments and Organizations. Structural Complexity and Individualism*. Thousand Oaks, CA: Sage.

Selznick, P. (1948) 'Foundations of the theory of organization', *American Sociological Review*, 13 (1): 25–35.

Selznick, P. (1949) *TVA and the Grass Roots*. Berkeley, CA: University of Berkeley Press.

Selznick, P. (1957) *Leadership in Administration*. New York: Harper and Row.

Selznick, P. (1992) *The Moral Commonwealth: Social Theory and the Promise of Community*. Berkeley, CA, University of California Press.

Steinmo, S., Thelen, K. and Longstreth, F. (eds) (1992) *Structuring Politics: Historical Institutionalism in Comparative Analysis*. Cambridge: Cambridge University Press.

Suleiman, E. (1978) *Elites in French Society*. Princeton, NJ: Princeton University Press.

Thoenig, J.C. (1987a) *L'Ere des technocrates*. Paris: L'Harmattan.

Thoenig, J.C. (1987b) 'Pour une approche analytique de la modernisation administrative', *Revue Française de Science Politique*, 4: 526–38.

Thoenig, J.C. (1996) 'Public sector organizations', in A. Sorge and M. Warner (eds), *Handbook of Organizational Behavior*. London: Thomson Business Press. vol. 5, pp. 421–32.

Tolbert, P.S. and Zucker, L.G. (1983) 'Institutional sources of change in the formal structure of organizations: the diffusion of civil service reform, 1880–1935', *Administrative Science Quarterly*, 30 (1): 22–39.

Weber, M. (1978) *Economy and Society* (eds G. Roth and C. Wittich). Berkeley, CA: University of California Press.

Wilson, W. (1887) 'The study of administration', *Political Science Quarterly*, 2.

11

Formal Theory and Public Administration

Jack H. Knott and Thomas H. Hammond

Formal theory involves the use of formal, mathematical logic to develop theories of individuals, groups, organizations and public institutions, and this chapter reviews the application of formal theory to public administration. Formalization can help us in a variety of ways to develop, explore and test theories of public administration (Hammond, 1996). First, formalization forces us to be as explicit as possible about the basic assumptions of our theories. Second, with our initial assumptions made explicit and expressed in some kind of symbolic notation, the rules of mathematics, such as calculus, geometry, or probability theory, can then be used to rigorously deduce the consequences of the assumptions. Third, formalization of a theory can help improve the quality of empirical tests since our formal theory gives us a clearer idea of precisely what should be tested and how to test it. Fourth, the greater capacity for formal theories to be empirically falsified, due to their greater explicitness, makes theoretical improvement more possible. Finally, for studies of especially complex problems only a formal representation, especially via computer simulation, may be able to capture some of the complexity and yet still allow the theory's implications to be rigorously explored, and thereby made amenable to empirical test.

Over the past three decades, applications of formal theory to public administration have proliferated, and it is impossible to review all the contributions. Hence, in this chapter we can only touch on a few of the contributions that formal theory has made. For example, scholars have used it to explain the existence of public agencies, which may be formed to address inefficiencies in voluntary market exchanges. Formal theory

demonstrates that public agencies do not necessarily solve these market failures, and that individually rational choices by agency employees do not necessarily produce rational policies for the agency as a whole. Clarifying the nature of these individual versus agency tensions helps explain the dysfunctional group dynamics identified in earlier sociological and psychological studies of organizational behavior. The emphasis in formal theory on individual preferences and institutional structures has improved our understanding of how agency structure affects agency policy. Additionally, formal theory helps explain why it is difficult to simultaneously pursue such desirable administrative values as accountability, efficiency and decentralization. Moreover, formal theory has contributed to our knowledge of how legislators and executives can gain some control over agencies via the use of administrative procedures and other controls. Formal theory also shows us, however, the way in which agencies can take advantage of asymmetric information and multiple principals to gain autonomy from their would-be overseers.

WHY DO PUBLIC AGENCIES EXIST?

Economists were the original developers of formal, mathematical theories in the social sciences, and in neo-classical economics the baseline model of social interactions has come to be the competitive market. Hence, one of the earliest questions asked by economists was this: why aren't *all* choices made through market exchanges? Several answers have been provided.

Transaction costs

One early answer was provided by Coase (1937), who was interested in explaining why economic agents sometimes organize themselves into hierarchically structured firms. His explanation is that under certain conditions hierarchy is more efficient than voluntary market exchange. The reason stems from the costs associated with production processes requiring multiple transactions among independent suppliers, owners, labor and experts; North (1990: 14) defines these costs as the 'cost of measuring and enforcing agreements'. Economic agents must bear the costs of gathering and evaluating information on their production processes, and must pay the costs of negotiating a contract for each market transaction. Self-interested rational agents will want to minimize these costs.

Coase's insight was that when market transactions entail these kinds of costs, central authority can more efficiently coordinate production processes. Coase (1937: 391) posited a relationship in the firm whereby the employer could direct the activities of employees within certain limits. This authority contract substituted for the myriad of negotiated contracts in the market.

Although Coase was largely ignored in the literature for decades, his work provided an important intellectual foundation for subsequent economic analyses of market failures, and it stimulated economists to examine whether government and public agencies could cope with these failures (Wolf, 1975).

Market failures and public goods

Several different aspects of production and exchange can lead to inefficient outcomes. One kind of inefficient outcome stems from transaction costs. If each street in a city were privately owned, travelers would need to pay a toll at many different intersections. The solution to this problem is for one firm to own all the streets, or for the government to own them. Such centralized authority would eliminate the transaction costs involved in traveling across the city.

A second kind of market failure occurs when transactions impose external effects on third parties. If someone purchases shoes, for example, the shoes affect only the feet of the purchaser. In contrast, the purchase of a dog which barks constantly affects the peace and quiet of neighbors. Producers and consumers generally do not take these kinds of 'negative externalities' into account when engaging in market exchanges. In judging the overall efficiency of market exchanges, the efficiencies due to the market exchanges are reduced by the costs imposed on third parties. In effect, then, since the costs to the producers and consumers are less than the overall costs to society, this means that the goods involved are overproduced.

A third kind of market failure involves the underprovision of public goods. A defense establishment provides everyone in a country with national security and not just the citizens who pay taxes. Other public goods include clean air, clean water and public broadcasting. Citizens have an incentive not to pay for such a good since they can consume it even if they do not pay for it. Since those producing the public goods are not completely compensated for their production, the goods are underproduced. As a result, governments are often called upon to provide these public goods.

A fourth kind of market failure occurs when consumption of a common resource affects others who use the resource. This social dilemma, known as the 'tragedy of the commons', derives from the example given by Hardin (1968) of a village with a common green for grazing cattle. Each herdsman has an incentive to graze as many cattle as possible, but over time the grass on the green is ruined, hurting all the herdsmen. To avoid this kind of dilemma, governments often establish public agencies to regulate use of the commons (Ostrom, 1999).

A fifth kind of market failure occurs when one firm monopolizes an industry. In such a situation, the monopolist can engage in predatory pricing or use other practices that prevent competitors from entering the market. Because the monopolist can raise prices to increase profits, this reduces the amount of the good that would otherwise be consumed, thereby causing market inefficiency. Government regulation of monopoly production offers the possibility of avoiding underproduction and overpricing of the good.

Finally, information asymmetries in transactions can also lead to market failure (Greenwald and Stiglitz, 1986). Because consumers often have limited information when making a purchase, consumers will not know whether the price charged for a product reflects the product's true value to them. Hence, sellers can take advantage of the consumers' ignorance by overcharging for the quality of the product sold. This problem especially occurs in the purchase of expert services, such as medical care, but can occur even in less technical markets as well, such as the market for used cars (see Akerlof, 1970).

Governments often regulate these kinds of transactions through occupational licensing and certification and other kinds of mandatory product quality standards.

In sum, the formal literature provides reasons why markets fail to operate efficiently under some conditions. These failures do not necessarily explain the existence of public agencies, but they do imply the need for some form of social action to mitigate the market failure. Nonetheless, citizens often ask governments to create public agencies which will perform the necessary tasks. Whether public agencies can perform these tasks more efficiently than private firms is a complex question that will be discussed next.

INTERNAL ADMINISTRATION

We now turn our attention to the internal operation of private firms and, especially, public agencies. What does formal theory have to say about supervision, control, coordination, motivation, organizational structure and communication in these organizations? We will consider three problems: team production, principal–agent theory and organizational structure.

Team production

Alchian and Demsetz (1972) argue that contractual arrangements within the firm may be more efficient than those occurring just within the market. When employees, professionals and managers work together as teams, they can produce more than when they work separately. This gain from cooperation gives them an incentive to coordinate their activities. A central task of public and private management, therefore, is to help organizations achieve the benefits of team production (Knott, 1993).

Interestingly, though, one resulting problem is how to allocate any surplus produced by team production (Miller, 1992). Team production often involves tasks that are interdependent, which means that assessing the marginal contribution of each team member is difficult. Since information about individual contributions is rarely available, the allocation of the surplus cannot be based on individual contributions. Instead, some other allocation rule must be used which depends on something other than each individual's contribution. The resulting rules for surplus allocation, such as equal sharing or seniority,

often produce inefficiency because each member then has an incentive to 'free ride' in the production of the team's product.

To produce efficient outcomes in the long run the individuals may thus have to act in ways that are contrary to short-term individual self-interest. Game theory offers a way to think about this problem. A game is a social interaction in which at least two players have at least two options for choice, and in which the players' choices of one action or another produce benefits or costs for the players (Miller, 1992: 21). The Prisoner's Dilemma (PD) game in particular is at the heart of the problem of team production. The dominant strategy in a PD game is for each team member not to cooperate with coworkers. The resulting outcome, know as a *Nash equilibrium*, comprises a set of choices in which no player could be made better off by choosing some other option. Each player is satisfied that he or she has made the correct choice once the other person's choice is revealed.

The problem in a PD is that this Nash equilibrium is *Pareto suboptimal*: an outcome is possible in which one or more players is better off and no one is worse off. The dilemma is that the players are satisfied that each has made the individually rational choice, but the resulting group choice is Pareto suboptimal. The two players can only achieve a Pareto optimal outcome if they somehow are able to coordinate their choices.

It is often thought that the creation of hierarchy will help solve the Prisoner's Dilemma and other social dilemmas: managers should impose an incentive system and monitor the resulting behavior so as to induce individuals to coordinate their activities in ways that produce group efficiency. While this function for management is consistent with early work on organizational behavior (Barnard, 1938), it turns out that implementation entails its own set of intractable dilemmas. For example, it is not clear that an ideal incentive system actually exists (Miller, 1992: 35), and it also appears that managers may lack the incentive to implement an ideal system even if one did exist (Miller and Hammond, 1994). It is thus to these incentive systems that we now turn our attention.

Principal–agent theory

The relation between superiors and subordinates in team production can be generalized to include principals who contract for services and agents who carry out the services (Bendor, 1988). The primary tasks for the principal are, first, to identify agents who are most likely to have the skills to achieve the principal's goals; second, to gain agreement on a contract with incentives such that the agents find it in their self interest to pursue the principal's goals; and third, to monitor the agents' behavior in carrying out the contract. Each of these tasks involves the potential difficulty of asymmetric information and conflicts of interest among the contracting parties (Moe, 1984: 754), both of which give the contracting parties incentives to hide their information and actions from each other (Arrow, 1974).

The concepts of 'adverse selection' and 'moral hazard', which derive from theoretical work on the economics of insurance, aid the understanding of hidden action and hidden information. Adverse selection is a concern in the recruitment and hiring of employees. Since the employer cannot directly observe the skills, values and work habits of applicants, he or she relies on indicators of these traits such as education or letters of reference. Of necessity, these indicators reflect others' estimates of how the applicant will perform on the job and are frequently unreliable. If the applicant meets the formal requirements but does not excel on the traits that are actually desirable (that is, the skills, values and work habits), the indicators may overstate the applicant's value to the organization. As a result, the employer may attract and unwittingly hire less qualified applicants.

Moral hazard occurs after an applicant is hired. The employer, who cannot costlessly monitor the employee's job performance, may have to use indirect, and often unreliable, measures of performance. Employees thus have an incentive to perform well on these proxy measures rather than on the actual goals of the organization; this is what Merton (1940) called 'goal displacement'. Employees also have an incentive to shirk because their behavior is not fully observable.

Thus, many of the social dilemmas that provide the rationale for hierarchy also plague the operation of the hierarchy once it is created. Moreover, incentive systems that actually induce employees to behave in ways that maximize team efficiency may lead to lower payments to the managers, and for this reason the managers may not adopt (or may not honestly implement) efficiency-enhancing incentive systems (Miller and Hammond, 1994). In other words, hierarchies appear to suffer from the same conflict between individual self-interest and the efficiency of the organization as occurs in markets plagued by externalities and the underproduction of public goods (Holmstrom, 1982; Miller, 1992). Which kind of institution is better at a given task cannot be answered in general.

One of the critical problems in any hierarchy involves the strategic misrepresentation of information by both principals and agents. In this strategic use of information, actors find themselves in a game where revealing the truth about their beliefs and preferences may give others an advantage. There are at least two different kinds of models which have been developed to explain the strategic use of information.

Signaling models focus on the transfer of information between the agents and the principal prior to any action by the principal. In signaling models the principal can modify her or his beliefs about the effect of a policy, based on the information received from the agents, and then take action accordingly. But the agents are assumed to not necessarily reveal to the principal their true beliefs and preferences or to convey information in an honest and complete fashion. There is an important implication from the resulting model: principals will receive better information if the agents have heterogeneous preferences (Gilligan and Krehbeil, 1989). This result supports the public administration literature on redundancy in which principals having multiple and heterogeneous agents can gain more reliable information (Landau, 1969; Bendor, 1985; Heimann, 1997).

Models of delegation (for a review see Bendor et al., 2001) also inform the creation and functioning of hierarchies. For example, Epstein and O'Halloran (1999) analyze the behavior of a boss who first receives a report from a subordinate and then, based on the information in the report, chooses whether to delegate authority for implementation to another agent. Their model provides insight into conflict between executive staff and a line agency. The more the staff shares preferences with the boss, the less likely is the boss to delegate authority to the line agency. The value of delegating to an informed subordinate is that the subordinate can condition his or her action on information unavailable to the boss. But if the boss becomes more informed through the signaling game with staff, the value of delegating authority to the line decreases or remains constant. The authors also find that if the line and staff in an agency have similar preferences, but are distant from the boss, the staff will transmit less information to the boss. The reason is that the more information the staff gives the boss, the less the boss will delegate to the line. If the line and staff are close, the staff prefers more rather than less delegation. Hence the staff will not transmit as much information.

In the real world, information provision and authority delegation often occur in repeated sequences over time. This raises the possibility of carrot-and-stick strategies of conditional cooperation. For example, if the subordinate cheats by shirking, the boss might retaliate by more tightly controlling the subordinate's behavior in the next period. Or if the boss cheats by grabbing credit, the subordinate might retaliate by shirking in the next period. Under certain assumptions, these actions might be individually rational for each player but produce a Pareto suboptimal outcome.

Axelrod (1984) has shown that a Tit-for-Tat (TFT) strategy in these repeated games can lead to a cooperative outcome in the long term if the future is important to both players. In a TFT strategy, both the boss and the subordinate would cooperate (delegate, work) in the first period. In further periods, the subordinate would cooperate if the boss delegated and would shirk if the boss controlled. The boss would delegate only if the subordinate worked, and control if the subordinate shirked. Axelrod shows that in repeated games of this kind there is the possibility of cooperation in the longer run, though it is not guaranteed.

Implications for public management

The fact that public agencies are established to deal with market failures, but are themselves subject to many of the social dilemmas that characterize market competition, suggests the challenge facing public officials. Several leadership strategies may help to establish cooperative solutions to the agencies' own social dilemmas.

While managers and employees may each be tempted to engage in suboptimal, self-interested behavior, if one side does behave in a trustworthy, committed and cooperative way, it makes it easier for the other side to behave that way as well (Miller, 1992). For example, a credible commitment by management to a cooperative solution signals to employees that they may act efficiently and communicate truthfully without negative repercussions. Recall that Barnard (1938) emphasized the 'moral example' that managers should give to employees, and experiments with TFT strategies in repeated Prisoner's Dilemma games (Axelrod, 1984) further show the potential for cooperation from this kind of signaling behavior.

The popular management literature emphasizes the importance of the motivations of employees and the internalization of norms of cooperation among the members of the team (Peters and Waterman, 1982). Team-building exercises, shared company myths, organizational missions and professional norms may help internalize cooperative behavior by managers and employees. For public agencies, professional core values (Knott and Miller, 1987) can play an especially important role by creating beliefs and expectations about proper behavior (Brehm and Gates, 1993).

Organizational structure

Governments periodically restructure their executive departments. These changes often group formerly separate agencies together or separate formerly integrated departments into smaller agencies (Gulick, 1937; Knott and Miller, 1987). Do these organizational changes affect the policies chosen by the agencies?

Because formal theory is concerned with how individual preferences interact with institutional rules to produce policy choices, we can hypothesize that the organizational structure of the agency can influence how the employees' preferences are aggregated to form agency choices. For example, Hammond (1986: 159–61) shows how organizing an agency by geography can produce different policy choices than organizing by function; two different structures populated by individuals with the same preferences can thus produce two different policy choices. Indeed, it may be impossible to design a hierarchy that does not affect policy choices (Hammond and Thomas, 1989).

This logic of preference aggregation in different organizational structures applies to other processes within an organization. The flow of information is organized by the agency's structure in similar fashion to individual preferences. At the most general level, hierarchy groups activities, information and people into categories that are then grouped into subcategories and sub-subcategories (Hammond, 1993). Different groupings may classify information differently, and thus decision makers may learn different things from the aggregated information presented to them. How information is categorized and grouped may thus affect what the agency learns from its environment.

Incompatible design criteria

The public administration literature identifies several different criteria which organizations may be designed to achieve. Kaufman (1956) focuses on neutral competence, representation and executive leadership, while Rourke (1984) discusses accountability and efficiency. Both authors identify the incompatibilities that occur among these various criteria. Hammond and Miller (1985) demonstrate how a paradox identified by Sen (1970) about the incompatibility of criteria governing individual rights and social welfare can be applied to organizations as well. Adapting Sen's criteria, four desirable organizational principles can be identified, and Sen's theorem shows that while designs can be found which satisfy three of the criteria, no organizational design can be guaranteed to satisfy all four.

For example, decentralized organizations may produce Pareto suboptimal decisions (for example, because different division heads do not find it in their interest to cooperate with each other), or exhibit preference cycles (for example, because an agency cannot settle on a final choice but continuously revisits previously rejected options).

Other organizational designs may avoid inefficiency and preference cycles but at the cost of imposing restrictions on the views and beliefs of employees. Recall that early organization theorists such as Gulick (1937) emphasized the importance of a 'dominant idea' in an organization as a way to achieve coordination, and Herbert Kaufman (1960) showed how recruitment and socialization processes and administrative procedures in the Forest Service created common norms, beliefs and behaviors. Such uniformity of belief has some advantages in a stable environment, but may leave the agency fatally unable to adapt to a changing environment.

Yet another kind of organizational design – the imposition of centralized management – avoids Pareto suboptimality, preference cycles and the uniformity of belief, but the traditional organizational theory literature, as well as the more recent literature on management (for example, Miller, 1992), are full of discussions of the hazards of dictatorial management.

Unfortunately, Sen's theorem demonstrates that the risk of at least *one* of these kinds of organizational pathologies will always be present. The lesson is that organizational design consists of choosing which bad consequence one most wishes to avoid and which other bad consequences nonetheless will be acceptable.

EXTERNAL RELATIONS

One of the unique features of public administration is the number and variety of institutions which influence the policy making process. A government agency head must interact with legislative committees, the chief executive, cabinet departments, the courts, interest groups, contractors, regional offices and state and local governments (Wilson, 1989). Since these institutions possess legal authority or political influence over the agency's activities, dealing with the external environment is a critical dimension of public administration and public management (Bozeman and Straussman, 1990). A number of formal approaches to this critical aspect of public administration have been developed.

Relations with the legislature and the chief executive

An important debate in public administration focuses on whether government agencies exercise much influence over policy. One scholarly tradition argues that bureaucracy dominates policy making through expertise, secret information and control over implementation (Behn, 1991; Doig and Hargrove, 1987; Lewis, 1980; for an extensive illustration see Caro, 1975). A contrary literature suggests that the legislature is able to dominate the bureaucracy (Banks and Weingast, 1992; Lupia and McCubbins, 1994; McCubbins and Schwartz, 1984; McCubbins, Noll, and Weingast, 1987; Weingast and Moran, 1983).

Legislators can be seen as principals who have public managers as their agents, and this perspective has generated a substantial number of arguments about, and insights into, legislative–agency relationships. Consider the influence of the bureaucracy over public budgeting. Niskanen (1971, 1975) argued that public managers have a monopoly over information on the supply side of the budget, which he defined as the amount of spending required to carry out agency programs. He also argued that public managers know the demand side of the budget, which he defined as the preferences of legislators for spending on government programs. Public managers, he suggested, are able to use this combination of information to propose budget options in the budget process. The legislature finds itself in a weak position to evaluate these options because it has little information about the 'true supply' requirements of the budget; hence the legislature is forced to simply accept or reject (but not modify) public agency budget proposals. The public managers' monopoly over budget information gives them agenda control in the budget process (for an empirical example see Romer and Rosenthal, 1978).

However, since legislators have authority to pass statutes and otherwise oversee the agencies, legislators possess several means for structuring these relations. These can help prevent the agency from exercising agenda control. For example, legislators can require the reporting of information which reveals agency supply and so they can monitor agency behavior in ways not foreseen by the Niskanen models. These revised models (see, for example, Miller and Moe, 1983; Bendor et al., 1987) tell a very different story of who controls the budgetary process.

The different means by which legislators can structure these legislative–agency relationships (Fiorina, 1977, 1982) have received considerable attention. Two broad classes of tools have been identified as useful in controlling public agencies:

First, *ex ante controls*. These controls are imposed prior to program design to influence policy choice and implementation. Some of these controls involve hearings, information gathering and 'burden of proof' requirements, and other controls involve administrative procedures that 'stack the deck' in agency decision making by giving some groups the legal right to be involved in selecting and reviewing agency actions (McCubbins, 1985; McCubbins et al., 1987, 1989).

Second, *ex post controls*. These controls are imposed on an agency after the agency has actually implemented a program. The controls are centered on budget and statutory actions to reward or punish agencies for positive or negative performance (Weingast and Moran, 1983; McCubbins and Schwartz, 1984; Calvert et al., 1987).

Multiple principals: political equilibria and agency autonomy

While principal–agent theory has provided a framework for analyzing the relations between public agencies, the legislature and the chief executive, and has helped scholars understand the incentives inherent in various budgetary and procedural requirements used to control agencies, this literature has not dealt adequately with the effect of multiple principals on the autonomy of public managers. As it turns out, though, the fact that multiple institutions may oversee an agency has substantial implications for agency autonomy.

Consider some 'decisive coalition', which consists of the actors (for example, the members of the legislative body and any independent chief executive) who collectively have the authority to overturn agency policies and impose one of their own. A policy is in equilibrium if there exists no decisive coalition which can replace the policy

with a new one. Define the 'core' as the set of equilibrium policies. Two factors determine the size of any set of equilibrium policies. The first factor is the number of veto points in the policy making system (Tsebelis, 1995); a veto point is some institution with the authority to reject a proposal to change policy. An increase in the number of veto points can increase the size of the set of equilibrium policies. The second factor determining the size of the set of equilibrium policies is the extent of preference heterogeneity among the veto points. If the members of the institutional veto points hold similar preferences, then preference heterogeneity is small and the impact of the multiple veto points is indistinguishable from only a single veto point; a small set of equilibrium policies is the result. In contrast, if preference heterogeneity among the veto points is large, then a large set of equilibrium policies is the result. Illustrations of political equilibria in a policy making system are shown in Calvert et al. (1989), Ferejohn and Shipan (1990), Hammond and Knott (1996), Krehbiel (1998) and Knott and Hammond (2000).

Note that as long as the agency considers only policies that are in the core, the agency can change from policy to policy without fear that any new choice will be upset by some decisive coalition. It follows that the larger the core, the greater the autonomy for the agency: with a larger core, the agency can consider a larger number of policies which are safe from upset by a decisive coalition.

Whether a public manager prefers a larger core or a smaller one depends in part on where the core is located in relation to a manager's own policy preferences. A larger core may give the manager more decision autonomy, but the policy choices the manager makes will not satisfy all the critical actors in the agency's political environment. With a small core, the manager may have much less autonomy, but because the other actors are not very far apart on policy preferences, they will be less likely to fight with each other over what they want agency policy to be. Moreover, if the manager's most-preferred policy is located inside this small core (and so is close to what the other actors want), the manager may not suffer unduly from the lack of autonomy. Thus, political equilibrium analysis suggests that for the public manager there may be tradeoffs between autonomy, policy satisfaction and involvement in intense conflicts over policy (Knott and Hammond, 1999).

Political equilibrium analysis also has implications for strategies that public managers might use to achieve their ideal policy. One important strategy is persuasion. If a public manager can persuade one or more of the actors to change what they consider to be ideal policies to something closer to the manager's ideal policy, the shape of the core may change enough so that the manager's ideal policy is now within the core. Redefining the nature of the policy problem (via 'agenda setting' or 'issue framing' rhetorical techniques) may also change the dimensions of the core, thus altering its shape. Consequently, understanding the shape of the core and the relative strengths of the actors' policy preferences are critical aspects of how a manager should handle the agency's political environment (Knott and Hammond, 1999).

Interest groups

The contributions of formal theory to an understanding of the role of interest groups in public administration stem from Olson (1965), which dealt with the problem of collective action (see also Moe, 1988). Olson argued that the dispersion of interests across the country gives any one interest little incentive to lobby the government. He developed a theory to explain how some groups overcome this collective action problem. If the number of entities affected by a government policy is small and if the impact is large enough, they will be motivated to work together to change government policy. Olson's theory explains cheap bulk mail rates, milk price supports and sugar subsidies, among other similar special interest policies (Knott and Miller, 1987). The impact of these policies on these firms is large relative to their profits, and there are far fewer of them than there are citizens. Second, associations of citizens concerned about a policy will not be able to gain enough members because of the free-rider problem. However, if the civic associations provide 'selective benefits' to potential members, such as life insurance, magazines, or travel packages, citizens will join because of the value of the selective benefits they receive from the association.

The major implication for public administration is that organized interests tend to represent producers, whereas diffuse interests in society have greater difficulty engaging in collective action to influence agency decision making. When citizens do organize, the resulting associations will tend to be organizations that provide selective benefits to their members and consequently may not actually represent the members' policy preferences.

SOME COSTS AND SOME CRITICISMS OF FORMAL THEORY

The development of formal theories of public administration, like any other research strategy, has some costs (Hammond, 1996). What are some of these costs?

First, because the development of formal theories is often difficult, their scope of application is usually narrower than that of informal theories. Unfortunately, it seems that there is a tradeoff between clarity and rigor, on the one hand, and sensitivity to richness, context and nuance, on the other.

Second, formal theorizing requires that particular technical skills be developed, involving various kinds of mathematics or computer languages. The time and effort required to learn these techniques is time that cannot be spent on other research activities.

Third, due to formal theory's technical languages, the audience for its results is sometimes small. Nonetheless, it is possible for formal theorists to do more than they have to date to make their results accessible to a broader audience.

Aside from these undeniable costs, other kinds of criticisms are sometimes leveled against formal theory as well. For example, it is sometimes argued that formal theories have little connection to real-world politics. However, lack of interest in the real world is not an inevitable or even widespread trait of formal theorists. Indeed, most formal theorists would agree that formal theorizing should not take place in an empirical vacuum, since they would otherwise have little idea as to what institutions or processes are worth modeling in the first place.

It is also sometimes argued that formal theories 'oversimplify reality'. While this is a complex philosophical issue, we would emphasize that every useful theory *must* simplify reality. A theory that is as complex as reality has no scientific value; such a theory could not be tested because testable hypotheses could not be derived from it. So to be useful for scientific purposes, any theory must leave things out.

Just because a theory is formalized, however, does not mean it is a good theory. It can be a poor theory in a lot of ways and formalization will not improve it. The best test of whether something allegedly important has been left out may be an empirical one: how well does the 'overly simple' theory predict key aspects of the real world, or otherwise account for actual events? If a simple theory works well empirically, then important things may not have been left out.

Another common criticism (see, for example, Green and Shapiro, 1994) is that formal theories are not subjected to empirical testing frequently enough. We would agree that many authors working in this area (including ourselves!) have too often 'tested by anecdote', that is, by finding a plausible story that matches the model. Much remains to be done in the conduct of systematic tests. However, as more and more students of public administration gain facility with both formal theorizing and empirical research methods, this problem is slowly resolving itself.

Finally, it is sometimes claimed that formal theories, especially rational choice theories, embody a conservative political agenda. This claim has no merit: there is nothing about the enterprise of formal theory (or rational choice theory) that is generically either 'conservative' or 'liberal', and many formal theorists (including rational choice theorists) would not consider themselves political 'conservatives' at all. At its best, formal theorizing is simply part of the enterprise of improving the quality of our theories about the real world.

Formal theorizing will never completely replace informal theorizing, nor should it: to the extent that formal theories originate in various kinds of informal theories, reducing the production of informal theories would ultimately reduce the quality and relevance of the formal theories as well. Thus, we would argue that formal and informal theorizing, along with empirical testing, all improve each other and rely on each other, and neglecting any of them would only serve to impoverish all of them.

CONCLUSION

Formal theory has contributed to public administration through introducing a formal logic which helps develop more rigorous theories of administrative institutions and behavior. It has contributed to our understanding of many of the core issues in public administration: incentive systems, teams, hierarchy, management, delegation of authority and relations between the legislature and agencies. While these theories have sometimes served to reinforce conventional understandings, they have also sometimes generated new, interesting and useful insights into the nature of public administration.

REFERENCES

Akerlof, George A. (1970) 'The Market for "Lemons": Quality Uncertainty and the Market Mechanism', *Quarterly Journal of Economics*, 84: 488–500.

Alchian, Armen A. and Demsetz, Harold (1972) 'Production, Information Costs, and the Economics of Organization', *American Economic Review*, 62: 777–95.

Arrow, Kenneth J. (1974) *The Limits of Organization*. New York: Norton.

Axelrod, Robert (1984) *The Evolution of Cooperation*. New York: Basic Books.

Banks, Jeffrey S. and Weingast, Barry (1992) 'The Political Control of Bureaucracies under Asymmetric Information', *American Journal of Political Science*, 36: 509–24.

Barnard, Chester (1938) *The Functions of the Executive*. Cambridge, MA: Harvard University Press.

Behn, Robert (1991) *Leadership Counts: Lessons for Public Managers from the Massachusetts Welfare, Training, and Employment Program*. Cambridge, MA: Harvard University Press.

Bendor, Jonathan (1985) *Parallel Systems: Redundancy in Government*. Berkeley, CA: University of California Press.

Bendor, Jonathan (1988) 'Formal Models of Bureaucracy', *British Journal of Political Science*, 18: 353–95.

Bendor, Jonathan, Glazer, Amihai and Hammond, Thomas H. (2001) 'Theories of Delegation', *Annual Review of Political Science*, 4: 235-69.

Bendor, Jonathan, Taylor Serge and Van Gaalen, Roland (1987) 'Politicians, Bureaucrats, and Asymmetric Information', *American Journal of Political Science*, 31: 796–828.

Bozeman, Barry and Straussman, Jeffrey D. (1990) *Public Management Strategies*. San Francisco: Jossey–Bass.

Brehm, John and Gates, Scott (1993) 'Donut Shops and Speed Traps: Evaluating Models of Supervision on Police Behavior', *American Journal of Political Science*, 37 (2): 555–81.

Calvert, Randall L., McCubbins, Matthew D. and Weingast, Barry R. (1989) 'A Theory of Political Control and Agency Discretion', *American Journal of Political Science*, 33: 588–611.

Calvert, Randall L., Moran, Mark J. and Weingast, Barry R. (1987) 'Congressional Influence over Policymaking: The Case of the FTC', in Mathew McCubbins and Terry Sullivan (eds), *Congress: Structure and Policy*. New York: Cambridge University Press.

Caro, Robert (1975) *The Power Broker: Robert Moses and the Fall of New York*. New York: Vintage Books.

Coase, Ronald (1937) 'The Nature of the Firm', *Economica*, 4: 386–405.

Doig, Jameson W. and Hargrove, Erwin C. (eds) (1987) *Leadership and Innovation: A Biographical Perspective on Entrepreneurs in Government*. Baltimore, MD: Johns Hopkins University Press.

Epstein, David and O'Halloran, Sharyn (1999) *Delegating Powers: A Transaction Cost Politics Approach to Policy Making under Separate Powers*. New York: Cambridge University Press.

Ferejohn, John A. and Shipan, Charles (1990) 'Congressional Influence on Bureaucracy', *Journal of Law, Economics and Organization*, 6: 1–27.

Fiorina, Morris P. (1977) *Congress: The Keystone of the Washington Establishment*. New Haven, CT: Yale University Press.

Fiorina, Morris P. (1982) 'Legislative Choice of Regulatory Forms: Legal Process or Administrative Process?', *Public Choice*, 39: 33–66.

Gilligan, Thomas and Krehbiel, Keith (1989) 'Asymmetric Information and Legislative Rules with a Heterogeneous Committee', *American Journal of Political Science*, 33: 459–90.

Green, Donald P. and Shapiro, Ian (1994) *Pathologies of Rational Choice Theory: A Critique of Applications in Political Science*. New Haven, CT: Yale University Press.

Greenwald, B. and Stiglitz, J.E. (1986) 'Externalities in Economies with Imperfect Information and Incomplete Markets', *Quarterly Journal of Economics*, 101 (2).

Gulick, Luther (1937) 'Notes on the Theory of Organization', in Luther Gulick and Lyndall Urwick (eds), *Papers on the Science of Administration*. New York: Institute of Public Administration, Columbia University.

Hammond, Thomas H. (1986) 'Agenda Control, Organizational Structure, and Bureaucratic Politics', *American Journal of Political Science*, 30: 397–420.

Hammond, Thomas H. (1993) 'Toward a General Theory of Hierarchy: Books, Bureaucrats, Basketball Tournaments, and the Administrative Structure of the National-State', *Journal of Public Administration Research and Theory*, 3: 120–45.

Hammond, Thomas H. (1996) 'Formal Theory and the Institutions of Governance', *Governance*, 9: 107–85.

Hammond, Thomas H. and Knott, Jack H. (1996) 'Who Controls the Bureaucracy?: Presidential Power, Congressional Dominance, Legal Constraints, and Bureaucratic Autonomy in a Model of Multi-institutional Policymaking', *Journal of Law, Economics, and Organization*, 12: 121–68.

Hammond, Thomas H. and Miller, Gary J. (1985) 'A Social Choice Perspective on Authority and Expertise in Bureaucracy', *American Journal of Political Science*, 29: 611–38.

Hammond, Thomas H. and Thomas, Paul A. (1989) 'The Impossibility of a Neutral Hierarchy', *Journal of Law, Economics and Organization*, 5: 155–84.

Hardin, Garrett (1968) 'The Tragedy of the Commons', *Science*, 162: 1243–8.

Heimann, C.F. Larry (1997) 'Understanding the *Challenger* Disaster: Organizational Structure and the Design of Reliable Systems', *American Political Science Review*, 87: 421–35.

Holmstrom, Bengt R. (1982) 'Moral Hazard in Teams', *Bell Journal of Economics*, 13: 324–40.

Kaufman, Herbert (1956) 'Emerging Conflicts in the Doctrines of Public Administration', *American Political Science Review*, 50: 1057–73.

Kaufman, Herbert (1960) *The Forest Ranger: A Study in Administrative Behavior*. Baltimore, MD: Johns Hopkins University Press.

Knott, Jack H. (1993) 'Comparing Public and Private Management: Cooperative Effort and Principal–Agent Relationships', *Journal of Public Administration Research and Theory*, 3: 92–119.

Knott, Jack H. and Hammond, Thomas H. (1999) 'Public Management, Administrative Leadership, and Policy Change', in Jeffrey L. Brudney, Lawrence O'Toole and Hal G. Rainey (eds), *Advancing Public Management: New Developments in Theory, Methods, and Practice*. Washington, DC: Georgetown University Press.

Knott, Jack H. and Hammond, Thomas H. (2000) 'Congressional Committees and Policy Change: Explaining Legislative Outcomes in the Deregulation of Trucking, Airlines, Banking and Telecommunications', in Carolyn J. Heinrich and Lawrence E. Lynn, Jr (eds), *Governance and Performance: New Perspectives*. Washington, DC: Georgetown University Press.

Knott, Jack H. and Miller, Gary J. (1987) *Reforming Bureaucracy: The Politics of Institutional Choice*. Englewood Cliffs, NJ: Prentice–Hall.

Krehbiel, Keith (1998) *Pivotal Politics: A Theory of U.S. Lawmaking*. Chicago: University of Chicago Press.

Landau, Martin (1969) 'Redundancy, Rationality, and the Problem of Duplication and Overlap', *Public Administration Review*, 29: 346–58.

Lewis, Eugene (1980) *Public Entrepreneurship: Toward a Theory of Bureaucratic Political Power – The Organizational Lives of Hyman Rickover, J. Edgar Hoover, and Robert Moses*. Bloomington, IN: Indiana University Press.

Lupia, Arthur and McCubbins, Mathew D. (1994) 'Learning from Oversight: Fire Alarms and Police Patrols Reconstructed', *Journal of Law, Economics and Organization*, 10: 96–125.

McCubbins, Mathew D. (1985) 'The Legislative Design of Regulatory Structure', *American Journal of Political Science*, 29: 721–48.

McCubbins, Matthew and Schwartz, Thomas (1984) 'Congressional Oversight Overlooked: Police Patrols Versus Fire Alarms', *American Journal of Political Science*, 28: 165–79.

McCubbins, Matthew, Noll, Roger G. and Weingast, Barry R. (1987) 'Administrative Procedures as Instruments of Political Control', *Journal of Law, Economics and Organization*, 3: 243–77.

McCubbins, Matthew D., Noll, Roger G. and Weingast, Barry R. (1989) 'Structure and Process, Politics and Policy: Administrative Arrangements and the Political Control of Agencies', *Virginia Law Review*, 75: 431–99.

Merton, Robert (1940) 'Bureaucratic Structure and Personality', *Social Forces*, 17: 560–8.

Miller, Gary J. (1992) *Managerial Dilemmas: The Political Economy of Hierarchy*. New York: Cambridge University Press.

Miller, Gary J. and Hammond, Thomas H. (1994) 'Why Politics is More Fundamental than Economics: Incentive-Compatible Mechanisms Are Not Credible', *Public Choice*, 6: 5–26.

Miller, Gary J. and Moe, Terry M. (1983) 'Bureaucrats, Legislators, and the Size of Government', *American Political Science Review*, 77: 297–322.

Moe, Terry M. (1984) 'The New Economics of Organization', *American Journal of Political Science*, 28: 739–77.

Moe, Terry M. (1988) *The Organization of Interests*. Chicago: University of Chicago Press.

Niskanen, William A. (1971) *Bureaucracy and Representative Government*. Chicago: Aldine.

Niskanen, William A. (1975) 'Bureaucrats and Politicians', *Journal of Law and Economics*, 18: 617–44.

North, Douglass C. (1990) *Institutions, Institutional Change and Economic Performance*. New York: Cambridge University Press.

Olson, Mancur (1965) *The Logic of Collective Action*. Cambridge, MA: Harvard University Press.

Ostrom, Elinor (1999) 'Coping with Tragedies of the Commons', *Annual Review of Political Science*, 2: 493–535.

Peters, Thomas J. and Waterman, Robert H. (1982) *In Search of Excellence: Lessons from America's Best Run Companies*. New York: Harper and Row.

Romer, Thomas and Rosenthal, Howard (1978) 'Political Resource Allocation, Controlled Agendas, and the Status Quo', *Public Choice*, 33: 27–43.

Rourke, Francis E. (1984) *Bureaucracy, Politics, and Public Policy*, 3rd edn. Boston, MA: Little, Brown.

Sen, Amartya (1970) 'The Impossibility of a Paretian Liberal', *Journal of Political Economy*, 78: 152–7.

Tsebelis, George (1995) 'Decision Making in Political Systems: Veto Players in Presidentialism, Parliamentarianism, Multicameralism, and Multipartyism', *British Journal of Political Science*, 25: 289–326.

Weingast, Barry R. and Moran, Mark J. (1983) 'Bureaucratic Discretion or Congressional Control?: Regulatory Policy Making by the Federal Trade Commission', *Journal of Political Economy*, 91: 765–800.

Wilson, James Q. (1989) *Bureaucracy: What Government Agencies Do and Why They Do It*. New York: Basic Books.

Wolf, Charles, Jr (1975) 'A Theory of Non-Market Failure', *The Public Interest*, 55: 114–33.

12

Environmental Perspectives
on Public Institutions

Karen M. Hult

'Beware', Charles Perrow warned, of 'unspecified "environments"' (Perrow, 1986: 278). His primary concern was that analysts should not ignore powerful actors and interests that might manipulate organizations or their members. More sharply delimited environments also are critical to myriad others, including public administration scholars seeking fuller understanding of the activities, evolution and impact of government organizations, and agency officials hoping to improve, or at least maintain, funding, performance or constituency support.

As in organization theory more generally, conceptions of organizational (and institutional) environments in public administration have been 'undergoing rapid and varied transformations' (Scott, 1995: 44). This chapter traces some of this development, directing particular attention to views of environmental dynamics drawn from theories of contingency, resource dependence, population ecology and institutionalism. Of interest throughout are the applicability of such ideas to *public* organizations, policies and decision making, especially in the more volatile settings of the past thirty years.

AN ANALYTICAL PRELUDE

Exploring the relations between 'environments' and 'public institutions' opens a Pandora's box of issues. Among those that are salient to the discussion here are the definitions of the two primary concepts, the levels of analysis at which they are examined and the assumptions made about environmental–organizational (or 'institutional') relationships and about change.

Definitions

Like organization theorists, many public administration scholars have 'shift[ed] from a focus on generalized attributes of environments to more specific interorganizational connections' (Scott, 1995: 45). Meanwhile, distinguishing between 'task' (or 'technical') and 'institutional' environments has become more common. The former, introduced by Dill (1958), focuses on environments as 'stocks of resources or sources of technical information; as foci of exchange relations ...' (Scott, 1995: 45); such a conception also encompasses other actors (both collective and individual) that affect the focal organization (Thompson, 1967: 28). Highlighting the task environment typically directs attention to conditions of external uncertainty, complexity and dependence. 'Institutional' environments 'are characterized by the elaboration of rules and requirements to which individual organizations must conform if they are to receive support and legitimacy ...' (Scott and Meyer, 1983: 140). Some analysts contend that institutional environments are especially critical when studying governmental organizations, which are 'subject to special pressures to conform to wider social understandings' of, for example, appropriate structuring and activities (Marsden et al., 1996: 60–1).

If treatment of the 'environment' has become more explicit and specific, the same cannot be said for the concept 'institution'. It routinely is used in numerous, not always consistent ways – for example, to refer to any formal organization, to a particular type of organization (Selznick, 1949), to 'governance or rules systems' ('rational choice theorists', in Scott, 2001: 32) and to 'formal structures and informal rules and procedures that structure conduct' (Thelen and Steinmo, 1992: 2).[1] Here, unless otherwise noted, W. Richard Scott's 'omnibus conception of institutions' (2001: 48) grounds discussion. It views institutions as 'social structures that have attained a high degree of resilience … [and] are composed of cultural-cognitive, normative, and regulative elements that … provide stability and meaning to social life.'

The last concept to be clarified is 'public'. Again, variations in usage emerge. Perhaps most common is to concentrate on 'ownership', that is, on formal governmental status. Alternatively, one can contend that 'all organizations are public', and explore the degree of 'publicness' (Bozeman, 1987). Below, the 'core' (or sector) and the 'dimensional' conceptions of publicness (Bozeman and Bretschneider, 1994) are included. Clearly, empirical support exists for both views (Beck Jørgensen et al., 1998; Bozeman and Bretschneider, 1994). Perhaps even more important, the rising incidence of partnerships, contracting and other arrangements linking governmental, for-profit and nonprofit actors – as well as the associated praise and criticism – suggest that the empirical and the normative significance of the two vantage points are growing more salient.

Levels of analysis

In the abstract, most public administration and organization scholars probably see the 'environment as a nested box problem; inside each box is a smaller box whose dimensions are constrained by the larger box' (Perrow, 1986: 192). Researchers have examined 'environments' at multiple levels of analysis, ranging from the global, sectoral, organizational field and population to the organizational and sub-organizational levels. Here, government organizations and their sub-units typically will be the 'targets' for potential environmental influences, but other possible foci include individuals, interorganizational networks and policy outcomes.

Assumptions

Finally, it appears important to highlight two key assumptions. First is whether organizations are seen as *adapting* to environmental influences or as being *selected* by the environment. Adaptive views are more common, although theories differ over the nature of the 'fit' they anticipate between environmental influence and

organizational response; perspectives with consonance or congruence assumptions expect closer matches than do those that assume 'equifinality'.[2] Approaches stressing adaptation typically focus at the organizational set level of analysis, while those emphasizing selection often work at the population level.

Second, and relatedly, theories differ in their 'locus of causality' (Pfeffer, 1997: 5). Sometimes referred to as the 'structure–agency problem', concern focuses on the sources or 'drivers' of organizational change, stability and activities. Not surprisingly many perspectives that emphasize adaptation tend to pay considerable attention to influences such as managerial skill and strategy or to internal age and race distributions, concerns stressed far less by those assuming stronger selection pressures.[3] Increasingly, analysts treat environmental, institutional and organizational influences as reciprocal and intertwined instead of unidirectional. Moreover, many view environments as 'enacted' by those within organizations.[4] In such situations, the very notion of cause-and-effect is likely to lose significance.

ORGANIZATION THEORY AND ENVIRONMENTAL RELATIONS

Scholars and practitioners of public administration (PA) frequently look to organization theory for guidance and insight. As helpful as those efforts can be, caution in application is warranted. Since Dwight Waldo (1961, 1978) compared organization theorists to the hapless blind folk grasping at an elephant, the field has grown ever more diverse.[5] Although this broadens the number of tools for those in PA to add to their analytical toolboxes, it can complicate both testing and communication across varying approaches.

Even more important, particularly for the 'Anglo-Saxon public administration scholars [who] typically use generic organization theory', such theory has 'strong roots in empirical studies of private firms' (Beck Jørgensen et al., 1998: 500). Nonetheless, little support exists for looking solely at governmental or only at for-profit organizations. Not only is there substantial 'public sector heterogeneity' in, for example, goals, responsibilities and openness to 'political' influences (Beck Jørgensen et al., 1998), but the boundaries between the sectors are increasingly blurred (Berman and West, 1998; Kalleberg et al., 1996; Rhodes, 1996).

Among the organization theoretic approaches PA scholars frequently rely on are contingency, resource dependence, population ecology and institutional perspectives. Although scarcely an exhaustive list, these perspectives differ on many of the dimensions delineated earlier.[6]

Contingency theories

Studies of diverse organizational arenas continue to produce findings that seem to be well captured by what can be termed *contingency* perspectives (Durant, 1998; Pfeffer, 1997).[7] That is, structuring, strategic choice, decision making and other activities and outcomes appear to vary with the environments (for example, the partisan, economic, or cultural contexts) in which organizational units are embedded or which they help enact.

Contingency theorizing, of course, has a relatively long history in organization studies, conventionally being traced back to the work of Burns and Stalker (1961), Lawrence and Lorsch (1967) and Woodward (1965). Flowing from the insight that organizations are 'open systems' (Katz and Kahn, 1966), contingency theorists explore the effects of aspects of environments on organizations. Usually, it is elements of the task environment (such as the levels of uncertainty, complexity or volatility) that receive attention. Typically, too, attention focuses on the organization set, and the unit of analysis is the organization or its sub-units.

Structural contingencies

A common variant is *structural* contingency theory, which proposes that organizational structuring adapts to fit, among other influences, environmental demands and conditions (for example, Donaldson, 2001; Pennings, 1992). When studying decision making in governmental organizations, for example, Hult and Walcott (1990) suggest that certain kinds of structures (recurring patterns of relations within or between organizations or organizational units) would emerge and stabilize to cope with (perceived) goal and technical uncertainty, controversy or consensus/certainty in particular decision settings. Testing these expectations (Walcott and Hult, 1995) by examining the decision processes in the White House Office in the Hoover through the Johnson presidencies, yielded a general pattern of 'congruence'.

Meanwhile, scholars focusing on 'high reliability organizations' (such as air traffic control systems and space shuttles) contend that structuring and decision processes vary with environmental demand. Under conditions of 'low and moderate demand ... when the task structure is complex and well known', authority is centralized and hierarchical and there is a clear division of labor. As demand rises, however, 'authority patterns shift to a basis of functional skill. Collegial authority patterns overlay bureaucratic ones ...' (LaPorte and Consolini, 1998: 849). These sorts of organizations may be 'harbingers of adaptive organizational forms for an increasingly complex environment' (Weick et al., 1999: 82).

Other work concentrates on organizational form and frequently is more prescriptive. Agranoff and McGuire (1998: 81) contend, for example, that since local 'economic development policy is designed and implemented under conditions of ambiguity and uncertainty,' it 'requir[es] network forms of organization rather than the traditional rational means of control that characterizes bureaucracies'. Drawing on the ideas of chaos theory (as articulated by Kiel, 1994), Neumann (1997: 96) adds 'great environmental turbulence' to the mix of conditions in most 'information environments'; he advises organizations to 'match the external complexity with ... internal complexity of [their] own'.

Performance contingencies

A second type of contingency theorizing shifts attention to the impact of the environment on *performance*. Much of this work also stresses activities of organizations embedded in particular, often policy-specific contexts (John and Cole, 2000). Christensen and Pallesen (2001: 197), for instance, report that the institutional 'microsettings' (for example, 'appropriations procedures and co-determination provisions in the public sector labor market') influenced the impact of several Danish reorganizations.

Others have explored the nature of implementation under differing environmental conditions. Meyers et al. (2001) found that the extent of goal congruence between local welfare organizations and US state-level agencies was positively related to the clarity and stability of policy directives and negatively linked to the number of implementing organizations, an influence heightened as integration declined. Meanwhile, Peters (2000: 42) usefully moves to the network level of analysis and argues that the 'probable effectiveness of networks in implementation' may be related to both the extent of network integration and, of interest here, the degree to which the focal network is influenced by other networks.

Strategic contingencies

A third strand of contingency reasoning looks for environmental effects on *strategy*. Nutt and Backoff (1995: 189), for example, present a 'framework in which types of strategies for public and third-sector organizations are matched to environments that are determined by the need for action and responsiveness'. The 'external' aspects of environments to which they direct attention include both policy (for example, new legislation) and electoral politics (for example, change in the party in power); the relevant 'authority networks' encompass key stakeholders (Nutt and Backoff, 1995: 210). Agency type and policy area are likely to be especially important when 'strategy' involves the selection of particular policy tools (for example, Peters and van Nispen, 1998: 2). If important external actors also select strategies for dealing with specific organizations, Waterman and Meier (1998) hypothesize that the nature of the relations between political 'principals' (such as ministers, legislative committees) and bureaucratic 'agents' may well vary with the degree of information symmetry and the level of goal conflict in their shared environment.

Contingency theorizing: tentative conclusions

Additional probing of contingency perspectives may well permit not only more careful empirical mapping of organizational and institutional terrains but also more systematic testing of the boundaries of particular theories. Clearly, such a strategy is not costless. One frequent objection is that contingency-based perspectives are inelegant, overly complicated. Certainly, problems like overdetermination, multi-collinearity and inclusion of 'irrelevant' variables need to be addressed. Yet, if one joins King, Keohane and Verba (1994: 30) in seeing parsimony as a 'judgment, or even assumption, about the nature of the world' rather than as a standard for evaluating theories, then one can contend that contingency perspectives may help in more usefully capturing the complexity and dynamics of 'real world' phenomena.

Even some who accept the general value of contingency approaches, however, debate the merit of restricting attention to particular policy areas.[8] Agranoff and McGuire argue, for example: 'Research that examines how and why networks emerge within the context of particular policy and program areas is necessary to better understand what can be expected from networks forms of governance and how to evaluate the

solutions that emerge from such forms' (2001: 322; cf. Scharpf, 2000). Yet others object, pointing to the interplay among issues, values and advocates across policy arenas and over time (Hood, 1996; LeGalès, 2001).

Resource dependence

Among the most crucial features of organizational (as well as network and other) environments are 'resources' (for example, information, statutory mandates). Resource dependence theorists often work at the organizational set level of analysis, exploring a specific organization's relations with actors in its (typically task) environment and examining resource exchanges and varying levels and types of interdependencies. Pfeffer and Salancik (1978), for example, found that organizational (or sub-unit) dependence on other organizations rose as the focal unit grew in size and visibility, as the needed resource became more critical, as the range of alternate suppliers declined, and as the provider's discretion over the resource mounted. At the same time, their studies demonstrate that in many circumstances organizations were able to manage dependencies.

Such adaptive capacity – although varying over time and space – makes the resource dependence view useful for identifying many of the 'strategies … employed by organizations to change and [adjust] to the environment' (Scott, 1998: 117). It appears, if only implicitly, in many discussions of strategic decision making (Pfeffer, 1981), public management (Heymann, 1987), 'policy partnering' (Lovrich, 2000) and 'network management' (Klijn et al., 1995).[9] Frequently, but not always explicitly, resource dependence studies may be cast in contingency terms.

Some explore resource dependence at higher levels of analysis. Applying the view to 'developing relations between local authorities and local non-elected public service agencies in England and Wales', Painter et al. (1997) argue, for instance, that 'organizational networks are … the appropriate unit of analysis when groups or clusters of organizations are tied together by their need to use and influence each other's resources, that is, where there are structures of resource-dependency' (1997: 225, 227). Others have used 'power dependence' models to examine the internal dynamics of central governments (Rhodes and Dunleavy, 1995; Smith, 1994).[10] Meanwhile, pointing to possible links between resource dependence and contingency perspectives, Matland (1995: 160) hypothesizes that (financial) resources may be most critical to implementation outcomes when environmental conflict and ambiguity are low.

In general, the accounts of individual, organizational and network dynamics that resource dependence models generate provide useful retrospectives of particular events (such as Margaret Thatcher's resignation; Smith, 1994), implementation outcomes (smallpox eradication; Matland, 1995) and network evolution (center–local relations; Rhodes, 1996). Even so, despite relatively high 'face validity,' many resource-based narratives risk becoming little more than *post hoc* reconstructions yielding few generalizations. The notion of 'resource' is often ill defined, applied to environmental features ranging from money to legitimacy. Moreover, as the diversity of resources and the complexity of relevant environments increase, the approach becomes cumbersome and hard to apply. As a 'meso-level' tool, it may have difficulty capturing micro and macro processes of change (Stoker, 1995: 109). Nonetheless, it does direct attention to the relations and the dimensions of dependence and interdependence among actors at multiple levels of analysis.

Population ecology

In rather sharp contrast, the population (or organizational) ecology approach spotlights the population level of analysis.[11] It emphasizes environmental selection rather than organizational adaptation; the role of 'chance' often receives special attention (Kaufman, 1985: ch. 4). Perspectives grounded in population ecology investigate the influence of the task and, increasingly, the institutional environments on the emergence of new organizations and organization forms, the death rates of organizations and organization forms, and the speed of change in organization forms (Singh and Lumsden, 1990: 162).

Although population ecology has produced considerable empirical research, most researchers have studied for-profit organizations such as newspapers and semiconductor firms. Even so, Canadian worker cooperatives (Staber, 1989), volunteer social service organizations (Tucker et al., 1990), healthcare organizations (Ruef, 2000) and units within US national and state executives (Meyer et al., 1985; Peters and Hogwood, 1991) also have received attention.

One of the most sustained recent research programs involving ideas drawn from population ecology, and one with potential relevance to those in public administration, is that of political scientists Gray and Lowery. They focus on state 'interest communities' in the United States.

Among their findings is that the diversity of interest systems 'ultimately depends on how environmental forces determine the carrying capacities of political systems within each interest guild [type of interest group]' (Lowery and Gray, 1998b: 940). The authors note as well that rising density of interest systems (characteristic of, for example, banking and public education) 'promotes higher rates of direct lobbying both because of its competitive exclusion consequences and because it encourages the use of multiple signal channels to communicate messages to government officials' (Lowery and Gray, 1998a: 251). They caution, however, that 'population characteristics of density and diversity do not bear in an obvious manner on policy outcomes'. More work needs to focus on 'specific interests at specific times, in specific places …' (Gray and Lowery, 1996: 241). The extent and nature of the influences of guilds like those in public education and local government, and the significance in other national contexts, appear to be promising places to begin.

Despite its relatively infrequent use in studying governmental organizations, population ecology may continue to hold promise for application to a variety of 'species' within the governmental, for-profit and nonprofit sectors. Among the subjects of interest might be comparisons across sectors or among governmental jurisdictions of units within similar 'niches' (Peters and Hogwood, 1991).

Institutional theories

To this point, the influences of the task environment have received much of the attention. By the 1980s, however, scholars relying on all three of the organization theoretical approaches just discussed began devoting greater emphasis to 'institutional' concerns. Although their uses and foci varied, many organization theorists broadened their conceptions of the environment to 'include symbolic elements' (Scott, 1995: 45) and started to pay systematic attention to the social, cultural and political aspects – not just the economic features – of environments. Some compared the technical and institutional environments to the two faces of Janus (Garud and Kumaraswamy, 1995), while another observed that 'even the social organization of technical practices is institutionally shaped' (Karnoe, 1995: 243). More generally, diverse versions of 'new institutionalism' swept through the disciplines of economics, political science and sociology, informing work in both public administration and business management.

Most forms of institutionalism highlight *legitimacy*. Legitimacy can be conceived as a 'generalized perception or assumption' that actions (or inaction) are 'desirable, proper, or appropriate within some socially constructed system of norms, values, beliefs, [rules], and definitions' (Suchman, 1995: 574). Although traditional resource-dependence models might include legitimacy as simply another resource, from the vantage point of institutional approaches it is 'a condition reflecting perceived consonance with relevant rules and laws, normative support, or alignment with cultural-cognitive frameworks' (Scott, 2001: 59).

'Institutional environments'?

Some variation, however, persists in treatments of 'institutional environments'. To an extent, the differences can be traced to disciplinary emphases. Referencing Selznick (1948), for instance, sociologist John J. Beggs views the 'institutional environment' as 'the institutional rules and norms of society' (1995: 613). Economists tend to see 'the institutional environment as created by entities such as markets and political systems' and reflecting the 'rules of the game' (Peters, 1999: 106). Even so, virtually all acknowledge the significance of rules (formal and informal) in discussions of institutions (Scharpf, 1997: 40).

At the same time, many appear to avoid the term 'institutional environment' altogether, referring instead to institutional 'settings' or 'conditions', or simply to 'institutions'. In part, this may reflect the ambiguous and multi-faceted nature of the concepts 'institution' and 'environment'. Yet the seeming avoidance also may highlight something about the analytical status of institutions and institutional influences. Scharpf notes, for instance, that in 'actor-centered institutionalism':

> 'institutional setting' does not have the status of a theoretically defined set of variables that could be systematized and operationalized to serve as explanatory factors in empirical research. Rather, we use it as a shorthand term to describe the most important influences on those factors that in fact drive our explanations – namely actors with their orientations and capabilities, actor constellations, and modes of interaction. (1997: 39)

In this view, institutions are critical to explaining which actors participate in policy making, in what sorts of ways, pursuing which goals and values. Meanwhile, actors socially construct these institutions; actors' policy decisions (and non-decisions), ideological orientations and preferences both shape and reflect institutions (see too Scott et al., 2000: 20ff.).

For most institutionalists, the result is a complex dynamic likely to vary over both time and space. More than minimally effective performance (presumably in competition with other organizations for scarce resources) is critical to organizational survival and prosperity; crucial as well is the capacity to become isomorphic with the relevant institutional environment(s) (Meyer and Rowan, 1977).

Institutional components

One way to distinguish among institutional theories is to probe the aspects of institutions that each highlights. Scott's (2001) framework includes three 'pillars'. The regulative pillar focuses on 'rule-setting, monitoring, and sanctioning activities'; rules, laws and sanctions signal its existence. The 'primary mechanism of control' involves coercion, which typically is legally sanctioned. Second, the 'normative' pillar emphasizes values and norms, which are 'both internalized and imposed by others' and can constrain and empower action. It can be indicated by, for example, professional licensing or organizational accreditation. Third, the 'cultural-cognitive' pillar 'stresses the central role played by the socially mediated construction of a common frame of meaning'. Evidence of common beliefs, orienting frames, or communication 'scripts' suggests this facet of institutions (Scott, 2001: 52–8).

Clearly, there can be considerable overlap and interplay among the pillars, and most studies grounded in institutional theories acknowledge the existence of all three. Nonetheless, particular approaches stress different mixes of institutional elements. For instance, those based in 'rational-choice institutionalism' (for example, Scharpf, 1997) typically focus on the regulative pillar, examining a variety of rules, incentives and sanctions.[12] By comparison, work grounded in 'sociological' (or 'normative') institutionalism (March and Olsen, 1989; Powell and DiMaggio, 1991) devotes more attention to normative and cultural-cognitive elements.[13] Edelman and Suchman (1997: 482), for example, describe a 'normative cultural' perspective that 'sees organizations as cultural rule-followers and sees the law [or 'legal environment'] as a system of moral principles, scripted roles, and sacred symbols. Thus, organizations look to the law for normative and cognitive guidance.' Employing these sorts of distinctions provides at least a crude way of organizing relevant scholarly work.

Regulative pillars

In an environment emphasizing the regulative pillar, 'institutional rules [are] understood as external constraints and incentives structuring the purposeful choices of self-interested rational actors' (Scharpf, 2000: 770). These rules become crucial parts of the environments (or 'institutional settings') for a variety of actors, with significant implications for governance.

The state issues most of these rules, although legal enforcement often is less important than actually operating in the 'shadow of the state' or the courts (both national and international). Examples of such rules include those delineating the extent of central bank independence and the nature of a senior career service. In addition, scholars continue to explore the apparent effects of electoral systems on policy performance (for example, Anderson, 2001).

Institutional factors also may override other influences. Examining the implementation of the EU's Packaging and Packaging Waste Directive, Haverland (2000: 83, 100) found that the country with the 'greatest misfit' between European provisions and national rules and practices – the United Kingdom – adapted more successfully than Germany, 'which only needed incremental adjustments'. Institutional rules – the number of veto points – evidently 'shaped the timing and the quality of implementation'. Meanwhile, Kelemen's study of environmental regulation in the European Union, Canada, the United States and Australia led him to conclude: 'the structure of the EU provides for a high fragmentation of power ... [A]s a fragmented power system, the EU is likely to head down the US path' of 'regulation characterized by detailed non-discretionary rules and a litigious approach to enforcement' (2000: 133, 135).

At a lower level of analysis (metropolitan areas), Klijn (2001) examines two local housing networks in the Netherlands. He stresses the 'cognitive aspects of rules' in structuring the 'meanings and creat[ing] the cognitive frames through which reality is viewed' as well as the importance of the prevailing 'social context' (2001: 136).

Normative and cultural-cognitive pillars

As insightful as examination of the regulative pillar may be, the two additional elements of institutions are associated with 'a more expansive view' of institutional environments, seeing them 'not just as a strategic context but as a set of shared understandings that affect the way problems are perceived and solutions are sought' (Thelen, 1999: 371). Organizations exist and operate amidst 'norms of appropriateness, rules, and the elaboration of meaning' (March and Olsen, 1989: 171). For instance, Marsh, et al. (2000: 469) paint senior civil servants as 'constrained by the political and social context in which they operate..., by the broader civil service culture, and by their construction of each of these...' Lægreid (2000: 879) adds 'international administrative doctrines' to 'national political-administrative culture and polity' in explaining the differences between the contract systems for top civil servants in New Zealand and Norway.[14]

Scholars working in this stream explore the influences of multiple aspects of institutions. Radaelli (2000) expects that normative and mimetic influences will be crucial in easing the policy transfer of many EU initiatives. The former may be induced by 'professionalization ... in those policymaking processes dominated by cognitive resources, expertise, and even technocratic aspects ...' (pp. 28-9). Mimetism (a mechanism of the cultural-cognitive pillar) may flow from imitating organizations within particular countries that are 'perceived to be more legitimate or more successful' (p. 28). Focused at the organizational field level, cross-national research (Arum, 2000) on schools finds school-level practices as being structured by coercive (for example, government regulations, court decisions), normative (professional associations, education schools) and mimetic (international baccalaureate degrees, vocational programs) influences.

Institutional environments: tentative conclusions

It is difficult to overestimate the contributions of exploring 'institutional' influences to an understanding of policy processes and organizational and network dynamics. 'Some common problems of governing – implementation, forming governments, and making effective decisions – [pop] up whenever we begin to think and write about institutions' (Peters, 1999: 150). A 'new awareness of the importance of history and of process' among institutional scholars has focused attention on the possible effects of changing contexts over both space and time (Scott, 2001: 207–8).

Still, numerous challenges remain. Institutionalists and their critics alike call for clearer and more consistent use of concepts as well as for better indicators and more testable hypotheses. Others hope that scholars will continue to engage in constructive dialogue about varying 'new institutionalisms' (Peters, 1999). Perhaps most important from the perspective of public administration, institutional analyses may well enrich understanding of the sources and limits of the power and persuasiveness 'of the state, professions, and international associations [and] identify alternatives in other eras and contexts' (Scott, 2001: 212).

CONCLUSIONS

Exploring even a modest portion of the scholarship on environments and public institutions produces a mosaic of diverse theoretical and empirical work. It may suggest as well topics deserving additional attention. Even if generalizations can be expected to be limited temporally and spatially, it may make sense to target areas in which patterns might usefully be sought. Examples include the influences (and actors' constructions) of policies, issues or program 'context' on public organizations, populations, networks and organizational fields.

The world public administration confronts is one of global, international, nation-state and local jurisdictions, organizations and social movements. More explicit attention might be paid to levels (and units) of analysis. Doing so might not only reduce unproductive exchanges (Knill and Lenschow, 2001), but also encourage sustained efforts at cross-level analysis (Goodman, 2000).

Self-conscious construction of environments replete with complex, reciprocal relations that shape and reflect rules, cognitions and norms may highlight both the constraints on and the opportunities for public actions. Being clearer about the aims of such analyses (the 'dependent' variables) is one way to avoid Perrow's concerns about vague, 'unspecified' environments.

NOTES

I am grateful for the comments and suggestions of Tom Christensen, Charles Walcott and the students in my doctoral capstone seminar in organization theory.

1 Similarly, Scharpf observes that '"institution" is an ill-defined concept' (1997: 38) before delineating how he employs it in 'actor-centered institutionalism'. For a useful overview of the range of uses of 'institution' and 'institutionalization', see, e.g., Scott (2001).

2 Drawn from biology, an equifinality assumption holds that there can be many adaptations to the same influence, and similar adaptations may produce variable outcomes (Katz and Kahn, 1966).

3 Knill and Lenschow (2001) observe that studies that are 'structure-based' tend to concentrate on more macro levels of analysis, while 'agency-based' examinations are conducted at more micro levels.

4 The notion of an 'enacted environment' suggests that 'instead of a "given" environment "out there", an environment is based on the continuous trading and juxtaposing of meaning and interpretations about the organization and its purpose' (Gabriel et al., 2000: 299).

5 Organization theorists differ over whether this is cause for alarm. Pfeffer, for example, criticizes what he sees as the relatively low level of 'paradigm development' in 'organization science' (1993), while other scholars celebrate the heterogeneity (e.g., Cannella and Paetzold, 1994).

6 Similarly, Rainey (1997: 84ff) includes resource dependence, population ecology and 'institutional processes' among the 'more recent' theories of organization relevant to public administration.

7 Examples include Alvesson and Billing (1997), Dooley and Van de Ven (1999), Nelson and Bridges (1999).

8 Reich (2000) proposes yet another orientation to contingency theorizing and policy, contending that the 'policy domain' being examined indicates the appropriate version of institutionalism to apply analytically.

9 Despite such similarities, Kraatz and Zajac (2001) observe that few exchanges have occurred between resource dependence and strategic change theorists.

10 Although explicit application of such power-dependence models mostly has appeared in studies of parliamentary systems, many examinations of dynamics within separation of powers, presidential systems (e.g., Aberbach and Rockman, 2000: 95ff) can be easily reconstructed along such lines.

11 'Organizational ecology' encompasses work at several levels of analysis. Singh and Lumsden distinguish among the organizational, population and community levels. 'These three levels of analysis are characterized respectively by developmental, selection, and macroevolutionary approaches to study evolution' (Singh and Lumsden, 1990: 162).

12 Increasingly, however, analysts in this stream pay attention to norms and culture as well as to contextualized preferences (Thelen, 1999: 376).

13 Such labeling is similar to that used by, for example, Scharpf (1997, 2000) and Thelen (1999). Peters (1999) treats 'normative' and 'sociological' institutionalism separately, although he too notes the overlap. Meanwhile, Thelen (1999: 370) observes that the 'walls dividing' the types of institutionalism 'have been … eroded by "border crossers"'. Conspicuous by its absence is 'historical institutionalism'; it was not included here since the focus of much work in this area is on the emergence and (path-dependent) evolution of institutions rather than on institutions as settings in which actors, relationships and events are embedded.

14 Aberbach and Christensen add: 'New Zealand's experience clearly challenges the idea that reform processes must be culturally sensitive and compatible, or that reforms are only likely to be implemented if they are the product of negotiation processes and consensus-building' (2001: 419).

REFERENCES

Aberbach, Joel D. and Christensen, Tom (2001) 'Radical Reform in New Zealand: Crisis, Windows of Opportunity, and Rational Actors', *Public Administration*, 79 (2): 403–22.

Aberbach, Joel D. and Rockman, Bert A. (2000) *In the Web of Politics: Three Decades of the U.S. Federal Executive*. Washington, DC: Brookings Institution.

Agranoff, Robert and McGuire, Michael (1998) 'Multinetwork Management: Collaboration and the Hollow State in Local Economic Policy', *Journal of Public Administration Research and Theory*, 8 (January): 67–91.

Agranoff, Robert and McGuire, Michael (2001) 'Big Questions in Public Network Management Research', *Journal of Public Administration Research and Theory*, 11 (July): 295–326.

Alvesson, Mats and Billing, Yvonne Due (1997) *Understanding Gender and Organizations*. Thousand Oaks, CA: Sage.

Anderson, Liam (2001) 'The Implications for Institutional Design for Macroeconomic Performance: Reassessing the Claims of Consensus Democracy', *Comparative Political Studies*, 34 (May): 429–52.

Arum, Richard (2000) 'Schools and Communities: Ecological and Institutional Dimensions', *Annual Review of Sociology*, 26: 395–418.

Beck Jørgensen, Torben, Hansen, Hanne Foss, Antonsen, Marianne, and Melander, Preben (1998) 'Public Organizations, Multiple Constituencies, and Governance', *Public Administration*, 76 (Autumn): 499–518.

Beggs, John J. (1995) 'The Institutional Environment: Implications for Race and Gender Inequality in the US Labor Market', *American Sociological Review*, 60 (August): 612–33.

Berman, Evan M. and West, Jonathan P. (1998) 'Productivity Enhancement Efforts in Public and Nonprofit Organizations', *Public Productivity and Management Review*, 22 (December): 207–19.

Bozeman, Barry (1987) *All Organizations Are Public: Bridging Public and Private Organization Theories*. San Francisco: Jossey–Bass.

Bozeman, Barry and Bretschneider, Stuart (1994) 'The "Publicness Puzzle" in Organization Theory: A Test of Alternative Explanations of Differences Between Public and Private Organizations', *Journal of Public Administration Research and Theory*, 4 (April): 197–223.

Burns, Tom and Stalker, G.M. (1961) *The Management of Innovation*. London: Tavistock.

Cannella, Albert A., Jr and Paetzold, Ramona L. (1994) 'Pfeffer's Barriers to the Advance of Organization Science: A Rejoinder', *Academy of Management Review*, 19 (April): 331–41.

Christensen, Jørgen Grønnegard and Pallesen, Thomas (2001) 'Institutions, Distributional Concerns, and Public Sector Reform', *European Journal of Political Research*, 39 (March): 179–202.

Dill, William R. (1958) 'Environment as an Influence on Managerial Autonomy', *Administrative Science Quarterly*, 2: 409–43.

Donaldson, Lex (2001) *The Contingency Theory of Organizations*. Thousand Oaks, CA: Sage.

Dooley, Kevin J. and Van de Ven, Andrew H. (1999) 'Explaining Complex Organizational Dynamics', *Organization Science*, 10 (May–June): 358–72.

Durant, Robert F. (1998) 'Agenda Setting, the "Third Wave", and the Administrative State', *Administration and Society*, 30 (July): 211–47.

Edelman, Lauren B. and Suchman, Mark C. (1997) 'The Legal Environments of Organizations', *Annual Review of Sociology*, 23: 479–515.

Gabriel, Yiannis, Fineman, Stephen and Sims, David (2000) *Organizing and Organizations: An Introduction*, 2nd edn. Thousand Oaks, CA: Sage.

Garud, Raghu and Kumaraswamy, Arun (1995) 'Coupling the Technical and Institutional Faces of Janus in Network Industries', in W. Richard Scott and Soren Christensen (eds), *The Institutional Construction of Organizations: International and Longitudinal Studies*. Thousand Oaks, CA: Sage.

Goodman, Paul S. (2000) *Missing Organizational Linkages: Tools for Cross-Level Research*. Thousand Oaks, CA: Sage.

Gray, Virginia and Lowery, David (1996) *The Population Ecology of Interest Representation: Lobbying Communities in the American States*. Ann Arbor, MI: University of Michigan Press.

Haverland, Markus (2000) 'National Adaptation to European Integration: The Importance of Institutional Veto Points', *Journal of Public Policy*, 20 (1): 83–103.

Heymann, Phillip B. (1987) *The Politics of Public Management*. New Haven, CT: Yale University Press.

Hood, Christopher (1996) 'Cultural Theory and Institutional Variety', *Journal of Public Policy*, 15 (3): 207–30.

Hult, Karen M. and Walcott, Charles E. (1990) *Governing Public Organizations: Politics, Structure, and Institutional Design*. Pacific Grove, CA: Brooks/Cole.

John, Peter and Cole, Alistair (2000) 'When Do Institutions, Policy Sectors, and Cities Matter?: Comparing Networks of Local Policy Makers in Britain and France', *Comparative Political Studies*, 33 (March): 248–68.

Jørgensen, Daniel J. and Klay, W. Earle (2001) 'Technology in Public Administration', in Kuotsai Tom Liou (ed.), *Handbook of Public Management Practice and Reform*. New York: Marcel Dekker. pp. 75–96.

Kalleberg, Arne L., Knoke, David, Marsden, Peter V. and Spaeth, Joe L. (eds) (1996) *Organizations in America: Analyzing Their Structures and Human Resources Practices*. Thousand Oaks, CA: Sage.

Karnoe, Peter (1995) 'Institutional Interpretations and Explanations of Differences in American and Danish Approaches to Innovation', in W. Richard Scott and Soren Christensen (eds), *The Institutional Construction of Organizations: International and Longitudinal Studies*. Thousand Oaks, CA: Sage.

Katz, Daniel and Kahn, Robert L. (1966) *The Social Psychology of Organizing*. New York: John Wiley.

Kaufman, Herbert (1985) *Time, Chance, and Organizations: Natural Selection in a Perilous Environment*. Chatham, NJ: Chatham House.

Kelemen, R. Daniel (2000) 'Regulatory Federalism: EU Environmental Regulation in Comparative Perspective', *Journal of Public Policy*, 20 (3): 133–67.

Kiel, L. Douglas. (1994) *Managing Chaos and Complexity in Government*. San Francisco: Jossey-Bass.

King, Gary, Keohane, Robert O. and Verba, Sidney (1994) *Designing Social Inquiry: Scientific Inference in Qualitative Research*. Princeton, NJ: Princeton University Press.

Klijn, Erik-Hans (2001) 'Rules as Institutional Context for Decision Making in Networks: The Approach to Postwar Housing Districts in Two Cities', *Administration and Society*, 33 (May): 133–64.

Klijn, Erik-Hans, Koppenjan, Joop and Termeer, Katrien (1995) 'Managing Networks in the Public Sector: A Theoretical Study of Management Strategies in Policy Networks', *Public Administration*, 73 (Autumn): 437–54.

Knill, Christoph and Lenschow, Andrea (2001) '"Seek and Ye Shall Find!": Linking Different Perspectives on Institutional Change', *Comparative Political Studies*, 34 (March): 187–215.

Kraatz, Matthew S. and Zajac, Edward J. (2001) 'How Organizational Resources Affect Strategic Change and Performance in Turbulent Environments: Theory and Evidence', *Organization Science*, 12 (September–October): 632–57.

Lægreid, Per (2000) 'Top Civil Servants Under Contract', *Public Administration*, 78 (4): 879–96.

LaPorte, Todd M. and Consolini, Paula (1998) 'Theoretical and Operational Challenges of "High-Reliability Organizations": Air-Traffic Control and Aircraft Carriers', *International Journal of Public Administration*, 21 (6–8): 847–52.

Lawrence, Paul R. and Lorsch, Jay W. (1967) *Organization and Environment*. Cambridge, MA: Harvard University Press.

LeGalès, Patrick (2001) 'Urban Governance and Policy Networks: On the Urban Political Boundedness of Policy Networks. A French Case Study', *Public Administration*, 79 (1): 167–84.

Lovrich, Nicholas P. (2000) 'Policy Partnering Between the Public and the Not-for-Profit Private Sectors', in Pauline Vaillancourt-Rosenau (ed.), *Public–Private Policy Partnerships*. Cambridge, MA: MIT Press.

Lowery, David and Gray, Virginia (1998a) 'The Dominance of Institutions in Interest Representation: A Test of Seven Explanations', *American Journal of Political Science*, 42 (January): 231–55.

Lowery, David and Gray, Virginia (1998b) 'Representational Concentration and Interest Community Size: A Population Ecology Interpretation', *Political Research Quarterly*, 51 (December): 919–44.

March, James G. and Olsen, Johan P. (1989) *Rediscovering Institutions: The Organizational Basis of Politics*. New York: Free Press.

Marsden, Peter V., Cook, Cynthia R. and Knoke, David (1996) 'American Organizations and Their Environments: A Descriptive Overview', in Arne L. Kalleberg, David Knoke, Peter V. Marsden and Joe L. Spaeth (eds), *Organizations in America: Analyzing Their Structures and Human Resources Practices*. Thousand Oaks, CA: Sage.

Marsh, David, Smith, M.J. and Richards, D. (2000) 'Bureaucrats, Politicians, and Reform in Whitehall: Analyzing the Bureau-Shaping Model', *British Journal of Political Science*, 30: 461–82.

Matland, Richard E. (1995) 'Synthesizing the Implementation Literature: The Ambiguity Conflict Model of Policy Implementation', *Journal of Public Administration Research and Theory*, 5 (April): 145–74.

Meyer, John W. and Rowan, Brian (1977) 'Institutionalized Organizations: Formal Structure as Myth and Ceremony', *American Journal of Sociology*, 83 (September): 340–63.

Meyer, Marshall W., in association with Stevenson, William, and Webster, Stephen (1985) *Limits to Bureaucratic Growth*. New York: Walter de Gruyter.

Meyers, Marcia K., Riccucci, Norma M. and Lurie, Irene (2001) 'Achieving Goal Congruence in Complex Environments: The Case of Welfare Reform', *Journal of Public Administration Research and Theory*, 11 (April): 165–201.

Nelson, Robert L. and Bridges, William P. (1999) *Legalizing Gender Inequality: Courts, Markets, and Unequal Pay for Women*. New York: Cambridge University Press.

Neumann, Francis X., Jr (1997) 'Organization Structures to Match the New Information-Rich Environments', *Public Productivity and Management Review*, 21 (September): 86–100.

Nutt, Paul C. and Backoff, Robert W. (1995) 'Strategy for Public and Third-Sector Organizations', *Journal of Public Administration Research and Theory*, 5 (April): 189–211.

Painter, Chris, Isaac-Henry, Kester and Rose, John (1997) 'Local Authorities and Non-Elected Agencies: Strategic Responses and Organizational Networks', *Public Administration*, 75 (Summer): 225–45.

Pennings, Johannes M. (1992) 'Structural Contingency Theory: A Reappraisal', *Research in Organizational Behavior*, volume 14. Greenwich, CT: JAI Press. pp. 267–309.

Perrow, Charles (1986) *Complex Organizations: A Critical Essay*, 3rd edn. New York: Random House.

Peters, B. Guy. (1999) *Institutional Theory in Political Science: A 'New Institutionalism'*. New York: Pinter.

Peters, B. Guy (2000) 'Policy Instruments and Public Management: Bridging the Gap', *Journal of Public Administration Research and Theory*, 10 (January): 35–47.

Peters, B. Guy and Hogwood, Brian W. (1991) 'Applying Population Ecology Models to Public Organizations', in James L. Perry (ed.), *Research in Public Administration*, Volume 1. Greenwich, CT: JAI Press.

Peters, B. Guy and van Nispen, Frans K. M. (eds). (1998) *Public Policy Instruments: Evaluating the Tools of Public Administration*. Northampton, MA: Edward Elgar.

Pfeffer, Jeffrey (1993) 'Barriers to the Advance of Organization Science: Paradigm Development as a

Dependent Variable', *Academy of Management Review*, 18 (October): 599–620.

Pfeffer, Jeffrey (1997) *New Directions for Organization Theory: Problems and Prospects*. New York: Oxford University Press.

Pfeffer, Jeffrey (1981) *Power in Organizations*. Marshfield, MA: Pitman Publishing.

Pfeffer, Jeffrey and Salancik, Gerald R. (1978) *The External Control of Organizations*. New York: Harper and Row.

Powell, Walter W. and DiMaggio, Paul J. (eds) (1991) *The New Institutionalism in Organizational Analysis*. Chicago: University of Chicago Press.

Radaelli, Claudio M. (2000) 'Policy Transfer in the European Union: Institutional Isomorphism as a Source of Legitimacy', *Governance*, 13 (January): 25–43.

Rainey, Hal G. (1997) *Understanding and Managing Public Organizations*, 2nd edn. San Francisco: Jossey–Bass.

Reich, Simon (2000) 'The Four Faces of Institutionalism: Public Policy and a Pluralistic Perspective', *Governance*, 13 (October): 501–22.

Rhodes, R.A.W. (1996) 'The New Governance: Governing Without Government', *Political Studies*, 44 (September): 652–67.

Rhodes, R.A.W. and Dunleavy, Patrick (eds) (1995) *Prime Minister, Cabinet, and Core Executive*. Basingstoke: Macmillan.

Ruef, Martin (2000) 'The Emergence of Organizational Forms: A Community Ecology Approach', *American Journal of Sociology*, 106 (November): 658–714.

Scharpf, Fritz W. (1997) *Games Real Actors Play: Actor-Centered Institutionalism in Policy Research*. Boulder, CO: Westview Press.

Scharpf, Fritz W. (2000) 'Institutions in Comparative Policy Research', *Comparative Political Studies,* 33 (August/September): 762–90.

Scott, W. Richard (2001) *Institutions and Organizations*, 2nd edn. Thousand Oaks, CA: Sage.

Scott, W. Richard (1998) *Organizations: Rational, Natural, and Open Systems*, 4th edn. Upper Saddle River, NJ: Prentice–Hall.

Scott, W. Richard. (1995) 'Symbols and Organizations: From Barnard to the Institutionalists', in Oliver E. Williamson (ed.), *Organization Theory: From Chester Barnard to the Present and Beyond*, Expanded edn. New York: Oxford University Press.

Scott, W. Richard and Meyer, John W. (1983) 'The Organization of Societal Sectors', in John W. Meyer and W. Richard Scott (eds), *Organizational Environments: Ritual and Rationality*. Beverly Hills, CA: Sage.

Scott, W. Richard, Ruef, Martin, Mendel, Peter J. and Caronna, Carol A. (2000) *Institutional Change and Healthcare Organizations: From Professional Dominance to Managed Care*. Chicago: University of Chicago Press.

Selznick, Philip (1948) 'Foundations of the Theory of Organizations', *American Sociological Review*, 13: 25–35.

Selznick, Philip (1949) *TVA and the Grass Roots*. Berkeley, CA: University of California Press.

Singh, Jitendra V. and Lumsden, Charles J. (1990) 'Theory and Research in Organizational Ecology', *Annual Review of Sociology*, 16: 161–95.

Smith, Martin J. (1994) 'The Core Executive and the Resignation of Mrs Thatcher', *Public Administration*, 72 (3): 341–63.

Staber, U. (1989) 'Organizational Foundings in the Cooperative Sector of Atlantic Canada: An Ecological Perspective', *Organization Studies*, 10: 381–403.

Stoker, Gerry (1995) 'Intergovernmental Relations', *Public Administration*, 73 (Spring): 101–22.

Thelen, Kathleen (1999) 'Historical Institutionalism in Comparative Politics', *Annual Review of Political Science*, 2: 369–404.

Thelen, Kathleen and Steinmo, Sven (1992) 'Historical Institutionalism in Comparative Politics', in Sven Steinmo, Kathleen Thelen and Frank Longstreth (eds), *Structuring Politics: Historical Institutionalism in Comparative Analysis*. New York: Cambridge University Press.

Thompson, James D. (1967) *Organizations in Action*. New York: McGraw–Hill.

Tucker, D.J., Singh, Jitendra V. and Meinhard, A.G. (1990) 'Organizational Form, Population Dynamics, and Institutional Change: A Study of Founding Patterns of Voluntary Organizations', *Academy of Management Journal*, 33: 151–78.

Walcott, Charles E. and Hult, Karen M. (1995) *Governing the White House: From Hoover through LBJ*. Lawrence, KS: University Press of Kansas.

Waldo, Dwight (1961) 'Organization Theory: An Elephantine Problem', *Public Administration Review,* 21 (Autumn): 210–25.

Waldo, Dwight (1978) 'Organization Theory: Revisiting the Elephant', *Public Administration Review*, 38 (November/December): 589–97.

Waterman, Richard W. and Meier, Kenneth J. (1998) 'Principal–Agent Models: An Expansion?', *Journal of Public Administration Research and Theory*, 8 (April): 173–202.

Weick, Karl E., Sutcliffe, Kathleen M. and Obstfeld, David (1999) 'Organizing for Reliability: Processes of Collective Mindfulness', in Robert I. Sutton and Barry M. Staw (eds), *Research in Organizational Behavior*, Volume 21. Stamford, CT: JAI Press. pp. 81–123.

Woodward, Joan (1965) *Industrial Organization: Theory and Practice*. New York: Oxford University Press.

Section 4

ADMINISTRATIVE HISTORY

Introduction

Jos C.N. Raadschelders

Governance and government have always been. Living their lives, people are generally concerned with 'bringing home the bacon' and 'raising the kids'. That form of daily life, with its routines, obligations, schedules and desires, would be impossible without government. People encounter 'government' in a variety of ways: through regulations, taxes, voting, hearings, direct participation in policy and decision making etc. There is hardly any area – if any – where government does not affect people's lives. The citizens and public servants of today all grew up in an 'administrative state' that their grandparents witnessed in the making. Given the pressures of day-to-day life it is no wonder that few citizens, public servants or even scholars will stop to wonder how it happened that government has come to penetrate society in all of its corners. And yet, history holds our collective memory and is inherent to studying public administration. We live in a society with a government that has been – how could it be otherwise? – profoundly shaped by the past. Contemporary public policy and organization is embedded in the past. Satisfying public solutions to contemporary social changes cannot but be pursued in the context of public policies, practices and structures that developed in the past. This is why the current generation of citizens, public servants and future leaders in politics and administration would benefit from knowledge

about the making of the administrative state and the role it played in shaping today's society.

Given that government is the only force left that binds most members of contemporary society, the social science and humanist disciplines have increasingly adopted a historical perspective in their pursuit of an understanding of the phenomenon of *government-in-society*. More specifically, there is a growing need in public administration and political science for a better understanding of the past for the sake of the present and the future. Ideally, the sub-field of administrative history combines the traditional interests of the studies of public administration and political science. The comparative and international interest in the administrative history of the Western world has been growing in the past two decades (for an overview see Raadschelders, 1998a). Many individual nation-states have a tradition in this field of research that goes back at least a century (on the United States, see Raadschelders, 2000a; on various Western and Eastern European countries see the bibliographic overviews published annually in the *Yearbook of European Administrative History*). However, administrative history within public administration appears as a sub-field next to other, mainstream areas of interest. In view of the embeddedness of the present in the past, the argument has been made, though, that the historical perspective should be a standard element in all of the sub-fields in public administration (for example, organization theory, human resource management, public policy, public finance, intergovernmental relations, public management etc.) (Raadschelders et al., 2000b).

ADMINISTRATIVE HISTORY: WHAT IT IS NOT AND WHAT IT IS

What is a 'historical approach' in the study of public administration? Let us first knock off some 'false starts'. First, it is not a *l'art pour l'art* exercise that details how 'things' have become. As valuable as such histories are, they are not necessarily what students of public administration and practitioners in government look for. Second, a historical perspective in public administration will not lead to *usable knowledge*, to use the concept that was coined over twenty years ago (Lindblom and Cohen, 1979). It would be wrong to assume that history provides lessons that can be used to avoid making mistakes now. And yet, history is used by decision makers, whether it taught them or not, who most likely draw upon misconceived analogies. To prevent the problems that decision makers create when using the past as an analogy for the present, Neustadt and May (1986) have developed a set of so-called 'mini-methods' to show where analogies go astray. Third, administrative history should not reconstruct the past in terms contemporary theories and models. Such *anachronism* does not do justice to the past in itself, and blinds us to understanding the conceptualizations of decision makers in their own time and context. Fourth, the past should not be interpreted in terms of contemporary outcome. Such *present-mindedness* only results in the reconstruction of developmental paths relevant to the present in which case we lose sight of paths that ended somewhere in the past. In that case, too, decision makers lose potentially valuable information about past policies and reforms.

Instead, a historical approach in the study of public administration testifies to the degree to which the past exists in the present (Fesler, 1982). *A historical approach in the study of public*

administration recognizes that the present is embedded in but is not predetermined by the past. It is in this italicized claim that we see the inherent historical nature of public administration emerge.

Historical knowledge will help students and decision makers recognize when and where it is wise not to re-invent the wheel and when to dissociate from the past. In an earlier publication I distinguished between two types of administrative history (Raadschelders, 1998a: 7–8). The first, *administrative history in the broad sense*, is concerned with the interaction between government and society at large as well as with processes of state making and nation building (which latter topics are generally studied in political science). Administrative history in the broad sense is relevant because societal developments have consequences for quality and quantity of public service delivery. Students and practitioners benefit from learning how and why government responded to societal change and what consequences this had for the internal structure and functioning of government. The second, *administrative history proper*, is concerned with 'the study of structures and processes in and ideas about government as they have existed or have been desired in the past and the actual and ideal place of public functionaries therein'. Important in this definition is that not only the topics of mainstream Public Administration are included (that is, the development of, for example, organizational structure, of HRM, of policy, etc.) but also the development of ideas about governance and government in relation to society (which is more often studied within political theory).

WHAT MAKES THE STUDY OF ADMINISTRATIVE HISTORY UNIQUE?

There are several features that make administrative history a unique study. First, administrative history is multidisciplinary, like the study of public administration, for it must work with theories and concepts from other social science and humanist (mono-disciplinary) studies (for example, economics, sociology, psychology, law, philosophy, history, theology etc.).

It must, because mono-disciplinary approaches cannot but provide only partial insight in the phenomenon of government-in-society.

Second, unlike several of the more mono-disciplinary social sciences, administrative historical research does not primarily look for law-like generalizations nor does it work from or strive for a unifying theory. The strength and the challenge of administrative history is in identifying the impact of general societal trends (for example, secularization, rationalization, industrialization, demographic growth, urbanization etc.) upon the structure and functioning of government and administration at large (for example, the welfare state, bureaucratization) and upon individual public organizations, policies and offices. If anything, administrative history confronts, sometimes sweeping, generalizations concerning the world regions or even the world with more in-depth study of cultural and national traditions.

Third, and related to the second feature, administrative history does not only study social change but focuses rather on the inter-play of continuity, diversity and change. The continuity of traditions provides stability during times of change. In fact, there has never been a period in history where social change was so total that it eradicated earlier prac-tices and traditions. In emphasizing diversity as well, administrative history helps in recogniz-ing that such a general trend as bureaucratiza-tion, for example, has manifested itself in various ways, that is, within particular national and cultural contexts. Thus, administrative history adopts an evolutionary rather than a social change perspective. The evolutionary perspective draws attention both to the inter-generational and intercultural *diffusion of ideas* (political theory, for example) and (adminis-trative) traditions and practices as well as to the phenomenon of *parallel evolution* (where comparable ideas and practices developed more or less independently from one another; which, *inter alia*, recognizes the importance of Galton's problem in quantita-tive-statistical studies of change over time).

Fourth, administrative history helps preserve collective memory with an eye for present needs. It can serve as a source of understand-ing and/or reinterpretation of (a) modernity, (b) our time as one of epochal change and (c) the discourse in public administration. It can

and has even served an emancipatory function ('setting the record straight'), for instance in highlighting the influence of women upon the making of the American welfare state (these four points are mentioned in Raadschelders, 2000a: 515).

DEVELOPMENT AND STATE OF THE ART OF ADMINISTRATIVE HISTORY

In the course of the nineteenth century the study of administrative history emerged in the United States and in Europe as a history of political and administrative institutions from national down to the local level. In the United States this endeavor was mainly embedded in departments of political science, while in Europe it emerged within the professorial chairs in public administration as they had existed since the early eighteenth century. At the turn of the last century United States scholars adopted theories and conceptualiza-tions from (business) management studies. White's monumental four-volume study (1948–1958) of American administrative history between 1789 and 1901 is the prime example of this approach. In Europe, on the other hand, administrative history became largely part of the study of legal history, given the inclusion of the professorial chairs in public administration into the departments of law.

After the Second World War it was within the context of structural functionalism that a variety of scholars published studies on the development of the (early) state. Characteristic for that (old) institutional approach was the development and use of taxonomies. Finer's conceptual prologue to his huge study is a fine example of this (1997). Somewhat linked to the American managerial focus, studies appeared that were organized around themes specifi-cally relevant to the study of public administra-tion (best example: Gladden, 1972). Until the early 1980s many studies of an administrative-historical nature were descriptive (see the next section below). The emergence of neo-institutionalism since the early 1980s has given the study of administrative history the poten-tial to develop itself on a more theoretical basis. Specifically, historical institutionalism (see, Peters, 1999) and its concepts of, for example, path-dependency and critical junctures, hold great promise for the further development of administrative history provided that the first is not used in an attempt to re-introduce a nineteenth-century notion of causality (Raadschelders, 1998b) and the latter does not prohibit the understanding of continuity amidst change.

The study of administrative history is in good shape. At the handbook level there are at least three studies that provide overviews of the development of government with extensive bibliographic references (for example, Gladden, 1972; Finer, 1997; Raadschelders, 1998a). There are two journals that specifically concern administrative history. The *Journal of Policy History* (*JPH*) (Pennsylvania State University Press) and the international, comparative and multidisciplinary *Yearbook of European Administrative History* (*YEAH*) (Baden-Baden: Nomos Verlagsgesellschaft), both published since 1989, contain a wealth of in-depth studies based on research in primary (oral and written) sources. Especially the forum section in *YEAH* contains bibliographic articles on the development and state of the art of administrative history in specific Western, Central and Eastern European countries. Finally, there are quite impressive national traditions in administrative history. As can be expected, England, France, Germany and Italy lead the way in terms of continuous research throughout the twentieth century. The bibliographic articles that have become available in the past decade (see above), however, indicate that most European countries enjoy a well-developed tradition of study in administrative history. Also, and perhaps a little unexpected, there is quite a tradition in the United States in this area, and that goes back further than one might expect (Raadschelders, 2000a). The various bibliographies contain references to numerous book- and article-length studies. The major challenge for administrative historians is to make these accessible to large audiences. While many studies are written in English, French or German, there is even more in other languages. Also, a large portion of publications relevant to administrative history, and perhaps even the majority of them, is generated within other studies than public administration and political science. Especially scholars of law, sociology and history have contributed greatly to our understanding of the development of government. Compartmentalization of knowledge (whether for epistemological or more mundane organizational reasons) is certainly a barrier for the multidisciplinary study of administrative history.

THEMES, METHODS AND CHALLENGES OF ADMINISTRATIVE HISTORY

In view of the two definitions of administrative history (see section two above), two main thematic categories of research can be distinguished. First, administrative history seeks to enhance understanding about the role and position of government in society, more specifically the interaction between government and society. Administrative history in the broader sense studies different types of political organization and the degree to which it includes the population. The questions when and why subjects turned into citizens has generated a fair amount of literature, as has the question what consequences this had for government. The emphasis in contemporary government on citizen participation (whether passive as voters or active as co-policy and decision makers) places the development of the intertwinement between interest groups, professional associations and so forth firmly on the agenda of administrative history.

The second category includes attention for the role of ideas, and for the structure and functioning of government. While, seemingly, the study of public administration is predominantly focused on management issues (the management of organization, of personnel, of revenue and expenditure etc.), many scholars recognize that it is imperative to understand the ideas that legitimize the structure and functioning of government. What is/has been the role of political and administrative ideas (such as about, for example, equality before the law, *Rechtsstaat*, sovereignty, distribution of power, but also about division of labor, unity of command etc.) in shaping formal public institutions (such as the executive, the legislative, the judiciary) and policies (such as welfare state policies)? Furthermore, it is increasingly acknowledged that it is important to understand the time and context in which certain ideas about government-in-society germinated, how they 'traveled' over time, and how they 'fit' in their current environment. Ideas, as expressions of deeply cherished values and norms about government-in-society determine the structure and functioning of the polity. In many countries all over the world representative democracy has become the standard practice and at least a coveted – sometimes externally imposed – ideal. As mentioned earlier, we find much on (the role of) political ideas in studies of political theory. Assuming that generally congruence exists between political and administrative ideas, that is, the latter ideally emanating from the former, it is striking that administrative ideas are generally discussed in their consequences for, and thus in an analysis of, public organization, public office and public policy. In other words, many of the administrative historical studies of a (particular) public organization, a (particular) public office (such as the presidency, the city manager, the prime minister, top civil servants), a (particular) public policy etc. will indirectly address the underlying ideas. Also relevant to administrative history proper is the study of the development of political–administrative relations. Most often this is pursued at the more abstract level of the development of ideas and practices in general. However, biographies of incumbents of public office (elected and appointed) might prove to be a rich mine to explore (as, for example, Finer, 1952; Stillman, 1998). It will be clear that in terms of object, administrative history is a vast area of research.

Methods in the study of administrative history are as diverse as in other subjects that interest social scientists. There are at least four ways in which we can shed some light on methods of administrative history.

First, we can consider the use of *quantitative-statistical* and/or *quantitative-descriptive* methods. The former, while very popular in political science and public administration (given the positivist aspiration to achieve scientific status), places almost impossible demands upon administrative history. Specifically, it is almost impossible to generate consistent time-series that span hundreds of years. Historical work relies upon what is available in archives, and the research questions that interest us now may not have been of any

concern to those who documented and preserved the past decisions and actions of public officials. The administrative historian in Europe will find that the archives hold much, but not enough, while his/her colleague in the United States will find that, to quote de Tocqueville:

> the acts of society [and of government: JR] in America often leave less trace than the actions of a simple family. [...] The only historical monuments of the United States are newspapers. [...] ...in fifty years it will be more difficult to gather authentic documents on the details of the social existence of Americans of our day than on the administration of the French in the Middle Ages ... (2000: 198)

Another, and equally challenging wrench in the attempt to generate time-series of a dependent variable is that they must be grounded in conceptualizations that travel well over time. By way of example, the concept of politician as we know it (that is, a popularly elected office-holder with an authority and responsibility that is distinct from that of appointed administrative officeholders) did not and could not exist before the Napoleonic era.

The third challenge for those who favor quantitative-statistical studies is, obviously, that generating relevant time-series for the independent, explanatory variables is even more daunting. Thus, quantitative-descriptive studies hold more promise, which means that we need to be content with nominal time-series. Often, such time-series are merely copied from data-generating institutions such as a national census bureau. Examples are data on public personnel size, on public revenue and expenditure, population size, GNP and so forth. I will gloss over the problem that we then need to know the collection rationale. More important is research aimed at creating new time-series on the basis of primary research of archival sources. This is very rewarding yet time-consuming. As a consequence, *qualitative-descriptive studies* appear to be preferred by administrative historians.

A second way of discussing methods of administrative history starts with recognizing that it is a type of comparative study. While cross-national, cross-level and cross-policy (the last two basically in the past two decades) studies are acknowledged types of the comparative approach, the fact that administrative history is a cross-time study raises the issue of *what* is being compared. This relates to the remark above regarding the usefulness of contemporary concepts in a historical time and place. There are a variety of studies that concern, for instance, bureaucratization of the public sector or even of society at large. But, as soon as the scholar provides sweeping generalizations with more in-depth observations relating to and illustrations from particular countries it quickly becomes clear that concepts are not easily commensurable between different countries, and even between different policies and levels of government.

Discussing methods in terms of *how* a cross-time study is conducted constitutes a third way in which methods can be discussed and challenges can be identified. The distinction that Skocpol and Somers outlined between comparison as *parallel demonstration of theory*, as *contrast of contexts* and as *macrocausal analysis*, that is, the three logics-in-use, is an excellent example of this (1980). From a scholarly point of view, the third one is intellectually the most challenging and theoretically the most satisfying. The second is more commonly used, and the first approach may attract attention given the advent of historical institutionalism.

A fourth way to look at methods of administrative history starts with recognizing that historical perspectives often use periodization as the way of organizing data and narrative (as used in the traditional, not in the post-modern sense). Periodization is expressed in stage models: for example, early, intermediate and/or transitory, and modern stages. Some years ago I suggested that stage models can be categorized in two main groups. In the *empirical group* there are four types of stage models, namely those based in *classifications* (for example, a typology of the development of the early state: inchoate, typical, transitional state), in mere *periodization* (for example, providing approximate start and end dates for stages/ phases of X, for instance stages in the development of the Western legal tradition), in *functional models* (that allow more for variation of a particular phenomenon across time and space: urbanization) and *interaction models* (that focus on the interplay between two compound variables. In the *theoretical group* we find stage models that are constructed on a theoretical basis rather than being derived

from and based in historical events. The distinction made by the population-ecology school between five units/levels of analysis (from the 'individual level' to the 'communities of (populations of) organizations' level) can serve well as a framework for analyzing the transformation from loosely connected to highly interrelated organizations in the public arena. It can also serve as a framework for analyzing how changes at the micro level (that is, that of the individual or single organization) are a reflection of changes at the macro level. Obviously, in this case one must confront the challenge of the *fallacy of the wrong level*. When focusing specifically on (social) change, and attempting to characterize the changes in the nature of change over time, the scholar could use such distinctions as Eisenstadt made between marginal, accommodable and total change or as Hernes made between simple reproduction, extended reproduction, transition and transformation (Raadschelders, 1998a: 69–72).

With these four ways the degree to which administrative historians have consciously elaborated and used methods appropriate to their object can be illustrated. To my knowledge, no one has ever attempted to analyze and 'count' publications in administrative history according to the method employed. It is thus only intuitively that I suggest that the dominating methods thus far are quantitative and qualitative descriptions, using cross-national, cross-level, cross-policy and (obviously) cross-time comparisons of contexts, and using empirical stage models.

OVERVIEW OF THIS SECTION

The three chapters in this section of the Handbook represent the wide range that administrative history roams. In the first chapter Larry Luton focuses on the development of state and government in the Western world and addresses the question of why and how it is that government has come to play such a central role in society (that is, an emphasis on administrative history in the broader sense). In the second chapter Fabio Rugge looks at the consequences of increased societal demand for the internal structure and functioning of government itself (that is, administrative history proper). More specifically, he addresses administrative traditions in Western countries, as they still play a role (such as the common law tradition in England, the *Rechtsstaat* tradition in continental Europe and the administrative state tradition in Scandinavia). Both the chapters by Luton and Rugge show how much the governmental penetration of society and the administrative traditions in government have made the world as we know it. Indeed, the last remark is not off base for Western traditions and models of government have disseminated across the globe. Hence, both the Luton and Rugge studies emphasize the diffusion of ideas and practices between countries and cultures. In contrast, and as the final chapter of this section, James W. Björkman discusses the parallel evolution of ideas about governance and government. Doing so we can develop a sense of the degree to which Western conceptions of democracy and management are not exclusive to it.

All three authors will start their chapters in general, comparative terms and illustrate their observations with developments in a particular geographic setting. Thus Luton will focus in on the United States, Rugge will consider some European countries in more detail (especially England, France, Germany and Italy), while Björkman will draw upon his in-depth knowledge of India when comparing the political theories of Kautilya with those of Machiavelli. Also, each provides at the conclusion of their chapter some observations about the degree to which remarks and conclusions regarding their specific topic and/or region are generalizable. The ambition of the authors of this section is not to be complete in their account of (an aspect of) administrative history. Rather, it is their desire to show through cross-time and cross-national analysis that historical knowledge is a benefit to students and practitioners alike. Of course, I preach to the converted, but I hope that others will come to recognize that a historical perspective in public administration is not a waste of time. It may not lead to usable knowledge but will make us aware of the *portée,* to use Montaigne's concept, or reach of our knowledge at present and over time, and – better still – it may make us to 'be lowly

wise ...', which Milton claimed in *Paradise Lost* to be the highest form of knowledge (Shattuck, 1996: 29, 72–3). In the same spirit Jacob Burckhardt wrote almost 150 years ago: 'Wir wollen durch Erfahrung nicht sowohl klug (für ein andermal) als weise für immer) werden' (in paraphrased translation: It is through experience that we will not so much aspire to cleverness for the next time, but wisdom for ever).

The authors of this section accepted with enthusiasm and without reservations my invitation to write a chapter. They have done a great job and I would like to thank them for the time and energy they have put into this project. As far as this introduction is concerned, it had to be brief but provides the kind of information that enables the interested reader to expand into administrative history.

REFERENCES

Fesler, James W. (ed.) (1982) *American Public Administration: Patterns of the Past.* Washington, DC: American Society for Public Administration.

Finer, S.E. (1952) *The Life and Times of Sir Edwin Chadwick.* London: Methuen.

Finer, S.E. (1997) *The History of Government From the Earliest Times.* Oxford: Oxford University Press.

Gladden, E.N. (1972) *A History of Public Administration.* London: Frank Cass.

Lindblom, Charles and Cohen, David K. (1979) *Usable Knowledge. Social Science and Social Problem Solving.* New Haven/London: Yale University Press.

Neustadt, Richard E. and May, Ernest R. (1986) *Thinking in Time. The Uses of History for Decision-Makers.* New York: The Free Press/London: Collier Macmillan.

Peters, B. Guy (1999) *Institutional Theory in Political Science. The 'New Institutionalism'.* London/New York: Pinter.

Raadschelders, Jos C.N. (1998a) *Handbook of Administrative History.* Brunswick, NJ: Transaction Publishers.

Raadschelders, Jos C.N. (1998b) 'Evolution, Institutional Analysis and Path Dependency: An Administrative History Perspective on Fashionable Approaches and Concepts', *International Review of Administrative Sciences,* 64 (4): 562–82.

Raadschelders, Jos C.N. (2000a) 'Administrative History of the United States. Development and State of the Art', *Administration and Society,* 32 (5): 499–528.

Raadschelders, Jos C.N., Wagenaar, Pieter Rutgers, Mark and Overeem Patrick (2000b) 'Against a Study of the History of Public Administration: A Manifesto', *Administrative Theory and Praxis,* 22 (4): 772–91.

Shattuck, Roger (1996) *Forbidden Knowledge. From Prometheus to Pornography.* New York: St Martin's Press.

Skocpol, Theda and Somers, Margaret (1980) 'The Uses of Comparative History in Macrosocial Inquiry', *Comparative Studies in Society and History*, 22 (2): 174–97.

Stillman II, Richard J. (1998) *Creating the American State. The Moral Reformers and the Modern Administrative World They Made*. Tuscaloosa, AL/London: University of Alabama Press.

Tocqueville, Alexis de (2000) *Democracy in America* (edited by Harvey C. Mansfield and Delba Winthrop). Chicago/London: University of Chicago Press.

White, Leonard B. (1948) *The Federalists: A Study in Administrative History, 1789–1801*. New York: Free Press.

White, Leonard B. (1951) *The Jeffersonians: A Study in Administrative History, 1801–1829*. New York: Free Press.

White, Leonard B. (1954) *The Jacksonians: A Study in Administrative History, 1829–1861*. New York: Macmillan.

White, Leonard B. (1958) *The Republican Era, 1869–1901: A Study in Administrative History*. New York: Macmillan.

13

Administrative State and Society:
A Case Study of the
United States of America

Larry S. Luton

If we are finally to come to terms with
the state in America ... we will need a
reassessment of the significance of our
distinctive past. (Skowronek, 1982: 3)

In the United States the relationship between
public administration and society has been an
uneasy one. Throughout their history Americans
have tried to pretend that the country could operate without public administrators. The United
States Constitution describes a limited government – one that has only those powers specifically assigned to it – and, as is often pointed out,
it does not directly address administrative issues
(for example, Rohr, 1986: 1; Stillman, 1999: 19).
Even scholars of public administration have had
a tendency to speak as if the history of public
administration in the United States did not begin
until the 1880s (Luton, 1999: 210–12).

In some ways, it is difficult to examine the
relationship between the administrative state and
society through a case study of a society that has
demonstrated throughout its history a tendency
to pretend that it does not have an administrative
state. Founded on a limited government principle, over the years the United States has sought
ways of governing itself that have to varying
degrees diminished and/or denied the role of its
public administration. Stillman sees the root of
this uneasy relationship in the founders' distaste
for a strong executive, enthusiasm for republicanism and belief that the machinery of government could run on its own without the assistance
of an administrative state. He has described the

early history of the United States as a 'stateless'
condition (1999: ch. 2). Skowronek's characterization of the same period is, perhaps, more
generous; in his view there was a 'sense of
statelessness' that affected the 'peculiar way
state power was organized' (1982: 5, 8).
Milward's examination of the way in which late-
twentieth-century America was creating more
and more complex approaches to governance in
which 'involvement by the state is indirect and
extremely limited', led him to coin the phrase
'hollow state' (Milward et al., 1993: 310).

Using the United States as a case study, this
chapter will review the relationship between the
administrative state and society. It will begin
with a review of the history of US public administration as it has been described in the academic
literature. Through that literature it will examine
the history of tension between America's defining value–self-governance – and its need for
institutions of public administration – an administrative state.

Finally, based on this case study of the United
States, it will reach some tentative conclusions
regarding relationships between administrative
states and the societies they serve. Because the
United States has been seen as an important
exception from the 'rules' relating to governance
of a complex society, one needs to qualify the
generalizability of any insights gained through
an examination of its history and sectoral
dynamics. It should be understood that there is
no single model to follow; European and other
states are significantly different (Kickert and

Stillman, 1999; Waldo, 1999). Still, because it is sometimes seen as a model for others to follow (Waldo, 1984: 15), some implication of generalizability is difficult, if not impossible to avoid.

GENTLEMANLY GOVERNANCE: THE FEDERALISTS AND JEFFERSONIANS

The field of public administration's understanding of American history has been criticized by persons convinced of its importance (such as Adams 1992; Stivers 1995; Luton 1999), but the resources needed to improve that understanding are more available than is sometimes recognized (Raadschelders 2000a; 2000b: 22, 356–63).

White's (1948, 1954, 1956, 1958) descriptions of administrative theories and practices covering 1789–1901 represent one of the richest sources on US federal administrative history. Even though they do not reach back to the period under the Articles of Confederation, they offer a reasonable place to begin exploring relations between the administrative state and society in the United States. The government founded on the 1789 Constitution was designed in response to the failures of the Articles of Confederation and represented recognition of the need to strengthen the federal government to better address the needs of the nation. Although the Constitution was clearly designed to limit the power of governmental institutions, the deliberate action taken in Philadelphia to reconstruct the foundation of governance signified grand confidence in the ability of humans to improve their lives through rational consideration of the design of social institutions.

In the debates that shaped the Constitution, a major line of ideological demarcation was between the advocates of centralized and public versus decentralized and private means of action. The Federalists favored public state action at the federal level to promote progress in manufacturing and industrialization, and the Republicans wanted to limit federal power and pursue progress though decentralized action promoting agriculture and household crafts.

The Federalists held dominance during the first years under the Constitution (1789–1801), so their views regarding the role of the state in society became the foundation upon which the nineteenth century administrative state took shape. Only a few of the leaders of the Federalist era thought systematically about administrative matters, so many of them 'operated on a consistent set of often unformulated rules'

(White, 1948: viii). Among their major positions was a belief that governance is best left to society's elite – in their view the 'gentlemen' (White, 1948: 508). Trusting the gentlemen to do their duty toward society, they favored delegation of authority and administrative discretion, but they also thought that officials were to be held responsible for doing their jobs conscientiously. Under skilled administrators, this approach has been judged to have worked superlatively, but more frequently the administrators were not terribly skilled. As a result, White has characterized the United States in the Federalist era as a 'relatively unadministered society' (White, 1948: 515).

When Jefferson and the Republicans defeated the Federalists, one might have expected that the change in party control would translate into a significantly different approach to public administration. However, White's evaluation was that the Federalists 'administrative system was adopted by their political rivals' (1952: vii). A man of great vision, Jefferson was not particularly interested in administrative problems and once wrote: 'There are no mysteries in it [public administration]. ... Difficulties indeed sometimes arise; but common sense and honest intentions will generally steer through them' (White, 1952: 4). The most significant change in public administration during his first term was that the gentlemen, who Jefferson saw as naturally superior in virtue and talents, were – because of the practice of patronage – increasingly Republican.

Other than the disputes that dependence upon patronage generated, Jefferson's first term seemed rather serene, but developments during it set the stage for important disputes to follow. For someone who favored decentralization, his contribution to increasing the authority of the federal government was remarkable. His purchase of the Louisiana Territory was admittedly without constitutional authority, but it may have done more than any other single decision to shape the character of US history. In his second term, conflict between Britain and France led Jefferson to impose a disappointingly ineffective embargo on shipment of American products to foreign ports. As ineffective as it was, it still represented an expansion of the federal government's authority to regulate commerce. Thus, while he attached no great value to public administration, and solidified the practice of patronage in federal appointments, Jefferson played no small part in expanding the importance of the state in American society.

As his successor, Madison was left the unenviable task of fighting the war that Jefferson was unable to avoid. According to White, 'The

War of 1812 was the great watershed in the Jeffersonian period [1801–29]' (1952: 10). After that war the American people seemed to sense that they were a nation and began to focus their attention on the huge expanse of territory that Jefferson had purchased for them. The state was viewed as a significant vehicle for progress, and a faction of Jefferson's party that came to be known as the 'new Republicans' were ready to lead the way: 'They stood for the broad construction of national power, for an active employment of those powers, for a strong navy, for a well-organized army, for a United States Bank, for a tariff, for internal improvements, and for a foreign policy that looked toward the further acquisition of territory' (White, 1952: 14). The last of the Jeffersonian era presidents, John Quincy Adams (1825–29), in his first annual message went even farther, saying it was the duty of the state to assist in the moral, political and intellectual improvement of its citizens (White, 1952: 14).

Though the proper institutional vehicles for the pursuit of national goals remained in dispute, and decentralized practices were the most common resolution of that dispute, the expansion of territory during the Jeffersonian era meant that the US federal government was gaining more responsibility.

GOVERNANCE BY THE COMMON MAN

The Republican Party disappeared as its factions split into the Whigs and the Jackson Democrats. Jackson won the election of 1828, and in response to the problem of superannuation, he introduced 'rotation' into the federal system, but he was not (as is too often asserted) the originator of 'spoils' (Eriksson, 1926–7; Van Riper, 1958: 34–6). In his deliberate democratization of the federal service, he removed the gentlemen's stranglehold and opened opportunities to participate in governance to other white males. Political parties were central institutions in effecting this transition.

To some this represented retrogression in administrative practice, but it was popular as an expression of the need to reassert self-governance into the US administrative state. Moreover, it operated on the thesis that public office 'is a species of discipline of no unimportant character. It extends the views of men, trains them to the performance of justice, and makes them act for others as well as for themselves' (Judge

Frederick Grimke, quoted in White, 1954: 558). In expanding participation in governance, the Jacksonians were expecting to facilitate moral, political and intellectual improvement of the citizens. According to Tocqueville, they were successful; writing about the political effects of America's decentralized and participatory approach to governance, he said it resulted in citizens having an attachment with the state similar to that with their families, and that 'everyone is ready ... to guide and support it' (1990: 94).

Jackson's views regarding the role of the state were similar to those of Jefferson, leaning strongly toward limited government and *laissez-faire*. Accordingly, he diminished the role of the state in promoting internal improvements, but he had a much larger interior which he had to provide with some administration. Consequently, despite their frugality and their antipathy toward large government, the Jacksonians found themselves in power while federal expenditures rose from $15.1 to $63.1 million (White, 1954: 9). But that was not sufficient to address the needs of the growing nation. Meeting some of the administrative challenges was made possible by technological innovations such as the telegraph, which made communication much easier. Of greater administrative significance were the development of the bureau system, field inspections and reliance on a system of dual sovereign and autonomous levels of public institutions – federal and state. The Jacksonians fully supported 'state governments as the principal public agency of the American people' (White, 1954: 507), but the trend still moved toward enhancement of the federal government's importance in people's lives.

INTRODUCING PROFESSIONAL GOVERNANCE

The War Between the States punctuated that trend, definitively settling any question about whether the United States was one nation. White's administrative histories skip over the years of the Civil War, and the final volume covers the Republic Era (1869–1901). According to White there were two major developments during that era: the rise in power of the president in comparison to Congress, and the beginning of professional public administration marked by the achievement of civil service reform in 1883. But it should also be noted that by the end of the era the public service payroll had grown to five times its 1871 size (White, 1958: 2). Much of this growth was due to continued expansion of the responsibilities placed on the administrative state in managing the affairs of the nation – for example, regulation of the railroads, protection against monopolies and the geological survey. Because the American people were focused on limiting governmental power by limiting the legislative and executive branches, for most of this era the United States was a state where the political parties organized and implemented administrative action and the courts set the rules of engagement (Skowronek, 1982).

The Republican era began with the presidency in a shambles. The greatest power in the federal government was the Senate. Though the president was the chief executive, he was expected to play no active part in public administration (White, 1958: 392). Department heads were to report to the president, but administrative responsibility was in their hands. By the end of the era, the presidency remained much weaker than it had been during the Jeffersonian and Jacksonian eras, but Hayes, Garfield and Cleveland had done much toward restoring it.

Civil service reform in this era represented a rejection of some Jacksonian principles, but to be successful as a challenge to patronage and rotation in office, civil service reform had to be presented as democratic – as a way for the common man to participate in governance. Though it promoted merit as the characteristic that should qualify people for public service jobs, it could not be sold as a return to elite management of the public business. The Civil Service Commission pointedly described the examinations that were required for civil service positions as practical in nature and pitched at a modest intellectual level, not aimed at establishing a college-trained aristocracy.

In adopting a civil service system, the United States was participating in an international trend toward merit systems; but in the United States such a system was a direct challenge to patronage and rotation. The patronage system had lost favor because of its participation in the general decline in morality found throughout American society. Still, in order to succeed the merit system had to offer more than a return to morality; it had to offer new values that could counter patronage's claims to democracy and responsiveness. Merit's new values were derived from business – economy, efficiency and the ability to deal with the increasingly complex affairs of an industrial and urban society.

The promotion of the ideal of a 'businesslike' government (White, 1958: 387) in the drive for civil service reform may have been the most lasting impact of the Republican era on public administration. According to Skowronek, it is this establishment of the business ideal that represents the historical origin of 'modern institutional politics in America' (1982: viii). However, that ideal had to find some way to work with the foundational ideals of limited government and self-governance. The establishment of the modern administrative state in the United States was affected by the approaches to public administration it adopted during its first 100 years under the Constitution: 'states change ... through political struggles rooted in and mediated by preestablished institutional arrangements' (Skowronek, 1982: ix). Those arrangements included political party domination, active federal courts and decentralization. Political parties were a key part of the nation's first answer regarding how to run a state without depending too much on governmental institutions. Beginning as voluntary associations led by the gentlemen, during the nineteenth century parties had become institutions capable of organizing and mobilizing the nation. During that same period, federal courts helped to 'define relations between state and society' by shaping the boundaries of intergovernmental relations in ways that favored decentralized power and molding 'the prerogatives of government into predictable but flexible patterns of policy' that were friendly to market dynamics and the economic activities of corporations (Skowronek, 1982: 27).

ESTABLISHING MODERN PUBLIC ADMINISTRATION

The Progressive movement and the New Deal were formative periods for the modern American administrative state. Unlike the party- and court-based approach to public administration of the nineteenth century, the modern administrative state sought to separate the functions of expressing the will of the state and executing it (Goodnow, 1900). Running government in a more businesslike fashion meant insulating the business of government from the politics of governance. Instead of relying on partisan political connections to determine administrative questions, this administrative state was designed to utilize science and rationality to pursue economy and efficiency, and top-down hierarchy to ensure that the rationality, economy and efficiency were effective at pursuing the preferred goals. Identification of the preferred goals was seen largely as an executive/administrative leadership function. Specific expressions of these new doctrines were found in the New York Bureau of Municipal Research (founded in 1907), the Taft Commission on Economy and Efficiency (1910–1912), the Brownlow Commission Report (1937) and Executive Order No. 8248 (1939) which established the Executive Office of the President.

Stillman has identified seven key features of the modern American administrative state: (1) unelected experts who (2) work within formal hierarchical organizations, using (3) impersonal rules and procedures, to implement (4) important governmental functions, often using (5) networks of nonprofit or for-profit firms, in ways that are dependent upon (6) soft technologies such as managerial competence and rational analysis, and (7) hard technologies such as typewriters, computers and paper documentation (1998: 5). Obviously, a key element of that administrative state was the civil service system. With it came political neutrality, tenure in office and merit-based selection, promotion and remuneration.

Because the merit system diminished the localized power of political parties by creating a nationwide federal service appointment system, it increased the potential for the president to establish a national political constituency. As the power of the presidency increased, so did the ability of the civil service system to withstand diminishment at the hands of Congress. The popularity of President Theodore Roosevelt (who had been a member of and championed the Civil Service Commission) helped to secure the foothold of the US civil service system, but a more lasting contribution of the Progressive era to the importance of the administrative state derived from the constitutional stalemate between the executive and legislative branches (Skowronek, 1982: 176). Weaker political parties meant that more power was available at the national level and, in the absence of a clear victor between the executive and legislative branches, the administrative state became vital for stability in governmental operations. Because of the increasing role of the state in regulating the dynamics of industrialization, it was also vital for the health of the economy.

NOT ORTHODOXY BUT MULTIPLICITY

But there was more to the modern administrative state than this orthodoxy – the institutional and procedures-oriented 'businessification' of

government and public service provision. As Stivers has shown, the era was driven by two impulses – one toward order and rationality, and the other toward social justice (2000: 5). Whereas businessification was generally the work of male leaders of the Progressive movement, social justice was a concern that women focused upon: 'Women who were increasingly restricted from partisan political work turned to activities directed at improving municipal services, ameliorating poverty, and calling for social and regulatory policies' (2000: 9). Both genders played a role in constructing the administrative state and the field of public administration, but until recently the women's role has been a 'buried heritage' (2000: 13). While men were focused on rationalizing and institutionalizing the procedures of the modern administrative state, the women were establishing its substantive purpose (see also Skocpol, 1992).

Rosenbloom (2001) has also identified an aspect of the modern American administrative state that has been largely overlooked. He calls it 'legislative-centered public administration.' Congress rejected the model of executive leadership found within the Brownlow Committee report, and that is why it was necessary to establish the Executive Office of the President through Executive Order No. 8248. Passing four important statutes in 1946 (including the Administrative Procedures Act), Congress established its model of the modern American administrative state, a model in which administrative agencies are expected to honor democratic-constitutional values not found in the businessification approach – values like 'representativeness, participation, openness, responsiveness, procedural safeguards, and public accountability' (Rosenbloom, 2001: xi). These values represent modern resolutions of the problem of how to administer a complex state in ways that are consistent with limited government and self-governance. Self-governance is approached through participation, representation, and responsiveness. Government is limited by the expectation that it should be accountable and operate in the open and in ways that protect individual rights. In this model, which has been reiterated and reinforced by Congress over the years through such statutes as the Freedom of Information Act (1966) and the Negotiated Rulemaking Act (1990), federal administrative institutions have important executive, legislative and adjudicative functions and relationships. Administrative institutions participate in executing the laws and the presidency serves to coordinate federal administration. Administrative institutions adopt regulations, and Congress is the authorizer, organizer, funder and overseer of federal administration. Administrative institutions adjudicate disputes, and federal courts review administrative actions for compliance with the constitution and legislation. Moreover, because it is involved in governance and the allocation of benefits and burdens, administration is not seen as separate from politics.

Another model of the modern administrative state is offered by Charles Lindblom. Actually, he describes his as a model of the relationship between the state and the market system, but in this model 'the market system is the major administrative instrument of the state' (Lindblom, 2001: 258–9). The intertwining of the administrative state and the market system is so complex that they are sometimes difficult, if not impossible, to distinguish. The state establishes the legal foundations for the society and supports the market system through such functions as managing money and credit, subsidizing market activities, facilitating research and development, and regulating international trade. It also is a direct (and key) participant in the market, as a buyer and seller. In some instances the state is a price setter, setting minimum and/or maximum prices for some goods and services and affecting prices through tariffs. In this model, whether it is through private institutions or within public administration institutions the inclination is to utilize market dynamics to achieve the purposes of the administrative state. Instead of 'command and control' approaches, the administrative state prefers to rely on incentives and other market devices.

So, the modern American administrative state was probably always more complicated than the orthodoxy, but by the late 1940s it was clearly 'a vastly broader, more enriched, and more dynamic field, infused with multiple doctrines' (Stillman, 1999: 131). By 1980, Frederickson had identified five basic models of modern American public administration: the classic bureaucratic model, the neobureaucratic model, the institutional model, the human relations model and the public choice model (Frederickson, 1980: 17). So, the accuracy of the orthodoxy's description of the American administrative state has been undermined, but the modern state has been challenged in a more practical way by those who prefer minimalist state institutions (such as Butler, 1985; Savas, 1987), by the 'New Public Management' movement (see, for example, Reich, 1990; Self, 1993; Lynn, 1996; Kettl and Milward, 1996), and by the increased utilization of nonprofit institutions to serve public purposes.

There is not sufficient space here to examine each of these challenges, but a brief review of the reasons for the rise of nonprofits may be sufficient. 'The private nonprofit sector … is a set of organizations that is privately incorporated but serving some public purpose' (Salamon, 2001: 163). In the United States, nonprofits derive some of their attractiveness from the reluctance of citizens to depend on government, but they also help to deal with the limitations of both our government institutions and our market system. They are credited with providing ways to deal with 'market failure' to adequately address collective consumption, with 'contract failure' where purchasers of a service are not the same as the consumers, and with 'government failure' flexibly to provide all of the collective goods and services that we may desire (Salamon, 2001: 164–6). In addition to addressing these 'failures', some of the contributions that nonprofits make include: helping governments meet some needs, providing a greater diversity of public goods, providing for pluralistic expression, providing for pluralistic preferences, encouraging action for the public good, providing a sense of belonging with others of a like mind, providing a capacity for joint action, and improving the lives of their members and supporters (through art, music, sports etc.).

Milward has labeled the result of these practical challenges of the administrative state a 'hollow state' situation (Milward et al., 1993; Milward, 1996). He uses that label to point to dynamics that result when governmental institutions become separated from the services that they fund because they have chosen to contract out service delivery to third parties. He offers the example of when 'health and human services are funded by public agencies, [but] the distribution of these funds is controlled and monitored by nongovernmental third parties, who themselves determine which agencies to subcontract with for the actual provision of services' (1993: 310).

There are many intellectually inspired names for this kind of arrangement – network organizations, service implementation networks, shadow government, government by proxy, the contracting regime, third-party government etc. But there are ways in which it all sounds rather familiar, as if we have found some way to go almost full circle to the days when we relied on the nongovernmental organizations known as political parties to control the distribution of funds and to determine who received the contracts. Not surprisingly, some of the problems we faced when we depended on political parties to organize the activities of the state also seem to be circling back. For example, without the control mechanisms like those found within hierarchical organizations, effective coordination is challenging.

So, over the past 200 years, the tension between self-governance and public administration in the United States has constantly been in evidence. Whether the United States is truly stateless or merely something of a hollow state, it certainly has a uniquely evolving administrative state. Only time will tell whether Stillman was correct when he concluded that the US version of the administrative state may be 'the most enduring and powerful variety' (1998: 174) ever devised.

CONCLUSION

It may be 'difficult to imagine how modern civilization would exist without the immense, complicated services and goods provided by the administrative state' (Stillman, 1998: 3), but the rise of privatization, the New Public Management and the popularity of nonprofits serves to remind us that those services and goods could be delivered by institutions other than those that constitute the orthodox modern administrative state. Each time we choose some other way of administering our democracy, we are choosing to weigh some values more heavily than technical rationality and economy. Every version of administrative state that has evolved in the United States has had to find a way to honor the American value preference for limited government. That value preference has played no small part in providing a niche for non-governmental institutions in serving societal needs and providing public services.

The desire to see ourselves as self-governing has found many ways to express itself – as a denial of the value of public administrators, through the use of political parties to organize the work of government, in an insistence that our merit system would be one in which everyone has an opportunity to participate, and in a preference for delivery of governmental services by non-governmental institutions. The American value base that has us constantly trying to find a way to be both self-governing and organized for effective action may look odd to some. We may be subject to the charge of being logically inconsistent, but it seems to be a deeply ingrained part of who we are.

Is it possible to generalize about the role of the administrative state from a review of the history of approaches to public administration in the United States? At this point in our development of the political theory of public administration, that would be rather difficult. As Rutgers has pointed out, the American tradition of administrative thought is a quite different 'flavor' from that found in Europe: 'US literature may ponder whether the United States has a state, but this is not the issue [in Europe]' (2001: 223). Still, neither he nor I would go so far as to describe the situation as 'paradigmatic incommensurability' (p. 234). We remain optimistic and consider this to be simply one among the many challenges of cross-cultural communication.

REFERENCES

Adams, Guy B. (1992) 'Enthralled with Modernity: The Historical Context of Knowledge and Theory Development in Public Administration', *Public Administration Review*, 52 (4): 363–73.

Butler, Stuart M. (1985) *The Privatization Option: A Strategy to Shrink the Size of Government*. Washington, DC: Heritage Foundation.

Eriksson, Erik M. (1926–7). The Federal Civil Service under President Jackson, *Mississippi Valley Historical Review*, 13 (4): 517–40.

Frederickson, H. George (1980). *New Public Administration*. University, AL: University of Alabama Press.

Goodnow, Frank (1900) *Politics and Administration*. New York: Macmillan.

Kettl, Donald and Milward, H. Brinton (1996) *The State of Public Management*. Baltimore, MD: Johns Hopkins University Press.

Kickert, Walter and Stillman, Richard (1999) 'Introduction', in Walter Kickert and Richard Stillman (eds), *The Modern State and Its Study: New Administrative Sciences in a Changing Europe and United States*. Northampton, MA: Edward Elgar. pp. ix–xii.

Lindblom, Charles E. (2001) *The Market System: What It Is, How It Works, and What to Make of It*. New Haven, CT: Yale University Press.

Luton, Larry S. (1999) 'History and American Public Administration', *Administration and Society*, 31 (2): 205–21.

Lynn, Laurence E., Jr (1996) *Public Management as Art, Science and Profession*. Chatham, NJ: Chatham House.

Milward, H. Brinton (ed.) (1996) 'Symposium on the Hollow State: Capacity, Control, and Performance in Interorganizational Settings: Introduction', *Journal of Public Administration Research and Theory*, 6 (2): 193–5.

Milward, H. Brinton, Provan, Keith and Else, Barbara (1993) 'What Does the "Hollow State" Look Like?', in Barry Bozeman (ed.), *Public Management: The State of the Art*. San Francisco: Jossey–Bass. pp. 309–22.

Raadschelders, Jos C.N. (2000a) 'Administrative History of the United States: Development and the State of the Art', *Administration and Society*, 32 (5): 499–528.

Raadschelders, Jos C.N. (2000b) *Handbook of Administrative History*. New Brunswick, NJ: Transaction Publishers.

Reich, Robert (1990) *Public Management in a Democratic Society.* Englewood Cliffs, NJ: Prentice–Hall.

Rohr, John A. (1986) *To Run a Constitution: The Legitimacy of the Administrative State.* Lawrence, KS: University Press of Kansas.

Rosenbloom, David (2001) *Building a Legislative-Centered Public Administration: Congress and the Administrative State, 1946–1999.* Tuscaloosa, AL: University of Alabama Press.

Rutgers, Mark R. (2001) 'Traditional Flavors? The Different Sentiments in European and American Administrative Thought', *Administration and Society*, 33 (2): 220–44.

Salamon, Lester M. (2001) 'What Is the Nonprofit Sector and Why Do We Have It?', in J. Steven Ott (ed.), *The Nature of the Nonprofit Sector*, Boulder, CO: Westview Press. pp. 162–6.

Savas, E.S. (1987) *Privatization: The Key to Better Government.* Chathan, NJ: Chatham House.

Self, Peter (1993) *Government by the Market? The Politics of Public Choice.* London: Westview Press.

Skocpol, Theda (1992) *Protecting Soldiers and Mothers: The Political Origins of Social Policy in the United States.* Cambridge, MA: Harvard University Press.

Skowronek, Stephen (1982) *Building a New Administrative State: The Expansion of National Administrative Capacities, 1877–1920.* Cambridge: Cambridge University Press.

Stillman, Richard J., II (1998) *Creating the American State: The Moral Reformers and the Modern Administrative World They Made.* Tuscaloosa, AL: University of Alabama Press.

Stillman, Richard J., II (1999) Preface to *Public Administration: A Search for Themes and Directions,* 2nd edn. Burke, VA: Chatelaine Press.

Stivers, Camilla (1995) 'Settlement Women and Bureau Men: Constructing a Usable Past for Public Administration', *Public Administration Review*, 55 (6): 522–9.

Stivers, Camilla (2000) *Bureau Men and Settlement Women: Constructing Public Administration in the Progressive Era.* Lawrence, KS: University Press of Kansas.

Tocqueville, Alexis de (1990) *Democracy in America, Volume 1: With a New Introduction by Daniel Boorstin.* New York: Vintage Books.

Van Riper, Paul P. (1958) *History of the United States Civil Service.* Evanston, IL: Row, Peterson and Company.

Waldo, Dwight (1984) *The Administrative State, 2nd edn.* New York: Holmes and Meier Publishers.

Waldo, Dwight (1999) 'Foreword: Modern Public Administration as Model and Portent', in Walter Kickert and Richard Stillman (eds), *The Modern State and Its Study: New Administrative Sciences in a Changing Europe and United States.* Northampton, MA: Edward Elgar. pp. ix–xii.

White, Leonard D. (1948) *The Federalists: A Study in Administrative History, 1789–1801.* New York: Free Press.

White, Leonard D. (1954) *The Jacksonians: A Study in Administrative History, 1829–1861.* New York: Free Press.

White, Leonard D. (1956) *The Jeffersonians: A Study in Administrative History 1801–1829.* New York: Macmillan.

White, Leonard D. (1958) *The Republican Era, 1869–1901: A Study in Administrative History.* New York: Macmillan.

14

Administrative Traditions in Western Europe

Fabio Rugge

It is the purpose of this chapter to trace some of the major historical developments that provide the background of today's public administrations. This will be done not for the sake of mere documentary information, but with the intention of delineating traditions and legacies of particular relevance to our contemporary scene. In other words, the following is an attempt to place the existing 'administrative order' in a *longue durée* perspective, regarding it as a continuation or an alteration of previous administrative regimes or – in some respects at least – as a reaction to them.

The account will focus on European public administrations in the four largest countries: France, Germany, Italy and the United Kingdom. This choice is not based on a hierarchical appreciation of the various European traditions, although at least two of these four cases represent generally acknowledged 'models' in public administration. The selection rather depends on the present state of the art in comparative administrative history (Raadschelders, 1998) – and on the limits set to this chapter, which oblige the author to climb dangerously the ladder of abstraction up to the highest rungs (Sartori, 1970), and to neglect even some traditionally acknowledged differences between the national cases under review (Heady, 2001; Peters, 1988).

In this account special attention will be paid to the governmental penetration of civil society as reflected in the history of the past two centuries. Thus, no illustration will be provided of the history of the civil service as a social group (educational backgrounds, lifestyles, prevailing ideological allegiances, public employees' associations and unions); nor will there be a description of the changing features of bureaucratic work (from the pen to the typewriting machine to the computer etc.). Instead of such 'bureau-history', an historical account will be offered concerning some critical aspects of the role played by public administrations within modern political institutions and within society at large.

In the first section, the emergence of what we can term a 'modern public administration' will be sketched, so as to point to its fundamental traits in comparison with previous administrative regimes. The next section will deal with the differentiation process, which has made two different spheres of politics and administration, without however bringing about a separation or a reciprocal autonomy of the two. The third section will recount how the state's civilian activities – and public administrations as a consequence – expanded continuously from about the 1880s up to the 1980s, when that expansion met with a severe opposition. The fourth section will look at the growing 'pluralism' in public administration, starting from the nineteenth-century dualism of central and local administration up to the entropy displayed by administrative systems of the late twentieth century. The last section will highlight the development of those devices meant to ensure that public administrations act according to the law and without impinging infringement upon the individual citizen's freedom and legitimate interests.

WHEN IT ALL BEGAN

How far into the past should one reasonably venture in order to trace the antecedents of today's administrative systems? It is difficult to answer, given the influence of a characteristic consistently considered typical of public administration: that of continuity.

Eminent authors have either maintained or proved[1] that, in contrast to political systems and constitutional arrangements, administrative regimes do not experience those thorough collapses or all-pervading transitions that enable historians to speak – as they love to – of 'new eras' or of 'turning points'. In other words, periodization, always a challenging task for historians, may become particularly controversial when administrative history is at stake. Even wars as 'total' as those fought in the past century often failed in producing clear-cut discontinuities (Burk, 1982; Rugge, 2000).

Nonetheless, no administrative system is isolated from the institutional framework, both political and constitutional, in which it operates. This means that major changes affecting that framework inevitably reverberate, in however an attenuated way, on the administrative structures. When those changes are – or appear to be – epoch-making for the political and constitutional history, they usually provide some sort of punctuation in administrative history too.

Now, it can be reasonably argued that the decades prior to 1850 witnessed crucial developments in the sphere of political institutions. Indeed, those decades were decisive for the establishment of a new constitutional era. To be sure, that era had been inaugurated as early as 1776 by the American constitution and, a few years later, by the French revolutionary instruments. Still, the whole first half of the following century had to pass by before a new generation of constitutions spread all over Europe, making constitutional government both a permanent feature of most polities and a model for all of them.[2] In the United Kingdom, where no written constitution was ever adopted and a parliament had been established long before the nineteenth century, reforms as important as the Reform Act of 1832 helped produce a new constitutional framework.

This great transformation brought about two processes crucial to the development of modern public administration: the end of the 'kingly' administrations (Dreyfus, 2000; Wilson, 1887) and the invention of the politics/administration dichotomy.

As to the first, the adoption of constitutional arrangements entailed that state administration would no longer hinge – as it had used to do – on the figure of the monarch. Indeed, until the end of the seventeenth century and possibly later, nothing resembling an administrative structure in the modern sense of the word had

actually existed (Maravall, 1972). In its place, a network of king's servants dispensed *his* justice (such activity being regarded as the essence of administration) and administered the state's finances (conceived of as the monarch's patrimony).

During the eighteenth century, as the state became increasingly de-personalized and the scope of its action came to coincide, at least ideally, with the common welfare, the crown's servants were gradually replaced by state's servants, whose personal dependence on the sovereign was coupled with – although rarely replaced by – an institutional relation to the state (Jakoby, 1973; Raadschelders and Rutgers, 1996; Rosenberg, 1958). Real administrative apparatuses developed and their activities and proper functioning became the subject of a large number of writings, soon to amalgamate into a body of knowledge defined as the administrative science(s). Notwithstanding all this restructuring, 'kingly administrations' were not superseded until the beginning of the nineteenth century.[3] Up to this time, monarchs largely retained their powers in shaping states' administrative structures, in controlling their action, in appointing their personnel.

In the new constitutional era, new 'princes' arose to claim command over public administration: elected parliaments, speaking in the name of 'the people'. Such a take-over caused – and was accompanied by – a number of relevant changes, some of them deeply affecting the history of public administration in Europe. In particular, three great administrative issues emerged from the crisis of the previous constitutional order.

First, just as the 'kingly administration' had served the sovereign's interests, the new 'constitutional administration' was to serve the interests of the 'people', as they were represented in the parliament. Now, in the presence of a liberal-democratic pressure to enlarge the franchise, a proliferation of the represented interests was inevitable in terms both of the issues and of the people concerned (Rokkan, 1970). That opened the question as to whether the constitutional administration should deal with those issues and look after those people through regulative action or through direct intervention. This question, and the solutions given to it, have been a leitmotiv of administrative history in the past two centuries. They will be more closely addressed later in the chapter.

Secondly, the end of the 'kingly administrations' and the rise of a new constellation of constitutional values meant that any autocratic vein had to be removed from administrative procedures and from the civil servant's attitude towards citizens. Administration should no longer act so as to follow to the monarch's arbitrary will, but only according to the law and *therefore* entirely respecting all individual rights enshrined in the constitution no less than the individual citizen's interests warranted by the laws. From that moment on, the question of how (public) authority and (private) freedom should be conveniently balanced accompanied the history of modern public administration and became an important aspect of its development. Special attention will be devoted to this 'great issue' in the final section of the chapter.

Finally, a third great issue was brought about by the new constitutional era with the establishment of sovereign parliaments: this concerned the differentiation between politics and administration. This issue will be addressed first, because it is logically antecedent to those concerning the extent and the modes of administrative action. Indeed, it has actually to do with the very identity of public administration within institutional traditions in Europe.

THE POLITICS/ADMINISTRATION DICHOTOMY

Traditionally, public administration has been conceptualized as distinct from and often as the opposite of politics: its virtuous sister to some, its dull servant to others. The concept of politics has been taken to indicate the sphere where public opinion is formed, social interests are debated and confront each other, political parties act, authoritative decisions are taken; administration has been conceived as a single integrated piece of machinery, unstirred by partisan passions, devoted to advisory, clerical and technical work. The distinction between the two spheres has been regarded as obvious; their separation deemed desirable and even preached as indispensable.

Although such a distinction is very problematic in theory and separation has proved more than problematic in practice,[4] no one can deny that these ideas have represented a mighty intellectual – or ideological – pattern, which strongly contributed to shaping and animating public administration throughout the past two centuries. For this reason, the pattern and the reality behind it deserve some scrutiny.

First, the separation of politics and administration found a long-lasting anchorage in the doctrine about the separation of powers, which received its most popular expression in Montesquieu's *De l'esprit des lois* (1748).

According to this doctrine, and to its subsequent adjustments and applications, the executive power, and therefore the administration, must be separated from the legislative and the judiciary powers, and be exclusively charged with the task of implementing the legislator's will.

Secondly – and paradoxically – the permanence of some *ancien régime* features fostered the new politics/administration dichotomy. In particular, the persistent influence of the crown over the bureaucracy (civil servants continued to take an oath of loyalty to the monarch into the twentieth century) helped permeate administration with a unitary, hierarchical spirit and shape the image of the deferential civil servants (the opposite of the allegedly quarrelsome and treacherous politician). This was far more evident in those countries, like Prussia, where parliament played a feeble role in the new constitutional arrangements and the king stood out as the pole star of state bureaucracy.

Thirdly, around the mid-nineteenth century, a new practical factor came to support the politcs/administration dichotomy: a growing functional differentiation between the profession of the politician and that of the bureaucrat. Such a differentiation was to emerge more clearly in the decades around the turn of the century.

For politicians, parliamentary life – inside and outside the Chambers – became more and more complex and demanding, while ministers found it increasingly difficult to deal with the details of state affairs (as they had used to do in the past). As to the civil servants, at least for those in the high and middle ranks of the bureaucratic pyramid, the complexity and technicality of their work intensified. The establishment of a permanent civil service was largely prompted by the want of personnel with an entire and stable devotion to the administrative work. In its turn, the general spread of the merit system, although the outcome of many other circumstances, clearly signalled that a certain educational background was required for this kind of work (Cassese and Pellew, 1987).

However, in spite of the three factors just recalled (constitutional prescription about the separation of powers, influence of certain legacies of the *ancien régime*, professional differentiation between politicians and bureaucrats), it would be hazardous to argue that in the past 150 years politics and administration have represented two entirely different enterprises and two thoroughly separate worlds.

From the mid-nineteenth century on, two major, convergent drives have urged the encroachment of politicians into the administrative arena: the need for loyal co-operation and the exercise of patronage. As an outcome of these two pressures, a sort of politico-administrative continuum has usually emerged, blurring the border between the two spheres. The reasons are clear (Raadschelders and Van der Meer, 1998).

As to the politician's need for loyal co-operation from the side of the civil service, this is an obvious precondition for any effective governmental action. In fact, it was felt to be critical in all parliamentary systems from the very outset of the new constitutional era (except perhaps in countries, like Prussia and later Germany where, until the Weimar Republic, the administration's loyalty to government was secured by the strict allegiance of both to the crown).

In the United Kingdom, a solution to possible frictions between politicians and bureaucrats was found relatively soon and consisted in the 'neutralizing' of the civil service: whatever the party in power, administration would steadfastly follow its policy. Such an arrangement, based on the acknowledgement of the civil servant's professionalism, is congruent with the politics/administration dichotomy, but removes the conflicting component from it, featuring in fact a sort of fusion of the political and the administrative spheres (Thomas, 1978).

A different tradition prevailed in countries like France and Italy, where the politicization of public administration became the rule. Basically, this was achieved in two ways. On the one hand, ministerial cabinets were created in order to reinforce the minister's grip over the bureaucracy (Antoine, 1975; Rugge, 1998; Thuillier, 1982). On the other hand, the higher administrative positions were covered through appointment by the government. Such was the case with the prefects – key figures in these two centralized states – whose appointments and transfers very often had clear partisan purposes (Le Clère and Wright, 1973).

In the case of France it could be added that educational institutions like the Ecole Nationale d'Administration (ENA, established in 1945), originally meant to develop an administrative elite detached from the political leadership, changed into a sort of forcing ground for producing an elite capable of filling leading positions in the administration as well as in the political system (often commuting between the two). The process further attenuated the politics/administration dichotomy.

But patronage has been the main breach in that dichotomy (although this practice has been traditionally blamed in European political discourse). Especially the rise of mass parties at the end of the nineteenth and the beginning of the twentieth century reinforced this tendency, creating new

stimulants for it. First, mass parties collected and drilled a host of potential seekers of administrative positions. Secondly, mass parties were based on political creeds, demanding unflinching loyalty. In this kind of polity, ideological affinity between political and administrative officeholders was considered crucial and indeed became critical.

The outcome of this change may be observed in its most acute manifestation in the authoritarian regimes of the 1920s and the 1930s. For instance, both Italian fascism and German national-socialism – the prototypes of that kind of regime in Europe – disclaimed the liberal tenet about the separation between politics and administration; both preached the ideal of a state entirely pervaded by one ideology and commanded by one leader. However, as far as the civil services of the two countries are concerned, the two regimes were not equally successful in their purposes.

In Germany, Hitler's coming to power brought about a far-reaching change (not to say purge) in the higher ranks of public administration; but that did not avoid persistent tensions between the Nazi party and traditional bureaucracy (for instance, as to the recruitment procedures) (Caplan, 1988; Hattenhauer, 1980; Mommsen, 1966; Wunder, 1986). In Italy, the attempt to produce a civil service in 'black shirts' ended up with a tacit compromise. On the whole, the ministerial bureaucracy was loyal to the government, but quite often paid only lip-service to the fascist ideology and the government in its turn had to renounce the goal of colonizing the administration and was obliged to blandish the civil servants' class instead (Melis, 1996; Salvati, 1992).

Where Mussolini had a free hand was in those administrative bodies that fascism itself had created in order to discharge some of the new tasks the state took upon itself throughout the interwar period. In this sort of parallel public administration (see the following section), primarily made up of welfare agencies, fascism could place new men with a special reputation for their ideological allegiance to the regime or their administrative talents (Melis, 1996).

Seemingly peculiar to the Fascist regime, this process in fact designs a pattern replicated elsewhere and later on too – in democratic and multiparty systems. Indeed, twentieth-century governments and leading politicians have often enough been confronted with a state bureaucracy they perceived – and sometimes denounced – as sclerotic, incompetent or inefficient. Often such complaints had to do with the lack of political affinity between the civil servants and their political masters or with the resistance put up by the bureaucrats to politicians' encroachments into 'their' administrative territory. In any event, governments frequently reacted to such situations by circumventing state bureaucracies perceived as insufficiently co-operative, and increasingly resorted, in order to implement their policies, to administrative apparatuses located outside the typical ministerial framework. In pursuing such an 'outflanking strategy', state executives probably responded to a true need for effectiveness as much to their drive for patronage (although the two reasons have blended in different proportions according to circumstances).

THE ROAD TO 'BIG GOVERNMENT' – AND BACK

The creation of administrative structures outside the typical ministries or departments is connected with a phenomenon that, although not exclusive of the European tradition, is doubtless an important feature of it: the growth of government. This expression may in the first instance indicate the increase in number and latitude of the socially relevant matters for which public institutions (that is, central and local government or other agencies) claimed themselves – and were acknowledged – to be responsible.

In fact, the idea that the state's responsibility towards society was not limited to matters relating to law and order had become a commonly shared view and an established practice long before the mid-nineteenth century, especially on the continent (following the dictates of the German doctrine on the Polizei-staat[5] or the principles proclaimed by the French Revolution[6]). Early enough the construction and maintenance of roads and canals as well as forestry or the post office had fallen within the province of public administration's activity (for example, Dorwart, 1971).

Yet it was neither obvious nor undisputed that further state intervention should mean direct operation of public services rather than regulation of the supplying of those services through private trading or voluntary organizations. In fact, in the years around 1850, the idea of regulative – instead of operative – state intervention probably reached the zenith of its popularity among European ruling classes (although hardly any task already assumed by the state was in those years relinquished to societal actors) (Ellwein, 1965). Also from this point of view,

Table 14.1   *Per capita public expenditure in selected European countries, 1880–1910*

	1880	1910
France	81	100
Prussia/Germany	48	100
Italy	51	100[a]
United Kingdom	67	100

[a]Year 1912

Sources: Mann, 1993: ch. 11; Italy, Cassese, 1977. See also n. 7

Table 14.2   *Percentage of total population engaged in all levels of public administration, 1880–1910*

	1880	1910
France	1.28	1.42
Prussia/Germany	1.56	2.35
Italy	0.97	0.99
United Kingdom	0.46	2.60

Sources: Mann, 1993: ch. 11; Italy, Cassese, 1977. See also n. 7

then, these years may well be considered a turning point, as the regulative approach was replaced by a more operative-oriented philosophy.

From that moment on, the ideals of the minimal state and of the free market began to decline. From the 1880s and 1890s on, the prevalence of the statist tendency became more and more evident and for the century to come practically irreversible (Ashford, 1986). Government grew bigger; and so did public administration. A good piece of evidence of the process is supplied by the figures concerning the public expenditures for civilian purposes.

Table 14.1 shows how, in the four countries considered here, the per capita public expenditure at constant prices grew in the period between 1880 and 1910 (1910 = 100). In the same period also the percentage of people employed in the civil service in all levels of public administration increased, especially in the United Kingdom and Germany, as shown in Table 14.2. The figures offered in Tables 14.1 and 14.2 are not totally reliable (the state's ability to 'count itself' was itself the product of the development under consideration);[7] nevertheless, they consistently point to an upward trend of the financial and personnel resources wielded by public administrations.

The numerical evidence of the growth of government is supplemented by morphological evidence (Rosanvallon, 1990). The design of public administrations in each country became increasingly differentiated and intricate: new ministries, departments, offices and authorities were established. Sometimes this was the result of a process of functional specialization, sometimes of the necessity to cope with an emergency, sometimes of merely symbolic purposes.

If we simply look at the central administration and at its typical units – the ministries or the departments – their very name and order of appearance are testimony to the process through which an ever-increasing number of social transactions or conditions were progressively forming the subject of public policies and public administrative action.

First to appear, often long before the period under consideration, were the ministries for internal and foreign affairs, war and justice – all bound to the state's classical task of preserving the country from internal and external threats – and the ministries of finance or the treasury set out to extract financial resources necessary for discharging the aforementioned task (Mayntz, 1982). In the decades after 1850 the establishment of new ministries was a rather occasional occurrence. But from the 1880s and for the following century – a statist century indeed – the government's engagement in a number of new fields was institutionalized, supported and displayed by the creation of a host of special ministries.

The path and pace of such a parade of ministries are to a large extent related to the idiosyncrasies of each country's economic, social and political development. Thus France had its Ministère de l'Instruction publique in 1830 (Lelièvre, 1990; Prost, 1968), whereas this was not the case for the United Kingdom until 1945. But cross-national comparison of ministerial ramifications is made problematic by the diversity of nomenclatures and organizational principles used in the different nations, as well as by the fact that sometimes administrative units were active in one country without attaining the status of a ministry given them in another. For instance, a general directorate for the *sanità pubblica* (public health) had existed in Italy, more or less continuously, since 1887, but it became a ministry only in 1958.

In this period a variety of departments and other administrative bodies were the result of international events and cross-national political movements, which produced 'generations of ministries'. In 1916 and 1917, with the establishment of the Ministry of Pensions and of Labour respectively, the UK inaugurated a wave of homologous institutions like the German Arbeitsministerium (1918–19), the Italian Ministero del lavoro e della previdenza sociale (1920), the French Ministère d'Hygiène et de la Prévoyance sociale (1920, while a Ministère du Travail had already been established in 1906) (Tournerie, 1971).

Similarly, at the local government level, in the early twentieth century, utility companies, owned and managed by the municipal corporations (in German *Gemeindebetriebe*, in Italian *aziende municipalizzate*), spread all over Europe. The Verein für Sozialpolitik, a think-tank of German scholars (comprising, among others, Max Weber and Adolph Wagner), organized its 1909 conference in Vienna on this issue and published a collection of national reports, which in their turn contributed to the spread of this form of public intervention.

In sum, from the mid-nineteenth century on, both the figures and the morphology of the administrative complex account for what appears as a relentless march towards 'big government'. Decade after decade, public administration became a common presence in the daily life of every citizen.

A discussion of the historical factors causing or supporting this progression lies outside the scope of this chapter. Nonetheless, a couple of those factors may be mentioned in passing, while detailing some aspects of the process.

First, there is no doubt that government reacted to direct or systemic pressure to provide the infrastructure necessary for economic development. On a nationwide scale, this meant that an often reluctant state got involved in the provision of such services as the post, the railways and the telephone. The post was a traditional state-operated service; but state railways and telephone services were the fruit of the blooming statist season between 1880 and 1914. Germany nationalized its railways from the 1880s, with Prussia as a forerunner in 1879; France, after a timid and almost forced beginning in 1878, purchased a more substantial network from a private company in 1908; the Italian government began to run the entire railway system in 1905 (while the United Kingdom chose the 'regulative option' until 1947). The nationwide telephone systems experienced a similar shift from private to public ownership and operation (France 1889, Germany 1892, the UK 1896–98, Italy 1907) (Bertho-Lavenir, 1991).

On a local basis – and in particular in the rapidly expanding cities – transportation means, as well as water, gas and electricity, were increasingly provided by local authorities all over Europe (as discussed in the following section).

In this policy area, public administration performed a role that was supportive and indeed propulsive of economic growth. Although conflicts occasionally arose with individual private companies running the mentioned utilities as licensees or grantees, overall industrial and commercial interests benefited from public ownership no less than did the general public.

In another policy area, connected with both cultural and social integration, the role of public administration was of a benevolent and protective rather than propulsive nature. Healthcare, social insurance and pensions became the terrain of welfare policies, which helped relieve poverty, reduce social tensions and enhance living standards (Alber, 1982). In fact, even before the First World War the democratization of the franchise had produced parliaments that were more inclined to legislate in favour of this sort of intervention than had been their predecessors (who were rather tended to pursue propulsive policies).

It goes without saying that the two policy areas and the two corresponding roles – the propulsive and the benevolent – although distinguishable in theory, were not separated at all in practice. Education is a typical case in point. Attendance at primary school was an occasion for children of the lower classes to improve their social condition, but general economic progress also depended on it, while parents in their turn did not always perceive their children's compulsory school attendance as a 'benevolent' measure.

It should also be noted that, although the commitment of governments was generalized in the course of the statist century, some of them were proactive and others tardier, some hastened to monopolize and centralize service provisions, others tolerated and even welcomed substitution by non-governmental actors (for example, the Church). To take education as an example once more, as early as 1882 German governmental schools at all levels employed about 115,000 people (Mayntz, 1982); comparable figures were attained in Italy only in 1931. And while in 1902 the UK parliament was ready (some say happy) to put independent School Boards under local authorities' control, the Italian parliament, a few years later (1911), dissatisfied with the way the communes were dealing with primary school matters, enlarged the central government's competence on those matters (De Fort, 1996).

It is generally acknowledged that the First and the Second World Wars provided a spur for further government growth. The two conflicts favoured and sometimes demanded state regulative and operative intervention in fields that either had been a traditional province of free enterprise or had so far remained immune from all legal constraints (for example, housing, price regulation etc.). Moreover, the wars brought about and fostered co-operation between public administration and corporate interests in ways that, although varying in scope and intensity, were to prove a permanent feature of twentieth-century public administrative systems.

Admittedly, the preceding account of the march towards 'big government' is to a certain extent one-sided. It has been assumed – albeit not always explicitly – that the expansion of public administration was the outcome of social pressures originated outside the politico-administrative system and that that system only reacted to them – no matter whether in a planned or a haphazard mode. Yet a different tale could be told. Other versions of the same story emphasize that, especially after the rise of mass parties, the growth of government became a vital concern of the politicians, because it was associated with an increase in power and patronage. Government and public administration then may have grown bigger independent of social demands or well beyond them (Dunleavy and O'Leary, 1987: ch. 3; Poggi, 1991: ch. 7).

Credit must be lent to this opinion, if only because of the authoritative sources that have shared it: from Benjamin Constant (who spoke of the politicians' *esprit de conquête* long before mass parties had come into existence) up to some versions of the public choice theory. However, from the point of view of the present account, the relevant question is: did civil servants share their political masters' alleged interest in the growth of government? As a matter of fact, bureaucrats earn their living from bureaucracy: hardly any of those civil servants who made a name as leaders in public administration[8] preached *laissez-faire* and none of them gained a place in history for having dismantled administrative apparatuses.

Some politicians did. It is well known that, in the early 1980s, British Conservative cabinets made the recurrently voiced demand to reduce government the crucial issue on their agenda. Other European governments followed in their steps. Public welfare administrations and provisions were downsized; privatization of public corporations and services was legislated; a regulative rather than operative role for public administration was designed. Both the desirability and the practical outcome of such policies have been largely questioned (for example, Clarke and Newman, 1997). At any event, they have been perceived as a clear and sometimes dramatic rupture of an apparently well-established European administrative tradition. This rupture also reverberated on the methods and criteria of administrative action (Savoie, 1994). Under the watchword of 'New Public Management' an effort has been made to renew the organization and the operation of public administration, basically on the model of the private corporation (Dunleavy and Hood, 1994).

Historical perspective may provide some grounds for de-emphasizing the novelty of both the regulative and the managerial state. As far as regulation is concerned, although partially yielding to direct intervention in the early twentieth century and after the Second World War, it has never ceased to play a decisive role in the relations between the state and relevant societal actors. And it was often abandoned because it had proven ineffective or costly or both (Rials, 1985).

As to managerialism, it has been a permanent goal of many administrative reformers in the last hundred years, starting with the attempt to introduce the teachings of Taylorism into the public office, an attempt labelled in Italy as *taylorismo della scrivania* (desk Taylorism) (Melis, 1988: 201–34) and strenuously preached in France by personalities like Henry Chardon (Kuisel, 1981; Pierrot, 1970; Rials, 1977). A few factors have made this goal elusive, not least the persisting cultural resistance to the assimilation of public administration and private corporations. However, even at the beginning of the twentieth century tendencies were already at work to the effect of blurring and confusing the public/private dichotomy, as the next section will show.

CENTRAL, LOCAL AND PARALLEL

Although metaphors traditionally used to represent public administration frequently refer to machines or armies, real 'public administration' is – and always has been – much less compact and integrated than that.

As the account in the previous sections should have already made clear, public administration has historically comprised a multitude of authorities, apparatuses and offices endowed with different sorts of powers, entrusted with a vast array of different functions and scattered on the national territory. Indeed, rather than a peninsula intruding into the sea of societal life, public administration has come to resemble an archipelago embracing numerous islands of various sizes – some of them, like oceanic islets, periodically sinking and then emerging again (to the great annoyance of the administrative historian trying to map them).

It is true, however, that at the outset of the period under consideration, the design of public administration was much less complex. After all, by the end of the nineteenth century, most European states had gone through a process of both unification and centralization.

Unification and centralization might have already been attained a long time before – as in the case of France – or be recent accomplishments – as in Italy; they might have been fulfilled on the basis of a unitary constitution or a federal one (the latter being the case for Germany) and have produced a more or less centralized administration. But, at the closing of the nineteenth century, some sort of state and state administration stood there, towering over all the other governing institutions of each and any country in Europe.

German legal doctrine was particularly vehement in praising the creature born of a long-fought battle against particularism and the outcome of a passionate quest for 'rational' government. In the United Kingdom such rhetoric would have sounded alien, if not repugnant. Nonetheless, also in that country, throughout the nineteenth century, central government kept striving, albeit not always resolutely and often unsuccessfully, to bring about some order and uniformity in the administrative system at large (Bellamy, 1988).

Moreover, at that moment, the march towards 'big government' had only just begun and had not yet brought about that need for functional differentiation in administration which was to become evident a few decades later. In sum, public administration was still fundamentally state administration and a rather cohering and essential construct.

To be sure, in that construct one could notice differences and inconsistencies, both cultural and functional, involving, for instance, ministries called to co-operate in the implementation of a policy, as well as the field services of different ministries operating in the same territorial area. However, differences and inconsistencies of this sort hardly led to real conflicts. On the contrary, conflict was a rather common occurrence in the relationship between central government and local administrations, that relationship offering the most evident instance of division and tension within national administrative systems in the context of the nineteenth-century state.

At the root of the strains in central–local relations lay the fact that, already in the first half of the century, local governments, especially at the municipal level, had become elective bodies. This had happened in France as early as 1789, during the revolution, but it was a short-lived measure. Abolished in 1795, elections of municipal councils were then resumed in 1831. In Prussia, the first German state to adopt communal elections, they were introduced in 1808, by a decree of Baron vom Stein. In England elective borough councils were established by the Municipal Corporations Act in 1835 for 178 boroughs and subsequently extended. In the Kingdom of Piedmont, the immediate antecedent of the Kingdom of Italy, elections of municipal councils were enacted in 1848.

As a result, local administrations had become primarily responsive to their own political masters. Although the scope of local councils' competencies differed from country to country, these elective bodies were commonly entitled to set their own policy agenda, to provide for their revenues and to recruit their officials and employees. On each of these points their choice might happen to collide with what central governments would suggest, demand or expect. Hence the aforementioned strain – or at least what we may term an unsteady balance – between central government and local self-government.

This fact is of a seemingly paradoxical nature. As we have seen, locally elected councils, and therefore the establishment of legitimated local governments, were a product of state legislation. And sometimes, as in the case of Prussia, such legislation was clearly conceived, designed and enforced from above. In other terms, elective local government was essentially a creature of the state. Yet, in the very moment they gave birth to this creature, central governments proceeded to bridle it with all sorts of restraints, retaining the right of appointment for some key positions, imposing tasks on it, variously interfering in its fiscal policy and setting up control authorities and procedures.

To be sure, state tutelage could be more or less penetrating. For instance, it was not until 1933 that a uniform system of external budget auditing through district auditors (rather than through locally appointed personnel) was imposed on English municipal corporations. But also in England, whose local liberties were highly reputed and often mythologized on the continent, restrictions on the use of the boroughs' funds were dictated (especially in 1872) and important tasks were assigned to the boroughs themselves – for example, in the educational field, with the Education Act of 1902 (which entailed that from that moment on at least 20 per cent of local government spending was absorbed by education) (Ashford, 1980; Bellamy, 1988; Dunleavy, 1984). In countries of the Napoleonic tradition, like France and Italy, interference and control from the central government were normalcy: *maires* and *sindaci*, (Agulhon, 1986; Aimo, 1992), the heads of municipal administration, were selected and appointed by the central

government respectively until 1882/1884 in France and 1888/1896 in Italy.[9]

Why then had the nineteenth-century states promoted self-government at all? What did they need it for? A comprehensive answer to these questions should take into account a large number of factors, pertaining both to constitutional and political history. For instance, it should be borne in mind that previous local institutions had never been totally eradicated by nation-state sovereignty – they could be given a new identity, but they could not be ignored. Furthermore, it should be recalled how sensitive nineteenth-century ruling classes were to any idea connected with freedom and that local liberties were among the most praised liberties.

From the point of view of the administrative historian, the establishment of elective local authorities proceeded from the experience that a centrally ruled public administration was not expedient and possibly not capable of properly implementing all of the public policies (starting with an effective maintenance of law and order and the exaction of fiscal revenues). Local self-government entailed the possibility of mobilizing local elites and involving them in administrative activities on an honorary basis – and that with at least a twofold gain. First, such involvement was likely to enhance local communities' acceptance of, and co-operative attitude towards, public policies; secondly, it secured for skills public administration skills, from literacy to more sophisticated expertise, which were relatively rare at that time and should otherwise have been paid for.

All this implies a systemic relation between central and local administration. They were distinct from one another, and at times opposed to one another, but in the end they were the two key elements of one governance system responsible for the still limited number of public policies.

In that system, however, the state was the dominating actor. Only at the turn of the century was its position threatened. Cities all over Europe turned into laboratories of new policies and administrative devices (Hietala, 1987). In the United Kingdom, by the Edwardian period, municipal enterprise had become 'big business', and the Fabian Society was actively and successfully diffusing the gospel of socially concerned town halls (Falkus, 1977; MacBriar, 1966: ch. 8). In Italy, socialists and radicals were governing cities as important as Rome and Milan, while a law passed in 1903 provided legal basis for the mushrooming municipal enterprises. Proactive German burgomasters applied the principles of municipalization and the prescriptions of municipal engineering (*Städtetechnik*) upon a far more extensive scale than any other country (Hofmann, 1974; Rugge, 1989). Even French *communes*, although under tighter state grip, undertook new important tasks, especially in the fields of water provision and sewerage (Cohen, 1998; Rugge, 1992).

In short, municipal government became the cradle of administrative innovations and the expression 'civic renaissance' was forged to characterize this development. But, during the interwar period, the 'civic renaissance' came to a sudden end. War had brought the state to the foreground again. Furthermore, in two countries where municipal activism had been utmost (Germany and Italy) the authoritarian rule reduced local administration to an articulation of the central government and of the party machinery.

Not before the end of the Second World War was the development of local government set in motion again. The most relevant changes, however, did not affect city government. They rather concerned the intermediate level of administration, that is, territorial sub-units of the state such as regions, departments and the like. In particular, between the 1960s and 1970s, regionalization emerged as an important issue in the political debate of the countries under review (with the partial exception of Germany, with its traditionally established federal fabric) (Meny, 1982).

The practical results of this regionalistic upsurge were different. In Italy, a process of devolution of both legislative and administrative tasks to the regions went ahead in the 1970s, in spite of considerable resistance from the ministerial bureaucracy (ISAP, 1984; Leonardi et al., 1987; Levy, 1996). In France, after the law of 1972 introducing a regionalization *en trompe-l'œil*, substantial decentralization was enacted only in 1982 (Hayward, 1973; Loughlin and Mazey, 1995). In the United Kingdom, a regional movement emerged in the early 1960s, went into hibernation about fifteen years later without producing remarkable or lasting outcomes (Regional Economic Planning Councils were established in 1964 and extinguished in 1979), and has only recently revived with major impact.

But the inner diversity and complexity of the contemporary public administration systems has not only resulted from the creation of new local authorities. In fact, as the state acquired new social and economic powers, these were increasingly vested in public boards or agencies, which were classifiable neither as government departments nor as local authorities. A new family of public administrations therefore developed.

The first appearance of this 'parallel' public administration did not coincide with the early steps of the march towards 'big government': it was rather an occurrence of the interwar period. Pending the First World War, the expansion of state intervention had reached a critical point, making clear that ministerial or departmental administrations were not entirely up to the challenges the conflict had imposed on them. That situation demanded more organizational flexibility, higher capacity to consult and sometimes integrate external stakeholders (especially corporate interests) and a single mission instead of multipurpose structures.

An ever-increasing number of authorities, agencies and commissions developed, which were ordinarily created by legislation, commonly supported by public funds and acted each in one special field, mostly with a national scope (social insurance, health care, education, information, highways, regulation and surveillance on public utilities etc.) (Rugge, 2000). These parallel administrations, although mostly entrusted to personnel appointed by central government, were indeed neither state nor governmental administrations, since their statutes warranted them extensive independence of action.

Because of this special position, in French and Italian legal languages these bodies were soon defined as *entités paraétatiques* or *enti parastatali*, whereas in English they were later described as 'fringe bodies' or 'quangos' (quasi non-governmental organizations) (Parliamentary Affairs, 1995). On the continent, they were considered – in conformity with their origins and purposes – as part of the public administration system, but they were mostly allowed to operate according to the civil law (that is, as if they were private persons). Since this aspect placed them in a sort of grey zone between the public administration and the private persons, Italian legal doctrine defined these agencies with the somewhat crude but perceptive expression of *enti ermafroditi* (hermaphrodite bodies) (Melis, 1988).

During the interwar period and soon after the Second World War, their growth was relentless and impressive,[10] especially in the economic arena (suffice it to mention the UK's massive nationalization in the aftermath of the war). Here the public/private interpenetration took the form of public corporations, usually created to stabilize key economic sectors, protect sensitive national interests, support the overall development and buttress governmental policies.

More generally, the reasons for establishing parallel administrations have been various. For example, in the above-mentioned experience of Italian fascism (which produced an extensive mixed economy), both the quest for efficiency and the need for patronage played a role. But the causes may have been different from efficiency and even opposed to patronage, as in those cases where entrusting an activity to autonomous bodies was meant to reduce the scope for direct political control. Such is the case with the so-called Independent Administrative Authorities, a more recent entity in the expanding universe of parallel administrations in Europe – often a counterpart to the publicly elected and politically ruled central and local administrations (see below).

As a result of the processes mentioned in this section, the image of the European administrative systems has undergone a profound change: from the state-centred design of the late nineteenth and early twentieth centuries, to a less orderly and recently almost enthropic pattern: an *administration en miettes* (Dupuy and Thoenig, 1985).

BETWEEN AUTHORITY AND FREEDOM

Nineteenth-century constitutionalism reshaped the relation between public authority and individual freedom in a way that was relevant for public administration too. According to the tenets of constitutionalism, public administration was a machinery that was meant to implement the people's will as enacted by the parliament. Consequently, it was bound to act according to the law, following the principle of the so-called *Rechtsstaat* (*Etat de droit*, *Stato di diritto*).

In theory, such a scheme left little room for conflicts between the individual citizen and the administration, as the latter would act according to rules agreed upon by all citizens through their representatives. To this effect an administration framed into a parliamentary system was much more legitimated to command compliance than any 'kingly administration' had been. As a matter of fact, however, conflicts did arise also in the new constitutional context, the most obvious ground for contrasts being the citizens' refusal to comply with administrative decisions they regarded as unfair or even illegal infringements of their interests and rights.

When this happened, two ways opened up before those citizens willing to protect their interests. On the one hand, they could address themselves to the administration with a request to change its decision (the so-called *gracious* way); on the other hand, citizens could resort to a judicial authority entitled to arbitrate the interests involved in the conflict and dispense justice.

Regarding the nature of such authorities, two different traditions, with some variations, prevailed in Europe. They are commonly represented through the contrast between the British and the French systems (although this contrast was largely the outcome of a misrepresentation of each of the traditions) (Cassese, 2000). The United Kingdom is taken as the model of those countries where public administration and officials acting on its behalf are considered equal to the citizen and therefore equally liable before the ordinary courts of law. They were therefore considered as the natural judge in litigation involving private persons and public officials. The French system was impregnated with a more acute sense of the speciality of public administration as a representative of the state and of the general interest, so that whenever the public authority's action collided with any private interest, it was understood that the case of the former should receive special consideration.[11]

Accordingly, already under Napoleon, in 1800, a special administrative body had been created (actually reorganized) to deal with administrative litigations: this was the Conseil d'Etat, coupled with the *conseils de préfecture* at the local level. It is important to note that the Conseil d'Etat had no right to give a decision of its own, it could only advise the executive's chief (that is, the head of the state), who was vested with ultimate responsibility for the fair operation of state bureaucracy (Wright, 1972a).

Such a solution was consistent with the doctrine of the separation of powers, since it forbade the judiciary's review over decisions taken by the executive. But it also originated from a political preoccupation: that the judiciary, being a conservative body, might take advantage of its review power to hinder the implementation of the executive's revolutionary policies.

Arrangements located somewhere between the French and the British systems were experienced elsewhere. In Italy, for instance, a reform passed in 1865 gave the ordinary courts full jurisdiction on conflicts between public administration and citizens only when a political or patrimonial right was at stake; on matters concerning mere interests (as opposed to rights proper) and on other matters specifically mentioned by the law, the Consiglio di Stato, reorganized in 1831 upon the French model, retained its jurisdiction.

The Italian solution, however, may well be considered as the late fruit of an early season in the history of the continental systems of administrative justice. Those systems were under stress. The expanding scope of the state's activities was providing new occasions for conflicts between citizens and public administration. The growth of government was increasing the number of those who, being the servants of public authorities, were not entitled to appeal to ordinary courts and were therefore at pains to defend their interests before authorities that were at the same time both their masters and their judges. In short, the need for administrative courts, independent from the executive although separated from the ordinary courts, became evident.

Hence a stream of reforms. In 1872, the French Conseil d'Etat received a statutory competence to issue final judgment instead of mere advice on administrative litigation, acquiring as a result broader autonomy from the executive (Wright, 1972b). In 1875, Prussia legislated the institution of the Oberverwaltungsgericht (Superior Administrative Court), staffed with personnel sharing the same status and protection as the ordinary judges (Rüfner, 1984). A few years later (1889), the Italian Consiglio di Stato was reformed, to the effect of rendering its functioning more similar to the proceedings of the ordinary courts. Moreover, its jurisdiction was extended to those cases where citizens could not claim that any of their own rights had been violated, but could nevertheless claim that the unlawful conduct of the public administration had resulted in some kind of damage to their interests (the so-called *interesse legittimo*) (Aimo, 2000).

As for the United Kingdom, its path was apparently different. On the Continent a specific branch of public law, administrative law (*diritto amministrativo, droit administratif, Verwaltungsrecht*) (Burdeau, 1995; Heyen, 1982; Mannori and Sordi, 2001; Stolleis, 1992/1999) had been elaborated in order to rationalize and systematize jurisprudence concerning the special relationship between citizens and public administration. This juridical doctrine served as a reliable term of reference for administrative courts in their mission to balance authority and freedom – the state administration's supremacy with the inviolable rights of the individuals.

Nothing of this sort had been produced in the UK – stated, somewhat proudly, one of the great British scholars, Albert Venn Dicey, as late as 1884: the British constitution, having put public officials and private citizens on an equal footing, had made any such elaboration superfluous. All administrative litigation was solved by application of the ordinary law of the realm through the ordinary courts.

Reality, however, differed from Dicey's idealized constitution – and it was to differ even more profoundly in the following decades. Indeed, public administration's tasks had been growing dramatically in the UK too, touching upon fields such as sanitation, education, urban planning, building etc. (see above). Moreover, very often when a new policy had been legislated, a corresponding new *tribunal* had been set up. Yet such tribunals were not judicial authorities in the continental sense of the term. Their procedures were not those of a judicial body; they were composed of lay members, were entrusted with functions of active administration and usually incorporated some technical expertise. Administrative tribunals of this sort were originated, for example, through the London Building Act in 1894 and the National Insurance Act in 1911. In sum, although in principle submitted to the ordinary court's jurisdiction, much litigation between citizens and public authorities increasingly became the province of a variety of administrative tribunals, especially around the turn from the nineteenth to the twentieth century.

This system had some advantages, particularly in terms of expediency and technical appropriateness. Most of all, it is dubious whether the welfare state itself could have ever come into existence had the ordinary courts been the sole authority in charge of arbitrating that 'new deal' between individual freedom and social concern which underpinned the emerging welfare state.[12] Ordinary courts' jurisprudence, deeply rooted in the common law tradition, interpreted private property and freedom of contract as 'inflexible rights', while socio-political circumstances at the beginning of the twentieth century demanded they be softened into 'qualified rights', protected in as much as they were considered compatible with the common weal.

On the other hand, administrative tribunals' procedures did not offer sufficient protection to the rights of private persons. For instance, the possibility of appealing to the courts against the tribunals' decisions was restricted by law so as to become exceptional (Arthurs, 1985). In 1929, the Lord Chief Justice, Lord Hewart, in a famous book carrying the only too eloquent title *The New Despotism*, characterized this situation, speaking of 'administrative lawlessness' (Hewart, 1929). A redressing tendency set in thereafter. Particularly since the Franks Committee's report of 1957, a number of safeguards in the tribunals' procedure and composition have been adopted (such as the right of appeal or the appointment of legally qualified chairmen) which has brought them closer to the functioning of ordinary courts.

Looking at such developments, a convergence can be discerned between the continental and the British systems for securing a reasonable protection of private interests against governmental action without subjecting the latter to the judiciary's alien and often conservative control. The solution has been found in the creation of a panoply of bodies, bearing a more or less evident resemblance to the ordinary courts, but still different from them.

Even the more recently developed Independent Administrative Authorities, exercising both regulative tasks and judicial functions, may be considered as belonging to that panoply (Amato, 1998; Colliard and Timsit, 1988). And it is surely not insignificant for the metamorphosis of European modern polities that the noun 'authority' has come to indicate an arbitrating agency different from both the judges and the responsive government.

NOTES

1 One can consider Alexis de Tocqueville as the most prominent supporter (and indeed creator) of this opinion, since he argued that the effects of the French Revolution on the developments of French Administration had commonly been 'exaggerated' (Tocqueville, 1964). Making reference to the Weimar constitution, Otto Mayer, the 'father' of German administrative law, stated: 'Constitutional law passes by, administrative law stands still' (Mayer, 1924: introduction). On the 'mechanics' of administrative evolution, see also Legendre (1968: ch. 1).

2 A list of the countries adopting new constitutions in the first half of the nineteenth century should include: Spain (in 1812, then 1837 and 1845); France (1814, then 1830 and 1848); Holland (in 1815, thoroughly revised in 1848); Portugal (in 1821, then 1826, repeatedly modified afterwards); Belgium (1831); Piedmont and Switzerland (1848); Prussia (1850).

3 According to Henry Parris, the expression 'permanent civil service' does not apply to the period prior to 1780–1830 (Parris, 1969: ch. 1) See also Harling (1996). Not before the mid-nineteenth century did the modern concept of 'fonctionnaire' prevail in France (Thuiller and Tulard, 1994: 42).

4 For a disclaimer of the 'ancient proverb' about the politics/administration dichotomy, see Peters (1995: 177–8).

5 This doctrine was meant to provide the sovereign with the conceptual frameworks and practical guidance necessary to achieve and safeguard the welfare of his subjects (Brückner, 1977).

6 See the constitutional provisions, establishing both the Secours publics and the Instruction publique (titre premier of the 1791 constitution).

7 Figures drawn from Mann (1993: ch. 11), who offers a convincing discussion of data collected by other authors and of their interpretations. Figures concerning Italy have been derived from Cassese (1977).

8 For the concept of leadership in administration, see the study by Chapman (1984).

9 For a discussion – also in an historical perspective – of different models of central–local relations, see Page (1991).

10 See the figures concerning Italy in Mortara (1972).

11 Upon the diffusion of the French, and particularly the Napoleonic model of administration, see Wunder (1995).

12 This point was first made in the seminal work by Robson (1928).

REFERENCES

Agulhon, Maurice (ed.) (1986) *Les Maires en France du Consulat à nos jours*. Paris: Publications de la Sorbonne.

Aimo, Piero (1992) 'La "sciarpa tricolore": sindaci e maires nell'Europa dell'Ottocento', in *Jahrbuch für europäische Verwaltungsgeschichte*, 293–324.

Aimo, Piero (2000) *La giustizia nell'amministrazione dall'Ottocento ad oggi*. Bari/Rome: Laterza.

Alber, Jens (1982) *Vom Armenhaus zum Wohlfahrtsstaat. Analysen zur Entwicklung der Sozialversicherung in Westeuropa*. Frankfurt a.M.: Campus Verlag.

Amato, Giuliano (1998) 'Le autorità indipendenti', in L. Violante (ed.), *Storia d'Italia. Annali 14: Legge, diritto, giustizia*. Turin: Einaudi.

Antoine, Michel (ed.) (1975) *Origines et histoire des cabinets des ministres en France*. Geneva: Droz.

Arthurs, Harry William (1985) *Without the Law: Administrative Justice and Legal Pluralism in the 19th Century*. Toronto/Buffalo, NY: University of Toronto Press.

Ashford, Douglas E. (1980) 'A Victorian Drama: The Fiscal Subordination of British Local Government', in Douglas E. Ashford, (ed.), *Financing Urban Government in the Welfare State*. London: Croom Helm.

Ashford, Douglas E. (1986) *The Emergence of Welfare States*. Oxford: Blackwell.

Bellamy, Christine (1988) *Administering Central–Local Relations 1871–1919. The Local Government Board in Its Fiscal and Cultural Context*. Manchester: Manchester University Press.

Bertho-Lavenir, Catherine (1991) *L'Etat et les télécommunications en France et à l'étranger 1837–1987*. Geneva: Droz.

Brückner, Jutta (1977) *Staatswisseschaften, Kameralismus und Naturrecht. Ein Beitrag zur Geschichte der politischen Wissenschaft in Deutschland des späten 17. und frühen 18. Jahrhunderts*. Munich: Beck.

Burdeau, François, (1995) *Histoire du droit administratif (de la Révolution au début des années 1970)*. Paris: Presses Universitaires de France.

Burk, Kathleen (1982) *War and the State: The Transformation of British Government, 1914–1919*. London: Allen and Unwin.

Caplan, Jane (1988) *Government Without Administration: State and Civil Service in Weimar and Nazi Germany*. Oxford: Oxford University Press.

Cassese, Sabino (1977) *Questione amministrativa e questione meridionale: Dimensioni e reclutamento della burocrazia dall'Unità ad oggi*. Milan: Giuffrè.

Cassese, Sabino (2000) *La Construction du droit administratif: France et Royaume-Uni*. Paris: Montchrestien.

Cassese, Sabino and Pellew, Jil (eds) (1987) *Le Système du mérite*. Brussels: Institut International des Sciences Administratives.

Chapman, Richard A. (1984) *Leadership in the British Civil Service: A Study of Sir Percival Waterfield and the Creation of the Civil Service Selection Board*. London: Croom Helm.

Clarke, John and Newman, Janet (1997) *The Managerial State*. London/New Delhi: Sage.

Cohen, William B. (1998) *Urban Government and the Rise of French City: Five Municipalities in the Nineteenth Century*. New York: St Martin's Press.

Colliard, Claude-Albert and Timsit, Gérard (eds) (1988) *Les Autorités administratives indépendantes*. Paris: Presses Universitaires de France.

De Fort, Ester (1996) *La scuola elementare dall'Unità alla caduta del fascismo*. Bologna: Il Mulino.

Dorwart, Reinhold August (1971) *The Prussian Welfare State before 1970*. Cambridge, MA: Harvard University Press.

Dreyfus, Françoise (2000) *L'Invention de la bureaucratie: Servir l'état en France, en Grande-Bretagne et aux Etats-Unis (XVIIIè–XXè siècles)*. Paris: La Découverte.

Dunleavy, Patrick (1984) 'The Limits to Local Government', in Martin Boddy and Colin Fudge (eds), *Local Socialism? Labour Councils and New Left Alternatives*. London: Macmillan.

Dunleavy, Patrick and Hood, Christopher (1994) 'From Old Public Administration to New Public Management', *Public Money and Management*, 3: 9–16.

Dunleavy, Patrick and O'Leary, Brendan (1987) *Theories of the State: The Politics of Liberal Democracy*. London: Macmillan.

Dupuy, François and Thoenig, Jean-Claude (1985) *L'Administration en miettes*. Paris: Fayard.

Ellwein, Thomas (1965) *Das Regierungssystem Der Bundesrepublik Deutschlands*, 2nd edn. Cologne/Opladen: Westdeutscher Verlag.

Falkus, Malcom (1977) 'The Development of Municipal Trading in the Nineteenth Century', *Business History*, 134–61.

Harling, Philip (1996) *The Waning of 'Old Corruption': The Politics of Economical Reform in Britain 1779–1846*. Oxford: Clarendon Press.

Hattenhauer, Hans (1980) *Geschichte des Beamtentums*. Berlin: Heymann.

Hayward, Jack (1973) *The One and Indivisible French Republic*. New York: Norton.

Heady, Ferrel (2001) *Public Administration: A Comparative Perspective*. New York/Basel: Dekker.

Hewart of Bury, Lord Gordon (1929) *The New Despotism*. New York: Cosmopolitan Book Corporation.

Heyen, Erk Volkmar (ed.) (1982) *Geschichte des Verwaltungsrechtswissenschaft in Europa*. Frankfurt a.M.: Klostermann.

Hietala, Marjatt (1987) *Services and Urbanisation at the Turn of the Century: The Diffusion of Innovation*. Helsinki: SHs.

Hofmann, Wolfgang (1974) *Zwischen Rathaus und Reichskanzlei: Die Oberbürgermeister in der Kommunal- und Staatspolitik des Deutschen Reiches von 1890 bis 1933*. Stuttgart/Berlin: Kohlhammer.

ISAP (Istituto per la Scienza dell'Amministrazione pubblica) (1984) *La regionalizzazione*. Milan: Giuffrè.

Jakoby, Henry (1973) *The Bureaucratization of the World*. Berkeley/Los Angeles: University of California Press.

Kuisel, Richard F. (1981) *Capitalism and the State in Modern France: Renovation and Economic Management in the Twentieth Century*. Cambridge: Cambridge University Press.

Le Clère, Bernard and Wright, Vincent (1973) *Les Préfets du Second Empire*. Paris: A. Colin.

Legendre, Pierre (1968) *Histoire de l'administration de 1750 à nos jours*. Paris: Presses Universitaires de France.

Lelièvre, Claude (1990) *Histoire des institutions scolaires, 1789–1989*, Paris: Nathan.

Leonardi, Robert, Nannetti, Raffaella and Putnam, Robert P. (1987) 'Italy: Territorial Politics in the Post-War Years. The Case of Regional Reform', *West European Politics*, 10 (4): 88–107.

Levy, Carl (ed.) (1996) *Italian Regionalism: History, Identity, and Politics*. Oxford: Berg.

Loughlin, John and Mazey, Sonia (eds) (1995) *The End of the French Unitary State? Ten Years of Regionalisation in France (1982–1992)*. London: Frank Cass.

MacBriar, Alan Marn (1966) *Fabian Socialism and British Politics, 1884–1918*. Cambridge: Cambridge University Press.

Mann, Michael (1993) *The Sources of Social Power. 2: The Rise of Classes and Nation-States, 1760–1914*. Cambridge: Cambridge University Press.

Mannori, Luca and Sordi, Bernardo (2001) *Storia del diritto amministrativo*. Bari/Rome: Laterza.

Maravall, José Antonio (1972) *Estado moderno y mentalidad social (siglos XI a XVII)*. Madrid: Revista de Occidente.

Mayer, Otto (1924) *Deutsches Verwaltungsrecht (1895)*. Leipzig: Duncker und Humblot.

Mayntz, Renate (1982) *Soziologie der öffentlichen Verwaltung*, 2nd edn. Heidelberg: Müller Juristischer Verlag.

Melis, Guido (1988) *Due modelli di amministrazione tra liberalismo e fascismo: Burocrazie tradizionali e nuovi apparati*. Rome: Ministero per i beni culturali e ambientali.

Melis, Guido (1996) *Storia dell'amministrazione italiana, 1861–1993*. Bologna: Il Mulino.

Meny, Yves (1982) *Dix ans de régionalisation en Europe. Bilan et perspective, 1970–1980: Belgique–Espagne–France–Grande Bretagne–Italie*. Paris: Cujas.

Mommsen, Hans (1966) *Beamtentum in Dritten Reich*. Stuttgart: Deutsche Verlags-Anstalt.

Mortara, Alberto (ed.) (1972) *Gli enti pubblici italiani: Anagrafe, legislazione e giurisprudenza dal 1861 al 1970*. Milan: Angeli-Ciriec.

Page, Edward C. (1991) *Localism and Centralism in Europe: The Political and Legal Bases of Local Self-Government.* Oxford: Oxford University Press.

Parliamentary Affairs (1995) *The Quango Debate.*

Parris, Henry (1969) *Constitutional Bureaucracy.* London: Allen and Unwin.

Peters, B. Guy (1988) *Comparing Public Bureaucracies: Problems of Theory and Method.* Tuscaloosa, AL: University of Alabama Press.

Peters, B. Guy (1995) *The Politics of Bureaucracy.* New York: Longman.

Pierrot, Roger (1970) 'Un réformateur de l'administration au service de la liberté: Henri Chardon', *Revue du Droit Public et de Science Politique en France et à l'étranger,* No. 4: 925–60.

Poggi, Gianfranco (1991) *The State: Its Nature, Development, and Prospects.* Stanford, CA: Stanford University Press.

Prost, Antoine (1968) *Histoire de l'enseignement en France, 1800–1967.* Paris: Colin.

Raadschelders, Jos C.N. (1998) *Handbook of Administrative History.* New Brunswick, NJ: Transaction Publishers.

Raadschelders, Jos C.N. and Van der Meer, Frits (eds) (1998) *Administering the Summit.* Brussels: International Institute of Administrative Sciences.

Raadschelders, Jos C.N and Rutgers, Mark Roland (1996) 'A History of Civil Service Systems', in A.J.G. M. Bekke, J.I. Perry and Th. A.J. Toonen (eds), *Civil Service Systems in Comparative Perspective.* Bloomington, IN: Indiana University Press.

Rials, Stéphane (1977) *Administration et organisation 1910–1930: De l'organisation de la bataille à la bataille de l'organisation dans l'administration française.* Paris: Beauchesne.

Rials, Stéphane (1985) 'Le contrôle de l'état sur les chemins de fer (des origines à 1914)', in M. Brugière (ed.), *Administration et contrôle de l'économie 1800–1914.* Geneva: Droz.

Robson, William Alexander (1928) *Justice and Administrative Law: A Study of the British Constitution.* London: MacMillan.

Rokkan, Stein (1970) *Citizens, Elections, Parties: Approaches to the Comparative Study of the Processes of Development.* Oslo: Universitetsvorlaget.

Rosanvallon, Pierre (1990) *L'État en France de 1789 à nos jours.* Paris: Le Seuil.

Rosenberg, Hans (1958) *Bureaucracy, Aristocracy and Autocracy. The Prussian Experience, 1660–1815.* Cambridge, MA: Harvard University Press.

Rüfner, Wolfgang (1984) 'Die Entwicklung der Verwaltungsgerichsbarkeit', in K. Jeserich, H. Pohl and G.-Ch. Von Unruh (eds), *Deutsche Verwaltungsgeschichte. 3: Das Deutsche Reich bis zum Ende der Monarchie.* Stuttgart: Deutsche Verlags-Anstalt.

Rugge, Fabio (1989) *Il governo delle città prussiane tra '800 e '900.* Milan: Giuffrè.

Rugge, Fabio (ed.) (1992) *I regimi della città. Il governo municipale in Europa tra '800 e '900,* Milan: Angeli.

Rugge, Fabio (1998) 'Administering the Summit: The Italian Case', in Jos C.N. Raadschelders and Frits Van der Meer (eds), *Administering the Summit:* Brussels: International Institute of Administrative Sciences.

Rugge, Fabio (ed.) (2000) *Administration and Crisis Management: The Case of Wartime.* Brussels: International Institute of Administrative Sciences.

Salvati, Mariuccia (1992) *Il regime e gli impiegati. La nazionalizzazione piccolo-borghese nel ventennio fascista.* Turin: Bollati Boringhieri.

Sartori, Giovanni (1970) 'Concept Misformation in Comparative Politics' *American Political Science Review,* 1033–53.

Savoie, Peter J. (1994) *Thatcher, Reagan, Mulroney: In Search of a New Bureaucracy.* Pittsburgh: University of Pittsburgh Press.

Stolleis, Michael (1992/1999) *Geschichte des öffentlichen Rechts in Deutschland,* vols 1 and 2. Munich: Beck.

Thomas, Rosamund M. (1978) *The British Philosophy of Administration: A Comparison of British and American Ideas, 1900–1939.* London/New York: Longman.

Thuillier, Guy (1982) *Les Cabinets ministériels.* Paris: Presses Universitaires de France.

Thuillier, Guy and Tulard, Jean (1994) *Histoire de l'administration française.* Paris: Presses Universitaires de France.

Tocqueville, Alexis de (1964) *L'Ancien Régime et la Révolution* (1856). Paris: Gallimard.

Tournerie, Jean André (1971) *Le Ministère du Travail (origines et premiers développements).* Paris: Cujas.

Wilson, Woodrow (1887) 'The Study of Administration', *Political Science Quarterly,* 2 (June). (Reprinted 1941 in Political Science Quarterly, 61 (December): 481–506.)

Wright, Vincent (1972a) *Le Conseil d'État sous le Second Empire.* Paris: A. Colin.

Wright, Vincent (1972b) 'La Réorganisation du Conseil d'Etat en 1872', *Etudes et documents du Conseil d'Etat,* No. 25.

Wunder, Bernd (1986) *Geschichte der Bürokratie in Deutschland.* Frankfurt a.M.: Suhrkamp.

Wunder, Bernd (ed.) (1995) *The Influences of the Napoleonic 'Model' of Administration on the Administrative Organization of Other Countries.* Brussels: International Institute of Administrative Sciences.

15

South Asian and Western Administrative Experience: The Past in the Present

James Warner Björkman

The task of this chapter, as posed by the section editor, is to discuss the intricate balance between and, sometimes merging of, Western with indigenous traditions of governance and government. By comparing the precolonial and colonial with the post-colonial state and administrative traditions, we can develop an understanding of the degree to which Western conceptions of democracy and management have influenced the non-Western world. My assignment here is to consider the experiences of India in this subtle sequence of recursive interactions in order to show, in Raadschelder's words in the Introduction to this section, through cross-time and cross-national analysis, that historical knowledge is a benefit to students and practitioners alike.

To extract meaningful generalizations about the macrocosmic patterns of administrative change in India is to court disagreement if not ridicule. The task reminds one of the apocryphal examination question required of would-be civil servants: 'define Truth; be specific'. In self-defense, the following discussion on administrative traditions in South Asia is both cursory and highly impressionistic. It derives from having been an 'India-watcher' for over forty years, with all the built-in subjective biases that such an enterprise entails.

India should occupy massive space in the study of administrative history due to its immense scope and long duration over millennia. India, of course, is not just the terrain within the boundaries of the current nation-state that was one of the several successors to the British Raj, but refers the entire subcontinental region with its complex history of well over 5,000 years. In other words, administrative experiences and traditions are derived from ancient Hindu kingdoms, from medieval Muslim empires, from

Western (especially British) colonialism, as well as the modern era of independent nation-states. Such a canvass cannot be painted in a single chapter.

The twentieth century is the most well known as well as the most influential era of administrative practices in India. Its first half spanned the heyday of the British Raj; its second half has been characterized by massive efforts toward socio-economic development. But in many ways, the distant past is equally intriguing when viewed from the types of administrative history distinguished by Raadschelders (1998). This chapter will explore indigenous traditions of governance and government that, despite the absence of clear causal connections, permeate and influence the practice (and one might even say the mindset) of public administration in South Asia. To do so, comparison will be made with one of the most well known and least admired theorists of Western political thought. First, however, the broad scene will be sketched.

A COLONIAL DUET

While it is always easy to identify behavior that falls short of some ideal-type, few countries had been so explicitly prepared for independent democratic development as were those in South Asia. For nearly a century, the institutions and practice of government had steadily evolved to produce civil and military services that were both experienced and professional. Of course, it would be naïve to suggest that mere administrative apparatus means sound administration or even good governance. But shortly after the Raj had ended, India was described as 'among the dozen or so most advanced governments in the world' (Appleby, 1953: 8). Despite difficulties during the past half-century, public administration in India has demonstrated as much coherence, awareness and balance between tradition and change as most Western nations.

In comparative terms, popular political organization in India is also well developed, with competitive elections and multiple parties. Having been founded in 1885, the Congress Party triumphed as a nationalist movement by achieving independence in 1947 and then dominated the party system during the next forty years by supplying most of the national and state-level governments. Over the decades, however, internal quarrels and splits plus organizational atrophy (Björkman and Mathur, 1996) saw the emergence of many more political parties. And these, coupled with an increasingly sophisticated electorate, have yielded a new phase of coalitional (that is, non-majoritarian) governments. Without strong central leadership, the importance of public administration has re-emerged, although without its self-confidence of yesteryear.

The British came to South Asia in the sixteenth century in search of commercial trade and their initial administrative practices served mercantile interests. In a simplistic phrase, the East India Company over-reached itself and had to be rescued by the political state from which it had obtained its original commission. From this perspective, the Raj was an accidental empire rather than a purposeful enterprise. Rather than intentionally introducing British administrative practice into India, the Raj inherited a system of administration that had been under way for centuries, even millennia.

This administrative system was based on geographic areas, very specifically the 'district' that had responsibility for maintaining law and order as well as extracting revenue. Sub-district units called *tehsils* or *talukas* facilitated the collection of revenue and the administration of justice, but the district remained the center of action. The collection of land revenue had been the primary purpose of field administration since pre-Mughal time. Despite episodic attempts at reform, revenue units at district and sub-district levels remain the best key to understanding almost all contemporary administrative arrangements in India – including 'development blocks' under the state-managed Community Development Program in the 1950s and its participatory successor called Panchayati Raj (Björkman, 1979).

Under the Mughals these administrative areas were assigned to political retainers and allies but, on the demise or removal of these incumbents, the areas reverted to the monarch for reassignment (Moore, 1967: 319). Although these areas could be rank-ordered by size and importance, their administrators had no specific training other than perhaps apprenticeship. In the eighteenth-century China trade, however, British merchants observed the value of well-trained Mandarins, and in the early nineteenth century the East India Company introduced specialized training for its apprentice officials by establishing Haileybury College (1806–57). Because recruitment was largely in Britain, where stiff competitive examinations for entry into the company were held, the embryonic civil service was dominated by the English. But from 1853 onwards, Indians became eligible as well (Braibanti and Spengler, 1963: 31–2).

In a reversal of the usual assumptions of colonial tutelage, Spangenberg (1976) argues that the British experimented with administrative arrangements in India, including specialized training for functionaries, long before eventually bringing those reforms to Britain itself in the late eighteenth century. There is modest irony in the argument that the colonial power was itself colonized by administrative practices from its colony – a point that, given considerations of power and status, has not been well publicized. Indeed, the issue of what was borrowed from and/or influenced each partner in the colonial duet – Britain and India – is best described as a symbiotic synthesis that neither can easily recognize nor acknowledge. Yet in many ways – at least from my perspective – the two nations have grown together over some 400 years of interaction.

THE SCIENCE OF POLITY FOR THE PRINCE

This is not to deny that the pattern of administrative change in India owes much to two centuries of enduring British emphasis on procedural means of attaining equity and probity. But the core structure of administration seems equally related to the statecraft enjoined in the *Arthasastra*. The term *artha* signifies 'wealth' and 'the earth which contains mankind'; the term *sastra* or 'science', when affixed to *artha,* designates the 'Science of Polity' because it describes how this earthy realm is acquired and maintained (Shamasastry, 1960). Transmitted through oral Sanskrit over the millennia, the *Arthasastra* was first published in 1909 (the first English translation appeared in 1915) and attributed to Kautilya, the chief advisor to the founder of the vast Mauryan empire at the close of the fourth century BC.

The Mauryan empire was founded by Chandragupta Maurya, commander-in-chief of the last Nanda king of Magadha (in modern day Bihar), whom he eventually overthrew. When Maurya's initial conspiracy with Kautilya was discovered, both fled to the Punjab 'where tradition attributes to them a meeting with Alexander the Great' (Bingham et al., 1974: 150) and perhaps an exposure to Western ideas. Some fifteen years after killing the Nanda king in 322 BC, Chandragupta defeated the Seleucid Greeks (successors to Alexander) and obtained all the lands that Alexander had conquered in India.

Given Chandragupta Maurya's further conquests in Bengal and Gujarat, his empire's sway over most of the subcontinent lasted for some 130 years (Basham, 1954: 50–7). At its height the Mauryan empire embraced much of India with a population of perhaps 100 million people – about as many as lived in Europe in 1600 AD. Yet even after the collapse of the Mauryan empire, Kautilya's manual continued to guide rulers and writers for over 1500 years (Prased, 1928: 245). As K.V. Rangaswami Aiyangar (1934: 6) remarks, 'In India more than in many parts of the world the past persists in the present.'

Kautilya's manual is a rich repository of factual information, but its orientation is descriptive, prescriptive and didactic rather than analytical, and its content is predominantly political. The first book is primarily concerned with how the king must proceed if he is to choose reliable ministers, with how he is to set up and operate effective internal and external spy networks, and how he generally must guard his internal and external security. Book 2 deals with political as well as with economic regulatory agencies, while the next three books deal with family regulations, criminal justice and public service. The ten remaining books concern bases of sovereignty, international relations, sources of national distress, invasion, war, the conduct of military operations and international intrigue.

As the manual includes many prevailing customs and rules, the *Arthasastra* represents an attempt to codify Indian laws and customs as the West later did under the late Roman republic. It also reflects Brahmanical ethics and ideas about authority as well as the sources of law for the social order. Being aware of the value of propaganda and of the extent of belief in the infallibility of the sacred *Vedas*, Kautilya found in these ideas a powerful source of social stability (Aiyangar, 1934: 40–1).

Kautilya was concerned to devise a statecraft that would keep the large Mauryan empire unified, guard its integrity against the intrigues of power-seeking nobles as well as attack from abroad, and prevent the dissolution of the state. Hence he found it necessary to dismiss unrealistic and world-rejecting values and practices that were unfavorable to the functioning of a great empire. While he may be said to have subordinated ethics to politics, Kautilya did not endorse principles that ran counter to the social law and coercive authority of the *Vedas*.

Kautilya's insistence on the importance of coercive authority (physical force) indicates that he conceived of the politico-economic world in essentially Hobbesian terms – as did many ancient authors. It indicates also that he underestimated the self-adjusting or homeostatic character of social systems, together with the mechanisms governing their behavior. Yet the *Arthasastra* contributed to the resolution of the problem of justice because Kautilya's concern was with the rules intended to produce sufficient certainty in various interpersonal relations in order to preserve social stability. His conception of law, although not wholly free of metaphysical content, was essentially empirical and man-made, and his conception of justice consisted in compliance with what the law sanctioned, on the ground that it promoted the common good (Choudhary, 1951: 284–8). In this regard, Kautilya's efforts provide a 'hidden' positive law in contrast to the overt products of Roman law.

In his 1950 introduction to *The Prince* and *The Discourses*, Max Lerner suggests that 'when [Niccolo Machiavelli] wrote his grammar of power he came close to setting down the imperatives by which men govern and are governed in political communities, whatever the epoch and whatever the governmental structure' (Lerner, 1950: xxxiv). To test such a proposition would require extensive scholarship and no satisfactorily definitive conclusion would ever be obtained. However, 'there do arise, from time to time, curious parallels between one period and another' (Muir, 1936: 1) so an examination of the theories of another political author totally unrelated to Machiavelli in culture, territory, or time would provide a measure of critical comparison for Lerner's suggestion.

ERA AND AREA IN CONTEXT

Twenty-three centuries ago, almost six times the span of years since Machiavelli wrote, an obscure Indian Brahmin composed a political treatise on government. Although the past does not willingly divulge its secrets, a fortunate discovery near the turn of the twentieth century placed a copy of this treatise in the hands of modern scholars. This treatise, the *Arthasastra*, and its probable author, Kautilya (also known as Chanakya), will be compared with Machiavelli and his works in order to explore their ahistorical parallels.

Before these political theorists can be compared, however, the similarities and differences of the widely disparate eras of each man must be sketched and a brief commentary provided on known biographical information in order to gain a contextual perspective. The political concerns and techniques of each can then be discussed and contrasted, with final attention being paid to the practical results and applications of these theories. It should be noted, too, that both theorists subscribe to a cyclical sense of time that repeats itself or turns back upon itself, rather than the linear sense of time that characterizes Western civilization.

The politics of the European Renaissance were at best unsettled, and the adjective 'chaotic' would be an appropriate characterization for Italy. The peninsula itself included five major city-states with their hinterlands plus other minor principalities. The political kaleidoscope involved the maintenance of a precarious and shifting balance of power among the Republics of Venice and Florence, the Kingdom of Naples, the Duchy of Milan and the Papal State. Astute observers naturally perceived that 'political absolutism was the necessary remedy for the chaos and anarchy of internecine strife among the Italian cities' (Elliott and McDonald, 1949: 425).

Although the wondrous creations of Italian art held imperial sway in contemporary European culture, other European nations reciprocated with imperialism of a political nature. The kingdoms of France and Spain through their subsidiary alliances with Milan and Naples respectively were intermittently at war over the possession of Italy (Schevill, 1936: 463). The Papacy, which over the preceding centuries had been a significant influence in European politics, had itself devolved into little more than a narrowly based temporal state and had become a political football that frequently changed hands by manipulation within the College of Cardinals. The crowning irony of the age was the sack of the sacred and eternal city of Rome in 1527 by that most Holy Roman Emperor, Charles V of Spain. Machiavelli understandably concluded that 'stability was an illusion, life was a flux, nothing is eternal and all must change' (Muir, 1936: 138).

During the fourth and fifth centuries before Christ pre-Mauryan India was also plagued by a substantial degree of political division and turmoil. A maze of principalities included some

ruled by Greek 'foreigners in the Punjab and the adjoining regions' (Saletore, 1963: 51) plus some eighteen separate republics in various stages of development. This potpourri of states 'represented a bewildering diversity of political and social existence, which necessitated the forging of a delicately balanced system of politico-economic relations among them' (Ramaswamy, 1962: 4).

The *Arthasastra* is generally conceded to be 'essentially genuine and … its author was the minister of the Maurya emperor Candragupta [sic]' (Konow, 1945: 65). Due to certain inconsistencies of internal evidence, some controversialists regard the manuscript as an elaboration by others of a simpler treatise by Kautilya (Basham, 1954: 79). But 'the work seems to be substantially of the Mauryan age and may be taken to embody the view of the great minister of Chandragupta' (Altekar, 1949: 7).

Evidence on the political career of the Brahmin Kautilya is sketchy and he has achieved an almost mythological status. German orientalist scholars have argued that Kautilya fulfilled a political role in the Mauryan empire comparable to that of Bismarck in Hohenzollern Germany (Mookerji, 1914: x). Although occasionally acting as a 'super-advisor' to the new emperor, however, Kautilya evidently went into semi-retirement after he had replaced the last Nanda ruler by Chandragupta (Ramaswamy, 1962: 3). Analogous to the logic of Thomas Hobbes 2,000 years later, the political treatise appears to be an attempted justification of the abolition of 'the anarchy and misrule due to the profligacy and unpopularity of the previous Nanda king, who was unable to discharge the primary functions of government, viz. the protection of the weak against the strong' (Mookerji, 1914: xxxiii). Having produced a political handbook for the perpetuation of the newly established regime, Kautilya apparently died beloved by his royal pupil and reasonably successful in all his endeavors.

Being much closer to ours in time, Machiavelli's life is well known and needs little elaboration. Born in 1469 to a Florentine family, Machiavelli experienced the rule of Savonarola, the Dominican friar, and after the latter's execution was elevated to public office under the Soderini. As secretary to the Second Chancery of Florence, he maintained immediate practical contact with all the military and diplomatic affairs of the Republic, subjects which would be of immense importance in his later writings (Gauss, 1952: 10). In 1512 the aristocratic Medici returned to power in Florence and Machiavelli was dismissed from office, tortured under a false pretext, and banished to his farm until 1526. There he wrote his political analyses, not from the viewpoint of a professional theorist, but from that of 'an active participant in the troubled and unstable political life of his native Florence' (Gauss, 1952: 9). *The Discourses* and *The Prince* were written by a miserable, bitter and desperate man who by chance of fate had been exiled from his one true love, the political arena. The books were primarily intended to elicit favor from the political powerful.

Although Machiavelli was distinctly unsuccessful in his projected goals, Europeans reduced him to a symbol of immorality and evil incarnate. While his suggestions were only operational within a moral void, perhaps his greatest offense was to display 'to the world the mechanisms of power which were behind the authority of the rule' (Lerner, 1950: xli). Kautilya was likewise charged with having intentions of malicious evil. He 'as much presented a picture of the immoral practices of the kings and Brahmin ministers in the fourth century BC as Machiavelli did of the immoral rulers and Christian statesmen in the fifteen [*sic*] century of his *Prince*' (Saletore, 1963: 535). Comparable to Machiavelli's experience, the '*Arthasastra* must have fallen into the hands of unscrupulous pretenders who would extract support for their misdeeds from Kautilyan precepts on statecraft' (Ramaswamy, 1962: 5). Political realism dictates a recognition that these corrupt conditions and practices had existed long before the respective book was compiled and that the authors had merely observed the facts, utilizing them in a pragmatic manner.

Only brief mention need be made of the fact that Machiavelli represented one more step in the development of Western political thought. To the idealism of Plato, the Stoic republicanism of Cicero, the universalism of Dante *et cetera*, was added the secular realism of Machiavelli. Even advice to tyrants was nothing new because, in the fifth book of his *Politics*, Aristotle was concerned with the unemotional preservation of the tyrant's power in order to maintain political order.

Kautilya, too, was preceded by a long chain of political philosophies whose theories, unfortunately, are not completely known. Evidence has accumulated, however, which indicates that at least nineteen distinct schools of political thought had flourished over the many centuries before Kautilya's massive compendium appeared and seemingly terminated all controversies (Saletore, 1963: 49). More will be said later of this abrupt ending of speculative thought on politics in India. Ancient Indian political philosophy presupposed 'an inherent propensity of man to encroach on his weaker neighbour, and to be prone to commit acts of disorder and

aggression' (Saletore, 1963: 68). The continual references to this and other theories of ancient Indian scholars in the *Arthasastra* seem to indicate that the latter political treatise is a compilation and synthesis of earlier thought plus information on the functional operation of government and state machinery (Altekar, 1949: 2–3).

POLITICAL CONCERNS AND TECHNIQUES

Idealism/realism

The *Arthasastra* opens with a verse submitting that 'this *Arthasastra* is made as a compendium of almost all the Arthasastras which, in view of acquisition and maintenance of the earth, has been composed by ancient teachers' (Shamasastry, 1951: 1). Apparently Kautilya selected his political formulas and principles on the basis of past usefulness instead of idyllic formulations (Salatore, 1963: 50). This selection of verified principles from the past and construction upon them is characteristic of the modern progressive view of history.

Machiavelli, on the other hand, had not 'the faintest conception of the doctrine of evolution; he held the orthodox view that history returned upon itself, that it was a cycle, and that in studying the past men would learn what was to come in the future' (Muir, 1936: 137). The appeal to antiquity for both justification and exemplification is best summed up in his reliance on Titus Livius, the Roman historian, and accounts of the glorious era of the Roman Republic. And yet, the 'search for general rules or principles ... [by] reducing the confusing multiplicity of events to compact generalizations ... makes the Florentine secretary not so much a historian as a political scientist' (Schevill, 1936: 500).

The sometimes derisive, sometimes laudatory terms 'pragmatism' and 'political realism' are trademarks of the cult of Machiavelli. And indeed, Machiavelli was 'of the temper the political idiom of our time terms "realist" [for he combined] a formal deference to "idealism" with contemptuous dismissal of idealist measures in practice' (Steward, 1948: 275). Perhaps due to his background of political activism, he prided himself on the 'stark realism and often the cynicism about human nature that seem to be the hallmark of the experienced diplomat ...' (Elliott and McDonald, 1949: 19). Undoubtedly the emphasis on results can be summed up by Machiavelli's view that the 'supreme law of politics is success' (Ferrero, 1939: 569). Later, it will be demonstrated that Machiavelli was inconsistent in his supposed rejection of idealism for he replaced the spiritual 'oughts' of the medieval era with secular 'oughts' of his own.

Kautilya's writings are also permeated by a concern for results and an evaluation of techniques in terms of success. The tenor of the *Arthasastra* is characteristic of 'the work of a consummate politician like Chanakya [another name for Kautilya], who knew very well what to express and what to suppress in writing about contemporary politics' (Mookerji, 1914: xxxiv). Many scholars have concluded that 'an idealistic tone [is not] applicable in the case of Kautilya, who was anything but an idealist' (Saletore, 1963: 626). Because of his preoccupation with factual matters, the *Arthasastra* has been viewed as 'a unique record of the secular aspects or developments of Indian civilization in that brilliant period of Indian history – the Age of Chandra Gupta' (Mookerji, 1914: 1). Other scholars credit Kautilya with a more flexible approach to political realism and contend that although the state envisaged in the *Arthasastra* was tremendously influential and omnipervasive in the political realm, it was probably not a complete reality even under the Mauryas (Basham, 1954: 80).

In considering the role that the idealism–realism tension played in the philosophies of both writers, I believe Kautilya more fully comprehended the immense practical influence that ideals exert on political reality. Machiavelli, an observer of the very conditions that immediately preceded the Reformation, failed to realize the political effects of morals and spiritualism (McCoy, 1943: 631). Furthermore, Kautilya may have perceived that certain realistic insights should not be committed to writing, and therefore paid lip-service to various historical ideals. Ironically, Machiavelli's depth of insight into the political affairs of man may have been the real reason he was not accepted by the Medicis with open arms; he had probed deep into the realm of Renaissance politics and probably, in the words of that trite saying 'knew too much to be trusted'.

As an extension of their realism, Kautilya and Machiavelli each emphasized the importance of empiricism as opposed to rationalism. Machiavelli, especially in his *Discourses*, sets out to discover the system of government possessing the greatest order, the highest efficiency and the probability of longevity (Muir, 1936: 137). His devotion to empiricism is remarkably in evidence as he advocates submission to a despot or tyrant as ruler, amazing because the desire for republicanism is strong in Machiavelli

and the only truly successful portion of his own career occurred under the aegis of the popular-rule Soderini family in the Republic of Florence. However, the social anarchy of his age compelled Machiavelli 'by his clearness of vision and uncompromising rectitude of mind to justify the armed enforcer of laws and the destroyer of parties, the prince' (Schevill, 1936: xx). Resolution in accepting the facts of observation and applying them politically is the mark of a committed empiricist.

The Kautilyan *Arthasastra* is widely considered to be empirically based. For example, much of our knowledge of that age of Chandragupta comes from Kautilya's writing 'which is born only of a living experience of actual problems and contact with facts' (Mookerji, 1914: xliv). Saletore (1963: 281) sums it up well in saying that there is an 'extraordinary thoroughness [in] Kautilya's work; its eminent inductiveness and practical character, its unflinching logic and heedlessness of adventitious moral or religious standards, and its wide range of subjects and interests – which give it a unique combination of features that, in European literature, we find only separately in an Aristotle, a Machiavelli, and a Bacon'. Emphases on the minutiae of organizational government machinery are as central to the *Arthasastra* as are the philosophic justifications.

View of man/worldview

As mentioned previously, earlier Indian political philosophers considered man to be basically evil and 'prone to commit acts of disorder and aggression' – a view shared millennia later by the authors of *The Federalist Papers*. Kautilya subscribed to this view and posited a rudimentary theory of a contractual origin of political society as he explained how the people of India, weary of social anarchy, had voluntarily submitted to a monarch (Basham, 1954: 83). But Kautilya also realized that man has a capacity for good and expressed this realization in terms contingent upon the activity of the monarch. Thus, if the king were good, the people would be likewise; if he were evil or even passive, the people's base instincts would appear (Shamasastry, 1951: 36).

As a prototype of Hobbes, Machiavelli 'based his theories on the essential baseness of mankind, and on his belief that, left to themselves, men always act from selfish and generally evil motives' (Muir, 1936: 76). For the Italian, man was 'an animal driven by the simpler motives of fear, vanity, lust for power, and scheming self-interest ... who made the best of brute necessity and by shrewdness and ruthlessness achieved his ends' (Elliott and McDonald, 1949: 421). Since Machiavelli had voided himself of moral considerations, the logical procedure in politics was to utilize and maximize these instincts. Yet man, 'when forced to do [otherwise] by law or the conventions of religion' (Steward, 1948: 277), could act in the interests of a common good.

This appeal for a transformation in a man when he is cognizant of a common good – in Machiavelli's case the governing of a unified Italy – presents a problem in the interpretation of his writings. Not only does he ignore the basically evil view of man's nature and provide a basis for constructive action, but he thereby presents the use of an ideal – the common good – in the philosophy of an avowed realist who had rejected idealism. Here, obviously, is the previously mentioned inconsistency in Machiavelli who had rejected idealism and had accepted humanity's basic selfishness, and yet declared that 'the ideal of a united and triumphant Italy ought to command universal allegiance' (Steward, 1948: 277). Certain authors, of course, contend that Machiavelli's conception of a 'common good' is 'purely ornamental' and its only value is symbolic, 'completely emptied of its content' (McCoy, 1943: 632). However, the goal of national unity in Italy remained the central doctrine of all Machiavelli's endeavors and this represents an ideal towards which all other efforts are subordinated.

Kautilya also refers to a common good, but apparently with tongue in cheek and completely aware of the emotional appeal of this term. For example, in the pre-Mauryan and Mauryan ages, the monarch was expected 'to be a virtuous ruler devoted heart and soul to the welfare of the people; if he was not such, then gods will punish him' (Altekar, 1949: 8–9). As the *Arthasastra* reads: 'The king must regard his own happiness as indissolubly connected with that of his subjects' (Shamasastry, 1951: 8). This common good between the ruler and his people, however, is almost sophistical in that, as in the case of Machiavelli, the over-riding concern is with loyalty to the state (Ramaswamy, 1962: 30) – not, seemingly, a bad end until one recognizes that normally the benefits will accrue only to those who control the state itself.

The common image evoked by the mention of Machiavelli is the passionless legitimization of force, fraud and violence. For several centuries, the remainder of his political precepts were ignored as Christian churchmen and pious statesmen employed this aspect of Machiavelli's politics as a straw dummy against which to compare their enlightened theories. There is little doubt, of course, that Machiavelli's proposed state

'dwells in a moral void' that judges the monarch's activities in terms of success and failure, not of right and wrong (Schevill, 1936: 502). *The Prince*, for example, may be regarded as a 'technical treatise on the means of gaining and keeping power ... [and being] less concerned with the uses to which power is to be put' (Hallowell, 1950: 53). But Machiavelli had a goal or end, albeit almost unconscious in nature, for the fulfillment of which he dispassionately applied the empirical data he had collected. Being a patriot of sorts who was intensely desirous of national unification, he viewed despotism as the only way 'to bring a state into existence *or to reform a corrupt one*' (Hallowell, 1950: 55; emphasis in the original). Then he vaguely alluded to the possible progression of the state into popular self-rule if the population became 'virtuous'.

Compared to the *Arthasastra*, the example selected – the reforming of a corrupt state – and the techniques to be used closely parallel those of Kautilya. The political background of Kautilya's era was the rule of a corrupt and inefficient Nanda king, and this Brahmin was instrumental in placing the new Mauryan house on the imperial throne. Since the original transformation of the social anarchy in India into a political state had been accomplished through voluntary submission to force, force was easily extended as a justifiable concept in promoting continued social order (Saletore, 1963: 69). Despite the advocacy in the *Arthasastra* of 'every dishonest expedient' for the acquisition and maintenance of power, the duties of the king towards his people were outlined in such detail and precision as to establish an ideal of which few ancient civilizations can boast (Basham, 1954: 89). Furthermore, the composition of the *Arthasastra* followed the success of a *coup d'état* whereas Machiavelli wrote in anticipation of such a transformation of political power. Following the *fait accompli*, Kautilya's role in the action became secondary and his renown was obtained 'for being the greatest Indian exponent of the art of government, the duties of kings, ministers, and officials, and the methods of diplomacy' (Fleet, 1951: i).

Imperial desires

The emphasis placed upon imperialism by the two writers further magnifies their respective relationships to the *fait accompli* of political unity. Machiavelli, desirous of unifying Italy, decided that since the fragmented political powers remained in flux and as of yet no single force had been strong enough to vanquish the rest, a dictatorship was essential (Sturmthal, 1940: 79). Thus he wrote his article 'for the purpose of eliciting the aid of a strong man in bringing the Italian people out of their condition of political corruption' (McCoy, 1943: 629). The Papal state, for example, had long been the most viable and stable Italian principality and logically the ruler of this domain, if he were not a theocrat, could expand and unify Italy through a series of imperialistic wars.

On the other hand, the 'Kautilyan strategy of state expansion is much more complicated than the Machiavellian counterpart' (Ramaswamy, 1962: 34). Having established a new dynasty, the Brahmin minister was faced with the necessity of initiating a program of imperialistic expansion to incorporate and to 'mauryanize' the various autonomous or semi-independent principalities across northern India. Therefore, Kautilya recommended two goals for diplomacy: world conquest and world unity. And contrary to pre-Mauryan political practices of formalized tribute, his *Arthasastra* approved of conquest with the intent of direct annexation and pacification (Basham, 1954: 124). Regarding imperialism, the treatise states that 'the king who is weaker than "the other" should keep the peace; he who is stronger should make war'. This recommendation, moreover, is compatible with the royal charge to maintain social order domestically; the wars are fought on the periphery of the state and, furthermore, they divert the interests of the people from their immediate problems. Of course, in light of the imperialism of the modern variety, the Kautilyan version could be said to end as a sort of 'humanitarian imperialism'.

Bureaucracy

Centralized state machinery as a mode of government marks the most sweeping variation of the Arthasastran state from the pre-Mauryan political order. The bulk of the treatise is actually more concerned with the minutiae of bureaucratic detail than with either the acquisition or maintenance of power *per se*. The *Arthasastra* is frequently described as more of 'a manual for the administrator than a theoretical work on polity discussing the philosophy and fundamental principles of administration or of the political science. It is mainly concerned with the practical problems of government and describes its machinery and functions, both in peace and war' (Altekar, 1949: 5). Great emphasis is placed upon the prescription of the correct secretariat for government administration, a concern that may be traced back to his long service under the

Nandas and, of course, the first Maurya. Kautilya's prescriptions went much further than merely describing the static institutions of government; he also recommended extensive economic planning (Ramaswamy, 1962: 27) and continual sampling of public opinion through an internal security system (Basham, 1954: 121). The scope of subjects discussed and upon which recommendation were made is extremely broad, including social class, the family, the individual, education, sexual relations and prostitution, crime, local government, sundry occupations and a variety of other topics (Basham, 1954: 122–36). These myriad regulations and recommendations in the *Arthasastra* provided Mauryan India with a strong, centralized state government complete with a vast bureaucracy (Saletore, 1963: 54).

Machiavelli differs substantially from Kautilya on the topic of practical government for the former's commitment to pragmatism appears solely preoccupied with suggesting the means to obtain power and preserve it. Common, daily functions of government are largely ignored in the *Discourses* and especially in *The Prince*; the greatest elaborations on any topics concern the execution of war, the role of the military and the function of diplomacy. Machiavelli probably wrote at least *The Prince* in a frenzy of activity that made it a bit patchy and disjointed (Hughes, 1951: 377). If the recommendations on duplicity, for example, were applied consistently to human affairs, the inevitable effect would be a direct contradiction of the goal sought plus obsolescence of the technique. The closest Machiavelli came to describing the administrative machinery of a unified political state was his blanket proposal that a position be created comparable to that of the ancient Roman *dictator* (Elliott and McDonald, 1949: 426–7) and this only for emergencies – like the initial establishment of the state. Machiavelli is concerned neither with the morality of the techniques used to obtain power nor with the specific employment of that power once the initial goal of state unity has been achieved.

Recommendations for state initiative and the central control of society in the *Arthasastra* imply a belief on Kautilya's part in a concept of man's innate abilities similar to Machiavelli's 'virtu'. 'Virtu' does not hinge solely on having a goal in mind towards which to direct one's energies, but includes the ability of man to act and to cause that goal to become reality (Muir, 1936: 150). This ability, which appears to contain the element of free-will, is primarily concerned with how to control and utilize that element of chance and fate called 'fortuna', that 'mysterious …

intangible external constraint which comes from above and guides events blindly, as it wills and where it lists' (Chabod, 1958: 21). One Machiavellian thesis revolves around how the 'virtu' of a tyrant can rectify the political corruption – disunity – of the Italian people by taking advantage of all means possible (Meinecke, 1957: 41). In the end, furthermore, Machiavelli recognizes that ultimate success will not depend solely upon the quality of the individual leaders, but inevitably upon the entire Italian culture (Lerner, 1939: 307).

Such centralization of authority as prescribed by Kautilya indicates that he regarded the monarchy as the pace-setter for Indian society in general. The qualities of government, which represents the ruler writ large, will determine whether or not the base instincts of the populace will be restrained and collective efforts channeled towards a common good. Chapter XIX of the *Arthasastra* lays the cause and effect relationship upon the proverbial line: 'If the king is energetic, his subjects will be equally energetic. If he is reckless, they will not only be reckless likewise, but also eat into his works' (Shamasastry, 1951: 36). Yet ultimately Kautilya, like Machiavelli, perceived that the final authority and results rested upon at least the political acquiescence of the populace for 'the character of [a nation's] people determines the destiny of a state more than any other fact of consideration' (Altekar, 1949: 27).

Republicanism

Republicanism as a form of government becomes a very legitimate alternative to the monarchy when the very structure of political society is ultimately seen to rest upon the 'virtu' of the people. The logical extension of the former premise would be the people can best rule themselves through an egalitarian form of government. Grounded as they are upon empiricism, however, both writers conclude that for their respective societies this solution would be untenable.

Machiavelli becomes particularly confusing and enigmatic on the issue of republicanism. His political sympathies, both in his early career and in his theoretical writings, obviously lay with a popular-rule form of government. Not only did he perceive that political power is founded upon the support of the governed (*Discourses* I. 16), but openly declared that to prevent the public good from being subverted to the enhancement of private advantage, a republic was necessary

(Meinecke, 1957: 43). The conclusion drawn from the *Discourses* is that the greatest wisdom 'lies in the deliberation of popular assemblies rather than in the edicts of a single man' (Elliott and McDonald, 1949: 420). However, despite the lip-service paid to the concept of republicanism *if* all political factors were functioning properly, Machiavelli persisted in advocating the institution of a tyrant or despot. Total rejection of his republican ideal was avoided by rationalizing that ultimately the deep-rooted prejudices and beliefs of the populace would circumscribe the limits over which even a tyrant may not transgress for fear of deposition (Corry, 1943: 289).

Kautilya was much less circumspect about his views toward republics. Northern India in the pre-Mauryan age had several flourishing republics with philosophic roots in imported Greek ideals as well as in indigenous philosophies. As the agent of a successful imperialist, however, the Brahmin minister could express his views with impunity. Republics are mentioned in the *Arthasastra* in a generally unsympathetic manner, although no specific reasons are provided unless it be that they were reluctant to submit to imperialism. Book XI proposes several techniques by which the inherent weakness of factionalism in republics may be intensified and exploited.

Our scanty knowledge of older South Asian philosophies indicates that deliberative legislative bodies were an important element of pre-Mauryan monarchical India as well as in the republics (Altekar, 1949: 94–100). But the detailed description of Mauryan political institutions includes no mention of such a central legislative body. Interestingly, those republics that submitted to Chandragupta apparently retained their internal institutions of government, at least in the early Mauryan era (Altekar, 1949: 234–5). Later versions of the *Arthasastra* (transmission, by the way, was always orally and verbatim from one generation to the next) omitted the original Kautilyan references to republics, probably because they disappeared with the decline of Buddhism throughout India (Altekar, 1949: 10).

In addition, comparable to the view of Machiavelli, the Indian emperor was decisively checked by social custom and established laws despite his preferential position in the political realm (Altekar, 1949: 67). While the author of the *Arthasastra* obviously preferred a monarchy, he realized that no ruler could long maintain control of a disgruntled, irritated people and, therefore, many ingenious devices were suggested to promote popular identification with the monarch.

Secular power

In his essay the 'Science of Power', Adolf Sturmthal (1940: 79) observes that 'as long as power seemed established forever, rooted in God, there was no reason to analyze how power was won or lost'. Conversely, the instability of power relationships and the temporal corruption of the Papacy virtually compelled consideration of that question in Renaissance Italy. Machiavelli, in his considerations of this subject, viewed the institutions of religion in Italy with particular displeasure. The temporal domain of the Papal State not only represented an immense obstacle to the unification of the peninsula because of its central location, but also provided a convenient excuse for other European powers to intrude upon Italian affairs. Furthermore, the Florentine disdainfully viewed the Christian faith as servile, listless and prone to repress 'virtu' in man.

Machiavelli is often characterized as totally secular in his philosophy and in his rejection of the traditional Christian approach; so he was. Yet the Italian, although he did not adequately perceive the effect of morality and idealism on political reality, did grasp the concept of using religion as 'an instrument of popular control' (Schevill, 1936: 501). Reminiscing back to the virile gods of ancient Rome, Machiavelli advocated the promulgation of 'a religion which would make men courageous and proud' (Meinecke, 1957: 35). Thus the Florentine sought to make the adoration of power a religion (Lerner, 1939: 306), a religion which today bears the modern appellation of nationalism.

The *Arthasastra* also interpreted and evaluated the political realm from a secular position because Kautilya, although he undoubtedly possesses great insight into the religious dogmas of the age due to his priestly Brahmanical status, refused to consider politics from either an ethical or a religious viewpoint (Saletore, 1963: 53). For example, Kautilya was not deluded by the common mystical notion that the king was divine. Yet, with seemingly characteristic perception, he 'recognized that legends about the origins of kingship had propaganda value' (Basham, 1954: 83). Perhaps the real key to the Kautilyan successes was the utilization of a 'balanced metaphysical perspective' (Ramaswamy, 1963: 7).

Equal patronage was granted by the state to all Indian religions and sects. This largesse not only prevented any single sacerdotal grouping from controlling the political power but also established through public projects an identification of the regime with a common good for all, namely spiritual assistance (Altekar, 1949: 31). The ecclesiastical equilibrium achieved did preserve popular loyalty for the government and thereby managed to maintain social order (Ramaswamy, 1962: 11). And for Kautilya, as for Machiavelli, though established religions were manipulated, the concept of the state became 'a "destiny" sanctified by accepted tradition' (Ramaswamy, 1962: 31), which development may also be regarded as a prototype nationalism.

Fürstenspiegel

Long before Machiavelli collected and set down his practical observations toward the education of a prince, political scholars of Europe had been engaged in formulating textbooks for rulers. There was nothing unique, for example, in Machiavelli politically suggesting to the Medicis how to execute their tasks of government properly. His production of a 'handbook for rulers' in Renaissance Italy was intended for immediate use. Much later his compositions were interpreted to provide a more universal application of his principles and recommendations. In fact, one of the most glaring errors Machiavelli committed was his conception of the state as the creation of a single, omnipotent man who could be privately tutored in statecraft (Passerin d'Entrèves, 1959: 25). Reiterating the point made several times previously, the proposed education was narrowly confined to the acquisition of political power and not to any long-range utilization of this power once achieved.

The *Arthasastra* also represented a training manual for monarchs, especially in their childhood and adolescence, in order to prevent an improper use of state power (Altekar, 1949: 67). But Kautilya realized that the governing of a state, especially an imperial state, was more than a single man could handle efficiently. Therefore, in order to succeed, the *Arthasastra* informs the king that he must be assisted by a cabinet of competent councillors (Shamasastry, 1951: 12–14). Furthermore, the inclusion of administrative materials transformed the rather commonplace notion of a royal textbook into a manual for statecraft, bureaucracy and administration for the entire Mauryan domain and for an extremely long period of time (Saletore, 1963: 50). Even today in certain parts of India, the structure of the village – the dominant form of political organization – closely parallels the suggestions made by Kautilya more than two millennia ago. In short, the Kautilyan *Arthasastra* appears to have been a more practical and universally applicable treatise on government than any of Machiavelli's works.

PRACTICAL RESULTS AND
APPLICATIONS

Ironically, although Machiavelli had prepared a reasonably accurate description of the political tenor of the Renaissance, his formulas and suggestions for the acquisition and maintenance of power were not readily accepted. Confronted by the princely revulsion at this exposé of their common political methods and also by the lingering influence of Christianity, Machiavelli's ideas really did not enter the main stream of politics for some 300 years (Gauss, 1952: 15). Part of the reason for his failure rested upon himself and his impolitic methods of presentation. However, a more substantial reason for his rejection probably was because 'the idea of political regeneration was altogether beyond the capabilities and the wishes of the people and the rulers of that time' (Meinecke, 1957: 45).

In one sense, his system is only another portion of the rich and varied Western political theory. In another sense, it forms the wellspring for the era of nationalism. In the interwar fascistic states where the despotic components of his suggestions came to fruition, political speculation was largely suppressed and/or manipulated. Perhaps, however, Machiavelli made his most significant contribution through his reintroduction of the conception of politics as an end in itself (Hallowell, 1950: 60).

The effect of the Kautilyan *Arthasastra* was apparently quite significant on the activities of Indian political speculation. Although a variety of schools of thought had preceded the Mauryan minister, the appearance of his treatise seemingly solved all possible controversies efficiently and effectively (Saletore, 1963: 49). In the pre-Mauryan era, the final appeal was generally to the *dharma* or holy law, but in the system prescribed by the *Arthasastra* imperial decree became supreme. The power of decision-making was thus clearly reserved for the political realm; certain scholars have ascribed this phenomenon to the almost prototypic totalitarianism of the Mauryan empire (Basham, 1954: 114). Whatever the reason, previously competitive political philosophies fell into disuse and little political speculation occurred in the centuries following Kautilya (Altekar, 1949: 7–9). One wonders what effects a triumphant Machiavellian philosophy might have had on the subsequent political development in the Renaissance, the Reformation, and modern Europe in general.

Whether or not the system of political realism recommended by Machiavelli and Kautilya in their respective eras actually provides the universal imperatives of Max Lerner remains a moot point. By almost any definition assigned, political relationships among humankind will remain unstable and, in a certain respect, unpredictable. Yet at least conclusions as to efficacy, consistency and applicability can be drawn from this topical comparison.

As advocated by Machiavelli, empiricism has become a requisite for the development of political science. Reliance upon observable and verifiable phenomena fulfills a basic requirement for the so-called scientific method. Rejection of idealism, on the other hand, does not appear to be the mark of an astute politician. Ideals, while they may be impossible to attain immediately, provide a reference point for the utilization of man's energies, as the example of Kautilya would demonstrate. Machiavelli himself established a certain specific idealist criterion for judging action – namely, success – and on a logical note would appear inconsistent. Much of the motivation for Machiavelli's recommendations stemmed also from the desire to promote a common Italian good – unity! The concern shown for a 'common good' would indicate the existence of another ideal for this Renaissance realist.

Promotion or apparent promotion of a commonweal increases the effectiveness and influence of the promoting government; the people, as it were, appear to have a stake in the regime's success. Machiavelli assumed that the unification of his national state would be inherently good and be accepted by all Italians; he misjudged his compatriots on the latter point. Perhaps comparison of Machiavelli's failure with Kautilya's successes is unfair for the latter apparently wrote after his goal had been accomplished. Nevertheless, it is obvious in the *Arthasastra* that the Brahmin had persuaded Indians in general that the most reasonable and productive action on their part was submission to his emperor's state.

Centralization of government, which Machiavelli in general ignored even as Kautilya elaborated, has become a characteristic of modern society. Again, we can only hypothesize that part of Kautilya's success emanated from this emphasis. Government no longer merely presented an arbitrator of man's basically violent nature; sheer maintenance of law and order had expanded into promotion of a complete way of life. Rapid accomplishment of ends became possible also as man's energies came to be directed by a central agency. Whether the ends accomplished serve the common good of man is, of course, a different question.

The use of force and fraud is an identifying feature of Kautilya and Machiavelli. Perhaps no better comment can be made on this issue than mention of the speedy demise of *The Prince*'s model ruler, Cesare Borgia. Yet the Mauryan emperors reigned successfully for several centuries and Indian civilization reached an early climax under their aegis. Perhaps the important aspect of force is not the immediate acquisition of power, but the long-range use to which it is put. Certain underdeveloped countries today, for example, insist their lower levels of education, industrial development and political maturity require an authoritative allocation of resources if any progress is to be made. In the long run, force is almost certain to turn upon itself and hence must be regulated carefully. But its utilization in short-range projects can achieve certain ends rapidly. The question hinges upon the rejection of force as an end in itself and the alternative acceptance of force as the means to some end, some ideal.

Emancipation of politics from the grasp of institutionalized religion represents the greatest advance for the realist position. Ideals are essential to the proper functioning of a political system. But dogma and doctrine, inflexibility and immutability have only dysfunctional roles in the heterogeneous world of politics. In addition, institutions of any kind tend to become ossified and corrupt, especially when they have special vested interests. Until an ideal society is reached, pluralism must be protected in order that truth may flourish where it will, and no single interest should obtain total control of society.

REFERENCES AND FURTHER READING

Aiyangar, K.V. Rangaswami (1934) *Aspects of Ancient Indian Economic Thought*. Benares: Motilal Banarsidass.

Altekar, A.S. (1949) *State and Government in Ancient India from Earliest Times to c. 1200 A.D.* Banares: Motilal Banarsidass.

Appleby, Paul H. (1953) *Public Administration in India: Report of a Survey*. New Delhi: Cabinet Secretariat, Government of India.

Arora, Ramesh K. and Goyal, Rajni (1995) *Indian Public Administration: Institutions and Issues*. New Delhi: Wishwa Prakashan.

Basham, A.L. (1954) *The Wonder that was India: A Survey of the Indian Sub-Continent Before the Coming of the Muslims*. New York: Grove Press.

Basu, Rumki (1986) *Public Administration: An Introduction to Concept and Theories*. New Delhi: Sterling.

Bhalerao, C.N. (ed.) (1972) *Administration, Politics and Development in India*. Bombay: Lalvani.

Bingham, Woodbridge, Conroy, Hilary and Iklé, Frank W. (1974) *A History of Asia: Formation of Civilizations from Antiquity to 1600*, 2nd edn. Boston, MA: Allyn and Bacon.

Björkman, J.W. (1979) *The Politics of Administrative Alienation in India's Rural Development Programs*. Delhi: Ajanta.

Björkman, J.W. and Mathur, Kuldeep (1996) 'India: How a Government Party Decays When Government Swallows Party', in J. Blondel and M. Cotta (eds), *Party and Government: An Inquiry into the Relationship between Governments and Supporting Parties in Western Liberal Democracies*. London: Macmillan. pp. 225–48.

Braibanti, Ralph and Spengler, Joseph J. (eds) (1963) *Administration and Economic Development in India*. Durham, NC: Duke University Press.

Chabod, Federico (1958) *Machiavelli and the Renaissance*. London: Boves and Boves.

Choudhary, Radha Krishna (1951) 'Kautilya's Conception of Law and Justice', *Bihar Research Society Journal*, 37, parts 1 and 2.

Corry, J.A. (1943) 'Machiavellian Politics', *Queen's Quarterly*, Autumn (Kingston, Ontario, Canada: quarterly journal of Queen's University).

Davies, C. Collin (1959) *An Historical Atlas of the Indian Peninsula*, 2nd edn. London: Oxford University Press.

Elliott, William Y. and McDonald, Neil A. (1949) 'The Secular State', *Western Political Heritage*. New York: Prentice-Hall.

Ferrero, Guglielmo (1939) 'Machiavelli and Machiavellism', *Foreign Affairs*, 18 (April).

Fleet, J.F. (1951) 'Introduction to 1914 edition', *Kautilya's Arthasastra*, trans. R. Shamasastry, 4th edn. Mysore: Sri Raghuveer.

Gauss, Christian (1952) 'Introduction to the Mentor Edition', *The Prince*. New York: The New American Library of World Literature.

Hallowell, John H. (1950) *Main Currents in Modern Political Thought*. New York: Henry Holt and Company.

Hughes, Serge (1951) 'The Science of Machiavelli', *Commonweal*, 53 (12 January).

Konow, Sten (1945) 'Kautilya Studies', *Avhandlinger Utgitt av det Norske Videnskaps-Akademi I Oslo, II Historisk-Filosofisk Klasse*. Oslo: I Kommisjon Hos Jacob Dybwab.

Lerner, Max (1939) 'The Father of Power Politics', *The New Republic*, 100 (18 October).

Lerner, Max (1950) 'Introduction', *The Prince* and *The Discourses*. New York: The Modern Library.

Maheshwari, S.R. (1996) *The Census Administration under the Raj and After*. New Delhi: Concept.

McCoy, Charles N.R. (1943) 'The Place of Machiavelli in the History of Political Thought', *American Political Science Review*, 37.

Meinecke, Friedrich (1957) *Machiavellism: The Doctrine of Raison d'Etat and Its Place in Modern History*. New Haven, CT: Yale University Press.

Misra, B.B. (1983) *District Administration and Rural Development in India: Policy Objectives and Administrative Change in Historical Perspective*. Bombay: Oxford University Press.

Mookerji, Radhakumud (1914) 'An Introductory Essay on the Age and Authenticity of the Arthasastra of Kautilya', in Narendra Nath Law (ed.), *Studies in Ancient Hindu Policy*. New York: Longmans, Green.

Moore, Barrington, Jr (1967) *The Social Origins of Dictatorship and Democracy: Lord and Peasant in the Making of the Modern World*. Boston, MA: Beacon Press.

Morgan, Kenneth O. (ed.) (1993) *The Oxford History of Britain*, updated edition. Oxford: Oxford University Press.

Muir, D. Erskine (1936) *Machiavelli and His Times*. London: William Heinemann.

Oommen, T.K. (1990) *State and Society in India: Studies in Nation-Building*. New Delhi: Sage.

Passerin d'Entrèves, Alexander (1959) *The Medieval Contribution to Political Thought*. New York: Humanities Press.

Prased, Beni (1928) *The State of Ancient India*. Allahabad: Triveni Books.

Raadschelders, Jos C.N. (1998) *Handbook of Administrative History*. Brunswick, NJ: Transaction Publishers.

Ramaswamy, T.N. (1962) *Essentials of Indian Statecraft: Kautilya's Arthasastra for Contemporary Readers*. Bombay: Asia Publishing.

Saletore, Bhasker A. (1963) *Ancient Indian Political Thought and Institutions*. Bombay: Asia Publishing.

Schevill, Ferdinand, (1936) *History of Florence from the Founding of the City through the Renaissance*. New York: Harcourt, Brace and Company.

Shamasastry, R. (1951) *Kautilya's Arthasastra*, 4th edn. Mysore: Sri Raghuveer.

Shamasastry, R. (1960) *The Arthasastra*, 6th edn. Mysore: Mysore Government Oriental Library.

Spangenberg, Bradford (1976) *British Bureaucracy in India: Status, Policy and the I.C.S. in the Late 19th Century*. Columbia: South Asia Books.

Stein, Burton (1998) *A History of India*. Oxford: Blackwell.

Steward, H.L. (1948) 'Machiavaelli and History', *Queen's Quarterly*, Autumn (Kingston, Ontario, Canada: quarterly journal of Queen's University).

Sturmthal, Adolf (1940) 'The Science of Power', *The Nation*, 150 (20 January).

Weidner, Edward W. (ed.) (1970) *Development Administration in Asia*. Durham, NC: Duke University Press.

Zwart, Frank de (1994) *The Bureaucratic Merry-go-round: Manipulating the Transfer of Indian Civil Servants*. Amsterdam: Amsterdam University Press.

IMPLEMENTATION

Introduction

Søren C. Winter

Implementation research grew out of evaluation research. The Great Society policy reforms in the United States in the 1960s and 1970s stimulated a lot of evaluation research in order to estimate the effects of the new welfare state programs and to suggest improvements. Classic evaluation analyses raised the question whether it could be documented that a given policy intervention had any effect, and if so what effect. However, evaluation analysts often became frustrated that most studies actually showed little or no effect (Albæk, 1988). The classic interpretation of such findings was that the program did not work; it was based on a wrong causal theory. However, gradually the apparent failures stimulated another interpretation that maybe nothing was wrong with the causal theory behind the planned policy intervention, but the intervention might not have taken place as intended. This stimulated an interest in studying the relation between planned and actual interventions and the administrative process in between policy making and effects.

Most implementation researchers would regard Jeffrey Pressman and Aron Wildavsky's book *Implementation* from 1973 as the first piece of implementation research. It was a case study of an economic development program in Oakland in California that had been created to stimulate minority employment. However, it failed to do so due to the complexity of many actors having to work together. The book certainly opened the field, but also a few pieces of earlier research (for example, Kaufman, 1960; Murphy, 1971) had actually focused on implementation problems. Pressman and Wildavsky's (1973) guiding research questions were: 'How well was this authoritative mandate (law, regulation, program, official pronouncement) implemented?' and 'How might it have been better implemented?' Later research redefined the question to focus on achieving the explicit or implicit values in a given mandate rather than its prescriptive details (Bardach, 2001). Accordingly, goal achievement has been the dominating standard and dependent variable for implementation research since the 1970s.

With inspiration from Pressman and Wildavsky and other pioneers, implementation research became one of the fads of political science and policy analysis and reached its peak in terms of number of publications in the mid-1980s. While research published under that explicit label has later decreased (Sætren, 1996), still a substantial amount of research focusing on implementation problems is being published, but often under other labels such as public administration, management (Bardach, 2001), regulatory enforcement (Kagan, 1994; Scholz and Wei, 1986; Winter, 1999), street-level bureaucracy (Lipsky, 1980), principal–agent theory (Brehm and Gates, 1999), new institutionalism, governance (Bogason, 2000), networks (O'Toole, 2000), policy design and instruments (Linder and Peters, 1989; Salamon, 1981) etc., with several of these labels representing more recent research fads!

Implementation research is part of two sub-disciplines of political science, public policy/policy analysis and public administration. Growing out of evaluation research, implementation studies tried to address the basic questions of policy analysis: What are the content, causes and consequences of public policies (Dye, 1976)? Implementation research focused on the consequences of those public policies that have been enacted as laws or other authoritative statutes. However, policy can also be conceived at an operational level as the delivery of public services and enforcement of regulations to citizens. Consequently, implementation research focuses on the content of such performances, their causes and consequences. Implementation research has become an established part of public policy research that focuses on different stages of the policy process, such as agenda-setting, policy formation, policy design, implementation, evaluation, knowledge utilization and policy change more generally (Parson, 1995).

However, implementation research also addresses the basic question of public administration research: How is legislation executed? While public administration traditionally had studied formal, institutional and normative aspects of this issue, implementation research offered a fresh empirical, behavioral perspective on execution of laws that fitted well with the behavioral and much more political science-oriented trend in public administration research that started accelerating in the 1970s (Peters, 1978). Implementation research has had a major role in bringing public administration and public policy research together, implying that several scholars are working in both fields. This is often reflected even at the single publication level. Joint public administration and public policy programs have been formed at many universities. Other research has been important in that bridging process. The policy perspective has crept into many aspects of public administration research, and new research approaches have contributed as well, for example, neo-rational and institutionalist approaches, but implementation research has certainly played an essential role, too.

THE DIVERSITY OF IMPLEMENTATION RESEARCH

During the barely thirty years of implementation research no general implementation theory has emerged, although many implementation scholars have had the development of such a theory as their ultimate, yet farsighted objective. The implementation sub-discipline has been characterized by many different approaches representing different research strategies, evaluation standards, methodologies, concepts and focal subject areas for research.

One of the major controversies among implementation analysts has been whether implementation should be studied from the top down as a control problem (Mazmanian and Sabatier, 1981) or from the bottom up starting at actors most proximate to the problems to be solved by policies (Hull and Hjern, 1987). Related to that discussion is the proper evaluation standard for implementation studies. While as mentioned above, goal achievement has been the dominating standard, some bottom-up scholars have suggested focusing on problem solving rather than goal achievement. Problem solving could be defined either from the perspective of the group affected by the problem or by the researcher himself (Elmore, 1982; Hull and Hjern, 1987). In the following chapter in this volume Winter suggests avoiding using goal achievement as a standard when analyzing the delivery performance of implementers by using behavioral performance categories instead.

In terms of methodology, implementation analyses have been dominated by single case studies allowing the complex phenomena of implementation to be studied in detail and context. In each case several data sources are often applied, such as reports and documents, qualitative surveys with implementers, quantitative data on coverage of the program, participation, outputs in terms of delivery performance and outcomes (Yin, 1982). Some even use qualitative or quantitative methods for detailed text interpretation in case studies. Other scholars have called for a replacement of single case studies by comparative and statistical research designs, which can increase the number of observations and control for third variables in order to allow more systematic

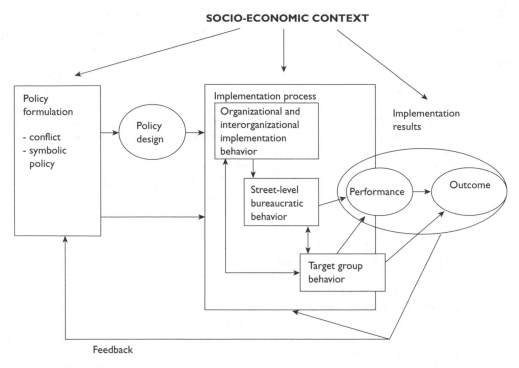

Figure 1   *An Integrated Implementation Model*

theory and hypothesis testing and generalization (Goggin, 1986).

Implementation scholars also disagree about the key concepts for implementation research. Some want to focus on the implementation *process* as the dependent variable (Lester and Goggin, 1998), while others examine implementation performance/output as the dependent variable (Lipsky, 1980) to be explained by process and organizational variables (Mazmanian and Sabatier, 1981; Winter, 1999). Some even include outcomes as dependent variables (Hull and Hjern, 1987; Mazmanian and Sabatier, 1981). According to Peter May (1999) conceptual ambiguity and confusion have severely hampered theory development in implementation research.

Somewhat related to the conceptual disagreement are differences in the subjects that implementation researchers study. Many implementation studies present long lists of variables that might explain implementation. A famous example is Mazmanian and Sabatier's (1981) list of seventeen variables. However, implementation scholars tend to focus on different variables and subject matters in their research, for example, hierarchical structuring,

tractability of problems, communication, commitment, political support, resources, interorganizational relations and coordination problems, decision and veto points, discretion at various levels (including discretion by street-level bureaucrats), contexts (including socio-economic conditions and target groups characteristics), empowerment of target groups, the role of policy design and instruments in shaping implementation.

AN INTEGRATED IMPLEMENTATION MODEL

One attempt to synthesize and integrate some of the most important and promising variables in implementation research in a common framework of analysis has been presented by Winter (1990, 1994) in his Integrated Implementation Model (see Figure 1). Some of the key factors in that model will be used as the main organizing principle for structuring the division among the following chapters in this implementation section.

As dependent variable and standard for evaluating the results of the implementation process the model focuses on both performance and outcome in relation to the official policy objectives. This standard was selected from a democratic point of view, as goals formulated in parliament and in laws have a particular legitimate status and are relevant for holding government accountable.

The first set of factors, which affects implementation results, is the *policy formulation process* and the *policy design*. Too many implementation researchers have erroneously put the whole blame for any lack of goal achievement on implementation. This is in sharp contrast to the early evaluation scholars who blamed the policy design for any lack of effect. As noted by Peter May in Chapter 17, well-designed policies are necessary but not sufficient for improving implementation prospects. Other implementation scholars have ignored or failed to conceptualize the connections between policy formulation, policy design and implementation.

The roots of implementation problems can often be found in the prior policy formulation process. For instance, conflicts in this process often create a policy that is marked by ambiguous goals as well as an invalid causal theory with a lack of connection between goals and means in the policy design concerned. Sometimes even symbolic policies are adopted to (appear to) address a problem without actually offering the means that could achieve the stated objectives. And as mentioned by Bardach (1977), the conflicts in policy formulation often continue in the subsequent implementation process. Not only conflict but also lack of attention among the coalition partners passing a law can lead to implementation failures (Winter, 1986).

A policy design typically contains a set of goals, a mix of instruments for obtaining these goals, a designation of governmental or non-governmental entities charged with carrying out the goals, and an allocation of resources for the requisite tasks (May, Chapter 17). Policy design, and particular policy instruments, have received substantial research interest since the 1980s. The basic claim of this literature is that any policy can be disaggregated to one or a mix of a limited number of generic policy instruments. The research

interest, however, has not led to agreement on any typology of instruments (Vedung, 1995). One simple classification consists of mandates, economic incentives and information, which aim at affecting the behavior of either target groups or intermediaries (implementers).

The policy design affects the implementation process and results in various ways. Different mixes of instruments are not equally effective in obtaining a given policy objective. May finds that policy design is important in affecting the incentives of intermediaries to carry out their requisite tasks, particularly through affecting their commitment and capacity and by signaling desired actions. However, while the validity of the causal theory linking instruments to objectives certainly is important, the research documentation of instrument effects is still meager (for another good attempt, see Gunningham and Grabosky, 1998). One reason is that effects of instruments on implementation are often determined by the context, including the political context as described by May in Chapter 17. Consequently, designing good policies is not a simple, technocratic process like selecting the best types of materials for building a bridge.

The instruments selected may also affect the overall implementation structure and process, as certain instruments favor the formation of particular implementation structures. Mandates aimed at regulating the behavior of target groups normally require a staff for inspecting and enforcing the mandate and a set of sanctions. Information strategies and use of economic incentives such as environmental taxes can sometimes be implemented with fewer staff, though there is no one-to-one relationship between instruments and staff requirements. Some taxes are relatively automatic and easy to collect, such as an environmental tax per liter of gasoline sold, while others require a substantial staff for inspection and enforcing, for example, taxing diffuse pollution.

It is important to understand that ineffective policy designs are not always due to lack of knowledge on the part of the policy designers. Policy design of instruments and organizational structure is first of all a political process, in which political actors – both policy proponents and opponents – try to maximize their interests, including selecting an organizational structure which will allow themselves to maximize long-term control of the implementation process (Moe, 1989). Peter May further develops the implications of policy design for implementation in his chapter.

The next set of factors of the model focuses on how the implementation process affects the results. Implementation processes are characterized by *organizational and inter-organizational behaviors* representing different degrees of commitment and coordination. Interorganizational implementation settings seem to become ever more important, as shown in O'Toole's Chapter 18 on 'Interorganizational Relations in Implementation', while Pressman and Wildavsky (1973) have focused on the typical 'complexity of joint action' according to which successful implementation is likely to be negatively related to the number of actors, the diversity of their interests and perspectives, and the number of decision and veto points.

However, according to O'Toole and Montjoy (1984; and see Chapter 18) that insight only applies to certain kinds of interorganizational implementation settings. Decision points are not independent of each other, but successful implementation results can be stimulated by an early agreement on basic understandings, which can promote 'bandwagon effects' in later decisions, and decisions can be merged by crafting 'package deals'.

The implementation prospects also depend on the type of resource-dependency among participating organizations. The 'complexity of joint action' applies best to a chain of sequential relations where one organization depends on outputs from another as input for its own contribution to implementation. Reciprocal relations where two organizations depend on each other for inputs can decrease the likelihood of veto points because both have incentives to cooperate. Pooled relations where multiple organizations can also produce and deliver implementation outputs independently of each other can produce relatively good implementation results even though the coordination may not be optimal. In the following chapters in this section of the Handbook O'Toole analyzes interorganizational relations in implementation in more depth, and both he and May discuss how interorganizational

coordination problems can be reduced by using policy design to increase commitment, build and use a common interest and facilitate cooperation via exchange.

The behaviors of *street-level bureaucrats* are also crucial for the implementation of most policies, and Lipsky's (1980) insights on 'street-level bureaucracy' are included in the Integrated Implementation Model. Street-level bureaucrats make important discretionary decisions in their direct contact with citizens, who tend to define public policies not as crafted in statutes, but as delivered to them by street-level bureaucrats. These bureaucrats work in situations characterized by many demands and limited resources. They cope with this situation by rationing services, making biased priorities among cases and clients, controlling clients and modifying policy goals and client-perceptions. According to Lipsky the coping behaviors of street-level bureaucrats systematically bias the delivery behavior in relation to the policy mandates.

While Lipsky's contribution was important for understanding implementation, the theory needs more specifications of the causal mechanisms that can explain variation in coping behaviors and their consequences (Winter, 2002). The concepts also apply better to social policies than regulatory policies with target groups who are stronger and less likely to demand more services. In later chapters Winter (Chapter 16) presents recent attempts to address these problems of conceptualizing and explaining behaviors of street-level bureaucrats, Marcia Meyer and Susan Vorsanger (Chapter 19) analyze the role of street-level bureaucrats in implementation more fully, while Steven Rathgeb Smith (Chapter 28), in another section in this volume, analyzes street-level bureaucracy from the citizens' perspective.

According to the Integrated Implementation Model, *target groups* of public policies, that is, citizens or firms, also play an important role not only on the effects of the policy, but also in affecting the performance by street-level bureaucrats through positive or negative actions in co-producing public services. Finally, the *socio-economic context* forms important framework conditions for implementation. For example, in employment policies both the types of employment offers and their effects depend heavily on ups and downs in the business cycle. The Integrated Implementation Model has been applied in studies of, for example, Australian domestic politics (Ryan, 1996) and Danish employment policy (Bonfils, 1998; Jensen et al., 1991). Obviously, it is not a model in the strict sense of a simple causal model. It is rather a framework of analysis presenting key factors and mechanisms that affect implementation outputs and outcomes. For each set of factors a number of more specific hypotheses can be developed (Jensen et al., 1991; Winter, 1990, 1994; see also the chapters by May, O'Toole, and Meyers and Vorsanger in this section).

As mentioned above, key parts of the model will be used for structuring this implementation section into the following four chapters. In 'Implementation Perspectives: Status and Reconsideration' Søren Winter offers an account of the development of implementation research. The field has been developed across and within three 'generations' of implementation research. Winter also performs a critical examination of the field and suggests new directions for implementation research. In his chapter Peter May examines the political role of policy design in shaping implementation results. Lawrence O'Toole analyzes the role of interorganizational relations in implementation and how these can be affected to improve implementation. Finally, Marcia Meyers and Susan Vorsanger give a critical account of the literature on the role of street-level bureaucrats in policy implementation.

REFERENCES

Albæk, Erik (1988) *Fra sandhed til information: Evalueringsforskning I USA – før og nu.* Copenhagen: Akademisk Forlag.

Bardach, Eugene (1977) *The Implementation Game.* Cambridge, MA: MIT Press.

Bardach, Eugene (ed.) (2001) 'Implementation, Political', *International Encyclopedia of the Social and Behavioral Sciences.* New York: Elsevier Science.

Bogason, Peter (2000) *Public Policy and Local Governance: Institutions in Postmodern Society.* Cheltenham: Edward Elgar.

Bonfils, Inge S. (1998) *Puljejobordningen. Implementeringen af puljejobordningen i kommuner og amter.* Copenhagen: Danish National Institute of Social Research.

Brehm, John and Gates, Scott (1999) *Working, Shirking, and Sabotage: Bureaucratic Response to a Democratic Public.* Ann Arbor, MI: University of Michigan Press.

Dye, T.R. (1976) *What Governments Do, Why They Do It, and What Difference It Makes.* Tuscaloosa, AL: University of Alabama Press.

Elmore, Richard F. (1982) 'Backward Mapping: Implementation Research and Policy Decisions,' in W. Williams, R.F. Elmore, J.S. Hall et al. (eds), *Studying Implementation.* Chatham NJ: Chatham House. pp. 18–35.

Goggin, Malcolm L. (1986) 'The "Too Few Cases/Too Many Variables" Problems in Implementation Research', *The Western Political Quarterly,* 39: 328–47.

Gunningham, Neil and Grabosky, Peter (1998) *Smart Regulation, Designing Environmental Policy.* New York: Oxford University Press.

Hull, Christopher J. with Hjern, Benny (1987) *Helping Small Firm Grow: An Implementation Perspective.* London: Croom Helm.

Jensen, T.P., Winter, S., Manniche, J. and Ørberg, P.D., with Thaulow I. (1991) *Indsatsen for langtidsledige – en undersøgelse af administration og effekt af arbejds- og uddannelsestilbud.* Copenhagen: AKF Forlaget.

Kagan, Robert A. (1994) 'Regulatory Enforcement,' in David H. Roosenbloom and Richard D. Schwartz (eds), *Handbook of Regulation and Administrative Law.* New York: Marcel Decker. pp. 383–422.

Kaufman, Herbert (1960) *The Forest Ranger.* Baltimore, MD: Johns Hopkins University Press.

Lester, James P. and Goggin, Malcolm L. (1998) 'Back to the Future: the Rediscovery of Implementation Studies', *Policy Currents – Newsletter of the Public Policy Section of the American Political Science Association,* 8 (3): 1–9.

Linder, Stephen H. and Peters, B. Guy (1989) 'Instruments of Government: Perceptions and Contexts', *International Public Policy,* 9: 35–58.

Lipsky, Michael (1980) *Street-Level Bureaucracy: The Dilemmas of the Individual in Public Services.* New York: Russell Sage Foundation.

May, Peter J. (1999) 'Toward a Future Agenda for Implementation Research: A Panelist's Notes'. Prepared for the annual meeting of the Western Political Science Association in Seattle. Department of Political Science, University of Washington.

Mazmanian, Daniel A. and Sabatier, Paul (1981) *Effective Policy Implementation.* Lexington, MA: Lexington Books.

Moe, Terry M. (1989) 'The Politics of Bureaucratic Structure', in John E. Chubb and Paul E. Peterson (eds), *Can the Government Govern?* Washington, DC: Brookings Institution. pp. 267–329.

Murphy, Jerome T. (1971) 'Title I of ESEA: The Politics of Administering Federal Education Reform', *Harvard Educational Review,* 42 (1): 35–63..

O'Toole, Laurence J., Jr and Montjoy, Robert S. (1984) 'Interorganizational Policy Implementation: A Theoretical Perspective', *Public Administration Review,* 44 (6): 491–503.

O'Toole, Laurence J., Jr (2000) 'Research on Policy Implementation: Assessment and Prospects', *Journal of Public Administration Research and Theory,* 10: 263–88.

Parson, Wayne (1995) *Public Policy: An Introduction to the Theory and Practice of Policy Analysis*. Aldershot: Edward Elgar.

Peters, B. Guy (1978) *The Politics of Bureaucracy: A Comparative Perspective*. New York: Longman.

Pressman, Jeffrey L. and Wildavsky, Aron (1973) *Implementation*. Berkeley, CA: University of California Press.

Ryan, Neal (1996) 'Some Advantages of an Integrated Approach to Implementation Analysis: A Study of Australian Industry Policy', *Public Administration*, 74: 737–53.

Sætren, Harald (1996): 'Whatever Happened to Implementation Research? A Diagnosis of the Decline, and Some Prescriptions for the Revival of a Once Popular and Still Important Research Field in Political Science'. Paper for presentation at the Conference of the Nordic Association of Political Science in Helsinki in August. Department of Administration and Organization Theory, University of Bergen.

Salamon, Lester M. (1981) 'Rethinking Public Management: Third-Party Government and the Changing Forms of Government Action', *Public Policy*, 29 (3): 256–75.

Scholz, J.T. and Wei, F.H. (1986) 'Regulatory Enforcement in a Federalist System', *American Political Science Review*, 80: 1249–70.

Vedung, Evert (1995) 'Policy Instruments: Typologies and Theories', in M.-L. Bemelmans-Videc, R.C. Rist and E. Vedung (eds), *Carrots, Sticks and Sermons: Policy Instruments and Their Evaluation*. New Brunswick, NJ: Transaction Books. pp. 21–58.

Winter, Søren (1986) 'How Policy-Making Affects Implementation: The Decentralization of the Danish Disablement Pension Administration', *Scandinavian Political Studies*, 9: 361–85.

Winter, Søren (1990) 'Integrating Implementation Research', in Dennis J. Palumbo and Donald J. Calista (eds), *Implementation and the Policy Process*. New York: Greenwood Press. pp. 19–38.

Winter, Søren (1994) *Implementering og effektivitet*. Aarhus: Systime.

Winter, Søren (1999) 'New Directions for Implementation Research', *Policy Currents – Newsletter of the Public Policy Section of the American Political Science Association*, 8 (4): 1–5.

Winter, Søren C. (2002) 'Explaining Street-Level Bureaucratic Behavior in Social and Regulatory Policies'. Paper prepared for the Annual Meeting of the American Political Science Association, 29 August – 1 September in Boston. Danish National Institute of Social Research.

Yin, Robert K. (1982) 'Studying the Implementation of Public Programs', in W. Williams et al. (eds), *Studying Implementation*. Chatham, NJ: Chatham House. pp. 36–72.

16

Implementation Perspectives: Status and Reconsideration

Søren C. Winter

Although the field of implementation research is barely thirty years old, implementation has already been analyzed from many different perspectives representing different research strategies, evaluation standards, concepts, focal subject areas and methodologies (see the Introduction to this section on Implementation). The purpose of this chapter is two-fold. It first performs a critical review of some of the major contributions to the literature. This examination will follow the development of the field. Commentators have already identified three generations of implementation research (Goggin, 1986), which will be presented and assessed below. These are the pioneers with their explorative case studies, the second generation studies with their top-down and bottom-up research strategies and synthesis models, and a third generation with more systematic tests based on comparative and statistical research designs. The nice thing about these generations is, however, that as a researcher you can belong to more than one, and thus stay alive and even get younger!

Second, based on a critical examination of the development and status of the research field, the chapter will suggest ways of moving ahead. It claims that implementation research can be improved by (1) accepting theoretical diversity rather than looking for one common theoretical framework; (2) developing and testing partial theories and hypotheses rather than trying to reach for utopia in constructing a general implementation theory; (3) seeking conceptual clarification; (4) focusing on output (performance of implementers) as a key dependent variable in implementation research; but also (5) including studies of outcomes in addition to outputs; and (6) applying more comparative and statistical

research designs rather than relying on single case studies in order to sort out the influence of different implementation variables.

THE PIONEERS

In several respects the book *Implementation* by Pressman and Wildavsky (1973) sets the stage for later implementation research. Most implementation research has focused on implementation problems, barriers and failures, and this pessimistic view of implementation was already reflected in the subtitle of the seminal work: 'How great expectations in Washington are dashed in Oakland; or, Why it's amazing that federal programs work at all …'

In this case study of the local implementation of a federal economic development program to decrease unemployment among ethnic minority groups in Oakland, the two authors focused on the 'complexity of joint action' as the key implementation problem. In that case – as in many others – federal, regional, state and local government actors, courts, affected interest groups, private firms and media had a role and stake in policy implementation. Implementation problems were amplified not only by the many actors but also by the many decision and veto points, which must typically be passed during the implementation process. Although they probably overemphasized the lack of conflict in their case, Pressman and Wildavsky convincingly showed that merely slightly different perspectives, priorities and time horizons among multiple actors with different missions in repeated and sequential decisions could cause delay, distortion and even failures in policy implementation.

However, the two authors also demonstrated that failures are not only caused by bad implementation but also by bad policy instruments. Many of the problems in the Oakland case would have been avoided had policy makers chosen a more direct economic instrument that would *ex post* have tied spending of public expenditures to the actual number of minority workers employed rather than relying on endless *ex ante* negotiations with affected parties and authorities.

Pressman and Wildavsky (1973) are good representatives for the first generation of implementation studies, which were typically explorative and inductive case studies with a theory-generating aim. Very few central theoretical variables were in focus, in this case the number of actors and decision points and the validity of the causal theory.

Another outstanding example is Eugene Bardach's (1977) *Implementation Games*, which placed more emphasis on the aspects of conflict in implementation, seeing implementation as a continuation of the political game from the policy adoption stage, though partly with other actors and other relations among actors. Bardach analyzed the types of games that various actors apply in the implementation process in order to pursue their own interests. However, these games tend to distort implementation from the legislative goals. Among other representatives from what has later been called the first generation of implementation research we find Erwin Hargrove (1975), who called implementation research 'the missing link' in the study of the policy process, and Walter Williams and Richard Elmore (1976).

SECOND GENERATION MODEL BUILDERS: TOP-DOWN, BOTTOM-UP AND SYNTHESES

Second generation implementation studies began in the early 1980s. While the first generation studies had been explorative and theory-generating, the ambition of the second generation was to take a next step in theory development by constructing theoretical models, or rather frameworks of analysis, which could guide empirical analysis. Some of these studies had more optimistic views on successful implementation.

The construction of models and research strategies, however, immediately led to a major confrontation between the so-called *top-down* and *bottom-up* perspectives on policy implementation. The predominant top-down researchers focused on a specific political decision, normally a law. Against the background of its official purpose, they followed the implementation down through the system, often with special interest in higher-level decision makers. They would typically assume a control perspective on implementation, trying to give good advice on how to structure the implementation process from above in order to achieve the purpose of the legislation and to minimize the number of decision points that could be vetoed.

The best-known and most frequently used (Sabatier, 1986) top-down analysis framework was developed by Mazmanian and Sabatier (1981). It contains seventeen variables placed in three main groups concerning the tractability of the problems addressed by the legislation, the social and political context, and the ability of the legislation to structure the implementation process. This structuring can be made by means of, for example, hierarchy, appointing of authorities and staff with a positive attitude towards the legislation/program, and use of incentives including competition among providers. By adding a long-term perspective of ten to fifteen years to implementation, the authors show that, over time, start-up problems are often ameliorated by better structuring of the implementation by policy advocates (see also Kirst and Jung, 1982). This gave rise to much more optimistic views of implementation in contrast to the pessimism introduced by Pressman and Wildavsky (1973) and joined by most implementation analysts.

Mazmanian and Sabatier's framework was met by two different kinds of criticism. According to one strand, the model was naive and unrealistic because it overemphasized the ability of policy proponents to structure implementation, thus ignoring the ability of policy opponents to interfere in this structuring process (Moe, 1989). Often policy opponents are able to make policy goals less clear and to increase their own long-term influence in the implementation process in order to avoid some of the effects intended by policy proponents. Conceptually, the model ignored the politics of policy formulation and policy design (Winter, 1986b; see also May, Chapter 17).

Another strand of criticism came from the bottom-up researchers who took special interest in 'the bottom' of the implementation system, the place where the public sector meets the citizens or firms. They all emphasized the influence that front-line staff or field workers have on the delivery of policies such as social services, income transfers and law enforcement in relation to citizens and firms. Field workers are crucial decision makers in these studies, and the disability of politicians and administrative managers to control field workers is emphasized.

Like top-down researchers and also most evaluation researchers, some bottom-up researchers use the official objectives of a given legislation as the standard of evaluation (Lipsky, 1980; Winter, 1986a). Michael Lipsky (1980) developed a theory on 'street-level bureaucracy'. It focuses on the discretionary decisions that each field worker – or 'street-level bureaucrat' as Lipsky prefers to call them – makes in relation to individual citizens when they are delivering policies to them. This discretionary role in delivering services or enforcing regulations makes street-level bureaucrats essential actors in implementing public policies. Indeed, Lipsky (1980) turns the policy process upside-down by claiming that street-level bureaucrats are the real *policy makers*. However, one ironic aspect of the theory is that although Lipsky emphasizes the individual role of street-level bureaucrats in implementing public policies, their similar working conditions make them all apply similar behavior. This means that street-level bureaucrats even across policy types tend to apply similar types of practices whether they are teachers, policemen, nurses, doctors or social workers.

Although trying to do their best, street-level bureaucrats experience a gap between the demands made on them by legislative mandates, managers and citizens on the one side and their high workload on the other. In this situation they apply a number of coping mechanisms that systematically distort their work in relation to the intentions of the legislation. They ration services, such as making it less attractive or more difficult for clients to turn up at their office. They make priorities between their tasks, for instance by upgrading easy tasks and cases where clients turn up themselves and exert pressure to obtain a benefit or decision, at the expense of complicated, non-programmed tasks and clients that do not press for a decision. For example, within the social services, acute casework and payment of benefits get higher priority than do rehabilitation and preventive work.

Street-level bureaucrats tend to apply few, rough standard classifications for grouping clients. By using rules-of-thumb for the processing of these categories, the action to be taken can easily be decided even if implying that part of the prescribed individual discretion is neglected. To prove successful, street-level bureaucrats tend to apply creaming in favoring relatively resourceful clients that might be in a good position to take care of themselves and downgrading the weaker clients. Street-level bureaucrats try to gain control over clients in order to make cases simpler to process, while difficult cases are passed on to other authorities. As time goes by, street-level bureaucrats develop more cynical perceptions of the clients and their intentions and modify the policy objectives that are the basis of their work.

Other bottom-up researchers go the whole length, rejecting the objective of policy mandates as an evaluation standard. Instead, their analysis departs from a specific problem such as youth unemployment (Elmore, 1982) or small firms' conditions of growth (Hull and Hjern, 1987). In practice it is the researcher himself, who in most cases defines the problem and thereby his evaluation standard. In my opinion this is acceptable if done explicitly, and it can be fruitful if the researcher is able to convince others about the appropriateness of his problem definition.

The next task in Hull and Hjern's bottom-up approach is to identify the many actors that are affecting the problem in question and to map relations between them. In these network analyses both public and private actors become essential, and the analyses often include several policies that affect the same problem whether or not it is intended in those policies. For instance, when defining youth unemployment as the focal problem, youth unemployment is affected by a great number of actors such as schools, high schools, educational and vocational training institutions, the social welfare system, employment service, unemployment foundations, employment providers as well as the social partners (for example, through fixing of wage rates).

Hull and Hjern (1987) focused on the role of local networks in affecting a given problem in the implementation process, and they also developed a way of identifying these networks. It is a combination of a snowball method and a sociometric method. Starting with the actors with most direct contact with people exposed to the problem, one gradually identifies more and more actors who are interacting with the first set of actors around the problem, and so on. In this way, the analysis maps the informal, empirical implementation structure around a given problem, while top-down research tends to look at the formal implementation structure related to one particular policy program. According to Hull and Hjern, empirical implementation structures tend to be far less hierarchical than formal ones, and they often cross organizational borders in forming collaborative networks at the operational level that may even take on an identity of their own relatively independent of their mother organizations. The bottom-up analyses by Hjern and associates is important in drawing attention to implementation activities and structures at the local operational level, but the perspective has more the character of guidelines for an inductive research strategy and methodology than a development of theory and hypotheses that can be empirically tested.

This also applies to Elmore's (1982) 'backward mapping' strategy, which has played an important role in the development of the bottom-up perspective. However, Elmore's perspective is more aimed at helping policy analysts and policy makers in designing sound policies than offering a research strategy and contributing to theory development. A recent example of the bottom-up approach is Bogason's (2000) study of local governance. It is inspired by Hull and Hjern but adds elements of institutional and constructivist analyses and points to the fragmented character of the modern state in policy making and implementation.

Suggested syntheses

The top-down and bottom-up perspectives were useful in drawing increased attention to the fact that both top and bottom play important roles in the implementation process, but in the long run the battle between the two approaches was not fruitful. Each tended to ignore the portion of the implementation reality explained by the other (Goggin et al., 1990: 12). Elmore (1985) actually recommends using both forward mapping – which is essentially a top-down analysis – and backward mapping for policy analysis as each tends to offer valuable insights for policy makers. He claims that policy designers need to consider the policy instruments and the resources they have at their disposal (forward mapping) as well as the incentive structure of the target group and street-level bureaucrats' ability to tip the balance of these incentives in order to affect the problematic situation of the target group (backward mapping).

Other scholars have tried to solve the controversy by specifying the conditions where one approach might be more relevant than the other. Sabatier (1986) claims that the top-down perspective is best suited for studying implementation in policy areas that are dominated by one specific piece of legislation, limited research funds, or where the situation is structured at least moderately well. Bottom-up perspectives, on the other hand, would be more relevant in situations where several different policies are directed towards a particular problem, and where one is primarily interested in the dynamics of different local situations.

Attempts were also made to synthesize the two models. Richard E. Matland (1995) suggests that their relative value depends on the degree of ambiguity in goals and means of a policy and the degree of conflict. Traditional top-down models, based on the public administration tradition, present an accurate description of the implementation process when a policy is clear and the conflict is low. However, newer top-down models, such as the Mazmanian–Sabatier framework, are also relevant when conflict is high and ambiguity is low, which makes the structuring of the implementation particularly important. In contrast, bottom-up models provide an accurate description of the implementation process when the policy is ambiguous and the conflict is low. When conflict as well as ambiguity is present, both models have some relevance according to Matland.

Other attempts at synthesizing the two approaches were made by the former main combatants. The previous bottom-up analyses, which were performed by the circle around Hull and Hjern (1987), focused on actors and activities at the bottom, while in practice their analyses had not risen very high above it. However, in their synthesis proposal – called 'an inductive approach to match outcomes of politics and their intentions' – Hull and Hjern recommend systematic interview analysis of relevant actors from the bottom to the very top, including mapping of implementation activities and structures, the actors' evaluation of the politically determined purposes of the relevant laws and their achievement, and also the actors' opinions on where it goes wrong and analyses of how various policies contribute to solve the *policy problem* in question. Obviously, it would require immense resources to carry out this research strategy, and I am not aware of any such study performed in practice. In addition – as was the case for their bottom-up analyses above – the proposed synthesis suffers from being methodological recommendations rather than theory-based expectations, which can be tested systematically.

Sabatier (1986) has also suggested a synthesis – the so-called *Advocacy Coalition Framework* (ACF). He adopts 'the bottom-uppers' unit of analysis – a whole variety of public and private actors involved with a policy problem – as well as their concerns with understanding the perspectives and strategies of all major categories of actors (not simply program proponents). It then combines this starting point with top-downers' concern with the manner in which socio-economic conditions and legal instruments constrain behavior (Sabatier, 1986: 39). The synthesis applies the framework to explaining policy change over a period of a decade or more in order to deal with the role of policy-oriented learning. It also adopts the top-down style of developing and testing hypotheses as a contribution to theory development. In conceptualizing policy change, Sabatier focuses on government action programs that in turn produce policy outputs at the operational level, which again result in a variety of impacts. The focus on legislative mandates as well as outputs and impacts could be potentially relevant for implementation research. In practice, however, the ACF framework was further developed to focus on policy change in mandates rather than implementation. Although making an important contribution to the public policy literature, Sabatier and his later associate, Jenkins-Smith (Sabatier and Jenkins-Smith, 1993), actually moved the focus of analysis away from implementation and towards policy change and formation.

Another kind of synthesis was suggested by Winter (1990, 1994) in his 'Integrated Implementation Model'. Unlike previous attempts, the purpose here is not to make a true synthesis between top-down and bottom-up perspectives, but rather to integrate a number of the most fruitful theoretical elements from various pieces of implementation research – regardless of their origin – into a joint model. Its main factors in explaining implementation outputs and outcomes are policy formation and policy design, inter-organizational relations, street-level bureaucratic behavior in addition to target group behavior, socio-economic conditions and feed-back mechanisms (cf. the Introduction to this section of the Handbook). The three first sets of key factors are elaborated in the following chapters by May, O'Toole, and Meyers and Vorsanger.

implementation. Malcolm Goggin (1986) pointed out that because implementation research had been dominated by single case studies, it was plagued by the problem of 'too few cases and too many variables' or by 'overdetermination', where two or more variables explain variation in the dependent variable equally well. The single case study approach did not allow for any control of third variables. According to Goggin, this problem had hampered the development of implementation theory. He therefore called for a third generation of implementation studies that would test theories on the basis of more comparative case studies and statistical research designs which could increase the number of observations.

Goggin followed up on these recommendations in a study with his associates (Goggin et al., 1990). The study was mainly based on a communications theory perspective on intergovernmental implementation but also included many variables from previous top-down and bottom-up research. The study focused especially on variation among states in the way they implement federal policies in three different social and regulatory policies and the extent to which they do so. The authors tried to encourage further research involving multiple measures and multiple methods, including quantitative methods. Later, Lester and Goggin (1998), in making a status for implementation research, called for the development of 'a parsimonious, yet complete, theory of policy implementation'. They suggested that such meta-theory might be developed by combining the insights of communications theory, regime theory, rational choice theory (especially game theory) and contingency theories. As dependent variable for implementation studies they proposed to focus on implementation processes rather than outputs and outcomes.

THIRD GENERATION: QUANTITATIVE RESEARCH DESIGNS

While the first and second generations of implementation studies have been helpful in directing attention to implementation problems and identifying implementation barriers and factors that might ease implementation, the research had not succeeded in sorting out the relative importance of the explanatory variables. A substantial part of the studies could be criticized as merely presenting – often long – checklists of variables that might effect

THE NEED FOR A NEW RESEARCH AGENDA

While agreeing with Goggin's (1986) call for using more comparative and statistical research designs based on quantitative methods, I disagree with several of the later methodological and theoretical recommendations made by him and his colleagues. As recognized by one of those co-authors (O'Toole, 2000), to follow the methodological suggestions given by Goggin, Bowman, Lester and O'Toole (1990) would involve at least outlining a research career's worth of work. This work would require applying research designs that involve numerous variables, across different policy types, across fifty states, over at least ten years, as well as measuring the relevant variables by a combination of content analyses, expert panels, elite surveys and expert reassessment of the data from questionnaires and interviews. As such a research strategy is too demanding, less demanding research strategies, which can still secure a sufficient number of observations, would be more realistic.

Given the many exploratory variables which have already been identified by various implementation scholars, the suggested development of a 'parsimonious, yet complete implementation theory' by combining theoretical elements from at least four different theories appears to be a *contradictio in adjecto* and is more likely to lead to theoretical mismatch. Rather than looking for *the* overall and one-for-all implementation theory, we should welcome diversity in both the theoretical perspectives and methodologies applied. Such diversity will give us new insights. Some of these may then later be integrated into broader analytical frameworks or models (Mazmanian and Sabatier, 1981; Goggin et al., 1990; Winter, 1990). It strikes me, however, as unrealistic to think that many scholars can agree on applying one common theoretical framework.

Although the general implementation frameworks presented by model builders so far have been helpful in giving an overview of some crucial implementation variables, the generality of such models may in fact be an obstacle for further development of our understanding of implementation. This is due to the fact that generality inhibits precise specification of variables and causal mechanisms (May, 1999). Consequently, it seems more fruitful to utilize research resources on developing partial theories and hypotheses about different and more limited implementation problems and on putting these to serious empirical tests.

My suggestions for further development of implementation research can be summarized in six points: (1) provide theoretical diversity; (2) focus on partial rather than general implementation theories; (3) seek conceptual clarification; (4) focus on the output (performance of implementers) as a key dependent variable but also (5) include studies of outcomes; and (6) make use of more comparative and statistical research designs. While the two first and the last points have been developed above, I will elaborate on the other points in the following and illustrate them by some of my recent research with Peter May on enforcement of and compliance with agro-environmental regulation in Denmark.

Conceptual clarification

As pointed out by Peter May (1999), most conceptual frameworks in the implementation literature are weakly developed, lacking adequate definitions of concepts and specification of causal mechanisms. The most important issue for the development of implementation research may be to reconsider what constitutes the object of the study. There has been some disagreement in the literature on the term 'implementation' and on what is the important dependent variable in implementation research.

One problem is that the concept 'implementation' is often used to characterize both the implementation process and the output – and sometimes also the outcome – of the implementation process. Lester and Goggin (1998) view implementation as a '*process*, a series of subnational decisions and actions directed toward putting a prior authoritative federal decision into effect'. Thereby, they reject focusing on the output of the implementation process as 'a dichotomous conceptualization of implementation as simply success or failure'.

Although agreeing that the success/failure dichotomy is problematic, I suggest that the two key dependent variables of implementation research should be the output of the implementation process in terms of delivery behavior and the outcome in terms of target group behavior. As mentioned in the Introduction to this section of the Handbook, implementation research can be conceived as public policy analysis at the delivery level of policy making. The classic foci of public policy research are the content of policy, its causes and consequences (Dye, 1976). Implementation output is policy content at a much more operational level than a law. It is policy as it is being delivered to the citizens. By the same token, outcomes are the consequences of the policy, which has been delivered. Accordingly, the key tasks for implementation analysis are to analyze the causes and consequences of delivery behavior.

However, we should conceptualize output and outcome in other ways than the common success/failure dichotomy or interval. The most common dependent variable in implementation research so far has been the degree of goal achievement, whether defined in terms of output or outcome. The first problem, however, is that goal achievement is a fraction. Output in terms of performance of the implementers or outcome in terms of effects on target population is the numerator, and the policy goal is the denominator. Yet, using a fraction as the dependent variable renders theory-building problematic when different factors explain variation in the numerator and the denominator. While the policy formation process is likely to account for variation in goals, the implementation process is likely to account for variation in the performance of implementers.

Therefore, a theory explaining variation in goal achievement requires a combination of three theories: a theory on goal-setting, a theory on performance and a theory on the relation between goal-setting and performance. Even if some implementation researchers have taken steps in that direction by incorporating the character of the policy adoption process in explaining variation in implementation (Winter, 1986b, 1990, 1994), such a combination of three different theoretical perspectives renders the construction and accumulation of implementation theory very complex.

Pushing it to extremes, the problem is that any attempt to make generalizations about goal achievement based on analysis of the behavior of implementers or target groups is dependent on the goal variable having a certain value. The generalization may become invalid if the goal changes. Therefore, generalizations about implementation output are extremely relativistic because statements are conditioned by the goals that are formulated. This is problematic when it is recognized that policy makers are often more interested in making decisions on means or instruments than goals, goals are often invented after decisions on the means have been made in order to legitimize the means adopted, and goals are not always expected or even intended to be achieved.

The second problem of using goal achievement as the dependent variable of implementation research is that such goals can be difficult to operationalize. Much has already been written in the implementation and evaluation literatures about the vagueness and ambiguity of policy goals and the difference between official and latent goals. In addition, while most policy statutes state some kind of goal for the outcome of the policy, many fail to specify any goals or standards for the behavior of the implementers.

This is often the case in regulatory policies. For example, Danish agro-environmental regulation has a general objective of reducing nitrate pollution of the aquatic environment to a certain level, and it specifies a large number of very specific rules for farmers' behavior in this respect. However, the only objective or requirement for the implementers – that is, the municipalities that are in charge of enforcement – is that they inspect farms for compliance with the rules. In this case it is hard to gauge implementation success unless we use the goals for changes in the farmers' behavior or in the physical environment as the standard. However, from the evaluation and implementation literature we also know that factors other than the implementation output may affect policy outcomes (Rossi and Freeman, 1989).

It is important that we make an analytical distinction between explaining implementation outputs and outcomes. Different bodies of theory are likely to be relevant for explaining the behaviors of implementers and target groups.

The performance of implementers

Because of the above problems of using goal achievement as a dependent variable, I suggest that we instead look for behavioral output variables to characterize the *performance* of implementers in delivering services or transfer payments to the citizens or enforcing regulations. One primary aim of implementation research then should be to explain variation in such performance. This will require substantial effort in conceptualizing and categorizing the performance of implementers at the level of agency, as well as that of the individual street-level bureaucrat.

One very intriguing question is whether we can find behavioral dimensions and classifications that are universally applicable in all policy areas, or if we should generate concepts and classifications that are different from one policy area to another. Lipsky's (1980) street-level bureaucracy theory represents an ambitious attempt to offer a universally applicable set of concepts for describing the coping behavior of street-level bureaucrats in all policy areas (see also Winter, 2002b). However, while coping is also relevant in regulatory policies, some of these mechanisms may be more relevant in social policies with weaker target groups. It is also a problem that the street-level bureaucracy theory only focuses on dysfunctional types of delivery behaviors. In addition, a universally applicable classification scheme may suffer from a lack of the precision that a more policy-specific set of concepts could offer. On the other hand, generalizations based on very policy-specific concepts and studies would have a rather narrow sphere of application.

A middle ground is to use sets of concepts that apply to very broad classes of policies. For example, concepts have been developed that are appropriate to classify the behavior of implementers in almost any kind of regulatory policy (Kagan, 1994). May and Winter (1999, 2000;

Winter and May, 2001) have developed concepts for regulatory enforcement at both agency and individual street-level bureaucrat levels. Agency enforcement choices are conceptualized as: *tools* (use of different enforcement measures: sanctions, information and assistance, and incentives); *priorities* (whom to target and what to inspect for); and *effort* (use and leveraging of enforcement resources).

The enforcement style of individual inspectors is defined as the character of the day-to-day interactions of inspectors with the target group. May and Winter expect and verify in a study of agro-environmental regulation in Denmark that enforcement style has two dimensions, comprising the degree of formality of interactions and the degree of coercion. They also identify distinct types of enforcement styles among inspectors along these two dimensions (May and Winter, 2000; see also May and Burby, 1998; May and Wood, 2003).

One advantage of creating such conceptualization of the behavior of implementers is that it is well suited for testing hypotheses for explaining variation in implementation behavior across time and space. Variables from implementation theory characterizing aspects of the implementation process would be an important basis for the development and testing of such hypotheses. However, another advantage of focusing on delivery performance as a dependent variable in implementation research is that we can integrate the study of implementation much more with theory on bureaucratic politics and organization theory. Implementation research can thereby gain inspiration from these research fields, which have a long tradition of studying the behavior of agencies and bureaucrats. In return, these sub-disciplines can benefit from implementation concepts that are much more policy-relevant than those behavioral variables applied in most bureaucracy and organization theory.

As an example, Winter (2000) analyzes the discretion of street-level bureaucrats in enforcing agro-environmental regulation in Denmark by applying a principal–agent perspective and its notion of information asymmetry in examining the extent to which local politicians control their street-level bureaucrats (Moe, 1984; Brehm and Gates, 1999). Regression analyses of 216 local inspectors show that local politicians' policy preferences have no direct impact on the behaviors of street-level bureaucrats. However, the politicians do control relatively visible kinds of performance, such as the number of inspections, through funding capacity for inspection. On the other hand, when it comes to less transparent street-level bureaucratic behaviors – such as

inspection styles and the strictness inspectors apply in reacting to violations of the rules – politicians' policy preferences and their funding of staff resources have little or no influence on these practices. On the contrary, the latter are dominated by the street-level bureaucrats' own values. The study also examines the impact of various types of attitudes on street-level bureaucrats' behavior. Their ideology does not have much effect, whereas their preferences for certain instruments and for less workload have strong impacts.

While relevant concepts for delivery performance/outputs have been developed for regulatory policies, such conceptualization seems to be underdeveloped in social policies apart from Lipsky's concepts of coping behavior. Some inspiration can be obtained from the above regulatory policy concepts at agency as well as individual field worker levels. In current research on the implementation of an employment training program for refugees and immigrants in Denmark (Winter, 2002b), similar behavioral concepts and typologies on agency actions and individual street-level bureaucratic coping behaviors and styles are being developed and tested. For other studies explaining variation in street-level bureaucratic behavior, see the chapter by Meyers and Vorsanger in this volume.

Need for outcome studies

My suggestion of using implementation output/ performance as one dependent variable in implementation research does not imply that outcome/ impacts are unimportant in public policy analyses. On the contrary, implementation scholars as well as other political scientists have paid far too little attention to explaining policy outcomes and to examining the relation between implementation output and outcome. As mentioned above, few implementation scholars include outcome in their implementation models or framework (Mazmanian and Sabatier, 1981; Elmore, 1982; Hull and Hjern, 1987; Goggin et al., 1990; Winter, 1990). It might, however, be fruitful to make a distinction between implementation output studies and outcome studies.

We do not have a complete understanding of the policy process unless we know how target groups respond to public policies. Despite the fact that 'the authoritative allocation of values for a society' (Easton, 1953) and 'who gets what, when, and how' (Lasswell, 1936) are among the most famous definitions of politics, very few political science studies focus on how citizens respond to public policies. Some would say that this is the province of evaluation research. However, evaluation is characterized by a focus on methods, whereas very little theory development has occurred, especially extremely little political science theory. Some law and society scholars have attempted to explain variation in compliance among citizens and to lesser degree firms. So far, very few political scientists and public policy researchers have tried to theorize and test hypotheses about variation in outcome and how the behavior of implementers affects outcomes. In political science journals the contrast between many studies of citizens' attitudes and behavior at the input side of politics and very few outcome studies is striking. Yet, the study of outcomes is as much, if not more, about policy than are most public opinion studies that relate to the input side of policy.

The suggested analytical distinction between implementation output and outcome does not only have the advantage of making it easier to explain variation in delivery performance. The conceptualization of performance is also likely to make it much easier to study the relation between implementation outputs and outcomes (May and Winter, 1999; Winter and May, 2001, 2002). In such studies delivery performance/output changes from being a dependent variable in implementation output studies to being an independent variable in outcome studies. Most likely, we need different theorizing for explaining implementation outputs and outcomes.

As claimed by Elmore (1982, 1985), to change target groups' problematic behavior requires an understanding of the incentives that are operating on these people as well as of how street-level bureaucrats can influence and build on these incentives. For example, in examining Danish farmers' compliance with environmental regulations, Winter and May (2001) map the regulatees' action model. In multiple regression analyses of survey data of 1,562 farmers, they show that compliance is affected by (a) farmers' calculated motivations based on the costs of complying and the perceived risk of detection of violations (while the risk of sanctions, as in most other studies, had no deterrent effect), (b) their normative sense of duty to comply and (c) social motivations based on adaptation to expectations from significant others. Inspectors signal such expectations through their style of interacting with target groups. Inspectors' formalism increases compliance up to a point by providing greater certainty of what is expected of regulatees, while coercive styles with threats of sanctions backfire for regulatees who are not aware of the rules. Willingness to comply is not enough if the ability to comply is not there. Thus,

awareness of rules and financial capacity increase farmers' compliance.

An understanding of the motivations and incentives of target groups is essential for specifying causal links between the delivery behaviors of implementers and target group responses. Further research along this line has shown that inspectors not only affect farmers' compliance directly through social motivation. They can also do so indirectly by using deterrence, as frequent inspections increase farmers' perceived risk of being caught if violating the rules (Winter, 2000a). Another effective, indirect strategy for inspectors is to use information provision for increasing regulatees' awareness of rules. Affecting their normative commitment to comply is, however, much trickier. Although inspectors often try to do so, they are unlikely to succeed because farmers do not trust them enough. In contrast, advice from credible sources – such as farmers' own professional trade organizations and consultants – is much more effective in fostering a sense of duty to comply. This demonstrates an important role for third parties – including interest groups and consultants – as intermediaries in affecting policy outcomes through information provision and legitimization (Winter and May, 2002). The findings from the Danish agro-environmental studies are likely to be valid in many other regulatory settings. They illustrate that delivery performance variables can be constructed that are fruitful both as dependent variables in explaining implementation outputs and as independent variables in explaining outcomes.

Although explaining variation in implementation outputs and outcomes are two distinct analytical processes, the combination of these insights can bring implementation research a major step forward. If we know (a) the motivations of the target group, (b) what kinds of implementers' performance trigger these motivations, as well as (c) the factors that account for variation in such implementation performance, our combined insight can be used to identify more effective ways of designing and implementing public policies.

CONCLUSION

Implementation is a relatively young research field in public administration and public policy. The field has made an important contribution in terms of adding a public policy perspective to public administration with a strong focus on how policies are transformed during the execution process till – and even after – the point of delivery. The research is valuable for our understanding of the complexities of policy implementation. The studies have revealed many important barriers for implementation and factors that may make success more likely.

The research has moved from explorative theory-generating case studies to a second generation of more theoretically ambitious models or frameworks of analysis with top-down and bottom-up research strategies and syntheses. However, while these frameworks presented lists of many relevant variables, the development of theory, specification of causal relations and tests were still hampered by overdetermination because the common reliance on single case studies did not allow any control for third variables.

Goggin (1986) offered a very valuable suggestion in terms of applying more comparative and statistical research designs to cope with this problem. However, this is hardly enough. There is also a need for more theory development and testing, and the development of partial theories seems more promising than continuing the search for *the* general implementation theory or model.

In addition to methodological improvements and the development of partial theories, we need more conceptual clarification and specification of causal relations in order to increase our understanding of implementation. This includes reconsidering the dependent variable in implementation research. I suggest that implementation studies should focus on separately explaining delivery output and outcomes. Achieving policy objectives has been the usual evaluation standard and dependent variable in implementation research. However, whereas this may sometimes be fruitful for examining outcomes, it is a poor standard and a poor dependent variable for explaining implementation outputs. Outputs in the form of delivery level performance are more adequate for such studies.

However, treating implementation outputs as a dependent variable in implementation research, does not imply that policy researchers should ignore studying and explaining outcomes or impacts. But making a distinction between implementation output and outcome studies might be fruitful, because different kinds of theorizing are needed. When implementation research was first identified, it was called the *missing link* in public policy research (Hargrove, 1975). Later on, the study of policy design and policy instruments was identified as a missing link between policy formation and implementation (Linder and Peters, 1989; see also May, in this volume). While we certainly need more

research on policy design and implementation outputs, it is now also appropriate to turn to the study of policy outcomes as a remaining missing link in our understanding of the policy process. If we return to the classic questions of public policy research formulated by Dye (1976), then the delivery level behavior of implementers is policy at its most operational level, policy design as well as the implementation process are important causes of such delivery level policies, and outcomes are the consequences of policy, which we should not ignore.

REFERENCES

Bardach, Eugene (1977) *The Implementation Game.* Cambridge, MA: MIT Press.

Bogason, Peter (2000) *Public Policy and Local Governance: Institutions in Postmodern Society.* Cheltenham: Edward Elgar.

Brehm, John and Gates, Scott (1999) *Working, Shirking, and Sabotage: Bureaucratic Response to a Democratic Public.* Ann Arbor, MI: University of Michigan Press.

Dye, T.R. (1976) *What Governments Do, Why They Do It, and What Difference It Makes.* Tuscaloosa, AL: University of Alabama Press.

Easton, David (1953) *The Political System.* New York: Alfred A. Knopf.

Elmore, Richard F. (1982) 'Backward Mapping: Implementation Research and Policy Decisions,' in W. Williams, R.F. Elmore, J.S. Hall et al. (eds), *Studying Implementation.* Chatham NJ: Chatham House. pp. 18–35.

Elmore, Richard F. (1985) 'Forward and Backward Mapping: Reversible Logic in the Analysis of Public Policy,' in K. Hanf and T.A.J. Toonen (eds), *Policy Implementation in Federal and Unitary Systems.* Dordrecht: Martinus Nijhoff. pp. 33–70.

Goggin, Malcolm L. (1986) 'The "Too Few Cases/Too Many Variables" Problems in Implementation Research', *The Western Political Quarterly,* 39: 328–47.

Goggin, Malcolm L., Bowman, Ann O'M., Lester, James P. and O'Toole, J., Laurence Jr (1990) *Implementation Theory and Practice: Toward a Third Generation.* New York: HaperCollins.

Hargrove, Erwin (1975) *The Missing Link: The Study of the Implementation of Social Policy.* Washington, DC: The Urban Institute.

Hull, Christopher J. with Hjern, Benny (1987) *Helping Small Firm Grow: An Implementation Perspective.* London: Croom Helm.

Kagan, Robert A. (1994) 'Regulatory Enforcement,' in David H. Roosenbloom and Richard D. Schwartz (eds), *Handbook of Regulation and Administrative Law.* New York: Marcel Dekker. pp. 383–422.

Kirst, M. and Jung, R. (1982) 'The Utility of a Longitudinal Approach in Assessing Implementation: A Thirteen Year View of Title 1, ESEA', in W. Williams, R.F. Elmore, J.S. Hall et al. (eds), *Studying Implementation.* Chatham, NJ: Chatham House. pp. 119–48.

Lasswell, H.D. (1936) *Politics: Who Gets What, When, How*. New York: McGraw–Hill.

Lester, James P. and Goggin, Malcolm L. (1998) 'Back to the Future: the Rediscovery of Implementation Studies', *Policy Currents – Newsletter of the Public Policy Section of the American Political Science Association*, 8 (3): 1–9.

Linder, Stephen H. and Peters, B. Guy (1989) 'Instruments of Government: Perceptions and Contexts', *Journal of Public Policy*, 9: 35–58.

Lipsky, Michael (1980) *Street-Level Bureaucracy: The Dilemmas of the Individual in Public Services*. New York: Russel Sage Foundation.

Matland, Richard E. (1995) 'Synthesizing the Implementation Literature: The Ambiguity-Conflict Model of Policy Implementation', *Journal of Public Administration Research and Theory*, 5 (2): 145–74.

May, Peter J. (1999) 'Toward a Future Agenda for Implementation Research: A Panelist's Notes'. Prepared for the annual meeting of the Western Political Science Association in Seattle. Department of Political Science, University of Washington.

May, Peter J. and Burby, Raymond J. (1998) 'Making Sense Out of Regulatory Enforcement', *Law and Policy*, 20: 157–82.

May, Peter J. and Winter, Søren (1999) 'Regulatory Enforcement and Compliance: Examining Danish Agro-Environmental Policy', *Journal of Policy Analysis and Management*, 18 (4): 625–51.

May, Peter J. and Winter, Søren (2000) 'Reconsidering Styles of Regulatory Enforcement: Patterns in Danish Agro-Environmental Inspection', *Law and Policy*, 22 (2): 143–73.

May, Peter J. and Wood, Robert (2003) 'At the Regulatory Frontlines: Inspectors' Enforcement Styles and Regulatory Compliance', *Journal of Public Administration Research and Theory*, in press.

Mazmanian, Daniel A. and Sabatier, Paul (eds) (1981) *Effective Policy Implementation*. Lexington, MA: Lexington Books.

Moe, Terry M. (1984) 'The New Economics of Organization', *American Journal of Political Science*, 28: 739–77.

Moe, Terry M. (1989) 'The Politics of Bureaucratic Structure', in John E. Chubb and Paul E. Peterson (eds), *Can the Government Govern?* Washington, DC: Brookings Institution.

O'Toole, Laurence J., Jr and Montjoy, Robert S. (1984) 'Interorganizational Policy Implementation: A Theoretical Perspective', *Public Administration Review*, 44 (6): 491–503.

O'Toole, Laurence J., Jr (2000) 'Research on Policy Implementation: Assessment and Prospects', *Journal of Public Administration Research and Theory*, 10: 263–88.

Pressman, Jeffrey L. and Wildavsky, Aaron (1973) *Implementation*. Berkeley, CA: University of California Press.

Rossi, Peter H. and Freeman, Howard E. (1989) *Evaluation*, 4th edn. Newbury Park, CA: Sage.

Sabatier, Paul A. (1986) 'Top-Down and Bottom-Up Approaches to Implementation Research: A Critical Analysis and Suggested Synthesis', *Journal of Public Policy*, 6 (1): 21–48.

Sabatier, Paul A. and Jenkins-Smith (eds) (1993) *Policy Change and Learning: An Advocacy Coalition Approach*. Boulder, CO: Westview Press.

Sætren, Harald (1996): 'Whatever Happened to Implementation Research? A Diagnosis of the Decline, and Some Prescriptions for the Revival of a Once Popular and Still Important Research Field in Political Science'. Paper for presentation at the Conference of the Nordic Association of Political Science in Helsinki in August. Department of Administration and Organization Theory, University of Bergen.

Williams, Walt and Elmore, Richard F. (eds) (1976) *Social Program Implementation*. New York: Academic Press.

Winter, Søren (1986a) 'Studying the Implementation of Top-Down Policies from the Bottom Up: Implementation of Danish Youth Employment Policy', in Ray C. Rist (ed.), *Finding Work: Cross National Perspectives on Employment and Training*. New York: Falmer Press. pp. 109–38.

Winter, Søren (1986b) 'How Policy-Making Affects Implementation: The Decentralization of the Danish Disablement Pension Administration', *Scandinavian Political Studies*, 9: 361–85.

Winter, Søren (1990) 'Integrating Implementation Research', in Dennis J. Palumbo and Donald J. Calista (eds), *Implementation and the Policy Process*. New York: Greenwood Press. pp. 19–38.

Winter, Søren (1994) *Implementering og effektivitet*. Aarhus: Systime.

Winter, Søren C. (2000) 'Information Asymmetry and Political Control of Street-Level Bureaucrats: Danish Agro-Environmental Regulation'. Paper for the Annual Meeting of the Association for Policy Analysis and Management in Seattle in November. Department of Political Science, University of Aarhus.

Winter, Søren C. (2002a) 'The Role of Enforcement and Social Norms in Shaping Deterrence'. Paper prepared for the Annual Meeting of the Law and Society Association, 30 May – 1 June in Vancouver, BC. Davish National Institute of Social Research.

Winter, Søren C. (2002b) 'Explaining Street-Level Bureaucratic Behavior in Social and Regulatory Policies'. Paper prepared for the Annual Meeting of the American Political Science Association in Boston, 29 August – 1 September 2002. Danish National Institute of Social Research.

Winter, Søren C. and May, Peter J. (2001) 'Motivations for Compliance with Environmental Regulations', *Journal of Policy Analysis and Management*, 20 (4): 675–98.

Winter, Søren C. and May, Peter J. (2002) 'Information, Interests, and Environmental Regulation', *Journal of Comparative Policy Analysis*, 4 (2): 115–42.

17

Policy Design and Implementation

Peter J. May

The realities of a policy in practice often differ from intentions on paper because of distortions in the process of implementing the policy. A central issue for implementation scholars is the extent to which noteworthy distortions can be anticipated and addressed as part of the design of a given policy. Some argue that modifications of policies during implementation to reflect particular circumstances are desirable adaptations that add value to policy intentions (Palumbo and Calista, 1990; Schneider and Ingram, 1997). Others argue that little realistically can be done to address such slippage, whether desirable or not, because of the inevitable ambiguities of policy goals and conflicts among implementers (Matland, 1995; Pressman and Wildavsky, 1973; Stoker, 1991). The perspective adopted in this chapter is that implementation difficulties can be partially ameliorated with the crafting of appropriate policy designs to build commitment and capacity of intermediaries and to signal policy intent to intermediaries and target groups.

Relatively little is known beyond broad generalities about what constitutes well-designed policies. This presents challenges for those who seek a better understanding of the relationships between policy design and implementation. Several strands of literature in public administration and political science address aspects of these challenges. One strand considers the assumptions and values that enter into policy design (Bobrow and Dryzek, 1987; Ingraham, 1987; Linder and Peters, 1984). A second strand catalogs policy instruments that make up the elements of policies (Hood, 1983; McDonnell and Elmore, 1987; Salamon, 1989, 2002; Schneider and Ingram, 1990). A third strand considers the way in which policies structure resources and send signals about desired courses of action (Elmore, 1987; Goggin et al., 1990; Smith and Ingram, 2002).

This chapter draws from these strands of literature in discussing the interplay of policy design and implementation. The first part of the chapter addresses the ways that policy design shapes the course of policy implementation. Those prospects, in turn, hinge in part on the political environment as discussed in the second part of the chapter. The third part of the chapter addresses choices for policy design that potentially affect implementation with particular attention to choices about policy instruments and implementation structures. The final part considers unresolved issues and future research questions.

INFLUENCE OF POLICY DESIGN ON IMPLEMENTATION

Public policies set forth courses of action for addressing problems or for providing goods and services to segments of society. Policies come in a variety of forms, including legislation, executive orders, or other official acts. Policies do more than simply announce a course of action. They typically contain a set of intentions or goals, a mix of instruments or means for accomplishing the intentions, a designation of governmental or nongovernmental entities charged with carrying out the intentions, and an allocation of resources for the requisite tasks. The intent is further signaled by the labeling of the policy, the language used to communicate policy goals and the particular mix of policy instruments.

The crafting of policies typically entails a long process of analysis of problems and options, give-and-take over politically acceptable courses of action, and an authoritative decision to enact a policy. Given the vagaries of the policy process, the design of a policy does not result from a single blueprint as if designing a house. Rather, policy design is both an art in identifying and working through feasible options and a science in analyzing the costs and impacts of different options. In one of the earlier writings on this topic, John Dryzek defines policy design as 'the process of inventing, developing and fine-tuning a course of action with the amelioration of some problem [in mind]' (1983: 346). The design perspective in particular calls attention to matching content of a given policy to the political context in which the policy is formulated and implemented (see Linder and Peters, 1984, 1989; May, 1991; Schneider and Ingram, 1997).

Different design contentions

It is undisputed that policies signal desired courses of action and structure implementation. Less settled, however, are the ways in which different policy designs either hinder or facilitate implementation. An extensive set of case studies of implementation shortfalls suggest that problems arise from inadequate specification of desired actions and from failure to include features that overcome basic conflicts among those carrying out policies. Building upon these case studies, an influential body of theorizing and research (Mazmanian and Sabatier, 1983; Van Meter and Van Horn, 1975) points to the ways that implementation is limited by key attributes of policies (that is, lack of goal clarity and inconsistency in goals), complex chains of implementing actions and indirect control (multiple actors, decision points and levels of action), and by other non-statutory factors (such as problem intractability, unsupportive political environments).

The message of these studies is not particularly optimistic about implementation prospects given that most policies lack goal clarity and have complex implementation structures. The basic prescription for enhancing implementation from this line of research is a call for 'statutory coherence' that is brought about by clear goals and simple implementation structures (Mazmanian and Sabatier, 1981, 1983). Although true, this prescription fails to recognize the political realities that account for policies with multiple goals, vague language and complex implementation structures.

A different perspective is offered by those (Elmore, 1987; Goggin et al., 1990; May, 1993, 1995; Stoker, 1991) who argue that the appropriate crafting of policies can overcome implementation difficulties attributable to vague goals and complex implementation structures. According to this viewpoint, implementation prospects are enhanced through three sets of policy provisions. One set are those provisions that build the capacity of intermediaries to carry out requisite actions and to cooperate. Capacity-building instruments include funding, education and training, and technical assistance. A second set are policy provisions that foster increased commitment of intermediaries to the basic policy goals. Commitment-building instruments include publicity about policy goals, authorization for citizen suits against inadequate implementation, sanctions for failing to act, cost-sharing requirements, and incentives to carry out programs. A third set are policy provisions that help to signal desired courses of action. These include oversight mechanisms and publicity about successful implementation practices. These mechanisms entail what Howlett (2000) labels procedural policy instruments aimed at intermediaries, rather than substantive provisions aimed at the targets of policy.

The prescriptions offered by this line of research are more complicated than the 'simplify and clarify' message of the earlier research. According to this perspective, the key to enhancing implementation is to build into policy designs incentives for appropriate actions by intermediaries and target groups. These may include such things as authority to undertake particular actions, enhanced status and funding or other forms of assistance.

Research about the different design contentions has been constrained by the generality of theorizing by implementation scholars and by other methodological issues that limit the ability to tease out effects of key variables (see critique by Goggin et al., 1990). The basic contention that poorly framed statutes and complex implementation structures are a source of implementation problems was established by research addressing the 'statutory coherence' framework (see Mazmanian and Sabatier, 1981, 1983; McFarlane, 1989; Sabatier, 1986). In contrast, Keiser and Meier's (1996) study of child support enforcement in the United States found only partial support for these key contentions. May's (1993) study of implementation of state environmental policies also found that statutory coherence is not a necessary condition for strong implementation efforts.

Several studies show that the thorny problems of intergovernmental implementation, highlighted in first generation case studies of implementation failures (e.g. Derthick, 1972; Pressman and Wildavsky, 1973), can be ameliorated by inclusion of appropriate features in intergovernmental policy designs. Goggin et al. (1990) find, in what they label as the 'communication model' of implementation, that differences in state-level implementation of federal programs can be explained by variation in clarity and consistency in the communication of policy intent. Stoker (1991) describes successful implementation by states and localities of reforms of the federal National School Lunch Program which attributes to the program's establishment of incentives for close cooperation among different implementers. In studying similar intergovernmental policy implementation for environmental management programs in Australia and New Zealand, May (1995; also see May et al., 1996) found that the historic mistrust of agencies at different levels of government was at least partially overcome through inclusion of capacity- and commitment-building mechanisms in the policy designs.

Policy instruments and policy design

The research findings that key features of policy designs can be altered to enhance implementation leads to consideration of the components of public policies. One of the conceptual shifts in implementation research from the 1970s to the 1990s is a shift from the study of policies and programs to a study of different policy instruments or tools that are part of policies and programs. With this, scholarly attention has shifted from addressing the content of a policy as a whole to understanding the workings and politics of the components of policy. These components are variously labeled as policy instruments or as policy tools. The basic notion is that any given policy incorporates a variety of means or tools for accomplishing objectives that include mandates, incentives (for example, grants, loans, tax expenditures), penalties (such as sanctions, fines) and provisions for sharing of information.

Although this change in focus from the study of policy content as a whole to the study of policy instruments provides a stronger analytic basis for unpacking policies, there is little agreement among policy scholars about the relevant components of policies. Over a dozen different typologies of policy instruments have been devised that vary in terms of their level of specification and their scope (for overviews see Salamon, 1989, 2002; Vedung, 1998). While there is conceptual agreement that policy instruments are the building blocks of policies, there is little agreement about the number of basic instruments. The more specific and comprehensive categorizations identify ten to fifteen

instruments. For example, one recent compilation (Salamon, 2002) addresses the following fourteen tools: direct government provision, governmental corporations and sponsored enterprises, economic regulation, social regulation, government insurance, public information, charges and special taxes, contracting, purchase-of-service contracting, grants, loans and loan guarantees, tax expenditures, vouchers and tort liability. The clear limitation of this type of classification is the *ad hoc* nature of the listing of tools.

Other taxonomies of policy instruments are more parsimonious in their classification of instruments in attempts to be more analytical in the distinctions among tools. Elmore (1987) draws a distinction among mandates as rules that are intended to produce compliance, inducements as conditional transfers of money for provision of specified services, capacity-building tools that invest in development of future services and system changing tools that transfer authority in order to alter service delivery. Schneider and Ingram (1990, 1997) provide a related analytic distinction among authority tools that prescribe desired behaviors, inducements and sanctions that alter calculated behaviors, capacity-building tools that enhance abilities and hortatory tools that are used to cajole action.

The shift in focus from studying different types of policy content to studying different policy instruments was expected to provide a stronger basis for theorizing about policy design and implementation. This expectation has not been fulfilled. Instead, the literature has taken a technocratic turn that emphasizes the mechanics of different policy instruments and attention to their fit with different problems, political settings and goals. Little has been written about how different tools can be combined to form policy strategies or about the political and policy logics of such combinations (for exceptions see Elmore, 1987; Gunningham and Grabosky, 1998).

More pointedly, the cataloging of policy instruments has not provided the hoped for basis for identifying unique sets of implementation challenges. Salamon and his coauthors (1989, 2002) have been influential in cataloging management and operational issues associated with different policy instruments. However, these lessons provide little insight about tradeoffs in choosing different mixes of instruments or about the impacts of different tools. This is because the managerial approach to the study of instruments fails to adequately address the policy context. Put differently, the broader lesson of policy design is that the value of a particular instrument is shaped as much by the political context in which it is employed as by the inherent features of the instrument.

POLITICAL ENVIRONMENTS AFFECTING DESIGN AND IMPLEMENTATION

One of the critiques of the implementation literature is that it depicts implementation as an administration of policy that is unrelated to the politics of policy formation. However, it is well documented that the political forces that shape policy design also greatly influence policy implementation (Bardach, 1977; Brodkin, 1990; Nakamura and Smallwood, 1980). As described by Maynard-Moody (1989), these same bureaucratic and interest group forces influence the design and implementation of administrative rules for carrying out policies.

Viewing implementation as policy politics alters how one thinks about policy design and implementation. Rather than treating design as a technocratic activity of finding the best design subject to certain political constraints, the political perspective views policy design as an art aimed at channeling energies of disparate implementers to foster agreement in working toward similar goals. Two aspects are relevant for this discussion. One is the way in which different political environments foster implementation and design challenges. The second is how politics shapes choices about policy instruments and implementation structures.

Implementation environments and policy design

It is useful to depict differing political environments that affect policy design and implementation. Drawing from the discussion of May (1991), a continuum of political environments can be depicted with one extreme labeled 'policies with publics' and the other extreme labeled 'policies without publics'. The notion of a continuum is useful in making the point that the differences are more matters of the degree of development of the relevant publics and related policy subsystems than of their existence or total absence. For 'policies with publics' there are well-developed coalitions of interest groups surrounding particular issues. For 'policies without publics' there is limited development of interest groups, usually restricted to technical and scientific communities.

Policies with publics

The dominant characterization of political environments for countries with democratic systems is that of policies with publics. According to this depiction, policy options are fashioned and choices are made in policy worlds comprised of multiple publics with competing interests and differential resources. In forming loosely connected, sometimes highly fragmented advocacy coalitions (Sabatier and Jenkins-Smith, 1993) the publics engage in a series of strategic interactions, often over a period of years, in attempting to dominate the processes of political problem definition, policy formation and implementation. Underlying these interactions are differing causal beliefs and belief systems (Stone, 1989). The ability to arrive at a stable consensus over problems or appropriate actions is undermined by the existence of strongly held, opposing core beliefs by relevant publics and those political actors they influence. In such instances, policy making takes place at the margins of solutions, and problems persist for many years.

The implementation challenges for policies with publics stem from the fact that relevant intermediaries and target groups who were active publics in defining the problem and shaping policy solutions also attempt to influence implementation (Bardach, 1977). In some settings, as discussed by Winter (1990) regarding policy implementation in Scandinavia, stable relationships among publics are helpful for policy legitimization and implementation. In the American setting, as discussed by Baumgartner and Jones (1993), existing ways of doing business and existing 'policy monopolies' become potentially powerful drags for policy change and implementation.

As long as the coalitions in support of business as usual are stable, fundamental changes are difficult to achieve. Similarly, in a given arena, policy instruments for new policies will differ little from those of the existing policy. Mandates get added to existing mandates. Regulations get piled on existing regulations. Grant-in-aid programs proliferate in areas where they already exist. As a consequence, it is not surprising that 'system changing' policy designs entailing new allocations of authority (McDonnell and Elmore, 1987) or 'roundabout methods' (Majone, 1989) entailing institutional redesign are little used instruments of policy design.

The policy design prescriptions for policies with publics emphasize structuring of relationships and coordinating behavior among the relevant publics that comprise intermediaries and target groups. The trick is finding a political logic as part of the policy design or policy debate that makes it possible to change policy thrusts (see Baumgartner and Jones, 1993; Elmore, 1987; Linder and Peters, 1984). This may consist of developing a policy design that is supported by a new coalition among interests, with the coalition based around a new combination of policy instruments. The political logic may also consist of a different political strategy than that used in past efforts to enact new policies. This may include creating a crisis, or the appearance of one, so as to make the case for new policies. Or, it may include finding a leader willing to take the blame for the negative impacts of the policy.

Policies without publics

A contrasting political world is that of policies without publics. This is the opposite end of the continuum of policy publics for which policy options are fashioned and choices made in what appears to be an apolitical environment. Publics surrounding the issue are neither extensive nor a source of major conflict. Issue networks or policy communities are only weakly developed. Belief systems concerning problems and solutions are tentative and dominated by technocratic expert opinions. Relevant policy discussions take place in the backwaters of political institutions. These include issues for which there is little incentive for organized interests to evolve in pursuit of a policy. This typically arises for public goods (or, conversely public bads) illustrated by dilemmas of achieving deficit reduction, maintaining biological diversity, addressing global environmental problems, addressing terrorism, or dealing with potential catastrophic disasters like major earthquakes.

The situation for policies without publics might appear to be beneficial for implementation. The lack of publics provides a greater degree of implementation autonomy than is the case for policies with publics. Under such circumstances, policy implementation is not likely to be actively thwarted by intermediaries or target groups. However, the relative absence of publics creates unique implementation challenges. Target groups are likely to be poorly delineated. Various intermediaries such as governmental organizations and street-level bureaucrats will exist, but are likely to be relatively uninterested.

Two broad strategies are potentially relevant to the design of policies when publics are lacking. One is direct governmental provision of programs without relying upon other intermediaries. In some instances, such as the response to terrorism, a centrally managed and implemented program is necessary for achieving rapid response to diffuse problems. In other instances, such as provision of terrorism insurance, direct government action is a necessary substitute for the faults of private markets. A second strategy is to stimulate the formation of publics. Mobilization of publics is appropriate when such participation of relevant stakeholders is necessary for successful policy implementation, as might be the case for protecting endangered species or for increasing awareness of civil rights. Provision information can be an important tool for mobilizing attention (Weiss and Tschirhart, 1994). Funds can be used to sponsor publics, as illustrated by the creation of Community Action Agencies as part of the War on Poverty in the United States.

Politics and tool selection

It is possible to identify the relevant considerations for selecting policy tools, but difficult to state how these will play out for any particular set of circumstances. Once again, the key issue is the context in which a given tool or set of tools is to be used. Three differing perspectives have been offered in recent years for thinking about selection of policy instruments. Peters (2002, also see Linder and Peters, 1989) suggests that five factors come into play: ideas (including ideologies), institutions, interests, individuals and the international environment. Peters suggests a basic understanding of tool choice can be gained from identifying the interests being advantaged or disadvantaged by the selection of a given policy instrument. From this perspective, those means favored by more powerful groups are more likely to be chosen than the means favored by less powerful groups. A more nuanced understanding of tool choice, according to Peters, requires consideration of the other factors that he identifies.

Schneider and Ingram (1997: 129–40) also focus on relevant interests in considering the role of policy makers' perceptions of the groups that are targets of a policy in affecting the choice of policy instruments. From this perspective, the social construction (that is, degree of social acceptance) and political power of potential policy targets constrain choices about relevant tools and implementation structures. From this perspective, 'advantaged groups' like farmers that have positive constructions and are powerful are more likely to be selected for subsidies or other inducements. In contrast, 'deviant groups' like drug users that have negative constructions and are powerless are more likely to be selected for penalties and coercive programs. Donovan (2001), in studying AIDS and drug policies in the United States, provides a more subtle perspective about the targeting of policies. He shows that legislators sometimes go to great lengths to obscure intended beneficiaries by crafting legislation that has hidden benefits.

Bressers and O'Toole (1998) focus on the source of policy ideas as an important basis for tool selection in arguing that characteristics of policy networks – the communities in which ideas evolve – shape the selection of relevant policy instruments. They provide a functional explanation of instrument choice in arguing that policy communities will advocate those instruments that help to maintain the existence of the community. In particular, they argue that the selection of instruments can be usefully analyzed by considering effects of instruments on the degree of cohesion and interconnectedness of a given policy network.

These differing perspectives about the politics of the choice of policy instruments and implementation structures emphasize how different interests and ideas influence policy design and authoritative decision-making. The reverse of this is the way in which policy tools affect various interests. Smith and Ingram (2002) suggest that the selection of tools can have a profound effect upon target groups by sending messages about their value to others and by shaping opportunities for participation and involvement in collective decision-making. They argue that these effects reverberate over time in shaping the ability and willingness of different groups to shape future policy choices.

SHAPING IMPLEMENTATION – CHOICES IN POLICY DESIGN

The process of policy design and implementation is not simply one of assembling parts and plugging in an implementation machinery. The compromises that are necessary to gain support for a given policy explain why policy designs and implementation structures are often so messy. Recognizing these facts, however, does not negate the value of considering how choices made when designing policies potentially shape policy implementation.

Policy intentions and philosophy

Perhaps the overriding considerations in shaping the contours of a policy are the intentions for and philosophy of the policy. Is the policy intended to provide benefits for particular segments of society, restrict behaviors in preventing a harm, mobilize action on the part of groups to address a problem, or something else? Policy intentions establish the goals and type of policy that is to be put in place. They also establish the contours of political debate that shape eventual politics of policy adoption and implementation.

A key lesson of efforts to classify different types of policies is the dual relationship between politics and policy. As discussed in a seminal article by Lowi (1972), not only does politics affect the design of policies, but the choice of policy affects the associated politics. Lowi demonstrated this in showing the different politics associated with distributive, redistributive and regulatory policies. Wilson (1973) further elaborated upon this framework in showing how the perceptions of the distributions of costs and benefits of a given policy affect politics by creating different challenges for policy enactment and implementation. The important point for implementation scholars of this research is that the political environment for policy implementation is a malleable landscape that can be affected by policy content.

The underlying philosophical or ideological glue provides an important policy rationale for linking solutions to problems, recognizing that any given intent can be justified and carried out in a variety of ways (Donovan, 2001; Stone, 1989). Linder and Peters (1984, 1989), among others, have argued that different national policy styles, reflecting cross-national differences in policy approaches, establish the foundations for such philosophies. Noteworthy studies of policy development concerning economic policy (Hall, 1993) and social policy (Heclo, 1974) highlight the role of ideas, ideology and social learning in shaping policy directions.

How does policy intention affect implementation? Rather than setting forth explicit direction for policy, it sets boundaries around choices of policy instruments and implementation structures. Thus, for example, a conservative ideological approach may favor use of tax incentives while a less conservative government may prefer direct subsidies to promote particular ends. One key lesson for policy design is to fashion instruments and implementation approaches (means) that are consistent with the policy intent (goals). Otherwise, the policy is working at cross purposes. A second key lesson is that the political environment, that is the target groups and field staff that implement the policy, must be supportive of the policy intention. Otherwise, they may exercise principled disagreement with the policy and work to subvert it. This is one reason why, as discussed below, it is important to build features into policies for building commitment to policy goals.

Scope of a policy

The scope of the policy addresses the scale of the undertaking. This can be characterized with respect to geographic scale (whether a policy is national or more limited in scale), with respect to the degree to which particular groups are targeted (a focused policy versus a more general one), with respect to the heterogeneity of the affected groups (whether they are similar or differ greatly), and whether the policy is new or an adaptation of existing policy.

How does the scope of the policy affect policy implementation? There are tradeoffs that present a basic dilemma for policy implementation. On the one hand, all else being equal, a more contained policy is easier to implement (Mazmanian and Sabatier, 1983). On the other hand, the likely impacts of a more contained policy are more limited, in that fewer are affected by the policy. This dilemma gets to the basic issue of the tractability of the policy that has been a key variable in thinking about prospective implementation success.

As the scope of a policy becomes more heterogeneous with respect to affected groups or other components, there is likely to be greater need and political pressure for policy adaptation in implementation. What constitutes appropriate adaptation has not been considered in the implementation literature beyond the observation that such adaptation can add value to policy. The topic of designing policies to promote learning about appropriate adaptation has been considered more generally in the literature concerning policy learning (see May, 1992) and the evolution of policies over time (Majone and Wildavsky, 1979). Adaptive management (Holling, 1978) and social experiments (Greenberg and Robbins, 1986) have been suggested as relevant mechanisms to foster such instrumental learning.

Policy instruments affecting target groups

The means for bringing about behavioral changes among affected groups or for delivering governmental services to segments of society entail choices about the appropriate means of intervention. As Majone and Wildavsky (1979) most clearly articulated, all policies contain hypotheses about how to bring about change – a theory of change – that may or may not be adequate (also see Linder and Peters, 1989; Schneider and Ingram, 1997). Part of the theory of change is presumptions about the workings of different policy instruments or tools that, as articulated by Salamon (2002), structure action in identifiable ways. It is beyond the scope of this discussion to identify the potential implementation problems associated with individual tools for which the literature noted earlier about policy instruments is a relevant resource.

Strategy, ideology and politics influence the ways in which different tools are combined into policy mixes. The strategic issues revolve around policy analysis considerations concerning the appropriate role of government and other actors, the potential means of intervention and the costs and feasibility of carrying out programs. The possible combinations of tools into policies provide a bewildering array of potential choices, but the practical issues often come down to the philosophical glue that holds together different potential mixes. The important lesson for policy design and implementation is that that the mix of instruments needs to adhere to an overall strategy for which the elements do not work at cross purposes. For example, it makes little sense that for a long time in the United States price support for tobacco farmers encouraged production of tobacco (and lower prices) while smoking cessation policies discouraged smoking.

Policy instruments affecting intermediaries

Although much of the discussion of policy design focuses on the intended targets or outcomes of policy, the intermediaries charged with carrying out policy are also relevant. The key advice of the literature is that policies should contain features that encourage or compel intermediaries to carry out requisite actions for implementing the policy. Weimer (1992) provides an instructive set of examples of how creation of desirable incentives, favorable structuring of decisions and instilling appropriate habits and norms can promote desired responses on the part of implementers.

Building the commitment to the basic policy goals and the capacity of intermediaries to accomplish those goals are important elements of this aspect of policy design. Commitment- and capacity-building provisions are best thought of as interactive features that reinforce each other in facilitating policy implementation (May, 1993). These features also serve important functions in signaling what is expected of intermediaries (see Goggin et al., 1990).

Implementation structures and third parties

The intermediaries that are charged with policy implementation and how they share responsibilities are important aspects that constitute the implementation structure for a given policy. The choice of a structure is rarely a simple matter of naming a governmental organization to carry out a policy. Hall and O'Toole (2000) show that as early as the mid 1960s the preferred implementation structure for American national policies was a multi-actor structure spanning governments, sectors and/or agencies. Indeed, one of the key themes of this Handbook is the increased role of networks of public and private actors in carrying out policies. To understand policy implementation it is no longer sufficient to understand how governmental agencies operate. As discussed by O'Toole in this volume (Chapter 18), it is now necessary to understand the dynamics and operations of a host of other types of institutions and how they relate to each other.

The guidance of the implementation literature about relevant structures has shifted from advice to clarify and simplify them (Mazmanian and Sabatier, 1983) to advice to develop implementation structures that 'mesh' with policy objectives (O'Toole, 1993). What the latter consists of is not well articulated in the literature. It can be thought of as a structure that both reflects the philosophy of the policy and engages entities that are committed to and have the capacity to carry out the policy. Stoker (1991) refers to this as the development of constructive patterns of cooperation. This is illustrated by New Zealand's intergovernmental approach to environmental management (see May et al., 1996). Regional and district councils are given latitude to carry out the spirit of the policy in ways they best see fit. This structure fits the policy intent of devolved policy making while the policy also incorporates mechanisms to ensure coordination of policies among layers of government.

It is important to recognize when the existing implementation structure is deficient or too rigid to adapt to new requirements of a given policy. Under such circumstances, Elmore (1987) reminds us that 'system changing' can be a useful policy tool. Changing the service delivery or regulatory responsibilities provides an opportunity to put in place a new, and hopefully more constructive, set of relationships. It also strongly signals a desire to do things differently. Lippincott and Stoker (1992) provide an example of how creation of a new institutional structure for resolving conflicts among local implementers of a county court reform in New York state helped overcome likely implementation barriers.

Policy oversight

Another ingredient in the policy design mix is the role of oversight in correcting difficulties that occur in implementing a policy. Bardach (1977) calls attention to the role of 'fixers', typically politicians with a vested stake in a policy by virtue of authorship of the policy, who have the power to investigate and fix implementation

problems. Other formal oversight mechanisms include committees, commissions, parliamentary offices and evaluation agencies charged with monitoring progress of a given policy or policy sector.

Stoker argues that oversight is important for encouraging cooperation among reluctant partners by 'assuring participants that those who exploit the process will be detected' (1991: 186). One assumption for such oversight is that relevant politicians have gained consensus on policy goals, which is not always the case. Torenvlied (1996) shows how lack of consensus over policy decisions in a Dutch municipality undermines implementation. More generally, the political science literature about oversight is less sanguine about the ability to detect problems but nonetheless recognizes the importance of different mechanisms for identifying and addressing problems (see Gormley, 1989; Gruber, 1987). Perhaps one of the most important functions of oversight is provision of repeated signals about policy intent and of the importance of particular policy goals.

Oversight clearly does not only occur through governmental mechanisms. The media, public interest organizations, trade groups, investors, insurers and citizen organizations can potentially play important roles in monitoring implementation actions. Gunningham and Grabosky (1998: 93–123) discuss a variety of such existing and potential roles as they relate to environmental regulation. Given this potential, an important issue of policy design is deciding the appropriate degree and form of oversight of policy implementation.

Discretion and accountability

Closely related to oversight is consideration of the amount of discretion that is granted to field-level implementers and the mechanisms that are employed to ensure accountability in program operations. Lipsky's (1983) seminal work on street-level bureaucrats sets out the basic dilemma. On the one hand, field-level personnel often need discretion in interpreting rules and implementing programs to be responsive to the special needs of diverse clientele. On the other hand, inconsistent use of discretion can result in de facto policies that differ greatly from policy intentions as well as inequitable policy implementation. Lipsky developed the notion of street-level bureaucrats in studying social service provision but the issue applies more generally to any program for which those at the frontlines of service delivery must have discretion to deal with complex situations. Thus, for example, Winter and May (2001) discuss how regulatory inspectors' choices about the style of enforcing regulations affect regulatory compliance.

There is a resurgence of literature in political science and public administration that addresses control of governmental agencies (for example, Golden 2000; Wood and Waterman, 1994) and control of bureaucratic discretion within governmental agencies (for example, Brehm and Gates, 1997; Vinzant and Crothers, 1998). The topics of street-level bureaucrats and bureaucratic control are addressed more fully in other chapters within this Handbook. Suffice it to note for the purposes of this chapter that a variety of mechanisms can be used to influence bureaucratic actions, but these are constrained by the beliefs, values and roles of the affected individuals.

UNRESOLVED ISSUES AND FUTURE DIRECTIONS

This chapter has addressed the interplay of policy design and implementation with particular attention to the extent to which noteworthy policy distortions can be anticipated and addressed as part of the design of a given policy. Implementation difficulties can be partially ameliorated with the crafting of appropriate policy designs. Such designs build the capacity of intermediaries to carry out requisite actions and to cooperate, foster increased commitment of intermediaries to the basic policy goals, and signal desired courses of action to intermediaries and target groups.

Policy design is not simply a technocratic task undertaken in a back room that entails the assembly of policy instruments to achieve some end. Nor is implementation simply an administrative task of handing over policy details to an organizational machinery. Policy design and implementation are tasks of policy and political problem solving that are subject to a variety of pressures. This chapter has considered how different political environments foster implementation and design challenges as well as how politics shapes choices about policy instruments and implementation structures.

The literature addressing the nexus of policy design and implementation provides important insights about policy design. Implementation scholars have developed a better understanding over time of the relevant factors that affect policy implementation. However, the scholars fall short of providing a theory of implementation that links different elements of policy designs to different implementation challenges. Instead,

implementation scholars offer a cataloging of potential problems and their sources (cf. Bardach, 1977) and a set of general prescriptions for improving implementation success. The prescriptions of the early implementation literature of 'clarify and simplify' policies have been replaced with more realistic advice about design of policies that create incentives for implementers to take requisite actions and to cooperate.

Despite these advances in understanding, key issues remain unresolved. Chief among these is a need for a better understanding of the interplay of different policy instruments. Much of the writing about policy instruments has emphasized the characteristics and issues that arise from the use of particular instruments. However, most policies contain a mix of instruments that emerge as a result of a variety of policy and political compromises. Little is known about the interplay of different instruments with respect to how they reinforce or contradict each other or with respect to the consistency of signals that they provide. Such discussion clearly requires that different political contexts are taken into account.

There is also a need for a better understanding of how we should think about different implementation structures. This may seem surprising given that a core aspect of the study of implementation is the way that different organizations and institutions shape how policies are carried out. Although the literature provides us with a good understanding of how bureaucratic and other forces shape incentives of implementers to carry out policies, it is less clear about the choices of alternative organizational arrangements and the implications of those choices for policy implementation. Stated differently, an effort akin to that of identifying policy instruments is required for identifying alternative implementation structures and associated problems. This would include attention to reliance on policy networks that involve private entities as third parties for service delivery and regulation.

Policy design is, of course, not the only factor that shapes implementation processes and outcomes. Although much of the implementation literature has moved on to address the role of context in shaping implementation, it is worth remembering the basic axiom that well-designed policies are necessary but not sufficient for improving implementation prospects.

REFERENCES

Bardach, Eugene (1977) *The Implementation Game: What Happens After a Bill Becomes Law*. Cambridge, MA: MIT Press.

Baumgartner, B. and Jones, B. (1993) *Agendas and Instability in American Politics*. Chicago: Chicago University Press.

Bobrow, Davis B. and John S. Dryzek (1987) *Policy Analysis by Design*. Pittsburgh: University of Pittsburgh Press.

Brehm, John and Gates, Scott (1997) *Working, Shirking, and Sabotage*. Ann Arbor, MI: University of Michigan Press.

Bressers, Hans T.A. and O'Toole, Laurence, J., Jr (1998) 'The Selection of Policy Instruments: A Network-based Perspective', *Journal of Public Policy*, 18 (Part III): 213–39.

Brodkin, Evelyn Z. (1990) 'Implementation as Policy Politics', in Dennis Palumbo and Donald Calista (eds), *Implementation and the Policy Process, Opening Up the Black Box*. Westport, CT: Greenwood Press. pp. 107–18.

Derthick, Martha (1972) *New Towns in Town, Why a Federal Program Failed*. Washington, DC: Urban Institute.

Donovan, Mark (2001) *Taking Aim: Target Populations and the Wars on AIDS and Drugs*. Washington, DC: Georgetown University Press.

Dryzek, John S. (1983) 'Don't Toss Coins in Garbage Cans: A Prologue to Policy Design', *Journal of Public Policy*, 3 (4): 345–68.

Elmore, Richard F. (1987) 'Instruments and Strategy in Public Policy', *Policy Studies Review*, 7 (1): 174–86.

Elmore, Richard F. (1979–80) 'Backward Mapping: Implementation Research and Policy Decisions', *Political Science Quarterly*, 94: 601–16.

Goggin, Malcolm L., Bowman, Ann O'M., Lester, James P. and O'Toole, Laurence J., Jr (1990) *Implementation Theory and Practice, Toward a Third Generation*. Glenview, IL: Scott Foresman.

Golden, Marissa Martino (2000) *What Motivates Bureaucrats? Politics and Administration During the Reagan Years*. New York: Columbia University Press.

Gormley, William T., Jr (1989) *Taming the Bureaucracy: Muscles, Prayers, and Other Strategies*. Princeton, NJ: Princeton University Press.

Greenberg, David H. and Robbins, Philip K. (1986) 'The Changing Role of Social Experiments in Policy Analysis', *Journal of Policy Analysis and Management*, 5 (2): 340–62.

Gruber, Judith E. (1987) *Controlling Bureaucracies, Dilemmas in Bureaucratic Governance*. Berkeley, CA: University of California Press.

Gunningham, Neil and Grabosky, Peter (1998) *Smart Regulation, Designing Environmental Policy*. New York: Oxford University Press.

Hall, Peter A. (1993) 'Policy Paradigms, Social Learning, and the State: The Case of Economic Policymaking in Britain', *Comparative Politics*, 23: 275–96.

Hall, Thad E. and O'Toole, Laurence J., Jr (2000) 'Structures for Policy Implementation: An Analysis of National Legislation, 1965–66 and 1993–94', *Administration and Society*, 31 (6): 667–86.

Heclo, Hugh (1974) *Modern Social Politics in Britain and Sweden*. New Haven, CT: Yale University Press.

Holling, C.S. (ed.) (1978) *Adaptive Environmental Assessment and Management*. Chichester: John Wiley.

Hood, Christopher C. (1983) *The Tools of Government*. London: Macmillan.

Howlett, Michael (2000) 'Managing the "Hollow State": Procedural Policy Instruments and Modern Governance', *Canadian Public Administration*, 43 (4): 412–31.

Ingraham, Patricia W. (1987) 'Toward More Systematic Consideration of Policy Design', *Policy Studies Journal*, 15 (4): 611–28.

Keiser, Lael R. and Meier, Kenneth J. (1996) 'Policy Design, Bureaucratic Incentives, and Public Management: The Case of Child Support Enforcement', *Journal of Public Administration Research and Theory*, 6 (3): 337–64.

Linder, Stephen H. and Peters, B. Guy (1984) 'From Social Theory to Policy Design', *Journal of Public Policy*, 4 (3): 237–59.

Linder, Stephen H. and Peters, B. Guy (1989) 'Instruments of Government: Perception and Contexts', *Journal of Public Policy*, 9 (1): 35–58.

Lippincott, Ronald C. and Stoker, Robert P. (1992) 'Policy Design and Implementation Effectiveness: Structural Change in a County Court', *Policy Studies Journal*, 20 (3): 376–87.

Lipsky, M. (1983) *Street Level Bureaucracy: Dilemmas of the Individual in Public Services*. New York: Russell Sage Foundation.

Lowi, Theodore J. (1972) 'Four Systems of Policy, Politics, and Choice', *Public Administration Review*, 32: 298–310.

Majone, G. (1989) *Evidence, Argument and Persuasion in the Policy Process*. New Haven, CT: Yale University Press.

Majone, Giandomenico and Wildavsky, Aaron (1979) 'Implementation as Evolution', in Jeffrey Pressman and Aaron Wildavsky (eds), *Implementation*, 2nd edn. Berkeley, CA: University of California Press.

Matland, Richard E. (1995) 'Synthesizing the Implementation Literature: The Ambiguity-Conflict Model of Policy Implementation', *Journal of Public Administration Research and Theory*, 5 (2): 145–74.

May, Peter J. (1991) 'Reconsidering Policy Design: Policies and Publics', *Journal of Public Policy*, 11 (2): 187–206.

May, Peter J. (1992) 'Policy Learning and Failure', *Journal of Public Policy*, 12 (4): 331–54.

May, Peter J. (1993) 'Mandate Design and Implementation: Enhancing Implementation Efforts and Shaping Regulatory Styles', *Journal of Policy Analysis and Management*, 12: 634–63.

May, Peter J. (1995) 'Can Cooperation Be Mandated? Implementing Intergovernmental Environmental Management in New South Wales and New Zealand', *Publius: The Journal of Federalism*, 25 (1): 89–113.

May, Peter J., Burby, Raymond J., Ericksen, Neil J., Handmer, John W., Dixon, Jennifer E., Michaels, Sarah and Ingle Smith, D. (1996) *Environmental Management and Governance: Intergovernmental Approaches to Hazards and Sustainability*. London and New York: Routledge.

Maynard-Moody, Steven (1989) 'Beyond Implementation: Developing and Institutional Theory of Administrative Policy Making', *Public Administration Review*, 49: 137–42.

Mazmanian, Daniel A. and Sabatier, Paul A. (eds) (1981) *Effective Policy Implementation*. Lexington, MA: Lexington Books.

Mazmanian, Daniel A. and Sabatier, Paul A. (1983) *Implementation and Public Policy*. Glenview, IL: Scott Foresman.

McDonnell, Lorraine M. and Elmore, Richard F. (1987) 'Getting the Job Done: Alternative Policy Instruments', *Educational Evaluation and Policy Analysis*, 9 (2): 133–52.

McFarlane, Deborah (1989) 'Testing the Statutory Coherence Hypothesis', *Administration and Society*, 20: 395–422.

Nakamura, Robert T. and Smallwood, Frank (1980) *The Politics of Policy Implementation*. New York: St Martin's Press.

O'Toole, Jr, Laurence J. (1993) 'Interorganizational Policy Studies: Lessons Drawn From Implementation Research', *Journal of Public Administration Research and Theory*, 3: 232–51.

Palumbo, Dennis J. and Calista, Donald J. (1990) 'Opening up the Black Box: Implementation and the Policy Process', in Dennis J. Palumbo and Donald J. Calista (eds), *Implementation and the Policy Process, Opening Up the Black Box*. Westport, CT: Greenwood Press. pp. 3–18.

Peters, B. Guy (2002) 'The Politics of Tool Choice,' in Lester Salamon (ed.), *The Tools of Government: A Guide to the New Governance*. New York: Oxford University Press.

Pressman, Jeffrey L. and Wildavsky, Aaron B. (1973) *Implementation, How Great Expectations in Washington Are Dashed in Oakland*. Berkeley, CA: University of California Press.

Sabatier, Paul A. (1986) 'Top-Down and Bottom-Up Approaches to Implementation Research: A Critical Analysis and Suggested Synthesis', *Journal of Public Policy*, 6 (1): 21–48.

Sabatier, Paul A. and Jenkins-Smith, Hank (1993) *Policy Change and Learning*. Boulder, CO: Westview Press.

Salamon, Lester M. (ed.) (1989) *Beyond Privatization: The Tools of Government Action*. Washington, DC: Urban Institute Press.

Salamon, Lester M. (2002) 'The New Governance: An Introduction', in Lester Salamon (ed.), *The Tools of Government: A Guide to the New Governance*. New York: Oxford University Press.

Schneider, Anne Larason and Ingram, Helen (1997) *Policy Design for Democracy*. Lawrence, KS: University of Kansas Press.

Schneider, Anne and Ingram, Helen (1990) 'Behavioral Assumptions of Policy Tools', *Journal of Politics*, 52 (2): 510–29.

Smith, Steven Rathgeb and Ingram, Helen (2002) 'Policy Tools and Democracy', in Lester Salamon (ed.), *The Tools of Government: A Guide to the New Governance*. New York: Oxford University Press.

Stoker, Robert P. (1991) *Reluctant Partners, Implementing Federal Policy*. Pittsburgh: University of Pittsburgh Press.

Stone, Deborah A. (1989) 'Causal Stories and the Formation of Policy Agendas', *Political Science Quarterly*, 104 (2): 281–300.

Torenvlied, Rene (1996) 'Political Control of Implementation Agencies, Effects of Political Consensus on Agency Compliance', *Rationality and Society*, 8 (1): 25–56.

Van Meter, Donald S. and Van Horn, Carl E. (1975) 'The Policy Implementation Process: A Conceptual Framework', *Administration and Society*, 6: 445–88.

Vedung, Evert (1998) 'Policy Instruments: Typologies and Theories', in Marie-Louise, Bemelmans-Videc, Ray C. Rist and Evert Vedung (eds), *Carrots, Sticks and Sermons: Policy Instruments and Their Evaluation*. New Brunswick and London: Transaction Publishers. pp. 21–58.

Vinzant, Janet Coble and Crothers, Lane (1998) *Street Level Leadership: Discretion and Legitimacy in Front-Line Public Service*. Washington, DC: Georgetown University Press.

Weimer, David L. (1992) 'Claiming Races, Boiler Contracts, Heresthetics, and Habits: Ten Concepts for Policy Design', *Policy Sciences*, 25 (2): 135–59.

Weiss, Janet A. and Tschirhart, Mary (1994) 'Public Information Campaigns as Policy Instruments', *Journal of Policy Analysis and Management*, 13: 82–119.

Winter, Søren (1990) 'Integrating Implementation Research', in Dennis J. Palumbo and Donald J. Calista, (eds), *Implementation and the Policy Process, Opening Up the Black Box*. Westport, CT: Greenwood Press. pp. 19–38.

Winter, Søren C. and May, Peter J. (2001) 'Motivation for Compliance with Environmental Regulations', *Journal of Policy Analysis and Management,* 20: 675–98.

Wood, B. Dan and Waterman, Richard (1994) *Bureaucratic Dynamics: The Role of Bureaucracy in a Democracy*. Boulder, CO: Westview Press.

18

Interorganizational Relations in Implementation

Laurence J. O'Toole, Jr

Policy implementation is an important and arduous task in many kinds of institutional settings. It is clear, nevertheless, that implementation issues are at their thorniest – and most interesting – in interorganizational contexts. This chapter frames the subject of implementation especially as it relates to public administration, with a particular focus on interorganizational settings. The analysis considers how interorganizational relations can influence the implementation process, and what some of the practical implications might be for those who are responsible for trying to manage for policy success.

The first section of the chapter frames the analysis by showing that interorganizational settings are both very common and also particularly challenging venues in which to effect implementation success. This section also indicates some of the reasons why interorganizational institutional settings are so often experienced – indeed, increasingly so. One implication is that public administrators need to develop an understanding about how to operate in such settings rather than hope or expect that they can be avoided. The section following then begins to offer a way of understanding the interorganizational setting for implementation, and how interorganizational relations can be mobilized for action on behalf of public policy. Here, the importance of structural relations themselves for implementation action is particularly emphasized. A third section sketches some of the ways that interorganizational cooperation can be encouraged, despite the daunting impediments often faced by implementers. Special attention is devoted to factors that may be useful for public administrators to consider in their efforts to improve implementation performance.

It should be emphasized at the outset that implementation in interorganizational settings is a complicated topic. While substantial research has been conducted on this subject, and while scholars can now say a considerable amount about how interorganizational relations shape implementation processes and what managers might do to improve their effectiveness, this chapter provides no 'cookbook' with unambiguous guidance. Policy implementation is shaped by many variables, and a valid general theory of the implementation process has eluded researchers (see O'Toole, 2000, for detailed discussion). The implications offered in this chapter, rather, should be considered of heuristic value. While offering guidance, therefore, implementation research nevertheless cannot tell a practicing manager just what to do in all situations.

INTERORGANIZATIONAL SETTINGS FOR POLICY IMPLEMENTATION

Aside from the very rare cases of virtually self-implementing public policy – for instance, interest rate changes by a central bank which reverberate through society via price signals, without any need for an elaborate enforcement apparatus – policy implementation requires institutions to carry the burden of transforming general policy intent into an array of rules, routines and social processes that can convert policy intention into action. This process is the core of what is meant by implementation.

The institutional settings for implementation can vary greatly in many ways. One important distinction is between implementation that can be accomplished by or through one organization (Torenvlied, 1996), on the one hand, and implementation that requires the cooperation and perhaps coordination of multiple organizations, or parts of organizations (Hjern and Porter, 1981), on the other. To the extent that implementation can be handled within the confines of a single formal organization, much of what is known about public administration in general can be applied to deliver policy results (O'Toole, 1996a). When public programs need to be executed through actions spanning two or more organizational settings, however, the implementation task is more complicated. Impediments to concerted action are greater, *ceteris paribus*, and inducements to work together are typically fewer. Between or among organizations, the differing routines and specialized languages, not to mention distinct ways of seeing the world, mean that interorganizational implementation poses particularly daunting challenges. Among other things, such situations call for public administrators to supplement what they know about managing within an organization with additional perspectives and options.

Interorganizational relations can be crucial for policy implementation. Two or more ministries of a single government may be tasked with handling a common program. Or so-called 'vertical' intergovernmental programs, such as those involving national and subnational authorities, require the development and administration of operations across organizational lines. 'Horizontal' intergovernmental programs are less obvious but increasingly significant. A set of governments within a large metropolitan area, for example, may jointly administer cooperative programs for transportation, economic development or emergency services.

Beyond these types are contracting ties and privatization, and many policy fields in numerous countries now use complicated cross-sectoral implementation arrangements. These may include one or more public agencies linked to for-profit companies and/or nonprofit organizations. Certainly, the impetus of the 'New Public Management' has further encouraged such developments in some parts of the world (see Hood, 1996). Additional stimuli include efforts peculiar to one country or another (an example here is the recent Presidential encouragement to involve 'faith-based' organizations in public problem solving in the United States). In other nations, public–private patterns for implementation are buttressed by long traditions of social

relations – such as the reliance on cooperation among 'social partners' in certain countries of Europe. And many public programs in several parts of the globe now include clients or target groups in the coproduction of policy action.

The proliferation of interorganizational connections has become so pronounced that scholars and practitioners increasingly emphasize themes like 'collaboratives' and collaboration (Bardach, 1998) along with the critical role of interorganizational relations in influencing program results. A particularly visible theme in recent years in this regard has been that of 'networks' and network management (for instance, Hufen and Ringeling, 1990; Kickert et al., 1997; O'Toole, 1997b). This last topic is covered more thoroughly elsewhere in this volume, but it is important to recognize the connection between its increasing salience and the interorganizational patterns that typify many implementation settings.

Some analysts suggest that the issue has been exaggerated (Kettl, 1993). A strong case can be made, however, that the implementation manager's world is a very heavily interorganizational one. Much of the systematic evidence on this point has been developed in Europe and the United States, although there are few reasons to expect that these parts of the world are especially distinctive in this regard. (A high-visibility conference during 2000 was convened by the city of Taipei, for example, to address the challenges of 'managing policy coherence', given that horizontal ties simultaneously encourage and complicate efforts to deliver results.) Indeed, the much-referenced forces of 'globalization' are likely to encourage still more, as interdependencies proliferate (Held, 1996).

Research in several countries of Europe shows clearly the importance of interorganizational phenomena for public administration. The works of Kickert, Klijn and Koppenjan (1997), Rhodes (1997) and Scharpf (1993) are illustrative; these studies document the complicated realities facing administrators and others in several countries (see also Klijn, 1996; Mayntz and Scharpf, 1995). Indeed, the phenomenon may be underattended to in such places (Hanf and O'Toole, 1992). Data developed in North America are also important (Milward, 1996).

Systematic studies of policy implementation are among the most telling kinds of evidence. In Europe, social scientists have shown that locally situated managers facing practical challenges like stimulating the growth of jobs and small-business economic activity confront an interorganizational terrain (Hull with Hjern, 1986). In the United States, research has shown that a substantial proportion of the public programs managed by public administrators are interorganizational (O'Toole and Montjoy, 1984; Hall and O'Toole, 2000). At the local level as well, interorganizational patterns are quite common (see Agranoff and McGuire, 2003).

Why is the world of policy implementation so structurally complex? One factor has been the increase in the number of public programs crafted to embrace multiple values. In the days when transportation programs focused solely on paving highways and adding lanes of traffic, maximizing the single objective of moving vehicles might have seemed relatively easy – an engineering problem to be solved by a department managed in the interests of expanding the highway system. But when such a unit also has to cope with environmental degradation, housing dislocations, noise pollution and other impacts of such a program, implementation problems – and institutional arrangements – become more complicated. A result is the expansion of implementation patterns to embrace additional actors and units and concerns.

The sheer expansion of the governmental agenda, furthermore, impels jurisdictional conflicts, overlaps and potential clashes. As the 'policy space' becomes increasingly filled with public programs and initiatives, it becomes ever more difficult to operate without finding a particular effort touching upon related programs and influences managed elsewhere by government – often by other departments of the same government. In such circumstances, it makes sense to try to link the operations in one way or another, or to provide some social infrastructure of mutual consultation and information sharing.

A related issue has to do with the fact that, increasingly, governments are being asked to address problems that cannot be neatly categorized into one niche or another. So-called 'wicked problems' (Rittel and Webber, 1973), which touch upon several arenas and considerations simultaneously, require governmental responses that involve multiple jurisdictions and departments for effective resolution. A consequence is greater cross-boundary institutional links: interdepartmental advisory committees, complex sign-off authorization procedures, multiple veto and approval points, and so forth. Sometimes the 'wickedness' of policy problems is recognized at the outset, and more complex managerial approaches are designed into policy responses. On other occasions, there is a gradual recognition of the second-order impacts that more constrained efforts can have. A consequence over the longer run can be to seek to 'internalize' the additional impacts and manage them by broadening the reach of the program and its administrative effort.

Another influence can be mentioned. Especially for governments facing budgetary stringencies, responses to new and pressing problems often take the form of 'mandates' directing an array of departments, governments or even outside parties to comply with orders. The purposes can be as varied as civil rights, sustainable development or the enactment of fair labor standards. The consequence can be that many units have additional objectives, and constraints, layered onto existing programs and activities. Such initiatives can constitute a particularly substantial catalyst for the proliferation of interorganizational patterns for implementing public policy.

A related stimulus derives from the forces of globalization, and in particular the impetus toward interorganizational patterning that emerges from the enactment of international agreements in policy fields from trade to weapons control to environmental protection. Once established, an international agreement can trigger reverberations at the national and subnational levels, as countries try to develop implementation patterns that can induce cooperation and compliance with commitments they have entered into. Oftentimes, the required actions encourage the forging of links across ministries, governments and sectors within a particular country – not to mention interorganizational ties between national bureaucracies and international secretariats, and transnational interorganizational links between and among cooperating national agencies. The fact that there are thousands of international agreements now in place, and many more on the agenda, suggests the importance of this phenomenon. And the European Union, despite emphases on subsidiarity and the lack of a sizeable bureaucracy thus far in Brussels, has also experienced and stimulated multi-level interorganizational relations as many policy fields become more complicatedly networked.

Two additional causal factors are directly related to the forces of politics *per se*. Sometimes managers can handle the technical needs of a policy problem during execution by using a relatively constrained set of actors in implementation, but political imperatives may encourage broadening the involvement to additional parties. This phenomenon is surely common in pluralisic systems, as public managers seek to maintain support for program execution following the enactment of policy. The addition of important institutions or other actors to the 'coalition' involved in program execution can stem criticism and enhance chances for implementation success, even if some of the additional parties are likely to contribute little to the program's performance *per se*. This point is hardly a new phenomenon. In fact, under the label of 'cooptation' (Selznick, 1949) the process of involving interested parties in public initiatives has long been widely discussed by analysts and practitioners.

A broadened coalition of participants during implementation increases the prospects that managers can achieve something significant during the less visible but still critical phases of program execution. Of course, interorganizational ties can also increase the chance that complexity and conflict will overwhelm efforts to make things happen. The trick is to promote the building of support while avoiding the tendencies toward confusion and excessive complexity. In more corporatist political systems, there may be little choice. Peak associations of interested parties that are involved during initial phases of decision making are also explicitly co-implementers and co-responsible parties during the latter phases of the process.

The second obviously political influence shaping interorganizational relations and policy implementation is that basic choices have been made, especially in nations with liberal commitments to the protection of a substantial private realm, that limits should be placed on the reach of public authority. In such settings, the demand that government should address pressing problems runs up against the preference for limited government. A 'solution' during implementation can be for government to commit to problem solving but limit its formal control by opting for more complex, 'partnered' approaches with private firms or not-for-profit organizations. The result is a considerably more complicated, networked institutional form.

Of course, there are additional forces impelling the waves of privatization, contracting and related phenomena. These may include pressures for cost-cutting, ideological agendas and weak management capacity in the public sector. In this regard, an irony can be briefly noted. To the extent that governments commit to contracting and privatization out of a concern that they lack internal management capacity, they are likely to be in for a nasty surprise. For public administration in such settings calls for great skill, effort and capacity – more so, probably, than management in the more traditional situations. Once dispersed, control is difficult to bring together for concerted, public-interested action (see for instance O'Toole, 1989, 1991).

For all these reasons, the layering of interorganizational implementation ties has developed apace. Almost none of these forces is likely to be short term. Rather, they signal a cluster of influences likely to complicate the operating environments of managers for the foreseeable future.

It seems clear, therefore, that the topic of interorganizational relations will remain important for administrators tasked with helping to make policy implementation succeed. Accordingly, it is critical to understand how to make sense of such institutional settings for improving prospects for implementation success.

UNDERSTANDING INTERORGANIZATIONAL POLICY IMPLEMENTATION

A review of any standard text in public administration shows that the assumption guiding much of the analysis and advice is that public managers possess at least formal authority over the actors they are responsible for guiding. While attention is devoted to notions like the 'informal organization', the need to generate support from subordinates, and the importance of the external 'environment', the framing principle behind much administrative advice is that managers can expect to have some significant ability to give orders and direct resources over the central part of their domain. But in a world of interorganizational relations, this premise is questionable.

The point can be put another way. Generating successful policy implementation means inducing cooperation, and perhaps even coordination, among interdependent actors in the face of impediments. In standard departments or ministries, the incentives to concert action would seem to be three: authority (B cooperates with A because B feels it is an obligation to do so), common interest (B cooperates with A because B feels that doing so toward the overall objectives would also serve B's own purposes), and exchange (B cooperates with A because B receives something else from A, or from elsewhere, that makes it worthwhile to go along). The formal hierarchy allows public administrators in departments to rely to some considerable extent on authority as an aid to coordination. But administrators working across boundaries typically do not possess this luxury. There may be formal points of authority across disparate departments – the chief executive's office, for instance, or the cabinet – but in practice such authority is almost never invoked. Central officials have little to gain from being dragged into interministerial disputes and typically expect organizations to work out their differences. And the time and authority of even central decision makers is strictly limited and usually rationed for the most compelling cases. Rare is the implementation manager who can operate informally as an authority figure across organizations. The result is that public administrators who wish to trigger policy implementation while working across organizational borders must turn to other options: finding or stimulating common interest – and its continuing salience – and developing and maintaining sensible exchanges (Gage and Mandell, 1990).

Behind these general and rather abstract statements lies a host of possibilities, and also complications. But the main point is that administering policy implementation in interorganizational contexts forces a reconsideration of the basic context of managerial choice, as well as the types and emphases accorded to managerial options. Administrators in interorganizational patterns can never assume support but must work to build it. They typically cannot rely on hierarchical institutional arrangements to congeal agreement, beyond their own formal unit, at any rate. Administrators working to implement in interorganizational settings often have to develop the infrastructure of communication – channels, language, signals and so forth – to help achieve the objective of policy-oriented cooperation. The interorganizational setting is not a whole new world, for managers have been operating to some extent across boundaries for quite a while. But assuming an interorganizational array as a core structural form means shifting approaches to implementation from those injunctions more typically emphasized.

Public administrators operating in such institutionally complex settings find themselves maneuvering in a world where there are *multiple* points of managerial influence and very different managerial roles across the departments and other units of the policy world. Few moves can be made unilaterally. The task is less one of directing and controlling and more that of assessing contexts of interdependence and seeking to influence these, often in subtle ways, to increase prospects for successful cooperation (see Stoker, 1991).

The implementation challenge faced by public administrators, then, consists of assessing the structural setting itself to determine its strengths and weaknesses for encouraging cooperative effort; and then to tap common interest and exchange, as appropriate and practical, to increase prospects for success. The remainder of this section considers the interorganizational structural setting itself. The next part of the chapter focuses on the inducements to cooperation that may be available within any given implementation setting.

Not all patterns of interorganizational relations are created equal. One of the most important aspects of implementation settings is the structure of interdependence required or encouraged among the organizations involved. For it is not the sheer number of units, but their pattern and the way they link to each other, that is most critical.

This point conflicts with an assertion made in one of the most well-known implementation studies, that by Pressman and Wildavsky (1984), who claim that the 'complexity of joint action' is the key impediment to successful implementation. By this term they mean the number of actors and decision points. Pressman and Wildavsky indicate that as the number of units involved in implementation increases, and particularly as the number of distinct decisions requiring collective agreement grows, the chance for action declines. Indeed, they seem to 'demonstrate' mathematically that in fairly typical circumstances involving multiple organizations and a set of decisions, implementation success is a near impossibility, even if the likelihood of agreement at any point is exceedingly high.

The contradiction between this deduction and the abundant real-world evidence that success is not only possible but frequent has been dubbed the 'Pressman–Wildavsky paradox' by specialists in implementation. As Bowen (1982), among others, has shown, there are significant flaws in the analysis conducted by Pressman and Wildavsky. For instance, in reality, probabilities of agreement among organizations are not impervious to events. Indeed, 'bandwagon effects' often develop: agreement on basic understandings at the outset of an implementation process can increase the odds of further agreement later. Organizations can also merge multiple decisions or decision points in a single set of negotiations. Doing so – bringing all the parties to the table to craft 'package deals' – can also dramatically enhance the odds of success. Putting many issues into play simultaneously generates possibilities for tradeoffs. And merging decisions into a more comprehensive set of negotiations reduces the number of separate hurdles.

These points suggest that the challenge of generating interorganizational cooperation toward implementation success, even in especially complicated cases, is not likely to be nearly so uniformly disappointing as the Pressman–Wildavsky analysis suggests. An especially important aspect of complex implementation contexts that Pressman and Wildavsky failed to take into account is the structuring among the organizations themselves. Some policy tasks require that organizations – public agencies, say, or an agency along with a few contractors and subcontractors – deal sequentially with the challenge of implementation. Other policy tasks might call on units to work together closely, with the outputs of each serving as inputs for the other, on a regular basis. Or perhaps a policy initiative might require several organizations to become active, but each one could act independently of the others – this might be the situation, for instance, if a national government were to try to stimulate economic development in certain urban areas by mandating several national ministries to focus their spending on such issues in those regions. These three different kinds of circumstances fit Thompson's notions of sequential, reciprocal and pooled interdependence, respectively (1967; see also O'Toole and Montjoy, 1984). Of course, in large, complicated interorganizational networks carrying out public programs, there may be instances of each of these types of interdependence within the same overall program array.

It should be clear that implementation is affected by the type(s) of interdependence in an interorganizational pattern, not simply the number of units or decisions. For example, in a sequential arrangement, a delay or impediment at any place in the chain will mean implementation problems at the point of intended impact. This assembly-line structure of interdependence creates, in effect, potential veto points at each link. Sometimes, interorganizational arrangements for implementation are structured to allow just one of the units involved to exercise potential veto power. This sort of arrangement is sometimes purposely chosen to make sure a particular organization, and its point of view and jurisdiction, are given special weight. An example would be an environmental agency charged with reviewing construction projects and disapproving those with significant adverse impacts.

In sequential arrangements, adding more organizational units in a chain increases the number of possible roadblocks to action. Here, Pressman and Wildavsky's proposition about the complexity of joint action rings true. But in other arrangements, for instance in programs that seek to pool the action of multiple organizations, adding units can *increase* prospects for some implementation action. In short, the structure of interdependence among the organizations can make a big difference in what happens. This point can be kept in mind when designing interorganizational patterns for implementation. For example, if reliability is of prime importance, multiple service-providing organizations arrayed in a pooled fashion can increase the probability of success via purposeful redundancy (Bendor, 1985; Chisholm, 1989). Note the vast number of organizations assisting the seriously mentally ill in mid-sized US cities (Provan and Milward, 1991); the overall pattern is highly

complex, but one result is that fewer clients slip entirely through the cracks. If a particular policy objective or value needs to be ensured in a complicated program setting, creating a veto point unit via sequential interdependence can be effective. If well-integrated interorganizational action is essential for policy-oriented problem solving, crafting interunit links framed around reciprocal interdependence can be important. And sometimes structural arrangements can be consolidated or reorganized to reduce coordination demands. This strategy has been invoked in Denmark as employment training implementation patterns were adjusted, in effect, from sequential to pooled – to allow both employment service and municipal welfare service units to contact private firms for their own clienteles rather than forcing all contacts through the former units.

ENCOURAGING INTERORGANIZATIONAL COOPERATION

Recognizing the significance of different interorganizational patterns is one step toward effective implementation. In addition, skillful implementation managers need to find ways of getting organizations to work together toward policy success. Inducing implementation success via interorganizational ties typically requires some combination of generating and tapping common interest, on the one hand, and/or utilizing exchanges to link units in productive ways for purposes of policy. Each of these themes deserves attention.

Building and using common interest

If organizations A and B each care about a policy objective, and if the participation of each is essential for success, their shared interest in the result may be enough to generate interorganizational efforts toward implementation. This statement is true, and important, but one should be careful to recognize as well the non-trivial impediments to joint action that may still remain. For one thing, different organizations very often have somewhat different goals and perspectives on matters like policy. Even where there are overlaps in interest and priorities, there are also likely to be some discrepancies. Second, one key reason why so much implementation involves interorganizational links is that complicated policy challenges often require consideration by different kinds of units reflecting distinct and partially competing goals. In such cases, which are quite common, it is unrealistic to expect common interest itself to be sufficient. At a minimum, it is likely that even shared goals will be differentially salient in separate units. Third, for a whole set of nitty-gritty implementation details, different organizations will have unique perspectives even if they share a common overall goal. For instance, matters like turf and budgets can trigger conflicts even among strongly committed units.

In addition, even if all relevant organizations share an interest in having the policy succeed, each may be reluctant to commit itself wholeheartedly without knowing that the others are doing so as well. Organizations involved in a complex enterprise, in short, may be cautious about the possibility of 'free riding' among their partners. When numerous organizations are potentially involved in an implementation effort, there may be a problem of collective action, even if there is common interest in the outcome (Ostrom, 1990). This issue can be quite vexing, since typically organizations are unlikely to signal publicly any plan to act as free riders, and virtually all can probably claim publicly that they are doing what they can for the overall objective – even if they are not. Particularly when levels of trust are low, it may be difficult to get a true interorganizational effort off the ground.

What can public administrators responsible for encouraging implementation success do to assist the process? A number of actions can he helpful.

One possibility is signaling. If different bureaus or departments have similar perspectives on the common endeavor, managers can help by simply making that important fact clear to all involved. The more that all understand that everyone shares the commitment, the less the chance that doubts and second thoughts will arise. A related point is 'framing' (see Kahneman and Tversky, 1984): interorganizational efforts are typically complicated. In the real world this complexity may cause doubts to form about the cooperative venture. Questions may arise about whether others are going to be cooperative, or whether differences will overwhelm the potential for success. Managers can help by highlighting the key points of common interest that could get lost from participants' attention amid a welter of detail and uncertainty. Focusing participants' perceptions on the accurate reality that they (mostly) do agree and that they are engaged with others in a valuable activity can help stem hesitation and increase trust (see further comments on this issue shortly).

Similarly, administrators working in interorganizational contexts can work to get parties on the record in public and obtain specific commitments to cooperate on certain observable tasks. Commitments on the part of some can facilitate the generation of commitments by others, as the risks of going it alone are substantially reduced. Similarly, iteration can help. Administrators can try to get the action going and keep it moving in relatively predictable, repeated interactions. Doing so reduces coordination costs, increases understanding and predictability, and also enhances trust (Axelrod, 1984). Moreover, administrators can craft transparent reporting systems, so that all parties can see what the others are up to on issues that matter for them (O'Toole, 1996b; 1997a).

None of these options really alters the 'natural' lineup of forces among the organizations; instead, the moves are aimed at facilitating the search for stable and cooperative approaches to the joint effort. Such actions can be consequential, particularly if the organizations involved share a substantial degree of common interest.

Additional steps can also be helpful. Administrators can make efforts to prevent some units from acting as free riders on the efforts of the others – for instance, by monitoring actions across multiple units, if all agree. Indeed, all may have an interest in assigning such responsibility to a particular unit or manager, given the shared interests in cooperative effort. Also, managers of interorganizational implementation can sometimes exercise discretion to design or shift the mix of units involved to ensure a substantial degree of overlap in perspectives; and implementation managers can use the art of persuasion, by finding ways to increase the perceived value associated with cooperative activities.

Cultivating norms supportive of cooperation can also be a valuable step (Weber, 1998). Norms of cooperation and respect for the needs of other participants can be critical as forms of 'social capital' that can pay dividends into the future, and, of course, administrators of programs crossing organizational lines can apply their own influence to help generate regard for those actions supportive of these norms.

Furthermore, administrators can generate increasing amounts of cooperation by disaggregating large, complicated and potentially risky commitments and decisions into smaller ones. If multiple departments, for instance, are being asked to commit time and substantial resources to a joint enterprise apparently fraught with risks – including the perceived risk that others will not do their part – implementation managers can sometimes make cooperation more feasible by rendering it less risky. By trimming a large commitment into a series of smaller bargains enforced over time, and with at least the potential for withdrawal (or retaliation), the costs of any particular move become less of an impediment, while the benefits of joint cooperation over limited tasks escalate over time. And beyond these direct contributions to achieving the collective task, there is another benefit. Organizations that have learned to work with others and to draw gradually on the contributions of others are very likely to increase their mutual trust. As this shift in expectations develops, additional agreements are easier to strike; the payoffs do not have to be as immediate. (Organizations that can expect others to contribute later may be willing to do their part now. There is a virtuous cycle, in other words, and successful management of the early stages can contribute to easier policy implementation over the longer haul.)

Common interest, in short, offers possibilities, despite the challenges and limitations outlined earlier. In particular, administrators have several moves at their disposal to tap common interest where it exists and to increase it where it is initially limited.

Facilitating cooperation via exchange

Beyond common interest as a kind of inter-organizational 'glue' that can congeal cooperation toward implementation action, exchange is a kind of social process that holds potential to shape implementation in productive ways. Organizations involved in interorganizational implementation typically need things from each other if they are to do their jobs. Just which ones are involved, and how the needs may be distributed depend on the nature of the policy tasks and the structure of interdependence, a topic discussed earlier. Exchanges between organizations involved in implementation can create sufficient inducements to congeal cooperation. Exchange here refers not simply to the use of funds to procure goods and services, but also to a broad array of types of trades among interdependent units.

The use of funds to cement concerted action, of course, is the most obvious kind of exchange to consider. Often, third party involvement in service delivery is desired by policy makers, for any of a variety of reasons. Contracting with such parties is a common instrument for linking organizations and framing the implementation arena, particularly when governments contract in a competitive context (Jensen et al., 1991). Indeed, a typical element of the 'New Public Management' visible in many countries now is an extensive set of contracting relations across organizations and sectors (Barzelay, 2001).

Many features of the exchange relations can be designed explicitly into the contracted understanding; and contract elements can be negotiated to try to ensure that incentives match desired behavior and/or outputs. Even here, nonetheless, there is considerable need for skillful public management. Contracts are not self-enforcing; they require talented administration to work well, and no set of incentives, no matter how carefully designed, is completely self-enforcing (Miller, 1992). Some degree of leadership must be employed to congeal support across the units for effective action.

Exchanges among organizations involved in policy implementation can extend considerably beyond formal agreements to trade money for effort or results (Bardach, 1998). Organizations need inputs from their environments on a regular basis, and they seek outlets for their products as well. The inputs can range from political support to human resources to information; and the outputs can be of myriad types as well. When implementation requires or encourages inter-organizational cooperation, those concerned about making the process work well are often advantaged by focusing on the kinds of exchanges that have developed, and could be encouraged to develop, among the interdependent units. Some of the possibilities are quite straightforward. Central government agencies can offer funding, discretion and information to subnational units, which can often, in turn, regulate or deliver services better than could central authorities within their territory. The success of the subnational effort also benefits the national agency, whose interest is served by smooth flows of funds and delivery of services. And so on.

Exchanges can extend considerably beyond the most obvious kinds of trades. Organizations typically have relatively complex agendas, and often they must deal with each other over many matters and through extended periods. While these facts of life can make negotiating complicated, they also render it more productive. Public administrators involved in policy implementation can use such circumstances to encourage successful policy action. Departments and other organizations are often interdependent on a number of tasks (Fountain, 2001). Even when they are not, it could be that what from one perspective looks like a single (potentially) cooperative endeavor – a joint program or proposal – can also be seen as a stream of interdependent decisions and joint efforts linked together, perhaps via a stream of exchanges.

This complexity can be an advantage, in the sense that the separable cooperative actions can be explicitly 'placed on the table' by creative public managers. Exchange might be built, and even built explicitly, across different tasks of interdependent units so as to facilitate more stable long-term cooperation. In a similar vein, large and long-term policy efforts that require management across boundaries can themselves be seen as a substantial set of less overwhelming potentially cooperative efforts. Almost inevitably, different parties will view the successful completion of these with different levels of salience or enthusiasm – the letting of a contract, the completion of a milestone, the involvement of certain outside interests, the incorporation of particular capital spending items into a larger plan, and so on. These discrete but related foci can offer a multitude of chances for tradeoffs in the interest of overall success.

Public administrators involved in interorganizational implementation can contribute to increasing the overall odds of success if they stay alert to such options, which provide the potential to cement exchanges and contribute to productive agreement. Often, the brokering of these possibilities does not happen without active effort on the part of managers focused on the overall effort. Identifying such exchange possibilities, proposing tradeoffs, helping to stipulate the terms of the interorganizational agreement, and then working to monitor and manage information flows so that all relevant parties can see what is happening and whether *quid pro quos* have remained viable – these kinds of managerial steps may be essential parts of any solutions over the longer term.

Sometimes exchange can be facilitated by public administrators who can effect a change in the set of alternatives for cooperation (and non-cooperation) under consideration. Sometimes, simply reminding organizations involved of the 'default option' – the consequences if no agreement is reached – can encourage productive exchange. Particularly if non-cooperation can result in another party (for instance, a higher level of government) enforcing its will on those involved in early stages of implementation, it can be helpful to alert such parties of the consequences of any lack of agreement. Public administrators can sometimes go beyond this point to identify new and creative options that may have escaped the notice of all other participants. The ability to see stable bargaining alternatives in highly conflictual situations has long been recognized as a key element of skillful diplomacy; and administrative diplomacy is often quite helpful in assisting exchange for interorganizational implementation. Crafting 'new' options, therefore, is often an important element of productive interorganizational relations.

Similarly, shifting the set of organizations involved in an interorganizational implementation setting can not only increase the degree of common interest among those in the program, as explained above, but can also facilitate exchange under certain circumstances. Which units ought to be a part of interorganizational implementation is only partially a technical matter. Stoker (1991) has pointed out that it may be possible to involve organizations that have enduring conflicts with each other and yet can find ways of cooperating on a particular program despite the persistence of such differences.

This consideration of exchange as a critical element of interorganizational implementation should not be taken to imply that interorganizational relations are always, or even usually, marked by totally voluntary agreements among organizational units. Despite the reality that formal authority is rarely invoked to force long-term, productive interorganizational cooperation, power relations among interdependent organizations can influence the flow of events during implementation (Bressers and Klok, 1988). Resource-dependence theory (Pfeffer and Salancik, 1978) suggests that those units in possession of critical resources needed by others can be more influential. Units involved in interorganizational implementation tend to try to manage their strategic contingencies to maintain some maneuverability, and certainly, organizations that are crucially important to the other units involved in an implementation effort can be expected to play a particularly significant role in shaping the kind and level of cooperation that develops.

Public administrators located in such agencies may be able to shape implementation processes meaningfully. It is useful for public administrators to be alert for circumstances in which their units are unusually influential; such situations can provide opportunity to institutionalize agreements and understandings in ways particularly favorable to successful implementation action.

CONCLUSION

The implementation of public policy occurs in highly varied settings, but it is clear that, quite often, interorganizational cooperation is called for to achieve successful results. The organizations involved include governmental departments and ministries, subnational agencies, nonprofit and for-profit units, and organizations of target groups – who may even be involved in coproducing the implementation action. Whether and how interorganizational cooperation emerges depends on a number of factors. Substantial impediments may be present, so cooperation must be developed; it cannot be assumed. The structure or pattern of interdependence among the organizations involved matters, although there is no 'one best' arrangement for all circumstances. More organizations add capacity and also constraints to any implementation system. Common interest among the units involved can help congeal cooperative action, as can opportunities for exchanges of various sorts among the participating units. In all these respects, the actions of public administrators acting on behalf of policy to effect cooperative action can be highly consequential.

This chapter has outlined these challenges and opportunities, with particular attention to the role of the administrator. Given the frequently interorganizational context of policy implementation, the importance of such a position is particularly deserving of attention and understanding.

REFERENCES

Agranoff, Robert and McGuire, Mark (2003) *Collaborative Public Management*. Washington, DC: Georgetown University Press.

Axelrod, Robert (1984) *The Evolution of Cooperation*. New York: Basic Books.

Bardach, Eugene (1998) *Getting Agencies to Work Together: The Practice and Theory of Managerial Craftsmanship*. Washington, DC: Brookings Institution.

Barzelay, Michael (2001) *The New Public Management: Improving Research and Policy Dialogue*. Berkeley, CA: University of California Press.

Bendor, Jonathan (1985) *Parallel Systems: Redundancy in Government*. Berkeley, CA: University of California Press.

Bowen, Elinor R. (1982) 'The Pressman–Wildavsky Paradox ...', *Journal of Public Policy*, 2 (February): 1–21.

Bressers, Hans and Klok, Pieter-Jan (1988) 'Fundamentals for a Theory of Policy Instruments', *International Journal of Social Economics*, 15 (3/4): 22–41.

Chisholm, Donald (1989) *Coordination without Hierarchy: Informal Structures in Multiorganizational Systems*. Berkeley, CA: University of California Press.

Fountain, Jane E. (2001) *Building the Virtual State: Information Technology and Institutional Change*. Washington, DC: Brookings Institution.

Gage, Robert W. and Mandell, Myrna P. (eds) (1990) *Strategies for Managing Intergovernmental Policies and Networks*. New York: Praeger.

Hall, Thad E. and O'Toole, Laurence J., Jr (2000) 'Structures for Policy Implementation: An Analysis of National Legislation, 1965–66 and 1993–94', *Administration and Society*, 31 (6): 667–86.

Hanf, Kenneth I. and O'Toole, Laurence J., Jr (1992) 'Revisiting Old Friends: Networks, Implementation Structures, and the Management of Inter-organizational Relations', *European Journal of Political Research*, 21 (1–2): 163–80.

Held, David (1996) *Democracy and the Global Order, From the Modern State to Cosmopolitan Governance*. Cambridge: Polity Press.

Hjern, Benny and Porter, David O. (1981) 'Implementation Structures: A New Unit of Administrative Analysis', *Organization Studies*, 2 (3): 211–27.

Hood, Christopher H. (1996) 'United Kingdom: From Second Chance to Near-Miss Learning', in Johan P. Olsen and B. Guy Peters (eds), *Lessons from Experience: Experiential Learning in Administrative Reforms in Eight Democracies*. Oslo: Scandinavian University Press.

Hufen, J.A.M. and Ringeling, A.B. (eds) (1990) *Beleidsnetwerken: Overheids-, semi-overheids-, en particuliere organisaties in wisselwerking*. The Hague: VUGA.

Hull, Chris with Hjern, Benny (1986) *Helping Small Firms Grow*. London: Croom Helm.

Jensen, Torben Pilegaard, Winter, Søren, Manniche, Jesper and Ørberg, Peter D. (1991) *Indsatsen for langtidsledige*. Copenhagen: AKF Forlaget.

Kahneman, Daniel and Tversky, Amos (1984) 'Choices, Values, and Frames', *American Psychologist*, 39: 341–50.

Kettl, Donald F. (1993) 'Searching for Clues about Public Management: Slicing the Onion Different Ways', in Barry Bozeman (ed.), *Public Management: The State of the Art*. San Francisco: Jossey-Bass. pp. 55–68.

Kickert, Walter, Klijn, Erik-Hans and Koppenjan, Joop (eds) (1997) *Managing Complex Networks: Network Management and the Public Sector*. London: Sage.

Klijn, Erik-Hans (1996) *Regels en Sturing in Netwerken: De Invloed van netwerkregels op de herstructurering van naoorlogse wijken*. Delft: Eburon.

Mayntz, Renate and Scharpf, Fritz W. (1995) 'Der Ansatz des akteurzentrierten Institutionalismus', in Renate Mayntz and Fritz W. Scharpf (eds), *Steuerung und Selbstorganisation in staatsnahen Sektoren*. Frankfurt a.M.: Campus Verlag.

Miller, Gary J. (1992) *Managerial Dilemmas: The Political Economy of Hierarchy*. Cambridge: Cambridge University Press.

Milward, H. Brinton (ed.) (1996) 'Symposium on the Hollow State: Capacity, Control, and Performance in Interorganizational Settings', *Journal of Public Administration Research and Theory*, 6 (2): 193–314.

O'Toole, Laurence J., Jr (1989) 'Goal Multiplicity in the Implementation Setting: Subtle Impacts and the Case of Wastewater Treatment Privatization', *Policy Studies Journal*, 18 (1): 3–22.

O'Toole, Laurence J., Jr (1991) 'Public and Private Management of Wastewater Treatment: A Comparative Study', in John Heilman (ed.), *Evaluation and Privatization*. San Francisco, CA: Jossey–Bass. pp. 13–32.

O'Toole, Laurence J., Jr (1996a) 'Implementing Public Programs', in James L. Perry (ed.), *Handbook of Public Administration*, 2nd edn. (San Francisco: Jossey-Bass, 1996). pp. 250–62.

O'Toole, Laurence J., Jr (1996b) 'Rational Choice and the Public Management of Interorganizational Networks', in Donald F. Kettl and H. Brinton Milward (eds), *The State of Public Management*. Baltimore, MD: Johns Hopkins University Press. pp. 241–63.

O'Toole, Laurence J., Jr (1997a) 'Implementing Public Innovations in Network Settings', *Administration and Society*, 29 (2): 115–38.

O'Toole, Laurence J., Jr (1997b) 'Treating Networks Seriously: Practical and Research-Based Agendas in Public Administration', *Public Administration Review*, 57 (1): 45–52.

O'Toole, Laurence J., Jr (2000) 'Research on Policy Implementation: Assessment and Prospect', *Journal of Public Administration Research and Theory*, 10 (2): 263–88.

O'Toole, Laurence J., Jr and Montjoy, Robert S. (1984) 'Interorganizational Policy Implementation: A Theoretical Perspective', *Public Administration Review*, 44 (6): 491–503.

Ostrom, Elinor (1990) *Governing the Commons: The Evolution of Institutions for Collective Action*. Cambridge: Cambridge University Press.

Pfeffer, Jeffrey and Salancik, Gerald R. (1978) *The External Control of Organizations: A Resource Dependence Perspective*. New York: Harper & Row.

Pressman, Jeffrey L. and Wildavsky, Aaron (1984) *Implementation*, 3rd edn. Berkeley, CA: University of California Press.

Provan, Keith G. and Milward, H. Brinton (1991) 'Institutional-Level Norms and Organizational Involvement in a Service-Implementation Network', *Journal of Public Administration Research and Theory*, 1 (4): 391–417.

Rhodes, R.A.W. (1997) *Understanding Governance: Policy Networks, Governance, Reflexivity and Accountability*. Buckingham: Open University Press.

Rittel, Horst W.J. and Webber, Melvin (1973) 'Dilemmas in a General Theory of Planning', *Policy Sciences*, 4: 155–69.

Scharpf, Fritz W. (ed.) (1993) *Games in Hierarchies and Networks*. Frankfurt a.M.: Campus Verlag.

Selznick, Philip (1949) *TVA and the Grass Roots*. Berkeley, CA: University of California Press.

Stoker, Robert P. (1991) *Reluctant Partners: Implementing Federal Policy*. Pittsburgh: University of Pittsburgh Press.

Thompson, James D. (1967) *Organizations in Action*. New York: McGraw–Hill.

Torenvlied, René (1996) *Besluiten in Uitvoering: Theorieën over beleidsuitvoering modelmatig getoetst op sociale vernieuwing in drie gemeenten*. Amsterdam: Thesis Publishers.

Weber, Edward (1998) *Pluralism by the Rules: Conflict and Cooperation in Environmental Regulation*. Washington, DC: Georgetown University Press.

19

Street-Level Bureaucrats and the Implementation of Public Policy

Marcia K. Meyers and Susan Vorsanger

The democratic control of implementing agents is a perennial public administration concern. Generations of scholars and practitioners have debated the appropriate relationship between the politics of the legislative processes and the administration of the resulting laws. More recently, scholars working with rational choice models have joined the debate, with particular attention to the incentive and contractual structures that align the interests of implementing agents with policy making principals. Similar concerns have been prominent in the scholarly literature on policy implementation, whether framed as a 'top-down' issue of fidelity to policy makers' goals or a 'bottom-up' issue of policy adaptation during the implementation process.

The control of 'street-level bureaucrats' raises a particularly interesting and thorny set of issues for scholars interested in bureaucratic control and policy implementation. In his seminal 1980 study of workers in schools, courts and welfare agencies, Michael Lipsky defined street-level bureaucrats as 'public service workers who interact directly with citizens in the course of their jobs, and who have substantial discretion in the execution of their work' (1980: 3). They include teachers, police officers, welfare workers, health and safety inspectors and other public employees who control access to public programs or enforce public laws and regulations. As such, they occupy a unique, and uniquely influential, position in the implementation process.

In this chapter we consider what is known, and some of what remains to be learned, about the role of street-level bureaucrats in policy implementation. We begin with a review of the most commonly discussed characteristics of those front-line workers who function as *de facto* bureaucratic policy makers. We next consider the questions of whether and how policy officials control the discretionary actions of these workers. This leads us to consider the normative questions that motivate concern about hierarchical control: the implications of the exercise of street-level discretion for democratic governance, treatment of citizens and policy achievement. Our review brings to the surface significant contradictions in the literature. In some studies these workers are portrayed as occupying a powerless position downstream of political and bureaucratic decisions; in others they emerge as loyal public servants who pursue the public good even when it means bending agency regulations; in still others they are described as self-interested bureaucrats whose coping mechanisms frustrate the will of elected officials.

We conclude the chapter by suggesting that these contradictory portrayals actually reveal much about the complexity of implementation processes and the influences of multiple, interacting factors on street-level workers. This complexity highlights the need for more sophisticated theoretical models that recognize the contribution of hierarchical control mechanisms, organizational constraints and individual incentives. And they raise important cautions about contextualizing our evaluations of front-line performance. Differences in the political, organizational, technical and other characteristics of implementation contexts preclude adoption of a single standard for 'successful' implementation. It is equally difficult to agree on a single standard for front-line 'cooperation' with democratic governance and policy achievement. If we fail to consider how the implementation context structures the job of front-line workers, we risk assigning them credit or blame for policy outcomes that are largely determined by features of the policy design, the organizational capacity or other implementation factors.

DEFINING THE STREET-LEVEL BUREAUCRAT

By virtue of their position at the interface between citizens and the state, street-level bureaucrats have significant opportunities to influence the delivery of public policies. Front-line workers are responsible for many of the most central activities of public agencies, from determining program eligibility to allocating benefits, judging compliance, imposing sanctions and exempting individuals and businesses from penalties. These front-line practices form the technical core of many public organizations.

Because these activities involve direct interactions with citizens, front-line workers also exercise considerable discretion. Much of the output of public agencies takes the form of intangible services and enforcement activities, the quality of which is difficult to assess and monitor. When this output involves direct contact with citizens, the ability of supervisors to monitor and direct staff activities is even more constrained. In contrast to other production processes, 'people changing' services and regulation require front-line workers to engage in a joint production process with their raw materials; workers can rarely produce desired policy outcomes without the active cooperation of the individuals who are beneficiaries of public services or the targets of public regulations (Hasenfeld, 1992). This interdependence introduces substantial variability and unpredictability into the work of street-level bureaucrats. It also greatly increases their need and their opportunities to exercise discretionary judgement.

Given their position at the interface of the state and the citizen, and their opportunities to exercise discretion, front-line workers exert influence well beyond their formal authority. They operate, in Michael Lipsky's (1980) term, as bureaucrats who not only deliver but actively shape policy outcomes by interpreting rules and allocating scarce resources. Through their day-to-day routines and the decisions they make, these workers in effect *produce* public policy as citizens experience it.

Some observers ascribe even more far-reaching influence to street-level workers. Lipsky (1980) argues that they act as 'agents of social control' by requiring behaviors of citizens with whom they interact. Vinzant and Crothers (1998) argue for a recasting of front-line workers as 'street-level leaders' whose choices about which outcomes to pursue, and how to achieve them, 'help to define what it means to be a citizen in America' (p. 19). Maynard-Moody and Musheno (2003) point out that front-line workers typically reject the term street-level bureaucrat, describing themselves instead as 'citizen-agents who help create and maintain the normative order of society' (p. 23).

THE EXERCISE OF DISCRETION AT THE STREET LEVEL

The potential for the discretionary decisions and actions of front-line workers to affect policy raises obvious questions of democratic control. In his study of Danish farm inspectors, Winter (2000) poses the question: 'Are street-level bureaucrats servants or masters?' The questions of whether, and how, policy making principals control the discretion of their implementing agents have dominated much of the empirical research on police, social service workers, health and safety inspectors, building inspectors and other front-line workers.

Researchers have examined a variety of political, organizational and professional factors that would be predicted to control street-level discretion. The findings from these studies have reached mixed and sometimes contradictory conclusions. Taken together, however, they suggest complexity rather than contradiction. Street-level bureaucrats are embedded in interacting policy, organizational, professional, community and socio-economic systems. The capacity of any single factor to influence their discretionary behavior – whether that factor is a policy official's directive or a local agency's culture – is mediated by the influence of other, oftentimes competing forces in the implementation system.

Political control

A number of scholars have taken up the question of whether political officials control the discretionary actions of street-level bureaucrats. This question has been particularly salient for scholars of the highly decentralized, federalist US system. Several studies using large, multi-state administrative datasets have found evidence that partisan political power (usually measured as the party composition of local legislatures) explains a significant portion of the variation in the performance of such front-line activities as determining eligibility for disability benefits (Keiser, 1999), granting good cause exemptions to child support cooperation requirements (Keiser and Soss, 1998), and conducting occupational health and safety inspections and imposing penalties (Scholz et al., 1991). Scholz and his colleagues reach the optimistic conclusion from this research that 'field office responsiveness to local electoral politics reintroduces a measure of local democratic control, which compensates for the failure of central institutions to provide sufficient democratic controls at the national level' (p. 84).

Because they rely on highly aggregated indicators of street-level behaviors, these studies provide, at best, indirect evidence for political control over the actions and decisions of street-level bureaucrats. Research that has been conducted closer to the front lines has yielded less optimistic conclusions about the ability of political officials to direct front-line workers. In his study of Danish agricultural inspectors, for example, Winter (2000) concludes that information asymmetries between street-level workers and their supervisors render important aspects of front-line work beyond the control of political executives. He suggests that political principals exert only 'differentiated and limited political control' of street-level bureaucracies. In particular, he concludes that actions that are visible, such as the number of inspections, are more readily subject to control by policy officials than less easily observed factors such as the strictness of inspections or harshness of penalties.

Studies of front-line workers in social welfare programs have reached similar conclusions. In a study of the delivery of information about welfare reforms in the state of California, for example, Meyers, Glaser and MacDonald (1998) conclude that the actions of front-line workers were consistent with easily observed program standards for claims processing but poorly aligned with the less easily observed and monitored program goals relating to new, employment-related activities. Lin (2000) also describes mixed outcomes in the implementation of prison educational programs. In one prison she observed a successful match of staff activities and policy goals; at others, she found that staff subverted policy goals by engaging in activities that were only weakly related to policy goals, neglected policy goals by failing to engage in a meaningful level of activities, or abandoned program implementation altogether. She argues that these outcomes are the sum of relatively difficult to observe and control 'program activities – the numerous little actions, like sleeping in class or being dressed down by correctional officers for missing class – that taken together *are* the substance of policy' (2000: 35).

Organizational control

Other researchers have focussed their attention on the role of organization in controlling front-line discretion. At the most basic level, the exercise of discretion by front-line workers has been linked to the structure of the task environment. For example, in their study of the failure of front-line staff to fully implement welfare reforms in California, Meyers and Dillon (1999) describe the 'paradox' that resulted when policy officials exhorted front-line staff to implement new employment-related policies but maintained existing performance monitoring systems and incentive structures that emphasized eligibility determination tasks.

The extent and direction of front-line discretion have also been linked to organizational and task complexity. Complexity increases the need for discretionary judgements by front-line workers along with the difficulty of overseeing and monitoring their actions. Also, political efforts to control discretion through the promulgation of detailed rules and procedures often produce the contrary result, forcing front-line workers to selectively apply rules that are too voluminous to enforce in their totality (Simon, 1983). As Maynard-Moody and Musheno (2003) observe: 'Street-level work is, ironically, rule saturated but not rule bound' (p. 8).

A number of studies have identified resource constraints as a key influence on the extent and direction of front-line discretion. Street-level bureaucrats have been observed to cope with chronically limited resources and unlimited client demands by rationing services, discriminating in the provision of services to more cooperative clients and rationalizing program objectives (Lipsky, 1980; Pesso, 1978; Winter, 2001). As Brodkin (1997) observes, 'Caseworkers, like other lower-level bureaucrats, do not do just what they want or just what they are told to want. They do what they can (p. 24).' Her studies of front-line welfare workers suggest that institutional resources and incentives establish the boundaries within which they can act. Ironically, efforts to cope with limited resource may lead to either inconsistent and particularistic treatment of similar clients, or routinized treatment of clients with dissimilar needs (Brodkin, 1995, 1997; Hagen, 1987; Pesso, 1978; Weatherley and Lipsky, 1977). The importance of resources has been noted also in studies of the regulatory effort of government inspectors (Winter, 2000), and studies that have used administrative data to study variation in such front-line activities as assigning child support benefits, granting disability benefits and exempting single parents from requirements to cooperate with child support enforcement (Keiser, 1999; Keiser and Soss, 1998).

In her study of the uneven implementation of education programs in various prisons, Lin (2000) refines the discussion of organizational factors by arguing that the implementation of new policies is likely to succeed only when the policies are congruent with the organizational context of implementing agencies. 'When policies are bent to purposes other than those that policymakers anticipated,' she observes, 'it is not because staff do not understand their work. Instead, it is precisely because they try to make sense of their work, and thus to understand their jobs as a series of related tasks all bent toward the same purpose. This naturally leads them to refer each new policy to the values that are most salient in their organization' (p. 162).

Worker ideology and professional norms

Other scholars argue that street-level bureaucrats are relatively immune to the power of both policy directives and formal organizational incentives. They point, instead, to the influence of individual interests, professional norms and the processes through which workers construct meaning in their daily work routines.

Numerous public administration scholars have described norms of public service as the most powerful incentive for bureaucratic performance. Some observers of street-level bureaucrats have reached similar conclusions. Examining survey and observational data on bureaucratic behavior, Brehm and Gates (1997) conclude that supervisors exert relatively little influence on the policy choices of bureaucrats – including those that work at the front lines of social services and policing. They conclude that bureaucrats are largely self-regulating. Bureaucrats 'work' – instead of shirking or sabotaging policy efforts – primarily because they embrace norms of public service and, secondarily, because these norms are shared and reinforced by their fellow bureaucrats. Their conclusions suggest that bureaucratic discretion depends first and foremost on the preferences of individual bureaucrats; 'fortunately for the public, the bureaucrats we have seen in our analysis prefer work and serving the public' (1997: 196).

Scholars have identified various aspects of worker ideology that may be consequential for discretionary behaviors, from their socialization into professional norms to their personal beliefs about policy instruments and targets. Winter's (2001) study of coping behaviors among front-line workers in a Danish social welfare program lends empirical support to the multidimensional

role of worker beliefs. His multivariate analyses capture significant, independent contributions from workers' beliefs about their work environment (including perceived workload and adequacy of professional support), their assessment of the potential effectiveness of the policy instruments at their disposal, and their beliefs about target populations.

In a study of front-line workers' engagement with collaborative, interagency activities, Sandfort (2000) extends the inquiry into professional norms by considering the role of the collective beliefs that front-line workers develop during the course of daily work. She describes front-line welfare workers as largely isolated from their external environment and resistant to new policy directives, and this held true whether they worked in rule-driven public agencies or at private contractors that employed outcome-based performance monitoring. She concludes that these street-level bureaucrats were guided largely by the shared knowledge and collective beliefs that staff developed to make sense of their day-to-day work. When management initiatives were consistent with these collective schemas, front-line workers found it reasonable to comply with new directives. But when initiatives appeared illegitimate or disconnected from the realities of daily work, workers' collective schemas legitimated workers' pursuit of alternative objectives and definitions of success.

In an innovative study of the 'stories' or narratives that front-line workers use to describe their work, Maynard-Moody and Musheno (2003) describe street-level bureaucrats in vocational rehabilitation, in schools and welfare offices as rarely bound by formal policy directives or regulations in their allocation of time and benefits to clients. Workers relied, instead, on their own moral judgements – judgements based on their personal knowledge of and interaction with program clients. In their own conception, workers did not see themselves as implementers of public policy, but as 'citizen agents' who acted in response to individual needs and circumstances. As a result, the authors conclude, 'street-level decisions and actions are guided less by rules, training, or procedures and more by beliefs and norms, especially beliefs and norms about what is fair' (p. 6).

NORMATIVE AND EVALUATIVE QUESTIONS ABOUT STREET-LEVEL DISCRETION

The salience of the question about control depends entirely on normative beliefs about democratic governance and policy delivery. We care about the extent to which policy officials direct and limit the discretionary actions of front-line workers to the extent that we believe it has implications for outcomes we value: democratic governance, fair and equitable treatment of citizens, or policy achievement.

Here, too, the literature is rife with contradictions. The belief that these outcomes are best achieved through a top-down, hierarchical model of control is a legacy of early public administration theory. A variety of competing perspectives suggest that the exercise of discretion by front-line workers is not only inevitable but desirable – for promoting democratic control over policy processes, tailoring policies to individual needs and increasing the effectiveness of policy efforts.

Democratic governance

The most obvious governance concern is the potential of street-level bureaucrats to undermine the goals of elected officials. Because street-level bureaucrats are neither elected nor appointed by elected officials, they are largely immune to electoral accountability. To the extent that elected officials cannot fully control their day-to-day decisions and actions, citizens have few mechanisms for assessing, much less controlling, their impact on policy. Policy goals may be displaced or distorted when front-line workers focus their energies on managing workloads, coping with job demands, or pursuing their own ideological, policy or political interests (for example, Lipsky, 1980; Sandfort, 2000; Winter, 2000). In the language of principal–agent theory, while some street-level bureaucrats may 'work' to achieve policy makers' goals, others may 'shirk' by pursuing other objectives or 'sabotage' policy by deliberately undermining the directives of their superiors (Brehm and Gates, 1997).

In other respects the exercise of discretion by street-level workers may actually contribute to democratic governance by bridging gaps between citizens and elected officials. Local program workers, inspectors and other front-line workers can serve as one more 'check and balance' on the exercise of power by legislators who are often far removed from the citizens who are the targets of their policies (for example, Ferman, 1990). The exercise of discretion by front-line workers may promote representative democracy by allowing for local influence on federal rules and bureaucracies (Scholz et al., 1991) and by creating opportunities for those most affected by policies to influence their delivery (Ferman, 1990). Vinzant and Crothers (1998) propose an even more important governance role for 'street-level leaders'

whose 'active, accountable and responsible' work at the interface of citizens, communities and the state can increase the legitimacy and responsiveness of government agencies.

Treatment of citizens

A second normative question concerns the implications of street-level discretion for the individuals who are affected by their actions. It is possible that front-line workers use their discretion to the benefit of the citizens with whom they interact. Workers who are closest to the citizen-client are arguably best able to take individual circumstances into account when allocating benefits, enforcing regulations, applying sanctions and the like. Street-level bureaucrats are also assumed by many to have professional expertise and knowledge that they can use to the advantage of clients (Vinzant and Crothers, 1998). Studies of welfare workers, rehabilitation counselors, police and teachers provide numerous examples of the exercise of 'positive discrimination' to assist those individuals that they consider most in need or most deserving of assistance (Goodsell, 1981; Maynard-Moody and Musheno, 2003).

Similar dynamics may create complicit relationships between regulators and the targets of regulation. Gormley (1995), for example, describes 'regulatory rituals' in US childcare arising from a combination of weak state regulations and regulators' unwillingness to punish poor quality providers by putting them out of business. As he describes, 'the cumulative effect of all these norms is that good and bad providers become virtually indistinguishable, judging from the regulatory agency's output. Inspectors know who has been naughty and who's been nice, that remains their little secret' (p. 56).

It is equally possible that the exercise of street-level discretion with minimal accountability gives workers undue power over the allocation of resource and enforcement of obligations. Street-level bureaucrats in gatekeeping roles may limit claimants' access to benefits to which they are entitled (Hill and Bramley, 1986). Other troubling possibilities arise when street-level bureaucrats are allowed to discriminate in their treatment of the beneficiaries or targets of public policy, introducing their own biases into the distribution of public benefits and the enforcement of penalties (Brodkin, 1997; Keiser and Soss, 1998; Lipsky, 1980). Brodkin (1997) and others argue that chronic resource limitations coupled with the difficulty of monitoring the quality of front-line services in public agencies create conditions in which workers are very likely to deliver government services that are inconsistent and of poor quality. And she notes that this is particularly likely for poor and involuntary 'clients' of the welfare state for whom 'rights are uncertain, "voice" is risky, and "exit" means forgoing basic income support' (p. 25).

Policy achievement

A third normative question concerns the implications of front-line discretion for the achievement of policy objectives. The ability of street-level workers to tailor policies to the realities of local communities and citizen-clients may improve both the responsiveness and effectiveness of public policies. When the technology for achieving policy goals is unknown or uncertain, front-line workers may also contribute to policy achievement through program experimentation, learning and adaptation (Ingram, 1990; Pressman and Wildavsky, 1973).

The influence of street-level workers also introduces considerable uncertainty into the achievement of public policies. The final achievement of policy goals depends on the cooperation of policy makers, workers and clients. The policy interests of these groups may be distinctly different (for example, Meyers et al., 2001). Even when all three share a long-term interest in the achievement of policy objectives, in the short term they usually operate with distinctly different priorities: policy makers, to satisfy stakeholder demands for visible results; front-line staff, to cope with the problems of managing work; clients, to survive and to manage the social bureaucracies (Lin, 2000; Lynn, 1993).

The attempts of policy makers, front-line workers and clients to satisfy these short-term objectives may result in achievement of policy officials' goals. Behn (1991), for example, describes successful welfare-to-work programs in which agency managers employed performance measures and incentives (such as, tracking and rewarding job placements) that aligned workers' interests with those of policy officials (to reduce welfare caseloads) and clients (to obtain stable employment). The attempts of each group to satisfy their own goals can result, however, in implementation that is inconsistent, at best, and incomplete, subverted or aborted at worst. In these cases, the achievement of policy objectives is partial at most: for example, routinization of 'individualized' educational plans (Weatherley and Lipsky, 1977); prison education programs that do not provide instruction (Lin, 2000); child-care inspections that become 'regulatory rituals' without sanctions or rewards (Gormley, 1995); or manpower training programs that 'train

students for unemployment' by directing them to overcrowded occupations or equipping them with outdated skills (Hjern and Porter, 1981) or that fail to deliver on promises to place them into meaningful training and employment (Winter, 2001).

Much of the empirical research on front-line discretion and policy achievement has relied on detailed case studies of one or a small number of programs. A handful of studies have used multivariate techniques to examine the link between the behaviors of front-line workers and policy achievement by capitalizing on cross-site variation in workers' approach and in program outcomes or outputs. Findings about the explanatory power of worker behavior from these have been mixed and suggest that results are sensitive to both model specification and to the measurement of the dependent variable.

Riccio and Hasenfeld (1996), for example, find only modest support for their hypothesis that the approach used by welfare-to-work staff influences client participation in employment-preparation activities. When they use a large sample of observations from similar welfare-to-work programs and employ multi-level estimation methods to control for individual as well as program-level characteristics, Bloom, Hill and Riccio (2001) find substantially stronger client-level effects associated with workers' description of the service approach in their office – such as the degree of personalization.

Multivariate studies also suggest that the same policy and organizational factors may have different effects on different aspects of target group behaviors. May and Winter (2000) find significant but weak effects of agency enforcement tools and inspectors' enforcement styles on perceived compliance of farmers with agricultural regulations. But May and Wood (2001) find evidence that while building inspectors' enforcement style does not influence homebuilders' compliance with building codes directly, it may do so indirectly through affecting their knowledge of code provisions and cooperation with inspectors.

STUDYING THE STREET-LEVEL BUREAUCRAT IN CONTEXT

The growing body of scholarship on street-level bureaucrats paints a contradictory portrait. In some studies these workers emerge as frustrated and powerless cogs in bureaucratic machines; in others, as self-interested bureaucrats whose coping mechanisms frustrate and distort the policy intentions of elected officials; in still others, as heroic local leaders who translate impersonal policy directives for the benefit of their clients.

Detailed case studies of the impact of street-level discretion on policy outcomes ascribe a powerful influence to front-line workers, while efforts to measure this impact using multivariate models have found relatively weak effects.

This contradictory portrait of street-level bureaucrats reflects both the lack of sufficient theory and methods for studying street-level workers and the failure to fully contextualize the evaluation of their performance. Front-line workers often wield influence that goes well beyond their official positions in implementing systems; but they are also constrained in important respects by those systems. Theoretical or empirical treatments of public policy that fail to account for the street-level adaptation of formal policy risk mis-specifying the 'policy' that was actually implemented; studies of front-line workers that fail to account for the context in which they work risk assigning to street-level workers credit (or blame) for policy outcomes over which they have little control.

Theory

Inconsistent findings about the extent of street-level discretion, and the factors that limit and direct the exercise of this discretion, underscore the need for more fully developed conceptual models that account for multiple, oftentimes competing sources of influence on front-line workers. As Winter illustrates in his chapter in this volume, implementation results from interactions among street-level bureaucrats, the organizations and interorganizational networks in which they work, and the target groups with whom they work; these interactions are themselves embedded in larger systems of policy design, political processes and socio-economic conditions.

As Hjern and Porter (1981) argued over two decades ago, given the complexity of implementation structures, neither organizational models of hierarchical control nor economic theories of individual incentives fully describe the influences on street-level workers. It is clear that hierarchical accountability structures and formal policy directives influence but only partially control the actions of front line workers. We need to develop theoretical models that explain how the power of these political tools is mediated by factors such as the congruence of new policies with existing organizational culture, as described in Lin's study of the introduction of educational programs into prisons, or with the collective schemas that staff develop to make sense of their task environments, as described by Sandfort in her study of interagency collaboration in welfare systems.

At the same time, it would be a vast oversimplification to describe street-level workers as utility maximizers whose actions are unconstrained by policy makers' preferences. Policy designs create some opportunities for action and foreclose others. The organizations in which street-level bureaucrats work function as policy instruments through resources, structures, performance standards, rewards and penalties that both reflect and enforce policy officials' goals. The professional and peer cultures into which street-level bureaucrats are socialized also embody and reinforce policy preferences. We need to develop more fully integrated theories of how these political, organizational and individual factors channel street-level discretion into specific directions through policy design, organizational features and professional norms and culture.

Methods

The complexity of the implementation context in which street-level bureaucrats are embedded also raises important issues for empirical research. Scholars have taken several approaches to the study of front-line workers. Some of the richest descriptive data has been collected by researchers who have used ethnographic, participant–observer and other qualitative methods. These case studies have provided both detailed information about the conduct and conditions of work at the front lines of public agencies and new conceptual models of the factors that turn front-line workers into street-level bureaucrats. These approaches are also extremely labor-intensive; their obvious limitations are sample size and generalizabililty. It is particularly difficult to isolate the causes and consequences of street-level activities, and to control for third variables with data drawn from one or a small number of sites.

Other analysts have turned to administrative data to construct measures of front-line activity in terms of observable units of action; examples include the number of health and safety inspections performed and penalties levied (Scholz et al., 1991) and the number of exemptions granted from child support collections (Keiser and Soss, 1998). These measures have the advantage of being available in large datasets that span multiple sites. But they provide, at best, an indirect measure of activities at the front lines. They are particularly likely to miss the critical and less easily observed discretionary decisions that give street-level bureaucrats such influence over policy. These studies have also been limited by the use of sometimes blunt proxies for explanatory variables. Establishing that the partisan makeup of local government is associated with the rigor of program eligibility decisions or imposition of penalties tells us that *something* associated with political hierarchies has shaped some aspect of front-line behaviors. But it does not tell us much about the mechanisms through which political control was exercised or about the influence on less easily quantified front-line behaviors.

A number of researchers are now moving beyond the limitations of both of these approaches, using multivariate methods to analyze more precise and robust measures of street-level performance. One promising line of research considers the contribution of political, organizational and individual factors to explaining variation in the behaviors of street-level workers. In one such study, Winter (2001) finds that the coping behaviors of workers in Danish social service programs are little affected by workers' understanding of explicit policy goals but are highly influenced by both actual and perceived program capacity and by workers' own beliefs about the effectiveness of policy instruments and about the targets of policy efforts.

In a study of the regulatory enforcement practices of Danish agricultural inspectors, Winter (2000) considers the influence of administrative capacity, politicians' policy preferences and street-level bureaucrats' own policy preferences on the regulatory enforcement practices of Danish agricultural inspectors. He finds evidence that though policy officials' preferences have no direct influence on the most highly visible aspects of inspectors' regulatory efforts (number of inspections conducted), officials have a relatively strong influence through funding administrative capacity. However, less-easily observed aspects of enforcement style (including stringency, level of coercion and formalism) are influenced not by policymakers' preferences or capacity but rather by inspectors' own policy values, beliefs about the effectiveness of various policy tools, and workload preferences. These studies nicely illustrate the value of multivariate models both for estimating the relative influence of multiple factors on street-level behaviors and for identifying the differential influence of these factors on different aspects of front-line behavior.

A second important line of research considers the extent to which variation in front-line behaviors explains variation in the achievement of desired target group behaviors. In one recent example, Bloom, Hill and Riccio (2001) model a variety of client-level outcomes in welfare-to-work programs as a function of local program model, local program capacity, consistency of beliefs between staff and managers and one aspect of front-line behavior (personalization of services), while controlling for both client-level characteristics and local economic conditions. Their use of multiple measures and multi-level estimation methods allows them to identify the substantial and positive contribution of personalized treatment to positive client outcomes.

Context

Normative debates about the influence of street-level bureaucrats on public policy have also made contradictory claims about their contribution to democratic governance and policy achievement. These contradictions reflect, in part, the failure of many observers to place their assessments in context. If street-level bureaucrats are embedded in complex implementation structures that both grant discretionary power and channel the exercise of that discretion, then it is impossible to evaluate their performance without considering the implementation context. This creates considerable difficulties for the analyst who hopes to evaluate the 'success' of implementation or the 'cooperation' of street-level bureaucrats with policy officials' goals. The same front-line decisions and actions that represent cooperation in one implementation context may reflect shirking or even sabotage in another.

Implementation contexts vary across countries and political systems. Hill (1997), for example, contrasts the acute concerns for hierarchical policy control that arise in the highly fragmented and competitive federalist system of the United States with the 'rather gentler and more consensual' debates about national and local collaboration that arise in the more cooperative political systems in Scandinavian countries. Policies are implemented in diverse political cultures and are embedded in a variety of existing political conflicts (Brodkin, 1990; Ferman, 1990).

Implementation contexts also vary with policy design. Delivering benefits to citizens, for example, raises very different implementation issues than regulating their behavior. Because policies designed to affect the behavior or circumstances of target groups must be co-produced with these targets, the implementation context also varies with characteristics of the target population. Regulating relatively powerless groups such as childcare providers, for example, is a very different job than regulating well-informed and politically powerful targets such as manufacturers.

Moreover, some social problems are simply easier to resolve than others because the technology is more certain, the desired outcomes are more realistic, or the interests and capabilities of the target population are more consistent with policy goals.

Politics and policy designs determine not only what will be done or provided to whom, but also the resources and authority that the implementing agencies will have at their disposal, the capacity of the organizational delivery system, the complexity of the interorganizational network that must cooperate to achieve policy objectives, the density and coherence of the existing policy framework, and other organizational factors. Policies based on strong political consensus, for example, or those with strong political champions, are likely to command thoughtful policy designs and appropriate resources for implementing agents. Unresolved political conflicts, on the other hand, often result in ambiguous policy directives, poorly supported programs, or policies with deeply flawed theories of action. Incremental reforms arising from political compromise often create dense systems of overlapping organizational responsibility and poorly coordinated or even contradictory policy directives.

Given the diversity of implementation contexts, resolving the normative questions of what street-level bureaucrats *should* do, and the empirical questions of what they *do* do have an often-overlooked indeterminacy. As Helen Ingram (1990) suggests, 'the challenge presented to implementers depends very much on the problems passed along to them by policy formulators' (p. 470). The problems passed on to implementing bureaucracies, and the solutions they adopt, become, in turn, the challenge presented to local agencies and their front-line staff – including the job they are asked to do, the resources they are provided to do it, the rewards for performance and the penalties for nonperformance. If the job of the street-level bureaucrat and his or her capacity to do that job depend on the implementation context, against what criteria do we judge their exercise of discretion?

Traditional public administration and implementation theory appears to provide an unambiguous answer: Are front-line workers carrying out the intentions of elected policy officials? In its most rigorous formulation, this would suggest that front-line performance be judged against the standard of policy achievement. Recognizing the limited control that many workers exercise over policy outcomes and impacts, some observers suggest that we judge fidelity in terms of street-level behaviors rather than policy results. Lin (2000), for example, suggests that implementation success be judged on the basis of staff activities that are 'plausibly related' to the achievement of policy objective. Winter, in this volume also argues for the evaluation of behavioral variables that characterize the *performance* of implementers. Whether this performance brings about desired behaviors among target groups depends on additional variables, including the validity of the underlying causal model, which may be beyond the control of street-level workers.

Fidelity to policy makers' intentions can provide a useful yardstick when the intentions of policy officials are clear, consistent and reasonable in light of agency capacity and expertise. But these implementation conditions are far from certain in democratic societies, and when policy goals or technology are less certain, this standard is incomplete at best. Consider the case, quite common in social policy, in which policy making officials achieve political consensus by adopting ambiguous or even contradictory policy directives. In this case we may judge the activities of front-line workers in terms of their successful negotiation of a clear set of directives.

In other cases, policy makers may solve political problems by passing on conceptually flawed policy directives or passing them to weak and inappropriate implementing agencies; the 'faithful' pursuit of policy makers' interests in this case might be measured by the extent to which front-line staff modify and improve on the legislative or administrative directive. When the technology required to achieve desired policy ends is uncertain or unknown, front-line cooperation might be judged by the extent and success of local program experimentation. In still other cases, front-line implementing agents may seek to faithfully pursue policy makers' interests but fail to achieve policy goals because they are not given the resources, or lack technical capacity, to achieve them. Under these conditions, success and cooperation might be viewed in terms of policy learning, with implementing staff informing decision makers about the mismatch between formal goals and actual capacity. Through a different lens, cooperation under these conditions could be defined as quiet complicity with the nondelivery of bold but essentially hollow promises that policy officials make to their constituents.

In short, in various implementation contexts, we might consider creativity, adaptation, learning, entrepreneurship, experimentation, or even complicity as the appropriate outcome against which to evaluate the exercise of discretion by street-level bureaucrats. Our failure to acknowledge this indeterminacy can lead us to assign both credit and blame for policy outcomes to street-level bureaucrats when our attention should be directed toward policy designs and other factors in the implementation context. As Hill (1997) observes about the assessment of recent decentralization efforts in Britain: 'The notion of the distinction between policy making and implementation provides a splendid vehicle for shifting the blame – there was nothing wrong with the policy but it was undermined, subverted, and so on' (p. 383).

CONCLUSION

Front-line workers in public agencies play an important but often-overlooked role in the shaping of policy delivery, output and impact. They have been overlooked by many policy officials, who are surprised by the nondelivery or distorted implementation of their policy directives. They have been overlooked by scholars of the policy process, whose interest often ends with the adoption of these directives. And they have been overlooked by program evaluators who mistakenly assume that the policy 'treatment' they are evaluating is accurately described by these directives.

The role of front-line workers is often ignored because studying these processes is exceedingly difficult. When we review the modest scholarly literature on street-level bureaucrats it is tempting to conclude that when scholars have examined these issues they have drawn fundamentally different conclusions – about the extent of discretion exercised by street-level workers and about whether this discretion is good or bad for democracy and policy achievement.

We have argued in this chapter that these apparent contradictions have more to do with limitations in theory, methods and the contextualizing of research than with more fundamental disagreements. Theory has been limited by the failure to specify the dimensions of street-level behavior that matter for governance and policy achievement, and to identify the ways in which hierarchical control (for example, through policy design and supervision) *and* individual-level incentives (such as professional norms and individual beliefs) interact to direct these behaviors. Empirical study has been limited by the difficulties of defining and observing relevant behaviors across diverse settings. Multi-site studies that capture variations in policy and organizational settings have typically employed weak proxies

for street-level behaviors, while studies employing richer measures have typically been conducted in one or a limited number of settings that do not provide variation in predictor variables.

Despite these difficulties, there is reason to feel optimistic about the future of research on street-level bureaucrats. A number of researchers are now employing multivariate methods to isolate the influence of contextual factors on street-level behaviors, policy outputs and even policy effects. Studies of service delivery and regulatory behaviors in multiple settings are identifying constructs that appear to be robust across different agency, policy and even national contexts. And more theoretically oriented scholars are improving our understanding of how street-level bureaucrats make sense of their environments – and how these 'sense making' processes inform and guide their day-to-day behaviors.

One of the most important challenges for these and other scholars will be to find commonalities across street-level workers while remaining cognizant of ways in which larger political, social and economic systems shape the context for their work. Giving more prominent attention to the activities and influence of street-level bureaucrats will enrich our understanding of implementation successes and failure. But crediting those successes or failures to street-level bureaucrats, alone, can easily distract us from an analysis of the political, policy design and organizational factors that shape their actions.

REFERENCES

Behn, R. (1991) *Leadership Counts*. Cambridge, MA: Harvard University Press.

Bloom, H.S., Hill, C.J. and Riccio, J. (2001) '*Modeling the Performance of Welfare-to-Work Programs: The Effects of Program Management and Services, Economic Environment, and Client Characteristics*'. Working paper. Manpower Demonstration and Research Corporation.

Brehm, J. and Gates, S. (1997) *Working, Shirking, and Sabotage: Bureaucratic Response to a Democratic Public*. Ann Arbor, MI: University of Michigan Press.

Brodkin, E.Z. (1990) 'Implementation as Policy Politics', in D.J. Palumbo and D.J. Calista (eds), *Implementation and the Policy Process*. New York: Greenwood Press.

Brodkin, E.Z. (1995) *The State Side of the 'Welfare Contract': Discretion and Accountability in Policy Delivery*. University of Chicago, School of Social Service Administration.

Brodkin, E.Z. (1997) 'Inside the Welfare Contract: Discretion and Accountability in State Welfare Administration', *Social Service Review*, 71 (1): 1–33.

Ferman, B. (1990) 'When Failure is Success: Implementation and Madisonian Government', in D.J. Palumbo and D.J. Calista (eds), *Implementation and the Policy Process*. New York: Greenwood Press.

Goodsell, C.T. (1981) 'Looking Once Again at Human Service Bureaucracy', *Journal of Politics*, 43: 763–78.

Gormley, W.T., Jr (1995) *Everybody's Children: Child Care as a Public Problem*. Washington, DC: Brookings Institution.

Hagen, J.L. (1987) 'Income Maintenance Workers: Technicians or Service Providers?', *Social Service Review*, (June): 261–71.

Hasenfeld, Y. (1992) 'The Nature of Human Services Organizations', in Y. Hasenfeld (ed.), *Human Services as Complex Organizations*. Newbury Park, CA: Sage pp. 3–23.

Hill, M. (1997) 'Implementation Theory: Yesterday's Issue?', *Policy and Politics*, 25 (4): 375–85.

Hill, M. and Bramley, G. (1986) *Analysing Social Policy*. New York, NY: Blackwell.

Hjern, B. and Porter, D.O. (1981) 'Implementation Structures: A New Unit of Administrative Analysis', *Organization Studies*, 2 (3): 211–27.

Ingram, H. (1990) 'Implementation: A Review and Suggested Framework', in L. Lynn and A. Wildavsky (eds), *Public Administration: the State of the Discipline*. Chatham, NJ: Chatham House. pp. 462–80.

Keiser, L.R. (1999) 'State Bureaucratic Discretion and the Administration of Social Welfare Programs: The Case of Social Security Disability', *Journal of Public Administration Research and Theory*, 9 (1): 87–106.

Keiser, L.R. and Soss, J. (1998) 'With Good Cause: Bureaucratic Discretion and the Politics of Child Support Enforcement', *American Journal of Political Science*, 42 (4): 1133–56.

Lin, A.C. (2000) *Reform in the Making: The Implementation of Social Policy in Prison*. Princeton, NJ: Princeton University Press.

Lipsky, M. (1980) *Street Level Bureaucracy: Dilemmas of the Individual in Public Services*. New York: Russell Sage Foundation.

Lynn, L.E., Jr (1993) 'Policy Achievement as a Collective Good: A Strategic Perspective on Managing Social Programs', in B. Bozeman (ed.), *Public Management: The State of the Art*. San Francisco: Jossey–Bass. pp. 108–33.

May, P.J. and Winter, S. (2000) 'Reconsidering Styles of Regulatory Enforcement: Patterns in Danish Agro-Environmental Inspection', *Law and Policy*, 22 (2): 143–73.

May, P.J. and Wood, R. (2001) 'Regulating Compliance in Inspector Behavior'. Paper prepared for the Annual Research Meeting of the Association for Public Policy Analysis and Management, Washington, DC (1–3, November, 2001).

Maynard-Moody, S. and Musheno, M. (2003) *Cops, Teachers, Counselors: Narratives of Street-Level Judgment*. Ann Arbor, MI: University of Michigan Press.

Meyers, M. and Dillon, N. (1999) 'Institutional Paradoxes: Why Welfare Workers Can't Reform Welfare', in G. Frederickson and J. Johnston (eds), *Public Administration as Reform and Innovation*. Tuscaloosa, University of Alabama Press.

Meyers, M.K., Glaser, B. and MacDonald, K. (1998) 'On the Front Lines of Welfare Delivery: Are Workers Implementing Policy Reforms?', *Journal of Policy Analysis and Management*, 17 (1): 1–22.

Meyers, M.K., Riccucci, N.M. and Lurie, I. (2001) 'Achieving Goal Congruence in Complex Environments: The Case of Welfare Reform', *Journal of Public Administration Research and Theory*, 11 (2): 165–202.

Pesso, T. (1978) 'Local Welfare Offices: Managing the Intake Process', *Public Policy*, 26 (2): 305–30.

Pressman, J.L. and Wildavsky, A. (1973) *Implementation*. Berkeley, CA: University of California Press.

Riccio, J. and Hasenfeld, Y. (1996) 'Enforcing a Participation Mandate in a Welfare-to-Work Program', *Social Service Review*, 70 (4): 516–42.

Sandfort, J.R. (2000) 'Moving Beyond Discretion and Outcomes: Examining Public Management from the Front Lines of the Welfare System', *Journal of Public Administration Research and Theory*, 10 (4): 729–56.

Scholz, J.T., Twombly, J. and Headrick, B. (1991) 'Street-Level Political Controls Over Federal Bureaucracy', *American Political Science Review*, 85 (3): 829–50.

Simon, W.H. (1983) 'Legality, Bureaucracy, and Class in the Welfare System', *Yale Law Journal*, 92: 1198–250.

Vinzant, J.C. and Crothers, L. (1998) *Street-Level Leadership: Discretion and Legitimacy in Front-Line Public Service*. Washington, DC: Georgetown University Press.

Weatherley, R. and Lipsky, M. (1977) 'Street-Level Bureaucrats and Institutional Innovation', *Harvard Educational Review*, 47 (2): 171–97.

Winter, S. (2000) 'Information Asymmetry and Political Control of Street-Level Bureaucrats: Danish Agro-Environmental Regulation'. Paper prepared for the Annual Research Meeting of the Association for Public Policy Analysis and Management, Seattle, WA (2–4 November, 2000).

Winter, S.C. (2001) 'Reconsidering Street-Level Bureaucracy Theory: From Identifying to Explaining Coping Behavior'. Paper for the Annual Meeting of the Association of Policy Analysis and Management held in Washington DC (1–3 November, 2001). Danish National Institute of Social Research.

LAW AND ADMINISTRATION

Introduction

Gavin Drewry

Law lies at the heart of both the theory and the practice of public administration. Max Weber (himself a lawyer by his early training, as Jacques Ziller reminds us in Chapter 20) associated the pervasiveness of his bureaucratic model of organization in advanced societies with the rational-legal authority that underpins such societies. Woodrow Wilson's famous essay on 'The Study of Administration' first published in 1887 propounded a working definition of public administration as 'detailed and systematic execution of public law'.[1] Even if this is perhaps a bit of an oversimplification, it is certainly the case that knowledge of the legal framework of administrative systems is crucial to an understanding of the nature and rationale of those systems.

Public law is often seen as being necessarily different from private law if only because states are states and governments have to govern. Public functions and obligations are in many ways intrinsically different from private ones – hence the fact that governments are often subject to the jurisdiction of constitutional courts; and state bureaucracies are usually subject to regimes of administrative law, of which there are numerous variations – some of them discussed in the chapters that follow – applied in many cases by specialized administrative courts and tribunals (complemented in many countries by ombudsman systems). And, increasingly, globalization has resulted in a growth in the impact of *international* law, which has both public and private aspects, for example in the domain of human rights. European readers will not need to be reminded of the pervasive significance of European Union Law and of the European Convention on Human Rights.

In one aspect, public law can be seen in this context as having a *restraining* effect – setting the boundaries of what government can legally do. The concept of constitutionalism – based upon a perception that 'a State powerful enough to maintain order may also be strong enough to suppress liberty', and that the machinery of government needs to be equipped 'with brakes as well as a motor'[2] – has been the source of much legal and political science discourse, particularly in the United States. Variants on the idea of a 'rule of law' are also relevant to this perception. Also, dispute resolution and redress of citizens' grievances are crucial aspects of judicial review.

But laws and constitutions also have a positive part to play in enabling governments to govern and as providing a *positive* framework for a good public service. In discussing the modern development of administrative law in the United Kingdom, Harlow and Rawlings have used the apt metaphor of the traffic signal – showing how a Diceyan 'red light' belief that rampant governments with collectivist ambitions need to be subjected to the restraints of the ordinary law gave way to a 'green light' perception that law should facilitate and not impede the necessary development and operation of public services; followed then by an inevitable 'forever amber' signal that recognizes law's dual function in this context.[3]

But the distinction between public and private law can never be completely watertight. Public bodies and state functionaries may, in the course of exercising public functions, be liable to private law actions in contract or tort (and/or to criminal prosecutions, for example, for corruption). The line between public and private conduct may be difficult to draw, and the distinctions have become much more problematical as variants of New Public Management have created new contractual and quasi-contractual modes of delivery of public services and hybrid relationships between public and private bodies. The boundary between public and private sector institutions and functions – and hence between public and private law – has become increasingly blurred. A leading treatise on UK judicial review summarizes the most important aspects of recent public service reform and concludes that:

> The legal relationships that arise out of these new forms of service provision are neither wholly 'public' nor 'private'. They involve a complex mixture of regulatory activity on the traditional 'command and control' model, intertwined with regulation based upon contractual-type arrangements between the direct provider of services and the ultimate purchaser, consumer or customer.[4]

In countries that have undergone variants of New Public Management reform, patterns of judicial review (and other mechanisms of accountability) have reflected a continuing struggle to keep abreast of the changing machinery of state functions and services, and to establish a workable line of demarcation between public law *per se* and private law (including the law of contract and tort) as it applies in the context of public functions and state power.

The three chapters that follow explore, from different standpoints, the nature and significance of the interactions between legal systems and public administration. In Chapter 20, Jacques Ziller looks at the development and influence of the two main continental European traditions of public law – the French *principe de légalité* and the Prussian/German *Rechtsstaat*. Both traditions (allied, in the case of post-revolutionary France, with the development of the Napoleonic system of administrative law, and in post-Nazi Germany with a growing concern about constitutional protection of human rights) have been enormously influential across most of Western Europe. Although there have been very big variations in the influence of the two models in different European countries – he dismisses the misleading perception of 'a homogeneous system of law relating to continental European public administration' – both models have resulted in continental public administration systems that are underpinned extensively by law. Ziller also shows that the legal arrangements of many European countries share more characteristics of the common law systems of the UK and/or of the United States than is commonly supposed.

Anglo-American public law traditions are explored by Paul Craig in Chapter 21. The author refutes the claim that administrative law is a recent development in the Anglo-American tradition: it has a long history, rooted in the common law and the development and adaptation of legal remedies by the courts. But although administrative law in the UK and the United States has common roots, there are major divergences, arising substantially from the fact that one country has a 'written' constitution and an Administrative Procedure Act, while the other has neither; however, the UK has gone down interesting new pathways as a result of its membership of the European Union, and the side-door introduction of European administrative law jurisprudence through authoritative judgments handed down by the European Court of Justice. The chapter discusses, with reference to both countries, the enforcement of 'process rights', the extent of a duty to consult in administrative rule-making and the extent to which courts have refrained (or not) from substituting their own judgment for that of policy makers and administrators.

Finally, in Chapter 22, David Feldman looks more generally at the extent to which law can and should constrain public administration. He examines the functions and characteristics of legal norms in relation to other normative systems, and the part they play in underpinning the legitimacy of democratic systems based on the rule of law. The author discusses the factors that lead administrators themselves to internalize legal norms, and the impact of legal rules and judicial review on the administrative process: 'it would be unreasonable', he concludes, 'to expect law, and judicial review in particular, to provide anything approaching a coherent guide to public administration'. But that conclusion does not mean that either the student or the practitioner of public administration can afford to ignore them. The chapters in this section should make that abundantly clear.

NOTES AND REFERENCES

1   Woodrow Wilson, 'The Study of Administration', *Political Science Quarterly*, 2 (1887), pp. 197–222.
2   William G. Andrews, *Constitutions and Constitutionalism*, 3rd edn (Princeton, NJ: Van Nostrand, 1968), p. 9. See also D. Greenberg et al. (eds), *Constitutionalism and Democracy: Transitions in the Contemporary World* (New York: Oxford University Press, 1993).
3   Carol Harlow and Richard Rawlings, *Law and Administration*, 2nd edn (London: Butterworths, 1997), Chs 2, 3 and 4.
4   Lord Woolf and Jeffrey Jowell, *Judicial Review of Administrative Action*, 5th edn (London: Sweet and Maxwell, 1995), p. 165.

20

The Continental System of Administrative Legality

Jacques Ziller

In continental Europe, until the last quarter of the twentieth century public administration studies were developed in most countries by scholars who had received their main education in law, and by legal practitioners of public administration.[1] For the large part, public administration studies have been primarily a by-product of administrative law. Even Max Weber,[2] the founder of sociology of administration, had been educated as a lawyer before becoming interested in economics and in sociology. This tradition contributes a great deal to a somewhat misleading perception of a homogeneous system of law relating to continental European public administration – as opposed to an Anglo-American system that would derive its features from *common law* heritage. A closer look at different countries would reveal a lot of common features between a number of European continental countries and the United States, other similarities between some European continental countries and the United Kingdom, and a lot of important differences between one European continental country and another. The purpose of this chapter is to describe and explain the role of law in the structure and functioning of public administrations across the Western part of continental Europe, taking into account the weight of two historically dominant models: the French *principe de légalité* and the German *Rechtsstaat* idea.

THE GERMAN AND FRENCH MODELS

The two main models of contemporary European continental public administration were developed in Prussia during the eighteenth century and in France at the turn of the nineteenth century, mainly during the time of Napoleon.[3] Whereas the Prussian model had an early influence on the Austrian administration, the attraction of the Napoleonic model has also been important for both countries, as well as for the Netherlands – and thus consequently for Belgium and Luxembourg – Italy and Spain. Only Sweden and Switzerland have kept an administrative system with structures very different from the rest of Western Europe, but with a strong role of law, as on the rest of the Continent.[4] As far as the role of law is concerned, the Prussian tradition of the *Rechtsstaat* and the French tradition of the *principe de légalité* both explain the importance of law for public administration.

The idea of the *Rechtsstaat* – literally 'the legal state', but usually translated in Europe by 'Rule of law' – was developed mainly during the nineteenth century by German writers,[5] as opposed to the *Poliziestaat* – police state. The latter corresponded to autocratic absolute monarchy. The *Rechtsstaat* idea has its roots in the *Siècle des Lumières* philosophy that influenced the Prussian enlightened despotism throughout the eighteenth century. In outline, the main feature of the *Rechtsstaat* idea is that a sovereign has to be bound by the rules they have made and which have to be stable, known by their subjects and applied in a fair manner to all of them by politically neutral judges and administrators. Until the twentieth century the idea of *Rechtsstaat* was centred on legal formalism as a safeguard for a fair social order and was closely linked with the existence of a bureaucratic apparatus as the main guarantee of the functioning of the system. It was therefore quite appealing to the European monarchies that had not yet been transformed into parliamentary regimes, mainly the German countries and, during its most enlightened periods, the Austro-Hungarian Empire. It also influenced Nordic countries and to a limited extent the Netherlands. The Nazi period and the perversion of German legal traditions that it fostered – with the help of renowned lawyers and academics like Carl Schmitt[6] – led to a deep transformation of the *Rechtsstaat* idea after the Second World War. Beyond legal formalism, which remains important in the perspective of procedural guarantees to the citizen, it now incorporates a very solid constitutional protection of human rights and non-discrimination, and above all the dignity of human beings. It relies on a sophisticated system of judicial protection centred upon a constitutional court – the model of which had already been developed in Austria in 1920 under the influence of Hans Kelsen.[7] This revived concept of the *Rechtsstaat* has had a growing influence in Europe, having met with developments of much the same kind in Italy as a reaction to the fascist period. German constitutional law has become a major source of inspiration in the transition to democracy in Europe, first for former autocratic regimes – Greece and Portugal after 1974 and Spain after 1976 – then for former communist countries after 1989.

The *principe de légalité* – principle of legality – is also rooted in the *Siècle des Lumières* philosophy. But whereas Voltaire's[8] sceptical philosophy of enlightenment had influenced the King of Prussia, Frederic the Great, it was mainly Rousseau's[9] theory of democracy which was adopted and developed by the political personnel of the French Revolution of 1789. Montesquieu's theory of the separation of powers[10] took more time to become part of French tradition: it needed the establishment of a parliamentary regime under the monarchy in 1816–20 and its acceptance by democrats as a feature of the republican regime in the last quarter of the nineteenth century. The main idea of the *principe de légalité* is that of *la Loi expression de la volonté générale* to put it into Rousseau's words: [statute] law as an expression of the general will. According to this idea linked to the concept of social contract, citizens are only to obey rules that they have accepted through decisions of their representatives. Whereas the idea of *Rechtsstaat* developed independently, and preceded that of democracy in German institutions throughout the nineteenth century, the *principe de légalité* has always been linked to the idea of representative democracy, even if reduced to mere formalism during the autocratic regimes of Napoleon Bonaparte (1799–1814) and Napoleon III (1852–70). From 1848 onwards it became also directly and permanently linked to the idea of universal suffrage. The *principe de légalité*, the principle of universal suffrage and the Declaration of Human Rights of 1789 were the three main concepts by which French revolutionary ideas influenced European liberal thinking; at the same time, the Napoleonic system of administration was even more influential as it impressed on one side liberals because of its links with the French Revolution, but also on the other side leaders of autocratic monarchies because of its efficiency.[11] In France the legal consequences of the *principe de légalité* have been developed mainly by the case law of the *Conseil d'Etat* (State Council). This institution was set up in 1799 in order to be the government's legal council, and it very soon became the highest appellate body in litigation between citizens and government – that is, public administration – as government did not depart from its advice. In 1872 it became an independent court making decisions in the name of the people. As early as the middle of the nineteenth century the case law of the *Conseil d'Etat* was the first developed body of modern administrative law. This body of law therefore has been a source of inspiration for the development of administrative law in most Western European countries and the model of the *Conseil d'Etat* has been used in a – smaller – number of countries for the establishment of supreme administrative courts.[12]

These differences in principle and origins account for a great deal in explaining differences from one European country to the other: the role of endogenous ideas and that of French and German influence differ in time and space. But the *Rechtsstaat* and the *principe de légalité* concepts have a number of common features – common also to some extent to the United States of America. These are mainly linked to the system of statute law based upon a written constitution. Nevertheless, there are important differences in the systems of courts across continental Europe, that account for the diversity to be found, in administrative law as a set of principles, as well as in statute law and in judge-made law. A good understanding of those common features and differences helps in gaining a better overview of the meaning and relevance of the Weberian model of public administration[13] at the turn of the twentieth century as well as a hundred years later.

THE CLOSE LINKS BETWEEN PUBLIC ADMINISTRATION AND STATUTE LAW

The written constitutions of European continental countries include a set of principles applying to public administration. Sometimes they are only vaguely spelt out – clear nevertheless due to jurisprudence and interpretation: this is the case with the more ancient constitutions like that of Belgium (1832), but is also true of the French constitution of 1958, in the drafting of which lawyers from the *Conseil d'Etat* had a dominant role. In most cases these principles are more precise. This is mainly the case for constitutions drafted after accession of or return to democracy – Austria 1920, Italy 1947, Germany 1945, Greece 1975, Portugal 1976, Spain 1978, a number of former communist countries in the 1990s – or in a move to rationalization and codification – the most recent examples being Switzerland in 1999[14] and Finland in 2000.[15]

According to these principles, the role of public administration is to apply the law – that is, a set of rather abstract general principles that have been written into statute law by the legislature (parliament) – to individual cases. It should be remembered that throughout Europe, including the British Isles, little distinction was made until the seventeenth or eighteenth century between administration and justice as a function, and that applied equally to staffing. The Swedish system of independent administrative agencies has long been an illustration of this lack of differentiation in functions.[16] The same holds true for the Prussian system of career civil service. The separation of judicial and administrative functions had a dominant role in the development of a modern administration, especially in the case of Spain during the sixteenth and France during the seventeenth centuries.

The continental European legal tradition is based partly upon Roman law, where a systematic construction of the law and codification had been very developed. It is also based upon a tradition of systematization of law in the framework of universities (Bologna, Montpellier etc.). From the seventeenth century onwards national codification developed in several countries. The main purpose had initially been to unify the law of the land (Denmark 1687, Sweden 1734, Prussia 1794), but codification also became a tool for social modernization, especially in the case of the French Napoleonic codes of 1804 (*Code civil*) and 1810 (*Code pénal*), and later the German civil code of 1901 (*Bürgerliches Gesetzbuch – BGB*). This has not only led to an important quantity of written statute law, a feature common to all industrialized countries, but also to a specific way of drafting statute law, which used to differentiate it from that of 'common law' countries.

According to this tradition there is a developed and systematized hierarchy of written law. At the top, the constitution, subject to specific rules for amendment – different from those applying to ordinary statute law – is supposed to set up the most general and structural principles of the country's political institutions and societal system. Then acts of parliament, the only ones which are called 'Laws' (*Lois, Gesetze, Legge, Leyes etc.*), are supposed to set up general principles by which the sovereign (the king or people's representatives) regulates society. According to a drafting tradition that is best illustrated by the French and German civil codes, statute law was thus not supposed to go into details, but only to set up principles and rules according to defined categories. This is why acts of parliament have usually to be complemented by more detailed general regulations (*règlements, Verordnungen*) that are adopted by the executive, and which differ from acts of parliament by their much more detailed character, providing for a set of specific solutions for predetermined circumstances. Incidentally, the best of this drafting tradition has been lost due to the abuse of professional jargon by bureaucracies and the interference of badly trained advisers. In order to apply the law as set up in acts of parliament and regulations to specific real-life cases, legally binding administrative decisions (*actes administratifs, Verwaltungsakte*) of the relevant members of the executive are necessary. Most of these administrative decisions are delegated to civil servants on a permanent basis. This hierarchy of sources of legal instruments defines the rules of legality: individual decisions, which have to be taken by the executive in order to apply the law, have to be consistent with general regulations, even if the same authority has the power to adopt both regulations and individual decisions. General regulations have to be consistent with acts of parliament, which in turn have to be consistent with the constitution.

According to both the *Rechtsstaat* tradition and the *principe de légalité*, a public authority can only take a decision with legally binding consequences if it has been duly authorized to do so by law. It has to be formally empowered by the constitution or by statute law, and there are very strict rules as to the conditions and limits to delegating decision making power, for general regulations as well as for individual decisions. The key concept of the continental European public law tradition is that of competency (*compétence, Zuständigkeit*) – meaning empowerment. A most decisions to be taken in order to implement public policies have legally binding consequences – even if based on a contractual agreement between public administration and a private party – policy making and implementation need statute law as a tool. According to the principle of legality any of these decisions is also subject to judicial review by independent courts, who will not only check whether the person who took the decision had legal authority to do so – if it did not act *ultra vires* in the Anglo-American wording – but also whether he or she has duly interpreted and applied the general rules set up by parliament and the executive. As will be elaborated below, judicial review of administrative action developed much earlier in continental Europe – and especially in France – than on the other side of the English Channel, thus greatly reducing the scope of actions and decisions of public administration which fall outside of law. This has important consequences on the formal structure of public administration and on policy making, as well as on working habits, education and training of civil servants, which are common to many continental European countries, although with some important differences in culture.

The general structures of government at central as well as at local level have to be set down in detailed legally binding instruments; the same applies not only to autonomous public bodies but also to the internal structures of ministerial departments and departmental agencies. Whereas in all countries only parliament has the power to set up the framework for local government structures, there are important differences from one country to another with regard to the competencies allocated by the constitution to different branches of government when it comes to setting up the structures of central government. In a country like Italy this is a competence of the legislature – normally of parliament or exceptionally of the cabinet acting upon powers of delegated legislation under strict parliamentary control. Therefore the Italian government needs to go through parliamentary procedure in order to create or suppress a ministerial department and also in order to change the broad structures of its internal organization; a ministerial department can also be suppressed by a referendum based on a people's initiative, as happened in 1993. The Italian system is probably the most rigid in Western Europe but it is representative of the most generalized system (to be found in countries as different as Austria, Germany, Portugal, Spain or Sweden), even if in most countries the degree of detail as to what has to be decided by parliament is less developed. In France, on the contrary, the internal organization of state administration lies in the sole power of the cabinet – that of local government being in the power of parliament; the same applies to as great extent to Belgium and the Netherlands. It has some connection with the British system

of royal prerogative. In both cases, whether the basis is laid down in acts of parliament or in government regulations, important procedural rules have to be followed for structural change, a feature that does not facilitate rapid reform in public management. These procedural rules go far beyond parliamentary procedure, as in most countries a number of opinions of consultative bodies have to be sought before government may adopt these types of regulations.

A further aspect of administrative action where law plays an important role is that of contractual relationships. A number of European continental countries, and specially France and Germany, developed at quite an early stage a specific law of public procurements, based on the application of the principle of equality to the tendering procedure. For this reason, public administration has been submitted to quite rigid and explicit procedural rules for contract management. While in some countries and in a number of cases this merely means an increase in bureaucracy, the purpose of those rules – often achieved in practice – has been to guarantee competition in a time where anti-trust law was only developed in the United States, and hardly in Europe. France furthermore – imitated by a number of other continental countries – developed a quite sophisticated law for contracting out public service activities (*concession de service public*) as early as the middle of the nineteenth century.

STATUTE LAW IN THE STRUCTURE AND FUNCTIONING OF THE CIVIL SERVICE

The same kind of reasons account for the existence of statutes or regulations setting up the career patterns and working conditions of civil servants. In most European continental countries – as well as in Ireland – parliament has acquired during the twentieth century regulatory power in a field that was traditionally in the competence of the executive. Only the Netherlands and Belgium have kept the former system (derived from the royal prerogative) as far as state civil servants are concerned. In all other continental countries, this competence has been transferred to parliament, either through a deliberate mention in the constitution or simply by the fact that parliament decided to legislate on the matter of civil service regulation.

The main reason for this change was the introduction or consolidation of a merit system for the management of civil servants. A number of countries have gone a step further and adopted a general regulation applying to all state civil servants – sometimes also to local government agents. The first country to adopt a general regulation of that kind was Spain in 1852, followed by Luxembourg in 1872 and Denmark in 1899. Italy followed in 1908, the Netherlands in 1929–31 and Belgium in 1937. Significantly, Germany adopted a first general regulation of this type in 1937 and France 1941: in both cases it was the work of an autocratic nationalistic government and one of the purposes of the general regulation was to exclude Jews and women from the civil service. It was only after the Second World War that for those two countries the concept of a general regulation of the civil service by statute law became linked to the idea of protecting democratic values for all state civil servants.

Non-specialists tend to confuse the legal nature of this kind of regulations – be they acts of parliament or government regulations – and their content. For about a century there have been two dominating different concepts of the content of civil service regulation in continental Europe. The first is based on the monarchic tradition, according to which state employees need a specific status due to the fact that they are the servants of the sovereign, to whom they owe a special fidelity and who in turn gives them a special protection; it is best illustrated by Germany. Thus civil servants are a specific category of state employees, empowered with very specific duties linked to the exercise of public authority. They are submitted to rules and employment conditions, which are very different from common labour law. In Germany about 40 per cent of government employees (federal, regional and local) have this position of a civil servant (*Beamter*) whereas the others are submitted to 'ordinary' law, that is, civil and labour law. This kind of system is also at the basis of civil service regulation in Austria, Denmark or Luxembourg.

The second tradition is linked to the idea of equal access of all citizens to state employment and equal conditions of employment for all government employees. It is best illustrated by France, and followed by a majority of European continental countries as different as Belgium, the Netherlands, Sweden, or Spain. This implies specific rules for recruitment and career, usually different from those of labour law – but not always, as the case of the Netherlands demonstrates, but in most other respects with variations in time and space, the content of civil service regulations need not be very different from that of labour law. In most countries labour law has come closer and closer to civil service law. The

fact that government employees enjoy tenure – but this is no longer the case in Sweden nor in Italy since a few years ago – should be put in relation to the labour law provisions which tend to protect employees with a contract without time limitation. In practice, however, almost all civil servants tend to enjoy lifetime appointments due to the combination of two factors: government activities are not linked to market performance and thus government jobs tend to be much more stable than private sector positions; and in most countries unions are quite powerful in public service and have the safeguard of tenured positions as one of their major goals.

At the end of the twentieth century, a tendency to suppress differences between civil service law and labour law appeared in a number of countries, according to two different formal schemes.[17] The most common trend, followed by Sweden and Finland first, then by the Netherlands, has been to transform the content of civil service regulations – making them similar to labour law – while formally keeping a specific statutory instrument for government employees. A much more radical change – from a formal point of view – has been made in Italy from 1992 onwards, where the general statute on government employees has been abolished, and where all – state as well as local government – employees are now employed under civil and labour law provisions. Along the same lines, Denmark has been gradually diminishing the part of state employees governed by a specific statute since the 1960s. In all those cases, the change took place at a time where employees in the private sector enjoyed a very high degree of protection as long as their company did not go bankrupt or restructure. A key explanatory factor for the change is also that it allowed a much more important role for trade unions and social dialogue in public administration.

As far as policy making is concerned, a consequence of the principles discussed above is that acts of parliament and regulations are also required even in cases where they have no binding effects on private parties, in order to allocate responsibilities as clearly as possible. Therefore, the idea that all civil servants with decision making powers should have some kind of legal training is common to all continental European countries; here again there are big differences in practice. The German system remains based on the Prussian model where civil servants were considered as part of the legal profession and thus received the same university education as judges and advocates. In most other European countries, the number of civil servants having a law degree has been quite high until the last decades of the twentieth century, but this does not mean that they had received a real professional legal training. Typically a large number of French civil servants who have been educated in the National School of Administration (*Ecole nationale d'administration – ENA*) have never studied civil or criminal law and even less civil or criminal procedure, whereas their German counterparts have. In the case of France it should be added that traditionally about half of the top administrative jobs are occupied by engineers who have been trained first in the *Ecole polytechnique* – created in 1794 and put in charge of training army engineers by Napoleon – than in more specialized *Grandes écoles* like the schools for *Ponts et chaussées* (bridges and roads), *Eaux et forêts* (waters and forests) or the mines school. This goes together with the monopoly of the *Conseil d'Etat* as legal adviser of the national government and ministerial departments, as opposed to the German system where almost all top civil servants are traditionally trained as lawyers, and where each section of a ministerial department has legal expertise.

ADMINISTRATIVE LAW IN THE ACCOUNTABILITY SYSTEM OF PUBLIC ADMINISTRATION[18]

Under the influence of Dicey,[19] British scholars and judges long believed that the main purpose of the French system of *droit administratif* was to protect the executive against the public. On the Continent, on the contrary, the French system of judicial review of public administration which developed during the nineteenth century has had a very important influence in the setting up of systems enabling independent scrutiny of the activity of the executive and especially public administration.

A key feature of the continental systems of administrative law lies in the sophisticated control by independent courts of the exercise of administrative discretion. This goes far beyond reviewing whether public authorities do indeed have under statute law the powers they claim to exercise – which would correspond to the review of *ultra vires* in common law systems. Through review of legality (*contrôle de légalité – Rechtsmässigkeitskontrolle*) courts have the power to check how public authorities exercise these powers, whether they have chosen the most appropriate means, whether the consequences of an administrative decision do not go beyond what was strictly necessary to achieve the goals set up

by legislation (*principle of proportionality*) and whether general principles such as equal treatment and the protection of human rights and civil liberties have been respected by public administration. As a sanction of this scrutiny the courts have the power to declare an administrative decision to be void and – to an extent that varies from country to country – to impose the content of a decision on the administration. This system was developed in France[20] during the nineteenth century under the very misleading title of *recours pour excès de pouvoir* (remedy for abuse of power – initially corresponding to the common law concept of *ultra vires*), and was then taken up with nationally specific features, usually under the title of 'remedy for review of legality', as in European Community law, or under a number of more specific remedies (*Rechtswege*), like in German law.[21]

A majority of continental European countries as different as Sweden, Italy, Germany, Belgium, Greece, France or Portugal have established a specific system of administrative courts – separate from the so-called *ordinary* courts that deal with civil and criminal litigation. The exception is Denmark, which always had only a single system of courts in charge of administrative as well as civil or criminal litigation. Usually this system of administrative courts is more closely linked to the activities of public administration, although their judges are as independent as so-called *ordinary* judges are. This allows for a specialization of administrative judges that enables them to review much more deeply the activities they are familiar with, and thus allows both for a better protection of citizens against the administration and a better understanding of the needs of policy implementation. Furthermore, in a number of countries, access of plaintiffs to administrative courts is easier and cheaper than to ordinary courts. However, this system is sometimes under suspicion for being too close to public administration and it has the major inconvenience of generating quite complex and delicate legal debates about the boundary between ordinary and administrative courts' jurisdiction; in a number of cases this leads to considerable delays in legal procedures. These reasons explain why Italy and Greece suppressed their administrative court system in the second half of the nineteenth century, before re-installing them at the turn of the century. In the middle of the twentieth century, Spain – to be joined by the Netherlands at the end of the century – chose a system of specialized chambers within a unified system of courts, thus hoping to combine the advantages of both systems.

The scope of judicial protection against unlawful or damaging decisions of public administration is not limited to declaring those decisions void. Courts can also allocate damages to be paid by the state budget or local budgets. In a majority of European countries these damages are allocated by ordinary courts applying general common principles of tort law as stated in the civil code, or principles and mechanisms set up by special legislation for specific public activities. In France, damages have been allocated by administrative courts since 1872 – even since 1806 as far as public works damages are concerned. The French system has allowed for the development of a number of principles unknown to civil tort law, like damages for breach of equality of treatment or damages for the consequences of statutory law – even sometimes for the consequences of acts of parliament. The main feature of these systems of damages[22] is that they are based upon the responsibility of public institutions as organizations, which is easier to establish and easier to finance than that of individual officials. Their employers can usually in turn sue the latter on a disciplinary basis in order to compensate for the damages paid by the institution if the wrongful activity of a specific official was at the basis of the claim.

In France, and later on in most other countries that adopted such a system of administrative law, the administrative courts system has led to building a set of principles to be followed in administrative decision making, or due process in administrative procedure – most of them resting upon judge-made case law. Letting this development happen on the sole basis of judge-made case law has nevertheless two major disadvantages: the principles are not easily known to the general public and they develop somewhat at random, due to the succession of proceedings which are started against public administration. Therefore a number of countries codified their administrative decision making procedure during the last quarter of the twentieth century. The German federal legislation of 1976 and the *Länder* legislation of the following years have long been considered as the most comprehensive system of codification of administrative procedure, providing much better protection of individuals against harmful actions or errors. Most continental countries adopted such general legislation during the last two decades of the twentieth century, sometimes for only some aspects of administrative procedure – Italy, France – sometimes on a very comprehensive basis – the Netherlands, the Nordic countries, Spain and Portugal. Quite interestingly, the general legislation on administrative procedure of both Sweden and Denmark has been developed mainly upon recommendations of their national ombudsmen, which were based on their own jurisprudence on cases of maladministration. This shows that the need for written legal principles in regulating public administration is deeply rooted in the European continental tradition, even in countries reputed for their pragmatism and their specific administrative institutions.

European Union law has been deeply influenced by the continental systems of judicial review of administrative action, mainly the French and German system, which accounts for most of the relevant provisions in the EC treaty. In turn, the European Court of Justice has started to set up a body of principles of European administrative law during the past fifteen years which apply not only to European institutions but also to national administrations whenever they implement European law.[23] These principles mainly are geared to a well-functioning and accessible system of judicial remedies against administrative action and are fostering some kind of harmonization of judicial review of administrative action in all European Union member states, the British Isles included. Some elements of this case law of the European Court of Justice are the basis of the right to good administration, which is guaranteed by article 41 of the European Union Charter of Fundamental Rights adopted in the year 2000.

LEGALITY AND PUBLIC MANAGEMENT REFORM

In the last quarter of the twentieth century the role of law in public administration came under attack as fostering bureaucracy, especially in the move to New Public Management. The focus on input and procedures supposedly characteristic of the Weberian model of public administration – as opposed to the managerial focus on output and achievement – is very often attributed to law itself by critics of bureaucracy as well as by public managers themselves. A comparative study of the role of law in public administration shows that these types of criticism rest upon a double misunderstanding of what law is today and what Max Weber meant when analysing the systems of public authority a century ago.[24]

Whereas public administration and public management studies easily identify perverse consequences of a too rigid application of the principle of legality, too little attention has probably been paid to what is inherent in the law applying to public administration, and to what is due to the well-intentioned zeal of badly trained administrators who do not differentiate law and detailed written regulation. This might be one of the reasons why there has been a trend in most European countries to increase the number of written regulations that go very deep into details. Too many civil servants whose main task is to write down regulations or general non-binding directives on how to apply the law have not received an appropriate training in drafting statutory law according to the best tradition of continental codification. Even more civil servants totally underestimate their own margins of manoeuvre in those cases where statute law empowers them with discretionary powers, that is, the possibility to adapt the application of legal principles to the circumstances of the case. Typically, the French administrative courts have often been led to declare void an administrative decision because its author did not exercise his or her discretionary power on the sole merits of a given case, but blindly applied general directives issued by ministerial departments.

This inflation of written regulation is being heavily criticized by politicians and also by a number of public institutions in most continental European countries. However, the same politicians who criticize it and recommend more deregulation very often contribute to this inflation by the mere fact that they want to present a good record of policy making to their constituents: in a number of continental European countries this is manifested through attaching one's name to a specific statute. This is why a number of public institutions like the French *Conseil d'Etat* insist on codification, simplification and better drafting of written law rather than on deregulation, a very ambiguous concept even in those countries where the language differentiates between regulation as a function (*Regulierung, régulation*) and regulation as a legal tool (*Regelung, réglementation*).

A number of criticisms addressed to the role of law in public administration seem to derive from a confusion between, on the one hand law as a set of tools and a limited number of general principles, and on the other, the law of the day as it is set down at a specific moment in a country's legislation. This confusion leads to a very conservative use of law that tends to justify immobility. A factor that increases the confusion is that one word, 'law' (*droit, Recht*), can be used to designate an academic discipline that has some ambition to being a social science and the profession of professors of law, and also to refer to the content of constitutions, to statute law and other written legal sources, the legislature, and to case law originated by courts or other public authorities and by practising lawyers as different as

advocates, judges or legal counsellors in public administration and business administration.

In the last decade of the twentieth century it has become fashionable to oppose the continental tradition of public administration based on law to a tradition of management sometimes qualified as the 'Anglo-Saxon tradition'. This also rests on a confusion between two very different features of British tradition. On the one hand, common law sometimes appears as very flexible to non-specialists, due to a legal culture where statutes do not have the same predominant value in law as in continental Europe; but in fact formalism is as high on the British side of the Channel, or even more so when it comes to judicial proceedings. On the other hand, the customary principles of the British constitution are also interpreted as corresponding to a tradition of flexible law. Indeed, the principle according to which the Cabinet has all powers under the *royal prerogative* to organize and to manage the civil service has no real equivalent in continental Europe; this places the British Prime Minister in a position that would be envied by all his continental counterparts, who are bound by their national constitutions to a set of principles and procedures. The President of the United States probably would also envy the British Prime Minister if he only knew about the prerogative; but he would also envy the French President and Prime Minister for all they can do without the interference of parliament.[25]

Nevertheless, even detailed written statute law can be changed in order to restructure public administration, as the reforms undertaken in Italy from 1992 to 2000 show, which have introduced in written law most of the elements of the structural reforms introduced into British government on the basis of government papers without legal value, like the 'Next Steps' reports.[26] For a government that has both the will to reform and the political means to do it, the only difference is really a matter of time – a very important factor indeed for the success of administrative reform. The time factor apart, law as such is not an obstacle to administrative reform, nor to the introduction of management: it is a set of tools which can be used well or badly according to the quality of legal education of those who have to set up and implement new modes of management.[27]

NOTES AND REFERENCES

1 One of the best examples is, for France, Auguste François Vivien de Goubert (1807–74), who has been a *préfet* and a member of the *Conseil d'Etat*, and whose *Etudes Administratives* (1845) have influenced

French public administration for generations. See Vivien, A.F. (1974) *Etudes Administratives* (Paris: Cujas, reprint).

2 1864–1920. His most famous work in this respect is usually know as *Economy and Society* (1920). One of the first translations was Weber; Max, Henderson, A.M. and Parsons, Talcott (1947) *The Theory of Social and Economic Organisation* (Oxford: Oxford University Press). See also Weber, Max and Anderski, Stanislav (eds) (1983) *Max Weber on Capitalism, Bureaucracy and Religion* (London: Allen and Unwin). Max Weber is also famous for his sociology of religions; see his famous work, published in 1905, Weber, Max (1976) *The Protestant Ethic and the Spirit of Capitalism* (London: Allen and Unwin).

3 See Wunder, Bernd (ed.) (1992) *The Influences of the Napoleonic 'Model' of Administration on the Administrative Organization of Other Countries* (Brussels: International Institute of Administrative Sciences).

4 See Ziller, Jacques, 'European Models of Government: Towards a Patchwork with Missing Pieces', *Parliamentary Affairs*, 54, 1 (2001), p. 102–19.

5 Especially Gerber (1823–91) and Laband (1838–1918). See Gerber, Carl Friedrich von (1852) *Über öffentliche Rechte* (Tübingen: Laupp); Gerber, Carl Friedrich von (1880) *Grundzüge des deutschen Staatsrechts*, 3rd edn (Leipzig: Tauchnitz); Laband (1876–82), *Das Staatsrecht des deutschen Reiches* (Tübingen: Laupp, vols 1 and 2, 1876 and Freiburg: Mohr, vols 2 and 3, 1882).

6 1888–1985. See Bendersky, Joseph W. (1983) *Carl Schmitt, Theorist for the Reich* (Princeton, NJ: Princeton University Press).

7 1881–1973. A renowned lawyer and academic, one of the Fathers of the Austrian Constitution of 1920, is best known for his 'Pure Theory of Law' – *Reine Rechslehre*. See Kelsen, Hans and Hartney, Michael (1991) *General Theory of Norms* (Oxford: Oxford University Press).

8 Francois Marie Arouet (pen name Voltaire), 1694–1778.

9 Jean-Jacques Rousseau 1712–78. His main work in political theory is *The Social Contract – Du contrat social*, 1762. See Rousseau, Jean-Jacques, Cress, Donald A. and Gay, Peter (1987) *Basic Political Writings* (Indianapolis: Hackett).

10 Charles de Secondat, Baron de la Brède et de Montesquieu, 1689–1755. His most famous work, which influenced the fathers of the US constitution is *The Spirit of the Laws* (*De L'Esprit des lois – 1748*). See Cohler, Anne, Miller, Basia and Stone, Harold (1989) *Montesquieu – The Spirit of the Laws* (New York: Cambridge University Press).

11 See Wunder (note 3 above).

12 See: International Association of Supreme Administrative Jurisdictions (IASAJ), http://www.iasaj.org

13 The analysis by Max Weber (above n. 2) of modern administration of the 'legal-relational' type is usually referred to as the Weberian model (of public administration).

14 See http://www.admin.ch

15 The constitutions of the Member states of the European Union can be found on http://www.iue.it/LAW/conseulaw

16 See: Ragnemalm, Hans, 'Administrative Justice in Sweden', in Piras, Aldo (1991) *Administrative Law – the Problem of Justice*, vol. 1 *Anglo-American and Nordic Systems* (Milan: Giuffré).

17 For an up to date survey of civil service law in the member states of the European Union, see Bossaert, Danielle, Demmke, Christoph, Nomden, Koen and Polet, Robert (2001) *Civil Services in the Europe of Fifteen: Trends and New Developments* (Maastricht: EIPA).

18 See Piras, Aldo, (1991–1997) *Administrative Law – the Problem of Justice*, vol. 1 *Anglo-American and Nordic Systems* (Milan: Giuffré) (vol. 1 *Anglo-American and Nordic Systems*; vol. 2 *Western European Democracies*; vol. 3 *Western European Democracies*).

19 Albert Venn Dicey (1835–1922) is famous in a number of continental European countries as exponent of the principles of the Rule of Law in Great Britain. See Dicey, Albert Venn (1885) *Law of the Constitution* (London: Macmillan; 9th edn, 1950).

20 See Brown, L. Neville and Bell, John S. (1998) *French Administrative Law*, 5th edn (Oxford: Clarendon).

21 See Singh, Marendra P. (2001) *German Administrative Law in Common Law Perspective* (Berlin: Springer).

22 See Bell, John and Bradley, Anthony W. (1991) *Governmental Liability: A Comparative Study* (London: UKNCCL).

23 See Schwarze, Jürgen (1992) *European Administrative Law* (Brussels/Luxembourg: Bruylant/OPOCE). As this book is based on a German version dating from 1988, see also Chiti, Mario (1999) *Diritto amministrativo europeo* (Milan: Giuffré).

24 See n. 2 above.

25 The gender of the pronoun used merely reflects the incumbents at the time of writing.

26 See: http://www.official-documents.co.uk/

27 See George, Alexandra, Machado, Pedro and Ziller, Jacques (2001) *Law and Public Management – Starting to Talk* (Florence: EUI Working Document).

21

Administrative Law in the Anglo-American Tradition

Paul Craig

HISTORICAL FOUNDATIONS

It is a common belief that 'administrative law' is a recent development in the Anglo-American tradition. This is mistaken. The Anglo-American tradition is not premised on the existence of a separate set of courts to adjudicate on public law matters, as is common within civilian jurisdictions. To reason from this premise, to the conclusion that there was, until recently, no administrative law is a *non sequitur*. English law has exercised procedural and substantive controls over the administration for well over 350 years. Three features of this control were of central importance.

First, the history of judicial review was inextricably bound up with the development of remedies as opposed to the creation of new heads of review (Craig, 2000; Henderson, 1963; Jaffe and Henderson, 1956). The elaboration of grounds for review took place within, and was framed by, the evolution of adjectival law. Mandamus was transformed into a general tool for the remedying of administrative error. Lord Mansfield (*R. v. Barker* (1762) 3 Burr. 1265) gave the seminal rationalization of mandamus. It was, he said, introduced to prevent disorder from a failure of justice, and defect of police. Therefore it ought to be used 'upon all occasions where the law has established no specific remedy, and where in justice and good government there ought to be one'. The evolution of certiorari into a generalized remedy capable of catching a variety of governmental errors occurred later.

Secondly, it was through the common law itself that these developments in judicial review occurred. The common law was seen as the embodiment of reason, which could be modified so as to meet the challenges of a new age. Coke and other lawyers 'disapproved of Parliament changing the common law, because they believed that the wisdom of a single Parliament was unlikely to surpass the wisdom embodied in laws shaped by the accumulated experience of many generations' (Goldsworthy, 1999: 119). The same relationship between statute and common law can be seen in the eighteenth century, as exemplified by the work of Blackstone and Mansfield. Blackstone's *Commentaries* were the pre-eminent statement of the law during this period. They also constituted the main teaching manual for law students in the eighteenth and nineteenth centuries (Lieberman, 1989: 64–5) Blackstone lamented the 'mischiefs' which had arisen from alterations in the law, and laid the blame for this squarely with Parliament, for its passage of imperfect and inadequate legislation. While he acknowledged the importance of certain legislation, such as that concerned with habeas corpus, his general stance was to venerate the perfection of the common law, and regret the manner in which its symmetry had been distorted by ill-conceived legislation. This vision of the common law was inherently conservative and idealistic, as forcefully pointed out by Bentham. The preference for the common law over statute was equally evident in the creative jurisprudence of Lord Mansfield.

Thirdly, the courts did not reason on the basis of any rigid dichotomy between public and private law. This did not mean that there was no administrative law until the mid-twentieth century. There was a wealth of case law dealing with all aspects of review, both procedural and substantive, from at least the seventeenth century onwards. It did mean that the constraints were fashioned on the basis of what were felt to be sound normative principles for the exercise of power. Whether the power was public, private or a hybrid of the two could be a factor in this determination, but there was no assumption that the conceptual rationale for such constraints, or the constraints themselves, had to be different depending on how the body was classified.

THE DICEYAN LEGACY AND BEYOND

It was Dicey's dislike of administrative law that cast a shadow over the subject in the early years of this century, at least in the UK, but also to some extent in the United States. The modern growth of administrative law was directly connected with the extension of governmental functions relating to the poor, the unemployed, trade regulation and the like. It became impossible to separate an evaluation of the agencies applying these laws from a value judgment of the social policies in the laws themselves. Those who disliked such social intervention, including Dicey, tended to view the agencies applying such laws with suspicion (Dicey, 1959). The predominance he accorded to the 'ordinary law', applied by the 'ordinary courts', was a means of controlling these agencies, and of maintaining judicial supervision over the substantive policies which they applied. The paramount function of the courts was essentially negative, to ensure that the agency did not make mistakes by exceeding the power granted to it.

These ideas of mistake avoidance and distrust came to be challenged as a direct consequence of changing attitudes towards the social policies which the agencies were applying. People perceived the positive contributions made by such policies. Academics such as Robson (1928: xv) approached the study of administrative justice without 'any ready-made assumption that every tribunal which does not at the moment form part of the recognized system of judicature must necessarily and inevitably be arbitrary, incompetent, unsatisfactory, injurious to the freedom of the citizen and to the welfare of society'.

The consequences of this change in attitude were important. Administrative agencies were not now viewed as perfect. Defects in their operation were readily apparent. However it was no longer taken for granted that the justice dispensed by the ordinary courts and the ordinary law was necessarily

better than that of agencies. Nor was it felt that the sole object of administrative law was to ensure that the agency avoided making mistakes by overstepping its boundaries. A more positive desire that the agency should successfully fulfil the policy assigned to it became the focus of discussion, and the courts were perceived as but one factor in fulfilling this objective (Aman, 1993: Ch. 1; Harlow and Rawlings, 1997: Ch. 1–3). Scholars differed in their approach.

Some advanced an explicitly pluralist vision of democracy, in place of the unitary view espoused by Dicey. They contested the idea that all public power was wielded by the state. Religious, economic and social associations exercised authority. 'Legislative' decisions would often be reached by the executive, after negotiation with such groups, and would then be forced through the actual legislature. Group power was applauded rather than condemned. The all-powerful unitary state was dangerous. Liberty was best preserved by the presence of groups within the state to which the individual could owe allegiance (Laski, 1917, 1919). This vision of political pluralism was complemented by a concern with the social and economic conditions within the state. There was a strong belief that political liberty was closely linked with social and economic equality. The scope of administrative law should not therefore be concerned only with those bodies to whom statutory or prerogative power had been given, but also with other institutions that exercised public power.

Others advanced a more market-based conception of pluralist democracy, which was manifest in governmental policy within the late 1970s and 1980s, both in the UK and the United States, (Craig, 1990: Ch. 3–4; Stewart, 1975). The market was viewed as the best 'arbitrator' of economic issues, and direct governmental regulation thereof was perceived as necessary only when there was market failure, the existence of which was narrowly defined. The sphere of legitimate governmental action was therefore closely circumscribed. The very fulfilment of the free market vision required, however, a strong central government. Different conclusions were drawn as to the bodies that should be run by the state. Deregulation and privatization were the consequences of this approach. Even where some continuing regulation of a privatized industry was required, the aim of the regulation was coloured by the market-oriented vision. The purpose was often to prevent an industry with monopolistic power from abusing its dominant position.

Yet others viewed administrative law through the lens of participatory democracy, and republicanism. This was particularly so in the

United States, where Sunstein (1985, 1988) and Michelman (1986) were prominent advocates of this underlying theory as to the purpose of administrative law. They rejected the view that administrative law was simply about the aggregation of interests. Republicanism connoted an attachment to deliberation, political equality, universalism and citizenship. The purpose of politics was not simply to aggregate private preferences, but rather to subject those preferences to scrutiny and review. Discussion and dialogue were central to this process.

DIVERGENT STRAINS WITHIN ANGLO-AMERICAN ADMINISTRATIVE LAW

It is self-evident that there will be points of divergence within the Anglo-American tradition, in terms of doctrine. Two points are, however, of more general importance in this respect.

The first is that doctrine in the United States is developed against the background of a written Constitution and a general statute, the Administrative Procedure Act of 1946 (APA). By way of contrast, there is no written constitution in the UK, and nothing equivalent to the APA. The greater part of UK administrative law has traditionally been judge-made common law. There have, however, been important statutes dealing with particular issues. The Human Rights Act 1998, which came into effect on 2 October 2000, is especially important in this respect. It brings the rights from the European Convention on Human Rights (ECHR) into UK domestic law, and allows individuals to rely on such rights in actions before national courts (Grosz et al., 2000).

The second point is that the UK is a member of the European Union. This has had a marked impact on its administrative law. EU law is binding on the Member States in those areas covered by the Treaties. Principles of judicial review developed by the European Court of Justice (ECJ) will therefore have to be applied by national courts in areas that fall within the remit of the EU. These principles will be fashioned by the ECJ drawing on concepts from Member State law. The great majority of states that are members of the EU have civilian legal systems. The consequence is that EU law, developed from these sources, will be binding on the UK. There is therefore a greater interplay between common law and civil law concepts in the UK than hitherto. It should moreover be noted that principles of EU law can have a 'spillover impact'.

They may be applied by UK courts in areas not covered by EU law in a strict sense, and thus influence the development of the general principles of judicial review (Andenas, 1998; Andenas and Jacobs, 1998; Ellis, 1999; Schonberg, 2000).

DOCTRINE: PROCEDURAL CONSTRAINTS IN ADJUDICATION

Foundations

Academic commentators and courts alike have, as in the United States, recognized two rationales for the application of procedural rights in adjudication. They perform an instrumental role in the sense of helping to attain an accurate decision on the substance of the case. They can also serve non-instrumental goals such as protecting human dignity by ensuring that people are told why they are being treated unfavourably, and by enabling them to take part in that decision (Galligan, 1996: 75–82; Hart, 1961: 156, 202; Mashaw, 1985: Ch. 4–7; Michelman, 1977; Rawls, 1973: 235; Resnick, 1977). These twin rationales for the existence of procedural rights have been recognized by the judiciary in the UK and the United States, (R. v. Secretary of State for the Home Department, ex p. Doody [1994] A.C. 531, 551; Goldberg v. Kelly 397 U.S. 254 (1970)).

The derivation of process rights varies from country to country. In the United States these rights will normally be grounded in the Constitution or the Administrative Procedure Act of 1946 (APA). There is, as seen above, no written constitution or Administrative Procedure Act in the UK. The common law courts have therefore largely developed procedural rights, although statute has had an impact in this area to some degree. The applicability and the extent of procedural rights have also been affected by the European Community law, and by the European Convention of Human Rights.

If an individual is aggrieved by the actions of government, a public body, or certain domestic tribunals or associations, he or she may claim that there has been a breach of natural justice. The phrase natural justice encapsulates two ideas: that the individual be given adequate notice of the charge and an adequate hearing (audi alteram partem), and that the adjudicator be unbiased (nemo judex in causa sua).

In the eighteenth and nineteenth centuries the audi alteram partem principle was applied to a wide variety of bodies. Deprivation of office (Bagg's Case (1615) 11 Co. Rep. 93b), and disciplinary measures imposed on the clergy (*Capel* v. *Child* (1832) 2 Cr. & J. 588) were two common types of case to come before the courts. The principle was also applied to private bodies such as clubs, associations and trade unions (*Abbott* v. *Sullivan* [1952] 1 K.B. 189). The generality of application of the principle was emphasized in *Cooper* v. *Wandsworth Board of Works* ((1863) 14 C.B. (N.S.) 180), where the court held that the omission of positive words in the statute requiring a hearing was not a bar since the justice of the common law would supply the omission of the legislature. This was further reinforced by Lord Loreburn L.C., who stated that the maxim applied to 'everyone who decides anything' (*Board of Education* v. *Rice* [1911] A.C. 179, 182).

The breadth of the *audi alteram partem* principle was, however, limited in the first half of this century. The courts held that a hearing would only be required if the body was acting judicially rather than administratively (*Errington* v. *Minister of Health* [1935] 1 K.B. 249); there was misunderstanding over remedies, particularly the scope of certiorari, which affected the applicability of natural justice; and some courts held that natural justice would only apply to protect rights and not privileges (*Nakkuda Ali* [1951] A.C. 66, 77–78; *Bailey* v. *Richardson* 182 F 2d 46 (1950)).

The principle of natural justice was revived in the UK by the House of Lords in *Ridge* v. *Baldwin* ([1964] A.C. 40), and in the United States by *Goldberg* v. *Kelly* (397 U.S. 254 (1970)). In *Ridge* the House of Lords swept away many of the limitations on the application of the principle which had been imposed by the case law of the early twentieth century. The applicability of natural justice was to be dependent on the nature of the power exercised and its effect upon the individual concerned. In *Goldberg* the Supreme Court was willing to apply Constitutional Due Process to a welfare claimant, and characterized the claimant's interest as being property for the purposes of the Fifth Amendment.

The applicability of procedural protection

The 'trigger' for the applicability of procedural protection varies in common law regimes, depending upon the more precise foundation for the process rights.

Thus, in the United States claimants can seek to base procedural protection on three different sources. If the claim is framed in constitutional terms, it will have to be shown that the claimant has a life, liberty or property interest that has been affected by the agency action complained

of. The interpretation of these terms is for the courts, and ultimately for the Supreme Court (*Board of Regents* v. *Roth* 408 U.S. 1972). A claimant can invoke the APA of 1946. Section 554 will apply to agency adjudication required by statute to be determined on the record after opportunity for an agency hearing. This statutory language has been interpreted in rather different ways by the courts (compare *Seacoast Anti-Pollution League* v. *Costle* 572 F. 2d. 872 (1978), and *Chemical Waste Management Inc.* v. *US Environmental Protection Agency* 873 F. 2d 1477 (1989)). Where neither the Constitution nor the APA is applicable, then an individual may be able to gain limited process rights through the reasoning in *Citizens to Preserve Overton Park* v. *Volpe* 401 U.S. 402 (1971). This provides a basis for the derivation of limited process rights in relation to informal agency action. The process rights must, however, be linked to enforcing substantive limits on the agency's power.

The position in the UK is somewhat different, precisely because there is no written Constitution and nothing equivalent to the APA of 1946. The courts have determined the applicability of procedural protection through the common law. The years since *Ridge* v. *Baldwin* have seen the development of the duty to act fairly. Some courts regard natural justice as but a manifestation of fairness. Others apply natural justice to judicial decisions, and reserve a duty to act fairly for administrative or executive determinations. As discredited limitations have been discarded, and natural justice has expanded to new fields, fairness is seen as a more appropriate label (*McInnes* v. *Onslow-Fane* [1978] 1 W.L.R. 1520). The courts determine what adjudicative procedures are required in particular areas. In some it may approximate to the full panoply of procedural safeguards including: notice, oral hearing, representation, discovery, cross-examination and reasoned decisions. In others it may connote considerably less. There will be a broad spectrum in between. The courts have therefore exercised control over procedural rights not by rigid prior classification, but rather by admitting that natural justice or fairness applies and varying the content of those rules according to the facts of the case.

The claimant will none the less have to show that he or she has an interest which is sufficient to trigger the applicability of procedural rights. There is therefore an analogy between the UK jurisprudence and that of the US courts when deciding on the applicability of constitutional due process (*Board of Regents of State Colleges* v. *Roth* 408 U.S. 564 (1972)). In the UK the claimant will have to show some right, interest or legitimate expectation in order to be entitled to procedural protection. The term *right* covers a recognized proprietary or personal right of the individual. The term *interest* is looser than that of right. It has been used as the basis for a hearing even where the individual would not be regarded in law as having any actual substantive entitlement or right in the particular case. This is exemplified by the application of natural justice in the context of licensing, social welfare, clubs, unions and trade associations. The concept of *legitimate expectations* can provide the foundation for process rights in circumstances where the individual does not possess the requisite right or interest in the preceding sense. Thus the courts have used the concept to protect future interests, such as licensing renewals (*McInnes* v. *Onslow-Fane*). It has also been used when a representation has been made by a public body, where in the absence of the representation, it is unlikely that the substantive interest would entitle the applicant to natural justice or fairness (*A.G. of Hong Kong* v. *Ng Yuen Shiu* [1983] 2 A.C. 629). The existence of a representation, and the consequential legitimate expectation which flows from it, may serve to augment the procedural rights granted to the applicant (*R.* v. *Liverpool Corporation, ex p. Liverpool Taxi Fleet Operators' Association* [1972] 2 Q.B. 299).

The content of process rights: the balancing process

In deciding upon the content of process rights the court will balance between the nature of the individual's interest, the likely benefit to be gained from an increase in procedural rights and the costs to the administration of having to comply with such process rights. This is the *Mathews* v. *Eldridge* calculus (*Mathews* v. *Eldridge* 424 U.S. 319 (1976)). The UK courts have reasoned in a similar manner, as exemplified by *Re Pergamon Press Ltd.* [1971] Ch. 388.

It is clear that balancing necessitates not only an identification of the individual's interest, but also some judgment about how much we value it, or the weight which we accord to it. For example, to take some position, as Megarry V.C. did in *McInnes* [1978] 1 W.L.R. 1520 as to whether the renewal of a licence is a 'higher' interest than an initial application, is not to engage in rigid conceptualism, but is rather a necessary step in reaching any decision.

It is clear also that valuing the other elements in the balancing process, the social benefits and costs of the procedural safeguards may be problematic. This is not simply a 'mathematical' calculus. Deciding what are the relevant costs and benefits is itself a hard task (Mashaw, 1976: 47–9).

Moreover, the existence of judicial balancing should not lead us to conclude that all such balancing is necessarily premised on the same assumptions. The premises that underpin a law and economics approach to process rights may be far removed from those that underlie a more rights-based approach to process (compare Posner, 1973, and Mashaw, 1985).

The content of process rights: particular process rights

This section will consider, albeit briefly, the most important process rights which applicants commonly claim.

The courts will protect the right to *notice* since as, Lord Denning said, if the right to be heard is to be a real right which is worth anything, it must carry with it a right in the accused man to know the case which is made against him (*Kanda* v. *Government of Malaya* [1962] A.C. 322, 337).

In terms of the *hearing* itself, the strict rules of evidence will not normally have to be followed (*Ex p. Moore*, [1965] 1 Q.B. 456, *Richardson* v. *Perales* 402 U.S. 389 (1971)). The tribunal is not restricted to evidence acceptable in a court of law; provided that it has some probative value, is relevant and comes from a reliable source, the court will consider it. Where there is an oral hearing, written evidence submitted by the applicant must be considered, but the agency may take account of any evidence of probative value from another source provided that the applicant is informed and allowed to comment on it. An applicant must also be allowed to address argument on the whole of the case. These general principles are, however, subject to the following reservation. The overriding obligation is to provide the applicant with a fair hearing and a fair opportunity to controvert the charge (*R.* v. *Board of Visitors of Hull Prison, ex p. St. Germain (No. 2)* [1979] 1 W.L.R. 1401, 1408–1412). This may in certain cases require not only that the applicant be informed of the evidence, but that the individual should be given a sufficient opportunity to deal with it. This may involve the cross-examination of the witnesses whose evidence is before the hearing authority in the form of hearsay.

The provision of *reasons* is of particular importance. Reasons can assist the courts in performing their supervisory function; they can help to ensure that the decision has been thought through by the agency; and they can increase public confidence in the administrative process and enhance its legitimacy. A duty to provide reasons can, therefore, help to attain both the instrumental and non-instrumental objectives which underlie process rights more generally (*R*. v. *Secretary of State for the Home Department, ex p. Doody* [1994] 1 A.C. 531). Reasons may also be required because of Community law. In EC law there is a duty to give reasons based on Article 253 EC (formerly 190). The extent of this duty will depend upon the nature of the relevant act and the context within which it was made. The duty is principally imposed upon the Community organs themselves, but it can apply to national authorities where they are acting as agents of the Community for the application of EC law.

The impact of the European Convention on Human Rights

In the UK, process rights are also influenced by Article 6 of the ECHR. Under the Human Rights Act 1998 (HRA), the courts have an obligation to interpret legislation to be in accord with these rights, and acts of public authorities which are incompatible with the rights are unlawful. Section 2 of the HRA provides that the national courts must take into account the jurisprudence of the Strasbourg institutions, although they are not bound by it. Article 6 provides, so far as relevant here, that 'in the determination of his civil rights and obligations or of any criminal charge against him, everyone is entitled to a fair and public hearing within a reasonable time by an independent and impartial tribunal established by law'.

The phrase 'civil rights and obligations' has been interpreted broadly so as to include: disputes concerning land use; monetary claims against public authorities; applications for, and revocations of, licences; claims for certain types of social security benefit; and disciplinary proceedings leading to suspension or expulsion from a profession. The European Court of Human Rights (ECtHR) has stressed a number of elements as integral to the requirement of a fair hearing pursuant to Article 6. There must be access to a court. There must be procedural equality or what is often termed 'equality of arms'. This implies that each party must be afforded a reasonable opportunity to present his case, including his evidence, under conditions that do not place him at a substantial disadvantage in relation to his opponent. There must be some proper form of judicial process, which will often take the form of an adversarial trial where the parties have the opportunity to have knowledge of, and comment on, the observations and evidence adduced by the other side. While there is no express requirement to give reasons the

ECtHR regards this as implicit in the obligation to provide a fair hearing. Reasons do not have to be given for every single point, but they must be sufficient to enable a party to understand the essence of the decision in order to be able to exercise any appeal rights. The requirements of a fair hearing do not have to be satisfied at every stage in the decision-making process. Where an administrative body does not comply with the duty imposed by Article 6 it will have to be subject to the control of a judicial body which does so comply.

DOCTRINE: PROCEDURAL RIGHTS IN RULE MAKING

There are considerable advantages to allowing some form of consultation or participation before rules are made. It enables views to be taken into account before an administrative policy has hardened into a draft rule. It can assist the legislature with technical scrutiny. It is hoped that there will be better rules as a result of input from interested parties, particularly where they have some knowledge of the area being regulated. A duty to consult allows those outside government to play some role in the shaping of policy. In this sense it enhances participation. It is moreover not immediately self-evident why a hearing should be thought natural when there is some form of individualized adjudication, but not where rules are being made. The unspoken presumption is that a 'hearing' will be given to a rule indirectly through the operation of our principles of representative democracy. Reality falls short of this ideal, both in the UK and in the United States.

It would be mistaken to think that according such participatory rights is unproblematic. It has been argued that the APA provisions on rule making can lead to 'paralysis by analysis', with interest groups opposed to the proposed rule using all available legal machinery to delay its implementation. Participatory rights can also lead to delay and extra cost. However, if all decisions were made by an autocrat they would doubtless be made more speedily. A cost of democracy is precisely the cost of involving more people. Moreover, the argument for increased participatory rights is based, in part at least, upon the idea that the people who are consulted may have something to offer the administrator. The rule that emerges will, it is hoped, be better. Whether this is always so may be debatable, but there is little reason to suggest that the argument does not hold in certain instances. Where it does have validity, then it is far less clear that the granting of such rights will entail an overall increase in cost. If a less good rule emerges where there is no consultation then the total costs may be greater because, for example, the rule fails to achieve its objective.

In the UK the rules of natural justice are not generally applicable to rule making, and in the United States Constitutional Due Process is not applicable in such instances. This is, however, where the legal analogy stops (Ziamou, 2001). In the UK a right to participate in rule making will exist only where parliament has chosen to grant it under a particular statute. In the United States the Administrative Procedure Act 1946 accords a general right to participate in rule making by the agencies covered by the legislation.

Notice of any proposed rule making is to be published in the Federal Register, including a statement of the time and place of the rule making proceedings and the terms or substance of the proposed rule. After notice the agency is to afford interested persons an opportunity to participate in the rule making. There are, in essence, three differing modes of participation, which have varying degrees of formality. Most administrative rules are subject to notice and comment: the proposed rules are published and interested parties can proffer written comments. Other rules are subject to formal rule making – a full trial-type hearing, which can include the provision of oral testimony and cross-examination. Yet other rules are governed by a hybrid process, which entails more formality than notice and comment, but less than the trial-type hearing.

DOCTRINE: SUBSTANTIVE CONSTRAINTS

General approach

It is clearly not possible, within the limits of available space, to set out all the doctrines of substantive review commonly found within the Anglo-American tradition. Certain foundational principles can none the less be enunciated.

The courts will maintain substantive control over agency determinations. The nature of this control will vary depending upon the nature of the issue that arises before the courts. Thus courts in the Anglo-American tradition will tend to maintain greater control over the conditions that set the jurisdictional limits for the agency, than they will over agency discretionary choices. The nature of these controls will be examined below. In relation to discretionary determinations

it is generally accepted that it is not for the courts to substitute their view as to how the discretion should have been exercised for that of the agency. The political branch of government has assigned this discretion to the agency, and it is not for the courts to intervene simply because they would, as a matter of first impression, have exercised the discretion differently from the agency. While courts in the Anglo-American tradition accept this dictate, there is considerably more discussion as to how intensive review of discretion should be. The fact that it is accepted that there should not be substitution of judgment does not mean that there is consensus about the intensity of review falling short of this. It would, for example, be possible for the courts to intervene only where there has been some manifestly unreasonable or arbitrary decision. They could, by way of contrast, exercise greater control over discretionary determinations, albeit falling short of substitution of judgment, through a hard look form of review, through a more exacting test of reasonableness, or through control framed in terms of proportionality. Courts in the UK, United States and elsewhere have grappled with these issues, and have reached differing conclusions as to the proper bounds of control over discretion. The intensity of review has ebbed and flowed over time. The principal factors that have affected the judicial choices have been the courts' perception of their relationship with agencies, their willingness to become involved in technically complex material, and the structural limits imposed by the nature of the review process itself.

It should not, moreover, be thought that courts in the Anglo-American tradition will always be of the same view as to the appropriate limits of judicial intervention. This can be exemplified by considering the contrasting approaches of the courts in the UK and the United States in relation to control over issues of law.

Control over law: a contrast

All agencies established through legislation will be given a statutory remit that defines the scope of their authority. A simple paradigm is of agency established on the following terms: if an employee is injured at work the agency may grant compensation. Courts will have to decide on the appropriate test for review when it is claimed that the agency adopted an incorrect meaning of the term employee, injury or work. The test adopted will reflect judicial choice as to the correct balance between agency autonomy and judicial control. Courts in the USA and in the UK have not always been of like mind on this issue.

The leading case in the UK is *Page* v. *Hull University Visitor* ([1993] 1 All E.R. 97). It was held that Parliament had only conferred the decision making power on the basis that it was to be exercised on the correct legal basis: a misdirection in law in making the decision therefore rendered the decision *ultra vires*. In general therefore, any error of law made by an administrative tribunal or inferior court in reaching its decision would be quashed for error of law.

The seminal modern case on this topic in the United States is *Chevron, U.S.A., Inc.* v. *Natural Resources Defense Council, Inc.* (467 US 837 (1984)). The case concerned the legality of regulations made pursuant to the clean air legislation. The Clean Air Act Amendments of 1977 imposed certain requirements on states that had not met the national air quality standards established by the Environmental Protection Agency (EPA). The requirements included an obligation on such states to establish regulatory regimes under which permits would be issued relating to 'new or modified major stationary sources' of air pollution. A permit could not be issued unless stringent conditions had been met. The EPA promulgated regulations designed to implement the permit requirement and these regulations allowed a state to adopt a plant-wide definition of stationary source. The effect of this was that an existing plant which had a number of pollution emitting devices could install or modify one piece of equipment without meeting the permit conditions, provided that the alteration did not increase the total emissions from the plant. The state was, therefore, allowed to treat all the pollution emitting devices within the same industrial grouping as though they were encased in a 'bubble'. It was this construction of the enabling legislation which was challenged by the National Resources Defense Council, the argument being that this interpretation was too generous to industrial users.

Justice Stevens gave the judgment of the Supreme Court. He adopted a two stage approach. First, if the intent of Congress is clear, that is the end of the matter; for the court, as well as the agency, must give effect to the unambiguously expressed intent of Congress. Secondly, if however the court determined that Congress had not directly addressed the precise question at issue, the court did not simply impose its own construction on the statute, as would be necessary in the absence of an administrative interpretation. Rather, if the statute was silent or ambiguous with respect to the specific issue, the question for the court was whether the agency's answer was based on a permissible construction of the statute. If Congress had explicitly left a gap for the agency to fill, there was an express delegation of authority to the agency to elucidate a specific provision of the statute by regulation. Such legislative regulations were given controlling weight unless they were arbitrary, capricious or manifestly contrary to the statute. Sometimes the legislative delegation to the agency was implicit rather than explicit. In such a case, a court should not substitute its own construction of a statutory provision for a reasonable interpretation made by the administrator of an agency. The court should defer to the agency's construction whenever a decision as to the meaning or reach of a statute involved the reconciliation of conflicting policies, in circumstances where the agency had particular expertise in the matters subjected to its regulatory remit.

Applying these principles the court then upheld the contested agency interpretation. It found that Congress did not have any specific intention with regard to the applicability of the bubble concept to the permit programme. Given that this was so, the question was not whether the reviewing court believed that the bubble concept was a good thing within the general context of a scheme designed to improve air quality. It was rather whether the agency's view that the bubble concept was appropriate within this scheme was a reasonable one. Looked at in the light of the objectives of the legislation in this area the court found that it was a reasonable interpretation which sought to balance the needs of the environment and those of business. The NRDC was, said Justice Stevens, seeking to wage a battle over policy in the courts on an issue which Congress had not specifically addressed, having lost that battle in the agency itself: these policy arguments should more properly be addressed to the legislators or administrators rather than the judges. There has been significant academic commentary on the case, (Aman, 1988; Farina, 1989; Pierce, 1988; Scalia, 1989; Sunstein, 1988).

The case law since the *Chevron* decision is itself of considerable interest as later cases have sought to test the metes and bounds of the principles set out above. There have been cases that give latitude to agency interpretations. There have been many cases where the court comes closer to substitution of judgment, drawing upon that part of the argument in *Chevron* that asserts the primacy of Congressional intent where that can be identified. It is clear moreover that judges possess considerable discretion as to how to characterize a particular case, in the sense of whether it comes within part one or part two of the *Chevron* formula. This is inevitable. What is less readily apparent is that there has been real disagreement among the judiciary as to the meaning that should be ascribed to the two parts of test, especially part one. This is particularly important, as can be appreciated by considering two contrasting views on this issue.

In *Immigration and Naturalization Service* v. *Cardozo-Fonseca* (480 U.S. 421 (1986)), the Supreme Court decided that the meaning of a particular statutory term was clear within the first limb of the *Chevron* test because the Court could divine this through the normal tools of statutory construction. This provoked a powerful separate opinion from Justice Scalia. He felt that the approach of the majority would radically undermine the purpose of the *Chevron* formula, given that a Court could always then hold that the meaning of a statutory term was clear through the use of 'normal tools of statutory construction'. The approach in the *Cardozo-Fonseca* case can be contrasted with that in *Rust* v. *Sullivan* (111 S. Ct. 1759 (1991)), where Chief Justice Rehnquist gave the leading judgment of the Court. His interpretation of the first limb of *Chevron* was markedly different. On his view a case would only fall under the first limb of the test if the Congressional meaning of the term really was evident on the face of the statute. If this was not so then the matter would fall to be determined under the rationality part of the formula. This in turn provoked a sharp dissent from Justice Stevens who argued that the majority was construing part one of the test too narrowly.

The contrast between the UK and US jurisprudence throws into sharp relief the judicial choices that are available in this area.

The courts can, as in the UK, substitute judgment for that of the agency on all issues of statutory interpretation. This will be so irrespective of the nature of the issue posed, and the relative expertise of agency and court to resolve it. The courts can, as in the United States, proceed via a two-part test. Issues coming within part one of the *Chevron* test would lead to substitution of judgment by the court for that of the agency. Issues that fall within part two of that test would be subject to control through the medium of the rational basis or reasonableness test. While there are bound to be some disagreements as to which of these tests should be applied in any particular case the nature of these should not be overstated. Substitution of judgment is suitable either where the legislature really has spoken to the issue, or where the challenged decision involves an issue on which the agency does not have any special expertise. In other instances the rationality test should be applied, particularly in relation to those matters of statutory interpretation that do fall within the agency's sphere of competence. It should not, moreover, be forgotten that agency determinations can be struck down even under this latter standard of review.

The choice between the two approaches outlined above has important implications for the more general relationship between agencies and courts. At base, the issue is whether agencies are to have any autonomy over the meaning to be ascribed to their empowering legislation. Under the UK approach the answer is essentially 'no'. Under the US approach the answer is a qualified 'yes'. It is clear that different commentators will have differing views as to which of these options is to be preferred, but at least the US jurisprudence enables us to see that there are ways of maintaining control over agency choices short of substituting judgment on each and every occasion.

REFERENCES

Aman, A. (1988) 'Administrative Law in a Global Era: Progress, Deregulatory Change and the Rise of the Administrative Presidency', *Cornell Law Review*, 73: 1101–247.

Aman, A. (1993) *Administrative Law and Process*. New York: Matthew Bender.

Andenas, M. (ed.) (1998) *English Public Law and the Common Law of Europe*. London: Key Haven Publications.

Andenas, M. and Jacobs, F. (eds) (1998) *European Community Law in the English Courts*. Oxford: Oxford University Press.

Craig, P. (1990) *Public Law and Democracy in the United Kingdom and the United States of America*. Oxford: Oxford University Press.

Craig, P. (2000) 'Public Law, Political Theory and Legal Theory', *Public Law*, pp. 211–39.

Dicey, A.V. (1959) *An Introduction to the Study of the Law of the Constitution*, 10th edn. London: Macmillan.

Ellis, E. (ed.) (1999) *The Principle of Proportionality in the Laws of Europe*. Oxford/Portland, OR: Hart Publishing.

Farina, C. (1989) 'Statutory Interpretation and the Balance of Power in the Administrative State', *Columbia Law Review*, 89: 452–528.

Galligan, D. (1996) *Due Process and Fair Procedures*. Oxford: Oxford University Press.

Goldsworthy, J. (1999) *The Sovereignty of Parliament, History and Philosophy*. Oxford: Oxford University Press.

Grosz, S., Beatson, J. and Duffy, P. (2000) *Human Rights, the 1998 Act and the European Convention*. London: Sweet & Maxwell.

Harlow, C. and Rawlings, R. (1997) *Law and Administration*, 2nd edn. London: Butterworths.

Hart, H.L.A. (1961) *Concept of Law*. Oxford: Oxford University Press.

Henderson, E. (1963) *Foundations of English Administrative Law*. Cambridge, MA: Harvard University Press.

Jaffe, L. and Henderson, E. (1956) 'Judicial Review and the Rule of Law: Historical Origins', *Law Quarterly Review*, 72: 345–64.

Laski, H. (1917) *Studies in the Problem of Sovereignty*. New Haven, CT: Yale University Press.

Laski, H. (1919) *Authority in the Modern State*. New Haven, CT: Yale University Press.

Lieberman, D. (1989) *The Province of Legislation Determined, Legal Theory in Eighteenth-Century Britain*. Cambridge: Cambridge University Press.

Mashaw, J. (1976) 'The Supreme Court's Due Process Calculus for Administrative Adjudication in *Mathews v. Eldridge*: Three Factors in Search of a Theory of Value', *University of Chicago Law Review*, 44: 28–59.

Mashaw, J. (1985) *Due Process in the Administrative State*. New Haven, CT: Yale University Press.

Michelman, F. (1977) 'Formal and Associational Aims in Procedural Due Process', in J. Roland Pennock and John W. Chapman, (eds), *Due Process*. New York: New York University Press. Ch. 4.

Michelman, F. (1986) 'Foreword: Traces of Self-Government', *Harvard Law Review*, 100: 4–77.

Pierce, R. (1988) 'Chevron and Its Aftermath: Judicial Review of Agency Interpretation of Statutory Provisions', *Vanderbilt Law Review*, 41: 301–14.

Posner, R. (1973) 'An Economic Approach to Legal Procedure and Judicial Administration', *Journal of Legal Studies*, 2: 399–458.

Rawls, J. (1973) *A Theory of Justice*. Oxford: Oxford University Press.

Resnick, J. (1977) 'Due Process and Procedural Justice', in J. Roland Pennock and John W. Chapman (eds), *Due Process*. New York: New York University Press.

Robson, W. (1928) *Justice and Administrative Law: A Study of the British Constitution*. London: Macmillan.

Scalia, A. (1989) 'Judicial Deference to Administrative Interpretations of Law', *Duke Law Journal*: 511–21.

Schonberg, S. (2000) *Legitimate Expectations in Administrative Law*. Oxford: Oxford University Press.

Stewart, R. (1975) 'The Reformation of American Administrative Law', *Harvard Law Review*, 88: 1667–813.

Sunstein, C. (1985) 'Interest Groups in American Public Law', *Stanford Law Review*, 38: 29–87.

Sunstein, C. (1988a) 'Constitutionalism after the New Deal', *Harvard Law Review*, 101: 421–510.

Sunstein, C. (1988b) 'Beyond the Republican Revival', *Yale Law Journal*, 97: 1539–90.

Ziamou, T. (2001) *Rulemaking, Participation and the Limits of Public Law in the USA and Europe*. Aldershot: Ashgate/Dartmouth.

22

The Limits of Law: Can Laws Regulate Public Administration?

David Feldman

BACKGROUND: SIX PLAUSIBLE PROPOSITIONS

There is little hard evidence about the relationship between law and public administration. The sociology of law movement has gradually provided information about the roles which law plays in society, and some more specialized studies have examined its impact on administration,[1] but current understanding of the subject relies heavily on a combination of largely untested hypotheses from theoretical analyses, fairly small-scale studies of particular administrative bodies or procedures, and anecdotal accounts. A number of studies of all these types have tried to assess the impact of applications for judicial review,[2] one type of legal procedure, on administrators, but the principles and procedures of judicial review form only a tiny aspect of the law applying to public administration. Other studies have examined the making and applying of rules, including legal rules, as a way of empowering and controlling administration, and have illuminated the conditions under which rules are more or less likely to achieve their drafters' objectives in practice. Although scholars and practitioners must still attempt to generalize from insufficient information, it is possible to offer some propositions that seem likely to be reasonably reliable, as a background to the account which follows.[3]

First, norms (a term encompassing standards, principles, policies and rules) have a pervasive effect on administration, shaping the activities undertaken, the way in which they are undertaken and the efforts of individual administrators

and groups of them (whether aimed at achieving the objectives enshrined in the norms or at frustrating them). Norm-based organization is an important aspect of the idea of bureaucratic rationality which the Weberian tradition sees as a hallmark of the modern state.

Secondly, it would be unwise to imagine that the impact of legal norms is distinctively different in practice from that of other norms, such as non-legal guidance and directions issued to or within the organization, and the morality of individual officers. Front-line staff with discretion may experience all norms in a rather similar way: 'cultural, social, political, psychological, institutional, and doctrinal forces may moderate that discretion'.[4] All forms of norm are subject to factors limiting their potential effectiveness. Legal norms are not special when seen from the perspective of administrators, although they may carry with them special risks and opportunities. Of course, law is special in the eyes of lawyers and legislators, but it would probably be wrong to assume that it offers a decisive way of influencing administrative behaviour.

Thirdly, many legal norms are institutionally enforceable by judicial action, although not all. A legal rule may contain a broad and imprecise standard, such as 'efficiency', which is not likely to be justiciable.[5] A typical legal rule which is not designed to be enforced by law is Section 1 of the UK National Health Service Act 1977, requiring the Secretary of State to promote a 'comprehensive health service designed to secure improvement (a) in the physical and mental health of the people of [England and Wales], and (b) in the prevention, diagnosis and treatment of illness'. This cannot give rise to judicially enforceable obligations owed by the Secretary of State to individual patients. The norm is politically, rather than legally, enforceable. Analogously, non-legal norms may also be institutionally enforceable, through managerial action (performance appraisal affecting pay and promotion prospects, budgetary penalties, or loss of contracts under contracting-out and compulsory competitive tendering regimes) or social pressure (the ethos of the department concerned).[6]

Fourthly, the most distinctive feature of legal norms is that virtually all power-conferring rules must be legal, because a non-legal rule cannot make lawful the action of a public authority which interferes with people's legal rights and freedoms. The most significant contribution of law to public administration is, therefore, to empower authorities to do things which would otherwise be unlawful. The legal and other norms which impose restrictions on the way in which an authority may exercise its powers are there to ensure that the powers are not used arbitrarily or inappropriately. In theory, the restrictions should strike a balance between preserving space for worthwhile discretionary action in pursuit of goals and ensuring that proper respect is shown to people affected by the pursuit.

Fifthly, law has a number of functions in common with other normative systems. It has a symbolic value when it enshrines the basic aspirations, values and objectives of a field of public administration, even if they are not expected to be enforced judicially. Law may also have educational value, helping to shape the attitudes as well as the activities of a public authority, for example to encourage respect for equality and for people's dignity. It may also seek to control excessive, unfair, misdirected or irrational behaviour, typically prospectively, but also on occasions retrospectively. Judicial review has a role in all these activities, although it is most likely to be most often concerned with seeking to rectify, retrospectively, improper action. But it is only one of a growing number of mechanisms for enforcing norms governing public administration.

Sixthly, for legal rules and procedures to command respect and support from administrators, there are at least three requirements. The substance of the rules must be compatible with the achievement of public objectives, and must be given effect predictably and in ways that take full account of the objectives of the public programme in which the administrators are engaged. It was suggested above that legal rules as applied in the courts usually have these characteristics. But in addition the rules themselves must be in a form which makes them appropriate to the task of regulating decision making and action in the context of the area of public administration in question. Rules have formal qualities which affect their capacity to influence administrative action. As Dr Julia Black has explained,[7] a rule has four dimensions: its content, its mandatory or permissive character, its legal status and any consequence attaching to non-compliance with it,[8] and its structure. The last three of these give rise to its 'rule-type'. The last dimension, the structure of the rule, itself has four aspects: its scope or inclusiveness; its precision or vagueness; the ease with which it can be applied to concrete situations (which Black calls its 'simplicity or complexity'); and its clarity or opacity, in terms of 'the degree to which the rule contains words with well-defined and universally accepted meanings'.[9] There are both tactical and strategic reasons for using particular rule-types, and the use of particular rule-types has certain consequences, which are independent of the content of the rules, for the ability of agencies to formulate and then achieve policy objectives. A rule may fail through being over- or under-inclusive. The search for precision may help to ensure consistency, but only at the cost of increasing the size of the rule-book, reducing the extent to which rules can be internalized, restricting potentially useful discretion, and making it harder for officials to implement policy flexibly. Clarity may make life easier for non-specialists, but create a barrier to the proper deployment of expertise (for example, in the field of medical assessments).[10] If the form of rules (legal or administrative) makes them difficult for administrators to read, comprehend or apply in practice, they are likely to have little influence over day-to-day decision making and practice, although they may still exercise an influence over high-level policy making which settles the general direction of administrative effort.

Finally, legality and respect for rights are two important bases for the legitimacy of all governmental action, and of public administration generally. There is a common belief that modern government derives its legitimacy from its democratic foundations, that is, from the ballot box.[11] However, this gives only a partial picture of the rich web of sources from which a public authority must seek to gain legitimacy in a civilized modern society. Other elements include respect for the constitution, respect for law, respect for fundamental rights, respect for international obligations and respect for members of society as citizens. An arm of government which does not display these forms of respect in its daily work is likely to be all the more illegitimate by reason of the fact that many decisions and actions of public administrators cannot be clearly linked to any expression of public support at the ballot box. Professor Robert Baldwin has gone further, identifying a number of different 'discourses' within which claims to legitimacy may be made. He identifies claims based on 'democratic mandate', 'accountability' or 'democratic voice', 'due process', 'expertise' and 'efficiency', to which one can add claims founded on recognition of the equality and dignity of the citizen. As Baldwin points out, each of these is problematic individually, but together they have justificatory force.[12] It should also be noted that they are capable of pulling in different directions, and not all are equally appropriate for assessing the legitimacy of any one institution or programme of public administration or law.

Against that background, we can consider, first, the relationship between legal norms and public administration, and, subsequently, the effect of judicial review and other legal proceedings in relation to public administration.

THE RELATIONSHIP BETWEEN LEGAL NORMS AND PUBLIC ADMINISTRATION

The doctrine of the Rule of Law imposes standards of governmental legitimacy which operate alongside, and complement, other standards of legitimacy, such as democratic accountability, representativeness, efficiency, expertise and respect for the rights of people who are subject to the power of the state. It has been commonplace at least since the seventeenth century in common law systems, and at least since the early nineteenth century in civilian systems, to believe that the power of the state should be checked by law, and accordingly that much, if perhaps not all, public administration should properly be a rule-governed and legally accountable activity. At the very least, legally enforceable standards provide a basis for independent courts or tribunals to protect people who suffer as a result of the failure of public institutions to meet minimum standards of legality. By enforcing fidelity to law, lawyers can play a part in combating arbitrary government, imposing at least a minimum level of procedural propriety, consistency and predictability on public institutions and programmes. In the growing number of states whose legal systems include certain fundamental rights, the Rule of Law may also substantively limit the ways in which public authorities can lawfully treat people (for example by making it unlawful to subject them to degrading

treatment), and by requiring actions which affect fundamental rights to be justified according to criteria laid down by law.

These objectives provide good reasons for asserting that legality is a necessary condition for the legitimacy of public administration. Nevertheless, it has never been clear how far legal standards can, and should, provide the basis for the day-to-day work of public officials. A number of factors have tended to reduce the importance of law as an influence on public administration in the estimation of commentators.

First, public administration is a goal-orientated activity. Administrators are required to pursue objectives. The law may set an objective, impose a duty to develop a programme to achieve it and confer the powers which are thought to be necessary to the aim. However, laws rarely specify in any detail what the objective means in practice, how the activity is to be carried on, or how powers are to be used. Those matters are left to the judgement of administrators, using their expertise and experience to respond to the infinitely changeable, and often quickly changing, circumstances which they confront. For example, law may require a public authority to take steps to reduce the incidence of homelessness by offering advice and support for homeless people, and if necessary by providing housing for them. Legislation may specify the categories of people who are entitled to be helped, and the kinds of help which can be made available from public funds. It may also specify the procedures that are to be followed in making decisions affecting individual homeless people. However, administrators will need to exercise judgement in deciding whether people meet the criteria of eligibility for assistance, and to find ways of accommodating needs to available resources. The social and economic conditions of different areas, including the available housing stock and the calls on it, will vary widely, as will the personal, family and financial circumstances and needs of individual claimants. The people administering the programme will have to decide how best to use their resources to discharge their duties and achieve their objectives.

In carrying out that task, the resource constraints are likely to be of more central concern to administrators, and are likely to have a stronger impact on their day-to-day behaviour, than the law.[13] Courts sometimes go out of their way to accommodate this. To take an example from the UK, in *R. v. Gloucestershire County Council, ex parte Barry*,[14] the House of Lords, by a majority, relieved the local authority of a duty to provide for the applicant's need for cleaning and laundry services under the Chronically Sick and Disabled Persons Act 1970 after a reduction in the council's budget forced it to prioritize. The majority in the House of Lords held that 'need' had to be assessed taking account of the resources of the body required to meet the need. In a vigorous dissent, Lord Lloyd pointed out that a person's need had to be assessed by reference to civilized standards, not public authorities' resources. By linking need to resources, the majority was relieving Parliament and central government of the need to provide adequate resources for the discharge of a duty which they had themselves imposed on councils. However, public authorities cannot rely on courts bailing them out in this way. Indeed, judicial decisions about public authorities' liability to provide services or benefits to people necessarily lead to the priorities between competing claims on authorities' resources being re-thought. This is as true of decisions about liability of public authorities for negligence as it is of decisions in judicial review proceedings. The balance between competing interests may change, but the rules will always have to be implemented in ways that reflect a judgement about the relative weighting appropriate to competing considerations in the context of a particular set of objectives.

Where a public authority seeks to achieve consistency and predictability and to exercise financial control in administering its programmes by providing directives and guidelines for its staff, compliance with them is likely to be monitored continuously through managerial and audit techniques, and may be part of the staff appraisal process. Staff are unlikely to be as conscious of the importance of purely legal rules as they are of the rules and practices of the public authority itself. To put it another way, there are fewer incentives for most staff to internalize legal rules than to internalize administrative ones. One needs to ask whether the relevant people are aware of a norm, and, if they are, how they use it. All norms, once accepted as such by those who have to operate them or are subject to them, can have a variety of effects. A study of police officers found that they treated rules purporting to govern the exercise of their discretion in one of three ways.

Working rules are those that are internalized by police officers to become guiding principles of their conduct. *Inhibitory rules* are those which are not internalized, but which police officers tend to take into account when deciding how to act and which tend to discourage them from acting in a particular way in case they should be caught and the rule invoked against them. *Presentational rules* are the ones that exist to give an acceptable appearance to the way that police work is carried out. … Most of the presentational rules derive from the law and

are part of a (successful) attempt by the wider society to deceive itself about the realities of policing.[15]

This is not unique to police officers. For example, where a norm would produce a result that is unacceptable to an official dealing with a case involving a homeless person, there is evidence that the official, if sufficiently experienced, may finesse the norm by way of procedural sleight of hand (in the case of legal norms) or by exploiting the case-worker's advantage over line manager in terms of familiarity with the case (in relation to institutional policies and managerial monitoring).[16] This clash of norms turns the institutional rules and policies in question into 'inhibitory rules': they are respected so far as they cannot be avoided. There is also strong evidence of case workers presenting cases to superiors in the way most likely to produce the result the case worker wants under the rules, making them 'presentational' rather than 'working' rules for the case worker (although for the superior officer, applying the rules to the story as constructed by the case worker, it may be a 'working rule').[17]

If norms are to be internalized, becoming 'working rules', individual officials must see them as being useful in discharging their responsibilities. Power-conferring rules will normally be perceptibly useful, although certain powers may not be exercised if their use would compromise other aspects of the job, or prejudice consensual working relationships (such as those between regulators and regulated enterprises) on which success depends.[18] Legal rules which restrict the way in which public authorities can operate (as opposed to those which confer additional powers) will then tend to be seen within the authorities merely as obstacles to be circumvented, or as hoops to be jumped through, unless staff appreciate how the standards which legal rules encapsulate can help them to do their jobs well. Norms specifying procedures to be followed are particularly likely to be seen as counterproductive if they demand additional paperwork and time spent in meetings, and come between the official and the objective. For example, social workers may see procedural protection for the rights of children and their parents in childcare investigations in this light. If the rules are regarded as 'inhibitory' rather than internalized as 'working' rules, they will be most fully implemented where the threat of review or reversal of decisions by another body is most potent. The perceived threat is likely to be heightened, in the case of legal rules, where the people affected are particularly likely to be able and willing to litigate; well-informed people who are eligible for legal aid are likely to be treated more carefully than less well-informed people who, despite limited means, are unlikely to be granted legal assistance out of public funds.

An active and well-publicized pattern of decisions by courts might make such 'inhibitory' rules more effective. It is unlikely to make them more accepted, however, unless accompanied by a programme of education to underline the inherent or instrumental value of the rules, together with assistance (in the form of additional resources or help with planning and implementation techniques) in overcoming the difficulties presented by the rules. In fact, any of the attitudes to rules mentioned above requires administrators to be conscious of the rules and aware of their demands. This must be imbued and maintained through training and communication within the public authority. It is not cheap or easy to establish, but it can help to avoid costly and time-consuming legal challenges, which distract attention and resources from an authority's prime task. For a legal norm to be accepted as a working rule, there must also be what Simon Halliday calls 'legal conscientiousness': 'a professional concern with being lawful, which includes both finding out about "what the law is" on a given question, and being concerned to apply that law'.[19] Legal conscientiousness is even more difficult to instil in an organization, unless its main function is to adjudicate on the basis of legal criteria, and even then legal conscientiousness may be difficult to maintain if some of the members of the organization have a different set of professional values, as has been shown in UK studies of social security adjudication officers and Mental Health Review Tribunals.[20] Strict procedures may be promulgated within the organization in line with legal advice, and difficult decisions may be checked with the legal department, rather than mainstreaming within the organization the values which the rules seek to advance. While the letter of the rules is generally observed, their spirit will be ignored, because front-line administrators will not be aware of it. Instead of informing everyday activities, legal rules become the specialized business of legal departments, even though this is unlikely to be as effective in avoiding legal disputes, in the long term, as making the values a pervasive element in the structure of decision making. Where the public authority in question is democratically accountable, the input of lawyers may have the incidental effect of reducing the range of options available to elected decision makers, at least if they want to avoid charges of illegality later.[21] Tactical decisions about the best way of approaching the challenges which new legal rules present to organizations are always difficult. The ability and willingness of a public authority to make the right choice for its own circumstances will considerably influence the success of a new body of rules affecting all public authorities, such as the Human Rights Act 1998 (which incorporated the European Convention on Human Rights into UK law) or the duty to enhance racial equality under the Race Relations (Amendment) Act 2000, in achieving the legislator's objectives and being judged to be legitimate.

One can conclude this part of the discussion by observing that law can never offer a complete, or even sufficient, set of standards to guide public administration. It can only effectively seek to ascribe functions to public authorities, to confer powers for those purposes, to circumscribe the circumstances in which a public authority may lawfully act and the purposes for which it may exercise its powers, to provide for the sources of funds on which the authority may lawfully draw, and to lay down a minimum set of procedural standards to be met when the authority is engaged in its work. The important roles for law are to uphold the principle of legality in respect of public authority action, and to ensure so far as is possible (given the limitations of enforcement possibilities) that people who are adversely affected by an authority's failure to respect the limitations on its powers or to measure up to its procedural obligations will have an effective remedy. At the same time, if the rules are to be effective in stimulating officials to accept them as either 'working rules' or 'inhibitory rules', neither the legal rules nor the enforcement procedures must interfere with the work of the authority to such an extent as to make it practically impossible for it to do its job properly (unless its job is intrinsically incompatible with some fundamental legal or constitutional principle, such as the separation or division of powers or a prohibition on interfering with rights of bodily integrity or human dignity so far as those principles operate within a given legal system).

Two questions follow from these observations. First, are the principles of administrative law and other legal restrictions on the powers of public administrators ever, or always, incompatible with the values of public administration? Secondly, do legal rules always provide minimum standards below which public administrators must not be allowed to drop, or are the standards ever, or always, to some extent negotiable?

I Are legal principles incompatible with good public administration?

The principles of public law which typically govern public administration have been discussed at length in the two preceding chapters. One can sum them up (albeit at the risk of over-simplifying them) as follows. First, there are requirements derived from the principles of legality and con-stitutionality, which form an essential part of the Rule of Law. Public bodies must stay within their powers. They must respect the limits imposed by their position under the constitution. Admini-strative or executive bodies must not trespass into the judicial or legislative sphere, at any rate without express authority to do so. Where power is divided between central and provincial bodies, each must stay within the limits of their constitu-tional authority. Where legislation imposes obligations on an administrative body, the body must discharge them. When legislation limits the powers of a body, the body must respect those limits, and must not exercise power for an unauthorized purpose.

Next, there are limits related to the manner in which a power is exercised or a duty is performed. These are of three kinds. There are requirements as to the procedures to be followed, designed to enhance fairness. This notion of procedural due process is a way of ensuring that people are allowed to participate in decisions affecting them, respecting their autonomy and self-respect, as well as tending to ensure that the decision is informed by as full an appreciation as possible of the relevant factors and arguments. Then there are requirements as to the way in which deci-sions must be justified and communicated to those affected by them and to the wider commu-nity. These ensure that relevant matters and arguments will be taken properly into account, and that the outcome will be demonstrably rational and non-arbitrary.

Legality is essential to good administration. As a matter of principle, impartiality, probity, professional competence, rationality, consis-tency, fairness, giving reliable advice and infor-mation, and reasonable expedition are not only compatible with, but are bench-marks of good administration. There may have to be careful judgements about the level at which each can be incorporated in an administrative institution, and tensions between them may have to be resolved (as well as other tensions with the competing standards of efficiency, effectiveness and eco-nomy), but they cannot but be regarded as goods to be respected. Pragmatically, good administra-tors sensibly try to avoid making decisions which are likely to turn out to be ineffective when tested in court. Respecting the limits of one's powers is as much an ordinary part of public administration as finding ways to work within budgetary con-straints. Similarly, no sensible administrator would be heard to argue that fairness and ratio-nality were unimportant in good decision making.

Like freedom of information and the availability of reviews or appeals, requirements of proce-dural fairness and rationality impose a discipline which is likely to enhance the quality of decision making and administrative action. Insofar as legal standards serve to underpin what are really principles of good administration, the law is capable of reinforcing desirable aspects of administrative practice.

Nevertheless, there may be tensions between the aims of administration and the ways in which legal standards manifest themselves in practice. Looking first at the substance of the legal rules, they may impose inappropriately restrictive limits on the freedom of administrators to pursue the goals of their programmes. Procedural requirements may be so demanding, time-consuming and inflexible as to make it effec-tively impossible for an authority to use its powers. This was the fate of the powers of the Commission for Racial Equality in the United Kingdom to initiate formal investigations into suspected cases of discrimination in employ-ment. As a result, the Commission has had largely to limit itself to informal investigations and to dealing with discriminators by way of negotiation and education rather than enforce-ment.[22] That is not to say that those techniques are necessarily unproductive; they can be used very successfully. (More will be said about this below.) But the legal conditions attaching to the formal powers, as interpreted by courts, greatly reduced their usefulness. Similarly, requirements of due process, rationality and legitimate expec-tation may make it so time-consuming and resource-intensive for a body to make a decision in a way that will pass judicial scrutiny, or to adapt policies and practices to changing circum-stances, that the effectiveness of the body is compromised. In particular, there is often said to be a risk of defensive administration:[23] surviving challenge takes precedence over achieving goals in the minds of officials, potentially frustrating the objectives of the institution. There is a paucity of scientific substantiation of these effects, and they may in any case be ameliorated by making officials better informed about the principles of judicial review and their practical operation, but anecdotal evidence suggests that they should not be too easily discounted.

However, this tendency to inhibit worthwhile, goal-directed activity is a feature of all proce-dural rules, not only of legal rules. Public admin-istration is, or tends to be, an hierarchically organized activity. Within the hierarchy of administrators, those in superior positions promul-gate vast quantities of rules in an effort to ensure that programmes are implemented consistently and in accordance with budgetary and other constraints. The plethora of codes of practice, directives, guidance and advice which flows down through and between the structures of public authorities is in principle just as capable as legal rules of stifling flexibility, initiative and dynamism in the pursuit of an organization's goals. As noted above, sometimes officials learn to subvert or evade institutional policies by using internally generated rules for presentational, rather than working or inhibitory, purposes in order to achieve their view of the right result in particular cases.[24]

Yet there is a difference between legal rules and other rules intended to influence action and decision making. It becomes clear when one examines the ways in which legal standards manifest themselves in practice. Drafters of legal rules made specifically for a particular institution or programme normally go to some trouble to relate them to its aims (although some rules are ill-considered, and even sensible rules may produce dysfunctional results when interpreted in particular ways by administrators or courts). Where the rules significantly interfere with the pursuit of a goal, it normally means that the rule making body has decided that the goal is not to be pursued at any price, and must sometimes be balanced against competing interests. For example, service provision may be limited by requirements of economy. Occasionally courts condone the tendency of public authorities (noted earlier) to give resource considerations a higher priority than the words of the statute which imposes a duty on the authority, as in *R. v. Gloucestershire County Council, ex parte Barry*,[25] mentioned earlier, but that will not always happen.

The question is often not 'Should a balance be struck?', but 'Who should strike it?'. In the UK, with its strong constitutional doctrine of parliamentary sovereignty, where Parliament has spoken unequivocally (as it appeared to have done in *ex parte Barry*), it would be wrong for courts or administrators to seek to undermine the legislature's assessment of priorities. Where administrators within the responsible authority have made a judgement, a court or tribunal outside the institution may have little direct experience of the impact of different decisions on the work of the institution. There is a danger that a judicial decision will reflect a judicial balance between competing interests, shaped by the concerns of the legal system, rather than a legislative balance. Judges may give a high priority to procedural fairness and adversarialism in decision making, because a high level of fairness in the context of an adversarial procedure is one of the distinctive

features of a good deal of legal procedure. Yet relatively little administrative decision making is of that kind: it usually neither determines vested rights nor represents the resolution of any dispute. The fact that legal rules are ultimately interpreted and enforced by judicial rather than administrative authorities can lead to situations in which they have a dysfunctional effect. One way round this is to reduce the content of legal rules and govern administration as far as possible by way of administrative rules or standards which have no, or limited, legal effect, such as value-for-money assessment, the UK Citizen's Charter programme or Codes of Practice. However, that will tend to undermine the protection for legal rights and values. In particular, in the context of some activities (such as policing or housing) it may make it difficult to ensure adequate legal protection for the right to be free of arbitrary detention, or to provide for the right to a fair hearing where that applies, as required by (for example) Articles 5 and 6 of the European Convention on Human Rights. Once the general law of the land assigns special significance to some values or rights, the task of adjusting their application to accommodate the needs of different programmes and contexts may prove difficult, and put some obstacles in the way of the pursuit of administrative objectives.

What is true of fundamental rights and freedoms is also true of other general principles of public law developed without relation to particular institutions or goals. The rule against sub-delegation is an aspect of the principle of legality which can support good administration but may sometimes make it unworkable, requiring to be relaxed by administrative practice sanctioned by judges.[26] For example, sub-delegation may be a practical necessity where a power is granted to a minister or a collective body such as a local authority to decide very large numbers of individual cases, for example in the land-use planning or social security systems. The effect of the principle and of its relaxation may then be very much changed when put in a new organizational context, such as that of New Steps agencies or contracting out.[27] The same is true of the principles of fairness or natural justice, the rule that discretions must not be fettered, and requirements that reasons be given for decisions, all of which are aspects of good administration in general, but in particular settings may be capable of hamstringing administrative bodies and interfering with desirable flexibility. Where there are many people making discretionary decisions about the same issues in different cases, it will often be essential to impose some limitation on the range of decisions available to each decision maker in order to make sure that decisions are properly directed towards the approved goal, and to achieve a reasonable degree of consistency and predictability, which are all desirable characteristics of administrative procedures from both administrative and Rule of Law perspectives.

In the same way, being required to give reasons for decisions is a useful way of ensuring that decision makers take account of relevant matters and exclude irrelevant matters from their consideration, thereby helping to maintain the quality of decision making. It also treats with proper respect those who are subject to the decision making power by requiring their treatment to be justified to them, and upholds the Rule of Law by facilitating appeals and judicial review. On the other hand, it is important to avoid demanding such detail in the reasons as to impose a crippling burden on decision makers, thus slowing down the process to a point at which it ceases to operate reasonably efficiently. On appeal or review, courts and tribunals need to ensure that they do not dissect the reasoning of non-legal decision-makers as if the writing of decisions were an exercise in statutory drafting by qualified lawyers, invalidating decisions that did not meet that demanding standard.

On the whole, courts and tribunals strike a reasonable balance between ensuring that decisions are rational and properly related to the purpose for which the power was conferred and allowing public administrators to get on with their jobs. The principle of due deference to the expertise of expert bodies and the democratic legitimacy of democratically accountable bodies allows judges to maintain that balance, upholding the Rule of Law without making it impossible for public administration to proceed. Nevertheless, a court may have a significantly different view from that of administrators of the reasonableness of the balance struck. It will often be difficult to persuade administrators of the appropriateness of judicial review of their actions and decisions, either in general or in relation to particular cases. Viewed objectively from the perspective of an outsider, the legal rules help to confer and shape the powers of administrators to ensure that they operate functionally and respect the dignity and interests of those with whom they deal. In other words, legal rules aid good administration, and appeal procedures and judicial review of decisions merely act as a safety-valve for those cases (often the most difficult ones) which deserve or need special consideration for some reason. Legal rules, administrative rules and procedures, and external review of decisions are, on this view, complementary, enhancing the quality of public administration both within organizations and in dealings between administrators and members of the public.

From the perspective of the organization, and *a fortiori* that of individual decision makers within it, the picture may look different. While administrators may accept that the principles of review are not intrinsically inconsistent with the demands of good administration, they are likely to view appeals to courts and judicial review as a threat, rather than a useful safety net in hard cases. Introducing any kind of review by an authority external to the organization may be perceived as a threat, in three ways. First, it affects the finality of decisions, making administration more uncertain and causing delay. This can be particularly awkward in relation to large-scale and complex programmes of public work affecting many people's diverse interests, such as road building or the siting of airports, and partly explains the UK Government's desire to change the planning process for such projects, using Parliament rather than quasi-judicial procedures for decision making. Secondly, public administrators may see themselves as having special competence in administering complex programmes that involve balancing public interest considerations such as quality of service, type of service, location of service, and cost in the context of competing claims by service users. They may not consider that courts or non-specialist tribunals have that sort of expertise; indeed, the essentially adversarial nature of much court procedure can be seen as ill-suited to deciding matters of that kind. Thirdly, public administration is an increasingly professionalized, largely rule-based activity whose practitioners have their own distinctive system of values and ways of operating. Law is another professionalized activity of the same kind. Both form part of the foundation of modern bureaucratic states, as Max Weber observed. It would be surprising if the two groups did not share a degree of mutual suspicion, if not rivalry. Professionals who see themselves as having distinctive skills are likely to be upset when their decisions and actions are reviewed by outsiders. They may feel particularly threatened if the outsiders are part of a rival professional group asserting special authority, even if that authority is exercised only in limited circumstances and according to principles which, objectively, can be seen generally to complement rather than compete with administrative values. In such circumstances, much is likely to be made of those cases in which the courts are considered to have made decisions which, from an administrative standpoint, are dysfunctional.

When an administrative body feels under threat from an external reviewing body, it is likely to affect the way it relates to that body and the principles it promulgates. An organization that sees itself as having a co-operative relationship with an outside body is likely to try to internalize the principles which the outsiders propound, giving effect to the values which they enshrine and making their spirit an integral part of their operations and decision making. By contrast, an organization that feels threatened by an outside body is likely to try merely to ensure that its decisions and actions are immune to external review, sticking to the letter of the rules and insulating pre-existing internal principles and procedures as far as possible from the influence of the external authority. This defensive approach to administration under law could be seen in the first edition of a UK Cabinet Office booklet, first issued in the mid-1980s, advising central government civil servants about the demands of principles of judicial review. Even the title, *The Judge over your Shoulder*, is redolent of a defensive attitude, and has survived in subsequent editions even though the content of the booklet has progressively encouraged administrators to accept that the principles and practices of judicial review are compatible with, and can even aid, good administration.[28]

2 Do legal rules always provide minimum standards below which public administrators must not be allowed to drop, or are the standards ever, or always, to some extent negotiable?

This will often depend as much on the nature of the activity in question and the attitude that administrators adopt to their tasks as on the form or substance of the rules and the way they are interpreted and applied by courts. In childcare programmes, the law normally provides that the best interests of a child are to be the paramount consideration. This would appear to require public authorities to give greater weight to the welfare of the child than to the interests of the parents and other members of the family. However, in practice there is a significant area of flexibility. If the child is living with the family, it is likely to be in the child's best interests to accommodate as much as possible the interests of other members of the family. It is not acceptable to subject the child to a real risk of long-term physical or mental harm, and the authorities must act to prevent that. But the law also provides that removing a child from the family should normally be seen as a temporary measure, because it is assumed that all members of the

family benefit from (and, under the ECHR Article 8, have a presumptive right to) the enjoyment of their familial relationships. A care plan for a child in local authority care should therefore aim to effect a reintegration of the family where that is possible, offering education and support to achieve it. This leaves a considerable area of judgement within which local authorities must assess the needs of the child as part of the family unit rather than as an individual, negotiating with the family to achieve as safe and nurturing an environment as possible rather than imposing a solution to advance the supposed best interests of the child alone.

Even where an authority is enforcing a legal regime rather than delicately balancing competing or complementary interests, a number of factors may lead to a flexible approach to the task. Take for example the work of environmental health officers. The ultimate objective of the authority is to protect people against unjustifiable threats to health. Resources do not permit officers to police all possible occasions on which there is a threat to ensure that the law is complied with. The most efficient way of achieving the ultimate goal is therefore often to work as far as possible with potential offenders, helping them to develop their own systems for safeguarding public health without making their activities uneconomic. This will tend to mean that officers will regard education, encouragement and negotiation as the best way of dealing with people with whom they deal on a regular basis. Enforcement and prosecution will be relatively rarely used against such people, and then only as a last resort, usually only in cases of egregious breaches of rules; more regularly deploying enforcement powers would tend to interfere with the co-operative relationship on which effective protection of the environment depends. Nevertheless, different departments and individual officers may strike a different balance between the use of what Dr Bridget Hutter has called 'persuasive' and 'insistent' strategies, and the existence of an implicit or express threat of legal enforcement at some future time provides a significant incentive for people to respond constructively to officers' exhortations.[29] A similar pattern was found in the 'enforcement' of anti-pollution law, where to some extent even the permissible level of pollution (and therefore the content of the applicable legal rules) is open to negotiation.[30]

Enforcement by negotiation creates a risk that an overly cosy relationship will develop between people who potentially threaten public interests and those who are supposed to protect the public interest. Such relationships can give rise to at least the appearance of undue flexibility, and the suspicion that developers exercise undue influence over the land use planning process, waste disposal operators over pollution regulators, and so forth. Nevertheless, authorities can use the threat of legal action to encourage people to co-operate in developing good practice, achieving a reasonable level of compliance and public protection without expending vast resources on policing and prosecuting likely offenders, particularly as the response of magistrates may be unpredictable. How the balance is struck between use of formal powers and informal encouragement, assistance and negotiation will depend on the nature of the activity, the extent of an authority's resources, the ethos of the authority and to some extent the personality of individual officers.[31] Disagreement about the appropriate approach to policing of laws against 'soft' drugs reflects a debate about the proper balance between negotiation and enforcement in that context; to put it another way, about the extent to which the legal rules should be regarded as laying down hard and fast standards in practice.

In other kinds of administrative programmes, such as tax gathering, social security provision and the investigation of serious crimes, there may be less scope for using law as a basis for negotiation rather than as dispositive rules. Where an entitlement to money from the state is set out in statute, there is little room for manoeuvre on the law. The relevant authority (such as the Benefits Agency) would act unlawfully if it paid too little, and would be acting beyond its powers if it paid too much. Where a benefit depends on an assessment or evaluation, such as a judgement about a claimant's degree of incapacity, the judgement is typically made professionally and is not subject to negotiation. None the less, if the claimant makes a good impression it may contribute to a favourable decision by predisposing the decision maker in his or her favour: many factual assessments appear to be made on the basis of intuitive judgements, coloured by an officer's previous experience, of the claimant's reliability or need.[32] Even so, if the decision requires different claimants' needs to be prioritized, there are likely to be some needs which are absolutely excluded from consideration by statutory regulations or authoritative directions, and the priorities between other needs are set by local management guidelines. In the context of the British welfare state, discretionary Social Fund payments are of this kind: a local office has to stay within its quarterly budget and meet claims so far as possible taking account of the seriousness of the need and the money remaining in its budget. The apparently discretionary decisions are thus principally rule-driven, the rules being derived from a variety of sources, some having legal force and others being wholly administrative, subject to review by the social fund inspectors of the Independent Review Service for the Social Fund, who in turn are subject to judicial review. It is not possible to distinguish adequately between the effects of rules coming from these different sources.

Payments due to the state are in a slightly different position. The maximum amount due is set by statute or statutory instrument, but the officials responsible for collecting the money (tax inspectors and tax and social security fraud investigators) typically have discretion to relieve those subject to the charges of some part of the amount due. Sometimes these remissions are formalized in administrative rules, such as the UK Inland Revenue's published extra-statutory concessions which are treated just as if they were binding rules of law. In other contexts, they are the subject of negotiation in individual cases: penalties or other payments may be staggered, or remitted in whole or in part, on the grounds of hardship, or because insisting on the full payment at once would drive the payer into insolvency and make it more or less impossible to recover any substantial amount, or as an incentive for a payer to provide information about other activities or other people. In these investigative settings, the relationship between the legal rules and the behaviour of officials is far more like that between regulators and the regulated, described above. Negotiations take place against the background of the often draconian legal powers which officials would in practice find it counter-productive to use to the full.

JUDICIAL PROCEDURES AND THEIR EFFECT ON PUBLIC ADMINISTRATION

The impact of legal procedures on public administration runs closely in parallel with the impact of legal rules. We can distinguish between legal proceedings brought by public authorities and those brought against them. An authority's power to bring enforcement proceedings may (as noted above) be used rarely, and when used it may be counter-productive if the court imposes a low penalty or none at all. Nevertheless, it will have a significant impact on negotiations between the authority and potential offenders.

Awareness of the possibility of a prosecution and uncertainty about the result affects the balance of power between the authority and a potential offender when they negotiate with each other. The threat of legal proceedings is, perhaps, more powerful than their deployment in controlling breaches of legal rules.

It is not entirely clear whether the same is true of the impact of judicial review on public authorities. Applications for judicial review are usually retrospective challenges to decisions or actions already taken. To that extent, the individual cases will, as Dr Hugh Rawlings suggested, normally be sporadic, peripheral and temporary.[33] So far as it is sporadic rather than regular and predictable in its incidence, it will not allow the principles of judicial review to operate effectively as 'inhibitory' rules. To be effective, they will have to achieve 'working rule' status; otherwise they will be, at best, 'presentational'.

Nevertheless, there are circumstances in which judicial review can have a significant future effect on the institution being reviewed. If the point at issue is one affecting a large number of cases, and the authority has adequate systems for ensuring that the lessons from the case are understood quickly by other officials dealing with them, it can lead to a change in practices. For example, the UK Independent Review Service for the Social Fund has systems for ensuring that the relatively small number of inspectors understands the implications of legal challenges to their decisions.[34] But in larger and less centralized decision making structures, or institutions where officials' functions are more diversified and where heavy workloads leave little time for training or reading, or in departments staffed largely by temporary staff who are less well inducted into the work of the department than permanent staff, it will be difficult to achieve that level of legal consciousness, let alone legal conscientiousness. In other words, the impact of judicial review on public administration will vary in part according to the nature, staffing, training and organization of the public authority in question. For judicial review to perform an hortatory or educational role, there must be appropriate systems of communication and education between the judges and those whose behaviour they seek to influence.

There are also features of judicial activity which affect the impact that judges' decisions can expect to have. So far as judicial review seeks to influence administrative activity, it can be seen as performing three different functions: directing, limiting and structuring decision making. A court may hold that a body has a duty to act in a particular way on the facts of the case,

and direct it to comply. *Directing* decision making in this way usually gives effect to legislative provisions. It may achieve a high public profile and have significant resource implications, especially where the case is one of a number of similar ones and the duty will be costly to fulfil, and to that extent it may affect a wide range of functions which the authority exercises by forcing it to re-examine its priorities.[35] (The same happens in decisions about tort liability of public authorities.) However, this is unlikely to affect day-to-day administrative practices very much. *Limiting* a public authority to keep it within the range of activities, powers or purposes allocated to it by statute can have a greater effect on day-to-day administration, and may make it more difficult to achieve its goals, but can be justified by the principle of legality. *Structuring* decision making goes further, and has the greatest potential for affecting administrative practices. It provides principles to guide decision making by providing for fair procedures, and reasoned and reasonable decisions. It is here that judicial review intrudes most closely into the field of good administration, for good or ill.[36] This is why it is not surprising that studies of the effect of judicial review on prison administration have concluded that the effect has been greatest where decisions relate to procedural matters, such as disciplinary procedures and the right to make representations in respect of parole decisions, and far less extensive in relation to the conditions of imprisonment and regimes of prison governance.[37] However, even in relation to 'structuring' decisions, the tendency of judicial review to focus on the facts of a particular case, rather than to examine the matrix of decisions and procedures from which it emerges, may distort judicial appreciation of the context and so limit the usefulness of the case in shaping future decision making practices.

Where a decision has an impact on the administration, the practical effect will depend on the nature of the decision, and the ease with which the public authority can respond to it. Particularly in the field of 'structuring', the principles of judicial review tend to be very flexible, varying their content with the context. As Professor Carol Harlow and Professor Richard Rawlings have pointed out, the flexibility of standards of 'procedural fairness' is essential if judicial attempts to fashion principles of general application to the whole of public administration are not to suffer from over- or under-inclusiveness, strangling administrators with impossible demands in some fields while giving inadequate protection to their clients in others; yet it adds to the uncertainty of judicial review, making it difficult for administrators to predict what is required of them, and so reducing the constructive and useful role that judicial review can play in helping authorities to structure their own procedures.[38]

This shows how the impact of judicial review, like the impact of legal rules, cannot be separated from the social and structural context of the public authority that is being reviewed. There are features of judicial review, and the principles on which it operates, which make it difficult for it to affect administration. Other problems stem from the nature of the organizations subject to judicial review, their receptiveness, the legal consciousness of staff, and their sometimes very limited awareness and memory of judicial review challenges to decisions of other parts, or even their own part, of the organization.[39] The picture is complex, and for that reason (among others) it would be unreasonable to expect law, and judicial review in particular, to provide anything approaching a coherent guide to public administration. The focus of law is on legality, which (as suggested at the beginning of the chapter) is valuable as a matter of principle and compatible in principle with good administration; but the value of legality may give rise to tension (constructive or destructive in different settings) with goal-driven principles of good administration.

NOTES AND REFERENCES

1   C. Harlow and R. Rawlings, *Law and Administration*, 2nd edn (London: Butterworths, 1997) is an outstanding example.

2   In this chapter the phrase 'judicial review' denotes mechanisms for challenging the legality or fairness of administrative action, in contrast to the American usage of the phrase to mean challenges to the constitutionality of legislative or executive action.

3   Although nearly all the illustrative examples in this chapter are drawn from the author's UK background and experience, most of the points they illustrate are of more general application to other legal and administrative systems.

4   C.E. Schneider, 'Discretion and rules: a lawyer's view', in K. Hawkins (ed.), *The Uses of Discretion* (Oxford: Clarendon Press, 1992), Ch. 2 at p. 87.

5   See, e.g., G. Zellick, 'The Prison Rules and the courts' Criminal Law Review, 1981, p. 602; 'The Prison Rules and the courts: a postscript', Criminal Law Review, 1982, p. However, it is possible for an apparently non-justiciable standard to become justiciable through subjection to judicial interpretation: for example, the adjective 'economic' as a requirement of the public transport system for London was surprisingly given legal teeth in *Bromley London Borough Council v. Greater London Council* [1983] 1 AC 768, HL.

6   See, e.g., M. Feldman, 'Social limits to discretion: an organizational perspective', in Hawkins (ed.), *The Uses of Discretion*, Ch. 5; G. Richardson with A. Ogus and P. Burrows, *Policing Pollution: A Study of Regulation and Enforcement* (Oxford: Oxford University Press, 1982), pp. 183–90; B.M. Hutter, *The Reasonable Arm of the Law? The Law Enforcement Procedures of Environmental Health Officers* (Oxford: Clarendon Press, 1988), Chs 5 and 6.

7   J.M. Black, '"Which Arrow?": rule type and regulatory policy', *Public Law*, 1995, pp. 95–118.

8   Black refers only to sanctions, but, as H.L.A. Hart, *The Concept of Law* (Oxford: Clarendon Press, 1961), pp. 26–49 demonstrated, not all rules have sanctions.

9   'Universally accepted' seems to refer to acceptance within a particular social culture or sub-culture, such as a given community or a legal or administrative sub-culture within it.

10 For a broadly similar, though less developed, analysis of the formal qualities of rule-types and their relationship to reasons for failure of rules to achieve compliance, see R. Baldwin, *Rules and Government* (Oxford: Clarendon Press, 1995), pp. 7–11, 159–92.

11 See, e.g., J. Griffith, 'Judges and the constitution', in R. Rawlings (ed.), *Law, Society and Economy* (Oxford: Clarendon Press, 1997), at p. 308.

12 Baldwin, *Rules and Government*, pp. 41–6.

13 I. Loveland, *Housing Homeless Persons: Administrative Law and the Administrative Process* (Oxford: Clarendon Press, 1995), Ch. 10; M. Sunkin and A. Le Sueur, 'Can government control judicial review?', Current Legal Problems, 44 (1991), p. 161.

14 [1997] AC 584, HL.

15 D.J. Smith and J. Gray, *Police and People in London: the PSI Report* (London: Gower, 1985), pp. 441–2.

16 S. Halliday, 'The influence of judicial review on bureaucratic decision-making', *Public Law* 2000, at pp. 110–15 and 118; and see Loveland, *Housing Homeless Persons*.

17 See, e.g., Halliday, 'Influence of judicial review', at p. 118.

18 This is discussed further below.

19 S. Halliday, 'The influence of judicial review on bureaucratic decision-making', *Public Law*, 2000, at p. 114. Of course, even legally conscientious authorities are not equally conscientious in relation to all legal rules, as Halliday shows ('Influence of judicial review', at pp. 114–15).

20 See J. Baldwin, N. Wikeley and R. Young, *Judging Social Security: The Adjudication of Claims for Benefit in Britain* (Oxford: Clarendon Press, 1992), Ch. 2; G. Richardson and D. Machin, 'Judicial review and tribunal decision making: a study of the Mental Health Review Tribunal', *Public Law*, 2000, p. 494.

21 L. Bridges, C. Game, O. Lomas, J. McBride and S. Ranson, *Legality and Local Politics* (Aldershot: Avebury, 1987), pp. 106–11; and on the value of legal advice, and its limitations, in avoiding subsequent liability, see *Porter v. Magill* [2001] UKHL 67, [2002] 2 WLR 37, HL, at paras. [34]–[40] *per* Lord

Bingham of Cornhill, [147]–[148] *per* Lord Scott of Foscote.

22 C. McCrudden, 'The Commission for Racial Equality: formal investigations in the shadow of judicial review', in R. Baldwin and C. McCrudden (eds), *Regulation and Public Law* (London: Weidenfeld and Nicolson, 1987), Ch. 11.

23 See, e.g., M. Kerry, 'Administrative law and judicial review: the practical effects of developments over the last twenty-five years on administration in central government', *Public Administration*, 64 (1986), p. 163; A. Barker, 'The impact of judicial review: perspectives from Whitehall and the courts', *Public Law* 1996, p. 612.

24 Halliday, 'Influence of judicial review', at pp. 118–19.

25 [1997] AC 584, HL.

26 *Carltona v. Commissioners of Works* [1943] 2 All ER 560.

27 See M. Freedland, '*Privatising Carltona*: Part II of the Deregulation and Contracting Out Act 1994', *Public Law*, 1995, 21; M. Freedland, 'The rule against delegation and the *Carltona* doctrine in an agency context', *Public Law*, 1996, p. 19.

28 Compare Kerry, *op. cit.*, n. 22 above with D. Oliver, 'The Judge over your Shoulder – Mark II', *Public Law*, 1994, p. 514.

29 Hutter, *Reasonable Arm of the Law*, Chs 4, 5 and 6.

30 Richardson et al., *Policing Pollution*, esp. Chs 5 and 6.

31 On the need to see rules in the context of the social organization of the authority, see M. Feldman, 'Social limits to discretion'.

32 See, e.g., Halliday, 'Influence of judicial review', at pp. 115, 119.

33 H.F. Rawlings, 'Judicial review and the "control of government"', *Public Administration*, 1986, p. 135.

34 T. Buck, 'Judicial review and the discretionary Social Fund', in T. Buck (ed.), *Judicial Review and Social Welfare* (London, 1998).

35 This is particularly likely to be the case in respect of public interest challenges, as to which see C. Harlow, 'Public law and popular justice', *Modern Law Review*, 2002, p. 1–18.

36 D. Feldman, 'Judicial review: a way of controlling government?', *Public Administration*, 66 (1988), p. 21.

37 See, e.g., S. Livingstone, 'The impact of judicial review in prisons', in B. Hadfield (ed.), *Judicial Review: A Thematic Approach* (Dublin: Gill and MacMillan, 1995), p. 180.

38 Harlow and Rawlings, *Law and Administration*, pp. 562–5, 574. See also S. James, 'The political and administrative consequences of judicial review', *Public Administration*, 74 (1996), p. 613; A. Le Sueur, 'The judicial review debate: from partnership to friction', *Government and Opposition*, 31 (1996), p. 8; A.H. Hammond, 'Judicial review: the continuing interplay between law and policy', *Public Law* 1998, p. 34.

39 See, e.g., Halliday, 'Influence of judicial review', at pp. 120–1.

POLITICS AND ADMINISTRATION

Introduction

Nicole de Montricher

Since the emergence of the democratic state, relations between politics and administration have been an issue. At stake is the balance between a fair implementation of public policies, voted by the elected bodies, and an exclusive appropriation of the state apparatus by a political coalition. In the real world, however, this result has been reached; each state organizes its own framework based on distinctive values and institutions to get this balance. During the nineteenth and twentieth centuries, the focus has been on the difficult compliance of the 'principle of neutrality' with the compelling domination of politics over administration. The concept meant that public administration was nothing but an instrument under the hierarchical authority of the executive power to implement the political will expressed by the legislative power. The substance of neutrality was professionalism and dependence. However, as pointed out by Lascoumes and Le Galès in their chapter in this section, disastrous decisions taken by accredited civil servants changed this point of view. The twenty-first century sees positively the powers that balance the possibly oppressive behaviour of a neutral administration. Technocracy and the hazardous tyranny of a political majority should be challenged. Recently, important changes show up at both ends of the spectrum. The top-level administration is becoming more political and ordinary citizens are getting involved in public decisions. Responsibility remains the sphere of politics. Bureaucratic accountability is becoming a central issue.

HISTORICAL CONTEXT

Public organizations regulate private behaviour and provide public services and goods. When democratic governments elaborate public decisions, they have to articulate them through specific organizations and processes that comply with desires expressed by the citizens. Politics frame the constraints, public policies set the rules and administration transforms them into individual cases. The first model so designed emerged in Europe during the nineteenth century. Employees claimed their professionalism and scholars saw 'neutrality' as the focus of their understanding of public administration (Vivien, 1845). According to Luc Rouban in his chapter, this quality is the founding myth upon which the civil service was built as an accurate occupation separated from politics. It has given shape to know-how in the public service and it has provided for the emergent status of the civil service. The same path was followed later in the United States, when the crucial implication of the theory was accepted, namely that positions in the civil service were no more to be considered rewards; they were to be distributed according to expertise, as was the case for any job. The bureaucracy was a tool in the hands of elected officials and its legitimacy followed from that. The rule of law regulated its actions. Publicness implied specificities, privileges and commitments. This classical view of the relationships between politics and administration was generally accepted at the end of the nineteenth century.

Based on these principles, two different approaches to bureaucratic action were promoted. In Europe, the mainstream position was derived from the 'State of Law' under the direction of German and French schools of law, law being understood as a science for action in the public sector (Duguit, 1903). A theoretical and ideological division between politics and administration characterized these developments. Their relationships were structured according to such concepts as control and hierarchy. Research methods were directed by the deductive thinking of lawyers and they concentrated on the conditions under which rules and regulations were enforced. On the other hand, during the same period, American students of public administration were urged by Woodrow Wilson (Wilson, 1887) to build on a true science of public administration, separated from politics and oriented toward the search for efficacy. He strongly recommended relying on the experience of private management. Consequently, scientific activity was based on observation to set up instructions.

At the beginning of the twentieth century the German sociologist Max Weber founded the classical model of ideal-type bureaucracy (Weber, 1922). Thus he transformed the concept of administration by rejecting the division between public and private organizations. Until the Second World War, the study of public administration was dominated by the examination of structures and processes to describe and classify them. The hypothesis here was a division between politics and administration on the one hand, and a separation between administration and society on the other. This was made to comply with neutrality, the use of hierarchy to accomplish domination and the rule of law to reach efficacy and efficiency. The work done over the period

is inward-oriented. Its contribution to the knowledge of public administration as implementing political decisions is a major one. It shows that authors were perfectly aware of the theoretical and practical difficulties. They often show the conditions under which the norms were actually activated, their true meaning, and elaborated on the rationality of the whole setting (Fayol, 1918; Taylor, 1911). All the authors of this period relied on a positivist view of scientific management and they believed in the feasibility of a 'one best way' to organize the relationships between politics and administration. This conviction gave rise to a planning, programming, budgeting system. The failure of that system arose precisely from the fact that it overshadowed the political nature of the relationships between governments and their agencies.

THE IMPACT OF PUBLIC POLICY STUDIES

Decisive changes in the knowledge of the workings of the civil service occurred from outside the field of public administration when political scientists took an interest in the mechanisms operating the Welfare State. The way was then open to clarify the complex nature of public action, although the legitimacy of bureaucratic intervention was still conceived as resulting exclusively from its function as an instrument of the government. The first step was taken with the manifestation of a new way to question the real world through the study of public policies. This approach intended to explain the logic underlying administrative processes and the influence of public organizations on public action. The area became the territory of public administration and political science, but it was highly fertilized by sociology, economy, history and law. As described in Gary Bryner's chapter, the change came primarily from the study of new themes, the analysis of real functioning, grass roots situations and street-level interactions, and secondarily the transformation came also from modern methods and techniques of research provided by the behavioural sciences allowing better collection and understanding of data.

To describe and explain the substance of public policies researchers focused on the impact of organizations in the bureaucracy. On doing so they discovered that the distinction between administration and politics was more problematic than was expected. Public administration was not a unified entity and agencies played a crucial part in political action. As stated by Luc Rouban, 'public administration is, in the broad sense, a political institution'. Similarly to politics, bureaucracy is the territory of power. It is the scene where interests conflict, as was established by Selznick for the Tennessee Valley Authority (Selznick, 1949) and analysed by Michel Crozier in his study of the French civil service (Crozier, 1963). During the same period, scholars tried to discover the relevant causes for the failures of the Welfare State and they studied the changing adjustments between the state and society, mainly through the search for efficacy (Simon, 1957). Thus, considering the bureaucracy as a political body and public policies as theories of social change, researchers started to do empirical work. They found that adversary individuals and organizations are at the head of the chain of command that connects politics and administration. New knowledge came also from the political arena in 1961, when President Eisenhower warned citizens against 'iron triangles', meaning the influence of politics and interest groups at various levels of the bureaucracy. In practice, boundaries separating the bureaucracy from politics were blurred, as described in the chapter written by Pierre Lascoumes and Patrick Le Galès.

Indeed, it is during the 1970s, when economic constraints put an end to the ongoing development of the Welfare State, that efficiency of the bureaucracy became an issue. This type of concern gave rise to a number of theoretical and empirical researches arguing that the public service uses public money for its own purposes (Tullock, 1970). Then political managers discovered that their authority over the bureaucracy was not unlimited. President Nixon, for example, as reported by Aberbach and Rockman (1976), endured the resistance of the staff in the Department of Health, Education and Welfare when he intended to redirect public action according to a line they did not trust. More generally, when civil servants are organized in unions, they play a crucial part in

the game. At the end of the twentieth century scholars contributed to the modification of the assumptions on which previous theory was based. First, the bureaucracy is not dominated by politics. On the contrary, most of the time political authorities rely on the expertise of civil servants and on the data that they provide (Allison, 1971; Heclo, 1974; Jobert and Muller, 1987). In addition, it is argued that politics gets bureaucratized. Secondly, the technical skills of civil servants are challenged by the horizontal and vertical fragmentation of the structures, thus causing unintended conflicts and delays. The classical work undertaken by Pressman and Wildavsky on the conditions under which the federal programme in favour of the unemployed in Oakland was implemented (Pressman and Wildavsky, 1973) is a good example of impediments arising from too long and heterogeneous a chain of command. Similarly, in France scholars highlighted the role of the préfets and local 'notables' in reshaping or blocking the intentions expressed by representatives of the central government in order to fulfil local demand (Gremion, 1976; Worms, 1966). Thirdly, the bureaucracy is not a uniform organization, partly because at the lowest level employees in operational positions have their own mode of reasoning. In the daily operation of public policies, they are confronted with problems and they solve them according to their own standards of action (Dupuy and Thoenig, 1985). Fourthly, public administration is not separated from society, as joint interests can link together private and public organizations (Heclo and Wildavsky, 1974; Lowi, 1979), and even the target groups can influence the implementation process (Sabatier and Mazmanian, 1980). During the whole period the role of interest groups both within and outside the bureaucracy is progressively included in the study of public administration, thus illuminating their impact on bureaucratic behaviour. As Lascoumes and Le Galès describe in their chapter, the emergence of European institutions has modified both the character of interest groups and their strategies. Thus the relationships between the bureaucracy and its environment have been transformed.

Scrutinizing the situation from a different point of view, Gary Bryner indicates in his chapter that a radical change has occurred in the relationships between politics and administration because the legitimacy of the bureaucracy is no longer limited to the technical implementation of governmental will. In making known that politics and administration do interact, studies in the field of public policies tell that public management is not the sole issue; substance is also at stake, because in implementing public policies the bureaucracy is answering to the citizen's expectations. This question was raised when it became clear that people were affected in their day-to-day life by perfectly legal public decisions that they resented. Research on the balance between general and special interests first focused on the capture of public agencies. During the 1960s and 1970s various works emphasized the conditions under which individuals and organizations gain access to the bureaucracy by lobbying from the top to the bottom, including the level of local government that implements national public policies. More recently, organized groups of citizens have emerged asking for democratization of the bureaucracy, arguing that it is part of the public sphere and as such it should face the political constraints of democracy. Accordingly, after considering the representative bureaucracy (Krislov, 1974) and its disagreements (Krislov and Rosenbloom, 1981), practitioners and researchers are in search of the participative structures and processes that would transform the nature of the Weberian bureaucracy (Callon et al., 2001).

RESEARCH ON POLITICS AND ADMINISTRATION

As described in the three chapters of this section, the field today is characterized by heterogeneity, dynamism and hybridization: heterogeneity of political and administrative systems, dynamism of scientific methods and research questions, hybridization of theories, concepts and definitions. It appears, however, that crucial ground was covered when scholars changed their perspective and started to study public policies not only as dependent variables but also as independent variables. Nevertheless, the field can still be distinguished as 'art and craft' in Wildavsky's words (Wildavsky, 1979).

The first observation is that uncertainty is the distinctive quality of definitions in the field. If neutrality is now generally regarded as an empty concept, bureaucracy is a polysemous word meaning either the specific organization described by Max Weber or public administration as a function, or a pejorative expression for an organization known for rigidity and conformism. Politicization is the name applied to the appropriation of public agencies by a specific political coalition or the strengthening of the top level of an administration to implement the commitments of the electoral campaign. Participation refers to the capture of public action by self-interest groups or new avenues for the development of democracy. Public management defines the search for an 'efficient and effective instrument for carrying out the will of the nation' (Brownlow et al., 1937) while New Public Management (NPM) specifically qualifies tools aimed at better service through privatization and decentralization to separate management from politics.

As assessed by Gary Bryner, theory and practice are closely linked to the ideological conflict separating the academic community and the political arena, between those who assume that the 'market rule' should be valued to promote democracy through 'value for money' services and those who believe that the specificity of public intervention still makes sense to reach this democratic goal through monopolies and public interest. Hence the relationships between politics and administration are central to the antagonism. Both groups consider that governments must control the bureaucracy, but the first envisages better performance through self-constraint by the construction of quasi-markets and the 'principal and agent' theory, while the latter values the general interest and the hierarchical chain of command. Whatever theory is adopted, there is now an agreement on the fact that the relationship between politics and administration is characterized by interaction. However, the rapidly growing influence of public management implies reflection on the conditions under which efficiency can be included among the principles of democratic governance.

This consideration has generated a great range of research in the field of public management. Some researchers are devoted to the mechanisms for action (Hood, 1983) while others focus on a revisited division between politics and bureaucracy. According to the most radical school of thought, the New Public Management, to achieve good-quality and efficient public services the bureaucracy should be separated from the government in order to optimize its resources once relieved of political interference (Pollitt, 1998). For the time being, most states have been reluctant to adopt this division, but theoretical and practical work is rapidly expanding in the field to balance bureaucratic autonomy and political domination. Other scholars explore new hypotheses, variables and modes of classification to test the relevance of the Weberian model in an era of political and administrative questioned legitimacy.

Reform is common but, as stated in each of the three chapters, contextual variables are often decisive. Specifically, political systems differ in important ways, making comparisons problematic. As clearly presented by Lascoumes and Le Galès, it is especially the case for interest groups, which deserve a highly different level of participation in the governmental system in the United States and in the European Union. Although comparative work is still in an early stage, the relationships between politics and administration have been illuminated by research on governmental work. Comprehensive research on public policies, which intends to embrace actors and systems, structures and interests, is in progress. Elaborating on the available knowledge, Guy Peters finds four models of governance that span the different types of coherence between politics and administration (Peters, 1996). In the 'market model' the government imposes its policy and ideological directives on quasi-autonomous organizations, thus producing more innovative programmes. In the 'participatory model' the lower echelons and their users deserve a substantial impact on policy decisions because they possess a higher level of information. In the 'flexible model' governance is characterized by an experimental approach giving senior officials an opportunity to test their own conceptions of good policy. Finally, in the 'deregulated model' the bureaucracy is liberated from its unnecessary rules and red tape to serve the goals of political leaders, which cannot be properly attained without professional civil servants taking an active role.

To measure phenomena is problematic, as pointed out by Luc Rouban, because concepts do not have the same meaning everywhere and classical tools are not suited, for example, to describe politicization or to assess the impact of interest groups. Consequently, the relative weight of specific facts is usually difficult to apprehend. On the other hand, case studies, when they are carefully undertaken according to clear dimensions, allow a reliable description of the real world. Today they constitute the major source of knowledge in the field, although crucial steps remain to be taken to set up methodological rules and theoretical hypotheses.

POLITICS AND ADMINISTRATION IN THE TWENTY-FIRST CENTURY

Since it emerged with decisive changes in the English bureaucracy at the end of the 1970s, the theme of 'administrative reform' has been running for twenty years in most states, with important implications for the relationships between politics and administration. What is the direction of change?

International organizations like OECD or the World Bank consider that governments face similar problems and consequently they try to influence institutional arrangements, the tendency being to unify guidelines and evaluate national patterns according to a standardized norm of efficacy and efficiency. In conformity with the institutional evolution observed recently, the modern connection of guidelines and institutions is dominated by regulation more than by direct provision. This tendency means more authority, rules and standard setting and more decentralization, contracting out and control, an orientation that opposes the previous value set on technically implementing the political will. Change is also oriented toward more interrelations between private professions and the bureaucracy, thus denying the founding division of the modern state between public and private sectors. In the European Union, for example, the model of independent agencies has been adopted and imposed to regulate public utilities. More generally, administrative law as a tool for implementing the governmental will in conformity with the Weberian model of bureaucracy is slowly being challenged by different instruments aimed at controlling the agencies (Hood et al., 1999).

Contemporary administrations are primarily confronted by developments in their interactions with politics. Recently, electoral pressure for rapid implementation of the commitments declared during the campaign has resulted in a strengthening of the political layer of the executive (Peters et al., 2000) and, more specifically, in increasing politicization. As stated by Luc Rouban, although research has not given way to general paradigms in the field, the phenomenon is proved. The weight of the centre is growing and its politicization is increasing because of the civil servants' involvement in the definition and implementation of public policies. Rouban argues that in Europe a new pattern is emerging in which more emphasis is given to the political and professional skill of bureaucrats. This observation is borne out by Lascoumes and Le Galès, who show the changing structure of interest groups to interact with the bureaucracy at the European level.

The second characteristic of modern bureaucracies is autonomy, either through decentralization of local governments and agencies or by allocation of extensive freedom to operational offices set up on a functional rationale. The tendency has been to give more trust to private enterprises. Typical of the renewed complexity of the relationships between politics and administration is the 'subsidiarity principle', implying that the chain of command should be as short as possible, at the same time diminishing red tape and limiting the capacity to equalize situations. Meant to protect the political autonomy of the states in the emerging European Union, subsidiarity will probably allow the European bureaucracy to negotiate directly with infra-state institutions, thus increasing the interconnection of politics and administration, in addition to the mutual involvement of different levels of government as described by Lascoumes and Le Galès. This development will give rise to new experiences, multiplying the number and configuration of arrangements organizing the relations between various public and private bodies, coordinating and allowing access to the bureaucracy through institutions and networks.

The third characteristic that both Bryner and Lascoumes and Le Galès bring out in their chapter is the central position of agencies subject to the pressure of conflicting interests as demand grows for participation among an increasing number of actors claiming consideration for their affected interests and thus challenging the political decision taken by the elected bodies. The first interest to be manifest is inward-oriented. Public servants are eager to perpetuate their employment and to maintain the services that they deliver to the public, even when the political authority intends to cut it down. The French government experienced this situation at the end of the 1990s when it was obliged to withdraw the reform of the Ministerial Department of Finances (Bert, 2000). Another group that tends to express its own view of what is suitable service is composed of street-level bureaucrats. They claim that as it is they who are doing the job they should control its substance. They often know the compelling complexities of the day-to-day confrontation with the demands of the citizen. However, as developed by Lascoumes and Le Galès, bureaucracies are now facing citizens organized in a constantly moving scene of interest groups with whom they have to deal as partners in seeking the identification of the common good, thus being exposed to the challenge of such groups' representativeness and expertise.

FUTURE RESEARCH

The three chapters in this section give shape to a new model of relationships between politics and administration. According to this pattern, public policies would result from the confrontation between mediated demands as expressed by elected bodies and direct formulation of the will of affected citizens. This change in the substance of 'politics' will bring about a correlative modification of 'administration' and a new orientation of the relationship between the two. Interaction will give rise to new types of hybridization and power to replace instrumentalism. Their constituents should be explored regarding the changing skills of civil servants, the evolving procedures of decision and the development of original modes of control to match new demands expressed by distinct actors. Finally, novel hypotheses should be produced to classify differently the actors, problems and behaviours involved in the relationships between politics and administration.

REFERENCES

Aberbach, J., Rockman, B. (1976) 'Clashing beliefs within the executive branch: the Nixon administration bureaucracy' *American Political Science Review*, 70 (June): 456–68.

Allison, G. (1971) *Essence of Decision. Explaining the Cuban Missile Crisis*. Boston, MA: Little Brown.

Bert, T. (2000) 'La réforme de Bercy', in R. Fauroux and B. Spitz (eds), *Notre état*. Paris: R. Laffont.

Brownlow, L., Merriam, C. and Gulick, L. (1937) 'Administrative management in the government of the United States, January 8 1937'. Washington, DC, US Printing Office. (Reprinted in J. Shafritz and A. Hyde (1978) *Classics of Public Administration*, 2nd edn. Chicago: Dorsey Press.)

Callon, M., Lascoumes, P. and Barthe, Y. (2001) *Agir dans un monde incertain: essai sur la démocratie technique*. Paris: Seuil.

Crozier, M. (1963) *Le Phénomène bureaucratique*. Paris: Le Seuil.

Duguit, L. (1903) *L'Etat, les gouvernants et les agents*. Paris: A. Fontemoing.

Dupuy, F. and Thoenig, J.C. (1985) *L'Administration en miettes*. Paris: Fayard.

Fayol, H. (1918) *Administration industrielle et générale*. Paris: Dunod.

Gremion, P. (1976) *Le pouvoir périphérique*. Paris: Le Seuil.

Heclo, H. (1974) *Modern Social Politics in Britain and Sweden*. New Haven, CT: Yale University Press.

Heclo, H. and Wildavsky, A. (1974) *The Private Government of Public Money, Community and Policy Inside British Politics*. London: Macmillan.

Hood, C. (1983) *Tools of Government*. London: Macmillan.

Hood, C., Scott, C., James, O., Jones, G. and Travers, T. (1999) *Regulation Inside Government*. Oxford: Oxford University Press.

Jobert, B. and Muller, P. (1987) *L'Etat en action*. Paris: Press Universities de France.

Krislov, S. (1974) *Representative Bureaucracy*. Englewood Cliffs, NJ: Prentice–Hall.

Krislov, S. and Rosenbloom, D. (1981) *Representative Bureaucracy and the American Political System*. New York: Praeger.

Lowi, T. (1979) *The End of Liberalism*, 2nd edn. New York: Norton.

Peters, Guy B. (1996) *The Future of Governing: Four Emerging Models*. Lawrence, KS: University of Kansas Press.

Peters, Guy B., Rhodes, R.A.W. and Wright, Vincent (eds) (2000) *Administering the Summit: Administration of the Core Executive in Developed Countries*. Basingstoke: Macmillan; New York: St Martin's Press.

Pollitt, C. (1998) 'Managerialism revisited', in B.G. Peters and D.J. Savoie (eds), *Taking Stock: Assessing Public Sector Reforms*. Montreal and Kingston: McGill-Queen's University Press.

Pressman, J.L. and Wildavsky, A. (1973) *Implementation*. Berkeley, CA: University of California Press.

Sabatier, P. and Mazmanian, D. (1980) The implementation of public policy: a framework for analysis', *Policy Studies Journal*, 8: 538–60.

Selznick, P. (1949) *TVA and the Grass Roots*. Berkeley, CA: University of California Press.

Simon, H.A. (1957) *Administrative Behavior: A Study of Decision-making Process in Administrative Organization*. New York: Free Press.

Taylor, F.W. (1911) *Principles of Scientific Management*. New York: Harper.

Tullock, G. (1970) *Private Wants, Public Means: An Economic Analysis of the Desirable Scope of Government*. New York: Basic Books.

Vivien de Goubert (1845) *Etudes administratives*. Paris: Guillaumat. (Quoted by Luc Rouban (1996) *La Fonction publique*. Paris: La Découverte.)

Weber, M. (1922) *Economie et société* (French translation, 1971). Paris: Plon.

Wildavsky, A. (1979) *Speaking Truth to Power. The Art and Craft of Policy Analysis*. Boston, MA: Little Brown.

Wilson, W. (1887) 'The study of administration', *Political Science Quarterly*, 2 (June). (Reprinted 1941 in *Political Science Quarterly*, 61 (December): 481–506.)

Worms, J.P. (1966) 'Le préfet et ses notables', *Sociologie du travail*, 8: 3.

23

Public Organizations and Public Policies

Gary C. Bryner

The primary task of public organizations is to implement the policies enacted by governments. How well government achieves important policy goals is, to a great extent, a function of the capacity of public administration. Other factors are critical, such as legislative commitments of authority and resources to policy goals, and executive decisions concerning priorities and tradeoffs among competing concerns, in determining whether or not policy goals are realized Public organizations play important roles in the shaping of political systems in general. But policy success is intertwined in particular with administrative capacity. A public policy-based approach to viewing public organizations suggests numerous avenues. I focus on three broad themes.

First, the tremendous growth in the range and scope of public policies governments undertake has generated correspondingly more expansive expectations for governments. Those expectations have largely fallen on the shoulders of public administrators to implement programs that solve public problems and achieve public purposes. Different kinds of public policies pose different kinds of challenges for public administration. Some policies tend to be associated with political arrangements that implicate bureaucracy in ways that are quite consistent with other strongly held values of democratic accountability and representation, while others are more problematic. More broadly, the policy making process illustrates that 'administration' and 'politics' cannot be clearly delineated. The legitimacy and acceptability of public bureaucracies has traditionally been a function of the idea that agencies simply implement political decisions made by others, and that the administrative process

is neutral and objective. But administration is politics: political choices are endemic to administration, and public bureaucracies need to be understood as nested within a network of political actors.

Second, as the scope and reach of public policies increases in democracies, there has been a corresponding demand for more participation by affected interests. Agencies that are responsive to these demands must balance participation with other demands on bureaucratic resources, and the tradeoffs between more efficient and expedient operation and more outreach and discussion with the public are difficult to make. Demands for participation challenge expectations that the task of public administration is primarily the non-political implementation of political will expressed in statutes, and that administration is the purview of experts and professionals. As participation expands, lines of accountability and political oversight are muddied.

Third, assessments of the outcomes of public policies also shape the way we think about public organizations. Those who believe outcomes are largely positive are for the most part supportive of existing bureaucracies; those who take a more critical view of those outcomes naturally conclude that changes in public administration are necessary. Public agencies are often blamed for being ineffective, unable to solve the problems they are expected to remedy, but bureaucratic successes and failures are ultimately a function of the distribution of power in the political economy of which they are a part. The effectiveness of public organizations is largely determined by the extent to which they are able to satisfy the demands and interests of broader forces. While much attention is focused on questions of administrative structure, bureaucratic behavior, process, management and inter-governmental politics, public organizations cannot be understood apart from the broader context of the state.

In sum, a public policy-based perspective on public administration focuses attention on the tremendous expectations aimed at public organizations and the tremendous challenges they face in trying to satisfy competing and often contradictory values. Those values clash within bureaucratic organizations, as they interact with other political institutions, and as they operate within the broader distribution of economic, social and political power.

PUBLIC ADMINISTRATION, ADMINISTRATIVE POLITICS AND THE POLICY MAKING PROCESS

Policy steps or stages

The traditional model of the policy making process describes it as a dynamic process, a 'complex analytic and political process to which there is no beginning or end, and the boundaries of which are uncertain' (Lindblom, 1968: 4). It is also a continual process of identifying problems, formulating governmental responses or policies, organizing administrative mechanisms for carrying out the policies, and evaluating the extent to which policy objectives are achieved. The process of making public policies is not particularly precise. Since it is often difficult to identify with precision the nature of the problems to be addressed or the policy response that would most likely lead to their resolution, a lot of action may be taken with little effect. Policies often help to move society away from some of the effects of a problem, yet do not really move it closer to a solution, or may treat symptoms of problems without addressing root causes.

Although the policy making process differs for different kinds of policies, some elements are present in all policy efforts. As outlined by Charles Jones and others, the policy process includes four major steps: initiation and definition, formulation and enactment, implementation, and impact and evaluation (Jones, 1984; Peters, 1991). This model does not explain why policies take the shape they do, but it provides a useful way of examining the different factors that shape the policy process and, in particular, the role of public bureaucracies in that process.

The policy process 'begins', or, perhaps more accurately, a new cycle commences when people identify social and economic problems that might be resolved by governmental efforts. After the problem is perceived and defined, interests are aggregated and organized in anticipation of presenting demands or proposals to government officials. (Government officials themselves, particularly administrative officials, are often involved early in this step of the process, as they seek to develop support for policies of interest to them.) Depending upon the strength of the political forces behind a proposal and government officials' perception of its importance, the proposal may become an element of the policy agenda. Getting on the policy agenda is a major challenge, given the tremendous number of problems clamoring for attention. Interest groups may organize, mobilize their resources and lobby elected officials, but action may not occur until a major event or 'crisis' focuses widespread attention on the issue. Innovative policies are possible when there is a convergence of public attention, political interest in responding to public concern and 'policy entrepreneurs' who are able to channel the political energy toward policy changes (Kingdon, 1984).

The way policy problems are identified and the assumptions and values that give shape to the definitions can have a number of important consequences for the administration of public policies. Misperception of the problem (attention directed toward symptoms rather than root causes, for example) may lead to a proposed policy response that is inadequate or lacks proper focus. The political support (or lack of it) generated during this initial stage of the process can have an important effect on policy development, implementation and evaluation. Some problems may be ignored – and attention given to other, less serious problems – simply because they fail to attract strong political support.

The second step in the policy process includes formulating a program to respond to the demand for action, getting it on the policy agenda of the governing body that is to take action, enacting legislation to authorize implementation of the program, and appropriating sufficient funds for implementation. This requires the interaction of the law makers (the legislature or parliament), the groups advocating the proposal, the executive and the agencies that will ultimately be responsible for implementing the policy.

The coalition building and compromise that is central to the legislative process often results in laws that are imprecise and leave much room for interpretation by administrative officials. Difficult choices might be deferred to the agency implementing the policy, thus deflecting the political controversy from the legislative process to the administrative process. The political environment in which agencies operate is thus highly charged because agencies end up making basic policy decisions that are expected to satisfy the various interests affected. Even legislation that is quite specific usually gives agencies responsibilities that greatly exceed their resources, requiring that they set priorities and make basic policy choices. The success of policy makers in accurately defining the nature and causes of problems and in developing and implementing effective solutions is a function of policy analysis as well as political acumen and luck.

Implementation, the third step in the policy process, is often a long, complicated procedure that includes interpreting legislative intent, balancing statutory and executive priorities, creating administrative structures and processes, reviewing congressional or parliamentary debates on policy formulation as regulations are devised, and building political support for enforcement of regulatory requirements. This model of the policy process assumes a simple relationship between policy formulation and implementation that largely mirrors the separation of powers: the legislature makes the policy choices and the executive branch (and local governments) implement them. It reflects a widely held perception that major policy decisions are the responsibility of elected representatives. In reality, the line between making and implementing policies is blurred and there is much overlap; those who implement laws are often required to make policy choices.

There are a great number of reasons why implementation is so difficult (Mazmanian and Sabatier, 1983). Some implementation fails to achieve its objectives because of a lack of political will or agreement. Other efforts suffer from inadequate funding or authority. Policy goals in one area, such as environmental protection, for example, must compete with social welfare, economic and other policy objectives. There are multiple goals, they often conflict and there are limited financial and other resources. The price of political compromise is often vagueness, and there may be little agreement over what exactly the goals are. Implementation is a continuation of the politics of policy formulation, but with some new actors, procedures and institutional settings. As implementation efforts proceed, we become aware of new problems, constraints and opportunities. Resources and goals are constantly in flux. Unintended consequences pervade policy implementation efforts (Pressman and Wildavsky, 1984: 168–80). At the heart of implementation are the inevitable tradeoffs such as more centralized control and consistency versus decentralized

flexibility, community control and efficiency (Pressman and Wildavsky, 1984: 232–3). As a consequence of these and other competing concerns, implementation often seems to be unsuccessful in accomplishing the policy goals expected of it.

It is somewhat misleading to say that policy evaluation or analysis is the last step in the policy making process; in fact, it occurs throughout the entire process. The legislature and the executive branch oversee the implementation of the law or policy and regularly assess the effectiveness of its major provisions, including the clarity with which policy goals are expressed. They also consider the extent to which policy objectives have been achieved and reformulate policies as necessary. Administrators are expected to make a politically neutral professional judgment, but policy evaluation by legislators is a very political undertaking, pursued by politicians for a variety of purposes.

Central to the policy making process is the ability of policy makers to assess the strengths and weaknesses of existing policies and alter them when necessary. Policy analysis in general rests on the expectation that the technical assessment of competing policy options will be separated from the political calculations of the policy makers, and that there will be an objective, non-political assessment of policy options before the inevitable political calculations shape the decisions eventually made. In theory, careful policy analysis precedes the application of narrow political pressure and ensures that policies producing the greatest net gains in social welfare will be pursued. In practice, of course, policy analysis is a very political exercise, and public organizations are caught in the middle of the political tug of war over evaluating and reshaping public policies. In theory, policy makers allow those responsible for implementing a law the flexibility to make the adjustments necessary to solve evolving problems and to learn from trial and error. Policy evaluation requires clear goals and standards against which policy implementation efforts can be measured. But that kind of clarity is often lacking, and when it exists, the policy tasks may overwhelm the resources available to public administrators.

Different policies, different politics

Some kinds of policies are particularly problematic for public organizations. One of the most important characteristics of policy making is that different kinds of policies tend to be associated with different kinds of political relationships and processes. Theodore Lowi has persuasively argued that there are three primary types of policies – distributive, redistributive and regulatory – and that each type of policy is associated with a particular political process (Lowi, 1972). All public policies, according to Lowi, are coercive because they seek to alter individual and societal conduct. There are different ways of controlling behavior, however, and they have different implications both for the way the policy making process works and for the implementation of the policies that result.

Distributive policies include grants and subsidies that give protection to certain interests against competition and underwrite or directly provide benefits. Legislation regarding implementation is likely to be quite specific and to allow little administrative discretion. The key decisions – who is to receive the benefits and how much they are to receive – are usually made by the legislators, who have a considerable interest in ensuring that recipients can clearly trace the origins of the benefits given them.

Redistributive policies are concerned with the economy and society. They include the actions that affect credit and the supply of money, as well as taxes and social security and transfer payments. Redistributive policies are ideological; they raise basic issues about the proper role of government in societal and economic matters. They usually capture the attention of elected officials and are formulated in a more centralized manner than other policies. Some redistributive policies are only vaguely defined by law and require considerable administrative expertise and discretion in implementation; other policies are clearly defined by law and require only routine methods of administration. In general, however, the task of public bureaucracies is to faithfully implement the details of the programs developed by elected policy makers.

Regulatory policies seek to alter individual behavior directly by imposing standards on regulated industries and are much more likely to arouse controversy. Private interests may be significantly constrained or have compliance costs imposed upon them by regulatory actions. Powerful interest groups are likely to be organized around regulatory issues, and the interaction of these policy advocates plays an important role in determining the nature of the policy. Regulatory policies often involve complex, technical decisions or concern areas of effort where appropriate policy actions cannot easily be determined; much time will be spent discussing technical issues, and the role of experts in administrative agencies and interested groups will be paramount. More broadly, Lowi criticizes the broad delegation of authority and discretion to administrative agencies that replaces vigorous political debate and a strong commitment to the rule of law, with an administrative process that is less politically partisan and uninformed by strong political debate (Lowi, 1979).

Government does not grow inexorably in every policy area. There are significant differences in growth in different policy arenas. For example, as public policy becomes more and more oriented toward social programs, the challenges to public organizations include balancing assistance to individuals with the demands of a competitive economy. In Europe, for example, social programs account for two-thirds of all public expenditures. The largest spending category, 44 per cent, is for transfer payments to the elderly, unemployed, disabled and others unable to work. Health and education are the next largest categories. Interest on funds borrowed to pay interest on current and past debt is the fourth largest category of expenditure, followed by defense and public order. The remaining spending is dispersed in pursuit of a great number of public purposes, such a promoting economic growth, trade, agriculture and industry; protecting the environment; providing public goods such as transportation and communications; and the cost of government itself. Since the 1950s, defense spending as a percentage of national product has fallen by 50 per cent and spending on social programs has more than doubled (Rose, 1996: 240–2). The pattern is similar in the United States. The debate over the welfare state in the United States and Europe has prompted a major reassessment of the compatibility of social assistance and economic prosperity in the global economy, and public organizations are key actors in efforts to find the right balance between these enduring policy goals (Bryner, 1998). The intractability of the problem creates tremendous expectations that these organizations are incapable of satisfying.

Policy makers, citizens and scholars alike ask whether the growth of government and the ambitious, detailed, comprehensive laws that accompany that growth are sustainable. These laws continually heighten public expectations, yet the government continually falls short in its attempts to meet them. Each law passed by the legislature has a cumulative impact on future efforts to devise effective solutions to public problems. Government's unwillingness or inability to succeed may ultimately erode the public's faith in collective efforts and the institutional capacity to resolve pressing public problems. Again, these pressures to achieve contradictory and competing goals are felt by government as a whole, but it is often public organizations that are caught in the middle of these conflicting demands and are unable to deliver on them.

PUBLIC ADMINISTRATION AND DEMOCRATIC PARTICIPATION

The argument for strong democratic participation in the policy making process begins with the view that normative deliberations about policy goals and outcomes are not inferior to scientific assessments, but merely different, and both have value. Frank Fischer (1995), for example, suggests that deliberations about public policies should take place at two levels. The first order evaluation raises traditional technocratic issues of examining outcomes – does the policy achieve its objectives and how appropriate are the objectives, given the nature of the problems at which they are aimed? These questions require technical information that is largely generated and evaluated by experts. The second level of analysis shifts to the larger social, political and economic system, the impact of policies on the system as a whole and to its underlying normative principles and values. Decision making requires different but interrelated discourses, from assessments of the impact of policies (or likely impacts of policy alternatives) to the compatibility of policies with public order, public values and norms, and the capacity of democratic institutions. Both experts and citizens have a role in generating and assessing information to be used in policy making and implementation.

Other scholars emphasize the essentially political nature of public policy choices. Deborah Stone argues that the essence of policy making is 'the struggle over ideas', a 'constant struggle over the criteria for classification, the boundaries of categories, and the definition of ideas that guide the way people behave' (Stone, 1997: 11). For every policy issue there is a 'contest over conflicting, though equally plausible, conceptions of the same abstract goal or value', the task of policy makers is to 'reveal and clarify the underlying value disputes so that people can see where they differ and move toward some reconciliation' (Stone, 1997: 12). Rather than seeing policy making as a process of moving from formulation to implementation, where things usually go wrong and policy experts try to devise new tools to fix them, Stone emphasizes that policy making is about changing people's behaviors, and each policy effort takes place within a particular political arena that operates on its own

peculiar ground rule. Successful policy making requires policy makers and the public alike to continually debate and redefine boundaries, the distribution of burdens and benefits, and examine the consequences for fundamental values and commitments. Such policy efforts are ultimately successful political processes that engage all relevant parties.

If these and other scholars are right, the primary challenge facing public administrators is learning how to function more effectively in a political environment in ways that promote strong democratic participation and engage a wide variety of actors in finding and implementing solutions that solve or at least ameliorate public problems. This challenge is not new. Public policies in the United States and other democracies have traditionally been judged on substantive and procedural grounds. From a substantive perspective, policies are evaluated on how well they solve the problems at which they are aimed: does government intervention make things better? From a procedural view, the analysis rests on how well the process of policy making takes place: was the process fair? Were all interests adequately represented or did 'special', narrow interests dominate?

A procedural-based approach to policy analysis is attractive for several reasons. There is often little agreement concerning the substantive successes of public policy making. The lack of consensus concerning what kinds of policies should be pursued and what role government should play in economic and social activities makes judging policies nearly impossible. Since there are no objective measures or widely agreed upon standards by which public policies can be evaluated, attention is directed toward procedural values of pluralism, openness and representation. If procedural norms are satisfied, then policies can largely be judged successful. Procedural concerns, always important in democratic theory, become even more critical as procedural adequacy and, more fundamentally, consistency with democratic values becomes the basis for evaluating public policies (Barber, 1984; Mansbridge, 1983). At the heart of these efforts are notions of strong democracy, suggesting a reinvigorated commitment to more extensive democratic participation in general, and participatory policy analysis, calling for more public involvement in assessing policy choices. But strengthening bureaucratic democracy is no simple task, and public administrators are confronted with difficult choices about how to proceed.

Democratic participation in administrative policy making and implementation ranges from minimal involvement in public hearings and meetings to collaborative decision making where stakeholders are authorized to generate proposals that can garner consensus among participation. Ideas about what exactly constitutes fair policy making procedures have evolved considerably over the past three decades. Public participation has become a central part of administrative agencies' decision making processes for several reasons. In the United States, the constitutional mandate of due process implies some right to participate in at least some administrative proceedings that affect our interests. Federal courts have expanded participation rights in federal agency decision making, and many states have taken the opportunity offered. In contrast, administrative politics has traditionally been less contested, as interests groups' participation in decision making has been recognized as legitimate and institutionalized, and administrative discretion to bring parties together to resolve differences and shape policies more accepted (Bryner, 1987).

As has happened in other countries, government managers and decision makers in the United States have seen it in their interest to expand participation in order to increase the diversity of information and views available to them. Participation is seen as a way to gain the support of those affected by public policies; the more they feel as though they have a voice in decisions affecting them, the more likely it is they will comply with whatever requirements are selected. If parties have a voice in the formulation of policies they will be less likely to challenge decisions in court. Proponents of more extensive participation argue that cooperation is better than conflict and cooperative efforts can contribute to a sense of community and foster social capital in ways that go beyond the resolution of the particular policy issues. There is increasing interest in fostering democratic discourse, in developing processes that increase discussion, facilitate the exploration of alternative views and give voice to those who in the past have been marginalized or ignored.

Different modes of public participation in public bureaucracies are either supplements to existing decision making processes, or alternatives to existing processes that are not working well. A thick version of participation, which includes the sharing of decision making power, is necessarily local in scale. In the United States, for example, there is great interest in community-based, collaborative decision making as a process for making natural resource policies. Collaboration seeks to avoid the conflict litigation, and other problems that have plagued other planning processes, and provide a forum for government officials from different levels of government and overlapping jurisdictions to work together. One of the best known examples of collaboration is the Quincy Library Group – stakeholders who met in the Quincy, California town library in the 1990s to devise a management plan for the nearby national forest. National environmental groups opposed the Quincy group's final plan, and Congress eventually intervened by passing legislation to codify the plan (Brunner, 2002). But the idea is not new: federal public land agencies have convened advisory groups for decades to solve problems and implement policy (Kenney, 2000).

Of particular importance is the role of experts in embracing strong democratic decision making and in committing to work with non-experts in assessing policy choices and pursuing policy decisions. Ensuring that bureaucratic officials represent diverse demographic and ideological affinities and reflect the variety of views within the societies in which they operate is essential. Identifying and inviting representatives from major interests is likewise critical. Much can be learned from the neo-corporatist form of European policy making in ensuring that broad interests are involved in policy making processes, and that mechanisms are in place to ensure decisions are reached even when there are strong differences of opinion. Technical experts can lend their expertise to different interests to ensure that all views have an adequate opportunity to contribute meaningfully and effectively to analyses, and public administrators can ensure that a diverse set of experts and citizens are involved in deliberations. Pay, status and other incentives to encourage experts to engage in democratic decision making are critical. Monitoring, feedback mechanisms, reviews and other structural provisions increase the chance that learning from experience will occur (Woodhouse, 1997).

Defenders of the public participation solution argue that if it is truly inclusive and grants access to decision makers, it can empower people to make their own decisions, and does not rely on paternalistic policy making by government. People can decide for themselves how to balance risks and benefits rather than having those decisions made by others. It is also attractive because it does not require policy makers to come up with a set of principles for making these decisions but only requires that they come up with a fair process. That is no easy task, but coming to an agreement over a fair process might be an easier administrative task than devising and imposing a solution on others.

Bureaucratic democracy is an ambitious agenda for public administration and there are numerous challenges as it seeks remedies for the flaws outlined above. Agencies must decide what kind of participation is to be provided, what interests to include in public proceedings, how public participation is to be reconciled with other expectations such as the rule of law and policy making that is subject to legal constraints (rather than the result of stakeholder bargaining), what to do if public participation conflicts with expertise and scientific assessments, and how to reduce conflict and delay. Conflict avoidance processes may emphasize consensus at the expense of a consideration of alternatives that might initially appear unpopular but may be valuable. Agreements fashioned among local participants may not be acceptable to broader interests or take their views into account. Procedural solutions to policy debates where there is little agreement over substantive ends are critical. While interests vigorously may disagree over what public choices we should make, if policy makers can devise a process that everyone can accept as fair and legitimate, then they may be able to come to accept whatever results come from that process.

PUBLIC ADMINISTRATION AND POLICY OUTCOMES

Public policy scholars rooted in democratic theory point to the size of federal agencies, their insulation from direct electoral politics, their inadequate provision of public participation, their physical separation from the communities and activities, and other essential attributes of bureaucracy that are inconsistent with democratic participation and accountability. For example, critics of liberal political thought that provided the underpinnings for public bureaucracy like Michael Sandel (1996) and Michael Walzer (1983) argue that liberal government fails to recognize the social networks, obligations, responsibilities and commitments that are at the heart of people's lives and fails to provide ways for those commitments and networks to flourish. A polity based on individual rights and utilitarian aggregation of preferences 'fails to cultivate the qualities of character that equip citizens to share in self-rule' (Sandel, 1996: 24).

Institutional theorists argue that bureaucrats are often able to maintain their independence by playing off against each other efforts to direct them by congressional and presidential overseers, or that agency officials are part of iron triangles and issue networks that are insulated from broader political scrutiny and influence. In both cases, bureaucracies flaunt their power at the expense of traditional democratic politics. In part, this is simply a function of time and resources: the range and reach of administrative activity far exceeds the ability of a relatively few elected officials to monitor, assess and, when necessary, redirect that activity. In other cases, politicians are so supportive of and committed to the agenda of agencies that they are unwilling or unable to provide penetrating and critical review. Iron triangles, issue networks, logrolling and deference to other politicians' agendas in exchange for their support, and other metaphors capture the sense that at least many bureaucracies are free from effective oversight (Fesler and Kettl, 1996; Lowi, 1979).

Bureaucratic fragmentation and discretion is seen as part of a larger structural problem of policy making deadlock that has prompted some scholars to call for replacing the American system of separation of powers with one that can produce coherent policies and ensure that once policies are selected they will be faithfully and effectively implemented. Using the United Kingdom and other parliamentary systems as a model, a group of scholars, elected officials and administrators who formed the Committee on the Constitutional System have suggested that while Americans have been quite innovative in developing new institutions of governance, such as administrative and regulatory agencies, they have resisted making changes in the basic governing structure to adapt to changing circumstances. As a result, government lacks the capacity to develop and implement coherent and effective policies (Sundquist, 1992). Other governments built around parliamentary systems that do not separate powers also face political fragmentation, the instability of coalitions and other challenges that make the tasks of public organizations difficult.

Public policy scholarship has reinforced this critical view of public bureaucracy in other ways as well. Few books and articles approvingly endorse the work of public agencies. Most scholars are dismayed at the shortcomings of agencies and their repeated failure to accomplish the tasks given them and to solve the problems at which they are aimed. Studies of specific policies almost always find that the failure to achieve policy goals is rooted in administrative failure. Sometimes these criticisms are quite sympathetic to bureaucracies: their disappointing performance is to be expected, given that the tasks they undertake are extraordinarily difficult and left to government because market-based institutions have not been able to perform them (Lindblom and Woodhouse, 1993: 63).

Even when the lack of success is understandable, dissatisfaction with public bureaucracies grows with each public policy effort that fails to remedy the problems at which it is aimed. Mancur Olson, for example, offers an analysis of societies throughout the world that are in decline because of the rigidity of their governing institutions and their responsiveness to powerful special interests that encourage them to pursue inefficient policies. Government agencies are at the heart of this decline of nations because of their inability to resist these pressures (Olson, 1982). Only occasionally do scholars write of policy successes and examples of the positive role that government plays in the lives of people, such as reducing poverty, creating educational and other opportunities, developing transportation and communications infrastructure, and improving environmental quality (Schwartz, 1988).

Implementation studies have concluded that government is destined to fall short in achieving its policy goals because of administrative complexity. Pressman and Wildavsky (1984), for example, concluded that the complexity of requiring participation by so many political actors destined most policies to failure or at least to delays and distortions. The assumption that implementation meant policy making could come from the top down, that agency heads could impose controls from above on a host of actors below them was simply unrealistic. Subsequent studies of implementation have concluded that governments can successfully implement programs (Mazmanian and Sabatier, 1983) and have suggested factors that appear to be associated with different outcomes (Ingram, 1990). Nevertheless, successful implementation of policies is so rare that the predominant view reflected in studies is that government does not work, and that has paralleled the decline of public confidence in the ability of governments to work effectively.

The scientific and technical basis of policy making reinforces administrative power and autonomy and makes democratic control all the more difficult in many areas of public policy. Bureaucratic expertise and professionalism insulate agencies from effective democratic control since non-experts are unable to provide competent, independent assessments of administrative activities and decisions. Langdon Winner has explored in detail the perception that technological policy making is beyond effective democratic control: 'rule by technically trained experts is the only kind of government appropriate to a social system based on advanced science and technology ... [and] its premises are totally incompatible with a central notion that justifies the practice of liberal politics: the idea of responsible, responsive, representative government' (Winner, 1976: 146). Others emphasize that the deference to experts fails to incorporate the diversity of relevant actors, issues and ethical values essential for democratic decision making (Hiskes and Hiskes, 1986). One problem emphasized by Charles Lindblom is that modern science, academic disciplines and social learning is fragmented into ever more narrow and specialized bits of knowledge, and it is increasingly difficult to reassemble the bits into an effective strategy for solving problems (Lindblom, 1990). Agencies fail to learn from experience and adapt in response to lessons that could be deduced from trial and error because they are often inflexible and resistant to change, because feedback fails to reach those in authority in a timely fashion, and because they are uncommitted to ensuring monitoring, assessment and reanalysis of their efforts (Morone and Woodhouse, 1986).

Public choice theorists emphasize the self-interested nature of bureaucrats and the decisions they make, arguing that bureaucrats are economically rational decision makers and pursue goals such as maximizing their power, resource base and authority, rather than being engaged in the disinterested pursuit of the public interest. These theories challenge the expectations of technical expertise, specialization and neutral administration on which the legitimacy of public bureaucracy rests. Bureaucrats become more conservative as they age, less likely to take risks, encourage innovations and solve problems, and they are more likely to rigidly preserve the status quo and their positions of power (Downs, 1967). Other theories rooted in rational choice theory argue suggest that bureaucracies are so difficult to direct and organizational effectiveness so hard to achieve because of the difficulties inherent in relationships between principals (policy makers) and their agents (bureaucrats) and the lack of control principals typically have over their subordinates (Moe, 1984). While some rational choice theorists argue that bureaucratic behavior can be shaped by elected officials (Wood and Waterman, 1991), the influence largely affects administrative activity rather than outcomes or effectiveness (Kettl, 1993: 417–18).

Critical theories deconstruct bureaucracy in ways that emphasize how economic interests dominate agency decision making, and how bureaucracies largely perpetuate the interests and advantages of economic and social elites. Bureaucracies are not independent actors as much as dependent ones, dominated by political forces in ways that may not be economically efficient or effective in solving problems. Charles Lindblom, for example, argues that business interests enjoy a privileged position in policy making and bureaucrats give great deference to their interests at the expense of broader, more democratic concerns (Lindblom, 1977). Marxists have long argued that governments are merely social superstructure, shaped and directed by the real driving forces of economic institutions. The failures of public organizations are rooted in the 'institutional and class context within which the state functions, in other words, the political economy of capitalism' (Fainstein and Fainstein, 1984: 309). While public administration may be criticized as weak or inefficient or ineffective because of internal flaws, these weaknesses are precisely what is prescribed by holders of private power who seek to insulate their activities from public regulation. Conversely, the agencies that appear to operate most smoothly are those that serve these powerful interests. More pessimistically still, post-modern public administration believes that bureaucrats seek to manage 'obsolete programs' because 'the modern is obsolete' and there are no shared assumptions or guiding principles in public administration because truth or theory are impossible (Rosenau, 1992: 86–7).

James Q. Wilson, in his conclusion to a comprehensive study of bureaucracy, observed that 'public management ... is a world of settled institutions designed to allow imperfect people to use flawed procedures to cope with insoluble problems' (Wilson, 1989: 375). Public bureaucracies are both too independent and too susceptible to external political control, too much a threat to individual liberty and too weak to solve problems efficiently and effectively. Criticisms vary over time and the life of an agency. Some agencies can do some things well but not other things. Administrative agencies in Europe are more likely than their American counterparts to be viewed as effective and competent, because of different traditions in the training of administrators and because of cultural factors that embrace positive government rather than promote distrust.

ASSESSING PUBLIC ADMINISTRATION THROUGH A PUBLIC POLICY LENS

The study of public organizations from the perspective of public policy contributes much to our understanding of how public organizations function and how they can contribute to effective policy making and implementation. Much public policy scholarship is descriptive as it seeks explanations for why public bureaucracy has taken the form it has and why its (rare) successes and (frequent) failures occur. But scholarship is also prescriptive and is shaped by the values and ideologies of the scholars themselves. Theorists and analysts who believe that government should do less, because it is undemocratic or inefficient or otherwise inferior to other forms of decision making and resource allocation will find much ammunition in political science and public policy writings to help make their case. This is entirely a legitimate and appropriate undertaking, and is quite potent because of the uneasy constitutional and political status of administration. If one has as a goal the limiting of the reach and power of government, attacking bureaucracy as illegitimate, ineffective, unaccountable and inconsistent with personal freedom is surely a rational and effective way to proceed.

In contrast, if one begins with the assumption that public bureaucracies can and must play a central role in achieving public policies, the question then becomes one of how political science and public policy scholarship might help address the conceptual and practical challenges to public bureaucracy. The agenda for improving governance and the functioning of public bureaucracies in particular mirrors some of the diagnoses summarized above. The solutions one prefers to the theoretical and practical shortcomings of public administration ultimately depend on which of these flaws are viewed as most problematic. Public administration cannot be studied and understood outside this broader framework of what is the appropriate scope and reach of the state.

Within that broader debate over what are the tasks of government is the challenge of enhancing the capacity and legitimacy of administration through increasing opportunities for participation by affected interests. But broadened participation must also be accompanied by a commitment by all parties to aggregate experience over time and learn from past efforts. It is clear that public organizations will continue to function in an environment of increasing uncertainty, unpredictably and complexity, and the key to their future success in contributing to better policy making is their ability to adapt and adjust. Public policy and public administration scholarship can contribute to the development of an expanded administrative capacity in several ways. Among the most important needs are finding ways for public bureaucracies to learn more from experience and apply that learning to improved policy design and implementation, helping agency officials find better ways to engage a broader range of interests in administrative proceedings, and suggesting how elected officials can delegate with more clarity and integration across policy tasks to public administrators.

REFERENCES

Barber, Benjamin (1984) *Strong Democracy.* Berkeley, CA: University of California Press.

Brunner, Ronald D. (2002) *Finding Common Ground: Governance and Natural Resources in the American West.* New Haven, CT: Yale University Press.

Bryner, Gary C. (1987) *Bureaucratic Discretion: Law and Policy in Federal Regulatory Agencies.* New York: Pergamon.

Bryner, Gary C. (1998) *Politics and Public Morality: The Great American Welfare Reform Debate.* New York: W.W. Norton.

Downs, Anthony (1967) *Inside Bureaucracy.* Boston, MA: Little Brown.

Fainstein, Susan S. and Fainstein, Norman I. (1984) 'The Political Economy of American Bureaucracy', in Frank Fischer and Carmen Sirianni (eds), *Critical Studies in Organization and Bureaucracy.* Philadelphia: Temple University Press. pp. 309–19.

Fesler, James W. and Kettl, Donald F. (1996) *The Politics of the Administrative Process,* 2nd edn. Chatham, NJ: Chatham House.

Fischer, Frank (1995) *Evaluating Public Policy.* Chicago: Nelson–Hall.

Hiskes, Anne L. and Hiskes, Richard P. (1986) *Science, Technology, and Policy Decisions.* Boulder, CO: Westview Press.

Ingram, Helen (1990) 'Implementation: A Review and Suggested Framework', in N.B. Lynn and A.B. Wildavsky (eds), *Public Administration: The State of the Discipline.* Chatham, NJ: Chatham House.

Jones, Charles O. (1984) *An Introduction to the Study of Public Policy.* Monterey, CA: Brooks/Cole.

Kenney, Douglas S. (2000) *Arguing About Consensus: Examining the Case Against Western Watershed Initiatives and Other Collaborative Groups Active in Natural Resource Management.* Boulder, CO: Natural Resources Law Center, University of Colorado School of Law.

Kettl, Donald F. (1993) 'Public Administration: The State of the Field', in Ada Finifter (ed.), *Political Science: The State of the Discipline II.* Washington, DC: American Political Science Association. pp. 407–27.

Kingdon, John W. (1984) *Agendas, Alternatives, and Public Policies.* Boston, MA: Little, Brown.

Lindblom, Charles E. (1968) *The Policy-Making Process.* Englewood Cliffs, NJ: Prentice–Hall.

Lindblom, Charles E. (1977) *Politics and Markets.* New York: Basic Books.

Lindblom, Charles E. (1990) *Inquiry and Change: The Troubled Attempt to Understand and Shape Society.* New Haven, CT: Yale University Press.

Lindblom, Charles E. and Woodhouse, Edward J. (1993) *The Policy-Making Process.* Englewood Cliffs, NJ: Prentice–Hall.

Lowi, Theodore J. (1972) 'Four Systems of Policy, Politics, and Choice', *Public Administration Review,* July–August. pp. 298–301.

Lowi, Theodore J. (1979) *The End of Liberalism,* 2nd edn. New York: W.W. Norton.

Mansbridge, Jayne (1983) *Beyond Adversary Democracy.* Chicago: University of Chicago Press.

Mazmanian, Daniel A. and Sabatier, Paul A. (1983) *Implementation and Public Policy.* Glenview, IL: Scott Foresman.

Moe, Terry (1984) 'The New Economics of Organization', *American Journal of Political Science,* 26: 197–224.

Morone, Joseph G. and Woodhouse, Edward J. (1986) *Averting Catastrophe: Strategies for Regulating Risky Technologies.* Berkeley, CA: University of California Press.

Olson, Mancur (1982) *The Rise and Decline of Nations: Economic Growth, Stagflation, and Social Rigidities.* New Haven, CT: Yale University Press.

Peters, B. Guy (1991) *American Public Policy: Promise and Performance,* 3rd edn. Chatham, NJ: Chatham House.

Pressman, Jeffrey L. and Wildavsky, Aaron (1984) *Implementation,* 3rd edn. Berkeley, CA: University of California Press.

Rose, Richard (1996) *What is Europe?* New York: HarperCollins College Publishers.

Rosenau, Pauline Marie (1992) *Post-Modernism and the Social Sciences: Insights, Inroads, and Intrusions.* Princeton, NJ: Princeton University Press.

Sandel, Michael (1996) *Democracy's Discontent: America in Search of a Public Philosophy.* Cambridge, MA: Harvard University Press.

Schwarz, John E. (1988) *America's Hidden Success: A Reassessment of Public Policy from Kennedy to Reagan,* rev. edn. New York: W.W. Norton.

Stone, Deborah (1997) *Policy Paradox: The Art of Political Decision Making.* New York: W.W. Norton.

Sundquist, James L. (1992) *Constitutional Reform and Effective Government,* rev. edn. Washington, DC: Brookings Institution.

Walzer, Michael (1983) *Spheres of Justice: A Defense of Pluralism and Equality.* New York: Basic Books.

Wilson, James Q. (1989) *Bureaucracy: What Government Agencies Do and Why They Do It.* New York: Basic Books.

Winner, Langdon (1976) *Autonomous Technology.* Cambridge, MA: MIT Press.

Wood, B. Dan and Waterman, Richard W. (1991) 'The Dynamics of Political Control of the Bureaucracy', *American Political Science Review,* 85: 801–28.

Woodhouse, Edward. J (1997) 'Toward a Theory of Success and Failure in the Design of Governmental Institutions', *Research in Social Problems and Public Policy,* 6: 11–43.

24

Politicization of the Civil Service

Luc Rouban

The politicization of the civil service has been the subject of considerable debate in Western democracies for at least the past two centuries. The matter is of particular importance in the eyes of both civil servants and theorists of the state. For civil servants at the start of the twenty-first century, politicization represents a threat to their professional status and the strategic balance that has gradually been achieved between public administration and politics. For theorists, politicization implies taking into consideration all dimensions of bureaucratic activity. In fact, public administration is, in the broad sense, a political institution. As Levine, Peters and Thompson point out: 'Since administrative activity invariably affects who gets what from government and cannot be value-free, all of public administration is in a sense political. But different observers see politics from different viewpoints.' (Levine et al., 1990: 103).

The scope and complexity of the subject explain why there is no general theory nor a major 'paradigm' of politicization but instead a series of limited theories that try to handle some of the variables and analyze the case of a few different countries. In political science, relations between bureaucrats and elected officials have mainly been studied in a very broad manner by theories of political development that attempt to explain the historical dynamics which led to the building of modern nation-sates or democratic regimes (such as Shils, 1960). But these very ambitious and often disputable theories have devoted no attention to administrative sociology. On the other hand, the public policy analysis literature has brought to light the underlying political arrangements of government programs

in the welfare state. Unfortunately, the frontiers between academic disciplines have caused public policy analysis to leave research on public administration by the wayside or devote only minor attention to it. The politicization of the civil service is an interdisciplinary matter that remains at the exploratory stage at the dawn of the twenty-first century. Some epistemological precautions must therefore be taken.

Today it is impossible to study the politicization of the civil service without taking into account the social evolution, political culture and the history of the various countries reviewed. Although major constitutional and political differences exist between the United States and Latin America countries, or between European Union and Eastern European countries, there are also major national differences that may differentiate countries in the same cultural area or sharing similar political regimes. For instance, the very nature of the relationship between the executive branch and senior civil servants is not the same in Australia, Canada and the United Kingdom, even if these three countries are part of the 'Westminster system' (Campbell and Halligan, 1992). Moreover, the politicization of the civil service is not only a complex phenomenon but also a changeable one that can evolve over time within a single country. For instance, politicization suddenly accelerated pace in France from 1981, whereas it had remained at a fairly low level since 1958 (Rouban, 2001). Any research on the politicization process should include a good assessment of the whole political environment.

Another question may be posed: is the politicization process based on the government will?

Is there any kind of a 'politicization policy'? Politicization can be the result of voluntary action, as was long the case in totalitarian political regimes, or a systemic effect, as is generally the case in Western democracies. Sweeping reforms were enacted in the nineteenth century to control the politicization of civil servants in the United States (Civil Service Reform Act of 1883) as well as in Britain (Northcote–Trevelyan Report of 1854). It was indeed a matter of containing a phenomenon that no one could or wanted to eradicate totally. The politicization of the civil service could be desirable in the context of the democratization of Western political systems, allowing governments to overcome bureaucratic resistance. So the question is: what are the boundaries within which the politicization process is politically affordable and profitable? And for whom?

Another problem lies in the lack of a precise definition, not of politicization this time, but of the civil service. First, Western countries do not all use the same defining criteria: in France, teachers are civil servants whereas they are not in the UK. Second, the legal status of civil servants may vary considerably. As a result, politicization can be on a very unequal scale, and especially, may have a very different meaning from one country to another. In a country with a weak administrative tradition, such as Greece, no policy decision was made until the 1990s to control the excesses of politicization (Spanou, 1996). Lastly, politicization can spread beyond the civil service strictly speaking into the entire public sector, affecting state-owned companies, agencies with an ill-defined legal status or even corporations or institutions working under government contract. The fact that the frontiers between public and private sectors are often somewhat blurred allows a number of political jobs to be created that escape the usual legal or political checks. In this case, any scholar is confronted with complex networks or informal arrangements that feed the politicization process.

The subject of politicization therefore raises important questions that touch as much on the nature of administrative models as on the real extent of democracy. The overlapping of these two registers gives rise to many clichés and much confusion. All public administration specialists (see, in particular, Aberbach et al., 1981; Peters, 1988; Pierre, 1995) agree on the point that the politicization of the civil service can refer to at least three distinct phenomena: politicization as civil servant participation in political decision-making; politicization as control over nominations and careers; politicization as civil servants' political involvement. These three phenomena can occur in combination.

In this chapter, the three dimensions of politicization will therefore be studied, as well as the theoretical and practical questions they raise.

POLITICIZATION AS PARTICIPATION IN POLITICAL DECISION MAKING

A first interpretation is that politicization is the result of the prevailing balance between the political control that governments exercise over the administrative machinery and civil servants' involvement in the definition and implementation of public policy. The politicization of the civil service is, in this case, synonymous with participation in political authority. In this sense, all civil servants are 'political' because they are called upon to carry out political decisions, adapt them and explain them, in other words to accomplish work of a political nature that obviously is not limited to the mere application of legal or economic rules. The fact that civil servants are thinking beings precludes considering them as machines having no freedom of judgment. However, there is a whole range of situations varying from intelligent interpretation of political decisions depending on the actual circumstances of implementation to technocracy, in other words a socio-political system in which decisions made by bureaucrats replace decisions that should normally be made by elected officials. The problem here lies in the fact that this sort of politicization is more a matter of degree than of qualitative threshold. Most public administration specialists, unlike politicians, consider that it is very difficult to distinguish between making rules and enforcing them, all the more so since Western democracies have produced complex public policies of which the normative effect has more to do with measures of implementation than with the decisions originally made by legislators or the executive branch. Thus it is possible to slip imperceptibly into technocracy by allowing civil servants more latitude in managing major public policies.

To a certain extent, all industrialized democracies are more or less technocracies, in that the political class is no longer the sole actor in the decision making process, and the decision is often difficult to identify and localize (Allison, 1971). Specific national situations can be identified. In certain countries, such as the UK,

Conservative governments have criticized the fact that senior civil servants were not sufficiently involved in defining public policy and hid behind total political neutrality (Hood, 1998). In France, on the other hand, a majority of politicians both on the left and the right have always been wary of technocracy and what they feel to be the excessive power of graduates of the Ecole Nationale d'Administration and the Ecole Polytechnique. In Japan, the senior civil service has controlled the entire political process up until the 1980s, orienting economic policy through a tight network of influences in the Diet as well as in industry. In the Japanese case, some scholars have mentioned a true 'iron triangle' interlocking the bureaucracy, the Liberal Democratic Party and the major state enterprises (Johnson, 1982). In the 1990s, state reform thus aimed mainly at reducing the influence of the bureaucracy (Nakamura, 1998). In the aforementioned cases, the 'politicization' of the civil service has only involved the senior civil service, whose role in public policy making also depends on its social status and its history.

The question is a different one in developing countries, because the civil service is almost always the only expertise and advisory resource for governments. In this case, the 'politicization' of the civil service must be interpreted differently, because civil servants are often the only organized social force on which governments can rely. The situation is sometimes also reversed in favor of the public service, especially the military, which may act as the only organized political force in the country. Relations between the government and the civil service in developing countries can be organized according to a variety of models depending on the relative strength of the political leadership and the social role assumed by the bureaucracy (Cariño, 1991). One model is that of a political domination provided by the party in power, either in democratic conditions (for instance, Corazon Aquino's government at the end of the 1980s in the Philippines), or in the context of an authoritarian regime that can literally organize purges in the civil service or submit it to an extremely restrictive political discipline (this was in particular the case of Korea between 1961 and 1963). In a contrasting model, bureaucracy shares power with the political leaders on the basis of an implicit 'arrangement'. The bureaucracy can then support democratic reforms as long as they allow it to increase its powers (this was Mexico's case in the 1970s). In some cases, civilian bureaucracy shares power with a military-style authoritarian regime (this was the case of the 'guided democracy' in Indonesia under Sukarno's administration between 1959 and 1965).

The respective role of civil servants and elected officials in defining public policy also depends on contextual variables. One essential variable is ministers' capacity to exercise real political leadership over their civil servants and advisors (Savoie, 1994). Some French ministers have complained of being dispossessed of their power by the senior civil servants in their entourage. At the opposite end of the spectrum, in the UK, senior civil servants have denounced the overly directive role of Margaret Thatcher's government, accusing it of wanting to politicize the senior civil service or at least make it espouse the Conservative ideology (Hennessy, 1990). There is no doubt that a politician must often assert himself to earn respect from professionals who have expertise and time on their side. Politicization becomes the result of a potentially perilous power struggle that depends as much on the networks on which senior civil servants can rely on as the political or personal legitimacy of politicians. The question of politicization became all the more sensitive in the 1990s since it raises a fundamental question about the respective roles that should fall to elected officials and civil servants at a time when public administrations seem to be losing control of the situation in the face of an increasingly fragmented civil society, infatuated with new technologies and quick to demand ever greater quality from the public service for lower taxes (Rouban, 1999).

Most public administration specialists have thus concluded that politicization cannot be treated in a broad manner but only on a case-by-case basis. Another series of variables in fact has to do with the fragmentation of today's administrative apparatuses. The most autonomous administrations are usually administrations that have a technical or scientific competence, whereas the most vulnerable are those with a fairly low level of expertise. Reinforcing administrative specialization or transforming civil servants into managers can contribute to weakening the political control exercised over these administrations. Some ministerial bureaucracies can also impose their viewpoint on ministers when powerful and well-organized lobbies in their economic sector back them: this is especially the case of the Agricultural Ministry in France (on this question, see the chapter on pressure groups). Here, cases of actual fusion of political, economic and administrative powers have been observed, since the minister himself has sometimes been chosen from among farmers' union leaders! The same type of situation has been noted in Japan. Politicization in this case leads to a blending of powers. Not only is there no longer a difference between political decision and administrative decision, but also, it is impossible to distinguish between public and private interests. But it is precisely this 'big difference' that has served as the historical basis for liberal democracies. Paradoxically, then, privatization can foster politicization. By privatizing state services ensuring economic development, and even, sometimes, sovereign functions such as customs or border control, some African states have been able to recover the political control of their economy (Zartman, 1995). Networks of personalized power then take over for bureaucracies too corrupted or independent to continue to serve as instruments for government decision making. We can also interpret Margaret Thatcher's attempt to submit the British administration to private management and subject it to the rules of competition as a means of recovering the political control of an administration regarded as too independent (Bouckaert and Pollitt, 2000).

The strategies deployed in European countries by politicians and civil servants alike to control the process of politicization have been partly transformed by the creation of the European Union. European integration, in fact, has had two main consequences: the first was to weaken the national political classes, which were forced to comply with decisions made in Brussels, particularly in the area of public sector privatization. The second consequence is the reinforcement of administrations, which have become the primary interlocutors for private interest groups in highly technical matters. The previous model, which posited that elected officials decided and civil servants carried out their decisions, has therefore disappeared: national civil servants henceforth adapt directives passed by the European Commission to the state or local level in the framework of a multilateral negotiation that politicians cannot fully control. The transformation of administrative work is a real challenge to the elite structure, because public policy is no longer designed only at the higher government levels between groups of decision makers generally from the upper classes of society and, like in the UK, France or Germany, who are graduates of the same schools (Derlien, 1990; Page and Wright, 1999).

POLITICIZATION AS PARTISAN CONTROL OVER THE BUREAUCRACY

The second, much more precise and more widespread, meaning of politicization of the public sector refers to government and nongovernment activities that subject the appointment and career of civil servants to political will. In this case, politicization means that not only a civil servant's activity but also his or her career depend more on political than professional norms defined by the administrations and ruled by law.

There is considerable confusion surrounding this point. The first misunderstanding has to do with the fact that politicization can be perfectly legal and legitimate, because democratic rule implies that the voters' choices should actually be implemented and not buried under the workings of bureaucracy. This is the whole logic of the spoils system that developed in the United States in the nineteenth century. It is also logical for certain positions to depend on a political choice that takes into consideration the ideas backed by the civil servants, because these positions have a particular strategic importance in the eyes of the government. Generally, these positions are limited in duration and involve very few senior civil servants who serve as a go-between for the political realm and the bureaucracy. All Western countries have created 'political positions' to give the executive branch some means of control over public policy.

Another source of confusion comes from the fact that the politicization of appointments does not necessarily imply a lack of professional competence. Politicization generally seems linked to the idea of an amateurish administration. This matter has always been at the heart of the debate in the United States. But in some countries, such as Germany and France, top-level positions are occupied by senior civil servants who are both highly qualified professionals drawing on an old tradition of professional autonomy and highly politicized, as they have been previously involved in political activities as advisors or party supporters. Actually, politicization connotes incompetence mainly when it affects not only appointments but careers. Politicization can then become a means of showing favor to some political allies to the detriment of others, whatever their level of performance or their merits, or of allowing trade unions to define personnel policies. On a historical level, there is no question that the fight against favoritism was one of the major labor demands of British and French bureaucrats in the nineteenth century. Today, for many developing countries, the only way to fight politicization connected with corruption practices, which can harm the country's economy, is to organize a truly professional civil service. For instance, in 1983 Mexico undertook a sweeping bureaucratic modernization program that aimed mainly to organize the public sector on the basis of a merit system (Haro Belchez, 2000).

The division between administration and politics is a central organizing principle in all Western political systems. This distinction is of course based on the principles Max Weber put forth in his classic analysis of bureaucratic legitimacy in modern societies (Weber, 1947). The creation of professional bureaucracies in the first half of the twentieth century stems from the simultaneous application of two principles: subordination to a hierarchy and separation of administrative careers from partisan influences. It is perfectly obvious, as many observers have already noted, that the separation principle has never been entirely enforced. In fact, an evolution in the interpretations of this principle can be noted: in the early twentieth century it implied that the political authority made decisions and bureaucrats merely carried them out. With the increasing complexity of the welfare system and public interventionism, it has become nearly impossible to distinguish the decision from its implementation and no longer are there any administrative 'details' that cannot be transformed into a real political issue. The principle of separation has thus gradually been interpreted as allowing civil servants some degree of professional leeway in their activities. This is naturally far more ambiguous. In fact, civil servants can thus be held responsible for the results of public intervention, both from a legal and a political standpoint. The separation between the political and the administrative world has created complex possibilities for strategic interplay between the two groups of actors depending on the circumstances, all the more so since, as Guy Peters points out, there are 'more invidious types of political influence … because they are difficult for the citizenry to identify and even more difficult to control' (Peters, 1995: 178).

The separation principle is therefore probably a myth, but a founding myth allowing all Western political systems to modernize, since it is useful from a functional standpoint. On the one hand, it allows civil servants to intervene in policy making in the name of their professional autonomy; on the other hand, it allows politicians to remove some decisions from citizens' control by entrusting them to public administrations, contending that they are too technical in nature to be debated publicly. The separation principle thus organizes the relative autonomy of the political and administrative worlds, an autonomy that paradoxically indirectly challenges the principle of accountability on which democratic regimes are based.

On the strictly administrative level, the separation principle should above all be understood as a professional norm on which the merit system can be organized. It is in this perspective that the major theorists of public administration, such as Woodrow Wilson and Frank Goodnow, have championed it. In the late nineteenth century, the professionalization of public administration was associated with the development of scientific management. In his famous 1887 essay, Woodrow Wilson declared: 'the field of administration is a field of business. It is removed from the hurry and strife of politics' (Wilson, 1887/1941: 493).

Therefore, another problem lies in the fact that this professionalization of civil servants has been conceived in very different ways in Western countries. Although professionalization was early on seen in the United States as a means of developing managerial standards, in France and Germany it was principally associated with the development of a vast body of administrative law. In the UK, professionalization implies the independence of civil servants from Parliament but, as agents of the Crown, their steadfast obedience to the decisions of the executive branch. Administrative traditions and culture are essential to understanding bureaucratic politicization, because the professionalization of the civil service has developed in significantly different political and constitutional contexts. On this point, there is no Western model of public administration, nor is there any reason to mention a European convergence.

Although all European systems are based on the merit system and equal access to the civil service, recruitment systems are rooted in very different philosophies. For example, even if all European countries organize the recruitment of professional civil servants on the basis of an objective procedure in order to guarantee equality among candidates, the criteria for selection vary considerably: in Germany, the good professional is above all a high-level legal specialist; in the UK the main quality is found in a generalist who has a feeling for team work; France prefers to measure the general level of education and intellectual brio. The very notion of civil servant does not, therefore, refer to the same type of culture or even the same type of professional practice. Consequently, it is logical that politicization is conceived and especially experienced in a very different manner from one country to another: in the UK, the politicization of a Permanent Secretary is unthinkable because it would threaten the professional status of the civil service; in France, politicization of ministerial departments heads is fairly accepted by senior civil servants who use politics to exercise their intellectual abilities as government advisors.

In most Western countries, specific rules have been set up to distinguish civil servants who are political appointees from civil servants whose career is entirely subjected to professional norms. In the United States, the corruption fostered by the spoils system, particularly under Richard Nixon's administration, led to reorganizing the senior civil service with the Civil Service Act of 1978, which created the Senior Executive Service (SES). The SES is made up of higher positions, 10 per cent of which can be politically appointed. The law also requires that 70 per cent of the positions of the entire SES must be attributed to career civil servants in order to avoid the massive recruitment of former political civil servants in career positions. In Germany, the *Politischer Beamter* are distinct from other civil servants: the *Politischer Beamter* can be appointed and revoked on the basis of political considerations but with career guarantees. France distinguishes 'positions at the government's discretion', in other words, a set of approximately 500 higher positions the holders of which can be appointed and revoked at the government's discretion. Here again, there are nevertheless professional guarantees because these positions are mainly occupied by career civil servants who can use particular legal provisions allowing them to return to their original agency after they are revoked. This distinction between political positions and career positions is far more recent in Eastern European countries. In Russia, it did not appear until 1995 because the concept of civil servant, in the Western sense of the term, did not exist.[1] Now, within the 'State offices', there is Category A, which in fact covers elected political officials, Category B, which applies to civil servants appointed on the basis of political criteria (1,300 positions at the federal level), and Category C, which is that of the career civil servants.

In many countries, politicization occurs through the multiplication of short-term contract positions. In the UK, there has been a marked rise in the number of personal ministerial advisors since the early 1980s. In Italy, political senior civil servant posts have been endowed with 'internal' fixed-term contracts since 1993. In Australia, the creation of 'ministerial advisers' in the late 1980s has provided a means to avoid politicizing senior jobs along the American model while reinforcing political control over career civil servants' activities (Campbell and Halligan, 1992). In most Latin American countries, government political advisors are recruited on a contractual basis (Farazmand, 1991).

Growing job instability can also provide governments with a ready means to politicize the civil service. This form of politicization is not used to control an administration's activity but much rather to hand out jobs to friends of the political party or parties in power, operating a shift from a relationship of *clientela* to one of *parentela* (Peters, 1995). This politicization has especially been observed in the 1970s in Italy where the Christian Democratic Party was used to distribute local jobs (the *lottizazione* system). This type of politicization is closer to the administrative models of developing countries, where it is above all regarded as a means to make political allies by giving jobs to the unemployed. Political deals of this kind can nevertheless be found in the most developed countries, especially at the local level, and fairly often lead to the spread of illegal practices. When this occurs, there are no longer any institutional barriers between government agencies and political parties. Such practices have developed in Europe but not in any systematic fashion. They range from outright illegality, as was in particular the case in Greece from 1974 when a democratic regime was set up, to 'arrangements' that are legal but hardly in keeping with administrative traditions, as was the case in France at the local level with the 1982 decentralization policy that resulted in a multiplication of overlapping administrative structures. This type of politicization quickly exhausts the limits of modern public administration theory, for it very often becomes impossible to distinguish in these public positions between what is due to politicization and what is due to personal loyalty. Weber's 'bureaucratic' model thus gives way to his model of 'traditional' authority. Furthermore, ties of personal loyalty appear to play an important role in setting up new administrations in Eastern European countries. In Russia, nearly 65% of the administrative management officials in the 1990s were former Communist Party members associated with networks of personal power that ran through major state enterprises such as Gazprom or the bureaucracies of large cities.

Politicization of the civil service does not only occur through appointments. It can also be exercised through the creation of specific structures at high state levels, which are charged with ensuring the link between government wishes and the implementation of public policy by professional bureaucracies. The White House Office in the United States, the Cabinet Office in England, the Federal Chancellery in Germany, the Prime Minister's Cabinet and the Secretariat General of the Elysée in France insure a very important role in defining and carrying out administrative activity. In general, these top-level administrations have developed considerably in Europe since the end of the 1980s, in small countries such as Denmark as well (Peters et al., 2000). They are usually made up of a few hundred top-level civil servants who are fairly highly politicized, and have connections in the administrative system either through the network of political advisors or ministerial offices. The strengthening of senior administrations is rooted in three factors: first, in Europe, the European integration policy has required the creation of coordinating agencies to harmonize national policy with European programs. Then, most of the national administrations have adopted a subsidiarity model, meaning that ministers and the executive branch have gone from 'doing things' to 'getting things done'. This has resulted in an increased demand for administrations specialized in policy implementation and evaluation as most major government programs are now handled by a wide range of public and private agencies. Finally, since the early 1980s, most Western governments undeniably have clearly sought to strengthen and centralize their political power in the face of changing societies that have become much more diversified than before. This is a possible interpretation for the development of the New Public Management reform in the UK that, by setting up institutional models borrowed from the private sector, aimed to reinforce the British government's control over an administrative fabric thought to be too independent. The same thing has clearly happened in Canada (Savoie, 1999).

It is obvious that the legal mapping of political positions or the institutional reinforcement of senior administrations does not always give a precise idea of the degree of politicization of the civil service because discreet networks of influence may exist allowing the political recruitments and promotions of career civil servants according to their ideological affinity with the government. It is always fairly difficult for scholars to measure the degree of politicization. We can take into consideration the turnover of staff appointed to 'sensitive' positions or analyze biographies so as to identify political networks within public administrations. The task is nevertheless a tricky one because, although it is possible to measure flows, it is impossible to measure intentions or ulterior motives. Interviews must always be interpreted with great caution, as it is obviously rare to find senior civil servants who will assert that their only qualification is to be a friend of the minister! In most cases, politicization can only be demonstrated through historical comparative data showing trends in recruitments and carriers.

In the early twenty-first century, politicization seems to have increased in most Western countries. This may appear paradoxical, because so many observers have drawn attention to the development of an economic orthodoxy that would inevitably lead all developed countries to follow the same model of 'good governance' on the basis of a single recipe: decrease in public deficits, tax reductions, better management of public spending and public policy evaluation. One of the most intriguing questions is: to what extent has the development of this 'good governance' led to new administrative practices? In particular, the effects of the New Public Management on the relations elected officials have with senior civil servants can be examined. Subjecting senior civil servants to managerial norms can just as much reduce their leeway, and thus subject them more to political authority, as it can increase the power they exercise on a daily basis on the running of administrative affairs and thus give them greater autonomy with respect to the government's political considerations. A comparative study shows that the new public management has had different effects in Europe in different countries: although senior civil servants are more tightly controlled by the political authorities in the UK, they are now more independent in the Netherlands and Finland (Revue Française d'Administration Publique, 1998). The blend of New Public Management and politicization has thus not had the same effects in all countries. The actual degree to which managerial norms have developed and how senior civil servants use them strategically must be taken into account.

It is easy to understand that in countries where democracy is fragile, such as in South America, governments try to win over the public service to their cause, especially the military. Civil servants' loyalty to the single party is also a *sine qua non* condition for survival in totalitarian countries like China. On the other hand, it is more difficult to explain the increasing politicization of the civil service in developed countries. One of the most satisfactory explanations seems to lie in the crisis running through representative democracies, characterized by a high abstention rate at elections and the rise in power of a social criticism condemning the political class (but not civil servants). The political class in most Western countries is constantly threatened by the risk of scandals or challenges to its usefulness given the growing independence of civil society. In the face of this criticism, the initial reflex is to make the senior civil service even more political, first by mounting 'political fuses' that will blow in the event of failure; second, by giving the impression that the government is still capable of coordinating public policy and making effective decisions, that is, simply of governing. Paradoxically, the development of pluralistic 'governance' has thus been associated with a greater will to politicize the civil service, directly or indirectly.

Politicization must therefore be conceived in developed countries as the effect of a general evolution of the political system. If governments attempt to control administrative activity better through politicization, there are nevertheless limits to this politicization other than legal ones. Management of the civil service by senior administrations has not always been an easy task. For instance, the setting up of the 'administrative Presidency' in the United States under Richard Nixon was thwarted by the fragmentation of the US administrative machinery. Moreover, direct intervention of political authorities in the professional life of civil servants requires daily effort and therefore considerable energy. Setting up 'parallel' political administrations also is a risk because they can create a screen between civil servants and elected officials, which leads to a widespread breakdown in communication within the government as well as the establishment of more or less autonomous systems of power.

Appointments are another means of politicization, but the political choice is usually considerably checked by the need to recruit competent individuals already having a great deal of experience in administrative affairs. If not, a political cast, or a 'government of strangers' (Heclo, 1978) is created, largely rejected by career civil servants. As Ball and Peters point out: 'Although their political "masters" may want to control the bureaucracy, the expertise of the bureaucracy is crucial for effective government and the success of any elected government' (Ball and Peters, 2000: 221). The fact that technical matters having to do with public health or the environment protection are becoming increasingly preponderant in politics reinforces the professional situation of civil servants who can use their expertise to counter the more or less demagogic plans of governments.

Another limit lies in the fact that political parties, particularly in the United States and in France, can be weakened and divided by internal movements. The political choice then must take into consideration the diversity of these viewpoints that are not necessarily reconcilable. In European countries where governments are very often elected on the basis of political coalitions (Austria, Belgium, the Netherlands), political positions must also be distributed in proportion to the election results of the various parties, which leads to a sort of 'parliamentarization' of the executive branch.

Lastly, there is a political limit to politicization, particularly in Europe, which has to do with the fact that civil servants inspire more trust among citizens than politicians or governments (Eurobarometer, 1997, 1999). A government's legitimacy can thus be seriously threatened if the press can attest to an overly politicized civil service.

POLITICIZATION AS POLITICAL INVOLVEMENT

Politicization of the civil service has a third meaning. In this case, politicization refers to the degree of civil servants' political involvement as citizens and voters. The question is thus the following: is the civil service a political force?

First, situations can be found in which the ideological commitment of civil servants is a crucial element in setting up a new political system: this is particularly the case in regimes born in Africa in the 1960s following decolonization. On the other hand, in India and Pakistan public administration served instead as a stabilizing element at the time of independence. In both cases, the civil service compensated for the lack of a sufficiently developed middle class to offer democratic governments an electoral base. This central position of the public service, particularly that of the military, is obviously a factor of weakness and political dependence: successive *coups d'état* have occurred in both Africa and Latin America, often following conflicts within the very state apparatus. In Europe, the civil service has rarely served as a social basis for major political change.

The fact that civil servants share political convictions obviously plays an essential role in a country's political life but also in the management of its administrations. It is hard for a government to ask civil servants to implement public policies that run counter to their ideological convictions, even if they are called upon to work as perfectly neutral professionals. Furthermore, if there is a high proportion of civil servants, it becomes obvious that civil service policy will be subjected to particularly strong constraints for electoral reasons. This is the case in France, where civil servants make up 22 per cent of the total workforce and one-sixth of the voters, but approximately one-third if one includes their family. All socialist governments since 1981 know that civil servants constitute their most loyal electorate. However, this loyalty began to crumble in the late 1990s when left-wing governments adopted the economically liberal measure of privatizing the public sector (Rouban, 1998).

Professional tradition

	LOW	HIGH
LOW	United States Russia	Australia Italy UK
HIGH	Austria Belgium Netherlands	France Germany Spain Sweden Japan

(vertical axis label: **Political involvement of civil servants**)

Figure 24.1   *Models of politicization by civil servant involvement in political life and the strength of the professional tradition*

In 1999, a national education minister was even dismissed because his reforms provoked strikes and demonstrations among the teachers, a corps of one million civil servants.

Do civil servants then make up a political force capable of influencing government policy? It can be contended that civil servants have all the more influence in a specialized sector when users particularly appreciate their work. This is true of corps such as firemen, the postal service, hospitals, etc. Politicization is all the stronger when it can draw support from close functional links with outside pressure groups and, on the other hand, a strong trade union that has more or less close links with a political party.

We do not have precise data on the political involvement of civil servants in various countries. This field of research has been neglected. The rare studies undertaken have shown that civil servants in Western countries usually maintain an affinity with the socialists in Europe and the Democrats or the 'center left' in North America (Blais and Dion, 1991; Rouban, 2001). They are more inclined than private sector workers to defend the welfare state and government intervention in economic and social matters. This propensity to defend the 'big government' can be considered perfectly normal among civil servants who are paid out of the state budget. Nevertheless, behind the global figures there are considerable differences that tend to make civil servants' vote and political attitudes vary according to their profession (police officers are usually more to the right than teachers) and their rank (senior civil servants are generally split into two groups corresponding to the left and the right whereas clerical workers are more often on the left of the political axis). It is also highly tempting to want to pit civil servants against private sector workers. But here again it is the profession that matters more than the legal status of the job, even if civil servants are generally more culturally liberal and less economically liberal than private business workers.

Depending on the country, civil servant politicization can also draw support in trade unionism. Trade union rights are generally acknowledged in all European countries (except for certain categories such as the military) whereas they are far more limited in the United States. Trade unionism can, however, vary in degrees of politicization as well as in its power of influence over government decisions. It is fairly highly politicized in Austria, France, Germany, Italy and Spain, where civil service unions are branches of national unions that group workers by political affinity. In the UK, trade unionism is, on the other hand, very profession-oriented and does not get involved in political debate. In fact, Margaret Thatcher's administration took advantage of its weakness to impose considerable managerial changes in the British civil service.

Another dimension of civil servant politicization has to do with the legal and social possibilities bureaucrats have of getting involved in political life. Though in the UK senior civil servants are barred from participating in political activity at the national level, there are no such restrictions in France, Germany and Spain. As a result, the political class of these three European countries is largely made up of former civil servants who can easily recover their posts and their rank in public administration if they lose an election. This professional freedom is often considered a privilege with regard to private sector workers who must give up their job to enter into politics. It is obviously a strong incentive for civil servants to play the political card if their career is at a standstill. On the other hand, the effects of this massive presence of civil servants in the ranks of parliament on political orientation should not be overestimated, because former civil servants very soon adapt to the rules of the political game and no longer consider themselves civil servants.

CONCLUSION

Any scholar will find difficult, if not impossible, to control all the variables that may influence the politicization of the civil service. In most of the cases, sociology will be called upon to support political science research. In particular, the effect of politicization on civil servants' switch-over to private enterprise needs to be studied, because in some countries, such as France, Japan and the United States, access to senior positions in the administration allows civil servants later to become CEOs of major private corporations.

However, two variables seem especially important: on the one hand, the strength of the administrative tradition, which can be measured by civil servants' degree of professional independence or 'corporatism' and, on the other hand, civil servants' involvement in political life, which can be measured by their capacity for collective mobilization or their presence within political parties. From these two dimensions, a diagram of politicization in the main developed countries can be drawn up (Figure 24.1) showing that political involvement of civil servants can very well go hand in hand with a strong administrative tradition (France, Germany, Spain) and that the lack of a strong professional culture does not necessarily imply any particular partisan involvement (the United States). It should especially be noted that there is no 'European model' and that the models of politicization do not fit into simple dichotomies, which, for instance, would divide countries of the northern hemisphere from the south, or federal countries from unitary countries.

What could be the avenues for further research? At first sight, it appears clearly that there is a huge need for quantitative data on civil servants' political behavior. Such data are difficult to obtain as civil servants are generally reluctant to give this kind of information, especially at the higher levels of public administration. This obstacle could be overcome partially through the use of interviews for senior civil servants and through the insertion of demographic questions in opinion polls. Until the 1990s opinion polls dedicated to political surveys did not include any question identifying civil servants from other kinds of wage earners. Only questions related to the social hierarchy were used, distinguishing employees and workers from free professions and white-collar workers. This kind of research may offer an opportunity for public administration specialists and political scientists to work together.

From another perspective, due attention should be paid to the historical evolution of the relationship between public administration and politics in each country in order to make good and useful comparisons. Too often, data are outdated or lacking even in Western democracies, giving room for misleading interpretations. Biographical studies and career stories are of a crucial interest in order to understand the dynamics of politicization. A legal knowledge is not sufficient to give a clear overview of what is going on. Legal structures may be used or interpreted in various ways by both governments and civil servants. Both individual and collective reactions to politicization depend upon how careers have been managed and how politics has influenced personal opportunities. This kind of research is needed as there is generally no separation between the inception or the implementation of public policies, on the one hand, and professional concerns on the other.

NOTE

1 I would like to thank Professor Michel Lesage from the Université de Paris I for this information.

REFERENCES

Aberbach, J., Putnam, R. and Rockman, B. (1981) *Bureaucrats and Politicians in Western Democracies*. Cambridge, MA: Harvard University Press.

Allison, Graham (1971) *Essence of Decision: Explaining the Cuba Missile Crisis*. New York: HarperCollins.

Ball, Alan R. and Peters, B. Guy (2000) *Modern Politics and Government*, 6th edn. London: Macmillan.

Blais, André and Dion, Stéphane (1991) *The Budget-maximing Bureaucrat: Appraisals and Evidence*. Pittsburgh: Pittsburgh University Press.

Bouckaert, Geert and Pollitt, Christopher (2000) *Public Management Reform: A Comparative Analysis*. Oxford: Oxford University Press.

Campbell, Colin and Halligan, John (1992) *Political Leadership in an Age of Constraint*. St Leonards: Allen & Unwin.

Cariño, Ledevina (1991) 'Regime Changes, the Bureaucracy, and Political Development', in Ali Farazmand (ed.), *Handbook of Comparative and Development Administration*. New York: Marcel Dekker. pp. 731–43.

Derlien, Hans-Ulrich, (1990) 'Continuity and Change in the West German Federal Executive Elite, 1949–1984', *European Journal of Political Research,* 18: 349–72.

Eurobarometer (1997, 1999) *Trust in Institutions*, *Survey*. Brussels: European Union Commission.

Farazmand, Ali (ed.) (1991) *Handbook of Comparative and Development Administration*. New York: Marcel Dekker.

Haro Belchez, Guillermo (2000) 'La fonction publique de carrière', *Revue Française d'Administration Publique*, special issue on 'La fonction publique au Mexique', 94: 205–12.

Heclo, Hugh (1978) *A Government of Strangers?* Washington, DC: Brookings Institution.

Hennessy, Peter (1990) *Whitehall*. London: Fontana.

Hood, Christopher (1998) *The Art of the State: Culture, Rhetoric and Public Management*. Oxford: Clarendon Press.

Johnson, Chalmers (1982) *MITI and the Japanese Miracle*. Stanford, CA: Stanford University Press.

Levine, Ch., Peters, B.G. and Thompson, Frank J. (1990) *Public Administration, Challenges, Choices, Consequences*. Chicago: Scott Foresman.

Nakamura, Akira (1998) 'Japan Central Administration at the Crossroads: Increasing Public Demand for Deregulation, Decentralization and De-Bureaucratization', *International Journal of Public Administration*, 10 (21): 1511–31.

Page, E.C. and Wright, Vincent (1999) *Bureaucratic Elites in Western Democracies*. Oxford: Oxford University Press.

Peters, B. Guy (1988) *Comparing Public Bureaucracies: Problems of Theory and Methods*. Tuscaloosa, AL: University of Alabama Press.

Peters, B. Guy (1995) *The Politics of Bureaucracy*, 4th edn. White Plains: Longman.

Peters, B.G., Rhodes, R.A.W. and Wright, Vincent (2000) *Administering the Summit: Administration of the Core Executive in Developed Countries*. Basingstoke: Macmillan, New York: Martin's Press.

Pierre, Jon (ed.) (1995) *Bureaucracy in the Modern State, An Introduction to Comparative Public Administration*. Aldershot: Elgar.

Revue Française d'Administration Publique (1998) *Les Fonctionnaires et la politique dans les pays de l'Union européenne*, 86. Paris: La Documentation française.

Rouban, Luc (1998) *The French Civil Service*. Paris: La Documentation française.

Rouban, Luc (ed.) (1999) *Citizens and the New Governance*. Amsterdam: IOS Press.

Rouban, Luc (2001) 'Les cadres du privé et du public: des valeurs sociopolitiques en évolution', *Revue Française d'Administration Publique*, 98: 329–44.

Savoie, Donald J. (1994) *Thatcher, Reagan, Mulroney, In Search of a New Bureaucracy*. Pittsburgh: University of Pittsburgh Press.

Savoie, Donald J. (1999) *Governing from the Centre*. Toronto: University of Toronto Press.

Shils, Edward (1960) *Political Development in the New States*. The Hague: Mouton.

Spanou, Calliope (1996) 'Penelope's Suitors. Administrative Modernization and Party Competition in Greece', *West European Politics*, 19 (1): 97–124.

Weber, Max (1947) *The Theory of Social and Economic Organization*. New York: Free Press.

Wilson, Woodrow (1887) 'The Study of Administration', *Political Science Quarterly*, 2 (June). (Reprinted 1941 in *Political Science Quarterly*, 61 (December): 481–506.)

Zartman, Ira (ed.) (1995) *Collapsed States. The Disintegration and Restoration of Legitimate Authority*. Boulder, CO: Rienner.

25

Interest Groups and Public Organizations in Europe

Pierre Lascoumes and Patrick Le Galès

Bureaucracies have to deal with interest groups. In relation to public administration, research has classically stressed the dependence of bureaucracy upon interest groups to get information, to legitimize its policies, to implement policies and to create a stable political order. The contrast between pluralism in the United States and corporatism in European societies seems to be gone to a large extent. Gone are the days (if they ever existed) of stable institutionalized interest groups regulating a policy domain.

This chapter reviews the changes in interest groups and the ways in which bureaucracies are adapted to the new scene. It stresses the remains of corporatism, the blurring of the frontiers between social movements and interest groups, and the rescaling of interactions between interest groups and bureaucracies in Europe.

FROM MEDIEVAL CORPORATIONS TO ORGANIZED CORPORATISM

Western Europe was for a long time seen as societies where capitalism was more institutionalized and territorialized than in the United States. The organization of interest groups revealed that pattern. There was a major tradition of research in the pluralist tradition in the United States (Dahl, 1967; Truman, 1971), contested by neomarxist and radical approaches. The comparison of European cases brought to light contrasting patterns of relations between national public administrations and interest groups, together with major differences in terms of procedures and norms within public administration to deal

with those (Lehmbruch, 1991). In Scandinavia powerful economic interests are included by the state in deciding upon major national issues, cutting across economic and social priorities. By contrast, in other countries, interest groups are associated with the policy process in a more limited way within the management of pillars or public policy sectors. The legitimacy given to interest groups in the policy process also varies immensely from Germany, where a close form of cooperation between labour and business organization today contrasts with a low profile after the second world war, and France, where the almighty state is supposed to be above the pressure of mean and narrow-minded interest groups.

Interest groups and public administration were therefore mainly considered within a macro framework. Attempts to establish national models focused on three dimensions: the characteristics of economic interest groups, the type of state and then the types of exchange and interaction between them. Comparative research led to the definition of 'styles of government' (Jordan and Richardson, 1979), administrative culture or national configuration of interest groups and to more precise definition of national models, from the Austrian corporatism to the *corporatisme à la française* (Jobert and Muller, 1987).

Along with many European scholars, Schmitter (1997: 397) concludes that 'continental Western Europe' is characterized by the role of a particularly dense and resilient cluster of 'intermediary', that is, non-market and non-state, mechanisms. One can speculate *ad definitum* about the reason for this: the persistence of 'precapitalist', guild-like institutions; the weakness of liberal, individualist ideology; the impact of repeated, large-scale international warfare;

the strength of organized labour and social democratic parties; the overriding importance of maintaining public order in societies polarized by class cleavages during industrialization. The fact remains, however, that associations of capital, labour and the professions, networks between social groups, alliances among firms and, especially, private interest governments engaging both producers and authorities, seem to occupy a much more significant place in descriptions of how 'business' is conducted in Europe than in comparable accounts of other industrial societies'.

This is a long story which dates back at least to medieval cities which were structured and run by urban corporations. Corporations, chambers of commerce and industry, trade and craft associations, shopkeepers' and employers' organizations, business start-up and professional associations have all formed a dynamic pillar of European cities for a long time, and this continued well after the Middle Ages, before the two forces of economic liberalism and the nation-state removed their privileges and rebalanced the scales of economic development at the national level in favour of state elites (Black, 1984). Although British economic liberalism and the French Revolution proved particularly effective in reducing the influence of corporations and chambers of commerce to almost nothing, the same did not apply to Germany or to the Netherlands. The belated making of the nation-state in Germany and Italy has enabled associations of this type to prosper for a very long time at the local and regional level.

Public administrations in Europe therefore have for a long time been involved in relations that Crouch and Dore defined as 'old corporatism' that is

> old medieval corporations ... were granted monopoly privileges (the right to decide who should and who should not be allowed to sell certain kinds of services) in exchange for promises to make sure that the professional standards of those who did sell those services – their skills and their morals – were what the public had a right to expect. (Crouch and Dore, 1990: 3–4)

Those corporations were to be dismantled under the twin forces of state formation and capitalism, but they have survived in different ways. Margaret Thatcher's political struggles in the 1980s against the legal or medical professions, or France's surviving *notaires* and medical associations (Suleiman, 1987; Hassenteufel, 1997), together with Germany's still influential chambers of commerce, indicate the remains of that tradition.

The rise of the nation-state went hand in hand with the nationalization of the main interest groups (see Crouch, 1993) and the making of a distinctive state–interest group structural pattern. In Europe therefore, interest groups' formation and their forms of action have been decisively shaped both by their role and then their embeddedness within particular nation-states. From the late 1960s onwards (Shonfield, 1965), a group of scholars started a research programme which led to the analysis of economic interest groups, their organization, discourses, types of action and exchanges within the nation-state (Schmitter and Lehmbruch, 1979; Streeck and Schmitter, 1985; Crouch, 1993). They identified different types of corporatist arrangements and compared trade unions and business organizations. That stream of work, focusing on economic interest groups, was influential in characterizing different types of states and relations between public administration and interest groups (Suleiman, 1979; Dyson, 1980), the diversity of capitalism (Crouch and Streeck, 1996; Hollingsworth and Boyer, 1997) and the dynamics of different worlds of welfare (Esping-Andersen, 1990).

This 'modern' form of corporatism attracted much interest, that is, the relationship and interaction between public administrations and organized economic interest groups, mainly business organizations and labour. As Therborn argued (1985), European societies' main characteristics derive from the importance of the Industrial Revolution and the importance of the working class (first in the UK, Germany, the north and much later the south of Europe), the rise of trade unions, labour or social democratic parties, their mobilization during the great wars and the development of the welfare state, that is, the making of the Keynesian compromise between state, labour and capital to organize capitalist economic growth together with increasing social redistribution within the state. 'Modern' corporatist arrangements could then be defined as

> An institutionalised pattern which involves an explicit or implicit bargain (or recurrent bargaining) between some organ of government and private interest groups (including those promoting 'ideal interests – causes'), one element in the bargain being that the groups receive certain institutionalised or ad hoc benefits in return for guarantees by the groups' representatives that their members will behave in certain ways considered to be in the public interest. (Crouch and Dore, 1990: 3)

At first more interested by the state, European scholars rediscovered the major issue of interest groups and public administration. Since the late nineteenth century, the influence of European states and their bureaucracy in society has grown considerably, especially with the development of the Welfare State. In most European countries, state expenditure has increased, particularly during and after the world wars, as has the proportion of GDP that it represents. In retrospect, the decades following the Second World War seem like a kind of golden age of the 'modernizing state', when, in a context of economic growth, state intervention grew and became more differentiated into increasingly diverse and complex sectors. EU countries' share of public administration expenditure in GDP is above 44 per cent (less for Ireland, the UK and Spain, more than 50 per cent for Scandinavian countries, Greece or France) compared with less than 30 per cent in the United States (OECD, 2001). This money goes to investment but also to a large group of public sector employees in welfare services in particular. Within each nation-state, some groups have organized to defend their interest within the bureaucracy. In many public policy classic studies, UK top civil servants, the Italian *dirigenza* and the French *grands corps* appeared as major interest groups within the policy process, able to frame a problem and to control the implementation process. At least since Allison (1991), different sections of the armed forces have appeared as interest groups in their own right. However, the context of the end of the Cold War and the restructuring of armed forces has rather signalled a decline of influence of these groups within the policy process, as figures about defence expenditure tend to show (Cohen, 1994; Boesne and Dandekker, 1997). Again, the contrast with the United States could not be more striking, as the US spends twice as much as Europe on defence.

It also follows that public sector interest groups such as social service workers or teachers are more entrenched within European nation-states and are likely to defend their interests. In some cases, such as education and agriculture, the regulation of the sector was the result of intimate structured interactions between trade unions and the bureaucracy (Jobert and Muller, 1987; Smith, 1993).

Within the sphere of politics, regional and local authorities' national associations remain powerful interest groups. Those national associations, once a powerful factor of centralization and professionalization within public services, remain a crucial interest to consult in order to implement public policies. In many respects, the restructuring of nation-states goes with pressure to territorialize public polices, hence the role of local authorities to implement various programmes.

Although those types of sectorial corporatism have not disappeared, a large body of literature has stressed the lack of governability of interest groups. This Handbook deals in many chapters with changes within bureaucracies, the influence of various types of new management ideas and the search for strategic capacities. Two points are stressed in relation to interest groups: first, the impact of the neoliberal turn and the growing role of market regulation at the expense of interest groups. Second, faced with increased fragmentation, bureaucracies have set up new mechanisms to deal with interest groups. From the 1980s onwards, neoliberal ideas more or less mixed within the vague normative framework of 'New Public Management' became more influential. From the point of view of bureaucracies, two priorities became central: first, to reduce the pressure of what Olson called the 'distributional coalitions' and to either cut public spending or stop the rise, together with an emphasis on efficiency and effectiveness; and second, to limit both fragmentation and the autonomy of interest groups, hence the need to design new policy instruments to steer interest groups and to involve them within the implementation process of public policies (Mayntz, 1993; Kickert et al., 1999). Beyond large and organized interest groups, bureaucracies have had to face a myriad of other movements and fragmented groups, hence the rise of queries about governance and governability (Kooiman, 1993; Pierre, 2000).

SOCIAL MOVEMENTS AND BUREAUCRACIES

Bureaucracies have to deal with a large body of organized interests, either general or single-interest groups. Beyond established interest groups and the focus on economic interests, a large body of research has gradually blurred the frontiers between interest groups and social movements, thus enlarging the conception of collective actors within European democracies (as in the United States). Social movements once seen in isolation from the pluralist tradition and characterized by little institutionalization, a different repertoire of action (including protest) and a progressive political line, are now also somewhat more institutionalized, while more classic interest groups have diversified their modes of action and become more fragmented. Bureaucracies have to face a myriad of single-interest groups which may mobilize for or against different programmes.

Meyer and Tarrow (1998) put forward the idea of 'social movement societies' characterized by four elements:

1   that social protest has moved from being a sporadic, if recurring feature of democratic politics to a perpetual element in modern life;

2　that protest behaviour is employed with greater frequency by a more diverse constituency and is used to represent a wider range of claims than ever before;

3　that professionalization and institutionalization may be changing the major vehicle of contentious claims, the social movement, into an instrument within the reach of conventional politics;

4　that state strategies have shifted from reliance on repression towards facilitation and that police practices have moved towards more sophisticated and subtle forms of the latter.

Most research work has highlighted the diversity of forms of involvement in groups or associations in Western societies. It is estimated that over half of all Europeans are part of an association or a group. Social movements and protest have become permanent elements of our societies, involving both disadvantaged groups and the middle classes (Della Porta and Diani, 1999; McAdam et al., 2001). They developed as urban movements in relation to issues of collective consumption and of public services, issues of quality of life in the neighbourhood, and opposition to planned physical changes, demands for transparency and for democratic participation in urban government, and challenges to elected representatives and parties (Pickvance, 1995: 199). Close inward-looking bureaucracies started to take into account these demands and to adapt to the pressures. Social movements became famous in the context of the great urban struggles of the 1970s, when the many politicized (left or extreme left) members of the new middle strata, together with sections of the working class, challenged major planning projects, demanded the transformation of cultural policies, or demonstrated in favour of opening up collective facilities. In Germany and Northern Europe, squatters' movements set up in districts destined for demolition and renewal mobilized young radical students and immigrants.

Apart from these movements defending living environments, former social movements transformed into different types of groups, among them parents' associations working for schools, immigrant community associations, anti-poverty associations, housing associations or associations fighting social services cuts, many and varied cultural associations, women's movements, family associations, churches, groups defending the rights of sexual minorities, pacifists, Third World and anti-racist associations, associations of illegal immigrants or of unemployed people. Leisure associations have also proliferated: sports clubs, pensioners associations, associations linked to a particular hobby. Some associations and movements have become institutionalized,

moving from protest to contractualization, participation and service provision. Public policies increasingly call on various groups, which are frequently brought together under the title of 'third sector' or the ambiguous 'civil society', which seems to cover indiscriminately the family, churches, associations, the extended family, the local community, non-market organizations etc. These groups actively help to implement public policies and local initiatives, for instance in the sphere of public management of the drugs problem or AIDS.

The relationship between interest groups and the various segments of the bureaucracy is therefore taking a less structured form. This may be yet more evidence of the individualization process. Citizens' behaviour is less oriented to and determined by large organizations; they are more distant from interest groups to which they relate. Individuals belong to or participate in a multiple informal set of interest groups across a wide range, including single-interest groups, for instance in the case of the environment.

Behaviour is less encapsulated at the macro level and is more fruitfully understood in terms of the sociology of collective action. Balme and Chabanet (2002: 4) define collective action as:

all the behaviours – engagement, mobilization, representation and negotiation – through which social interests are constituted, and through which their political influence is exercised. Thus, this is a complex range of behaviours, with differences between individual and collective actors, most often bringing together cooperation and conflict, identification and transaction. The social dimension of these interests contrasts them with more specific political mobilizations, such as the vote or partisan commitment. Their nature may differ according to how diffuse or concentrated the interest is, how material or ethical, how particular or attached to a definition of the common good, how private or public, and according to how far it is a separable good or a collective good, to use economic terminology. Repertoires for promoting interests – whether based on protest or instituted – and the interpretative focus of stakes, actors and procedures define the mode of involvement of mobilizations in the political field, as well as the relational dynamics of public policy during the phases when it publicizes issues and draws up timetables for decision-making and implementation.

Even in the more economic sphere, the development of 'coordination' beyond established trade unions has become a major trend to signal the erosion of the stable corporatist model and the opposition to more institutionalized interactions between interest group leaders and bureaucracies. One of the major problems for bureaucracies derives from the fact that these groups have a radical or critical stance towards them, hence making it a difficult world to comprehend or to enlist, in contrast to the established trade unions. At first, bureaucracies mainly opposed such groups. However, repression by the public authorities merely provoked broader mobilizations. The radicalization of some movements, changes in local policies and modes of interaction with these mobilizations, and the institutionalization of some movements all contributed to the decline of this first wave, in the context of an economic crisis that delegitimized some programmes. The claim to act in the name of the general common good is not so easily followed, even in the realm of the majestic '*intérêt général*' of the once heroic French Jacobin state.

In the field of environment, anti-globalization, anti-poverty and immigration, young radicals do not easily negotiate following established patterns. The social movement literature has analysed the wider repertoire of action they use, including forms of protest and distance towards political organizations and bureaucracies alike. Although they often start as a single-issue group, organized on a firm local base, many groups then begin to relate to wider issues, to some wider common good, which takes them towards political issues. It follows that J. Berry's distinction between private interest groups and public interest groups is called into question. Again, the concept of public interest group takes on a more diverse meaning (Jordan et al., 1994). In the health sector for instance, associations fighting against AIDS have questioned the power of hospital bureaucrats and doctors alike (Pollack, 1988; Epstein, 1996). Local anti-nuclear protesters have made the link with more general issues of energy policy (Barthe, 2000).

This diversity of groups goes hand to hand with public policy changes in EU states. Many new areas of public policy are less concerned with well-defined issues controlled by entrenched sectorial interest groups. By contrast, new areas of public policy are characterized by three levels of heterogeneity: that of the issues, which are not easily defined or framed, not until the end of the implementation, that of the programmes themselves; and that of the actors. In various domains, from health to the environment, from support to economic development to consumption issues, from protection of minority rights to sexual equalities, bureaucracies have to deal with fragmented and diverse interest groups and problems. In those areas, bureaucracies have often been attacked, as they fail to defend what comes to be seen afterwards as the general common good. Failures to consult, to elaborate collectively something such as a common good, are no longer accepted.

On the one hand, bureaucracies are learning to deal with this shifting scene of interest groups. On the other hand, they bitterly attack the representativeness of those groups and their claim to defend views of the common good.

Interest groups closer to social movements have developed a repertoire of three main types of action in their interaction with bureaucracies: protest, mediation and participation. The more they interact with bureaucracies, the more they tend to move toward mediation and participation. Again, exchange and interaction are crucial in those dynamics. It is crucial to stress the fact that bureaucracies themselves have learned to deal with these groups. For instance, in order to create new infrastructure, such as an airport, rules on consultation with different interests are more and more codified. In the welfare field, bureaucracies have learned from their failures and they are more likely to provide incentives, including some to protest groups to join forces, for instance to fight poverty. German urban bureaucrats even gave funds to squatters to develop urban renovation programmes. Regular interaction and mediation with bureaucracies tends to lead radical groups to institutionalize these interactions. In many cases, radical protest groups are progressively associated with the management of public policy programmes, up to the point when they lose some of their negotiating capacity.

RESCALING OF INTERACTIONS ACROSS NATIONAL BOUNDARIES

Patterns of interaction between interest groups and central government were organized within the nation-state. A large body of research has now emphasized the twofold fragmentation of the state and the policy process, from both the sociology of organizations and the public policy approach. It appears to be fragmented in to a myriad of organizations (agencies, networks, individuals, differentiation of political arenas) where public policies do not work in terms of hierarchies or coherent policy stages but rather in terms of negotiation, flexibility and *ad hoc* arrangements, sometimes suggesting a dissolution of the state. This fragmentation also has a multi-tier dimension: the EU, the international and the sub-national levels of government. Local and regional governments are more differentiated within the political system and therefore contribute to the fragmentation of the state and of the public policy process.

Classic arguments on interest groups suggest that bureaucracies need interest groups and that interest groups enter into interaction with bureaucracies to capture resources and to influence public policy. The redistribution of authority within the multi-level European governance in the making is closely related to the reorganization of interest groups at different levels the, supranational and the subnational.

Institutionalization of EU–interest group interactions

The making of a European political space has created a movement towards the redistribution of authority. Power relations and hierarchies have not disappeared; they are re-aligning and redeploying. The EU now has a developed system of governance that has, among other things, a fairly small civil service with limited capacities and low tax receipts, which cannot rise above a certain ceiling, but also a substantial rule-making and conflict-resolution capacity through the European Court of Justice. European supranational modes of governance have now come into being, structured by systems of rules that apply to the whole territory of the Union and by transnational networks of actors (Sandholz and Stone Sweet, 1998: Introduction).

The term 'European governance' has been widely used to describe this strange 'polity'. The use of this term originates from three features of the EU: (1) the interpenetration of different levels of government; (2) the proliferation of actors and organized non-state interests, and the existence of public policy networks that display varying degrees of organization, alongside political and social sub-systems with many forms of interdependence; (3) the fact that, even though responsibility for decision making and policy has not been delegated to an elected government, decisions are made and rules are imposed on all citizens. 'European governance' takes into account multiple interactions and the production of rules and public policies. In other words, the term 'governance' is used to describe the process of government at the European level 'because authoritative allocation takes place without or outside government' (Kohler Koch, 1999: Ch. 1).

At an early date, the field of European integration gave prominence to the role of interest groups in a neofunctionalist perspective (Haas, 1968). Interest groups were seen as dynamic agents of transnationalization and legitimized many EU policies before the states did. Also, the EU Commission has always presented itself as open, and dependent upon interest groups to gather information that states did not make easily available. For instance, in the late 1950s once the first economic treaty about steel and coal became implemented, leading national firms in Europe quickly organized as a powerful interest group. This well-entrenched interest group in Brussels gradually extended its coverage. It is today a key actor in the energy policy currently on the agenda, concerning for instance electricity, gas and oil. Over time, it has supported the move toward liberalization and has provided the Commission with detailed expertise and programme proposals.

The EU Commission has estimated that there are about 3,000 interest groups seeking influence over policies in Brussels, employing between ten and fifteen thousand persons, more or less as many as the staff of the Commission itself (Greenwood, 1997). There is now a general agreement to devise original European modes of action for interest groups, resulting from the hybridization of existing national or regional models (Greenwood, 1997; Lequesne, 2001). However, some authors suggest that what the Germans call 'the joint multi-level decision making' gives incentive to interest groups to be present at different levels of the policy process and thus dilutes their influence. By contrast, others suggest that the dense concentration of interest group representatives in Brussels gives them far more influence on the policy process than within national systems, in particular for those groups that were not so central. Women's groups were not always highly considered as powerful interest groups by central bureaucracies within most European nation-states. Now, in the still emerging European social policy, significant changes have been achieved to establish equal opportunities for men and women in different areas. Women's interest groups organized in Brussels a successful group to make, first, several changes within EU social legislation (labour market policy, for instance), second, to establish specific programmes to enhance women's interests, and third, to introduce a new set of rules and norms within mainstream EU policy which impose women's representation within the policy process. Last but not least, national women's groups have used these new opportunities to appeal to the European Court of Justice to establish these norms in their own countries against the wishes of their domestic national governments (Cichowky, 2001).

Most of the literature is now working on the distinction between different forms of Europeanization processes for interest groups (Balme et al., 2002). The institutionalization of European governance is generating tensions with national arenas for regulating public policy. Interactions entail processes of transfer, adaptation and hybridization, as well as dynamic conflicts that produce new rules and help to structure a new public policy space. Any representation of European governance that stressed only interconnected public policy hierarchies would fail to address the power of reshaped states and the institutionalization of Europe, which lend stability to actors' behaviour. Structures are starting to appear. European institutions provide a stable frame work within which anticipation reduces uncertainties. Regularity in the behaviour of European interest groups is achieved through cognitive and normative matrices, coordinated sets of values, beliefs and principles of action, assimilated by the actors to varying degrees and guiding their practices (Pierson, 1998; Stone Sweet et al., 2001). New repertoires of action are also in the making (Marks et al., 1996).

After the creation of the Single European Market, the Commission could not cope with the flow of demands from the myriad interest groups. A process of institutionalization of the relations between the Commission and interest groups was started, including the production of a directory and the writing of procedures to consult interest groups at different stages of the policy process (Mazey and Richardson, 1993). In some sectors, the EU may be described as a regulatory state (Majone, 1996). Majone gives public health, the environment and safety, as examples of collective goods. European agencies, such as the Environmental Agency (created in 1994) or the Agency for the Evaluation of Medicinal Products, for example, promote integration by non-regulatory means, relying instead on national administrative bodies. This indicates a new avenue for interest groups to organize and become part of the policy process within the EU. Greenwood (1997) identifies nine types of 'bargaining chips' for interest groups in Brussels: information and expertise, economic muscle, status, power in implementation, the organization of the interest into a non-competitive form, coherent organization, ability to help the overloaded Commission with carrying policies, ability of an interest group to influence its members.

As a result of the institutionalization of Europe, the category 'European interest groups' makes greater political sense. European public policies, rules, procedures, conflict-solving mechanisms, debates and norms are now relevant to all public administrations within the EU. Europeanization processes provide a new structure of opportunities for interests groups, and incentives to engage with other actors to promote their spatial or sectoral interests through both vertical and horizontal networks. But it also represents a new structure of constraints, of rules which limit their autonomy and overlap with national or regional institutions. This opening of the field offers new potential for interest groups: lodging appeals against state decisions through the European Court of Justice, organizing lobbying in Brussels to influence decisions and policies, acquiring resources and expertise independently of the state, developing horizontal transnational relationships with other interest groups, getting deeply involved in various sectoral networks, questioning the state's formulation of the common interest. The more the EU – and, in particular, certain of its policies – becomes institutionalized, the more the actors tend to react by organizing to contest and defend their interests; and, in doing so, they contribute to the production of new rules that foster the institutionalization dynamic (Stone, et al., 2001). This fundamental trend within the European context grows stronger with globalization.

Research on interest groups at the EU level has given a new impetus to the analysis of interest groups in the policy process, in relation to different types of public bureaucracies and agencies, at different levels. Most research stresses the fact that, in Brussels, two types of interest groups have been the main winners in the European integration process: business interests first and foremost, which share the agenda of the Commission of eradicating barriers to exchanges to create a market, and interests such as environmental groups, which used to be less influential at the national level. However, both in terms of organization and action, and parallel to the dynamics of transnationalization, a trend towards subnationalization has modified interactions between bureaucracies and interest groups.

Interest groups and bureaucracies at the local and regional level

Decentralization trends in Western Europe are giving more prominence to local and regional governments. In most European countries, some subnationalization of interest groups and increased demands from local and regional bureaucracies have been observed. Regional and city councils, elected politicians, are under pressure to deal with a set of problems that used to come within state control: economic development, law and order, social exclusion. In organizational terms, the developments outlined above reveal increased horizontal, contractual relationships between bureaucracies and interest groups.

Keating (1998) has shown in detail the importance of the EU in structuring the 'new territorial politics' in Western Europe, within and beyond the state: 'The new territorial politics is focused less on territorial management and national integration, and more on territorial competition, within national arenas but also within Europe and the wider market' (1998: 185). In most European regions and cities, attempts are made by political leaders to create coalitions with interest groups, to organize modes of governance. Cities and regions are increasingly becoming sites of aggregation and representation of different interests, integrating them within a more or less shared cognitive framework – a set of priorities which may seem to represent the city's or region's common good.

Cities' political and administrative elites are benefiting from their increased autonomy, creating more innovations and experiments in organizing and running services. The key words are now experimentation, managerialism, leadership, governance in close connection with interest groups within and outside their territory (John, 2001). In relations between elected representatives and citizens, and between the makers of political regulation and interest groups, something is shifting towards more autonomy for the various actors, increased legal control over relationships and conflicts, and more consultation. For instance, by comparison with American public–private partnerships, which frequently vest most power in the private sector, European public–private partnership experiments remain fairly limited, except in the UK, and city councils still have strong capacities for initiative and control. City councils have developed their mode of action in two directions in particular: consideration of group, neighbourhood and residents' demands, and management of urban services. Major reshaping is taking place in many of them, directed towards diversifying modes of management of different services, confirming the role of mayors and their deputies, and professionalizing the management of local government.

At the scale of medium-sized European cities, social movements, associations and private interests are most often highly visible and identifiable. They fall within different time scales, sometimes long-term ones. They deploy to organize the defence of their interests, to accumulate legacies and, in distinctive social strategies (schools, housing, cultural practices, clubs), in political groups, in public policy networks, in property and commercial investment strategies (Le Galès, 2002). In general, they are divided, rather than integrated into a single organization or under a legitimate leadership. From north to south across Europe, mayors and bureaucracies complain about the unadventurous nature of residents and about systematic opposition to their major projects: stations, airports, shopping centres, property complexes, leisure parks, regeneration activities, and – last but by no means least – the construction of service networks. Bureaucracies and politicians must systematically compromise with district associations, tenants' committees, environmental groups and groups protecting their living environment, all more or less institutionalized and taking part in numerous types of activity: demonstrations and petitions accompany systematic legal appeals, brawls with the constabulary, or the heckling of elected representatives (Lascoumes, 1994).

Relations between economic interest groups and politics have appeared, first, in terms of exchanges between groups in the pluralist tradition and then in the urban growth coalitions and urban regimes tradition where powerful economic interests allied to local bureaucracies and politicians organize urban development (Logan and Molotch, 1987). In many cases, fragmentation prevails rather than integrated modes of governance. But it has also appeared in governance, less in terms of domination and more in terms of mobilization and organization of interests.

Regional levels of government also now have more resources, more legitimacy, more room for manoeuvre within European governance in the making. When corporatist or national neocorporatist models became weak, the hypothesis that similar forms would emerge at a subnational territorial level was put forward, for instance as regional meso-corporatism (Streeck, 1992). Interest groups were considered as important. However, it remains a fact that these organizations are not very evident or structured at this level, barring notable exceptions, for example in the German *Länder*, in Scotland and Wales, Catalonia, the Basque Country and Brittany, where the identity dimension gives rise to regional mobilization. Consequently, in most European countries, on the one hand, interests are relatively weakly organized at a regional level and, on the other hand, there is no significant empirical proof of the reorganization of interest organizations at regional level, unlike at the European level. Most research underlines the multiplication of networks, including interest groups crossing territorial boundaries on different scales.

The rise of yet another buzzword, 'partnership', was first used to describe cooperation between public and private actors and different bureaucratic organizations. But in many countries it also encompasses wide-ranging cooperation between public actors and interest groups (Benington and Geddes, 2001). The whole issue of coordination of public policy involves various schemes to bring together different levels of government. Policy instruments addressing this question are on the rise: for instance, contracts, pacts and partnership. The development of new policy tools provides evidence of the ambiguity of the interactions between bureaucracies and interest groups. It reveals attempts to redefine public policy in a flexible way in order to face ill-defined problems, to cope with difficult heterogeneous goals or to manage different types of networks (Kickert et al., 1997).

CONCLUSION

At the micro level, policy processes reveal fragmentation, adjustments between representations, goals and policies which are made through interactions on a day-to-day basis, with progressive elaboration of some views of general interest and institutionalization of collective action.

General arguments about the restructuring of politics in Europe tend to indicate the decreasing salience of state regulation (in the sense of hierarchy, authority being the driving force and the state playing the central role of coordination and resource allocation, a focal point for conflicts) in favour of the loose coupling between different levels through networks of various kinds, that is, more interactions between a larger range of actors at different levels. Interest groups, once mainly organized within nation-states, reorganize, bypass the state and organize transnational networks with representatives in Brussels. The redistribution of authority goes hand in hand with the multiplication of different networks, including some policy networks, and the development of regulation mechanisms through negotiation and cooperation based on interests but also on trust or values. The European multi-level governance in the making is seen through pluralist lenses.

As mentioned elsewhere in the Handbook, the literature on state and administrative reform has stressed the fragmentation and differentiation of states which have become splintered and incoherent, thus reinforcing the fragmentation of interest groups. The state seems to be a series of interconnected agencies, organizations, flexible rules and negotiations, where an increasing number of actors and interests play a part in public policy, in one way or another. Public policy is often characterized by *ad hoc* or contingency

arrangements, enmeshed networks, the blurring of boundaries between sectors, a proliferation of actors, various constraints, multiple aims, heterogeneity, cross-linking of issues, the coming together of heterogeneous actors, changing scales of reference territories, adjustments between contradictory social interests and the increasing complexity of instruments for intervention. All this blurs the boundaries between public and private, and suggests a picture of a crumbling state where access points for interest groups have multiplied.

The neoliberal turn of the 1980s signalled the end of the Keynesian compromise, a more fragmented pattern of interest groups and the restructuring of nation-states and public administrations. Attention focused on the wider view of interests and social movements, on the micro dimension of mobilization, on the meso and micro analysis of interest groups and public administrations, hence raising issues of the governance of networks of different interests.

REFERENCES AND FURTHER READING

Allison, G. (1991) *Essence of Decision: Explaining the Culson Missile Crisis*. New York: Harper Collins.

Balme, R. Chabanet, D. and Wright, V. (2002) *Les Intérêts organisés en Europe*. Paris: Presses de Sciences Po.

Barthe, Y. (2000) 'La mise en politique des déchets nucléaires'. Thesis, Ecole des Mines, Paris.

Benington, J. and Geddes, M. (eds) (2001) *Local Partnership and Social Exclusion in the European Union*. London: Routledge.

Berger, S. (ed.) (1981) *Organizing Interests in Western Europe: Pluralism, Corporatism and the Transformation of Politics*. Cambridge: Cambridge University Press.

Black, A. (1984) *Guilds and Civil Society in European Political thought from the Twelfth Century to the Present*. London: Methuen.

Boesne, B. and Dandekker, C. (eds) (1997) *Les Armées en Europe*. Paris: La Découverte.

Boyer, R. and Hollingsworth, R. (eds) (1997) *Contemporary Capitalism*. Cambridge: Cambridge University Press.

Cichowsky, R. (2001) 'Judicial rulemaking and the institutionalization of EU sex equality policy', in A. Stone Sweet, N. Fligstein and W. Sandholz (eds), *The Institutionalization of Europe*. Oxford: Oxford University Press.

Cohen, S. (1994) *La Défaite des généraux*. Paris: Fayard.

Crouch, C. (1993) *Industrial Relations and European States Traditions*. Oxford: Clarendon Press.

Crouch, C. and Dore, R. (1990) *Corporatism and Accountability, Organized Interests in British Public Life*. Oxford: Oxford University Press.

Crouch, C. and Streeck, W. (eds) (1996) *The Diversity of Capitalism*. London: Sage.

Dahl, R. (1967) *Pluralist Democracy in the United States.* Chicago: Rand–McNally.

Della Porta, D. and Diani, M. (1999) *Social Movements, an Introduction.* Oxford: Blackwell.

Dyson, K. (1980) *State Traditions in Western Europe.* Oxford: Martin Robertson.

Epstein, S. (1996) *Impure Science: AIDS, Activism and the Politics of Knowledge.* Berkeley, CA: University of Berkeley Press,

Esping-Andersen, G. (1990) *The Three Worlds of Welfare Capitalism.* Cambridge: Polity Press.

Grande, E. (1996) 'The state and interest groups in a framework of multilevel decision making: the case of the EU', *Journal of European Public policy,* 3 (3): 318–38.

Greenwood, E. (1997) *Representing Interests in the European Union.* London: Macmillan.

Haas, E. (1968) *The Uniting of Europe.* Stanford, CA: Stanford University Press.

Hassenteufel, P. (1997) *Les Médecins face à l'état.* Presses de Sciences Po.

Jobert, B. and Muller, P. (1987) *L'Etat en action.* Paris: Presses Universitaires de France.

John, P. (2001) *Local Governance in Europe.* London: Sage.

Jordan, G. and Richardson, J. (eds) (1979) *Government and Pressure Groups in Britain.* Oxford: Clarendon Press.

Jordan, G., Maloney, W. and Bennie, L. (1996) 'Les groupes d'intérêt public', *Pouvoirs,* 79: 69–85.

Keating, M. (1998) *The New Regionalism in Western Europe.* Aldershot: Edward Elgar.

Kickert, W., Klijn, E.H. and Koopenjan, J.F.M. (eds) (1997) *Managing Complex Networks.* London: Sage,

Kohler-Koch, B. and Eising, R. (eds) (1999) *The Transformation of Governance in the European Union.* London: Routledge.

Kooiman, J. (ed.) (1993) *Modern Governance.* London: Sage.

Lascoumes, P. (1994) *L'Éco-pouvoir.* Paris: La Découverte.

Lehmbruch, G. (1991) 'The organization of society, administrative strategies and policy networks: elements of a development theory of interest systems', in R. Czada and A. Heritier (eds), *Political Choice: Institutional Rules, and the Limits of Rationality.* Frankfurt Campus.

Lequesne, C. (2001) *L'Europe Bleue.* Paris: Presses de Sciences Po.

Le Galès, P. (2002) *European Cities, Social Conflicts and Governance.* Oxford: Oxford University Press.

Le Galès, P. and Thatcher, M. (eds) (1994) *Les Réseaux de l'action publique.* Paris: L'Harmattan.

Logan, J. and Molotch, H. (1987) *Urban Fortunes. The Political Economy of Place.* Berkeley, CA: The University of California Press.

Majone, G. (1996) *Regulating Europe.* London: Routledge.

Marks, G., Sharpf, F., Schmitter, P. and Streeck, W. (eds) (1996) *Governance in the European Union.* London: Sage.

Marsh, D. and Rhodes, R. (eds) (1992) *Policy Networks in British Government.* Oxford: Clarendon Press.

Mayntz, R. (1993) Governing failures and the problem of governability, in J. Kooiman (ed.), *Modern Governance.* London: Sage.

Mayntz, R. (1999) La teoria della governance: sfide e prospettive', *Rivista Italiana di Scienza Politica,* XXIX, no.1.

Mazey, S. and Richardson, J. (eds) (1993) *Lobbying in the European Community.* Oxford: Oxford University Press.

McAdam, D., Tarrow, S. and Tilly, C. (eds) (2001) *Dynamics of Contentions.* Cambridge: Cambridge University Press.

Meyer, D. and Tarrow, S. (eds) (1998) *The Social Movement Society, People, Passions and Power.* Lanham, MD: Rowman & Littlefield.

OECD (2001) *Economic Outlooks,* no. 69. Paris: Organization for Economic Co-operation and Development.

Pickvance, C. (1995) 'Where are urban movements gone?', in C. Hadjimalis and D. Sadler (eds), *Europe at the Margins: New Mosaics of Inequality.* London: Wiley.

Pierre, J. (ed.) (2000) *Debating Governance, Authority, Steering and Democracy,* Oxford, Oxford University Press.

Pierson, P. (1998) 'The path to European integration: a historical-institutionalist analysis', in W. Sandholz and A. Stone Sweet (eds), *European Integration and Supranational Governance.* Oxford: Oxford University Press.

Pollack, M. (1988) *Les Homosexuels et le sida, sociologie d'une épidémie.* Paris: Métaillé,

Richardson, J. (1993) *Pressures Groups.* Oxford: Oxford University Press.

Sandholtz, W. and Stone Sweet, A. (eds) (1998) *European Integration and Supranational Governance.* Oxford: Oxford University Press.

Schmitter, P. (1997) 'The emerging Europolity', in J. Hollingsworth and R. Boyer (eds), *Contemporary Capitalism.* Cambridge: Cambridge University Press.

Schmitter, P. and Lehmbruch, G. (eds) (1979) *Trends Towards Corporatist Intervention.* London: Sage.

Shonfield, A. (1965) *Modern Capitalism.* Oxford: Oxford University Press.

Smith, M. (1993) *Power and Pressure Politics.* London: Macmillan.

Stone Sweet, A., Fligstein, N. and Sandholz, W. (eds) (2001) *The Institutionalization of Europe.* Oxford: Oxford University Press.

Streeck, W. (1992) *Social Institutions and Economic Performance.* London: Sage.

Streeck, W. and Schmitter, P. (eds) (1985) *Private Interests Government: Beyond Market and States.* London: Sage.

Streeck, W. and Schmitter, P. (1995) 'The emerging Europolity and organised interests', *European Journal of International Relations,* 1 (2): 191–218.

Suleiman, E. (1979) *Les Elites en France, grands corps, grandes écoles.* Paris: Le Seuil.

Suleiman, E. (1987) *Les Notaires,* Paris: Le Seuil.

Therborn, G. (1985) *European Modernity and Beyond.* London: Sage.

Truman, D. (1971) *The Governmental Process.* New York: Knopf.

ADMINISTRATION AND SOCIETY

Introduction

Bo Rothstein

The central question to be addressed in this section is how public support and legitimacy for the public administration affects its ability to conduct its role in society, especially to implement policies according to the intentions of political rulers. Such a society-centered perspective on public administration is broader and to some extent different from the classical 'tool' questions that focus on the possibilities for politicians to steer the bureaucracy according to their intentions. Empirical research in this society-centered approach is relatively young while the theoretical questions were posed long ago. It should be remembered that both Karl Marx and Max Weber took a stand on this problem. After the fall of the Paris Commune in 1871, Marx wrote that it had become obvious to him that the working class could not simply take over the existing state apparatus and use it for its political purposes; rather, thorough changes in the government machinery would be necessary first. Just what changes would be needed he never specified, for no fourth volume of *Das Kapital* (which was meant to be about the state) was ever written.

Max Weber, the founder of the theory of the modern bureaucracy, had a similar view about the relation between society and the state. At a meeting in Mannheim in 1907 with the German Society for Social Policy (the Verein für Sozialpolitik), he entered into a debate with some conservative scholars about extending the suffrage to the working class. The conservatives feared that if democracy was introduced, the Social Democrats would come into power and capture the state and use it to pursue their own narrow class interests. Weber argued against this, saying that if the Social Democrats were to come into power by such a process of democratization, it would not be they who conquered the bureaucratic state; quite the contrary, the bureaucratic state would in the long run conquer the Social Democrats. It is safe to say that research about the impact of Social Democracy still ponders on these questions. The problems taken up in this section of the Handbook, about, for example, the social and political representation of the public administration and its direct interactions with citizens, thus have a long history in the social sciences.

The four chapters in this section analyze this problem from different theoretical angles. The chapter by Rothstein stresses the importance of social capital and trust. The central idea in this new discussion has been that social capital, defined as interpersonal and trust and social networks, are one of the central ingredients that make the administrative part of the democratic machinery work. Rothstein turns this around and argues that it may be the case that a well-functioning public administration is an important causal factor for the generation of social capital. If citizens perceive that they cannot trust the police, the judges, teachers, they will infer that nor can people in general in their society be trusted.

The chapter by Wise on representative bureaucracy poses a number of interesting dilemmas as to how to make the administration more legitimate by changing the pattern of recruitment. Since bureaucrats are not elected but wield power, the question about their representativeness becomes important. She makes the important distinction between passive representation, which is when the bureaucracy statistically has a social, ethnic and demographic background setup that is similar to the population at large, and active representation, which is when civil servants are recruited because they have a certain ideological orientation or background that will make their decisions go in a particular direction. One of the dilemmas is how the demand for neutrality and impartiality can come into conflict with the idea that the different interests should be represented in the recruitment of civil servants. Another problem is of course which type of background should be counted as a legitimate reason for bureaucratic representation. Here we can think of age, social class, ethnicity, gender, sexual orientation, language, geography, religion and quite a few others. Deciding which of these should be recognized is a politically charged problem in many countries. In international organizations such as the EU, national representation in the bureaucracy has become standard.

The chapter by Smith stresses the importance of street-level bureaucrats. In many ways, these are the direct link between the administration and society and they are thus central for questions about legitimacy. The basis for the theory about the importance of street-level bureaucrats is their discretionary power in making the numerous micro-decisions that mount up to the public

policy that is actually implemented. Smith analyzes several ways in which many countries during the past two decades have tried to manage their street-level bureaucracies. One of them is the 'New Public Management Approach' (NPM), another has been to increase the influence of organizations rooted in the surrounding community. The NPM approach has taken most of its intellectual influence from the *logic of exchange* and market ideology, while the community-based approach is rooted in a fundamentally different normative agenda based on theories about *civil society*. While the NPM approach centers on making street-level bureaucrats more responsive by using contracts, voucher-systems, benchmarking and competition, the civil society approach stress the importance of involving user-groups such as neighborhood associations or other types of voluntary associations. Smith points out the implications for the relation between citizenship rights and street-level bureaucracies of both these approaches.

The last chapter in this section analyzes what the new electronic and communication technologies (ICT) have meant for changing the interface between the administration and society. Is the Bureaucratic State finally to be replaced by the 'Digital State'? Helen Margetts contrasts the optimistic and pessimistic views set by the hyper-modernists and anti-modernists respectively, with the more cynical approach put forward by the postmodernists. None of these predictions has been borne out by developments so far. The new technologies have neither made discretionary judgments by individual bureaucrats less frequent, nor have they created an electronic Leviathan. In many cases, the new technologies empower citizens as much as the administrators, because access to information and documents has become easier and cheaper. The chapter concludes with a discussion of a number of possible future scenarios in this interesting field of public administration development.

26

Political Legitimacy for Public Administration

Bo Rothstein

From a comparative perspective, systems of public administration vary tremendously in their relation to societal actors and the public at large. One could mention variation in degrees of patronage, clientelism and corruption, patterns of recruitment, and the ways in which the bureaucracy coordinates its activities with various civic networks and organized interests. One perennial question in this research is, of course, why do some countries have more efficient systems of public administration than others? One answer may be that this is determined by the amount of trust citizens have in the bureaucracy in their country, region or city. Simply put, it is easier to govern, coordinate, control, steer and/or manage a complicated system if one is trusted by the ones that are supposed to be governed, coordinated, controlled, steered and/or managed. If the legitimacy and trustworthiness of the civil service is low, it will be difficult for them to implement many policies, which in its turn may spur even more distrust between citizens and the administrative agencies.

If, for example, tax bureaucrats are known to be corrupt and/or inefficient, it makes little sense for citizens to correctly report their income/taxes (Scholz, 1998; Thorp, 1996). They will draw conclusions such as (a) most of their taxes will not reach their proper addresses or (b) most other people will get away with cheating the system (Putnam, 1995: 111). Such vicious circles have proved to be hard to break and seem to be determined by long historical trajectories (Bardhan, 1997; Treisman, 2000). An expert on the economic problems in Latin America interviewed in the *New York Times* stated that, 'I don't think there is any more vital issue in

Latin America right now ... It's a vicious cycle that is very hard to break. People don't want to pay taxes because they say government doesn't deliver services, but government institutions aren't going to perform any better until they have resources, which they obtain when people pay their taxes' (Rother, 1999). Without legitimacy and trust, it is difficult to obtain economic and political resources necessary for the state to implement policies in a competent way. But citizens who perceive the state as incompetent or untrustworthy are less likely to provide such resources, not to mention political support (Levi, 1998a, 1998b). To use game-theoretical language, such an inefficient equilibrium is re-enforcing and thereby stable (Bendor and Swistak, 1997).

Several prominent social scientists have recently argued that this 'quality of government' variable is crucial in explaining differences in standard of living and economic growth among nations. For many developing countries, not to mention the countries formerly belonging to the Soviet bloc, this may be the most difficult problem to solve for consolidating democracy and economic growth (Olson, 1996; North, 1998). As one expert from the World Bank stated:

Rampant corruption, frustrating bureaucratic delays, suppressed civil liberties, failure to safeguard property rights and uphold the rule of law, forces communities back on themselves, demanding that they supply privately and informally what should be delivered publicly and formally. Accordingly, in countries where these conditions prevail, there should be little to show for even the most well-intentioned efforts to build schools, hospitals and encourage foreign investments. (Woolcook, 2001: 16)

This 'quality of government' factor has recently received a fair amount of attention in research outside the traditional areas of public administration studies. The problem is that creating a high-quality public administration requires a fair amount of resources that a low-quality administration is less likely to obtain. As one study using data from between 60 and 209 countries concluded: 'we have consistently found that the better performing governments are also larger, and collect higher taxes' (La Porta et al., 1999: 234). The authors' conclusion is that 'identifying big government with bad government can be highly misleading'. But they would not have been economists if they had not immediately added that this result 'does not of course imply that it is often, or ever, socially desirable to expand a government of a given quality'.

THE THEORETICAL ASPECT OF BUREAUCRATIC LEGITIMACY

The reason why legitimacy and trust is central to any system of public administration is simple. Civil servants usually wield political power because there is room for discretion in the decisions they make (Rothstein, 1996; Brehm and Gates, 1997). Also, unlike elected officials, bureaucrats are neither voted into, nor can they be voted out of office. There are of course public policies that can be implemented by the use of general and precise rules and regulations, in which case the discretionary power of the bureaucracy is very small. For example, universal child allowances, universal tax credits or pensions systems may work in this way, in which case there is hardly any room for bureaucratic discretion which in its turn makes the problem of citizens' trust and legitimacy for the civil service less salient (Rothstein, 1998).

In many other areas that call for state intervention, it is more difficult to use precise laws and regulations. Instead, laws can only be created which state the general aim of the policy while the actual implementation has to be made according to the specific circumstances of the situation of the actual case. Such policy areas are, for example, labor market policy, industrial policy, workers' protection policy and environmental policy (Kelman, 1981; Offe, 1986; Moe and Chubb, 1991; Rothstein, 1996). Other areas are tax policy, the legal system (that is, the police and the courts) and educational policy. In fact, Aristotle himself noted that written laws cannot be applied in all situations, since legislators,

'being unable to define for all cases, ... are obliged to make universal statements, which are not applicable to all but only to most cases'. Aristotle concluded therefore that 'equity is justice that goes beyond the written law' (Aristotle cited in Brand, 1988: 42). Thus we can conclude that the need for situational adjustment in policy areas is often so great in many situations as to render impossible any centralized, uniform decision making process (Lipsky, 1980; Friedman, 1981). The more dynamic the policy area into which the government wants to intervene, and the more they have to rely on the judgment of various professional or semi-professional groups such as doctors, environmental specialists or social workers, the greater the problem with discretionary power (cf. Vinzant, 1998).

The father of bureaucratic theory, Max Weber, stressed the importance of analyzing the state not only as a system of representation but also, and maybe foremost, as a *form of administration*:

> For the state to endure, then, the persons living under its rule must submit to the authority to which the wielders of power lay claim. When and why do they do this? On what bases of internalized legitimacy, and on what outward instruments, do the rulers ground their authority? (Weber, 1989: 28)

Weber's analytical focus was, in the first instance, on the *legitimacy* of the established order (Barker, 1980; Beetham, 1985). How could the governing class most effectively uphold popular respect for its right to rule? The answer lay in ensuring that the governed – the citizens – regarded the exercise of power as *legitimate* (Friedman, 1981: 6). In contrast to most other social theorists, Weber viewed political legitimacy as depending not just on the political system's input side. For Weber, the output side – the implementation of policy by bureaucrats – was at least as important, for it was this side of the state with which citizens came into direct contact, and on which they were dependent. Weber thought, for example, that the state's legitimacy was more dependent on tax collectors' relations with citizens than on whether or not suffrage was universal (Barker, 1980; Beetham, 1985: 265ff). The central idea in Weber's theory of bureaucratic legitimacy was that the strict neutral implementation of codified universal and precise laws would make the decisions of the administration predictable for the citizens. However, Claus Offe has underlined that 'as soon as legal norms become disposable from the standpoint of their suitability for concrctc tasks, they lose their capacity to legitimate the choice and fulfillment of these tasks on the basis of any substantive validity' (Offe, 1984: 308).

This problem is especially acute in the modern welfare states, because of the extended responsibility they have for the welfare of their citizens. The distribution of childcare places, the placement of patients in the queue for medical operations, support for industries located in sparsely populated parts of the country, admission to higher education, to vocational training programs or to clinics for drug abusers – state personnel in such areas must make discretionary decisions *continually*; doing so is part of the day's work for a teacher in a classroom, for instance, or a doctor at an emergency ward. The scope for democratic control through the representative system over decisions of this kind is very slight because such decisions require a specific knowledge of each case. The need for *situational adjustment*, in other words, is so great in many situations as to render impossible any centralized, uniform decision making process. Other policy areas in which this problem is known to be acute include aid to developing countries and in international organizations (Hydén, 2000).

The central problems are thus the following. Given that, in many cases, it is necessary to entrust the administrative agencies and/or individual civil servants with large amounts of discretionary power, how can the public, and especially the various 'target groups' to which the policy in question is directed, trust the administrative agencies not to misuse that power? This 'trust in the state' problem is one of the main questions in the burgeoning research on trust as a general social problem (Braithwaite and Levi, 1998; Sztompka, 1998; Tyler, 1998; Warren, 1999; Cook, 2001; Uslaner, 2001). The policy question that follows is this: In what way can the public administration be organized or interact with the surrounding society so as to increase confidence that power entrusted in its hands will not be misused? This is a difficult policy problem because public images of 'the government' seem to have very deep historical roots that are hard to change (Rothstein, 2000). Citizens in contemporary Scandinavia have very different views and images of the very concept 'the government' compared to those in, for example, Romania.

SOCIAL CAPITAL AND PUBLIC ADMINISTRATION

There are few concepts that have had such a remarkable and instant success in the social sciences as *social capital* (Brehm and Rahn, 1997; Knack and Keefer, 1997; Hall, 1999;

Newton, 1999b; Uslaner, 1999; della Porta, 2000; Rothstein and Stolle, 2003). Although the concept and the theory behind it has a longer history, the credit for making social capital into a very useful and important tool in empirical research goes to Robert D. Putnam. His book *Making Democracy Work – Civic Traditions in Modern Italy*, published in 1993, has had a very substantial impact in political science as well as in many other disciplines such as economics and sociology. It is also a theory that has had a substantial impact on public policy in many countries. Important international organizations such as, for example, the World Bank, have become interested in the theory, especially in how it can be used to spur democratic development and economic growth in developing countries.

As the title suggests, *Making Democracy Work* presented an empirically grounded theory about what rightfully can be seen as the 'million dollar question' in political science. The answer given by Putnam and his research team was that the amount and quality of a society's *social capital* is the most important cause behind a well-functioning democracy (Putnam, 1993: Ch. 4). Following sociologist James Coleman, the major idea in the social capital theory is that social networks, informal as well as formal, creates norms of trust and reciprocity among citizens (Coleman, 1990). These norms are important because it makes it less difficult to solve problems of collective action, such as the provision of various forms of public goods. If the stock of social capital in a society or in a group is low, a situation metaphorically known as a *social trap* may occur (Platt, 1973).[1] Situations such as these are very common and range from helping to protect the environment by sorting your garbage (or not), to paying your taxes (or not), or to giving/taking bribes (or not). It makes no sense to be the only one who sorts your garbage, pays taxes or refrains from corruption if you are convinced that most other citizens cannot be trusted to do the same, because the good that is going to be produced will then not materialize (Ostrom, 1998).

From a public administration perspective it can be noted that the correlation between 'generalized trust' as measured in the World Value studies and indexes of corruption is high ($r = 0.65$). In a recent empirical study also using cross-national data, it is stated that '[t]rust is relatively strongly correlated with "judicial efficiency", "anticorruption", "growth" and "bureaucratic quality"' (La Porta et al., 1997: 336). In yet another recent study, the conclusion is that 'at the aggregate level, social trust and confidence in government and its institutions are strongly associated with each other. Social trust can help build effective social and political institutions, which can help governments perform effectively, and this in turn encourages confidence in civic institutions' (Newton, 1999b: 12). The problem, however, is the usual one that arises when using aggregate data. We don't know if there is a causal mechanism at the individual level, and we don't know how such a causal mechanism might actually work (Inglehart, 1999: 104).

The main thrust of Putnam's argument is that social capital is produced if citizens engage in horizontal voluntary organizations such as choral societies, parent–teacher's associations, sports clubs etc. In this Tocquevillian notion of the good social order, it is a vibrant civil society that generates social capital. In such a society, citizens engage in local grass root organizations where they learn the noble art of overcoming social dilemmas by getting to know people and learn that they can be trusted. At the aggregate level, Putnam is able to show very impressive correlations between the density of the world of voluntary organizations and democratic efficiency (Putnam, 1993).

Several scholars have questioned this society-centered approach to how social trust is created. Is it agents who already trust other citizens who join organizations, or is it the activity in the organizations that increases trust? Work by Dietlind Stolle and others seems to support the former thesis more than the latter. From her very interesting micro-level data, she concludes that 'it is not true that the longer and the more one associates, the greater one's generalized trust' (Stolle, 1998: 521). Eric Uslaner and Paul Whiteley have independently of each other also given empirical support to the thesis that it is not activity in voluntary associations which creates high levels of social trust. Instead they argue that social trust is a moral orientation and as such is a consequence of different socialization processes within the family (Whiteley, 1999; Uslaner, 2002).

The major counter-argument to Putnam's theory about trust among citizens is that it can also be created 'from above', that is, from the state. The argument is that governments can realize their capacity to generate trust only if citizens consider the state itself to be trustworthy. States, for example, enable the establishment of contracts in that they provide information and monitor legislation, and enforce rights and rules that sanction lawbreakers, protect minorities and actively support the integration and participation of citizens. If the legal and administrative institutions are perceived as fair, just and (reasonably) efficient, this increases the likelihood that citizens will overcome social traps (Brehm and Rahn, 1997; Levi, 1998a; Newton, 1999b). The causal mechanism at the individual level between the 'quality of public administration' and social trust may hypothetically run as follows.

1   If public officials are known to be corrupted, citizens will infer that even individuals given the responsibility to guard the public interest are not to be trusted, and if they cannot be trusted, then nor can 'most people' be trusted.
2   Following this, citizens will infer that most people cannot be trusted because they are engaged in direct or indirect corruption of these government institutions.
3   In order to 'survive' under such a system, each citizen will find himself forced to engage in corruption, even if it is against his moral orientation. But because she cannot trust herself to behave according to the rules, she is likely to infer that nor are 'other people' likely to play by the rules, and thus they cannot be trusted (Rothstein and Stolle, 2003).

If this is the 'cognitive map' of what can be expected from public authorities and fellow citizens that parents transfer to their children, this will mount up to what Uslaner and Whitley (above) mean by childhood socialization. If other citizens in general cannot be trusted as above, it makes of course little sense to join with them in different voluntary associations. The causal mechanism I want to specify here is that social trust may run from trust in the quality of government institutions responsible for the implementation of public policies to trust in 'most people' (cf. della Porta, 2000). It makes no sense to trust 'most people' if they are generally known to bribe, threaten or in other ways corrupt the impartiality of government institutions in order to extract special favors. One reason 'most other people' may be trusted is that they are generally known to refrain from such forms of behavior (Putnam, 1993: 111).

More casually, here is a 'true story' that helps to illustrate our argument. *Lonely Planet* is one of the world's largest companies in the guidebook industry. This is how the police are described in its latest guide to the Yucatan peninsula in Mexico.

> Be advised that the federal police have been implicated in rapes and murders … so don't turn to them for help if you have been assaulted. Obviously, if you survive an attack and go to the police, only to recognize an officer as one of your assailants, he won't be likely to give you the chance to identify him in a court of law.

The point I want to make is that in a society where such a perception of public officials is common, people will also trust other people in general to a much lower extent. If public officials, who are supposed to provide citizens with protection, cannot be trusted then what are the grounds for trusting people in general? Even visitors from countries where the population is known to have unusually high levels of trust in other people will quickly change their mind about how wise it is to trust other people, let alone the police. In addition, they will of course also feel vulnerable and unprotected, which makes them fear strangers even more. No wonder that the wonderful beaches at the Yucatan peninsula are being occupied to an astonishing degree by 'all inclusive resorts', which is the name for 'gated communities' in the tourist industry.

As stated above, public programs can be designed so as to give more or less discretionary power to bureaucrats. When it comes to social programs, the more universal they are the less room for discretion. Selective programs, on the other hand, must be implemented in a case-by-case manner, with considerable amounts of bureaucratic discretion. The difficulty of handling the discretionary power of administrators in selective programs has two important consequences. These consequences are often thought to be opposites, but in fact they are two sides of the same coin. They are the bureaucratic abuse of power, and fraud on the part of clients. Applicants in a selective system, if they are rational, will claim that their situation is worse than it actually is, and will describe their prospects for solving their problems on their own as small to non-existent. The administrators in such a system, for their part, often have incentives from their superiors to be suspicious of clients' claims. In game theory, this is known as 'the control game', a rather sad game because it has no stable equilibrium and thus no solution. Fraud by a few clients feeds into increased control by the bureaucrats which, in its turn, feeds into increased fraud by more clients, and so on (Hermansson, 1990).

Working with Swedish survey data, Staffan Kumlin has divided the population according to whether they have had personal contacts with selective welfare state institutions or not (Kumlin, 2000). The analyses show that experience with selective client-based public authorities (such as means-tested social assistance) has a sizeable and significant negative effect on generalized trust. This is not so surprising given that this category probably belongs to the 'have-nots' in Swedish society, which are generally low on trust (cf. Putnam, 2000: 193f). What is surprising, is that the negative impact on social trust from contacts with client-based selective public institutions holds when controlling for not only social class and income, but also for membership in voluntary associations, satisfaction with the way the Swedish democracy works, political interest, life satisfaction and trust in politicians (Rothstein and Kumlin, 2001). One reason for the low levels of corruption and high levels of social trust in the Scandinavian countries may thus be that most of their social programs have been universal, not selective.

There are thus good arguments, both theoretical and empirical, for seeing the standard of a nation's public administration not only as caused by the level of social capital in that country, but also as a causal factor in its own right behind high or low levels of social trust. As has been argued by Eric Uslaner, people who in surveys report high levels of social trust are likely to think that not only will most other people play by the rules in 'person-to-person' contacts, they will also 'play by the rules' in their contacts with government institutions. It has also been shown that people who in surveys report high levels of social trust also have a stronger confidence in public institutions, particularly in the legal system (Uslaner, 2002: 112). As Putnam states in his Italian study, the regions with the lowest amounts of social capital 'are the most subject to the ancient plague of political corruption' (Putnam, 1993: 111).

As in many other areas in the social sciences, what is cause and effect is often dependent on which time horizon is chosen. Even if Putnam's analysis stresses the importance of citizens' civic engagement and social trust for well-functioning government institutions, he also recognizes that the causal mechanism is difficult to measure and opens up the possibility that well-functioning institutions may also influence social capital in a society. For example, the strength of various forms of organized crime in the southern Italian regions is, according to Putnam, based on traditional patterns of clientelism, which in its turn has been caused 'by the weakness of the administrative and judicial structures of the state, in turn further undermining the authority of those structures' (Putnam, 1993: 146). While the correlation between social trust and corruption at the aggregate level is strong, it is very difficult to discern how it works at the individual level. Is it already trusting individuals who refrain from engaging in corruption, or is it corruption that breeds distrust?

This has important policy implications, not least when it comes to how to organize international aid to developing countries. One of the key debates in the social capital approach is between a more sociological approach, arguing the social trust grows 'from below' when people come together in various voluntary associations. On the other side we find the political approach, which stresses the importance of government institutions, not least the public administration (Hooghe and Stolle, 2003). If the sociological theory about social capital is correct, then the rich nations should try to find ways to channel aid to voluntary associations who organize people at the grass-roots level and thereby increase trust and norms of reciprocity in society. The risk with this strategy is of course not only that the theory can be wrong, but that groups that discriminate on ethnic grounds or use their power to undermine the integrity of government institutions by resorting to clientelism, patronage and outright corruption, will benefit from these resources. It could be argued that societies like Rwanda, Bosnia–Herzegovina and Northern Ireland have 'too much social capital' but of the wrong type. There is, as Putnam recognizes, also a 'dark side' of social capital and it is far from certain that it is at all possible to increase social capital in a society by supporting voluntary associations. The alternative approach would be to give support for increasing the 'quality of government' factor in developing countries. But where in a society where corruption and patronage is ingrained in the administrative culture can you find or create uncorrupted civil servants?

A case in point is Gary Miller's and Thomas Hammond's discussion of the use of the so-called 'city managers' as a successful way to get rid of corrupt party machine politics in American cities during the interwar period. These were highly trained civil servants known for their high moral standards and for being disinterested, selfless servants of the public good. They had a reputation that, as a rule, they could not be bribed. But as Miller and Hammond state, '[t]o the extent that such a system works, it is clearly because city managers have been selected and/or trained not to be economic actors' (Miller and Hammond, 1994: 23). And, of course, there is then no collective action problem in the first place, because it is 'solved' by blurring the assumption about human behavior on which the model is built. Due to what is known about bureaucratic discretion, the possibility of solving this problem by implementing controls from above is very limited (cf. Miller, 1992; Brehm and Gates, 1997). Miller and Hammond's advice to our Russian friend mentioned above is thus very simple, namely: 'to find out how such disinterested altruistic actors are created, and then reproduce them throughout the political system' (Miller and Hammond, 1994: 24). Well,

what more can you say, than 'good luck'. Barry Weingast has made a very important comment concerning this standard 'rule of law' solution, namely that '[a] government strong enough to protect property rights is also strong enough to confiscate the wealth of its citizens' (Weingast, 1993: 287). If a government has the power to establish the institutions to implement a 'rule of law' system, they would abuse that same power to break the 'rule of law' (that is, infringe on property rights) if acting as agents in game theory are supposed to act. Without some kind of social norms against such behavior, there is no solution to this problem (cf. Elster, 1989).

NEO-CORPORATIST STRUCTURES AND BUREAUCRATIC LEGITIMACY

Another way to ensure legitimacy and trust is to give interest groups direct influence over the implementation process. These interest groups can be very different, from loosely formed networks to centralized national interest organizations. The influence that these are given can also vary from informal consultation to formal representation in the boards of the public agencies in question. In some cases, the implementation of public policies has been entirely taken over directly by interest organizations. Research in this area started in the 1970s under the label 'neo-corporatism', which was launched by Philippe Schmitter in a seminal article in 1974 as an alternative to the pluralist understanding of how modern Western democracies actually operated (Schmitter, 1974).

The neo-corporatist model assumes that representatives from interest organizations that participate in the implementation of government policies are chosen because they enjoy the *confidence* of their constituents. A further assumption is that policy implementation is often successful only when the group towards which the policy is directed cooperates willingly. One way to elicit the group's collaboration is to grant the organization representing it an exclusive right to participate in the policy's execution (Lembruch, 1991). One of the reasons for allowing such organizational representatives to participate in administration is precisely that they

are closer to the target group (their members) than state bureaucracies, and they have more intimate knowledge of its situation and concerns. It is likely that this enables them to apply rules less formalistically and to take the specific conditions of individual cases better into account – which, in turn, tends to increase the acceptance of regulation by those affected by it. (Streeck and Schmitter, 1985: 22)

It may be argued that, in addition to its suitability for legitimizing administrative decisions, this neo-corporatist model has one more advantage. The state can organize the representation from societal groups so as to create an arena for negotiation and compromise between different organizations. In the Northern European countries, this has often been the case in the implementation of labor market and industrial policies. By granting representation on administrative bodies to both sides of industry, state leaders hope to encourage decisions marked by compromise rather than confrontation (Lewin, 1992). This means, however, that, in the neo-corporatist model, the distinction between politics and administration is virtually erased, for neo-corporatism is characterized precisely by the institutional fusion of policy conception and execution, of political representation and intervention (Cawson, 1986: 185). Scholars in legal sociology and in law have noted that this fusion produces a new legal form, which they have termed 'reflexive law'. Such law does not govern the disposition of material things, but rather regulates the areas of competence of different societal systems, their organizational and institutional structures, and their forms for decision-making (Brand, 1988; Lijphart and Crepaz, 1991).

Claus Offe has called attention to a critical distinction in this model, namely that between different types of interest organizations. Certain organizations, on the one hand, may be said to generate their strength outside the state (Offe, 1986). They may represent producers with a strong market position (for example, trade unions, employer organizations and other *producer organizations*) or popular groups held together by strong ideological bonds (ethnic and religious organizations). Other interest organizations, by contrast, arise as a result of political programs, and acquire their revenues almost exclusively from public sources (for example, patient associations, pensioners' organizations and student unions). Organizations of the former kind naturally occupy a position of much greater strength as against the state, since they possess resources over which the state has no direct control. They may in fact be so strong as to be able, when dissatisfied, to prevent implementation of the policies in question. Organizations without such resources obviously find themselves in a much weaker position as against the state (Olsen, 1992).

For both the state and the organizations, the efficiency of the neo-corporatist model rests on what seems to be a difficult balancing act. Over time, the organizations may risk losing their members' confidence if they come to be seen as defending the interests of the state first and foremost. The individual representatives may, over time, come to identify themselves more with the bureaucracy than with their organization. Their constituency may then start seeing them as co-opted, transformed into harmless instruments of state policy. Thus, if their collaboration with the state becomes too close, the model will lose its basis for creating legitimacy (Lewin, 1992; Rothstein, 1996).

Public bureaucracies also sometimes form alliances with powerful interest organizations so as to increase their political clout against politicians who may want to influence them (or shut them down). Such bureaucratic strategies are known to be very effective and an important source of bureaucratic strength. Such alliances, sometimes known as policy networks or 'iron triangles', are known to be very powerful (that is, the military–industrial complex). While such strategies may be efficient to increase the administration's legitimacy with some parts of society and some societal actors, it has also been known to decrease legitimacy within society as a whole (Offe, 1986).

There are certainly several other problems with this model. A central debate is whether or not neo-corporatist arrangements are harmful for democratic ideals. On the one hand there are scholars arguing that such arrangements make it possible for a democratic government to solve important policy questions which could not be handled if interest organizations were not given influence over the implementation process. By this argument, inviting interest organizations in to the implementation process can extend the democratic scope. The counter-argument is that neo-corporatism harms democratic ideals because they come into conflict with the principle of political equality. Simply put, some citizens (that is, those who are members of interest organizations) get more influence than others do.

A second debate has to do with economic and managerial efficiency. Extended representation may create short-sighted 'rent-seeking' by interest organizations and bureaucracies thereby harming the 'general interest' (Öberg, 1994). One or several interest organizations may 'capture' the bureaucracy in which they are represented and transform its operations so that it mostly serves 'special interests' (Rothstein and Bergström, 1999). Contrary to this, there are studies showing that this model actually increases economic efficiency by making it possible to create working compromises between different societal actors for finding solutions to common problems, especially when it comes to industrial policy and the labor market (Katzenstein, 1994; Visser and Hemerijk, 1997).

USING USER GROUPS TO CREATE LEGITIMACY

Another way to increase legitimacy and handle the problem of discretion is to let the citizens who *directly* use a public service exercise influence over its operations. We may then say that the service is organized according to the user-oriented model. In some advanced welfare states, the typical areas in which this model is applied are childcare, education and care of the elderly. In some countries, students at universities have the right to participate in certain decision making organs. The hope is that services applying the user-oriented model will appear legitimate in the eyes of their users, since, it is thought, users cannot lack confidence in an institution over which they have been able to exercise influence.

The users are those persons (or in case of children, parents) that are physically present when a service is provided. This presents the user-oriented model with its first problem – such persons may feel inhibited from criticizing the service in question. Clients may find it difficult, for instance, openly to criticize the staff on whom they are dependent for the daily satisfaction of their needs. It is clear that staff persons – who sometimes entertain specific professional notions about how to run things – enjoy an advantage over users. The precise relation between the influence of personnel and that of users is difficult to establish. In some cases, it is not clear who is to be regarded as a user, in what form decisions should be taken, what areas users have the right to decide over, and what responsibility they bear for their decisions. In some areas, such as sport and cultural facilities, local government agencies sometimes create networks with voluntary associations who are invited to take part in operating the facilities. In the Scandinavian countries, this model of user-influence has been motivated by the need to get more people interested in participating in the representative democratic process, but the results so far are mixed (Jarl, 1999; Dahlberg and Vedung, 2001).

Several other problems exist with this way of creating legitimacy. For example, it is unclear what should be done in the case of conflicts among users. Should the minority submit to the will of the majority? Yet another problem with this model is that it tends to favor persons with (a) abundant time resources, who are (b) highly interested in influencing the program and who (c) possess abundant resources in terms of information, education and experience in decision making organs. In relation to the democratic ideal – that all citizens possess equal worth – this makes the user-group model problematic.

CONCLUSION

The public administration in a country has different sources of legitimacy. One, of course, is connected to the 'tool' question. As stated by Schmuel Eisenstadt, the central question in this approach is 'whether the bureaucracy is master or servant, an independent political body or a tool, and if a tool, whose interests it can be made to serve'. A bureaucracy that cannot be steered by elected officials will sooner or later get into legitimacy problems. However, this 'legitimacy from above' is not the only form, and may not even be the most important source of legitimacy for government agencies. Its relation to the surrounding society – individual citizens as well as various organizations – may be even more crucial. In this chapter I have pointed out three such sources of 'legitimacy from below'. The one that recently has attracted most attention is the approach connected with research in social capital and social trust. Although this approach usually has been connected to the importance of civic networks and voluntary associations, it also has important implications for the study of various dimensions of the public administration. First, the 'quality of government' factor may be a result of the amount of social capital in a society. Secondly, the structure and operations of the civil service may also be a cause behind the existence of social trust and social capital in a society. The causal logic behind this process is yet to be analyzed. Two other sources of legitimacy have also been discussed, neo-corporatism and systems user-influence. All these three ways of connecting the public administration to the society it is supposed to serve may very well be connected. It may, or may not, be an accidental occurrence that the countries which score highest in surveys about social trust, namely the Scandinavian nations, are among those where neo-corporatist arrangements (and to a lesser extent, models of user-influence) have been most elaborated. However, the relations between these different systems for creating legitimacy for the public administration remain to be investigated.

NOTE

1 The problem has been given many other names, such as the tragedy of the commons, the *n*-persons prisoner's dilemma, the problem of collective action, the problem of the provision of public goods or the social dilemma.

REFERENCES

Bardhan, Pranab (1997) 'Corruption and Development: A Review of the Issues', *Journal of Economic Literature*, 35 (3): 1320–46.

Barker, Rodney (1980) *Political Legitimacy and the State*. Oxford: Clarendon Press.

Beetham, David (1985) *Max Weber and the Theory of Modern Politics*. Cambridge: Polity Press.

Bendor, Jonathan and Swistak, Piotr (1997) 'The Evolutionary Stability of Cooperation', *American Political Science Review*, 91 (2): 290–307.

Braithwaite, Valerie and Levi, Margaret (eds) (1998) *Trust and Governance*. New York: Russell Sage Foundation.

Brand, Donald (1988) *Corporatism and the Rule of Law*. Ithaca, NY: Cornell University Press.

Brehm, John and Gates, Scott (1997) *Working, Shirking, and Sabotage. Bureaucratic Response to a Democratic Public*. Ann Arbor, MI: University of Michigan Press.

Brehm, John and Rahn, Wendy (1997) 'Individual-Level Evidence for the Causes and Consequences of Social Capital', *American Journal of Political Science*, 41 (3): 999–1023.

Cawson, Alan (1986) *Corporatism and Political Theory*. Oxford: Blackwell.

Coleman, James S. (1990) *Foundations of Social Theory*. Cambridge, MA: The Belknap Press of Harvard University Press.

Cook, Karen S. (ed.) (2001) *Trust in Society*. New York: Russell Sage Foundation.

Dahlberg, Magnus and Vedung, Evert (2001) *Demokrati och brukarutvärdering*. Lund: Studentlitteratur.

della Porta, Donatella (2000) 'Social Capital, Beliefs in Government, and Political Corruption', in S.J. Pharr and R.D. Putnam (eds), *Disaffected Democracies*. Princeton, NJ: Princeton University Press.

Elster, Jon (1989) *The Cement of Society*. Cambridge: Cambridge University Press.

Friedman, Kathie V. (1981) *Legitimation of Social Rights and the Western Welfare State*. Chapel Hill, NC: The University of North Carolina Press.

Hall, Peter (1999) 'Social Capital in Britain', *British Journal of Political Science*, 29 (3): 417–64.

Hermansson, Jörgen (1990) *Spelteorins nytta. Om rationalitet i politik och vetenskap*. Uppsala, Statsvetenskapliga föreningen.

Hooghe, Marc and Stolle, Dietlind (eds) (2003) *Generating Social Capital: The Role of Voluntary Associations, Institutions and Government Policy*. New York: Palgrave/Macmillan.

Hydén, Göran (2000) 'The Governance Challenge in Africa', in G. Hydén, D. Olowy and H.W.O. Okoth-Ogendo (eds), *African Perspectives on Governance*. Trenton, NJ: African World Press. pp. 5–32.

Inglehart, Ronald (1999) 'Trust, well-being and democracy', in M.E. Warren (ed.), *Democracy and Trust*. New York: Cambridge University Press. pp. 88–120.

Jarl, Maria (1999) Brukardeltagande på gott och ont. *Det unga folkstyret*. E. Amnå: Stockholm, Demokratiutredningen.

Katzenstein, Peter J. (1994) *Corporatism and Change*. Ithaca, NY: Cornell University Press.

Kelman, Steven (1981) *Regulating America, Regulating Sweden*. Cambridge, MA: MIT Press.

Knack, Stephen and Keefer, Philip (1997) 'Does Social Capital Have an Economic Payoff? A Cross-Country Investigation', *Quarterly Journal of Economics*, 112 (4): 1251–88.

Kumlin, Staffan (2000) 'Welfare State Institutions and Generalized Trust'. Göteborg, Department of Political Science, Göteborg University.

La Porta, Rafael, Lopez-de-Silanes, Florencio et al. (1997) 'Trust in large organizations', *American Economic Review*, 87 (2): 333–8.

La Porta, Rafael, Lopez-de-Silanes, Florencio et al. (1999) 'The Quality of Government', *Journal of Law, Economics and Organization*, 15 (1): 222–79.

Lembruch, Gerhard (1991) 'The Organization of Society, Administrative Strategies and Policy Networks', in R. Czada and A. Windhoff-Héretier. *Political Choice: Institutions, Rules and the Limits of Rationality*. Boulder, CO: Westview Press.

Levi, Margaret (1998a) *Consent, Dissent, and Patriotism*. New York: Cambridge University Press.

Levi, Margaret (1998b) 'A State of Trust', in V. Braithwaite and M. Levi (eds), *Trust and Governance*. New York: Russell Sage Foundation. pp. 77–101.

Lewin, Leif (1992) 'The Rise and Decline of Corporatism', *European Journal of Political Research*, 26: 59–79.

Lijphart, Arend and Crepaz, M.M.L. (1991) 'Corporatism and Consensus Democracy in Eighteen Countries', *British Journal of Political Science*, 21 (2): 235–56.

Lipsky, Michael (1980) *Street-level Bureaucracy: Dilemmas of the Individual in Public Services*. New York: Russell Sage Foundation.

Miller, Gary J. (1992) *Managerial Dilemmas. The Political Economy of Hierarchy*. Cambridge: Cambridge University Press.

Miller, Gary and Hammond, Thomas (1994) 'Why Politics is More Fundamental Than Economics: Incentive-Compatible Mechanisms are not Credible', *Journal of Theoretical Politics*, 6 (1): 5–26.

Moe, Terry M. and Chubb, John E. (1991) *Politics, Markets and American Schools*. Washington, DC: Brookings Institution.

Newton, Kenneth (1999a) 'Social and Political Trust in Established Democracies', in P. Norris (ed.), *Critical Citizens: Global Support for Democratic Government*. New York: Oxford University Press. pp. 323–51.

Newton, Kenneth (1999b) 'Social Capital and Democracy in Modern Europe', in J.W. van Deth, M. Maraffi,

K. Newton and P.F. Whiteley (eds), *Social Capital and European Democracy*. London: Routledge. pp. 3–25.

North, Douglass C. (1998) 'Economic Performance Through Time', in M.C. Brinton and V. Nee (eds), *The New Institutionalism in Sociology*. New York: Russell Sage Foundation. pp. 247–57.

Öberg, Per-Ola (1994) *Särintresse och allmänintresse: Korporatismens ansikten*. Stockholm: Norstedts.

Offe, Claus (1984) *The Contradictions of the Welfare State*. London: Hutchinson.

Offe, Claus (1986) *Disorganized Capitalism: Contemporary Transformations of Work and Politics*. Cambridge: Polity Press.

Olsen, Johan P. (1992) *Organized Democracy: Political Institutions in a Welfare State: The Case of Norway*. Oslo: Universitetsforlaget.

Olson, Mancur, Jr (1996) 'Big Bills Left on the Sidewalk: Why Some Nations are Rich, and Others Poor', *Journal of Economic Perspectives*, 10 (1): 3–22.

Ostrom, Elinor (1998) 'A Behavioral Approach to the Rational Choice Theory of Collective Action', *American Political Science Review*, 92 (1): 1–23.

Platt, John (1973) 'Social Traps', *American Psychologist*, 28: 641–51.

Putnam, Robert D. (1993) *Making Democracy Work: Civic Traditions in Modern Italy*. Princeton, NJ: Princeton University Press.

Putnam, Robert D. (1995) 'Tuning In, Tuning Out: The Strange Disappearance of Social Capital in America', *PS Political Studies*, 28 (4): 664–83.

Putnam, Robert D. (2000) *Bowling Alone: The Collapse and Revival of American Community*. New York: Simon & Schuster.

Rother, Larry (1999) 'Where Taxes Aren't So Certain', *New York Times*, 4: 3.

Rothstein, Bo (1996) *The Social Democratic State: The Swedish Model and the Bureaucratic Problem of Social Reforms*. Pittsburgh: University of Pittsburgh Press.

Rothstein, Bo (1998) *Just Institutions Matter: The Moral and Political Logic of the Universal Welfare State*. Cambridge: Cambridge University Press.

Rothstein, Bo (2000) 'Trust, Social Dilemmas and Collective Memories', *Journal of Theoretical Politics*, 12 (4): 477–503.

Rothstein, Bo and Bergström, Jonas (1999) *Korporatismens fall och den svenska modellens kris*. Stockholm: SNS Förlag.

Rothstein, Bo and Kumlin, Staffan (2001) 'Demokrati, socialt kapital och förtroende', in S. Holmberg and L. Weibull (eds), *Land du välsignade: SOM-rapport 2001*. Göteborg, SOM-institutet, Göteborgs universitet.

Rothstein, Bo and Stolle, Dietlind (2003) 'Social Capital, Impartiality, and the Welfare State: An Institutional Approach', in M. Hooghe and D. Stolle (eds), *Generating Social Capital: The Role of Voluntary Associations, Institutions and Government Policy*. New York: Palgrave/Macmillan.

Schmitter, Phillipe C. (1974) 'Still the Century of Corporatism?', *Review of Politics*, 36: 34–76.

Scholz, John T. (1998) 'Trust, Taxes and Compliance', in V. Braithwaite and M. Levi (eds), *Trust and Governance*. New York: Russell Sage Foundation. pp. 135–66.

Stolle, Dietlind (1998) 'Bowling Together, Bowling Alone: The Development of Generalized Trust in Voluntary Associations', *Political Psychology*, 19 (3): 497–526.

Streeck, Wolfgang and Schmitter, Philippe C. (1985) 'Community, Market, State – and Associations? The Prospective Contribution of Interest Governance to Social Order', in W. Streeck and P.C. Schmitter (eds), *Private Interest Government: Beyond Market and State*. London: Sage. pp. 1–29.

Sztompka, Piotr (1998) 'Trust, Distrust and Two Paradoxes of Democracy', *European Journal of Social Theory*, 1 (1): 19–32.

Thorp, Rosemary (1996) 'The Reform of the Tax Administration in Peru', in A. Silva (ed.), *Implementing Policy Innovations in Latin America*. Washington, DC: Inter-American Development Bank. pp. 34–51.

Treisman, Daniel (2000) 'The Causes of Corruption: A Cross-National Study', *Journal of Public Economics*, 21 (2).

Tyler, Tom R. (1998) 'Trust and Democratic Governance', in V. Braithwaite and M. Levi (eds), *Trust and Governance*. New York: Russell Sage Foundation. pp. 269–314.

Uslaner, Eric (1999) 'Democracy and Social Capital', in M.E. Warren (ed.), *Democracy and Trust*. New York: Cambridge University Press. pp. 121–50.

Uslaner, Eric (2001) 'Trust and Corruption'. Salford, Conference on Political Scandals, University of Salford.

Uslaner, Eric (2002) *The Moral Foundation of Trust*. New York: Cambridge University Press.

Vinzant, Janet Coble (1998) *Street-level Leadership: Discretion and Legitimacy in Front-line Public Service*. Washington, DC: Georgetown University Press.

Visser, Jelle and Hemerijk, Anton (1997) *'A Dutch miracle': Job Growth, Welfare Reform and Corporatism in the Netherlands*. Amsterdam: Amsterdam University Press.

Warren, Mark (ed.) (1999) *Democracy and Trust*. New York: Cambridge University Press.

Weber, Max (1989) *The Profession of Politics* (edited, translated and introduced by Simona Draghici). Washington, DC: Plutarch Press.

Weingast, Barry R. (1993) 'Constitutions as Governance Structures – The Political Foundations of Secure Markets', *Journal of Institutional and Theoretical Economics*, 149: 286–311.

Whiteley, Paul F. (1999) 'The Origines of Social Capital', in J.W. van Deth, M. Maraffi, K. Newton and P.F. Whiteley (eds), *Social Capital and European Democracy*. London: Routledge. pp. 25–45.

Woolcook, Michael (2001) 'The Place of Social Capital in Understanding Social and Economic Outcomes', *ISUMA – Canadian Journal of Policy Research*, 2 (1): 12.

27

Representative Bureaucracy

Lois R. Wise

REPRESENTATIVE BUREAUCRACY IN HISTORICAL CONTEXT

Representative bureaucracy pertains to the extent to which the bureaucracy responds to the preferences of society. Pitkin (1967) identified different forms of substantive representation, including the relatively common forms of trustees, delegates and politicos. A trustee is someone who uses his or her discretion to make decisions on behalf of, and in the best interests of the represented; a delegate is someone who tries to discern the desires of the represented; and a politico is someone who acts to maximize a political position or status. Last, symbolic representation involves the general public's belief that it is fairly represented. It is achieved by visible evidence of salient group members in government rather than by proportional representation or policy congruence. In this form, bureaucrats act as neutral agents and actors for the state. Policy congruence between the bureaucracy and the general public is less important than the placement of group members in policy making positions. A government might pursue symbolic representation by appointing an equal number of women in high-level policy positions.

Scholarship on representative bureaucracy is grounded in political legitimacy. In administrative states, the bureaucracy functions as a linkage between political bodies and the people. As administrative complexity deepens, civil servants gain more responsibility for interpreting and applying public policies and their potential impact on the quality of citizens' lives increases (Anton, 1980; Dogan, 1975). As Weber (1968: 1393) observed, 'In a modern state the actual ruler is necessarily and unavoidably the bureaucracy ...' To safeguard the integrity of the state, bureaucracies often incorporate elements to assure neutrality and professionalism. The reasoning is that when bureaucrats follow procedures, rules and regulations, citizens can anticipate the outcomes of decisions and actions taken by public agencies (Rothstein, 1992). Others, however, warn against the dull governance and moral inertia that stem from placing rule following above human values (Gawthrop, 1998). Thus, the administrative state and its career service of professional bureaucrats presents a classic dilemma for governance: How can society's demands for representation and responsiveness be reconciled with administrative demands for neutrality, rules and structure, professional competence and efficiency?

The representativeness of the bureaucracy can also be seen as a vehicle for advancing liberty and equality in a society (Van Riper, 1966: 350) and the act of participation as a form of self-empowerment and acceptance of civic responsibility (Bachrach, 1967; Lewin, 1980; Wise, 1990). Concerns for the representativeness of the public bureaucracy can also be linked to distributive justice, since public employment is a benefit in itself and it offers rewards that can contribute to a citizen's economic circumstances and human development (Rawls, 1971). Where government is the principal employer, civil service employment policies contribute to the level of socio-economic equality by providing opportunities for social mobility and equitable pay (Mosher, 1968; Wise, 1990; Wise and Jonzon, 1991).

The remainder of this section of the chapter discusses the meaning of the key concepts of passive and active representation and different criteria used to determine representativeness. The next section examines new areas of research that are offshoots of the original theoretical work on representative bureaucracy. The third section examines the relationship between the theory and underlying assumptions of representation and current trends and practices.

Passive and active representation

Responsiveness is achieved in passive representation by the extent to which the bureaucracy is similar to the populace on key demographic attributes, such as ethnicity or gender. For active representation, responsiveness is achieved when the actions taken and policy preferences expressed by bureaucrats are congruent with the preferences of people they are demographically like in the populace.

One definition of the construct of passive representation is that it pertains to the extent to which the demographic origins of the members of the bureaucracy mirror those of the whole society (Mosher, 1968). For different reasons, groups may not always recognize themselves as outside the power elite or experiencing political inequality and make no demands for inclusion (Dahl, 1971). Thus a broader definition of passive representation might be useful: *A bureaucracy whose demographic profile mirrors that of the population on politically salient characteristics achieves passive representation.* Individuals are complex and may consider themselves affiliated with several underrepresented groups. The pursuit of passive representation requires that the system be attribute-conscious to some degree. The state may determine and record who possesses these characteristics in both the population and the public workforce. In some countries such documentation is the norm, while in others it raises sensitive issues of liberty and civil rights and is considered inappropriate (Rothstein, 2000).

On one level, passive representation and the appearance of inclusiveness give government legitimacy. Passive representation suggests that the opportunity for admission exists and in turn implies a commitment to equal access to government (Meier, 1993b; Mosher, 1968; Wise, 1990). On another level, passive representation gives the possibility for active representation, to the extent that inclusion of representatives from lower status groups in the bureaucracy provides an avenue for their unique values, preferences and moral principles to be represented in public administration.

Studies in the American tradition, where the individual is typically prioritized over the group, generally define representation at the individual level and compare the numbers or proportions of group members in the populace and bureaucracy or other elected bodies. In other contexts, inclusion of diverse others or representatives of their social groups may be considered sufficient for representation since those actors aggregate and channel citizens' preferences and opinions. In fact, Kingsley's (1944) original work on the subject was focused on the group as an opinion source. A bureaucracy in which the opinions of different groups were present could be judged representative. This notion of group opinion representation has resonance in a range of national contexts (Egeberg, 1995a, 1999; Carroll and Joypaul, 1993; Subramaniam, 1967).

Active representation is an assumed consequence of passive representation. The underlying premise is that people's demographic characteristics determine their attitudes and values. Bureaucrats have the advantage of knowing the preferences and values of a particular group as a consequence of their own affiliation with that group. When members of politically salient groups enter the bureaucracy, they bring their knowledge of the values and preferences of these groups with them. A related assumption is that bureaucrats act in a manner responsive to the preferences they represent when they implement public programs and make decisions.

The validity of this last assumption is a focus of contemporary research, but scholars have long been skeptical about the reliability of this linkage (Krislov, 1974; Pitkin, 1967). Lane (1995) reviews different models and perspectives on how bureaucrats might respond to private and public interests. The notion that bureaucrats can set aside their private interests is partly rejected by some and fully rejected by others. Trust and human nature are at the core of this debate (Hyneman, 1950: 15; March and Olsen, 1989). Two useful definitions of active representation are:

> Behavior actively represents a community when it increases resources ... associated with belonging to that community. (Thompson, 1976)

> *A* is responsive to *B* if *A* acts as *B* would act if *B* were in *A*'s position. (Meier, 1975)

The first assumes that groups primarily want to maximize their resources and status in the community. It implies that responsiveness may come from someone not directly affiliated with the benefited group. For example, it may be that members of one minority are expected to be more responsive to minority group members in general than are those from the majority group. Meier's second definition expands the concept of responsiveness because it implies that groups may have altruistic motives and preferences that go beyond economic benefit to their individual group.

Some would reject these definitions of representation on the grounds that those who are excluded from power are 'right in feeling unjustly treated' even though they may have gained from the efforts made on their behalf by those in positions of power (Rawls, 1971). Contemporary feminists, for example, would argue that women need to express their own ideas and present an independent voice in the bureaucracy (Jónasdóttir, 1987; Kelly, 1998). Participation in the public bureaucracy is a form of political participation. The significance of different forms of political participation depends upon the context in which they occur (Kimber, 1989: 206). Similarly, when participation for members of a disadvantaged group is channeled into certain agencies or lower ranks of the civil service, the benefits for citizenship that might come from participation in the public workforce are diminished (Wise and Jonzon, 1991). Policies to advance one type of equality, such as inclusion, run the risk of creating a minority ghetto within the ranks of the civil service if issues of status are not taken into consideration. Such practices may give the appearance of representation without voice and at the same time may create economic dependence upon the state as an employer (Wise, 1990).

Criteria for representativeness

Governments establish many different criteria for eligibility for membership in the bureaucracy either by statute or by informal norms. Informal social filters, including education and family background, are powerful determinants of who pursues and who wins a career in the public bureaucracy (Anton, 1980; Mellbourne, 1979). Since one of the most common formal criteria for membership in the national bureaucracy is citizenship, the manner in which citizenship is defined is fundamental to the attainment of representativeness (Kelly, 1998; March and Olsen, 1989). 'By limiting who has standing, we limit who has rights of representation. By limiting who has full rights to be represented, we limit the range and scope of the societal problems that will become policy issues and get on the agenda' (Kelly, 1998).

The notion of geographic or regional representation is another criterion (Aucoin, 1985). Although more typical of legislative bodies, the idea that the bureaucracy gains legitimacy by including or excluding people from certain geographic areas is found in some civil service systems. For example, Article 101 of the United Nations' charter stipulates that its civil service must be geographically representative of the member states (Macy, 1970). The European Commission recognizes the same criterion. Even in Norway, geographic origins can be seen as a factor associated with shared values that have policy impacts (Egeberg, 1995b: 568). Geographic representation as a principle for membership in the national bureaucracy also has historic roots and can be found in Korea (Kim, 1993) and India (Tummala, 1999), for example.

Concerns for representation based on a wider set of factors are apparent. For example, during their rule the British organized the Indian public service to assure representation of both Hindus and Muslims (Tummala, 1999). Linguistic differences related to ethnicity or geographic region (Hondeghem, 1997; Wilson and Mullins, 1978) and social class differences (Sjoberg et al., 1966) may also be seen as appropriate criteria for civil service membership and a determinant of representativeness. In addition to Kingsley's (1944) early study of the role of the British upper classes in government, others have examined the extent to which the civil service reflects a particular social class in Australia, France, India, Sweden and the United States (Anton, 1980; Lingard, 1993; Subramaniam, 1967; Tummala, 1999; Yeatman, 1990). Similarly, a civil servant's age may be an indicator of representativeness, with some systems preferring to recruit younger people who can be socialized into the organizational culture (Millar and McKevitt, 1997; Savoie, 1994) and others dominated by a particular generation with distinct values and preferences (Hondeghem, 1997; van der Meer et al., 1997). These different criteria for representativeness may compete with one another, as is the case between the United Nations' goals of equal representation of the sexes and geographic regions. Criteria for representativeness may compete with other eligibility standards, such as competence or merit.

NEW AREAS OF RESEARCH DEVELOPING FROM REPRESENTATIVE BUREAUCRACY

Many new areas of research stem from the literature on both passive and active representation. Research connected to the construct of passive representation includes the body of work that attempts to discern the factors and circumstances that affect inclusiveness and offers models of facilitators and barriers to inclusion. A substantial body of work attempts to address the dilemma of how to reconcile the tenets of representative bureaucracy with the demands for professionalism, neutrality, structure and rules that are the underpinnings of an administrative state.

We turn first to the work stemming from passive representation, which mainly involves studies describing the distributions of different groups in the bureaucracy and analyzing factors affecting inclusiveness. A second set of studies comprises a larger body of work investigating issues related to active representation and the inclusion of values in public administration.

Work stemming from passive representation

Both empirical and theoretical studies attempt to identify factors and models that determine why members of certain groups are excluded from the bureaucracy or are hindered in their efforts to advance to upper-level positions. Studies point to psychological, institutional and social barriers that impede women's access to policy positions (Cayer and Sigelman, 1980; Gidengil and Vengroff, 1997; Hede, 1995). The term 'glass ceiling' was coined to account for the vague and unseen force that seemed to prevent women's advancement into top management in the United States (Morrison et al., 1987). The metaphor has been found useful in other national contexts (Gidengil and Vengroff, 1997; Hede, 1994, 1995; Randell, 1994). One model of facilitators and barriers to career success for women in government employment describes an interactive effect between individual and organizational variables and demonstrates the many factors that affect women's job status (Hale and Kelly, 1989). The conclusion that obstruction and resistance from status quo leadership are key factors in defeating equality efforts is supported by many scholars (Cockburn, 1991; Dahlberg, 1986; Stone, 1990; van der Ros, 1997; Pincus, 2000).

Work stemming from active representation

One segment of work stemming from active representation examines the nature of bureaucratic discretion and the conditions under which bureaucrats are likely to use their own discretion in decision making (Aberbach and Rockman, 1988; Banks and Weingast, 1992; Bawn, 1995; Durant, 1991; Finer, 1941; Keiser and Soss, 2000; Meier, 1997; Meier and Smith, 1994; Meier et al., 1995; Redford, 1969; Sabatier et al., 1995; Schneider, 1993; Wood and Waterman, 1994). The underlying premise of representative bureaucracy, that bureaucrats will act on the knowledge of the special preferences and values of the groups they represent, creates a fundamental tension with the norm of administrative neutrality which is a key tenet of Weberian bureaucracy. The norm of neutrality means that bureaucrats should not use opportunities for discretion as an occasion to introduce their own values or moral principles and should remain emotionally disaffected by the problems they face. Many important paths of scholarship explore this fundamental tension.

A core question is whether the experience of being a member in an organization reduces the linkage between a person's background characteristics and value preferences. The social and educational processes involved in becoming qualified for a civil service position as well as the socialization process a person experiences upon entering a particular organization might replace earlier experiences, norms and values and reshape attitudes and behaviors. Perhaps some background characteristics are more resilient and more likely than other characteristics to explain behavior on the job (Pitkin, 1967).

Many scholars have looked for trends in the amount of discretion exercised by bureaucrats (Banks and Weingast, 1992; Bawn, 1995; Meier, 1997; Meier and Smith, 1994; Meier et al., 1995; Sabatier et al., 1995; Schneider, 1993; Wood and Waterman, 1994). Administrative structure provides numerous formal control mechanisms, but bureaucrats can retain significant autonomy in policy making processes (Egeberg, 1999; Meier, 1993a; Shumavon and Hibbeln, 1986). Some research suggests that the amount of discretion exercised is cyclical (Durant, 1991). Management reform trends, for example, would affect the extent to which accountability and steering of the bureaucracy are emphasized in a particular time period (Kickert, 1991; Winkler, 1981).

One approach to controlling bureaucratic discretion emphasizes external controls, including those found in other branches of government. Work in this tradition operates on the assumption that abuses of power are inevitable and external checks and controls are necessary to limit abuse (Finer, 1941; Redford, 1969). An alternative perspective to controlling discretion emphasizes internal administrative and normative controls, on the assumption that bureaucrats should be able to balance objectivity and professionalism with the public's needs and wishes (Friedrich,

1940; Gilbert, 1959). Bureaucrats' self-interest may be harnessed by the organizational incentive system, supervision, or organizational norms (Lægreid and Olsen, 1984; March and Olsen, 1989). Some think that bureaucrats eventually adopt some of the collective values found within the organization, its mission, policy area, or programs they administer, and this reduces the likelihood that they will act solely on the basis of self-interest (Meier, 1993a; Meier and Nigro, 1976; Romzek, 1990; Simon, 1957; Wilson, 1989). But others assert that bureaucratic values have a significant beneficial effect on policy and programs (Frederickson, 1976; Gawthrop, 1998; Kaufman, 1960).

Professionalization can be seen as a competitor with representativeness (Guy, 1985; Mosher, 1968; Willbern, 1966); the values and preferences of people's groups of origin may be replaced by the norms and values of their professional interests. Others (Egeberg, 1995a; Hodges and Durant, 1989; Kearney and Sinha, 1988) suggest that organizational and professional values become inextricably intertwined in many agencies. Some work finds a beneficial relationship between professionalism and bureaucratic responsiveness (Hodges and Durant, 1989; Kearney and Sinha, 1988). These studies challenge the notion that professionalism hinders direct citizen input into policy making and distorts or limits public discourse (Hummel, 1987; Price, 1965; Stillman, 1991).

Administrative structure may have consequences for democratic outcomes and representativeness affecting, for example, discourse and deliberation in decision making (Jenssen, 2001; White, 1969). Administrative structure defines choices and the capacity to respond to different policy or programmatic areas. Thus interests are partly endogenous to administrative structure and rational behavior can be seen as occurring within a given institution and context (Egeberg, 1995a; March and Simon, 1993; March and Olsen, 1996; Scharpf, 1977; Scott, 1995; Simon et al., 1950; Simon, 1957).

In the context of the representative bureaucracy literature, shared values are mainly viewed as a positive feature. Through shared values, for example, the views and concerns of those who are absent are represented in the decision making process. The existence of shared values can be seen as the cornerstone of cohesive and representative organizations (Downs, 1967; Meier, 1993b). Not only must the public and the bureaucracy have common values, those values must also be relevant to the mission of the bureau, useful in shaping bureaucratic behavior, and officials must be able to use shared values as

an incentive for shaping bureaucratic behavior. An opposite view is that shared values hinder new ideas and new solutions to policy and programmatic problems and that human diversity provides an advantage to government bureaucracies (Lindblom, 1959).

Many scholars argue that the determinants of bureaucratic behavior are more complex than models of representative bureaucracy allow; separating public interest from private interest is not an easy task for scholars or bureaucrats (Lane, 1995; March and Olsen, 1989). One alternative to the notion that bureaucrats act as trustees on behalf of the groups from which they come is found in the public choice school. The underlying premise of this school of thought is that government workers are motivated by self-interest and personal gain. They seek to maximize their self-interest, and expanding bureau size is conducive to meeting private interests (Buchanan and Tullock, 1962, 1977; Niskanen, 1971). The assumption that bureaucrats act on the basis of having calculated the potential gains and losses of different public policies and programs in terms of their own self-interest leads to the expectation that public employees will try to maximize the payoffs they receive from public actions. These payoffs may be in the form of bigger budgets and more benefits or less difficult work. Concerns about self-interested behavior among bureaucrats are magnified by evidence showing that public employees are more politically active than other citizens, which gives the opportunity for their preferences to have greater impact in the political arena (Lipset, 1960). Scholars challenge the idea that public employees can be presumed to be only self-interested (Aucoin, 1991; Seligman, 1986; Wade, 1979).

A counter-argument is that public employees' motives are more complex and factors other than self-interest determine their behavior (Downs, 1967; Hill, 1991; Kelman, 1987; Lane, 1995). Contextual and institutional factors may account for rational behavior among some civil servants in some national governments (Peters, 1991). Self-interested behavior may be limited in situations where bureaucrats act in their capacity as public officials (Blais and Dion, 1991; Egeberg, 1995a), thereby reducing the potential impact of self-interested behavior on the public interest.

RELATIONSHIP BETWEEN THEORY, PRACTICE AND RESEARCH

In this last section of the chapter, three main questions about linkage between theories and models of representative bureaucracy and actual practice are considered. The first asks what evidence exists to demonstrate that passive representation has been or can be achieved. The second asks what factors affect inclusiveness in the public bureaucracy. The third question is, what evidence exists of a link between passive and active representation?

Evidence about existence of and trends in passive representation

Research provides some insight into the conditions and trends for representative bureaucracy in different national contexts. In general, it appears that conditions for women have improved over the past twenty years both in terms of general representation in the bureaucracy and in some national contexts in terms of their likelihood for occupying positions of higher status (Dahlerup, 1988; Dolan, 2000; Wise and Jonzon, 1991). Apparently, economic factors, including declining parity in public and private sector compensation, partly account for the growing feminization of the civil service in many cases (Verheijen, 1999; Wise, 1990).

The continued lack of parity for women in leadership positions creates a political dilemma for governments that espouse equality as policy (Wise, 1992). Although there are many cases where women and men have achieved parity in terms of general public sector employment at the start of the twenty-first century, top leadership positions are more likely to be dominated by men and women's progress into the top ranks can at best be described as slow. A study of Anglo-American systems, for example, predicts that Australia and Canada will achieve gender equity in top civil service positions by about 2020, and the United States and United Kingdom by around 2035 (Hede, 1995). The same conclusion of slow progress for women into the upper ranks in local government is made for Scandinavia, Belgium, the UK, Ireland, North America and the Netherlands (Cockburn, 1991; Dahlberg, 1986; Gidengil and Vengroff, 1997; Pincus, 2000; Stone, 1990; van der Ros, 1997). Weak representation in the upper ranks of the bureaucracy and a tendency to cluster in the service ministries or departments is a common experience shared by women on different continents and not limited by regime type, level of economic development, or declared equality policies (Bayes, 1991; Hondeghem, 1997; Millar and McKevitt, 1997; van der Meer et al., 1997; Wise, 1992; Yishai and Cohen, 1997). But in some

countries, women are better represented than minority groups in these ranks (United States General Accounting Office, 2001; Wise, 1990).

What factors affect inclusiveness in the public bureaucracy?

We have limited empirical evidence upon which to draw conclusions about the factors that affect inclusiveness. Findings for various demographic, political and economic factors are mixed and it is hard to draw conclusions. This body of work is predominantly not based on central government administration, limiting the generalizability of such findings to national government administration. The way national governments allocate work may affect the educational requirements and skill distributions in central and local authorities. Similarly, labor markets may be segregated in such a way that occupations are associated with a certain gender, race, or ethnicity (Hale and Kelly, 1989; Peters, 1985).

Certain contextual factors may suppress representativeness. Internal labor market rules may reduce opportunities for admission and advancement. Similarly, employment policies regarding opportunities for leave and part-time employment may affect patterns of employment among social groups (Hale and Kelly, 1989). Women's greater likelihood of taking advantage of the right to work part time may account for the lower proportion of women in upper-level positions since management positions are less likely to have reduced hours (Wise, 1992). Studies at the central government level support the relationship between workforce skill distribution and female employment that is evident in local government research (Kellough, 1990; Peters, 1985; Saltzstein, 1986; Wise, 1990).

Greater access to education among disadvantaged group members may have a positive effect on representativeness (Lewis and Nice, 1994; Meier, 1975; Wise and Jonzon, 1991). For example, the Swedish civil service was transformed from one with upper and middle class origins to one with members of middle and working class roots who had obtained university degrees at public institutions (Anton, 1980).

What evidence exists of a link between passive and active representation?

Evidence linking passive to active representation has been mixed. Other factors appear more important than a civil servant's social background in accounting for his or her value preferences or attitudes. For example, a study of French and US bureaucrats found that status in the bureaucracy was more likely than personal characteristics to account for decision making behavior in both countries (Rouban, 1995). Institutional affiliation may be more important than social background or regional origins in accounting for value preferences among public servants (Egeberg, 1996; Lægreid and Olsen, 1984; Meier and Nigro, 1976).

Some work indicates that bureaucrats may successfully promote their own ideological values. For example, Swedish bureaucrats were found to successfully advance their social agendas during the 1970s (Anton, 1980). Similarly, ideological interests were shown to be more likely than status in the bureaucracy to account for policy preferences among Swedish national and local government bureaucrats (Wise and Szücs, 1996).

Interpretations of the evidence about the relationship between gender and policy preference differ (Kelly, 1993, 1998; Saltzstein, 1989), but there is little empirical research testing the relationship between representativeness and responsiveness in central government (Dolan, 2000). Since the late 1980s, however, studies based on both Third World and US public servants at various levels of government have reported that race and ethnicity were positively associated with active representation of a group's interests (Hindera, 1993; Selden et al., 1998).

One conclusion from this work is that passive representation operates for race and ethnicity but not for gender or other personal characteristics (Egeberg, 1999; Keiser et al., 2000). Other studies, however, suggest that the relationship between passive and active representation may also hold for women if more sophisticated models taking into account institutional and other contextual factors and using more developed definitions of key constructs are employed (Dolan, 2000; Keiser et al., 2000; Selden, 1997).

CONCLUSION

The theoretical underpinnings of the field of representative bureaucracy are based on certain key assumptions about the political and democratic consequences of representation of politically significant groups within the public bureaucracy. A critical assumption is that bureaucrats function as representatives or trustees advocating the value preferences and policy choices of people who share their social origins and group affiliations. This posture of advocacy, however, is in conflict with traditional notions of the way the administrative state should function and the so-called norm of administrative neutrality. It is also at odds with theories based on rational behavior that assume that individuals are primarily motivated by self-interest. Scholars call for a reexamination of the role of values, the consequences of shared values, the role of discourse, the effects of different administrative structures and the impact of professionalization on democratic responsiveness.

Achievement of a bureaucracy that mirrors the population on salient group characteristics proceeds slowly and often unevenly. Many studies explore the extent to which the presence of group members in the bureaucracy converts into active representation for the special interests and values of their social groups but the body of research is still too shallow and the models of investigation too simplistic to draw strong conclusions about the nature of these relationships and the circumstances under which passive representation produces a more responsive bureaucracy.

Practical knowledge and advice for policy makers that can be drawn from this body of work is limited. On the one hand, it is apparent that policies to increase inclusion may have unanticipated consequences that do not serve the interests of underrepresented groups and offer a limited and segmented form of equality. On the management side, we need much more empirical research to understand the behavior of complex human beings in different situations and organizational environments.

REFERENCES

Aberbach, J.D. and Rockman, B.A. (1988) 'Mandates or mandarins? Control and discretion in the modern administrative state', *Public Administration Review*, 48 (2): 606–12.

Anton, T.J. (1980) *Administered Politics: Elite Political Culture in Sweden*. Boston, MA: Martinus Nijhoff.

Aucoin, Peter H. (1985) *Regional Responsiveness and the National Administrative State*. Toronto: University of Toronto Press.

Aucoin, Peter H. (1991) 'The politics of management of restraint in budgeting', in A. Blais and S. Dion (eds), *The Budget-Maximizing Bureaucrat: Appraisals and Evidence*. Pittsburgh: University of Pittsburgh Press.

Bachrach, P. (1967) *The Theory of Democratic Elitism*. Boston: Little, Brown.

Banks, J.S. and Weingast, B.R. (1992) 'The political control of bureaucracies under asymmetric information', *American Journal of Political Science*, 36 (2): 509–25.

Bawn, K. (1995) 'Political control versus expertise: Congressional choices about administrative procedures', *American Political Science Review*. 89 (1): 62–73.

Bayes, Jane (1991) 'Women in California executive branch of government', in M.M. Hale and R.M. Kelly (eds), *Gender, Bureaucracy and Democracy*. New York: Greenwood Press. pp. 103–42.

Blais, Andre and Dion, Stephanie (eds) (1991) *The Budget-Maximizing Bureaucrat. Appraisals and Evidence*. Pittsburgh: University of Pittsburgh Press.

Buchanan, James M. and Tullock, G. (1977) 'The expanding public sector', *Public Choice*, 31 (1): 147–50.

Buchanan, James M. and Tullock, G. (1962) *The Calculus of Consent*. Ann Arbor, MI: University of Michigan Press.

Carroll, Barbara Wake and Joypaul, S.K. (1993) 'The Mauritian senior public service: Some lessons for developing and developed nations', *International Review of Administrative Sciences*. 59 (3): 423–40.

Cayer, Joseph and Sigelman, Lee (1980) 'Minorities and women in state and local governments', *Public Administration Review*, 40 (5): 443–50.

Cockburn, Cynthia (1991) *In the Way of Women – Men's Resistance to Sex Equality in Organizations*. London: Macmillan.

Dahl, Robert A. (1971) *Polyarchy, Participation and Opposition*. New Haven, CT: Yale University Press.

Dahlberg, Anita (1986) 'Aktivt jämställdhetsarbete – frigörelse med förhinder', *Kvinnovetenskaplig tidskrift*, 3: 16–32.

Dahlerup, Drude (1988) 'From a small to a large minority: Women in Scandinavian politics', *Scandinavian Political Studies*, 11 (4): 275–98.

Dogan, M. (1975) 'The political power of the Western Europe Mandarins: Introduction', in M. Dogan (ed.), *The Mandarins of Western Europe: The Political Role of the Top Civil Servants*. New York: Halstead. pp. 3–24.

Dolan, Julie (2000) 'The senior executive service: gender, attitudes, and representative bureaucracy', *Journal of Public Administration Research and Theory*, 10 (3): 513–29.

Downs, Anthony (1967) *Inside Bureaucracy*. Boston: Little, Brown.

Durant, R.E. (1991) 'Whither bureaucratic influence: a cautionary note', *Journal of Public Administration Research and Theory*, 1 (4): 461–76.

Egeberg, Morten (1995a) 'Bureaucrats as public policy-makers and their self-interests', *Journal of Theoretical Politics*, 7 (2): 157–67.

Egeberg, Morten (1995b) 'The policy administration dichotomy revisited: The case of transport infrastructure planning in Norway', *International Review of Administrative Science*, 61 (4): 565–76.

Egeberg, Morten (1996) 'Organization and nationality in the European Commission services', *Public Administration*, 74 (4): 721–35.

Egeberg, Morten (1999) 'The impact of bureaucratic structure on policy making', *Public Administration*, 77 (1): 155–70.

Finer, H. (1941) 'Administrative responsibility in democratic government', *Public Administration Review*, 1 (4): 335–50.

Frederickson, H. George (1976) 'Public administration in the 1970s: Developments and directions', *Public Administration Review*, 36 (5): 564–76.

Friedrich, C.J. (1940) 'Public policy and the nature of administrative responsibility', in C.J. Friedrich and E.S. Mason (eds), *Public Policy*. Cambridge, MA: Harvard University Press. pp. 3–24.

Gawthrop, L.C. (1998) *Public Service and Democracy*. New York: Chatham House.

Gidengil, Elizabeth and Vengroff, Richard (1997) 'Representative bureaucracy, tokenism and the glass ceiling: the case of Quebec municipal administration', *Canadian Public Administration*, 40 (Fall): 457–80.

Gilbert, C.E. (1959) 'The framework of administrative responsibility', *Journal of Politics*, 21 (3): 373–407.

Guy, M.E. (1985) *Professionals in Organizations: Debunking a Myth*. New York: Praeger.

Hale, Mary M. and Kelly, Rita Mae (1989) 'Women in management' in M.M. Hale and R.M. Kelly (eds), *Gender, Bureaucracy and Democracy*. New York: Greenwood Press. pp. 19–37.

Hede, Andrew J. (1994) 'The 'Glass Ceiling' metaphor: Towards a theory of managerial inequity', Canberra Bulletin of Public Administration, 76 (April): 79–85.

Hede, Andrew (1995) 'Women managers in the civil service: The long road toward equity in Britain', *International Review of Administrative Science*, 61 (4): 587–600.

Hill, Larry B. (1991) 'Who governs the American administrative state?', *Journal of Public Administration Research and Theory*, 1 (3): 261–94.

Hindera, John J. (1993) 'Representative bureaucracy: Imprimis evidence of active representation in the EEOC district offices', *Social Science Quarterly*, 74 (2): 95–108.

Hodges, D.G. and Durant, R.F. (1989) 'The professional state revisited: Twixt Scylla and Charybdis', *Public Administration Review*, 49 (5): 474–84.

Hondeghem, Annie (1997) 'The national civil service in Belgium'. Paper presented at Civil Service Systems in a Comparative Perspective, School of Public and Environmental Affairs, Indiana University, Bloomington (USA), 5–9 April.

Hummel, R.P. (1987) *The Bureaucratic Experience*, 3rd edn. New York: St Martin's Press.

Hyneman, Charles S. (1950) *Bureaucracy in a Democracy*. New York: Harper.

Jenssen, Synnove (2001) 'Transforming politics: Towards new or lesser roles for democratic institutions', in T. Christensen and P. Lægreid (eds), *New Public Management*. Aldershot: Ashgate Publishing Ltd. pp. 289–300.

Jónasdóttir, Anna (1987) 'Women's interests and other values', in A. Jónasdóttir and K. Jones (eds), *The Political Interests of Gender*. London: Sage.

Kaufman, Herbert (1960) *The Forest Ranger: A Study in Administrative Behavior*. Baltimore, MD: Johns Hopkins University Press.

Kearney, R.S. and Sinha, C. (1988) 'Professionalism and bureaucratic responsiveness: conflict or compatibility', *Public Administration Review*, 48 (5): 571–9.

Keiser, Lael R. and Soss, Joe (2000) 'With good cause: bureaucratic discretion and the politics of child support enforcement', *American Journal of Political Science*, 42 (4): 133–56.

Kellough, J. Edward (1990) 'Integration in the public workplace: determinants of minority and female employment in federal agencies', *Public Administration Review*, 50 (5): 557–66.

Keiser, Lael R., Wilkins, V., Meier, K.J. and Holland, C. (2000) 'Lipstick and logarithms: gender, identity, institutional context, and representative bureaucracy'. Paper presented at the American Political Science Association Meeting, Washington, DC, August.

Kelly, Rita Mae (1993) 'Diversity in the public workforce: new needs, new approaches', in Frank J. Thompson (ed.), *Revitalizing State and Local Public Service*. San Francisco, CA: Jossey–Bass. pp. 197–224.

Kelly, Rita Mae (1998) 'An inclusive democratic polity, representative bureaucracies, and the new public management', *Public Administration Review*, 58 (3): 201–8.

Kelman, Steven (1987) 'Public choice and public spirit', *Public Interest*, 87 (Spring): 80–94.

Kickert, W. (1991) 'Steering at a distance: A new paradigm of public governance in Dutch higher education'. Paper presented to the European Consortium for Political Research, University of Essex, March.

Kim, Pan Suk (1993) 'Public bureaucracy and regionalism in South Korea', *Administration and Society*, 25 (2): 277–92.

Kimber, R. (1989) 'On democracy', *Scandinavian Political Studies*, 12 (3): 199–219.

Kingsley, J.D. (1944) *Representative Bureaucracy*. Yellow Springs, OH: Antioch.

Krislov, S. (1974) *Representative Bureaucracy*. Englewood Cliffs, NJ: Prentice–Hall.

Lane, Jan-Erik (1995) *The Public Sector*, 2nd edn. London: Sage.

Lægreid, Per and Olsen, Johan P. (1984) 'Top civil servants in Norway: Key players on different teams', in E.N. Suleiman (ed.), *Bureaucrats and Policy Making*. New York: Holmes and Meier. pp. 206–42.

Lewin, Leif (1980) *Governing Trade Unions in Sweden*, Cambridge, MA: Harvard University Press.

Lewis, Gregory and Nice, David (1994) 'Race, sex and occupational segregation in state and local governments', *American Review of Public Administration*, 24 (December): 393–410.

Lindblom, H. (1959) 'The science of muddling through', *Public Administration Review*, 19 (1): 79–88.

Lingard, Bob (1993) 'Managing democracy in the public sector', *Social Alternatives*, 12 (2): 10–14.

Lipset, Seymour Martin (1960) *Political Man*. New York: Doubleday.

Macy, John W. (1970) 'Towards an international civil service', *Public Administration Review*, 30 (3): 260–70.

March, J.G. and Olsen, J.P. (1996) 'Institutional perspectives on political institutions', *Governance*, 9 (3): 247–64.

March, James G. and Olsen, Johan P. (1989) *Rediscovering Institutions: The Organizational Basis of Politics*. Toronto: Free Press.

March, J.G. and Simon, H.A. (1993) *Organizations*. Oxford: Blackwell (1st edition, 1958: Wiley).

Meier, K. (1975) 'Representative bureaucracy: An empirical analysis', *American Political Science Review*, 69 (June): 526–42.

Meier, K. (1993a) 'Representative bureaucracy: A theoretical and empirical exposition', *Research in Public Administration*, 2 (1): 1–35.

Meier, K. (1993b) 'Latinos and representative bureaucracy', *Journal of Public Administration Research and Theory*, 3 (3): 393–415.

Meier, K.J. (1997) 'Bureaucracy and democracy: The case for more bureaucracy and less democracy', *Public Administration Review*, 57 (3): 193–9.

Meier, K. and Nigro, L.G. (1976) 'Representative bureaucracy and policy preferences: a study of the attitudes of federal executives', *Public Administration Review*, 36 (4): 458–69.

Meier, K.J. and Smith, K.B. (1994) 'Representative democracy and representative bureaucracy: Examining the top-down and bottom-up linkages', *Social Science Quarterly*, 75 (4): 790–803.

Meier, K.J., Wrinkle, R.D. and Polinard, J.L. (1995) 'Politics, bureaucracy, and agricultural policy: An alternative view of political control', *American Politics Quarterly*, 23 (4): 427–61.

Mellbourne, A. (1979) *Byråkratins ansikten*. Stockholm: LieberFörlag.

Millar, Michelle and McKevitt, D. (1997) 'The Irish civil service'. Paper presented at Civil Service Systems in Comparative Perspective, School of Public and Environmental Affairs, Indiana University, Bloomington, 5–8 April.

Morrison, Ann M., White, R.P. and Van Velsor, E. (1987) *Breaking the Glass Ceiling*. Reading, MA: Addison–Wesley.

Mosher, F.C. (1968) *Democracy and the Public Service*. New York: Oxford University Press.

Niskanen, W.A., Jr (1971) *Bureaucracy and Representative Government*. New York: Aldine–Atherton.

Peters, B. Guy (1985) 'Sweden: The explosion of public employment', in R. Rose (ed.), *Public Employment in Western Nations*. Cambridge: Cambridge University Press. pp. 203–27.

Peters, B. Guy (1991) 'The European bureaucrat: The applicability of bureaucracy and representative government to non-American settings', in A. Blais and S. Dion (eds), *The Budget-Maximizing Bureaucrat*. Pittsburgh: University of Pittsburgh Press.

Pincus, Ingrid (2000) 'Male resistance and ambivalence in gender equality: Reforms in local authorities'. Paper presented at Workplace Diversity Research; A Research Perspective on Theory and Practice, Brussels, May.

Pitkin, Hanna (1967) *The Concept of Representation*. Berkeley, CA: University of California Press.

Price, D.K. (1965) *The Scientific Estate*. Cambridge, MA: Harvard University Press.

Randell, S. (1994) 'The glass ceiling: Six strategies', *Canberra Bulletin of Public Administration*, 76 (April): 128–30.

Rawls, John A. (1971) *A Theory of Justice*. Cambridge, MA: Harvard University Press.

Redford, E.S. (1969) *Democracy in the Administrative State*. New York: Oxford University Press.

Romzek, Barbara S. (1990) 'Employee investment and commitment: The ties that bind', *Public Administration Review*, 50 (3): 374–82.

Rothstein, Bo (1992) *Den Korporativa Staten*. Stockholm: Norstedts.

Rothstein, Bo (2000) 'Messing ger mig rysningar', Stockholm, Aftonbladet, 18 March, p. 3.

Rouban, L. (1995) 'The civil service culture and administrative reform', in B.G. Peters and D.J. Savoie (eds), *Governance in a Changing Environment*. Montreal: McGill–Queen's University Press.

Sabatier, P.A., Loomis, J. and McCarthy, C. (1995) 'Hierarchical controls, professional norms, local constituencies, and budget maximization: An analysis of U.S. Forest Service planning decisions', *American Journal of Political Science*, 39 (1): 204–42.

Saltzstein, G.H. (1986) 'Female mayors and women in municipal jobs', *American Journal of Political Science*, 30 (2): 140–64.

Saltzstein, G.H. (1989) 'Black mayors and police policies', *Journal of Politics*, 51 (August): 140–64.

Savoie, Donald (1994) *Thatcher, Reagan, Mulroney: In Search of a New Bureaucracy*. Pittsburgh: University of Pittsburgh Press.

Scharpf, F. (1977) 'Does organization matter? Task structure and interaction in the ministerial bureaucracy', in E. Burack and A. Negandhi (eds), *Organization Design*. Kent, OH: Kent State University Press.

Schneider, B.R. (1993) 'A comparative analysis of bureaucratic preferences and insulation', *Comparative Politics*, 25: 331–51.

Scott, W.R. (1995) *Institutions and Organizations*. Thousand Oaks, CA: Sage.

Selden, S.C. (1997) *The Promise of Representative Bureaucracy: Diversity and Responsiveness in a Government Agency*. Armonk, New York: M.E. Sharpe.

Selden, S.C., Brudney, J.L. and Kellough, J.E. (1998) 'Bureaucracy as representative institution', *American Journal of Political Science*, 42 (July): 716–29.

Seligman, Lee (1986) 'The bureaucrat as budget maximizer', *Public Budgeting and Finance*, (Spring): 50–9.

Shumavon, D.H. and Hibbeln, H.K. (1986) 'Administrative discretion: Problems and prospects', in D.H. Shumavon and H.K. Hibbeln (eds), *Administrative Discretion and Public Policy Implementation*. New York: Praeger.

Simon, Herbert A. (1957) *Administrative Behavior*. New York: Macmillan.

Simon, H.A., Thompson, V.A. and Smithburg, D.W. (1950) *Public Administration*. New York: Alfred A. Knopf.

Sjoberg, G., Brymer, R.A. and Farris, B. (1966) 'Bureaucracy and the lower class', *Sociology and Social Research*, 50 (April): 325–77.

Stillman, R.J. III. (1991) *Preface to Public Administration*. New York: St Martin's Press.

Stone, Isabella (1990) 'Institutionalising feminism – a contradiction in terms?'. Paper presented to the Friedrich-Ebert-Stiftung, Anglo-German Conference on Equality Policies for Women in Local Government, Bonn, 2–3 April.

Subramaniam, V. (1967) 'Representative bureaucracy: A reassessment', *American Political Science Review*, 61 (December): 1010–19.

Thompson, Frank (1976) 'Minority groups in public bureaucracies: Are passive and active representation linked?', *Administration and Society*, 8 (2): 201–26.

Tummala, Krishna K. (1999) 'Policy of preference: Lessons from India, The United States, and South Africa', *Public Administration Review*, 59 (6): 495–508.

United States General Accounting Office (2001) 'Senior Executive Service: Diversity Increased in the Past Decade', GAO-01-377. Washington, DC: Government Printing Office.

van der Meer, Frits M., Dijkstra, Gerrit S. and Roborgh Renk, J. (1997) 'The Dutch Civil Service System'. Paper presented at Civil Service Systems in Comparative Perspective, School of Public and Environmental Affairs Indiana University, Bloomington, 5–8 April.

van der Ros, Janneke (1997) *Et femokratisk prosjekt: organisering av likestilling – Slutrapport av forskningsprosjektet: Organisering av kommunal likestilling i 1990-årene*. Forskningsrapport nr. 28/1997, Lillehammer: Högskolen i Lillehammer.

Van Riper, Paul (1966) 'The senior civil service and the career service', in C.E. Hawley and R.G. Weintraub (eds), *Administrative Questions and Political Answers*. New York: Van Nostrand. pp. 342–53.

Verheijen, Tony (ed.) (1999) *Civil Service Systems in Central and Eastern Europe*. Cheltenham: Edward Elgar.

Wade, I.L. (1979) 'Public administration, public choice, and the pathos of reform', *Review of Politics*, 41 (5): 543–55.

Weber, Max (1968) 'Bureaucracy', in Gunther Roth and Claus Wittich (eds), *Economy and Society: Max Weber*, volume 3. New York: Bedminister Press.

White, Orion F., Jr (1969) 'The dialectical organization', *Public Administration Review*, 29 (1): 32–42.

Willbern, York (1966) 'Professionalization in the public service', in C.E. Hawley and R.G. Weintraub (eds), *Administrative Questions and Political Answers*. New York: Van Nostrand. pp. 333–41.

Wilson, James Q. (1989) *Bureaucracy*. New York: Basic Books.

Wilson, S. and Mullins, W.A. (1978) 'Representative bureaucracy: Linguistic/ethnic aspects in Canadian public policy', *Canadian Public Administration*, 21 (5): 513–38.

Winkler, J. (1981) 'The political economy of administrative decision', in M. Adler and S. Asquith (eds), *Discretion and Welfare*. London: Heinemann.

Wise, Lois Recascino (1990) 'Social equity in civil service systems', *Public Administration Review*, 50 (5): 567–75.

Wise, Lois R. (1992) 'Schwedisches Dilemma: Karriere mit Grenzen', *NORDEUROPAforum*, 4 (December): 3–6.

Wise, Lois R. and Jonzon, B. (1991) 'The Swedish civil service as a vehicle for social equality', in Ali

Farazmand (ed.), *Handbook of Comparative and Development Public Administration*. New York: Marcel Dekker. pp. 625–37.

Wise, Lois R. and Szücs, Stefan (1996) 'The public/private cleavage in a welfare state: Attitudes toward public management reform', *Governance*, 9 (1): 43–70.

Wood, B.D. and Waterman, R.W. (1994) *Bureaucratic Discretion: The Role of Bureaucracy in a Democracy*. Boulder, CO: Westview.

Yeatman, A. (1990) *Bureaucrats, Technocrats, Femocrats: Essays on the Contemporary Australian State*. Sydney: Allen and Unwin.

Yishai, Yael and Cohen, Aaron (1997) '(Un)representative bureaucracy: Women in the Israeli senior civil service', *Administration and Society*, 28 (4): 441–65.

28

Street-Level Bureaucracy and Public Policy

Steven Rathgeb Smith

In the past twenty years, a broad rethinking of the principles of public administration and management has been underway. Traditional public management has been criticized as rigid, inflexible, ineffective and unresponsive to the needs of citizens. To restore the legitimacy and effectiveness of government, a 'New Public Management' paradigm has been proposed (Behn, 2001; Feldman and Khademian, 2000; Moore, 1995; Osborne and Gaebler, 1992). Central to this New Public Management is an emphasis on performance and outcomes and greater responsive to citizens and their needs. To achieve these goals, attention has been focused in part on directly or indirectly changing the behavior of 'street-level bureaucrats' – the front-line workers who serve as the connection between public service and the citizenry (Lipsky, 1980). These street-level bureaucrats include the police, welfare caseworkers, teachers, physicians, nurses, mental health counselors and correctional officers. Through new performance standards, it is hoped that the effectiveness of street-level bureaucrats will be greatly enhanced. Others propose taking advantage of the knowledge and expertise of street-level bureaucrats to improve performance – in essence, to empower street-level bureaucrats by freeing them from some of the more onerous and unproductive rules and procedures characteristic of more traditional approaches to public administration (Schorr, 1997). This strategy can include empowering workers in public agencies or shifting the responsibilities of street-level bureaucrats in public agencies to private nonprofit and for-profit organizations through contracting, with the intention of stimulating competition in services.

In general, a marked diversification of policy tools including contracting for services, vouchers, tax credits and loan guarantees has occurred, spurred by the New Public Management that stresses competition, efficiency and effectiveness.

Arguably then, the role of street-level bureaucrats and their importance to the implementation of public policy has never been more important and more scrutinized. It is not an overstatement to argue that the success of these New Public Management strategies rests on street-level bureaucrats in public, nonprofit and for-profit agencies providing public services. As noted by Lipsky (1980: 13), the power of street-level bureaucrats to influence public policy implementation derives substantially from their discretion and their relative autonomy from organizational authority. This discretion and autonomy gives street-level bureaucrats substantial power actually to make policy, rather than simply to implement the directives of superiors (Bardach, 1977; Behn, 2001; Brehm and Gates, 1997; Carroll and Siegel, 1999; Elmore, 1979–80; Lipsky, 1978, 1980; Maynard-Moody and Musheno, 2000: Rothstein, 1996; Sandfort, 2000; Vinzant and Crothers, 1998; Wilson, 1978).

The challenges posed by the discretion and autonomy of street-level bureaucrats to effective program implementation, particularly in the new performance-oriented practices of today, is covered elsewhere in this volume (see Meyers and Vorsarger, Chapter 19). The focus of this chapter is different. This chapter examines the performance of street-level bureaucrats from the citizen's perspective with an emphasis on the crucial gatekeeper functions of street-level bureaucrats to the access of individuals to full citizenship rights. As a consequence, street-level bureaucrats also are critical to the legitimacy and trust in government. (For fuller discussion of legitimacy and trust in government in this volume see Rothstein, Chapter 26.) The relationship between street-level bureaucrats and citizens is especially important since most of the New Public Management literature tends to focus on performance issues rather than the citizenship and democracy implications of the work of street-level bureaucrats. Further, public management is in the midst of sometimes dramatic changes throughout the world. Contracting for services, privatization, devolution, community partnerships, local advisory councils and tax credits can quite dramatically change the relationship of street-level bureaucrats to local citizens.

CITIZENSHIP AND STREET-LEVEL BUREAUCRATS

Citizenship theory

Two key strands of citizenship theory have the most relevance to street-level bureaucrats and public policy. One theoretical perspective was initially developed over fifty years ago by T.H. Marshall, a British social scientist who argued that the transition of society from the Middle Ages to the modern industrial world redefined citizenship (Marshall, 1964).[1] He argued that the spread of the market economy and industrialization required the extension of citizenship rights to all citizens. He divided citizenship rights into three categories: civil, political and social. Civil rights such as freedom of speech, religion and assembly are protections against the state. Political rights include the right to vote and the secret ballot. Social rights are the government-protected minimum standards of health and welfare, including health and unemployment insurance, public pensions and social services.

Marshall considered these rights to build upon each other in a logical progression. Civil rights created the opportunity for more extensive political rights which then spurred a demand for social rights (Janoski, 1998; King and Waldron, 1988; Marshall, 1964; Rowe et al., 2001; Seligman, 1992; Turner, 1990; Waddington, 1999). Each of the rights was essential to full citizenship, which Marshall (1964) defined as follows:

Citizenship is a status bestowed on those who are full members of a community. All who possess the status are equal with respect to the rights and duties with which the status is endowed. (1964: 84)

Government was at the center of these rights since it was government that was needed to enforce these rights (civil and political) or provide the resources and/or access to resources necessary for people to enjoy full social rights.

Implicit in Marshall's framework was a certain relationship between citizens and the market, community and government. If citizens depend upon the market, they are required to pay for the services; individuals without adequate income will thus lack access to services. In the community sphere, individuals will depend upon voluntary organizations including churches, food banks, shelters and the American Red Cross. These agencies typically provide short-term and/or emergency relief; disadvantaged individuals with longer term or more intensive needs are often inadequately served by these agencies since these agencies typically do not have the resource base to provide for longer-term needs. Their mission may also only focus on short-term relief (Chaves, 2001; Sosin, 1986). The provision of civil, political and social rights is intended to sever the dependence of individuals on the market and private charity.

A different strand of citizenship theory dates to Alexis de Tocqueville (1956), who viewed the state with suspicion and considered voluntary organizations and their capacity to serve as a vehicle for citizen participation as essential to democracy and freedom (Janoski, 1998; Rowe et al., 2001; Smith, 1993). de Tocqueville places much greater emphasis on civil and political rights and much less on government-guaranteed social rights. In the past few decades, this perspective has been embraced by scholars and policy makers from across the political spectrum. For instance, Peter Berger and Richard John Neuhaus (1977) and Nathan Glazer (1988) have tended to emphasize the value of community organizations and voluntarism as alternatives to state programs, in part because they view these organizations as protectors of individual freedom and responsibility. Other scholars have developed the de Tocquevillian perspective as a complement rather than as a substitute for government programs (King and Waldron, 1988; Rowe et al., 2001). For example, Janoski (1998) argues that in addition to the three rights articulated by Marshall, a critical component of citizenship is 'participation rights', that is, the right of individuals to participate in local decision making. Also, Boyte and Kari (1996), Sirianni and Friedland (2001) and Lappe and Du Bois (1994) have written widely about the value of citizen participation in local affairs as a crucial aspect of full citizenship. Stivers (1990) contends that public administration has often neglected citizenship issues and calls for 'active citizenship', including participation of citizens in agency decision making. Racine (1995) calls for 'immersed civil servants' who would have close linkages to their local communities and tap citizens to help solve social problems.

Citizenship then cannot simply be reduced to a narrow perspective emphasizing the right to vote and certain legal protections; instead, full citizenship hinges on a full array of rights that support and indeed encourage full participation of individuals in societal affairs. In these realms, street-level bureaucrats play a critical role.

Citizenship theory and street-level bureaucrats

Marshall's progression of civil, political and social rights was predicated on the assumption of the growth of a large-scale public bureaucracy to guarantee these rights. This certainly fits with the experience of his own country, the United Kingdom, which built an extensive public bureaucracy in the post-Second World War period to offer these rights. Indeed, the National Health Service, as a public entity, comprised of thousands of 'street-level bureaucrats' from physicians to nurses to social workers, was emblematic of the type of bureaucracy Marshall conceptualized as crucial to citizenship rights. The United Kingdom also pioneered the development of an extensive array of personal social services that would be provided through local authority welfare bureaucracies (Ellis et al., 1999).

This framework has been very influential in thinking about the role of government, the bureaucracy and comparative welfare state policies. Wilensky and Lebeaux (1958) suggested that large-scale bureaucracy to provide social programs was an inevitable consequence of industrialization and modernization. The United States 'lagged' behind other advanced industrial countries since it had not devoted the resources to public sector bureaucracies that were characteristic of many postwar Western European countries. Esping-Anderson (1990) proposed an innovative typology of welfare states that divided advanced industrial countries into three 'regime' categories: social-democratic, conservative and liberal. He argued that a country's social policies varied depending upon their regime type, with countries such as Sweden in the social-democratic category and the United States and United Kingdom in the liberal camp.

But Esping-Anderson's focus was on income maintenance programs as measured by spending in the public sector. Importantly, he did not focus on what Hasenfeld (1985, 1987) called 'the bureaucratic encounter'. Through these encounters, street-level bureaucrats wield considerable influence on the access of citizens to full citizenship rights, especially social rights. Two separate critiques have emerged on the capacity of street-level bureaucrats to effectively respond to citizen needs and, more generally, to act as a guarantor of citizenship rights. Lipsky (1980, 1984) contends that street-level bureaucrats have great difficulty in responding adequately to citizens because they are always faced with escalating service demands and insufficient resources to respond. To cope with this conundrum, street-level bureaucrats are forced to use their discretion and relative autonomy from agency authority to ration services to bring the level of services in line with resources. They pursue a number of strategies to ration services, including limiting access and demand for services through classification, queuing and service routines. Citizens are not provided with social rights, instead they are processed as clients (Lipsky, 1980; Prottas, 1979; Weatherley, 1979). In part, service can be rationed since so many clients of street-level bureaucracies are not truly voluntary clients due to a serious power differential between street-level bureaucrats and their clients (Hasenfeld, 1985). Examples include children in public schools, welfare recipients, patients at community mental health clinics and criminals or suspected criminals. Many of these users of the services of street-level bureaucrats are in an inherently weak relationship *vis-à-vis* street-level bureaucrats such as teachers and the police. Consequently, clients are often unable to effectively challenge the rationing practices of street-level bureaucrats. The effect of service rationing is profound service inequality; thus individuals are routinely denied their full citizenship rights. Moreover, the street-level bureaucrats themselves suffer from serious alienation since they often find themselves severely constrained in their ability to respond to individual need, despite a genuine commitment to social justice and quality services.

By implication, the inequities in services also alienate the users of public service from government itself. The welfare office or the police are the face of government for many people, especially those on low incomes. To the extent they are discouraged from using public service or receive poor service, they may become alienated from the political system in general. Thus, the problems with street-level bureaucrats who provide social and health services for instance may affect more than just social rights; it may also affect the willingness of individuals to exercise their political rights.

The discretion and autonomy of street-level bureaucrats is justified in part because of their professional training. Ideally, this training is supposed to embue street-level bureaucrats with a commitment to universality and quality services. But the chronic shortfall in resources often means that street-level bureaucrats use their discretion protectively rather than to advance professional ideals or respond flexibly to people's individual needs. Indeed, studies of British social services provided by local authorities found that social workers often adopted a 'siege mentality' to deal with the lack of resources to deal with rising demand for services. As a result, workers tended to manage their work flow according to their own priorities rather than the needs of the clients (Ellis et al., 1999).

The standard approach to 'fixing' the problems of street-level bureaucrats from a traditional public administration perspective was to try to control the discretion of street-level bureaucrats through the imposition of more rules and procedures governing their work. For example, in the UK, legislation was passed in the 1970s that specified in great detail the duty and responsibility of street-level workers in local authorities to provide specific services (Doyle and Harding, 1992; Ellis et al., 1999). This effort in the UK and similar efforts elsewhere represented an attempt to control street-level bureaucrats through rules and procedures that typically entailed hierarchical controls imposed from the top down.

Elmore (1979–80) called this approach 'forward-mapping' and argued that it was destined to fail because it assumed that policy makers actually controlled (or could control) the work of street-level bureaucrats. He suggested that policy makers should instead adopt a 'backward-mapping' approach to policy implementation that focused on the transaction between street-level bureaucrats and their clients. By tapping the knowledge of street-level bureaucrats about their communities and clients, policy makers could develop more effective programs and more successful program implementation. Lipsky (1978) also challenged the top-down implementation approach when he urged policy makers to undertake a bottom-up approach to understanding policy implementation and program design. Further, attempts to control street-level bureaucrats through standardization and rules are likely to encounter serious difficulties because street-level bureaucrats possess many different tools to subvert rules and procedures put in place by high-level administrators (Lipsky, 1980). Street-level bureaucrats, for example, often control the information necessary to comply with rules and procedures governing their jobs. Wilson (1978) echoed this skepticism about hierarchical controls when he observed that many circumstances faced

by the police cannot be specified in advance; too many circumstances requiring police intervention call for discretionary judgment.

Logically following from the work of Elmore, Lipsky, Wilson and others, the conditions of work of street-level bureaucrats and the expectations placed upon them will have an enormous impact on the access of citizens to services and even the extent to which individuals are regarded as deserving of service. From a comparative perspective, great variation exists in pay levels and working conditions of street-level bureaucrats. Moreover, different countries have different social and health policies, labor markets and expectations on the appropriate role of the state. All of these factors are critical to the performance of street-level bureaucrats in their job (see Handler, 1996). For instance, Deborah Stone (1984) discusses the gatekeeper role of street-level bureaucrats in the awarding of disability benefits in advanced industrial countries. Variation in disability benefit participation across countries inevitably involves examining the different expectations of street-level bureaucrats who control access to disability benefits. Rothstein (1998) observed that selective (as opposed to universalistic) social policies tend to exacerbate the problems of inequality and bias in service delivery. Thus, countries such as the United States and the United Kingdom with many selective social policies are likely to have the most severe problems with street-level bureaucratic autonomy and discretion.

The work of Lipsky, Wilson and others also leads to a very challenging and difficult dilemma for managers and policy makers: discretion and autonomy are an inevitable and necessary part of the job of street-level bureaucrats; but many top-down efforts to control discretion are often doomed to failure because street-level bureaucrats can use their discretion to undermine efforts to control or manage their work and performance. In a sense, the public management reform initiatives of the past twenty years have been devoted to trying to solve this dilemma. The next section analyzes these reforms with particular reference to the impact of these reforms on citizens, their access to services, and more generally their citizenship rights and obligations.

PUBLIC MANAGEMENT REFORM, CITIZENS AND STREET-LEVEL BUREAUCRATS

During the 1980s and 1990s, widespread concern developed on government performance throughout advanced industrial countries. Many policy makers and citizens worried that public spending was increasing (sometimes quite sharply) but the performance of government agencies was lagging significantly. This concern crystallized in the work of David Osborne and Ted Gaebler, who published their book *Reinventing Government* in 1992. In their book, they called for a complete restructuring of the role of government and the work of street-level bureaucrats in particular. This general position has been broadly supported by policy makers and scholars in many different countries, even in countries with a very strong tradition of comprehensive public services.

In general, the reforms implemented in the wake of the call to 'reinvent government' tend to be collectively referred to as the 'New Public Management'. These reforms tend to cluster into two sometimes contradictory categories: the empowerment approach and the market-based competition strategy. The former also has two components that often overlap: empowering street-level bureaucrats and/or empowering citizens to become more active in monitoring, evaluating and delivering public services, essentially transforming citizens at least in part into street-level bureaucrats. The next section discusses this empowerment approach in more detail. The subsequent section focuses on the market approach and its implications for street-level bureaucrats and their relationship with citizens.

Empowering street-level bureaucrats and citizens

The approach builds upon the work of Elmore and others who argue that the expertise necessary for effective performance is at the street level; top-down reform is destined to fail (Behn, 2001: 30). The way to better performance is essentially to allow street-level bureaucrats to do their job using their professional training and expertise. This approach is rooted in an optimism that street-level bureaucrats can effectively address serious public problems and deal with the public in a fair and equitable fashion if only they are provided with the resources and the opportunity to use their talents and abilities. Lisbeth Schorr (1997: 65), a noted US social welfare advocate, called for 'taming the bureaucracy to support what works'. Similarly, Christopher Hood (1991) dubbed this approach the 'free to manage' strategy because it rests on a view that managers and their front-line workers have been hamstrung by restrictive regulations that prevent them from providing effective, quality service. The front-line workers are the people with the knowledge of the local

community and individual client needs; thus it is appropriate to tap their expertise.

This approach usually involves some decentralization from the 'center' to the 'periphery' or from the headquarters to the field offices. A good example is public education, where in the United States a broad movement has been under way to support 'site-based' management whereupon principals and teachers are given more authority over curriculum and program implementation (see Schorr, 1997). In environmental policy, regional offices of the US Environmental Protection Agency have been given greater authority to decide how to comply with environmental protection objectives.

In practice, this 'empowerment' strategy (Behn, 2001) has often met a very different relationship between street-level bureaucrats and citizens because empowerment has often met – apropos of Elmore – greater involvement of citizens in local decision making on public services and the implementation of public policy. Lipsky observed that street-level bureaucrats actually make policy; the shift toward empowerment and decentralization increasingly means offering citizens a role in making policy as well. Many different examples exist but it is appropriate to think about this citizen involvement along a continuum. At one end is traditional forms of citizen involvement with street-level bureaucracies – public meetings and serving on advisory committees.[2] Many public agencies, for example, held public hearings on proposed policy changes. Also, public schools, public welfare agencies and local environmental agencies have often had local advisory committees. Arguably though, the emphasis on empowerment has meant an increase in these more consultative forms of public involvement as street-level bureaucrats have used their discretion and increased responsibility to reach out to the community.

To be sure, citizen participation has always been part of service delivery to an extent. As Gordon Whitaker (1980) argued, public services are often 'co-produced' by street-level bureaucrats and citizens because the 'delivery' of so many public services such as child protection and police enforcement require input and cooperation of citizens. As a result, public services are substantially influenced by citizens, even if it is not formally structured input.

It is this more formal structuring of the bureaucrat–citizen relationship that is on the rise throughout advanced industrial countries. At the mid-point in this continuum, more intense and ongoing participation initiatives are characteristic. For instance, citizens and street-level bureaucrats may be engaged in a deliberative process on the needs of the community or region and the most appropriate way to meet these needs. Many examples of this new development exist: public–private partnerships, community coalitions to prevent teenage pregnancy, community and neighborhood planning.

These more deliberative forms have increased in many different countries. In the UK, community regeneration initiatives are predicated in part on active involvement of the target community in the planning and implementation of the regeneration projects (Smith and Beazley, 2000). In the United States, similar urban economic redevelopment projects called Enterprise Zones are designed with a governance structure that includes local public agency staff and representatives of the local community. In Germany, local participation has included 'territorial decentralization to committees or councils representing neighborhoods in particular towns' and new advisory committees of local citizens on planning issues (Hendriks and Tops, 1999: 142). In the Netherlands, citizen participation in zoning and land use decisions has increased markedly in the past ten years (Hendriks and Tops, 1999). One American effort for the homeless mentally ill involves a broad and diverse collaboration of citizens and professionals to help fully integrate these clients into the community; full citizenship for these clients was not possible without a full community effort (Rowe et al., 2001).

Importantly, many of these more deliberative processes involve a more direct and ongoing role for non-profit organizations. For example, in the United States many public–private partnerships on issues such as teen pregnancy and public health are comprised of institutional representatives of public and nonprofit agencies. Citizens without an organizational affiliation may or may not be represented in the partnership. Indeed, in many partnerships pertaining to social and health services most of the partnership members are organizational representatives. In many of these partnerships, citizens are given a formal role but it is often difficult to engage them on an ongoing basis, reflecting the challenge of enlisting citizen participation in the absence of strong institutional incentives.

This problem of collective action has been addressed in part by providing more formal, authoritative, and structured roles for citizens through initiatives that can be placed at the other end of the continuum. These initiatives include: forums, citizen juries, using citizens to evaluate the quality of public services provided by street-level bureaucrats, employing local residents and users as program staff, and user management (also see Rothstein, Chapter 26 in this volume).

Many examples of formalized public forums exist. In Munich, Germany, the 'Munich Forum' comprised of citizens, was created to evaluate planning proposals. Citizen juries to provide counsel and a specific recommendation to local government still tend to be rare; but citizen panels are much more common (Lowndes et al., 2001a). In Australia, government officials have consciously sought the feedback of citizens on the timeliness, accessibility, reliability and responsiveness of public services provided by street-level bureaucrats (Kettl, 1997). In the United States, cities such as Portland, Oregon have used 'benchmarking' by citizens as a way of evaluating the quality of services and citizen satisfaction with existing services.

In an effort to make services more responsive, a variety of initiatives have now tried to consciously include residents as staff and volunteers of the programs, essentially transforming them into street-level bureaucrats. For instance, several American foundations and government agencies have funded a major nationwide initiative called, 'Jobs-Plus' that in part employs the residents of low-income public housing units to provide workforce-related services (Kato and Riccio, 2001). This trend is also evident in many services provided to immigrant communities in different countries as well as in mental health services.

User management essentially shifts the street-level role to the citizen. For example, a local public park may now be maintained (sometimes with the support of public funds) by the local neighborhood association. Or homeless individuals may actually be employed to help maintain the shelter. In these arrangements, street-level bureaucrats may shift to a more administrative role and thus play a much less direct role in managing and allocating the services available to the public. A variation on user management that has gained favor within many health and social services is to have clients from specialized populations, such as those who are developmentally disabled, chronic mentally ill or physically handicapped, represented in the governance and management of the public services. For example, many nonprofit agencies offering social and health services have clients on their boards. Public agencies may have citizen panels comprised in part of clients of the services.

In essence, the range of options on this continuum are an implicit and explicit effort to transform the role of street-level bureaucrats and more broadly citizenship as it is understood by policy makers and citizens. These changes represent an effort to move toward more active citizenship (King and Stivers, 1998; Stivers, 1990) and the participation rights proposed by Janoski (1998). In these situations, citizenship is not a bundle of rights with their access controlled by street-level bureaucrats but a 'process' by which citizens actively participate (Mullard, 1997: 242). Street-level bureaucrats actively participate with users of public services to provide them with a process by which they can be intensely involved in public policy and the decisions affecting the provision of public services. In part, this involvement is aimed at making street-level bureaucrats more accountable. The critique of street-level bureaucrats from Lipsky, Wilson and others was based in part on the premise that they were 'unaccountable' to policy makers and high-level managers because of their relative autonomy and broad discretion. Greater involvement of citizens in decision making has the effect of increasing the transparency of the decisions of street-level bureaucrats, theoretically increasing the extent to which street-level bureaucrats are held accountable for their performance.

Competition and the New Public Management: the implications for citizens and street-level bureaucrats

The goals of participation and active citizenship have often been made more difficult to achieve by the push for more competition in public services. This latter, market-based approach to transforming public services has many manifestations: government contracting for public services with nonprofit and for-profit organizations, using vouchers to access services such as housing and education, using performance measures to spur increased competition between public, nonprofit and public agencies and increase accountability, and tapping private revenue to support public services. These strategies have been widely adopted throughout the world. In New Zealand, one of the pioneering countries in the implementation of market-based reforms, senior government officials are hired on performance contracts to manage agencies whose work is defined in purchase-of-service agreements. New Zealand and the United Kingdom have also aggressively privatized public services and made extensive use of government contracting with private and public agencies (Kettl, 1997). These contracts have specific performance targets that contract agencies need to reach if they hope to keep the contract. In the Netherlands, contract management, measurable policy objectives and the discourse of market discipline have become central to reforms of local government management (Hendriks and Tops, 1999). In the United States,

performance-based contracting has also increased greatly in the past twenty years, although unlike New Zealand and the United Kingdom, most of the increase in contracting does not represent a shift from public services to private agencies; instead, contracting has grown primarily as a vehicle to expand services. Examples such as job training, welfare-to-work, community mental health and residential care for the mentally ill and developmentally disabled are overwhelmingly new services provided by nonprofit and to a lesser extent for-profit agencies with public funds (Smith and Lipsky, 1993; Smith, 2002).

Contracting and performance measurement is also tied in some countries and communities to greater empowerment of local service organizations and citizens. In the United Kingdom, reforms in social services have entailed devolution to the local government authorities and much greater use of contracting. Local needs assessment involving local professionals and citizens is part of this process since ideally contracted services are supposed to be provided in accordance with local needs (Ellis et al., 1999). The emphasis on local needs assessment has also been a key part of many initiatives in the United States. The theme of local empowerment is often reinforced by the discourse on these reforms in social policy. In the UK, community care refers to the government's privatization and devolution strategy in social and health services. The widespread use of community organizations to provide services under government contract is also consistent with this theme (Ellis et al., 1999).

In practice, however, performance-based contracting and outcome-based management more generally has generally *not* been an empowering strategy for local citizens and communities. Part of this problem stems from the underlying philosophy of performance contracting. This form of contracting fits with the 'make the managers manage' strategy of the New Public Management (Behn, 2001; Hood, 1991). Theoretically, performance contracting is supposed to achieve this goal through the use of market competition among service providers and the requirement that managers meet identified performance targets. The emphasis is on efficiency and results. An unintended side-effect of this focus, however, is the creation of a variety of obstacles or challenges to citizen participation. These obstacles are three-fold. First, performance contracting with nonprofit community-based organizations often involves a process of local priority setting. Sometimes only the nonprofit grantees are involved; in other situations (for example, workforce development programs in United States) a variety of public, nonprofit and for-profit stakeholders are involved in a process of needs assessment and priority setting. Ideally, this local priority setting would prompt greater citizen participation in decision making pertaining to public services and policy. However, performance contracting is frequently implemented as a 'top-down' strategy where the targets are essentially set by high-level administrators or in some cases the legislature or political executive. This mismatch between the goal and rhetoric of local input and top-down decision making can be very disempowering at the local level. Community organizations and their representatives, including lay board members, will not participate in a local decision making process for very long if they do not feel as if they are able to influence the eventual performance goals and priorities.

Put another way, it has been argued that the new public management will lead to less emphasis on traditional hierarchical organizations and more on locally focused horizontal organizations that are based on cooperative networks of relationships between street-level bureaucrats in public and private organizations. This is the basic theme of the many of the empowerment strategies mentioned earlier. But performance contracting as it is currently implemented often recreates the vertical hierarchical relationships of traditional bureaucracies. As one commentator observed, 'there is a basic contradiction between pressure to seek collaboration and an infrastructure designed to stimulate a competitive market' (Flynn, as quoted by Kirkpatrick et al., 2001: 68). This contradiction is likely to be most severe in countries with selective welfare programs under financial pressure. Countries with more universal norms of access are likely to have more collaboration and less market competition for services (Considine, 2000).

Second, contracting is supposed to work on the basis of market competition whereupon public and private agencies compete with each other for government contracts. The market is supposed to work 'automatically' whereupon agencies face incentives to be efficient; the most efficient providers will win the contract and provide the best service. But to the extent contracting is implemented as an automatic policy tool, citizens may face high hurdles in trying to influence it (Smith and Ingram, 2002). In order to provide an opportunity for citizen input, administrators need to provide structured opportunities for the input of local organizations and citizens.

Third, contracting also tends to reduce the visibility of public policy and decision making about key policy and program priorities. In conventional public agencies, street-level bureaucrats are the face of government. While imperfect, a system exists to hold these bureaucrats accountable. Their role in policy implementation is often highly visible, especially in very sensitive policy areas such as child protection and policing. But contracting tends to mask the public role by shifting service to private agencies with their own separate governance structures. For instance, contracting with private, nonprofit agencies means that many ongoing management decisions are now made by nonprofit organizations. The new street-level bureaucrats are the front-line workers and their managers in these agencies. The relationship between the citizen and government though is much more indirect and the mechanisms by which a citizen might exercise 'voice' to hold the nonprofit agency receiving public funds accountable is not often clear or obvious.

The visibility of government has become even more obscure under devolution and privatization because in some cases it is not simply that government is contracting with a nonprofit or for-profit entity. Government may also contract with a third party intermediary which then sub-contracts with a private agency. This is the case with managed care programs in mental health and health care in the United States for example. Or alternatively, the national government may devolve funding responsibility to local government which then contracts with a local private service provider. In each of these situations, the relationship between the citizen and the state may become much more complicated, with a corresponding reduction in the visibility and transparency of government action. To be sure, the shift to local decision making can often help increase the visibility of government, but often the shift to local control is only partial, leaving the overall decision process more complex, creating obstacles to ongoing citizen involvement.

The visibility of street-level decision making is not only consequential for citizenship because it may affect the willingness and/or ability of citizens to participate in the policy process; it also directly influences the ability of individuals to access social benefits. Lipsky (1984: 3) calls attention to 'bureaucratic disentitlement' that takes place in the 'hidden recesses of routine or obscure decision making'. He further notes that the autonomy and discretion of street-level bureaucrats can allow them to incrementally reduce benefits (or the access to benefits and services) without generating public outcry or scrutiny because their actions lack visibility. Stone (1999, 2000a, 2000b) describes how regulatory changes designed to curtail expenditures in the

American Medicare program were implemented at the local level by caregivers working primarily in private agencies. Many caregivers were forced to operate within a new regulatory framework that greatly restricted their ability to develop a compassionate, effective relationship with their clients. In the UK, Rummery and Glendinning (2000) report that street-level bureaucrats working under devolved, reduced budgets resulting from the Community Care legislation are forced to ration care, in part by making it more difficult for citizens to receive community care assessments; thus the access of many citizens to community care benefits is more difficult since they cannot obtain the assessment necessary to trigger benefit eligibility.

Recent comparative research on contracting in advanced industrial countries also suggests that apropos of Esping-Anderson (1990), Rothstein (1998) and others, the characteristics of a country's overall social policies and political structure play a central role in the implementation of contracting in different countries. For instance, Considine (2000: 637) studied contracting for workforce development services in four countries and concluded that the Netherlands and the UK had markedly different approaches to contracting, with the latter much more likely to adopt 'a neo-bureaucratic paradigm' with performance targets limiting access. In Denmark, government officials have emphasized so-called 'soft contracting' that relies upon cooperation and relations among different public and private entities instead of strict market competition; this focus on cooperation fits with the consensual culture of Danish society (Greve, 2000).

Access to social rights is such a volatile and controversial issue in part because of the relationship between social rights and civil and political rights. Marshall (1964) argued civil and political rights preceded social rights. But in an interesting reversal of Marshall, many countries (and sub-national government units) are very worried that access to social rights broadly defined may be the prelude to civil and political rights. Street-level bureaucrats are problem-solvers who often develop a relationship with their clients (Stone, 1999, 2000a, 2000b). Since street-level bureaucrats are usually faced with high demand for their services, they are very interested in solving a problem and then moving on to the next problem. For this reason, they are much less concerned with larger political and social questions, especially since they are the people who must directly interact with people in need. For example, in Israel, the government has become concerned that many non-citizens are receiving social benefits such as job training and education. The worry is that the receipt of social benefits may then generate pressure for these non-citizens to receive full civil and political rights. Precedent for this development exists in many other countries, including the United States where the long-term receipt of social benefits by immigrants then helped legitimize the drive to grant these immigrants full citizenship status. Another example is in the provision of home healthcare, where caregivers tend to be quite sympathetic to the client, a tendency that can collide with more macro-policy goals such as limiting health expenditures (Stone, 1999).

Both of these examples also underscore the more general point on the role of street-level bureaucrats across countries. Contracting and other market strategies of providing public services tend to reduce the visibility of street-level bureaucrat decision making. But the specific impact of this shift will be dependent upon the prevailing welfare state policies and the social norms governing the provision of care.

LOOKING AHEAD

Brodkin (1997), Lipsky (1980), Prottas (1979), Wilson (1978) and others have argued that street-level bureaucrats are inevitably put in a position of rationing services due to a lack of resources to meet demand. The result is inequality, bias, alienation and a denial of citizenship rights as street-level bureaucrats adopt coping mechanisms to deal with their ongoing resource and demand problems. Trust in government and the overall legitimacy of government action is threatened. Reforming street-level practice to enhance citizenship rights including participation in agency decision making and access to social benefits is complicated and challenging. One strategy is enhancing the professionalism of street-level workers – essentially hoping that professionalization will provide workers with the tools to resist the imperatives of bureaucratic rationality. One strand of the New Public Management – empowering managers and front-line workers – is broadly consistent with this professionalism theme. But as noted, the other major thrust of the New Public Management – performance contracting and market competition in public services – tends to run in the opposite direction of empowerment; restricting professional discretion rather than celebrating it as an ongoing theme of many performance contracting initiatives. Indeed, the regulatory restrictions embedded in many contracts between government and private agencies make formal the rationing that was previously informal.

To be sure, many innovative strategies are being undertaken by street-level bureaucrats to actively promote citizenship rights, including more participation rights in local decision making. The range of initiatives from public–private partnerships to citizen forums to community coalitions is quite striking, especially in comparison to public service delivery of twenty years ago. But many of these initiatives ultimately are disappointing from a citizen's perspective; often, street-level bureaucrats are individually supportive of new programs and policy priorities, but are constrained by regulatory and funding policies from acting upon citizen recommendations and goals.

This situation calls attention to the need for policy makers and researchers to understand and examine the institutional context in which street-level bureaucrats operate. Thus, significant differences are likely to exist in the behavior of street level bureaucrats and their interaction with citizens depending upon the norms governing service delivery (for example, universal vs selective) and the prevailing funding and regulatory policies as they pertain to street-level workers. This perspective, however, also suggests the possibility for reform and a positive role for street-level bureaucrats and their impact on citizens. Street-level bureaucrats in countries with funding and regulatory structure encouraging equity and fairness in service delivery are more likely to behave in accordance with these norms. Government contracting with nonprofit agencies is not in and of itself a policy of retrenchment; it depends upon the type of 'contracting regime' (Considine, 2000; Smith and Lipsky, 1993) that governs the implementation of the contracting process. A crucial part of the regime is the extent to which the contracting process is visible and opportunities for professional and citizen input are offered.

Finally, the central role of street-level bureaucrats as the face of government to the citizenry and the gatekeeper to the government benefits and an array of citizenship rights once again calls attention to the necessity of re-conceptualizing our approach to provision of public services. Almost forty years ago, American legal scholar Charles Reich (1964) observed that government benefits had become the 'new property' and thus deserved the same procedural protections traditionally accorded to real property. While this perspective never achieved the revolution in American law that Reich might have hoped, it nonetheless helps explain why street-level bureaucrats are so important in contemporary society. Access to government benefits and programs – either provided directly by government agencies or indirectly through private nonprofit and for-profit entities – is crucial to citizenship, both in terms of providing tangible services that affect a citizen's life opportunities but also, more indirectly, in that the services of street-level bureaucrats and the benefits that they control confer legitimacy and status on individuals and groups that can then lead to more robust and extensive citizenship rights. Moreover, government benefits and programs can provide an opportunity to organize by groups and individuals interested in specific policies and programs.

All too often, reform in the way in which street-level bureaucrats provide services to citizens has not included consideration of the citizenship issues that are at the core of the political debate surrounding public services, especially in the health and social welfare arena. Instead, the focus of many of the New Public Management reforms has been on efficiency and effectiveness. These goals are, of course, important but an analysis of the implications of management reform on the relationship between street-level bureaucrats and citizens can also reveal the implications of management reform for other important goals of public policy including equity, responsiveness and access. More generally, attention to the effect of street-level practice on citizens would also help enhance the accountability of public services by increasing the visibility and transparency of the actions of street-level workers to the citizenry.

NOTES

The author thanks research assistant Stacy Holmes as well as Yeheskel Hasenfeld, Peter J. May, David J. Olson, Stephen Page, B. Guy Peters and Bo Rothstein for comments on earlier versions of this chapter.
1   This section is based in part on Smith (1993).
2   This continuum is based in part on Lowndes, Pratchett and Stoker (2001a, 2001b) and also on Timney (1998).

REFERENCES

Bardach, Eugene (1977) *The Implementation Game: What Happens After a Bill Becomes Law*. Cambridge, MA: MIT Press.

Behn, Robert D. (2001) *Rethinking Democratic Accountability*. Washington, DC: Brookings Institution.

Berger, Peter and Neuhaus, Richard John (1977) *To Empower People*. Washington, DC: American Enterprise Institute.

Boyte, Harry C. and Kari, Nancy N. (1996) *Building America: The Democratic Promise of Public Work*. Philadelphia: Temple University Press.

Brehm, John and Gates, Scott (1997) *Working, Shirking, and Sabotage: Bureaucratic Response to a Democratic Public*. Ann Arbor, MI: University of Michigan Press.

Brodkin, Evelyn Z. (1997) 'Inside the Welfare Contract: Discretion and Accountability in State Welfare Administration', *Social Service Review*, 71 (1): 1–34.

Carroll, Barbara Wake and Siegel, David (1999) *Service in the Field: The World of Front-Line Workers*. Montreal: McGill–Queen's University Press.

Chaves, Mark (2001) 'Congregations and Social Services: What They Do, How They Do It, and With Whom', *Nonprofit and Voluntary Sector Quarterly*, 30 (3): 660–83.

Considine, Mark (2000) 'Contract Regimes and Reflexive Governance: Comparing Employment Service Reforms in the United Kingdom, the Netherlands, New Zealand and Australia', *Public Administration*, 78 (3): 613–38.

Doyle, Nick and Harding, Tessa (1992) 'Community Care: Applying Procedural Fairness', in Anna Coote (ed.), *The Welfare of Citizens*. London: IPPR/Rivers Oram Press. pp. 69–82.

Ellis, Kathryn, Davis, Ann and Rummery, Kirstein (1999) 'Needs Assessment, Street-Level Bureaucracy and the New Community Care', *Social Policy and Administration*, 33 (3): 262–80.

Elmore, Richard F. (1979–80) 'Backward Mapping: Implementation Research and Policy Decisions', *Political Science Quarterly*, 94 (4): 601–16.

Esping-Anderson, Gosta (1990) *The Three Worlds of Welfare Capitalism*. Princeton, NJ: Princeton University Press.

Feldman, Martha S. and Khademian, Anne M. (2000) 'Managing for Inclusion: Balancing Control and Participation', *International Journal of Public Management*, 3 (2): 149–68.

Glazer, Nathan (1988) *The Limits of Social Policy*. Cambridge, MA: Harvard University Press.

Greve, Carsten (2000) 'Exploring Contracts as Reinvented Institutions in the Danish Public Sector', *Public Administration*, 78 (1): 153–64.

Handler, Joel F. (1996) *Down From Bureaucracy: The Ambiguity of Privatization and Empowerment*. Princeton, NJ: Princeton University Press.

Hasenfeld, Yeheskel (1985) 'Citizens' Encounters with Welfare State Bureaucracies', *Social Service Review*, 59 (4): 622–35.

Hasenfeld, Yeheskel, Rafferty, Jane A. and Zald, Mayer N. (1987) 'The Welfare State, Citizenship, and Bureaucratic Encounters', *Annual Review of Sociology*, 13: 387–415.

Hendriks, Frank and Tops, Pieter (1999) 'Between Democracy and Efficiency: Trends in Local Government Reform in the Netherlands and Germany', *Public Administration*, 77 (1): 133–53.

Hood, Christopher (1991) 'A Public Management for All Seasons?', *Public Administration*, 69 (Spring): 3–19.

Janoski, Thomas (1998) *Citizenship and Civil Society.* Cambridge: Cambridge University Press.

Kato, Linda Y. and Riccio, James A. (2001) *Building New Partnerships in Employment: Collaboration Among Agencies and Public Housing Residents in the Jobs-Plus Demonstration*. New York: MDRC.

Kettl, Donald (1997) 'The Global Revolution in Public Management: Driving Themes, Missing Links', *Journal of Policy Analysis and Management*, 16 (3): 446–62.

King, Cheryl Simrell and Stivers, Camilla (1998) 'Citizens and Administrators: Roles and Relationships', in Cheryl Simrell King and Camilla Stivers (eds), *Government is Us: Public Administration in an Anti-Government Era*. Thousand Oaks, CA: Sage. pp. 49–67.

King, Desmond S. and Waldron, Jeremy (1988) 'Citizenship, Social Citizenship and the Defence of Welfare Provision', *British Journal of Political Science*, 18: 415–43.

Kirkpatrick, Ian, Kitchener, Martin and Whipp, Richard. (2001) '"Out of Sight, Out of Mind": Assessing the Impact of Markets for Children's Residential Care', *Public Administration*, 79 (1): 49–71.

Lappe, Frances Moore and Du Bois, Paul Martin (1994) *The Quickening of America: Rebuilding Our Nation, Remaking Our Lives*. San Francisco: Jossey–Bass.

Lipsky, Michael (1978) 'Standing the Study of Public Policy Implementation on Its Head', in Walter Dean Burnham and Martha Weinberg (eds), *American Politics and Public Policy*. Cambridge, MA: MIT Press. pp. 391–402.

Lipsky, Michael (1980) *Street-Level Bureaucracy*. New York: Russell Sage Foundation.

Lipsky, Michael (1984) 'Bureaucratic Disentitlement in Social Welfare Programs', *Social Service Review*, 57 (1): 3–27.

Lowndes, Vivien, Pratchett, Lawrence and Stoker, Gerry (2001a) 'Trends in Public Participation: Part 1–Local Government Perspectives', *Public Administration*, 79 (1): 205–22.

Lowndes, Vivien, Pratchett, Lawrence and Stoker, Gerry (2001b) 'Trends in Public Participation: Part 2–Citizens' Perspectives', *Public Administration*, 79 (2): 445–55.

Marshall, T.H. (1964) 'Citizenship and Social Class', in *Class, Citizenship and Social Development: Essays*. New York: Doubleday. pp. 71–134.

Maynard-Moody, Steven and Musheno, Michael (2000) 'State Agent or Citizen Agent: Two Narratives of Discretion', *Journal of Public Administration Research and Theory*, 10 (2): 3–29.

Moore, Mark H. (1995) *Creating Public Value: Strategic Management in Government*. Cambridge, MA: Harvard University Press.

Mullard, Maurice, (1997) 'Discourses on Citizenship: The Challenge of Citizenship', in Maurice Mullard and Simon Lee (eds), *The Politics of Social Policy in Europe*. Cheltenham: Edward Elgar. pp. 237–57.

Osborne, David and Gaebler, Ted (1992) *Reinventing Government*. New York: Plume.

Prottas, Jeffrey Manditch (1979) *People-Processing*. Lexington, MA: Lexington Books.

Racine, David P. (1995) 'The Welfare State, Citizens, and Immersed Civil Servants', *Administration and Society*, 26 (4): 4–34.

Reich, Charles (1964) 'The New Property', *Yale Law Journal*, 72 (April): 733–87.

Rothstein, Bo (1996) *The Social Democratic State: The Swedish Model and the Bureaucratic Problem of Social Reforms*. Pittsburgh: University of Pittsburgh Press.

Rothstein, Bo (1998) 'The Universal Welfare State as a Social Dilemma', Unpublished paper.

Rowe, Michael, Kloos, Bret, Chinman, Matt, Davidson, Larry and Boyle Cross, Anne (2001) 'Homelessness, Mental Illness, and Citizenship', *Social Policy and Administration*, 35 (1): 14–31.

Rummery, Kirstein and Glendinning, Caroline (2000) 'Access to Services as a Civil and Social Rights Issue: The Role of Welfare Professionals in Regulating Access to and Commissioning Services for Disabled and Older People under New Labour', *Social Policy and Administration*, 34 (5): 529–50.

Sandfort, Jodi (2000) 'Moving Beyond Discretion and Outcomes: Examining Public Management from the Front Lines of the Welfare System', *Journal of Public Administration Research and Theory*, 10 (4): 729–56.

Schorr, Lisbeth B. (1997) *Common Purpose*. New York: Doubleday.

Seligman, Adam B. (1992) *The Idea of Civil Society*. New York: Free Press.

Sirianni, Carmen and Friedland, Lewis (2001) *Civic Innovation in America*. Berkeley, CA: University of California Press.

Smith, Mike and Beazley, Mike (2000) 'Progressive Regimes, Partnerships, and the Involvement of Local Communities: A Framework for Evaluation', *Public Administration*, 78 (4): 855–78.

Smith, Steven Rathgeb (1993) 'The New Politics of Contracting: Citizenship and the Nonprofit Role', in Helen Ingram and Steven Rathgeb Smith (eds), *Public Policy for Democracy*. Washington, DC: Brookings Institution. pp. 163–97.

Smith, Steven Rathgeb (2002) 'Social Services', in Lester M. Salamon (ed.), *The State of the Non-profit Sector*. Washington, DC: Brookings Institution. pp. 149–86.

Smith, Steven Rathgeb and Ingram, Helen (2002) 'Implications of Choice of Policy Tools for Democracy, Civic Capital and Citizenship', in Lester M. Salamon (ed.), *The Tools of Government*. New York: Oxford University Press. pp. 565–840.

Smith, Steven Rathgeb and Lipsky, Michael (1993) *Nonprofits for Hire: The Welfare State in the Age of Contracting*. Cambridge, MA: Harvard University Press.

Sosin, Michael R. (1986) *Private Benefits: Material Assistance in the Private Sector*. Orlando, FL: Academic Press.

Stivers, Camilla. (1990) 'The Public Agency as Polis: Active Citizenship in the Administrative State', *Administration and Society*, 22 (1): 86–105.

Stone, Deborah (1984) *The Disabled State*. Philadelphia: Temple University Press.

Stone, Deborah (1999) 'Care and Trembling', *The American Prospect*, 43 (March–April): 61–7.

Stone, Deborah (2000a) 'Rationing Compassion', *The American Prospect*, 11 (13): 16–17.

Stone, Deborah (2000b) 'Why We Need a Care Movement', *The Nation*, 13 March: 13–15.

Timney, Mary M. (1998) 'Overcoming Administrative Barriers to Citizen Participation: Citizens as Partners, Not Adversaries', in Cheryl Simrell King and Camilla Stivers (eds), *Government Is Us: Public Administration in an Anti-Government Era*, Thousand Oaks, CA: Sage. pp. 88–101.

Tocqueville, Alexis de (ed.) (1956) *Democracy in America*. New York: New American Library.

Turner, Bryan S. (1990) 'Outline of a Theory of Citizenship', *Sociology*, 24 (2): 189–217.

Vinzant, Janet Coble and Crothers, Lane (1998) *Street-Level Leadership: Discretion and Legitimacy in Front-Line Public Service*. Washington, DC: Georgetown University Press.

Waddington, P.A.J. (1999) *Policing Citizens: Authority and Rights*. London: UCL Press.

Weatherley, Richard (1979) *Reforming Special Education: From the State Level to the Street Level*. Cambridge, MA: MIT Press.

Whitaker, Gordon P. (1980) 'Coproduction: Citizen Participation in Service Delivery', *Public Administration Review*, 40 (3): 240–6.

Wilensky, Harold L. and Lebeaux, Charles N. (1958) *Industrial Society and Social Welfare*. Glencoe, IL: Free Press.

Wilson, James Q. (1978) *Varieties of Police Behavior: The Management of Law and Order in Eight Communities*. Cambridge, MA: Harvard University Press.

29

Electronic Government: A Revolution in Public Administration?

Helen Margetts

The potential for 'electronic government' or 'e-government' to transform public administration has been heralded at various points throughout the past half-century. Even by the 1960s and 1970s, as computers started to appear in government organizations, some public officials and commentators predicted that information technology would bring a revolution to public administration. As increasingly sophisticated information and communication technologies (ICTs) spread across all organizations during the 1980s and 1990s, politicians jostled to claim credit for 'information age government'. By the beginning of the twenty-first century, as use of the Internet became increasingly widespread, claims for the transformative power of ICTs became correspondingly enthusiastic. Earlier ICTs were largely internal to organizations, doing little to enhance interactions with citizens. But the widespread use of the Internet by both society and government seems to offer real possibilities for change in citizen–government relationships, just as new channels of communication and transaction have opened up new possibilities for the relationship between shops and banks and their customers in countries with high levels of Internet penetration.

This chapter briefly reviews the various approaches to analysing the impact of ICTs on public administration. Politicians' enthusiasm for ICTs has its source in a particular tradition of political thought: modernism. Computers and communications have long been cited as the key to bringing public administration up to date, just as domestic appliances modernize the home. They were viewed as a force for rationalization, as was Weberian bureaucracy in the first half of the twentieth century. The various approaches can be grouped according to their degree and direction of enthusiasm for the modernizing effect of ICTs, as hypermodernists, antimodernists and postmodernists. Alongside these commentaries lies mainstream public administration, which in general has underplayed or ignored the possible impact of ICTs. Fifty years after the first computers appeared in government, this chapter assesses the claims of these writers in light of the history of government ICTs. First, with respect to pre-Internet technologies, largely internal to public administration, and secondly, looking at web-based technologies which offer new opportunities for public agencies to communicate with citizens using new technologies. Both types of technology are relevant to the concept of e-government, which includes both 'providing public access via the Internet to Government services' as well as 'harnessing new technology to transform the internal efficiency of government departments' National Audit Office (NAO, 2002).

APPROACHES TO ICTS AND PUBLIC ADMINISTRATION

Working from the widely held premise that computers are a rationalizing tool, one possible role for ICTs in public administration would be to provide a strengthening of bureaucratic organization, to 'out-Weber Weber' as Christopher Hood once put it (Hood, 1994). For Weber, the road to modernity through rationality was facilitated by the development of bureaucracy.

Bureaucracy would allow the control of the world through calculation, the systematization of meaning and value into an overall consistent, ethical view (Kolb, 1986: 10). ICTs, at first glance, would appear to facilitate this modernization process still further. ICTs allow the formalization of rules and procedures and enhance the scope for increasing rationality into decision making. Ethical schemata are easier to implement using computers, for example the calculation of quality-adjusted life years in health care has become increasingly sophisticated. Long accepted problems of rational decision making such as 'bounded rationality' (Simon, 1955) can be tackled, as computers are used to simulate policy alternatives. The way that some writers have perceived the impact of ICTs is directly analogous to Weber's vision of administrative modernization: 'Informatization in public administration is a process of continued modernization' (Frissen, 1995: 8). It is in reaction to this perspective of ICTs as a modernizing force – either positive or negative – that most approaches to the phenomenon of ICTs are based and may be categorized.

Thus hypermodernists are technological utopians who see ICTs as the central enabling element of a utopian vision of public administration. A longstanding and popularly influential example is Alvin Toffler who in a trilogy extending over twenty years (Toffler, 1970, 1980, 1990) revelled in the notion of transition, transformation and revolution. *The Third Wave* would bring a new civilization with the electronics revolution at its technological base, peopled by 'information workers' in 'intelligent buildings' full of 'electronic offices', organized in networks rather than formal hierarchies. Political systems would not be able to cope with this wave of change and by 1990, Toffler claimed, governments would begin to 'bypass their hierarchies – further subverting bureaucratic power' (Toffler, 1990: 255). Management gurus followed Toffler in enthusiastically pronouncing the end of bureaucracy *per se*, with titles like *Intelligent Enterprise* (Quinn, 1992) and *The End of Bureaucracy and the Rise of the Intelligent Organisation* (Pinchot and Pinchot, 1994), based on the premise that technology would challenge the very basis of organizational theory. As use of the Internet rose steeply during the 1990s, this group of writers expanded to form a positive multitude, predicting the end of organizations, both private and public, that did not adapt radically to the Internet age (see for example, Lord, 2000). Politicians have been keen to follow this line of thought, seeing Internet-based technologies as a potential cheap and effective solution to long-standing administrative problems, with the potential to cover any manifesto for administrative reform with a modernist gloss. In the United States during the 1990s, when Al Gore was promising to replace 'industrial era bureaucracy' with 'information age government' as part of the 1994 National Performance Review, Alvin Toffler himself was in the pay of both the Democrats (Clinton and Gore) and the Republicans (Newt Gingrich). Belief in the ability of computers to empower citizens in relation to government led to a surprising element in Gingrich's programme – otherwise distinctive for the slashing of social welfare provision – that all citizens be given a laptop computer free. At the same time, in the UK, politicians of both Conservative and Labour parties were assuring voters that they were the 'British Al Gore' (Margetts, 1999: xiii). By 1997, an influential pamphlet by the head of Labour's Business Unit entitled *Information Age Government: Delivering the Blair Revolution* (Byrne, 1997), outlined a cornucopia of benefits to be gained from information technology and castigated the Civil Service for being 'quite unfit' to deliver the Prime Minister's vision of an 'information age' society.

In contrast, an 'antimodernist' stream of writing has seen computers as having an equally transformative but malign effect on public administration, bringing in the 'Control Revolution' (Beniger, 1991) or the 'Computer State' (Burnham, 1983), where massive databanks would be used as instruments of control. Beniger (1991: 388), for example, claimed that 'the progressive convergence of information processing and communications technologies in a single infrastructure of control is sustaining the "Control Revolution" – a concentration of abrupt changes in the technological and economic arrangements by which information is collected, stored and processed'. Other writers saw information technology bringing about the new Leviathan, 'integrating the state through the backdoor of information management' (Lenk, 1994: 313). Others predicted that computers would lead to a 'cyborg world' (Levidow and Robins, 1989) in which 'infotech systems promote new models of rationality, cognition and intelligence', or a 'military revolution' (Goure, 1993). Such views were founded on the pursuit of a logic of total control, both internal and external: 'The military information society involves internalizing a self-discipline, technologies of the self, in ways that come to be seen as normal, rational and reasonable' (Levidow and Robins, 1989: 8). Wright (1998) presented a 'worst case' scenario, where a 'range of unforeseen impacts are associated with the process of integrating these technologies into society's social political and cultural control systems', for example the 'militarization of the police and the para-militarization of the army as their roles, equipment and procedures begin to overlap' (Wright, 1998: 4). These views belong to a wider anti-utopian view that also has its roots in the Weberian tradition. Just as Weber feared unbridled bureaucratic domination, Orwell (1954) and Huxley (1932) warned of a rule of impersonal officialdom disastrously strengthened by technological advance. The human 'machine' of Weberian bureaucracy would be delivered first by systematization of human procedures, followed by the replacement of humans with automated machines.

Finally, ICTs have also caught the attention of another group of writers who viewed it as an essential element of postmodern society, fuelling equally radical changes in public administration. Frissen for example, argued that in a post-modernized public administration 'fragmentation will lead to an emancipation of the bureaucratic organization – beyond central control' (Frissen, 1995: 9). This enthusiastic welcoming of technology to public administration was echoed in other postmodernist analyses: 'where modernist organization was premised on technological determinism, postmodernist organization is premised on technological choices made possible through "de-dedicated" micro-electronics equipment' (Clegg, 1990: 181). These writers are in general optimistic about the influence of ICTs on public administration, seeing a strong increase in fluidity and flexibility where 'fragmentation will lead to an emancipation of the bureaucratic organization – beyond central control' and 'the pyramidal nature of public administration' changes into 'an archipelago of network configurations' (see Frissen, 1995, 1999). But more pessimistic postmodern observers have characterized the 'military information society' as postmodernist: 'current US Defense policy is creating a post-modern army of war machines, war managers and robotized warriors' (Gray, 1989: 44). In general, however, as with most postmodernist analyses, this group of commentators are stronger and more in agreement in their criticism of the modernist mainstream than on any outline of what a postmodern ICT-based public administration would look like.

In contrast to all the above, the vast majority of writers on public administration have ignored the widespread introduction of computers across government, appearing to regard ICTs as a neutral administrative tool, with little or no implications for public administration or policy. Most books on public administration have very little mention of computers or information technology and even textbooks ignore the phenomenon; see for example, Lynn and Wildavsky (1990) or Rhodes (1997), neither of which has any mention of computers, ICTs or the Internet in its indexes. Small groups of researchers – most notably the URBIS group at the University of California in Irvine in the United States, the Kassel group in Germany (see Lenk, 1992) and a European group based in the Netherlands (see Snellen, 1994 for a review) and the UK (see for example Bellamy and Taylor, 1998 or Pratchett, 1994) – have taken what might be called a 'critical modern' approach, carefully monitoring and recording the changes at work. But these groups of writers have tended to be somewhat 'ghettoized' within mainstream public administration. Even in the age of the 'dot.com' boom, when Internet trends would be the top story in almost every area of commerce and a vast range of edited collections appeared with the word 'virtual' or 'digital' in the title, books on public administration remained relatively impervious to the trend. Pollitt and Bouckaert (2000), for example, a comprehensive analysis of public administration across ten countries, offer only a couple of (disparaging) references to ICTs.

THE POLICY IMPACT OF ICTs

This belief that ICTs make no difference to public administration is challenged by the extent to which they are now embedded within all types of organization. In the period from the 1950s to the 2000s ICTs pervaded every corner of public administration across OECD countries, with real relevance for policy. There are few government offices without a computer, few administrative operations that do not rely on the processing by a complex network of ICTs. And ICTs now form a significant proportion of the budgets of government agencies. In the US expenditure on ICTs (including staff costs, consultancy, hardware and software) had reached around 6 per cent of the federal operating budget by the 1990s. In the UK, ICTs amounted to 11 per cent of running costs by 1995 (Margetts, 1999: 39–40).

ICTs can be shown to be policy critical. Margetts (1998, 1999) has shown how all the 'tools' of government policy identified by Hood (1983) – nodality, authority, treasure and organizational capacity – are now heavily reliant on ICTs. First, with respect to nodality – the extent to which government is at the centre of information and social networks – ICTs play a clear role, facilitating information channels both within government organizations and between government organizations, private sector companies, voluntary organizations and citizens. With respect to treasure – that is, money or 'fungible chattels' – all moneys processed within governmental organizations have since the 1960s been processed via computer systems. With respect to the legitimate authority that government has by virtue of being government, research suggests (Margetts, 1999) that authority wielding organizations have been among the most innovative. Police databases with massive search capacity have long facilitated a move towards more pre-emptive policing; more recently, widespread use of Closed Circuit Television (CCTV), DNA testing and the creation of searchable databases of DNA samples offer the potential to revolutionize policing strategies. In addition to the heavy reliance now placed upon them in all streams of government activity, ICTs, particularly in the area of law and order, open new policy windows. The electronic tagging of prisoners has made possible new policies, such as the early release of prisoners and curfew orders, which are forcing policy makers to re-evaluate traditional notions of punishment.

For the more general 'organizational capacity' of government, information systems have played a key role in replacing tranches of government bureaucracy; government organizations at the beginning of the twenty-first century can process more transactions more rapidly with less staff than they could before computers were introduced. The computer technologies of the 1970s, mainframe computers designed for heavy transaction loads were particularly well suited for taking over bureaucratic operations within the largest of government organizations processing large quantities of dealings with citizens, particularly those processing tax and social security. But these new technologies required new staff with different skills and have introduced new armies of technical specialists into government. In this sense, ICTs have brought a shift in resources from organizational capacity to 'organized expertise' (Dunleavy, 1994; Margetts, 1995; Dunleavy and Margetts, 2000). While traditionally government has marshalled its organizational resources through the operation of large-scale bureaucracies, now information technology is used by government to marshal other resources. Bureaucracy has traditionally been viewed as something that government organizations are 'good at', but now such organizations find themselves involved in large scale and complex ICT-based development tasks, not something that government has a reputation for being good at. The evident difficulty in the design, development and maintenance of information systems engenders a transfer from organizational capacity to organized expertise. All government bureaucracies must now maintain a division dedicated to the development of new technology-based projects, with new risks and new dangers.

As well as facilitating new and existing policies, ICTs can prevent policies being implemented, can constrain policy development and become a negative feature of public administration. The history of government computing in the UK is littered with high profile projects that have gone wrong and seriously hampered policy implementation. The introduction of computers into the UK social security agency involved a number of large-scale projects that ran over-budget, took longer than anticipated to implement and resulted in inadequate, inflexible and outdated systems. In 1998 the UK Passport Agency reached virtual collapse when a new system was introduced at the same time as a new policy requiring children under five to have their own passports was introduced, the resultant backlog brought the agency to virtual collapse. Throughout the second half of the 1990s, the Arthur Andersen company battled to replace the huge National Insurance system; the new index system failed to work for a year after the old system had been rendered non-operational. Even small agencies traditionally perceived as completely non-technical can be affected: in 1989, the UK Foreign and Commonwealth Office was severely incapacitated when its small accounting system crashed disastrously causing the Office to produce the most serious qualification of a department's accounts that the Comptroller and Auditor General had ever made (Margetts, 1999: 17). In the United States the history of government computing also includes failures in the most crucial of civilian agencies. In the 1970s, the US Social Security Administration experienced a major disaster which ground the agency to a halt in implementing a new system for Social Security Income and blackened the agency's reputation (and consequentially, Congressional funding) for managing technology over the next thirty years. The long-running series of projects to modernize the computer systems of the US Internal Revenue Service – Tax Systems Modernization – has absorbed spiralling budgets over twenty years with few tangible benefits and resulted in a tax system that is increasingly difficult to manage, with some parts of the system still dating back to the 1960s.

It is the problems in managing technology-based projects and the consequent need for organized expertise that has led to one of the key changes brought to public administration by ICTs – that of drawing into government a bewildering array of information technology experts, by now most usually in the form of huge global computer services providers. In the early days of computers, during the 1960s and 1970s, government organizations gained expertise in ICTs through employment of specialist staff or IT contractors on an individual basis. During the 1980s and 1990s, however, the trend was for contracts for IT expertise to become larger and larger. Particularly in the UK and the United States, great tranches of government work were contracted out in this way in the name of 'systems integration'. At the time of writing, almost all government departments and agencies are involved in a range of partnerships with large global private sector computer services providers. Some of these contracts represent major chunks of public expenditure: for example, the UK Inland Revenue's contract with Electronic Data Systems was worth £1 billion over 10 years when it was first signed in 1996 and £4 billion for the next ten years by the time contract re-tendering was considered in 2001 (KableDirect, November 2001). The companies that hold such contracts are major new players in public administration. And most of the major disasters with ICTs, some of which were mentioned above, have been linked with a significant partnership between a government agency and a major computer services provider.

The tendency towards private provision of ICTs in government has in some countries been both fuelled and shaped by New Public Management-style change, of which increased contracting and privatization is a key theme. In the UK, where NPM trends were particularly strong, and in the United States, where NPM rhetoric was used by the Reagan administration during the 1980s and during the second Clinton term in the 1990s (and in any case contracting out has been used as an administrative tool throughout the twentieth century), the vast majority of ICT-related tasks have been out-sourced. In other countries where NPM trends have been particularly strong, such as Australia and New Zealand, the US and UK patterns of oligopolistic computer services provision to government can also be observed (Dunleavy et al., 2001), with contracts showing a tendency to increase in size, with a concurrent increase in the size of companies able to tender for them. In the UK, research during 2000 showed that of the thirty-seven very large-scale government ICT contracts with individual values greater than £50 million covering the period 1990 to 2000, three companies (Electronic Data Systems, ICL and Siemens) held nearly 80 per cent of the contract value (Dunleavy et al., 2000). The

company Electronic Data Systems (EDS) has had particular success in winning UK government contracts, with a 1997 report produced by the US Embassy claiming that EDS had over 50 per cent of the total UK government IT services business while the government market research firm Kable suggested that this figure was 80 per cent (Dunleavy et al., 2000). In the United States, the market is less concentrated with the top four companies holding only around 20 per cent of major ICT contracts (Margetts, 1999; Dunleavy et al., 2002) but large global computer services providers have long been major players in both federal and state administrations. Garvey (1993), for example, has illustrated how the newer 'shadow bureaucracy' of 'beltway bandits' – largely ICT-based companies – operates along-side the more traditional 'formal bureaucracy' in Washington. In European countries outside the UK, NPM trends have been far less extreme and these countries have turned less to outsourcing to solve ICT problems. Where it is used, these countries have tended to adopt a different model of contracting, the so-called Rhineland model where contracts are smaller and based on a more consensual style.

Whatever the individual style of a country's contracting regime, computer services providers are major new policy actors in most administra-tions. Management of long-term ICT contract relationships and large-scale technology projects have become a permanent feature of contempo-rary public administration. Control of these major new players, many of them global companies with turnovers equivalent to the GDPs of small countries, will remain a continual challenge for government agencies of all kinds, with potential for such companies to influence policy innova-tion, shape policy development and import policy solutions across national boundaries (see Dunleavy, 1994; Margetts and Dunleavy, 1995).

SO WHO WAS RIGHT?

Although the policy-critical nature of ICTs chal-lenges the low profile accorded to them by public administration literature, the predictions of the hypermodernists have yet to be realized. For the hypermodernists, there have been many disasters and disappointments. There has been no overar-ching transformation of government through information technology that lends support to, for example, Toffler's claims that technology would bring the end of bureaucracy. The fact that ICT systems up to the 1990s were almost entirely internal to government organizations meant that they did little to change government–citizen relationships in the way that utopian modernists had hoped. Furthermore, the new risks and dangers inherent in the task of embarking upon large-scale, technology-based projects, unforeseen by hypermodernists, remain with government rather than appearing as a temporary 'glitch' in progress to a fully modernized state. Few would claim that the beginning of the twenty-first century saw 'the end of bureaucracy' and it is hard to discern the rise of 'the intelligent organization' from the experience of government agencies with ICTs.

The worst nightmares of the antimodernists also appear unfulfilled. As noted above, the authority-wielding agencies have been innovative in their use of technology. There remains potential for a 'control state', just as bureaucracy presented possibilities for totalitarian states of the past. Computer systems provide new opportunities for governments to take a government-wide approach, but such an approach would have been out of line with all recent administrative trends and, for example, in neither the United States nor the UK have government-wide databases emerged from fifty years of ICT development. The continual pressure to innovate, the opening up of new policy windows and the difficulty of controlling high technology projects means that technology seems to have introduced new irrationality as well as rationality into public administration. ICTs are revealed by various studies to be as much a control *problem* as a control *solution*. In general, ICT developments take place independently of each other, with transfers between systems remaining surprisingly limited. Furthermore, government holds no monopoly on technological innovation. Technologically sophisticated, control-wielding agencies encourage the tactics of the 'smart citizen', in turn necessitating further (and more difficult to attain) technological efforts from government agencies in a spiral of innovation. For example, as governments developed radar speed guns during the 1980s, companies started to market 'radar-gun detector devices', and so on. Authority-wielding agencies also find themselves under continual pressure to innovate in response to 'smart criminals'. Fingerprinting techniques transformed criminal detection when first developed, but became progressively less useful as criminals became aware of the necessity of wearing gloves or removing prints. DNA testing overcomes that problem – but already, the Human Genetics Commission is asking ministers to consider criminalizing the theft of DNA material, which could lead to criminals leaving false evidence at scenes of crime (*The Times*, 19 March 2002).

In general therefore there has been substantive change, but it has fulfilled neither the wildest dreams of the hypermodernists or the worst nightmares of the antimodernists. Up until the 1990s, this change was largely internal to public administration, part of the hidden world of government as bureaucracy. To citizens, it makes little difference whether the passport agency runs massive electronic databases or a large bureaucracy – except that when something goes wrong, it will probably be blamed on 'the computer system' rather than 'it's the rules'. And if the computer system is actually run by Electronic Data Systems rather than the UK Department of Employment, Work and Pensions or the US Social Security Administration, then citizens are unlikely to be made aware unless there is some high profile disaster. Until the 1990s, it was such disasters – the near total collapse of the UK Passport Agency in the summer of 1998 for example – rather than the clear benefits that ICTs have brought to government organizations that came to the attention of citizens.

THE INTERNET AND E-GOVERNMENT

The 1990s brought a new technological development with much greater potential to impact upon the citizen–government relationship – rapidly rising usage of the Internet across society, particularly in commerce – and a consequently higher profile for information technology in general, with ICTs being widely credited as a key driver of productivity and economic growth, particularly in the United States (see OECD, 2001a). Over 50 per cent of US citizens were using the Internet by 2001, while in Europe the Scandinavian countries lead Europe at around 55 per cent (OECD, 2001b: 77). In contrast to earlier technologies, the widespread use of the Internet offers more 'real' promise of transformation of the relationship between government and citizen. As noted above, earlier information technologies were largely internal, with few possibilities for external interactions, while Web-based technologies can open up organizations to external users. In the private sector, real transformation of some organizations relationship with their customers have taken place. Internet banking for example, was used by around 16 per cent of UK citizens by 2001 (Dunleavy and Margetts, 2002) and nearly 20 per cent of US citizens ordered goods or services over the Internet during 2000 (OECD, 2001a). New organizations with no shopfront opened up, such as the Amazon bookstore, which dashed to the frontiers of their markets (in terms of transaction volume if not in profits). Although the 'dot.com' crash of 2000 stilled the rush for Internet gold (and dampened political enthusiasm for e-government), there is no doubt that the Internet has proved a major new channel of communication by which increasing numbers of citizens are making transactions with a wide range of organizations.

Internet technologies are qualitatively different from earlier information technologies. As well as offering new potential for organizations to become externally facing, they lend themselves to different development styles. Private sector companies at the forefront of Web-based developments have found that such developments lend themselves to a 'build-and-learn' technique (Dunleavy and Margetts, 1999), whereby Web-based developments become part of a process of continual organizational learning and customers' reactions – for example, to new Web pages or facilities – can be quickly and continually assessed before further developments are made. This style contrasts with the 'big bang' approach applied to many of the large long-term computer projects noted above.

So how has public administration responded to this new challenge? At the height of the dot.com boom, politicians became particularly keen that government should maximize the potential of the new Internet technologies. Many countries introduced targets for the percentage of government services that would be available on the Internet. The US was the first, when as part of the 1994 National Performance Review Al Gore promised to provide all citizens with electronic access to government by 2000, by connecting every classroom, library, hospital and clinic to a national information infrastructure. In the UK in 1997 the then new prime minister Tony Blair pledged that by 2002 at least 25 per cent of all government interactions with citizens would be 'electronic'. By April 1999 the *Modernizing Government* White Paper put in place later targets of 50 per cent 'electronic' interactions by 2005 and 100 per cent by 2008 (see Dunleavy, Margetts, 1999, Parts 1 and 4) and this latter commitment was later brought forward to 2005. In Australia, also in 1997 the Prime Minister pledged that by the end of 2001 'all appropriate services' would be available on-line via the Internet.

In response to these targets and to increasing use of the Internet more generally, there has definitely been Internet driven change across government organizations, to varying degrees across and within governments. By 2002, most governments in OECD countries had developed central portals intending to offer citizens a coherent 'front-end' to government. Most government agencies now have websites which provide at least basic information about the agency and figures have grown rapidly in recent years. In the UK, for example, a survey for the National Audit Office showed that 81 per cent of government bodies (92 per cent of Whitehall departments) had a website by the end of 2001 compared with 60 per cent for a similar survey in 1999 (Dunleavy and Margetts, 1999, 2002). Most sites facilitate the e-mailing of officials with queries, basic information about the organization, the downloading of documents and accessing press releases and annual reports. Key civilian agencies in some countries are undertaking major percentages of transactions with citizens on-line. For example, in Australia by 2001 70 per cent of tax returns were being filed electronically and in the US, electronic filing had reached 23 per cent by 1999 (Dunleavy and Margetts, 1999). The Australian Department of Employment, Workplace Relations and Small Businesses runs a Web-based jobs placement service that has regularly been amongst the most heavily used Australian Web sites and offers both employers and employees a searchable database of nationwide details of vacancies updated daily. There have been some significant single agency developments in the UK, for example the 2001 census data provided for open access by the Public Records Office was tremendously popular – in fact, a victim of its own success, as early in 2002 the site had to be removed due to its failure to cope with heavy demand. In the UK, the displacing of major transaction loads for tax or social security has not reached the levels of the US or Australia, but between 1999 and 2001 the proportion of agencies with sites allowing users to fill in and submit forms on-line increased from one in seven to one in four (Dunleavy and Margetts, 1999, 2002).

Some such changes have led to a more open style of government where relationships between citizens and government have qualitatively changed. In the UK, a high proportion of government publications are now available free on line, in strong contrast with the pre-Internet era where they had to be purchased with difficulty and at significant expense from Her Majesty's Stationary Office. The HMSO resisted the change, but in an environment where so much Web content is free, their strict interpretation of copyright policy proved unsustainable. In

Australia for example, the website of the Australian tax office gives users some access to the organization's database of tax legislation, so that they can see on what basis decisions about their tax affairs have been made. In the Netherlands, the taxation authority has experimented with using the Web to encourage more widespread involvement in policy making. In January 2001, there was a change in the tax law and the first draft of the legislation was put on the Web before going to parliament. The taxation authority found themselves deluged with advice from tax consultants as to how to improve the draft law and those who wrote the law were impressed – the advice was good and the legislation much improved.

However, the brave intentions of the target regimes in most countries have proved problematic to follow. A report commissioned by the National Audit Office in 1999 (Dunleavy and Margetts, 1999) found that the UK government in particular was lagging behind the private sector. A second report two years later (Dunleavy and Margetts, 2002) noted an across the board improvement but it remained unlikely that the 2005 target for all services being available on the Internet would be attained and take-up levels were still extremely low. In fact, in spite of the clear potential of Web-based technologies, government organizations in countries with high Internet penetration rates have been in general slow, in comparison with the private sector, with voluntary organizations or with society in general, to capitalize on the possible advantages of the Internet (Margetts and Dunleavy, 2002). Ironically, among liberal democracies it is in some countries where public administration is less developed, such as Estonia and Lithuania, where government agencies have been more innovative in their use of Web-based technologies – possibly because they were able to leapfrog over some stages of technological development that occurred while these governments were still under the control of communist administrations and without access to newer technologies.

One possible explanation for the relatively slow development of e-government is that organizations' ability to manage Web-based technologies appears to be shaped by earlier experience with earlier ICTs. For this reason, the extent to which governments make use and benefit from Web-based technologies seems to be marked by the history of government computing. Cultural attitudes to technology engendered by previous bad experiences with IT projects or procurements can mean that organizations approach web development in a 'fatalist' way (Margetts and

Dunleavy, 2002). Previous experience of ICT projects that ran over budget, brought few costs savings or even failed to work altogether can lead to reluctance to invest in Web-based technologies. For example, many UK NHS managers were scared off entering into ICT contracts in the 1990s after a series of high-profile failures and became increasingly reluctant to spend even budgets already allocated. The poor reputation of NHS computing led to an extremely low Treasury threshold for ICT expenditure in the NHS, further exacerbating the problem. Such a background is unlikely to foster an environment in which managers explore possibilities for innovation via Web-based technologies. This barrier to e-government is ironic, because Web-based technologies tend to be cheaper and easier to develop than earlier technologies.

Another organizational response to previous bad experiences with IT can be a 'hands-off' approach by all staff outside the IT department, because they do not want to have their careers tainted through association with any more disasters. This response will tend to result in almost complete reliance on technical experts to deal with the problems presented by technology. In such an organization, a traditional style IT department will tend to dominate all the agency's technological developments – including e-government. This hangover from earlier management experience of IT is also unfortunate, because widespread private sector experience has shown that a traditional IT department can be the worst unit to lead an electronic service initiative – partly because such units have a large amount of intellectual capital invested in earlier technologies and may be resistant to the potential of Web-based technologies to render their existing expertise and training obsolete. Another approach can be to leave Web-based development to whichever computer services provider delivers other ICT developments to the organization – which can be equally problematic. Many of the big companies undertaking government contracts were slow to develop Web-based technologies themselves and have hampered those agencies dependent upon major partnerships in their attempts to develop Internet capability.

THE FUTURE OF E-GOVERNMENT

There is nothing inevitable about the interaction of government and technology and the future of Web-based government remains open. So will the Internet, finally, bring about the predictions of the hypermodernists, the antimodernists or the postmodernists? The most prevalent model across the IT industry for the development of electronic services in organizations is the 'stages model' (see Dunleavy and Margetts, 2002). Like the approaches to earlier ICTs discussed above, the stages model is also based on the modernist idea of progression towards some utopian ideal of e-government. It suggests that there is a natural progression from the most basic services – the provision of information and documentation on-line – to more advanced interactive facilities and transactions on-line – such as making and receiving payments – through to full 'account management' where a customer's account history is maintained, as in Internet banking. Translated to government, account management would represent an organization storing information about citizens' history of dealings with the agency. Some commentators have used this model to assess progress towards e-government across OECD countries (for example, Accenture, 2001) or at the local government level (SOC-ITM, 2001). The problem with this model is that there may be no reason why some agencies would need to implement, say, account management: it will depend, for example, upon the activities they undertake. Dunleavy and Margetts (2002) have developed an alternative model which presents a more realistic picture of how agencies might proceed, suggesting that between a basic Web-based services and full 'e-government' there are a variety of routes. e-publishing, interactive facilities, electronic transactions and full account management style can either co-exist or be developed into a full 'e-government' style of the agency and there is no automatic reason why government strategy should favour any one of these routes over others for all agencies. Instead each agency should ask: 'Given the type of organization that we are, and the kind of functions that we have, our fundamental mission and role, how far can we and should we move towards fully electronic or digital operations?' (Dunleavy and Margetts, 2002).

Variation across countries illustrates some of the possible futures for the development of e-government. Dunleavy and Margetts (2000) suggested a variety of scenarios for the 'Digital State', the beginnings of which can be identified as emerging in different countries. Variations may reflect concerted political commitment from the centre, in the form of a strongly resourced central target regime, for example. But variation will also depend upon the relationship between e-government initiatives and other characteristics of governmental administration, such as institutional patterns and the extent to which NPM type changes have been introduced. Singapore seems to be an example of the digital state in its strongest form, where e-government and NPM change reinforce each other. The small size and authoritarian governmental structures of Singapore facilitate an especially centralized approach in which citizen participation can be mandated (government measures to push citizens onto the Internet contributed to Internet penetration rates rising from 16 per cent in November 1999 to 53 per cent in March 2000.) and a 'strong vision' of electronic government (Lawson, 1998) pushed forward, unhindered by dissenting interests (Dunleavy and Margetts, 2000). It is in Singapore that you see the potential for implementation of the 'Control State' predicted by the antimodernists in the 1970s, but there seems more evidence that Web-based technologies are used for relentless pursuit of e-commerce.

In another scenario we might see the digital state actually replacing the New Public Management as a paradigm for contemporary public administration, in a more modest version of the hypermodernist utopia. In this scenario Web-based technologies become the central operating tool of the organization rather than a mere administrative add-on (Dunleavy and Margetts, 2000). With more developments towards a Web-based opening up of government agencies of the kind described above, we might see a new 'open-book' governance, with citizens more involved in public decisions and new forms of public accountability. In its most radical form, this type of Web-based change would involve drastic organizational change and re-engineering towards public organizations existing as the support mechanism for Web-based services: a government agency would 'become its web site' as one official from the Australian Tax Office put it (Dunleavy and Margetts, 2000). Democratic innovations such as electronic voting and deliberation would further involve citizens in policy-making.

In Britain, the United States and most European countries, however, neither of these two scenarios can yet be identified. In some, such as Germany at the federal level, there is little evidence of transformation, just as German public administration literature has in general ignored the phenomenon (see Lenk, 1994 as an exception). In the UK, there is an uneasy interaction between the relics of NPM-induced change and progress towards e-government. The logic of Web-based change works against the decentralizing and fragmenting tendencies of NPM

(Dunleavy and Margetts, 2000). Where NPM changes continue to be implemented at the same time as e-government initiatives, the two can work against each other. In the United States, an enormous proliferation of websites might also lead to 'a policy mess' (Dunleavy and Margetts, 2000), whereby government becomes more, rather than less confusing, in complete contrast to the rationalizing effect originally anticipated for ICTs. However, the new portal firstgov.gov has gone some way towards making it easier for citizens to find their way around the electronic offerings of the federal government and its usage figures, particularly in response to the terrorist attacks of September 11, 2001, have risen steeply since it was first introduced in 2001.

At the beginning of the twenty-first century, electronic government is a clear theme of public administration. There is no doubt that the presence of ICTs – both inside government and among society more generally – brings a continual source of change to public organizations. This continual pressure for innovation now felt by all government agencies challenges the absence of ICT issues from mainstream public administration. But the rationalizing power of ICTs, predicted by those commentators who have concentrated on ICTs, is less evident, either in terms of ending bureaucracy or in strengthening it disastrously. Even in the age of Internet and the dramatic new possibilities offered by Web-based technologies for transforming government–citizen and government–business relationships, the influence of ICTs remains unpredictable and uncertain with a range of viable scenarios for the future. In the sense that no modernist analysis seems to fit and ICTs remain as a continual source of uncertainty within public administration, perhaps the postmodernists were nearest to being right. It may be that to understand the relationships between public administration and ICTs we need a new approach which disregards the modernist assumption that government is embarked on a continuing process of rationalization, modernization and progress towards some paradigm of e-government but steers away from the wide abundance of 'postmodernisms' which have been used to 'try and shape, define, characterize and interpret the indeterminate, pluralistic, ever more globalized period in culture from 1945 on' (Bradbury, 1995: 766). Such an approach might be called 'ante-postmodernism', beyond modernism but before postmodernism. In the 'ante-postmodernist' era, ICTs are a vital and changing part of any organization, introducing new risks and new dangers but also new sources of creativity and innovation.

REFERENCES

Accenture (2001) e-Government Report. May 2001.

Bellamy, C. and Taylor, J. (1998) Governing in the Information Age. Buckingham: Open University Press.

Beniger, J. (1991) 'Information Society and Global Science', in C. Dunlop and R. Kling (eds), Computers and Controversy: Value Conflicts and Social Choices. London: Academic Press.

Bradbury, M. (1995) 'What was Post-Modernism? The Arts in and after the Cold War', International Affairs, 71 (4): October.

Burnham, D. (1983) The Rise of the Computer State. London: Weidenfeld and Nicolson.

Clegg, S. (1990) Modern Organizations Organization studies in the Postmodern World. London: Sage.

Dunleavy, P. (1994) 'The Globalization of Public Services Production: Can Government Be "Best in World"'?, Public Policy and Administration, 9, (2).

Dunleavy, P. and Margetts, H. (1999) Government on the Web. London: National Audit Office. HC 87.

Dunleavy, P. and Margetts, H. (2000) 'The Advent of Digital Government: Public Bureaucracies and the State in the Internet Age'. Paper to the Annual Conference of the American Political Science Association, Omni Shoreham Hotel, Washington, 4 September.

Dunleavy, P. and Margetts, H. (2002) Government on the Web II. HC764. London: National Audit Office.

Dunleavy, P., Margetts, H., Bastow, S. and Tinkler, J. (2000) 'The Digital State and Government–Business Relations in the Information Age'. Paper to the Annual Conference of the Political Studies Association of the UK, London School of Economics, April.

Dunleavy, P., Margetts, H., Bastow, S., Tinkler, J. and Yared, H. (2001) 'Policy Learning and Public Sector Information Technology: Contractual and E-government Changes in the UK, Australia and New Zealand'. Paper for the American Political Science Association's Annual Conference 2001, 28 August–1 September, Hilton Hotel, San Francisco.

Frissen, P. (1995) 'The Virtual State: Postmodernization, Informatization and Public Administration'. Paper to the Governance of Cyberspace Conference at University of Teeside, 12–13 April.

Frissen, P. (1999) Politics, Governance and Technology: A Postmodern Narrative on the Virtual State. Cheltenham: Edward Elgar.

Garvey, G. (1993) Facing the Bureaucracy: Living and Dying in a Public Agency. San Fransisco: Jossey Bass.

Goure, D. (1993) 'The Military-Technical Revolution', Washington Quarterly, 16 (4).

Gray, C. (1984) 'The Cyborg Soldier: The US Military and the Post-Modern Warrior', in L. Levidow and K. Robins (eds), Cyborg Worlds: The Military Information Society. London: Free Association Books.

Hood, C. (1983) The Tools of Government. London: Macmillan.

Hood, C. (1994) 'Economic Rationalism in Public Management', Explaining Economic Policy Reversals. Buckingham: Open University Press.

Huxley, A. (1932) *Brave New World: A Novel*. London: Chatto and Windus.

Kolb, D. (1986) *The Critique of Pure Modernity: Hegel, Heidegger and After*. London and Chicago: University of Chicago Press.

Lenk, K. (1992) 'Informatics and Public Administration: Towards a Research Programme'. Paper to the ESRC/PICT programme on ICTs in Public Administration, National Institute of Social Work, Tavistock Place, London, 12 March.

Lenk, K. (1994) 'Information Systems in Public Administration: From Research to Design', *Informatization and the Public Sector*, 3 (3/4).

Levidow, L. and Robins, K. (1989) 'Towards a Military Information Society?', in L. Levidow and K. Robins (eds), *Cyborg Worlds: the Military Information Society*. London: Free Association Books.

Lord, R. (2000) *The Net Effect*. London: Random House.

Lynn, N. and Wildavsky, A. (eds) (1990) *Public Administration: The State of the Discipline*. New Jersey: Chatham House.

Margetts, H. (1995) 'The Automated State', *Public Policy and Administration*, 10 (2).

Margetts, H. (1998) 'Computerising the Tools of Government', in I. Snellen and W. van de Donk (eds), *Public Administration in an Information Age*.: IOS Press.

Margetts, H. (1999) *Information Technology in Government: Britain and America*. London: Routledge.

Margetts, H. and Dunleavy, P. (1995) 'Public Services on the World Markets', *Missionary Government: Demos Quarterly*, (7): 30–32.

Margetts, H. and Dunleavy, P. (2002) 'Cultural Barriers to e-Government'. Paper to the National Audit Office at www.nao.gsi.gov.uk and www.governmentontheweb. org

National Audit Office (2002) *Better Public Services through e-Government*. London: NAO. HC704.

OECD (2001a) *OECD Science, Technology and Industry Scoreboard: Towards a Knowledge-based Economy*. Paris: OECD.

OECD (2001b) *OECD Science, Technology and Industry Outlook: Drivers of Growth: Information Technology, Innovation and Entrepreneurship*. Paris: OECD.

Orwell, G. (1954) *Nineteen-Eighty-Four*. Harmondsworth: Penguin.

Pinchot, G. and Pinchot, E. (1994) *The End of Bureaucracy and the Rise of the Intelligent Organization*. San Francisco: Berrett-Koehler Publishers.

Pollit, C. and Bouckaert, G. (2000) *Public Management Reform: A Comparative Analysis*. Oxford: Oxford University Press.

Pratchett, L. (1994) 'Open Systems and Closed Networks: Policy Networks and the Emergence of Open Systems in Local Government', *Public Administration*, 72 (1).

Quinn, J. (1992) *Intelligent Enterprise*. New York: Macmillan.

Rhodes, R. (1997) *Understanding Governance: Policy Networks, Governance, Reflexivity and Accountability*. Buckingham: Open University Press.

Simon, H. (1955) *Models of Man*. New York: Wiley.

Snellen, I. (1994) 'ICT: A Revolutionising Force in Public Administration?', *Informatization and the Public Sector*, 3 (3/4).

SOCITM (2001) *Local e-Government Now*. London, IDEA in conjunction with SOCITM.

Toffler, A. (1970) *Future Shock*. London: Pan Books.

Toffler, A. (1980a) *The Third Wave*. New York: Bantam Books.

Toffler, A. (1980b) *Power Shift*. New York: Bantam Books.

Wright, S. (1998) *An Appraisal of Technologies of Political Control*. Luxembourg: Directorate General for Research, European Parliament.

BUDGETING AND FINANCE

Introduction

Frans K.M. van Nispen

THE CALL FOR A BUDGETARY THEORY

The appeal of V.O. Key for a budgetary theory is a landmark in interest in public budgeting in modern history. Key clearly referred to a *normative* theory, raising the question: 'On what basis shall it be decided to allocate X dollars to activity A instead of activity B?' (Key, 1940/1978: 20). Early efforts to develop such a theory failed before Aaron Wildavsky took over the relay baton, issuing the first edition of his seminal *The Politics of the Budgetary Process*, which changed the budgetary landscape almost completely.[1] He argued that the allocation of scarce resources is not a matter of arithmetics or calculation, but a matter of power. Furthermore, he claimed that the concept of incrementalism offered both the best description of and prescription to for the budget process, introducing such now common words as the 'base' and 'fair share' into the vocabulary of budget watchers (Wildavsky, 1964).[2] Soon, incrementalism became the dominant theory of public budgeting in America and, strangely enough, also in Europe, where the power of the purse is with the executive rather than the legislative branch of government. Moreover, empirical support was at best mixed, if not to say weak (LeLoup, 1978; Rubin, 1988).

The incremental nature of the budget was further challenged in the period of economic decline in the 1980s due to the oil crises. It turned out that decrementalism is not simply the mirror image of incrementalism, since the base is under attack (Schick, 1983: 23). The various interest groups and stakeholders will fight the spending cuts, giving the budget process a highly political profile. The traditional way of budgeting – across-the-board cuts[3] – did not provide much relief, requiring more targeted spending cuts. Consequently, micro-budgeting was counterbalanced by macro-budgeting (LeLoup, 1988), setting norms for the reduction of the budget deficit and/or public expenditures, changing the rules of the game and this is noteworthy, changing the relative strengths of the players of the game.[4] The advocates suddenly faced strong guardians, playing down the upward pressure on the budget. The success and failure of these budgetary reforms and their predecessors, like the Planning, Programming, Budgeting System (PPBS) and Zero-Base Budgeting (ZBB), has gained much more attention than the design of a grounded theory. Unfortunately, we have to conclude that our insight into the process of public budgeting and cut-back management is still anecdotal and fragmented (Van Nispen, 1993), though we know a lot more than Valdimer Key when he issued his call for a budgetary theory.

THE BATTLE ON THE BALANCED BUDGET

The attempt to balance the budget is still relatively young, though James Savage has argued that the idea of balance is deeply rooted in American history (Savage, 1988). In the mid-1980s the GRH Amendment (1985), creating the sequestration procedure, prepared the ground for a reduction of the budget deficit. The impact may have been modest, but it is quite clear that the more effective spending caps of the Budget Enforcement Act (of 1990) (BEA) would not have passed without the GRH Amendment. The movement only became serious when the budget became an issue in the mid-term elections during the first Clinton administration (1994). The *constitutional* amendment, as promoted by the Noble Prize winner James Buchanan, may have failed, but both parties reached a *statutory* arrangement to balance the budget (Buchanan, 1995).

A few years later the European countries followed when the heads of state came to terms about a target for the budget deficit and a procedure for the reduction of excessive budget deficits at the Maastricht summit (1991). The reference value as one of the standards for qualification for the Economic and Monetary Union (EMU)[5] was first set at 3 per cent of GDP and later, at the Amsterdam summit (1997) reinforced to a *'budgetary position close to balance or in surplus'*. In five out of twelve EMU countries the revenues now outnumber the outlays. The same is true for the three non-EMU countries. The overall figure for the EU as a whole is slightly below zero (that is, in deficit).

Many differences can be identified, but the similarities between the American and European case are striking: in America the Republican party tried to amend the constitution; in Europe the heads of state changed the treaty. In both cases limits have been imposed on the budget deficit (Anderson, 1999). Besides, new procedures have been established for the reduction of the budget deficit and, even more important, the budget deficit made way for a budget surplus, mainly thanks to the recovery of the world economy. Finally, on both sides of the Atlantic a dispute has been going on about the utilization of the budget surplus for current priorities or for a reduction of the public debt, and as such for the retirement of the Baby Boomer generation.[6] It seems apt to point out that, as Bernard Pitsvada has stated correctly (1996: 221), there is no simple device to cut the Gordian knot between the demands for guns and for butter.

ORGANIZATION OF THIS SECTION

The first chapter in this section, by John Mikesell, deals with the revenue side of the budget. He raises four basic questions that each government, particularly a government of a developing country or one in transition, has to answer in the design or redesign of their system of taxation and their revenue base. He argues that governments miss opportunities to pursue more effective and efficient alternatives than those represented by the status quo by assuming that revenue policies will not change.

In the following chapter Mark Hallerberg looks at the changing role of institutions, and more precisely at rules to deal with the principal–agent problem, moral hazard and common pool resources, using empirical data collected for a report commissioned by the Dutch Minister of Finance about the European member states. He concludes that the selection and the effectiveness of institutions may be affected by the characteristics of the political system.

Rita Hilton and Phil Joyce take a historical angle in their chapter, looking at the current revival of performance budgeting or rather performance-informed budgeting. A survey of OECD countries shows that a lot is going on in the field, but that might only be lip service. The authors identify five critical factors, notably that participants must have incentives to use performance information.

The final chapter is about the latest trend in budgeting, and has to do with accrual budgeting. It has its roots in accounting and control rather than in budgeting. The ins and outs are discussed by Leonard Kok, drawing on the evidence of a survey of the OECD member countries, recording a growing interest. However, one may question the utility since only a small portion of the budget is applicable for accrual budgeting.

NOTES

1 It is hard to find a book on public budgeting without reference to his work.
2 In all fairness, I should note Verne B. Lewis already mentioned incrementalism in his contribution to (the discussion about) a budgetary theory (Lewis, 1952).
3 The sequestration introduced by the Gramm–Rudman–Hollings (GRH) Amendment in the United States was built upon automatic across-the-board cuts.
4 The incoming minister of Finance, Zalm, successfully launched a norm, named after him, to curb public spending at the start of the so-called Purple Coalition in the Netherlands (1994).
5 The other criteria being participation in the Exchange Rate Mechanism for more than two years and the reduction of inflation rates, interest rates and the public debt.
6 The dispute has faded away as snow under the sun, at least temporarily, since the terrorist attacks on the World Trade Center in New York and the Pentagon in Washington.

REFERENCES

Anderson, Barry (1999) *Budgeting in a Surplus Environment*. OECD/PUMA/SBO 1999/3/Final. Paris: OECD.

Buchanan, James M. (1995) 'Clarifying Confusion about the Balanced Budget Amendment'. Paper presented at a conference of the National Taxpayers Association, Chrystal City, Virginia, 22 May.

Key, Valdimer O., Jr (1940) 'The Lack of a Budgetary Theory', *American Political Science Review*, pp. 1137–44, reprinted in Albert C. Hyde and Jay M. Shafritz (eds) (1978) *Government Budgeting: Theory, Process, Politics*. Oak Park, IL: Moore Publishing. pp. 19–24.

LeLoup, Lance T. (1988) 'From Microbudgeting to Macrobudgeting: Evolution in Theory and Practice', in Irene S. Rubin (ed.) (1988) *New Directions in Budget Theory* [wrongly titled *Budget History*]. New York: State University of New York Press.

LeLoup, Lance T. (1978) 'The Myth of Incrementalism: Analytic Choices in Budgetary Theory', *Polity*, 10 (4): 488–509.

Lewis, Verne B. (1952) 'Toward a Theory of Budgeting', *Public Administration Review*, 12 (1): 42–54.

Pitsvada, Bernard T. (1996) 'A Call for Budget Reform', *Policy Sciences*, 29 (3): 213–26.

Rubin, Irene S. (ed.) (1988) *New Directions in Budget Theory* [wrongly titled *Budget History*]. New York: State University of New York Press.

Savage, James D. (1988) *Balanced Budgets and American Politics*. Ithaca, NY/London: Cornell University Press.

Schick, Allen (1983) 'Incremental Budgeting in a Decremental Age', *Policy Sciences*, 16 (1): 1–25.

Van Nispen, Frans K.M. (1993) *Het dossier Heroverweging* [The Reconsideration Files]. Delft: Eburon.

Wildavsky, Aaron (1964) *The Politics of the Budgetary Process*. Boston, MA: Little, Brown.

30

Critical Choices for Design and Operation of Public Revenue Systems

John L. Mikesell

Taxation is at the heart of democratic government in a modern market economy. Such a government requires resources to deliver services decided upon by representatives of the people and these resources must be purchased from private owners on the open market, not commandeered in the fashion of feudal lords or modern dictators. Those purchases require money and, although national governments have the power of seigniorage, money creation usually represents an economically unacceptable option. The history of horrendous inflation generated by uncontrolled money creation as a means of finance – the American Confederate States, post-First World War Germany, the countries of the former Soviet Union in the early transition period, even recently in Turkey, among the more infamous episodes – demonstrate the economic disaster that stems from its use as a tool of finance.[1] Neither will the money come from sales of basic government services (primary and secondary education, public safety, redistributive and safety net, etc.); these public goods are such that attempting to finance them from their sales will lead to underprovision of those services and an undermining of the civil society that the government is responsible for maintaining.[2] With other options generally unavailable, a government must resort to the ultimate and distinguishing power of the sovereign – the coercive power of taxation. Hence, taxation is the elemental power of government in a market democracy which distinguishes government from the ordinary, beneficially inclined nonprofit organization and from proprietary enterprises, and is the favored free market tool for government finance – not seizure, not seigniorage and not sales. Taxation policies establish who pays for

government services and whether desired public services can be afforded.

This tool of free market government finance must be used with extreme care: United States Chief Justice John Marshall properly observed that 'the power to tax involves the power to destroy'.[3] Nevertheless, it is the purpose of the tax system to harm the private economy – the system has not done its necessary job if it does not move resources from private use to public use. The concern for tax policy is damage control – how can resources be moved to valuable public use with least collateral damage to society and the private economy? This is the central challenge of tax policy and its administration in all market-oriented democracies. It also represents a crucial test for nations undergoing transition from central plan to market, because when boundaries are drawn between public and private ownership, the government then requires a tax system to finance the purchase of resources required for the delivery of government services.

The revenue problem is not simply that of ensuring that governments have sufficient revenue capacity to finance their service responsibilities. It is the problem of *how* that revenue is to be raised, in terms both of structure (the set of laws establishing tax liability) and collection (the mix of administrative procedures and compliance responsibilities that link the tax structure to revenue production). In developing such a system, a nation faces four critical decisions. These decisions are:

1   Selection of tax bases: the choice of taxes will establish the distribution of the cost of government services across the private economy and, along with the structure of the

tax applied to each base, the incentive effects of the revenue system.

2 Degree of fiscal autonomy: the determination as to what government or governments will be responsible for adopting taxes and determining their rates and structures, regardless of whether the adopting government retains collections or transfers them to other governments.

3 Degree of administrative autonomy: the decision on administration establishes what governments will collect taxes, regardless of what unit levies them.

4 Extent of co-production in tax collection: the co-production decision determines the distribution of responsibilities between tax authorities and taxpayers in revenue generation. Each represents a distinct planning choice and the best options for a government may change with economic, political, social, technological, or legal developments.

These decisions are, of course, not made every year; the pattern in each nation at any point in time is normally the product of legal, administrative, economic and social choices made over many years. When countries are undergoing major transformation and transition, however, as has been the case recently in South Africa and in the countries of the former Soviet Union, all these revenue system choices are on the table.[4] Moreover, as mature democracies work through the global wave of decentralization and privatization, they too must recognize the alternative revenue system options available to them and not assume that the historic choices that have been made are necessarily the only or the optimal alternatives for financing government. While recent practice is the best empirical predictor of current revenue system practices in a country, that does not mean that other structures are unthinkable, unworkable, or contrary to the best interests of the population.[5] Hence it is useful and appropriate to examine this infrequently examined set of revenue system alternatives.

THE SELECTION OF REVENUE BASES

Once lawmakers have established how big the government will be, they must decide how to distribute its cost across private entities. This question of 'Who pays?' is one of the most difficult ones that government faces because payment of taxes is not pleasant.[6] Some government services can be sold and a rational scheme for selling goods and services that benefit only a few, easily identifiable businesses or individuals should be part of any government's revenue system. That prevents subsidization of the few by the many and preserves the capacity of the general tax system to support broad public goods. However, it is not reasonable to expect general purpose governments in even countries most devoted to use of free exchange for resource allocation to support a preponderance of their services through charge finance for two reasons. First, it is not possible to identify direct beneficiaries of many basic public services – national security, the judicial system, public safety, basic education, public health etc. – with the degree of precision needed to calculate a tax bill; the extent of 'publicness' or benefit externality is too great. Second, many government services are intended to redistribute from affluent to the less well off, so charging beneficiaries would defeat the purpose of the program. Nevertheless, few governments fully exploit the revenue potential of charges, often out of the political desire to protect vulnerable segments of society for paying for services, even though that means giving away much more of the service to the affluent than the poor would ever consume.

General purpose governments rely on tax revenue to support the services they provide. The principal tax alternatives, following the classification of the International Monetary Fund, are:

1 Goods and services taxes, either selectively (for example, excises on tobacco products) or generally (as with retail sales or value added taxes).

2 Income taxes (individual and corporate).

3 Social insurance contributions (collected from employer or employee or both and usually based on payroll or employment) and payroll taxes.

4 Property taxes (recurrent taxes on property or wealth and taxes on property transfer).

5 Taxes on international trade (duties on import or export of goods or services).

The alternatives chosen by the government determine the distribution of governmental cost across taxpayers – for instance, heavy reliance on the consumption base distributes the cost of government differently than would heavy reliance on wealth. Each base has its own economic, social and political limitations and adverse effects generally are magnified as exploitation of any base is greater. Consequently, most governments resort to a mixture of the various bases, rather than relying exclusively on a single base. Diversity spreads the risk in economic downturn and reduces the draw placed on any base. However, spreading the cost of government over several bases also contributes to opacity about the true cost of government, thereby complicating responsive governance and providing political cover for lawmakers.

Devising and reforming revenue systems presents difficult challenges for any democratic government because the tax paid by an individual or business typically has no impact on the type or amount of government service that the individual or business receives. Each entity would prefer taxes paid by others – and that creates great political conflict. Decisions about the tax base determine which sectors of the private economy will bear the cost of government services, what production and consumption incentives will emerge from application of the tax system, how revenue production will vary with changes in the economy, and how much revenue will be lost by the cost of its collection.

Governments choose different taxes in their quest for revenue. Tables 30.1 and 30.2 show the extent to which governments distribute governmental cost across the alternative tax bases. Table 30.1 presents data for the high-income countries of the Organization for Economic Co-operation and Development and Table 30.2 presents comparable data for a group of larger developing countries (those with gross domestic product over $100 billion at purchasing power parity in 1999). Both within and across these groups it is apparent that countries employ different tax mixtures for support of their governments.

Several patterns appear in these tables. First, governments in the more developed countries tend to rely heavily on taxes on income and on payrolls (including social security contributions). On average, these countries collect around 60 per cent of their tax revenue from such taxes; only Finland, Greece, Iceland and Spain do not rely on these taxes for at least half of their tax revenue. Japan, Sweden, Switzerland and the United States raise more than 70 per cent of their tax revenue from these taxes. The mean for the developing group is only 41 per cent; only eight (the Czech Republic, Hungary, Indonesia, Poland, the Russian Federation, the Slovak Republic and South Africa) collect as much as half their revenue from such taxes.

Second, governments in developing countries rely on taxes on domestic goods and services and on international trade. The developing countries raise roughly half their tax revenue from the taxes on trade (domestic and international). Only Algeria, Argentina and the Czech Republic do not raise at least one-third of their revenue from these sources. Eight countries

(Chile, China, Morocco, Peru, Thailand, Venezuela and Vietnam) collect more than 60 per cent of their revenue from them. The mean is only 31.4 per cent for the developed group; only Finland and Greece collect as much as half their revenue from such taxes. The difference is particularly striking in regard to international trade taxes: the median for the high-income OECD countries is less than 1 per cent of total revenue, against 8 per cent for the developing group.

Greater reliance on taxes on goods and services, that is, consumption taxation, has been an international trend of the past quarter-century. Among members of the OECD, revenue from consumption taxes has increased by four percentage points as a share of gross domestic product. Much of the increase is the result of adoption of national value added taxes. However, the United States, one of the few countries in the world and the only OECD member with no value added tax, shows no inclination toward such a tax. The desire to integrate with the European Community induced countries of the former Soviet bloc to adopt value added taxes, at least in rudimentary forms, because such taxes are a condition for membership.[7] Among the countries listed in Tables 30.1 and 30.2, only the United States, Canada and the Russian Federation levy a general consumption tax other than the value added tax; lower tier governments in each of these countries levy retail sales taxes.[8]

Third, governments in the high-income OECD countries collect much more of their total tax revenue from payroll and social insurance taxes than do the developing countries, with comparable medians of 23.8 per cent and 1.58 per cent. Social insurance programs are not well developed in the latter group, thus explaining much of the difference. However, the share is less than 5 per cent in some high income countries (Australia, Denmark, Greece, Iceland, New Zealand and Spain), largely because of choices made in these countries in regard to finance or extent of social insurance programs. Among the developing countries, reliance on these taxes is above 20 per cent in Brazil, the Czech Republic, Hungary, Poland, Russia and the Slovak Republic.

Fourth, taxes on property contribute a relatively small share of total tax revenue for each group. However, the median for the high income group – 4.82 per cent – is more than double that of the developing country group – 2.07 per cent. The property tax share is above 10 per cent in Canada, Spain, the United Kingdom and the United States, generally because local governments rely upon it as their means for fiscal autonomy.

Table 30.1 *Tax systems of high income members of the OECD (percentage of total tax revenue from each tax base)*

Country (year of data)	Income	Social security contributions	Income plus social security	Goods and services	International trade	Goods and services plus international trade	Property	Other
Australia (98)	58.30	1.97	60.27	26.54	2.23	28.77	6.04	4.93
Austria (97)	29.42	37.38	66.80	28.54	0.29	28.84	1.37	2.99
Belgium (97)	36.86	32.24	69.10	27.98	0.00	27.98	2.92	0.00
Canada (95)	46.19	14.36	60.55	22.45	1.02	23.47	10.58	5.39
Denmark (95)	60.52	3.57	64.09	32.00	0.04	32.04	3.46	0.42
Finland (97) (C)	33.83	12.57	46.40	50.96	0.00	50.96	2.45	0.19
France (97)	20.34	41.11	61.45	28.43	0.00	28.43	5.78	4.34
Germany	28.56	40.91	69.48	27.47	0.00	27.47	3.03	0.02
Greece (98)	32.76	2.27	35.03	56.81	0.07	56.87	4.51	3.59
Iceland (97)	37.26	8.30	45.56	43.98	1.06	45.04	7.32	2.07
Ireland (96)	41.88	14.89	56.77	38.34	0.00	38.34	4.89	0.00
Italy (98) (C)	32.44	33.34	65.77	30.98	0.18	31.17	1.98	1.08
Japan (93) (C)	43.07	31.53	74.61	17.18	1.48	18.67	4.82	1.91
Luxembourg (97)	39.30	24.79	64.09	25.78	0.00	25.78	7.27	2.86
Netherlands (97)	25.51	42.27	67.78	23.73	0.00	23.73	4.48	4.01
New Zealand (98)	62.21	1.01	63.21	27.89	2.46	30.35	5.95	0.49
Norway (97)	38.69	21.24	59.93	36.81	0.54	37.34	2.72	0.00
Portugal	29.68	26.78	56.46	39.14	0.00	39.15	1.92	2.48
Spain (96)	15.59	0.01	15.59	39.58	0.00	39.58	40.25	4.57
Sweden (98)	43.12	31.23	74.34	21.67	0.05	21.73	3.83	0.10
Switzerland (97)	36.63	37.26	73.89	17.67	0.73	18.40	7.71	0.00
UK (98)	39.48	17.81	57.30	31.79	0.00	31.79	10.89	0.02
US (97)	48.67	23.82	72.49	15.91	0.81	16.71	10.80	0.00
Median	37.26	23.82	63.21	28.43	0.05	28.84	4.82	1.08
Mean	38.27	21.77	60.04	30.94	0.48	31.42	6.74	1.80

C: Central government only; local tax revenue not disaggregated by type of tax.

Source: International Monetary Fund (1999)

Table 30.2 *Tax systems of economically larger developing countries (percentage of total tax revenue from each tax base)*

Country (year of data)	Income	Social security contributions	Income plus social security	Goods and services	International trade	Goods and services plus international trade	Property	Other
Algeria (96)	71.64	0.00	71.64	10.94	16.25	27.19	0.00	1.16
Argentina (97)	18.70	17.66	36.36	27.82	4.88	32.71	5.50	25.44
Brazil (94)	12.45	33.51	45.95	49.76	1.79	51.55	1.61	0.88
Chile (98)	20.47	7.10	27.57	55.47	8.76	64.24	3.58	4.61
China (97)	15.64	0.00	15.64	74.19	3.86	78.05	1.89	4.42
Columbia (98)	41.21	0.00	41.21	47.54	11.11	58.65	0.00	0.14
Czech R (98)	24.68	40.84	65.52	30.82	2.07	32.89	1.57	0.02
Egypt (97)	34.37	0.00	34.37	27.24	19.93	47.17	1.27	17.20
Hungary (98)	24.43	30.15	54.58	38.48	3.68	42.16	2.22	1.03
India (96)	21.38	0.00	21.38	53.52	21.27	74.78	0.52	3.32
Indonesia (93)	57.01	0.00	57.01	31.76	5.95	37.71	4.20	1.08
Korea (93)	30.97	10.84	41.82	39.08	7.39	46.47	2.03	9.69
Malaysia (97) (CR)	43.28	1.46	44.74	32.04	15.05	47.09	2.60	5.57
Mexico (97)	27.50	10.99	38.48	53.39	3.44	56.83	1.52	3.16
Morocco (95)	23.67	8.15	31.82	46.90	17.64	64.54	2.41	1.22
Pakistan (99)	27.82	0.00	27.82	35.32	16.08	51.41	1.56	19.21
Peru (98) (C)	24.47	1.56	26.03	59.41	11.37	70.78	0.00	3.18
Philippines (92)	32.38	0.00	32.38	30.58	31.71	62.30	2.02	3.30
Poland (98)	30.73	29.97	60.71	33.09	3.06	36.15	3.10	0.04
Russia (95)	32.61	20.12	52.73	32.23	5.97	38.20	4.26	4.82
Slovak R (98)	28.33	30.68	59.01	32.95	5.65	38.60	2.39	0.00
South Africa (98)	56.30	1.59	57.89	34.96	0.25	35.21	6.13	0.77
Thailand (97)	33.35	1.58	34.93	49.66	12.70	62.36	2.12	0.59
Turkey	41.23	0.00	41.23	49.51	2.67	52.18	2.53	4.05
Venezuela (98)	29.12	5.30	34.42	50.80	14.59	65.39	0.19	0.00
Vietnam (99)	23.54	0.00	23.54	38.43	28.98	67.41	8.18	0.87
Median	28.73	1.58	39.84	38.46	8.08	51.48	2.07	2.19
Mean	31.82	9.67	41.49	41.00	10.62	51.62	2.44	4.45

CR: Central and regional. No tax breakdowns available for local.

C: Central. No tax breakdowns for regional or local.

Note: The Czech Republic, Hungary, Korea, Mexico, Poland, the Slovak Republic, and Turkey are members of the Organization for Economic Co-operation and Development.

Source: International Monetary Fund (1999)

Finally, no single tax system seems to fit all countries, as shown by the considerable differences in tax-by-tax reliance within both developed and developing countries. The pattern is the result of a complex interplay of historical precedents (there is an adage that 'an old tax is a good tax'), economic opportunities, public decisions about the equitable basis for distributing governmental cost, and other factors.

REVENUE AUTONOMY

Which levels of government may tax? Will governments be expected to raise the revenue that they spend or will they rely on revenues transferred to them by other levels of government? A system that assigns significant taxing authority to regional or local government affords these governments greater flexibility for response to the interests of their citizenry and places on them much greater accountability and responsibility than does a system in which those governments spend revenue raised by others. Furthermore, voters are likely to hold their governments more closely accountable when there is a close link between money spent and taxes to be paid, assuming that the adopted taxes are visible to voters, substantial enough to be economically meaningful, and cannot be easily exported outside the jurisdiction. Of course, politicians prefer that others levy the taxes or, if they must tax, that the visible burden on their voters be minimized; neither improves the efficiency of the government sector because they conceal the true cost of service provision. To operate as if resources are costless will not yield sound public choices.

It may be argued that the principle of subsidiarity should apply in assignment of tax options among levels of government. In other words, discretionary revenue sources should be assigned to the lowest feasible level of government because satisfactory subnational options are few. In general, subnational government taxes should apply to tax bases that are not highly unstable, are not extremely mobile and are not so narrow as to require a high rate to yield meaningful revenue. However, higher tiers of government usually control what taxes regional or local government may levy and often retain the best options for themselves.[9] As Bird (2000: 2069) points out, the standard model of tax assignment 'assigns most productive revenue sources to the central government.' Local governments are frequently left with real property taxes, always politically unpopular, and user charges, a source with limited yield potential (Bahl and Linn, 1992; Fisher, 1996; Messere, 2000).

Table 30.3 shows how countries in the industrialized and developing groups distribute tax levying power by presenting the percentage of all tax collections in the country that the central government receives. The range is substantial. For instance, more than 90 per cent of tax collections are central in Ireland, Luxembourg, the Netherlands, New Zealand, Portugal, the United Kingdom, Chile, Hungary, Indonesia, Malaysia, Peru, the Philippines, Poland, the Slovak Republic, South Africa and Thailand. This means that any significant government service responsibility decentralized to local (or regional) government will need to be supported by central government transfers, not regional or local tax effort. However, in other countries regional and local governments raise a significant share of all taxes collected. These countries provide greater fiscal autonomy to subnational governments, even though those governments may still operate within considerable fiscal limits.[10]

Countries organized as federal states typically raise a smaller percentage of tax collections at the central level than do unitary states. Even among federal states there is considerable variation, with Australia, Austria, and Mexico, for example, raising around 80 per cent of tax revenue at the central level, a considerably higher share than in some unitary states in Scandinavia, while the central share is only 50 per cent in Canada. In Germany, federalism is strictly limited to the expenditure side of the budget; a single German state has no competence to alter any tax rate, making revenue generation entirely a national concern and preventing any tax competition between the states (Kirschgasser and Pommerehne, 1997). Obviously, the assignment of taxing authority among tiers of government is not rigidly linked to the federal/unitary decision. Federal states like Germany, Russia and Australia concentrate revenue generation at the central level, then support subnational government operations through transfers; federal states like the United States and Canada give subnational units greater responsibility for raising the money they spend. Similarly, some unitary states give local governments taxing authority for partial support of services they provide.

Revenue autonomy has been accommodated through mixes of three administrative models, presented here in increasing order of lower-tier discretion provided. First, the system may be one of tax surcharges (piggybacking): governments may levy their own rate on a centrally determined and centrally administered tax base. The

Table 30.3 *Distribution of tax revenue to central government in selected industrialized and developing countries (percentage of total tax revenue)*

Country (year of data)	Central government
Industrialized	
Australia (98)	77.4
Austria	79.8
Belgium (97)	95.0
Canada (95)	48.9
Denmark (95)	68.5
Finland (97) (C)	72.8
France (97)	89.2
Germany (96)	70.7
Iceland (97)	76.6
Ireland (96)	97.7
Italy (98) (C)	88.5
Luxembourg (97)	94.1
Netherlands (97)	95.9
New Zealand (98)	93.7
Norway (97)	81.3
Portugal	96.3
Spain (96)	85.7
Sweden (98)	68.2
Switzerland (97)	64.5
UK (98)	96.1
US (97)	67.8
Larger developing countries	
Argentina (97)	58.9
Brazil (94)	68.7
Chile (98)	92.2
China (97)	51.4
Czech R (98)	87.3
Hungary (98)	90.1
India (96)	64.6
Indonesia (93)	97.1
Malaysia (97) (CR)	97.6
Mexico (97)	78.7
Peru (98) (C)	97.8
Philippines (92)	96.6
Poland (98)	90.7
Slovak R (98)	95.3
South Africa (98)	94.7
Thailand (97)	93.9

C: Central. No tax breakdowns for regional or local.
CR: Central and regional. No tax breakdowns available for local.

Source: International Monetary Fund (1999)

taxing government receives revenue based on point of collection or location of taxpayer from the administering government. For example, local personal income taxes applied as supplements to the national tax are used in Nordic countries, local governments in Switzerland often supplement the canton income taxes, and local retail sales taxes piggybacked on state taxes are common in the United States. In these instances, the taxing government selects the rate that it will apply to the base defined and administered by a different government. This arrangement provides great revenue autonomy without the complications – for government or taxpayer – of defining the base or collecting the tax and allows governments access to tax bases that would ordinarily be administratively impossible for them to tax.

Second, the central government may provide assistance for a tax actually levied by the lower tiers: lower-tier governments have the choice of rate and base, but a higher-tier government 'co-administers' some parts of collection (for example, registration, assessment, collection, enforcement, etc.) for lower tiers. In a number of countries the central or regional government does assessment of the real property base, the technically most demanding task in levying such a tax, while local governments are responsible for collection of the rates they levy on that base (McCluskey and Williams, 1999). For example, Australian municipalities levy and collect real estate taxes (rates) on taxable values of property established by state government valuation offices, an arrangement that affords high technical capacity uniformly available to municipalities in the state while providing local flexibility and responsibility for application of the tax.

Finally, the lower tier may be assigned certain tax bases for independent levy (tax base assignment): governments have separate authority to levy and administer taxes on certain bases. There may be fundamental laws that assign certain bases to certain tiers of government, as is the case in the Russian Federation, for instance, or the options may be generally open, as is the case in the United States.

Each model provides lower tiers of government with authority and capacity for taxation. They differ in the extent of coordination and in how collection occurs. The latter topic is discussed later in this chapter.

The advantages from decentralizing taxing authority are several. First, revenue authority gives regional and local governments flexibility to respond to the demands of citizenry for services. Authority and responsibility for raising revenue gives these governments the capacity to decide how much will be spent, not just how to spend money provided by the higher levels of government.

Second, autonomous revenue authority gives a government greater capacity to determine how the cost of providing its services will be distributed. Revenue policies of the government providing the services, not those of a higher tier, will determine that distribution. For example, in the United States, if a function is to be the responsibility of the federal government, its cost will be distributed according to incomes; if it is to be the responsibility of state or local government, the distribution will be more heavily driven by consumption and by ownership of real property. Unless tax reliance is the same at each tier, the choice of tier for service responsibility will determine the distribution of the cost of providing that service.

Third, the closer relationship between choices about receiving services, that is, spending money, and paying for those services that revenue autonomy facilitates should improve government efficiency and responsiveness to citizen interests. Voters will hold their governments more accountable if a considerable share of the cost of local government services is visibly financed from locally imposed taxes and charges, as opposed to being financed from central transfers. The local governments are not spending 'other people's' money.

Fourth, local revenue authority gives local governments a greater reason to support economic development. Development can bring complications to local residents and their governments – traffic congestion, noise, pollution, unattractive infrastructure etc. – and, unless there are clear gains to the existing community, resistance to development is likely. Giving local governments a clear fiscal return from that development – not simply the return that might or might not flow as a transfer from the central government – can provide a useful incentive for otherwise unattractive development. And the prospect of lower tax burdens or more public services may make local residents more likely to accept the inconveniences ('negative externalities') that growth can bring.[11]

There are some problems from giving regional and local governments greater responsibility and authority for raising their own revenue. First, not all areas are equally endowed with taxable resources, causing differences in revenue potential and, accordingly, in the public services provided by the locality. This fiscal disparity means that people in high-capacity areas will enjoy greater yield and superior public services from a given tax rate than will those in lower-capacity areas. The degree of disparity will be great whenever there are considerable differences in levels of regional economic activity. For example, Tannenwald (1999) estimates that, in the United States, the fiscal capacity of the state with highest revenue potential is 2.5 times that of the state with the lowest, creating a considerable difference in the government services that could be provided with comparable tax effort in the states. But this disparity is mild in comparison with that found in the Russian Federation: Martinez and Boex (1998: Table 3–11) find the highest per capita regional government (*oblast* or other subnational subject of the federation) revenue in 1997 to have been ninety times that of the lowest.[12]

Second, central governments with control over revenue assignment may be reluctant to allow local governments to tax fiscally significant sources, leaving them with an array of minor nuisance taxes and charges. In that instance, the cost of collection may be so large as to negate any advantages from the autonomy. Being assigned too many taxes of insignificant yield increases collection cost, disguises the true cost of government operations and, because of compliance burdens, discourages economic development.

Third, local authorities may get caught in tax competition in an effort to influence business decisions and local economic development. Tax concessions – offered in a desire to meet relief extended by competitive localities – can become so great as to cripple the local revenue system. Furthermore, there is fiscal competition among local governments for economic development. This competition limits their capacity to adopt policies dramatically at variance with those of their neighbors. Even if the actual effect of taxes on economic development is minimal, political leaders are fearful about the effects and want to avoid blame for adverse results.

Does decentralization of responsibility for raising revenue systematically lead to smaller government, as likely would be the case if tax competition paralyzed lower tiers, causing them to fear to increase taxes because of potential economic loss to lower tax neighbors? Kirchgassner, after a laborious review of three decades of literature on the issue, concludes that there is some evidence that decentralization of revenue raising authority leads 'to a smaller size of government, but the evidence is far from being overwhelming' (2001: 20). The evidence, both across and within nations, mixed as it is for impact on size of government, is such that one may conclude that revenue authority decentralization indeed provides a means for better accommodating public preferences for government services, in terms of both size of tax burden and how that burden is distributed.

DEGREE OF ADMINISTRATIVE AUTONOMY[13]

Will the government that levies a tax also be responsible for its collection? In federal systems, national, regional and local governments may levy taxes; in unitary states, national and local governments may have taxing authority. But in no case is it necessary that administration be by the government that levies the tax. Some technical parts of administration may even be handled through contract with private firms. For example, in the United States, states have experimented with contract auditors for sales and corporate income taxes, localities regularly contract with private appraisal firms for the difficult task of real property assessment, and all levels frequently contract with private firms on more difficult collection assignments. The decision about administration hinges on a combination of technical and political factors (Veehorn and Ahmad, 1997: 109; Veehorn and Brondolo, 1999; McLure, 2001).

These assignments of tax administration may be arrayed into three groups.[14] First, a single, central government agency may administer all taxes. When a tax is centrally administered, staff of the administrative unit – regardless of posting – are central employees and geographic subunits are subordinated to the national administration. The National Tax Board/regional Tax Authorities structure in Sweden offers an example of decentralization of organization within a national system. Each of the ten national authorities (one for each county) has a County Tax Director and a governing council, but all are under National Tax Board guidance. With centralized administration, the national administration collects taxes levied by the national government, the revenue from which may finance national government services, may be distributed to regional or local governments through conditional or unconditional grant programs, or may be shared by formula with those lower governments.[15] Furthermore, that central administration would also collect any taxes levied by regional or local governments, if those governments have been granted taxing authority.

Second, each government that levies a tax independently administers that tax. Independent subnational power both to enact tax legislation (choose taxes, define bases, set rates etc.) and to administer the taxes that have been enacted affords the ultimate in fiscal autonomy for these subnational units. Some taxes – like the standard value added tax or a corporate income tax – are less technically suitable for subnational administration than

others and not all administrative functions for those that might be administered at lower tiers are efficiently performed by smaller governments. But where lower tier governments are otherwise technically competent, subnational administration can be considered. State sales and local property taxes in the United States are good examples of fully independent administration (Penniman, 1980; Due and Mikesell, 1994). In general, countries are wary of permitting subnational administration of any major taxes; user charges, minor excises and licenses are frequently the limit of such responsibility.

Finally, government may arrange to cooperate and share administrative functions. Tax administration can divide tasks among central and subnational government, with lower units choosing tax base and rate and conducting certain functions in administration while the central government 'co-administers' other functions. They will be performed for each tax, but not necessarily by the government levying the tax and not necessarily all by the same government. Functions requiring greater technical competence or exhibiting economies of scale in production may be the responsibility of higher governments; functions requiring greater knowledge of local conditions and business practices may be the responsibility of lower governments. Shared administration allows independence while permitting administrative specialization. It provides many of the advantages that fully centralized administration might afford, while permitting some autonomy and advantages of small, local operations. The decision to cooperate and to share is entirely that of each state (Duncan and McLure, 1997).

Administrative formats may vary for different taxes within a nation. Canada offers one of the more striking examples of that variation, with different administrative assignments for individual income, corporate income and retail sales taxes. The provinces levy personal income taxes administered by Revenue Canada, although each province designs and adopts its own tax base and rates.[16] Each province adopts and administers its corporate income tax; the various provinces even use different formats for their taxes. Finally, the provincial retail sales taxes are collected in three different arrangements in regard to national administration and connection with the federal Goods and Services (value added) tax: five provinces levy and administer their own sales tax that is independent of the national tax; one province levies its own sales tax and administers both that tax and the Goods and Services tax in its jurisdiction; and three provinces levy a sales tax that is fully harmonized with the national tax and is administered by Revenue Canada.[17]

Evidence from international experience suggests the following conclusions about centralized administration. First, centralized administration offers uniformity throughout the country. With good administrative controls, the same procedures and processes will be followed everywhere in the nation. That permits a single information system for tracking taxpayers and their economic activity; a single master file could encompass all relevant data to provide a strong tool for enforcement and collection. It will also improve the chances that taxpayers will receive uniform treatment by the tax authority, without regard to where the entity or its taxable activities are located. This uniformity is critical for fair, non-distorting application of a national tax. It is less critical when subnational units have fiscal autonomy, although it can be comforting for businesses that operate in many jurisdictions. Furthermore, a national organization can facilitate rotation of personnel, a critical component of internal control to reduce the potential for corruption.

Second, with a single administrative authority, taxpayers will not be confused about which tax authority can answer questions, distribute forms, receive filings etc. When there are multiple administrative agencies involved, some payments, correspondence, appointments etc. inevitably get misdirected. This will not happen if there is only a single tax authority. Furthermore, a single audit assignment can cover central and subnational taxes; there need not be multiple audit visits in a single audit cycle.

Third, large centralized administrative agencies may afford more qualified personnel and more sophisticated and newer technology and may enjoy economies of scale for some administrative functions. Small units may not be able to afford specialized and more costly equipment and technology used in tax administration, personnel capable of handling more complex issues, or specialized training programs for their small numbers of staff.

Finally, a single administration can be better equipped – legally, technically and economically – and have greater clout to deal with national and global business entities than smaller subnational authorities. That authority will have the weight of the national government behind it, including tax treaty powers not available to subnational governments, and can sometimes intermingle tax enforcement with international agreements in ways that lower governments legally cannot manage. The large single administration is less likely to be swamped by the force of a transnational corporation than is an authority from a lower-tier government.

Experience with independent regional and local tax administration suggests the following. First, higher-level administration of a tax levied by a lower level of government can reduce transparency. Taxpayers receiving a consolidated tax bill often cannot discern which level of government is levying which portion of the total tax. When administration is separate, it is much easier for taxpayers to see the tax and then to hold governments accountable for the taxes they levy.

Second, independent tax authorities can act as experimental laboratories for tax administration. They can innovate new approaches and techniques, exploiting the nimbleness that often characterizes smaller organizations. The impact of confusion and mistakes is also localized and limited, should experiments not work out. The innovations will not put the nation at risk – as would attempts at new practices at the national level – and those that are successful can become a 'best practices' model for the rest of the country. Because there are multiple authorities working for the best interests of their citizenry, there will be strong competitive incentives for these units to strive for efficiency and effectiveness: the citizens will see what other governments are doing and will demand similar or better responses from their own leaders.

Third, when subnational governments may adopt independent tax bases, independent administration allows the design of organizational structures best suited for the tax in place. A national structure need not be reshaped to meet the peculiarities of the subnational tax. The independent local administration can use its familiarity with local markets, local business practices and other local peculiarities to improve compliance.

Fourth, independent administration may provide quicker and more certain control over collections for the taxing government. The government levying the tax has control over funds as soon as the taxpayer pays and does not have to await distribution from some other tax authority. Subnational governments also like the government employment power that independent administration provides, as well as the assurance that full and appropriate diligence will be given to the collection of its taxes.

Finally, local revenue administration can bring special knowledge and expertise about the local economy and business practices into the process of tax enforcement and administration. In large and economically diverse countries, there may be enough difference in regional economies and commercial practices to warrant considerable difference in administrative structures from one area to another.

EXTENT OF CO-PRODUCTION IN REVENUE COLLECTION[18]

How much responsibility in the tax collection process will the tax authorities place on the taxpayer? Revenue collection mixes both tax administration, the work of the government tax administrators, and tax compliance, the efforts by private taxpayers to comply with the tax laws, but any system of collection involves a constant set of functions, regardless of available technology, structure of the tax, or level of government responsible for administering the tax law. The core functions of tax administration – taxpayer registration and taxpayer service, tax declaration or assessment, accounting for taxpayers and revenue, delinquency control, audit, enforcement, and appeal or protest – have, as Baldwin observes, 'been essentially constant since at least biblical times' (Baldwin, 1996: 1105). How the authorities perform the functions has changed with technological development and the resources available in the administering nation, but their spirit has not changed. The process works to transfer revenue from private entities so that it may be used to finance government services. However, it must 'make the transfer so that the distribution of tax burdens reflects what the tax law intended, so that economic activities are distorted as little as possible, and so that the cost of collecting that revenue is as low as is consistent with achieving the other economic and social goals of taxation' (Mikesell, 1998: 196).

The most interesting policy issues involve the division of collection responsibilities between administration and compliance – the extent to which collection is privatized, that is, how much of the collection task will be the responsibility of private entities rather than the tax authorities. Some governments may design tax collection on a taxpayer active system, in which much responsibility for revenue production is placed on the taxpayer (or the taxpayer's representatives: employer, financial institutions making payments to the taxpayer etc.). In this instance, revenue administrators must design implementation structures to encourage voluntary compliance with tax requirements; in a taxpayer active scheme, revenue encouraged voluntarily is much cheaper to collect than revenue directly collected by the authorities. Some governments may design collection on a taxpayer passive system, in which responsibilities of the taxpayer are essentially non-existent; in this system, revenue authorities can focus attention on efficient means of directly collecting revenue from the taxpayers, not on inducing voluntary payment of tax owed.

There is no unique way in which any tax must be collected, so the division is an important policy choice. For example, taxes on real property are typically collected in a manner that places little responsibility on the taxpayer: tax authorities maintain records, establish the taxable value of properties, determine what rates and relief apply to a property parcel, and calculate bills for the individual property. However, the same tax could involve significantly greater taxpayer activity by requiring taxpayers to estimate the taxable value of their property, to return calculation and filing, and to carry out other compliance tasks.[19] In the other direction, individual income taxes in the United States place considerable requirements for recordkeeping, calculation and return preparation on the taxpayer. However, roughly thirty countries operate virtually return-free income taxes, in which the government calculates tax bills on the basis of information supplied by employers and others making payment to the individual (US General Accounting Office, 1996). The division of responsibility can change. For instance, in 1996, the United Kingdom changed its personal income tax system to one allowing taxpayers to calculate their tax liability on current-year earnings (a self-assessment) from one based on an Inland Revenue assessment based on previous year's income, although taxpayers could continue to ask Inland Revenue to calculate their tax liability. That represents a considerable privatization of the collection process and a considerable shock to a system that had been in place for more than half a century.

The distribution of responsibilities between tax authority and taxpayer in revenue generation is a policy decision. Choice of tax base does not determine the appropriate division of responsibility. Collection scheme choices should be established according to criteria involving collection cost, equity of burden distribution and control of adverse economic incentives. In general, governments give inadequate attention to the possibility of alternative collection schemes.

CONCLUSION

Just as governments do not dramatically change their budget system or the broad outline of government services they provide from one year to the next, neither do they change their revenue systems much across budget years. Nations generally make their tax structures and revenue systems part of their permanent law, so they stay in place. Politicians, analysts and taxpayers even seem little aware of the range of alternative systems open for distributing the cost of government and how those systems can be implemented. The preceding chapter shows that public revenue policy involves four discrete policy choices: tax base, degree of revenue autonomy, administrative responsibility, and division of responsibility between tax authorities and taxpayers. Furthermore, there are alternatives within each of these policy choices: a given tax base can be used with different tax handles, revenue autonomy can be provided through various mechanisms, responsibility for tax administration can be devolved or centralized through several options, and the extent of revenue co-production can be wide-ranging. Economically and politically prosperous countries do indeed use significantly different revenue systems. Unfortunately, however, there is a tendency to presume that the tax policy choices in place at a particular time in a particular country are the only options available, are the best options available, or, most discouragingly, that no positive change is possible. The permanence of revenue law helps implement that presumption.

Major revisions – like the switch from sales tax to value added tax in Switzerland in 1995 or the privatization of income tax administration in the United Kingdom in the late 1990s – are notable because of the very rarity of significant change. More typically, the system in place is the product of choices made over many years and usually they do not change dramatically or quickly. But it is wrong to assume that change in revenue system, even major change, is impossible or even unwarranted. The financing of a given expenditure budget can be raised using many different combinations of revenue policy choices and the choices should be conscious ones, not simply the result of political, economic and social inertia. By assuming that revenue policies will not change, governments miss opportunities to pursue more efficient and effective alternatives than represented by the status quo.

NOTES

1 Seigniorage was a normal means of finance in Soviet times, but could no longer function when administered prices ended with the fall of Soviet controls (Kravchuk, 1998). Neumann (1992) provides estimates of the more modest seigniorage revenue of the United States.

2 Ancillary, amenity and utility services provided by governments to particular individuals or businesses – without significant third party effects – may be financed from sales revenue, but these operations typically represent only a small element of a general purpose government.

3 *McCulloch* v. *Maryland*, 4 Wheaton 316 (1819).

4 For example, Martinez-Vasquez and McNab (2000) trace the history of tax system transformation in the countries making the transition from plan to market in the 1990s.

5 Privatization ('self-assessment') of income tax collection in the United Kingdom in 1996–97 and the global switch to value added taxation are two important counter-examples of big-bang, not gradual, change in the revenue choices in mature democracies.

6 Two excellent studies of the important influences and determinants of the choices countries make are works by Peters (1991) and Sandford (2000).

7 The early versions of these value-added taxes included several features not consistent with the European model (Summers and Sunley, 1995). They are gradually being revised to the international standard in terms of crediting, destination principle and so on.

8 The taxes levied by subjects of the Russian Federation typically apply at both retail and wholesale levels (Mikesell, 1999).

9 Even in the United States, where states are virtually unconstrained by the federal government in designing their tax systems, the states usually limit the tax alternatives available to their localities.

10 Ter-Minassian (1997) offers an excellent source on the range of national options and how they are implemented.

11 Metropolitan tax base sharing programs reduce the returns to the host locality from economic development and hence the compensation for negative externalities the host must face. While these programs may reduce fiscal disparity between communities, their overall impact may not be desirable (Fox, 1981).

12 The Russian data include all revenues collected in the subject, federal as well as subnational. Because all major subnational taxes had rate and base features set by the federal government, it was not necessary to adjust for tax effort differences to examine disparity there.

13 This section is based on Mikesell (2001).

14 User charges are almost always administered by the government providing the service, regardless of how taxes may be administered.

15 Tax sharing of the type practiced in many countries of the former Soviet Union and in Germany is a formula transfer. In these systems, the central government adopts the tax and shares with other governments on a derivation basis, the shares being established by the central government. Tax sharing provides no more fiscal autonomy than a general purpose grant program, because tax structure, rates, administration and sharing rates are controlled by the central government.

16 Until recently, Canadian provinces levied their personal income taxes as a percentage of national liability.

17 One province and all the territories do not levy a retail sales tax, exercising the revenue autonomy that characterizes the Canadian system.

18 Rather than view the private role in revenue collection as one of co-production, Harvey and McCrohan (1988) suggested an application from the literature of philanthropy: compliance by the taxpayer would be modeled as a form of 'helping', taking from the language of volunteerism. Compliance behavior and philanthropic volunteerism would thus have similar roots.

19 Self-assessment is the rule for personal property taxes in the United States – and that assessment is seldom subject to audit.

REFERENCES

Bahl, Roy W. and Linn, Johannes F. (1992) *Urban Public Finance in Developing Countries.* Washington, DC: Oxford University Press for the World Bank.

Baldwin, John (1996) 'Evolving Taxpayer Information Systems', *State Tax Notes,* 10: 1105–14.

Bird, Richard M. (2000) 'Rethinking Subnational Taxes: A New Look at Tax Assignment', *Tax Notes International* 20: 2069–97.

Due, John F. and Mikesell, John L. (1994) *Sales Taxation, State and Local Structure and Administration.* 2nd edn. Washington, DC: Urban Institute Press.

Duncan, Harley T. and McLure, Charles E., Jr (1997) 'Tax Administration in the United States of America: A Decentralized System', *Bulletin of International Fiscal Documentation,* 51: 74–85.

Fisher, Glenn W. (1996) *The Worst Tax? A History of the Property Tax in America.* Lawrence, KS: University Press of Kansas.

Fox, William F. (1981) 'An Evaluation of Metropolitan Area Tax Base Sharing: A Comment', *National Tax Journal,* 34: 275–80.

Harvey, James W. and McCrohan, Kevin F. (1988) 'Is There a Better Way of Improving Compliance With the Tax Laws? Insights from the Philanthropic Literature', *Journal of Public Policy and Marketing,* VII: 138–51.

International Monetary Fund (1999) *Government Finance Statistics Yearbook 1999.* Washington, DC: IMF.

Kirchgasser, Gebhard (2001) 'The Effects of Fiscal Institutions on Public Finance: A Survey of the Empirical Literature', Center for Economic Studies and Ifo Institute for Economic Research Working Paper Series No. 617 (December 2001) ONLINE (http:// papers.ssrn.com/abstract=292219).

Kirchgasser, Gebhard and Pommerehne, Werner (1997) 'Public Spending in Federal Systems: A Comparative Econometric Study', in P. Capros and D. Meulders (eds), *Budgetary Policy Modelling: Public Expenditures.* London/New York: Routledge.

Kravchuk, Robert (1998) 'Budget Deficits, Hyperinflation, and Stabilization in Ukraine, 1991–6', *Public Budgeting and Finance,* 18 (Winter): 45–70.

Martinez, Jorge and Boex, Jameson (1998) *Fiscal Decentralization in the Russian Federation: Trends, Issues, and Options for Reform.* US Government Technical Assistance Team in the Russian Federation, December.

Martinez-Vasquez, Jorge and McNab, Robert M. (2000) 'The Tax Reform Experiment in Transitional Countries', *National Tax Journal,* LIII (June): 273–98.

McCluskey, William and Williams, Brendan (1999) 'Introduction: A Comparative Evaluation', in W. McCluskey (ed.), *Property Tax: An International Comparative Review.* Brookfield, VT: Ashgate Publishing. pp. 1–31.

McLure, Charles E., Jr (2001) 'The Tax Assignment Problem: Ruminations on How Theory and Practice Depend on History', *National Tax Journal,* 54 (June): 339–63.

Messere, Ken (2000) 'Evaluating the Taxing Powers of Sub-Central Governments', *Bulletin for International Fiscal Documentation,* 54 (March): 133–45.

Mikesell, John L. (1998) 'Tax Administration: The Link Between Tax Law and Tax Collections', in Fred Thompson and Mark T. Green (eds), *Handbook of Public Finance.* New York: Marcel Dekker. pp. 173–98.

Mikesell, John L. (1999) 'Decentralizing Government Finances in the Russian Federation: The Regional Sales and Imputed Income Taxes'. *Proceedings of the Ninety-second Annual Conference on Taxation of the National Tax Association.*

Mikesell, John L. (2001) 'Administration of Local Taxes'. Topical Brief on World Bank Group Tax Policy and Administration Website (www1.worldbank.org/public-sector/tax/adminlocal.htm) [ONLINE] April 2001.

Neumann, Manfred J.M. (1992) 'Seigniorage in the United States: How Much Does the US Government Make from Money Production?', *Federal Reserve Bank of St Louis Monthly Review* (March/April): 29–40.

Penniman, Clara (1980) *State Income Taxation.* Baltimore, MD: Johns Hopkins University Press.

Peters, B. Guy (1991) *The Politics of Taxation: A Comparative Perspective.* Cambridge, MA and Oxford: Blackwell.

Sandford, Cedric (2000) *Why Tax Systems Differ – A Comparative Study of the Political Economy of Taxation.* Bath: Fiscal Publications.

Summers, Victoria P. and Sunley, Emil M. (1995) 'An Analysis of Value Added Taxes in Russia and Other Countries of the Former Soviet Union', IMF Working Paper WP/95/1. Washington, DC: International Monetary Fund.

Tannenwald, Robert (1999) 'Fiscal Disparity Among the States Revisited', *New England Economic Review* (July/August): 3–25.

Ter-Minassian, Teresa (ed.) (1997) *Fiscal Federalism in Theory and Practice.* Washington, DC: International Monetary Fund.

US General Accounting Office (1996) *Tax Administration: Alternative Filing Systems.* GAP/GGD-97-6. Washington, DC: GAO.

Veehorn, Charles L. and Brondolo, John (1999) 'Organizational Options for Tax Administration', *Bulletin for International Fiscal Documentation,* 53 (November): 499–512.

Veehorn, Charles L. and Ahmad, Ehtisham (1997) 'Tax Administration', in Teresa Ter-Minassian (ed.), *Fiscal Federalism in Theory and Practice.* Washington, DC: International Monetary Fund.

31

Fiscal Rules and Fiscal Policy

Mark Hallerberg

Formal rules in budgeting are designed to address certain problems. This chapter classifies formal rules according to the problems some rules are meant to solve. It begins with a consideration of the common pool resource problem, which develops when spending is targeted to a specific group but the taxes used to pay for it come from general revenues. It then considers a related issue that can exist when there are multiple levels of government, namely the moral hazard problem. Lower levels of government are prone to spend more when they expect that higher levels of government are going to bail them out. The third topic is the 'principal–agent' problem. Budgets inevitably involve some form of delegation of authority. The problem arises when 'agents' do not do what 'principals' wants them to do. In practice the literature discusses problems that arise when voters delegate authority to elected officials, and when elected officials delegate authority to bureaucrats. The final section discusses who chooses fiscal rules. An important question is whether the institutions themselves matter. If persons with preferences for tighter fiscal discipline always choose certain fiscal rules over others, there is a question whether the preferences or the institutions drive the results. The section concludes that the rules continue to matter, but that the field is underdeveloped in addressing this question.

THE COMMON POOL RESOURCE PROBLEM: RULES THAT CENTRALIZE THE BUDGET PROCESS

One of the fundamental problems of budgeting is what is known as the common pool resource (CPR) problem. The 'common pool' in a budgeting framework consists of government revenues. Policy makers draw from this pool when they spend money. The problem arises when policy makers consider fully the consequences of their spending decisions but do not consider fully how their decisions affect the common pool.[1] Theoretical work indicates that under such a situation policy makers will spend more than the case where they consider completely the tax implications of their decisions. In a multi-period framework, the budget deficits of the government will also be larger and governments will carry larger debt burdens (Hallerberg and Von Hagen, 1999; Velasco, 1999, 2000).

A question to ask is why policy makers do not consider the full tax implications of their decisions. There are two reasons, one that concerns the preferences of decision makers and one that concerns the budget process. First, there may be incentives for policy makers not to consider the full tax burden. Weingast, Shepsle and Johnsen (1981) provide a nice example from the US Congress. Voters elect Representatives to Congress in electoral districts where only one candidate wins and the candidate with the most votes is declared the winner. Candidates appeal to voters in their district through budget policy. Voters like additional spending on projects like bridges, new museums and the like where they live, but they do not like additional taxes. The would-be Representative knows that additional spending is financed by a tax base that includes the entire country, not just the electoral district. In the US House of Representatives, where there are 435 members, this means that each member of the House worries about only 1/435 of the tax burden (assuming that the tax burden is evenly distributed in the country when making budget decisions). Representatives will therefore support more spending in their districts than they would if their district alone had to pay for the spending. It should be noted that this type of incentive structure is not limited to the US Congress nor even to legislatures. A minister of defense may consider more the benefits of new planes than their cost implications, while a member of a green party may worry more about cleaning up toxic waste sites than where the money is coming from to pay for the clean-up.

Whether policy makers who do not have reasons to consider the entire tax burden make decisions that increase the CPR problem is the second issue to consider, which concerns the decision making process itself. The classic article by Weingast, Shepsle and Johnsen (1981) details how the CPR problem can encourage 'log rolls' among Congress members, who make informal agreements among themselves to back each other's spending proposals for their districts. The way members vote on the spending determines whether the log rolls happen. Note that, if bills for spending in districts are voted on sequentially and separately, members should vote for no bill but their own. The reason is that other bills simply increase the tax burden on one's voters without providing any tangible benefits. Some sort of institutional rule is needed to maintain log rolls in legislatures with many members. In other work, Shepsle and Weingast (1994; see also Baron, 1991) argue that 'closed rules' (simple up or down votes on bills with no possibility of amendment) as well as votes on packages of bills in the form of omnibus bills allow log rolls. In settings with fewer decision makers, informal rules to support each other may be all that is necessary for a log roll to function. Drees, Jr (1955) argues that in the Netherlands log rolls were simply implicit and required no formal discussion. Von Hagen (1992) finds that full cabinet votes on budget bids from different ministries encourage log rolling behavior. The problem can therefore arise in both parliaments and in cabinets.

It is also possible that the decision making process itself hides the full tax implications of additional spending. One policy maker may have a mandate only to increase security at airports while another policy maker is given the task to improve air quality. If their budget requests are simply aggregated into the total budget, there will be little consideration of the tax implications of their decisions and the CPR problem will be endemic. This pattern of decision making is referred to as 'bottom-up' budgeting. A second possibility is that the policy makers do not know how much others in the government are spending. If all relevant actors understood the true dimensions of their spending decisions they

might modify their own behavior. Empirical studies indicate that 'fragmented' decision making leads to higher levels of spending and to higher budget deficits than in 'unfragmented' systems (for discussions of OECD countries see Kontopoulos and Perotti, 1999; Volkerink and de Haan, 2000; for a discussion of fragmentation in American cities see Baqir, 2001).

These two sources of the CPR problem lead to several suggestions for how to solve it, but they all have the following in common – the goal is to assure that the decision taken is one that considers the full tax implications of any spending. A first solution is to assure that an important budget player has reason to care about the entire budget. Finance ministers at the national level and city managers at the local level can serve as this actor. In one of the classic texts on budgeting, Wildavsky (1975) conceives of the finance minister as the 'guardian' of the treasury who keeps the spending of 'advocates' (or spending ministers) in check. Building upon this logic, one could argue that the stronger the finance minister, the more fiscal discipline (Hahm et al., 1996). The Inter-American Development Bank (1997), while noting that most Latin American countries have 'strong' finance ministers already, nevertheless argues that strengthening the finance minister would lead to higher budget discipline. Measures a government can take to strengthen the finance minister include: having the finance minister propose the annual budget; requiring that budget negotiations be between the finance minister and a relevant spending minister and not before the full cabinet; and allowing the finance minister to cut spending during the execution of the budget. The key is to have budget rules that increase the discretionary power of the actor who considers the entire tax burden.

Not all scholars recommend stronger finance ministers in all cases, however. Hallerberg and Von Hagen (1999) and Hallerberg, Strauch and Von Hagen (2001), while noting that stronger finance ministers play a critical role in some countries, caution that the coalition structure of governments may make such 'strong' ministers impractical. A given coalition partner may not be willing to delegate decision making powers to one central player who is not from this partner's party, and this unwillingness increases if the parties in government expect to face each other in the next election. Hallerberg and Von Hagen (1999) propose an alternative approach for parliamentary democracies with multi-party coalition governments. Parties should negotiate 'fiscal contracts' as part of their coalition agreement that provide detailed spending targets for every ministry. In a country like the Netherlands, for example, parties agree to the budget figures before they agree which party should head which ministry. This process assures that the actors consider the tax burden of their decisions on the entire coalition. It is also a process that is most successful when a series of rules exist to reinforce the original contract. Rules for what to do when revenues are too high or too low, for example, allow the actors to avoid contract renegotiations that can spell the end of the coalition.

A second solution proposed is that budget processes be 'top-down' instead of 'bottom-up'. Decision makers in a top-down approach first decide on a total spending figure, then they consider how the total should be divided among the different ministries and departments. An agreement first on the total level should lead decision makers to consider tradeoffs among different spending priorities, which would not occur if the process were 'bottom-up' (Schick, 1986; OECD, 1987; see also Wicksell, 1896, for the earliest exposition). Many countries have since instituted some form of a top-down procedure, from the Congressional Budget and Impoundment Control Act of 1974 in the United States that required the Congress to pass aggregate spending targets before a vote on specific appropriations, to sweeping budgetary reforms in Sweden in the mid-1990s that require parliament to pass aggregate targets for the following three years (Wildavsky and Caiden, 1997; for Sweden see Molander, 2000).

Not all scholars agree, however, that a move to a 'top-down' approach is helpful. In an influential article, Ferejohn and Krehbiel (1987) argue that politicians who want more spending can simply pad the aggregate figures, and they provide examples where top-down decision making would lead to more spending than bottom-up. In assessing the discussion, it is important to remember the problem that is being solved and to ask whether the process is forcing the actors to consider the entire tax burden when they make decisions. Changes in the budget procedure in Sweden may be instructive. Following a 'top-down' logic, the reforms of the mid-1990s introduced a parliamentary vote on aggregates in the spring and more specific votes on budget items in the fall. In summer 2001, and in the face of clear opposition from the Finance Ministry, the parliament voted to move the consideration of the aggregates to the fall, or just before consideration of the specific parts of the budgets. Finance Ministry officials are concerned that this move constitutes a *de facto* return to bottom-up budgeting. The rationale the parliamentary majority used to move the consideration of aggregates, however, was that parliamentarians needed so much information on the budget in spring on individual programs to feel confident enough to vote on the aggregates that, in practice, they were debating the entire budget twice. This argument for the move suggests that simply moving the timing of votes may not be enough to ensure a true 'top-down' process.

MORAL HAZARD: RULES ON SUBNATIONAL GOVERNMENTS

The second issue, known as moral hazard, is closely related to the CPR problem. The argument once again is that policy makers do not consider the full implications of their spending decisions. The root of the problem, however, is different. Instead of an ignorance of a (local) government's own tax burden, the (local) government expects to be able to draw upon a wider (national) tax burden for its financing. It also expects that another government body will bail it out if it gets into trouble. Subnational governments therefore engage in riskier fiscal behavior. For example, Italian regional and local governments routinely ran large deficits in the 1980s with the knowledge that the national government would, and did, rescue them from fiscal insolvency (Bordignon, 1999). Fiscal problems at the subnational level have arisen in developing countries as well (De Mello, Jr, 2000). Within the European Union, there is a concern that the introduction of a common currency under Stage III of Economic and Monetary Union in 1999 will lead to a moral hazard problem among its states. The argument is that a given state will enjoy the full benefits of additional spending, but will anticipate that its partners will bail it out if it gets in financial trouble. The states participating in EMU would then bear the costs of the bail-out.

There are a series of fiscal rules proposed to eliminate the moral hazard problem, but they have one thing in common – they try to make it unlikely that any government can anticipate a bailout. This is more difficult than one may think. The European Union, for example, agreed to a 'no bail-out clause' in the Treaty of Maastricht, but most observers, and for that matter most governments, do not consider the clause credible. The reason why is simple: states participating in EMU will likely suffer less from bailing out a country in need than from letting that country go bankrupt. The European Union has since established its 'Stability and Growth Pact', which sets minimum budget balances states should maintain unless they are experiencing a serious recession. If a state's budget balance slips below −3 per cent of GDP and is not soon corrected, the European Union will fine the state. The basic idea is that minimum budget balance standards should guarantee that no state finds itself in danger of defaulting (for a critical discussion see Eichengreen and Wyplosz, 1998).

The European Union's requirement that states have certain deficit targets is not new, although the usual arrangement in more traditional national–subnational governmental forms is that the higher-order government imposes some form of budget balance requirement on the lower-level governments. In France and Germany localities are required to abide by the 'golden rule', which means that borrowing in a given year should not exceed total capital outlays (Seitz, 1999; see also Rodden, 2000). In Sweden since 2000, local governments are required simply to run balanced budgets. In other states, such as Ireland, Spain and the United Kingdom, the central government has the (formal) power to limit subnational borrowing.

Unlike in some European countries, where the central government imposes restrictions on local governments, most US states developed balanced budget requirements of their own. These requirements range in practice from an obligation that state governors propose a balanced budget to a ban on state governments from carrying over deficits from year to year. Empirical work indicates that not all balanced budget requirements are created equal – only the carryover ban leads in practice to tighter fiscal discipline in the form of higher average surpluses and faster elimination of outstanding deficits (Alt and Lowery, 1994; Bohn and Inman, 1996). Rattsø (2000) comes to the same conclusion for Norway, where there are formal budget balance requirements but where local governments can carry over deficits from year to year.

There are other fiscal rules common at the subnational level that target something other than the budget balance. In the United States, twenty-five state governments face either tax and/or expenditure limitations and another twelve have supermajority requirements that mean that the state legislature must approve any new taxes by more than a simple majority (Knight and Levinson, 2000). In the United Kingdom, the central government formulates 'standard spending assessments' (SSAs) that represent attempts by the central government to calculate the costs of 'standard' local public services. It then uses these assessments to set expenditure limits on localities (Duncan and Smith, 1996). In Argentina, the focus is the availability of financing. The central

bank must approve any provincial bonds issued in foreign currency or issued abroad, although to the detriment of the general government's budget performance the bank in practice rarely intervenes (Dillinger and Webb, 1999).

There have been several reservations about the use of such limitations in the literature. Eichengreen and Von Hagen (1996) argue that 'no bail-out' clauses are credible when governments have revenue sources (such as significant tax bases) at their disposal. If revenues come only from central government transfers, central government bail-outs are likely because there is no other way for local governments to get out of financial difficulties. Strict rules on subnational governments, therefore, are needed only in cases where subnational governments do not have their own tax bases. Empirically, Eichengreen and Von Hagen (1996) examine the circumstances under which upper levels of governments impose debt restrictions on lower levels of government in a sample of thirty-six countries. They find that such restrictions are most common when subnational governments do not have the ability to generate additional revenues through taxes of their own. Sbragia (1996) reinforces this finding in her work on the United States. Most US states limited the borrowing of their communities during the period after the American Civil War, with the restrictions on borrowing often corresponding to a certain percentage of the taxable property base of a given community. These restrictions were meant to assure markets that the locality had enough resources at its disposal to bail itself out of any financial difficulty.

Others suggest that markets can discipline states so that formal rules are not necessary. Someone must lend governments money, and markets will balk at providing financing to states and localities with real default risks. Bird and Tassonyi (2001) find that market pressure plays a significant role in maintaining fiscal discipline in Canadian provinces, even in the absence of formal rules that limit provincial borrowing. Inman (1995) recounts how the city of Philadelphia, Pennsylvania, failed to find buyers for its bonds when bond traders perceived that the city's finances were in disarray. Yet the effects of market pressure do not seem to be consistent across all governments. Willett (2000), for example, indicates that markets tend to respond to fiscal problems relatively late and, when they do respond, tend to overreact and make fiscal corrections more difficult. Mosely (2000) interviewed market participants and found that they pay closest attention to large swings in government policy. Only half of her sample followed government debt levels. This evidence reinforces the impression that markets are not effective at preserving fiscal discipline by themselves, and that effective fiscal rules do serve an important purpose.

There are also concerns about whether such formal restrictions do nothing more than encourage creative accounting. Strauch (1998) finds that US states that impose the strictest expenditure limits lead simply to a shift from the expenditure to the investment budget. Von Hagen (1991) finds that the stringency of expenditure constraints has no effect on total debt. He speculates (Von Hagen, 2000) that other studies find significant effects of these limitations because the studies look at state-guaranteed, rather than total, debt. Stringent expenditure constraints lead to a shift from guaranteed to unguaranteed debt instruments. To the extent that these shifts obscure what the government is doing, they may increase the severity of our next issue, namely the principal–agent problem.

PRINCIPAL–AGENT PROBLEM: RULES THAT STRENGTHEN ACCOUNTABILITY

Budgets inevitably involve some form of delegation. There are two forms common in the literature. The first involves voter delegation of authority to elected politicians, while the second is from elected politicians to (generally unelected) bureaucrats. The problem arises when the 'agent' (or the person delegated authority) does not do what the 'principal' (or the delegator of authority) wants that person to do. Politicians ignore the directions of voters and spend more money on defense when the electoral mandate seemingly was to improve the environment; bureaucrats hide the true costs of their work so that politicians give bureaucrats more money than it costs to produce a given public good. The general prediction of principal–agent models of budgeting is that the worse the problem, the higher the public spending. This is because agent preferences are somehow different than principal preferences. Politicians may, for example, like to spend money on the perks of office such as first class plane tickets that populations do not want (Niskanen, 1971; for a theoretical argument see Banks, 1989). Bureaucrats may not place the same value in finding and eliminating inefficiencies in spending where they exist because they have different priorities for their time.

One solution to the problem is to design a contract between principals and agents that brings

the incentives for the agent more in line with what the principal wants. This is not that easy, however: contracts can provide perverse incentives (for examples from budgeting see Kiewiet and McCubbins, 1991). Another option is for principals to screen individuals before they select them as agents. Public debates among candidates for office may allow some screening of future politicians. Similarly, the confirmation process for top bureaucrats in some democracies allows the legislature to evaluate whether future heads of departments have preferences that differ greatly from the median in the legislature. Finally, principals may actively monitor agents to learn what the agents are doing.

Monitoring agents is simpler when the actions of agents are observable, and this insight has led to an emphasis in recent years on the benefits of a transparent budget process. A system is transparent when all relevant information on the budget is made available in both a timely and a systematic fashion (OECD, 2001: 3). The critical actor then becomes the public. The easier it is for the public to understand what members of the government are doing, the more accountable the public will hold politicians (IMF, 1998: 16). This accountability tightens the relationship between the first set of principals (public) and agents (elected politicians). It also brings in the public as a monitor to check the second set of principals (elected politicians) and agents (bureaucrats). If agents are doing what principals want, there should be better budget performance.[2]

What budget rules in practice increase transparency? International organizations, such as the IMF, the OECD and the World Bank, actively encourage governments to increase transparency levels. The IMF has prepared a Manual on Fiscal Transparency that spells out best practices states should follow. The international organization also encouraged officials from member states to take a voluntary survey that would allow the level of transparency to be assessed across different countries. Similarly, the OECD (OECD 2001) published a list of 'best practices' based on the experiences of its member states.

While emphasizing that some variation across countries should be expected, and for that matter even encouraged, there is general agreement across the international organizations on a set of fiscal practices governments should approximate. The first general category of recommendations concerns the annual budget. States should make budget documents comprehensive, which means that it should include all government revenue sources as well as all expenditures. They should also provide commentaries that explain each part of the budget. The second category concerns assumptions underlying the annual budget. These should be made explicit so that readers can assess for themselves how the budget would change under alternative assumptions. The assumptions should be quite detailed: how many recipients should receive unemployment benefits, the model for making macro-economic forecasts, etc., should be explicit. A third category concerns timing. The annual budget should be presented as one document. It is not possible for someone to get a clear sense of policy trade-offs if different parts of the budget are presented throughout the year. The government should present the budget with enough lead-time before the end of the current fiscal year so that the legislature can evaluate fully the different parts of the budget.[3] Similarly, the government should develop medium-term budget forecasts that provide estimates of future budgets. It should also publish a series of reports during the execution of the budget that allow persons outside of government to evaluate whether the government is sticking to the budget law. Finally, the international organizations provide a series of technical recommendations on how to increase control and accountability in accounting practices.

Some initial empirical work indicates that increases in the level of transparency that such fiscal rules provide have beneficial effects on fiscal policy. Alt et al. (2001) test eleven of seventy-six measures of transparency that appear in an OECD survey on spending levels and on budget deficits in 19 OECD countries.[4] In their empirical analysis, they find that the most transparent states have both lower spending and lower budget deficits than states with lower transparency. Similarly, in a theoretical paper, Milesi-Ferretti (2000) argues that increases in transparency reduce the creative accounting often found in countries with formal rules discussed in the previous section. This suggests that a combination of rules that guarantee transparency and that limit spending is beneficial. It should be noted that this emphasis on fiscal transparency accompanies a more general call for greater transparency throughout the economy. The lack of transparency in financial markets and financial institutions may have contributed to the worsening of the Asian financial crisis of the latter part of the 1990s. Fiscal *and* financial rules that increase transparency should consequently be introduced together (Vishwanath and Kaufmann, 1999).[5]

Another way to increase transparency is to bring the level of government closer to voters. There has been a wave of fiscal decentralization around the globe the past decade, from the creation of regional parliaments with, in Scotland's case, some fiscal powers in the United Kingdom, to an increase in the fiscal responsibilities of states and localities in countries as diverse as Colombia, Russia, Scandinavia and the United States. One reason for these decentralizations has been to bring the government closer to a people dissatisfied with the provision of public goods at the national level (Tanzi, 1999). While decentralization may potentially reduce the scale of the principal–agent problem, the previous section indicated that new difficulties in the form of the moral hazard problem may arise.

Even if the principal has some sense of what the agent is doing, there is also a concern whether the agent is meeting the principal's goals. The tasks the agents do may not seem to accomplish much of anything. A poverty reduction program, for example, could spend a lot of money on what seem like worthy projects, but in the end not reduce poverty. This concern has led to what is known as 'performance budgeting' or 'results focused management' (OECD, 2002). Governments should include both 'output' evaluations of performance, or what amount is actually spent, as well as 'outcome' evaluations, which consider the impact of the budget on the relevant target group, environment etc. One way to implement results focused management is to establish performance contracts that define explicit targets for the government to achieve. In Denmark, for example, since 1992 departments and agencies agree to contracts that define targets and required results within a set period of time (Thorn and Lyndrup, 2002). In terms of accounting rules, accrual-based accounting facilitates a more accurate consideration of the costs of both outputs *and* outcomes. To date, however, within the OECD only the three Anglophone countries of Australia, New Zealand and the United Kingdom budget on a full accrual basis (OECD, 2002: 10).

A final issue to consider is a possible difference in the time horizon between voters and politicians.[6] Politicians want to get re-elected, and they therefore prefer fiscal policies that yield immediate electoral payments. Governments may run larger budget deficits in pre-electoral periods in the hope of stimulating the economy. They may also front-load the benefits of a given governmental program in the first year or two after the program passes while they back-load the costs of a given program into years further in the future. This problem can be the opposite of the re-election incentive because the politicians expect to lose office. In this case, they are trying to get what they can for their supporters while trying to leave the costs of their policies with their successors (Grilli et al., 1991).

One proposed solution is to force governments to propose and, under 'normal' conditions, to maintain multi-annual budget programs. Such programs are meant to force governments to think longer term. Under the Stability and Growth Pact, for example, all EU member states must submit a budget program to the European Commission each year that includes five years of data (year −1 to year +3). As noted earlier, such programs also increase transparency. It is doubtful, however, that simply imposing medium-term budget plans will change the incentives politicians face to think short-term.

WHO CHOOSES FISCAL INSTITUTIONS?

Another issue concerns what the literature calls the endogeneity of institutions. That is, why do some countries select a given set of fiscal rules while others do not? This question is important. It may be that countries that are predisposed to combat certain types of problems are the ones most likely to adopt fiscal rules that address them. A population that prefers lower taxes, for example, may support a formal rule that limits tax collections while a population that will support higher taxes will not support the same rule. This line of inquiry begs the question of whether it is the underlying preferences, rather than the formal rules themselves, that are critical.

There has been little work that takes seriously the question of why the use of fiscal rules differs across countries. Baqir (2001), in his study of American city budgeting, hypothesizes that cities with many electoral districts have greater common pool resource problems and are more likely to choose a strong executive veto to control the problem. Yet he is concerned that some external effect may explain a change both in the presence of an executive veto *and* in the number of districts. To get at this problem, he finds an instrument – the number of streams, which are likely to be natural boundaries for electoral districts – for one institutional feature he cares about, namely the number of electoral districts. Once this correction is introduced, he finds both that cities with many districts are more likely to have executive vetoes, and that increases in the veto power of the mayor decrease the level of spending.[7]

As mentioned briefly previously, Hallerberg and Von Hagen (1999) and Hallerberg, Strauch and Von Hagen (2001) are concerned about the effectiveness of certain types of rules given the presence of other political institutions. Some scholars argue that proportional representation electoral systems, for example, lead to poorer budgetary performance than plurality (or first-past-the-post) electoral systems because proportional representation leads to unstable governments (Grilli et al., 1991), while others contend that multi-party coalition governments lead to larger budget deficits (Roubini and Sachs, 1989) because coalition governments cannot make the quick changes to budget profiles that one-party governments can. The counter-argument is that these institutions by themselves do not affect the budget. Rather, they *do* affect the type of fiscal rules that are most effective in enforcing fiscal discipline. The 'strong finance minister' model mentioned before works best under one-party majority governments, which are usually found in countries with plurality electoral systems. Detailed 'fiscal contracts' among coalition partners can serve the same purpose of maintaining fiscal discipline in countries with multi-party coalition governments. Hence, underlying factors found in a country's political system may affect both the choice of a given set of fiscal rules as well the effectiveness of those institutions once they are introduced.

Recent scholarship that attempts to correct for the endogeneity question therefore indicates that formal rules still matter, but scholars are just beginning to explore this issue. More work in this area clearly needs to be done.

CONCLUSION

This chapter reviews three problems that fiscal policy makers commonly face: the common pool resource problem, the moral hazard problem and the principal–agent problem. It also discusses several proposed solutions in the literature. While the chapter treats the problems separately for expositional purposes, it also indicates that solutions to one problem may affect the severity of other problems. Fiscal decentralization may decrease the principal–agent problem, for example, but increase the severity of a moral hazard problem. Changes in fiscal rules should therefore not be considered in isolation of one another, but rather as a complete package. Only in this way can one assess the true costs and benefits of using one set of fiscal rules over another.

NOTES

1 This problem is not limited to budgeting situations. The best theoretical discussions are found in Elinor Ostrom's work (see Ostrom, 1990).

2 There is a growing literature that considers what actions the government can take to strengthen the role of the public as a watchdog. Freedom of information acts, laws that give the press wide berth to investigate the government and to publish reports as the press sees fit, and guarantees that persons who are critical of the government are not charged easily with treason, all improve the ability of the public to monitor the government. This literature is not directly relevant for an essay on fiscal rules, but it is important for the reader to understand that one cannot simply assume that the public will be able to serve its watchdog function unless other types of 'rules' are in place.

3 The OECD suggests that budgets go to the legislature at least 90 days before the end of the fiscal year; see OECD, 2001: 4.

4 They include any measure that increases information on the budget in fewer documents; increases the level of independent verification of the government's figures; uses non-arbitrary language, such as the use of accrual accounting; and offers more justification of what the government does with budgeting, such as a legal requirement that the government must present an ex post report of how it spent the budget.

5 Joseph Stiglitz (2000) provides a good discussion in general of information economics and, more specifically, of the role of transparency as applied to corporate governance.

6 In the central banking literature one talks about a 'time inconsistency' problem. The idea is that politicians have different time horizons than their populations. Governments pledge to have low inflation, but before elections they are tempted to push up inflation. Populations anticipate this response, and they factor in higher inflation in their wage demands. A country then gets a suboptimal policy that leads to higher levels of inflation. If the agents delegate the setting of inflation to a (conservative) central bank, the country will experience the optimal policy that leads to lower inflation.

7 See Knight and Levinson (2000) for a similar type of analysis for the US states.

REFERENCES

Alt, James E., Dreyer Lassen, David and Skilling, David (2001) 'Fiscal Transparency and Fiscal Policy Outcomes in OECD Countries'. Paper presented at the 2001 American Political Science Association Meetings, San Francisco, CA.

Alt, James E. and Lowery, Robert C. (1994) 'Divided Government, Fiscal Institutions, and Budget Deficits: Evidence from the States', *American Political Science Review*, 88 (4): 811–28.

Baldassare, Mark (1997) *When Government Fails*. Berkeley and Los Angeles: University of California Press.

Banks, Jeffrey S. (1989) 'Agency Budgeting, Cost Information, and Auditing', *American Journal of Political Science*, 33 (3): 670–99.

Baron, David P. (1991) 'Majoritarian Incentives, Pork Barrel Programs, and Procedural Control', *American Journal of Political Science*, 35: 57–90.

Baqir, Reza (2001) 'Government Spending, Legislature Size, and the Executive Veto'. Paper presented at the 2001 American Political Science Association Meetings, San Francisco, CA.

Bird, Robert M. and Tassonyi, Almos T. (2001) 'Constraints on Provincial and Municipal Borrowing in Canada: Markets, Rules, and Norms', *Canadian Public Administration – Administration Publique du Canada*, 44 (1): 84–109.

Bohn, Henning and Inman, Robert P. (1996) 'Balanced Budget Rules and Public Deficits: Evidence from the U.S. States'. NBER Working Paper No. 5553.

Bordignon, Massimo (1999) 'Problems of Soft Budget Constraints in Intergovernmental Relationships: The Case of Italy'. Unpublished manuscript.

De Mello, Luiz R., Jr (2000) 'Fiscal Decentralization and Intergovernmental Fiscal Relations: A Cross-Country Analysis', *World Development*, 28 (2): 365–80.

Dillinger, William and Webb, Steven B. (1999) 'Fiscal Management in Federal Democracies: Argentina and Brazil'. World Bank Working Paper.

Drees, W., Jr (1955) *On the Level of Government Expenditures in The Netherlands after the War*. Leiden: Stenfert Kroese.

Duncan, Alan and Smith, Peter (1996) 'Modelling Local Government Budgetary Choices under Expenditure Limitation', *Fiscal Studies*, 16 (4): 95–110.

Eichengreen, Barry and Wyplosz, Charles (1998) 'The Stability Pact: More than a Minor Nuisance?', *Economic Policy*, 26: 65–104.

Eichengreen, Barry and von Hagen, Jürgen (1996) 'Federalism, Fiscal Restraints, and European Monetary Union', *American Economic Review*, 86 (May): 134–8.

Ferejohn, John and Krehbiel, Keith (1987) 'The Budget Process and the Size of the Budget', *American Journal of Political Science*, 31: 296–320.

Grilli, Vittorio, Masciandaro, Donato and Tabellini, Guido (1991) 'Institutions and Policies', *Economic Policy*, 6: 341–91.

Hahm, Sung Deuk, Kamlet, Mark S. and Mowery, David C. (1996) 'The Political Economy of Deficit Spending in Nine Industrialized Parliamentary Democracies: The Role of Fiscal Institutions', *Comparative Political Studies*, 29 (1): 52–77.

Hallerberg, Mark, Strauch, Rolf and von Hagen, Jürgen (2001) 'The Use and Effectiveness of Budgetary Rules and Norms in EU Member States'. Report Prepared for the Dutch Ministry of Finance, July 2001. Available for download at http://www.minfin.nl

Hallerberg, Mark and von Hagen, Jürgen (1999) 'Electoral Institutions, Cabinet Negotiations, and Budget Deficits within the European Union', in James Poterba and Jürgen von Hagen (eds), *Fiscal Institutions and Fiscal Performance*. Chicago: University of Chicago Press. pp. 209–32.

Inman, Robert (1995) 'How to Have a Fiscal Crisis: Lessons from Philadelphia', *American Economic Review*, 85 (2): 378–83.

Inter-American Development Bank (1997) *Latin America After a Decade of Reform*. Washington, DC: Johns Hopkins University Press.

Kiewiet, D. Roderick and McCubbins, Mathew D. (1991) *The Logic of Delegation. Congressional Parties and the Appropriations Process*. Chicago: University of Chicago Press.

Knight, Brian and Levinson, Arik (2000) 'Fiscal Institutions in US States', in Rolf Strauch and Jürgen von Hagen (eds), *Institutions, Politics, and Fiscal Policy*. Boston/Dordrecht/London: Kluwer. pp. 167–90.

Kontopoulos, Yianas and Perotti, Roberto (1999) 'Government Fragmentation and Fiscal Policy Outcomes: Evidence from OECD Countries', in James Poterba and Jürgen von Hagen (eds), *Fiscal Institutions and Fiscal Performance*. Chicago: University of Chicago Press. pp. 81–102.

Milesi-Ferretti, Gian Maria (2000) 'Good, Bad, or Ugly? On the Effects of Fiscal Rules with Creative Accounting'. IMF Working Paper No. 172.

Molander, Per (2000) 'Reforming Budgetary Institutions: Swedish Experiences', in Rolf Strauch and Jürgen von Hagen (eds), *Institutions, Politics, and Fiscal Policy*. Boston, MA: Kluwer. pp. 191–214.

Mosely, Layna (2000) 'Room to Move: International Financial Markets and National Welfare States', *International Organization*, 54 (4): 737–73.

Niskanen, William A. (1971) *Bureaucracy and Representative Government*. Chicago: Aldine Atherton.

Organization for Economic Co-operation and Development (1987) *The Control and Management of Government Expenditure*. Paris: OECD.

Organization for Economic Co-operation and Development (2001) *OECD Best Practices for Budget Transparency*. Paris: OECD.

Ostrom, Elinor (1990) *Governing the Commons*. Cambridge: Cambridge University Press.

Persson, T. and Svennson, L. (1989) 'Why a Stubborn Conservative Would Run a Deficit: Policy with Time Inconsistent Preferences', *Quarterly Journal of Economics*, pp. 325–46.

Rattsø, Jørn (2000) 'Fiscal Adjustment with Vertical Fiscal Imbalance: Empirical Evaluation of Administrative Federalism in Norway'. Manuscript, Norwegian University of Science and Technology, October.

Rodden, Jonathan (2000) 'Breaking the Golden Rule: Fiscal Behavior with Rational Bailout Expectations in the German States'. Prepared for the Workshop European Fiscal Federalism in Comparative Perspective Center for European Studies, Harvard University, 4 November 2000.

Roubini, Nouriel and Sachs, Jeffrey D. (1989) 'Political and Economic Determinants of Budget Deficits in the Industrial Democracies', *European Economic Review*, 33: 903–38.

Schick, Alan (1986) 'Macro-Budgetary Adaptations to Fiscal Stress in Industrialized Democracies', *Public Administration Review*, 46: 124–34.

Shepsle, Kenneth A. and Weingast, Barry R. (1994) 'Positive Theories of Congressional Institutions', *Legislative Studies Quarterly*, 29: 149–79.

Shepsle, Kenneth A. and Weingast, Barry R. (1987) 'Why are Congressional Committees Powerful?', *American Political Science Review*, 81: 929–45.

Seitz, Helmut (1999) 'Subnational Government Bailouts in Germany'. Center for European Integration Studies (ZEI) Working Paper.

Stiglitz, Joseph E. (2000) 'The Contributions of the Economics of Information to Twentieth Century Economics', *Quarterly Journal of Economics*, 115 (4): 1441–78.

Strauch, Rolf (1998) 'Budget Processes and Fiscal Discipline: Evidence from the US States'. Center for European Integration Studies (ZEI) Working Paper.

Tanzi, Vito (1999) 'The Changing Role of the State in the Economy: A Historical Perspective', in L.R. de Mello, Jr and K. Fukasaku (eds), *Fiscal Decentralization, Intergovernmental Fiscal Relations and Macroeconomic Governance*. OECD: Paris.

Thorn, Kristian and Lyndrup, Mads (2002) 'The Quality of Public Expenditure – Challenges and Solutions in Results Focused Management in the Public Sector. Denmark'. Manuscript, OECD.

Velasco, Andrés (2000) 'Debts and Deficits with Fragmented Fiscal Decision-making', *Journal of Public Economics*, 76: 105–25.

Velasco, Andrés (1999) 'A Model of Endogenous Fiscal Deficits and Delayed Fiscal Reforms', in James Poterba and Jürgen von Hagen (eds), *Fiscal Institutions and Fiscal Performance*. Chicago: University of Chicago Press. pp. 37–58.

Vishwanath, Tara and Kaufmann, Daniel (1999) 'Towards Transparency in Finance and Governance'. Manuscript, World Bank.

Volkerink, Bjørn and de Haan, Jakob (2000) 'Fragmented Government Effects on Fiscal Policy: New Evidence'. Manuscript, University of Groningen.

Von Hagen, Jürgen (2000) 'Budgeting Institutions and Public Spending'. Manuscript, Center for European Integration Studies, University of Bonn, December.

Von Hagen, Jürgen (1992) 'Budgeting Procedures and Fiscal Performance in the European Communities', *Economic Papers*, 96.

Von Hagen, Jürgen (1991) 'A Note on the Empirical Effectiveness of Formal Fiscal Restraints', *Journal of Public Economics*, 44: 199–210.

Weingast, Barry, Shepsle, Kenneth A. and Johnsen, Christopher (1981) 'The Political Economy of Benefits and Costs: A Neoclassical Approach to Distributive Politics', *Journal of Political Economy*, 89: 642–64.

Wicksell, Knut (1896) *Finanztheoretische Untersuchungen*. Jena: Gustav Fischer.

Wildavsky, Aaron (1975) *Budgeting: A Comparative Theory of the Budget Process*. Boston, MA and Toronto: Little, Brown.

Wildavsky, Aaron and Caiden, Naomi (1997) *The New Politics of the Budgetary Process*, 3rd edn. New York: HarperCollins.

Willett, Thomas D. (2000) 'International Financial Markets as Sources of Crisis or Discipline', *Princeton Essays in International Finance*, No. 218. Princeton, NJ: Princeton University Press.

32

Performance Information and Budgeting in Historical and Comparative Perspective

Rita M. Hilton and Philip G. Joyce

Public sector budgets are used to allocate scarce resources. Because these budgets are the direct result of political processes they will always be surrounded by some degree of contention. Dissatisfaction that policy makers or others may have with public sector budgets – either on the allocation or on the outcome side – often lead them to propose changes. Changes may be focused on the process of deciding on allocations, or it may relate to managing expenditures for efficient outcomes.

Reforms can range from those genuinely intended to promote better use of public resources, to efforts aimed at gaining political advantage. One view is that a budget process reform is 'a proposal put forth by losers in an attempt to become winners' (Kliman and Fisher, 1995: 27). The reform that presently has most widespread currency worldwide is an effort designed to increase government effectiveness by introducing more information on actual performance into decisions on allocation of public resources.

Performance-oriented budget reforms have been attempted across settings, with varying degrees of success, for the past half century. So-called 'performance-based budgeting' is hard to carry out in practice because: it is conceptually difficult; it requires extensive changes in practice; and supporters of the status quo often raise significant constraints to implementation.

This chapter offers a comprehensive view of the relationship between performance information and government budget processes. The chapter is organized into three broad sections. We first provide a framework for considering the use of performance information in government budgeting.

We prefer the term performance-*informed* budgeting, noting that the relationship between performance and resources has been an abiding concern of budget reformers and that performance information can be used in many ways in many different stages of the budget process.

Second, we discuss the preconditions for the use of performance information in government budgeting. We first cover the necessary conditions for effective budgeting in general. Conditions necessary for successful implementation of more sophisticated techniques – that is, performance-informed budgeting – include clarity of mission, appropriate performance and cost measurement, and the incentives are present for using this information to make budget decisions.

Third, the chapter reviews the current state of performance-informed budgeting, with a primary focus on practice in the United States (state/local and national governments) and relatively wealthy countries that are a part of the Organization for Economic Co-operation and Development (OECD) – complemented by information on selected efforts under way in developing countries.

USING PERFORMANCE INFORMATION FOR BUDGETING: HISTORICAL AND CONCEPTUAL FRAMEWORK

One of the major criticisms that has been leveled at government budget processes is that they stop short (perhaps far short) of asking – and in turn answering – outcome questions. At most the focus is on outputs purchased; often the questions don't get past the question of inputs ('How many dollars are flowing into my state, or legislative district?'). For this reason, efforts to make the budget process relate more directly to demonstrable results have been central to budget reform over at least the past 40 years.

The range of initiatives tried – for example, Planning, Programming, Budgeting Systems (PPBS) Management by Objectives (MBO), etc. – largely failed to deliver on their promise. PPBS, for example, 'died of multiple causes, any of which was sufficient' (Schick, 1973: 148). A comprehensive review of PPBS and other systems at both the national and state levels in the United States (Harkin, 1982) noted that there were several reasons that these reforms tended to fail. First, budgeting systems had a difficult time overcoming opposition from those who feared that the reforms might interfere with the flow of funds to key electoral constituencies. Second, there were many difficulties in agreeing on the goals and objectives of many programs, which interfered with the ability to develop valid performance measures. Finally, the almost overwhelming need for data tended to kill the systems, particularly when it became clear that the data were not being used. Indeed, Aaron Wildavsky indicated that the PPBS reform not only failed but was destined to fail, because 'its defects are defects in principle, not in execution. PPB does not work because it cannot work … it requires ability to perform cognitive operations that are beyond present human (or technical) capacities' (Wildavsky, 1984: 199).

The failure of these systems, however, did not extinguish interest in the genre of reform. The logic of budgeting for results is so intuitively appealing that it has remained a primary focus for budget reformers. The 1990s, in particular, saw renewed attention, first in OECD countries such as Australia and New Zealand (Holmes and Shand, 1995), then in state and local governments in the United States (Osborne and Gaebler, 1992; General Accounting Office, 1993), then in the national government in the United States (Congressional Budget Office, 1993) and finally in the developing world. These reform efforts, often described under the rubric 'performance-based budgeting', aim to relate budget allocation to demonstrated performance.

Measuring government performance requires specifying and quantifying a complex set of relationships involving inputs (the resources used by government programs), outputs (the activities or work performed by the government organization itself) and outcomes (the broader societal results that are to be achieved as a result of these inputs and outputs). Efforts to base budgets on measures of performance stem from a variety of motivations, which span a spectrum of perspectives. At the simplest level, there is a desire to improve public sector efficiency – how can less expensive or fewer inputs be used to achieve a given output/outcome? This view assumes that relations between inputs, outputs and outcomes are identifiable – or implicitly assumes that outcomes are assured, independent of input mix. From a more complex policy perspective, reforms may be motivated by questions regarding the nature of relations between inputs, outputs and outcomes – the question might be how to improve outcomes by changing the input mix. For example, in the education sector, an input-focused process would ask the question 'how many teachers do we have?'. An output-oriented process would ask 'how many days of instruction are we delivering?'. An outcome-focused process would ask 'how much are students learning?'.

An underlying problem with so-called performance-based budgeting involves the challenge of clarity. The term is one of many (but the most common) different descriptors that are used to describe the connection of performance information, on the one hand, and government resources, on the other. In some circles, however, this term has come to connote the replacement of 'political' resource allocation with some magic algorithm that allocates resources based solely on performance data. It is not, in our view, either desirable or useful to encourage adherence to such a simplistic model. There will always be a political and a judgment-based dimension to allocation of public resources. The goal should be to have performance information brought to the table when political decisions are made. For this reason, we prefer not to use the term performance-*based* budgeting, but focus on the use of performance information throughout the budget process, or what could be called performance-*informed* budgeting.

Using a scheme first articulated by Joyce and Tompkins (2002) permits a more robust view of the role of performance information in the budget process. We look at the full budget process, recognizing that there are important questions regarding the availability and use of performance information to be asked at each stage of the traditional budget process – that is, budget preparation, budget approval, budget implementation or execution, as well as audit and evaluation.

Why does taking a more comprehensive view of the process matter? Simply put, most research into 'performance-based budgeting' has looked

Table 32.1   *Dimensions of performance measurement in the budget process*

Stage of budget process	Measures available	Use of measures to:
Budget preparation *Agency level*	Agency strategic planning and performance planning Cost accounting Performance (outcome) measures	Make tradeoffs between agency subunits to allocate funds strategically Build budget justification for submission to central budget office Determine overlapping services within agency
Budget preparation *Central Budget Office*	Government-wide strategic planning and performance planning Cost accounting Performance (outcome) measures	Make tradeoffs between agencies to allocate funds strategically Build budget justification for submission to legislative body Determine overlapping services between agencies
Budget approval *Legislative*	Performance measures, accurate cost estimates, and strategic/performance plans included with budget justifications	Compare costs to marginal effects on performance during legislative funding process Make performance expectations clear as part of budget allocation
Budget approval *Chief Executive*	Implications of legislatively-approved budget for achieving government strategic objectives	Make decisions on signature, veto, or line item veto/reduction informed by performance implications
Budget execution	Agency and government-wide strategic plans Performance (outcome) measures Cost accounting	Use spending discretion and flexibility to allocate funds in line with strategic priorities and consistent with achievement of agency performance goals
Audit and evaluation	Agency strategic goals Actual performance data Cost accounting information	Shift focus of audits/evaluations to include performance questions, rather than only financial compliance

Source: Joyce, P.G. and Tompkins, S. (2002) 'Using Performance Information for Budgeting: Clarifying the Framework and Investigating Recent State Experience', in K. Newcomer et al. (eds), *Meeting the Challenges of Performance-Oriented Government*. Washington, DC: American Society for Public Administration.

only at selected stages of the budget process. Most particularly, they have been preoccupied with questions of legislative and central budget office use. Since performance information may be used in important ways at other stages of the process – agency budget preparation, budget execution, and audit and evaluation – such a limited scope of inquiry risks missing important opportunities for applying and capturing the benefits from performance-informed budgeting.

The typology presented in Table 32.1 (from Joyce and Tompkins, 2002) embraces such a comprehensive approach to thinking about the connection between performance information and the budget. The table illustrates that there are many possible decision points at which performance information can be incorporated into the budget process. At each of these decision points, the twin questions of availability and use are equally relevant. A given government or agency might have or make use of performance information at one stage of the process, independent of what might happen at other stages of the process. For example, agencies might make substantial use of performance information in building the budget, while other actors (central budget offices, legislatures) make little or no use of that information at subsequent stages. Conversely, the absence of performance concerns in preparation and approval would not prevent a given agency from using its discretion to execute its budget by considering the effects of different execution strategies on its goals and objectives (that is, applying outcome measures).

NECESSARY CONDITIONS FOR PERFORMANCE-INFORMATION BUDGETING

Outlining a framework for understanding the role of performance information in budgeting is not enough. In our view, successful implementation of a performance-informed budgeting system cannot occur unless two sets of conditions are present. First, certain fundamental institutional and technocratic prerequisites to effective budgeting and financial management must exist. These prerequisites simply do not exist in all settings at all times. For example, some are much more likely to be present in OECD countries than in developing ones. It is important not to be too enthusiastic about replicating systems across countries, without due regard to institutional realities. Second, even if these institutional and technical prerequisites are in place, it is unwise to underestimate the practical difficulties that can be encountered in implementing performance-informed budget reforms.

Fundamental prerequisites for effective budgeting and financial management

There are a number of important characteristics of budgeting and financial management systems that enable them to perform the most basic functions of allocating and tracking public resources. Several attempts have been made in the United States to try to identify useful financial management practices (Meyers, 1997; Strachota, 1996; Ingraham et al., 2003). It is our view that these characteristics, in addition to representing the necessary conditions for effective budgeting and financial management systems, must be present before a given country attempts more sophisticated reforms, such as performance-informed budgeting. Briefly, these characteristics include:

- *The rule of law* – budgets are assumed to be adopted by duly constituted authorities (legislatures and governors, city councils and mayors, parliaments, etc.).
- *Budget adherence* – Once agreed to, spending and revenue plans are assumed to be carried out as enacted (or close) – they are not remade in a room by the minister of finance and several close associates. If remade, they should be revised by the same legitimate authorities who made them in the first place.
- *Transparency* – the government should make information about the budget available to the public. In addition, there should be a free press that has access to information on government resources.
- *Publicly expressed preferences* – the government should have the capability of collecting information on the preferences of the electorate. In the absence of reasonable information on preferences, it is very difficult for resources to be allocated efficiently.
- *Avoidance of structural deficits* – over a number of years, the budget should bring in sufficient revenues to match expenditures. This recognizes that financial management is a long-term, rather than a single-year, proposition. For example, it is a cause for concern if a government uses non-recurring revenues (transfers from other funds, short-term borrowing) to finance continuing expenditures.
- *Timely budget adoption* – adherence to budget timetables can be an important contributor to effective financial management and government performance. In particular, the failure to adopt budgets by the start of the fiscal year creates massive uncertainty and therefore tends to promote inefficiency.
- *Forecasting competence and predictability* – revenues and expenditures need to be estimated accurately. If revenues are chronically overforecast or expenditures are underforecast, mid-year corrections are often necessary, and this compromises the ability of program managers and other recipients of government funds to have predictable funding flows.
- *A functioning accounting system* – at a minimum, a government or government agency should have the ability to know how much money is available and how much has been spent. Many developing countries, in particular, have a history of being unable to provide even the most rudimentary accounting information. But this problem is not necessarily limited to developing countries.
- *Audit capacity* – governments should have the capacity to ensure accountability through effective auditing. First, a 'preaudit' capacity should exist – this has to do with controls, up front, on expenditures to guard against overspending. Second, a 'postaudit' capacity should be present – governments should know, after the fact, what money was spent for and (perhaps) what was obtained as a result of that spending.

In our view, these are the basics – the building blocks, if you will – which must be in place if budget reforms are to be implemented. If a government cannot establish these basic prerequisites, the chances are slim that a successful marriage of performance information and the budget can be carried out. Perhaps as importantly, those governments without the basic building blocks are probably better served through developing basic budgeting capacity than by embracing more ambitious reforms.

Necessary characteristics for successful performance-informed budgeting

Even if these building blocks are present, it does not mean that performance-informed budgeting is easy to carry out. While, as noted earlier, it is hard to argue against bringing more performance information into government decision processes, it is easy to ignore the real constraints that exist (even in wealthy OECD countries) that make such reforms difficult to carry out in practice. There are at least five conditions for successful use of performance information in the budget process, each of which is difficult to achieve.

1 *Public entities need to know what they are supposed to accomplish.* Holmes and Shand noted that a key condition for performance management in government is 'clarity of task and purpose' (Holmes, 1996). Strategic planning (preferably government-wide), to the extent that it enables decisions to be made that establish clear direction for government programs, is crucial. This is often quite difficult to carry out in practice, particularly in countries like the United States that have a fragmented political structure. It is relatively easier in parliamentary systems, where the majority party or coalition actually runs cabinet ministries.

2 *Valid measures of performance need to exist.* It is hard to measure outcomes in the great majority of public programs, and far easier to measure outputs. For example, the US National Aeronautics and Space Administration (NASA) has claimed that the goal of its Space Science Program is to 'chart the evolution of the universe from origin to destiny'. Quite understandably, NASA has no performance measures that would enable it to determine whether it has met this objective. It does have a great number of output indicators: for example, number of missions successfully launched. Beyond conceptual challenges of defining relevant indicators, most public sector organizations resist being held accountable for outcomes, since they are influenced by so many factors that are outside of agency – or even government – control.

3 *Accurate measures of cost need to be developed.* Connecting resources with results implies knowing how much it costs to deliver a given level of outcome. Most public organizations cannot even track how much it costs to deliver an output, largely because of problems with allocating indirect costs. In such situations, extrapolating from output to outcome cost is simply not feasible.

4 *Cost and performance information need to be brought together for budgeting decisions.* There is no simple decision rule for relating cost and performance in the public sector, at least at a macro level. A simple, but incorrect approach (embraced by some members of Congress in the United States) would be to take money from those who fail to meet performance targets, and give more money to those who meet targets. While this may sound good in theory, it relies on heroic assumptions, one of them about the causal link between money and results. In fact, for any program, sorting out the contribution of funding versus other factors would require a full understanding of the logical relationship between inputs, outputs and outcomes.

5 *Finally, participants in the budget process must have incentives to use performance information.* Successful performance-informed budgeting occurs only when those involved in the budget process move beyond the production of information to the use of information. This can only occur if all budgetary actors have effective incentives (and resources) to collect and use information. This is not the case in all situations. In fact, the incentive question is probably the most important one to focus on in determining the possibility that performance information will actually be used as an input in the various stages of budget decision-making.

In short, understanding performance-informed budgeting requires that we determine the extent to which each of these conditions is met. They are additive, in the sense that failure to identify a strategic direction imperils the development of appropriate performance measures, and the lack of appropriate measures of performance and cost undermines the appropriate use of information for budgeting purposes.

PERFORMANCE-INFORMED BUDGETING IN PRACTICE

As noted above, the introduction of more performance information into government budgeting processes is a phenomenon that not only has historical currency, but also is getting worldwide attention. While there is a great deal of activity, it does not necessarily translate into progress in achieving the goals that advocates of performance-informed budgeting are pursuing. This next section of the chapter will survey the current state of performance-informed budgeting:

1   in the United States, both in state and local governments and in the federal government;
2   in other industrialized countries in the OECD, particularly Australia, Canada, Great Britain and New Zealand; and
3   across a limited sub-set of developing countries.

The United States

In the United States, recent efforts to better connect performance information and the budget started in state and local governments, and have more recently been transferred to the national government.

State and local governments

Measures designed to promote performance measurement and share good practices. States and localities were on the cutting edge of implementing reforms to incorporate performance measurement in budgeting. Local governments, including Sunnyvale, CA, Charlotte, NC, Dayton, OH, and Phoenix, AZ, were frequently cited as examples of places where performance measurement was alive, well and influential. The best-seller *Reinventing Government* (Osborne and Gaebler, 1992) took many of its anecdotes from local governments and used them to define principles for other governments/agencies to follow. The International City/County Management Association (ICMA) has had an ongoing Center for Performance. It is, however, very difficult to generalize about local governments, given there are more than 80,000 (of uneven size and purpose) in the United States.

State governments have also been quite active. Statewide initiatives, such as the Oregon Benchmarks or Minnesota Milestones, have focused on strategic planning (Broom and McGuire, 1995). A recent report indicates that nineteen states had a statutory requirement for agencies to develop strategic plans as of the end of 2000 (Urban Institute, 2001: 5). A study of state performance-based budgeting requirements (Melkers and Willoughby, 1998) indicated that, as of 1997, forty-seven of the fifty states

indicated that they had some kind of requirement for strategic planning and performance measurement, which these authors defined as performance-based *budgeting*. This is, in our view, an overly broad definition, but the significance of the result is that it indicates just how widespread the movement toward measuring performance in the public sector actually is in the United States. While reports of activity are extensive, assessments of effectiveness are more limited.

Joyce and Tompkins (2002) attempted to address the question of the use of performance information for budgeting explicitly, by reviewing the experiences of states studied by the Government Performance Project (GPP) in 1999. (The GPP is a collaborative project between Syracuse University and *Governing* magazine which evaluates management practices in state and local governments.) This research found widespread availability of performance information, but very few actual uses of performance information throughout the budget process. Only four states – Missouri, Texas, Louisiana and Virginia – reported extensive use of performance information in the budget office; only Louisiana reported extensive use by the legislature. State agencies, on the other hand, reported substantial use of performance measures to support internal management: that is, in the course of budget implementation or execution.

Another recent study of states viewed as leaders in performance-oriented budget reform concluded that 'neither the executive branch or the legislature appear to have systematically used outcome data for budgeting' (Urban Institute, 2001: 12). Texas and Louisiana prove partial exceptions to this pattern, since the legislature appears to be incorporating performance targets in the budget. One concern expressed by managers in these six states is that performance information may be used solely to punish agencies that have not met targets, as opposed to assisting in a broader understanding of the factors contributing to agency performance. A number of additional challenges were identified as well, including the problem of dealing with results that do not happen until after the budget year, the incentives for legislators to use performance information, and the problem of multiple agencies with shared performance measures.

The federal government

The US federal government has been the subject of reform efforts at least since the 1960s, when the Planning, Programming, Budgeting System was the *reform du jour* (Schick, 1966). During the 1990s, there was renewed emphasis on the marriage of performance information and the budget, exemplified by the Government Performance and Results Act of 1993 (GPRA). GPRA requires agencies to develop strategic and performance plans, and to report on actual performance achieved. It also anticipates an eventual move to 'performance-based budgeting'.

Agencies have produced some very impressive strategic and performance plans. Most notable have been the plans produced by the Department of Transportation and the Department of Veterans' Affairs, which have been praised by the General Accounting Office. On the other hand, the GAO and others have found implementation to be a bit patchy (General Accounting Office, 1997; General Accounting Office, 2001). In particular, a number of agencies have experienced great difficulty in developing valid performance measures (Laurent, 2000).

Further, although it is clear cost accounting has not taken off in a comprehensive way across all federal agencies, there are some examples of federal agencies that have made significant strides in cost accounting. Agencies funded primarily through user fees have incentives to specifically identify their costs. For example, the United States Patent and Trademark Office, which is entirely funded through fee revenue, has invested considerable resources in determining costs. This allows them to set their fees to cover – or closely approximate – the cost of processing applications for patents and trademarks (*Government Executive,* 1999b; Peters, 2001). Other agencies have generally not made as much progress, in particular because substantial studies have not been made in reforming financial systems (Peters, 2001).

While progress has unquestionably been made in strategic planning, performance measurement and cost accounting, substantial room continues to remain in terms of the use of performance information, particularly for budgeting. The Bush Administration's recent budget evaluated the success of twenty-six federal agencies, including all of the cabinet departments in 'budget and performance integration' – one of the administration's five key management initiatives. This scheme classifies agencies into three categories, giving 'red lights' to those with significant problems, 'yellow lights' to those with mixed records and 'green lights' to those who had fully accomplished the objective of budget and performance integration. The result – no agencies in the 'green' category, eight agencies in the 'yellow' category and eighteen in the 'red' – suggests that much room for progress remains (Office of Management and Budget, 2003).

When performance information has been used in the federal budget process, it has tended to be at the budget execution stage. For example, the Veterans Health Administration has developed a sophisticated formula-driven system to allocate resources based on actual health needs, rather than on hospital location. However, reluctance of Members of Congress to close facilities constrains the agency's ability to apply the system (*Government Executive,* 1999a; Laurent, 2000). To the extent that there is flexibility to manage and commitment of managers, it is reasonable to assume that agency management of budgets will continue to look to performance concerns.

Use of performance information by elected officials for allocating resources is likely to come slowly, for three reasons. First, agreement on clear objectives – necessary for defining performance measures – does not exist in many cases. Second, systems for collecting and monitoring necessary performance and cost data are still under development. Third, and perhaps most significant, elected officials have (at best) limited incentives to use performance information in allocating public resources. Until there are electoral penalties for failing to make performance-informed decisions, it is naïve to expect the US Congress to embrace performance-informed budgeting.

Other OECD countries

The United States is not alone among industrialized countries in attempting performance-oriented budget reform. Many OECD countries are pursuing similar efforts. The general consensus is, in fact, that other countries may have progressed farther and faster than the United States. Four countries in particular are most frequently mentioned as being at the forefront of public budget reform efforts: Australia, Canada, Great Britain and New Zealand.

In 2002 the OECD published a document that reviewed the success of member countries in implementing 'results-focused management and budgeting'. In all, the OECD reported the responses of twenty-seven member countries to surveys conducted between 1999 and 2001. Several of the results reported in this document are of direct relevance to the issues raised in this chapter.

First, three-quarters of these countries reported that they routinely include performance information in their budget documentation, although only 36 per cent are legally required to do so.

Second, eleven of the twenty-seven countries (40 per cent) reported that they make a distinction between outputs and outcomes in most or all government organizations. The five that reported making such a distinction in *all* organizations included Italy, Japan, Sweden, the United States and Chile. (Australia, which probably makes this distinction in all organizations, did not respond to the survey.)

Third, the countries seem to have made much less progress in accounting than in performance measurement. The OECD analysis reviews experiences with accrual accounting and budgeting, noting that 'some see accrual accounting and budgeting as a prerequisite for accurate costing of outputs and outcomes'. The majority of OECD countries are budgeting and accounting on a cash basis. The report indicates that only 'Australia, New Zealand, and the United Kingdom reported to be budgeting on a full accrual basis and only the first two of these countries use accruals as an accounting basis for the consolidated financial statements.' In total, twenty-one of the countries reported that they continue to budget on a full cash basis; the equivalent number for accounting is eighteen.

Fourth, twenty-four of the countries responding (all but Austria and Hungary) reported that they routinely show output targets in budget justifications submitted to legislative bodies, while nineteen reported that they show outcome targets in these justifications. A total of fifteen countries reported that they systematically report on how public organizations have performed against outcome targets.

Finally, the OECD asked senior budget officials in member countries whether there was 'evidence that performance data were regularly used in determining budget allocations'. While 50 per cent of these officials answered affirmatively (40 per cent answered 'no' while 10 per cent did not respond), most of those answering yes viewed this information as being used to influence allocations within programs and agencies. Only one in three (of the affirmative responders, or one in six overall) thought that there was evidence of performance data influencing allocations between programs or ministries. In other words, agencies are much more likely to use performance information in budget preparation or execution, and the information is much less likely to be used for government-wide resource allocation.

A more detailed review of these OECD experiences cannot be attempted here due to space constraints, but certainly this survey only scratches the surface in terms of reviewing the experiences of OECD countries. The two countries most frequently highlighted as leading the way in this effort are New Zealand and Australia. The two countries have taken related, but different approaches to budget reform. (See Premchand, 1999, for a review of the experiences of these countries.)

New Zealand

In New Zealand, an important focus of the reform effort was so-called 'load shedding'; that is, as the government had previously delivered a great many goods and services with the characteristics of private goods, there was a strong argument for transferring many of those responsibilities to the private sector. Public choice theory strongly influenced other government reform efforts. According to Holmes and Shand there was a 'clear separation of policy and implementation' (Holmes and Shand, 1995: 571). The budget in New Zealand is a contract between the parliament and the delivering agency, but (significantly) that contract specifies the outputs to be delivered by the agency. The connection between outputs and outcomes is to occur at the level of the parliament. Further, a significant characteristic of this reform was the definition of inputs in accrual, rather than cash, form. So in short, in New Zealand performance-informed budgeting is characterized by explicit contracts wherein the accrued costs are incurred by the ministries in order to deliver the agreed upon outputs, which then are assumed to deliver the expected results.

Australia

The Australian reform effort differs from that of its neighbor on the other side of the Tasman Sea in two significant ways. First, there is much less of an emphasis on privatization in Australia, in large part because Australia did not have the kind of bloated public sector that was present in New Zealand. This does not mean, however, that private sector incentive systems, such as introducing more competition for government services and increasing user charges, were not an important element of the Australian reform; they were. Second, the explicit emphasis in the agencies is not on outputs, but on outcomes. Put another way, in Australia the agencies are encouraged to make the linkages between outputs and outcomes, but all along it is clear to them that their responsibility transcends just the delivery of outputs. In Australia, the system was designed to a much greater degree to match accountability with results, with the removal detailed controls over inputs; this implied a much greater level of trust in and autonomy of bureaucracies in budgeting than exists in New Zealand.

The developing country setting

Non-OECD countries vary greatly. In 2000, there were over 150 countries falling into either the 'low income' or 'middle income' categories, based on gross national income per capita (International Bank for Reconstruction and Development, 2002). As a group, these countries face greater challenges in public budgeting than high income countries. The fiscal constraints and service demands facing these countries tend to be greater than in OECD or high income countries. The lack of basic financial management systems and the often ambiguous and confusing goals and incentives faced by these countries often make it quite difficult for them to assess public sector performance.

The poorest developing countries often lack many, if not most, of the basic reform prerequisites suggested earlier in this chapter – that is, adherence to the rule of law; transparent publicly expressed preferences; absence of structural deficits (excessive debt financing has been a chronic problem for the poorest countries); timely and conclusive budget adoption; basic institutional capacity (forecasting, systems); and availability of data. In some countries, the most basic links between macro realities, revenue flows and budget documents may not be in place. In other countries, budgeting and financial systems are more fully developed and steps needed to incorporate use of performance information in budgeting are correspondingly more limited – for example, to improving capacity in certain prerequisites (e.g. forecasting, data systems).

In the past ten years, a variety of developments have simultaneously resulted in conditions that are not only favorable to reform of public budgeting practices – but essentially require it. First, the broad-based movement to improve transparency and require good governance throughout economies directly addresses some of the key prerequisites for budget reform (that is, rule of law, timely budget adoption, improved access to available data). Second, a strong trend among donors towards working with developing country policy makers to focus on a viable medium-term economic outlook addresses a most basic prerequisite, that is, establishing a framework within which planning is feasible. Third, there has been a widespread movement across donors towards focus on monitoring and evaluating development efforts, which places attention squarely on outcomes.

Government administration and fiscal management in developing countries has been influenced by practice in OECD countries, for two reasons. First is the natural process of learning across countries. Second, development programs – whether of OECD countries or multilateral organizations – focus on assisting developing countries to implement what is viewed as successful experience. A variety of examples of a developing country experience with use of performance information in allocation of public resources is emerging. Time lag is inevitable, and it is too early to judge success, but there is a wide field to watch.

Virtually without exception, budget reform in developing countries is an integral means towards the general objective of modernizing government. It is not, as in OECD countries, a step towards accomplishing marginal technical improvements in the use of public resources. Selected examples give a sense of the type of reforms promoting the use of performance information in public budgeting in developing countries.

- **Ghana**, in 1995, launched a Public Financial Management Reform Program (Kusek and Rasappan, 2001). In addition to focusing policy makers' attention on outcomes and promoting buy-in to public expenditure management, the reform was aimed at simply putting key administrative prerequisites in place, that is, an adequate accounting system, auditing, monitoring and information management systems.
- **Brazil**, following on challenges experienced in the wake of the 1997 Asian financial crisis, embarked upon an extensive fiscal reform program. The government committed itself to reforms extending beyond short-term solutions, to address structural causes of fiscal imbalance. Initially, a modern legal framework was established, and related institutional and administrative changes were implemented to focus agencies and subnational governments on fiscal discipline. Subsequently, the government has moved forward towards enhancing transparency in public expenditure management, improving forecasting and instituting a multi-year expenditure planning process – thereby incorporating performance information in the allocation of public resources.
- **Benin** committed to a path of budget reform in 2000, in order to allow it to achieve its poverty reduction objectives. The reform plan covered financial systems and controls. In addition, it very explicitly addressed linking budget allocations with programs and sector priorities. The government very explicitly chose to begin a multi-year effort aimed at building its capacity to collect, manage and apply performance information in the budget process.

Recent budget reforms in transition economy countries differ from experience in other regions primarily only in starting point. These countries, in particular, face significant challenges in adopting the use of performance information. Moving from central planning to a more outcome-oriented resource allocation model requires substantial change. The practice of using standard formulae or 'norms' to calculate input–output relationships has proven difficult to abandon in many cases. Countries across the region are at varying stages of reform.

The Ukranian case is notable because of complementary civil society interest. Not all budget reform efforts come exclusively from the public sector. One of the most interesting developments – implicitly focused largely on the execution and evaluation stages of budgeting – is the emergence of civil society movements for improved accountability in allocation and use of public resources. Such efforts have emerged in a wide variety of countries, for example, India, Brazil, South Africa. While these popular movements are frequently focused at local levels of government, they generally are implicitly calling for use of, and public access to, performance information in public budgets.

While experience continues to unfold in developing countries, two common lessons can be drawn from the early stages, irrespective of countries' political starting point or relative wealth. First, because measures aimed at incorporating performance information into the process of allocating public resources are not only technical reforms, but have political implications, significant political will is required in order for the reforms to take hold and become effective. Second, because of the stringency of resource constraints – financial and human – in developing countries, attention to selection and sequencing of manageable reforms is particularly critical.

CONCLUSION

The introduction of more performance information into government budget processes is a laudable goal. It is very difficult, however, to carry out in practice. Four conclusions seem particularly worth keeping in mind as governments continue to struggle with whether – and how – to put performance-informed budgeting into practice.

1 Performance-informed budgeting is not a substitute for sound financial management and budgeting practice. Many countries would do well to focus on building basic budgeting capacity before attempting more sophisticated reforms.

2 Even where necessary conditions for good budgeting in general exist, there are certain building blocks for successful integration of performance information into the budget process. Governments need to know where they want to go, they need to have appropriate measures of performance and cost, and they need to create incentives for relating performance information to budget decisions. The incentives to use performance information may be lacking across some or all stages of the budget process.

3 Performance-informed budgeting can pay real benefits, even if it doesn't apparently pay significant dividends. Government budget processes have many stages, and there are many ways to use performance information to improve government effectiveness at each of these stages. While it seems more difficult (and less likely) for performance measures to make government-wide resource tradeoffs, they can be (and are being) used quite successfully for managing resources during budget implementation. Since the management of resources does involve their allocation, this is a potentially significant development.

4 Further, the development of better performance and cost information can itself spur greater attention to performance, even in places where an input focus has been ascendant. Transparency concerning the relationship between funding and results can shine a light on practices that result in failing to allocate resources toward desired societal ends.

In short, past reforms have frequently been viewed as failures, in part because they have been oversold; Light (1997) suggests that the problem has been too much reform, rather than not enough. We would argue that the failure of these reforms only looks like failure through a narrow lens. If one looks at the experience of governments over the past 40 years, it is more likely that the trend is upward, both in terms of the availability of performance information and the use of that information. Viewed through this lens, the current wave of reform is consistent with the general trend and is consistent with a general shift in culture and change in budgetary practice that – while operating in fits and starts – has been under way since the middle part of the last century.

NOTE

The authors wish to thank Jody Zall Kusek and William Doritinsky for invaluable advice and assistance. The findings, views, and interpretations expressed in this paper are those of the authors, and should not be attributed in any way to others – either individuals or organizations.

REFERENCES

Broom, C.A. and McGuire, L. (1995) 'Performance-Based Government Models: Building a Track Record', *Public Budgeting and Finance*, 15 (4): 3–17.

Congressional Budget Office (1993) *Using Performance Measures in the Federal Budget Process*. Washington, DC.

General Accounting Office (1993) *Performance Budgeting: State Experiences and Implications for the Federal Government*. GAO/AFMD-93-41 (February). Washington, DC.

General Accounting Office (1997) *The Government Performance and Results Act: 1997 Governmentwide Implementation Will Be Uneven*. GAO/GGD 97-109. Washington, DC.

General Accounting Office (2001) *Managing for Results: Federal Managers' Views on Key Management Issues Vary Widely Across Agencies*. GAO-01-592. Washington, DC.

Government Executive (1999a) 'Healthy Accomplishments', February, pp. 66–8.

Government Executive (1999b) 'Patent Answers', February, pp. 81–4.

Harkin, J.M. (1982) 'Effectiveness Budgeting: The Limits of Budget Reform', *Policy Studies Review*, 2 (3), pp. 112–26.

Holmes, M. (1996) 'Budget Reform: Experiences from the Past 15 Years'. Notes for a presentation to the South African Conference on Expenditure Budget Reform, Pretoria, South Africa, 1–2 April.

Holmes, M. and Shand, D. (1995) 'Management Reform: Some Practitioner Perspectives on the Past Ten Years', *Governance*, 8 (4): 551–78.

Ingraham, P., Joyce, P. and Donahue, A. (2003) *Government Performance: Why Management Matters*. Baltimore, MD: Johns Hopkins University Press.

International Bank for Reconstruction and Development (2002) *World Development Report 2002*. Washington, DC: The World Bank.

Jones, L.R. and McCaffery, J.L. (1992) 'Federal Financial Management Reform and the Chief Financial Officers Act', *Public Budgeting and Finance*, 12 (4): 75–86.

Joyce, P.G. (1999) 'Performance-based budgeting', in Roy Meyers (ed.), *Handbook of Government Budgeting*. San Francisco: Jossey-Bass. pp. 592–617.

Joyce, P.G. and Tompkins, S. (2002) 'Using Performance Information for Budgeting: Clarifying the Framework and Investigating Recent State Experience', in K. Newcomer et al. (eds), *Meeting the Challenges of Performance-Oriented Government*. Washington, DC: American Society for Public Administration.

Kamensky, J. (1996) 'Role of the "Reinventing Government" Movement in Federal Management Reform', *Public Administration Review*, 56 (3): 247–55.

Kettl, Donald F. (1995) 'Building Lasting Reform', Chapter 2 of *Inside the Reinvention Machine*. Washington, DC: Brookings Institution.

Kliman, A. and Fisher, L. (1995) 'Budget Reform Proposals in the NPR Report', *Public Budgeting and Finance*, 15 (1): 27–38.

Kusek, J.Z. and Rasappan, A. (2001) 'Outcomes-Based Budgeting Systems: Experience from Developed and Developing Countries'. Special Paper prepared for the World Bank for the Government of Egypt, November.

Laurent, A. (2000) 'The Tyranny of Anecdotes', *Government Executive*, March, pp. 36–9.

Light, P. (1997) *The Tides of Reform: Making Government Work*. New Haven, CT: Yale University Press.

Liner, B., Hatry, H., Vinson, E., Allen, R., Dusenbury, P., Bryan, S. and Snell, R. (2001) *Making Results-Based State Government Work*. Washington, DC: The Urban Institute.

Melkers, J. and Willoughby, K. (1998) 'The State of the States: Performance-Based Budgeting Requirements in 47 out of 50', *Public Administration Review*, 58 (1): 66–73.

Meyers, Roy T. (1997) 'Is There a Key to the Normative Budgeting Lock?', *Policy Sciences*, 29 (3): 171–88.

Organization for Economic Co-operation and Development (2002) *Overview of Results Focussed Management and Budgeting in OECD Member Countries*. Paris: OECD.

Osborne, D. and Gaebler, T. (1992) *Reinventing Government*. Reading, MA: Addison–Wesley.

Peters, K. (2001) 'Money Pit', *Government Executive*, April, pp. 16–20.

Premchand, A. (1999) 'Budgetary Management in the United States and in Australia, New Zealand, and the United Kingdom,' in Roy Meyer (ed.), *Handbook of Government Budgeting*. San Francisco: Jossey-Bass. pp. 82–115.

Schick, A. (1966) 'The Road to PPB: The Stages of Budget Reform', *Public Administration Review*, 26 (4): 243–58.

Schick, Allen (1973) 'A Death in the Bureaucracy: the Demise of Federal PPB', *Public Administration Review*, 33 (2): 146–56.

Strachota, D. (1994) 'A Blueprint for State and Local Government Budgeting', *Government Finance Review*, April, pp. 48–50.

United States, Office of Management and Budget (2003) *Budget of the United States Government, Fiscal Year 2004*. Washington, DC: US Government Printing Office.

Wildavsky, A. (1984) *The Politics of the Budgetary Process*, 4th edn. Boston, MA: Little, Brown.

33

Accrual Budgeting in a Comparative Perspective

Leonard Kok

Since the introduction of New Public Management (NPM), there has been increasing emphasis within the public sector on working more like a business. Those who consult *Reinventing Government* (Osborne and Gaebler, 1992) as the handbook of New Public Management, are confronted on almost every page with the agenda for more business-like government. A few examples include a focus upon service delivery, a results orientation, a focus upon client needs, market orientation etc. It is not surprising that the countries that have attempted to introduce the ideas of NPM in the public sector sooner or later also confront the issue of how the budgetary system, that in many countries is a cash-based budgeting and accounting system, can also accommodate these more business-like goals.

Why is this topic of budgeting and accounting so important? The answer is that budgeting and accounting are at the heart of the administrative process of a government – and this administrative process is also the basis of the power of the purse in representative democracies. The type of budgeting and accounting system may influence the way in which administrations and parliament decide about policy that has budgetary consequences; and almost each policy decision has budgetary consequences.

The two main systems of budgeting and accounting are the cash-based and the accrual system, which is common in the market sector. It is not possible to say that one system is better than the other. It totally depends on the use of the system within the governing bodies. But one thing must be clear: if you want to introduce more entrepreneurial elements in the public sector, a cash system creates many problems and a business-line system will fit much better.

First, a number of central concepts of business accounting are introduced and discussed. This is a general overview and should not be read as a speed course in book-keeping. Secondly, a sketch is offered of developments in this area in a number of OECD countries. Finally – as a case study – a more detailed description of the experiences of the Netherlands with business accounting is presented. The plans for the implementation of business accounting in the Netherlands has been described by an OECD report (2002) as an example of best practice in the OECD member countries. The Dutch approach illustrates an interesting combination of both strengthening results orientation and also increasing effectiveness, without disrupting the ability to command and control the budget.

OVERVIEW

Concepts

It is desirable first to clarify a number of concepts. This chapter is about business accounting or – as it is often called – accrual accounting. As has already been stated, there were and continue to be a number of countries that have not adopted the accrual principle within their public sectors, and rather continue to conduct their budgetary activities according to the principles of the cash-based system. In the cash-based system, expenditure is deducted in full from the moment when the expenditure is made. A salary payment to a public servant for example would be deducted from the books and would thus effect the budget in the year and month that the payment took place. Similarly, payment for a road would be deducted in the budget at the moment that the expenditure took place. The difference between the salary payment and the expenditure for a new road is that the payment of wages would have to be paid again and again every month, unless of course the employee has stopped working, while alternatively the payment for the road is in principle a one-off expenditure, even though the road would continue to provide services for many years after the payment is made. The accrual principle allows the expenditures that are made today and that will provide benefits over a number of years to be deducted at small amounts over a longer period of time. The expenditure for a road for example would be included in the book-keeping at the time that the services of the road are used. Due to wear and tear, the road loses value over time and this reduction in value is described by a technical term: depreciation.

The system of depreciation and calculation of expenditure over time is common practice in the private sector, but this system is clearly also much more complicated than the cash-based system of accounting. How do you determine the rate of wear and tear for example and thereby also the yearly depreciation of goods? This is more difficult to calculate than the total cash expenditure that is made at the time the road is laid down. The cash expenditure is simply the concrete payment made to the contractor.

The accrual system provides very useful extra information that its user can draw upon in decision making – for example, whether it is financially better to buy or rent an office. In the cash system buying is always more expensive than hiring because the one-off purchase will be deducted at the time of purchase and thus will always be a greater deduction than the yearly expenditure for renting an office. But the actual costs of purchasing an office are obviously not the same as the purchase price and the cash expenditure that was made at the time of that purchase. To identify the costs of buying an office it is first of all importance to know the reduction in the value of the office that occurs in a year, the depreciation. In addition, there is also another type of costs that need to be considered when buying an office, and that is the financial costs of the purchase or rather the sequestration of one's property. This requires additional explanation. For example, consider that you did not buy the office but instead put the money in the bank; this would have provided you with a financial return in the form of interest. By not putting the money in the bank and receiving this income from the interest, one incurs a capital charge. A requirement of efficient investment decisions is making

visible this lost return, or rather the – hidden – costs of the sequestration of one's property.

In order to be able to calculate the capital charges that the public sector is subject to, it is necessary to be able to get an insight into the value of government property and possessions. In business accounting these possessions (and debts) are included in the balance of the book-keeping. Therefore in addition to the financial overview that is provided by an accrual accounting system, business accounting also provides an overview of possessions and debts. These two aspects of the financial accounts should connect seamlessly. The balance of the accounts will in this respect give insight into the financial position of the organization or the nation. If the balance is compared to the previous year, one is also able to see how the financial position has changed – whether a nation is becoming wealthier or poorer.

Another element of budgeting and accounting for governments is related to the nature of government: there is no market that sets prices, so you need a budgeting system. The budgeting system is the base for providing departments with money. This system must be clear and tight, otherwise it will lead to budgetary problems. A cash system is from this point of view the most suitable system; the only way to manipulate a cash-based system is at the end of the year by shifting cash from one year to another. The ways of manipulating an accruals system are more difficult to understand, but there are many more opportunities: by making provision for spreading out costs, by making reservations, by changing depreciation periods, etc. These sorts of things must of course be declared in the annual accounts, but that does not make the accounting system more transparent.

Certainly there are also other aspects that are associated with an accrual accounting system and these will be discussed later in this chapter, when the case of the Netherlands is presented. To summarize, Table 33.1 provides an overview of arguments in the debate on cash and accruals.

DEVELOPMENTS IN OECD COUNTRIES

The countries in the OECD that have introduced some kind of accrual accounting system have generally done so in combination with broader management reforms of the public sector. The most interesting OECD countries will be discussed here but first, information on the systems used by OECD countries is given in Table 33.2 and planned future developments are detailed in Table 33.3.

Table 33.1   *Main elements of accounting systems*

	Cash-based system	Accruals system
Main characteristic	Shows payments and receipts	Shows profits and losses
What is administered	Cash as it occurs	Spreads costs over years
Main purpose	Treasury information	Information on costs and property
Main advantage	Easy to understand	More information
Main disadvantage	Less information	Complexity
Main risk	End of the year cash manipulation	Manipulation of figures
Budget control	Solid base	More room for manoeuvring

Table 33.2   *Accounting basis applied for budget approved by legislature*

	Full accrual basis	Accrual basis, except no capitalization or depreciation of assets	Cash basis, except certain transactions on accrual basis	Full cash basis
Australia	X			
Austria				X
Belgium				X
Canada		X		
Czech Republic				X
Denmark			X[1]	
Finland		X[2]		
France				X
Germany				X
Greece				X
Hungary				X
Iceland		X		
Ireland				X
Japan				X
Korea				X
Luxembourg				X
Mexico				X
Netherlands			X	
Norway				X
New Zealand	X			
Poland				X
Portugal				X
Spain				X
Sweden				X
Switzerland				X
Turkey				X
United Kingdom	X[3]			
United States			X[4]	

1 Denmark – Interest expenses and employee pensions treated on accrual basis.
2 Finland – Transfer payments not on accrual basis.
3 United Kingdom – Budget on full accrual basis effective fiscal year 2001–02.
4 United States – Interest expenses, certain employee pension plans, and loan and guarantee programmes on accrual basis.

Source: OECD

Full accrual basis

New Zealand

New Zealand is the most renowned example. In 1984, against the background of serious economic problems, fundamental reforms were introduced. In New Zealand these reforms included both privatization and the reduction of the public sector, as well as increasing the effectiveness, cost consciousness and accountability of the public sector. Inside public sector organizations

Table 33.3   *Plans to move budget to accrual basis*

Country	Full accrual basis budgeting to be introduced	Additional accrual basis information to be presented
Canada	X[1]	
Denmark		X
Germany		X
Korea	X[1]	
Netherlands	X	
Portugal		X
Sweden	X[1]	
Switzerland	X[1]	

1 Under active consideration.

Source: OECD

contracts for goods and services over a five-year period were made between ministers and the responsible managers. An accrual accounting system was seen as an essential instrument for supporting these contract arrangements. In the first place accruals promoted the clarification of concrete products and services and secondly they made possible the calculation of the costs of these products and services. In New Zealand a number of big changes and reforms were introduced at the same time: big reductions in government finances were made, a new organizational structure within the public sector was created, a new system of book-keeping was introduced and the privatization wave swept across a number of formerly government organizations.

Australia and Canada

In Australia the changes have been more incremental. The creation of units within the public sector that were granted more independence (agencies) occurred in combination with the introduction of accruals. These reforms were, as in New Zealand, intended to make managers more accountable for their management and to hold them responsible for their results. In order to meet these intentions in a consistent and comparable way and at the same time to improve the effectiveness, efficiency and performance of these independent units, the information from an accrual accounting system was central. The developments in Canada were, although somewhat later, quite similar to Australia. In Canada improvements in quality and efficiency were also high on the government's agenda.

United Kingdom

Agencies were also created in the United Kingdom, but in the UK the structure of the public sector maintained core departments with a steering role. Only some organizations responsible for the implementation of policy were granted agency status. Reforms to improve the performance of the public sector had already begun in the 1980s. It was quickly recognized that these reforms could be promoted and strengthened by the replacement of the cash-based accounting system with business accounting methods. The latter would also enable comparisons to be made between the public and private sector and it would also promote cooperation, or rather what has been referred to as public–private partnerships. Therefore in the UK the process began with making organizations accountable for their financial activities according to an accrual basis and since that time accrual budgeting has been introduced. In the UK this arrangement is referred to as Resource Accounting and Budgeting (RAB).

The objectives of this operation in the UK can be shortly summarized thus:

- Faster and clearer accountability
- Improved implementation of the budget and planning
- Better management of assets and working capital
- Improvement in cost price information
- Improvement in the way decision making and investment decisions are taken
- Connecting performance, outputs and outcomes.

Partial accrual basis

The arguments in the UK can also be seen in all of the countries that have, in one way or another, been occupied with the introduction of accruals. Table 33.4 presents the accounting basis that OECD countries use at the present time.

Some countries, such as the United States and France, have made only partial use of accruals. These countries do not allow accrual information

Table 33.4   *Accounting basis applied for consolidated (whole of government) financial statements*

	Full accrual basis	Accrual basis, except no capitalization or depreciation of assets	Cash basis, except certain transactions on accrual basis	Full cash basis
Australia	X			
Austria				X
Belgium				X
Canada		X		
Czech Republic				X
Denmark			X[1]	
Finland	X			
France			X[2]	
Germany				X
Hungary				X
Iceland		X		
Ireland				X
Japan				X
Korea				X
Luxembourg				X
Mexico				X
Netherlands				X
Norway				X
New Zealand	X			
Poland			X[3]	
Portugal				X
Spain				X
Sweden	X			
Switzerland				
Turkey				X
United Kingdom				X
United States			X	X[4]

1 Denmark – Interest expense and employee pensions treated on accrual basis.
2 France – Interest expense and certain other transactions treated on accrual basis. Full accrual basis to be introduced.
3 Poland – Employee pensions treated on accrual basis.
4 United Kingdom – statements on full accrual basis effective fiscal year 2005–06.

Source: OECD

to be primary in the budget (ex-ante), but use it rather as a way to account for financial expenditure (ex-post). This is an important point because the rules for reporting on an accrual basis originate from the private sector. Standards for reporting have been developed in the private sector, but it is ultimately accountants that define how the different aspects of this accounting should be included within the budget. In some countries it is deemed acceptable to use these methods in the process of accounting for organizational activities and performance, but not as a way to set up the budget. This is because setting up both the budget and reporting of expenditure according to the rules of accrual accounting involves the transfer of decision making power to accountants. This effect has led to some countries preferring to maintain a budget organized according to cash-based principles.

In the Netherlands this problem – of reporting requirements that at some point could lend accountants influence over what is primarily a political process, the budget – has been resolved in a very creative way. This is discussed in the next section of this chapter. In addition, the IMF and World Bank have shown – against the background of improved transparency and good government – increased interest in administration on an accrual basis.

THE DUTCH CASE

Since the beginning of the 1990s the Netherlands has introduced diverse initiatives to promote the results orientation of the public sector and increase its effectiveness. Over the years a number of instruments have been adopted to make the cash-based system of accounting less rigid (for example, the year end margin, the savings facility etc.), and to promote more flexibility in the management rules, for example through the creation of agencies. (Agencies are government bodies that implement policy and may use business accounting methods.)

At the end of the 1990s initiatives were introduced to encourage the public sector to become more results orientated. This was primarily promoted by making the budget more transparent, so that on the one hand the relation between policy goals and policy results, and on the other hand that between policy instruments and financial resources, were central. The policy goals and policy results formed the spine of the budget and accounting to the parliament, but it also strengthened the results orientation inside government organizations themselves. The creation of the budget and the yearly accounting reports to parliament are not just loose facades but are concretely related to the results of policy activities within the government. The agencies represent the jewels in the crown of a government that will be more results orientated.

Owing to the introduction of agencies (from 1994), the situation has arisen where two budget systems are used side by side: the cash-based accounting system in the (core) ministries and the accrual accounting system in the agencies. This has been the subject of an increasing degree of criticism from, among others, the Court of Audit in the Netherlands. In 1997 a sketch was drawn of the actual growth in agencies and other organizations that used an accrual accounting system (at the moment there are more than twenty agencies and another anticipated twenty in preparation). Given this growth, it has become logical to allow the national budgetary system to change from a cash-based system to an accrual accounting system. Not least because the provinces, local government and businesses all work with (a form of) accrual accounting. Since the end of the 1990s it has become less a question of whether the public sector would adopt a national accrual accounting budget system and more a question of when this turning point would take place. The pace of this reform is still uncertain.

Goals of an accrual accounting system

The goals behind the introduction of an integral accrual accounting system in the Netherlands are to a large degree equivalent with those identified in the UK.

1. Improvement in (decision making over) efficiency and effectiveness through:
2. better insight into (integral) costs of policy instead of just having information on cash payments and
3. improvements in investment decisions by making cash restrictions less important.
4. Improvement in allocation at the cabinet level.
5. Introduction of a sustainable and unequivocal budget norm.

These goals are briefly discussed below.

Improvement in (decision making over) efficiency and effectiveness of government expenditures

The most important motivation for introducing an accrual accounting system in the Netherlands was the improvement of (decision making over) efficiency and effectiveness of government expenditure. This can be realized in two ways.

Better insight into the (integral) costs of a policy
In the accrual accounting system the integral costs of policy are made transparent. Costs and cash expenditures can vary from each other, for example in the investment expenditure. The accrual accounting system delivers information that makes it possible to make more efficient decisions and promote a better command of fixed assets.

Improvement in investment decisions
By working with more integral costs, it becomes possible to make considerations of future costs in investment decisions (life cycle costs approach). For example, an investment in a road becomes both the cost of building it and the costs of maintaining it. In the current system investments are funded on a 'pay-as-you-go-basis'. This encourages cheaper roads that require expensive maintenance to be chosen instead of more expensive roads with cheaper maintenance. In the accrual accounting system these considerations can be looked at differently because there is not a one-off total payment for the road made but rather the structural costs become central. This promotes more efficient decision making.

Improvement in allocation

The second motivation for an integral accrual accounting system is improvement in allocation at the macro level. The new budget system enables a more balanced consideration of investment expenditure versus possible running costs, and also in times when economic and budgetary conditions are tight. There is thus an end to the relative judgement of consumption expenditure when making budget decisions.

A sustainable and unequivocal budget norm

The third motivation for the integral introduction of an accrual accounting system is the realization of an unequivocal budgetary norm. In the Dutch situation a budgetary norm in cost terms was put in place as part of the introduction of agencies. In contrast, the rest of the national public sector used a budgetary norm that was calculated in cash terms. As a result of this distinction an intended effect arose whereby it became attractive to be selective about which norm to use, depending upon which calculation provided the better outcome (double norm, double morale). With the increasing growth of agencies and other organizations that use an accrual accounting system in the Dutch public sector, this situation is expected to present greater problems in the future. With the introduction of a national budget that is integrated in terms of cost, the possibility of shopping between different budgeting norms is eliminated.

Contours of an accrual accounting system in the national public sector

In the new budgetary system that is based upon accruals, the budget will obtain the new character of a cost budget. This is in contrast to the cash budget that had characterized the previous budgetary system and it places primary emphasis on costs. Costs can be equivalent to cash expenditure, such as is the case for running costs and expenditures like wages or subsidies etc. Costs can also be characterized as long-term investments with depreciation costs; this is the case with capital expenditure. Similarly, costs may also consist of interest. In the annual report of a ministry, the accounting of the cost budget is presented and included in the balance of the budget.

Why choose a variant of accrual accounting administration and not a standard type of administration that is used in the private sector? There are two reasons. The first is that government services and production, unlike in the private sector, often lack a clear relationship between costs and benefits. This can be seen, for example, in the (lack of) relationship between tax receipts and defence expenditure. From the receipts perspective, it is therefore not desirable to make a clear relation with costs. There are some exceptions to this example, such as organizations that are set up to cover their own

costs. Similarly, it is just as undesirable to speak of profit and loss when considering the state of a department's costs and receipts.

Secondly, decisions about the national budget are often made against a background of endless social questions that require extra expenditure, therefore it is desirable that a tight budgetary regime is in place. The budget should, to work effectively and also be governable, be able to manage different aspects of expenditure with respect to the cost of policy.

These two explanations also have consequences for the way that the budgetary system in the Netherlands will continue to be constructed. In setting up the budget, the possessions of the state play an important role. Where there is no 'correction from the market place', the 'correction of the budget' is absolutely necessary. In contrast to the, for the most part, flexible reporting conditions of the market sector, within the public sector the reporting should be conducted according to tight budgetary regulations. This applies also to the definition of capital expenditure and the basis upon which it is valued. These two somewhat more technical aspects are further described below.

Defining capital expenditure and the basis of valuation

In an accrual-based budget, the steering accountability regulations and the introduction of a norm for government expenditure are based upon costs. Therefore it is necessary that the definition of capital expenditure (that is, expenditure where the cash price and the costs per definition are not the same) is unequivocal and sustainable. The definition of capital expenditure determines which expenditure can be included within the balance and whether that expenditure may be deducted over a period of time. Beside the requirement that the definition of capital expenditure be unequivocal and sustainable, this definition must also be economically useful, practical and transparent. The European System of National and Regional Accounts '95 (ESR '95) presents a good option in this respect.

In addition, with regard to the issues of the basis for valuation, the ESR '95 has been explicitly chosen as a starting point. This means that, where possible, valuations are calculated according to actual value. Where ministries own stocks, for example TNT Post Group N.V, the calculation of actual worth can be simply made according to the rates on the stock market. However, it is much more difficult to calculate the value of some of the fixed assets of the public sector. In these cases the actual worth is calculated according to an indexed historical cost price. Where it is desirable, fixed assets can also be periodically revalued in order to correct for differences in the actual worth of an asset and its indexed value.

Guarantees in the system

Since it is generally recognized that an accrual administration offers more possibilities for 'budgetary manipulation' than a cash administration, it is necessary to implement and formulate tight regulations. In the Netherlands such regulations have been developed for the national accounts. This is also clearly advantageous from an efficiency perspective. However, the risk exists that in times of prosperity opportunistic demands may be placed upon valuation, depreciation etc. in contrast to times when there is greater budgetary flexibility. Therefore it is useful to establish an authority that is able to judge the legitimacy of regulations and exceptions. In order to promote reliability and transparency, it is obvious that this authority should be independent.

Implementation

The implementation of an accrual accounting system demands an extensive transformation process. It is therefore important to connect to this process a number of factors which, if adequately attended to, offer a greater chance that the implementation will be visibly successful. These critical success factors are:

- Availability of (expert) personnel
- Adequate provision of information
- Adequate adaptation of the law and regulations
- Valuation of current fixed assets
- Support from important politicians.

When is adequate attention is granted to these factors, the introduction of an accrual administration can contribute significantly to a more effective and transparent public sector. Also, where stringent regulations are chosen to support the budget and accountability more generally, the risks to budgetary control can be avoided.

CONCLUSION

This chapter has examined budgeting and accounting in the government sector, looking at the two main systems, which we can refer to as 'cash' and 'accruals'. In a cash based accounting system the expenditures and receipts are calculated in the accounts at the moment that the cash is deducted or received. This is simple, but also provides little information. Alternatively, in the accruals system expenditure and receipts are calculated and included in the budget in the relevant *period* that these transactions take place. We therefore call these expenditures costs and refer to the receipts as benefits. The balance of the costs and benefits at the end of the year is calculated in the balance. The balance is a yearly overview of the possessions and the debts. This system is much more complicated, but also gives much more information. In many OECD countries, there is a transformation from cash systems to more or less accrual standards.

It is not possible to state that one system is better than the other; it depends on the purpose a government has with its budget. A budget system must fit to a government's purpose. This is also the reason why the government of the Netherlands has developed plans for an alternative system, which can be described as a 'third way', between cash and accruals. It combines elements of budget control of cash budgeting with elements of real cost information of an accruals system. It also provides information for better budgetary decision making: it offers more efficiency, as in a private enterprise.

REFERENCES

Blöndal, Jón R. and Kromann Kristensen, Jens (2002) 'Budgeting in the Netherlands', *OECD Journal on Budgeting*, 1 (3): 43–78.

Commonwealth of Australia (1999) 'Fiscal Policy Under Accrual Budgeting'. Information Paper.

General Audit Office (2000) *Accrual Budgeting: Experiences of Other Nations and Implications for the United States*. Washington, DC: GAO.

Her Majesty's Treasury (1999) *Resource Accounting and Budgeting, A Short Guide to the Financial Reforms.* London: HMSO.

Ministerie van Financiën (2002) 'Eigentijds Begroten (Modernizing the Budget)', in Ministerie van Financiën, *Miljoenennota 2002* (Budget Memorandum 2002). The Hague, pp. 106–27, (www.minfin.nl).

Norman, Richard (1997) *Accounting for Government*. University of Wellington, Victoria Link Ltd.

OECD (2002) 'Overview of Results Focussed Management and Budgeting in OECD Member Countries'. Paper prepared for an Expert Meeting on the Quality of Public Expenditures, Paris, 11–12 February 2002.

Osborne, David and Gaebler, Ted (1992) *Reinventing Government: How the Entrepreneurial Spirit is Transforming the Public Sector.* Reading, MA: Addison-Wesley.

Van den Berg, J.W. and Kok, L.H. (2001) 'Eigentijds Begroten (Modernizing the Budget)', *Openbare Uitgaven*, 33 (5): 211–16.

Section 10

COMPARATIVE AND INTERNATIONAL PUBLIC ADMINISTRATION

Introduction

Edward C. Page

The comparative study of public administration is hardly new. Raadschelders' (1998: 45) analysis of administrative history includes Herodotus, Aristotle and Ibn Khaldun as comparativists. Looking at the modern period only, Weber's ([1920] 1972) analysis of bureaucracy, one of the landmarks in the whole area of public administration and management, is based on a comparative cross-national and historical perspective. And among the early modern social science pioneers in the field one could include Lowell (1896), Otto Hintze ([1911a] 1962), Herman Finer (1932) and Brian Chapman (1959). Yet the field is commonly regarded as something of a laggard when compared to other areas of political science such as the study of elections and parties (see Derlien, 1992).

Brans' chapter helps put this laggard reputation in perspective. The slogan 'compare or perish' underlines the importance of comparative research for explanation, theory development and the generation of practical advice. Despite the major constraints involved in comparison – complexity of subject matter, availability of data, and definition and specification of data – the field has managed to produce a respectable volume of work. What has been missing is a 'grand theory', to give the field focus and sets of common questions.

Instead, the discipline has travelled along two tracks – one reflecting changing practical concerns and another, changes in theoretical concerns in the field.

Perhaps it is no more reasonable to expect comparative public administration to evolve a grand theory than to expect it of public administration as a whole. As Brans' discussion of the empirical focus of comparative public administration shows, comparison is a method used to understand key issues and variables (internal administrative structures and processes, politico-administrative relations and relations with civil society) of public administration as a whole. The comparative method in public administration, as elsewhere, is a tool that can be used to analyse substantive questions rather than a field in itself.

Some questions in public administration can, however, only be understood by reference to cross-national experience. One such theme is the increasingly popular question of the development of convergence between administrative systems. Issues connected with Europeanization and globalization as well as common administrative developments such as New Public Management have driven this topic along, to use Brans' terms, the policy track. 'New institutionalist' theory, such as the discussion of 'isomorphism' by diMaggio and

Powell (1989), has given the whole area of policy transfer a strong impetus in the past decade (see Rose, 1993; Dolowitz and Marsh, 1996).

Dimitrakopoulos and Passas point in their chapter to the apparent paradox that the supranational organization with some direct authority of its own over its members, the European Union, has a rather indirect influence in national administrative development. More direct influence on administrative structures comes from intergovernmental organizations such as the OECD and its PUMA programme. Dimitrakopulos and Passas show that while such organizations exert different kinds of 'pressures', this says little about responses to such pressures, still less whether they will produce the same response in different nations and thus convergence in administrative systems. International influence and its impact on the administrative structures and processes in individual states is highly contingent on a wide range of variables that make it impossible to predict growing 'isomorphism' in administrative development.

The range of variables that make administrative systems distinctive and which prevent any confident predictions of a convergence in administrative structures, processes and styles is addressed in this section by Martin Lodge. Administrative structures are embedded in national patterns of politics. These patterns are so diverse that attempts to classify and group states with some similar characteristics (such as 'strong' and 'weak' states) can at best be regarded as crude descriptions. To conclude, however, that diversity and the difficulties involved in making cross-national generalizations make each country unique and comparison impossible, is not only pessimistic, it is inaccurate.

Lodge shows the range of features of the national political system in which bureaucracies are embedded – historical origins, political institutions and the autonomy and ability of the bureaucratic system to resist political control – can be and have been fruitfully compared. Rather than seeking to imply that bureaucracies fit neatly into 'families' sharing broad characteristics (Page, 1995), Lodge shows that we need more discriminating comparison of the discrete components of national politico-administrative systems.

'Path dependence' is the contemporary term used to describe the way in which inherited politico-administrative structures, processes, constraints and patterns shape national reactions to common issues and stimuli. This of course has been a central notion in administrative history since its inception (Raadschelders, 1998). Lodge shows that path dependence does not involve relinquishing comparison since, if we specify the paths carefully enough, they are comparable. In fact one can go further and suggest that we only know what is a distinctive path if we compare it with others.

To recognize path dependencies should not itself become a theoretical rut. It was conventional at the beginning of the last century to argue that German politico-administrative development was distinctive – that it developed along a monarchical path and in this deviated from much of the rest of Europe, and that policy prescriptions appropriate to states with more liberal paths of development were not appropriate there (Hintze, [1911b] 1962). The fact that Germany's administrative system has for nearly sixty years been entirely integrated in the theoretical, empirical and practical literature on public administration as another democratic and pluralist system indicates that developmental paths are not straight lines – they cross, merge and in some cases radically change directions.

So is comparative public administration a laggard? There is a growing volume of material that is comparative in Brans' more relaxed definition of the term. There are increased publication outlets for comparative material in the field. Even more encouraging, studies and collections analysing administrative issues using a comparative method tend to include a wider range of countries – while US and West European comparisons still tend to dominate in the literature, increasingly comparative analyses include countries such as Australia, Canada, New Zealand and Japan. There is certainly some way to go before comparative scholars manage to realize the hopes for much wider comparisons taking in less developed nations. Yet the fact that comparative studies have not yielded one dominant paradigm, or been based upon a common or even widely shared theoretical focus, is more likely to be the result of the pluralism of social science research in general rather than any specific defect in comparative public administration.

REFERENCES

Chapman, B. (1959) *The Profession of Government*. London: Allen and Unwin.

Derlien, H.-U. (1992) 'Observations on the state of comparative administration research in Europe – rather comparable than comparative', *Governance*, 5 (3): 279–311.

DiMaggio, P.J. and Powell, W.W. (1989) 'The iron cage revisited: institutional isomorphism and collective rationality in organizational fields', *American Sociological Review*, 48 (1): 47–60.

Dolowitz, D. and Marsh, D. (1996) 'Who learns what from whom', *Political Studies*, 14 (2): 343–57.

Finer, H (1932) *The Theory and Practice of Modern Government*, 2 vols. London: Methuen.

Hintze, O. ([1911a] 1962) 'Der Beamtenstand', in Otto Hintze, *Staat und Verwaltung*. Göttingen: Vandenhoeck and Ruprecht.

Hintze, O. ([1911b] 1962) 'Das monarchische Prinzip und die konstitutionelle Verfassung', in Otto Hintze, *Staat und Verwaltung*. Göttingen: Vandenhoeck and Ruprecht.

Lowell, A.L. (1896) *Government and Parties in Continental Europe*. London: Longmans Green and Co.

Page, Edward (1995) 'Administering Europe', in J.E.S. Hayward and E.C. Page (eds), *Governing the New Europe*. Cambridge: Polity Press.

Raadschelders, J.C.N. (1998) *Handbook of Administrative History*. New Brunswick, NJ: Transaction Books.

Rose, R. (1993) *Lesson Drawing in Public Policy*. Chatham, NJ: Chatham House.

Weber, M. ([1920] 1972) *Wirtschaft und Gesellschaft*, 5th edn. Tübingen: J.C.B. Mohr.

34

Comparative Public Administration: From General Theory to General Frameworks

Marleen Brans

ON VALUE, DEFINITIONS AND PROBLEMS OF CPA

'Compare or perish', or the value of CPA for PA and p.a.[1]

'Compare or perish' is perhaps too strong a motto for founding the rationale of comparative public administration (CPA) research. However, comparison has long since been acknowledged as the 'very essence of the scientific method' in political science in general and Public Administration in particular (Almond and Powell, 1966: 878; Verba, 1967; Lijphart, 1971; Pierre, 1995: 4; Landman, 2000).[2] For Dahl (1947: 6) the construction of a science of administration depended upon the success in establishing propositions which transcended national boundaries. This development of concepts and generalizations at a level between what is true of all societies and what is true for one society at one point in time and space (Antal et al., 1987: 14; Korsten, 1995: 33) takes place along systematic inquiries of cross-national and cross-time similarities and differences. Systematic comparison not only allows for assessing the effects of different environments upon organizational structure and behaviour, but also for analysing why organizational structure and behaviour may matter in producing different outcomes that are relevant for society (see Peters, 1988).

The theoretical and empirical specification of individual cases in comparative frameworks is not only important for the more ambitious goals of building and testing theories that make us understand and, even more ambitious, predict structures and performances of public administration in the world. It is multifunctional and not only serves some more modest scientific goals, but also less modest practical purposes. At a low level of ambition, the least cross-national comparison can do is reveal and point at possible exaggerations within the parochial scientific discourse (for instance on the alleged huge public sector size in the Netherlands and Sweden, or the alleged unique character of conflict resolution in Belgium). In such a view, the aims and pretensions of comparative research are reduced to something like putting national results into perspective (Van Deth, 1994: 2).

International examples are also important for the practice of public administration, as they enable both researchers interested in practical recommendations and practitioners seeking to adopt them to investigate a broader range of ideas about what constitutes good structure and best practices. Institutional and policy transfer is by no means new. In the nineteenth century, institutional transfer, as constitutional consulting, was not merely an academic pastime but an actual export and import business between different nations. To be sure, several authors in the 1960s and 1970s warned against the limits of institutional transfer (see Siffin, 1976), mostly associated with the export of administrative technology to the newly decolonized worlds. Their warnings remain valid 30 years later, since the break-up of the Soviet Union, and more generally processes of globalization have given a new impetus to transfers between different jurisdictions being big business once more, supported by major funding institutions and policy diffusers such as the OECD, the World Bank and the IMF. Comparative frameworks for understanding political and cultural variables of administrative behaviour and performance beyond listings of best practices are indispensable before considering transfers (Tummala, 2000).

Stringent and relaxed definitions of CPA research

As will be shown further, assessments of the development and state of CPA are strongly dependent on the definition of CPA research. Stringent definitions emphasize uniformity of research approach and structured design. In essence, such definitions call for research in several countries, with data being collected according to a certain regime, guided by a central research question. If not quantitative in nature, cases are chosen according to a most similar systems design (MSSD) or most different systems design (MDSD) or carefully replicated along the relationship between dependent and independent variables in order to control intermediate variables and produce robust evidence or counter-evidence. The goal of such comparative design is most ambitious in that it seeks to test hypotheses from certain theoretical perspectives and rule out rival explanations. Such a design already relies heavily on cognitive simplifications of complex realities, which are exactly the subject of research captured by more relaxed definitions, or what Derlien (1992) would call weaker variants of CPA. Much comparative research is indeed reported in edited volumes, the co-operative effort of which combines the construction of classifications such as dichotomies or more complex typologies, and contextual description. The extent to which such research is lifted to the level of theory testing will often depend on the strength of editorial hands (see also Page, 1995). Such co-operative efforts clearly demand skilled research management in which editorial rigour and the avoidance of hobbyism is balanced with making allowances for contextual richness and the prevention of ethnocentrism.

Another so-called weak variant are secondary analyses, for which monographs and journal articles have provided a mass of information, with the admitted flaw of possible reduced validity by not always offering to discern which statements are really based on empirical evidence and which are more loosely founded on works that are primarily theoretical and impressionistic in nature (see Egeberg, 1999: 160). Another variant of CPA, and by some not perceived as part of CPA at all, are single case studies, the material of which can be the subject of the above mentioned secondary analysis. Some single case studies are themselves theory testing in that they represent unique or critical cases, beyond the Zanzibar flaw. This implies of course that they use concepts that apply in other countries, or seek to make larger inferences (Landman, 2000: 23). Alternatively, they provide the contextual description without which the higher aims of classification and theory testing cannot be reached. Contrary to what some observers claim, and following what the comparative sections of major Public Administration journals contain, single case studies should be considered as part of the larger CPA research enterprise.

Problems and opportunities

CPA research is subject to recurrent criticism. From the late 1960s to date, in both the United States and Europe, assessments of the state of the discipline are not enthusiastic and the sharpness of critiques is to some extent related to the kind of definitions of CPA reviewers explicitly or implicitly hold. Disappointments are greatest among those reviewers with the most ambitious definition of CPA as a hypothesis testing enterprise (Heady, 1979: 41; see also Feick, 1987). Edited volumes would lack a comparative design and their conclusions on country juxtapositions would remain too impressionistic, depending too heavily on vague notions of differences of political culture (see Derlien, 1992; Page, 1995). Much of our understanding of the comparative dimensions of public administration would remain descriptive (Peters, 1988: 1–2), and an integrative and cumulative capacity to move the mass of case study findings up the hierarchy into meaningful classifications appears to be lacking.

Why is it so difficult to move from description onto classification and eventually to theory testing? The reasons are multiple. It is commonplace to refer to the lack of time, money and institutional support. The accepted discourse on the rise and decline of American CPA is telling in this respect (see Riggs, 1998). The underlying reasons for the costliness of CPA research are more interesting. They relate to the complexity of the subject matter and the lack of method to reduce this complexity into meaningful typologies and dimensions which allow for a structured set of dependent and independent variables, the relationships between which are central building blocks for theory testing.

The subject matter is indeed complex. Public administration is complex and the environment of administrative systems is complex. Even if there is basic agreement on the nature of dependent variables, such as structures, actors and actions of administrative systems (Aberbach and Rockman, 1987), they are not easily researched in a comparative perspective. There are many kinds of agencies and actors doing many kinds of things (see Fried, 1990: 322), at different levels of government and in different formal settings, which of course challenges researchers to find functional equivalents and use concepts that travel across space (see Pierre, 1995: 6–7; Maor and Lane, 1999: xiv). Classical examples include the problems of classifying agents as civil servants, or ministries, departments and agencies into the basic administrative structures of central government, or the great variety of local government structures. In addition, administrative systems are not easily characterized in a general fashion, given that there is much sub-system variability (Aberbach and Rockman, 1987: 477, 484). For some features of administration, within-system variance may be greater than between-system variance. Moreover, administrative arrangements are in a constant flux, and concepts should thus also be able to travel over time. So are their environments, which, irrespective of change, already consist of many possible variables.

Problems of operational definition and measurement hamper singling out the basic dependent variables of administrative systems, and their cross-national and cross-time comparison. Turning the nature of these variables into independent variables for exploring the impact of different institutional arrangements makes things even more difficult: outputs and outcomes are not easily defined and measured either, and are complicated by further problems of data collection.

The availability and reliability of data is indeed a sore point in the development of CPA. Data may be scarce but also vulnerable to manipulation, as they are often the constructs of actors and agencies involved (see Fried, 1990: 323). There are relatively few independent data sets, particularly when compared to what comparative politics has available for the issues it tends to focus on (or does comparative politics focus on issues for which data sets are available?). CPA researchers are generally more eclectic in their use of data, which has the advantage of corroboration from multiple sources of evidence. Some data, however, are legally or ethically warranted, and hence are embargoed also by researchers, the limited opportunities for replication of which

may reduce the validity of their inferences (Gill and Meier, 1999: 4–6).

Some critiques go beyond the traditional methodological flaws addressed in reviews and render the prospects for CPA research even bleaker. To be sure, language skills and sensitiveness to translating concepts across cultures have long since been acknowledged as necessary ingredients for cross-national research. But it is clear that the far reaching ontological conclusions postmodernist assign to the role of language, seriously threaten CPA as a post-positivist endeavour (for an overview of postmodern approaches to Public Administration see Heady, 2001: 53). A further but less existentially threatening source of relativism is related to the alleged process of globalization in general, and European convergence or eurocompatibility pressures in particular. These forces would reduce the relevance of nation-states as units of analysis, in that their environments are increasingly shared by nations, no longer confined to them (see also Heady, 1979: 64).

Leaving aside postmodern relativism, there are many sources of optimism and opportunities for CPA. Moving up from the flaws mentioned above, studies of globalization have not produced indicators of powerful forces for institutional convergence (Chandler, 2000: 264). Integration and the loss of sovereignty should not be a brake on CPA research in a cross-national context (Korsten et al., 1995: 31–2). National states remain useful contexts of comparative analysis, if given only the importance of the path dependency of change, and the meaning major actors keep assigning to national structures and processes. As mentioned above, sub-system variation may also make national level generalization difficult. The challenge for CPA then becomes to distinguish the conditions under which there is greater variation across national administrative systems than within systems (see Aberbach and Rockman, 1987: 477).

Globalization does seem to contribute to the rapid spread of information and data, and major policy diffusing institutions such as the OECD, Worldbank and United Nations, have since the late 1990s increased their efforts to collect public sector data. Bearing in mind that the magnitude of data does not compare with the comparability of data, data collection for CPA purposes calls for sustained vigilance as to reliability and validity. The absence of large, independent data sets is not an overall bad thing, in that CPA, unlike much of comparative politics, is not 'trapped in them', and limited to investigating just those variables for which data is readily available (see Page, 1995).

The availability of increased data and the bulk of case studies and secondary analyses may not have contributed to a general theory of administrative systems, but leaving aside for now the question of whether such a general comparative theory of administrative systems is possible or even desirable, an optimist analysis of CPA research would certainly not miss the following points. First, advances in the comparative documentation and analysis of major sub-questions in Public Administration are multiple, having produced meaningful typologies and classifications. These include comparative studies on general and senior civil service systems in OECD countries, Central and Eastern Europe, and Asia (Bekke et al., 1996; Page and Wright, 1999; Verheijen, 1999; Burns and Bowornwathana, 2001); local government structures and functions (Harloff, 1987) and public service delivery systems (Hood and Shupert, 1988). Second, even if not fully comparative by design, we can notice a more informed use of analytical strategies for theory testing. Triangulation (Webb et al., 1966; see Peters, 1988: 3), for instance, or the method of running theoretically predicted patterns of rival theoretical lenses through cross-national evidence seems a fruitful strategy to enhance our understanding of certain administrative phenomena, such as local government reorganization (Dente and Kjellberg, 1988), decentralization (Page and Goldsmith, 1987) or public sector pay (Hood and Peters, 1994). Time series too, on condition data are available, provide quite straightforward tests of theoretical propositions, as in, for instance, Rose's (1985) study of the growth and decline of big government, or Hood and Peters (1994) on self-interested behaviour in the dynamics of public sector pay. The promising small N analysis or QCA (Ragin, 1989) has been taken up by many research institutes, but is still awaiting a broader reception by CPA. A final path for apparently fruitful research is to look back, with comparative historical analyses of major features of civil service systems (see, for example, Silberman, 1994) carrying important lessons for studying the comparative dimensions of administrative reform today.

FROM GENERAL THEORY TO GENERAL FRAMEWORKS

Parallel and intersecting tracks of middle range theory development

The theoretical advances aided by the above mentioned research strategies are not situated at the level of grand theory development, attempting broad, cross-cultural explanations and concerned with the definition of clusters of concepts helpful in classifying administrative systems around the world in terms of rich and poor bureaucracies or weak and strong states (see Presthus, 1959; Heady, 2001: 17). This kind of general systems modelling was at the heart of the American CPA movement in the 1950s and 1960s, with its leading exponent F. Riggs articulating its strong scientific ambitions, drawing upon structural functional concepts as an alternative for functionalist analysis such as Almond's (Almond and Coleman, 1960). The story of the decline of the American CPA movement is partly an institutional story, with references to plummeting funding and the shrinking interest of development agencies in administrative arrangements as levers for social and economic development (see Fried, 1990: 326). But the strongest disenchantment derived from unfulfilled scientific promises or the failure to produce a general theory of administrative systems. Several observers advised CPA to move its theoretical efforts from grand theory development of cosmic dimensions (Prestus, 1959: 26; Jreisat, 1975: 663; both in Heady, 2001: 33) to a more incremental production of middle range theories. It seems this advice was, consciously or not, taken up, since much of the theoretical and conceptual advancement of the CPA discipline developed around the consequent study of defined sub-fields within the larger discipline.

At the risk of oversimplification, the development of middle range theory can be seen as running along two tracks, at times separated or one catching up with the other, at times intersecting and giving momentum to comparative research in certain sub-fields. Of the tracks, one can, to a large extent artificially, distinguish the first as problem-driven. Here, theory development seeks to codify, classify and understand structural or behavioural phenomena of public administration, or developments in its environment that are politically and socially perceived as problematic or in a state of flux.

The first track: problem-driven

The problem of the 1980s, following the economic world crisis of the 1970s and given extra salience by the advent of neo-liberal discourse, was undoubtedly scarcity. The problem of scarcity, and the emerging concerns with efficiency and economy, favoured an agenda for comparatively investigating public sector size and growth (see Rose, 1985), with a further two-fold spin-off. First, accounting for public sector growth became a focal point in theories on bureaucratic power, which were influential in modifying the traditional bureaucratic model (see further). Second, problems with regard to measuring the size of government called for comparative studies of public sector variance, a development that was given a further impetus by the downsizing bureaucracy movement towards privatization and deregulation in the late 1980s (Vickers and Wright, 1988) and its effects in the early 1990s (Wright, 1994b). Privatization was comparatively noted as a dominant trend, with the public sector becoming leaner and the inter-actions between public and private actors increasing, one of the results of which was the emergence of a range of new public–private institutional arrangements for service delivery (Hood and Schuppert, 1988). The managerialist 'revolution' in several countries further compli-cated the issue of variance by introducing inter-nal privatization. The wide-spread practical and political acclaim of the new managerialism trig-gered off a great deal of comparative research on the variance of administrative reform over time, not only in the Western world, but gradually also for developing countries (Crozier and Trosa, 1992; Wright, 1994a; Aucoin, 1995; Naschold, 1995; Massey, 1997; Verheijen and Coombes, 1998; Barzelay, 2000; Pollitt and Bouckaert, 2000; McCourt and Minogue, 2001), which so far confirm, against the claims of globalization, the persistence of national administrative tradi-tions. Also personnel policies, particularly per-formance-based systems and the profile of the New Public Managers, received compara-tive attention (see Derlien, 1992: 291; Farnham et al., 1996).

Meanwhile, administrative reform at other levels of government has established a compara-tive research tradition for itself. The large-scale nature of local government structural reform in the post-war era suggested that common causes and efforts to account for cross-national variance led to fruitful theorizing and operationalization (Sharpe, 1979, 1993; Batley and Stoker, 1991; Dente and Kjellberg, 1988; see also Page and Goldsmith, 1987). Federalism, or more generally devolution, also enjoyed renewed attention, with the unification of (the traditionally already federal) Germany, the federalization of Belgium, region-alization in France, Spain and Italy, devolution in the UK, and the 'new federalism' in the United States (Walker, 1995; Hesse and Wright, 1996; Keating, 2001; EZF, 2001; Stepan, 2001).

Much of the administrative reform agenda of the 1980s and early 1990s was concerned with the pursuit of economy and efficiency, and to a lesser extent with effectiveness, the latter receiving more attention towards the second half of the 1990s. The concern of politicians to produce policies that make a difference (or that make themselves differ) can be viewed as being part of the larger concern to restore declining levels of trust in government, of which several indicators are noted (Klingeman and Fuchs, 1995; Norris, 1999; Rouban, 1999). Real or perceived problems of declining trust have triggered efforts to reaffirm the position of citizens (Pierre, 1995: 12–13) and to find ways to create democratic legitimacy that are not elective in character (see Marini, 1998: 369). Even the OECD, after having focused for years on managerialist aspects of public administration, now promotes ways to engage citizens in the policy-making process. Systematic research on the different modes of administrative mediation of citizens' perspectives in both policy formulation and implementation is still lacking, as are structured explorations of the effects the outward-looking behaviour of civil servants will produce for administrative organiza-tion and politico-administrative relations.

Meanwhile, quite a bit of comparative research on trust-related issues has materialized. For a long time, corruption was parochially thought to be endemic to the developing world, and looked upon as a sign of immaturity of developing nations. In the United States, the issue surfaced with Watergate, and pushed the issue of admini-strative ethics on to the agenda. But comparative research on the many faces and causes of corrup-tion only gained real momentum after much reported scandal and sleaze in Europe in the late 1980s and early 1990s and subsequent concerns with standards in public life (Della Porta and Meny, 1997; Williams, 2000a, 2000b; Williams and Robin, 2000; Rohr, 2001).

A final issue in this problem-driven chronology, is the problem and challenge for public adminis-tration associated with the informatization of society. If we may believe the OECD as a major problem spotter and trend setter, e-government is a top priority of governments at the start of the new millennium. The use of new information and communication technologies by government may drastically transform the structures and operations of government and alter the latter's interactions with civil society. E-government has many faces and the range of concerns for Public Administration is broad. How can ICT facilitate governments' capacity to respond to clients and customers? How does e-communication impact on hierarchies within government and on the relations between superiors and subordinates? What does e-government mean for equality of citizens' access? Finally, will the integration of management and policy information systems reinvent rationalist models by increasing the cognitive capacity of government, the limits to which were central in conceptualizing bounded rationality? The exploration of these questions will no doubt benefit from comparative studies that go beyond listing good practices.

The second track: discipline-driven

The single most dominant conceptual framework surviving the CPA heyday of the 1950s and 1960s was the bureaucratic one (see Arora, 1972 quoted in Heady, 1979: 14, 60), either conceived as a checklist instrument or a broader model for comparing the chief structural and functional characteristics of different administrative systems (see Waldo, 1964). Middle range theory development in the CPA discipline was much informed by applications and alterations to the bureaucratic model.

Several important developments came from translating generic organization theory to bureaucratic organization and bureaucratic behaviour (Peters, 1989: 7; see Jørgensen, 1998: 500). Organizational theory did much to articulate the role of environmental differences, perhaps a bit too much. Contingency theory, for instance, tried to match characteristics of the environment of organizations and their mode of production to the most appropriate structures. It was criticized, however, for not acknowledging incidences of organizational closure due to environmental influences (also at the heart of autopoietic theory of organizations) and for overinsulating structural variables from institutional transfer (Peters, 1989: 7). Ecology theory, in turn, was interesting in that it offered a perspective on organizational inertia, change and transformation (Kaufmann, 1976; see also Hogwood and Peters, 1983). Other lasting influences come from organization theory that emphasized cross-national differences in organizational culture. In the United States, Presthus (1959) preceded this development. In Europe, Lammers and Hickson (1979) offered comparative perspectives on organizational cultures. Crozier (1963), in his study on the bureaucratic phenomenon, also drew on organization theory. Although his study was not comparative by design, and his observations on differences between the French, US and Soviet bureaucracies were not systematic, the importance of Crozier's work should not be underestimated for the development of European CPA, since it paved the way for a theoretical and methodological break with the administrative sciences which mainly focused on descriptions of institutions and public law (see Smith, 1999).[3] Other influential work from organization theory was produced by Hofstede (1984), whose four dimensions of culture, which were also appreciated for their avoidance of ethnocentrism, offered ways to discern and typify cross-cultural values. Particularly his dimension of power distance has much in common with the often used dichotomies between Latin and Nordic or Catholic and Protestant politico-administrative cultures (see for instance Page and Goldsmith, 1987), and deserves to be integrated in other conceptions of politico-administrative cultures such as the one that distinguishes between Anglo-Saxon, Germanic Rechtstaat, French Napoleonic and the mixed Scandinavian traditions (Rhodes and Weller, 2001: 244).

Another important source of modifying the traditional bureaucratic model came from formal theorizing on the dysfunctions and ills of bureaucracy, the public choice tradition of which received much impetus from the bureaucracy-bashing climate that emerged from concerns with the inefficiencies of big government. These accounts (see Peters, 1996) of bureaucrats as shirkers and budget-maximizers and of bureaucratic monopolies (Downs, 1967; Niskanen, 1971; Moe, 1984) translated concepts from the new organizational economics, primarily principal–agent models. Dunleavy's (1991) bureau-shaping model was original, in that its institutional public choice approach did not draw on principal–agent models. Another influential, empirical study was Allison's (1971), which not only presents a good example of the method of triangulation but greatly helped in conceptualizing bureaucratic power and politics (Kettl, 1993: 412).

These theories seriously challenged the traditional bureaucratic model in two ways. They offered ways to conceptualize bureaucratic power over state policies, and helped bureaucracy be seen as an arena in which conflicts are played out, two neglected issues in the accepted version of the traditional model.[4] The notion of bureaucratization of politics prompted a revisiting of the classic dichotomy between politics and administration, which was, to a great extent unjustifiably, associated with the Weberian bureaucratic model. Meanwhile other theoretical developments and comparative research came to demonstrate the politicization of bureaucracy. Aberbach, Putnam and Rockman's seminal study (1981) on cross-national variation of bureaucratic roles and Aberbach and Rockman's' (1987) conceptualization of the ways in which politics penetrates bureaucracy further helped erode the theoretical and empirical claims of the dichotomy. The relationship between policy makers and bureaucrats has become a chief variable in the comparative study of administrative systems, both in terms of dependent and independent variables, and in terms of their formal and behavioural manifestations. The four types of politico-administrative relations identified by Putnam and associates, and the fifth type added by Peters (1988), lend themselves to capturing cross-national variation, and also to monitoring shiftings over time (see Golembiewski, 1996: 14).

That administration is highly political was also shown by Pressman and Wildavsky's (1973) empirical study of implementation. Their study was very influential in the development of implementation theories in both the United States and Europe (Hjern and Hull, 1982; Hanf and Toonen, 1985; O'Toole, 1986; Sabatier, 1986). Whether best understood from a bottom-up or top-down perspective, the complexities of implementation pointed at the multi-actor character of turning legislation into working programmes, no longer conceptualizing public administration as embedded in a single, monolithic organization (Peters, 1989: 8).

Assumptions of increased complexity would get increasing attention from then on (Kickert et al., 1997; see Teisman, 2000). In Europe, the implementation of European legislation, and particularly of structural funds, became a focal point for comparative research on networks (Heinelt and Smith, 1996; Marsh, 1998), and so did many public–private and public–public arrangements at different levels of government all over the world. The British network approach, which was originally conceived as an account of interest intermediation, moved to accounting for the patchwork organization of the public sector, involving many different public–private actors in different arrangements (Rhodes, 1996; Börzel, 1998). In Germany, the concept of *Politikverpflechtung* of Frits Scharpf and the network studies of his Max Planck school was much used in examining a whole range of policies (Hanf and Scharpf, 1978; Scharpf, 1993; Windhoff-Héritier, 1993; see also Marin and Mayntz, 1991; Knoke et al., 1996; Daugbjerg, 1998).

Comparative research on policy networks offers strong theoretical perspectives and analytical frameworks, but still shows a lack of operational definition (O'Toole, 1997; see Benz, 1999), which makes it difficult not only to judge their properties in terms of open or closed, or even more the relationship between their characteristics and their consequences, for instance in terms of producing private or collective benefits (see Börzel, 1998; Pierre, 1998).

The involvement of third parties in public administration, whether private sector actors, agencies at different government levels, or groups or individuals from civil society, emphasizes once more the need to conceptualize public sector diversity, or rather the institutional and societal embedding of the tools of implementation (see Ashford, 1978), for which the growing interest in policy instrumentation can help, particularly when conceptualized as representing relationships between the state and civil society or along a dimension from coercion to voluntarism (Hood, 1986; Doern and Phidd, 1992; Howlett and Ramesh, 1995; Bemelmans-Videc, 1998).

Some theory development is cumulative, often building upon sets of empirical studies. But several observers have pointed out the occurrence of pendulum-type development in Public Administration theory, with periods of temporary amnesia or blindness for already established theory and evidence, or for the wisdom of old masters (Kettl, 1993: 408; Page, 1995: 138–9; Golembiewski, 1996; Holden, 1998; Hood, 1999). Explanatory factors here include the cognitive limits of the discipline and the use of binary schemes or dichotomies on the one hand, and normative clashes and turf conflicts on the other.

In 1979, Heady, for instance, was doubtful about the longevity or impact of the new public administration movement (1979: vii). He was not able to predict the forcefulness with which the issues at the heart of that movement would resurface in the 1990s, in reaction to the alleged normative consequences and the intellectual foundations of the NPM. Indeed, NPM should be credited for having done a great job for Public Administration, not only in triggering efforts to define its subject matter, or the publicness of public administration, but also for re-emphasizing classic issues in Public Administration, such as accountability, control and co-ordination, and re-awaking such dormant issues as the role of lower civil servants, and citizens' empowerment. The new public service movement today indeed has much in common with the new public administration movement of yesterday (see i.a. Walmsley and Wolf, 1996).

A similar development can be noted in the reaction to the intellectual school with which NPM's intellectual tradition is related. Reaction to the public choice 'revolution' reconfirmed the role of institutional arrangements, which underpins the very rationale of comparative analyses of structural variables. The role of culture, of which individualism is just one variant, is also reconfirmed, and comparative applications of cultural theory produce fruitful avenues for explaining cross-national differences (see Hendriks, 1999 on transport; Hood and Peters, 1994 on public sector pay; or Verweij, 2000 on environmental protection).

General frameworks for CPA

Accounts of problem-driven and discipline-driven theory development for CPA reflect the absence of a single paradigm, a variety of questions, and a variety of approaches. Such accounts are one way to structure the discipline and identify the main questions and ways to answer them. But these narratives are no doubt incomplete, and also biased, for other observers may tell a different story, with different sequences and emphases. Another, and possibly more fruitful way of structuring the discipline of CPA, and thus to give it purpose and coherence, is to seek agreement on what to study, and organize comparative data collection and theory development around core dependent variables. Such an approach clearly departs from CPA as a grand theory exercise, as it no longer has administrative systems or transformations as a whole as its subject, but more narrowly defined subjects. It has, however, the advantage of allowing for a structured collection of comparative evidence and more feasible in-depth comparative analyses across countries, time and government levels, while not excluding broader theoretical explorations of relations between variables.

The usefulness of such an approach to CPA is recognized by many comparativists, but views differ as to which variables to include. Having acknowledged that grand theory was to be substituted by middle range theory, some thought progress was best achieved by studying 'the backgrounds, attitudes, and behaviours of bureaucrats and those with whom they interact' (Sigelman, 1976: 624, in Heady, 2001: 33). This view recognizes the environment of those with whom bureaucrats interact, but it remains quite narrow in that its focus on individuals is behavioural only. Heady (1979, 2001) takes a broader view. He specifies the environment of public administration by identifying the arena in which bureaucrats interact with others, that is, the broader political system and society in general. He also adds an organizational focus and emphasizes the importance of relying on several levels of analysis for understanding the complexity of public administration (Heady, 2001: 34). Maor and Lane (1999) take actors, structures and behaviour as building blocks for comparative public administration, but do not explicitly mention relations with the environment. Neither does Peters (1988), for whom the candidate

dependent variables are public employees, public organizations, bureaucratic behaviour and politico-administrative relations. Pierre's approach (1995) to CPA is probably the most comprehensive in taking three sets of variables. He adds an explicit focus on the administration's relations with civil society, which in Peters' scheme are not absent but captured under bureaucratic behaviour. The three sets of variables in Pierre's CPA project are: the intra-organizational dynamics of bureaucracy, which comprises such variables as actors, structures and behaviour; politico-administrative relations; and the relations between administration and civil society.

Internal dynamics: actors, structure, behaviour

The building blocks for theory building on the internal dynamics of the pubic sector are individuals, organization and behaviour. Of these, the first two are the most tangible, although it is acknowledged that the operationalization of public employees and public organizations are not automatic and require careful judgements. The operationalization, classification and explaining of behaviour, however, is more problematic because of the absence of a theoretical paradigm on the nature of human behaviour in general.

The study of the individuals that operate in the public sector has established a research agenda for itself (Peters, 1988). The results of comparative civil service studies, either focusing on the civil service in general or the top, provide a mass of material for secondary analysis. Comparisons of the numbers of public employees, their socio-economic background and characteristics, and the socio-economic conditions of their employment support theory development on public sector employment, recruitment and career patterns in the civil service, and the pay and perks of public office. They present answers to central explanatory and normative questions in public administration. The number and nature of public employees serve as indicators for the size of the public sector and the way in which the latter pervades society. The characteristics and background of public employees addresses such issues as the representativeness of the civil service, and the degree of equality, while the level and method of their payment gives insights into the social status of the civil service.

The reasons for comparing organizations and structures as units of analysis are multiple. Comparing the number and nature of public organizations, as more than aggregates of the individuals that operate within them, provides a composite picture of the public sector.

Comparisons over time and across countries are revealing in that they help to put such issues as the size and modes of public service delivery in perspective, beyond what conventional wisdom might suggest. A focus on organizations as units of analysis also provides perspectives on change and transformation (Kaufmann, 1976; Peters, 1988), government priorities (Rose, 1985), and the ways in which differences in the environment of administrative systems are translated onto the organizational make-up of the state (population ecology). But bringing organizations and organizational structure to the centre of analysis may also serve goals that are more ambitious than explaining public sector size and change only.

As acknowledged in different variants of neo-institutionalism, organizational structure, as a composite of culture, path-determining institutions, or equilibrium outcomes, will constrain or enable behaviour and strategic interactions within the public domain. This articulation of structure over agency is reflected in studies that address the conditions for effective implementation or in network approaches for understanding complexity, and increasingly also for understanding the scope and nature of public sector reform (Hood, 2001). Comparisons of organizations and structures are thus not only a necessary ingredient for understanding the complexity of the internal dynamics of the public sector, or for judgements on the size, diversity, transformation and 'publicness' of the public sector. They are also central building blocks for institutional design since various structural arrangements of hierarchies and specialization may produce various outcomes that matter for public administration: co-ordination, information exchange, the smoothness of implementation, professional autonomy, transparency ... (Egeberg, 1999).

Together with public employees, organizations and structures are relatively tangible units of analysis, although operational definition and the search for functional equivalents will not always be straightforward, particularly when the boundaries of public and private actors and sectors are blurred. But the third core variable for understanding the internal dynamics of the public sector presents a bigger problem of operational definition and data collection and is more demanding for the interpretation of data and the avoidance of supply-and-demand-side bias. Data on behaviour is less easily accessed and verified, and requires contextual interpretation, the latter of which is further complicated by the absence of a behavioural paradigm. An important strand of theory development has chosen to ignore the latter problem, by formally modelling behaviour on the universal assumption of utility maximization.

Although such assumptions remain questionable, formal theories of bureaucratic behaviour are useful for CPA, in that they provide a vehicle for hypothesis formulation and heuristic tools for structured empirical comparisons. Particularly when used in triangulation with other theoretical perspectives, they may generate explanatory power.

The foci of other, more empirical theory developments on bureaucratic behaviour reflect the diversity of actions and interactions that public administrators may be involved in. Fruitful theorizing came from empirical work on their behaviour toward clients (street-level bureaucracy, Lipsky, 1980), the conversion of decisions into actions (bottom-up and top-down implementation literature), their interactions as superiors and subordinates (management studies), and decision making (contending models of rational, incremental, or even irrational decision making). There is no overarching conceptualization of the various ways in which administrators use their discretion, and most available theories cast the nature of discretionary behaviour in negative terms. This is definitely the case for the formal models of bureaucrats as shirkers, budget-maximizers or leisure seekers, but also in empirical studies of coping behaviour, policy failures and, even more explicitly, with studies on corruption and ethics. The normative purport of studies of bureaucratic behaviour is apparent, and the importance of comparative approaches for administrative transfer are hence obvious. Comparative analyses of bureaucratic behaviour not only help to explain how public administration actually functions but may also support informed considerations of what works, how, and under which conditions.

Politico-administrative relations

Consistent with the erosion of the dichotomy politics–administration, the relations between politicians and bureaucrats are now an important set of variables. Their cross-national documentation and the investigation of central shiftings over time are important. They are 'at the centre of many issues' (Kettl, 1993: 421; see also Golembiewski, 1996: 144), the most pressing concern of which is the blending of political control with policy capacity. The bureaucratization of politics or politicization of bureaucracy can take on many faces and produce outcomes that matter for institutional design.

Cross-national comparisons of politico-administrative relations are not simple and require data collection on a number of analytical units. Many advances have already been made, however, and the prospects for further advances are bright. One established way of approaching comparative politico-administrative relations comes from role theory (Aberbach et al., 1981). In this tradition, attitudes, roles and behaviour are investigated by interviewing large samples of administrative and political elites in a number of countries. These studies have empirically helped to erode the classic dichotomy, have provided insights into the differential policy role of administrators, and have documented the many faces of politicization of civil servants. The research methodology is robust and deserves to be applied to cases still uninvestigated, and repeated for analysing and theorizing shifts over time.

An additional way to approach politico-administrative relations is the construction of ideal types, as furthered by Peters (1988), which provides a structured means to identify empirically and classify the interactions between politicians and bureaucrats in such terms as the tone of relations, the likely winners, and the mode of conflict resolution between the two sets of actors. Divergence from idealized patterns of relationships can then be used to refine the models, and give a further theoretical impetus to the future research agenda, as Verheijen's (2001) study of Central and Eastern European cases shows.

Explaining variance of types and hybrids requires careful institutional analysis, and an investigation of a range of variables that impact on the interactions between politicians and civil servants. Such a research programme, however, should not be scary, because many of the candidate variables have already been documented, hence reducing the need for original research. Understanding politico-administrative relations indeed relies on knowledge about civil servants and political executives, and the impact of broader systemic or structural factors. Our comparative knowledge of the background, careers and position of civil servants has advanced greatly, and comparative political science has a lot of data to offer for what we need to know about political executives. Lacking still is a consistent data set on the structural interfaces between the two groups of actors, and more work needs to be done on the role of formal rules and co-ordination mechanisms through which responsibilities are allocated and interactions structured. These data, together with that on a range of systemic factors such as partitocracy, consensus democracy, majoritarianism or trust, may be combined by applying small N analysis, from which great progress is anticipated in establishing causality.

A comprehensive research programme on politico-administrative relations not only challenges the discipline's quest for theory building, it also carries great normative appeal for institutional designs that seek to avoid the various negative effects of conflicts over power and policy, ranging from inertia, through ineffectiveness to outright policy failure. The nature of these relations matters greatly for reconciling electoral mandates for political direction with professional policy making, as they present a trade-off between two classic values for designing institutions and allocating responsibilities between them (Peters, 1988: 178).

Relations between public administration and civil society

Parallel with the rise and resonance of the governance debate in the 1990s, a range of buzzwords (re-)emerged, such as transparency, consultation and participative or interactive policy making. These and similar concepts serve to highlight the changes or challenges to contact points between public administration and civil society broadly defined. Attention to the relations between public administration and civil society are not new and neither are certain tools to reduce the distance between them (see Lasswell, 1960). Classifications such as weak–strong states, for instance, have been useful in comparing the bureaucratization of society or the encroachment of society on the autonomy of the state. Another established research tradition comes from studies that compare differences in trust and consent (Almond and Verba, 1965) and, more recently, of the value of social capital for government performance (Putnam et al., 1994).

Approaching the contact points between public administration and civil society involves disaggregating the relation into several components: tools, direction and subjects. Useful classifications and conceptual frameworks come from political theories on citizenship, communitarianism and discursive democracy, from the literature on policy instrumentation, policy networks and policy making models, as well as from empirical comparative work on public–private partnerships and the characteristics of the so-called third sector.

The nature and types of contact points seem to vary according to the nature of the tools that are employed, the directions of contacts and the subjects with which public administration is rendered in contact. Tools for reducing the distance between public administration and civil society may be legal, when rights are created by freedom

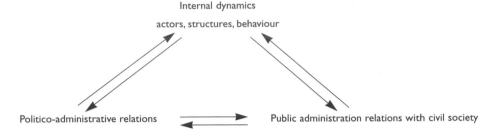

Figure 34.1

of information acts or citizen's charters. They may also be communicative and, for instance, involve enhanced IT-supported information and communication or the use of citizen's and client surveys. Contact points may also be anchored in institutions (such as partnerships) or political procedures for access of citizens and groups to one or more steps in the policy cycle. At least as important is the direction of interactions. Information and consultation may be confined to bureaucracy's control over society and the wish to secure effective implementation. Participation, in turn, means more in terms of empowerment, and creates access for citizens and groups beyond the ballot box. A comparative analysis of the relations between public administration and civil society also involves a narrowing of what is meant by civil society and the third parties that are being engaged. Are the subjects (although in less active conceptions, mere objects) individual citizens, profit-seeking actors or not-for-profit organizations? Cross-national comparison here can benefit from work on conceptions of individual citizens. Interactions will differ if administrations conceive of individuals with whom they interact as customers, clients, or active citizens (Sjöblom, 1999), giving them different opportunities in terms of choice, dialogue and intervention. As for the operational definition of other subjects, advances have been made by work on public–private partnerships (Pierre, 1998) and on defining the third sector (Salamon and Anheier, 1997).

The normative input from understanding the relationship between public administration and civil society is obvious, since several important guiding values for institutional design are at stake. Suffice it here to refer to the debate on the digital divide that may reduce the distance from government for some, but not a great deal for others, or to the reconciliation of policy co-production by active citizens with electoral

policy mandates and accepted standards of representativeness, or to the challenge of steering process towards products.

CONCLUSION: GENERAL FRAMEWORKS FOR GENERATING AND INVESTIGATING CORE QUESTIONS

With the three sets of variables shown in Figure 34.1 a comprehensive framework is constructed with which to approach a comparative public administration research agenda that fosters accumulation through structured data collection, the creation of a common language and the development of meaningful theories. The agenda can help to identify the need for original research for cases where information is still lacking or in need of updating. The framework is also helpful in generating questions about the relationship between the three sets of variables. Generating the questions that are challenging for both theory development and institutional design can indeed proceed by treating each of the sets of variables as independent variables for the others.

One can, for instance, explore the impact of the nature and changes within the internal dynamics of public administration on politico-administrative relations and public administration's contact points with civil society. Public sector personnel and organization are recognized as systemic factors influencing the nature of politico-administrative relations. How then are changes to organizational structure, career paths and the socio-economic conditions of office induced by managerialist reform, impacting upon the balance between political executives and civil servants? Comparative designs can test hypotheses on the relaxation or strengthening of political control over policy, or the reduction or increase in the degree of separation between the two sets of players. Does top-level recruitment from outside the bureaucracy for instance break into the cosy world of highly integrated interactions between politicians and civil servants and how do political executives deal with the insecurity this may impose upon them? Equally interesting are designs that explore the impact of organizational and behavioural change on the way public administration interacts with civil society. Do greater pressures for service responsiveness, for instance, lead to different conceptions of citizenship, and what do enhanced particularist client relationships mean for the autonomy and the 'publicness' of bureaucracies?

Comparative designs may also reverse the relationships between these variables. The nature of politico-administrative relations affects the internal dynamics of bureaucracies. It impacts on the behaviour of civil servants in policy making and the various ways in which they apply administrative discretion. It may also determine bureaucratic initiatives for change, and may help account for variance in terms of weaker or stronger vertical integration of politico-administrative elites. The nature of politico-administrative relations may thus be conceived as an explanatory factor in accounting for variance in public sector reform. Just as the differential need for political control accounted for various designs of bureaucracies in the nineteenth century (Silberman, 1994), differences in politico-administrative relations may help explain who carries out what kind of public sector reform and why (see Hood, 2001).

Public administration's contact points with civil society may also be theorized as affecting bureaucrats' roles and behaviour, as well as the nature of relations between the administrative and political components of bureaucracy. Some of the interesting questions such designs may help to answer are whether the reduction of the distance between public administration and citizens and groups increases the distance with political executives; what it means for civil servants to do the great split in serving two masters; and how greater access and transparency break up information monopolies and challenge civil servants to act upon competencies other than technical expertise; or what the enhanced involvement of third parties, private or not-for-profit, means for the publicness of bureaucracy, and its commitment to the common good.

There is no grand theory to answer all these and other central questions of both public administration and Public Administration. Such theory is neither possible, nor desirable. The questions are better approached from general frameworks in which the core dependent variables are agreed upon, the collection of the required original and secondary evidence is feasible, and the theoretical exploration of interconnectedness between variables is meaningful.

NOTES

1 This chapter follows the convention of referring to the academic discipline of Public Administration (PA) in upper case and to the practice of public administration (p.a.) in lower case. 'Compare or perish' is translated from the Dutch 'Vergelijk of verga', a provocation to the community of social scientists in 1992 by the Dutch political scientist De Beus regarding the sorry state of comparative research (Korsten, 1995: 15).

2 Public Administration is seen here as a sub-discipline of political science.

3 Although having an earlier disciplinary tradition with eighteenth-century cameralism and policy studies, European Public Administration was, from the late nineteenth century, firmly rooted in the discipline of public law (see Rutgers, 1994).

4 This is not the place to give a full critique of the assimilation of the Wilsonian dichotomy with Weberian bureaucracy. Suffice it to say that re-reading Weber makes his concepts valid for capturing the intricate relationship between political authority and bureaucratic power, of which the accepted checklist model is but one variant.

REFERENCES AND FURTHER READING

Aberbach, J.D. and Rockman, B.A. (1987) 'Comparative Administration: Methods, Muddles and Models', *Administration and Society*, 18 (4): 473–506.

Aberbach, J.D., Putnam, R.D. and Rockman, B.A. (1981) *Bureaucrats and Politicians in Western Democracies*. Cambridge, MA: Harvard University Press.

Allison, G. (1971) *Essence of Decision*. Boston, MA: Little, Brown.

Almond, G.A. and Bingham Powell, G. (1966) *Comparative Politics*. Boston, MA: Little, Brown.

Almond, G.A. and Coleman, J.S. (eds) (1960) *The Politics of Developing Areas*. Princeton, NJ: Princeton University Press.

Almond, G.A. and Verba, S. (1965) *The Civic Culture: Political Attitudes and Democracy in Five Nations*. Princeton, NJ: Princeton University Press.

Antal, A.B., Dierkes, M. and Weiler, H.N. (1987) 'Cross-national Policy Research. Traditions, Achievements and Challenges', in M. Dierkes, H.N. Weiler and A.B. Antal (eds), *Comparative Policy Research*. Aldershot: Ashgate, pp. 13–31.

Arora, R.K. (1972) *Comparative Public Administration*. New Delhi: Associated Publishing House.

Ashford, D. (ed.) (1978) *Comparing Public Policies: New Concepts and Methods.* London: Sage.

Aucoin, P. (1995) *The New Public Management. Canada in Comparative Perspective.* Montreal: Institute for Research on Public Policy.

Barzelay, M. (2000) *The New Public Management: Improving Research and Policy Dialogue.* Berkeley, CA: University of California Press.

Batley, R. and Stoker, G. (1991) *Local Government in Europe: Trends and Developments.* Basingstoke: Macmillan.

Bekke, H.A.G.M., Perry, J.L. and Toonen, T.A.J. (eds) (1996) *Civil Service Systems in Comparative Perspective.* Bloomington, IN: Indiana University Press.

Bemelmans-Videc, M.-L., Rist, R.C. and Vedung, E. (1998) *Carrots, Sticks, and Sermons. Policy Instruments and their Evaluation.* New Brunswick, NJ: Transaction Publishers.

Benz, A. (1991) 'Book Review', *Public Administration,* 77 (1): 223–4.

Bonazzi, G. (1983) 'Scapegoating in Complex Organisations: The Results of a Comparative Study of Symbolic Blame-giving in Italian and French Public Administration', *Organization Studies,* 1: 1–19.

Börzel, T.A. (1998) 'Organizing Babylon – On the Different Conceptions of Policy Networks', *Public Administration,* 76: 253–73.

Braun, D. (ed.) (2000) *Federalism and Public Policy.* Aldershot: Ashgate.

Burns, J.P. and Bowornwathana, B. (2001) *Civil Service Systems in Asia.* Cheltenham: Edward Elgar.

Chandler, J.A. (ed.) (2000) *Comparative Public Administration.* London: Routledge.

Collier, D. (1993) 'The Comparative Method', in A.W. Finifter (ed.), *The State of the Discipline.* Washington: ASPA. pp. 105–19.

Crozier, M. (1963) *Le Phénomène bureaucratique.* Paris: Le Seuil.

Crozier, M. and Trosa, S. (1992) *La Décentralisation: reforme de l'etat.* Boulogne: Pouvoirs Locaux.

Dahl, R. (1947) 'The Science of Public Administration: Three Problems', *Public Administration Review,* 7 (1): 1–11.

Daugbjerg, C. (1998) *Policy Networks Under Pressure: Pollution Control, Policy Reform and the Power of Farmers.* Aldershot: Ashgate.

Della Porta, D. and Mény, Y. (1997) 'Conclusion: Democracy and Corruption: towards a Comparative Analysis', in *Democracy and Corruption in Europe.* London: Pinter. pp. 166–80.

Denhardt, R.B. and Denhardt, J.V. (2000) 'The New Public Service: Serving Rather than Steering', *Public Administration Review,* 60 (6): 549–59.

Dente, B. and Kjellberg, F. (1988) *The Dynamics of Institutional Change: Local Government Reorganization in Western Democracies.* London: Sage.

Derlien, H.-U. (1992) 'Observations on the State of Comparative Administration Research in Europe – Rather Comparable than Comparative', *Governance,* 5 (3): 279–311.

Derlien, H.-U. (1996) 'The Politicization of Bureaucracies in Historical and Comparative Perspective', in B.G. Peters and B.A. Rockman (eds), *Agenda for Excellence 2. Administering the State.* Chatham: Chatham House Publishers. pp. 149–62.

Doern, G.B. and Phidd, R.W. (1992) *Canadian Public Policy: Ideas, Structure, Process,* 2nd edn. Toronto: Nelson Canada.

Downs, A. (1967) *Inside Bureaucracy.* Boston, MA: Little, Brown.

Dunleavy, P. (1991) *Democracy, Bureaucracy and Public Choice.* Brighton: Harvester Wheatsheaf.

Egeberg, M. (1999) 'The Impact of Bureaucratic Structure on Policy Making', *Public Administration,* 77 (1): 155–70

EZF (Europäisches Zentrum für Föderalismus-Forschung Tübingen) (2001) *Jahrbuch des Föderalismus 2001 – Föderalismus, Subsidiarität und Regionen in Europa.* Baden-Baden: Nomos.

Farazmand, A. (1999) 'Globalization and Public Administration', *Public Administration Review,* 59 (6): 509–22.

Farnham, D., Horton, S., Barlow, J. and Hondeghem, A. (1996) *New Public Managers in Europe: Public Servants in Transition.* London: Macmillan.

Feick, J. (1987) 'Vergleichende Staats- und Verwaltungswissenforschung'. *In Jarhbuch zur Staats- und Verwaltungswissenschaft.* Baden-Baden: Nomos. pp. 473–83.

Fried, R.C. (1990) 'Comparative Public Administration: The Search for Theories', in N.B. Lynn and A.B. Wildavsky (eds), *Public Administration: The State of the Discipline.* Chatham, NJ: Chatham House Publishers. pp. 318–47.

Gill, J. and Meier, K.J. (1999) 'Public Administration Research and Practice: A Methodological Manifesto'. Paper at the 5th National Public Management Research Conference, Texas, A&M University, December 1999.

Golembiewski, R.T. (1996) 'The Future of Public Administration: End of a Short Stay in the Sun? Or a New Day A-dawning?', *Public Administration Review,* 56 (2): 139–48.

Hanf, K. and Scharpf, F.W. (eds), *Interorganizational Policy Making: Limits to Coordination and Central Control.* Beverly Hills, CA: Sage.

Hanf, K. and Toonen, T.A.J. (1985) *Policy Implementation in Federal and Unitary Systems.* Dordrecht: Martinus Nijhoff.

Harloff, E. Martin (1987) *The Structure of Local Government in Europe: Surveys of 29 Countries.* The Hague: IULA.

Heady, F. (1979) *Public Administration in Comparative Perspective,* 2nd edn. (Public Administration and Public Policy/6.) New York: Marcel Dekker.

Heady, F. (2001) *Public Administration. A Comparative Perspective,* 6th edn. New York: Marcel Dekker.

Heinelt, H. and Smith, R. (eds) (1996) *Policy Networks and European Structural Funds.* Aldershot: Avebury.

Hendriks, F. (1999) *Public Policy and Political Institutions. The Role of Culture in Traffic Policy.* Cheltenham: Edward Elgar.

Hesse, J.J. and Wright, V. (eds) (1996) *Federalizing Europe? The Costs, Benefits and Preconditions of Federal Political Systems*. Oxford: Oxford University Press.

Hjern, B. and Hull, C. (1982) 'Implementation Research as Empirical Constitutionalism', *European Journal of Political Research*, 10 (2): 105–15.

Hofstede, G. (1984) *Culture's Consequences. International Differences in Work-Related Values*. London: Sage.

Hogwood, B.W. and Peters, B.G. (1983) *Policy Dynamics*. Brighton: Wheatsheaf.

Holden, M. (1998) *Continuity and Disruption: Essays in Public Administration*. Pittsburg: University of Pittsburg Press.

Hood, C.C. (1986) *Tools of Government*. Chatham, NJ: Chatham House Publishers.

Hood, C.C. (1999) 'British Public Administration: Dodo, Phoenix or Chameleon?', in J. Hayward, B. Barry and A. Brown (eds), *The British Study of Politics in the Twentieth Century*. Oxford: Oxford University Press. pp. 287–311.

Hood, C.C. (2001) 'Public Service Bargains and Public Service Reform', in B.G. Peters, and J. Pierre (eds), *Politicians, Bureaucrats and Administrative Reform*. London, Routledge. pp. 13–23.

Hood, C.C. and Dunsire, A. (1981) *Bureaumetrics*. Farnborough: Gower.

Hood, C.C. and Peters, B.G. (eds) (1994) *Rewards at the Top. A Comparative Study of High Public Office*. London: Sage.

Hood, C.C. and Shuppert, G.F. (eds) (1988) *Delivering Public Services in Western Europe*. London: Sage.

Howlett, M. and Ramesh, M. (1995) *Studying Public Policy: Policy Cycles and Policy Subsystems*. Toronto: Oxford University Press.

Ingraham, P.W. (1997) 'Play It Again, Sam; It's Still Not Right: Searching for the Right notes in Administrative Reform', *Public Administration Review*, 57 (4): 325–31.

Jones, L.R., Schedler, K. and Wade, S.W. (eds) (1997) *Advances in International Comparative Management* Greenwhich, CT: JAI Press.

Jørgensen, T.B., Antonsen, M., Hensen, H. and Melander, P. (1998) 'Public Organizations, Multiple Constituencies, and Governance', *Public Administration*, 76 (3): 499–518.

Jreisat, J.E. (1975) 'Synthesis and Relevance in Comparative Public Administration', *Public Administration Review*, 35 (6): 663–71.

Kaufman, H. (1976) *Are Government Organizations Immortal?* Washington, DC: Brookings Institution.

Keating, M. (2001) *Nations against the State. The New Politics of Nationalism in Quebec, Catalonia and Scotland*, 2nd edn. London: Palgrave.

Kettl, D.F. (1993) 'Public Administration: The State of the Field', in A.W. Finifter (ed.), *Political Science. The State of the Discipline II*. APSA: Washington. pp. 407–28.

Kickert, W.J.M., Klijn, E.-H. and Koppenjan, J.F.M. (1997) *Managing Complex Networks*. London: Sage.

Klingemann, H.D. and Fuchs, D. (1995) *Citizens and the State*. Oxford: Oxford University Press.

Knoke, D., Pappi, F.U. and Broadbent, J. (1996) *Comparing Policy Networks: Labor Politics in the U.S., Germany, and Japan*. Cambridge: Cambridge University Press.

Korsten, A.F.A., Bertrand, A., de Jong, P. and Soeters, J. (eds) (1995) *Internationaal vergelijkend onderzoek*. The Hague: VUGA.

Lammers, C.J. and Hickson, D.J. (eds) (1979) *Organizations Alike and Unlike. International and Inter-institutional Studies in the Sociology of Organizations*. London: Routledge and Kegan Paul.

Landman, T. (2000) *Issues and Methods in Comparative Politics: an Introduction*. London: Routledge.

Lasswell, H.D. (1960) 'The Technique of Decision Seminars', *Midwest Journal of Political Science*, 4: 213–36.

Lijphart, A. (1971) 'Comparative Poltics and the Comparative Method', *American Political Science Review*, (1965): 682–93.

Lipsky, M. (1980) *Street-Level Bureaucracy: Dilemmas of the Individual in Public Services*. New York: Russell Sage Foundation.

Maor, M. and Lane, J.E. (1999) *Comparative Public Administration, Volume 1*. Aldershot: Ashgate (The International Library of Politics and Comparative Government).

Marin, B. and Mayntz, R. (eds) (1991) *Policy Networks: Empirical Evidence and Theoretical Considerations*. Frankfurt a.M.: Campus.

Marini, F. (1998) 'Foundation Under Innovation: Proceed with Care!', *Public Administration Review*, 58 (4): 369–73.

Marsh, D. (ed.) (1998) *Comparing Policy Networks*. Buckingham: Open University Press.

Massey, A. (ed.) (1997) *Globalization and Marketization of Government Services: Comparing Contemporary Public Sector Developments*. Houndmills: Macmillan.

McCourt, W. and Minogue, M. (2001) *The Internationalization of Public Management. Reinventing the Third World State*. Cheltenham: Edward Elgar.

Meyers, F. (1985) *La Politisation de l'administration*. Brussels: IIAS.

Moe, T. (1984) 'The New Economics of Organizations', *American Journal of Political Science*, 28: 739–77.

Naschold, F. (1995) *The Modernisation of the Public Sector in Europe: A Comparative Perspective on the Scandinavian Experience*. Helsinki: Ministry of Labour.

Needham, B. (1982) *Choosing the Right Policy Instruments*. Aldershot: Ashgate.

Nelissen, N. (1998) 'Megatrends in Public Administration Science in Europe', *De Europese Gemeente*, 33 (1): 19–24.

Niskanen, W.A. (1971) *Bureaucracy and Representative Government*. Chicago: Aldine Publishers.

Ostrom, V. and Ostrom, E. (1997) 'Cultures: Frameworks, Theories, and Models', in R. J. Ellis and M. Thompson (eds), *Culture Matters. Essays in Honor of Aaron Wildavsky*. Boulder, CO: Westview Press.

Norris, Pippa (1999) *Critical Citizens: Global Support for Democratic Governance*. Oxford: Oxford University Press.

O'Toole, L.J. (1986) 'Policy Recommendations for Multi-Actor Implementation: An Assessment of the Field', *Journal of Public Policy*, 6: 181–210.

O'Toole, L.J., Jr (1997) 'Treating Networks Seriously: Practical and Research-Based Agendas in Public Administration', *Public Administration Review*, 57 (1): 45–52.

Page, E.C. (1987) 'Comparing Bureaucracies', in J.E. Lane, (ed.), *Bureaucracy and Public Choice*. London: Sage. pp. 230–55.

Page, E.C. and Goldsmith, M.J. (1987) *Central and Local Government Relations. A Comparative Analysis of Western European Unitary States*. London: Sage.

Page, E.C. (1995) 'Comparative Public Administration in Britain', *Public Administration*, 73 (1): 123–41.

Page, E.C. and Wright, V. (1999) *Bureaucratic Elites in Western European States: A Comparative Analysis of Top Officials*. Oxford: Oxford University Press.

Peters, B.G. (1988) *Comparing Public Bureaucracies. Problems of Theory and Method*. Tuscaloosa, AL: Alabama University Press.

Peters, B.G. (1989) *The Politics of Bureaucracy*, 3rd edn. New York: Longman.

Peters, B.G. (1978) 'Public Policy and Public bureaucracy', in D. Ashford, *Comparing Public Policies: New Concepts and Methods*. London: Sage. pp. 283–315.

Peters, B.G. (1996) *The Future of Governing: Four Emerging Models*. Lawrence, KS: Kansas University Press.

Pierre, J. (ed.) (1995) *Bureaucracy in the Modern State. An Introduction to Comparative Public Administration*. Aldershot: Edward Elgar.

Pierre, J. (1998) *Partnerships in Urban Governance*. Basingstoke: Macmillan.

Pollitt, C. (1990) *Managerialism and the Public Service: The Anglo-American Experience*. Oxford: Basil Blackwell.

Pollitt, C. and Bouckaert, G. (2000) *Public Management Reform. A Comparative Analysis*. Oxford: Oxford University Press.

Pressman, J.L. and Wildavsky, A.B. (1973) *Implementation*. Berkeley, CA: University of California Press.

Presthus, R.V. (1959) 'Behavior and Bureaucracy in Many Cultures', *Public Administration Review*, 19: 25–35.

Putnam, R.D., Leonardi, R. and Nanetti, R. (1994) *Making Democracy Work: Civic Traditions in Modern Italy*. Princeton, NJ: Princeton University Press.

Ragin, C.C. (1989) *The Comparative Method: Moving Beyond Qualitative and Quantitative Strategies*. Berkeley, CA: University of California Press.

Rhodes, R.A.W. (1996) 'From Institutions to Dogma: Tradition, Eclecticism, and Ideology in the Study of British Public Administration', *Public Administration Review* 56 (6): 507–16.

Rhodes, R.A.W. and Weller, P. (eds) (2001) *The Changing World of Top Officials. Mandarins or Valets?* Buckingham: Open University Press.

Riggs, F.W. (1998) 'Public Administration in America: Why our Uniqueness is Exceptional and Important', *Public Administration Review*, 58 (1): 22–39.

Rohr, J.A. (2001) 'Constitutionalism and Administrative Ethics. A Comparative Study of Canada, France, the United Kingdom and the United States', in T.L. Cooper (ed.), *Handbook of Administrative Ethics*, 2nd edn. New York: Marcel Dekker.

Rose, R. (1985) *Understanding Big Government. The Programme Approach*. London: Sage.

Rouban, L. (ed.) (1999) *Citizens and the New Governance: Beyond New Public Management*. Implementation Research as Empirical Constitutionalism, Amsterdam: IOS.

Ruscio, K.P. (1997) 'Trust in the Administrative State', *Public Administration Review*, 57 (5): 454–8.

Rutgers, M.R. (1994) 'De Bestuurskunde als "Oude" Wetenschap', *Bestuurswetenschappen*, 5: 386–405.

Sabatier, P. (1986) 'Top Down and Bottom Up Approaches to Implementation Research', *Journal of Public Policy*, 6: 21–48.

Salamon, L.M. and Anheier, H.K. (1997) *Defining the Nonprofit Sector. A Cross-national Analysis*. Manchester: Manchester University Press.

Sharpe, L.J. (1979) *Decentralist Trends in Western Europe*. London: Sage.

Sharpe, L.J. (ed.) (1993) *The Rise of Meso-Government in Europe*. London: Sage.

Scharpf, F.W. (1993) *Games in Hierarchies and Networks: Analytical and Empirical Approaches to the Study of Governance Institutions*. Frankfurt a.M.: Campus.

Sigelman, L. (1976) 'In Search of Comparative Administration', *Public Administration Review*, 36 (6): 621–5.

Silberman, B.S. (1994) *Cages of Reason. The Rise of the Rational State in France, Japan, The United States, and Great Britain*. Chicago: University of Chicago Press.

Siffin, W.J. (1976) 'Two Decades of Public Administration in Developing Countries', *Public Administration Review*, 36 (1): 61–71.

Sjöblom, S. (1999) 'Transparency and Citizen Participation', in L. Rouban (ed.), *Citizens and the New Governance: Beyond New Public Management*. Amsterdam: IOS. pp. 15–27.

Smith, A. (1999) 'Public Policy Analysis in Contemporary France: Academic Approaches, Questions and Debates', *Public Administration*, 77 (1): 111–31.

Stepan, A. (2001) 'Toward a New Comparative Politics of Federalism', in *Arguing Comparative Politics*. Oxford: Oxford University Press.

Teisman, G.T. (2000) 'Models for Research into Decision-Making Processes: On Phases, Streams and Decision-Making Rounds', *Public Administration*, 78 (4): 937–56.

Tummala, K.K. (2000) 'An Essay on Comparative Administration', *Public Administration Review*, 60 (1): 75–80.

van Deth, J. (1994) *Comparative Politics in an Incomparable World*. IPSA Paper, Berlin, 1994.

Verba, S. (1967) 'Some Dilemmas in Comparative Research', *World Politics*, 1 (20): 111–27.

Verheijen, T. (ed.) (1999) *Civil Service Systems in Central and Eastern Europe*. Aldershot: Ashgate.

Verheijen, T. (ed.) (2001) *Politico-administrative Relations: Who Rules?* Bratislava: NISPAcee.

Verheijen, T. and Coombes, D. (1998) *Innovations in Public Management: Perspectives from East and West Europe*. Cheltenham, Edward Elgar.

Verweij, M. (2000) *Transboundary Environmental Problems and Cultural Theory: The Protection of the Rhine and the Great Lakes*. New York: St Martin's Press.

Vickers, J. and Wright, V. (1988) *The Politics of Privatisation in Western Europe*. London: Cass.

Vogel, D. (1987) 'The Comparative Study of Environmental Policy: a Review of the Literature', in M. Dierkes, H.N. Weiler and A.B. Antal (eds), *Comparative Policy Research*. Aldershot: Ashgate. pp. 99–171.

Wachendorfer-Schmidt, U. (ed.) (2000) *Federalism and Political Performance*. London: Routledge.

Waldo, D. (1964) *Comparative Public Administration: Prologue, Problems, and Promise*. Chicago: ASPA.

Walker, D.B. (1995) *The Rebirth of Federalism*, 2nd edn. Chatham, NJ: Chatham House Publishers.

Walmsley, G.L. and Wolf, J.F. (eds) (1996) *Refounding Democratic Public Administration: Modern Paradoxes, Postmodern Challenges*. Thousand Oaks, CA: Sage.

Webb, E.J., Campbell, D., Schwartz, R. and Sechrest, L. (1966) *Unobtrusive Measures*. Chicago: Rand–McNally.

Welch, E. and Wong, W. (1998) 'Public Administration in a Global Context: Bridging the Gaps of Theory and Practice between Western and Non-Western Nations', *Public Administration Review*, 58 (1): 40–9.

Williams, R. (ed.) (2000a) *Explaining Corruption*. Cheltenham: Edward Elgar.

Williams, R. (2000b) *Corruption in the Developed World*. Cheltenham: Edward Elgar.

Williams, R. and Robin, T. (eds) (2000) *Corruption in the Developing World*. Cheltenham: Edward Elgar.

Wright, V. (1994a) 'Reshaping the State: Implications for Public Administration', *West European Politics*, 17 (3): 102–34.

Wright, V. (1994b) *Privatization in Western Europe: Pressures, Problems and Paradoxes*. London: Pinter.

Windhoff-Héritier, A. (1993) 'Policy Network Analysis: A Tool for Comparative Political Research', in H. Keman, (ed.), *Comparative Politics*. Amsterdam: VU University Press. pp. 143–61.

Ziamou, T.T. (2001) *Rulemaking, Participation and the Limits of Public Law in the USA and Europe*. Aldershot: Ashgate.

35

International Organizations and Domestic Administrative Reform

Dionyssis G. Dimitrakopoulos and Argyris G. Passas

This chapter focuses on the role of international organizations as promoters of administrative reform at the national level. Typically, international organizations are placed in two broad categories. *Intergovernmental organizations* involve a type of membership whereby the legal autonomy of states remains largely intact primarily because of the subordinate role of the organization's institutional actors. *Supranational organizations* are characterized by an increasing delegation of powers by their members to an autonomous set of institutions whose output penetrates into national legal orders, domestic administrations and operational codes.

So far as the impact of the two types of international organizations upon national administrations is concerned, at first sight there seems to be a paradox: whereas supranational organizations are typically associated with a more indirect influence on national administrations, and thus a more covert type of reform, some intergovernmental organizations exert a more direct influence.

In supranational organizations – a category that essentially includes the European Union (EU) – the need for reform is an indirect consequence of membership. It stems primarily from the twin necessities of effective participation in policy making and the implementation of common policies. Intergovernmental organizations take a different approach. They either

1 regard domestic administrative reform as a formal *and* a functional condition for the effective pursuit of the material advantages that they offer, such as loans etc. (this is the case with the World Bank and the IMF); or

2 foster specific (market embracing) administrative policies, although they do not necessarily rely on legally binding instruments or other equally coercive mechanisms (for example, the OECD).

The first section of this chapter focuses on the pressures exerted on national administrations as a result of membership of the EU. The second section discusses the responses adopted at the national level. The third section examines the types of reform typically promoted by intergovernmental organizations. The final section outlines the main themes regarding the fostering of administrative reforms by international organizations and highlights some ideas about future research.

Ours is a rather *sceptical* view, which stresses – at least in the context of the EU – the conceptual and the empirical limits of the 'convergence thesis', namely: the lack of a specific model (Lippert et al., 2001); the resistance which promoters of reform typically face; the persistence of historically defined *national* characteristics; and the difficulty in clearly distinguishing between the pressures on domestic administrations stemming from international organizations and those from other sources. In short, we argue that, despite the significant formal and functional pressures exercised upon domestic administrations by the process of European integration, there has been no convergence. Rather, domestic administrations have responded through their own standard operating procedures and institutional repertoires. These responses exemplify *existing* patterns of success and failure in dealing with public policy issues. In turn, success and failure display clear *national* traits.

Second, we highlight the fact that pressure for administrative reform differs across international organizations. The idea that our sceptical view regarding 'Europeanization' may apply to the impact of other organizations on domestic administrations as well is appealing. Nevertheless, empirical research is needed before a conclusion can be reached. Indeed, the comparative analysis of the impact of various types of international organizations on domestic administrations is the challenging next step in this area.

SUPRANATIONAL ORGANIZATIONS AND NATIONAL ADMINISTRATIONS: THE CHALLENGE OF MEMBERSHIP

Membership of the EU entails a number of challenges for domestic administrations. First, an increasing number of sections of the domestic *central* government apparatus are involved in the management of EU-related business. Second, *subnational authorities* are increasingly involved in the conduct of EU-related business. Third, in *procedural* terms the nature of 'EU business' differs radically from traditional international affairs in that it transcends the boundaries between ministerial domains. Indeed, it permeates and affects almost every aspect of the state's operation. Fourth, in *substantive* terms, the 'product' of this process is legally binding and supersedes domestic legislation, thus significantly affecting the operational capacity of the state and its agents. Furthermore, this product (EU policies) is frequently premised on policy ideas, public philosophies and frames of reference that differ significantly from those that prevail in the domestic arena.

Pressures for reform

The issue of the pressures that national administrations face as a result of membership of the EU is not new (Wallace, 1971, 1973; Davies, 1973; González Sánchez, 1992; Institut International des Sciences Administratives, 1990; Toonen, 1992; Spanou, 1998). One can identify a number of sources of pressure for administrative reform at the national level. They are all inextricably linked to *membership* of the EU and are, therefore, to be distinguished from the pressures for reform generated by other international organizations (see below).

The first indication of pressure for reform stems from the formulation stage of the EU policy process because of the intensive involvement of national civil servants therein (Kassim and Wright, 1991). In quantitative terms, this type of pressure is demonstrated by the growth (by 22.8%) of the number of sessions that these officials attended between 1975 and 1985 – that is, even before the relaunch of the single European market project and the intensive legislative activity that followed it – in the context of the Council of Ministers (Wessels, 1990: 234). In qualitative terms, this pressure generates two types of functional imperatives: the recruitment and training imperative and the co-ordination imperative. Both are permeated by the idea that failure to influence the content of EU policies will generate increased adaptation costs, not least because of the legally binding nature of EU law.

National civil servants and the EU decision making process

Unlike in the domestic arena, where key administrative actors share the same frame of reference and policy style, the role of national civil servants in the context of the EU is more complex, not least because of the language barrier and the different – and frequently competing – national policy traditions and frames of reference. This added complexity highlights three types of needs in terms of the training that national civil servants should receive. First, there is an increased need for language training. Second, the nature of the EU decision making process – in particular the involvement of a variable number of actors and its unpredictable pace – highlights the need for knowledge of the policy styles that prevail in other member states, advanced negotiation skills and techniques, and thorough knowledge of 'Community procedures' (Polet, 1999). Indeed, the last of these is further highlighted by the increasing use of qualified majority voting (QMV): on the one hand, QMV undermines the capacity of individual member states to shape the course of negotiations; on the other hand, it highlights the need for 'coalition-building'. Third, the EU is a law-intensive organization. Indeed, the operation of EU institutions relies on an increasingly complex web of EU-specific legal provisions, for example, treaties, directives, regulations, decisions, the jurisprudence of the European Court of Justice (ECJ), in addition to domestic legislation. Knowledge of the domain-specific EU (and, ideally, national) legislation and the relevant jurisprudence of the ECJ is an inherent part of the profile of the 'perfect national administrator' who is involved in the management of EU business (González Sánchez, 1992; Pertek, 1993).

The 'co-ordination imperative'

The need for such knowledge stems from the expansion of the number of national ministries and subnational state actors that are involved in the EU policy process, including the implementation of EU policies. This imperative (Wallace, 1971; Davies, 1973; Kassim et al., 2000; Kassim et al., 2001; Peters and Wright 2001) has a horizontal as well as a vertical dimension. The horizontal dimension concerns the co-ordinated activity of administrative actors at the same level of (usually central) government that is required to promote a coherent, specific and workable set of policy 'preferences' expressed in a timely manner both in the various levels of the Council of Ministers and in the preparatory meetings organized by the Commission (that is, in the agenda-setting stage of the EU policy process).

The vertical dimension of co-ordination refers to the need for the central administrations of the member states to be aware of potential and actual problems regarding the implementation of EU policy at street level and to (a) provide the necessary means for corrective action (in implementation) or (b) devise flexible and pragmatic policies (in policy formulation). This need is enhanced by the attitude of the Commission that promotes the involvement of subnational authorities in the formulation and, naturally, the implementation of national plans for regional development.[1] Finally, the system of rotating presidencies and the increasing frequency of intergovernmental conferences place additional burdens on national administrations (Kassim, 2000: 4–5).

RESPONSES: NATIONAL PATTERNS OF LEARNING?

How did the member states of the EU respond to these pressures? (Debbasch, 1987; Mény and Wright, 1994; Rideau, 1994: 745–864; 1997; Rometsch and Wessels, 1996; Mény et al., 1996; Hanf and Soetendorp, 1998; Kassim et al., 2000; Kassim et al., 2001) Most of the existing literature directly or indirectly emphasizes the changes brought about in national administrations as a *result* of membership of the EU (see below). Crucially, these changes were produced despite

the enunciation by the ECJ of the *principle of institutional autonomy* (Rideau, 1972; Debbasch, 1990: 19), whereby the member states are formally obliged to fulfil the obligations that stem from membership of the EU but remain *formally* free to do so on the basis of their *own* legal and administrative arrangements. Despite this formal element, *functional* pressures that result from membership of the EU have eroded the formal autonomy of the national administrative systems. Below we discuss the patterns of national administrative reform and the mechanisms that have affected them.

The so-called 'convergence/adaptation' thesis (Hanf and Soetendorp, 1998; Mény et al., 1996; Börzel, 1999) – also known as the 'Europeanization' thesis, whereby national administrations are *thought* to converge towards a similar structure (or even 'model') as a result of membership of the EU – is attractive but not convincing. Arguably, more subtle and theoretically informed analyses of administrative reform at the national level (see Passas and Makridimitris, 1994; Passas and Stephanou, 1997; Harmsen, 1999; Kassim et al., 2000; Kassim et al., 2001; Goetz, 2001; Page, 2003) convincingly establish that

1 the *pace* of reform is slow (that is, incremental change prevails);
2 the *direction* of reform remains path-dependent (that is, national administrations evolve along the lines of previously established patterns); and
3 *learning* is the mechanism that drives this process whereby member states come to identify the type of pressure that they face, but they then go on to 'respond' *individually*.

Co-ordination mechanisms

Both successful and unsuccessful attempts to change the mechanisms whereby central governments co-ordinate their policies on EU affairs (Kassim et al., 2000; Peters and Wright, 2001) are illustrative of the *national* patterns of institutional development. Indeed, the French (Lequesne, 1993) and the British (Bender, 1991; Bulmer and Burch, 1998; Kassim et al., 2000: ch. 1) models, which rely essentially on strong central mechanisms that co-ordinate the increasing number of administrative actors involved in the *formulation* stage of the EU policy process, are widely regarded as the most effective systems of co-ordination in the EU. Their effectiveness relies on three essential elements:

1 the large number of co-ordination meetings that bring together pro-actively a significant number of officials in Paris and London;
2 the culture of diffusion of information that prevails in these central administrations; and, most importantly,
3 the establishment of strong mechanisms that provide solutions to conflicts (over competence and policy) between ministerial departments.

Although the British system has been influenced by the French, it essentially relies on the assumptions and the wider logic that permeate the Whitehall machinery in general (Bulmer and Burch, 1998). The three aforementioned elements were parts of the manner in which Whitehall departments managed government business even *prior* to the accession of the UK to the then EC. Also, the success of the French system explains why the British looked at it in the first place. However, the *compatibility* of the assumptions and logic that permeate the French and the British systems of co-ordination explain why the latter was influenced by the former. The EU-specific mechanisms, in turn, reflect wider similarities in both the management of government business in London and Paris (especially the strong core executive) and the two respective polities (in particular the centralized nature of the two states).

Other member states, such as Greece, that have considered the adoption of the Franco-British model have soon abandoned these ideas (Passas and Makridimitris, 1994, 1997; Spanou, 2000). The efforts of the Greek government to establish an effective system for the co-ordination of EU policy in the early 1980s eventually led to the reconfirmation of established patterns of interorganizational relations in the Athenian bureaucracy. The system that was established formally was backward-looking in the sense that it relied on the traditional distinction between domestic and foreign affairs. It relied on the Ministry of Foreign Affairs for the co-ordinated *presentation* of the views of the Greek government in the institutions of the EU, and the Ministry of National Economy for the co-ordinated *transposition* of EU law into the national legal order. Both aspects of the system have since proved to be problematical.[2] Both the idea of a centralized system and its institutional expression – that is, the committees that were aimed at imposing some sort of co-ordination – were soon abandoned. Recent empirical research has highlighted the fact that the co-ordination of national policies on EU affairs follows 'pre-existing domestic institutional structures and values' (Kassim, 2000: 26; Kassim et al., 2000; Kassim et al., 2001).

The gradual adaptation of training programmes for national civil servants and the extensive practical experience that they gain in Brussels have undermined the validity of the aforementioned argument. Nevertheless, the increased interest in the development of the political aspects of European integration (illustrated primarily through the development of a Common Foreign and Security Policy) reaffirms the importance of Ministers of Foreign Affairs at both the national and the European levels.

The profile of the national civil servants

Incremental and path-dependent changes in the national structures (and the interactions that take place therein) are mirrored by the persistence of national patterns of recruitment to the national civil service. This is demonstrated by the slow progress made in the liberalization of access of EU nationals to the wider public sector of other member states (Commission, of the European Communities, 1988; European Commission, 1999). However, as far as senior (policy making) posts are concerned, existing patterns of recruitment remain unchallenged (Burnham and Maor, 1995). For example, the British administration is still dominated by Oxbridge graduates, the German, Italian and Greek administrations are still dominated by lawyers, etc., whilst the procedures used for the recruitment remain *varied* (Ziller, 1988).

Furthermore, training and secondment programmes that are designed to facilitate the management of EU-related business at the national level – typically by explaining how the EU works – have not produced a *systemic* impact. Discussing the introduction of such programmes in the Scottish Office, Smith argues that while they have 'led to limited cultural change in the sense that they facilitated the ability of civil servants to develop working practices which met the demands of EC/EU membership, *they did not herald wider changes in bureaucratic emphasis or approach*. In particular, there was no identifiable transformation of approach from domestic to "European"' (2001: 162; emphasis added; see also Christoph, 1993: 534). More importantly, a recent study of three Whitehall departments highlights the fact that 'only limited importance is attached to training in Eurocratic skills until they are needed', but the importance of formal training for language skills has increased (Maor and Stevens, 1997: 541–2).

The limits of the convergence thesis

Kassim, a critic of the convergence thesis, notes that 'it has an intuitive appeal. Members belonging to the same organization are subject to common rules, share common obligations and interact with common structures. Facing the same demands and the same difficulties, it would seem logical to suppose that their responses would also be the same' (Kassim, 2000: 3).

The convergence thesis relies on three cardinal ideas. First, a *causal* link is thought to exist between membership of the EU and the convergence of national administrative systems towards a specific model. Arguably, there is very little, if any, evidence to support this view. Although the administrations of the member states are called upon to perform the *same roles*, a number of models continue to exist (Rometsch and Wessels, 1996; Spanou, 1998: 472; Kassim et al., 2001). Detailed qualitative case studies of specific countries reveal that national administrations use their *own*, historically defined, standard operating procedures and institutional repertoires so as to manage the necessities of membership, and so remain largely unaltered. This is so because they successfully perform their new roles[3] (Harmsen, 1999) and also because resistance to change remains strong and implementation is undermined by conflict and the lack of determined, powerful and resourceful 'fixers' (Passas and Makridimitris, 1994, 1997).

The second assumption upon which the convergence thesis is based relates to a mechanism that is thought to drive convergence, namely, *learning*. Although learning does occur in national administrations (Olsen and Peters, 1996), in the case of EU-related administrative reform it appears to relate to the identification of the pressures that stem from membership of the EU rather than to the spread of a specific set of ideas as to how one should deal with them.

Third, both the convergence and the related (wider) 'Europeanization' thesis – which concerns the patterns of intergovernmental relations – rely implicitly or explicitly (Börzel, 1999) on

1   the idea that the source of the impetus for change, namely 'Europe', is *exogenous* to the member states; and
2   the so-called 'goodness of fit' between national institutions and the EU.

This mode of analysis calls for two comments. First, it is extremely hard to draw a clear distinction between the effects of *membership* of the EU and those of other concurrent developments upon national administrations (Christoph, 1993: 535; Kassim, 2000: 27). Such developments include most notably the advent of New Public Management that is promoted either directly, by organizations such as the OECD (see below), or indirectly by other organizations and international fora such as the WTO (Kleitz, 2001). Second, the logic that underpins the argument about the 'goodness of fit' is inherently static since it ignores the well-documented[4] (Harmsen, 1999; Passas and Makridimitris, 1994) capacity of national administrations to perform new tasks by means of their existing standard operating procedures and institutional repertoires, which they modify marginally in an incremental and piecemeal manner. More importantly, it ignores the fact that 'Europe' *is not exogenous*. Rather, what the EU *is* and what it *does* is largely shaped by national civil servants, who manage EU-related business in Brussels, national capitals and at the subnational level.

INTERGOVERNMENTAL ORGANIZATIONS AND DOMESTIC ADMINISTRATIVE REFORM

Pressures for domestic administrative reform stem from intergovernmental, that is, more traditional, organizations where the erosion of state power is much less evident. Whereas the influence exerted by supranational organizations is an integral element of membership, without necessarily being an area where, for example, the EU has a clearly defined, specific and deliberate *policy*, intergovernmental organizations, by contrast, have a clear *policy* regarding domestic administrative reform. It focuses on the diffusion of more or less specific neo-liberal principles, ideas and logics that are seen as 'optimal' solutions to 'common problems' such as the quest for operational efficiency, optimal service delivery and accountability.

These pressures exhibit three cardinal features. First, their form differs across intergovernmental organizations: for example, whereas administrative reform is a *formal condition* for the provision by the World Bank and the IMF of heavily needed financial assistance, the OECD promotes the same kind of reforms through the much more subtle means of the diffusion of ideas, 'best practice' and the provision of advice. Second, these reforms appear to be 'blanket solutions' to seemingly 'common problems'. Finally, they have not led to the homogenization of domestic administrative structures.

A useful organizing principle for the discussion of these pressures can be derived from the literature on 'isomorphism', which, stemming from sociological institutionalism, highlights three factors – coercion, mimetism and normative pressures – that are thought to lead to increasingly similar organizational *forms* (DiMaggio and Powell, 1983) – as well as *outcomes* (DiMaggio and Powell, 1991).

Indeed, there are three types of 'isomorphic pressures'.[5] First, *coercive pressures* can be formal or informal. They essentially rely on relations of dependence which are, by definition, asymmetrical. They entail the direct or indirect imposition of either structures or a specific logic that must underpin a set of structures. Second, *mimetism* provides a useful rule of thumb in cases where uncertainty and ambiguity reign. The ambiguity of preferences and a poor understanding of a given context or problem frequently lead decision makers to choose organizational structures and logics that imitate those found in other areas of activity, countries or regions. They do so because these structures are (or are thought to be) successful and legitimate in tackling the same or similar problems. Finally, *normative pressures* essentially rely on professionalization. This entails both the formal education of decision makers (that is, politicians and civil servants) and the establishment of networks of professionals that operate as carriers of both a common terminology and approach to problem-solving and ideas and logics which are meant to resolve common problems.

Our discussion in the next two sub-sections focuses on two intergovernmental organizations, namely, the World Bank and the Organization for Economic Co-operation and Development (OECD). Both play a prominent role in the diffusion of policies for administrative reform on the basis of the 'New Public Management'. The key characteristics of New Public Management (Aucoin, 1990) include (Hood, 1991: 4–5) hands-on professional management in the public sector, the introduction of explicit standards and measures of performance, emphasis on output controls, disaggregation of public sector units, and a focus on competition and private sector management styles (including a strong emphasis on the disciplined use of resources) in the public sector.[6]

Isomorphism and the diffusion of New Public Management: the case of the World Bank

The key feature of the World Bank's role in the diffusion of New Public Management amongst borrower countries is the *conditional* nature of these loans. In other words, the loans are disbursed on condition that specific reforms will be implemented according to a fixed timetable. In particular, the funds that are related to the so-called 'adjustment lending' – typically needed in conditions of extreme financial pressure – are released 'when the borrower complies with stipulated release conditions, such as the passage of reform legislation, the achievement of certain performance benchmarks, or other evidence of progress toward a satisfactory macroeconomic framework' (World Bank, 2001d).

The key characteristics of New Public Management are evident in the reforms promoted by the World Bank (2001a). Adjustment lending has largely focused on short-term cost-containment measures that were part of a wider effort to contain the public sector in the recipient countries – including the number of public employees, construed by the World Bank as an endemic problem (World Bank, 2001c) – the introduction of performance-orientated budget systems, a flexible civil service, increased accountability and fiscal transparency (World Bank, 2001a: 46, 48). This process was underpinned by attempts to quantify policy targets as well as service delivery by means of benchmarks, and by the use of fiscal performance tests (World Bank, 2001c). Moreover, the establishment of semi-autonomous bodies within the public sector was also promoted. These bodies perform sector-specific tasks previously performed by central government departments, in an effort to improve operational efficiency through greater managerial discretion and flexibility as well as operational autonomy from politicians' short-term orientations.

The conditional nature of loan provision to countries in desperate need of funds exemplifies the importance of *coercive* isomorphism in the transfer of New Public Management through the World Bank. However, this is not the only form of isomorphic pressure exerted by this intergovernmental organization. Growing criticism of its 'heavy-handed' approach has led the World Bank to develop other (much more subtle) forms (most notably *normative*) of isomorphic pressure. This is exemplified by its 'learning programmes' which focus on themes such as 'decentralization and governance' (involving the diffusion of knowledge about 'a creditworthy government', 'efficient and client-orientated service delivery' and 'techniques of public expenditure management'), 'controlling corruption and improving governance', and, more importantly, the 'training of trainers' with regard to the implementation of development projects (World Bank, 2001b). In addition, the World Bank provides 'analytic and advisory services' to client countries in the form of 'tailored' economic and sectoral programmes, as well as the opportunity for the establishment of 'knowledge networks'.

Isomorphism and the diffusion of ideas and best practices in public management: the case of the OECD

Since 1989 the OECD has developed a wide range of activities in administrative reform through its Public Management (PUMA) programme directed by the Public Management Committee, which consists of senior national officials. The Council of the OECD (1999), in its recent resolution on the mandate of the Public Management Committee, stipulates that its mission is to facilitate the efforts of member countries and interested non-member states regarding good governance and public management. The objective is to improve the effectiveness, efficiency, transparency and accountability of public institutions.

The PUMA group (Public Management Committee and Public Management Service), established in 1990, acts primarily as a forum for the exchange of ideas among government top officials on how to adapt public sector governance to the changing needs of the fast-moving modern world. For that purpose PUMA

*   produces various materials (studies, comparative analyses, annual reports, country reviews, evaluative benchmarking, guidelines for the evaluation and the design of policies – for example, in regulatory decision making, etc.) on various policy issues, such as public sector budgeting and management (OECD, 2002); e-government, knowledge management and the use of IT; sustainable development; government–citizen relations; human resources management; regulatory management and reform; territorial governance; ethics and corruption;
*   convenes and manages a large network of working groups, for example, working party of Senior Budget Officials, working party on Human Resources Management, working

party on Regulatory Management and Reform, working group on Strengthening Government–Citizen Connections, the annual meeting of Senior Officials from Centres of Government; and
*   shares the results of the existing work with interested non-member countries through the Governance Outreach Initiative.

In organizational terms, the reforms promoted by PUMA (Matheson, 2001: 6; Cordova-Novion, 2001) focus on the enhancement of the managerial autonomy of specialized regulatory bodies as well as the decoupling of policy implementation and advice from policy making. Although the delegation of powers to these bodies is thought to have been 'a largely positive experience', significant problems have arisen (Matheson, 2001: 7): the lack of institutional clarity, the inability of central governments to monitor and control these bodies, weaknesses in the governance structure and reporting mechanisms, and difficulties in implementing performance management.

In particular, these reforms have revealed an increased risk of capture, weakened the efficiency and effectiveness of the public sector and undermined citizens' trust (Matheson, 2001: 8). Nevertheless, the intensity of the pressure for this particular type of reform is exemplified by the fact that the solutions to these problems are sought in the same vein: the quest for a clear division of responsibility between the autonomous institutions and the ministries, the establishment of clear reporting mechanisms, the enhancement of a 'quasi-contractual relationship', and enhanced capacities for audit bodies (Matheson, 2001: 9–10).

PUMA relies on continuous interactions between the members of a large group of senior government officials. Thus, it represents an example of normative isomorphic pressure exerted on member states (transfer of ideas, model solutions, best practices etc., among professionals, knowledge networks/communities). Indeed, although senior officials of the OECD do not challenge the idea that the same solutions should not necessarily be implemented in differing national contexts, 'modern governance structures in fact are an important determinant of business confidence in all countries participating in the globalized economies'(Kleitz, 2001: 3). In other words, these ideas and practices are depicted as being at least more *au fait* with the challenges of modern governance. Hence, even if modifications are needed, they cannot and should not challenge the core principles that underpin the ideas and practices promoted by the OECD.

As far as the *actual* impact of those pressures is concerned, there is limited empirical evidence to draw on. PUMA reports are the main source of information. Indeed, the dominant view is that 'no universal practices exist: viability [of reforms] is related to the *political, economic, administrative and social contexts; capacities are as important as the basic setting*' (Cordova-Novion, 2001: 14; emphasis added). As Guy Peters notes, '[f]urther research will be required to understand how the learning from other administrative systems takes place, what the role of international organizations such as the OECD is, and who learns directly from whom' (Peters, 1997: 85–6).

Moreover, one can identify other forms of (especially informal) coercive isomorphic pressures in the activity of another OECD group, Support for Improvement in Governance and Management in Central and Eastern European Countries (SIGMA). Established in 1992, SIGMA is a joint initiative of the OECD and the European Union and comprises two teams: (1) ten European Union candidate countries of Central and Eastern Europe (Bulgaria, the Czech Republic, Estonia, Hungary, Latvia, Lithuania, Poland, Romania, Slovakia and Slovenia, in cooperation with the EU's Twinning Programme) and (2) the western Balkan countries (Albania, Bosnia and Herzegovina, Croatia, the former Yugoslav Republic of Macedonia, and the Federal Republic of Yugoslavia). SIGMA advises transition countries on improving good governance and administrative efficiency, and promoting adherence of public sector staff to democratic values, ethics and respect for the rule of law, and helps to build up indigenous capacities at the central governmental level to face the challenges of globalization and to prepare the first team's accession to the European Union. For that purpose SIGMA provides information and expert analysis to policy makers (see, e.g., OECD/SIGMA, 1998) and facilitates contact and exchange of experience amongst public sector managers.

EU membership is conditional on the implementation of these reforms. This programme, in tandem with other EU actions – such as the Twinning Programme – benefits from the OECD/PUMA experience and expertise in administrative reform in order to improve results in the pre-accession period. Hence, this joint programme has become an instrument through which the EU exerts coercive isomorphic pressures on the Central and East Europe candidate countries. However, in these countries, too, 'reactions and solutions do not converge' (Lippert et al., 2001: 980).

CONCLUSION: RESISTANCE AND CONVERGING PRESSURES

The concept of isomorphism and a significant part of the wider debate about the impact of international organizations on national administrative systems imply, explicitly or not, that membership of those organizations entails a gradual process of *convergence* (but see, *inter alia*, Page, 2003). In this chapter, we have outlined the sources and nature of these pressures and have linked them to two types of international organization.

We have argued that membership of the EU entails a significant *informal* pressure for administrative reform. This concerns primarily – but not exclusively – the need for co-ordination, the improved training of national civil servants and the *de facto* gradual shift in the balance of power between foreign and 'technical' ministries. On the other hand, intergovernmental organizations exert two kinds of pressure:

1 *Direct* pressures for the adoption of neo-liberal, market-embracing reforms. This is typically a condition for the approval of loans and other benefits (World Bank and IMF).
2 *Indirect* pressures. The OECD is an example of an intergovernmental organization that performs the subtle role of a forum for the diffusion the principles, ideas and norms that permeate market-based reforms.

The distinction between supranational and intergovernmental organizations has provided a useful organizing principle for the discussion of the impact of international organizations upon domestic administrative structures. Nevertheless, there is evidence that the two types of organizations exert increasingly *similar* pressures. Indeed, the European Union's strategy to embrace the candidate countries of Central and Eastern Europe relies on a set of principles – the 'Copenhagen criteria' – amongst which the capacity to implement the '*acquis communautaire*' and the adoption of market economy figure prominently. These are *conditions for membership*. In that sense, the EU exercises a new type of *direct coercive* pressure similar to the pressure for reform exercised by the World Bank.

Further, we have argued that existing analyses are much more useful in identifying *pressures* (and the sources thereof) and the *prevailing discourse* regarding administrative reform than in outlining the *model* towards which national administrative structures and practices are thought to converge. This sceptical view highlights both the role of culture (*administrative* culture in particular) that conditions any reform (established patterns of behaviour and accepted lines of resistance) and the idea that reform depends on the timely and effective combination of three cardinal factors, namely, *opportunity* (which is country-specific), the existence of a coherent *strategy* (government goals) and *tactics* (the capacity to mobilize support in an effective manner). In addition, we have argued that there is little empirical evidence that supports the 'convergence' thesis.

We conclude by highlighting a number of interesting avenues for future research. The 'administratization' (Timsit, 1987) of traditional international organizations in conjunction with their proliferation (Virally, 1973; Cassese, 1985; Argyriades, 1988) are key features of the modern international political environment. The increasing complexity of the relations between international organizations and their member states has raised a number of issues regarding the management of overlapping issues, in particular the need for co-ordinated action between various international organizations (Ferretti, 1984), the cohesion of the member states' policy expressed within international organizations (Valticos, 1988) and the organizational and functional cohesion of the member state (Cohen Jonathan, 1988). Indeed, as a result of membership of international organizations states face a number of pressures at both the political and the administrative levels, including the *explicit* politicization of seemingly 'technical' issues[7] which blurs the lines between departmental responsibilities and thus changes the nature of the relations between government departments. Moreover, as a result of its organizational and administrative fragmentation, the state is now acting as a 'federation of agencies' rather than a unit (Cassese, 1985: 178), due not least to the direct involvement of various government departments in the operation of international organizations. Further, the traditional role of foreign ministries and their predominance in the management of a state's international relations is challenged by the increased involvement of economic and 'line' departments in the day-to-day handling of business associated with specialized international organizations. Virally has termed this phenomenon 'dediplomatization' (Virally, 1973: 24). This is especially obvious in some specialized international organizations (such as the ILO, IMF) (Cassese, 1985: 178). The increasing direct involvement of 'line' departments in the management of membership of international organizations necessitates an internal/intraministerial administrative re-organization (Hopkins, 1976) and an effort of co-ordination

(horizontal/interdepartmental and vertical/intradepartmental) in order to ensure that the state's 'foreign policy' is coherent. In this context, the increased role of national permanent representations in international organizations is of particular importance (Virally et al., 1971; Hayes-Renshaw et al., 1989; Kassim et al., 2001). Naturally, the analysis of the impact of these trends upon national administrations requires empirical research.

NOTES

1 The implication (in terms of workload and the need for expertise) for the staff of these authorities is thus evident.
2 The failure of the Greek Ministry of Foreign Affairs to perform this role was indicative of a wider pattern that was identified in most member states. This pattern concerns the declining importance of these ministries in the conduct of government (as well as EU-related) business.
3 A quantitative analysis regarding the UK has revealed a similar pattern (see Page, 1998).
4 The same sceptical view has been shown to apply to the wider pattern of intergovernmental relations. Indeed, discussing the case of Germany, Goetz (1995) argues convincingly that European integration has 'tended to affirm, if not reinforce key structural principles of German federalism'.
5 Also, the transfer of Western models to Central and East European countries has been promoted by domestic political elites who have benefited from it (Jacoby, 2001).
6 This was elegantly termed 'the diminishing publicness of public service' (Haque, 2001).
7 In other words, international politics entails much more than the management of 'high politics': 'technical' issues (for example, economic and environmental development, social and labour issues) have a clear political dimension. Hence, all government departments are directly involved in the management of political matters.

REFERENCES

Argyriades, Demetrios (1988) 'The administrative problems of international organizations', in *Mélanges en l'honneur de Phedon Vegleris*. Athens: Sakkoulas.
Aucoin, Peter (1990) 'Administrative reform in public management: paradigms, principles, paradoxes and pendulums', *Governance,* 3 (2):115–37.
Bender, Brian G. (1991) 'Whitehall, central government and 1992', *Public Policy and Administration,* 6 (1): 13–20.
Börzel, Tanja A. (1999) 'Towards convergence in Europe? Institutional adaptation to Europeanization in Germany and Spain', *Journal of Common Market Studies,* 37 (4): 573–96.

Bulmer, Simon and Burch, Martin (1998) 'Organizing for Europe: Whitehall, the British state and European Union', *Public Administration*, 76 (4): 601–28.

Burnham, June and Maor, Moshe (1995) 'Converging administrative systems: recruitment and training in EU member states', *Journal of European Public Policy*, 2 (2):185–204.

Cassese, Sabino (1985) 'Relations between international organization and national administrations', in *Proceedings of the XIXth International Congress of Administrative Sciences, Berlin (West) 1983.* Deventer/Netherlands: Kluwer.

Christoph, James B. (1993) 'The effects of Britons in Brussels: The European Community and the culture of Whitehall', *Governance*, 6 (4): 518–37.

Cohen Jonathan, Gerard (1988) 'L'état face à la prolifération des organisations internationales', in Société Française pour le Droit International (ed.), *Les Organisations internationales contemporaines. Crise, mutation, développement.* Paris: Pedone.

Commission of the European Communities (1988) 'Free movement of workers and employment in the public service of the member states'. Communication of the Commission with regard to the implementation of article 48 paragraph 4 EEC Treaty, *OJEC*, C 72, 18 March.

Cordova-Novion, Cesar (2001) 'Regulatory governance'. Paper read at the Conference on Devolving and Delegating to More Autonomous Bodies and Controlling Them. Bratislava, 22–23 November, http://www.oecd.org/pdf/M00023000/M00023692.pdf.

Davies, John (1973) 'National governments and the European Communities', *New Europe*, 2: 24–8.

Debbasch, Charles (ed.) (1987) *Administrations nationales et intégration européenne.* Paris: Centre National de la Recherche Scientifique.

Debbasch, Charles (1990) 'L'influence des transferts de compétence vers les instances communautaires sur les compétences des administrations', *Administration*, 149: 17–20.

DiMaggio, Paul J. and Powell, Walter W. (1983) 'The iron cage revisited: institutional isomorphism and collective rationality in organizational fields', *American Sociological Review*, 48 (2): 147–60.

DiMaggio, Paul J. and Powell, Walter W. (1991) 'The iron cage revisited: institutional isomorphism and collective rationality in organizational fields', in W. Powell and P. DiMaggio. (eds), *The New Institutionalism in Organizational Analysis.* Chicago: University of Chicago Press.

European Commission (1999) 'Commission takes further steps against Luxembourg for failing to comply with ECJ ruling in the social field and Spain for discrimination in access to employment in the public service'. http://www.europa.eu.int/comm/dg05/fundamri/movement/news/infring_en.htm (26 April).

Ferretti, Raymond (1984) *La Coordination de l'action des organizations internationales au niveau européen.* Brussels: Bruylant.

Goetz, Klaus (1995) 'National governance and European integration: intergovernmental relations in Germany', *Journal of Common Market Studies*, 33 (1): 91–116.

Goetz, Klaus (2001) 'European integration and national executives: a cause in search of an effect?', in K. H. Goetz and S. Hix (eds), *Europeanised Politics? European Integration and National Political Systems.* London: Frank Cass.

González Sánchez, Enrique (1992) 'La négotiation des décisions communautaires par les fonctionnaires nationaux: les groupes de travail du Conseil', *Revue Française d'Administration Publique*, 63: 391–9.

Hanf, Kenneth and Soetendorp, Ben (eds) (1998) *Adapting to European Integration: Small States and the European Union.* London: Longman.

Haque, Shamsul M. (2001) 'The diminishing publicness of public service under the current mode of governance', *Public Administration Review*, 61 (1): 65–82.

Harmsen, Robert (1999) 'The europeanization of national administrations: a comparative study of France and the Netherlands', *Governance*, 12 (1): 81–113.

Hayes-Renshaw, Fiona, Lequesne, Christian and Mayor Lopez, Pedro (1989) 'The permanent representations of the member states to the European Communities', *Journal of Common Market Studies*, 28 (2): 119–37.

Hood, Christopher (1991) 'A public management for all seasons?', *Public Administration* 69 (1): 3–19.

Hopkins, Raymond (1976) 'The international role of "domestic" bureaucracy', *International Organization*, 30 (3): 405–32.

Institut International des Sciences Administratives (ed.) (1990) *Les Implications administratives de l'intégration economique régionale: L'exemple de la CEE. Approche comparative.* Madrid.

Jacoby, Wade (2001) 'Tutors and pupils: international organizations, central European elites, and Western models', *Governance*, 14 (2): 169–200.

Kassim, Hussein (2000) *The National Co-ordination of EU Policy: Must Europeanisation Mean Convergence?* Cahiers Européens de Sciences Po 5/2000. Paris: Presses de la FNSP.

Kassim, Hussein and Wright, Vincent (1991) 'The role of national administrations in the decision-making processes of the European Community', *Rivista Trimestrale di Diritto Pubblico*, 31 (3): 832–50.

Kassim, Hussein, Menon, Anand, Peters, B. Guy and Wright, Vincent (eds) (2001) *The National Co-ordination of EU Policy: The European Level.* Oxford: Oxford University Press.

Kassim, Hussein, Peters, B. Guy and Wright, Vincent (eds) (2000) *The National Co-ordination of EU Policy: The Domestic Level.* Oxford: Oxford University Press.

Kleitz, Anthony (2001) 'Experience and best practices in achieving regulatory efficiency and open markets'. Paper read at the Regulatory Management and Reform Seminar, Moscow, 19–20 November, http://www.oecd.org/pdf/M00023000/M00023229.pdf.

Lequesne, Christian (1993) *Paris–Bruxelles: Comment se fait la politique européenne de la France?* Paris: FNSP.

Lippert, Barbara, Umbach, Gaby and Wessels, Wolfgang (2001) 'Europeanization of CEE executives: EU membership negotiations as a shaping power', *Journal of European Public Policy,* 8 (6): 980–1012.

Maor, Moshe and Stevens, Handley (1997) 'Measuring the impact of new public management and European integration on recruitment and training in the UK civil service', *Public Administration,* 75 (3): 531–51.

Matheson, Alex (2001) 'The Public Management Service of the OECD (PUMA)'. Paper read at the Conference on Devolving and Delegating to More Autonomous Bodies and Controlling Them, Bratislava, 22–23 November, http://www.oecd.org/pdf/M00023000/M00023675.pdf

Mény, Yves and Wright, Vincent (eds) (1994) *La Riforma Amministrativa in Europa,* Bologna: Il Mulino.

Mény, Yves, Muller, Pierre and Quermonne, Jean-Louis (eds) (1996) *Adjusting to Europe: The Impact of the European Union on National Institutions and Policies.* London: Routledge.

OECD (2002) Overview of results-focused management and budgeting in OECD member countries. PUMA/SBO(2002)1, 11–12 February 2002.

OECD (1999) Resolution of the Council concerning the mandate of the Public Management Committee, 964th Session of the Council, C(99)175/FINAL.

OECD/SIGMA (1998) 'Preparing Public Administrations for the European Administrative Space'. SIGMA Paper No. 23.

Olsen, Johan P. and Peters, B. Guy (eds) (1996) *Lessons from Experience: Experiential Learning in Administrative Reforms in Eight Democracies.* Oslo: Scandinavian University Press.

Page, Edward C. (1998) 'The impact of European legislation on British public policy making: a research note', *Public Administration,* 76 (4): 803–9.

Page, Edward C. (2003) Europeanization and the persistence of administrative systems', in *Festschrift Vincent Wright.* Oxford: Oxford University Press.

Passas, Argyris and Makridimitris, Antonis (1994) *The Greek Government and Co-ordination of European Policy.* Athens: Sakkoulas [in Greek].

Passas, Argyris and Stephanou, Constantine (1997) 'Grèce', in J. Rideau (ed.), *Les États membres de l'Union Européenne. Adaptation – mutations – résistances.* Paris: LGDJ.

Pertek, Jacques (1993) 'La formation des fonctionnaires et des juristes aux questions européennes', *Revue da Marché Commun et de l'Union Européenne,* 371: 746–53.

Peters, B. Guy (1997) 'Policy transfers between governments: the case of administrative reforms', *West European Politics,* 20 (4): 71–88.

Peters, B. Guy and Wright, Vincent (2001) 'The national co-ordination of European policy-making: negotiating the quagmire', in J. Richardson (ed.), *European Union: Power and Policy-Making,* 2nd edn. London: Routledge.

Polet, Robert (ed.) (1999) *Formation à l'intégration Européenne.* Maastricht: IEAP.

Rideau, Joël (1972) 'Le rôle des états membres dans l'application du droit communautaire', *Annuaire Français de Droit International,* 18: 864–903.

Rideau, Joël (1994) *Droit institutionnel de l'Union et des Communautés Européennes.* Paris: LGDJ.

Rometsch, Dietrich, and Wessels, Wolfgang (eds) (1996) *The European Union and Member States: Towards Institutional Fusion?* Manchester: Manchester University Press.

Smith, James (2001) 'Cultural aspects of Europeanization: the case of the Scottish Office', *Public Administration,* 79 (1): 147–65.

Spanou, Calliope (1998) 'European integration in administrative terms: a framework for analysis and the Greek case', *Journal of European Public Policy,* 5 (3): 467–84.

Spanou, Calliope (2000) Greece. A truncated pyramid?', in H. Kassim, B.G. Peters and V. Wright (eds), *The National Co-ordination of EU Policy: The Domestic Level.* Oxford: Oxford University Press.

Timsit, Gerard (1987) *Administrations et états.* Paris: Presses Universitaires de France.

Toonen, Theo (1992) 'Europe of the administrations: the challenges of '92 (and beyond)', *Public Administration Review,* 52 (2): 108–15.

Valticos, Nicolas (1988) 'Institutions nationales et institutions internationales: facteurs et problèmes d'un rapprochement', in *Mélanges en l'honneur de Phedon Vegleris.* Athens: Sakkoulas.

Virally, Michel (1973) 'L'état face à l'organisation mondiale', in *Actes du IIe Colloque.* Geneva: Georg/ Librairie de l'Université.

Virally, Michel, Gerbet, P. and Salmon, J. (1971) *Les Mission permanantes auprès des organisations internationales.* Brussels: Bruylant.

Wallace, Helen (1971) 'The impact of the European Communities on national policy-making', *Government and Opposition,* 6 (4): 520–38.

Wallace, Helen (1973) *National Governments and the European Communities.* London: Chatham House.

Wessels, Wolfgang (1990) 'Administrative interaction', in W. Wallace (ed.), *The Dynamics of European Integration.* London: Pinter for the Royal Institute of International Affairs.

World Bank (2001a) *Adjustment Lending Retrospective.* Final report, 15 June. Washington, DC: The World Bank, mimeo.

World Bank (2001b) *Catalogue of Learning Programs: Public Sector Development.* http://WBLN0018.world-bank.org/

World Bank (2001c) *Civil Service Reform: A Review of World Bank Assistance.* Sector study No. 19599. Washington, DC: World Bank Operations Evaluations Department.

World Bank (2001d) *World Bank Lending Instruments.* http://www.worldbank.org/whatwedo/svc-lendintro.htm

Ziller, Jacques (1988) *Égalité et mérite: l'accès à la fonction publique dans les états de la Communauté Européenne.* Brussels: Bruylant.

36

Administrative Patterns
and National Politics

Martin Lodge

Any assessment of the dynamics between administrative patterns and national politics reflects on a number of perennial debates in the field of public administration. Foremost, it relates to different conceptions of the roles, functions and relationship between politics and administration. Such distinctions build on Max Weber's diagnosis of the rise of bureaucratic legal rationality which challenges other types of authority, and Woodrow Wilson's often dismissed distinction between politics and administration (Wilson, 1887: 209–11). The dichotomy between politics and administration, where elected politicians decide and professional administrators implement political choices and maintain political authority, continues to attract much interest (Campbell and Peters, 1988; Aberbach and Rockman, 1994; Rutgers, 2001). While the normative (liberal democratic) argument and the self-perception of politicians and administrators seem to add weight to the dichotomy, empirical analysis has pointed to an often close, although varying extent of intermeshing between administrative and political levels and roles (Pierre, 1995: 207). It is therefore difficult to differentiate clearly between administrative and political functions. While, on the one hand, the two roles are based on different conceptions of recruitment and legitimization, on the other hand, in terms of functions, both roles substantially overlap.

A second concern relates to the question whether observed or predicted administrative patterns reflect commonalities across territories and national political cultures. For example, claims concerning the 'rise' of bureaucratic rationality and commonality are often used to

point to international changes from assumed 'public bureaucracy' towards 'New Public Management' states (Aucoin, 1990). In contrast, studies stressing national or sectoral diversity point to the importance of national institutions and veto points, political and administrative cultures, as well as of sectoral characteristics.

A third concern relates to the nature of administrative or bureaucratic capacity in transposing political preferences and in formulating and adjusting state–society relations, for example in the diverse interfaces between bureaucracy and society, such as the terms of recruitment and representativeness, administrative coordination and policy responsiveness (Subramaniam, 2000: 564–8).

Any attempt to account for the multidimensional complexity of the relationship between national politics and administrative patterns encounters a diversity of approaches within the public administration literature. These range from the distinction between 'weak' and 'strong' states, 'entrepreneurial' or 'bureaucratic' societies, discussions as to how national political cultures impact on administrative patterns and the relationship between national cultures and organizational cultures (see for example, Hofstede, 1980, 1991, 1993; Tayeb, 1988), the supposed wider societal value shift towards a post-industrial society leading to different types of citizen-demands on administrations (Inglehart, 1997), difference in civil servants' values (Putnam, 1974; Aberbach et al., 1981; Aberbach et al., 1994), accounts stressing the importance of party political concerns ('do parties matter?'), arguments relying on political and administrative institutional factors in exploring the relationship between national politics and administrative patterns (Hall, 1986), to formal models of legislative delegation to executive agencies under different types of constellations (Epstein and O'Halloran, 1999; Huber et al., 2001).

The following does not aim to provide a complete overview of all these arguments, but attempts to highlight dimensions in which traditional debates on the politics/administration dichotomy continue to inform analysis. It is centered on a discussion of civilian administration in the (European) developed world, given that region's particular exposure to 'transnationalization' effects. It is therefore less concerned with transition, developmental or military administration. First, this chapter assesses the different national patterns through which administration is politically controlled. Second, it explores the impact of national politics and administrative patterns on policy change, to highlight the importance of administrative patterns in informing the orientation of political and policy change. Third, the changing nature of the politics–administration relationship is considered, in the light of themes of transnationalization and 'de-hierarchization'. Such developments arguably challenge the traditional conception and study of *national* politics and administration relationships. The conclusion suggests that in order to move beyond the comparison of single state studies, analysis needs to operate either within united frameworks and assess the impact of these factors, or to identify particular trends and enquire about the effect of particular patterns on such developments. Such a strategy allows one to move the analysis beyond the broad stereotyping of particular political systems (Peters, 2000: 351).

NATIONAL POLITICS AND ADMINISTRATIVE PATTERNS: CONSTRAINTS AND DISCRETION

Among the most widely discussed themes in public administration are the various means through which relationships between national politics and administrations are patterned. The asymmetric power of bureaucracies, based on expertise and permanence, has traditionally been associated with incomplete political control leading to self-interested bureaucratic activity, both in terms of shaping and implementing political decisions. The necessities of operating within a legal-rational code, superior resources, professionalization and specialization effects are all said to have led to a 'bureaucratization' of

political life (Eisenstadt, 1958). Incomplete political control, as suggested in the transaction cost literature on legislative delegation to administrative bodies, points to 'agency drift', the agent's self-selected activity due to incomplete control by the political principal (McCubbins et al., 1987; Horn, 1995). In contrast, the issue of 'political drift', the politically motivated shirking by legislative action at a later time period, points to methods of insulating administrative activity from political intervention, a concern which had already been prominent in nineteenth-century administrative reform debates.

To come to a better understanding how different literatures have dealt with the issue of political control of administration, the following section sets out three perspectives on factors molding the so-called 'politico-administrative relationship' (Pierre, 1995: 207). These perspectives can be distinguished between historical-cultural, political-institutional and less 'macro-level' approaches on how national politics shape and control political control.

Historical-cultural origins

The historical development of national public administration has occurred in distinct contexts, primarily driven by the increasing political centralization of emerging states and their need to organize and administer tax collection and the military (Mayntz, 1985: 17–32). A prime example is France, with its early development of a centralized administration in the sixteenth century, which after further reforms under Napoleon became an organizational 'template' for continental European public administration. As in the case of Prussia, this involved the (gradual) centrally driven 'crowding out' of previously existing local patterns of administration, despite the persistence, in certain domains, of corporatist-type governance arrangements. While across the German states bureaucracies were dominant sources for economic and policy reform, England relied largely on self-regulation. Central government only became prominent in the course of industrialization in the nineteenth century, without, however, following the continental pattern of administrative organization. Similarly, Silberman (1993) has shown that instead of witnessing a unifying march of bureaucratization according to 'legal rationality', bureaucratic development across countries has been diversely path-dependent, set by the way critical institutional design dilemmas were handled at major historical turning points, in particular with regard to recruitment of senior civil servants.

Cultural perspectives draw on historical foundations and events in accounting for diversity in administrative patterns and relationships between politics and administration. Thus, 'civic culture' bureaucracies are often distinguished from 'continental' bureaucracies. National political cultures are said to influence the way in which public organizations recruit and operate as well as their public perception (Borre and Viegas, 1995), while particular administrative cultures operate (either cross-departmentally and/or within a single department) in shaping policies, recruitment and internal operating procedures (Page, 1995). Hofstede (1980) reports distinct patterns of national cultures (measured in terms of power distance, uncertainty avoidance, individualism and masculinity) which impact on organizations. However, while it is important to investigate potential cultural differences at the national and at the administrative level as well as the continued impact of different historical foundations of administrative systems, it is also necessary to analyze why these factors continue to persist and how they resist demands for change.[1]

Political institutions

While the context of political institutional frameworks and the broader national constitutional settlement are shaped by historical-cultural conditions, these factors also more directly shape both political and administrative patterns. So-called 'macro-level' factors, such as the distribution of functions and responsibilities across levels of government, differences between and among both unitary and federal political systems (making national administration far more pervasive in unitary systems – Page 1995: 259), the nature of the government, whether single-party, coalition or consociational, linkages of particular interests to certain political parties as well as broad access points for lobbying and opposition, are significant in defining the role of national administrations.

At one level, such national differences provide spaces for administrative discretion, and establish different requirements of the civil servants' political craft (in addition to technocratic and managerial skills) in understanding and operating within a national political system (Goetz, 1997). Thus, national administration in unitary systems faces fewer co-ordination problems in implementing centrally formulated policy, in contrast to systems such as Germany's system of 'cooperative federalism', which relies not only on the regional and local delivery of federal policies, but also on a large degree of executive-driven bargaining and compromise-seeking. Furthermore, apart from different types of interest-group universes and their access to the political system, national systems are also shaped by dominant departments – for example the overarching role of the British Treasury in economic and social policy – as well as by particular sectoral agencies.

At a broader level, political-institutional frameworks also establish the incentives for particular administrative strategies, whether in terms of different types of 'bureau-shaping' activities (Dunleavy, 1991; Dolan, 2002) in contrast to 'budget-maximization' (Niskanen, 1971) or in terms of the emergence of the 'regulatory state' (Majone, 1994, 1997), where budgetary constraints are said to establish an incentive to maximize influence over policy content rather than expenditure. The wider political economy literature has also stressed the importance of the institutional and constitutional framework for explaining regulatory 'commitment' and 'credibility' (Levy and Spiller, 1994). Thus, particular administrative patterns are chosen to insulate against particular political influence, for example by establishing semi-independent regulatory agencies or supposedly autonomous interest-rate setting central banks. However, the example of central banks and regulatory agencies highlights the importance of an understanding both of the 'rational' incentives provided by an institutional framework, and of the wider historical and cultural setting of these institutions. For example, the German Bundesbank (pre-Euro) and the German Federal Cartel Office have played far more important roles in shaping national economic policy than their formal status would suggest due to their ability to mobilize particular resources through coalition-building and the management of public perceptions (such as claiming the guardian role against 'hyper-inflation' or for the 'social market economy'). The significance of such reputational factors, as well as the evolved understanding of that role across political, administrative and societal actors, suggests that any analysis of administrative patterns and their relation to national politics requires, on the one hand, an analysis of the distribution of formal powers and functions, while on the other hand, it demands thorough understanding of the 'appropriate' role associated with any particular organization and how such perceptions are being mobilized and maintained in order to advocate or oppose initiatives that are perceived to affect the organization's standing.

Political control and administrative resources

While historical, cultural and broad political institutional arrangements provide the context within which both political and administrative actors pursue their strategies, the analysis of inter-action patterns between 'politics' and 'adminis-tration' suggests not only a long-established tradition of a politicized role of administrative interlocutors with politics (Campbell, 1988), but also distinct patterns across both federal as well as unitary systems (Pierre, 1995). Thus, organi-zational structures, career patterns and political control arrangements within national administra-tive systems seem to be unrelated to the overall political institutional framework, such as unitary or federal systems (Pierre, 1995: 208–10). Focusing on methods of political control of administrations, two types of control, internal and external, can be distinguished.

Internal controls to make administrations 'compliant' with political preferences deal with the relationship between political and senior administrative officials, the degree of civil service cohesion and its shared 'corporate iden-tity'. National patterns suggest substantial vari-ety, for example the large-scale politicization of senior positions in the case of the United States, the mixed German system which distinguishes between political civil servants (mostly with an established 'technical' career background) who can be retired early and 'technical civil servants' who remain the intellectual backbone of the federal executive (similar arrangements exist in France and Sweden), the more party-membership dominated appointment system in Austria (and also Belgium, Greece and to a lesser extent Spain) to the UK (and Danish, Irish and partly Dutch) type of a seemingly 'neutral' civil service, operating under the assumption that the civil service will operate loyally to any government of the day (see Page and Wright, 1999: 270–2).

The degree of civil servant cohesion and per-ceived 'corporate identity' across the administra-tive system establish a significant counterweight to attempts of political control. In this respect, substantial differences exist between the US-type 'government of strangers' (Heclo, 1977), the (although increasingly diversifying) 'Whitehall village' (Heclo and Wildavsky, 1974), the French grands corps or the departmentalism of the German federal executive (Page, 1995: 261–5). At the same time, the German higher civil service, while predominantly having a legal academic background and operating within a shared legal framework, has been designed to establish a relatively heterogeneous workforce

(Goetz, 1999), in contrast to France where the members of the grands corps, across private and public sectors, are formed as an elite, or the United Kingdom with its homogeneity of recruit-ing mostly from selected universities.

External controls, apart from courts, are political devices to increase the ability to control administrative action. Such devices include junior ministers or the German parliamentary state secretaries, French-style Cabinets (also very prominent in the European Commission, but also in Germany in terms of ministerial Leitungsstäbe) or the more extensive usage of political advisors (Page and Wright, 1999: 277–9). Moreover, the duration of ministers in office, varying substantially across countries, offers a further political control over administra-tions, with a longer period in office encouraging some form of domain expertise among political actors. Further political 'controls' are exercised through legislatures. While the role of parlia-ments in controlling the executive is said to have been increasingly challenged, substantial differ-ences exist between systems with a strong legis-lature due to committee systems (in particular the United States), or the German system with its relatively (and arguably increasingly) powerful committees (Goetz, 1999), in contrast to the rather weak parliamentary oversight in the UK. However, while there has been a shared percep-tion of a decreasing trust in the competence of administrations and a parallel trend towards increasing mainly external political controls, differences in national 'original positions' have led to different response patterns across national contexts (Page and Wright, 1999; for China, see Huang, 2002). While these measures mainly present mechanisms supporting political over-sight and so-called 'police controls', the involve-ment or additional support given to potentially affected interests, which then act as so-called 'fire alarms' to raise political interest, offers a further way in which national politics can control administrative agents.

Linking issues of the relationship between politics and administration to themes of historical development and reform opportunities, Christopher Hood has utilized the notion of 'public service bargain' to highlight different patterns through which the civil service has 'contracted' either formally through law or infor-mally through convention with the political system and has thereby established its 'appropri-ate' role in the policy process (Hood, 2000). These so-called 'public service bargains' are broadly distinguishable between systemic 'trustee' (establishing the civil service as a quasi-autonomous position and making it part of a wider constitutional settlement) and a variety of more pragmatic 'agency' bargains (establishing a principal–agent type relationship). These 'bargains' establish different types of managerial spaces and opportunity structures for reform. They provide an insight both into the historical national circumstances through which the role of the national administration has been positioned *vis-à-vis* national politics and into the incentives and understandings which influence the extent to which types of reform are adopted to alter existing patterns of political-administrative relations. Furthermore, it illustrates the foundations for the emergence of particular normative values which lead to different degrees of public esteem associated with the *Beamtenethos* of the *Rechtsstaat* tradition and the more managerial understandings in the Anglo-American context.

This brief overview of a large body of literature suggests that the relationship between administrative patterns and national politics is defined not by an outright dominance of the one over the other, but rather by a continuous tension between the two. The examples of national interaction between the administrative and political levels provide a picture of diversity of control mechanisms and influence of wider rule and historical-cultural arrangements, in particular the importance of the existing wider institutional arrangement. It also suggests a shared understanding of the close involvement of administrative actors in politics as well as of political actors in administration.

ADMINISTRATIVE PATTERNS AND POLICY CHANGE

Closely related to the different means of control and different institutional settings of public administration have been debates regarding the capacity for change of administrative patterns. This section is primarily concerned with discussing how administrative patterns (that is, not only organizational structures, but also 'standard operating procedures') shape processes of political and policy reform. The following section first sets out why public sector reform provides insights into the dynamics between national politics and administrative patterns and then provides an overview of different approaches towards explaining the character of public sector reform, which can be broadly distinguished between political-institutional and 'administrative pattern' accounts. The former is more interested in the capacity for the exercise of political

leadership (and the ability of an administration to react, possibly in a dynamic conservative way), while the latter is more concerned with the orientation of change.

While for some administrative and regulatory reforms represent an eventual convergence of forms cross-nationally, others argue that regulatory reforms represent 'catching up' effects, similar themes which are interpreted, however, in culturally distinct ways or represent persistent diversity due to path dependencies (Hood, 2000: 3–4). Research on national administrative reform has therefore stressed the significance of different patterns and reform trajectories (Hood, 1995; Pollitt and Bouckaert, 2000; Schröter, 2001; for an analysis of 'agencification', see James, 2001). At the same time, the public sector reform agenda is directed at clarifying (as so often before) the relationship between political control and administrative autonomy, with New Public Management arguably being directed at both the enhancement of managerial autonomy and the assertion of political control. Furthermore, it addresses questions as to the capacity of political leadership *vis-à-vis* administrations. For example, Bezes (2001) has stressed the importance of different leadership strategies for explaining different degrees of 'success' in French prime ministerial attempts to reform public administration, distinguishing ineffective 'offensive' strategies (aiming to 'shatter' existing arrangements) and more successful 'defensive' (and internally generated) strategies for administrative reform.

The most prominent accounts for explaining how 'politics matters' in administrative and wider public sector reform have stressed the importance of national political institutions, given that these define the extent of political leadership, that is, the way through which policy is formulated and administered, as well as provide the opportunity structure for those affected to oppose the policy's implementation. In the past two decades, it has become increasingly popular to argue that the number of veto points in a political system explain the degree of a state's capacity for policy change (see Grande and Schneider, 1991; Immergut, 1992; Weaver and Rockman, 1995). Such accounts have been employed to explain why neoliberal ideas were successful in Britain under the administration of Margaret Thatcher in contrast to other supposedly market-liberal governments in Western Europe in the 1980s and 1990s.[2] For example, differences between public sector reform in the United Kingdom and Germany are linked to different levels of 'reform capacity', with the existence of a unitary state with single party government arguably offering more scope for reform at the national level, whereas German administrative reform has, for constitutional reasons, primarily occurred at the 'delivery end' of public administration, namely local government, while the privatization of the few federally owned utilities (rail, telecommunications and post) required extra-large majorities to engineer constitutional amendments.

Others have concentrated on different types of incentives provided by national political institutional systems. Steinmo (1993), for example, compared the development of tax systems and related these to the underlying ways in which political decision making was conducted in the United States, the United Kingdom and Sweden. Hall (1983: 57; 1986: 273–6) suggested in the case of the UK that innovation in economic policy was primarily driven by political parties, while Hayward (1976), in his analysis of French and British civil servants, stressed the importance of cultural values, in particular with regard to understandings of the appropriate authority of the state *vis-à-vis* society, in order to explain differences in civil service engagement in major policy innovation. However, wider political attitudes seem less powerful in explaining public sector reform: in the case of Britain and Germany, findings in political culture and attitude surveys offer little explanatory support for differences in public sector reform (Schröter, 2000).

Besides this interest in the impact of political institutional frameworks and cultural conceptions of the appropriate role of the state *vis-à-vis* society for explaining how national politics motivate change in administrative patterns, other accounts regard administrative patterns themselves as crucial in facilitating and constraining innovation. For example, Weir (1989) stresses in particular the significance of administrative patterns in terms of recruitment patterns, career promotion and standard operating procedures in order to account for differences in receptiveness to Keynesian ideas. Comparing the 'Keynesian' responses of the 1920s in Sweden, Britain and the United States, Weir and Skocpol (1985) highlight the importance of the 'openness' of the administrative system to external advice and the importance of institutional division of ministerial responsibilities.

Knill (1999) has offered two ideal types of bureaucracies which respond to political demands for change in distinct ways (resembling to some extent the distinction between 'strong' and 'weak' states). He distinguishes between 'autonomous' and 'instrumental' bureaucracies, where the former represents highly entrenched administrative patterns that prove self-adaptive to challenges for change, generating reform

strategies internally in the face of largely absent executive leadership, whereas 'instrumental bureaucracies' are characterized by their limited influence on policy formulation and by a larger extent of external leadership and 'inspiration'. Knill points to three dimensions explaining administrative change 'capacity', namely the capacity for executive leadership, the institutional entrenchment of administrative structures and procedures, and the influence of the bureaucracy on policy making. Such ideal type comparisons are likely to encounter evidence that will not only mostly lie in the 'grey area' of the continuum between the two ideal types but also vary significantly across time and domains.

Nevertheless, such accounts highlight the role of administrative patterns and their interaction with political constellations in contributing to policy change, in particular in terms of the orientation of policy change. Among the crucial factors for explaining the orientation of policy change are, therefore, national civil servants, their recruitment and their career paths. Substantial differences exist between the 'in- and outsider' patterns of the United States, with recruitment undertaken by the agencies themselves, the widespread (although increasingly regulated) system of *pantouflage* in the French public administration, with its administratively educated elite civil servants (Rouban, 1999: 87–8), the German civil service, with its still dominantly legal expertise which is shaped by a primarily *Ressort*-based career, in contrast to the British 'generalist' with a service-wide character of an open career structure. Thus, apart from different types of prior education (and differences in legal education), it is the type of 'learning on the job' (defined by Weber as *Dienstwissen*) that allows for different degrees of specialization and establishes different patterns of institutional memory (Page, 1992: 48). Similarly, Hood (1996) has pointed to the importance of 'second learning' effects from British civil servants moving from one domestic public sector reform to another. For example, in the case of the British railway privatization, it was a 'reform community' of civil servants with experience of privatizations which brought forward a model relying on vertical separation and horizontal fragmentation of service operations in the face of increasing reluctance by politicians (see Lodge, 2002: ch. 7). While political motivations and preferences are therefore clearly crucial in motivating change, the context of existing administrative patterns is not only likely to shape the extent of reform ambitions and opportunities, but also the nature of such policy change, with even supposedly 'instrumental' bureaucracies including substantial capacity to internally generate and manage reform processes.

While discussing primarily the impact of particular political and administrative factors on policy change, rather than policy change itself, this section has aimed to stress the relevance of public sector reform for exploring the relationship between national politics and administrative patterns, not only in terms of outcome, but also in terms of impact on the extent and orientation of reform. Broader institutional and cultural predispositions that enhance or constrain the exercise of political leadership and concentrate on the existing initial conditions are utilized to point to different reform outcomes. In contrast, an emphasis on administrative patterns provides insights into why particular reform templates were chosen rather than others. Utilizing either approach has informed and continues to inform the study of the 'politico-administrative relationship' and moves the analysis beyond the description of changes in terminology and organizational architecture towards questions of accounting for the extent and orientation of diagnosed policy change.

CHANGING ADMINISTRATIVE PATTERNS AND NATIONAL POLITICS

Existing administrative patterns and the selection of policy instruments are said to be shaped by the dominant national 'policy style' (Jordan et al., 1982). The notion of policy styles refers to a dominant procedural ambition which reflects the preferred choice of instruments and mirrors normative values in how to achieve accommodation. While it is difficult to make any predictive claims about 'policy styles', and such notions often raise more questions than answers, the notion of 'style' in this context relates to national preferences for particular administrative patterns and policy instruments. Similarly, Linder and Peters (1989) suggest that political culture shapes the degree of acceptance of a population of the imposition of particular measures of centralized government intervention. They highlight that particular organizational features are of crucial importance for understanding the appropriateness or non-appropriateness of particular policy choices, which besides reflecting on the internal organizational predisposition towards particular measures also relates to the character of the 'target population' and to the surrounding policy network. For example, Vogel

(1986) has pointed to the significance of cultural aspects when comparing the cooperative enforcement style in environmental regulation in Britain with the adversarial process in the United States. Thus, any wider understanding of administrative patterns and their relationship to national politics needs also to include societal actors and their involvement in both the formulation and delivery of policy within particular policy domains or sectors.

Two developments are said to increasingly challenge traditional interaction patterns between national politics and administrative patterns, transnationalization and 'de-hierarchization'. Both developments challenge the centrality of the state and its capacity to act in a 'sovereign' way in its internal or external affairs. On the one hand, national administrations are increasingly exposed to transnational themes, in particular in the context of the European Union, where the large majority of national economic regulation merely represents the transposition of EU provisions. On the other hand, national politics are said to be increasingly required to obtain the consent of particular stakeholders for initiating policy in particular domains. Thus, in the light of increasing difficulties in obtaining societal legitimacy for particular policy measures, new means of legitimization are required which move beyond the traditionally distinct national administrative patterns of interaction with interest groups and associations (see Sacks, 1980; Lehmbruch, 1991; Page, 1992: 108–19). Among these attempts to sustain legitimacy are instruments such as delegation or negotiation, which potentially challenge traditional interaction patterns between administration and societal actors. This section looks first at issues of 'transnationalization' (focusing on EU member states), before turning to issues of 'de-hierarchization'. Both advance the complexity of the relationship between national politics and administrative patterns.

The perceived transnationalization of administrative patterns relates to several commitments through which national states have traded in parts of their formal sovereignty in order to cooperate in international or regional agreements, the most prominent being membership of the European Union. While the logic of 'delegation' is often associated with functional dynamics, such as enhanced problem solving capacity, the impact of membership on national politics and administrative patterns is characterized in cross-national perspective both by commonalities of interests and by diversity of responses.

Membership in the EU requires diplomatic skills and institutional arrangements for effectively representing and negotiating with other member state administrations. It also demands the capacity to transpose and implement transnational provisions and to monitor their implementation (Menon and Wright, 1998). A further aspect is the administration of EU provisions given the European Commission's reliance on national (and subnational) administrations in the execution of its policies. These activities have meant that large areas of national public administration have increasingly come to operate at both the national and the EU level. Wolfgang Wessels (1997) claims that this tendency has led to an 'administrative fusion', with civil servants no longer distinguishing between their national and EU-related activities. This fusion, however, operates largely within established national administrative and political patterns, thus leading to a Europeanization of policy content and a potential change in the allocation of legal authority, but not necessarily in terms of structure. For example, Bulmer and Burch (1998: 606) report that European integration 'has been absorbed into the logic of the Whitehall machinery'. A similar diagnosis has been made by Goetz (1995) in the case of German federalism. At the policy level, however, the interaction between EU policies and national administrations is leading to a diversity of responses due to different degrees of coercion, adaptation pressures and incentive structures (Knill, 1998). The level of adaptation pressure is said to depend on the institutional fit between national administrative patterns, in particular the embeddedness and degree of flexibility of the existing national arrangements, and EU measures. The importance of national conditions also holds for cases of 'voluntary imports' of European 'models', for example in the case of the European competition law framework, which was, with qualifications, adapted also at the British and the German national level in the late 1990s. In both cases, however, policy change was driven primarily by national actors for national reasons, with national issues dominating the legislative process (Eyre and Lodge, 2000). In contrast, most areas of domestic telecommunications regulation are now effectively prescribed through European provisions.

Besides this transnationalization of administrative activity, national politics remain almost solely based on the electoral legitimization at the national level with elections to the European Parliament mainly presenting an opportunity to hold a referendum on the national government of the day. For national politics, transnationalization of government activity places a constraint on pursuing particular options, either due to the formal requirements of European law or because of the enhanced potential for regulatory competition within the Single Market (Scharpf, 1999). The latter is said to limit the ability to impose costly policy options on potentially mobile constituencies. On the other hand, politics at the EU level provide national politics with an additional level to pursue strategies, for example by allowing them to 'export' particular policy 'solutions' or by aiming to initiate policy change, which would potentially be vetoed at the domestic level.

So far the analysis has assumed that administrative patterns define the activities of *public* administration. However, it is not necessarily a new insight that administration, both in terms of policy formulation and implementation, involves 'public' and 'para-public' as well as 'private actors', for example churches in health care, corporatist arrangements between trade unions, employers and governments in macro-economic policy in the 1970s, or more recently in 'social pacts' (see Teague, 1999), industry associations in standard setting (Werle, 2001) or even proposals favoring 'faith-based' policies. The degree to which interest groups influence or dominate administrative patterns depends both on the problem constellation as well as national traditions. Thus, Wilson (1980) has suggested that the distribution of costs and benefits between affected interest groups largely determines how policy is developed, with a pattern of concentrated costs and diffuse benefits most likely to lead to a 'clientalist' relationship between a particular interest and the responsible bureaucracy. Interactions between interest groups and bureaucracies vary accordingly across sectors, but also across countries. Thus, the United States is arguably characterized by a trend towards 'issue networks' with a strong influence of particular interests in certain domains; in Germany, there is still a reliance on the established associations for consultation and implementation; Sweden has been characterized by technocratic concertation, while in France, the administration is said to stand aloof from the partiality of interest groups. While to some extent this national variation in terms of 'negotiable space' can be explained by the organization of the national interest group universe and the (declining) power of associations over member companies, particular concertation styles and the extent to which political authority is shared are a consequence of historical developments, for example the (transformed) persistence of guild structures or state–church relations (Crouch, 1993).

Despite these historical precedents, political actors are arguably increasingly required, in order to obtain legitimacy for their activities, to receive the consent of particular actors inside certain policy domains (Schneider, 2000).[3] The primary cause for this perceived increase in need to accommodate domain-based organizations is said to rest in the functional differentiation of society which challenges the primacy of politics and in the perceived increase in complexity of policy problems that require involvement of experts. This perceived change in national politics towards negotiation also requires change in administrative patterns, moving towards an emphasis on co-ordination and negotiation rather than 'traditional' executive acts, for example in environmental policy.[4] Thus, political as well as (public) administrative activity is said to be increasingly concerned with interaction and negotiation between political, administrative and large societal organizations (Windhoff-Héritier, 1996) and requires increased incentive-setting and 'tipping of balances' rather than hierarchical acts of government.

Given this increased importance of negotiation as a key political and administrative tool to achieve compliance, patterns beyond the 'traditional' tools of hierarchy and market have emerged, usually described as 'networks'. Mayntz and Scharpf highlight the prevalence of different types of control (or 'governance' – see Pierre, 2000) across 'sectors close to the state', distinguishing between 'hierarchist', 'colonized', 'corporatist', 'market' as well as 'network' type arrangements (Mayntz and Scharpf, 1995). Streeck and Schmitter (1985) discuss mechanisms of community, market, state and associations and the regulatory literature distinguishes between hierarchical, delegated, self-regulatory and market-type modes of regulation. Similarly, Hood (1996, 1998) utilizes the grid-group cultural theory framework to discuss different (pure and mixed) patterns of control over bureaucracies.

Nevertheless, besides normative questions that debate the political legitimacy of domain-based governance and the privileged access of partial interests in the context of a further 'de-parliamentarization' of national policy making (see Schneider, 2000), there is still a lack of analysis across countries and sectors that debates whether and to what extent administrative patterns in terms of governance mechanisms are changing and how deep such changes are, whether these are changing in similar ways and whether these are changing for similar or opposite reasons (for administrative reforms in Germany, see Wegrich, 2001). Furthermore, while it is widely argued that there has been a shift from hierarchical to network and market-type modes of governance, such tendencies also include so-called reverse and mirror-image effects. For example, Hood *et al.* (1999) suggest

that in the areas of regulation within British government an increased use of market-type arrangements went hand-in-hand with an extension of (hierarchical) oversight. Nevertheless, a historical institutional perspective would suggest that existing administrative patterns and wider political institutional frameworks shape the way in which both political as well as administrative actors operate under these diagnosed changing conditions, what type of responses they prefer and what type of 'new' modes will be regarded as most 'appropriate' and 'functional'.

COMPARING ADMINISTRATIVE PATTERNS AND NATIONAL POLITICS

Arguably one of the key difficulties in comparing administrative patterns is their national distinctiveness. Despite the perceived presence of supposedly 'global' pressures, the supposed convergence of political platforms as well as the rise and fall of doctrinal fads and fashions in administrative design (and subsequent organizational re-arrangements), the responses by public administrations have arguably been the replication of diversity rather than emerging convergence, in particular due to the institutional inertia caused by embedded standard operating procedures, strictly guarded distributions of authority, constitutional and historical functions and dominant 'policy styles'. This chapter has attempted to provide a brief (and by no means, exhaustive) overview of three general themes in the literature which are concerned with the dynamics between administrative patterns and national politics. This concluding section considers attempts to move beyond the reformulation of the politics–administration 'dichotomy' in order to account for both the spread of common themes and the (often diverse) responses by national politics and administrative patterns.

Across national contexts, similar problems and challenges highlight not so much the dichotomy between politics and administration (which seems largely artificial given the inherent political activity of any senior civil servant regardless of the supposed spread of managerialism), but rather relate to problems inherent to the so-called 'administrative state', which has been defined as a political system largely governed by the bureaucracy but with elected officials ultimately responsible for public policy (Pierre, 1995: 207). Nevertheless, how the systems respond to shared concerns and deal with similar issues – for example, the perceived increase of political control attempts over administrations – the way in which administrative and wider public sector reforms have been and continue to be implemented and the operation of both administration and politics at different levels, offer grounds for genuine comparative research. Furthermore, extending the analysis of the relationship between national politics and administrative patterns within the administrative state to issues of policy change, transnationalization and de-hierarchization adds to the challenges to a literature that has evolved from the analysis of relationships within individual states.

Attempts to make sense of the national diversity of administrative patterns and national politics have resorted to grouping particular countries together in order to highlight particular commonalities across states. Page (1995), in the context of Europe, differentiates administration types between the German continental (characterized by its federal composition based on Roman law, *Ressort*-particularism and moderate politicization), French continental (defined by its aloofness from politics), South European (characterized by its legal, but nevertheless politically weak status and patronage), Scandinavian (defined by professionalization, its fragmented character and corporatist cooperation), 'British–Irish' (defined by its 'neutrality') as well as East European administration.[5] Such analysis has also been supported by Hofstede's work on cultural values and country clusters and seems to fit well with the dominance of historical institutionalism in the field, which stresses the importance of tradition, both historical and legal, and so-called path dependencies in shaping subsequent developments. However, while the notion of path dependency has gained increased currency in both economics and political science (see Pierson, 2000), the challenge for comparative public administration is not only to describe and evaluate whether change is leading to increasing similarity (as a weaker case of convergence) or whether diversity remains dominant, but also to point to the sources for such national continuities in administrative patterns and to explain how these are being sustained and to assess how formal as well as informal resources (such as attitudinal understandings) are being employed to maintain particular arrangements. At the same time, utilizing Teubner's (1998) notion of 'policy irritant' offers a way towards studying the 'import' of legal (and other) instruments into different national, legal and political contexts. It predicts 'unintended consequences' of adverse reactions owing to different institutional

'national production regimes' (Soskice, 1999) or 'varieties of capitalism' (Hall and Soskice, 2001), thus leading to renewed diversity.

One aim of this chapter has been to highlight the importance of particular administrative patterns and the character of national politics for policy change, especially in respect of the *direction* or *orientation* of policy change, in contrast to accounts relying on broader historical-cultural and political institutional constellations. Such accounts offer insights into potential political and administrative strategies. Moreover, this chapter has aimed to point to the increasing difficulty in clearly defining not only the borders between politics and (public) administration in the context of multi-level governance, but also to what extent societal actors are part of political and administrative arrangements in diverse areas of policy making and implementation.

The challenge for comparative public administration is to combine an awareness of particular cross-national trends and tendencies, while at the same time accounting for differences, and locating both in the formal and the historical-cultural context of the particular object of study. A further task is to explore the causes and strategies which allow for the maintenance of particular patterns of public authority. Apart from exploring traditional concerns with regard to public sector recruitment, the receptiveness and interaction between administration and society, implementation patterns and internal administrative arrangements (Subramaniam, 2000: 564), such accounts start from commonly observed phenomena (for example, public sector reform or the transposition of legislation) and investigate how and why particular political and administrative factors mattered cross-nationally; or they can utilize particular analytical concepts and 'ideal types' to investigate how different systems process and update their administrative and policy performance 'intelligence', address particular problems of the relationship between politics and administration or aim to 'hardwire' particular administrative design ideas. Such approaches allow for the extraction of salient features of different administrative patterns and the impact of national politics and highlight how they matter.

While these suggestions are far from establishing a universal theory of the dynamics between national politics and administrative patterns (and they could be accused of cultural bias – Subramaniam, 2001: 338), they, nevertheless, inform wider debates within public administration and political science, while being attentive to the changing environment in which the so-called administrative state is supposed to operate.

NOTES

I thank Christopher Hood, Ed Page, Colin Thain, Kai Wegrich and the anonymous reviewer for most valuable comments and suggestions.

1 Apart from the difficulties to come to a definite view as to what constitutes a 'culture', especially a 'national culture'.

2 It should be noted that prior to the 1980s, the British state was regarded as immobile to change. For example, Hayward (1976: 436) questions whether 'in Britain the undoubted muddle that usually ensues [in decision making] eventually gets through'.

3 Admittedly, the literature lacks a clear measure of how much 'network-ization' of state activity differs from previous administrative patterns, such as 'iron triangles' or 'policy communities'.

4 Such challenges have led to claims which diagnose a shift from the 'welfare state' to the 'regulatory state' (Majone, 1997) or the 'supervision state' which is primarily responsible for contextual steering and infrastructure provision and access (Willke, 1995). Apart from negotiation, further means of 'de-hierarchization' are arguably the privatization of particular policy functions or the decentralization of executive functions to either lower tiers of government or to agencies (such as so-called 'quangos'). This overall phenomenon has been labelled as a 'hollowing-out' effect.

5 Similar differences have been established for developmental administration (see Subramaniam, 2001).

REFERENCES

Aberbach, J.D. and Rockman, B.A (1994) 'Civil Servants and Policymakers: Neutral or Responsive Competence', *Governance*, 7 (4): 461–9.

Aberbach, J.D., Derlien, H-U. and Rockman, B.A. (1994) 'Unity and Fragmentation, Themes in German and American Public Administration', in H-U. Derlien, U. Gerhard and F.W. Scharpf (eds), *Systemrationalität und Partialinteresse*. Baden-Baden, Nomos.

Aberbach, J.D., Putnam, R.D. and Rockman, B.A. (1981) *Bureaucrats and Politicians in Western Democracies*. Cambridge, MA: Harvard University Press.

Aucoin, P. (1990) 'Administrative Reform in Public Management: Paradigms, Principles, Paradoxes and Pendulums', *Governance*, 3 (2): 115–37.

Bezes, P. (2001) 'Defensive versus Offensive Approaches to Administrative Reform in France (1988–1997): The Leadership Dilemmas of French Prime Ministers', *Governance*, 14 (1): 99–132.

Borre, O. and Viegas, J.L. (1995) 'Government Intervention in the Economy', in O. Borre and E. Scarbrough (eds), *The Scope of Government*. Oxford: Oxford University Press.

Bulmer, S. and Burch, M. (1998) 'Organizing for Europe: Whitehall, The British State and European Union', *Public Administration*, 76: 601–28.

Campbell, C. (1988) 'Review Article: The Political Roles of Senior Government Oficials in Advanced Democracies', *British Journal of Political Science*, 18: 243–72.

Campbell, C. and Peters, B.G. (1988) 'The Politics/Administration Dichotomy: Death or Merely Change?', *Governance*, 1 (1): 79–99.

Crouch, C. (1993) *Industrial Relations and European State Traditions*. Oxford: Clarendon Press.

Dolan, J. (2002) 'The Budget-Minimizing Bureaucrat? Empirical Evidence from the Senior Executive Service', *Public Administration Review*, 62 (1): 42–50.

Dunleavy, P. (1991) *Democracy, Bureaucracy and Public Choice*, Hemel Hempstead: Harvester Wheatsheaf.

Eisenstadt, S.N. (1958) 'Bureaucracy and Bureaucratization', *Current Sociology*, 7 (2): 99–124.

Epstein, D. and O'Halloran, S. (1999) *Delegating Powers*, New York: Cambridge University Press.

Eyre, S. and Lodge, M. (2000) 'National Tunes and a European Melody? Competition Law Reform in the UK and Germany', *Journal of European Public Policy*, 7 (1): 63–79.

Goetz, K.H. (1995) 'National Governance and European Integration: Intergovernmental Relations in Germany', *Journal of Common Market Studies*, 33: 91–116.

Goetz, K.H. (1997) 'Acquiring Political Craft: Training Grounds for Top Officials in the German Core Executive', *Public Administration*, 75 (4): 753–75.

Goetz, K.H. (1999) 'Senior Officials in the German Federal Administration: Institutional Change and Positional Differentiation', in E. Page and V. Wright (eds), *Bureaucratic Elites in Western European States*. Oxford: Oxford University Press.

Grande, E. and Schneider, V. (1991) 'Reformstrategien und staatliche Handlungskapazitäten in der Telekommunikation in Westeuropa', *Politische Vierteljahresschrift*, 32 (3): 452–78.

Hall, P.A. (1983) 'Policy Innovation and the Structure of the State: The Politics–Administrative Nexus in France and Britain', *Annals of the AAPSS*, 466 (3): 43–55.

Hall, P.A. (1986) *Governing the Economy*, Cambridge: Polity Press.

Hall, P.A. and Soskice, D. (2001) 'An Introduction to Varieties of Capitalism', in P.A. Hall and D. Soskice (eds), *Varieties of Capitalism: The Institutional Foundations of Comparative Advantage*. Oxford: Oxford University Press.

Hayward, J.A.S. (1976) 'Institutional Inertia and political impetus in France and Britain', *Journal of European Political Research*, 4: 341–59.

Heclo, H. (1977) *A Government of Strangers: Executive Politics in Washington*. Washington, DC: Brookings Institution.

Heclo, H. and Wildavsky, A. (1974) *The Private Government of Public Money: Community and Policy Inside British Politics*. London, Macmillan.

Hofstede, G. (1980) *Culture's Consequences – International Differences in Work-Related Values*. Beverly Hills, CA: Sage.

Hofstede, G. (1991) *Cultures and Organizations: Softwares of the Mind*. New York, McGraw–Hill.

Hofstede, G. (1993) 'Europe', in D.J. Hickson (ed.), *Management in Western Europe*. Berlin: Walter de Gruyter.

Hood, C. (1995) 'The "New Public Management" in the 1980s: Variations on a Theme', *Accounting, Organizations and Society*, 20 (2/3): 93–109.

Hood, C. (1996) 'Control Over Bureaucracy: Cultural Theory and Institutional Variety', *Journal of Public Policy*, 15 (3): 207–30.

Hood, C. (1998) *The Art of the State*. Oxford: Oxford University Press.

Hood, C. (2000) 'Paradoxes of Public-sector Managerialism, Old Public Management and Public Service Bargains', *International Public Management Journal*, 3 (1): 1–22.

Hood, C., Scott, C., James, O., Jones, G. and Travers, T. (1999) *Regulation Inside Government*. Oxford: Oxford University Press.

Horn, M. (1995) *The Political Economy of Public Administration*. Cambridge: Cambridge University Press.

Huber, J.D., Shipan, C.R. and Pfahler, M. (2001) 'Legislatures and Statutory Control of Bureaucracy', *American Journal of Political Science*, 45 (2): 330–45.

Huang, Y. (2002) 'Managing Chinese Bureaucrats: An Institutional Economics Perspective', *Political Studies*, 50 (1): 61–79.

Immergut, E. (1992) 'The Rules of the Game: The Logic of Health Policy-making in France, Switzerland, and Sweden', in S. Steinmo, K. Thelen and F. Longstreth (eds), *Structuring Politics: Historical Institutionalism in Comparative Politics*. Cambridge: Cambridge University Press.

Inglehart, R. (1997) *Modernization and Postmodernization: Cultural, Economic, and Political Change in 43 Societies*. Princeton, NJ: Princeton University Press.

James, O. (2001) 'Business Models and the Transfer of Businesslike Central Government Agencies', *Governance*, 14 (2): 233–52.

Jordan, G., Gustafsson, G. and Richardson, J. (1982) 'The Concept of Policy Style', in J. Richardson (ed.), *Policy Styles in Western Europe*. London: Allen & Unwin.

Knill, C. (1998) 'European Policies: The Impact of National Administrative Tradition', *Journal of Public Policy*, 18 (1): 1–28.

Knill, C. (1999) 'Explaining Cross-national Variance in Administrative Reform: Autonomous versus Instrumental Bureaucracies', *Journal of Public Policy*, 19 (2): 113–39.

Lehmbruch, G. (1991) 'The Organization of Society. Administrative Strategies and Policy Networks', in R. Czada and A. Windhoff-Héritier (eds), *Political Choice – Institutions, Rules and Limits of Authority*. Frankfurt a.M.: Campus.

Levy, B. and Spiller, P. (1994) 'The Institutional Foundations of Regulatory Commitment: A Comparative Analysis of Telecommunications Regulation', *Journal of Law, Economics and Organization*, 10: 201–46.

Linder, H. and Peters, B.G. (1989) 'Instruments of Government: Perceptions and Contexts', *Journal of Public Policy*, 9 (1): 35–58.

Lodge, M. (2002) *On Different Tracks: Designing Railway Regulation in Britain and Germany*. Westport, CT: Praeger.

Majone, G. (1994) 'The Emergence of the Regulatory State in Europe', *West European Politics*, 17: 77–101.

Majone, G. (1997) 'From the Positive and to the Regulatory State', *Journal of Public Policy*, 17 (2): 139–67.

Mayntz, R. (1985) *Die Soziologie der öffentlichen Verwaltung*, 3rd edn. Heidelberg: C.F. Müller Juristischer Verlag.

Mayntz, R. and Scharpf, F.W. (1995) 'Steuerung und Selbstorganisation in staatsnahen Sektoren', in R. Mayntz and F.W. Scharpf (eds), *Gesellschaftliche Selbstregelung und politische Steuerung*. Frankfurt a.M.: Campus.

McCubbins, M., Noll, R.G. and Weingast, B.R. (1987) 'Administrative Procedures as Instruments of Political Control', *Journal of Law, Economics and Organization*, 3: 243–77.

Menon, A. and Wright, V. (1998) 'The Paradoxes of "Failure": British EU Policy Making in Comparative Perspective', *Public Policy and Administration*, 13 (4): 46–66.

Niskanen, W. (1971) *Bureaucracy and Representative Government*. Chicago: Aldine, Atherton.

Page, E.C. (1992) *Political Authority and Bureaucratic Power*, 2nd edn. Hemel Hempstead: Prentice–Hall.

Page, E.C. (1995) 'Administering Europe', in J. Hayward and E.C. Page (eds), *Governing the New Europe*. Cambridge: Polity Press.

Page, E.C. and Wright, V. (1999) 'Conclusion: Senior Officials in Western Europe', in E. Page and V. Wright (eds), *Bureaucratic Elites in Western European States*. Oxford: Oxford University Press.

Peters, B.G. (2000) 'Explaining Success in Administrative Reform', in H. Wollmann and E. Schröter (eds), *Comparing Public Sector Reform in Britain and Germany. Key Traditions and Trends of Modernisation*. Aldershot: Ashgate.

Pierre, J. (1995) 'Conclusion: A Framework of Comparative Public Administration', in J. Pierre (ed.), *Bureaucracy in the Modern State: An Introduction to Comparative Public Administration*. Aldershot: Edward Elgar.

Pierre, J. (2000) 'Introduction: Understanding Governance', in J. Pierre (ed.), *Debating Governance*. Oxford: Oxford University Press.

Pierson, P. (2000) 'Increasing Returns, Path Dependence, and the Study of Politics', *American Political Science Review*, 94 (2): 251–67.

Pollitt, C. and Bouckaert, G. (2000) *Public Management Reform*. Oxford: Oxford University Press.

Putnam, R.D. (1974) 'The Political Attitudes of Senior Civil Servants in Western Europe: A Preliminary Report', *British Journal of Political Science*, 3: 257–90.

Rouban, L. (1999) 'The Senior Civil Service in France', in E. Page and V. Wright (eds), *Bureaucratic Elites in Western European States*. Oxford: Oxford University Press.

Rutgers, M. (2001) 'Splitting the Universe: On the Relevance of Dichotomies for the Study of Public Administration', *Administration and Society*, 33 (1): 3–20.

Sacks, P.M. (1980) 'State Structure and the Asymmetrical Society', *Comparative Politics*, 349–76.

Scharpf, F.W. (1999) *Governing in Europe: Effective and Democratic?* Oxford: Oxford University Press.

Schneider, V. (2000) 'Organisationsstaat und Verhandlungsdemokratie', in R. Werle and U. Schimack (eds.), *Gesellschaftliche Komplexität und kollektive Handlungsfähigkeit*, Frankfurt a.M.: Campus.

Schröter, E. (2000) 'Culture's Consequences? In Search of Cultural Explanations of British and German Public Sector Reform', in H. Wollmann and E. Schröter (eds), *Comparing Public Sector Reform in Britain and Germany. Key Traditions and Trends in Modernisation*. Aldershot: Ashgate.

Schröter E. (2001) 'Staats- und Verwaltungsreformen in Europa: International Trends und nationale Profile', in E. Schröter (ed.), *Empirische Policy- und Verwaltungsforschung*. Opladen: Leske and Budrich.

Silberman, B.S. (1993) *Cages of Reason*. Chicago: Chicago University Press.

Soskice, D (1999) 'Divergent Production Regimes: Coordinated and Uncoordinated Market Economies in the 1980s and 1990s', in K. Kitschelt, P. Lange, G. Marks and J.D. Stephens (eds), *Continuity and Change in Contemporary Capitalism*. Cambridge: Cambridge University Press.

Steinmo, S. (1993) *Taxation and Democracy*. New Haven, CT: Yale University Press.

Streeck, W. and Schmitter, P.C. (1985) 'Community, Market, State – and Association?', *European Sociological Review*, 1 (2): 119–38.

Subramaniam, V. (2000) 'Comparative Public Administration: From Failed Universal Theory to Raw Empiricism – a Frank Analysis and Guidelines Towards a Realistic Perspective', *International Review of Administrative Sciences*, 66 (4): 557–72.

Subramaniam, V. (2001) 'Comparative Public Administration: The Prismatic Approach versus the Political Economy Approach', *International Review of Administrative Sciences*, 67 (2): 335–42.

Tayeb, M.H. (1988) *Organizations and National Culture*, London: Sage.

Teague, P. (1999) 'Reshaping Employment Regimes in Europe: Policy Shifts Alongside Boundary Change', *Journal of Public Policy*, 19 (1): 33–62.

Teubner, G. (1998) 'Legal Irritants: Good Faith in British Law or How Unifying Law Ends Up in New Divergences', *Modern Law Review*, 61: 11–32.

Vogel, D. (1986) *National Styles of Regulation: Environmental Policy in Great Britain and the United States*. Ithaca, NY: Cornell University Press.

Weaver, R.K. and Rockman, B.A. (1995) *Do Institutions Matter? Government Capabilities in the United States and Abroad*. Washington, DC: Brookings Institution.

Wegrich, K. (2001) 'Verwaltungsmodernisierung im Mehrebenensystem der deutschen Bundesländer – Verwaltungspolitik und Wandel der Steuerungsformen'. Paper presented to the joint DVPW, OEGPW and SPW conference 'Changes in federal structures', Humboldt University, Berlin, 8–9 June 2001.

Weir, M. (1989) 'Ideas and Politics: The Acceptance of Keynesianism in Britain and the United States', in P.A. Hall (ed.), *The Political Power of Economic Ideas*. Princeton, NJ: Princeton University Press.

Weir, M. and Skocpol, T. (1985) 'State Structures and the Possibilites for "Keynesian" Responses to the Great Depression in Sweden, Britain, and the United States', in P. Evans, D. Rueschemeyer and T. Skocpol (eds), *Bringing the State Back In*. Cambridge: Cambridge University Press.

Werle, R. (2001) 'Institutional aspects of standardization – jurisdictional conflicts and the choice of standardization organizations', *Journal of European Public Policy*, 8 (3): 392–410.

Wessels, W. (1997) 'An Ever Closer Fusion? A Dynamic Macropolitical View on Integration Processes?', *Journal of Common Market Studies*, 35: 267–99.

Willke, H. (1995) *Die Ironie des Staates*. Frankfurt a.M.: Suhrkamp.

Wilson, J.Q. (1980) 'The Politics of Regulation', in J.Q. Wilson (ed.), *The Politics of Regulation*. New York: Basic Books.

Wilson, W. (1887) 'The Study of Administration', *Political Science Quarterly*, 2 (2): 197–222.

Windhoff-Héritier, A. (1996) 'Die Veränderung von Staatsaufgaben aus politik-wissenschaftlicher-institutioneller Sicht', in D. Grimm (ed.), *Staatsaufgaben*. Frankfurt a.M.: Suhrkamp.

Section 11

ADMINISTRATIVE REFORM

Introduction

Theo A.J. Toonen

Reform

Reform is about bringing about change. More so, reform is about the promise of bringing innovation and, hopefully, improvement. Reform is about becoming better through the removal of faults and errors or by abolishing or correcting malpractice, especially of a moral or political or social kind. Reform is therefore about values and quality. Administrative reform is about the administrative quality, constituted by administrative values, of public sector institutions, of public policy decision-making processes and of public organization and management.

Public Administration

We follow the definition of Public Administration provided by the *Blackwell Encyclopaedia of Political Institutions*:[1]

> **Public administration** In the lower case (p.a.) institutional arrangements for the provision of public services; in the upper case (P.A.), the study of those arrangements. 'Institutional arrangements' is a general term to denote the complex of agencies, authorities and enterprises, the formal rule structures, mixes of instruments, and conventions of behaviour which describe the organisational means of public services.

This implies that administrative reform is about improvements suggested or improvements made. Reform is on the one hand about PA: ideas, visions, analytical concepts and theoretical promises. The debate on administrative reform is a debate on concepts, models and 'paradigms' of reform: the way to look at and understand actual or proposed reforms; the 'theory' or *focus* of reform. Reform is, on the other hand, about p.a.: deeds, realizations, empirical developments, actual activities and achievements within a broad spectrum of institutional arrangements for public services delivery. Reform is a debate on the art and nature of the empirical subject matter of administrative reform in any specific context or episode – the p.a. *locus* of reform.

Studies of the focus of reform – the idea – are more common than studies of the locus – implementation – of reform. In the study of administrative reform the two dimensions often become confused. Many studies and reports claim to address the issue of reform, whereas actually they merely concentrate on the pros and cons or the feasibility of the timely and fashionable concept, approach or 'paradigm' of reform in a given episode. On the other hand, many criticisms of the public administration practice are often gauged in terms of a criticisms – or support – of the current paradigm of reform, without even studying and analysing empirically the degree to which this paradigm has become a reality or is de facto being pursued in practice at all.

As a consequence, people often think the realities of public administration in terms of a locus of action have changed because the conceptual language of PA in terms of a focus of research has changed. On the other hand, reform and transformation of public administration often goes undetected if the concepts and language of PA in a given period or country stay the same. On balance, the study of administrative and public sector reform is still more a study of focus than of the locus of government in action. There is ample reason to shift the balance in future PA studies of reform.

Concept and process

Reform is about content and process. Different types or visions of reform may be and have to be distinguished. Yet, there is no uniformly accepted language, conceptualization or categorization of types of reform, inside or outside the field of Public Administration. Many differences in vision or definition, however, may be attributed to either differences in a focus on *content of reform* or reform movements – in terms of core values, goals and programmes – or to differences in a focus on the *process of reform* – in terms of the distinction between (mechanistically) 'planned' versus (organic) 'emerging' change in many analytical guises – or to conceptual uses of a specific combination of both.

Concepts and outcomes

Reform is about promise and performance. Reform, by definition, has to be subject to cycles and fashion. Administrative concepts symbolize administrative practices and policy consequences. Changing governmental, market or third sector practice often has to start by changing symbols, labels and concepts. Ideas are powerful reform tools. The call for or announcement of 'Reform' is often a highly politicized response to a socially undesired practice, disaster or crisis. The debate on reform is constantly walking the thin line between substantial impact and hollow rhetoric.

Field of study

Many reform movements and reform efforts are value loaded or have an ideological nature and background. 'Reform' is also a political and economically profitable industry. It is a marketplace for advisers, consultants, academics and politicians alike. Each has the incentive to underscore the innovative, unique and distinct character of the proposed or opposed model of reform. From a broader PA perspective, these different reform movements, reform paradigms, or reform processes do not necessarily contradict each other. They may very well address different and complementary aspects of public sector governance. A mission for PA theory could be to provide a more balanced and contingent overview of modes and models of reform, their contradictions and complementarities. From a PA point of view, the quality of government is a multifaceted phenomenon, the debate on which has a long history and tradition in the field of both academic Public Administration (PA) as the praxis of government and public administration (p.a.).

ORGANIZATION OF THE SECTION

The next three chapters try to provide an overview in a complementary way. Theo Toonen addresses the analytical, conceptual and theoretical aspects and puts the more recent developments in administrative and public sector reform in the broader perspective of the field of Public Administration. Elke Löffler and Tony Verheijen address the experiences with public administration reform in two rather different historical, social and institutional contexts. Löffler presents and analyses the topic on the basis of experiences with the reform of public administration in the context of Western liberal democracies. Verheijen addresses the reform of public administration in the context of the transitional systems of the post-communist countries in Central and Eastern Europe.

NOTE

1   Vernon Bogdanor (ed.), The Blackwell Encyclopaedia of Political Institutions (Oxford, 1987), p. 504.

37

Administrative Reform: Analytics

Theo A.J. Toonen

REFORM ACTIVITY: AN OVERVIEW

A superficial glance at reform activities in the 'Western world' over the past two decades might easily give the impression that in the 1980s, continued into the 1990s, many countries, irrespective of their political and administrative systems, have embarked upon a similar type of public sector reform, some sooner, others later. There has been much talk of a 'global paradigm shift' in the approach of government and governance (Aucoin, 1990; Osborne and Gaebler, 1992, Lane, 1993).[1]

It soon became clear a business oriented approach to government does not necessarily also lead to a preference for markets over governments. The question of what government ought to do may be divorced from the question how government manages its affairs. By the middle of the 1990s, however, more and more people started to pose methodological questions (Flynn and Strehl, 1996: 4; Naschold, 1996; Toonen, 1997). The managerial perspective had not only become an empirical locus for research; it implicitly became 'the model' to study reform and public administration in a comparative way (Chandler, 2000). The paradigm developed from a locus into the focus of research. As a consequence, but often unintentionally, observers sometimes seemed happy to overlook historical and spectacular examples of administrative public sector reform. The German unification, the Italian wars on corruption, the French decentralization, Spanish economic consolidation efforts or Belgian federalization are just a few examples. From the managerial angle these countries were often even perceived as 'laggards' or cases of non-reform.

From a PA perspective, the neo-managerial approach to government and governance is precisely what it is: a *neo*-managerial approach. Organization and Management studies constitute a tradition within the development of the field of PA, as do institutional analysis, policy studies and decision making analysis. The reform of organization and management has been a key concern to the field of PA ever since the invention of modern organization theory, beginning with the Scientific Management Movement and the Science of Administration in the first half of the twentieth century (Burrell and Morgan, 1979: 118; Henry, 1995). The utilitarian, instrumental and technocratic character which some contribute to New Public Management has also been very typical for earlier administrative reform movements, stressing for example 'the Rationalization and Democratization' of administrative systems, like various forms of 'rational policy analysis' or Programming, Planning, Budgeting System (PBBS) approaches in the 1960s and 1970s. However, even if we restrict ourselves to the past twenty years, the reality of international public administration manifests a much larger variety of models and modes of reform.

NPM reform

In the current literature, England is still standing out as the model case in terms of the reception and implementation of the neo-managerial types of reform of the late twentieth century. The only other country that seems to meet the English model equally, if not more radically, is New Zealand (Halligan, 1996; Schick, 1996) – another Westminster-type government system.

The Republic of Ireland proves, however, that there is obviously room for choice and that a (unified) Westminster model need not be equated with NPM-type reforms, despite – or perhaps because of – the remarkable economic achievements of the Irish economy in the 1990s.

If one widens the perspective to include, for example, the United States, and other former Commonwealth nations like Canada, the picture gets even more diverse, particularly if one bothers to look at the issue of the implementation of 'managerial reforms'. In contrast to the United States, where business management was – and still is – 'normal science' in Public Administration, the New Public Management (NPM) approach indeed constituted a kind of 'paradigm shift' in the more pragmatic and historically and policy oriented Oxbridge civil service context. As a consequence, the real impact of NPM, in many accounts, has been bigger in England than was, for example, that of the 'Reinventing Government' Movement and the Gore Report (National Performance Review, 1993) in the United States (PAR, 1996).

Welfare state policy reform

Cutting back expenditure was a major goal of the reforms. Reform may aim at reducing the volume – not necessarily the nature – of government involvement by reducing policy entitlements, changing welfare schemes and introducing policy savings programmes of various sorts. Retrenchment, trimming down programmes and ambitions and a more distant, harsh and robust (that is, 'powerful') operation of government towards citizens (welfare recipients for example) and society in general, have been more common in many countries than 'rolling back the state' by wholesale policy termination. In the process, these reform movements and programmes have used updated or 'modern' managerial notions and associated institutional reforms in adapting their public sector structures to the new economic and European conditions.

The main vehicle for public sector reform in welfare states has been to redesign policies, budgets and policy programmes. If one 'cuts back' policy programmes and expenditures long enough, there comes a point at which policy reform spills over into a reform of management structures or institutional reform and may amount to the reconstitution of the welfare state (Lane, 1995: 511). Managerial reform, then, is the consequence, not the origin of administrative reform.

Institutional reform

In countries like Belgium, France and Italy, privatization, debureaucratization, customer-orientation and decentralization have been striking reform processes. There are reports on improved public service delivery and a greater awareness of the citizen–client as recipient of the policy process. But these movements have hardly been fuelled by an explicit neo-managerial reform philosophy. The French regions have proved able to master the techniques of public sector marketing and entrepreneurship quite well. As an administrative reform phenomenon in itself, however, it was regionalization of the unitary state as such – Belgium, Spain, France, Italy – which was a striking and Europe-wide reform development at the end of the twentieth century (Sharpe, 1993). In several cases the development is not likely to stop short of a total state reform.

Regime reform

The political and administrative transformation of the former Eastern block countries[2] can obviously not be excluded by any definition of administrative reform (Baker, 2002: 7). But Southern Europe also presents special cases of public sector reform in systems that have faced a regime transformation from dictatorial or semi-dictatorial systems into civil democracies, such as Greece, Portugal and Spain.

In Italy, but also in other countries of southern Europe, reforms have long been motivated by a concern for a 'proto bureaucratic' administrative culture, particularly the wish to push back traditional clientalistic patterns and legalistic cultures in favour of more quality- and performance-oriented approaches. In France, administrative bodies have been modernized using notions such as service responsiveness, 'single service windows' and citizen orientation (Claisse, 1995). But more traditional concerns also had to be addressed, like problems of administrative integrity and corruption, clientalism and the transparency of administration. By now, in the internationalized 'trust society' administrative integrity is becoming of increasing concern to administrative reform movements all over the world, not only the 'developing countries' (Fukuyama, 1995). Cases like ENRON and WorldCom illustrate how this concern is not restricted to the public sector.

Comprehensive reform

It goes without saying that the British and Antipodean reform policies since the late 1970s and early 1980s have been characterized by a high degree of visibility, vigour and radicalism. They stand out as examples of a comprehensive, non-consensual, centrally guided and legislated process of public sector reform. This has been the case even though the process was perhaps not being designed as such and things were often invented along the way (Wright, 1994: 109). Most countries, however, have been more gradualist and differentiated in their efforts, despite the occasional 'grand design', 'blueprint for reform' or 'big operation' that is issued in about every country once every few years. If 'Reinventing Government' in the United States is classified as a blueprint operation, then, indeed, there would be many of these operations in Western Europe as well. More accurate, however, is to stress the piecemeal, experimental and gradualist nature of most reform processes that we have witnessed, particularly the seemingly more effective and fundamental one's.

Gradualist reform

The gradualist reform processes are characterized by consensual and step-by-step experimental proceedings. Comprehensive reforms of sub-sections of government and public administration occasionally do take place within an overall context of experimental and gradualist processes. Germany is generally seen as the prototype of the gradualist category, as Löffler further outlines in Chapter 38. However, many countries are forced into more consensual and therefore gradualist reform strategies. Consensus democracies in general, pair 'gentle democracy' to performance, but are typically slow to reform in the process (Lijphart, 1994, 1999). Political parties of the Left and the Right often supported welfare state policy reforms. The electorate in many countries has temporarily forced them into 'cohabitation', 'purple-' and 'rainbow coalitions' (Toonen, 2001: 186).

Gradualism does not exclude comprehensive reform. Germany has faced and is still facing the formidable task of a comprehensive state reform, by the incorporation of the former East German *Länder*. Other countries have managed to bring about rather fundamental changes in evolutionary development strategies. The Belgian State Reforms (Delmartino, 1993) or the Dutch 'Polder Model' (Hendriks and Toonen, 2001) may serve as examples. Yet, due to the high degree of necessary consensus, these types of gradualist reform systems do permanently run the risk of fall back, stagnation and deadlock. It often needs a crisis of some sort to trigger and sustain the process.

Non-reform

Germany shared a seeming lack of attention for managerial issues and structural reform with other Germanic systems like Austria and Switzerland. Also Luxembourg has shown little sign of far-reaching administrative or public sector reforms. Perhaps it is the concern for prudence and stability that is so cherished by the world of financial *haute culture* that makes these systems cautious in tinkering with their state institutions. But these countries, and particularly Germany, still cannot be depicted as immobile or petrified and incapable of modernization. In a comparative perspective it would also be unwise to see the reliable and stable administrative bureaucracies of these countries as lagging behind, as, for example, the British, New Zealand or Australian government apparatus on the basis of the mere fact that the latter have more recently experienced more change and fanatic reform.

Transformation without reform

In some countries there has been much transformation and little reform, as Verheijen observes in his chapter on developments in the post-Communist systems. The relationship might also be the other way around. In many countries well-established, historical and sometimes very traditional or even ancient institutions – like Auditing Chambers, Inspectorates or Tax Administrations – have transformed from within and developed from a 'formal' into an 'effective' working part of the constitution of modern administrative systems. This often occurred in an entrepreneurial instead of a 'reformist' way.

French regions were not developed or designed in the 1980s, but already existed as former administrative units in the abandoned French central planning model of the 1950s. They were simply 'inflated' with a functional regional and urban development mission and corresponding tasks and budgets. The emergence of a 'New Regionalism' (Keating, 1998) and the changing nature of urban systems over the past ten to twenty years provides another example of fundamentally changing administrative patterns and systems, mostly without an explicit reform strategy, but as a by-product of other strategic and structural developments.

The position of once very well established institutions like national ministries and administrative systems in Europe has changed drastically, in a relatively short period of time, under the impact of social, economic and institutional developments like internationalization, the ICT revolution and the new demographics in the multicultural society. The developments of policy networks and intergovernmental bargaining systems inherent to the transformation of 'Europe of the Administrations' has over time sometimes contributed to a drastic change in the position and power of local and regional governments, mostly in the absence of any official 'decentralization' of 'local government reform policy' (Toonen, 1992; Benz, 1995; Bogason, 1996; Peters and Pierre, 2001).

Important changes in governance structures are easily missed if one wants to restrict the concept of 'administrative reform' to intentional, centrally planned or legislated changes.

GOALS AND VALUES

There are and always have been many reasons to reform, or to announce reform. Administrative and public sector reform involves thinking about values, norms and principles. Very often it is not very helpful merely to rely on stated goals and purposes. Administrative and public sector reforms are certified domains for sweeping political symbolism and bureaucratic rhetoric.

Core values in Public Administration

The language differs from era to era. At the same time, one encounters similar types of goals and values, which, upon close inspection, often reveal quite a different operational meaning. The same political goals and administrative values may give rise to different activities and programmes, dependent on time and place. Reconstructions of administrative theory (Ostrom, 1973; Henry, 1986 (1975); Bogason and Toonen, 1998) and of administrative argument (Hood and Jackson, 1991) are rather consistent in the type of administrative values, which over time are being stressed as of importance to the quality of government. The emphasis may change from time to time and country to country, but in the long run administrative reform seems to serve a rather stable set

of administrative values. On the basis of a reconstruction of the history of administrative argument, Hood (1991) has identified three 'families' of related administrative core values, which may represent the value-oriented PA concern – the focus – in studying administrative reform as a locus of research and advice.

Responsiveness and satisfaction

The first group of values, stresses *parsimony and economy*. It adheres to the mission to 'keep government lean and purposeful'. These values reflect the concern in all organization theory for 'efficiency and productivity'. These values belong to the world of public management. Optimal results have to be produced with given resources, or given goals have to be achieved at a minimum of organizational cost and effort. These managerial values have been present in the debate on administrative reform ever since modern organization theory developed at the beginning of last century.

In this perspective, the administrative organization is easily conceived as a tool of government that needs to be instrumental in achieving given goals. Once within the field of PA this approach has not only been applied to managerial levels, but also tried out in reforms to 'rationalize' policy making or reduce and minimize 'transaction costs' – the economist's term for institutionalization, organization and administration.

The conceptual development over time in pursuit of the mission to keep it lean and purposeful has been the discovery and acceptance of the principle that, in the classic words of Tulock (1976): 'The most efficient government is not the most orderly looking government, but the government that comes closest to carrying out the wishes of its masters.' What started out as an ambition to rationalize and streamline 'messy' organizational structures in the 1920s and 1930s has developed into administrative reform strategies to increase the external *responsiveness* of public service, public management and public administration to the needs of the relevant external environment in order to increase the *satisfaction* with government performance among citizens and other major stakeholders in society.

Integrity and trust

The second group of administrative core values, in terms of Hood (1991), are: *fairness, equity and rectitude*. They relate to the mission 'to keep government honest and fair'. These values refer to the world of public *governance*. In institutional terms, we are talking about the organization of collective action, joint policy and decision making, and public accountability. These processes provide the structure and context in which the 'given' managerial goals (and resources) are defined, standards for managerial performance may be set and evaluation procedures designed and implemented.

This family of values easily extends into values and related instrumentalities that have become close to being administrative values in themselves, such as legality – the *Rule of Law* – bureaucratic loyalty, unimpeachable behaviour and lack of corruption. Democracy may be treated as an important institution for political mobilization and social participation. From a PA perspective, the inherent transparency and openness, at least implied by the concept of democracy, also serves as a set of administrative quality procedures. 'Due process' and *Legimation durch Verfahren* are the classic terms. The democratic procedures of the administrative state try to secure the validity and fairness of the governance process, respecting justified entitlements, guiding the operation of the system of administrative responsibility and accountability, and seeing to the proper operation and discharge of public duties.

The administrative values of this second family all serve efforts to secure the *integrity* of public administration in order to create and maintain *trust* in government officials and procedures. More than client satisfaction perhaps, public trust has proved itself over time to be an indispensable resource for governmental support and long-term economic development.

Reliability and confidence

The third set of administrative values includes: *robustness, resilience and sustainability*. The mission is 'to keep government robust and resilient'. This set of values refers to the usually more hidden constitutional dimension of government and administrative reform (Ostrom, 1982; Lane, 1996). They refer to the 'constitutional quality' of administrative systems, not only in a legal sense, but also to the state of the governmental system in more general terms of vitality, health, strength, etc. They apply to the *institutional design, redesign and (re)development* levels of governance. Institutions provide an administrative infrastructure of normative and empirical constraints to processes of governance and thus hamper or facilitate joint decision making and managerial behaviour.

The values represent longstanding and very traditional concerns in the PA study of public administration, symbolized by the old Weberian 'reliable bureaucracy' and the loyal and 'reliant civil servant'. Over time, stability and robustness increasingly have become interpreted as social and dynamic concepts. The 'limits of government' have been duly acknowledged. In the long run, governments can achieve very little in the way of substantial results without broad social support. This makes, for example, attention to mass communication and relations between government and the civil society important concerns for the future of administrative reform. Respect for human rights gradually submerges the traditional 'right of life and limb' as a universal manifestation of good government. Research on 'normal accidents' (Perrow, 1999) and 'the risk society' (Beck, 1986) has convinced many that a reliable, stable and robust administrative system is not a system that is able to resist change and reform, but which is resilient, able to learn and adapt to meaningful changing circumstances.

The administrative values in this group serve to secure the *reliability* of the administrative system in order to secure the *reliance* of citizens and the *confidence* of society in governmental institutions. As a concern for administrative reform, this domain constitutes a difficult category. Institutions often represent the 'common good' in public administration, and are equally vulnerable to degeneration and 'tragedies of the commons' as are other common pool resources (Ostrom, 1990). Here we enter the domain of political leadership and statesmanship. In the managerial world a popular conception of administrative reform is that 'if it ain't broke, don't fix it'. At governance levels, politicians and general administrators are typically hesitant, to touch issues that are not yet publicly recognized as a problem. Both attitudes hamper warranted 'constitutional' or 'institutional' administrative reform, sometimes until it is too late. Public reliance is like (social) capital or the stock market: once confidence is lost, it is difficult to get it back.

Quality of government

Various interdependent layers of administrative value constitute the quality of government. In the long run, administrative reform has to serve different administrative value systems, creating obviously different modes and models of reform depending on time, context and 'logic' of reform. Seemingly similar reform might serve quite different value systems in different cases. There is a huge difference, for example, whether a privatization programme serves to increase the responsiveness and management of public service

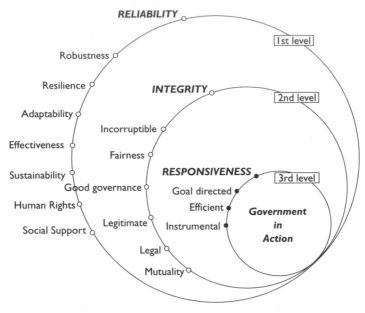

Figure 37.1   *Quality in public administration*

delivery – as in the Western reforms – or whether it serves the institutional design – the constitution – of a reliable market system, as in the post-Communist countries (Toonen, 1993). Failures to distinguish these different levels in administrative reform will have high price in practice. It will also be detrimental to learning processes of reform (Olson and Peters, 1995), as the experience with many privatization programmes in both East and West may testify.

In systems theory the three layers distinguished in Figure 37.1 are sometimes identified as functional legitimacy (administrative responsiveness), procedural legitimacy (administrative integrity) and regime legitimacy (administrative reliability). The sets of values presuppose each other, but may in specific situations and contexts very well put different demands on a reform programme. This tension makes administrative reform a highly dynamic process, full of contradictions, conflicts, ambiguity and inherent strategic paradoxes (Wright, 1994; Hood Hesse et al., 1996). The value systems may reinforce each other, either in a detrimental or in a constructive way. The way in which reforms are conducted may make the difference.

REFORM MODES

The debate on reform, both political and academic, is often a debate with rather rationalistic,

normative and sometimes even moralistic undertones. 'Reform' should be identified at the outset and attached to a formal government programme. The reality of administrative reform as a process, however, is that it constantly circles around two principles. These invariably are referred to with a large number of different words and concepts, exemplifying a deeply rooted theoretical, if not philosophical controversy on how administrative systems change and develop (Leemans, 1970; Rottleuthner, 1988). The empirical study of public administration suggests that administrative reform as a process is best conceived of as somewhere on a continuum between *Planned* (Synoptic, Comprehensive, Rational, Blueprint, Mechanistic, Centrally Guided, Consciously Designed, Modernizing) *Change* on the one hand, and *Emerging* (Incremental, Piecemeal, Intuitive, Organic, Mutually Adjusted, Garbage Can, Post-Modernizing) *Strategy* on the other.

In many cases, reform is often presented as the outcome of 'planned' effort, politicized to some degree, and in intent and presentation certainly not incremental in nature. Ambitious reform plans do, however, often only constitute the beginning of a complex, and sometimes cumbersome, process of consultation and negotiation among various institutionalized interests and administrative powers. The 'implementation of reform' usually shapes the policy. A process of negotiated reform turns grand schemes easily into pragmatic and step-by-step processes of change and transformation. Grand stated ambitions are modified to modest, but sometimes determined and irreversible changes with large long-term consequences.

At the beginning of the 1980s, for example, French decentralization policy created a pattern of administrative negotiation and renegotiations, which resulted in incremental but irreversible changes of the former, rather immobile administrative system (Crozier and Thoenig, 1976). The 'next steps' were never clearly indicated or presented as such, unlike, for example, John Major did in the context of the British reforms. In the French case, there was less political gain to suggest more coherence than actually existed. But a process with a fundamental decentralization (1982), subsequent and substantial privatization (1986), efforts to mobilize the administrative system from below (1989), followed by an attempt at (national) state reform (1995) and a clear intensification of attention to managerial issues throughout the system at the beginning of the new decade, cannot be denied a certain degree of 'logic', 'consistency' and 'comprehensiveness'.

It even becomes the question whether the overall nature of the reform process in both countries is so much different as is often stated, or that France and the UK merely took different paths in the same overall direction (Crouch and Marquand, 1989). From the perspective adopted here, both countries, at about the same moment in time – the early 1980s – started to work on the opposite sides of the administrative value system outlined earlier. France started out by introducing institutional reform (regionalization and decentralization), soon followed through with governance reforms by the democratization of *départments* and regions and the redesign of political (*cumul des mandats*) and administrative intergovernmental relations (position of *préfet*; regional administrative courts; *contrats du plans*) (Le Gales and Lequesne, 1997). More recently this is being backed up by clear attention to the *autogestion*, that is, managerial innovation of administrative units at various levels within the system.

The United Kingdom, on the other hand, started out at the managerial levels, with the NPM reforms, and followed through with the governance reforms inherent to the functional decentralization, fragmentation, agentification and service charters of the Next Steps programmes. This inevitably resulted in a call for structural reform serving coordination and integration at local and regional levels. The 'Rejoining Administration' initiatives of the Blair government might quite well amount to a reform of constitutional proportions as far as the federalization of the United Kingdom and regionalization in England is concerned (Toonen, 2001).

Retrospective rationalizations have to be avoided. But cases like these illustrate that reform is best conceived of as a long-term, less rationally designed, piecemeal and cyclical process. A process that is full of inconsistencies, and self-induced consequences, but also with unexpected serendipities, which, in the long run, may actually generate some decent results, next to the misses inherent to any experimental and learning process. The question of convergence or divergence of administrative reform has to be studied in the long run, not on the basis of a particular reform programme in a particular country at a particular moment in time.

UNDERSTANDING VARIATION

Reforms are often associated with lack of results and undelivered promises. The evaluation of reform, however, is by far the weakest developed step of all of the public sector and administrative reform programmes, both from a PA and public administration perspective. Although often called upon, evaluations of reforms are virtually never conducted in a systematic, let alone comparative way (OECD, 1995: 81; Ingraham, 1996: 262). There is clearly a research agenda here, as both Löffler and Verheijen elaborate in the following chapters.

Reforms bring about multiple effects, which are appreciated in different ways. Observers and analysts may still see very much what they want to see. In the midst of cynicism, there are cases that are internationally recognized to show that attempts to reform, at least for a certain period, may quite well be successful and yield effects. The Japanese model, the Scandinavian model, the New Zealand model, the British model, the Belgian State Reform, *Modell Deutschland*, the Dutch 'Polder Model', the Wisconsin model, the Tilburg model, the Asian and Celtic Tigers, the 'New Steering Model', or more recently, the Spanish reforms as an example of the European modernization strategy, are just a few to mention. Each country seems to be allowed its short moments of glory in the international hall of fame of administrative reform – but often only temporarily.

An obvious outcome of public sector reforms in both West and Central and East European state systems is the bewildering convergence as well as variety exemplified by the practice of public administration. What the countries have in common is that they have all been involved in reform processes over the past decade, and that there are marked differences in the way in which public sector reform has proceeded in various countries. The overall pattern seems to be that common external pressures and general constitutional constraints are, with time and place specificity, and moulded by institutional characteristics, turned into differential reform processes that over a longer period in time reflect several common features in a context of varying state traditions.

The elaboration and understanding of different patterns of administrative reform, and the way they interconnect, seems to set another agenda for future research. In analysing commonalties and variations it seems that we need to look at five different but rather traditional explanatory factors, which in combination seem to account for much of the variation and convergence uncovered by this exploration (cf. Castels and McKinlay, 1979; Hesse and Benz, 1990; Toonen, 2001).

External pressures

The best explanation for reform is still the need to cope with some kind of crisis, deficit, failure or external pressure. The economic problems of the end of the 1970s and the beginning of the 1980s forced governments in the Western world into a series of institutional and budgetary reforms. Since then, within the domestic process, international developments, or 'Europe' (or the *acquis*), are consistently used to legitimize reform and overcome resistance to reforms that, according to many specialists, would have had to take place anyway.

Political choice

Economics has provided the pressure and urgency, institutions and traditions the nature of response. We cannot, however, disregard the importance of politics, ideology and leadership. 'Politics matters' in administrative reform, particularly in terms of politically framing the problem, timing initiatives and setting the reform agenda. In the context of an overall reform process 'strong leadership' does not guarantee 'reform', nor does 'weak leadership' prohibit reform. It seems that in countries with 'strong leadership' it is more likely that this leadership has to become involved in the reforms to be successful. In countries with 'weak leadership', reforms may be conducted in a more decentralized fashion. '[L]eaders may change the course

of history, but only if and to the degree that the environment permits it' (Elgie, 1995: 8). Leadership is a fashionable topic, but comparative analysis of structural underpinnings, or what it takes to go against the social and political current may be developed much further.

Reform logic

Reform policy is, as we have illustrated, often its own cause. Reforms at one level induce or trigger reforms at other levels of action within the administrative system. There are no clear-cut stages in a 'reform-logic'. There may, however, be a path dependency constituted by a conditional logic. Not every reform starts at the same level of departure in terms of administrative capacity. Certain problems need to be resolved before certain types of reform may take place effectively. The CEE experience illustrates that there are some 'nuts and bolts' of administrative systems to be respected in order for any system to work (Hesse, 1993). This experience has probably even partly saved the word 'public administration' on the European continent, after it was nearly – if not completely, as in the UK – washed away during the international managerial fashion of reform (Hood, 1990; Lane, 1994). Managerial reforms presuppose some minimal institutional administrative infrastructure, but what is the minimal package in administrative reform?

On the other hand, the experience with performance management practices in OECD member countries (Bouckaert, 1996) indicates that changes at the managerial level will, in the longer run, have consequences for the governance and institutional levels of the administrative state. Attention to quality and performance in government requires new forms of supervision: from the traditional (legal) compliance control to quality control. Methodologies to 'benchmark' countries in their administrative development are lacking. The internal and self-generated dynamics of administrative reform and the relationships – instead of the differences – between different kinds of reform deserve more attention.

Institutional constraints

The institutional features, which affect paths and forms of reform and institutional development, are deeply rooted in more general traditions. Institutional constraints provide opportunities and barriers to reform. In the development of the British welfare state, the non-executant role of central government was translated into strong executive powers for local authorities. This made them the predictable target for any effort to 'roll back the state'. In other countries policy domains and their third sector organizations were the more likely 'victims of reform'. In the German context, leadership, for historical reasons, is not a reform concept easily adopted. In Italy in matters of contracting-out and 'market testing' considerations of legality for all the right reasons were sometimes considered to be more important than considerations of efficiency (Dente, 1988: 181). Law and legislation do play very different roles in reform processes in different countries. Reforms in some systems are – have to be – 'legislated' in order to be effective; others do not, or in a different – framework – way.

Administrative traditions

In this varied overall reform context it is striking that contrary to a much encountered assertion, it is analytically not very helpful to contrast continental European reforms with an ill-perceived type of Anglo-Saxon or Anglo-American managerialism as over and against continental European styles of administration. There are many structural and institutional differences, which set American public administration apart from European administrative systems (Page, 1985) and their impact on administrative reform needs to be elaborated. Many of the continental systems do, however, have long 'management' traditions, be it that the managers are often lawyers or people with a technical professional background. The no nonsense, businesslike, pragmatic and practical approach to government and administration has been for ages by far the most popular approach within the practice of European public administration. Over time they have acquired what Max Weber called *Dienstwissen* – generalized practical knowledge about how to run government. Experience shows that the military, the police, civil engineering and physical planning units of many continental systems will, after some retraining, have few problems in incorporating modern business management concepts into their standard operating procedures if they feel the need or are being urged to modernize. The same applies to large public service organizations in welfare, healthcare, social policy or social assistance. If seeking to grasp the richness, diversity and depth of the subject, Public Administration would be ill advised to study administrative reform only in managerial terms, whether one is in favour of or against the approach.

NOTES

1 Löffler explores the topic more fully in her contribution.
2 More fully treated by Verheijen in Chapter 39.

REFERENCES

Aucoin, P. (1990) 'Administrative Reform in Public Management, Paradigms, Principles, Paradoxes and Pendulums', *Governance*, 3 (2): 115–37.

Baker, Randall (ed.) (2002) *Transitions from Authoritarianism: The Role of Bureaucracy*. Westport, CT: Praeger.

Beck, U. (1986) *Risikogesellschaft: auf dem Weg in eine andere Moderne*. Frankfurt, a.M.: Suhrkamp.

Benz, Arthur (1995) 'Institutional Change in Inter-governmental Relations: The Dynamics of Multi-Level Structures', in Joachim Jens Hesse and Theo A.J. Toonen (eds), *European Yearbook of Comparative Government and Public Administration*. Baden-Baden/Boulder, CO: Nomos/Westview Press. pp. 551–76.

Bogason, Peter (1996) 'The Fragmentation of Local Government in Scandinavia', *European Journal of Political Research*, 30 (1): 65–86.

Bogason, Peter and Toonen, Theo A.J. (1998) 'Networks in Public Administration', *Public Administration*, 76 (Summer): 201–28.

Bouckaert, Geert (1996) 'Overview and Synthesis of the Secretariat'. Paper on Performance Management Practices in Eight OECD Member Countries. PUMA/PAC (95)24.

Burrell, Gibson and Morgan, Gareth (1979) *Sociological Paradigms and Organisational Analysis*. London: Heineman.

Castels, F.G. and McKinlay, R.D. (1979) 'Public Welfare Provision, Scandinavia and the Sheer Futility of the Sociological Approach to Politics', *British Journal of Political Science*, 9: 157–71.

Chandler, J.A. (ed.) (2000) *Comparative Public Administration*. London: Routledge.

Claisse, A. (1995) 'La Modernisation Administrative en France: Au delà des Réformes, le Changement', in Joachim Jens Hesse and Theo A.J. Toonen (eds), *The European Yearbook of Comparative Government and Public Administration*. Baden-Baden/Boulder, CO: Nomos /Westview Press. pp. 409–37.

Crozier, Michel, J. Thoenig (1976) 'The Regulation of Complex Organised Systems', *Administrative Science Quarterly*, 21 (4): 547–70.

Crouch, Colin, and Marquand, David (eds) (1989) *The New Centralism: Britain Out of Step in Europe?* Oxford: Basil Blackwell.

Delmartino, F. (1993) 'Belgium: In Search for the Meso Level', in L.J. Sharpe (ed.), *The Rise of Meso Government in Europe*. London: Sage. pp. 40–60.

Dente, Bruno (1988) 'Local Government Reform and Legitimacy, in Bruno Dente and Francesco Kjellberg (eds), *The Dynamics of Institutional Change. Local*

Government Reorganization in Western Democracies. London: Sage. pp. 171–86.

Elgie, Robert (1995) *Political Leadership in Liberal Democracies*. London: Macmillan.

Flynn, Norman and Strehl, Franz (eds) (1996) *Public Sector Management in Europe*. Brighton: Harvester Wheatsheaf Prentice Hall.

Fukuyama, Francis (1995) *Trust: The Social Virtues and the Creation of Prosperity*. New York: The Free Press.

Halligan, John (1996) 'New Public Sector Models: Reform in Australia and New Zealand', in J.E. Lane (ed.), *Public Sector Reform*. London: Sage.

Hendriks, Frank and Toonen, Theo A.J. (eds) (2001) *Polder Politics: Re-inventing Consensus Democracy in the Netherlands*. Aldershot: Ashgate.

Henry, Nicholas (1995) *Public Administration and Public Affairs*, 2nd edn. Englewood Cliffs, NJ: Prentice Hall.

Hesse, Joachim Jens (1993) 'From Transformation to Modernisation: Administrative Change in Central and Eastern Europe', *Public Administration*, 71: 219–57.

Hesse, Joachim Jens and Benz, Arthur (1990) *Die Modernisierung der Staatsorganisation. Institutionspolitik im internationalen Vergleich: USA, Groszbritanien, Frankreich, Bundesrepublik Deutschland*. Baden-Baden: Nomos.

Hesse, Joachim Jens, Hood, Christopher, Peters, B. Guy (1996) 'Paradoxes in Public Sector Reform: Soft Theory and Hard Cases', in Joachim Jens Hesse and Theo A.J. Toonen (eds), *European Yearbook of Comparative Government and Public Administration*. Baden-Baden/Boulder, CO: Nomos /Westview Press.

Hood, Christopher (1990) 'Public Administration: Lost an Empire, Not Yet Found a Role?', in A. Leftwich (ed.), *New Developments in Political Science; An International Review of Achievements and Prospects*. Aldershot: Dartmouth.

Hood, Christopher (1991) 'A Public Management for all Seasons?', *Public Administration*, 60: 3–19.

Ingraham, Patricia (1996) 'The Reform Agenda for National Civil Service Systems: External Stress and Internal Strains', in Hans A.G.M. Bekke, James L. Perry and Theo A.J. Toonen (eds), *Civil Service Systems in Comparative Perspective*. Bloomington, IN: Indiana University Press. pp. 247–67.

Keating, Michael (1998) *The New Regionalism in Western Europe: Territorial Restructuring and Political Change*. Cheltenham: Edward Elgar.

Lane, Jan-Erik (1993) *The Public Sector, Concepts, Models and Approaches*. London: Sage.

Lane, Jan-Erik (1994) 'Will Public Management Drive Out Public Administration?', *Asian Journal of Public Administration*, 16 (2): 139–51.

Lane, Jan-Erik (1995) 'End and Means of Public Sector Reform', in Joachim Jens Hesse and Theo A.J. Toonen (eds), *The European Yearbook of Comparative Government and Public Administration*. Baden-Baden/Boulder, CO: Nomos /Westview Press. pp. 507–21.

Lane, Jan-Erik (1996) *Constitutions and Political Theory*. Manchester/New York: Manchester University Press.

Leemans, A.F. (1970) *Changing Patterns of Local Government*. The Hague: International Union of Local Authorities.

Lijphart, Arend (1994) 'Democracies: Forms, Performance and Constitutional Engineering', *European Journal for Political Research*, 25 (1): 1–17.

Lijphart, Arend (1999) *Patterns of Democracy: Government Forms and Performance in Thirty-Six Countries*. New Haven, CT/London: Yale University Press.

Naschold, F. (1996) *New Frontiers in Public Sector Management: Trends and Issues in State and Local Government in Europe*. Berlin/New York: de Gruyter.

National Performance Review (NPR) (1993) *The Gore Report on Reinventing Government*. Washington, DC.

OECD (1995) *Governance in Transition. Public Management Reforms in OECD Countries*. Paris: OECD.

Olson, Johan P. and Peters, B. Guy (eds) (1995) *Lessons from Experience. Experiential Learning in Administrative Reforms in Eight Democracies*. Oslo: Scandinavian University Press.

Osborne, David and Gaebler, Ted (1992) *Reinventing Government: How the Entrepreneurial Spirit is Transforming the Public Sector*. Reading, MA: Addison–Wesley.

Ostrom, Elinor (1990) *Governing the Commons: The Evolution of Institutions for Collective Action*. Cambridge: Cambridge University Press.

Ostrom, Vincent (1973) *The Intellectual Crisis in American Public Administration*. Tuscaloosa: Alabama University Press.

Ostrom, Vincent (1982) 'A Forgotten Tradition: the Constitutional Level of Analysis', in J.A. Gillespie and P.A. Zinnes (eds), *Missing Elements in Political Inquiry: Logic and Levels of Analysis*. Beverly Hills, CA: Sage.

Page, Edward C. (1985) *Political Authority and Bureaucratic Power*. Brighton: Wheatsheaf.

PAR (1996) *Public Administration Review*, special issue on 'Reinventing' Public Administration, 56 (3): 245–304.

Perrow, C. (1999) *Normal Accidents: Living with High Risk Technologies*. Princeton, NJ: Princeton University Press.

Peters, B. Guy and Pierre, Jon (eds) (2001) 'Intergovernmental Relations and Multi-Level Governance', Special Issue of *Policy and Politics*, 29 (2).

Rottleuthner, Hubert (1988) 'Biological Metaphors in Legal Thought', in G. Teubner (ed.), *Autopietic Law: A New Approach to Law and Society*. Berlin: DeGruytes.

Schick, Allan (1996) *The Spirit of Reform: Managing the New Zealand State Sector in a Time of Change*. Wellington: State Services Commission.

Sharpe, L.J. (ed.) (1993) *The Rise of Meso Government in Europe*. London: Sage.

Toonen, Theo A.J. (1992) 'Europe of the Administrations: The Challenges of '92 (and Beyond)' *Public Administration Review*, 52 (2): 108–15.

Toonen, Theo A.J. (1993) 'Analyzing Institutional Change and Administrative Transformation:

A Comparative View', *Public Administration*, 71 (1/2): 151–67.

Toonen, Theo A.J. (1997) 'Public Sector Reform in Western Europe: a Paradigm Shift or Public Administration as Usual?', in Joachim Jens Hesse and Theo A.J. Toonen (eds), *The European Yearbook of Comparative Government and Public Administration*, Vol III/1996. Baden-Baden: Nomos. pp. 485–98.

Toonen, Theo A.J. (2001) 'The Comparative Dimension of Administrative Reform', in B. Guy Peters and Jon Pierre (eds), *Politicians, Bureaucrats and Administrative Reform*. London: Routledge. pp. 183–202.

Wright, Vincent (1994) 'Reshaping the State: The Implications for Public Administration', *West European Politics*, 17 (35): 102–37.

38

The Administrative
State in Western Democracies

Elke Löffler

At the beginning of the twenty-first century Western countries face new and different challenges from those with which they were confronted in the 1980s. Current reform programmes in Western countries are now increasingly focused on governance issues, which cannot be solved by the 'administrative state' alone but require the involvement of a wide array of stakeholders in the public, private and non-profit sectors. Most literature has focused on New Public Management (NPM) reforms whereas other public sector reforms such as the process of European integration and its impact on the public administration of EU member states (see, for example, Knill, 2001) have been largely neglected. Most attention has focused on the reform of central governments (or state administration as continental Europeans would call it) rather than the lack of reforms in the political sphere and the intense reforms often taking place at regional and local levels. In assessing public sector reforms, many authors have been guided by rhetoric and often confused the causes and the results of reforms.

THE EVOLUTION OF
PUBLIC SECTOR REFORMS

Recent public sector reforms in Western countries can be dated to the late 1970s when many Western countries faced major economic problems. The Great Depression of the 1930s produced a similar wave of changes to the role of the public sector. However, the reactions of governments from the early 1980s onwards do seem to be rather different in nature to what had gone before. The worldwide economic recession of the mid-1970s meant a mismatch between increasing public expenditure and declining tax bases. Of course, there were different trajectories of public spending (in total and on particular services) within these overall trends.

The OECD statistics in Table 38.1 show the evolution of budgetary positions of selected Western countries from the mid-1970s until 2000. As the table shows, the oil crisis hit different countries at different times and with different severity. However, in almost all cases the need to save money became a very strong reform motive (Pollitt and Bouckaert, 2000: 159). Nevertheless, it would be inappropriate to say that public sector reforms were only driven by financial motives. Apart from the budgetary squeeze, other forces with a dramatic effect upon public management practice included:

- The social value change that has seen core values of 'public duty' and 'individual responsibility' being replaced by values of individual self-realization and rights (Klages, 1993: 191–4).
- Rising expectations both of citizens and staff in the public sector which has led to an 'expectations gap' on the part of the public (Davis, 1998: 106–9).
- Rapid increase in applications of ICT to processes and activities in the public sector (Willcocks and Mark, 2000).

Most Western countries responded to these challenges with an increasing focus on making the public sector 'lean and more competitive while, at the same time, trying to make public

Table 38.1 Budget deficits and surpluses in percentage of the nominal GDP

	1985	1986	1987	1988	1989	1990	1991	1992	1993	1994	1995	1996	1997	1998	1999	2000	2001	2002	2003
Australia	-5.1	-4.2	-2.2	-0.4	0.0	-1.2	-3.8	-6.0	-5.6	-4.6	-3.7	-2.2	-0.5	0.6	1.1	0.3	0.1	0.2	0.5
Austria	-2.6	-3.8	-4.4	-3.5	-3.1	-2.4	-3.0	-2.0	-4.2	-5.0	-5.2	-3.8	-1.9	-2.4	-2.2	-1.1	0.0	-0.4	0.1
Belgium	-10.2	-10.1	-7.9	-7.3	-7.6	-6.7	-7.3	-7.9	-7.3	-5.0	-4.4	-3.7	-2.0	-0.8	-0.6	0.1	0.0	0.0	0.2
Canada	-8.6	-7.1	-5.4	-4.3	-4.6	-5.8	-8.3	-9.1	-8.7	-6.7	-5.3	-2.8	0.2	0.5	1.6	3.2	2.8	2.1	2.2
Czech Republic	—	—	—	—	—	—	—	—	-0.4	-1.2	-1.1	-2.0	-2.4	-2.4	-3.9	-5.5	-6.0	-9.3	-5.8
Denmark	—	—	—	1.5	0.3	-1.0	-2.4	-2.2	-2.9	-2.4	-2.3	-1.0	0.4	1.1	3.1	2.8	2.0	1.4	1.7
Finland	3.3	3.7	1.3	3.8	6.0	5.3	-1.1	-5.6	-7.3	-5.7	-3.7	-3.2	-1.5	1.3	1.9	6.9	3.7	1.9	2.1
France	-3.0	-3.2	-2.0	-2.5	-1.8	-2.1	-2.4	-4.2	-6.0	-5.5	-5.5	-4.1	-3.0	-2.7	-1.6	-1.4	-1.5	-1.8	-1.4
Germany	-1.1	-1.3	-1.8	-2.1	0.1	-2.0	-3.0	-2.5	-3.1	-2.4	-3.3	-3.4	-2.7	-2.2	-1.6	1.2	-2.5	-2.5	-1.8
Greece	-11.6	-9.6	-9.6	-11.4	-14.2	-15.9	-11.4	-12.6	-13.6	-9.9	-10.2	-7.4	-4.0	-2.4	-1.8	-1.1	0.2	0.6	1.3
Hungary	—	—	—	—	—	—	—	—	-6.6	-11.0	-7.6	-5.9	-7.2	-8.3	-5.2	-3.0	-4.9	-4.8	-4.5
Iceland	-1.1	-4.0	-0.8	-2.0	-4.5	-3.3	-2.9	-2.8	-4.5	-4.7	-3.0	-1.6	0.0	0.5	2.1	2.3	-0.2	-0.8	-0.9
Ireland	-10.3	-10.2	-8.2	-4.2	-1.7	-2.8	-2.9	-3.0	-2.7	-2.0	-2.2	-0.2	1.2	2.3	2.3	4.6	3.2	2.2	1.9
Italy	-12.2	-11.4	-11.0	-10.7	-9.8	-11.8	-11.7	-10.7	-10.3	-9.3	-7.6	-7.1	-2.7	-2.8	-1.8	-0.3	-1.4	-1.1	-1.1
Japan	-0.6	-0.7	0.3	1.1	1.8	1.9	1.8	0.8	-2.4	-2.8	-4.2	-4.9	-3.7	-5.5	-7.0	-6.6	-6.4	-6.7	-6.6
Korea	1.1	1.6	2.6	3.5	3.4	3.5	1.8	1.4	2.5	3.1	4.2	3.8	3.6	1.9	3.1	6.9	5.7	5.1	5.5
Luxembourg	—	—	—	—	—	5.1	1.5	0.7	2.1	2.9	2.3	2.0	3.4	3.4	3.6	6.1	5.3	3.2	2.9
Netherlands	-4.1	-5.7	-6.6	-5.1	-5.3	-5.7	-3.2	-4.4	-3.6	-4.2	-4.2	-1.8	-1.1	-0.8	0.4	2.2	1.1	0.6	0.7
New Zealand	—	-6.4	-2.1	-4.6	-3.4	-4.6	-3.5	-3.1	-0.4	3.1	2.9	2.9	1.6	-0.2	0.9	1.9	1.3	0.1	-0.3
Norway	9.9	5.9	4.6	2.7	1.8	2.6	0.1	-1.7	-1.4	0.4	3.5	6.6	7.9	3.5	5.9	14.8	14.3	11.5	11.7
Poland	—	—	—	—	—	—	—	—	-4.5	-3.5	-2.5	-2.9	-2.8	-2.3	-2.0	-2.2	-4.4	-4.9	-4.9
Portugal	-7.3	-6.2	-5.5	-3.4	-2.3	-5.0	-5.9	-2.9	-6.3	-5.9	-4.6	-4.0	-2.7	-2.3	-2.1	-0.5	-1.7	1.5	-1.4
Spain	-5.6	-6.1	-3.7	-3.3	-3.6	-4.2	-4.3	-4.0	-6.7	-6.1	-6.6	-4.9	-3.2	-2.6	-1.2	-0.3	0.0	-0.4	0.0
Sweden	-3.9	-1.4	3.9	3.0	4.9	3.8	-2.0	-7.8	-11.9	-10.8	-7.7	-3.1	-1.6	2.1	1.7	4.1	3.8	1.6	1.8
United Kingdom	-2.9	-2.6	-1.8	0.5	0.8	-1.6	-3.1	-6.4	-7.9	-6.7	-5.8	-4.4	-2.2	0.4	1.1	1.9	1.1	0.0	-0.7
United States	-5.0	-5.3	-4.3	-3.6	-3.2	-4.3	-5.0	-6.9	-5.0	-3.6	-3.1	-2.2	-0.9	0.3	0.8	1.7	0.6	-0.1	-1.3

Source: OECD Economic Outlook No. 70 (December 2001), p. 232

administration more responsive to citizens' needs by offering value for money, choice flexibility, and transparency' (OECD, 1993: 9). This was later referred to by the scientific community as 'New Public Management' or NPM (Hood, 1991).

New Public Management (NPM)

NPM is generally recognized as being a bundle of concepts – in Pollitt's term 'a shopping basket' (Pollitt, 1995). Typically, it includes elements such as (OECD, 1993: 13):

- A move towards performance management
- A related tendency towards more flexible and devolved financial management
- More devolved personnel management with increasing use of performance-related pay and personalized contracts
- More responsiveness to users and other customers in public services
- Decentralization of authority and responsibility from central to lower levels of government
- Greater recourse to the use of market-type mechanisms, such as internal markets, user charges, vouchers, franchising and contracting out
- Privatization initiatives of public enterprises.

Different countries chose different elements from this shopping basket, influenced by their socio-economic context and their budget situation. Consequently, it is not easy to claim that OECD countries have been pursuing the same reforms. Pollitt and Bouckaert (2000: 176) identify four very different strategies, which OECD countries have adopted in order to deal with the pressures outlined above:

- Maintain – 'tightening up traditional controls' in order to achieve savings
- Modernize – more flexible, efficient and customer-oriented ways of public management and service delivery
- Marketize – institutionalization of as many market-type mechanisms as possible in order to foster competition in the public sector
- Minimize – transferring as many tasks as possible to the private sector through contracting-out and privatization.

Interestingly, no OECD country (or non-OECD country) can be clearly categorized under just one of these basic strategies. The four 'M's' may be considered as ideal-types that have never existed as such in administrative practice. Nevertheless, they highlight a set of reform strategies between which a country must choose as it establishes its direction and priorities over time.

By the beginning of the twenty-first century, the budgetary position of many Western countries had improved. In 2000, the United Kingdom and the United States and various other countries even had a budget surplus. As a result, the financial driver for managerial reforms has become weaker.

New challenges

In the meantime, other external challenges have emerged to drive public sector reforms, typically in a different direction to the managerial reforms of the 1980s and 1990s (Bovaird and Löffler, 2002):

- Political pressure from unresolved 'wicked issues', such as crime and vandalism, terrorism, asylum, economic deprivation, the problem of pensions and quality of life for an ageing population, etc.
- The use of ICT ('e-government', 'e-democracy') not only in relation to service delivery but also in dealing with public policy issues more generally
- Greater pressure from the media as there is a rapid proliferation of private press, radio and television channels and people have access to much greater information from the Internet
- Increasing globalization which makes governments an important economic player but which also exposes them to a volatile global economy
- The development of a differentiated civil society, in which many (very vocal, and usually well educated) people are using the new media to engage in debates on 'quality of life' issues and controversial national public policy issues, while others are increasingly isolated by the digital divide.

REFORM TRAJECTORIES

Whereas introducing (private sector) management principles in the public sector in the 1980s meant realizing the three 'E's' – economy, efficiency and effectiveness – the focus shifted to quality and customer orientation in the 1990s (Walsh, 1995). At the beginning of the new century there is a much bigger concern about institutions and other administrative values. To the original three 'E's' another three 'E's' can now be added: 'ethics, equalities, and equity'.

Public sector reform programmes have also changed their contents, as is evident from the changing public sector reform agendas in different OECD countries. Given that it is not possible to cover all OECD countries in this chapter, three countries are considered in detail.

Following John Loughlin and Guy Peters' (1997) categorization of administrative traditions in Europe, the selection includes one country from the so-called 'Anglo-Saxon' countries (United Kingdom), one country from the Germanic countries (Germany) and one country representing the Napoleonic tradition (Italy).

UK: from the 'market testing state' towards 'Best Value'

The managerial changes in the UK in the early 1980s have been described by one of their progenitors 'as the most important reform of the British civil service since Northcote-Trevelyan in 1845' (Kemp, 1990: 196). The radical changes in the British civil service under Margaret Thatcher were partly driven by a cost-reduction imperative. They were also influenced by neo-liberal market ideology and public choice theory.

The first radical reform was the massive privatization of national enterprises starting in 1979, which transferred almost 50 per cent of the 1979 state sector and 800,000 employees to the private sector by 1990 (Richardson, 1994: 70).

Efficiency units

In order to secure value for money in the remaining civil service a series of scrutinies were launched by the newly established Efficiency Unit. Their objective was to see how particular areas of activity could be performed more efficiently and indeed whether they were necessary at all. These scrutinies paved the way for the Management Information Systems for Ministers (MINIS), out of which emerged the Financial Management Initiative (FMI) in 1982 (Barberis, 1995: 39). This initiative forced all departments to set targets, measure outputs and report performance against those targets. In return and as an encouragement to enhanced performance, civil servants were given greater delegated authority, in order to circumvent the disabling effects of hierarchy and 'to release the energies of enterprise' (Barberis, 1995: 40).

Next Steps

The Next Steps initiative was the logical structural conclusion of the processes set in motion by the FMI, since the creation of agencies was intended to allow for more flexible, customer-oriented service delivery outside the rigid behaviours of a unified civil service. In Next Steps Executive Agencies, the policy making and policy implementing functions of the civil service were separated, with semi-autonomous agencies set free to undertake the executive functions of government within a policy and resources framework set by their sponsoring department (Kemp, 1990: 188). While no long-term assessment of the Next Steps initiative has yet been published, the annual report on executive agencies in 1999 showed that there had been an increase in the meeting of targets and that targets were being set at more ambitious levels than before (Cabinet Office, 1999).

In 1988 parallel initiatives for locally delivered services saw the creation of an internal market in the National Health Service and the introduction of Compulsory Competitive Tendering (CCT) in both local government and the health service, which meant that the service delivery arms of local health bodies and local authorities were placed in an arm's-length relationship with their policy development arms.

Citizen's Charter

An admission that the 'minimizing' element of the governments reform strategy may have gone too far was evident in the next major initiative – John Major's Citizen's Charter in 1991, which, in conjunction with market testing, aimed at making 'public services answer better to the wishes of their users, and to raise their quality overall' (Cabinet Office, 1991: 2). The Citizen's Charter Mark Award, organized for the first time in 1992, was another instrument to foster customer-orientation in public agencies.

Value of public services

Since 1997, the Blair government has partly continued the agenda of the previous Conservative government, particularly on the improvement of service quality (Prime Minister and the Minister for the Cabinet Office, 1999). Indeed, it has hugely increased the levels of inspection of all public services and has intervened more often in public organizations, which inspectors have deemed to be providing 'failing services'. However, the new Labour government has – after a two-year hesitation period – increased the level of investment in public services and greatly increased funding to both health and education services (which were recognized to be severely underfunded in comparison to their EU counter-parts). At the same time, it has reduced the pre-vious emphasis on competition. Moreover, it has emphasized that it wishes to bring about a renewed sense of the value of public services, both by providing a new deal for staff and by embracing a co-production philosophy with service users and partner organizations in the voluntary and private sectors.

'Best Value' initiative

The new direction of public sector modernization in the United Kingdom is well illustrated by the current local government modernization pro-gramme, many elements of which have acted as pilots for the modernization programme in the health services and other parts of government. The first part of this programme, the 'Best Value' initiative, was introduced in local govern-ment in 1997 to replace the much-hated CCT legislation, first as a pilot initiative, then as a statutory duty from 1 April 2000. In practice, 'Best Value' means (DETR, 1999):

- Every part of the council's budget must be reviewed at least once every five years.
- Every review must apply the '4Cs' methodol-ogy to the service or the cross-cutting issue, which consists of the following steps:

  Challenge the need for the service and the way it is carried out
  Consult with all relevant stakeholders
  Compare the performance of the service with other providers
  Compete – test the competitiveness of the service.

- Each local authority must plan to improve its performance so that, within five years, it has reached the level currently attained by the upper quartile of authorities (subsequently amended in 2002 to give more emphasis to 'stretch targets' agreed by each local author-ity with government departments across a range of priority issues).

Local government modernization

Other aspects of the local government modern-ization agenda have gradually attained greater significance – including role of the local authority in community leadership (within statutory Local Strategic Partnerships, which have a duty to prepare Community Strategies), the new power of economic, social and environmental well-being (which means that local authorities are no longer restricted in how they can act to improve conditions in their local areas). In other words, local authorities are no longer just perceived as a public agency for service delivery but also important leaders of the new governance agenda of the Blair government.

Germany: from the 'lean state' towards the 'activating state'

In Germany, as in many other federal countries, the modernization of the public sector has to be understood as a 'bottom-up evolution' (Klages and Löffler, 1995: 132). In the early 1990s some pioneering local authorities initiated NPM reforms within their own organization to deal with a pressing fiscal crisis in the wake of German Reunification. Reform at national and *Land* level was slow by comparison with the local level. At national level, of course, the government was involved in one of the largest 'modernization' programmes in recent European history, as it managed the absorption of 15 million new citizens in the *Neue Länder*.

The German version of NPM was strongly shaped by a comprehensive performance manage-ment model which was developed by a nonprofit local government association in the early 1990s – the so-called 'New Steering Model' (Wollmann, 2001: 226), adapted from the model used by the Dutch city of Tilburg since the mid-1980s (http://www.tilburg.nl/english/modeluk.htm). It is directed towards the radical reorganization of local authorities in order to improve their managerial capacity as a service provider.

New Steering Model

After more than ten years of the New Steering Model in German local government, the question arises what has been accomplished. Various sur-veys by the German Association of Cities show that most German local authorities (but, in particular, the large and medium-sized cities) are still running pilot experiments with one or other elements of the model. In spite of this, there are hardly any cases in which the New Steering Model has been fully implemented. Consequently, the results achieved so far are rather sobering. Nevertheless, there is evidence

(Banner, 2000: 15) that, in those local authorities that implemented the NSM to the greatest extent, customer-orientation has improved and efficiency gains have been made. However, the German case shows that there are limits as to what 'bottom-up' experiments can achieve without central support.

Debureaucratization

Paradoxically, this model became the 'blueprint' for managerial reforms at the state and federal level even though it had never been designed for public agencies dealing with policy making rather than service delivery. It was only in 1995 that the Kohl government developed a reform programme for the federal level by setting up an expert commission, which was labelled the 'Lean State Commission' (*Sachverständigenrat 'Schlanker Staat'*). In contrast to previous reform commissions, the Lean State Commission did not first undertake lengthy research; it took a very pragmatic approach and made concrete recommendations for immediate implementation. The working programme of the Commission focused very much on debureaucratization and cutbacks in the number of public tasks. The final report (*Sachverständigenrat*, 1998) resembled a shopping list of piecemeal reforms more than a well-designed and coherent programme. Moreover, the relocation of the government from Bonn to Berlin was not used as an opportunity to overhaul the federal bureaucracy.

Activating state

The 'Red–Green' successor government headed by the social democratic Gerhard Schröder put even greater weight on budgetary consolidation and the reduction of skyrocketing public debt. Nevertheless, the social-democratic government could not accept the neo-liberal *Leitbild* of the 'lean state' and came up with the label 'activating state' to describe the eventual goal of public sector reforms. The change was meant to emphasize that the new government was opposed to the simple retreat of the state as a means for modernizing public administration. According to a government decision of December 1999, this implied a 'new division of responsibility between state and society' as well as a 'new balance between the duties of the state, individual initiatives, and the engagement of civic society', both of which have to be activated. The 'activating state' therefore corresponds to a state 'which is less a decider and a producer and more of a mediator and activator of social development, which the state cannot and should not determine itself'.

An evaluation of the 'activation potential' of the fifteen lead projects and twenty-three other projects, which are supposed to deliver the 'activating state', suggests that the new vision has not been translated into action (Reichard and Schuppan, 2000: 89). Indeed, the present reform agenda (Federal Ministry of the Interior, 2002) includes a wide variety of unconnected themes, which are still largely influenced by the New Steering Model borrowed from local government:

- Greater effectiveness and acceptance of the law
- The Federation as a partner, in particular in relation to the *Länder*, local authorities and the private sector
- A high-performance, cost-effective and transparent administration
- Motivated staff.

A comparison with the reform agendas of other OECD countries shows that many issues, such as increasing the diversity of the civil service or strengthening public sector leadership, appear still to be non-issues in the current public sector reforms in Germany. Indeed, in some cases, they even appear to be taboos, as in the case of leadership, where the very concept of 'leader' has unpleasant historical connotations.

In general, public sector reform policies are still not considered a priority on the federal level, which has even watered down implementation of the scattered reforms that have been carried out and has made it hard for 'reform pioneers' at the *Länder* and local level to achieve their goals. However, there are now signs that managerialism has begun to take root in some *Länder*, at least in relation to financial management (Reichard and Bals, 2002) and performance management (Horvath and Kühnle, 2002).

Italy: from 'muddling through' towards a 'federalist administration'

Italy has never lacked public sector reform initiatives, although these have typically been little noticed in the English-speaking world. The problem with most past reform efforts was that they were imposed through legislation and not negotiated with the target groups. The result of 'management by decree' (Panozzo, 2000) was that the application of new public management and governance instruments and processes became more an issue of compliance rather than a mechanism for promoting change. There was, therefore, often a big gap between stated reform goals and reality.

Pressure

The political, social and financial crisis in Italy in the 1990s marked a turning point in the Italian administrative tradition. In particular, the Maastricht criteria put strong pressure on the Amato and Ciampi governments in 1992 and 1993 to reduce public debt, restarting a discussion about the role of the central government which was already on the agenda in the 1980s. For Franco Bassanini (then Minister of Public Administration) it was obvious that a comprehensive reform was needed but that it was also necessary to seek the consensus of key players, in particular the trade unions. Without any doubt, Bassanini gave the reforms a new momentum and today Italy is moving faster than many other countries in its reform process, which incorporates a major regulatory reform (OECD, 2001a), the normalization of public labour law, and the implementation of freedom of information laws addressing apparent weaknesses of transparency and accountability of public agencies to the public.

Decentralized decentralization

Bassanini believed that there was a need for effective decentralization of power and financial resources to the regions, provinces and municipalities (Bassanini, 2000). Consequently, the third round of administrative decentralization in Italy, which started in 1997, has become known as the 'Bassanini reforms'. They differed from previous (rather unsuccessful) decentralization reforms in three respects: first, the necessary legislation could be passed quickly as the parliament authorized the government to issue a large number of legislative decrees; secondly, instead of defining the tasks which had to be passed to local levels, the 'Bassanini reforms' identified the areas which must remain the responsibility of the central government. Thirdly, the responsibilities that were affected by decentralization were allocated to the various levels of government in two steps:

- An initial transfer of responsibilities from the central government to the regions
- A second transfer in which each region used its legislative power to determine which responsibilities were assigned to the

provinces and municipalities, including mountain communities.

As a result of this 'decentralized decentralization' process, local authorities now exercise very different tasks from region to region. Whereas some Italian regions have been hesitant to transfer parts of their recently acquired portfolio of tasks on to local levels, regions such as Tuscany have taken the process of decentralization a long way.

It is obvious that this far-reaching reform process has dealt a new hand of cards between the political and administrative actors in Italy. On the one hand, it gives local and regional levels of government more power and flexibility to consider local needs and problems. Most important has been the direct election of local mayors and regional presidents since 1995, which has given municipalities and regions some real political accountability. Some municipalities and regions have taken advantage of these new opportunities to initiate innovations, which go well beyond the legislative decrees.

One example is the Province of Siena, which is now nationally and even internationally considered a model of good governance, since it has initiated a wide range of different partnerships, most of which were established before national government promoted such initiatives in provinces through national legislation and funding (OECD, 2002). Other local areas, such as the municipality of Modena, took advantage of decentralization opportunities by piloting an integrated approach to electronic networks (Mele and Forghieri, 2002). The resultant Web-based system, MoNet, represents a unique tool for involving minorities and other local interest groups in civic and social issues, and it offers enormous potential for establishing public–private partnerships and other forms of co-operation, as the basis of effective local governance.

Co-operation and co-ordination

The decentralization process has increased the need for better co-operation and co-ordination between levels of government. Since the early 1990s, there has been a whole series of laws aimed at promoting horizontal and vertical co-operation between government agencies, but also with private and nonprofit sectors in policy fields such as infrastructure, urban planning and local development – commonly referred to as 'negotiated planning instruments' (see OECD, 2001b: 129–31). Many governments have readily made use of these instruments – for example, by 2001 nearly 100 territorial pacts, concentrating mainly on economic development, were in operation throughout Italy (OECD, 2001c: 9). This marks a clear reversal from past practices where policy making was fragmented and each administration imposed a hierarchy of controls on lower levels.

Results

In the field of regulatory reform, by December 2000 the number of procedures needed to create a new corporation or an individual business had been reduced from twenty-five to five. The maximum time needed for the whole process had fallen from twenty-two to ten weeks (OECD, 2001a). Nevertheless, it will take time until the Bassanini reforms have a comprehensive effect on behaviours. There is an ongoing temptation for central government 'to estimate progress in terms of legal changes rather than concrete outcomes' (OECD, 2001a).

Differences and similarities of the reform trajectories

Clearly, the UK, Germany and Italy have changed their reform strategies over time. At present, the German strategy at the federal level mainly emphasizes maintenance of the status quo, whereas the *Länder* and local level pursue a mix of modernization and marketization. In Italy, the national level has recently implemented modernization programmes, while there are now more and more reform champions at the regional and local levels, which have gone beyond legal requirements and initiated innovative modernization and marketization reforms from the bottom. In the UK, central government and local authorities have shared an interest in modernization strategies, but the local level has been much less interested in marketization than has Whitehall.

In each of the three countries we may observe that administrative reforms have become broader over time, no longer encompassing only internal organizational issues but now including also the modernizing of interorganizational relationships and even the reform of civic society. The 'foci and loci' of public sector reforms have changed.

The emergence of new governance agendas such as partnership working, citizen involvement, social exclusion, transparency and ethics does not mean that all the 'bread and butter issues' of the NPM agenda have become irrelevant. It is clear that public sector productivity and service quality still need to be improved further. In deciding the priority between the 'old' NPM agenda and the 'new' governance agenda, it is important to assess what has been achieved so far, what has worked and what has not worked, so that the direction of future reform can be decided.

THE ACHIEVEMENTS: IMPACT AND OUTCOMES

The impact of rhetoric should not be underestimated. In the long term, it changes the way in which people think and act. As Clarke and Newman (1997: 92) argue, 'the adoption of managerial and business language both serves to legitimate organizations and to change roles and goals within them'. At the same time, rhetoric should not be mistaken for reality. The existence of corporate and business plans does not mean that the organization has a firm grasp of its destiny. The various waves of managerial reform in the UK public sector do not imply that British public services are the best in the Western world. Indeed, the countries that have been highlighted by OECD or the World Bank as 'reform laggards' may actually have higher starting points in terms of service quality than the more active NPM pioneers.

Intended consequences of public sector reforms

The main goal of the public sector reforms in Western countries of the late twentieth century was often to save money, at least initially. Many Western countries seem to have achieved this goal since their fiscal positions improved. However, the cause and effect relationships are unclear. The economic boom in the United States and other Western countries has helped to increase tax incomes and to reduce social expenditures such as welfare benefits. The Swedish government claims that NPM-oriented budgeting reforms have been a major factor in improving its fiscal position (OECD, 1998), but it has also considerably reduced the size of its welfare programmes.

At the level of 'reform strategies', claims have been made that 'marketization' has brought about greater efficiency of service delivery. International studies have consistently shown that permanent cost savings of around 20 per cent can be achieved by contracting out activities,

Table 38.2   *Cost savings from contracting out (%)*

Australia	15–20
Denmark	5–30
Iceland	20–25
Sweden	9–25
United Kingdom	20
United States	20

Source: OECD, 1998: 70

while maintaining or improving service levels (Table 38.2). However, it is not clear whether the OECD statistics include the transaction costs of specifying and monitoring performance contracts. Therefore, the jury is still out on whether greater managerial autonomy has led to improved organizational performance.

Nevertheless, it is clear that recent public sector reforms in Western countries have changed the nature of the state, which in most Western countries has now become much more diversified. This was a declared reform goal in the UK and in some other strongly centralized Western countries. For example, in the United Kingdom more than 75 per cent of the previously unified civil service now works in 140 executive agencies, with different HRM systems and even different organizational cultures.

Unintended consequences

Critics of NPM predicted increasing corruption in the new 'contract and agency state' where public sector organizations and individual public sector employees have more discretionary freedom. Again, it has been argued that NPM unilaterally promotes economic values at the expense of other values such as the common good. These perceptions and fears are, however, not yet backed up by much empirical research comparing ethical conduct before and after reform programmes.

Public management reforms have challenged traditional public sector value:

- Reforms have often changed the status of public sector organizations – to what extent should public corporations and agencies fall under the same ethical and behavioural guidelines as the core public sector?
- Reforms have also sometimes produced (semi-)autonomous bodies, which have used their managerial freedom to define their own ethical standards, often reinforced by increased recruitment from the private sector to leading positions. Will the former coherent

public service 'ethos' break down and progressively fragment?

- Increased managerial freedom within public sector organizations allows for more opportunities for 'irregular' behaviour – not an ethical problem when it produces innovation rather than misconduct, but potentially problematic when management information systems and accountability structures have not kept pace.
- Reforms have also tended to blur the frontier between the public and private sector, with political consequences. For example, does competition between public and private sector organizations imply that public organizations have the right to withhold information from citizens if it might have a negative impact on their ability to compete?

Western countries have responded to these challenges in different ways. While Westminster-type countries have tended to introduce 'codes of conduct' which give public sector staff guidance on how to behave properly, continental European states with a fully developed body of disciplinary law for different parts of the public administration (like Germany) or an administrative tradition of training in ethics (so-called *déontologie*) and strong hierarchical control (such as France) chose to reinforce controls – either through new regulations or better enforcement (PUMA, 2000).

Non-reforms

While public managerial reform programmes have been very comprehensive in some Western countries, little corresponding reform of political institutions – whether parliaments or judicial systems – has taken place. An international survey on the implications of NPM in 1993 revealed that most respondents saw no need for any reform activities in relation to parliaments (Löffler and Hofmeister, 2001: 181). Parliamentarians have only recently woken up and taken steps to respond to the reform agenda – for example, there have been some parliamentary reforms involving the budgetary function, as in Sweden (OECD, 2001c). On the one hand, reforms of budget laws have tended to reduce the level of detail at which the legislature controls expenditure. On the other hand, the executive now often has to give MPs better performance information on outputs.

It seems that, generally, the focus on inputs (financial perspective) suits most politicians better than the focus on results (performance perspective). Therefore, the shift in administrative reform from inputs to outputs and outcomes will be challenging for politicians, especially those part-time politicians who predominate in local and regional parliaments. Yet, from a governance perspective, a high-performing state needs to be more than an excellent administrative state or service provider. It must also be excellent in the way in which it discharges its political and social responsibilities in the local, national and international community.

REFERENCES

Banner, Gerhard (2000) 'From Government to Governance: German Local Authorities between Regulation, Service Provision and Community Development', *Annals of Public Administration Research*, 17: 9–26.

Barberis, Peter (1995) 'The Civil Service from Fulton to Next Steps and Beyond – Two Interpretations, Two Epistomologies', *Public Policy and Administration*, 10 (2): 34–51.

Bassanini, Franco (2000) 'L'Italie. Notre révolution silencieuse', in Roger Fauroux and Bernard Spitz (eds), *Notre Etat. Le Livre vérité de la fonction publique.* Paris: Robert Laffont. pp. 148–73.

Bovaird, Tony and Löffler, Elke (2002) 'Moving from Excellence Models of Local Service Delivery to Benchmarking of "Good Local Governance"', *International Review of Administrative Sciences*, 67 (1): 9–24.

Cabinet Office (1991) *The Citizens' Charter: The Facts and Figures.* Cm. 2970. London: The Stationery Office.

Cabinet Office (1999) *Executive Agencies 1999 Report.* Cm. 4658. London: The Stationery Office.

Clarke, John and Newman, Janet (1997) *The Managerial State.* London: Sage.

Davis, Evan (1998) *Public Spending.* London: Penguin Books.

DETR (1999) *Local Government Act 1999 Part One: Best Value.* Circular 10/99. London: DETR.

Federal Ministry of Interior (2002) *Modern State – Modern Administration. Progress Report 2002.* Berlin.

Hood, Christopher (1991) 'A Public Management for All Seasons?', *Public Administration*, 69 (1): 3–19.

Horvath, Peter and Kühnle, Boris Alexander (2002) 'Using the Balanced Scorecard for Implementing Political Strategies: The Case of a German Bundesland', in A. Neely, A. Walters and R. Austin (eds), *Performance Measurement and Management: Research and Action.* Cranfield: Cranfield Business School. pp. 257–66.

Kemp, Peter (1990) 'Next Steps for the British Civil Service', *Governance*, 3 (2): 186–96.

Klages, Helmut (1993) *Traditionsbruch als Herausforderung. Perspektiven der Wertewandelsgesellschaft.* Frankfurt a.M. and New York: Campus.

Klages, Helmut and Löffler, Elke (1995) 'Administrative Modernization in Germany – a Big Qualitative Jump in Small Steps', *International Review of Administrative Sciences*, 61 (3): 373–83.

Knill, Christoph (2001) *The Europeanisation of National Administrations.* Cambridge: Cambridge University Press .

Löffler, Elke and Hofmeister, Albert (2001) 'Implications of Contract Management for Cantonal Parliaments in Switzerland: Observers become Players', in Peter, Falconer, Colin Smith and C. William R. Webster (eds), *Managing Parliaments in the 21st Century. EGPA Yearbook*, Vol. 7. Amsterdam: IOS Press. pp. 181–95.

Loughlin, John and B. Guy Peters (1997) 'State Traditions and Administrative Reform and Regionalisation', in Michael Keating and John Loughlin (eds), *The Political Economy of Regionalism.* London: Frank Cass.

Mele, Valentina and Forghieri, Claudio (2002) 'The Modena e-Network for Strengthening Local Governance and Citizen Participation', in Tony Bovaird, Elke Löffler and Salvador Parrado Diez (eds), *Developing Local Governance Networks in Europe.* Baden-Baden: Nomos. pp. 165–81.

OECD (1993) *Public Management Developments. Survey 1990.* Paris: Organization for Economic Co-operation and Development.

OECD (1998) 'Contracting Out Government Services: Best Practice Guidelines and Case Studies', *PUMA Occasional Papers*, No. 20, Paris: Organization for Economic Co-operation and Development.

OECD (2001a) *Regulatory Reform in Italy.* Paris: Organization for Economic Co-operation and Development.

OECD (2001b) *OECD Territorial Reviews Italy.* Paris: Organization for Economic Co-operation and Development.

OECD (2001c) *Local Partnerships for Better Governance.* Paris: Organization for Economic Co-operation and Development.

OECD (2001d) 'Budgeting in Sweden', *OECD Journal on Budgeting*, 1 (1).

OECD (2002) *OECD Territorial Reviews: Siena, Italy.* Paris: Organization for Economic Co-operation and Development.

Panozzo, F. (2000) 'Management by Decree. Paradoxes in the Reform of the Italian Public Sector', *Scandinavian Journal of Management*, 16 (4): 357–73.

Pollitt, Christopher (1995) 'Justification by Works or by Faith? Evaluating the New Public Management', *Evaluation*, 1 (2): 133–54.

Pollitt, Christopher and Bouckaert, Geert (2000) *Public Management Reform. A Comparative Analysis.* Oxford: Oxford University Press.

Prime Minister and the Minister for the Cabinet Office (1999) *Modernising Government.* Cm. 413. London: The Stationery Office.

PUMA (2000) 'Recent Developments in the Field of Professionalism and Ethics in the Public Administration: The Case of France'. HRM Working Party Meeting, Paris, 3–4 July (available on Olis as PUMA/HRM (2000)8).

Reichard, Christoph and Schuppan, Tino (2000) 'Wie ernst ist es der Bundesregierung mit dem Thema

"Aktivierender Staat" '?, in Erika Mezger and Klaus-W. West (eds), *Aktivierender Sozialstaat und politisches Handeln*. Schüren: Marburg.

Reichard, Christoph and Bals, Hansjürgen (2002) 'Resource-based Accounting and Output-Budgeting as Common Patterns of Public Sector Financial Management Reforms', in Dietmar Bräuning and Peter Eichhorn (eds), *Evaluation and Accounting in Public Management*. Baden-Baden: Nomos. pp. 137–51.

Richardson, J.J. (1994) 'The Politics and Practice of Privatization in Britain', in Vincent Wright (ed.), *Privatization in Western Europe. Pressures, Problems and Paradoxes*. London: Pinter Publishers. pp. 57–82.

Sachverständigenrat 'Schlanker Staat' (1998) Bonn: Abschlußbericht.

Walsh, Kieron (1995) *Public Services and Market Mechanisms. Competition, Contracting and the New Public Management*. Basingstoke and London: Macmillan.

Willcocks, L. and Mark, A. (2000) 'IT Systems Implementation: Research Findings from the Public Sector', *Journal of Information Technology*, 4 (2).

Wollmann, Hellmut (2001) 'Public Sector Reforms and Evaluation in Germany – Advances and Lags', in 'Evaluating Public Sector Reforms: An International and Comparative Perspective' (special issue) *Revista Internacional de Estudios Publicos*.

39

Public Administration in Post-Communist States

A.J.G. Verheijen

The post-Communist states of Central and Eastern Europe and the former Soviet Union provide a microcosm of the problems inherent in comprehensive public administration reform processes. These states range from EU candidate states to states that have slid to extreme levels of poverty and have fallen back to the level of economic development of the lower strata of some developing countries. At the same time they are all in one way or another 'post-Communist states' that needed to re-build systems of public administration virtually from scratch after the collapse of the previous regimes. They also share the inheritance of the former systems of governance as far as systems of public administration are concerned, an inheritance which has proved extremely difficult to shake off. As a result, more than a decade after the start of the transition the process of developing modern and professional systems of state administration cannot be said to be completed and irreversible in any of the states that are covered in this chapter

The limited achievements of post-Communist states in the area of public administration reform may come as a surprise if one considers the overall achievements in institutional reform in the region, especially in Central and East European states. With few exceptions, the states in the region have created generally accepted constitutions and have built the political institutions provided for in these constitutions. This is valid also for the newly independent states of Central Asia and the Trans-Caucasus,[1] many of which may not yet meet international standards of democracy, but most of which have nevertheless created the foundation for the development of democratic institutional systems in the future. Virtually all states in Central and Eastern

Europe, as well as several members of the Commonwealth of Independent States (CIS), have also undergone one or more peaceful changes of government and leadership and a majority of these are universally recognized as democratic states.

Reform of public administration however, is an area where, as a rule, much less progress has been made than in any other area of institutional reform. There are certainly 'islands of success', but generally these are partial, and in any case they cannot be considered irreversible (Verheijen, 2001: 7). The question why this is the case has increasingly started to raise interest among politicians and academics. The main reasons for this are concerns about the administrative preparedness for EU membership among the ten candidate states in the region, and the perceived link between failure in public administration reform and economic underperformance of several of the states in the region.

First, in this chapter the conditions in which states have attempted to implement reforms will be explored, followed by a review of reform methods applied. This will be followed by an assessment of progress, which will discuss the relevance of traditional notions of administrative reform to the region.

THE NEED FOR COMPREHENSIVE CHANGE

Before reflecting on the process and approaches to reform applied in Central and Eastern Europe, it is important to first reflect on the nature of the task that states in the region faced. There are two important issues to be considered in this respect. The first relates to the nature of reform processes, which has two aspects:

- The comprehensive and holistic nature of reform that needed to be undertaken
- The type of reform process that states needed to engage in, which showed more resemblance to a process of public administration *development* than public administration *reform* in the classical sense of formal reorganization.

The second issue is the context of the reform process, in particular the ideological environment of public administration development in the region, which has been far from conducive to success.

The need for holistic and developmental approaches

The first important point to take into account when reflecting on the process of public administration reform in post-Communist states is that following the start of the transition, states were left with administrative systems that were both irrelevant and inadequate for providing the framework-setting role that systems of public administration are expected to perform in a market economy.

First, systems of public administration as they functioned in the previous system of governance were at best an 'implementation machine' for decisions taken by the Communist Party apparatus, and at worst a means of suppression of citizens by the state. In this respect systems of public administration were fundamentally different from, for instance, systems in Southern European states before the transition in the late 1970s (Verheijen, 1995). A fundamental re-orientation of the role of the administration in relation to citizens and in relation to politics was therefore required. The reform of policy processes is of particular importance in this respect.

Second, the role of systems of public administration under the previous regime was one of at least direct control of economic processes and in most economic areas direct delivery of goods and products. An overhaul of the structure and functions of the state administration was thus needed.

Third, the notion of a professional civil service, different from the private sector both in terms of legal framework and organization, had been eliminated in most states, with the exception of Yugoslavia, where this notion at least

formally remained in place until the late 1980s. This has fundamental implications for the 'usability' of the staff that was in place when the transition started and thus required the definition of a new legal framework as well as a new training and socialization system.

These three reform requirements can only be successfully addressed if reform processes are defined in a holistic manner, built on integrated strategies and approaches. In addition, the emphasis in addressing the systemic problems of the system of the public administration in the region needs to be developmental rather than reformist. However, the need to build modern and professional systems of public administration rather than to reform existing systems was not well understood at the start of the reform process.

The context of public administration development in post-Communist states

The start of the transition coincided with a period in which neo-liberal concepts of public administration were dominant in thinking about the state. More importantly, neo-liberal views were predominant in those countries from which initially inspiration was drawn, especially the USA and the UK, and when post-Communist states faced multiple priorities in difficult economic conditions. The dominant focus of the international reform movement became more important than an empirical assessment of the needs of the empirical locus of reform, which the post-Communist state experience actually constituted. Therefore it is not surprising that public administration development was not considered a priority. Later on, in the second half of the 1990s, when different views on the role of the state started to prevail and EU conditionality was defined also in terms of administrative capacities, priorities started to shift, but by then further, and some would argue almost irreversible damage had already been done both to systems of public administration and to their perception of society. Public administration development became even more difficult than it would have been in the early 1990s.

THE REFORM PROCESS

As stated above, the prevailing conditions in post-Communist states required a holistic and developmental approach. In reality the history of public administration development has been one of piecemeal and ill-sequenced attempts to reform existing systems, with limited success thus far.

Limited use of strategic approaches

A comprehensive approach to public administration development needs a strong strategic underpinning. Without a strategic vision, possibly embodied by a strategic document and related implementation plan, it is unlikely that comprehensive change can be brought about. Strategic documents, however, remain a rare commodity in the region. The Bulgarian government strategy for 'creating a modern system of public administration', adopted in 1997 and currently under revision, is one of the few examples of a comprehensive approach, including an assessment, objective and a discussion of tools to be used to achieve the state objectives. The Bulgarian case is still ill-publicized, but is certainly worth more in-depth study. The Slovak government strategy on decentralization and modernization of the public administration (1999) is another interesting example of a well-designed strategic document, even if its orientation was more towards decentralization. The implementation of the strategy has been fraught with difficulties, due to the vagaries of coalition politics in the state, but it still offers a rare case of a strategic framework that has been at least partially implemented. Finally, the Hungarian government's Public Administration Modernization Strategy (1995) is worth mentioning as a more managerially driven reform strategy, even if its implementation was abandoned after the change of government in 1998. These are possibly the three best cases of nationally driven and at least partially implemented strategic reform processes.

Other attempts at drafting strategies have often been externally driven (for example, Albania) and as a result have lacked ownership. In other cases strategy development was stopped at a halfway point, for example in Ukraine, where the development of the public administration reform concept (1999) has so far been the end point rather than the intended intermediate stage in the development of a comprehensive strategy. Moreover, there are many cases of strategies not implemented (for example, Bulgaria's earlier strategy, a New Administration, 1995).

In some other states, such as Kazakhstan and Kyrgyzstan, strategic approaches were embedded in wider institutional development strategies (the 'Kazakhstan 2030' national development programme and the Comprehensive Development Framework in Kyrgyzstan), with different degrees of success, ranging from a rather encouraging record in Kazakhstan to limited progress in Kyrgyzstan. Strategic approaches have been applied in a rather limited fashion, contrary to the developmental needs in the region.

However, even if piecemeal, issue-by-issue approaches that have been generally used are sub-optimal in the context of post-Communist states, it is still important to review what has been achieved in the crucial areas of civil service development, structural reform and policy process reform.

In this respect it should be noted that structural reform should logically precede civil service reform if the latter is to be effective. Yet, it is interesting to note that post-Communist states have generally tried to apply these two reform steps in the inverse sequence, starting civil service reform before a structural overhaul of the administration.

Civil service reform: law first, people later

The creation of a new civil service system is an obvious key element of the development of new systems of public administration in post-Communist states. Of the different elements of reform and development in the region, this is the area that has seen much more intensive activity than the one discussed above. At first glance this seems an odd reversal of the logical sequence of public administration reforms: structures first, staff afterwards. However, it should be stressed that even if more attention has been paid to this element of reform, civil service development has in most states been limited to the development and adoption of civil service legislation. The adoption of laws was considered the panacea for addressing problems such as politicization, fragmentation and instability.

The adoption of civil service laws in a large number of states in the region, however, has not resolved the problems of instability and politicization and has rarely led to the development of a well-working system of long-term career development (see national case studies in Verheijen, 2001). Even where the basis for such systems has been created, as in Hungary, Poland and Kazakhstan, civil service systems cannot be considered irreversible as yet and often remain incomplete. The following examples provide an illustration of the fragility of civil service legislation and the systems laws have tried to create.

In *Hungary* a Civil Service Law was adopted as early as 1992, creating some stability in the civil service. However, the development of a well-balanced recruitment and promotion system has still not been completed. Politicians have made extensive use of loopholes in the law, such as the fact that the civil service law does not make it mandatory to advertise vacancies. The question that remains is how the impact of the civil service law can be taken beyond stabilization. Amendments to the 1992 law have been developed, but as yet have not been implemented. The lack of a strong civil service management structure that could have 'carried' the implementation of the previous law and break the autonomy of the line ministries is often quoted as a key reason why the system failed to develop further (Vass, 2001).

Poland adopted its second civil service law since the start of the transition in 1998, replacing, mainly for political reasons, the previous civil service law that had been adopted two years earlier. The new system that has been put in place is arguably the least prone to politicization among those in the region, and is often quoted as a textbook example. It is based on an independent civil service office, which has a high degree of control over decisions regarding top-level administrative appointments (Czarnecki, 2000). It should be said, though, that the new government that took office after the September 2001 elections is planning an overhaul of the civil service system. In addition the system only applies to a relatively limited number of civil service positions as yet.

A further illustration of the short-lived nature and low level of impact of civil service laws is provided by the cases of *Estonia*, *Latvia* and *Lithuania*. All three states adopted civil service legislation within a relatively short time span in 1994–95, but the impact of the laws has as yet been limited. In Latvia and Lithuania the adopted civil service laws were never fully implemented. Latvia adopted a fundamentally revised law in 2000, without ever having implemented the earlier law. In Lithuania a new civil service law was adopted in 1999, replacing the earlier law adopted in 1994. In Estonia the civil service law, adopted in 1995, entered into force in January 1996. Unlike in the other two Baltic States, the Estonian civil service law has been implemented. However, since the implementation of the civil service law was not enshrined in a clear public administration reform concept, the overall impact of the law has remained limited (Sootla, 2001).

An interesting contrasting case is that of *Kazakhstan*. Kazakhstan adopted a civil service law in 1999, and has since pursued a consistent policy of professionalization of the civil service, paired with the development of a new training system and, most important, a fundamental reduction in ministerial discretion over appointments, promotions and dismissal. A highly professional civil service agency has been created to manage the implementation process and has so far enjoyed strong backing from the political leadership. Even if the implementation of the new system has met a lot of resistance from line ministries, high-level support for the agency as well as skilled management of the implementation process by the agency has so far limited the impact of such resistance (Verheijen, 2001). However, it should be stressed that also here the process is not yet irreversible. Arguably, the general political stability that characterizes Kazakhstan is a factor in the successful implementation of the reform process so far. At the same time, however, many states of the former Soviet Union have similar or higher levels of stability and yet have not engaged in a comprehensive reform of the civil service system. A combination of political will, combined with the development of a strong, independent and well-managed civil service agency seems to have made the difference.

In conclusion, the positive picture one could have when one considers the development and adoption of civil service legislation in an increasing number of post-Communist states[2] at face value, is really a false impression. In reality, civil service laws seldom have had the impact they were expected to have, which was to be a catalyst for the stabilization, de-politicization and professionalization of the central administration. Even in the few cases where they have fulfilled this role, their impact is not yet sure to stretch beyond the next change of government.

Training and staff development, the lack of structural achievements

A further element of the improvement of public administration staff is the development of training systems. This is true in particular for post-Communist states, where the new institutional system has to rely at least to some degree on officials that had worked under the previous regime, which needed to be trained rapidly in new skills and work methods. Furthermore training systems can help to create the 'glue' that holds fragmented administrations together. Joint pre- or post-entry training of new recruits can help create a sense of community among new civil servants. This sense of community could play a role in reducing fragmentation. Joint training of top level officials can have a similar effect. However, the lack of developed human resource development policies, as well as the lack of progress in creating suitable new training structures in post-Communist states can be considered key elements of failure in the development of new administrations. There is no space here for an in-depth review of the various failed attempts to create viable civil service training systems,[3] it suffices to state that there are few, if any, successful examples to discuss here.

There are three main reasons why the use of training as a reform and development tool has failed so dismally. The first is the general lack of openness of politicians in the region towards using any reform tools except legislation. Functional review, albeit with difficulty, was gradually accepted as a reform tool. The acceptance of training as a 'serious' reform tool has been even more difficult. As a consequence of this, most governments have no training policy or programme. The general scepticism among politicians about the usefulness of training as a reform has thus become a self-fulfilling prophecy. A second important reason is the lack of indigenous training capacities, which leads to a lot of training still being 'imported', and as a consequence, not tailor-made to the needs of the administration. As a third reason, governments have often been unwilling to invest in the development of training systems for budgetary reasons. Unless the development of training institutions was funded by outside sources, there was little willingness to support the idea of creating them. Even where institutions were created, they often closed down or faded into irrelevance once funding dried up.

Designing new administrative structures: the first thing last?

Among the numerous weaknesses of the old system of public administration it may well be the problems with administrative structures and their interrelations that will prove most difficult to repair. Recent studies (UNDP, 2001) identify various structural problems in central state administrations:

- A clear conception of the role of the state is missing
- Leftover elements of the previous system are still present
- Mechanical and technical approaches to public administration continue to prevail, with low priority assigned to strategic thinking
- Intra- and inter-sectoral co-ordination systems are not functioning
- Public administration systems remain opaque, with a lack of clarity in lines of accountability.

This is a complex set of interrelated problems, which has not been fully addressed by any state in the region. Apart from the more generic explanations offered in the previous sections, one should also consider the following, more specific reasons.

First, there is the multi-faceted nature of structural reform. Structural reform involves the re-definition of the role and position of ministries, their subordinated organizations and the core executive unit.[4] This is of particular importance in Central and East European states, since the core executive units of the administration used to 'shadow' line ministries under the previous regime and play a dominant role in the process of policy co-ordination. Policy processes were therefore 'top heavy', based on co-ordination at the top, and ultimately controlled by the Communist Party. Core executive units also tended to manage large numbers of subordinated institutions. Ministries in turn had direct responsibility for the management of a plethora of subordinated bodies, including often state enterprises and other institutions that in a market economy either belong in the private sector or, at the very least, in the 'third' sector.

A second element of complexity is the need for radical change in accountability systems, which has both institutional and cultural implications. In the past, accountability lines were directed towards the leading political party. Changing a system based on a single hierarchy with single accountability lines to a complex accountability system with various 'centres' to which institutions report is a highly difficult task.

Early attempts to address at least some elements of structural reform were made in Poland and Hungary in the mid-1990s. Poland carried out a substantial reform of the Council of Ministers' administration, with the objective of creating a small core Prime Minister's Office, among others, by, 'pushing down' co-ordination tasks into the administration. In Hungary attempts were also made to 'slim down' the Prime Minister's office, though the current government has again expanded the number of substantive shadow units in the office (Meyer-Sahling, 2001). However, these partial reforms proved to be insufficient for driving the necessary deep systemic change.

During the past few years initiatives have been taken in several states to come to a more comprehensive approach to structural reform. One method applied has been the use of framework laws to regulate the role and function of the different institutions in the administration and to rationalize their operation. For instance, in Bulgaria a Law on Public Administration was adopted in 1998, defining the type of institutions that can exist in the state administration, and their relations of accountability. Other states have also taken initiatives of this kind in recent years, such as Latvia and Lithuania. Slovakia has defined a package of laws and regulations, which is in the process of being adopted, and the Ukraine has initiated a similar process, though political instability has made this a slow process in the latter country. Further east, Kazakhstan and Kyrgyzstan have both been engaged in processes to reform administrative structures and rationalize accountability systems, using a step-by-step approach.

The significant shift in attention to structural reforms is interesting to note and begs the question why it has occurred. The answer is closely linked to the shift in reform tools applied in various states in recent years, away from across-the-board budget cuts and full reliance on legislation as a reform tool, towards a more managerial approach, based on functional reviews as a diagnostic tool.

Functional review

Functional review is fast becoming a remarkably universal reform tool in post-Communist states. At the last count, some ten states in the region have conducted some form of comprehensive functional review in the past four years, and in several other states the use of this reform tool is being considered. For a region that for a long time ignored structural reform and relied on budget cuts and legislation as tools of administrative reform, the 'sudden' use of functional reviews on such a large scale is rather odd.

There are various possible explanations for the increasingly widespread use of functional reviews. The first reason is pressure by international donors, in particular the World Bank. The World Bank has often 'prescribed' functional reviews as a condition for the delivery of structural adjustment loans. It should be noted that the World Bank approach to functional reviews is predominantly sectoral in nature, with system analysis playing a secondary role, if conducted at all. This has led in some countries, such as for instance Latvia, to successful structural reform processes in individual ministries, without, however, leading to significant improvements in the public administration system overall. In other states, such as in the Ukraine, where the World Bank, DFID and UNDP have worked together in this area, a more balanced approach has been chosen, without, however, having led to much better results, due to the lack of sufficient national commitment to the process.

A second reason for the increasing use of functional review has been the realization by politicians that across-the-board staff cuts, which have often been applied in the face of budgetary crises, have had a strongly negative effect on the functioning of the administrative system as a whole. Across-the-board cuts 'freeze' structural problems and arguably even aggravate their effect (UNDP, 2001). Governments in states such as Bulgaria, Lithuania, Slovakia and Kyrgyzstan have tried functional review as an alternative way of achieving staff/budget cuts, while simultaneously reforming the structure of the administration. It is early yet to judge whether the latter form of using functional reviews has brought significantly better results than the externally driven form, as the implementation of proposed reforms in Slovakia and Kyrgyzstan is still ongoing, and in Lithuania the implementation process has stalled after a change of government. On the basis of the Bulgarian case, however, it would seem that the nationally driven approach has more chances of success: the results of the review and its recommendations were enshrined in a reform strategy and a package of legislation that has generally been judged to have been implemented successfully. It is certain that a fundamental and widespread change is taking place in the way the reform of administrative structures and processes is being perceived and approached.

It should be said that, so far, the use of functional reviews has rarely led to fundamental changes in the situation in central state administrations in the region. Problems in design of reviews and also limited commitment from national governments have made the implementation of proposed changes problematic in many states. However, the fact that governments have accepted, in several cases voluntarily, the use of very untraditional reform tools, may well reflect a gradual change in perception regarding the importance of the development of fundamentally different administrative structures and processes in the overall administrative development process.

REFORM IN POST-COMMUNIST STATES: LESSONS?

The limited academic writing on public administration reform in post-Communist states uses a variety of explanations for the relative failure of reforms (Nunberg, 1998; Verheijen and Coombes, 1998). Apart from the difficult legacy of history, which was already mentioned above and is well documented, there are three further reasons why reforms have generally failed to produce results:

1 Lack of political consensus on reforms
2 The problem of reform design
3 The changing and often contradictory signals of external organizations.

The relative importance of these three reasons for reform failure is important to understanding what may be achieved in the future and through what means.

Lack of consensus: political polarization and a lack of continuity

Political consensus (or the long-term continuity of one political force) and consistency in reforms policies are generally considered to be key conditions for successful administrative reform. These conditions have not been met in large parts of Central and Eastern Europe and the former Soviet Union. In states where there is political consensus or where one political force dominates the political scene, there has often been a remarkable lack of consistency in administrative development policies.

In Central and East European states, voters have virtually on every occasion thrown out the government in office. This affects administrative development policies in particular, since these are not 'vote-winning policies'. As an aggravating factor, political party systems remain highly polarized, often around the Ex-Communist–Former Opposition dichotomy,[5] which further reduces the potential for continuity in policies. Interestingly, this appears to affect economic policies much less than administrative development. However, the reversal of administrative development measures, strategies and even laws remains common practice throughout this part of the region. The absence of long-term policies to stimulate administrative development therefore does not need to come as a surprise.

States in the eastern part of the former Soviet Union have a much higher degree of political stability, and often a not fully developed political party system. Paradoxically, this could have created the conditions to build long-term and consistent administrative reform policies. However, it seems that so far only in one state has this to some degree worked as a beneficial factor. Between 1998–2002 Kazakhstan developed a legislative framework for the development of a professional civil service, pursued a consistent policy of investment in capacity development in the state administration, and simultaneously conducted a functional review process as a basis for the reorganization of the state administration. No other state in the CIS has pursued a similarly consistent policy of administrative development, regardless of the relatively high level of political stability.

The problem of reform design

Lack of sound judgement in reform design is the second reason for the lack of progress in administrative development. Politicians and foreign experts alike have made mistakes, both in sequencing reform measures and in choosing reform tools. The over-reliance on legislation as the main reform instrument, which is not surprising taking into account the legalist tradition of most of the states discussed here, an over-emphasis on civil service reform and the lack of attention to the reform of administrative structures and processes are all key to an understanding of the lack of success in administrative reform. The recent history of administrative development in post-Communist states provides a textbook illustration that legislation is not an appropriate reform tool on its own. Furthermore it proves that the development of civil service systems cannot succeed without the necessary accompanying structural reform measures, which in turn need to be based on a well-elaborated assessment of organizational structures and capacities. The recent change in approach to administrative reform in the region shows that this realization is finally dawning. However, the experience with functional review processes, as the basis for structural reform, has so far been mixed. Much of the explanation for this may lie in the role of international donors thus far, which often have not shown a good understanding of the nature of administrative development processes in the region.

The role of international actors

At first glance, external pressure to carry out administrative reform seems to be considerable. The EU is the main organization to have important political leverage in a majority of the states discussed here. EU membership conditions include the creation of a stable, professional and accountable administration,[6] which should provide incentives to Central and East European governments. However, the EU has been far from consistent in the signals it has sent to the candidate states (Dimitrova, 2001; Verheijen, 2000), even if in recent years the emphasis on both horizontal and sectoral administrative capacities has increased.

Other institutions, in particular the World Bank and the IMF, have also increasingly put pressure on Central and East European governments to give more priority to administrative development. The interest of the World Bank, and to a lesser degree the IMF, in promoting public administration development is still quite recent and it is early yet to predict to what degree these institutions will be able to have a significant impact in this area. However, it should be noted that the work of the World Bank in particular has generally focused on improving management in public administration, rationalizing central government structures[7] and the development of fair and sustainable reward systems. These are some of the core issues identified earlier on as crucial to the success of public administration development. In this respect the work of the World Bank has the potential to become a catalyst for administrative development in years to come.

Lessons learned?

There are various lessons to be drawn from the so-far unfortunate experience of administrative reform and development in post-Communist states. First, those involved in administrative reform processes have often underestimated the deeply rooted nature of the problems the public administration systems in the region are facing. An over-simplification of proposed recipes for change, combined with a general indifference on the side of politicians, largely explain the failure of the first five years of reform. Where political institutions were reformed and started to operate, administrations were left behind. Second, even when and where the diagnosis of the problems in the systems was correct, and politicians could be convinced that reform was after all really needed, the medicines applied were not the right ones, or at least they were not applied in the right sequence. Designing and adopting civil service legislation without attacking the root causes of the problems in the administration first has proved to be a highly inadequate reform strategy, all the more so because the right of interference in appointments and promotions has been one thing that politicians have in most cases refused to give up. Only in the past few years has a more comprehensive approach to reform been tried in some states, using more than one type of reform instrument and addressing more than just one set of problems. Initial results in states like Bulgaria, Kazakhstan and, to a lesser degree, Poland and Slovakia, show that progress is possible and that both reformers and advisers have learned some lessons. However, it should also be stressed that in three of these four states reform processes are highly vulnerable to political changes. Experience will have to show whether initiated reforms will 'hold'. Even if this risk is less pronounced in Kazakhstan, continuity in reform policy is also not fully guaranteed there.

The not-so-exciting truth remains that convincing political leadership remains the key condition for progress to be made. Definitely there is a much greater understanding in the region of the need and complexity of administrative reform than there was ten years ago, and this is true across the board. However, a continuous effort to educate politicians that administrative change is to their benefit is needed if a review of administrative reform in post-Communist states undertaken in ten years' time is to yield more than a few partial illustrations of success and a sometimes demoralizing large number of cases of reform failure.

NOTES

The opinions and analysis presented in this chapter represent the personal views of the author only and do not constitute in any way the official view of the World Bank.

1 See for an in-depth discussion of the political systems in Central Asia and the Trans-Caucasus, David Hayhurst, 'Building Castles on Shifting Sands'. *Local Government Brief*, January 2001, and Tony Verheijen, Sergei Sirotkin and Anastazia Kozakova, 'Government in Central Asia', *Local Government Brief*, June 2001.

2 All EU candidate states except Slovenia and the Czech Republic, for instance, have adopted civil service legislation.

3 See, for instance, the discussion in Verheijen (2000) for further details.

4 For instance, Chancelleries, Prime Minister's Offices, Cabinet Offices or Councils of Minister.

5 The election compaign in Poland provides a good illustration of this.

6 As defined in the so-called SIGMA baseline criteria (SIGMA, 1999).

7 In particular in Latvia.

REFERENCES

Czarnecki, R. (2000) *Building a Professional and Merit-based Civil Service: The Experience of Poland*. Warsaw. Office of Civil Service.

Dimitrova, A.L. (2001) 'Governance by Enlargement? *The Case of the Administrative Capacity Requirement in the EU's Eastern Enlargement'*. Paper presented at the ECPR General Conference, 6–8 September 2001, University of Kent at Canterbury.

Meyer-Sahling, J. (2001) 'Methodological Frameworks for the Study of Politico-Administrative Relations and their Applicability in Post-Communist States', in T. Verheijen (ed.), *Politico-Administrative Relations, Who Rules?* Bratislava, NISPAcee. pp. 45–64.

Nunberg, B. (1998) *The State After Communism.* Washington, DC: World Bank.

Sootla, G. (2001) 'Evolutions of Roles of Politicians and Civil Servants during the Post-Communist Transition in Estonia', in T. Verheijen (ed.), *Politico-Administrative Relations, Who Rules?* Bratislava, NISPAcee. pp. 109–47.

UNDP (1997) *The Shrinking State.* New York: UNDP/RBEC.

UNDP (2001) *Rebuilding State Structures, Methods and Approaches.* Bratislava: UNDP/RBEC.

Vass, L. (2001) 'Civil service Development and Politico-Administrative Relations in Hungary', in T. Verheijen, (ed.), *Politico-Administrative Relations, Who Rules?* Bratislava: NISPAcee. pp. 147–75.

Verheijen, T. (1995), *Constitutional Pillars for New Democracies.* Leiden: DSWO Press.

Verheijen, T. and Coombes, D. (1998) *Innovations in Public Management.* Cheltenham: Edward Elgar Publishers.

Verheijen, T. (1999) *Civil Service Systems in Central and Eastern Europe.* Cheltenham: Edward Elgar.

Verheijen, T. (2000) *Administrative Capacity Building for EU Membership. A Race against Time?* WRR Working Paper 109. The Hague: WRR.

Verheijen, T. (2001) *Politico-Administrative Relations, Who Rules?* Bratislava: NISPAcee.

PUBLIC ADMINISTRATION IN DEVELOPING AND TRANSITIONAL SOCIETIES

Introduction

Goran Hyden

This section of the Handbook highlights the issues associated with administering public services in societies undergoing economic and political reform. Although such reforms tend to be ongoing in all regions of the world, including industrial societies, their implications and outcomes differ from region to region largely because of differential legacies of state–society relations. They differ also among countries within a single region. Thus, it is important to point out from the outset that the authors in this section are understandably unable to cover everything. We have made a decision to try to capture the essence of what has occurred in each region in recent years and wherever appropriate point out some of the more salient differences that exist in each region. There are obvious gaps that the critical reader may discern. For instance, we do not cover the issues of public administration associated with the countries in the Middle East, nor those that specifically pertain to the many small island countries around the world.

Public administration in developing countries was once referred to as 'development administration', implying that there is something special about administering development. Although the term is still in use, it has lost its analytical specificity. Thus, in this section, we do not specifically discuss development except to the extent that shifting perceptions of the

concept bear on how public administration in developing and transitional societies has been affected and reformed in order to correspond to these shifting notions.

More specifically, the chapters in this section highlight both similarities and differences in the way public administration has evolved in recent decades, partly in response to changing domestic conditions, partly as a result of fresh ideas having been introduced from the outside. The two principal challenges that seem to come out of the individual contributions are (1) the task of emancipating public organizations from their embeddedness in social and political circumstances that curtail their performance, and (2) the exercise of finding models and instruments of reform that really work in developing or transitional societies. In this brief introduction I shall place these issues in a broader and comparative context and highlight important points that the four authors in this section of the Handbook make.

STATE–SOCIETY RELATIONS

A prevalent attribute of the state in developing and transitional societies is the discretionary power that is associated with occupying public positions. This may be most apparent at the top level where heads of state or cabinet ministers use their position of authority to make decisions that are often against even the faintest sense of public good. A similar type of discretion is also evident at lower echelons in the government hierarchy. Members of the public often find it difficult to obtain services or decisions from 'street-level' bureaucrats without first paying them a bribe. The point that the authors make in this section is that this kind of behavior is not just incidental but part of a system that they call 'patrimonial' or 'neo-patrimonial'. In making this point, they echo an argument that is quite common in the literature on politics and administration of developing and transitional societies (see, for example, Riggs, 1964; Clapham, 1982; Migdal, 1988; Bratton and van de Walle, 1997).

One can take this point as support for the position that missing in these societies is a culture that prioritizes legality and rationality in the sense that Max Weber described modern bureaucracies (Weber, 1947). Politicians are to blame for not allowing legal-rational forms of organizations to evolve. Dwivedi, with reference to Asia, Nef, in discussing Latin America, and Olowu, in examining Africa, see politicians as the root of the problem. Although Ágh does not give this observation the same weight as the other authors, there is evidence in parts of the region that he covers – Eastern and Central Europe – of the same kind of tension between organizational ideals, on the one hand, and societal values, on the other. Given that the authors come to this conclusion from very different vantage points, this is interesting in itself. The considerably longer state tradition in Asia has not evolved beyond patrimonialism; nor has the now quite old post-colonial state in Latin America. As Olowu points out with reference to Africa, the absence of a state tradition on the continent translates into not only patrimonialism but also immobilism, or inadequate executive capacity. Eastern and Central Europe, according to Ágh, manifests similar features, although there is variation, with Eastern Europe and the Balkan countries being more deeply affected by inadequate public services than Central Europe.

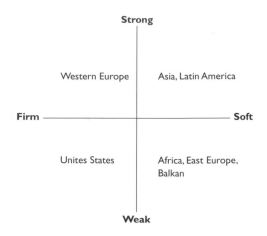

Figure 1   *Typology of public administration systems*

In order to fully understand how public administration in developing and transitional societies compares with that of industrial societies, it may be helpful to distinguish public administration systems along two parameters, the first dealing with executive capacity, the second with adherence to rules, or legality. With regard to the former, systems can be placed along a continuum from 'strong' to 'weak'; with regard to the latter, along a continuum from 'firm' to 'soft'. Drawing on the contributions made here and the literature at large, it is possible to use the matrix in Figure 1 to locate public administration systems in different parts of the world.

REFORM LESSONS

The second issue of special significance in this section concerns the reform efforts. The history of reform is long in developing and transitional societies, but the results are very meager. Ever since 'development administration' was invented by Western organization theorists in the 1960s as the preferable way of conceiving of the role of public services in promoting national development, the story has been rather dismal. As Schaffer (1969) noted over thirty years ago in one of the first assessments of this movement, bureaucracy is not really suited for tasks that involve coping

Table 1 *Sources of pressure within public administration systems in developing and transitional societies*

Dimension/source	Patrimonialism	Routinization	New Public Management
Organizational objective	Power maintenance	Law-and-order	Development
Service rationale	Ruler	Rule	Result
Organizational structure	Patriarchal	Hierarchical	Team-based
Operational mode	Discretionary	Mechanistic	Organic
Staff orientation	Upward	Inward	Outward
Career system	Favoritist	Fixed and closed	Flexible and open
Handling of wrongs	Blaming others	Denying responsibility	Learning lesson

with change. Because of its rule orientation, it tends to look inwards rather than outwards; it is better at maintaining law-and-order than promoting social or economic development. In short, there is a poor 'fit' between bureaucracy and development.

A similar situation seems to prevail with regard to more recent efforts to reform the public services. The New Public Management (NPM) approach that has accompanied structural reforms aimed at reducing the size of the public service has encountered criticism for lack of suitability to the conditions in developing and transitional societies. The contributors to this section all report an adverse attitude to the principles of reform associated with NPM. It is not clear how far this criticism is inherent in the public service itself, but there is evidence that neither the public nor the political leaders seem to appreciate it. Much of this has to do with the fact that NPM is part of a broader reform package that is being introduced – sometimes imposed upon – developing and transitional societies on the assumption that economic policy changes need the support of administrative reform in order to be sustainable.

The points made in this section raise an issue that previous analysts of public administration have often returned to: is administrative reform best carried out from within or does it need the 'push' from outside? Earlier studies, for example, by Montgomery (1987), have come to the conclusion that managers and administrators in developing societies are not different from those in Europe or North America. They hold most of the same values.

The problem with studies of this type, however, is that they rely on interviews with managers without seeing them in their operational context. As Hofstede (1991) emphasizes, if administrators are studied in their cultural context, significant differences do occur because they are induced or forced to behave in ways that may differ from their own values. They simply cannot avoid the pressures of the societal culture in which they live – and work. Hofstede does not rule out the possibility of change from within, but he is skeptical of the idea that large-scale training programs in combination with organizational restructuring, whether along the lines of NPM or any other approach, will produce the expected results. Henderson (1990) suggests that globalization is bringing people and societies closer together; hence the importance of greater emphasis also on internationalization of the effort to build stronger public administration systems. While the chapters in this section do not rule out the prospect for change, they are all cautious, if not outright critical, in their evaluation of the inputs from the outside.

Administrative reform is likely to be both slow and incremental. Public administration systems will continue to be pulled in opposite directions – both forward and backward. There is little room for a 'big bang' approach to progress. Ágh's study of Eastern and Central Europe confirms that even in those countries where the old system literally collapsed and a new one had to be built from scratch, the legacy of the past continues to hang over the present. If one disaggregates the story that the four chapters in this section tells, it is possible to argue that public administration in developing and transitional societies is being caught in a triangular hold where influences come from political sources in the shape of patrimonialism, from within professional civil service cadres in the direction of routinization of rules, and from international consultants and finance institutions in the form of the urge to adopt a 'new' type of public management. Table 1 summarizes the principal differences between these three approaches and indicates the long distance that often exists between practice and reform promise.

CONCLUSION

In a book similar to this published over ten years ago (Dwivedi and Henderson, 1990), Gerald and Naomi Caiden argued in a concluding chapter that comparative studies of administration abound, but comparative administration barely progresses (Caiden and Caiden, 1990: 396). This is not the place to enter into an argument with their position, but it seems that one reason for such a conclusion is that public administration theorists tend to assume that their particular theory has universal value and application. Their ambition is to accommodate all systems of public administration under a single theory or model. The empirical reality of developing and transitional societies defies such an approach, as the authors in this section point out. A more inductive approach, for example, along the lines suggested in Table 1 above, which acknowledges that public administration systems are subject to competing pressures from several sources, seems a more realistic and helpful approach, whether the objective is purely academic or practical in terms of offering prescriptive advice.

REFERENCES

Bratton, Michael and van de Walle, Nicolas (1997) *Democratic Experiments in Africa*. New York: Cambridge University Press.

Caiden, Gerald and Caiden, Naomi (1990) 'Towards the Future of Comparative Public Administration', in O.P. Dwivedi and Keith M. Henderson (eds), *Public Administration in World Perspective*. Ames, IO: Iowa State University Press.

Clapham, Christopher (1982) *Private Patronage and Public Power*. New York: St Martin's Press.

Dwivedi, O.P. and Henderson, K.M. (eds) (1990) *Public Administration in World Perspective*. Ames, IO: Iowa State University Press.

Henderson, Keith M. (1990) 'Rethinking the Comparative Experience: Indigenization Versus Internationalization', in O.P. Dwivedi and K.M. Henderson (eds), *Public Administration in World Perspective*. Ames, IO: Iowa State University Press.

Hofstede, Gert (1991) *Cultures and Organizations*. London: McGraw–Hill.

Migdal, Joel (1988) *Strong Societies and Weak States*. Princeton, NJ: Princeton University Press.

Montgomery, John D. (1987) 'How African Managers Serve Development Goals', *Comparative Politics*, 19 (2): 347–60.

Riggs, Fred (1964) *Administration in Developing Countries: The Theory of Prismatic Society*. Boston, MA: Houghton–Mifflin.

Schaffer, Bernard (1969) 'The Deadlock of Development Administration', in Colin Leys (ed.), *Politics and Change in Developing Countries*. Cambridge: Cambridge University Press.

Weber, Max (1947) *The Theory of Economic and Social Organization* (ed. T. Parsons). London: Unwin Books.

40

The Crisis in African Public Administration

Dele Olowu

This chapter reviews the performance of African public administration systems and focuses on reform efforts since these countries became independent around the 1960s. As noted by Hyden in the Introduction to this section, reform efforts have been aimed at making African public administrations *developmental, managerial and democratic*. Such a multiple transformation represents a paradigm shift from the present preoccupation with rule maintenance and autocracy. This change is necessitated by the challenges confronting the continent and its people in the twenty-first century. They are part of wider governance of reforms, which have been pursued in the continent since 1990 – a trend, which is not confined to Africa – although least internalized there (Hyden and Bratton, 1992; Hyden et al., 2000: Kiggundu, 1998; Pereira and Spink, 1997).

The crisis in Africa that has given rise to these reforms is multiple in nature. Economically, even though growth has resumed in the continent, poverty has also increased at a time when estimates for other regions of the world report a decline in the numbers of the poor. Average income per capita is lower than it was in the mid-1960s; thirty-eight of the world's least developed populations are African. Over one half of the countries in the region have average annual incomes less than US$1 a day – the international definition of poverty (World Bank, 2000). Such figures only reflect the dire problem of the continent's flagging performance – declining export shares in traditional exports, low trading activity and growing indebtedness, rising from US$5.7 billion to US$12.4 billion between 1980 and 1998. Africa's share of foreign domestic investment has declined at a time when other developing

countries have made spectacular gains. Socially, Africa has lost ground it gained earlier. There have been shortfalls in primary school enrollments. Child mortality and endemic diseases, including malaria and HIV/AIDS, have risen phenomenally. Total roads–to-population fell from 3,100 km to 2,500 km per 1 million people between 1980 and 1996 (the figure for Sub-Saharan Africa (SSA) was from 3,400 km to 2,400 km within the same period). This further reduces opportunities for economic development. Continuing instability, conflict and corruption in all its forms – grand and petty – signify that Africa's political institutions remain largely un-institutionalized. Fundamental concerns on how to bridge the wide gulf between the rulers and the ruled, exotic and indigenous organizations remain unresolved (Dia, 1996; Hyden et al., 2000; Olowu and Erero, 1996).

The rest of this chapter will examine more closely the crisis of public administration in Africa by focusing on its principal components. It will subsequently discuss the reform efforts and the problems encountered in implementing them.

THE PUBLIC ADMINISTRATION CRISIS

The crisis of public administration in Africa can be said to have three major components. The first concerns the mission of this system, the second its performance and the third its internal managerial qualities. These three components have contributed to calling into question the legitimacy of the state itself, an institution that has become increasingly alienated from society (Ekeh, 1975; Joseph, 1999). I shall briefly discuss each of these components.

The crisis of mission

This crisis largely stems from the dramatic shift that has taken place in the role of the state and its public service since the time of independence. African countries have gone from being almost exclusively dependent on the state to a situation at present where the state is expected to be responsible for only a few basic functions. This has inevitably had ramifications both for state employees and the public.

At the time of independence, the role of the state was systematically viewed as being that of development manager. Indeed, initial efforts at creating development administration institutions were premised on the colonial idea that the state had the responsibility for managing development, being the only modern credible institution of governance. In the post-colonial period, this idea was given great prominence, as the public service became not only a regulator but also an active player in the economic realm, as a financier and entrepreneur of development. As a result, a large number of parastatal agencies were created and the dominance of the state over all other institutions was reinforced through administrative reforms, which subordinated them to the central executive branch and politicians. For instance, semi-autonomous local government systems were transformed into field administrations of the central government, cooperatives were directed by civil servants and, in extreme cases where they could not be controlled, as in Tanzania, were abolished. All economic and social institutions (trade unions, universities, civil services, parastatals etc.) were brought under one party or legislated out of existence. The state was to be supreme and its role comprehensive. The topmost positions in the civil service were politicized and merit was largely abandoned.

The resulting lack of fit between developmental expectations and administrative capacity led to a sharp decline in performance. As a response, most countries in the region, with the assistance of International Finance Institutions (IFIs), initiated programs of structural adjustment (SAP). Fiscal balance, macroeconomic stabilization and economic liberalization were SAP's key components. This meant the pursuit of economic outward-looking rather than inward-looking strategies, the exposure of their economies to international competition rather than protection. They were encouraged to develop an exportable agriculture rather than promote import-substituting industrialization. The mission of the state was reduced to its classical notion – a residual one, whatever the private sector could or would not do. Indeed, in the earlier version of these reforms, the state was perceived as the obstacle to development and growth. The strategy was to get the state out of the way – so that productive forces in society – the private sector, recognized as the engine of development – could lead the development process.

This minimalist state doctrine incorporates major reforms of the civil service, in the parastatals sector and the local governments. Later, a much more restrained liberal view of the state was advanced in the 1997 World Development Report. But the principles of the minimalist state continue to provide the framework for institutional reforms in the public sector. These are reviewed in greater detail below.

Even though there are now efforts to give the state a more positive role again by expecting it to become an enabler by stimulating other actors to get involved in development (Osborne and Gabler, 1993; Premchand, 1999), there is still much uncertainty about its future mission. Is the state ready to play such a role?

The performance crisis

The public service has been made one of the main culprits behind the fiscal crisis that engulfed the state in the 1980s by virtue of not having performed its role as a producer of goods and services. Revenues tended to decline as the numbers of public servants and payroll rose. State payroll, for instance, in seven West African countries averaged 62 per cent of GDP (ranging from 51 per cent in Togo to almost 80 per cent in Benin) from 1980 to 1993. This compares with an average of 15 per cent for many OECD and East Asian countries (Doe, 1998: 135). A sharp decline in recurrent and capital expenditure reflects poor quality infrastructures, neglected basic services and poor security for citizens. Savings as a proportion of GDP were 21 per cent in 1970 and fell to 17 per cent in 1997. In contrast, comparable figures for South and East Asia show an upward trend: from 17 to 20 per cent in South Asia and from 22 to 38 per cent in East Asia. Similarly, investment per capita fell from US$130 in 1970 to US$92 in 1997 while it rose in Asia: from US$48 to 105 per capita in South Asia and from US$ 37 to 252 in East Asia.

Africa's tax revenue is still dominated by indirect compared to direct taxes. Although experiments with tax management reforms in many countries underscore the possibilities that remain unexplored at the national level, students of African political economy argue that the reluctance to develop direct revenue sources is a rational strategy of reducing the pressure on government for transparency and accountability from a tax-paying citizenry (Guyer, 1991; Moore, 1998).

Perhaps the most serious evidence of the performance crisis, however, is the growing realization that African governments are no longer responsible for developing and advocating policy initiatives of their own (Court et al., 1999). African public services thus fail on each of the three indicators that have been suggested for measuring the performance of any public sector organization. These are – policy capacity, implementation authority and operational efficiency (Polidano, 2000).

The crisis of internal management

Public administration systems in Africa are also in a serious disequilibrium. Some of the most serious symptoms of this state of affairs include absence of reliable information systems on staffing levels, sense of mission, or sense of performance or achievements over a period of time. Other administrative routines that are necessary for keeping the system going, like the system of monitoring and appraising the activities of personnel and units, rules relating to personnel management – hiring, training, deployment and separation, the civil service procedures, financial regulations, and code of conduct for public officers – have virtually collapsed. The result today is a service which in many countries has all the manifestations of bureaupathology: low competence levels, inconsistency in upholding standards of performance, absence of sound financial systems and practices, failure to exact accountability, ineffective organization systems, pay and compensation systems that do not reflect market realities, low morale and inertia among public officials etc. (Kiggundu, 1998; Olowu, 1995). It is no surprise that in this kind of setting corruption is rampant (Hope and Chikulo, 2000; Moody-Stewart, 1997).

This sense of public sector failure has instigated the search for alternative approaches for constituting/reforming these public service systems. In the next section, reform directions in each segment of the African public sector are evaluated.

REFORM DIRECTIONS

Reforms of public administration in Africa were initially very ambitious in terms of what could be done. A first generation of reform efforts in the late 1960s and early 1970s clearly aimed at making the public service a more effective instrument of development. More recently, the level of ambition has changed. It has focused more on cutting the service to size and simply allowing it to perform basic public services that cannot be delegated to private and voluntary institutions. I shall start by analyzing what has happened in the civil service, and then proceed to discuss the public enterprise sector, and finally local government.

Civil service reforms

In addition to making the public service an instrument of development, post-independence civil service reforms sought to indigenize the personnel of the civil services, replacing the colonial masters. Making the service more performance-oriented, however, turned out to be a challenge beyond what reform consultants and policy makers could achieve. These services remained wielded to the rule-oriented structures, a confession that comes from the African civil servants themselves (AAPAM, 1984).

An assumption of the administrative reforms of the 1960s and 1970s was that the public sector must provide leadership to other sectors in overall national development. Unfortunately, administrations generally and in particular in the African context could more easily protect the status quo than promote developmental change.

In contrast, civil service reforms from the 1980s focused on macro-economic stabilization goals (and hence key activities such as organizational restructuring and ministerial reviews, downsizing, pay reform and budgetary and financial management reforms) have been the recurring elements of the exercise. These post-1980 reforms came in two sequential streams.

With their preoccupation with quantitative rather than qualitative aspects of reform, it is not surprising that both streams have been successful at improving inputs and processes. In contrast, they have not been very successful with respect to outcomes and impact – improved services delivered to the people, higher customer/citizen satisfaction, ownership, accountability, transparency and good governance (Kiggundu, 1998).

Several reasons have been suggested for this outcome. One view, advanced by African governors of the World Bank is that these reforms only deal with one side of the problem (fiscal imbalance – leading to the emphasis on the downsizing elements of civil service reforms but scant attention to the more important challenge of building critical capacity for development) (World Bank, 1996). Since the Bank issued this report, it has articulated a renewed concern with capacity building and this led to the launching of a new initiative aimed at further strengthening the African Capacity Building Foundation (ACBF) based in Harare, Zimbabwe. Again, it has been noted that the problem may not just be with building capacity but with retaining scarce skills in view of the wide disparity in the wages paid to professionals by competing institutions, including international ones (Cohen and Wheeler, 1997). Some countries have resorted to building enclaves – which ensure that people with critical skills are paid higher salaries tied to their performance or given 'top-ups' in donor-financed projects (Wuyts, 1996). The problem is that this tends to dampen incentives to improve the overall quality of the civil service. At the same time, it is obvious that there are severe limits on the ability of many of these countries to increase salaries given the parlous state of their treasury. In one country, Tanzania, it is estimated that it would take 35 years to restore public service pay to the real level enjoyed by civil servants in the mid-1970s (Klitgaard, 1997).

A balance sheet of the achievements and failures of civil service reform in Africa in the post-1980 period would include the following key elements. First, on the positive side, additional information has become available on African civil services. Such information has led to improvements in the design of reform. The Uganda civil service reform is regarded as one of the best examples of second-generation reforms, because it has demonstrated that it is possible to do more than just ensure fiscal balance. Public services in that country have improved considerably also in terms of efficiency and effectiveness (Langseth, 1995; Olowu, 2001).

Second, the reforms have led to large reductions in the numbers in the civil and public services through a combination of measures – the busting of ghost workers, deletion of empty posts, enforcing of retirement ages guaranteed entry to the civil service from the education system, voluntary and compulsory retirement, frozen salaries, privatization and contracting out government services to other organs. Within 10 years, six countries in the region reduced their civil services by more than 10 per cent – the

Central African Republic, Guinea, Madagascar, Mali. Uganda took out 50,000 workers while Tanzania, which started much later, removed 65,000 workers from its payroll. Ghana identified 10,000 ghost or fictitious workers in its payroll. The idea was to produce a leaner civil service that would reduce the fiscal burden on the system as a whole. A third achievement of these reforms, at least in a macro-economic perspective, has been the lowering of nominal and real wages. Lienert (1998) estimates that the average wage bill for thirty-two African countries fell from 7 per cent to 6 per cent of GDP between 1986 and 1996. Schiavo-Campo (1998) also concurs that among the world's regions, only in Africa has there been so much reduction in the central government employment as well as in the wage bill as a proportion of the GDP.

Cost recovery, however, has sometimes been more fictitious than real. Central government departments are responsible for recruiting workers for other parts of the civil and public services. In some instances, the reductions in numbers, as in Uganda, Tanzania and Ethiopia, meant the re-allocation of these workers to the local government (Beyene, 1999; Mccourt, 1998). Moreover, the savings in numbers have not always led to reduction in cost – because of the nature of many African civil services. They are bloated at the junior levels but short-staffed at the professional and upper levels. Although too much effort seems to have been spent on the quantitative rather than the qualitative side of the public service, a few interesting qualitative improvements should be noted. One is the introduction of independent executive agencies based on experiences from countries like Denmark, Sweden and the United Kingdom. Another is the re-introduction of systems of personnel control and monitoring that had been lost. With the help of computerization, personnel management has become more effective. A third innovation is the introduction of autonomous revenue authorities. Countries that have adopted this model have witnessed considerable improvements in revenue collection (Adamolekun and Kiragu, 1999; Hubbard et al., 1999). Also worth mentioning here is the improvement in other public institutions on which the civil service depends, for example, the judiciary, local government, the legislature and the creation of anti-corruption organs (Olowu, 1999b).

In spite of this list of achievements of African civil service reforms in the past twenty or so years, it must be said that they have not adequately addressed two key issues: those of pay and incentives and capacity retention that results in substantial productivity improvements by the civil services in Africa. I have argued elsewhere that these two serious shortcomings are due to three closely related factors (Olowu, 1999a). First, the reforms are based on a wrong premise – that what matters is an affordable rather than a required civil service. By focusing on affordable service, fiscal issues dominate the reform process rather than the equally important concerns of governance capacity and improvement. A focus on the needs of democratic, developmental states, as articulated in the World Development Report of 1997, will lead countries to search for short-, medium- and longer-term solutions to resolving affordability of the civil service without making this the major preoccupation of reform.

Secondly, reforms have been based on a wrong diagnosis that African civil services are bloated – a fact that cannot be empirically established for the whole of the civil service. As already suggested above, the civil service is poorly structured: it has surpluses at the base and in the administrative cadres but is seriously short-staffed in the professional levels. It also tends to be highly concentrated in the central government and urban centers with lots of vacancies in local governments and rural areas, where they are most needed. The real problem, therefore, is not being oversized, but lacking the right incentives for better performance (Adedeji et al., 1995; United Nations, 1992).

Thirdly, the recipe of reducing numbers and cost is wrong-headed. African countries actually need to increase the civil service numbers and their costs – for the simple reason that highly skilled staff cost money. There might be savings through retrenchment but there cannot be net savings in cost and numbers (Lindauer and Numberg, 1994; McCourt, 1998). If the goal is to build stronger civil service systems that can assist the policy process, regulate and stimulate other organizational actors, and ensure the delivery of quality services to a discerning and demanding public, increased costs are inevitable.

In sum, inadequate attention to two critical factors of civil service decline – incentives and pay – has belied the huge efforts at civil service reform in the region. Even though impressive numbers of people have been taken out of the civil service, the expectation that this would lead to substantially improved pay for those left behind has proved illusive. Many observers have linked this failure to the increased incidence of petty and institutionalized corruption in civil services (Chew, 1990; Klitgaard, 1989, 1997; Yahaya, 1993). Perhaps, as Grishanker (1999) argues, the problem with these second-generation civil service reforms is that multiple objectives

that should have been kept separate have been conflated. The result is a situation in which many civil services are in worse shape today than they were at independence (Haque and Aziz, 1999; Olowu, 1999a).

Public enterprise reform

Public enterprises or parastatals are organizations that are dedicated to the promotion of entrepreneurship in the public sector. They combine 'publicness' (in terms of ownership, price setting and management) with 'business'. They are public in the sense that: (a) major decisions are made by non-private agencies on criteria that often transcend financial returns; (b) net returns accrue to the public, not private persons and in most instances the government owns the majority of equity capital; (c) the enterprise is accountable to the society. On the other hand, a public enterprise is expected to operate as any other private enterprise, subject to market discipline – take risks, search for innovations in factor and product markets, and charge prices relative to costs. Public enterprises in African countries came about for a variety of reasons. Some were inherited from the colonial powers, others were established on ideological grounds, yet others were seen as public investment outlets.

An IMF study showed that African countries had the highest share (32 per cent) of public enterprise investments as a proportion of gross capital formation in their countries – the figures for Latin American and Asian countries were 11 per cent and 22 per cent respectively (Short, 1984). Another study showed that in the 1980s, thirty African countries had a total of 3,000 such enterprises, the number ranging from a low of seven for Lesotho to a high of 400 for Tanzania. African public enterprises were dominant in the capital markets borrowing but not adding value to manufacturing or employment (Nellis, 1986).

Unfortunately, public enterprises in Africa have failed to live up to the high expectations their people or their leaders had of them. Wamalwa (1987), a former senior civil servant in Kenya, described them as 'bottomless pits gobbling up scarce national resources', saying 'many of them have been accused of being incapable of discharging these services'.

The problems that have faced public enterprises in Africa fall into two main categories: external and internal. Among the external problems are (a) unclear and contradictory objectives; (b) excessive political interference in operational decisions, and weak accountability structures; and (c) a poor macro-economic framework which discourages competition and the attainment of high levels of productivity – controls on prices, exchange mechanisms, imports, subsidies etc. The three internal problems are (a) the quality of the board members appointed by the government, their composition, tenure and size; (b) lack of personnel management, control and incentives; and (c) under-capitalization. Instead of attempting to resolve the constellation of internal and external problems, many countries imposed even more controls on their parastatals with the result that even the few that were performing well started to show declining performance (Grosh, 1991; UNECA, 1996).

Structural adjustment programs in the 1980s tried to tackle these problems. The most important instruments utilized in reforming them have included reform of the macro-economic framework, divestiture and financial rehabilitation, as well as reform of institutional and managerial framework. Generally, African countries have found it easier to liquidate poorly performing enterprises than to restructure them, even though effort has been made in this respect as well. In reality, many of these enterprises had actually stopped functioning before they were formally declared liquidated.

Privatization across African countries had proceeded quite far by 1999. Most of the privatizations occurred before 1995 and the impetus for privatization has generally tapered off since that time. Those countries that have gone the furthest in privatizing public enterprises tend to be those that also had the largest number of such institutions, for example, Tanzania, Mozambique and Angola. The fact that most of these were small operations means that value obtained from such sales was quite modest. Only in Tanzania, Zambia and Kenya were large value sales carried out.

Privatization has confronted a number of problems in Africa. These can be classified into political, economic and managerial. The political problems include the weak political constituency for reforms. In many cases, privatization meant selling off the family silver to foreigners. There has also been a fear that privatized firms would be sold to opponents of the regime, thus strengthening the hands of the opposition. In order to avert such prospects, countries like Ethiopia, for example, have sold public enterprises to the ruling party on the assumption that they will generate income.

The economic problems have revolved around the fact that privatization has most often not led to increased levels of efficiency or solved fiscal crises. First, severance benefits were often quite high and had to be paid by government before privatizations could go through. Second, in many

countries, with only a few buyers, public enterprises faced a buyers' market – most buyers are interested not in loss-making parastatals but only in profitable ones. Some countries have therefore had to 'fatten' their public enterprises before disposing of them, making them as attractive as possible to buyers. Buyers have received several favors – tax benefits, duty free imports, tariff protection, priority access to credit and other scarce inputs – which reduced social benefits. Prices of some enterprises were set so low that it became possible for some of the original buyers to resell with huge profits. Examples from Togo and Uganda are cases in point. The most serious challenge, however, has been to create conditions conducive to improved performance of the enterprises. The absence of a competitive environment and essential financial institutions such as a capital market – there are only sixteen in the whole of the continent – have been severe constraints.

Management problems have also adversely afflicted privatization. The latter requires high professional auditing and legal skills, which were often unavailable in African countries. The cost of hiring foreign consultants proved prohibitive in many instances. Moreover, the existing financial institutions are constrained by bad financial practices and a poor regulatory environment. This touches on a very important issue in the African context: the contention by some scholars that the private sector is not the paragon of efficiency that it should be: first, most are heavily dependent on a decadent public sector, and second, large private enterprises rarely operate within a competitive environment nor the small and medium ones within the framework of legality (Ariyo and Jerome, 1999; Ukaegbu, 2000). Unfortunately, most of the efforts at privatization reform have focused on public sector rather than private sector improvement. There is evidence from the Tanzanian case, which has been extensively reviewed, that where these problems are confronted through reforms of the banking system, state-owned enterprises, the civil service and the taxation system, remarkable changes can result not only for privatization but for the whole economy (Temu and Doe, 2000). Another management problem in a number of countries (Ghana, Nigeria, Guinea, Sierra Leone, and Zambia) is that the sale of public enterprises has not been transparent. This has led to allegations of corruption in several instances (Tangri, 1999).

Besides privatization, many countries have discovered that they must develop other approaches for managing the public enterprises that remain in the public sector. The most utilized alternative has been the management contract.

Unfortunately, the contract plan has not been particularly successful in many countries for a variety of reasons. These include lack of commitment by the two parties to the plan's requirements, absence of capital for restructuring the firm, absence of enforceable targets, incentives or sanctions for failure, especially given the weak financial audit regimes, information on fiscal transfers and productivity indices.

In spite of the extensive sales of public enterprises, some continue to operate. At least one study that compared successful and unsuccessful public enterprises concluded that the former tended to be 'free from government interference, accountable to government and subject to government sanctions and rewards, whereas the bad performers had the opposite characteristics' (Knight, 1994: 330). Most countries in Africa, however, have still to take this insight into account in improving the now much leaner public enterprise sector.

Local governance

Compared to all other regions and continents of the world, African countries are the least formally decentralized. This is the case whether we look at relative expenditure or employee size of local governments vis-à-vis the rest of the public sector (Schiavo-Campo, 1998; Steffensen and Trollegaard, 2000). Africa's formally centralized status is best understood within the framework of state decentralization. State formation in most countries required centralization of resources and responsibilities. Whereas this process took place ahead of the efforts at state dencentralization in many industrialized countries, in Africa and many other developing countries the twin processes are taking place concurrently. This, therefore, sets off contradictory impulses, which students of the subject have referred to as the 'rhetoric of decentralization and the reality of centralization' (Subramaniam, 1980) and or as 'the pendulum swing thesis', whereby a period of strong decentralization initiatives is followed by reversals and re-centralization (Mawhood 1983). The rationale for centralization was initially articulated in terms of the need for national integration, incipient democratization and prudent economic management. The earliest studies of corruption argued that corruption would be rife in local governments for two reasons: the limited bureaucratization and the face-to-face contacts between the governors and the governed (Wraith and Simpkins, 1963; Wunsch and Olowu, 1990).

Among development scholars and policy makers alike, the strong preference in the early days was for deconcentration if there was to be any decentralization in developing countries. Fred Riggs (1964), for example, argued that decentralization in developing countries only tended to aggravate poverty, an argument that has been taken up with a different emphasis recently by Prud'homme (1995). Contrary to general expectations at the time, centralized rule only aggravated the governance crisis in many countries (Wunsch and Olowu, 1990). While the reality of the historical forces pushing in the direction of centralization must be recognized, the real explanations for reluctance to decentralize lay in the absolute power enjoyed by political power holders and the threat that democratic decentralization could pose to this entrenched governance mode. In addition, there were problems concerning institutional design, alternative institutional options and the lack of information on local government systems.

Since the late 1980s, a constellation of internal and external influences have led many African countries to adopt a more democratic form of decentralization, indeed in many countries it is an attempt to restore a system of local governance which seems to have worked fairly well in the late colonial period (Steffensen and Trollergaard, 2000). It is also significant that many of these countries had existed in pre-colonial times as parts of extensive empires, for centuries using the principles of subsidiarity and local governance (Davidson, 1993; Coulibaly, 1999).

A number of countries in the continent, however, have continued with the old approaches to decentralization which exacerbate central control over all local activities for reasons – weak local capacity, fear of local level corruption, communal and ethnic insurrection – which seem sound and reasonable at first sight, but really are counter-productive to development.

We can summarize this sub-section by suggesting that by the end of the 1990s the picture with regard to local administration and governance had become quite varied. These countries could be classified along a continuum from conventional administrative decentralization (deconcentration) to various forms of political decentralization, including federalism. It is significant that the majority of countries have still been very cautious in taking decisive steps to decentralize authority. Table 40.1 gives an indication of the spread and the steps taken by various countries.

What has emerged from the analysis of decentralization reforms in Africa is that democratic decentralization is a long and often complicated process. It takes a considerable amount of time before the objective of local self-governance is realized. There are several reasons for this, but

Table 40.1   *Types of decentralization in Africa*

Type of decentralization	Country examples
Deconcentration with nominal devolution	Cameroon, Ghana, Kenya, Malawi, Zambia
Partial devolution (urban areas only)	Botswana, Mozambique, Namibia
Devolution	Cote d'Ivoire, Mali, Mauritius, Senegal, Tanzania, Uganda
Federalism	Ethiopia, Nigeria, South Africa

one of the most important considerations is the need to reconcile the motivating factors for devolution with the dilemmas with which the process is confronted in many countries. These dilemmas are political, economic and managerial.

The political ones include the unwillingness of political and administrative officials to share the power that they inherited from the colonial powers. There is a tendency to view devolution of authority to local levels as a zero-sum game in which local actors gain at the expense of the center instead of a positive-sum game in which all players, national and local, stand to win. Another problem with devolution is that power tends to be captured by local elites at the expense of the broader masses. This power is often used to strengthen local patronage and, in some instances, to discriminate against local minorities. In spite of these hurdles, countries like Ethiopia, Nigeria and Uganda have developed elaborate systems of fiscal transfers, which ensure that substantial national resources are made available to cash-starved local organs (Smoke, 1999).

On the economic side, the dilemmas include the possibility that a more democratic form of decentralization compromises economic stabilization and distribution goals (Litvack et al., 1998; Smoke, 1999). Another issue is the cost of decentralization. It is typically not done as a cost-saving measure, but in situations where the public budget is tight, the room for devolutionary forms of governance is not necessarily there.

The managerial dilemmas start with the challenge of what constitutes a proper institutional design for democratic local governance. Should institutions be the same all over the country or should they be allowed to vary according to specific criteria (Steffensen and Trollergaard, 2000)? How much should central oversight be developed as compared to local accountability? Various authors, for example, Haque (1997) and Olowu (1997), have pointed to the fact that central officials often abuse their right to audit local governments.

CONCLUSION

The continent's public administration systems have functioned under the shadow of the colonial model of the state since their development in the early parts of the twentieth century. The colonial state was a state of conquest. Hence, public policies were externally imposed, the bureaucracy was not only elitist but also authoritarian with minimal participation of the public or their opinion in governance. Most Africans knew the colonial state as an instrument of repression. Protective care was available only for the wealthy and influential (Mamdani, 1996). The post-colonial state was meant to be different, but forty years of experience shows that it has really failed in that sense. The state continued to dominate the polity and economy from above also after independence. All that happened in the first two decades of independence was that civilian and military elites, sometimes using the instrumentality of the political party, tried to perpetuate the system of control established in colonial days (Potter, 2000). This meant, as this chapter has tried to argue, that public administration was often humiliated by being subordinated to ad hoc and often flimsy political considerations that had the effect of undermining the role that senior civil servants could play in policy formulation and implementation.

Forces of globalization, democratization and economic liberalization have changed the political and economic parameters of African development in the past two decades, but it is not clear that the state, and by implication, therefore, public administration, has kept pace with the new challenges. To be sure, the civil service has been cut to size, some public enterprises have been sold, and steps toward local governance may have been taken, yet, much of the same culture that inhibited reform in earlier days still prevails. Politicians want to dominate in a zero-sum fashion. Professionals are being confined to enclaves, often kept breathing by their access to professional colleagues in the international development community, the very people that many African leaders are ready to accuse of interfering in their affairs. There is so much that well-intentioned professionals, both Africans and expatriates, would like to do – and many have tried for decades – but what they may experience as success in the short term rarely becomes viable in the long run. It is for this reason that it must be concluded that public administration in Africa will not be reformed in an effective manner as long as politics remains based on patronage and is allowed to dominate public affairs at the expense of other spheres. State–society relations continue to be in need of reformation along structural, managerial and ethical lines.

Looking ahead, it is clear that mainstream efforts at reforming the public service, such as better monetary incentives and new personnel management approaches, will make little, if any difference in the African context. The measures that are needed imply the creation of public institutions that are as much as possible protected from the influence of patronage politics. This type of reform is more far-reaching and therefore potentially more controversial, but it is hard to see any other way forward. International agencies can continue to play a useful role in strengthening public management in Africa provided they are ready to explore this avenue and support the re-professionalization of the public service (Koehn and Ojo, 1999).

REFERENCES

AAPAM (African Association of Public Administration and Management) (1984) *African Public Services: Challenges and a Profile for the Future*. New Delhi: Vikas Publishing House.

Adamolekun, L. and Kiragu, K. (1999) 'Public Administration Reforms', in L. Adamolekun (ed.), *Public Administration in Africa: Main Issues and Selected Country Studies*. Boulder, CO: Westview Press. pp. 159–76.

Adedeji, A., Green, R. and Janha, A. (1995) *Pay, Productivity and Public Service: Priorities for Recovery in SubSaharan Africa*. New York: UNICEF and UNDP.

Ariyo, A. and Jerome, A. (1999) 'Privatization in Africa: An Appraisal', *World Development*, 27 (1): 201–13.

Beyene, A. (1999) 'Ethiopia', in L. Adamolekun (ed.), *Public Administration in Africa*. Boulder, CO: Westview Press. pp. 227–49.

Chew, D. (1990) 'Internal Adjustments to Falling Civil Service Salaries: Insights from Uganda', *World Development Report*, 28: 1003–14.

Cohen, J.M. and Wheeler, J.R. (1997) 'Building Sustainable Professional Capacity in African Public Sectors: Retention Constraints in Kenya', *Public Administration and Development*, 17: 307–24.

Coulibaly, B. (1999) 'The African State in Transition'. Unpublished typescript, Leiden University.

Court, J., Kristen, P. and Weder, B. (1999) *Bureaucratic Structure and Performance: First Africa Survey Results*. Tokyo: United Nations University.

Davidson, B. (1993) *Blackman's Burden: Africa and the Curse of the Nation-State*. Oxford: James Currey.

Dia, M. (1996) *Africa's Management in the 1990s and Beyond*. Washington, DC: The World Bank.

Doe, L. (1998) 'Civil Service Reform in the Countries of the West African Monetary Union', *International Social Science Journal*, 155: 125–44.

Ekeh, P. (1975) 'Colonialism and the Two Publics in Africa: A Theoretical Statement', *Comparative Studies in Society and History*, 17 (1): 91–112.

Grishanker, R. (1999) 'Civil Service Reform: A Review of World Bank Assistance', in Peter de Haan (ed.), *Reader Workshop Reform*. The Hague: Ministry of Foreign Affairs and Development Cooperation.

Grosh, B. (1991) 'Kenya: A Positive Politics of Parastatals Performance', in B. Grosh and R.S. Mukandala (eds), *State-Owned Parastatals in Africa*. Boulder, CO: Lynne Rienner. pp. 45–62.

Guyer, J.I. (1991) 'Representation without Taxation: An Essay on Democracy in Rural Nigeria, 1952–1990'. Working Papers in African Studies No. 152. Boston, MA: African Studies Center, University of Boston.

Haque, S. (1997) 'Local Governance in Developing Nations: Re-Examining the Question of Accountability', *Regional Development Dialogue*, 18 (2): iii–xvi.

Haque, N. and Aziz, J. (1999) 'The Quality of Governance: "Second Generation" Civil Service Reforms in Africa', *Journal of African Economies*, 8: 68–106.

Hope, K.R. and Chikulo, B.C. (eds) (2000) *Corruption and Development in Africa: Lessons from Country Case Studies*. London: Macmillan. pp. 17–39.

Hubbard, M., Delay, S. and Devas, N. (1999) 'Complex Management Contracts: The Case of Customs Administration in Mozambique', *Public Administration and Development*, 19: 153–63.

Hyden, G. and Bratton, M. (1992) *Governance in Africa*. Boulder, CO: Lynne Rienner.

Hyden, G., Olowu, D. and Okoth-Ogendo, H.W.O. (eds) (2000) *African Perspectives on Governance*. Trenton, NJ: Africa World Press.

Joseph, Richard (1999) *State, Conflict and Democracy in Africa*. Boulder, CO: Lynne Rienner.

Kiggundu, M. (1998) 'Civil Service Reforms: Limping into the 21st Century', in M. Minogue, C. Polidano and D. Hulme (eds), *Beyond the New Public Management: Changing Ideas and Practices in Governance*. Cheltenham: Elgar. pp. 155–71.

Klitgaard, R. (1989) 'Incentive Myopia', *World Development*, 27 (4): 447–59.

Klitgaard, R. (1997) 'Cleaning Up and Invigorating the Civil Service', *Public Administration and Development*, 17: 487–509.

Knight, J.B. (1994) 'Public Enterprises and Industrialization in Africa', in F. Stewart, S. Lall and S. Wangwe (eds), *Alternative Development Strategies in Sub-Saharan Africa*. London: Macmillan. pp. 321–35.

Koehn, P. and Ojo, O.J.B. (eds) (1999) *Making Aid Work: Innovative Approaches for Africa at the Turn of the Century*. Lanham, MD and Oxford: University Press of America.

Langseth, P. (1995) *Civil Service Reform in Uganda*. Working Paper No. 95–05. Washington, DC: EDI.

Lienert, I. (1998) 'Civil Service Reform in Africa: Mixed Results After 10 Years', *Finance and Development*, 35 (2): 1–7.

Lindauer, D. and Numberg, B. (eds) (1994) *Rehabilitating Government: Pay and Employment Reform in Africa*. Washington, DC: The World Bank.

Litvack, J., Ahmad, J. and Bird, R. (1998) *Rethinking Decentralization in Developing Countries*. Washington, DC: World Bank Sector Study Series.

Mamdani, M. (1996) *Citizen and Subject: Contemporary Africa and Legacy of Late Colonialism*. Princeton, NJ: Princeton University Press.

Mawhood, P. (1983) *Local Government in the Tropics: The Experience of Tropical Africa*. Chichester: John Wiley.

McCourt, W. (1998) 'Civil Service Reform Equals Retrenchment? The Experience of "Rightsizing" and Retrenchment in Ghana, Uganda and the UK', in M. Minogue et al. (eds), *Beyond the New Public Management*. Cheltenham: Edward Elgar. pp. 172–87.

Moody-Stuart, G. (1997) *Grand Corruption: How Business Bribes Damage Developing Countries*. Oxford: World View Publishing.

Moore, M. (1998) 'Death Without Taxes: Democracy, State Capacity and Aid Dependence in the Fourth World', in M. Robinson and G. White (eds), *The Democratic Developmental State: Politics and Institutional Design*. Oxford: Oxford University Press.

Nellis, R. (1986) *Public Enterprises in Sub-Saharan Africa*. Washington, DC: World Bank Discussion Papers.

Olowu, D. (1995) 'The Challenge of Productivity Improvement', in S. Rasheed and D. Luke (eds), *Development Management in Africa*. Boulder, CO: Westview Press. pp. 45–54.

Olowu, D. (1997) 'Comment', in *Regional Development Dialogue*, 18 (2): 107–18.

Olowu, D. (1999a) 'Redesigning African Civil Service Reforms', *Journal of Modern African Studies*, 37 (1): 1–23.

Olowu, D. (1999b) 'Combatting Corruption and Economic Crime in Africa: An Evaluation of the Botswana Directorate of Corruption and Economic Crime', *International Journal of Public Sector Management*, 12 (7): 604–13.

Olowu, D. (2001) 'Pride and Performance in African Public Services: Analysis of Institutional Breakdown and Rebuilding Efforts in Nigeria and Uganda', *International Review of Administrative Sciences*, 67 (1): 117–34.

Olowu, D. and Erero, E.J. (eds) (1996) *Indigenous Governance Systems in Nigeria*. Local Institutions for Sustainable Development, Ile-Ife: Obafemi Awolowo University Press.

Osborne, D. and Gaebler, R. (1993) *Reinventing Government*. Reading, MA: Addison–Wesley.

Pereira, L. and Spink, P. (eds) (1997) *Reforming the State: Managerial Public Administration in Latin America*. Boulder, CO: Lynne Rienner.

Polidano, C. (2000) 'Measuring Public Sector Capacity', *World Development*, 28 (5): 805–22.

Potter, D. (2000) 'The Power of Colonial States', in T. Allen and A. Thomas (eds), *Poverty and Development into the 20th Century*. Oxford: Oxford University Press. pp. 271–88.

Premchand, A. (1999) 'Public–Private Partnerships: Implications for Public Expenditure Management', in M. Mackintosh and R. Roy (eds), *Economic Decentralization and Public Management Reform*. Cheltenham: Edward Elgar. pp. 48–77.

Prud'homme, R. (1995) 'The Dangers of Decentralization', *World Bank Research Observer*, 2 (10): 201–10.

Riggs, F. (1964) *Administration in Developing Countries: The Theory of Prismatic Society*. Boston, MA: Houghton Mifflin.

Schiavo-Campo, S. (1998) 'Government Employment and Pay: The Global and Regional Evidence', *Public Administration and Development*, 18 (5): 457–78.

Short, R.P. (1984) 'The Role of Public Enterprises: An International Statistical Comparison', in R.H. Floyd et al. (eds), *Public Enterprises in Mixed Economies: Some Macroeconomic Aspects*. Washington, DC: International Monetary Fund.

Smoke, P. (1999) *'Fiscal Decentralization in Developing Countries: A Review of Current Concepts and Practice*. Geneva: United Nations Research Institute for Social Development.

Subramaniam, V. (1980) 'Developing Countries', in D.C. Rowat (ed.) *International Handbook of Local Government Reorganization*. Westport CT: Greenwood Press. pp. 582–93.

Steffensen, J. and Trollegaard, S. (2000) *Fiscal Decentralization and Sub-National Government Finance in Relation to Infrastructure and Service Provision*. Synthesis Report of 6 Sub-Saharan African Country Studies, Washington, DC: The World Bank.

Tangri, R. (1999) *The Politics of Patronage in Africa: Parastatals, Privatization and Private Enterprise*. Oxford: James Currey.

Temu, A.E. and Doe, J.M. (2000) 'The Business Environment in Tanzania after Socialism: Challenges of Reforming Banks, Parastatals, Taxation and the Civil Service', *Journal of Modern African Studies*, 38 (4): 683–712.

Ukaegbu, C.C. (2000) 'Working Conditions and Employee Commitment in Indigenous Private Manufacturing Firms in Nigeria: Managing Business Organizations for Industrial Development', *Journal of Modern African Studies*, 38 (2): 295–324.

UNECA (United Nations Economic Commission for Africa) (1996) 'Enhancing Accountability in the Management of Public Enterprises in Africa'. ECA/PHSD/PAM/96/6 (3b). Addis Ababa: UNECA.

United Nations (1992) *Size and Cost of the Civil Service: Reform Programmes in Africa*. New York: Department of Economic and Social Development.

Wamalwa, W.N. (1987) 'Managerial Autonomy and Accountability in Public Enterprises', in African Association for Public Administration and Management (ed.), *Public Enterprises Performance and the Privatization Debate: A Review of the Options for*

Africa. New Delhi: Vikas Publishing House. pp. 112–27.

World Bank (1996) *Partnership for Capacity Building in Africa: Strategy and Programme of Action.* Report of African Governors. Washington, DC: World Bank.

World Bank (1997) *World Development Report 1997.* New York: Oxford University Press.

World Bank (2000) *Can Africa Claim the 21st Century?* Washington, DC: World Bank.

Wunsch, J.S. and Olowu, D. (eds) (1990) *The Failure of the Centralized State: Institutions and Self-Governance in Africa.* Boulder, CO: Westview Press.

Wraith, R.E. and Simpkins, E. (1963) *Corruption in Developing Countries.* London: Allen & Unwin.

Wuyts, M. (1996) 'Foreign Aid, Structural Adjustment and Public Management'. ISS Working Paper Series No. 206.

Yahaya, A.D. (1993) 'The Economic Crisis, Resource Scarcities and the Decline in Ethical Standards in Public Agencies', in S. Rasheed and D. Olowu (eds), *Ethics and Accountability in African Public Services.* Addis Ababa: UNECA. pp. 63–74.

41

Challenges of Culture and Governance in Asian Public Administration

O.P. Dwivedi

Mapping the history of public administration of a vast region such as Asia is indeed an enormous task, especially since the region consists of nations that demonstrate significant racial, ethnic, cultural and political differences. Such a diverse group defies generalizations but some common features are nonetheless identified in this chapter. In order to provide a little more specificity and as a way of providing examples from countries that are especially important in Asia, I have chosen to focus my attention primarily on China, India and Pakistan. The first part of this chapter deals with the historical legacy, since it is my belief that it is important for understanding contemporary public administration systems in the region. Drawing on that introductory section, I proceed to discuss administrative culture and style of governance before analyzing the impact of Western ideas of public administration that for the past fifty years have been significant in shaping approaches to reforming and improving the administration of public services.

THE HISTORICAL LEGACY

The case of China

China has the world's oldest and most continuous administrative system. E.N. Gladden (1972) traces Chinese public administration back to the Qin dynasty (221–206 BC), while the introduction of competitive merit examinations in order to qualify for bureaucratic positions started during the Han dynasty (206 BC – 220 AD). According to Harris (1989: 228), these exams became the standard form of recruitment from

165 BC. Heady (1984) calls the bureaucratic system the most sustaining element of Chinese civilization. The traditional Chinese bureaucracy consisted of an educated and highly motivated elite of scholar–administrators, with the imperial mandarinate acting as the steel frame of the whole administrative system. Governance was highly centralized and hierarchical, with provinces being answerable to the central authority while, within provinces, administration was stratified into prefectures, districts and numerous functional areas.

Although the practice of recruiting mandarins came to an official end in 1904, and there had been other changes in the ways the Chinese emperors had administered their country, the most important point to make here is that there has been a remarkable continuity in the way the Chinese have looked upon the role of public officials. The culture of China encompassed many diverse and competing philosophies, including Taoism, Buddhism, Legalism and a whole lot of other 'little traditions'. Transcending all these philosophies has been Confucianism. As Shenkar and Ronen (1987) note, it is the foundation of Chinese culture, and Confucian values continue to provide the basis for the norms of Chinese inter-personal behavior. The Confucian tradition has a concern for the correct and well-mannered conduct of one's duties, based on sound respect for the social conventions of a patrimonial system. It stresses order, hierarchy, quality of relationships and obligation to social collectivities (Smith, 1974; Lockett, 1988). Education is very important because it is seen to give individuals all the virtues of life, thus allowing them to literally stand above the law. The latter, in Chinese tradition, is reserved only for the uneducated masses.

In this kind of culture, it is not surprising that the mandarins or their successors as public servants tended to see themselves as akin to Plato's philosopher-kings. They were privileged, remained aloof and deliberately created a mystique surrounding their role. Ordinary people were fearful in approaching them. As long as they loyally served the regime's policies and programs, they could continue enjoying their privileged status. The idea of being politically neutral in the Weberian sense never arose in the Chinese tradition of rule.

The Communist revolution that brought Mao Zedong and his comrades to power in 1949 brought about a major change at the top political level. The old feudalist and the budding bourgeois systems of organizing the economy were replaced with a socialist system that annihilated private property and placed all commercial and productive operations under state control. The role of the state expanded tremendously during this period. In effect, with the exception of farmers, practically every salaried working Chinese adult became a state employee (Kwong, 1997: 9). In spite of this significant change in both economy and polity, the system of administering the country remained remarkably similar to the earlier imperial days. It kept being organized hierarchically in the same way into provinces, prefectures and counties, the principal difference being that the Communist Party was organized in a parallel fashion to exercise oversight and control. The same applied to the public enterprise sector, where each medium-size and larger organizational unit also contained a party branch (Laaksonen, 1988: 31). The Cultural Revolution in the late 1960s and early 1970s temporarily disrupted the operations of this system by accusing managers and bureaucrats of being 'enemies of the revolution'. Nonetheless, it was eventually restored and did not change until the 1980s after a policy of market reform had been adopted by the government in Beijing. The Chinese version of 'market socialism' had gradually given more autonomy to administrative and managerial organs in the state. For example, party, government and enterprises have been formally separated in order to make the economic system work more efficiently, and allowing economic managers to become more capable of achieving stated targets of performance.

The case of South Asia

Public administration in South Asia does not have the same long tradition as in China, although the indigenous rulers, notably the Moguls, had their own system of administering the affairs of their societies. Nonetheless, none of them laid the same stable foundation of rule as did the emperors of China. The historical legacy in South Asia, therefore, tends to be primarily associated with the colonial era. The British colonial masters were the architects of the system that was inherited by the Indians at the time of independence in 1947. India, like the other countries in the region that had been under British colonial rule, inherited a monolithic, highly stratified and strictly hierarchical administrative system. The line of command ran unimpeded from the Viceroy and Governor-General in New Delhi, the capital, to the farthest village head. Created during the time of Warren Hastings and Lord Cornwallis, it had four distinguishing features: (a) the district serving as the basic unit of administration, with the District Collector or Deputy Commissioner acting as the alter-ego of the vice-regal authority, controlling, directing, and coordinating all administrative activity in his district; (b) authority being centralized both territorially and functionally in virtually all policy areas; (c) the civil service being unified, with the Indian Civil Service (ICS) occupying the top policy and management positions by virtue of its elite status; and (d) a system of elaborate rules and regulations designed by the British to enable them to control their vast number of Indian subjects, dispersed far away from the administrative capitals of the central and provincial governments. This system had served the colonial objectives of control and law-and-order very well.

At the time of independence, a politically divided India faced overnight the movement of millions of refugees across what was to become the border between India and Pakistan. This exodus of Muslims to Pakistan and Hindus to India, perhaps the largest ever in history, created great problems of relief and rehabilitation in societies already plagued by poverty, disasters, inflation and food shortages. These problems put the inherited and emergent political and administrative structures to severe test (Dwivedi et al., 1989). In spite of these strains, political leaders successfully managed the transition to parliamentary democracy and an economic system devoted not only to growth but also to promoting the social welfare of the citizens and industrializing with a view to solving the problems of poverty, unemployment and want. In the social field, the government committed itself to changing the caste-ridden stratified society into a progressive community oriented toward social justice. Finally, there was also a determination to have modern science and technology light up the lives of the many conservative rural people. In order to fulfill these ambitious independence goals, the new government in South Asian countries adopted the Five-Year Plan as the major instrument of economic and social policy.

The adoption of planned economic development inevitably led to an increase in the size of the bureaucracy. The planning system placed heavier responsibilities on the district as the traditional unit of administration. However, the British-devised administrative system could not carry on, and eventually suffered from (a) the rigid adherence to, and inflexible dependence upon rules; (b) a focus on top-down decision making with a lack of delegation of authority and a generalized rigidity that prevented the organization from adapting readily to the changing demands placed upon it; and (c) the structuring of human reactions in rigid hierarchical terms, a tendency encouraged by the caste system and by the tradition of deference toward authority (Taub, 1969). It was no surprise that in a few years' time, the administrative system adopted 'ad hocism', resulting in low levels of efficiency, integrity and public trust.

The political leaders of the South Asian nations tried to govern too much, as compared to the British who governed too little and did not concern themselves enough with changes in the social and economic order. Perhaps it was inevitable, mainly because the political leaders were in a great hurry to reach a level of development akin to the West. Nevertheless, this seeming haste had a negative influence on the administrative process, especially its efficiency, effectiveness and standard of conduct. South Asian governments became more intensively involved in regulating, planning, stimulating and placing under direct government control many economic, commercial and banking activities, thereby stifling market forces. Over time, citizens also became overly dependent upon the initiative and the bestowal of governmental largesse in all spheres of their lives.

ADMINISTRATIVE CULTURE

The case of China

China is a very interesting case study of the contradictions inherent in modernization. While it has allowed for significant reforms in the direction of a market economy, it has retained its centralized political system. The Chinese have so far considered this a great advantage because it has allowed them to retain political stability while at the same time enjoying one of the fastest levels of economic growth in the world. The ordinary Chinese are increasingly aware of this contradiction between economic liberalization and autocratic rule. The events on Tianamen Square in 1989 were obviously a shock to the Chinese leaders, who since then have become increasingly cautious when it comes to loosening the political reins. In all this, the continued presence of Confucian values in Chinese society is likely to have a dampening effect on how the public will respond to the growing gap between economic and political liberties. These values call for submission to authority and a belief that governance and administration can be improved, not by checks and balances, but by raising the level of individual devotion to the virtues of life. Thus, Communist leaders believe that there is an indigenous Chinese way of coping with corruption and other forms of maladministration. Westernization of how the system of governance and administration works is seen not only as a threat to stability but also as being foreign to how the Chinese interact with each other.

Although the system of managing enterprises in China is increasingly being influenced by Western ideas because so many of them are now joint enterprises or wholly owned by foreigners, the system of public administration remains relatively intact. Child (1994), for example, notes that Chinese managers tend to take initiatives of their own only when they know that they believe their political superiors support them. They do not wish to take any risks. This is even more salient in the bureaucracy where red tape continues to be notorious. Chinese organizations, especially in the public sector, face major problems of collaboration and communication of a horizontal kind between different departments. Identities and loyalties are vertical in direction, and reflect the high respect that Chinese people have for their hierarchies. This problem is often further exacerbated by a group orientation, that is, an inclination to shed individual responsibility in favor of the group. Losing face because of having made a mistake is disastrous in the perspective of most Chinese. 'Face' is essentially the recognition by others of a person's social standing and position. There are two Chinese concepts of face – *lien* and *mianzi*. Whereas the latter stands for prestige and personal success, the former refers to the confidence others have in the moral character of a person. Losing *lien* can literally incapacitate a person as a member of his or her community. Any form of idiosyncratic behavior carries the risk of losing face and is more or less culturally inhibited in China. This idea of preserving face is linked to a strong sense of group identity. Conflicts within a group must remain private; if publicized, the whole group is demeaned (Bond and Hwang, 1986).

The culture that prevails in public organizations in China today does little to encourage innovation and what Schumpeter called learning from 'disequilibrium' situations, that is, when things are not in balance. China provides a favorable context for the social acceptance of a paternalistic public bureaucracy. Both the culture and the political system emphasize unified leadership and authority, mutual dependence, moral incentives and conformity of thought. These characteristics sharply contrast with the pluralism of ownership, competition, individualist entrepreneurship, economic incentives and innovation, which have generally been associated with Western modernization. Compared to most other modernizing countries in the world, China has remained remarkably true to its own cultural and historical origins. That is why external reforms have been difficult to introduce in the public sector and why the bureaucracy remains paternalist and often discretionary in its relations with the public.

The case of South Asia

The case of South Asia differs sharply from the experiences in China in the past fifty years. While the political transition in the early days of independence was quite smooth, cracks began to show up in the 1950s. A new generation of politicians emerged for whom the old liberal democratic traditions and morality were a mere hindrance, which could be sacrificed for political expediency, status and private gain. What Pakistan faced with respect to a weakening of democratic governance and effective administration in the 1950s and 1960s, India did in the 1970s and 1980s (Islam, 1989). The emergence of this new breed of politicians brought in its wake an erosion of many of the fundamental values of the governing system that had been consolidated during the earlier years of independence. Furthermore, political interference, influence peddling and muscle-flexing unions of government employees made even the most legitimate means of accountability meaningless in the administrative parlance (Dwivedi and Jain, 1988).

With this kind of politicization, the fundamental canons of a reliable and effective administration were undermined. For example, politicians would be found acting as brokers between business and commercial interests, on the one hand, and government, on the other; the interpretation and enforcement of laws was politicized; interference in normal personnel administration to secure the appointments of friends and supporters, or the promotion of local civil servants, became commonplace; the sale of government property and the issuing of contracts and licenses came under political sway; political intervention became evident in the purchase of machinery, equipment and services for government departments; official and confidential information was misused by politicians for private gain; and extra-constitutional and legal authority was placed in the hands of favored individuals who did not hold elected positions. Naturally, this type of environment influenced the conduct and attitudes of public servants who, by and large, saw the benefit of accommodating themselves to the prevailing winds.

The elite cadre in India, Pakistan and Sri Lanka tried to maintain its dominant position in policy making and governance, but its power and prestige was constantly undermined by the measures mentioned above. The result has been that the public service ethics has declined to the point where practically all aspects of public life appear to be engulfed in unethical activities. Officials, like politicians, have acquired dual personalities; their private actions ill match their public pronouncements. A parallel 'black administration' has emerged in which influence, favors, money, privileges, misuse of public funds, falsification of records, the bending of rules and regulations prevail (Dwivedi, 1989: 249).

This insidious subculture does not encourage citizens to even attempt seeking what is legally due to them. Instead of facing the ordeal themselves, those who can afford to do so hire the services of 'agents' who are ready to pay the 'fee' for whatever service is being requested. This has become very common at the lower echelons where citizens interact with bureaucrats.

In spite of the prevalence of these malpractices, there are public servants in South Asia who refuse to be corrupted. This core of exceptionally hard-working and dedicated individuals in the bureaucracy, however, is outnumbered and has a very tough task to get anything done. This contributes to eating away the public trust in effective governance. Convinced that the political and administrative system seems to be beyond improvement, most people have become too tired to even ask questions. Reform of the public services in the South Asian nations seems to be a monumental challenge.

THE IMPACT OF WESTERN IDEAS

I have already suggested above that the public administration system in China has remained remarkably stable over time, anchored as it is in Confucian ethics. No such philosophy has been at work in South Asia, where instead these systems have been treated as major laboratories for testing fashionable ideas about how to improve the quality and efficiency of public services. This section, therefore, will focus exclusively on the experiences of South Asia, although these may also apply in varying degrees to other countries in Asia that have allowed Western management ideas to guide their reform efforts in recent years.

The first wave of Western management ideas coincided with the launching of the development administration movement in the late 1950s and early 1960s. The premise was that public administration systems had to be reformed in order to deal with the government's new development efforts. The idea was not only that the bureaucracy in developing societies had to be modernized, but it also had to be made more attuned to change. For instance, in India development administration became closely associated with the objectives of community development. As Schaffer (1969) has observed, no one took notice of the contradictions inherent in having a government department conduct what was essentially meant to be a 'bottom-up' effort by the local communities themselves. The attempt, therefore, to boost ambitious development objectives set by the first generation of nationalist leaders through administrative reform ideas brought in from the West became a dismal failure. This happened not only in India but elsewhere in Asia and in Africa where the same movement pushed for these ideas (Dwivedi and Nef, 1982).

More recently, South Asia has been bombarded by the ideas associated with what is called the New Public Management movement. It is an outgrowth of the same effort that has brought to the global economy the need for economic reform, typically called 'Structural Adjustment'. The latter reflects a sense of inadequacy felt with the Keynesian economics that had dominated the international development community in the 1960s and 1970s. It places emphasis on results, greater attention to cost and the use of private sector approaches to motivate employees (Dwivedi and Gow, 1999: 130).

This paradigm is based on the premise that by reducing the opportunities for incompetence and corruption through narrowing down the scope of government activities, efficient, transparent, effective and accountable governance would

come into place. The rationale appears to be that with less bureaucratic structure there would be fewer bureaucratic problems. Once more, a heavy emphasis is being placed on the objective criteria of responsibility and accountability with a blind faith in structures, processes and procedures but with total disregard for the moral (or subjective) dimension. Asian nations as well as other developing nations are being urged to have market-friendly governance and administration. And since administration is posited more as a problem than a solution, New Public Management in the garb of 'development management' is recommended as a cure-all medicine. International aid is being made conditional upon accepting this prescription. It includes shrinkage of the bureaucracy, the elimination of subsidies and protectionism, the acceptance of currency devaluation, and other changes in monetary and fiscal policy (Dwivedi, 1994).

There is no doubt that the emphasis on result-based management is of value, but there is a danger of neglecting political as well as legal dimensions and other subjective criteria of responsibility which come under the umbrella of moral values. At the same time, faced with the complexities of day-to-day administration and the conflicting values that the system has thrust upon them, the administrators need some fundamental reference point to which they may turn in case of doubt. In this respect public managers differ from private ones. While the latter may regard the law as a constraint, something they must obey, the public manager must also uphold it. To be sure, New Public Management proponents usually say that they are aware that the state is not a business, and that the classic values of accountability and respect for the law tend to be eclipsed by it. In practice, however, very few public servants actually believe that government should be thought of as a corporation. Finally, 'the greatest charge against managerialism is its reductionism and its lack of imagination. It tries to reduce a complex phenomenon to a single model drawn from business' (Dwivedi and Gow, 1999: 178).

The problem with these reform ideas is that they do not really speak to the practical problems on the ground in South Asian bureaucracies. They overlook the importance of fitting management ideas into a cultural context where they can be understood and acted upon by administrators and the public alike. The result is that the problems facing public administration systems in South Asia are on the increase. Few of them are being effectively tackled, let alone solved. It is important, therefore, to look at what the challenges are for public administration in the Asian region.

REMAINING CHALLENGES

I shall now turn to a discussion that is more generally about the Asian region as a whole. I am the first to admit that problems vary from country to country. They also vary in degree. Yet, there are at least two that are common to virtually all countries, namely corruption and governance. I shall briefly discuss each in turn.

Corruption

Although the leaders of most newly independent nations in Africa and Asia started off with very high standards of probity and accountability, their successors have ended up deep in the cesspool of corruption. This is not to suggest that corruption is confined to these new nations. They exist in most places. The difference between corruption in industrialized nations and the developing world is that in the former, a high public office does not sanctify the misdeeds of the office-holder as is often the case in the latter.

The three major causes of corruption are: (a) delay in government decisions, (b) concentration of regulatory and discretionary power in the hands of a few government officials and (c) cumbersome procedures in dealing with public needs. We already know that where there is a concentration of power and discretion there is always the possibility of abuse. This becomes accentuated in the context of scarcity of resources, with a high demand exceeding services, and control and pressure to spend public money. I shall now look more closely at the situation in China, India and Pakistan.

The case of China

In Chinese society corruption has always been practised but also condemned. The moral argument has been persuasive, especially when the political forces have enforced it. Thus, in the 1970s when China opened its doors to outsiders, visitors found 'a utopia' where a safe and honest society appeared to exist. They offered a euphoric evaluation of a clean, efficient and transparent system. There is no doubt that, in general, socialist values are more puritanical than capitalist ones. By the end of the 1980s, however, when a market element was introduced into socialism, a contrasting account began to appear. With the monopoly of power at both the national and grass-roots levels, state ownership of property, and central planning, the opportunity

for corruption increased in the following four-fold manner (Kwong, 1997: 54):

1 An absolute dependence on the higher authority for funds encouraging lower level managers to inflate their needs in order to obtain more resources.
2 Strong pressure from the top to conform inducing state and lower echelons to falsify reports on their productivity to please superiors.
3 With supervisors having absolute control over resources, subordinates being ready to use bribes to receive resources for their own benefits.
4 The public's dependence on these officials discouraging them from reporting illegal activities, thus enhancing the anonymity of corrupt officials.

Monopoly of power and efforts to exact conformity would result in exaggerated reporting on production or task performed because the negative consequences of non-conformity were too high while the payoffs from meeting results were great. Kwong, for example, reports that between 1972 and 1979, the Guocai Furnace Company won several prizes for using less steel, less coke and less electricity when in reality it was using twice the national norm of steel, and its heating capacity was 14 per cent less than reported (Kwong, 1997: 56). In a restrictive environment, inflated output reports are made by lower echelons in order to make a good impression on their superiors, or to receive some tangible benefits. As happened in the former Soviet Union, various administrative units in many ministries tried to minimize their accountability and maximize their resources.

There is no doubt that until the 1970s, government took severe measures to punish all those found guilty of corrupt practices; such swift actions struck fear among employees.

> More importantly, the political leaders projected the image of honesty, dedication and self-sacrifice; their constant ideological campaigns instilled pride in the civil service for asceticism, discipline, altruism, and success in overcoming the temptation of breaking the organizational and legal rules ... Conformity bred conformity. In such a social climate, individuals would find it easier to follow than to break state regulations and laws or to indulge in questionable behaviour to benefit themselves materially ... (Kwong, 1997: 134–5)

With the advent of a materialistic orientation in the 1980s, however, many new opportunities for enrichment emerged while the ascetic code of public service ethics was disregarded. Those, who acquired wealth, were admired, envied and became socially acceptable by the rest as long as they were not caught. In such a situation, those who enriched themselves from corrupt practices would shy away from reporting similar transgressions by their colleagues or subordinate employees. Slowly, a climate of corruption developed; at the same time, honest officers became materially poor compared to their colleagues and were ostracized as stupid. The principle of leadership by virtue, which is so deeply ingrained in the Confucian tradition, no longer applies with the same degree of consistency. The market reforms have brought in new values that seem to undermine the old principles. This is increasingly an issue in China that the political leadership is grappling with.

The case of India and Pakistan

The Santhanam Committee (India, Republic of, 1964) acknowledged that there were two major contributory factors for the growth of corruption in the country: government's unwillingness to deal drastically with corrupt and inefficient public servants, and an iron-clad protection given to public servants under Article 311 of the Constitution, whereby a permission to prosecute an accused public official must come from the authority that appointed him in the first place. Thus, if a public servant belonging to an All India Service received a letter of initial appointment in the name of the President of India, permission to prosecute that person must be secured from the same authority. But securing permission is so cumbersome, and delays are so drawn out, that cases are not pursued. Elected members of parliament and legislative assemblies are given the same protection. The situation in Pakistan is equally alarming: 'Corruption in Pakistan is so pervasive that it cannot be viewed merely as a structural issue ... Pakistani society and culture reveal an inherent contradiction in their attitude towards corruption' (Islam, 1989: 282).

It is no surprise that by the mid 1990s the Transparency International designated both India and Pakistan among the highly corrupt nations in the world. By 1999, the Transparency International Corruption Perceptions Index (CPI) placed India and Pakistan 72nd and 88th respectively among 99 countries, while China was listed at 59th place.

Is corrupt governance the ultimate destiny of South Asian countries? Corruption has not only become a fact of life but is fast approaching becoming a way of life. There exists in the public a total indifference or cynicism towards corruption. So long as there are corrupt politicians, corruption will keep on flourishing because it has become a high profit industry with low risk. This is so because: (a) corrupt people at the top are rarely punished, even if caught; (b) the wealth so amassed is not confiscated (thus permitting the corrupt to enjoy the benefits) even when a person is under judicial investigation; and (c) when the size of a ministry increases to double its previous size (about 100 ministers were appointed in the State of Uttar Pradesh, India in 1998–99 in order to entice representatives from many splinter political groups), such an over-bloated cabinet sets a bad example to all levels of bureaucracy and sends a message that politicians are out to loot rather than administer. And as long as such politicians keep holding ministerial portfolios, any prosecution or criminal proceeding against them is held in abeyance. With such a situation, corruption becomes an absolutely open-ended process. The fact remains that the entire cycle of corruption begins and ends with corrupt politicians. They are the epicenter of it all.

Governance

Governance has become a very fashionable way of talking about reform in government and its relations with society. It is now a central part of international development discourse. More specifically, it has provided Western consultants and organizations with a justification for emphasizing the need for developing nations to adopt and replicate ideas and institutions that have a proven track record in industrialized societies. The result of efforts to date, however, does not suggest as much success as it indicates a hodgepodge of techniques superficially imposed on already ineffective bureaucracies. The world of the twenty-first century may be ready for the American style of fast food chains, denim blue jeans and Madonna, *but hardly for the Western notion of 'one size fits all' in the field of governance and administration*. Of course, the developing world will have to set its house in order by controlling corruption, discontinuing unproductive public enterprises, and reforming the inefficient administrative system. East and South Asian countries have a lot to do to improve their systems of administration, but this will not happen merely with the introduction of new techniques from the West.

Missing in the missionary activities of Western economists and organization theorists working in the developing world is a sense of how their prescriptions fit into the existing moral fabric of society. Governance principles are not only a set of techniques that can be peddled from one corner of the world to another. They need to be developed in the local context of the societies where they are meant to apply. These principles include a call for individual moral responsibility and obligation, sacrifice, compassion and justice, and an honest effort to achieve the highest good. It is morality rather than technique that provides the foundation for the governing process. Public confidence and trust in liberal democracy can be secured only when the governing process exhibits a higher moral value. Yet that moral value is only one of several prerequisites of good governance. A broader list includes the following values: democratic pluralism, legitimacy, consensus and socio-economic equity, popular participation, rule of law, responsiveness to stakeholders, the strategic vision of leaders, accountability of public officials, and transparency in governmental operations, in addition to moral governance. Good governance and sustainable human development, especially for developing nations, also require conscientious attempts at eliminating poverty, sustaining livelihoods, fulfilling basic needs, and offering an administrative system that is clean and open.

A holistic approach to good governance requires that public officials be held responsible and accountable not only for the procedure (following rules and regulations, keeping away from illegal activities) but also for the ethical and moral consequences of their deeds. But those who believe in procedural accountability, asserting that the means, processes and procedures in government administration are just as important as purposes or ends, overlook the importance that ethics play in determining the quality of governance and administration. 'Thus the emphasis is on the effects observed, results achieved, and ends met' (Dwivedi and Gow, 1999: 168).

Public officials who believe in this approach feel that in public policy and administration, most choices are not moral absolutes, but depend on calculations of costs and benefits, not only to the public, but also to politicians and public servants. This approach emphasizes creating institutions of external control (such as the office of auditor general, parliamentary committee on public accounts, vigilance commission, etc.) and procedures to check financial mismanagement and corruption. However, the main weaknesses of this approach are its emphasis on reductionism and lack of a moral imperative. We know that no matter how comprehensive the rules and procedures to check the misuse of power and authority, people will invent the means to bend the rules or use legal loopholes in order to engage in unethical activities.

Insisting on morality in public policy and decision making is a condition for strengthening the ethical obligations of the people. Without politicians and government administrators behaving in an ethical manner, the chances for national development in a sustainable manner are seriously compromised. Echoing the recipes of Barnard (1948), one is inclined to say that public administration reform in developing nations needs to be taken back to the drawing board and reinvented with some of the classical concerns about the behavior of the executive in mind. Public servants must be moved by a higher cause, believing they have been entrusted with the stewardship of the state, and therefore owe special obligations, have specific expectations and reside in a fiduciary world. It is here where the moral approach acquires a holistic tone; ultimately, our public servants exist for the public they are employed to serve. This approach needs to be revitalized in public service in Asian countries. Unless public officials are guided *also* by a sense of vocation, service to others and accountability, we cannot expect moral government (Dwivedi, 2002).

CONCLUSION

I conclude this chapter by returning to two points that are of special significance not only for the three countries discussed above, but also most other countries in Asia. The first issue concerns the cultural discontinuity between the values prevailing in society and those that are imported from outside in the name of such 'fancy' innovations as New Public Management or Good Governance. Although it may be an oversimplification to talk about a set of distinctive Asian values, it is true that a good number of Asians do not subscribe to the set of Western values that dominate global discourse about administration and governance. For example, the notion of duty and community rights, sacrifice for the family and other communal needs, respect for authority, and consensual decision making are deeply rooted in Asian societies, but they do not feature at all in the prescription for improved public administration or better governance that the international development community advocates today. It is a rather sad comment on the state of the discipline of public administration that half a century after the notion of development administration was first launched to bring developing countries out of poverty and backwardness, the same mistakes that were made then in terms of replicating Western models are being repeated today. The gap between what

Asians consider important values, on the one hand, and what administration or governance experts regard as their priority, on the other, remains as large today as it was fifty years ago.

The second issue concerns what can be done to bridge this gap in the future. This chapter has argued that it is necessary to transcend the technocratic approach to public administration reform and accept that the underlying problems are ethical and thus go beyond the walls of the public service *per se*. The issues of corruption and other forms of abuse of public office have their roots in society, in general, and in politics in particular. It is in this context that governance, viewed as reforming the rules of public conduct, bears on what takes place in public administration. The relationship between politics and administration needs to be reviewed not merely in terms of cost-effectiveness but, above all, in terms of how they can enhance public trust in public authority. Forty years ago, this issue was analyzed in terms of capacity to administer development (for example, Riggs, 1964). As we move into the twenty-first century, it is being examined in terms of the legitimacy – and credibility – of all public institutions, whether officially labeled political or administrative. Public administration, more than ever before, can be fully analyzed and understood only in its political context. This is a lesson that can convincingly be drawn from the cases discussed above, but applies also to other Asian countries such as Indonesia, Malaysia and Thailand, all of which are confronting issues of legitimizing the role that public institutions play in society.

NOTE

The generous assistance by Goran Hyden in editing and completing this chapter is gratefully acknowledged.

REFERENCES

Barnard, Chester I. (1948) *The Functions of the Executive*. Cambridge, MA: Harvard University Press.

Bond, M.H. and Hwang, Kwang-kuo (1986) 'The Social Psychology of the Chinese People', in M.H. Bond (ed.), *The Psychology of the Chinese People*. Hong Kong: Oxford University Press.

Child, John (1994) *Management in China During the Age of Reform*. Cambridge: Cambridge University Press.

Dwivedi, O.P. (1987) 'Moral Dimensions of Statecraft: A Plea for an Administrative Theology', *Canadian Journal of Political Science*, 20 (4): 699–709.

Dwivedi, O.P. (1989) 'Administrative Heritage, Morality and Challenges in the Sub-Continent since the British Raj', *Public Administration and Development*, 9 (3): 245–52.

Dwivedi, O.P. (1994) *Development Administration: From Underdevelopment to Sustainable Development*. London: Macmillan.

Dwivedi, O.P. (2002) 'On Common Good and Good Governance: An Alternative Approach', in D. Olowu and S. Sako (eds), *Better Governance and Public Policy: Capacity Building for Democratic Renewal in Africa*. Bloomfield, CT: Kumarian Press. pp. 35–51.

Dwivedi, O.P. and Nef, Jorge (1982) 'Crises and Continuities in Development Theory and Administration: First and Third World Perspectives', *Public Administration and Development*, 12 (9): 894–911.

Dwivedi, O.P. and Gow, James Iain (1999) *From Bureaucracy to Public Management: The Administrative Culture of the Government of Canada*. Peterborough, Canada: Broadview Press.

Dwivedi, O.P. and Jain, R.B. (1988) 'Bureaucratic Morality in India', *International Political Science Review*, 9 (3): 205–14.

Dwivedi, O.P., Jain, R.B. and Dua, B.D. (1989) 'Imperial Legacy, Bureaucracy, and Administrative Changes: India 1947–1987', *Public Administration and Development*, 9: 253–69.

Gladden, E.N. (1972) *A History of Public Administration*. London: Frank Cass.

Harris, Peter (1989) 'China: The Question of Public Service Accountability', in Joseph G. Jabbra and O.P. Dwivedi (eds), *Public Service Accountability: A Comparative Perspective*. West Hartford, CT: Kumarian Press. pp. 227–49.

Heady, Ferrel (1984) *Public Administration: A Comparative Perspective*. New York: Marcel Dekker.

India, Republic of (1964) *Report of the Committee on Prevention of Corruption*. (K. Santhanam Committee). New Delhi: Ministry of Home Affairs, Government of India.

Islam, Nasir (1989) 'Colonial Legacy, Administrative Reform and Politics: Pakistan 1947–1987', *Public Administration and Development*, 9 (3): 271–86.

Kwong, Julia (1997) *The Political Economy of Corruption in China*. New York: M.E. Sharpe.

Laaksonen, Oiva (1988) *Management in China During and After Mao in Enterprises, Government and Party*. Berlin and New York: Walter de Gruyter.

Lockett, M. (1988) 'Culture and the Problems of Chinese Management', *Organization Studies*, 9: 475–96.

Riggs, Fred (1964) *Administration in Developing Countries*. Boston, MA: Houghton Mifflin.

Schaffer, Bernard (1969) 'The Deadlock of Development Administration', in C. Leys (ed.), *Politics and Change in Developing Countries*. Cambridge: Cambridge University Press.

Shenkar, O. and Ronen, S. (1987) 'The Cultural Context of Negotiations: The Implications of Chinese Interpersonal Norms', *Journal of Applied Behavioral Science*, 23: 263–75.

Smith, D.H. (1974) *Confucius and Confucianism*. London: Paladin.

Taub, Richard P. (1969) *Bureaucrats Under Stress*. Berkeley, CA: University of California Press.

42

Public Administration and Public Sector Reform in Latin America

Jorge Nef

This chapter intends to provide a general overview of Latin America's public sector restructuring in the context of the broader economic, social and political changes in the past two decades. Administrative reform may evoke a worldwide trend, yet its circumstances, outcomes and effects are region- and country-specific and are conditioned by the current pattern, as well as legacy, of state–society relations. Most analysts of public administration in the region view administrative systems as inseparable from politics: administrative changes have to be studied as driven by particular political interests and with specific political implications for the relationship between state and society.

Six basic questions will be addressed. First, what changes can be noticed in administrative structures, culture and behavior in Latin America as a result of economic and political reforms in the past two decades? Second, to what extent do the administrative systems increasingly present legal-rational characteristics? Third, is public administration becoming more efficient and/or effective in delivering services as a consequence of the above-mentioned reforms? Fourth, are government agencies more – or less – client- or service-oriented? Fifth, what is happening to public probity, and more specifically to corruption? Finally, to what extent does public administration contribute to national and regional development?

Despite the great diversity among the countries, there are sufficient structural commonalities (Burns, 1998: 71) as to configure an identifiable set of nations, especially by contrast to the developed states of North America. Conventionally, Latin America has been seen to encompass eighteen Spanish-speaking countries, as well as Brazil and Haiti. It does not include the 'newer' microstates of the Caribbean, which are also members of the Organization of American States (OAS). To build a 'model' that portrays Latin American public administration as a whole with rigor and precision is a daunting task. Yet, it is possible to sketch a general outline of the structural, behavioral and attitudinal traits present in the various executive agencies across the region. These agencies comprise diverse national administrations in the central government, functionally decentralized agencies and territorially decentralized units, such as state and local governments. It is important to recognize too that the public and the private sectors, and their cultures, tend to intersect, especially at the level of the power elite (Mills, 1957).

THE HISTORICAL LEGACY

Public administration in the region has experienced induced transformations since the days of colonial rule. It has passed through protracted phases of nation building (1850s to 1880s), early institutionalization (1880s to1930s), bureaucratization (1930s to 1970s) and authoritarianism (1970s to the mid 1980s). In the latter phase, technocratic and militaristic values dominated the relationship between state and society.

However, in the past fifteen years, a transition to limited democracy has reduced to some extent the influence of what some call the 'praetorian guards', that is, the bureaucratic autocrats. In conjunction with that, neoliberal economic reforms have further reshaped the role of the state: it has been downsized, while reducing its past centrality in socio-economic development. In addition to these challenges, the public sector has also confronted emerging social movements and a more complex and trans-nationalized type of political and economic context.

Any profound understanding of public administration in Latin America must by necessity explore the long run cycle (Braudel, 1980). Moreover, the study of administrative reform and change is, by its very nature, historical analysis, where the past is always present. The New World was born as a dependency of Madrid and Lisbon (Jaguaribe, 1964). An imitative and ritualistic administration emerged. Even, the seemingly 'modern', yet schizophrenic, patterns of administrative behavior of today's Latin America can be traced back to a colonial tradition of obedience without compliance (Moreno, 1969).

Independence in the early 1800s was more the result of European conflicts and big-power politics than widespread nationalism and liberal ideas among New World aristocrats (Keen, 1992). Emancipation did not result from bourgeois revolutions and homegrown ideas of liberty, equality, civil rights or effective citizenship. The severance of colonial ties, though difficult and violent, maintained almost intact the property and privilege of the same landed oligarchy who profited from colonialism.

Constitutional and legal forms transplanted from Europe and North America were often a measuring rod of 'modernity' by imitation, not a substantial rendering of a public service. Government jobs constituted mostly rewards for loyalty to a faction in power, or to members of the ruling classes, not the manifestation of a neutral, representative and responsible bureaucracy. Even, when efforts at the professionalization of the civilian and military cadres of the state began in the 1880s, this seemingly non-partisan body of state employees was at best an elitist stratum to which ordinary people had little access. Bureaucratic and authoritarian traditions intersected in a political and social order that was patrimonial at its core and only superficially legal-rational. Equally embedded, and seemingly contradictory traditional attitudes towards authoritarianism, formalism, patrimonialism and venality coexisted with more universalistic orientations as distinct cultural layers within this

incipient state class. The ideological amalgam described here was particularly noticeable among one of the most typical fractions of the Latin American middle classes: the officer corps (Nun, 1968).

The administrative state

The social contract resting upon the export economy, as discussed above, collapsed with the Great Depression. The consequence of the catastrophic 1929–34 economic recession on the Latin American state was two-fold. On the one hand, and virtually in all of the states, the role of the military as conflict-managers and enforcers of last resort (and as ultimate protectors of elite privilege) was enhanced. On the other, in the relatively more developed countries (such as Argentina, Brazil, Uruguay, Chile and Mexico), the dramatic downturn expanded the mediating and brokerage function of a middle-class-controlled and relatively autonomous state to arbitrate social conflict by means of economic management. Thus, to the early law and order, educational and social and welfare functions of the state, a new mission was added: economic development. A technocratic and productivity-oriented bureaucracy emerged side-by-side with the more traditional patrimonial and legal-rational central administration. This 'state of compromise' with strong populist overtones manifested itself in the creation of numerous parastatals with broad functions in planning, regulating, financing and covering fields as diverse as energy, industry, transportation and marketing. It also meant a Keynesian policy of induced development, known as Import Substitution Industrialization (ISI) (Furtado, 1976). In the lesser-developed countries, however, the civil service remained ineffectual and mostly patrimonial, while the commanding heights of the state were in the hands of military rulers. But even the above-mentioned state of compromise was short-lived. As chronic deficit financing, inflation and paralysis signaled the exhaustion of induced development policies, tensions between labor and business increased, this time in the context of the Cold War. Lower-class defiance grew in scope and intensity. Populism of the kind espoused by ISI was simultaneously under attack by both ends of the ideological spectrum. Political and administrative immobilism, deadlock and hyperinflation fed on each other. Crises of legitimacy affected the relatively more institutionalized administrative states, while those under protracted military rule faced crises of domination (Cox, 1982) – the inability of the repressive apparatus to control by force.

In the context of UN First Development Decade, the US-sponsored Alliance for Progress (1961), a reaction to the Cuban revolution, belatedly attempted to stabilize the region by means of development assistance. Development administration and administrative development (Pérez-Salgado, 1997) were part of a strategy using modernization as counter-insurgency (Nef and Dwivedi, 1981). Foreign aid, professionalization and development planning played an important role in a broad effort at refurbishing the administrative cadres of Latin America. Under USAID sponsorship, increasing numbers of Latin American students and trainees were exposed to American ways. Western European assistance followed a similar course. Money was also pouring in to carry on domestic programs on educational, agrarian and tax reforms, and also for the training and rationalization of the civil service under the principles of Scientific Management, Program Budgeting and Organization and Methods. These civil service reforms were predicated under the logic of induced development ('development administration') and the supremacy of the bureaucratic model ('administrative development'). More important, however, were the modernization and retooling of the security apparatus along national security and counter-insurgency lines (Barber and Ronning, 1966). While the reforms of the civil service, though extensive, remained largely unfocused, 'technical' and piecemeal, the thoroughgoing transformation of the security apparatus had an enormous and long-term systemic impact. With the failure of liberal reformism, the officers and their National Security Doctrine would occupy center stage to secure the maintenance of the domestic and regional status quo.

Despite rhetoric, the military regimes of the 1970s were objectively not only parasitic, but also instrumental in undermining the precarious sovereignty of the Latin American nations. The 'managers of violence' also proved to be incompetent conflict and development managers in the long run (Burns, 1986). Yet, they succeeded in radically restructuring the nature of the Latin American state, as well as the latter's relations with both civil society and the Inter American system. The US-sponsored transitions to democracy in the 1980s, and the so-called Washington consensus (Vilas, 2000), occurred in the context of these profound alterations (Black, 1998).

While military rule floundered in the midst of staggering debt burdens and mismanagement, critics within the West began to perceive such regimes as a liability for the survival of their economic and political interests, as clearly outlined in the Linowitz Report of 1975. A carefully orchestrated transition to restricted democracy, superintended by the regional superpower, ensued (Nef, 1998). This 'return' had strict limits and conditionalities. On the whole, it maintained the socio-economic and political forces that had benefited by decades of military rule, while excluding radical and popular sectors. The exiting security establishment was to be both the warrantor of the process and the central authoritarian enclave, or insurance policy, of the new institutional arrangement. This 'low-intensity' democracy (Gil et al., 1993) also preserved the basic neoliberal economic agendas of the authoritarian era. Chief among these legacies was a 'receiver state', whose prime goal was to manage the fiscal bankruptcies and facilitate IMF-inspired structural adjustment packages (Vilas, 1995).

Incomplete transition, restricted democracy and the receiver state have had significant effects upon the administrative systems in Latin America. Privatization, budget cuts, downsizing, deregulation and denationalization – especially in the social and developmental areas – have reduced the scope and function of the state. As profit and personal gain, on the one hand, and the national interest, on the other, become blurred in the new ideological domain, the notion of public service appears increasingly irrelevant. Furthermore, as the status and income levels of civil servants sink, and with a thriving illegal economy, such as the drug trade (Lee, 1988), systemic corruption is on the rise and reaches the highest levels of government and administration. Under these circumstances, externally induced efforts to make public administration more accountable, responsible, universalistic, effective, client-oriented and less corrupt become as formal and ineffectual as the Development Administration prescriptions of the 1960s.

THE STRUCTURAL CONTEXT OF PUBLIC ADMINISTRATION

The historical continuities and discontinuities discussed above have resulted in the coexistence of numerous and often incongruous traits. These include foreign and domestic influences, attempted and failed reforms and persistent crises. The aforementioned legacy manifests itself into three deep and interconnected structural contradictions.

The first is the persistent and unresolved tension between expanding social expectations and shrinking economic capabilities. For all the talk about Latin America's emerging markets and reinsertion in the global economic order, the region is still characterized by extreme vulnerability and weak and unstable growth. The second tension is that between 'haves' and 'have-nots'. Constricted generation of surplus, compounded by extreme forms of wealth and income inequality, has reduced the possibilities for consensual conflict-management. In fact, Latin America exhibits the paradox of being simultaneously the most favorably endowed region of the globe in terms of the balance of resources to population and the worst in income distribution. While contemporary social conflict does not outwardly present the subversive characteristics of the revolutionary confrontations of the Cold War, social unrest has not subsided. As its underlying causes persist, so does its intensity, irrespective of the changing manifestations of mass–elites relations. This proclivity for disequilibria connects to the third systemic tension: that between the formality of sovereignty and the reality of dependence. The Latin American nation-states are penetrated political systems with ever-more precarious control over actors, events and policies. Their economic foundations are still built upon a skewed and exogenous mode of development, with boom and bust cycles, compounded by massive debt burdens, current conditionalities and rapid transnationalization. In addition, external constituencies – political, military and economic – are essential to maintain adequate support (Easton, 1957) in systems whose internal legitimacy is weak.

Both public disillusionment with government and the increasing meaninglessness of the restricted democracies are ubiquitous. If the state cannot maintain political and economic sovereignty, protect the life and well-being of its citizens, safeguard democratic rights and assure participation – in brief, provide for human security – its very reason for existence becomes problematic. Furthermore, as the prevailing neoliberal ideological and policy packages reduce the state role to that of protecting business interests, there is little room for a public sector, no matter how efficient, effective or transparent. The New Public Management (NPM) formula, with its corollaries of privatization, downsizing, deregulating, localizing and outsourcing, in the absence of a strong and legitimate political order and community, has potentially destabilizing effects. Moreover, without a pre-existing cohesive and vigorous civil society, administrative modernization is simply a means to a vacuous end.

ADMINISTRATIVE CULTURE

Public servants' attitudes towards public service in the region are imbedded in an alienated set of orientations towards public life reflective of the prevailing social tensions. This administrative culture constitutes a rational adaptation and functionalization of conflicting traits present in the context of public organizations. A sketchy interpretative profile of these predispositions would suggest a superimposition of various cultural 'layers'.

Seen from afar, the administrative culture of Latin America presents significant universalistic and achievement-oriented traits. After all, Latin America is squarely in the domain of Western culture. The drive for efficiency, effectiveness, technological innovation and probity by means of public management is pervasive in theory and discourse. Yet in practice, the core component of Latin America's administrative culture is defined by the persistence of ascription and influence peddling. Primary groups, especially extended families and friends, play a fundamental role in social life, even in the allegedly 'modern' confines of urban and organizational life. The endurance of patrimonialism, 'amiguismo' and 'compadrazgo' are manifestations of this built-in particularism. So is the overall level of inwardness, lack of transparency and distrust of strangers surrounding the performance of public functions.

The Latin American state classes have been, since their origins, a 'status officialdom' (Morstein-Marx, 1963: 63), derived from their possession of official titles. A bureaucrat (even a white-collar employee in a private corporation) or an officer, irrespective of the discredit in which the service may find itself, is a 'somebody'. In a hierarchical social order, being middle class confers a degree of respectability and recognition. This accounts for the extreme formalism present in administrative behavior. Ritualism, hyper-legalism and the codification of language in deductive law (rooted in Civil and Roman Law) makes the behavior and expectations of officials depend upon detailed interpretations of norms. There is a fundamental double standard: a public 'facade' for outsiders and a private zone of exceptionality for insiders (Riggs, 1967). The same applies to the use of time: delays, waiting and slowness are selectively used to define the importance of the relationship and delineate power and hierarchy.

Under the mantle of formalism described above, paradoxically, there is a high degree of operational autonomy. Formalism and particularism ostensibly clash. The former becomes a mechanism for avoiding responsibility, or for justifying dynamic immobilism and aloofness. The flip side of this contradiction is that it transforms the role of the civil servant into one of dispensing personal favors as well as facilitating exceptions from existing norms. Such exceptionalism gives rise to recurrent nepotism, corruption, patronage and abuse.

The official's perception of the relations between state and society is influenced by the weak brokerage and associational representation for most of the public *vis-à-vis* the government. This enhances an almost 'natural' form of corporatism and authoritarianism (Malloy, 1977). Moreover, the recognition of an entrenched, elitist socio-economic structure enhances a self-perception of autocracy, where the bureaucracy acts as a mediator and arbiter of the social conflict (Heady, 1984), but with extremely limited accountability. There is a profound schism between 'insiders' and 'outsiders'. Clientelism, patrimonialism, the ubiquitous use of 'pull' and the persistence of episodes of military intervention, reinforce the aforementioned characteristics. Though the white-collar military and civilian state classes are not part of the landed, financial and commercial oligarchy, public officials dwell in the confines of the elites and a few of them are able to ascend into the upper crust. Their connection with essentially undemocratic practices and governments makes the functionaries prone to assume an attitude of arbitrariness and disregard for the public. This demeanor towards the outsiders, especially the lower strata, is pervasive not only in government but also in the private sector.

Most administrative structures and processes in Latin America, irrespective of the level of territorial or functional operation, are heavily concentrated at the top. The institutional mold is one of centralism (Véliz, 1980). Most states are unitary; only Mexico, Venezuela, Brazil and Argentina have limited forms of federalism. Moreover, the attempts at territorialization and localization do not necessarily make administration more accountable, democratic and 'closer to the people'. This centralism is even more manifest with regards to the pattern of executive–legislative relations. Without exception, the form of government is one of presidential dominance, where the legislature is a weak instrument for checks and balances. Parliamentary control and parliamentary supremacy, concepts generated in the US presidential and the British parliamentary systems, are not significantly entrenched. Nor is there a word for 'accountability' in the lexicon. Only in recent years the word *'responsabilización'* has been coined, but may authors still prefer to use the English idiom. The administrator's values, behavior and expectations tend to reflect a view of 'things public' defined by high levels of concentration of power. Decisions normally flow up to the 'top'; so does responsibility (Campos, 1967). Though operational autonomy – as mentioned – is not uncommon, propensity to delegate is rather infrequent. Therefore, it is extremely difficult to attain coordination. This, in turn, enhances the propensity to further concentrate authority.

The ideological 'software' of the Latin American public sector is the result of an ongoing process of immersion, acculturation and socialization, whose structural drivers are both implicit and induced. Reform projects and other innovations originated in the realm of international technical cooperation, are adopted to the extent that they fit pre-existing cultural molds. Thus, diverse views of administration coexist but do not necessarily fuse into a cultural synthesis. The primary vehicles for reproducing administrative culture are, at their most basic levels, the family, the educational system, peer groups and direct experience with the public service. As indicated earlier, the fundamental class identification of civil servants is with the middle strata. There is a sort of circular causation: the middle strata produce employees, while becoming a white-collar worker confers the attribute of middle classness. Class distinctions are very important in Latin America, social identity being a function of ancestry, neighborhood, education, tastes, gender, ethnicity and language. The educational system, especially in its secondary and tertiary levels, is quite exclusive and discriminating. High school and university education are in general the points of entry for employee roles. More specific training may occur at the post-secondary levels either in public service schools or in university careers geared to administrative postings. Academic curricula in these educational institutions are connected to law, business and economics, and also to a very narrow view of public administration. All these professions are characterized by a strong and largely uncritical social engineering orientation. Beyond programmatic declarations, few countries have developed an administrative class, in the sense understood in North America, the UK and continental Europe (Heady, 1984). Many observers point at Costa Rica, Uruguay and Chile as possible examples approaching the model of a 'neutral', 'effective' and relatively more transparent bureaucracy. But even these exceptional cases appear problematic when closely scrutinized.

In the case of the military, officer academies at the secondary and post-secondary levels give specificity to a distinct body of doctrine and *ésprit de corps*. National security and counter-insurgency doctrines define a predominantly antidemocratic and ultraconservative view of the world, heavily dependent upon ideological and material support from the North. In fact, the officers and their external constituencies exercise a kind of relational control, or 'metapower' (Baumgartner et al., 1977) over the domestic political process. Underneath a veneer of nation-alism, most security forces act as occupying forces of their own countries. Civilian and military roles are sharply divided, with military professionalism being largely defined by the control over the instruments of force, institu-tional autonomy, verticality, rigidity, secrecy, high transnational integration, institutional arro-gance, isolation and corporate identity (Black, 1986). With the shrinkage of the developmental function of the state, by design and by default, security management, combined with the above-mentioned receivership have evolved into the most ostensible functions of the state (Nef and Bensabat, 1992). With the Cold War over, the content of national security has been redefined to fit other concerns: 'wars' on drugs, 'terrorism', or whatever justifies the paramountcy of the institutional interests of the security forces.

ORGANIZATIONAL FEATURES

A primary feature of organizational life is the already-mentioned coexistence, side by side, of patrimonial and bureaucratic tendencies. In this sense, the administrative machinery of the state cannot be seen as merely an instrument for policy implementation. It is also a pivotal, albeit highly fragmented, socio-political actor with a multiplicity of latent functions related to the maintenance of the sociopolitical order. Another is organizational syncretism: from an 'archeologi-cal' point of view, Latin America's public administration presents a complex overlay of actually existing structures and practices. Some of these can be traced as far back as the colonial and post-independence period; others are the out-croppings of more recent reorganizations, policy orientations and political allegiances.

Most significant within this organizational legacy is the presence of numerous agencies and activities inherited from the Keynesian adminis-trative state. In the relatively more developed Latin American countries the scope and depth of state involvement was impressive. It included mass education, health, social security, housing, popular credit, marketing boards and commercial monopolies, public utilities (especially electricity, water and sewage), mass transportation (trains, sea transport and airlines), strategic industrial enterprises (cement, steel, hydrocarbons, petro-chemicals, aeronautics) and in some instances even the film industry. In Chile, Costa Rica, Uruguay, Brazil, Mexico and, to a lesser extent, Venezuela, there existed national development corporations to finance and hold numerous state enterprises, or semi-private ventures financed with government funds or credit. Though many of these entities and activities have been either priva-tized or eliminated under the policies of structural adjustment, a good number still persist. Successful state corporations, like Mexico's oil monopoly PEMEX, Costa Rica's power and telecommuni-cations monopoly INE, or Chile's Copper Corporation CODELCO, have been spared the privatizing wave. In numerous cases, either the pace of liberalization has been too slow or the institutional and symbolic entrenchment of the corporations too strong to privatize.

A third ostensible trait – already discussed under culture – is the strong influence of legal-ism in every aspect of organizational life. There is an elaborate and quite similar body of public law – both constitutional and administrative – as well as abundant jurisprudence regulating virtually every aspect of Latin American bureau-cracy. Legalism and formalism are terms virtu-ally synonymous with public administration. Government entities are formal organizations whose origin, mission, instrumentalities and *modus operandi* are explicitly prescribed by law; and this is particularly strong in societies where notary publics have to certify every action or intent.

A fourth important characteristic is the high autonomy of the military and security apparatus. (The only exception is Costa Rica, which does not have a military force.) The armed bureaucrats are, for all intents and purposes, a virtual state within the state. Furthermore, there are numerous authoritarian enclaves throughout the non-military public service – inherited from the times of bureaucratic authoritarianism – that remain outside the realm of effective political control. In some instances, like Chile's main state copper mining conglomerate, CODELCO, a substantial part of the proceeds (9 per cent of revenue) go directly to the military. In other cases (Brazil and Chile), the military are integrated into 'military–industrial complexes' of their own, which include the highly profitable area of international arms sales.

A fifth, significant and enduring characteristic of Latin American public administration is the formal co-habitation of two administrative systems, one central and the other decentralized. The central, or 'fiscal' apparatus is made of Ministries, agencies and services, under the helm and budgetary control of the Chief Executive. These units are usually departmentalized by major purpose and operate under the general provisions of public service legislation. The other is the decentralized sector, constituted by the semi-autonomous control and regulatory agencies, functionally decentralized services, state enterprises and corporations of many kinds. A distinct component of the 'autonomous' sector is territorially decentralized and involves local government and administration. Decentralized bodies are chartered in special legislation that grants them relative operational, statutory, budgetary and personnel independence from the central agencies, and in some cases they operate under the provisions of private law. Until recently, the distribution of personnel between these two sectors was roughly similar, while in the budgetary area, the decentralized sector's share was slightly higher than that of the central administration. However, in recent years there have been some significant changes. Functional decentralization has been steadily replaced by privatization, deregulation and downsizing. Meanwhile, under the banner of localization, territorially decentralized agencies (in particular municipalities) have increased in numbers, functions and importance.[1]

A final characteristic is the institutionalization of a myriad of newer horizontal functions, in addition to the more conventional horizontal operating systems – that is, planning, budget, financial and personnel management, and legal and accounting controls (for example, the Comptroller General's office). Most of these new agencies are coordinating units, cutting across the more conventional vertically departmentalized ministries and government agencies. One type of these newer structures are those dealing with emerging issues such as environment, privatization, export-promotion, interaction with the civil society (that is, 'the public'), or gender equity. Another type of integrated functions are those pertaining to administrative and institutional reform itself. Since the 1990s, almost all the governments in the region have embarked on the implementation of strategic plans for the modernization of the public sector.

To accomplish this mandate, presidential level agencies have been established. In some cases, such as in Argentina, Under-Secretariats of Public Management and Modernization have been created, along with an office to fight corruption. Mexico, under the PAN administration

of President Fox, initiated a similar program of its own. In most countries, inter-ministerial and inter-agency committees, charged with computerization and technological innovation, quality control, program evaluation, user satisfaction, performance assessments and de-bureaucratization have been in existence for at least a decade. An example of this arrangement is Chile's Inter-ministerial Committee for the Modernization of the State, with a broad mandate and housed in the strategic Ministry of the Secretary General of Government.

A feature of the current approach to administrative modernization, unlike the 'rationalization' efforts under the rubric of development administration, is that it uses a broader definition of the public sector. Besides central agencies, the object of reform encompasses local governments, the judiciary and the process of privatization. Most countries, notably Brazil, Argentina, Bolivia, Chile, Colombia, Panama, Ecuador and the Dominican Republic, have created agencies and formulated plans to transfer and download governmental functions at the communal level. These regional development offices and under-secretariats are also mandated to enhance administrative skills and build managerial capabilities in local government. In addition, a great deal of effort has been devoted to modernizing the judiciary, simplifying procedures and attempting to give more agility and transparency to the judicial process, one identified by external observers as being not only slow but also corrupt. Finally, the issue of transferring public ownership to the private sector has been addressed. This is a major ideological and fiscal tenet of the institutional reforms contained in the conditionalities attached to debt relief. The discourse behind this practice refers to a 'leaner but meaner' state, where regulation and leadership replaces direct ownership or management. To this effect, all the countries have established mechanisms (in the form of commissions) to expedite the privatization process.

THE DYNAMICS OF REFORM: PROCESSES AND EFFECTS

Administrative change in Latin America has been for the most part either externally induced, or heavily assisted by external actors (Wharlich, 1978). Colonial reforms, the desire of local elites to modernize, the presence of international missions and consultants (like the Kemmerer Commission in the 1920s), development administration (Crowther and Flores, 1984), and today's New Public Management with structural adjustment programs (SAPs) are all cases in point. The instances of administrative reform from within have been fewer, piecemeal, heavily localized and mostly reactive to deep discontinuities. One such instance was the already-mentioned development of the post-First World War welfare state with limited social security and medical coverage, which preceded its counterparts in Europe and North America by at least a decade (Mesa-Lago and Witte, 1992). The other was Import Substitution Industrialization (ISI) in the 1930s, the only experience to become codified and theorized upon in the works of ECLA and other regional agencies. A third example has been the rare attempts at radical reorganization resulting from revolutionary changes, such as in Cuba (1960s) and the aborted Sandinista experiment in Nicaragua (1980s). Rhetoric aside, these experiences have been largely improvizations in the face of dramatic international conjunctures and nearly impossible odds. Rene Dumont has referred to this style of management as 'creative chaos'. Finally, a most remarkable exception is the set of micro experiences in autonomous mobilization, such as the Christian Base Communities in Central America and Brazil, the now-defunct Popular Economic Organizations in Chile, the self-managed urban communities in Peru (Nef, 1991) and the still vital Landless Rural Workers' Movement (MST) in contemporary Brazil (Robles, 2000; MST, 2001).

The common denominator of all administrative reform in Latin America, whether internally or externally induced, is its distinct political character (Marini Ferreira, 1999). For such reforms, irrespective of the technical language in which they are couched, in the last analysis strengthen, weaken, consolidate or challenge existing power relations. Furthermore, they all operationalize in organizational and managerial terms a broader political, social and economic project.

Administrative modernization in the 1990s has been predicated in a very different domestic and international environment – and programmatic objectives – from those of the structural reforms of the 1960s. The policy framework for international cooperation present in the West today (and a decade ago) was, and continues to be, distinctively neoliberal, not Keynesian. MERCOSUR, NAFTA and the proposals for a Free Trade of the Americas (FTA) are part of the new regional environment. Markets, rather than planning and government intervention, are central, though paradoxically this policy switch is contingent upon strong state enforcement. Latin America came out of the Cold War through a transition to a limited and not very transparent form of democracy brokered by external agents. The countries were also saddled with enormous and unmanageable debt burdens. The international financial community and its international bodies used debt-management to impose stringent conditionalities. The latter included a number of measures for attaining macroeconomic equilibrium via debt reduction, open market policies and institutional reforms.

It is precisely in the context of these structural adjustment policies that the bulk of the prescriptions for the current administrative reform have to be seen. The administrative corollary to the neoliberal package contained in the SAPs is fundamentally the New Public Management (NPM) paradigm (Ormond and Löffler, 1999). The latter is well known in the United States through the work of Osborne and Gaebler, *Reinventing Government* (Jones and Thompson, 1999). Yet, its lineage can be traced back to the conservative administrative reforms in the 1980s in the United Kingdom, New Zealand, Australia and Canada, which materialized in what was then called a 'neo-conservative' agenda. Its administrative corollary has been a movement from civil service to public management (Bonifacio, 1995). Downsizing government, making it publicly more accountable and transparent, turning it into a more efficient mechanism for delivering services on its own or in partnership with private and/or voluntary organizations are not purely isolated measures to secure 'better' administration. They are all manifestations of a broader neoliberal ideological rationale (Nef and Robles, 2000). The role of the state under this model is mainly subsidiary; that is, its main directive is to protect the functioning of the market, and private property. The basic 'social contract' is post-Fordian, in the sense that reduces and fragments the role of workers in the system of labor relations, enhancing instead the uncontested hegemony of capital, both foreign and domestic. The notion of popular and national sovereignty is replaced by the sovereignty of capital. This manifests itself in labor, taxation and welfare policy.

Over the past two decades, there has been a redefinition of the role of the state throughout Latin America, as in most of the globe, along the lines mentioned above. This has manifested itself in a transition between two models. One was the Keynesian 'administrative state', whose central mission was the attainment of national development. The other is the 'receiver' state, whose principal role is the management of structural adjustment and whose subsidiary role is the implementation of palliative development. Such development refers to targeted programs to address the plight of those who fall as a result of orthodox economic policies, by means of micro-credit, capacity building and the like. This transformation, as mentioned earlier, came on the heels of the bureaucratic authoritarian restructuring of the 1970s and was largely facilitated by it.

Since the 'return to democracy', there has been a reduction in the scope and size of the public sector.[2] This has been accomplished by closures, privatization of many activities – especially in public utilities, health, social security and education – and also by outsourcing in the private sector. A myriad of private entities have emerged to take on these downloaded public functions with captive clienteles and low elasticity: Pension Management Funds (AFPs), 'health service' entities (like Health Management Organizations), sanitary services firms and the like.

The record of privatization has shown mixed results, ranging from greater quality and rationalization of service, to more effective costing and profitability, to situations of exclusion and manifest decline in the quality, coverage and accessibility. In some cases, it has given an impetus for modernization, improved standards and generated sources of new investment, and even cheaper and better products (for a while this was the case in telecommunications). However, in many others (as in power utilities) it has spearheaded at best speculative appropriations at the public expense and widespread fraud. Downsizing the civil service has led to a proliferation of personnel on limited service contracts and a large quantity of private consultants. It also means a resurgence of patrimonialism (Robin, 1995). It is not uncommon to see a parallel structure to the officially downsized agencies, made of contractual and external personnel. More often than not, this 'temporary' structure evolves into a persistent clientele conditioned to the ups and downs of patronage politics. Loss of employment, labor vulnerability and declining incomes, as in the case of schoolteachers and other civil servants, has had a generalized deleterious effect on service quality and human security in the region.

Fiscal management has moved to the center stage of public administration. On the one hand, the financial base for public programs has been significantly reduced; on the other, budgetary processes have been streamlined. Budget cuts have been geared to attaining fiscal balance, facilitating the management of structural adjustment policies. Institutionally, this has translated into the primacy of the ministries of finance as the key actors and regulators of the administrative process. These ministries increasingly represent the paramountcy of the central banking authorities and the international financial institutions, such as the IMF, the World Bank or the Inter-American Development Bank.

In addition to the macro issues of privatization and fiscal management, the administrative reform under NPM has had some remarkable achievements, especially when it comes to the 'micro' and efficiency-oriented aspects of administration. Of all the activities implemented, the most clearly successful have been the efforts to streamline procedures, de-bureaucratize and computerize services. The quality and time of service rendered to customers has clearly improved in many of the countries. This applies especially to licenses, certificates, filing income taxes and a reduction of red tape. More substantial structural reforms have met with less success, ranging from limited accomplishments (such as localization), to mere cosmetic changes, to complete ineffectiveness, or worse. This realization has prompted some participants and analysts of the reform process in Latin America to call for a redefinition of NPM principles along the lines of a more socially oriented version of institutional reform. Many point at the European social democracies, and Anthony Giddens' *Third Way* (Giddens, 1998) as an alternative to the economic and ideological orthodoxy of neoliberalism. In this sense, CLAD's own document, 'A New Public Management for Latin America' (CLAD, 1999), constitutes a call to reconstruct an administrative paradigm. It proposes a 'third way' of implementing market reforms with a human face: putting people first, revitalizing civil society and emphasizing a more active and democratic state.

CONCLUSION

This interpretative and tentative exploration makes it possible to hypothesize on the relationships between administrative culture, structure and functions sketched above and the larger social and political order. It has also suggested some conjectures regarding the dynamic relationship between such patterns and strategies of reform, which can be summarized into six propositions.

1 The administrative systems of Latin America reflect the distinctiveness and complexity of the various national realities and the common regional trends. The latter include persistent dependence, the perpetuation of rigid and particularistic social structures, chronic economic vulnerability, weak and unstable growth, social marginalization, low institutionalization and

acute social polarization. The above translates into high levels of ambiguity and uncertainty. Administrative change in the region is conditioned more by these circumstances than by the declared goals of 'technical' reform. Ostensibly, structural transformations have taken place, yet administrative culture and behavior have persisted, producing syncretistic adaptations rather than profound reorganizations. The political economy of reform has been characterized by a bias for the maintenance of the domestic and regional status quo.

2　The administrative systems in Latin America, unlike other peripheral areas, have long exhibited the formal attributes of bureaucracy, and successive reforms have entrenched these traits. Yet, under the circumstances described here, the presence of 'legal-rational' characteristics do not constitute substantive indicators, let alone predictors, of responsiveness, effectiveness or democratic accountability. Rather, the formality of the legal-rational model often hides the reality of a 'mock' bureaucracy (Gouldner, 1954.), where complex procedures and technical trappings are geared to a dysfunctional mixture of issue non-resolution and non-issue resolution. Public administration in Latin America has been distinctively derivative. As a reflection of an entrenched center–periphery regional and global order, it has tended to follow vogues, recipes and solutions manufactured in the developed societies. In this sense, it has been exogenous in its motivations, problem identification and prescriptions (Crowther and Flores, 1984). The tendency to define problems and questions from the vantage point of rather standard answers and solutions has provided for a rather mechanistic and acritical approach. The scientific and technological institutions in the region have been more interested in reproducing the prevailing modes of social engineering than addressing larger contextual – and politically contentious – issues. Technical cooperation has not fared any better.

3　In the past two decades there have been ostensible improvements in 'de-bureaucratizing', 'de-cluttering', reducing waiting-times and cutting down red tape. This has been accompanied by deregulation, a reduction of the size of the civil service and a transfer of many public functions into private agencies. The incomplete transition to democracy of the 1980s, debt crises and structural adjustments have altered the content and instrumentalities of public policy (Nef, 1997). The region's administrative systems have been directly affected by current circumstances and challenges derived from a concerted effort at

modernization along the lines of the prescriptions of Western governments and international agencies. However, this alteration has not resulted substantively into greater efficiency, let alone effectiveness to 'get things done' for the public; nor does it seem to effect a deep transformation of administrative practices and behavior.

4　The same applies to the question of administrative responsiveness to public demands. In a narrow technical sense, the transformation of the recipient into a 'client' – as has been attempted in numerous reforms – does not alter substantially the intrinsic quality of the service. A key problem in Latin America is the absence of citizenship in the public arena. The irony is that, while social demands on the public sector to tackle mounting problems and to provide more services are growing, the state apparatus is shrinking. What is happening instead is a revolution of rising frustrations resulting from the inability of the political systems and their bureaucracies to tend to the most basic problems people face in their daily lives.

5　In this, the inability to control corruption is indicative, and indeed the very logic, of the current prescriptions. Administrative practices in Latin America are immersed in a larger cultural matrix, containing values, behaviors and orientations towards the physical environment, the economy, the social system, the polity and culture itself. Corruption in Latin America is not only public: it is systemic. A predatory attitude towards resource extraction (often fueled by the foreign debt), possessive individualism, amoral familism, a weak civic consciousness and a tendency to imitate 'the modern', configures a conservative mind-set with ethical double standards. This also engenders irresponsibility and a lack of capacity (and will), to anticipate and make strategic policy shifts. Administrative reforms promoting privatization, a smaller role for the state, deregulation, downsizing, outsourcing and formal decentralization have failed to address the fundamental issues of inequality, lack of democracy and abuse that underpin the region's administrative structures and practices. They may have also encouraged official corruption (Robin, 1995).

6　Historically, the administrative experience of Latin America has been molded by numerous failed attempts at modernization and cyclical crises. This results in a protracted condition of institutional underdevelopment. It has also contributed to perpetuating a self-fulfilling prophecy of immobility (Adie and Poitras, 1974). Without political and institutional development, addressing real issues such as poverty, unemployment or lack of effective citizenship, administrative reforms – even couched in the current rhetoric of public sector modernization – are mere epiphenomena (Martner, 1984). The contribution of the current reform vogue to development – and democracy – are mostly marginal, as the protection of market forces, not development (let alone democracy), is its prime directive.

Any profound administrative reform involves both structural and attitudinal (as well as value) changes. Efforts at administrative restructuring, 'modernization' and the like, need to address first, either directly or indirectly, the nature of administrative culture and the issue of democracy,

or rather lack of democracy, in the region. Administrative culture is something heterogeneous, dynamic and syncretic. But, above all, culture is *an agent, not an impediment for change* (Maturana and Varela, 1980). It contains the seeds to bring about a critical awareness (Freire, 1971) of the multiple contextual factors – environmental, economic, social, political and ideological – that affect public policies and administration. The contradiction between liberalism and democracy (Macpherson, 1977) lies at the core of the governance problem of Latin America. Administrative modernization without real political democratic reform, beyond purely formal facades, is an interesting but often fruitless exercise.

NOTES

1 A comparison of national, functionally and territorially decentralized administrations in a number of countries indicates the following variations between 1991 and 1997:

Country*	(A) National admin. 1991	1997	(B) Functional 1991	1997	(C) Local 1991	1997	% change (A) 1991–97	% change (B) 1991–97	% change C 1991–97
Argentina	534	462	242	51	1159	1317	−13.5	−89.0	13.6
Chile	120	134	56	37	23	23	11.7	−32.3	0.0
Costa Rica	127	133	6	3	6	8	4.7	−50.0	33.3
Nicaragua	89	81	15	11	41	47	−9.0	−26.6	14.6
Venezuela	238	197	99	28	193	208	−17.3	−71.8	2.3

*Figures refer to thousands of civil servants and are in absolute values. If they were calculated as proportion of population, or economically active population, declines would be larger and increases smaller. The 'local' comprises municipal, or provincial, or both, depending upon data available. *Source:* CLAD/SIARE, web address http://www.clad.org.ve/siareweb

2 A comparative table, calculated on the basis of data provided by CLAD, between 1987 and 1998–99, indicates a declining trend in civil service employment, *vis-à-vis* the economically active population EAP.

Country	Civil service (×1000) 1987	1998/99	% change	% EAP 1990	1999	% change
Argentina*	1.973	1.829	−7.3	14.53	12.23	−26.0
Venezuela	975	374	−61.7	—	—	—
Mexico*	3.751	4.422	17.8	19.46	18.38	1.0
Costa Rica*	272	146	−46.4	13.95	11.20	−19.8
Chile	215	172	−20.0	2.09	1.60	−44.9
Panama	157	136	−13.3	—	—	—
Uruguay*	272	230	−15.5	18.12	16.14	−11.00

*Observations for Argentina are 1991–97: for Mexico, 1990–96; Costa Rica, 1990–98; and Uruguay, 1995–98. *Source*: CLAD 2001: http://www.clad.org.ve//siareweb

REFERENCES

Adie, Robert and Poitras, Guy (1974) *Latin America. The Politics of Immobility*. Englewood Cliffs, NJ: Prentice–Hall. pp. 250–71.

Barber, William and Ronning, Neale (1966) *Internal Security and Military Power: Counterinsurgency and Civic Action in Latin America*. Columbus, OH: Ohio State University Press. pp. 217–45.

Baumgartner, Thomas, Burns, Tom and DeVille, Philippe (1977) 'Reproduction and Transformation of Dependency Relationships in the International System. A Dialectical Systems Perspective', *Proceedings of the Annual North American Meeting of the Society for General Systems Research*. pp. 129–36.

Black, Jan (1998) 'Participation and the Political Process: The Collapsible Pyramid,' in Jan Black, *Latin America. Its Problems and its Promise. A Multidisciplinary Introduction*. Boulder, CO: Westview Press. p. 226.

Black, Jan (1986) *Sentinels of the Empire: the United States and Latin American Militarism*. New York: Greenwood Press.

Bonifacio, José Alberto (1995) 'Modernizacion del servicio civil en el contexto de la reforma estatal', *Revista centroamericana de Administracion Publica*, Nos. 28 and 29 (January–June), pp. 5–26.

Braudel, Fernand (1980) 'History and the Social Sciences: the *longue durée*', in Fernand Braudel, *On History*. Chicago: University of Chicago Press. pp. 25–54.

Burns, E. Bradford (1986) *Latin America. A Concise Interpretive History*, 4th edn. Englewood Cliffs, NJ: Prentice–Hall. pp. 96–101, 134–53, 313–24.

Burns, E. Bradford (1998) 'The Continuity of the National Period,' in Jan Black (ed.), *Latin America. Its Problems and its Promise. A Multidisciplinary Introduction*. Boulder, CO: Westview Press. pp. 70–6, 77–8.

Campos, Roberto de Oliveira (1967) 'Public Administration in Latin America', in Nimrod Raphaeli (ed.), *Readings in Comparative Public Administration*. Boston, MA: Alwyn and Bacon. pp. 286–7.

CLAD's Scientific Council (1999) 'A New Public Management for Latin America'. CLAD Document in *Revista del CLAD, Reforma y Democracia*, No. 13 (February).

Cox, Robert (1982) 'Gramsci, Hegemony and International Relations: An Essay on Method', *Millennium: Journal of International Relations*, 12 (2): 162–75.

Crowther, Win and Flores, Gilberto (1984) 'Problemas latinoamericanos en administración pública y dependencia de soluciones desde Estados Unidos', in Gilberto Flores and Jorge Nef (eds), *Administración Publica: Perspectivas Criticas*. San José, Costa Rica: ICAP. pp. 59–89.

Easton, David (1957) 'An Approach to the Analysis of Political Systems', *World Politics*, 9 (3): 384–5.

Freire, Paulo (1971) *Pedagogy of the Oppressed*. New York: Herder and Herder.

Freire, Paulo (1976) *Education, the Practice of Freedom*. London: Writers and Readers Publishing Cooperative.

Furtado, Celso (1976) *Economic Development of Latin America*, 2nd edn. Cambridge: Cambridge University Press. pp. 107–17.

Giddens, Anthony (1998) *The Third Way: the Renewal of Social Democracy*. Cambridge: Polity Press; Walden, MA: Blackwell.

Gil, Barry, Rocamora, Joel and Wilson, Richard (1993) *Low Intensity Democracy: Political Power in the New World Order*. London: Pluto Press, pp. 3–34.

Gouldner, Alvin (1954) *Patterns of Industrial Bureaucracy*. Glencoe, IL: The Free Press. pp. 117–30.

Heady, Farrel (1984) *Public Administration. A Comparative Perspective*, 3rd edn. New York: Marcel Dekker. pp. 174–221, 338–42.

Jaguaribe, Helio (1964) *Desarrollo económico y desarrollo político*. Buenos Aires: EUDEBA, pp. 122–9.

Jones, Lawrence and Thompson, Fred (1999) 'Un modelo para la nueva gerencia publica: leciones de los sectores publico y privado', *Revista del CLAd Reforma y Democracia (Caracus)*, 14 (June) (electronic version, pp. 1–26).

Keen, Benjamin (1992) *A History of Latin America*, 4th edn. Boston: Houghton-Mifflin. pp. 158–62, 182–3.

Kliksberg, Bernardo (1987) 'Nuevas fronteras tecnológicas en materia de gerencia en América Latina' *Revista de la CEPAL*, No. 31 (April): 179–99.

Lee, Rensselaer W. (1988) 'Dimensions of the South American Cocaine Industry,' *Journal of Interamerican Studies*, 30 (3): 87–104.

Macpherson, Crawford Brough (1977) *The Life and Times of Liberal Democracy*. Oxford: Oxford University Press.

Malloy, James (1977) 'Authoritarianism and Corporatism in Latin America: the Modal Pattern', in James Malloy (ed.), *Authoritarianism and Corporatism in Latin America*. Pittsburgh: Pittsburgh University Press. pp. 3–19.

Marini Ferreira, Caio, Marcio (1999) 'Crise e reforma do estado: uma questão de cuidadania e valorização do servidor'. Rio de Janeiro: Escola Nacional de Administração Pública, pp. 1–37.

Martner, Gonzalo (1984) 'El papel de la reforma administrativa en la estrategia del desarrollo', in Bernardo Kliksberg (ed.), *La reforma de la administración pública en América Latina. Elementos para una evaluación*. Alcalá de Henares, Spain: Instituto Nacional de Administración Publica. p. 62.

Maturana, Humberto and Varela, Francisco (1980) *Autopoiesis and Cognition. The Realization of the Cognitive*. Boston and Dordrecht: T. Reidell. (Boston Studies in the Philosophy of Science, Vol. 42.)

Mesa-Lago, Carmelo and Witte, Lothar (1992) 'Regímenes previsionales en el Cono Sur y en el area andina', *Nueva Sociedad*, No. 122 (November–December): 19–34.

Mills, C. Wright (1957) *The Power Elite*. New York: Oxford University Press. pp. 3–29.

Moore, Barrington (1966) *Social Origins of Dictatorship and Democracy. Lord and Peasant in the Making of the Modern World*. Boston, MA: Beacon Press. pp. xvii.

Moreno, Francisco José (1969) *Legitimacy and Stability in Latin America. A Study of Chilean Political Culture*. New York: New York University Press. pp. 34–7.

Morstein-Marx, Fritz (1963) 'The Higher Civil Service as an Action Group in Western Political Development', in Joseph LaPalombara (ed.), *Bureaucracy and Political Development*. Princeton, NJ: Princeton University Press. p. 63.

MST (Landless Rural Workers Movement) (2001) Manifesto, 'Fundamental Principles for the Social and Economic Transformation of Brazil', *Journal of Peasant Studies*, 28 (2): 153–61.

Nef, Jorge (1991) 'Development Crisis and State Crisis: Lessons from Latin American Experience', in O.P. Dwivedi and P. Pitil (eds), *Development Administration in Papua New Guinea*. Boroko: ADCOL-PNG. pp. 10–33.

Nef, Jorge (1997) 'Estado, poder y políticas sociales: una visión crítica,' in Raúl Urzúa (ed.), *Cambios sociales y política públicas en América Latina*. Santiago: Andros. pp. 233–62.

Nef, Jorge (1998) 'The Politics of Insecurity,' in Jan Black (ed.), *Latin America. Its Problems and its Promise. A Multidisciplinary Introduction*. Boulder, CO: Westview Press. pp. 239–40.

Nef, J. and Bensabat, R. (1992) '"Governability" and the Receiver State in Latin America: Analysis and Prospects', in Archibald Ritter, Maxwell Cameron and David Pollock (eds), *Latin America to the Year 2000. Reactivating Growth, Improving Equity, Sustaining Democracy*. New York: Praeger. pp. 171–5.

Nef, J. and Dwivedi, O.P (1981) 'Development Theory and Administration: A Fence Around an Empty Lot?', *The Indian Journal of Public Administration*, XXVIII (1): 42–66.

Nef, Jorge and Robles, Wilder (2000) 'Globalization, Neoliberalism and the State of Underdevelopment in the New Periphery', *Journal of Developing Societies*, XVI (1): 27–48.

Nun, José (1968) 'A Middle-Class Phenomenon: The Middle-Class Military Coup,' in James Petras and Maurice Zeitlin (eds), *Latin America: Reform or Revolution? A Reader*. Greenwich, CT: Fawcett. pp. 145–85.

Ormond, Derry and Löffler, Elke (1999) 'Nueva Gestión Pública ¿Que tomar y que dejar?', *Revista del CLAD. Reforma y Democracia*, No. 11 (February): 141–72.

Pérez Salgado, Ignacio (1997) 'El papel de la cooperación técnica internacional en el proceso de modernización del Estado y la gestión en América latina', *Revista del CLAD. Reforma y Democracia*, No. 8 (July): 247–70.

Riggs, Fred (1967) 'The Sala Model: An Ecological Approach to the Study of Comparative Administration', in Nimrod Raphaeli (ed.), *Readings in Comparative Public Administration*. Boston, MA: Alwyn and Bacon. pp. 415–16.

Robin, Theobald (1995) 'Globalization and the Resurgence of the Patrimonial State', *International Review of Administrative Sciences*, 61 (3): 424.

Robles, Wilder (2000) 'Beyond the Politics of Protest: The Landless Rural Workers Movement of Brazil', *Canadian Journal of Development Studies*, XXI (3): 657–91.

Véliz, Claudio (1980) *The Centralist Tradition of Latin America*. Princeton, NJ: Princeton University Press.

Vilas, Carlos (1995) 'Economic Restructuring, Neoliberal Reforms, and the Working Class in Latin America,' in Sandor Halebsky and Richard Harris (eds), *Capital, Power, and Inequality in Latin America*. Boulder, CO: Westview Press. pp. 137–63.

Vilas, Carlos (2000) 'Más allá del Consenso de Washington? Un enfoque desde la política de algunas propuestas del Banco Mundial sobre reforma administrativa', *Revista del CLAD. Reforma y Democracia*, No. 18 (October): 25–76.

Wharlich, Beatriz (1978) 'The Evolution of Administrative Science in Latin America', *International Review of Administrative Sciences*, No. 12: 70–92.

43

Public Administration in Central and Eastern Europe

Attila Ágh

THE HISTORICAL LEGACY

Given their Communist heritage, the countries of Central and Eastern Europe have had an especially long distance to travel to reach a market economy and a democratic system of governance. After more than ten years, it is time to take stock of these reforms as they apply to the field of public administration. The purpose of this chapter is to make up a preliminary balance sheet, identifying both the positive and negative side of what has happened so far. After a brief introduction to the geographical diversity of the three regions here referred to as the countries of Central and Eastern Europe, the chapter also briefly introduces the principal features of the Communist system of governance and administration. The substantive part then deals with the basic issues that these three regions have encountered in their efforts to carry out public administration reforms. Special attention will be paid to two countries – Hungary and Russia – which represent the two poles of high achievers and laggards in public administration reforms. It concludes with a brief discussion of the lessons learned and what these portend for the future.

The term 'Central and East European states' covers three regions:

1　Central Europe: Poland, Czech Republic, Slovakia, Hungary, Slovenia, Croatia, Estonia, Latvia and Lithuania
2　The Balkans: Albania, Bulgaria, Romania, Bosnia, Macedonia, Yugoslavia
3　Eastern Europe proper: Russia, Belarus, Ukraine and Moldova.

History matters in many ways, since it reinforces and blurs the regional borders at the same time. First of all, the collapse of Communism has laid bare the underlying historical legacies of each region. In their thousand-year history, the Central European countries have always been closely integrated with Western Europe, in both trade and culture, and they had before Communism been exposed to some democracy. The Balkan countries belonged to the Ottoman Empire and were cut off from Western Europe for many centuries, so democratic structures and patterns of culture have appeared rather belatedly. The deep authoritarian traditions of the Russian Empire have not really been broken by the recent efforts for democratization. The Communist system was imposed upon the Central European and Balkan states with a forced convergence among different countries from various regions. As the past has come to play a greater role in post-Communist society, this applies also to the field of public administration.

Most spectacularly, the three Baltic states have gradually re-joined the Central European region, even in the field of public administration reforms (Noergaard and Johannsen, 1999; Horváth, 2000; Nunberg, 2000). On the other side, the post-Yugoslav states still have some common features in their political as well as public administration systems, although the former Yugoslavia has completely fallen apart into the Central European (Slovenia and Croatia) and the Balkan (Bosnia, Macedonia and Yugoslavia) successor states. The EU factor is crucial for public administration reforms, since it predetermines the major directions of the transformation of the new democratic polity as a whole. For those Central European and Balkan countries that are associate members, the application and implementation of a particular type of public administration that meets EU standards is mandatory. For all the others, there are some general efforts at democratization, for example, along the lines formulated by the Council of Europe – on the agenda without a single applicable model and with milder external pressure. All in all, public administration reforms appear in Central Europe as a process in early consolidation and Europeanization, in the Balkan region as part of a still ongoing democratic transition and in Eastern Europe as transformations without a clear, unambiguous direction.

Despite their regional divergences, systemic change has triggered public administration reform in all Central and East European countries. However, there is a paradoxical situation in the analysis of these reforms. On the one hand, there has been an increasing international literature on this topic (for example, Galligan and Smilov, 1999), with many reports for international agencies (for example, Nunberg, 1999, 2000) that give a good basis for summarizing the main features of public administration reforms in these countries. On the other hand, it has become more and more difficult to describe the general process of public administration reforms in these 'post-Communist' countries because of their growing diversity. Actually, there were more common features in their polities and public administrations at the beginning of the nineties because of their common Communist legacy and also in their effort to remove and replace the old structures as an attempt at 'creative destruction'. These initial years were followed by an 'original institutional chaos', because this period came with a mixture of old and new institutions, regulations and patterns of behavior. In a more recent third period, however, the institutional vacuum has recently been partly filled with increasingly region-specific approaches. Consequently, while it is relatively easy to describe the common negative features of their administrative structures, the present diversity makes it more difficult to find some common features that apply to all Central and Eastern European states.

The collapse of the 'Communist' or 'state socialist' system took place not only in the political sphere but also in the overwhelming and omnipresent public sector of administration and management. What the public sector is, escapes a clear definition even in advanced democracies, but the term becomes especially complicated to define in state socialism where the public sector is 'everything', and the public–private dichotomy hardly exists at all. As a common Communist

legacy, the ruling party exercised a power monopoly over society and economy. Simply formulated: the central organs of the party and government dealt with everything and decided everything. The basic principle of state socialism was unitary power, that is, state ownership meant at the same time political control over all spheres of social life. There was no such thing as the separation of powers or the autonomy of the various social fields and the actors, including those of the public sector, as has been a tradition in Western countries. Hence, the political reform process has included an element of democratization in the sense of separation and devolution of power as well as privatization in its economic meaning of privatization of state assets. The complementariness of these two processes is important in the case of Central and Eastern European countries because both have been necessary to establish a new legal order in which private property rights are recognized and new local government bodies take over public ownership from central organs. From a functional or institutional aspect, these processes have led to a differentiation at various levels of public administration as well as the creation of a new mode of intergovernmental coordination.

The public administration reforms in the Central and Eastern European countries have come from a combination of external challenges, pressures and assistance, and privatization has served as a prime domestic mover for the structural differentiation of the public sector. In an issue-oriented approach, I discuss first the Western assistance, then the privatization in order to see their impact on the main issues of the institutionalization and professionalization of the public administration in the countries concerned.

WESTERN ASSISTANCE AND THE NEW ADMINISTRATIVE STRUCTURES

The Central and Eastern European countries have joined the Council of Europe and the European Charter of Local Self-Government – opened for signature on 15 October 1985 – which has become pivotal for their public administration reforms. It has provided these countries with both the constitutional framework and the basic structure for the new public administration. The Council of Europe has always recognized the overriding importance of democracy at local and regional level. In 1994 it organized the Congress of Local and Regional Authorities of Europe

(CLRAE) as a consultative body that has become vital in public administration reforms for these countries through its detailed advice in the practical management of public administration. Among other tasks, CLRAE prepares – under Statutory Resolution (2000) 1 of the Committee of Ministers of the Council of Europe – regular country reports on the situation of local and regional democracy in all member (and candidate) states. In particular, the CLRAE monitors how the principles of the European Charter of Local Self-Government are implemented and this control function has had a particular significance for all Central and East European countries.

This intensive attention paid by the West to public administration and management among its Eastern neighbors has led to various forms of technical assistance and conditionalities (see for example, Treen and Madsen, 2000). The Council of Europe, in fact, already in 1992 designed a special program, LODE (Local Democracy Program), to promote local democracy and to develop local and regional authorities, in principle for all member states, and in particular for the new democracies. The LODE program draws inspiration from the European Charter of Local Self-Government and is developed every year on the basis of the needs expressed by the beneficiary countries. This program operates at both intergovernmental and local–regional levels in order to create central government structures capable of cooperating with the autonomous local self-governments and to develop local and regional authorities capable of efficiently managing public affairs. Given the fact that the cultural factor is the real bottleneck in public administration reforms, the professionalization of public administration is the biggest task for the Central and East European countries. Thus, LODE puts a special emphasis on the training of local and regional authority elected representatives and officials in the framework of ENTO (European Network of Training Organizations for Local and Regional Authorities). In addition, Local Democracy Agencies were established in 1993 as part of the peace process in former Yugoslavia to form a partnership between a particular local authority and local counterparts elsewhere in Europe. As an example of what this kind of collaboration has produced, it is worth mentioning that in Kosovo it has helped to recruit international administrators for its thirty municipalities, to draft legal texts on municipalities and elections, and to monitor the municipal electoral process.

In addition to the Council of Europe and its various assistance programs, the World Bank has provided assistance and conducted research on public administration reforms in the Central and East European countries. In its series of Regional and Sectoral Studies, a report on the State After Communism was published by the Public Sector Group (Nunberg, 1999). This comprehensive document has served as the basis for a detailed analysis of the administrative capacity of the states that are applying for EU membership. Also of prime importance is the Strategy Paper prepared by the World Bank Group's Public Sector Board in May 2000 on Reforming Public Institutions and Strengthening Governance, which in its Section Three deals with Europe and the Central Asia Region. Because it tries to outline the general situation in the Central and East European and Central Asian countries, it tends to deal more with the laggards in the latter two sub-regions than with the high performers in Central Europe.

This document distinguishes between three separate periods of technical assistance to public sector reform in Central and Eastern Europe that coincide with the stages of institutional development mentioned above. For the World Bank assistance, the early years of public sector transformation meant Institution-Building/Technical Assistance (IBTA) projects that usually suffered from weak client commitment and turned into information technology projects with a limited prospect of sustainable impact on institution-building. In the mid-1990s the World Bank initiated broader institutional reforms, such as public resource management and specific functions of state administration – tax administration, treasury system, etc. – in order to build up both technical and organizational foundations for modern public administration. In the last couple of years there has been an expansion in the scale, scope and depth of public sector reform according to the World Bank Strategy Paper in the fields of fiscal management, public administration and civil service, as well as legal, regulatory and judicial reform. In reviewing its own experience, the Bank paper refers to two separate strategies, one 'top-down' approach that starts with the needs as viewed holistically from a central government perspective, another 'bottom-up' approach that places more emphasis on the importance of locally initiated changes and feeds on the energy of civic associations. The Bank experts do not necessarily argue that one supersedes the other, but its prescriptions for the future lean more towards the importance of strengthening popular participation and control in Central and East European countries.

Beyond the Council of Europe and the World Bank assistance programs – but connected with them in many ways – there are other specific programs aimed at strengthening public administration and/or local governance in these countries. First of all, the Organization for Economic Co-operation and Development (OECD) has supported the SIGMA program (Support for Improvement in Governance and Management in Central and East European Countries). More specifically, it has developed the PUMA (Public Management and Governance) program. It has also edited the bimonthly *Public Management Forum*, advising and informing public managers and administrators in 'transition countries'. From among the civic organizations, the Local Government and Public Service Reform Initiative may deserve special attention as part of a program run by the Budapest-based Open Society Institute. The latter, in turn, has been closely connected with other forms of organization, such as LOGIN (Local Government Information Network on the internet) and NISPAcee (Network of Institutes and Schools of Public Administration in Central and Eastern Europe, Bratislava). LOGIN has developed close cooperation with the national associations in Bulgaria, Hungary, Latvia, Lithuania and Poland, and with some other research centers.

NISPAcee, for its part, has produced a series of relevant publications and conferences about public administration reforms in the Central and East European countries. Two recent books deserve to be mentioned because they offer a broad overview of public administration reform in many countries of the Central European, Balkan and East European regions. The first, edited by Jak Jabes (2000), deals with the experience of public administration during the first ten years of transition. Contributors to the volume provide a detailed description of the reforms in individual countries in the three regions. While thin on theory, it provides a solid ground for further study of these reform efforts. The second – more theoretically oriented – book is edited by Tony Verheijen (2001). It focuses more specifically on the relations between politics and administration. Verheijen himself provides a useful summary of the main efforts and new approaches 'to the classification and comparative study of politico-administrative relations' in the new democracies. These books also complement other efforts, such as the recent volume by Peters and Pierre (2001), which place the regional reforms in the new democracies of Eastern and Central Europe in a broader international perspective. As this brief overview suggests, the public administration reform efforts in Central and East European countries provide a fertile ground for research and comparison with similar programs in other regions of the world.

PRIVATIZATION AND PUBLIC SERVICE REFORMS

The basic precondition for all public administration reforms is the structural differentiation of the public sector. However, the various sub-systems of the public sector became really separate and visible in the Central and East European countries only during its decomposition. The overcentralized and overwhelming public sector disintegrated with the Communist political system as the transition was initiated. Privatization has been both the result and the prime mover of all public sector reforms. The drastic reduction of the state sector brought about the essential differentiation of its major components. In general, there are three sub-systems of the public sector that have become separated in the process of complete disintegration of the Communist state. At the same time, there has been a radical transformation of the political meso-system of social actors such as interest organizations and micro-system as a network of civic associations. Altogether, a complete reorganization of public–private relationships has taken place that has changed the social environment of public administration beyond recognition – for instance, its relationship to NGOs, nonprofit organizations, or the public–private 'twinning' in public service deliveries, etc. – but several of these points go beyond what can be covered in this chapter.

The largest and dominant part of the former public sector (PS-1) was the State Owned Enterprises. These organizations controlled both production and exchange. Privatization has left very few of these enterprises in the most advanced Central and East European market economies, while a drastic reduction and decomposition has taken place in all countries. The new public enterprise sector has not yet been stabilized and made productive enough. Nonetheless, there has so far been no complete separation of business and politics, a state of affairs that has given rise to a high level of corruption in most states. Public procurement or acquisition has also opened new opportunities to blur the necessary borderline between business and politics. Nonetheless, by and large, this process of PS-1 transformation may be considered as almost completed.

The second major sub-system of the public sector (PS-2) is the provision of public services in the fields of education, health care, social services, public transport and communication, etc. The decline of GDP in the early 1990s in the Central and Eastern European countries was between 25 and 50%. Since the power transition took place in all countries under conditions of a severe economic crisis and huge state foreign debt, the public service sector has suffered major budgetary restrictions. It was oversized compared to the economic capacity of the countries concerned and cutbacks have been rather haphazard and ad hoc. Hence, there has been no real reform, just a transition without a comprehensive strategy or detailed plan of action. The best achievements are partial reforms, for example, in the pension system. Without a purposeful, intentional change the Central and East European states simply have abandoned or drastically reduced the delivery of public services under budgetary pressures. For instance, in Hungary, according to the Central Statistical Office, public service delivery was reduced between 1991 and 1999 from 38.2% to 27.0% of the state budget. Yet, Hungary is still among the countries from the three regions with one of the best service delivery coverages. The lack of comprehensive planning of the reform process in this sub-sector means that many issues still remain unresolved.

The third sub-system of the public sector (PS-3) is public administration in the largest sense, as all state administration functions. Public administration in the Central and East European countries has been re-designed, so one can speak in this respect about conscious reforms and not only about random transformations. In 1992 the Central European governments established special public administration reform committees. Some such public body, however, has been set up in all countries concerned. Changes in this sub-system resulted in ambitious projects, but most of them have not been fully implemented or not yet completed. Yet PS-3 has been much more successful in public administration reforms than PS-2 and this chapter focuses on the reform of public administration in this narrower meaning.

We have briefly presented the basic transformation in three fields, separated for the first time, since the public service sector and public administration have emerged as special systems as a result of democratization. Earlier they were secondary and subjected to the workings of the State Owned Enterprises. The three sub-systems overlapped and were closely connected, since the State Owned Enterprises were managed as part of the state administration. The public managers as 'apparatchiks' moved easily – following political decisions – between these three sub-systems and had similar patterns of behavior. With the collapse of state socialism they were replaced and/or retrained, but since then the various sub-systems have required different kinds of public managers. Also, the tasks of the central governments and local administrations have changed beyond recognition. They were drastically reduced when the State Owned Enterprises became completely or partially privatized. The conscious attitude in public administration reform comes from this situation, since with the 'shrinking state' the reform of public administration has proved to be the center of political fights and public discourse. After the power transition, the reform of central government and its administration was absolutely necessary and started immediately, while the reform of local and territorial self-governments has lagged very much behind. All the same, it is the democratization of patron–client relations and an improved relationship between public employees and the citizens that have emerged as a set of especially salient reform issues.

THE MAIN ISSUES OF SYSTEMIC CHANGE

Democratization in terms of public administration in the Central and Eastern European region means basically devolution of decision-making powers and deconcentration of the administrative responsibilities for implementation. In the initial period of systemic change the basic transformation of public administrations appeared at two levels.

First, constitutional provisions with general rules were established. This created a separation between the competencies of the central government and local (and territorial) self-governments. Through this legislation both state-controlled administrative and self-governing units have emerged parallel, first of all in meso-structures. Second, basic changes occurred in the early 1990s in local–territorial power relations. Passing a new municipal electoral law was among the first actions of the democratic governments. The first free and fair local or municipal elections resulted in great changes in the local elites. For example, in Estonia the first three municipal elections in the postwar period after a fifty-year break produced a breakthrough to a new public administration. The first, semi-free elections took place on 10 December 1989, almost two years before independence and preparing it to a great extent. The next municipal elections were held on 17 October 1993, when also the Constitution was approved by referendum. The subsequent municipal elections were organized on 20 October 1996, which produced the necessary routine of local public administration for the development of grassroots democracy and civil society. In 1990–91 there were municipal elections in all Central and Eastern European states and since then they have become as regular as the parliamentary elections. Municipal elections and public administration reforms may have played the biggest role in political mobilization and democratization in the Baltic states (Noergard and Johannsen, 1999: 161–5), but they have proved to be an important factor of political change everywhere in the region.

These constitutional and electoral changes were, in fact, the first steps toward reform of the public administration systems. In general, there have been three stages or steps in the democratic institution building that I have described in detail elsewhere (for example, Ágh, 1997). The first step included the constitutional and legal changes mentioned above, which meant a historical turning point but produced only very general and abstract provisions about the separation of state and public administrations and about the autonomy of local self-governments. It produced the creative destruction of the powers inherent in a system of democratic centralism. The paradox is that the state has played a great role in its own deregulation from 'super-state' to 'mini-state'.

The second period, which I prefer to call that of 'original institutional chaos', emerged with a mix of some newly established and some remaining old institutions. This institutional chaos was, and in some cases has been, more characteristic in meso-politics, that is, at the middle level of functional and territorial organizations, than in macro-politics. In most cases the administrative units as divisions of state administration were reorganized earlier – and had more resources – than the new self-governing units of public administration. As a consequence, they continued to dominate, even when the new self-governments had come into being. After the first years of this period, public administration reforms lost momentum everywhere and the initial ambitious plans were not carried out. The resistance of many former institutions (such as the deconcentrated state organs in counties or districts) and previous patterns of – over-politicized, rigid and hierarchical – administrative behavior was much bigger than expected in the moments of the initial great changes. Last but not least, the economic crisis and the following drastic crisis management were not favorable for the second step in the institution-building, first of all because of the ensuing economic and budgetary re-centralization. Also, the political volatility in most new regimes contributed to the slowdown of administrative changes and the conservation of some former institutions.

In the most recent period of the early 2000s an institutional vacuum has come into being, since some structures are now permanently missing in the new polities. Basically, in all Central and East European states asymmetrical institution-building has taken place, although the degree of asymmetry varies from country to country. After the emergence of macro-politics with its power centers (government, president, parliament and Constitutional Court) and major actors (parliamentary parties), the creation of meso- and micro-political institutions has been delayed everywhere. What is more, it has been prevented and distorted not simply by the overwhelming power of macro-political institutions but also consciously by the actors in macro-politics. The micro-structures such as local self-governments and civic associations have suffered most from the dominance of the new macro-politics, since, for example, the legal-political autonomy of local self-governments has been fatally damaged by budgetary re-centralization. Meso-structures such as functional and territorial interest organizations have also remained half-baked, that is, not completely organized and/or regulated.

It seems as if the top-down process of reform in public administration that was necessary in the early years of transition has now reached its limits. Pressures are building from below to create more elbow room for popular initiatives. The most important actors here are not the local government structures at the meso-level but increasingly stronger organizations in civil society. It is no coincidence that the relationship between government and civil society was the main topic at the 2001 NISPAcee conference in Riga, Latvia (Wright, 2001).

Europeanization has recently introduced a new factor into the transformation process in countries seeking access to the European Union. The latter is increasingly insisting on the need for development of 'administrative and judicial capacity', regional structures and a social dialogue among principal stakeholders. The Spanish presidency of the Union announced in early 2002 that these developments would be monitored. All these efforts are seen as measures to accelerate the EU convergence of the accession countries. Whether this is a wise move or not is certainly a matter of debate given that the transformation of national public administration is a complex process and depends very much on the peculiarities of existing structures (Knill, 2001). Nonetheless, with the added pressure from the EU, it is possible that this process of homogenizing public administration within the Union may actually take place quicker in the accession countries than in the more established member countries.

Regardless of how effective this process of transformation is, however, the tasks ahead in public administration reforms are tremendous in both policy and political terms. There is still a big gap between the demand for a significant role of public administration in managing democratic transition or consolidation and the actual administrative capacity of most states. Basically, there are two main issues of all public administration reforms as democratization processes. The first is the transformation of the objective/institutional side, the second is that of the subjective/personal side, with the two key terms of decentralization and professionalization. Consequently, the keywords for institutional reform are the decentralization of decisions and deconcentration of implementation that have been briefly outlined above. For these tasks, Samuel Huntington offers four criteria: 'The level of institutionalization of any political system can be defined by the adaptability, complexity, autonomy, and coherence of its organizations and procedures' (1968: 12). These criteria have also provided a point of departure for the institutional change in the new democracies. Put simply, *adaptability* presupposes the ability of an institution to meet challenges from a changing environment. *Complexity* relates to the level of internal differentiation and the creation of an internal structure appropriate for the given functions or tasks. *Autonomy* is the capacity of an institution to act without control by other actors. Finally, *coherence* is the capacity of the institution to produce integrated and coordinated decisions. These are good criteria for assessing institutionalization in the countries of Central and Eastern Europe. In my view, autonomy is the most and coherence is the least developed feature of the new public administrations. That is, most institutions have gained their legal-political autonomy but are still to a great extent unable to produce coherent policies. Institutions have shown degrees of adaptability, since these institutions have been drawn into a flux of changes but their complexity and internal/external coordination capacity is still really weak.

All these institutional deficiencies have their counterparts on the managerial side of public administration. Drawing on a World Bank survey (Nunberg, 2000: 6–21), one can provide two sets of criteria. The first may be called human resources management as composed of (a) the legal and ethical framework, (b) employment and pay policy and (c) training and career development. The second set is about the policy formulation and coordination capacity, which consists of (a) decision making processes and procedures, (b) organizational culture and management practice and (c) openness and readiness to Western

policy transfer and its implementation (as for example, the EU accession management). The first set of criteria is more about the individual administrator, the second more about the collective unit or the organizational performance of an institution.

In principle, all Central and East European countries can be characterized by this set of criteria, but usually the data are scarce and the information provided by the national agencies is sometimes distorted. One can say about the human resources management, however, that while the legal and ethical framework has been set everywhere, the pay for public administration has declined drastically. This has created a mass exodus to the private sector, although the job security is still a big advantage in public administration. On-the-job training has become a standard part of public administration, with regular exams and merit-based career opportunities, but administrative careers have often still been blurred and distorted by the practice of making appointments based on political criteria. As far as policy making and coordination are concerned, public administration systems have a lower performance level than their employees individually. The reason is that the decision making processes and procedures in most places have not been clearly regulated in the rapidly changing world, although computerization is facilitating a more systematic and holistic approach to management. The organization culture is still very rigid, and a transfer of new management practices from the more modernized private sector is still in an initial stage. Finally, countries vary greatly in their inclination and capacity to learn from Western practices and to develop contacts with Western partners as well as international organizations. The Central European countries have an interrupted Western tradition in public administration and they quickly re-established both their normatives and contacts, as have the Balkan states, although to a lesser extent. The East European countries, however, have shown at best an ambiguous attitude, sometimes welcoming and at other times refusing institutional and policy transfers from the West. These institutional and professional criteria can be best illustrated through two case studies, which provide a contrast in realizing these criteria of institutionalization and professionalization.

A HIGH ACHIEVER AND A LAGGARD

The increasing diversity among the states concerned can be illustrated by two case studies, reflecting the two opposites of performance to date when it comes to executing public administration reforms. The top performers or 'high achievers' are typically found in Central Europe among the countries that are getting 'ready for Europe'. I shall use Hungary as an example of a high achiever. The opposite end is occupied by countries in Eastern Europe, where reforms have achieved little and their legitimacy is still in question. I use Russia as the case in point.

Hungary

Hungary has been described by Barbara Nunberg as a pioneer in building up strong administrative capacity in order to be 'ready for Europe' (Nunberg, 2000: 7). In the same way, Martin Brusis has suggested that Hungary is 'exceptional' in its efforts in territorial reorganization and regional development funds (Brusis, 2001: 230). The reform of central government began in Hungary in the late 1980s with extended legislation on the free market. The further reduction of competencies of the central government reached another milestone in the early 1990s with accelerated privatization.

Government reorganization began in 1990 when all economic branch ministries were eliminated, leaving only three ministries dealing with the economy. The next government, in 1994, reduced them to two: the Ministry of Economy and Ministry of Finances. In the 1990s the Ministry of Finances was the more important but in 1998 the third government made the Ministry of Economy the decisive actor, since the economic crisis management was over. With the elimination of the Central Headquarters of the former ruling party (Hungarian Socialist Workers Party) the central government received a new function. It had to deal with the policy planning and policy coordination of ministries. Hungary has developed a German type of chancellor democracy, in which the central role in policy coordination is played by the Prime Minister's Office. The Orbán government completed the process of institution-building in central government through the creation of the Prime Minister's Office into a major body for coordination of all the other ministries and also intergovernmental relations.

Traditionally Hungary has had nineteen counties and the capital (Budapest) as the major administrative units. In addition to these twenty units, the 1989 Constitution stipulates three administrative levels for parliamentary and municipal elections: (1) settlements below and (2) those above 10,000 inhabitants and (3) the

capital (see Temesi, 2000 for details). All the above-mentioned administrative units have self-governing elected bodies, paralleled with the lower level of state administration in the counties and Budapest. These de-concentrated offices of ministries and other national authorities ('decos') have represented the lower level state administration. The decos have been organized in one common county (or capital) office and, combined with the territorial state administrative office, monitor the legality of the territorial and local self-governments. The basic constitutional principle is that the territorial and local self-governments are completely autonomous; the only function of state administration is the legal control of their activities. The state administration of central government and the public administration of territorial and local self-governments meet at the level of meso-politics in the twenty major administrative units. This parallel working and cooperation has not been without conflicts since 1990 but certainly has improved a lot as both sides have learned their new functions (the same parallel structures exist in the Czech Republic and elsewhere in Central Europe; see Lacina and Vajdova, 2000: 263).

The first autonomous territorial and local self-governments were elected in autumn 1990 and since then there have been regular elections. Nowadays all mayors are directly elected and the election of the council members proceeds according to a proportional system with a compensation list. On 7 July 1993 the Hungarian parliament passed an Act on the Rights of National and Ethnic Minorities (Act LXXVII/1993). These rights were secured already in the Constitution but were specifically regulated by this law, including the rights of ethnic-national communities to their own elections in the framework of the municipal elections. In Hungary there are thirteen ethnic minorities, most of which are very small but two minorities (Roma and German) exceed 100,000 inhabitants. Their elected representatives may represent them in local self-governments in two ways. First, they may form a settlement municipality government if they elect the majority of councilors in a given settlement. Second, if they are only a minority in a given settlement, they can form a local minority self-government, which will be part of the municipal council in its own right. In the regular minority elections, as part of municipal elections, the thirteen minorities have elected as many as one thousand minority self-governments from both types. Beyond this, the two forms of minority self-governments elect their National Councils on a nation-wide basis, which are the partners of the Minority Office of the central government in regulating minority matters and allocating government funds for the activities of ethnic-national minorities (see Ágh and Kurtán, 1996).

The workings of the territorial and local self-governments have been regulated by two major legislative packages of 1990 and 1994. The main direction of these amendments has been the extension of the rights and competencies in favor of mayors towards the municipal councils to strengthen the stability of self-governments. But the major change in 1994 was the abolition of incompatibility between the posts in the local–regional and the national political representations. According to the Act on the Mayors (Act LVII/1994, passed on 5 July 1994) the mayors and the councilors of the territorial and local self-governments may also be elected to the Hungarian parliament. This has meant the unification of the national and the regional–local political elites, and it has made the territorial–local politics a preparation stage for national politics. As a result, more than one-third of the MPs in the Hungarian parliament have usually also a post in local politics, and altogether more than half of them have past experiences of this type.

In the Hungarian public administration system, politics has been separated from administration. The mayor and the councilors are elected, but the civil servants are 'selected', that is, they are career public servants and the 'notary' heads their staff, a pattern that is common in Central Europe (see Horváth, 2000: 41). The civil service is governed by the Act XXXII/1992 on the Legal Status of Civil Servants, and public servants or employees (health, education and social services) are covered by the Act on Public Employees (Act XXXIII/1992). Civil servants have to pass an exam, which has recently been regulated by a government decree (35/1998) on the Act on the Special Administrative Exam. The Civil Service Department, which controls 60% of civil servants and 80% of public employees, is within the Ministry of the Interior. In the late 1990s there were about 104,000 civil servants (out of which there were 52,000 in both state and public administrations), around 13% of public sector employment in general (814,000). These figures correspond to those, for instance, in the United Kingdom. Although repeated efforts have been made to improve the salary level for both civil and public servants, it is still very much below the level for the same experts in the private sector. It is no surprise, therefore, that the public sector has suffered huge losses in human resources since 1990.

Regionalization has also come to the fore in Hungarian public administration reforms since the mid-1990s, mostly as part of the EU adaptation process. The Act on Regional Development (Act XXI/1996) has identified seven regions in Hungary, six of which have been formed from clusters of adjacent counties, and one forming a central region with the capital. However, these regions are still only territorial-statistical units for regional development and not yet self-governing territorial units. Thus, all regions have organized Regional Development Councils for allocating funds and for regional planning. The Hungarian parliament has also decided on the Concept for National Regional Development by a parliamentary resolution (Resolution 35/1998). The Orbán government further developed the National Council for Regional Development and the Regional Development Councils (Act XCII/1999). But this was a half-step back, since – unlike the Polish case (Kowalczyk, 2000: 223) – this law did not facilitate the creation of regions with their elected bodies, but instead strengthened the influence of central government in the Regional Development Councils. Under the former Hungarian government a new debate began about the advantages and disadvantages of decentralization. This debate has also been going on in the international political science literature (see recently De Vries, 2000).

On the domestic side, the major problems of the Hungarian public administration are fragmentation and financing, which open the way for political intervention by the governing parties or state administration. The 1989 Constitution created about 3200 (3187) settlements, with one-third of them having less than one thousand inhabitants. This fragmentation has led to a general situation where many local self-governments are unable to provide those basic public services they are supposed to deliver according to the Constitution. They are too small and also too poor for doing so. Although the Constitution also stipulates that the local self-governments are entitled to state financial support for these public services, the drastic crisis management in the 1990s with a permanent reduction of the public sector budget prevented these allocations. The percentage allocation for local self-governments has declined in the state budget between 1990 and 2001 from 13.7 to 11.2 per cent and has produced a relative impoverishment of local self-governments. The result is that major social conflicts have become deconcentrated in this way from the national to the local levels.

The bottlenecks of the Hungarian public administration reforms in the process of European integration have been in policy making and professionalization. First, policy coordination appears to work efficiently but policy formulation is still too legalistic and often lacks economic assessment for making good decisions. Second, despite many efforts, the preparation of public administrators (and politicians, including MPs) for accession to the EU is not yet satisfactory in the field of language and legal training. Nonetheless, the management of Hungary's accession to the EU has been quite good and the detailed National Program for the Adoption of Aquis (March, 1998) has been considered positively by the EU Commission. Summarizing the description I have relied on so far, Barbara Nunberg states that 'In general, the structures and procedures used to coordinate EU integration are satisfactory, and have already been seen to be effective in positioning Hungary in a strong position for EU membership' (Nunberg, 2000: 316).

Russia

At the other pole, Russia can be considered as a model case of the less successful public administration reform in Eastern Europe. In discussing Russia, Nunberg asks the question in her title 'A New Administrative Order for Post-Soviet Russia?', and her answer is very skeptical. Russia faces four specific problems in reforming its public administration:

1   A long Communist legacy with virtually no living memory of law and public administration from times prior to the Communist state that could be usefully retrieved, even those traditions that are different from what is mainstream in the rest of Europe.
2   With a loss of empire and prestige there has been a new unease and resistance to change, and, as a result, some Russians are not ready to learn from abroad and import foreign institutions.
3   Russia in its Communist period was completely isolated, not only from the West but to a great extent also from the countries in its external empire as far as administrative systems were concerned.
4   No drastic transformations have taken place, only adaptation of existing structures.

Russia's volatile politics (political infighting, extreme dominant figures and fragile presidential system) has slowed the country's effort at civil service and public administration reform, leaving its performance and modernization low on the political agenda. In sum, 'Russian idiosyncrasy and instability pose formidable difficulties for would-be civil service reformers' (Nunberg, 1999: 156).

One has to add here that the size of the country also matters. It is not by chance that Nunberg describes first of all changes in public employment in general and civil service employment in particular. Public employment at large includes the larger state administration as well as the administrative apparatus of sectoral organizations (trade unions and professional associations) and economic management of public enterprises, both of which increased between 1990 and 1992 from 0.87 to 1.07 million, that is, from 1.2 to 1.5 per cent of all employment. This increase came with the decentralization, since most of the increase of personnel was due to the organization of regional and local levels (from 325,600 to 468,700 employees). At the same time, employment in the management of public enterprises declined in the early 1990s from 36,000 to 12,600 employees, which indicates the impact of the privatization process on public employment. Civil service employment proper grew in this period from 666,000 to 881,000 employees, that is, from 0.9 to 1.2 per cent of all employment and shows the strengthening public administration apparatus (Nunberg, 1999: 159–61). From her account, it is clear that understanding the full dimensions of the transformation of the multi-level administration structures is not easy because there is little information about the institutional changes in this huge country. The overall impression at this point is that the central government has weakened, the administrative units have gained some autonomy, but without clear legal regulations. A process of re-centralization under President Putin, therefore, has not been surprising.

This does not mean that efforts at regulating the public administration system have been totally absent. First of all, the Civil Service Act was passed in 1995. It has been a big step towards the improvement of performance in public administration but the law has serious disadvantages. For instance, it has not delineated the civil service from the rest of the public sphere, since it embraces the employees of military, judicial, banking and parastatal organizations. It establishes a rigid and steeply hierarchical grading structure, with no flexibility for talent and performance, and also fails to draw clear distinctions between political and administrative appointments. All in all, this description of the Russian public administration reforms illustrates the rather chaotic changes in Eastern Europe, where the political reform process has yet to produce institutional consolidation.

There is a more detailed picture about some sectors of the Russian public administration reforms, for example about the local administration of social assistance programs, that opens up a broader perspective about the whole administrative structure of Russia. This picture reinforces the general impression of the high level of heterogeneity and the lack of transparency. First, the sharp decentralization of fiscal and administrative responsibilities is one of the cardinal characteristics of the transition period in Russia. Second, decentralization has been much greater in program administration and service delivery than in program design and funding. Furthermore, the decentralization and reorientation of government functions have required or will entail both the modification of existing local government agencies and the creation of new offices to administer programs transferred to localities, as well as some newly established programs. There is a general recognition that in Russia the administration of social protection programs has been weak. The situation in general may be characterized by the passing of laws, which are severely hampered by an implementation deficit and enforcement gaps. In Russia the highest level of sub-national government is called Subjects of the Federation, of which there are eighty-nine, mostly republics, in addition, the two large cities (Moscow and St Petersburg), some *'oblasts'* (provinces), autonomous *'okrugs'* (regions) and one autonomous *'raion'* (district). These organizations at different territorial levels are formally equal in their powers and they have some budget autonomy as well, and some Subjects of the Federation signed separate treaties under President Yeltsin. What is more, not only these bigger units but also each municipality is organized in a different way and they administer and deliver public services also in a different way (see Richman and Struyk, 2001: 3–7). Obviously, Russia still has a long way to go before it has completed public administration reforms in this huge country by satisfying both the regional–local specificities and the requirements of homogeneity of public administration.

CONCLUSION: REGIONS MATTER

In drawing my conclusion, I wish to borrow insights from three other scholars (Hesse, Hood and Peters, 1997), who suggest that there are sub-regional idiosyncrasies that stand out in Central and Eastern Europe. With reference to the Central European region, they describe the public administration reform situation as 'effectiveness plus jeopardy'. The main goal of public administration reforms has been achieved but

there have also been many negative side effects. The 'effective state' and efficient public administration has already been established to quite an extent but new dysfunctions have also appeared in intergovernmental relations and the mass exodus of professionals from the public to the private sector has basically damaged the public sector.

Their characterization of the Balkan region is 'futility plus jeopardy'. The main goal of public administration reforms has not yet been achieved, only attempted. The half-transformed public sector has produced only an insufficient control of public affairs. Some measures have been successful and the long-term trend of democratization can be noticed but the chaotic, incoherent features of public administrations are still dominant, principally in the post-Yugoslav states. The administrations of both the central government and local self-governments are weak and inefficient in the Balkan states. Although both democratization and professionalization have been promoted, power has remained over-centralized at the level of the central government and vertical–horizontal accountability mechanisms have not yet worked properly. The performance criteria have only very slowly penetrated public management.

The East European region is described as 'perversity plus jeopardy'. No consequent systemic change can be noticed in democratization in general or in public administration in particular, since the public sector has in many ways collapsed. There has been stagnation or at most a slow recovery of the economy, but no reconstruction yet of the delivery of basic services. The public administration and civil service is still halfway between reform and regression. Therefore, the new public administration as a system is rather unstable in the East European states and its legitimacy has also been weak and fragile, since the 'retreat of the state' from public services and has caused widespread dissatisfaction among the populations.

In the 'miraculous year' (1989), or in the initial period of systemic change, the emphasis was on the 'Great Transformation', and it was rightly so. By now, more than ten years later, the emphasis has to be put on the half-completed public administration reforms with missing institutions and patterns of behavior in most countries, which gives a rather gloomy picture. Only the Central European states, which are catching up with Western standards, have developed professionalism and accountability in a rather stable system of public administration. They have increasingly improved the delivery of public services as well, but it is still very far, not only from the high demands of their populations but also from the minimum EU requirements.

The state was largely absent in the analysis of democratization in the early 1990s and the almighty market was mystified. Now, the significance of the 'effective state' is back, both in East and West. This is reflected in the new philosophy of international organizations such as the UN and the World Bank in the spirit of 'Reinventing Government' (see the UNDP Regional Report, 1997 and World Development Report, 1997). The late Herbert Simon, before his death, formulated this new philosophy very markedly. In his message 'Public Administration in Today's World of Organization and Markets', delivered at the Annual Meeting of the American Political Science Association (APSA), Simon emphasized that the market is a rather limited coordinating mechanism and often needs the 'visible hand' of the state or public administration for regulation. Large – both governmental and business – organizations, in fact, 'are more effective than markets' (2000: 753).

Consequently, state capacity, including administrative capacity, is vital in the present globalized world. Increasingly, the interest of analysts in the democratization processes in Central and Eastern Europe turns to the public administration reforms. Governments in this region are concerned, but not yet mobilized and committed enough to thorough reforms. First of all, the Balkan and East European states do not yet see its significance because, to a great extent, they are still preoccupied with economic stability, although that is not possible in a globalized world without an effectively performing state and public administration. The Central European states have already completed their economic stabilization and have embarked upon the tasks of social construction of democracy. The creation of an effective state has been almost completed by the Central European countries under EU pressure, but public administration reforms as a foundation of citizen-friendly, participatory and multi-level governance are still outstanding challenges in these countries.

REFERENCES

Ágh, Attila (1997) 'Actors of Systemic Change: The Political Context of Public Sector Reform in Central Europe'. Discussion paper No. 19, European Centre for Comparative Government and Public Policy.

Ágh, Attila and Kurtán, S. (1996) 'Parliaments and Organized Interests in Civil Society: Local Government Legislation and Elections in Hungary (1990–1995)', in Attila Ágh and Gabriella Ilonszki (eds), *Parliaments and Organized Interests in Central Europe: The Second*

Steps. Budapest: Hungarian Centre for Democracy Studies.

Brusis, Martin (2001) 'Institution Building for Regional Development: A Comparison of the Czech Republic, Estonia, Hungary, Poland and Slovakia', in Jürgen Beyer, J. Wielgohs and H. Wisenthal (eds), *Successful Transitions: Political Factors of Socio-Economic Progress in Postsocialist Countries*. Baden-Baden: Nomos.

De Vries, Michiel (2000) 'The Rise and Fall of Decentralization', *European Journal of Political Research*, 38 (2): 193–224.

Hesse, J.J., Hood, C. and Peters, B.G. (1997) 'Paradoxes of Public Sector Reform: Soft Theory and Hard Cases'. Working Papers of the European Centre for Comparative Government and Public Policy (Berlin).

Horváth, Tamás (ed.) (2000a) *Decentralization: Experiments and Reforms – Local Governments in Central and Eastern Europe*. Budapest: Local Government and Public Service Reform Initiative (Login).

Horváth, Tamás (2000b) 'Directions and Differences of Local Changes', in Tamás Horváth (ed.), *Decentralization: Experiments and Reforms – Local Governments in Central and Eastern Europe*. Budapest: Local Government and Public Service Reform Initiative (Login).

Huntington, Samuel (1968) *Political Order in Changing Societies*. New Haven, CT and London: Yale University Press.

Jabes, Jak (ed.) (2000) *Ten Years of Transition: Prospects and Challenges for the Future of Public Administration*. Bratislava: NISPAcee.

Knill, Christopher (2001) *The Europeanization of National Administrations: Patterns of Institutional Change and Persistence*. Cambridge: Cambridge University Press.

Kowalczyk, Andrzej (2000) 'Local Government in Poland', in Tamás Horváth (ed.), *Decentralization: Experiments and Reforms – Local Governments in Central and Eastern Europe*. Budapest: Local Government and Public Service Reform Initiative (Login). p. 223.

Lacina, Karel and Vajdova, Z. (2000) 'Local Government in the Czech Republic', in Tamás Horváth (ed.), *Decentralization: Experiments and Reforms – Local Governments in Central and Eastern Europe*. Budapest: Local Government and Public Service Reform Initiative (Login). p. 263.

Noergaard, Ole and Johannsen, L. (1999) *The Baltic States after Independence*. Cheltenham: Edward Elgar.

Nunberg, Barbara (1999) *The State After Communism: Administrative Transitions in Central and Eastern Europe*. Washington, DC: The World Bank.

Nunberg, Barbara (2000) *Ready for Europe: Public Administration Reform and European Union Accession in Central and Eastern Europe*. Washington, DC: The World Bank.

Peters, B. Guy and Pierre, J. (eds) (2001) *Politicians, Bureaucrats and Administrative Reform*. London: Routledge.

Richman, Burton and Struyk, R. (2001) 'Local Administration of Social Assistance Programs in Russia', *NISPAcee Occasional Papers in Public*

Administration and Public Policy, Vol. II, No. 1, Winter 2001.

Simon, Herbert (2000) 'Public Administration in Today's World of Organizations and Markets', *PS – Political Science and Politics*, 33 (4): 753.

Temesi, István (2000) 'Local Government in Hungary', in Tamás Horváth (ed.), *Decentralization: Experiments and Reforms – Local Governments in Central and Eastern Europe*. Budapest: Local Government and Public Service Reform Initiative (Login). pp. 343–84.

Treen, Nick and Madsen, J.M. (2000) 'EU Candidates Preparing to Manage Pre-Accession Funds', *Public Management Forum*, 6 (4): 4–5.

UNDP Regional Report (1997) *The Shrinking State: Governance and Human Development in Eastern Europe and the Commonwealth of Independent States*. New York: UNDP.

Verheijen, Tony (ed.) (2001) *Politco-Administrative Relations: Who Rules?* Bratislava: NISPAcee.

World Development Report (1997) *The State in a Changing World*. Oxford: Oxford University Press published for the World Bank.

Wright, Glen (ed.) (2001) *Government, Market and the Civic Sector: The Search for a Productive Partnership*. Bratislava: NISPAcee.

ACCOUNTABILITY

Introduction

Paul G. Thomas

Accountability has always been a central concern of both the study and the practice of public administration. This key concept has also been elusive and controversial, with theoretical debates under way almost constantly. In the realm of practice, critics have seldom been hard pressed to find fault with existing accountability arrangements and procedures, regardless of the type of political and bureaucratic system under examination. Because accountability is such a prized political and administrative value, the usual assumption has been that there can never be too much of it. Also, there has been a reluctance to acknowledge that accountability must at times adjust to, compromise with and even yield to other important political and administrative values, such as representation, responsiveness, efficiency, equity and legitimacy.

While controversy swirls around the concept of accountability, there is a core meaning on which most commentators agree. Accountability is a formal relationship governed by a process. As a relationship, it involves a person or body in a position of authority assigning or negotiating with others the performance of certain responsibilities, ideally based on agreed-upon expectations and standards. Those persons and bodies who are assigned responsibility are obliged to answer for their performance and it is usually assumed that they are potentially subject to penalties for

non-performance or the beneficiaries of rewards for successful performance. The sanctions and rewards that underpin an accountability relationship can be tangible and/or symbolic. Loss of office, demotions or reduced autonomy are examples of tangible penalties, while the assignment of blame, guilt, humiliation and loss of reputation represent more symbolic penalties. The potential impact of such psychological costs on the thinking and behaviour of public officials should not be underestimated.

For accountability to be fairly enforced requires that the responsible persons or bodies be given the capacity to deliver results through some combination of authority, resources, control over events and, in general, a supportive environment. Accountability also assumes that the authoritative party in the relationship has an obligation to monitor performance to ensure compliance with assigned directions and expectations. Accountability breakdowns can occur, not only because individuals and organizations fail to perform, but also because authorizing bodies lack the will and/or the capacity to provide direction for and/or scrutiny of performance. In summary, accountability represents both a constraint and an opportunity. While it limits freedom of action and requires justification for behaviour, it also entails the delegation of authority and resources that empower persons and organizations to act. Robert Behn (2001) neatly captures the balance between delegating and checking with his comment that accountability means 'trust but verify'.

The meaning of accountability has consistently widened over the years. The term is now frequently used to describe situations where the core features of an authoritative relationship and a formal process of enforcement are not necessarily present. Certainly, the public no longer sees accountability in strictly legal and organizational terms. For them, accountability is a broader professional, ethical and moral construct that is achieved only when public officials, both elected and appointed, serve with a commitment to do the right things. Reflecting its growing prominence in public debates, the term accountability may be used to describe: a general, subjective sense of responsibility, the upholding of professional values and standards even in the absence of external scrutiny, a demonstrated responsiveness to particular clients or to the community at large, and to the requirement for openness, a democratic dialogue and public participation in governance.

The expansion of the meaning of accountability has caused a number of academic commentators to develop interpretative frameworks and typologies to compare how accountability is enacted in various contexts. Resisting this tendency, other academics have called for more precision and consistency in the use of the term, insisting that it should be reserved for those situations where an authoritative relationship exists (Mulgan, 2000). Some writers have also argued that the aims and means of accountability should not be conflated and confused. For example, transparency is a highly prized value, but on a strict interpretation it is a means to achieve ultimate democratic accountability rather than an end in itself.

Government officials recognize that they are facing more diverse and more demanding accountability expectations, but many believe that in practice the essence of accountability has not changed all that much. For them accountability still comes down to a process of 'naming' and 'blaming'. Widespread cynicism towards government pervades most societies, the media and political debate. The prevailing public perception is that governments are not accountable and that no one pays a serious price when misdeeds or errors occur. Governments are blameworthy, but the avoidance of blame is seen as the standard operating practice. Most of the blame is targeted at politicians, but public servants also come in for their share of criticism. In response to public disillusionment and as a reaction to revelations of untoward events, governments have tended to layer new accountability requirements on top of existing accountability rules, in part as a way to prevent a recurrence of events and in part as a symbolic gesture to restore public confidence. The result has been to create over time multiple criteria, institutions and processes intended to strengthen accountability. An ironic consequence of the proliferation of accountability requirements has been to create even greater confusion about who is accountable for what in government.

Focusing responsibility and accountability within government is becoming more and more difficult. The underlying assumption of the practice of accountability (in contrast to emerging theories) is that identifiable individuals and institutions have independent, reasonably complete and predictable control over actions and outcomes. However, this assumption corresponds less and less to the realities of public sector decision making today. The external and internal environments of public sector organizations have become more complicated, interdependent, turbulent and unpredictable. Activities undertaken by governments are increasingly collaborative in nature, whether that collaboration takes place across programs, departments, governments or with other institutions within society. In an era of collaborative government no one individual or institution can be singled out as being fully in charge. In summary, the traditional, vertical, straight line and individualistic interpretation of accountability does not fit with the emerging reality of a horizontal, interconnected and collective approach to problem solving (Considine, 2002; Wilkins, 2002).

Under these conditions a strong case can be made for a shared or collective approach to accountability. In his recent book *Rethinking Democratic Accountability* (2001), Robert D. Behn calls for the development of a new

'360-degree' approach to accountability based on 'a compact of mutual collective responsibility'. Such an approach would be cultural and values-based, rather than legal. It would require reciprocal trust and obligation among individuals and institutions. It would involve acceptance of collective responsibility and abandonment of the search for an individual scapegoat when something goes wrong. It would rely more on a self-imposed sense of responsibility than on externally imposed accountability requirements.

Behn is obviously not suggesting that we scrap existing legal and organizational approaches to accountability, but he does acknowledge their limits. It must also be recognized, however, that a shift to a collective culture of accountability will conflict with the ideas of individual fault, blame, liability and punishment that remain at the heart of popular understanding of what accountability means in practice. There is, therefore, still a need to develop formal accountability mechanisms for the collaborative arrangements that are becoming so common in the public sector. Such mechanisms must include the clearer delineation of roles and responsibilities, well-defined management structures, performance expectations that are balanced with capabilities, appropriate monitoring, measurement and evaluation regimes, procedures to deal with non-performance and dispute resolution mechanisms for when the partners operating in a collaborative arrangement disagree (Office of the Auditor General of Canada, 1999).

The rise of 'joined up' governments (the phrase popularized by the Labour Government of Tony Blair in the UK) is one of the factors pushing governments away (rhetorically at least) from 'compliance' accountability in favour of 'performance' accountability. Other factors that have made performance measurement and performance reporting the newest, 'ideal' model of accountability are:

- The New Public Management approach, with its collection of strategies and techniques intended to enhance performance
- The financial difficulties of governments and the desire to eliminate or reduce ineffective programs

- The need in an era of rapid and unpredictable change to capture signals from the external environment about what works and what doesn't
- The widespread adoption of alternative organizational designs (such as executive agencies) and new service delivery methods (such as widespread contracting out)
- The opportunity to use information technologies and new analytical techniques
- The concern to reverse declining trust and confidence in governments
- The desire to reduce the scope of politically driven decision making by making 'objective' evidence play a more important role.

In theory, the gathering, analysis and publication of relevant, valid, reliable and timely information on what was achieved within the new partnership and networked relationships will enable the respective governing bodies and the public to hold the institutions and individuals involved more accountable. In practice, despite such structural and procedural safeguards, the result is still likely to be a kind of 'fuzzy accountability' (akin to fuzzy logic) that sacrifices a measure of precision but permits more flexible approaches to complex problems solving (Wilkins, 2002).

In a democratic state, the key accountability relationships are between citizens and the holders of public office, both elected and appointed, and between elected politicians and appointed public servants. The emergence of a wide variety of approaches to accountability has somewhat obscured and displaced the central importance of these key accountability relationships. Inside and outside of government, the sources of accountability are many – the constitution, laws, the daily political process, executive–legislative relationships, the organizational arrangements of various public bodies, administrative rules and procedures, reporting requirements, contracts with other governments and third parties, the rulings of courts, the activities of pressure groups, public debates and, of course, elections. All of these mechanisms shape and reinforce, to some not easily measured extent, an internalized subjective sense of responsibility and accountability felt by both

Table 1   *Accountability dichotomies*

Political accountability versus administrative accountability
Formal, objective accountability versus informal subjective accountability
Procedural/compliance accountability versus performance/results
Hierarchical accountability versus non-hierarchical (e.g. contracting out/partnerships)
Retrospective versus prospective accountability
Blaming/punitive accountability versus learning/remedial accountability
Internal versus external accountability
Centralized versus devolved accountability
Accountability for actions versus accountability for inaction
Top-down bureaucratic accountability versus bottom-up bureaucratic accountability (answerable to Politicians and citizens) versus customer accountability (answerable to clients and customers)
Legal versus moral accountability
Symbolic versus real accountability

elected politicians and appointed public servants. The norms and practices of accountability are deeply rooted in particular societies and in particular policy communities. National differences in constitutional arrangements, political processes and political/administrative cultures can have a profound impact on definitions of culpability and approaches to the enforcement of accountability.

At times public officials will face conflicting accountability expectations and requirements. There is at this point very little practical theory to design different accountability procedures and standards of accountability for different types of action by an increasingly diverse range of organizations that comprise the kaleidoscopic world of the modern public sector broadly defined. Nor do we have a good sense of the cumulative impact of the various accountability requirements upon the thinking and acting of public officials, especially which of the many different types of accountability requirements public servants find most compelling to obey on a daily basis.

A certain amount of overlap and redundancy in accountability systems can provide protection against untoward events because the breakdown of one mechanism might be compensated by the effectiveness of another. The simultaneous and repeated failure of all accountability processes is probably a rare occurrence; although this is what appears to have happened during and after the tragic events leading to the deaths of twelve infants in a pediatric cardiac surgery program in Winnipeg, Canada (Manitoba Health, 2001).

That case illustrated the danger of confusing the different models of accountability that operated in the public health care system. The three dominant models of health care accountability were political, professional and economic, with a consumer-based model gaining growing currency. As in other fields, the public was not prepared to rely simply on one model of accountability or to restrict accountability to formal relationships where there was a prior act of delegation from one party to another. In most instances, the formal and the informal dimensions of accountability relationships are not easily or appropriately separated, especially when blame for untoward events is being assigned.

As in other areas of public administration analysis, dichotomies involving accountability are popular. Table 1 lists the main dichotomies employed in relation to accountability. Restricting the debate over accountability to a choice between two options is a simplistic and unrealistic description of the world of practice where multiple meanings exist. Not only is accountability multidimensional, it is also dynamic. This can be seen in the impact of new public management (NPM) thinking during the past decade. NPM calls upon 'public managers' to become entrepreneurial, innovative risk-takers who are prepared to accept occasional failures. In contrast, the 'old' public administration (OPA) traditional approach to accountability required 'public servants' to follow rule-bound, standardized behaviour as a basis for providing their elected political masters with 'error-free government' and citizens with procedural and substantive fairness. The tension between the OPA and the NPM perspective is documented for the UK public sector in a book with the intriguing title *Regulation in Government: Waste Watchers, Quality Policy and Sleaze-Busters* (Hood et al., 1999). The reform rhetoric of UK governments promised a complementary shift in which compliance accountability reduced and performance accountability increased. But, in practice public sector organizations faced 'double jeopardy' in which there was both more accountability for results and more procedural regulation. Increased internal regulation came from new accountability enforcers in the areas of performance measurement, service quality initiatives, auditing, employment equity, etc. Exemplifying 'the rule of unintended consequences', the drive for more accountability ended up reducing administrative efficiency and responsiveness – presumably two values that the new accountability rules were meant to strengthen.

OVERVIEW OF THE SECTION

The three chapters presented in this section of the Handbook reflect the complexities, controversies and continuing evolution of the concept of accountability and closely related ideas like responsiveness, responsibility and legitimacy. Robert Gregory's chapter leads off by insisting on more careful definition and use of these related, but not synonymous terms. He argues that in the current context there are two main problems involved with restricting accountability to its original meaning of answerability for one's actions. First, multiple, other meanings of accountability are involved in public life. Second, there is the so-called principal–agent problem involving the difficulty for the authorizing party in ensuring the truthfulness of the accounting provided by those who are delegated authority and resources. Governments, he suggests, are better at using accountability mechanisms to prevent mistakes than they are at finding the means to ensure success. Also, focusing on the obligation to answer says little about the attention that should be paid to ethics,

morality and integrity in the actions of governments. Accountability is a relatively objective check on behaviour whereas these other broader values are more subjective and applied in a voluntary manner by people and institutions. Behaviours that are legal and accountable can be unethical and immoral, and vice versa. It is my own view that confusing accountability with ethical responsibility leads to the deflation of ethics, especially when statutes and ethical codes become the focal point for promoting virtue in public office. Focusing narrowly on particular offences leads to a downplaying of a higher level of moral discussion and development in public life.

Gregory was one of the first commentators to warn of the dangers for accountability arising from the ideas of NPM, which is perhaps not surprising given that he was writing from New Zealand, the country in which those ideas were being tested in their purest and fullest form (Gregory, 1998). The New Zealand state sector reforms of the late 1980s were intended to clarify and reinforce accountability by creating new types of organizations with clearer mandates and placing the relationships between politicians and senior public servants on a contractual basis that assigned responsibility for outcomes to politicians and responsibility for outputs to senior public servants. According to Gregory, the New Zealand model incorporated a false assumption that all public management can be seen as a form of 'production' in which the 'production function' is well understood and both the 'outputs' and the 'outcomes' are observable and measurable. Contrary to the expectation of the reformers the result was to blur accountability and to encourage blame avoidance when adverse events took place. When embattled ministers attempted to unload blame onto public servants, the latter did not always meekly fall on their swords but instead fought back by accusing ministers of backdoor interference and/or inadequate resources. Rather than represent an improvement on the admittedly vague and problematic notions of ministerial responsibility and administrative anonymity, the new framework of political-bureaucratic relationships presented its own problems.

In his chapter, Gregory warns of the danger of an unduly rationalistic and technocratic conception of accountability. It is not clear, he concludes, whether NPM has offered any conclusive resolution to the perennial issues of responsibility and accountability. In short, there is no 'one best' approach to accountability and accountability cannot be treated as a problem to be resolved once and forever.

The second chapter, by Linda deLeon, examines the links between administrative responsibility and the personal ethics of individuals. She argues that responsible behaviour in government and elsewhere must be based upon both an internalized subjective concern to do the right thing, as well as on the presence of external accountability requirements. The relative reliance upon internal, normative versus external, formal controls will vary depending upon the type of organizational setting involved. Four types of settings – hierarchies, competitive pluralism, community and anarchy – are identified, mainly on the basis of the extent to which goals and means are identifiable and consensual. Bureaucracies, markets, communities and anarchies each encourage somewhat different ethical responses from individuals.

Turning to administrative responsibility in government, de Leon asks where public servants obtain their values. Admitting such values are a complex amalgam, she discusses four sources of values – human nature, community values, professional socialization and personal philosophy. All four value systems interact with and are shaped by institutional norms of behaviour and culture.

Operating in a turbulent, and unpredictable, world, where there is a lack of consensus on the future role of governments, creates profound ethical ambiguity and anxiety for public officials. Professional public servants have to be more self-consciously aware of the ethical dilemmas they face. In reading this discussion, I was struck by the similarities to *A Strong Foundation* (Canadian Centre for Management Development, 1996), a Canadian report from a national task force on public service values and ethics. That report identified four 'families of values' – democratic values, professional values, ethical values and people values – that should comprise a public service ethos for the future. The task force recognized what Professor de Leon concludes: in a disorderly and problematic world, responsible administrative behaviour depends more upon committed and collaborative ethical discourse than it does upon the multiplication and more stringent enforcement of external controls.

Kevin P. Kearns argues in the final chapter in this section that the blurring of the line between the public, the private-for-profit and the not-for-profit sectors of society has compounded the challenges of responsibility and accountability. Use of the private sector to deliver services previously provided directly by government does not mean that we necessarily obtain the best of both worlds: the efficiency and effectiveness of the private sector along with representativeness and accountability of government. At the same time that the public was becoming more demanding in terms of ethical and accountable behaviour, authority and power were becoming more dispersed and shared, within governments and with outside entities of various kinds. The new accountability environments created by these trends present unprecedented accountability challenges for governments and their private sector partners.

Kearns presents a conceptual framework that illuminates four modes of accountability. He challenges organizational leaders to act strategically when dealing with the more complicated accountability environments they face. He recommends a 'learning approach' to strengthening accountability based upon a three-pronged strategy:

- The adoption of a broader definition of accountability that goes beyond compliance to embrace responsiveness to stakeholders
- The use and refinement of this conceptual framework to develop strategic and tactical approaches to accountability
- Making a commitment to the development of an interorganizational culture of accountability in which all stakeholders continuously learn from each other.

Trust, discretion, self-discipline, voluntary followership, dialogue and systems thinking will be integral features of the accountability culture proposed by Kearns.

These brief summaries cannot adequately capture the complexities and nuances of the analyses presented in the three chapters that follow this introduction. All the authors endorse a broad, multidimensional approach to accountability. They recognize the strain on the traditional understandings of accountability arising from such developments as: the emergence of new types of public sector organizations, the transformation of public service cultures through the infusion of new values, the increased reliance on private sector organizations to deliver public programs, the public's insistence on stricter and higher standards of ethical and accountable behaviour by public officials, and the rising demands for more direct public involvement in both policy development and program delivery. All of these developments are making accountability a very elastic term, which is being applied more and more loosely to a wide variety of situations.

My own preference would be for a more restricted and precise use of the term to describe situations where an authoritative relationship exists. Accountability should be seen as a formal relationship governed by a process and shaped in practice by the surrounding environment and culture (Thomas, 1998). Distinctions could then be made between accountability and related, but different concepts, such as responsibility, answerability, liability, responsiveness, transparency etc. Some degree of terminological confusion is inevitable, but it should not be compounded by the synonymous and often erroneous use of a number of related concepts.

During the past two decades, the study and practice of public administration has moved significantly away from the founding disciplines of political science and law and more into the domains of economics and management. One result of this shift has been to downplay the importance of accountability. New Public Management emphasizes responsibility and freedom to manage and denigrates control and procedural accountability. Privatization, commercialization, contracting out and the use of market-type mechanisms within government are meant to promote efficiency,

effectiveness and responsiveness, mainly by reducing the need for centralized political and administrative direction, control and monitoring. It is not clear however, whether responsiveness to market signals by independent or semi-independent institutions and individuals constitutes an effective and appropriate substitute for the traditional mechanisms of democratic accountability.

The challenges and paradoxes of accountability in practice will only increase in the future. Over the past twenty years there have emerged new theoretical models that seek to capture the more complicated, kaleidoscopic and unpredictable realities of the contemporary public sector where authority, finances, power and risks are increasingly shared both inside government and with outside entities. Clear accountability relationships and processes are rarely possible and there is a need to invent credible approaches to the assignment and enforcement of collective accountability. In the dynamic world of today's public sector, accountability is best approached not as a problem to be solved permanently, but rather as a condition to be continuously monitored. Accordingly, we must promote an accountability culture of continuous learning since accountability issues will always be present and will be complex.

REFERENCES

Behn, Robert D. (2001) *Rethinking Democratic Accountability*. Washington, DC: Brookings Institution.

Canadian Centre for Management Development (1996) *A Strong Foundation*. Report of the Task Force on Public Service Values and Ethics, Ottawa.

Considine, Mark (2002) 'The End of the Line? Accountable Governance in the Age of Networks, Partnerships, and Joined-Up Services', *Governance*, 15 (1): 21–40.

Gregory, R. (1998) 'A New Zealand Tragedy: Problems of Political Responsibility', *Governance*, 11 (2): 231–40.

Hood, C., Scott, A., James, C., Jones, O. and Trawers, T. (1999) *Regulation Inside Government: Waste Watchers, Quality Police and Slease Busters*. Oxford: Oxford University Press.

Manitoba Health (2001) *The Report of the Review and Implementation Committee for the Report of the Pediatric Cardiac Surgery Inquest*. Winnipeg: Government of Manitoba.

Mulgan, R. (2000) '"Accountability", an Ever-expanding Concept?', *Public Administration*, 78: 555–74.

Office of the Auditor General of Canada (1999) *Involving Others in Governing: Accountability at Risk.* Ottawa: Office of the Auditor General.

Thomas, Paul G. (1998) 'The Changing Nature of Accountability', in B. Guy Peters and Donald Savoie (eds), *Taking Stock: Assessing Public Sector Reforms.* Montreal and Kingston: Canadian Centre for Management Development/McGill-Queen's University Press. pp. 348–93.

Wilkins, Peter (2002) 'Accountability and Joined-up Government', *Australian Journal of Public Administration*, 61 (1): 114–19.

44

Accountability in Modern Government

Robert Gregory

ACCOUNTABILITY AS CONTROL

In Britain in the mid-1990s a major political controversy arose over the respective account-abilities of prison management and ministers of the crown (Barker, 1998; Polidano, 1999). In the United States, serious issues of accountability were identified in the wake of the *Challenger* space shuttle disaster (Romzek and Dubnick, 1987). More recently, the collision between the *USS Greeneville* and the Japanese fishing trawler *Ehime Maru* focused public attention on the accountability of the *Greeneville's* commander. In Canada, twelve children died as a result of shortcomings in a Manitoban paediatric cardiac surgery programme (Manitoba Health, 2001). In New Zealand fourteen people were killed by the collapse of a wilderness viewing platform built by a government department (Gregory, 1998); and a few years later the shortcomings of a national cancer screening programme generated widespread concern (Ministry of Health, 2001). Such cases represent a few among many, and are witness not necessarily to the increasing failure of governmental systems and processes, but to widespread and intense public concern over accountability.

Few words are more widely used in the par-lance of modern government than 'accountabil-ity'. The word continues to excite a great deal of academic debate and practical application. It trips readily from the lips of citizens and news media observers of governmental action, but as Thomas reminds us, it remains 'an elusive phenomenon' (1998: 387).

The word embraces a number of different mean-ings, and is commonly used in close association with other ideas, particularly responsiveness, answerability, fault and blame. It is often used – mistakenly, as argued below – synonymously with responsibility. As the above examples suggest, issues of accountability are most commonly raised when events go awry, when there is some failure of public authority, for which particular institu-tions or individuals are expected to be 'held to account'. Romzek and Ingraham (2000) call this the 'gotcha' mentality, whereby accountability means some sort of 'witch hunt' for those who are culpable, and punishable, when things go wrong. They argue that American political culture empha-sizes this approach to accountability, but this is undoubtedly so across a broader spectrum of political systems.

This attitude reflects the synonymity of accountability and control, as in Klitgaard's (1997: 500) formulaic $C = M + D - A$ (corrup-tion equals monopoly plus discretion minus accountability). When public power is abused or misused – and not used when it is believed that it ought to have been – in the name of accountabil-ity politicians or officials (or both) may be seen to have failed in their fulfilment of some duty of public obligation, and are likely to be sanctioned for their failures. As Thomas points out, 'Preventing the potential abuse of power is the ultimate goal of the numerous accountability arrangements and procedures adopted by con-temporary governments ...' (1998: 348). These arrangements are intended to ensure both the constitutionally appropriate use of elective politi-cal power itself, and the coordinated, systematic and planned bureaucratic implementation of the policy purposes defined through the exercise of that power. A long history of Western political philosophy attests to and underpins the centrality of accountability in liberal democratic political systems, but the concept is central to all forms of modern, bureaucratized, government, including totalitarian regimes.

Because accountability concerns are most commonly apparent when public power and authority have been abused or misused the term tends to have negative connotations. It is more likely to be used in public discourse when consequences flow from actions or inactions that are generally considered to be deleterious to the polity as a whole or to particular groups or individuals within it. As with Klitgaard, people frequently express concerns over accountability when they believe there has been none or too little of 'it'. What is usually meant is that certain persons or organizations are illegitimately evading at least one of three things, if not all three: their need to explain events and circumstances; their own complicity in them; or blame and sanction for that complicity. Thus, accountability is identified with the demand that when things go wrong, 'heads should roll'.

Demands for more accountability are much less likely to be heard when governmental systems are seen to be working well (for example, effectively, economically, efficiently, humanely, justly). While there are often calls for heads to roll, there are seldom demands that heads should be crowned. Those who wield public power can readily be punished for the one per cent of things that go wrong while being deprived of praise for the ninety-nine per cent of things that go right.

Accountability as the ineluctable quest for control means that governmental policy making is often more devoted to avoiding worst outcomes than to achieving the best ones. As Lucas has put it:

> Accountability is a form of quality control. We avoid the really bad, but have to forego the really good. It is a price well worth paying to avoid the great evil of misgovernment, but always there will be some question whether we are not fettering discretion too much, and insuring too heavily, at the cost of making it impossible for the decision-makers ever to discharge their commission, against dangers that can be adequately guarded against in other ways. (1976: 84)

The study of governmental institutions and processes probably has more to say about how wrong-doing can be prevented (and corrected when it occurs) than about how to generate outstanding success. So many of the tasks that governments perform are inherently politically contentious and technologically uncertain, involving continuing efforts to alter citizens' behaviour, as distinct from producing tangible 'products'. Much more is known, for example,

about how to prevent prison inmates from escaping than is known about how to ensure they will not reoffend when released; much more about paying out welfare benefits than about preventing the abuse of children.

For these sorts of reasons public agencies in Western democracies are subject to a plethora of externally imposed institutional and statutory arrangements, in the name of accountability. These include legislative processes and committees, constitutional and other foundational statutory requirements (such as a Bill of Rights), official information and privacy enactments, ombudsmen, parliamentary auditing offices, not to mention the news media's 'watchdog' role in public affairs. These are some of the main sources of the 'red tape' that binds bureaucratic authority and tends to make many public organizations risk-averse, or constraint-driven (Kaufman, 1977; Wilson, 1989). It is why politicians and officials are concerned to 'cover their backsides', to insist first and foremost on procedural regularity and correctness, in the knowledge that they are likely to be sanctioned far less for failing to achieve often difficult, ambiguous and uncertain outcomes than for failing to do so correctly (according to specified procedures). It is as if about ninety per cent of organizational members cannot be trusted in an effective pursuit of organizational purpose.

ACCOUNTABILITY AS DISTINCT FROM RESPONSIBILITY

In popular parlance the two words accountability and responsibility are frequently used as if they were synonymous. They are not. By comparison, accountability is a matter of political and organizational housekeeping, whereas responsibility is often about moral conflicts and issues of life and death.

As Uhr (1993) has explained, the etymology of accountability in government is traceable to the requirement that the expenditure of public money be verifiable and controllable. Literally, expenditure of taxpayers' money should be rigorously accounted for. The formal procedures of government financial accounting arose out of this requirement. The notion of accounting, however, applied not just to control over the use of money, but also over the consumption of time, energy and other official resources, and discretionary authority. Aucoin and Heintzman (2000) refer to this as 'accountability as assurance'. In this endeavour the central idea of accountability has been than of answerability, in both the political and bureaucratic domains, to secure control and provide assurance.

Objective responsibility: accountability as answerability

This idea of accountability as answerability was captured in Mosher's (1968) conceptual distinction between what he called objective responsibility and subjective responsibility. Objective responsibility addresses the formal institutional framework within which those who exercise public authority work. It can be envisaged as a formal map, or organization chart, which depicts the constitutional and organizational lines of answerability, or – in the terminology of agency theory – the chain of principal–agent relationships that constitutes the formal structure of constitutional and organizational authority. For example, in Westminster parliamentary systems, the theory of ministerial responsibility depicts a formal arrangement whereby bureaucratic officials are answerable to their ministers, who in turn are answerable to parliament and thus (but not solely through this formal channel) to the sovereign citizenry. Under the American presidential system, where the political executive is institutionally separable from the legislature, the federal bureaucracy is answerable to the President (through the cabinet) and thence to the public, while members of the Congress are directly answerable to the public.

Objective responsibility primarily means that someone is answerable *to* someone else for the carrying out of specified tasks with commensurate authority and resources. It requires agents (politicians or bureaucrats) to give an account of their actions to specified others, who have the right and capacity to monitor performance and to invoke sanctions and rewards, and to answer to these with an account of how and why decisions were made, discretion exercised, and actions taken.

There are two main sources of the practical problems commonly associated with the idea of accountability as answerability. First, as illustrated by Romzek and Ingraham (2000), there are multiple types of accountability. They identify four: hierarchical, legal, professional and political. Respectively, these emphasize the values of efficiency, the rule of law, expertise and responsiveness. Hierarchical accountability relationships are characterized by close supervision of individuals who have little work autonomy; legal relationships entail detailed oversight from external bodies such as legislatures and courts; professional relationships are marked by high

levels on operating autonomy on the part of those who have internalized norms of appropriate practice; and the political type gives managers the choice of responsiveness primarily to key stakeholders, such as elected officials, the public at large, or client groups. The last form, sometimes referred to as 'dual accountability', speaks to the answerability of officials to particular 'client' groups as well as their formal accountability to hierarchical superiors. Romzek and Ingraham argue that, 'The fact that public managers face diverse expectations and work under several accountability relationships simultaneously creates a significant challenge of how to manage the various accountability systems.' Agencies usually work under one or two of these systems on a daily basis, with the others being underused, even dormant, but in times of crisis, failure, or reform there is often a shift in priority among the different types.

Similarly, Stone (1995) has argued that in Westminster systems ministerial responsibility as 'the dominant principle of administrative accountability' sits uneasily with five 'subordinate' conceptions of accountability, which have arisen out of several interrelated and long-term stimuli for administrative change. These conceptions correspond to different sets of institutional arrangements, and there is considerable potential for conflict among them. The five conceptions he identifies in Westminster-style democracies are: parliamentary control, managerialism, judicial/quasi-judicial review, constituency relations and market. Parliamentary control is the traditional Westminster understanding of accountability, as provided for in the doctrine of ministerial responsibility. In recent years, as will be discussed below, 'managerialist' conceptions of accountability have gained prominence in parliamentary democracies such as the UK, Australia and New Zealand. Processes of judicial review of public administration have been increasing markedly in parliamentary democracies, and have historically been a central feature of West European jurisdictions. Accountability as constituency relations is close to the 'dual accountability' referred to above, embodying not just 'upward' accountability to ministers and parliament but 'downwards' and 'horizontal' accountability to peers and other reference groups. Market accountability emerges from reformist moves in recent years to render many public agencies more 'customer-driven' (that is, more 'responsive') in the ways they deliver goods and services, as with the Citizen's Charter introduced in the UK in the early 1990s (Doern, 1993; Lewis and Birkenshaw, 1993; Pierre, 1998). It is also central to 'third party' government, involving the increasingly widespread contracting-out of public services, a development which is replete with issues concerning the public accountability of both government agencies and service providers (see, for example, Kettl, 1993; Martin, 1995).

The second problem of accountability as answerability is that of veracity. If accountability is to be secured through the upward flow of information through organizational hierarchies it is often very difficult, sometimes impossible, for superiors (principals) to be certain about the truthfulness of the accounts given by their subordinates (agents), especially when supervision is not immediate and direct and when answerability is exercised after the event. For example, police officers on duty in patrol cars necessarily exercise discretion in how they spend their time on the job. They often cannot be directly monitored by their superiors, who must rely on ex-post accounts given by the officers of what they have been doing. And the need for superiors to know what is actually going on leads to other, often informal, ways of checking.

Subjective responsibility and individual moral choice

Issues of veracity and trust are raised by Mosher's second notion, that of subjective responsibility. The idea of accountability as answerability through formally prescribed channels is too restrictive, and often does not connect well with the lived experiential reality of public administration.

Unlike his objective responsibility, or accountability as answerability, Mosher's concept of subjective responsibility focuses attention not on the external, formal, procedures through which politicians and officials answer for their actions, but on the moral dimensions of those actions. It is a psychologically-oriented idea, focusing on moral conflict and choice among the subjectively felt duties of obligation confronting politicians and administrators. Accountability as formal answerability is therefore a necessary but insufficient component of responsibility, in that there is a moral obligation on the individual to answer *for* (explain, justify), both honestly and openly, his or her decisions and actions. But answerability *per se* says little about the morally responsible exercise of discretionary choice among conflicting obligations (including, some ~~might~~ argue, the choice to dissemble to protect ~~rather~~ than truthfulness).

~~...~~ of responsibility does not assume the ~~...~~ of accounts offered under formal ~~...~~lity processes. Rather, it acknowledges

what everyone knows to be so: the opportunistic desire to hide the truth, to put the best complexion on bad outcomes, to engage in the deceptive practices which often characterize the unending pursuit of political advantage. It affirms, on the other hand, that truthful answerability depends ultimately on the moral character of those who are required to be accountable; that accountability obligations need to be fulfilled responsibly.

Ideas of accountability and responsibility become fused in the notion that a person should be *held* accountable – that is, be found blameworthy and punishable when something goes wrong. Bovens (1998: 28–31) refers to this as 'responsibility-as-accountability' or 'passive responsibility'. As he puts it, to be responsible in this sense means that every one of four elements must be present: 'You are either accountable or you are not. There is no middle way, you cannot be "somewhat" or "fairly" accountable, and you cannot call someone a little bit to account.' The idea embraces the elements of human conduct (action or inaction) leading to a harmful or shameful event or situation; a causal connection between individual conduct and damage done; there must be personal liability; and a relationship with the agent, particularly in cases where one is held to account for the (in)actions of another.

Hence, politicians or administrators can be fully accountable but irresponsible. Nazi officials, for example, may have been fully and openly accountable, behaving with full procedural regularity, reporting honestly, yet at the same time profoundly irresponsible in their instrumental complicity in the pursuit of evil purposes. Individuals might answer for their actions fairly and truthfully, yet be irresponsible in their incompetence or unreliability. Or they might be trustworthy in doing the job competently and reliably yet be irresponsible in their inability or unwillingness to exercise individual reflective judgement about the moral legitimacy of their work. In speaking of the mental attitudes and moral qualities demanded of public servants Stephen K. Bailey (1964) thoughtfully teased out some of the qualities subsumed within this concept of responsibility as individual virtue, or character.

Whereas accountability is primarily concerned with making bureaucratic organizations function efficiently and effectively, the moral dimensions of responsible individual and group action can be inherently subversive of bureaucratic control. Organization members are generally rewarded for obedient conformity rather than critical dissent. As C.P. Snow once averred,

When you think of the long and gloomy history of man you will find far more, and far more hideous crimes have been committed in the name of obedience than in the name of rebellion ... Yet the duty to question is not much of a support when you are living in the middle of an organised society.[1]

In many subtle ways bureaucratic organizations desensitize the moral sensibilities of their members and make it difficult for them to engage in the reflective judgement which lies at the core of individually responsible behaviour and enables a person to determine for themselves the limits to organizational obedience. Forty years on, Stanley Milgram's experiments remain open to interpretation (Milgram, 1974; Miller, 1986). But issues of bureaucratic accountability and responsibility cannot be adequately examined without serious reference to them, while vast numbers of governmental officials, whether they choose to acknowledge it or not, are obliged to grapple with moral and ethical conflicts.

'THE RULE OF NOBODY'

Hannah Arendt (1963: 289) described bureaucracy as 'the rule of Nobody'. A former New Zealand Director-General of Health typically expressed the sentiments behind such a description when answering, in a national radio interview, for his role in the failure of a national programme of cervical cancer screening.[2]

Interviewer: Shouldn't some individual take responsibility for what's happened to the women?

Former Director-General: I can understand people feeling that way. The problem though that I see is that if that was pinned on an individual many people would breathe a sigh of relief and say, 'Ah, we've caught the person who is to blame for this. It will now be alright because they've gone.' And that is not the situation that we're in here. This is a complex programme. There's been a host of people involved with it over fifteen years. There have been many – some may call them mistakes – changes in the direction of the health system or restructuring of the system. Staff have moved in and out of key positions in this system and to some extent all of us share a collective responsibility, and unless we all together look at what happened and what went wrong and seek to learn from that, simply blaming it on an individual and then quietly moving on misses the point.

This response illustrates well the distinction drawn by Thomas (2001: 23) between accountability as 'blaming' and accountability as 'learning' (a remedial model). The former, akin to the 'gotcha mentality' referred to by Romzek and Ingraham, is commonly expressed as a public demand that someone be found culpable and punished when something goes seriously wrong.

Thomas points out that such a retrospective 'punitive model' of accountability, often expressed in parliamentary systems as a call for ministerial resignations, may contradict a more desirable prospective, learning approach to accountability. Dowding and Won-Taek Kang (1998) show that in the UK the number of ministerial resignations increased dramatically over the half-century to 1997, with sexual scandals, policy disagreements and personality clashes being the most common reasons for resignation. The argument that in some jurisdictions ministerial responsibility has lost its force because ministers seldom resign overlooks the real impact of the doctrine in enforcing a powerful discipline on political and administrative behaviour.

Political controversies over accountability and responsibility (with the two terms usually being conflated in public discussion) generate a great deal of public posturing, most of which is driven by the rational desire to avoid blame and sanction when something goes wrong. Such posturing often appears to be cynical and does little to engender public respect for political institutions. In Westminster systems the theory of ministerial responsibility, for example, often occludes as much as it clarifies, when it comes to determining questions of responsibility as accountability (as distinct from answerability as accountability). Consequently, the doctrine becomes transmuted into a convenient rationalization whereby when something goes wrong there is no moral obligation on the part of ministers and officials other than to ensure that it will not happen again. This is ministerial responsibility primarily if not exclusively as technical rectification: 'The constitutional doctrine of individual ministerial responsibility is primarily about requiring ministers to answer in parliament and fix up mistakes' (Palmer and Palmer, 1997: 72).

All the more reason, therefore, for the grand gesture of self-sacrifice in various, perhaps symbolic, forms. Such gestures might include official apologies, ex gratia compensatory payments and individual resignations, all as a means of reassuring citizens, albeit paradoxically, of the ultimate humaneness of profoundly impersonal governmental systems.

Issues of this sort demonstrate a fundamental difficulty with the notion of 'holding people to account' in the governmental realm. In the complex world of public policy making it is often extremely difficult to trace cause and effect; all sorts of endogenous and extraneous factors combine to produce outcomes that are seldom finite and change over time. Power, authority, resources and risks are shared; 'co-production' inevitably supersedes production; bureaucratic organizations are, by definition, collective not individualist systems; formal policy evaluation is usually driven as much by political judgement as scientific calculation; and the contributions of particular individuals to policy 'success' and 'failure' can seldom be demonstrated conclusively. On top of all this, it is not at all clear that the increasing 'out-sourcing' or contractualization of governmental services in quasi-markets can be easily reconciled with quests for accountability in individualistic terms.

A major challenge is to develop practical means and public expectations of collective rather than individual accountability and responsibility. This might be more compatible with the political ethos of parliamentary systems, where the political executive is collectively and individually accountable to parliament and voters, than with that in a presidential system like the United States, where the public mind is more likely to be concentrated on individual executive accountability. Whatever the case, there is no easy way of reconciling punitive and individual approaches to accountability on the one hand, and remedial and collective ones on the other.

'THE PARADOX OF ACCOUNTABILITY': A PERENNIAL DEBATE

Issues of conflicting moral obligation revolve around what Harmon (1995) has called 'the paradox of accountability'. This stems from the two views of accountability already mentioned: accountability as (mere) objective responsibility, and as subjective responsibility, embodying a fuller appreciation of the moral dimensions of individual choice and action. Harmon distinguishes between 'hard' rationalism and 'soft' rationalism. The former, derived from logical-positivist distinctions between facts and values, means and ends, sustains a mechanistic model of rational-linear control linking the purposes of government action clearly and directly to the instruments of their fulfilment, the bureaucratic apparatus. Soft rationalism, on the other hand, while acknowledging the general validity of hard rationalism's conception of accountability as organizational and political control, recognizes that the political process (embodying the administrative pursuit of political purpose) is infused with a great deal of uncertainty, ambiguity and contingency. All of this renders inevitable the discretionary exercise of public authority on the part of all of those engaged in this process.

Hard rationalism's conception of top-down hierarchical bureaucratic control (accountability) constitutes an important constraint on official activity, and may be justified as an important fiction that helps to sustain a sense of instrumental efficacy and political legitimacy. But in another sense it is largely illusory. Instead, soft rationalism recognizes the inevitability of administrative and managerial discretion and the concomitant view of the public official, not primarily as a technically instrumental and amoral functionary, but as an autonomous moral agent individually responsible for his or her actions.

Harmon's paradox of accountability holds that if government officials are accountable solely for the achievement of goals mandated by political authority then as mere instruments of that authority they cannot be held personally responsible for the consequences of their actions. This argument was rejected at the Nuremberg Trials. On the other hand, the soft rationalist view holds that because officials are political actors in their own right, involved in shaping public purposes through the discretionary authority they necessarily exercise, then their instrumental accountability is compromised and political authority undermined.

This has been a perennial issue in the history of public administration theory, and has been the wellspring of seminal theoretical debates. The first view represented in the paradox was fundamental to the emergence through the late nineteenth century, and the first half of the twentieth, of the foundational concept of a professional, politically 'neutral' public service, in the Anglo-American tradition, and in the tradition of administrative law that has underpinned public administration in continental Europe. In this conception, strongly influenced by Weberian bureaucratic and political theory, public servants are accountable for the degree of technical competence they employ in the efficient, economic and effective implementation of public policy purposes determined by the elective political authorities whom they serve. Their accountability is ensured through their compliance with the institutionally, constitutionally and legally mandated rules and processes under and within which they carry out their functions. Since, in the purest sense, they are not engaged in the political (value-laden) task of shaping public purposes they are answerable, as agents, to their political principals.

The importance of this conception, articulating what has become known as the 'politics–administration dichotomy', was emphasized by Woodrow Wilson (1887) and Goodnow (1900) in their influential prescriptions for modern, professional, governance. It helped to inspire the idea of 'scientific management', as promoted by Taylor (1911). It was also the linchpin of Finer's (1941) response to Friedrich (1940), in their famous exchange. Friedrich had argued that the rise of professionalism in government administration, together with the growth of administrative discretion and complexity, meant that formal and externally imposed mechanisms of ensuring administrative responsibility (or accountability), while still necessary, were no longer adequate. Instead, responsible official action depended upon officials also being responsive to technical knowledge tempered by 'popular sentiment'. For Friedrich, as later for Appleby (1949), a conceptual distinction between policy and administration was unsustainable in practice: 'Public policy is being formed as it is being executed, and it is likewise being executed as it is being formed' (Friedrich, 1940: 6). Friedrich seemed to be more prescient of the growth through the later part of the century of professional power and influence in government than did Finer, who responded by asserting the primacy of formal external controls.

About ten years after the Friedrich–Finer debate, two other seminal figures in organization and public administration theory, Herbert Simon (1952) and Dwight Waldo (1952), locked swords. Waldo challenged Simon's positivist commitment to a science of administration based on a decisional separation between facts and values, policy and administration. In Waldo's view, administration should not be treated as a science, since values infused the choices that administrators made and could not be corralled within the political or policy domain. Moreover, in his view a quest for pure, scientifically grounded, efficiency constituted a threat to the democratic process.

Over the decades these debates resonated in the halls of academe. Meanwhile, politicians and administrators grappled with a huge variety of policy issues, in an increasingly complex policy environment. Accountability and responsibility, while capable of intellectual definition, derived practical meaning mainly from the disputatious world of political interaction.

The most pervasive response to perceived 'problems of accountability' is usually drawn from the school of hard rationalism. Formal mechanisms of bureaucratic control are 'tightened up', in an attempt to cater even more rigorously for whatever contingencies may arise in the exercise of discretionary authority. There is a positive correlation between the scope of administrative discretion and the thickness of bureaucratic operating manuals. This imperative constitutes the

stuff of what the sociologists of bureaucracy have called 'goal displacement', seminally depicted by Merton (1940). The means of accountability become ends in themselves; regulation and control tends to be self-reinforcing; effective purpose is displaced by unintended consequences and reverse effects (Hood et al., 1999).

Although one person's red tape is 'another's treasured safeguard' (Kaufman, 1977: 4), the popular image of constraint-driven, ruleobsessed, bureaucracy has virtually everywhere proved to be both a source of public scorn and an object of reformist intent. In most Western democracies throughout the twentieth century there were major efforts to strike some new balance between these two horns of the administrative dilemma, with some more conscious than others of the issue's inherent intractability. These included the 1937 Brownlow Committee set up by President Franklin Roosevelt in America, and the two Hoover Commissions during the Truman administration; the 1968 Fulton Committee on the British Civil Service; the Glassco Commission in Canada in 1962; the 1976 Coombs Commission on Australian Government Administration; the Gore National Performance Review in America, 1993; and the 1994 'Next Steps' review in Britain. There were managerial nostrums, replete with acronyms such as PPBS, MBO and ZBB, and TQM; and wider reformist movements, however short-lived – like New Public Administration, which sought to institutionalize a practical commitment to equity, justice and fairness, rather than efficiency and economy. Managerial approaches developed in corporate business were applied in the public sector well before the advent of New Public Management (NPM, below) in the 1980s.

Corporate planning, however, could not satisfactorily resolve its inherent paradox. Rational control requires the specification of clear objectives, but organizational effectiveness is continually jeopardized by the realities of a rapidly changing, uncertain and politically charged, environment. Thus, a conundrum: if objectives must be clearly specified to ensure accountable and effective performance, then how often do they need to be revised in the face of pervasive societal change, lest they become obsolete and an impediment to (rather than a component of) effective administration? And if they need to be changed frequently why try to specify them in the first place? The fact that public policy objectives are often 'multiple, conflicting, and vague' (Wildavsky, 1979: 215), is a political necessity as much as a rationalistic vice. Moreover, no rationalistic 'buzzwords' are an effective substitute for careful thought about accountability in the face of the real exigencies of change (Thomas, 1996).

Effective politicians and bureaucrats instinctively understand this paradox. They respond by acknowledging the constraints placed on them by formal 'planning', while putting the plan in the bottom drawer and getting on with the job of dealing with the 'situational imperatives' that confront them (Wilson, 1989: 169).

It is helpful to see accountability and responsibility as two sides of the same coin, one fettering performance, the other enhancing it. As Uhr (1993: 4) puts it:

> Accountability is about compliance with authority, whereas responsibility is about empowerment and independence. Accountability is the negative end of the same band in which responsibility is the positive end. If accountability is about minimising misgovernment, responsibility is about maximising good government.

In other words, responsible proactive commitment, based on justifiably high levels of trust, is at least as desirable as accountable reactive control, which assumes and even breeds mistrust.

THE IMPACT OF NEW PUBLIC MANAGEMENT

The NPM movement which emerged in the 1980s and 1990s tends to focus its attention on accountability rather than responsibility. Founded upon the theoretical base of institutional economics it has used public choice theory, agency theory and transaction costs analysis, together with management theory, to reshape public institutions. These reforms have been adopted in many countries, at different governmental levels, and with varying mixes of components. Whereas countries like the United States, Australia, New Zealand, Britain, Thailand, Switzerland, Sweden and Brazil have keenly embraced a range of various NPM ideas, others like Norway, France and Germany (especially at the federal level) have been less enthusiastic. The movement has been strongly influenced by US concerns over the accountability of government officials operating within a framework of separable executive and legislative powers and a whole raft of quasi-autonomous governmental agencies whose answerability to the citizenry at large has been a matter of obvious contention. As Thomas (1998: 368) has put it:

> The more pluralistic, permeable, and open nature of the American bureaucracy leads to an emphasis on the personal responsibility of individual public servants and to a preference for publicity surrounding the exercise of bureaucratic authority. This contrasts with the parliamentary emphasis on public service anonymity and the insistence on secrecy concerning internal decision making.

NPM has sought a shift away from traditional Weberian, rule-bound, bureaucracies to results-oriented organizations. It has tried to free up innovative managerial capability, to have it much less constrained by the demands of compliance-based mechanisms of control. And it has generated its own paradoxical quest: to 'let managers manage', and to 'make them manage'.

This school of thought seems almost obsessed with technical arguments about how to enhance accountability in government. NPM speaks of how to ensure that managerial systems link 'outputs' to 'outcomes', and how governmental budgeting processes can be connected more efficaciously to both; about how duties and responsibilities can be more clearly delineated between the political executive, executives, and managers; about how public policy can be better 'coordinated' in the pursuit of strategic and operational objectives; about the complexities of specifying operational objectives and evaluating performance against them; about how legal contractual arrangements can best be designed for both executive appointments and the 'out-sourcing' of public goods and services; about how executive performance can best be assessed; and about the ways in which all of these endeavours will render managers more accountable for organizational performance. In short, NPM has generated a raft of micro-management processes.

The NPM movement, of the hard rationalist school, is grounded in the logical-positivist foundations of orthodox economic theory. It has promised more precision, clarity, certainty and 'transparency' in the pursuit of results-oriented public management, with managers 'freed' to manage without the unnecessary fetters of rule-driven compliance, yet 'made' to do so by apparently rigorous accountability mechanisms, and with citizens as consumers 'empowered' to exercise a degree of choice in order to compel greater responsiveness (direct accountability) to consumers on the part of those who provide public goods and services.

In some parliamentary democracies, such as the UK, Australia and New Zealand, agency theory has been invoked to replace 'relational contracts' between ministers and their former permanent heads with fixed-term contractual appointments of departmental chief executives.

These are supported by a complex apparatus of rules and processes designed to make top public officials directly accountable not only for their own personal performances but for the general performance of the agencies they head. In New Zealand, a country which has been a foremost exponent of NPM, contractual appointments of top officials were intended to dissipate the so-called 'enveloping haze' surrounding the theory of ministerial responsibility (Palmer, 1987: 56). The political executive would be held responsible for, and accountable to parliament for, the achievement of policy 'outcomes'. Departmental chief executives would be accountable to their ministers for the production of those departmental 'outputs' deemed necessary for the successful pursuit of outcomes. However, this distinction often proves artificial, of little help in clearly delineating respective responsibilities. It also enhances goal displacement, by encouraging a focus on measurable and tangible outputs rather than on less quantifiable, more ambiguous, outcomes.

NPM's theoretical armoury has little to say about the nature of responsibility, and its mechanistic and technocratic propensity to (re)create artificial bifurcations like policy and management, outputs and outcomes, purchasers and owners, seems out of touch with the organic ebb and flow of political and administrative power. It is doubtful that it has firmly shifted the balance of the bureaucratic paradox in favour of effective policy fulfilment away from the procedural apparatus of bureaucratic accountability. The trade-off between managerial discretion and accountability has generally been made in favour of the latter. Complex performance review procedures and a legalistic culture of contractualism have generated transactions costs which are at least equivalent to those produced under former rule-driven bureaucratic systems.

This is not surprising, since red tape tends to multiply because public organizations are public, rather than because they are bureaucratic. Control as accountability takes precedence over purposeful initiative, since whatever is accomplished must be achieved within constraints intended to safeguard such values as fairness, impartiality, openness, responsiveness, honesty, equity, efficiency and economy. Rather than having produced a genuinely results-oriented governmental system NPM has largely replaced one form of bureaucratic control with another. Schick (1996), a commentator not opposed to NPM tenets, found in New Zealand a potential for the emergence of a 'checklist mentality' in the fulfilment of specified accountability requirements.

COUNTING OR PROBING?

NPM's rationalist foundations have generated a drive to measure all things, even those which by their nature are not easily measurable. However, the belief that accountability will be enhanced to the extent that political and administrative/managerial performance and policy 'outcomes' can be measured in increasingly precise ways produces perverse effects. What is measured is what can most easily be measured, rather than what might be the most important dimension of governmental capacity or policy outcome. Politicians and officials can be rigorously accountable for irresponsible or irrelevant outcomes (Schön, 1983). The perennial question endures: is it better to be roughly right than precisely wrong? T.S. Eliot can be rephrased: 'Where is the responsibility we have lost in accountability? Where is the accountability we have lost in answerability?'[3]

Nor does the quest for precise results acknowledge political preferences for inconclusive outcomes. As Thomas asks, 'What are the benefits and costs for ministers and public servants in publicizing their policy and program shortcomings? Won't parliamentarians, interest groups, and the media focus on the imperfections more than the successes?' (1998: 380).

Structuralist/quantitative approaches are certainly a necessary means of sustaining accountability of those who exercise public power. But more is needed. Although he was not directly addressing issues of accountability in public policy making, Lindblom (1959, 1990) has shown why accountability cannot be guaranteed, and may be subverted by an over-commitment to performance measurement. Instead, he has argued for a multi-faceted and eclectic form of 'probing' to help ensure that public power is wielded responsibly.

Harmon (1995: 195) acknowledges the importance of legitimate political constraints that officials must not violate – the notion of accountability as control. But these set the framework for accountability as 'a dialogue involving the mutual interpretation of people's actions in the process of cooperatively discovering what sorts of practices are worth engaging in'. A similar view is found in Aucoin and Heintzman's third purpose of accountability (apart from that of control and reassurance): 'to encourage and promote learning in pursuit of *continuous improvement* in governance and public management'. They recognize the tensions existing among the three purposes, arguing that the pursuit of continuous improvement demands that, 'those who audit, inspect and review public service management acknowledge the constraints that affect the realization of outputs and outcomes *and* over which public servants have little or no control' (2000: 45, 54; emphases in the original). Organization theorist Chris Argyris (1980, 1990) has examined another dimension of the accountability paradox: how demands to render information more open impel more creative ways of keeping it hidden, and how organizational defences inhibit the capacity to learn from mistakes and respond and adapt to changing circumstances. Ideas such as these might seem a bit fuzzy when compared with apparently hard-edged, calculative, if not punitive approaches. But they probably connect better with governance realities.

The idea of accountability as the quest for continuous improvement addresses capacities for public discourse about the shape, scope, purpose and impacts of policy through the widest possible range of institutional arrangements – from parliamentary scrutiny and debate, the sharing of official information, the testing of administrative law, citizens' charters and referenda, journalistic investigation, academic research and so on. What it lacks in measurable precision it compensates for in the facilitation of informed 'public judgement' over time (see Yankelovich, 1991).

MEETING NEW ACCOUNTABILITY CHALLENGES

Stone (1995: 523) argues that, 'The identification of multiple options for administrative accountability ... raises questions about how the different accountability systems are to be chosen and combined to maximize accountability without impairing the effectiveness of different sorts of administrative work.' De Leon (1998: 554) has similarly argued that, 'the challenge for government is to identify the varying task environments in each sphere of action and use mechanisms of accountability that are appropriate in that arena.'

One size does not fit all, and there can be no last word written on these complex issues. The last decades of the twentieth century saw a widespread shift to the contractual 'out-sourcing' of public goods and services; the adoption of market and quasi-market approaches to service delivery; the increase in 'adhocracy', with more and more state agencies working in an 'arm's length' relationship with their respective political executives; the general emergence of what has been referred to as the 'shadow state' or the 'hollow state' (Wolch, 1990; Rhodes, 1994); and the development of e-government technologies.

The growth of discretionary authority has demanded increasingly higher levels of responsible action in the exercise of public power. But reliance on formal accountability procedures, essential as they are, is unlikely to guarantee these levels. Reliance on them alone will diminish rather than enhance them. New, more positive, arrangements and expectations need to be established between what Aucoin and Heintzman (2000) see as the on-going dialectical relationship between accountability as control and verification and accountability as continuous improvement in governmental performance. Robert Behn vigorously advocates a new paradigm of democratic accountability 'to create some new cooperative institutions that can promote accountability for performance', in order to offset too strong a preoccupation with rule-bound accountability for 'finances and fairness' (2001: 217).

John Uhr (1993: 13) is undoubtedly correct in his description of accountability as 'probably one of the most basic yet most intractable of political concepts'. As the meaning and practical application of the term are endlessly worked through, in different governmental jurisdictions, further structural and legalistic innovations and reforms will be made in its name. But 'problems of accountability' are essentially 'wicked' rather than 'tame' (Rittel and Webber, 1973) – messy, complex, and paradoxical rather than clearly defined, logically consistent and unilinear. They are to be resolved over time, in changing circumstances, rather than solved once and for all.

Attention will be focused on the capacities of legislative institutions and their offices, freedom of information legislation, ombudsmen, news media and the whole apparatus of bureaucratic control in attempts to ensure that public power is exercised legitimately. Some advocates will stress the mechanistic and structural means of ensuring accountability, while others will emphasize more organic approaches to ensure that governmental authority is exercised by trustworthy people of good character, within institutions imbued with a strong culture of ethical probity (see OECD/PUMA, 1996).

In pursuit of this aim it is important that accountability be considered as a component of, but often in a paradoxical relationship to, the multi-faceted idea of responsibility. Weber's 'ethic of responsibility', which speaks to an individual's need to reconcile impersonal bureaucratic realities with individual moral and political choice, can be instructive. It helps in understanding the relationship between accountability and responsibility in modern governmental systems increasingly run according to managerial strictures. Narrowly defined concerns over accountability can inhibit reflection on how to enhance responsibility. Politicians and officials who wield public power need institutional space within which to think and act as morally responsible individuals, not just as agents of constitutionally and hierarchically aligned superiors.

The twentieth century provided ample evidence that bureaucratic organizations, in whatever form, tend to facilitate the pursuit of inhumane purposes and impede the quest for humanitarian ones. Issues of accountability, therefore, like those of responsibility, are as much moral and ethical as they are technical in nature, and impinge firmly upon the trust needed to underpin a democratically healthy relationship between politicians, bureaucrats and citizens.

NOTES

I am grateful to Paul Thomas for comments on an original draft of this chapter.

1 From an address to the American Association for the Advancement of Science, New York, 27 December 1960; reported in *The New York Times*, 28 December 1960, p. 14, and quoted in Frankel (1962: 152).

2 Excerpt from Radio New Zealand interview, National Programme, 2 May 2001.

3 From a chorus in 'The Rock' (1934):

Where is the wisdom we have lost in knowledge?
Where is the knowledge we have lost in information?

REFERENCES

Appleby, Paul (1949) *Policy and Administration.* University, AL: University of Alabama Press.

Arendt, Hannah (1963) *Eichmann in Jerusalem: A Report on the Banality of Evil.* Harmondsworth: Penguin.

Argyris, Chris (1980) 'Making the Undiscussable and its Undiscussability Discussable', *Public Administration Review*, 40 (May/June): 205–13.

Argyris, Chris (1990) *Overcoming Organizational Defences: Facilitating Organizational Learning.* Boston, MA: Allyn and Bacon.

Aucoin, Peter and Heintzman, Ralph (2000) 'The Dialectics of Accountability for Performance in Public Management Reform', *International Review of Administrative Sciences*, 66 (1): 45–55.

Bailey, Stephen K. (1964) 'Ethics and the Public Service', *Public Administration Review*, 24 (December): 234–43.

Barker, Anthony (1998) 'Political Responsibility for UK Prison Security – Ministers Escape Again', *Public Administration*, 76 (1): 1–23.

Behn, Robert (2001) *Rethinking Democratic Accountability.* Washington, DC: Brookings Institution.

Bovens, Mark (1998) *The Quest for Responsibility: Accountability and Citizenship in Complex Organisations.* Cambridge: Cambridge University Press.

De Leon, Linda (1998) 'Accountability in a "Reinvented" Government', *Public Administration*, 76 (3): 539–58.

Doern, G. (1993) 'UK Citizen's Charter: Origins and Implementation in Three Agencies', *Policy and Politics*, 21 (1): 17–29.

Dowding, Keith and Won-Taek Kang (1998) 'Ministerial Resignations, 1945–97', *Public Administration*, 76 (3): 411–29.

Eliot, T.S. (1934) 'Choruses from "The Rock"', in *Collected Poems, 1909–1962.* London: Faber and Faber (1963).

Finer, Herman (1941) 'Administrative Responsibility in Democratic Government', *Public Administration Review*, 1 (Summer): 335–50.

Frankel, Charles (1962) *The Democratic Prospect.* New York: Harper and Row.

Friedrich, Carl J. (1940) 'Public Policy and the Nature of Administrative Responsibility', *Public Policy*, 1: 3–24.

Goodnow, Frank (1900) *Politics and Administration.* New York: Macmillan.

Gregory, Robert (1998) 'Political Responsibility for Bureaucratic Incompetence: Tragedy at Cave Creek', *Public Administration*, 76 (3): 519–38.

Harmon, Michael M. (1995) *Responsibility as Paradox: A Critique of Rational Discourse on Government.* London: Sage.

Hood, C., Scott, C., James, O., Jones, G. and Travers, T. (1999) *Regulation Inside Government: Waste-Watchers, Quality Police, and Sleaze-Busters.* Oxford: Oxford University Press.

Kaufman, Herbert (1977) *Red Tape: Its Origins, Uses, and Abuses.* Washington, DC: Brookings Institution.

Kettl, Donald F. (1993) *Sharing Power: Public Governance and Private Markets.* Washington, DC: Brookings Institution.

Klitgaard, Robert (1997) 'Cleaning Up and Invigorating the Civil Service', *Public Administration and Development*, 17: 487–509.

Lewis, N. and Birkenshaw, P. (1993) *When Citizens Complain: Reforming Justice and Administration.* Buckingham: Open University Press.

Lindblom, Charles E. (1959) 'The Science of Muddling Through', *Public Administration Review*, 19 (2): 79–88.

Lindblom, Charles E. (1990) *Inquiry and Change: The Troubled Attempt to Understand and Shape Society.* New Haven, CT: Yale University Press.

Lucas, J.R. (1976) *Democracy and Participation.* Harmondsworth: Penguin.

Manitoba Health (2001) *The Report of the Review and Implementation Committee for the Report of the Manitoba Pediatric Cardiac Surgery Inquest.* Winnipeg: Government of Manitoba.

Martin, John (1995) 'Contracting and Accountability', in Jonathan Boston (ed.), *The State Under Contract.* Wellington: Bridget Williams Books.

Merton, Robert K. (1940) 'Bureaucratic Structure and Personality', *Social Forces*, 17: 560-8.

Milgram, Stanley (1974) *Obedience to Authority: An Experimental View*. New York: Harper and Row.

Miller, A.G. (1986) *The Obedience Experiments: A Case Study of Controversy in Social Science*. New York: Praeger.

Ministry of Health (2001) *Report of the Ministerial Inquiry into the Under-Reporting of Cervical Smear Abnormalities in the Gisborne Region*, Wellington: Ministry of Health.

Mosher, Frederick C. (1968) *Democracy and the Public Service*. New York: Oxford University Press.

OECD/PUMA (1996) *Public Management Occasional Papers: No. 14 – Ethics in the Public Service: Current Issues and Practice*. Paris: Organization of Economic Co-operation and Development.

Palmer, Geoffrey (1987) *Unbridled Power: An Interpretation of New Zealand's Constitution and Government*, 2nd edn. Auckland: Oxford University Press.

Palmer, Geoffrey and Palmer, Matthew (1997) *Bridled Power: New Zealand Government Under MMP*. Auckland: Oxford University Press.

Pierre, Jon (1998) 'Public Consultation and Citizen Participation: Dilemmas of Policy Advice', in B. Guy Peters and Donald Savoie (eds), *Taking Stock: Assessing Public Sector Reforms*. Montreal and Kingston: Canadian Centre for Management Development/ McGill–Queen's University Press.

Polidano, Charles (1999) 'The Bureaucrat Who Fell Under a Bus: Ministerial Responsibility, Executive Agencies and the Derek Lewis Affair in Britain', *Governance*, 12 (2): 201–29.

Rhodes, Rod (1994) 'The Hollowing Out of the State: The Changing Nature of the Public Service in Britain', *The Political Quarterly*, 65 (2): 138–51.

Rittel, H.W. and Webber, M.M. (1973) 'Dilemmas in a General Theory of Planning', *Policy Sciences*, 4 (2): 155–69.

Romzek, Barbara S. and Dubnick, Melvin J. (1987) 'Accountability in the Public Sector: Lessons from the *Challenger* Tragedy', *Public Administration Review*, 47 (3): 227–38.

Romzek, Barbara S. and Ingraham, Patricia W. (2000) 'Cross Pressures of Accountability: Initiative, Command, and Failure in the Ron Brown Plane Crash', *Public Administration Review*, 60 (3): 240–53.

Schick, Allen (1996) 'The Spirit of Reform: Managing the New Zealand State Sector in a Time of Change'. A report prepared for the State Services Commission and the Treasury, Wellington, NZ.

Schön, Donald A. (1983) *The Reflective Practitioner: How Professionals Think in Action*. New York: Basic Books.

Simon, Herbert A. (1952) 'Development of Theory of Democratic Administration: Replies and Comments', *American Political Science Review*, 46: 494–6.

Stone, Bruce (1995) 'Administrative Accountability in the "Westminster" Democracies: Towards a New Conceptual Framework', *Governance*, 8 (4): 505–26.

Taylor, Frederick W. (1911) *Principles of Scientific Management*. New York: W.W. Norton.

Thomas, Paul G. (1996) 'Beyond the Buzzwords: Coping With Change in the Public Sector', *International Review of Administrative Sciences*, 62: 5–29.

Thomas, Paul G. (1998) 'The Changing Nature of Accountability', in B. Guy Peters and Donald Savoie (eds), *Taking Stock: Assessing Public Sector Reforms*. Montreal and Kingston: Canadian Centre for Management Development/McGill–Queen's University Press.

Thomas, Paul G. (2001) 'The Institutional Context and the Search for Accountability', in Manitoba Health, *The Report of the Review and Implementation Committee for the Report of the Manitoba Pediatric Cardiac Surgery Inquest*. Winnipeg: Government of Manitoba. Ch. 2.

Uhr, John (1993) 'Redesigning Accountability: From Muddles to Maps', *Australian Quarterly*, Winter: 1–16.

Waldo, Dwight (1952) 'Development of Theory of Democratic Administration' [and Replies and Comments], *American Political Science Review*, 46: 81–103, 501–3.

Wildavsky, Aaron (1979) *Speaking Truth to Power: The Art and Craft of Policy Analysis*. Boston, MA: Little, Brown.

Wilson, James Q. (1989) *Bureaucracy: What Government Agencies Do and Why They Do It*. New York: Basic Books.

Wilson, Woodrow (1887) 'The Study of Administration', *Political Science Quarterly*, 2 (June): 481–506.

Wolch, Jennifer R. (1990) *The Shadow State: Government and Voluntary Sector in Transition*. New York: The Foundation Center.

Yankelovich, Daniel (1991) *Coming to Public Judgment: Making Democracy Work in a Complex World*. Syracuse, NY: Syracuse University Press.

45

On Acting Responsibly in a Disorderly World: Individual Ethics and Administrative Responsibility

Linda deLeon

Although the words 'accountability' and 'responsibility' mean similar things and are often used as synonyms, students of public administration have long distinguished between them. Accountability is used to refer to systems of external controls on individual behavior, which may be formal or informal. Responsibility, on the other hand, refers to the internal controls on behavior that are exerted by an individual person's beliefs and feelings. In common parlance, 'responsibility' has various shades of meaning. It can indicate the capacity to cause something – which Harmon (1995) terms *agency*: 'Jones was responsible for our victory over Collingwood.' It can mean a task assignment (or *accountability* in Harmon's terms), as in 'This week, I'm responsible for cleaning up the coffee room.'[1] Finally, and it is this meaning that the word most usually carries in public administration, it connotes *obligation*: 'I feel responsible for ensuring that no one will be hurt.'

This chapter will address the linkages between the concept of administrative responsibility and personal values and ethics. It first presents a theoretical framework organizing the varieties of organizational settings and the kinds of accountability systems that can be associated with them. Next, the special characteristics of these various settings create issues that invoke particular kinds of ethical questions and responses. One of the major themes of this section of the chapter is that no system of human endeavor can forego either the use of external controls (accountability) or a reliance on the internalized restraints imposed by a sense of responsibility. In the third section, the

sources of ethics are considered; the theme of this discussion is that responsibility, an internal impulse to consider the needs of things and people other than oneself, is a complex compound formulated from many different sources, but it is primarily rooted in an individual's sense of belonging to communities of various sorts. Finally, the essay concludes by paying particular attention to the ways in which contemporary trends, such as administrative reform, raise a characteristic set of questions concerning ethical, responsible action for public administrators.

SOME PROBLEMS

Carl Friedrich (1940) and Herbert Finer (1941), in their justly renowned exchange of views concerning accountability, delineated a key issue for administration: is it enough that public servants should have a keenly felt sense of responsibility for the public welfare (Friedrich), or is it also necessary (and perhaps even more important) that they be subject to external, formal controls (Finer)? The question they framed remains a very important one, because there are many situations where the work of administrators cannot be closely and constantly monitored: they work in the field (Kaufman, 1960; Lipsky, 1980), or they have technical expertise exceeding that of their supervisors (Raelin, 1986). In fact, as we shall see, to the extent that we want public sector employees who are empowered, creative, flexible, entrepreneurial etc. – qualities often praised in the rhetoric of reinvention and reform – we are also required to give them the freedom to act independently. This in turn means we need to trust them to make decisions in the public interest, constrained (to some degree) by the prospect of the day of accounting, but also (in the short run) by their own inner sense of responsibility.

Harmon (1995) points out the paradoxical nature of administrative responsibility: administrators' actions cannot be simultaneously the result of their own personal intentionality and of their responsiveness to the will of others (hierarchical superiors, elected political representatives, citizens). Although under favorable conditions the two may reinforce each other, the problem remains that personal morality does not provide a basis for administrative legitimacy under a theory of overhead democracy (Redford, 1969). In fact, conflicts between personal and organizational responsibility frequently cause ethical problems for public servants. Cooper (1998) makes this issue his subject in *The Responsible Administrator*, analyzing the competing responsibilities that may face administrative actors. These include three 'realms of obligation and virtue', such as the obligation to pursue the public interest, the obligation to authorize processes and procedures, and an obligation to colleagues (Cooper, 1987). Eschewing to offer any ethically 'correct' solutions or actions, Cooper asks administrators to pass each ethical choice past four filters: moral rules,[2] ethical principles, rehearsal of defenses ('How will the proposed action be viewed if it becomes public knowledge?') and anticipatory self-appraisal ('How will I feel about myself if I act thus?').

A THEORETICAL FRAMEWORK

Clearly no organization, not even the most coercive, can function well if it must obtain compliance solely on the basis of external controls. It simply takes too much time and energy on the part of the controllers to monitor behavior and enforce compliance. Furthermore, repressing natural impulses and constantly toeing a tight line demand a great deal of energy on the part of the subordinate individuals, too. On the other hand, to the extent that people can trust each other to behave in predictable, desired ways, a dual sense of group cohesion *and* individual initiative is produced, and many desirable organizational consequences (productivity, creativity) flow from it. For this reason, 'trust' is constantly invoked by organization theorists as a basic precondition for the effectiveness of most organizational processes:[3] a sort of organization-level version of Tolstoi's famous observation that 'happy marriages are all alike'.

In a loose sense, there is probably a trade-off between external controls and internal ones. Where persons can be trusted to act responsibly, fewer rules are needed, monitoring need not be so close, and sanctions will be required only rarely. Where individuals do not act responsibly, of course, constraints must be applied to keep them within the bounds of what is acceptable.

In a series of earlier articles, I have used a scheme to categorize work situations, one based on the work of organization theorist James Thompson (1967; Thompson and Tuden, 1959). Organizational tasks can be arrayed along two dimensions: whether the goals toward which action is to be directed are clear or conflicting/ambiguous, and whether the means to be used (more precisely, the cause-and-effect relationships specifying how a goal may be reached) are certain or uncertain. Making the assumption, for purposes of simplicity, that each dimension can be treated as a dichotomous variable produces a four-fold grid, (Figure 45.1). The terms used in the table have been modified slightly from Thompson's original, to reflect the language used in contemporary scholarship to capture the fourth-cell condition, which has been variously labeled 'organized anarchy' (Cohen and March, 1986) or 'the garbage can' (Bolman and Deal, 1990; Cohen et al., 1972).

Categorizing types of accountability, Romzek and Dubnick (Dubnick and Romzek, 1991; Romzek and Dubnick, 1987, 1991) have generated a rather similar typology, identifying two dimensions – whether accountability is internal or external, and whether it is tight or loose – resulting in four types: bureaucratic, legal, professional and political. (Figure 45.2).[4]

In Cell 1 of Figure 45.1, goals are clear and means are certain: therefore decisions are relatively codified or routine, and bureaucratic structures are appropriate. In these hierarchical systems with a clear chain of command, accountability is to rules and procedures, and the supervisor's job is to monitor subordinates' behavior, rewarding the good and correcting whatever is wrong. Even here, however, individuals are expected to *internalize* the rules and procedures (as well as the informal norms of the agency) and to have the self-discipline to follow them without constant oversight.

In Cell 2, means are known, but the goals toward which action should be directed are ambiguous or conflicting. Such decision systems are essentially political – before action can take

GOALS (preferences regarding possible outcomes)

		Clear	Ambiguous or conflicting
MEANS (knowledge of cause/effect relations)	Certain	CELL 1: *Hierarchy* Decisions by computation Bureaucratic structure	CELL 2: *Competitive pluralism* Decisions by bargaining Representative structure
	Uncertain	CELL 3: *Community* Decisions by consensus Collegial structure	CELL 4: *Anarchy* Decisions by 'inspiration' Network structure

Figure 45.1 *Decision and organization structure*

SOURCE OF CONTROL

		Internal	External
DEGREE OF CONTROL	High	Bureaucratic	Legal
	Low	Professional	Political

Figure 45.2 *Types of accountability*

place, a goal must be chosen, either in a winner-take-all game (competitive pluralism) or through bargaining, negotiation and compromise. The parties to the conflict compete to win primacy for their own ideas, candidates or programs. In this sort of decision arena (examples are partisan politics, law and, of course, professional sports), accountability is to the rules of the game. Participants in the game are allowed, even expected, to do everything not explicitly forbidden in order to win. External control is through political or legal oversight, which is performed by 'referees' (the courts or their authorized delegates) – and also, informally, by spectators (for example, interest groups and the media) who observe the contest and report violations. Even where competition is fierce, however, participants are nevertheless supposed to internalize the rules of the game (avoiding infractions), and to act so as to protect the game itself. This latter stricture is well illustrated by the censure errant athletes endure from fans and sports writers who point out that their behavior (even if it were off the field) disgraces the sport as a whole.

Administrative organizations are kept responsive to the goals of the political system in two ways. Where political appointees to a public agency serve at the pleasure of the appointing authority, they may be dismissed if they are not responsive to its programmatic goals. Also, a variety of techniques can be used to bring informal pressure (as opposed to formal authority or appeal to professional standards) to bear on public managers. In addition, legal accountability can apply both at the organizational level – as when a school district is subjected to court oversight to ensure that it complies with the law – or at the individual level. In the United States, the latter has been increasingly common since the 1970s: whereas public officials used to have absolute immunity from civil suits arising out of actions in pursuit of their official duties, now most federal and local government employees can be sued for damages by individuals who believe their constitutional rights have been violated by the official's actions.

In Cell 3, the goal is clear but the means are uncertain. This is the realm of the traditional professions: in medicine, for example, physicians unambiguously want to preserve life and health, but the body's complexity makes it difficult to know how best to achieve this result. In such situations, accountability is loose, relying upon the integrity and trustworthiness of the expert tasked with getting the job done.[5] These experts are permitted considerable freedom of action (that is, they are more likely to be held accountable for *results* but given the authority to make their own decisions about work *methods*), even when they work in a bureaucratic setting, for they are expected to have internalized a strict code of professional conduct during their professional training. External control, to the extent that it is present, is exercised through the informal medium of peer opinion and (more rarely) through the formal processes of professional review boards. In addition, professionals may be required to 'give an account' of their actions and results, justifying their decisions and outcomes.

The last type of situation, called 'anarchic' here (cf. deLeon, 1994), occurs when goals are conflicting and means uncertain. Cohen, March and Olsen called this sort of decision situation a 'garbage can' because it is one in which problems and solutions (goals and means) churn about until, occasionally, ones that fit meet, and organizational action is possible. Note that 'anarchy' is not used here in its common sense of 'disordered' or 'chaotic' but as a term for a particular kind of decision situation. According to Taylor (1982), anarchies are systems in which there is (a) no specialization of political roles (in other words, everyone participates equally in the making of political decisions) and (b) no enforcement of collective decisions. Examples of anarchic systems in public administration include some organizational networks (those that have no umbrella agency with authority over the participants), such as those described by Chisholm (1989) or Radin (1993; Radin and Romzek, 1994), and organizations of self-managing individuals (professionals in group practice, collectives).

It would seem that in a 'garbage can' there is no accountability at all. Theorists of anarchic systems such as international relations, however, point out that there is a sort of external control on behavior, which in an evocative phrase they have called 'the shadow of the future' (Axelrod and Keohane, 1985). This simply means that every party has an incentive to refrain from harming others today for fear of how the others would retaliate tomorrow. Taylor also argues, however, that anarchic systems can only be stable and well-ordered if they are based upon something more benign than fear of retaliation: there must also be shared norms and values to form the basis for trust and reciprocity among members. (Thus responsibility, a term being used in this chapter to indicate *internal* controls on behavior, would therefore be possible in anarchies, even though accountability would not.) To be a viable and desirable state, then, an anarchy must also be a community.

In summary, each kind of organizational setting – hierarchies, competitive pluralism, community and anarchy – uses external controls to constrain behavior within acceptable limits, but each also relies on internalized controls, the sense of individual responsibility. Not even the most coercive system can function without at least some cooperation from participants (Goffman, 1990), and even in the anarchy of perfectly competitive markets, buyers and sellers trust each other to fulfill their bargains and contracts without court enforcement (Solomon, 1992). On the other hand, no system can function entirely without some means of bringing errant participants into line, whether it is the strictness of close supervision or the implicit shadow of the future. Some mixture of accountability and responsibility is required to keep social, political and economic systems on an even keel.

ADMINISTRATIVE RESPONSIBILITY AND PERSONAL ETHICS

Just as organization structure is in part shaped by the kind of decision that is most common and/or central to its key function, and just as accountability systems are shaped by the organization's structure and function, the structure of the organization in turn affects the ethical problems faced by individuals within it. Bureaucracies, competitive arenas, communities and anarchies each place a premium on somewhat different ethical responses.

Bureaucracies

The preceding discussion suggests that the accountability of bureaucracy is to rules and procedures, and it is monitored and enforced by hierarchical superiors. The bureaucratic form of organization emphasizes the moral rule, 'Discipline, obedience and service' (deLeon, 1993); everyone in a bureaucracy has a duty of followership to those in the chain of command above him/her. Although leadership receives much more attention, followership is an equally important concept. Chaleff (1995) describes the leader-follower relationship as a 'dance', in which both share a common purpose and core values (cf. Follett, 1992 [1926], who makes the point that work flows best not when followers take orders from leaders, but when both see themselves as taking 'orders' from the 'law of the situation'). Courageous followers, Chaleff says, have five kinds of courage. First is the courage to assume responsibility, which means that they are willing to initiate values-based action in order to correct or improve the organization's internal processes or external actions. The courage to serve includes willingness to assume additional responsibilities in order to protect the leader's time and energy, as well as to stand up for the leader and the organization when they are misunderstood. Another sort of courage is required in order to challenge leaders who behave inappropriately. In organizations beset by a turbulent environment, the courage to participate in organizational transformation means that followers need to be champions of change, supporting the leader and group while the struggle to cope with it continues. Finally, followers must have the courage to leave when it is necessary, whether because the leader or organization is pathological, because a leader is ineffective, or even because a leader is enlightened but personal values lead the follower to a higher calling (see also Hirschman, 1970 for his provocative explication of the follower's choices among exit, voice and loyalty).

Competitive arenas

Capitalist, pluralist societies abound with examples of competitive arenas. Sports and games offer many excellent analogies, while partisan politics, legal proceedings and economic markets institutionalize competitive interactions. In competitions, there must be rules (as there are in bureaucracies) and governors (referees) who are charged with spotting and stopping foul play. For politics, law and markets, rules are set by law and custom; judges play the role of referees. Accountability, then, is by legal oversight (see Figure 45.2).

The situation of the player in a game with respect to the team captain or coach is similar to that of an official in a bureaucracy, for the relation is subordinate. With respect to competitors, however, the relationship is quite different. The basic moral rule operative in a game is 'Play by the rules', but implicit in this admonition is the notion that whatever is not forbidden is permitted – players are expected and encouraged to do everything they can to win, using all their skill, power and craftiness to overcome the opposition. Often, however, spectators do not know and understand the rules nearly so well as do participants (players, coaches, referees), and since they judge conduct by the standards of everyday morality, some permitted plays may seem highly unethical. This reaction is shared by observers of politics, law and business as well: political parties engage in both honorable campaigning and 'dirty tricks', lawyers badger witnesses and make full use of technicalities if they can, and business competitors engage in spying, hostile takeovers and a wide variety of other sharp practices.

There are other ways to view adversarial relationships, however. In a wonderful, offbeat book entitled *The Inner Game of Tennis*, Gallwey (1974) draws analogies from his Zen Buddhist practice to his tennis matches. He suggests that quieting the mind and developing single-pointed concentration are essential, but more importantly, he prescribes thinking of one's opponent with gratitude and affection:

> [T]rue competition is identical with true cooperation. Each player tries his hardest to defeat the other, but in this use of competition it isn't the other *person* we are defeating; it is simply a matter of overcoming the

obstacles he presents. In true competition no person is defeated. Both players benefit by their efforts to overcome the obstacles presented by the other. Like two bulls butting their heads against one another, both grow stronger and each participates in the development of the other. (p. 123)

The great games of politics, law and business are not the only competitive arenas, to be sure. Bureaucratic politics can be as cut-throat as partisan contests, and an ethic of caring competition would be as beneficial within organizations as in the struggles among them.

Communities

Two kinds of communities are of particular interest for our purposes here. First are organizations that are themselves communities (such as small cooperative associations, professionals in group practice, faculties, and so on). These groups are characterized by shared values, frequent direct interactions, and relatively equal status among members. The second sort of community to which many public administrators belong is a profession, an affiliation which may complement or compete with membership in a bureaucratic organization (Ben-David, 1957; Engel, 1970; Hall, 1968, Mosher, 1968: 18; Scott, 1966).

The moral rule of communities is 'One for all, and all for one' (deLeon, 1993). Although there is much that is appealing in the vision of a cohesive group based on shared values, there are also problems. One of the most often cited is that communities can repress dissent, enforcing conformity to shared norms. Burke (1996: 599) asserts that, 'fundamentally communitarians … do not like it when moral differences emerge: difference, debate, and moral discord are not [for them] the starting point of democratic politics and political accommodation but a sign of disordered practices and of social fragmentation'. Also communities may be exclusive, even building cohesion by creating outside enemies or relieving tension by expelling scapegoats. Thus the critical ethical challenge for communitarian systems is inclusion. For administrators, this may require rising above a shared but wrongheaded community consensus on enmity toward a minority or toward outsiders; it may require courageous leadership to bring about a more just and compassionate society (Alexander, 1997). For administrators in communities of professionals, the challenge of inclusion means respecting diversity of opinion – a willingness to make the profession open to all who can achieve expertise and honor the service ideal – furthermore, it also means having humility enough to solicit and respect the views of stakeholders who are not also experts.

At a more quotidian level, community calls forth what Gilligan termed 'an ethic of care', which is 'an activity of relationship, of seeing and responding to need, taking care of the world by sustaining the web of connection so that no one is left alone' (1982: 62). Within organizations, this would entail a very strong emphasis on administrative benevolence (Denhardt, 1991). Gilligan proposed that differential gender socialization in Western cultures may have resulted in men and women approaching moral judgments differently. In work based on small samples[6] and often criticized (Moore, 1999; Wilson, 1993: 180n.) but of far-reaching impact, Gilligan found that women were more likely to employ the 'ethic of care' and men to use an 'ethic of justice'.[7]

Anarchies

While political and organizational theorists have focused much attention on bureaucracies, pluralism, and community, they have largely neglected anarchies. Both international relations and markets that are perfectly (in theory, at least) competitive, however, are examples of such systems that have been extensively analyzed by political scientists and economists, respectively.

Several forms of anarchic structures have recently become more common in the public sector as well as the private. At the organizational level, networks are increasingly utilized as a flexible structure for cooperation among various kinds of actors: organizations (Chisholm, 1989; Radin, 1993; Radin and Romzek, 1994) or mixtures of individuals, groups and organizations (Heclo, 1978; Meltsner and Bellavita, 1983). Within organizations, self-directed work teams may display anarchic features, although in most cases they do have the power to enforce collective decisions (since entry and exit from teams is constrained by the organization in which they exist).

In an anarchy, the basic moral rule is 'Live and let live' (deLeon, 1993). The catchphrase suggests both that individuals feel a positive moral duty to seek their own self-actualization (or groups to seek their collective ends) and that they must allow other individuals or groups the freedom to do the same thing. Fictional characters such as the heroes of Ayn Rand's books, or countless artists such as Hemingway or Picasso, offer examples of this position, which is not one that is unambiguously admired by most people.

Anarchies, unlike communities, are prone to conflict and contention. They are not necessarily chaotic, although the popular usage of the term implies that they are; but the fact that anarchies do not enforce collective decisions indicates that they do not have formal systems of accountability. The difficulty of imposing formal accountability mechanisms results from the nature of the anarchic decision situation (Cell 4 in Figure 45.1), which is characterized by conflict over goals, and uncertain knowledge of means. These attributes imply that since goals are in conflict, administrators cannot be held responsible for 'results'. And since means are poorly understood, no one knows exactly what to do, and therefore administrators cannot be held accountable for 'process', either.

Because formal accountability is not possible, the importance of informal controls becomes correspondingly greater. Informal external controls can be of two types: peer pressure and the prospect of retaliatory action (the shadow of the future). The vehicle for exerting control is participation. In order to have a share in decisions, to exert pressure, or to hint at retaliation, it is necessary to be present and fully engaged. Like employees in an organization in crisis, no one can afford to go on vacation for fear of what may befall their interests while they are absent.

Anarchic conditions are inevitably very uncomfortable unless all participants consistently act with honor, benevolence and justice toward their fellows. That is to say, they must subject their own behavior to strong *internal* control – self-control – although they cannot enforce their personal standards upon others. More than in any other setting, anarchy requires individuals to have a strong personal code of ethics, a deeply held sense of administrative responsibility. In the next section, the sources of such a code will be explored.

THE SOURCES OF THE SENSE OF RESPONSIBILITY

Each individual public servant's sense of responsibility is a complex amalgam of many basic elements. In this section, we will discuss four of them: human nature, community values, professional socialization and personal philosophy. These elements produce endless combinations, which then interact with organizational norms and values to create responsible public administrators.

Human nature

James Q. Wilson (1993) offers, in his book *The Moral Sense*, an intriguing argument that human morality has its source in the fact that man is a social animal (and, as Darwin argued, that any animal would develop a conscience were it to attain to the same intellectual level as man, cf. de Waal, 1996). He proposes that there are at least four fundamental values that are so functional for human species survival that they have been hard-wired, so to speak, into our genetic code: sympathy, fairness, self-control and duty.[8] As he puts it,

> Sociability dominates in man because individuals have evolved in ways that place their most self-centered instincts under some kind of higher control. The success families have in socializing their children would be impossible if it were not for both the prosocial instincts of the infant and the central nervous system's favoring of society-regarding impulses. (1993: 132)

Wilson also finds the sources of the moral sense in families (meaning such experiences as bonding and discipline), gender (the imperatives of sexual selection) and culture. While he concludes that there is probably no single moral principle upon which moral or political philosophy can be based, Wilson does suggest that the impulse to *create* moral principles – to justify one's actions in terms of something more than self-interest – is probably universal. So the first source of individual ethics and morality lies in community, that is, our origins as social beings, as members of the human community.

Community values

Tightly knit communities are very effective at inculcating values. Communities that share religious beliefs are an example; military units (especially elite ones), fraternities and gangs are others. Professions are, in effect, another kind of community, but since their special features have important implications for the world of work (including public administration), they will be discussed separately, below.

Entrepreneur Joseph J. Jacobs, who founded Jacobs Engineering, a California firm, provides a fine illustration of how community values constrain behavior, even in the anarchic setting of the competitive marketplace. In his words, 'The strong emphasis upon character, morality, and the sanctity of one's "reputation" that I learned from my parents and the Lebanese ethnic enclave in which I grew up was a source of strength that nurtured the entrepreneurial accomplishment' (Jacobs, 1991: 2). He also tells how, during the Second World War, his father had an opportunity to make extraordinary profits on goods he traded, since the war had cut off supplies to his competitors. Jacobs, Sr chose to ration supplies to his regular customers instead of allowing demand from others to force the price of his goods upward. 'The lesson,' writes Jacobs, Jr, 'was clear. To take inordinate advantage of a temporary situation was as reprehensible as not making a profit' (p. 25). The audience for this laudable self-restraint was the Lebanese-American community, and its regard frequently motivated Jacobs to go to great lengths to correct deficiencies in his company's projects, even when there was no legal obligation to do so. 'Honor and principle are not as incompatible with success in business as many people think' (p. 27).

Administrators develop their ethics and values long before they begin their working life, beginning in the local embrace of family, church and school. The influence of these communities is the more entrenched for being developed early and before one is aware of it; like water to fish, it is invisible for most people, awareness being the product of wider experience, education and sustained critical reflection.

Professional socialization

In contemporary society generally, even the traditional professions suffer from decreasing public confidence. We want to believe in the power of modern medicine, but we joke about how our surgery or our teenager's dental braces fund the cardiologist's trip to Paris or the dentist's Porsche.

Nevertheless, professional status is highly valued and therefore professional occupations have considerable power over those in them and those seeking admission.

Professions tend to display certain features, such as a body of specialized knowledge, rigorous training to develop both cognitive knowledge and practical skills, and a professional culture and code of ethics (Greenwood, 1966), but the fundamental attributes of every profession are (a) claims to autonomous expertise and (b) a 'service ideal' (Wilensky, 1964). The service ideal is not only desirable but necessary, because professionals have knowledge of sensitive information about their clients (Seymour, 1966) and also because professions have, in terms coined by sociologist Everett C. Hughes (1959) a 'license' and a 'mandate'. The mandate that society gives a profession is to make risky decisions (that is, those where means are uncertain, as in medicine) about important matters. The license is a grant of special exemption from legal punishment for non-negligent failures, and the profession itself has the right to decide what constitutes malpractice.

As the modern era of specialized knowledge has developed, expertise has become relatively more important than the service ideal as the basis for trust in professionals. We obey doctors' orders because they know more about our bodies than we do; we trust lawyers (grudgingly) because they know the law. At the same time, however, the necessity of placing our welfare in the hands of educated strangers also means that we want to believe in their adherence to the service ideal: that they will put our interests above their own and that they will earnestly strive first, to do no harm, but also to offer help.

For public administrators, professional socialization occurs in the course of professional education and continues in the occupational 'community' of the workplace and professional associations. In most schools of public administration – in all of those accredited by the National Association of Schools of Public Affairs and Administration – ethics courses are targeted at exposing students to systematic ethical reasoning. They also develop students' appreciation for key moral principles, such as honor, benevolence and justice (Denhardt, 1991). Honor implies adherence to the highest standards, benevolence is a disposition to do good and promote the welfare of others, and justice signifies fairness and regard for the rights of others. In addition, the profession (the American Society for Public Administration) has a well-publicized Code of Ethics (Van Wart, 1996), which receives constant critical attention in its publications.

Personal philosophy

Many, if not most, public servants also have developed their normative theory of public administration as part of a personal philosophy. Of course, for many – perhaps most – administrators, the personal philosophy is not explicit or even well-developed; it may contain contradictions or be based on incorrect theories about causes and consequences. Piaget describes the moral development of children as moving from 'moral realism', a belief that morality is something parents impose on them, to an idea of justice that is the product of social conventions, rules of the game (Piaget, 1965). Kohlberg (1981) adds a further, adult stage, in which individuals reason out their ethical positions using abstract ideas such as human dignity and equality. The development of this level of ethical reasoning does not seem to happen naturally (Stewart and Sprinthall, 1991), but it can be facilitated by study of philosophy as

well as by reflection on practical experience (Denhardt, 1993, particularly his instructions for keeping an Administrative Journal; Schon, 1983). Importantly, however, such reflection should be disciplined and penetrating, based on careful and honest critical assessment of ideas and their implications. Schools accredited by the National Association of Schools of Public Affairs and Administration (United States) are required to offer course work in ethics, providing students with a structured opportunity to develop a personal philosophy and to understand the criteria for choosing among alternatives.

THE CONTEMPORARY CHALLENGE FOR PUBLIC ADMINISTRATORS

In recent years, public management reform has been undertaken in countries worldwide (Kettl, 2000). In the words of the National Performance Review initiative in the United States, the goal has been to improve government so that it 'works better and costs less' (Gore, 1993). Prompting these efforts was a pervasive sense that public organizations need increased flexibility and maneuverability in order to respond creatively to changed and still changing conditions. More than that, the conventional view of the nature of government's tasks (deLeon, 1997) is that they are 'wicked' problems (Rittel and Webber, 1973), where goals are conflicting and means are uncertain.

It is important to emphasize that the belief that public problems are particularly and increasingly difficult is socially constructed, because socially constructed beliefs are not necessarily isomorphic to real conditions, although they are certainly affected by them. Not long ago, in the postwar world, most people in the Western democracies perceived that there was a fairly broad consensus on social goals, and they believed that science had tremendous untapped capacity to generate solutions to social problems. As time has passed, however, the diversity of opinion concerning objectives has increased, both as a result of demographic changes in national populations and in consequence of a growing realization that the previously apparent consensus had merely masked a silence of divergent voices. Now, we see polarities of opinion even when consensus does exist. For example, despite the American mass media's portrayal of the abortion debate as a contest between 'pro-life' and 'pro-choice' ideologues, public opinion polls find that in fact most Americans *agree* on the issue, believing that abortion should be both legal and yet rare (Rosenblatt, 1992). Similarly, science has proved incapable of solving deadly social problems such as crime, drug abuse, domestic violence, pollution and so on. The net result is a widespread conviction, among citizens and elites alike, that life is chaotic and problems intractable.

The conviction that all problems are 'wicked' ones may be incorrect in many cases, however; there are still many of the other sorts of problems described in Figure 45.1. So although bureaucracy is widely disparaged (Goodsell, 1994), it is a perfectly appropriate structure for organizing to do 'routine' problem solving. The current emphasis on creativity and entrepreneurship in public management, however, is evidence of a belief that these skills are essential to devising programs to meet more challenging issues. Thus public management reform can be seen as a response to the view that most public problems lie in Cells 3 and 4 of Figure 45.1.

One of the key strategies of Westminster-style reform is the use of contracts to delegate responsibility for deciding *how* work should be done, while holding the organization or employees accountable to the terms of the contract ('making managers manage'). The agent is held responsible for results, while the principal is faced with the challenges inherent in monitoring the activities of the agent, such as information asymmetries (the agent knows more about the task than the principal) and moral hazard (the agent may not have the principal's interests at heart, and may instead serve his/her own, despite the terms of the contract). Contracting is a strategy appropriate to Cell 3 conditions, where a goal can be agreed upon, but where means are unclear and thus a matter of discretion.

Empowerment ('letting managers manage') is a Cell 4 strategy. In agencies that value creativity, most likely because they handle non-routine tasks where innovation is constantly required, allowing managers considerable autonomy with respect to decisions as to how to perform their jobs is common. Empowerment is thought to provide benefits other than unleashing employee creativity, too: in an era where working for the sake of work is old-fashioned, workers are more likely to prize jobs that give the opportunity for personal growth and interesting activity, even more than they value security, high status, or even pay.

Self-management, for both individuals and teams, and even for divisions within an agency, is another Cell 4 strategy that is touted as improving morale, productivity and innovation.

Self-directed work teams are defined as teams (groups of persons, working interdependently toward a common goal) that have been given a significant slice of what are normally managerial responsibilities – scheduling, staffing and perhaps even hiring, discipline, performance evaluation and compensation decisions. The concept of self-management places a high premium on responsibility toward others in the work unit (team) as well as in the organization as a whole. Even in organizations where self-management has not been essayed, there has often been significant flattening, in which layers of middle managers have been eliminated, thus widening the span of control of the managers who are left, necessitating that managers allow their subordinates more responsibility for the work.

In short, current trends in public management require more responsibility on the part of individuals than in the past. Yet internal and external controls stand in inverse relation to each other; increase in the use of one is linked to a decrease in the other. Does this have to mean that accountability is diminished, and citizens must rely solely on the hope that the personal ethics of administrators will keep them acting responsibly?

Beginning with Carl Friedrich, those who have considered the nature of administrative responsibility have noted that the ethics that govern an individual administrator's discretionary choices should not be based on purely personal values. Instead, they are a product of the interaction of personal ethics, professional expertise and 'proper regard for existing preferences in the community' (Friedrich, 1940: 403). Alexander (1997) distinguishes three versions of the role of a responsible administrator, which roughly correspond to the terms of Friedrich's equation. The administrator who has professional expertise functions as a 'neutral technician', by adhering to organization rules and procedures (and trying thus to live out the separation of administration from politics). This role is, as Alexander points out, ill-suited to the many situations in which administrators exercise considerable autonomy. Administrators can also function as delegates, in much the same way that political representatives may do: they can, on the basis of their own demographic characteristics or by imaginatively entering into the situation of their clients, act on behalf of those whom they serve (in Friedrich's terms, they can 'hold in proper regard' the majority opinion of the community). Or, and this is the role for which Alexander obviously has the most sympathy, the responsible administrator can act as an 'enlightened trustee', whose ethics are principle-driven and in service to the public interest. A key to this suggestion, however, is the importance placed upon interaction with citizens as a way in which administrators can not only learn and thus reflect citizen preferences, but also as a way in which their own ideas can shape and be shaped by these exchanges.

Because Alexander's analysis of responsibility is focused on race, one of the most difficult, touchstone problems of American life (and a problem for other Western democracies too, as immigration creates diversity in other relatively well-off countries), she is prompted to ask an especially significant question: how can administrators act as enlightened trustees except by rising above their own socialization? In the case of racial issues, administrators – like other citizens – have been socialized in a racist society; how can they step outside their conditioned responses and act to achieve social equity? How can they encourage public morality toward a higher ethical level?

The possibility of an answer lies in the willingness of administrators to reflect on their own subjective values and ethics, in combination with a sensitivity to the social context in which their action takes place (and the community values that are operative therein). In 'conversations' with others – both citizens and reflective colleagues and collaborators – administrators may generate a shared understanding of public policy problems and of their organization's responses. In praxis, defined as action and reflection on the world to change it, they can help create the consensus, the shared values, upon which community can be based. And, as the foregoing discussion has attempted to show, when community is present, the freedom and creativity and flexibility of anarchic models can flourish with benign effect.

Administrative responsibility in a disorderly and problematic world can be achieved if citizens and administrators engage in committed discourse and collaborative action together. In closing, three central implications of this principle should be noted. First, discourse flourishes precisely where collaborative action is happening, far more than in meeting rooms or mass media. An ethic that supports administrative responsibility therefore places a high value on inclusion and effective participation. Second, trust is the precondition for administrative discretion, which in turn is necessary for entrepreneurship and innovation. Therefore an ethic for contemporary administrators must be firmly founded on honor, benevolence and justice in order to win public trust and support the legitimacy of administrative action. Third, external controls – whether formal or informal – are not as efficient nor as effective as internalized ones.

Ethics and values that serve a democratic public administration must therefore be a sustained and central focus of our theory, our teaching and our practice.

NOTES

1 Using this sense of the term, an official could say, without irony, 'I am responsible, but I am not to blame' (cf. Chapter 44 by Robert Gregory in this volume).
2 Cooper defines moral rules as 'axioms or proverbs that we hold as moral guides' (1998: 9). They are a level above simple expressions of approbation or distaste, but below ethical analysis and post-ethical reflection (which last is the development of a world-view that allows us to answer the question, 'Why should I be moral?').
3 The term has received sustained analytical attention (Fukuyama, 1995; a symposium in the *Academy of Management Review*, 1998), featuring debates over conceptual and operational definitions as well as discussions of the processes by which trust is built and broken and its effects on other organizational processes.
4 The theoretical reasons why these two typologies are so similar is beside the point of this chapter, but their fit may be apparent from the following discussion.
5 Thomas (2001) notes that the deference shown to physicians and other professionals has slipped badly in recent years. They are not seen to have a monopoly on relevant knowledge nor on the most altruistic motive.
6 Three studies form the basis for the book: the 'college student study' had 25 respondents, the 'abortion-decision study' involved 29 women and the 'rights and responsibilities study' interviewed 36 people (a survey was administered to 144 persons).
7 By contrast, the ethic of justice, which Gilligan's studies found to be characteristic of most male respondents, is based on principles such as equality, emphasizing rights not relationships. In terms of the analysis here, it would be appropriate to both Cell 1 hierarchies and Cell 2 pluralist systems.
8 Additional candidates, according to Wilson, might include integrity, courage, or modesty, but he chooses 'to write about [sympathy, fairness, etc.] because I have something to say about them' (p. xiii).

REFERENCES

Alexander, J. (1997) 'Avoiding the issue: Racism and administrative responsibility in public administration', *American Review of Public Administration*, 27 (4): 343–61.

Axelrod, R. and Keohane, R.O. (1985) 'Achieving cooperation under anarchy', *World Politics,* 38 (3): 226–53.

Ben-David, J. (1957) 'The professional role of the physician in bureaucratized medicine: A study in role conflict', *Human Relations*, 10 (2): 255–74.

Bolman, L.G. and Deal, T.E. (1990) *Modern Approaches to Understanding and Managing Organizations*. San Francisco: Jossey–Bass.

Burke, J.P. (1996) 'Responsibility, politics and community', *Public Administration Review*, 56 (6): 596–9.

Chaleff, I. (1995) *The Courageous Follower*. San Francisco: Berrett–Koehler.

Chisholm, D. (1989) *Coordination without Hierarchy*. Berkeley, CA: University of California Press.

Cohen, M.D. and March, J.G. (1986) *Leadership and Ambiguity*, 2nd edn. Boston, MA: Harvard Business School Press.

Cohen, M.D., March, J.G. and Olsen, J.P. (1972) 'A garbage can model of organizational choice', *Administrative Science Quarterly*, 17: 1–25.

Cooper, T.L. (1987) 'Hierarchy, virtue, and the practice of public administration: A perspective for normative ethics', *Public Administration Review*, 47: 320–8.

Cooper, T.L. (1998) *The Responsible Administrator: An Approach to Ethics for the Administrative Role*, 2nd edn. San Francisco: Jossey–Bass.

de Waal, F. (1996) *Good Natured: The Origins of Right and Wrong in Humans and Other Animals*. Cambridge, MA: Harvard University Press.

deLeon, L. (1993) 'As plain as 1, 2, 3 … and 4: Ethics and organization structure', *Administration and Society*, 25 (3): 293–316.

deLeon, L. (1994) Embracing anarchy: Network organizations and interorganizational networks', *Administrative Theory and Praxis*, 16 (2): 234–53.

deLeon, L. (1997) 'Accountability in a "reinvented" government', *International Journal of Public Administration*, 76 (3): 539–58.

Denhardt, K.G. (1991) 'Unearthing the moral foundations of public administration: honor, benevolence, and justice, in J.S. Bowman (ed.), *Ethical Frontiers in Public Management*. San Francisco: Jossey–Bass. pp. 91–113.

Denhardt, R.B. (1993) *Theories of Public Organization*, 2nd edn. Belmont, CA: Wadsworth.

Dubnick, M.J. and Romzek, B.S. (1991) *American Public Administration: Politics and the Management of Expectations*. New York: Macmillan.

Engel, G.V. (1970) 'Professional autonomy and bureaucratic organization', *Administrative Science Quarterly*, 15: 12–21.

Finer, H. (1941) 'Administrative responsibility in democratic government', *American Political Science Review*, 1: 335–50.

Follett, M.P. (1992 [1926]) 'The giving of orders', in J.M. Shafritz and A.C. Hyde (eds), *Classics of Public Administration*, 3rd edn. Pacific Grove, CA: Brooks–Cole. pp. 66–74.

Friedrich, C.J. (1940) 'Public policy and the nature of administrative responsibility', *Public Policy*, 1: 3–24.

Fukuyama, F. (1995) *Trust: The Social Virtues and the Creation of Prosperity*. New York: Free Press.

Gallwey, W.T. (1974) *The Inner Game of Tennis*. New York: Random House.

Gilligan, C. (1982) *In a Different Voice: Psychological Theory and Women's Development*. Cambridge, MA: Harvard University Press.

Goffman, E. (1990) *Asylums*, 2nd edn. New York: Doubleday.

Goodsell, C.T. (1994) *The Case for Bureaucracy*, 3rd edn. Chatham, NJ: Chatham House.

Gore, A. (1993) *From Red Tape to Results: Creating a Government that Works Better and Costs Less*. New York: Penguin Books.

Greenwood, E. (1966) 'The elements of professionalization', in H.M. Vollmer and D.L. Mills (eds), *Professionalization*. Englewood Cliffs, NJ: Prentice–Hall. pp. 9–19.

Hall, R.H. (1968) 'Professionalization and bureaucratization', *American Sociological Review*, 33: 92–104.

Harmon, M.M. (1995) *Responsibility as Paradox: A Critique of Rational Discourse on Government*. Newbury Park, CA: Sage.

Heclo, H. (1978) 'Issue networks and the executive establishment', in A. King (ed.), *The New Political System*. Washington, DC: The American Enterprise Institute for Public Policy. pp. 87–124.

Hirschman, A.O. (1970) *Exit, Voice and Loyalty*. Cambridge, MA: Harvard University Press.

Hughes, E.C. (1959) 'The study of occupations', in R.K. Merton, L. Broom and L.S. Cottrell, Jr (eds), *Sociology Today*. New York: Harper & Row. Vol. II, pp. 442–58.

Jacobs, J.J. (1991) *The Anatomy of an Entrepreneur*. San Francisco: ICS Press.

Kaufman, H. (1960) *The Forest Ranger*. Baltimore, MD: Johns Hopkins University Press.

Kettl, D.F. (2000) *The Global Public Management Revolution*. Washington, DC: Brookings Institution.

Kohlberg, L. (1981) *The Philosophy of Moral Development: Essays on Moral Development*, Vol. I. San Francisco: Harper and Row.

Lipsky, M. (1980) *Street-Level Bureaucracy*. New York: Russell Sage Foundation.

Meltsner, A.J. and Bellavita, C. (1983) *The Policy Organization*. Beverly Hills, CA: Sage.

Moore, M. (1999) 'The Ethics of Care and Justice', *Women and Politics*, 20 (2): 1–16.

Mosher, F.C. (1968) *Democracy and the Public Service*. New York: Oxford University Press.

Piaget, J. (1965) *The Moral Judgment of the Child* (trans. Marjorie Gabain). New York: Free Press.

Radin, B. and Romzek, B. (1994) 'Accountability in an Intergovernmental Arena: New Governance and the National Rural Development Partnership'. Paper presented at the Annual Meeting of the American Political Science Association, New York City, NY.

Radin, B.A. (1993) 'Managing Across Boundaries: The Monday Management Group of the National Initiative on Rural Development'. Paper presented at the National Public Management Research Conference, Madison, Wisconsin.

Raelin, J.A. (1986) *The Clash of Cultures: Managers and Professionals*. Boston, MA: Harvard Business School Press.

Redford, E.S. (1969) *Democracy in the Administrative State*. New York: Oxford University Press.

Rittel, H. and Webber, M. (1973) 'Dilemmas in a General Theory of Planning', *Policy Sciences*, 4 (2): 155–69.

Romzek, B.S. and Dubnick, M.J. (1987) 'Accountability in the public sector: Lessons from the *Challenger* tragedy', *Public Administration Review*, 47 (3): 227–38.

Romzek, B.S. and Dubnick, M.J. (1991) 'Accountability, Professionalism and Leadership: The Los Angeles Police Department and the Rodney King Beating'. Paper presented at the National Public Management Conference, The Maxwell School, Syracuse University, Syracuse, New York.

Rosenblatt, R. (1992) *Life Itself: Abortion in the American Mind*. New York: Random House.

Schon, D.A. (1983) *The Reflective Practitioner*. New York: Basic Books.

Scott, R.W. (1966) 'Professionals in bureaucracies – areas of conflict', in H.M. Vollmer and D.L. Mills (eds), *Professionalization*. Englewood Cliffs, NJ: Prentice-Hall. pp. 265–75.

Seymour, F.J.C. (1966) 'Occupational images and norms – teaching', in H.M. Vollmer and D.L. Mills (eds), *Professionalization*. Englewood Cliffs: Prentice-Hall. pp. 126–9.

Solomon, R.C. (1992) *Ethics and Excellence*. New York: Oxford University Press.

Stewart, D.W. and Sprinthall, N.A. (1991) 'Strengthening ethical judgment in public administration', in J.S. Bowman (ed.), *Ethical Frontiers in Public Management*. Washington, DC: American Society for Public Administration. pp. 243–60.

Taylor, M. (1982) *Community, Anarchy and Liberty*. Cambridge: Cambridge University Press.

Thomas, P.G. (2001) 'The institutional context and the search for accountability', in Manitoba Health, *The Report of the Review and Implementation Committee for the Report of the Manitoba Pediatric Cardiac Surgery Inquest*. Winnipeg: Government of Manitoba. Ch. 2 (www.gov.mb.ca/health/cardiac, accessed 10 October 2001).

Thompson, J.D. (1967) *Organizations in Action*. New York: McGraw–Hill.

Thompson, J.D. and Tuden, A. (1959) 'Strategies, structures and processes of organizational decision', in J.D. Thompson (ed.), *Comparative Studies in Administration*. Pittsburgh: University of Pittsburgh Press.

Van Wart, M. (1996) 'The sources of ethical decision making for individuals in the public sector', *Public Administration Review*, 56 (6): 525–34.

Wilensky, H.L. (1964) 'The professionalization of everyone?', *American Journal of Sociology*, 60 (2): 137–58.

Wilson, J.Q. (1993) *The Moral Sense*. New York: Free Press.

46

Accountability in a Seamless Economy

Kevin P. Kearns

CONTEXT

Today, more than ever before, the delivery of public services is diffused among a menagerie of organizations, including national, regional and local government agencies, private nonprofit organizations and for-profit enterprises. This is true in the United States where the federal government has essentially divested responsibility for direct service delivery, assigning greater responsibility and flexibility to state and local governments which in turn are contracting with nonprofit and for-profit firms for the provision of public services. Other countries as well, including the United Kingdom, New Zealand, Australia and many European countries, have also experienced a blurring of the boundaries between government, nonprofit organizations and the private sector (Kramer et al., 1993; McDonald, 1997). There is no evidence to suggest that this trend will soon be reversed in any of the countries where devolution has taken root. We are now operating in a *seamless* economy, where government, nonprofit (or nongovernmental) organizations (NGOs) and businesses interact, and sometimes compete, as never before. Even the boundaries between church and state, long sacrosanct in the United States, have been probed by the Bush Administration with its program to provide faith-based social service agencies with easier access to government funding.

A diffused and privatized approach to public service delivery represents a frontal assault on centrally entrenched bureaucratic structures, which many citizens, pundits and politicians believe are the root cause of government inefficiency and lethargy. Certainly, from a managerial perspective, there are many valid arguments in favor of privatization and contracting out, including:

- Reduced overhead and fixed costs for government agencies because these arc now borne by contractors
- Greater flexibility in the allocation of resources and the design of services
- Increased efficiency due to competition for contracts
- The opportunity to bring public services 'closer to the people' and to give citizens greater input in the design and delivery of programs that affect them
- Potential for more innovation in program design and delivery because of private sector investment in research and development
- Holding the line on government payrolls
- And, from a conservative ideological perspective, weakening public sector unions and reducing the vulnerability of public programs to strikes.

THE PROBLEM

Despite the apparent managerial benefits of privatization, we must remind ourselves that the new approach to public service delivery brings with it a fundamental shift in how we think about and practice accountability (Terry, 1993; Moe, 1994). The bureaucratic structures and procedures that have been denounced so blithely by the *Reinventing Government* movement (Osborne and Gaebler, 1992) have also been the primary instruments for holding government officials accountable for their actions and, thereby, creating a powerful check on abuses of power and administrative discretion. For all of their shortcomings, traditional bureaucracies are in fact designed to pinpoint responsibility, sometimes very narrowly, so public officials can be held accountable for their actions (Goodsell, 1985).

Thus, if we dispense with the centralized delivery systems and bureaucratic structures in favor of diffused and privatized systems of service delivery, what accountability tools and mechanisms will we put in place to ensure that the public's interests are well served? How will the public (or even elected officials) know whom to hold accountable when services are not delivered as promised, when funds are misspent, when intended outcomes are not achieved? What kinds of checks should we place on *entrepreneurship* in public and nonprofit organizations? The advocates of privatization have offered no detailed proposals for strengthening accountability beyond some rather vague notions of how to empower citizens for greater involvement and oversight (Bellone and Goerl, 1992), or how to promote more responsible and ethical entrepreneurship by public officials (Cohen and Eimicke, 1999).

CURRENT APPROACHES TO THE PROBLEM

Current approaches to maintaining accountability in a diffused system of public service delivery are based primarily on principal–agent theory, which brings with it accountability measures like competitive bidding, performance contracting, mandated quality controls, outcome measurement, program evaluation and independent financial audits (Pope, 2001). These accountability instruments focus exclusively on *compliance* and address the most narrow definition of accountability – requiring service providers to literally 'account' for expenditures and activities to ensure that they are in accordance with legal, regulatory and contractual agreements (White, 1926: 221; Shafritz, 1992: 4). Within the narrow confines of this purpose, these oversight tools work reasonably well, although like any compliance mechanism they are subject to abuse, neglect and poor enforcement (McDonald, 1997). For example, in the managed care environment, physicians and health care institutions have come under scrutiny for manipulating the system in order to increase their reimbursement, sometimes for services they never rendered. And, it is not

difficult to uncover cases where entrepreneurship and privatization of public service delivery have produced spectacularly *bad* results, such as the bankruptcy of Orange County, California (Kearns, 1995), the theft of millions of dollars from investors in a Ponzi scheme known as the Foundation for New Era Philanthropy (Kearns, 1996), and the infamous abuses of power by William Aramony, former chief executive of the United Way of America.

Nonetheless, if the accountability instruments currently in place help regulators uncover these abuses (even *after they occur*), then according to a strict definition of accountability they have done their job because they have forced service providers to 'account' for their behavior and they give overseers the tools they need to properly assign blame when things go wrong. Presumably, these accountability instruments also serve as deterrents to abuse of the system, but this is difficult to verify.

The problem with an approach to accountability that focuses exclusively on compliance is two-fold. First, such an approach is out of sync with the economic rationality that pervades the private sector, including the nonprofit sector. When an accountability instrument focuses only on compliance in a contractual sense, the incentive is for private contractors to comply only with the 'letter of the law'. If private contractors employ traditional economic rationality, they will try to minimize their compliance costs by doing no more than is absolutely necessary to meet the expectations of their overseers. This is especially true among for-profit contractors but this economic philosophy also governs the behavior of the nonprofit sector, especially those that rely heavily on reimbursements to generate revenues. Under these conditions, private providers lose interest in developing standards of performance that exceed what is minimally expected of them. They are even less interested in trying to strategically anticipate and position themselves to respond to new expectations from citizens, oversight agencies, or elected officials. Certainly, it is not in their best interest to advocate new and more demanding accountability measures. Rather, from an economic perspective, it is advisable to simply await each new wave of regulatory measures imposed on them from above and then do their best to react with minimal effect on their bottom line.

Second, and related, the compliance instruments alone do very little to encourage the development of a *professional ethos* of accountability among commercial and nonprofit providers of public goods and services. This is not to suggest that private contractors are inherently less ethical than their government counterparts. Rather, the whole notion of accountability as we know it is rather new to the nonprofit sector and very new to commercial organizations that are now engaged in the 'business' of social service delivery. Businesses typically think of accountability only in terms of fulfilling their promises and obligations to shareholders, not to the general public or government overseers. Aside from the relatively recent appearance of MBA courses on topics like business ethics and social responsibility, there has not been a strong academic tradition supporting the notion of accountability (as we have come to know it) in educational centers that are producing tomorrow's business leaders.

These two problems – economic disincentives and the absence of a professional ethos of accountability – present a daunting challenge for which there is no quick and easy answer. We cannot simply re-engineer the economic incentives of private sector contractors regarding accountability, nor can we construct an ethos of accountability with a snap of the fingers. Indeed, we probably should *not* think in terms of achieving a 'solution' to these problems, but rather building the foundation for a 'learning organization' (Senge, 1990; Senge et al., 1994) or in this case a 'learning system' that continuously makes progress toward improvement. Toward this end, the modest proposal presented here suggests a three pronged strategy:

1 Embrace a broader definition of accountability, including but not limited to compliance, and a shared vocabulary that can be equally understood by all stakeholders – government, nonprofit and commercial organizations as well as citizens and consumers who must be part of the dialogue.
2 Design a conceptual framework that can help public and private providers to envision *strategic* as well as *tactical* approaches to accountability.
3 Make a commitment to building an interorganizational culture and climate in which all stakeholders continuously learn from each other about how to maximize accountability in a diffused and privatized system of service delivery.

These three approaches are briefly described below.

A BROADER DEFINITION OF ACCOUNTABILITY

A strict definition of accountability focuses on literally providing an 'account' of one's activities, typically with respect to agreed-upon performance standards or outcomes. It is an unapologetic bureaucratic concept that requires four things: a higher authority vested with responsibility for oversight or supervision; a criterion or measure used by the higher authority to assess performance or compliance; a mechanism for reporting compliance to the higher authority; and, the prospect of penalty or reward based on performance. In this respect, accountability is technically distinct from related concepts like *ethics*, *responsibility* or *professional obligation*, but precise semantic distinctions are difficult to maintain. Citizens, watchdog agencies and the news media simply do not adhere to strict, academically precise definitions of accountability. To them, accountability means much more than reporting one's compliance through an established chain of command. These stakeholders believe that accountability extends to broader goals such as serving the public interest and preserving the public trust. In their view, compliance with technical contractual obligations is only part of the equation. They want to ensure that *their* standards of appropriate behavior, as well as the standards of the enforcing agency, are adhered to.

For example, following the terrorist attacks of September 11th, the American Red Cross came under intense public criticism for having allegedly misled people who made donations to a relief fund that they believed would be dispensed *directly* to the victims and their families. The media, the politicians and the donors themselves were in no mood to hear the national president of the organization engage in a technical discussion of how the relief fund was intended to serve 'emerging needs' arising out of the attacks as well as immediate relief to families. The controversy was cast in terms of the accountability of the American Red Cross to its many publics, even though the accounting for the fund was never an issue. Ultimately, the president was forced to resign and the board of trustees essentially yielded to the public pressure. Purists don't like it, but subjective performance criteria and public perceptions of proper behavior (such as fairness, equity, prudence) have been subsumed under the general banner of 'accountability'. Thus, if citizens, watchdog organizations and representatives of the news media are to be part of a public discourse on accountability in the new, privatized system of service delivery, then these broader interpretations of accountability must be taken into account.

Even in the academic literature, there is no shortage of broader definitions of accountability. For example, Mansfield (1982: 61) says, 'The notion of accountability reaches beyond obeying instructions faithfully to include a responsibility for behavior and actions that are judged by standards [such as] … competency, integrity, judgement, prudence, vision, courage, and other like qualities.' Kingsley (1944: 282) and Krislov and Rosenbloom (1981: 22) argue that accountable organizations are those that respond to the needs of society. Shafritz proposes the following definition:

> Administrative accountability: The concept that officials are to be held answerable for general notions of *democracy and morality as well as for specific legal mandates.* (1992: 10; emphasis added).

There is yet another perspective that suggests that accountability involves not only reactive responses to public expectations, but also involves efforts to *anticipate* emerging performance standards in order to take *proactive* steps to ensure that the public trust is served. In an insightful analysis of the disaster of the *Challenger* space shuttle, Romzek and Dubnick conclude that 'accountability involves the means by which public agencies and their workers *manage the diverse expectations* generated within and outside the organization' (1987: 228; emphasis added). This definition of accountability implies that public expectations can be *managed* proactively, not just reacted to after the fact. Thus, according to Romzek and Dubnick, accountability may require providers of public services to take proactive steps to actually define and shape the public expectations in the environment in which they operate. By extension, we can argue that service providers should strategically position themselves by implementing accountability systems that build on their strengths and are appropriate for the environment in which they work.

So, the scholarly literature presents us with some alternative definitions of accountability that incorporate democratic and moral principles as well as a strategic perspective that goes beyond mere compliance to the development of proactive steps to shape and meet the expectations of the public. The broader definitions add some 'fuzziness' to the concept of accountability, but they also address important aspects of accountability that are essential to the current context of diffused and privatized systems of service delivery.

A broader approach to accountability is based on several important guiding principles (Kearns, 1996):

1   Accountability, in essence, is the obligation of public service providers (whether government or private sector organizations) to serve a higher authority – the public trust – which ultimately is the source of their mandate, their authority and their legitimacy.

2   While the standards of accountability sometimes are formally codified in laws and regulations, they can also be defined by *subjective standards* and *expectations* of citizens, clients, donors, the media, self-appointed watchdog organizations and other stakeholders.

3   Whether the standards of accountability are objective or subjective, formal or informal, they are dynamic components of an organization's strategic environment.

4   Public agencies and their contracted service providers can respond to their accountability environment with either tactical (reactive) or strategic (proactive) actions.

5   Like all other components of the strategic environment, the standards of accountability should be continuously monitored and incorporated into the organization's strategic management process.

These principles certainly broaden the meaning of accountability beyond compliance, but they are not intended to suggest that there are no boundaries whatsoever on how we think about accountability. The conceptual framework presented in the next section places some boundaries on the concept that allows the various stakeholders to develop a shared vocabulary and a common strategic tool for anticipating and responding to accountability challenges and opportunities.

A CONCEPTUAL FRAMEWORK FOR ACCOUNTABILITY IN A DIFFUSED DELIVERY SYSTEM

The discussion thus far can be summarized in a visual representation (Figure 46.1) of four distinctly different types of accountability, each with its own implications for how service providers can enhance their accountability to the public trust. Each cell of Figure 46.1 is described briefly below.

Legal accountability: compliance (Cell 1)

The upper left quadrant of Figure 46.1 (Cell 1) refers to the most familiar, and most narrowly interpreted, form of accountability – compliance by service provider with an explicit standard of performance, operational procedure, output measure, or reporting requirement. In a principal–agent

Standards of accountability

	Explicit and legally binding performance and reporting requirements	Implicit and non-binding expectations of citizens, donors, watchdog organizations, news media, and other constituencies
Tactical responses by the organization (reactive, forced)	**Cell 1** Legal accountability (Compliance)	**Cell 2** Negotiated accountability (Reaction)
Strategic responses by the organization (proactive, voluntary)	**Cell 4** Anticipatory accountability (Advocacy)	**Cell 3** Discretionary accountability (Professionalism)

(Organizational response, at left of the two organizational response rows)

FIgure 46.1   *Four types of accountability affecting providers of public services (Kearns, 1996: 67)*

relationship, the accountability standards in this cell are formally codified or embedded in contractual obligations and, therefore, carry the force of law. The enforcement mechanism may be the contracting agency or an oversight agency that has the power to impose sanctions on the lower organization for noncompliance or nonperformance or rewards for superior performance. Performance contracts, audits, mandatory program evaluations and many other accountability mechanisms fall into this category. They are the compliance-focused accountability tools discussed at length earlier in this chapter.

Negotiated accountability: responsiveness (Cell 2)

Cell 2, in the upper right corner of Figure 46.1, describes the accountability challenges facing service providers in several different circumstances. First, as we noted above, providers of public services are often held accountable for performance standards that are implicit – reflecting the beliefs and values of consumers, watchdog agencies, news media and other stakeholders. For example, a nongovernmental organization (NGO) engaged in relief activities might be under pressure to show that a certain percentage of its resources are spent directly on relief services, not administrative overheads. There may be no specified criterion or benchmark percentage specified in a performance contract or other legally binding agreement. But if the pressure is intense, perhaps coming from a powerful political group or arising

out of a recent controversy, then the NGO might be forced to *negotiate* with the stakeholders for a mutually acceptable response. Again, the case of the American Red Cross comes to mind. When the public outcry emerged, the Red Cross first tried to explain their policy (including technical semantics around the term 'emerging needs'). But ultimately the organization reached a kind of 'negotiated' solution with a shake-up of the top executive staff and a public apology and articulation of a new policy regarding disbursement of the disaster relief fund.

A second circumstance described by this cell is the need to be accountable for standards that are, in fact, codified, but where the laws and regulations are vaguely worded and, therefore, subject to interpretation by administrators who are charged with their implementation or oversight. A good illustration of this circumstance is given by the recent wave of consolidations, mergers and conversions in the United States health care industry. Let's say that the board of a community-based nonprofit hospital has decided to sell the hospital to a for-profit chain. The sale of the hospital must be approved by the State Attorney General who, in most states, is guided by a rather vague set of standards regarding the conversion of nonprofit organizations to for-profit status. In most cases, the Attorney General must engage in negotiations with the nonprofit board of trustees and with the for-profit corporation to decide whether the asset has been fairly valued. The Attorney General will also try to determine whether the community will be adequately served by the new for-profit hospital and, finally, will try to ensure that the community assets that have been invested in the nonprofit hospital continue to work in perpetuity for the benefit of the community. Inevitably, these discussions involve intense negotiations because there is no clear-cut formula or procedure for resolving these important issues, all of which have direct bearing on the accountability of the nonprofit hospital to the community it has served and to thousands of donors who have financed it over the years. In effect, the accountability of the nonprofit board of trustees to protect and preserve a valued community asset (the hospital) will be negotiated, not prescribed with precise rules or algorithms.

As described above, the accountability standards in this type of environment are vague and usually dynamic. As such, reasonable people will disagree about what types of organizational behavior constitute 'accountable' performance, often adding to conflict between the organization and its environment. Conflict, in turn, generally involves risk and uncertainty because the outcome of the dispute and its long-term effects cannot be controlled or predicted. On the other hand, negotiations may provide the opportunity to clarify expectations and performance standards, thereby reducing uncertainty and risk. As such, there may be an opportunity for the service provider to actively participate in defining the criteria by which they will be judged and, perhaps, to educate oversight agencies, the public, the media and other stakeholders about their constraints.

Discretionary accountability: professionalism (Cell 3)

Cell 3, at the bottom right in Figure 46.1, reflects the situation in which accountability standards and reporting mechanisms are not well defined or highly structured *and* where the pressure exerted on the organization is not sufficiently powerful to demand immediate tactical negotiations. Indeed, in this context there may be no identifiable parties with whom to negotiate, no specific oversight agency, and no formalized reporting mechanism. This portion of the accountability environment gives organizations great latitude to act strategically and to exercise professional judgment and, therefore, is labeled *discretionary accountability*. Under these circumstances accountability takes on its broadest meaning, blending with concepts like *obligation*, *responsiveness*, *ethics* and *professional responsibility*.

For example, several scandals in the nonprofit sector have involved governance boards or other oversight bodies that made the fatal mistake of placing far too much faith and trust in charismatic executives who abused that trust by undertaking questionable (or even illegal) activities on their behalf. 'Where was the board?' has become a familiar lament in the wake of several high-profile débâcles in the nonprofit sector. Not surprisingly, a growing number of nonprofit organizations are now taking governance much more seriously than before, and many have voluntarily established mechanisms to help prevent abuses of power by the CEO. These include policies to protect whistle-blowers, more elaborate orientation sessions for new board members, periodic reviews of board responsibilities, and more carefully prescribed processes for reviewing the performance of the CEO. The point here is that these organizations are undertaking new and more rigorous accountability measures *voluntarily*, not because of any focused pressure from outside constituencies. Preventive measures are taken by enlightened organizations, either to avoid débâcles that have crippled other organizations or to simply set a higher standard that they believe is in their strategic best interest.

In many circumstances there are incentives for organizations to act proactively by implementing more rigorous accountability measures on their own. A particularly powerful incentive is that the organization is free to develop accountability mechanisms that are tailored to its mission and to its unique context. One of the key shortcomings of almost all bureaucratic or legal standards of accountability is that they tend to follow a 'one size fits all' philosophy by lumping disparate organizations (and perhaps disparate consumers) into large categories to ensure identical treatment of all. But in Cell 3 of our conceptual framework, organizations have substantial freedom to define standards of accountability that are appropriate for their context, their mission and their clients.

Anticipatory accountability: advocacy (Cell 4)

Finally, Cell 4, the bottom left cell of Figure 46.1, reflects situations in which providers of public services must try to anticipate changes in the standards to which they may soon be held accountable. They may try to prepare themselves for compliance with these emerging standards or, perhaps, actively participate in the legislative or regulatory processes leading to their design and implementation. Thus, this cell is labeled *anticipatory accountability*.

Suppose a state legislature is considering steps to tighten regulatory controls on certain types of nonprofit fundraising strategies. Their purpose is to protect consumers by making nonprofit organizations accountable for the claims they make in their marketing literature and fundraising appeals. The lawmakers will need to address many questions: What is the desired outcome of the stricter regulations? What types of controls will achieve these outcomes? What enforcement mechanisms should be established? How should compliance be reported and through what chain of accountability? In this cell, the affected organizations should try to anticipate the formulation of these new standards in order to prepare for eventual compliance. In addition, these organizations may even play an advocacy role in shaping and defining the standards they believe eventually will be (or should be) imposed.

The notion of anticipatory accountability requires service providers in the nonprofit and commercial sectors to prepare for likely changes in their accountability environment. It also places added responsibility on managers to educate elected officials, board members and other policy actors on emerging public needs and the risks and benefits associated with contemplated legal or regulatory actions. Thus, the notion of anticipatory accountability is consistent with the concept of 'administrative advocacy' (Shafritz, 1992: 10), wherein public managers not only are responsible for implementing policy initiatives dictated from above, but also for advocating legislative or administrative initiatives to serve the public interest.

Clearly, this responsibility implies additional burdens of accountability. Stephen Baily (1983: 480) says that 'politics and hierarchy induce the public servant to search imaginatively for a public-will-to-be. In this search, the public servant is often a leader in the creation of a new public will, so he is in part accountable to what he in part creates.' The concept is also consistent with the work of Mark Moore (1995), who has suggested that the public manager's job is to search imaginatively for ways to 'create' public value.

SOME SUGGESTIONS ON PROCESS AND PROCEDURE

So, the four-cell framework presented in Figure 46.1 provides operational and strategic meaning to the several aspects of accountability that must be considered in today's diffused and privatized system of public service delivery. This framework can serve as a strategic planning tool, helping leaders of the organization scan their accountability environment in the same way they scan their technological environment, competitive environment, and so on. In other words, as the organization looks outward for threats and opportunities related to its overall corporate strategy, it should also use methods like those described here to focus specifically on the accountability environment.

The process described above provides a good opportunity for service providers to seek input from a variety of sources – citizens, clients, special interest groups, media representatives, peer organizations, regulatory agencies. Importantly, the four-cell framework provides a context in which to convene and conduct those discussions, rather than holding totally open-ended discussions that can easily degenerate into vague generalities. The framework is also useful for enhancing the dialogue between government contracting agencies and private sector providers.

Government agencies that contract with nonprofit and commercial firms could encourage them to utilize this or some other framework to clarify the accountability challenges and opportunities related to the contract. But mandating use of such a framework would likely defeat the purpose, because it would become yet another contractual obligation with all of the associated shortcomings and pitfalls discussed earlier. Instead, the conceptual framework presented in Figure 46.1 might better serve as an organizing device to facilitate constructive (and voluntary) civic discourse among service providers – government, nonprofit, commercial organizations – and also concerned stakeholders such as citizens, watchdog organizations, news media and others. The concluding section of this chapter sketches the outline of such an approach.

BUILDING AN INTERORGANIZATIONAL CULTURE OF ACCOUNTABILITY

The last section of this chapter will be brief, for the ideas expressed below are in their embryonic stage and, admittedly, represent an idealized vision that is a long way from operational implementation. The premise has been presented above but is worth repeating: in a diffused and privatized system of public service delivery, there are inherent problems with traditional notions of accountability. Compliance-focused accountability mechanisms will need to yield to (or at least accommodate) a broader definition of accountability that reflects the interests and perspectives of the many actors and stakeholders involved in the new delivery system. The new vision, proposed below, is simply this: actors and stakeholders in the new diffused system must make a commitment to a higher level of civic discourse about accountability, with the ultimate goal of collectively creating an interorganizational system that continuously *learns* about its accountability environment and adapts accordingly.

Over the past fifteen years, a growing number of organizational theorists have probed the question: Is it possible to create an organization that continuously 'learns' about and responds to its environment, just as human beings learn and adapt? These experts, including a growing number of senior executives, suggest that we are in the early stages of a sea change with respect to the factors that account for organizational success. William O'Brien, former CEO of Hanover Insurance Company, says that through most of the twentieth century organizations based their success on efficient production and distribution, effective mass marketing, quick adoption of new technology, financial expertise, and successful application of 'Theory Y' management. At the dawn of the twenty-first century, however, a new set of practices are needed for sustained performance (O'Brien, 1994).

- *Successful organizations will find ways to distribute power in decentralized organizations while increasing self-discipline.* Organizations that blindly 'empower' their employees (or their contractors) are likely to create chaos. Command and control bureaucracies cannot simply be abandoned without designing something to replace them. Organizations that invest in building a culture of *self-discipline* will succeed, while those that try to hold on to their bureaucratically designed systems of *imposed discipline* will likely fail to keep pace with their competitors.
- *Systemic thinking will be essential in the new environment.* Reductionist logic works well in stable environments, but is not sufficient for the kind of global complexity we are witnessing today. Successful organizations will be those that learn to recognize and even anticipate the interdependencies in their environment, making sense of and adapting successfully to a complex interplay of factors rather than solving one problem at a time.
- *Successful organizations will encourage and master the art of conversation, both internally and externally.* Learning takes place through conversation and conversations are most stimulating when they bring to light new information, new ideas and new assumptions.

Most organizational cultures today are not conducive to this type of conversation, either among their employees or with external stakeholders.

- *In decentralized organizations, success depends on securing voluntary followership.* In bureaucracies people are induced to follow by mandates and sanctions. In the new environment, success will require deeper levels of commitment from those who are charged with pursuing the mission of the organization. Mandates alone will not suffice.

Applying each of these principles to the problem of accountability yields propositions like the following:

- *In a diffused and privatized system of public service delivery, accountability will be enhanced to the extent that self-discipline accompanies decentralization and empowerment.* Imposed discipline, via compliance mechanisms, works only for certain types of accountability challenges. Many others require service providers essentially to police themselves. But chaos will rein if nonprofit and commercial providers are simply 'empowered' to police themselves. Government agencies and legislatures must promote a concerted effort to change the 'principal–agent' culture and replace it with a team oriented value system that builds self-discipline. A framework like that presented in Figure 46.1 above may help initially to channel accountability initiatives in a disciplined way while not confining these efforts to compliance alone.
- *Accountability will be enhanced to the extent that players can embrace systemic thinking about how to serve the public interest and preserve the public trust.* Traditional accountability mechanisms are based on reductionist logic that is not well suited to the new environment. A systemic approach continuously recognizes and adapts to changing standards of performance. A framework like that presented in Figure 46.1 embraces, rather than ignores, the systemic forces that continuously affect the way accountability is defined and acted upon.
- *Accountability will be enhanced to the extent that players engage in meaningful conversation about challenges and opportunities in the new system of public service delivery.* The current system for maintaining accountability is based on one-way flows of communication – from government agencies to nonprofit and commercial contractors. There are few, if any, opportunities for meaningful

dialogue among key players, including citizens, watchdog organizations, news media and others. A framework like that presented in Figure 46.1 could be used to facilitate dialogue, including efforts to surface and criticize the assumptions embedded in each of the four cells.

- *Accountability will be enhanced to the extent that mandates are tempered with voluntary followership.* Mandates may never cease being a central part of any accountability system, but, in a diffused and privatized system, command and control systems lose much of their power. Voluntary followership is essential to strengthening accountability.

The vision expressed above is quite distant conceptually and operationally from the current strategies for promoting accountability in public service delivery. Indeed, most of the current public debate on this topic seems to be focused on the development of new and more rigorous mandates for nonprofit and commercial firms, not empowering them to be team players in a collective learning process. Therefore, it may seem far-fetched to envision a model based on principles like those outlined above. But, the public sector has undergone a remarkable transformation over the past twenty years, and the apparent trajectory of that evolution may make the vision expressed here more and more plausible over the next twenty years.

REFERENCES

Baily, S.K. (1983) 'Ethics and the Public Service', in R.J. Stillman (ed.), *Public Administration: Concepts and Cases*, 4th edn. Boston, MA: Houghton Mifflin.

Bellone, C.J. and Goerl, G.F. (1992) 'Reconciling Public Entrepreneurship and Democracy', *Public Administration Review*, 52 (2): 130–4.

Cohen, S. and Eimicke, W. (1999) 'Is Public Entrepreneurship Ethical?', *Public Integrity*, Winter: 54–74.

Goodsell, C.T. (1985) *The Case for Bureaucracy: A Public Administration Polemic*, 2nd edn. Chatham, NJ: Chatham House.

Kearns, K.P. (1995) 'Accountability and Entrepreneurial Public Management: The Case of the Orange County Investment Fund', *Public Budgeting and Finance*, 15 (3): 3–21.

Kearns, K.P. (1996) *Managing for Accountability: Preserving the Public Trust in Public and Nonprofit Organizations*. San Francisco: Jossey–Bass.

Kingsley, J.D. (1944) *Representative Bureaucracy.* Yellow Springs, OH: Antioch University Press.

Kramer, R., Lorntzen, H., Melief, W.B. and Pasquinelli, S. (1993) *Privatization in Four European Countries: Comparative Studies in Government–Third Sector Relationships.* Armonk, NY: Sharpe.

Krislov, S. and Rosenbloom, D.H. (1981) *Representative Bureaucracy and the American Political System.* New York: Praeger.

Mansfield, H. (1982) 'Accountability and Congressional Oversight', in B.L.R. Smith and J. Caroll (eds), *Improving Accountability and Performance of Government.* Washington, DC: Brookings Institution.

McDonald, C. (1997) 'Government, Funded Nonprofits, and Accountability', *Nonprofit Management and Leadership*, 8 (1): 51–64.

Moe, R.C. (1994) 'The "Reinventing Government" Exercise: Misrepresenting the Problem, Misjudging the Consequences', *Public Administration Review*, 54 (2): 111–22.

Moore, M. (1995) *Creating Public Value.* Cambridge, MA: Harvard University Press.

O'Brien, W. (1994) 'Why Bother? (A CEO's Perspective)', in P. Senge, A. Kleiner, C. Roberts, R. Ross and B. Smith (eds), *The Fifth Discipline Fieldbook.* New York: Doubleday. pp. 13–15.

Osborne, D. and Gaebler, T. (1992) *Reinventing Government: How the Entrepreneurial Spirit is Transforming the Public Sector from Schoolhouse to Statehouse, City Hall to the Pentagon.* Reading, MA: Addison–Wesley.

Pope, T. (2001) 'Nonprofits Face Regulation, Enforcement From Several Areas', *The Nonprofit Times*, 1 August, pp. 1, 8.

Romzek, B.S. and Dubnick, M.J. (1987) 'Accountability in the public sector: Lessons from the *Challenger* tragedy', *Public Administration Review*, 47 (3): 227–38.

Senge, P. (1990) *The Fifth Discipline: The Art and Practice of the Learning Organization.* New York: Doubleday.

Senge, P., Kleiner, A., Roberts, C., Ross, R. and Smith, B. (eds), *The Fifth Discipline Fieldbook.* New York: Doubleday.

Shafritz, J.M. (1992) *The HarperCollins Dictionary of American Governnment and Politics.* New York: HarperCollins.

Terry, L.D. (1993) 'Why We Should Abandon the Misconceived Quest to Reconcile Public Entrepreneurship with Democracy', *Public Administration Review*, 53 (4): 393–5.

White, L. (1926) *Introduction to the Study of Public Administration.* New York: Macmillan.

INTERGOVERNMENTAL RELATIONS AND PUBLIC ADMINISTRATION

Introduction

Martin Painter

As a field of study, intergovernmental relations (or central–local relations as it was conventionally labelled in unitary states) has a number of dimensions, including the division of powers and functions among levels of government; the administrative and political relations between levels and between the units of subnational government; and the 'interstitial' activities, relationships and organizations that arise between levels and units (an aspect that has received growing attention). In turn, each of these areas has been studied from a variety of perspectives or disciplines – administrative, fiscal, legal, political and sociological.

With the growth of government in the twentieth century, the field became an increasingly significant one for scholars of public administration, as it was apparent that the practical complexities of public policy – for example, the interdependence of problems and sectors, with their 'spillovers' and 'externalities' – increasingly resulted in an intergovernmental dimension to most problems of administration. Secular trends such as growing urbanization and changing technology resulted in new spatial dimensions to policy problems, with consequences for existing arrangements in the division of powers and functions between levels. In the latter part of the century, the reordering of spatial relations

and policy problems increasingly took on a supranational or global dimension, calling into question the most fundamental building block of systems of intergovernmental relations, the nation-state itself (Elazar, 1998), and hence challenging state-centric views of government and politics (Rosenau, 2000).

Conceptual and theoretical developments in the field have tended to be uneven and fragmentary, with different traditions and approaches overlapping, but evolving in parallel. In the United States, intergovernmental relations is close to being coterminous with the study of federalism, which draws on diverse fields including political theory (Ostrom, 1987), studies of political culture (Elazar, 1994) and public finance (Oates, 1972). Deil Wright (1983: 418) went so far as to argue that intergovernmental relations (or IGR) was to be preferred to federalism as a less value-laden way of 'referring to the multiple, complex, and interdependent jurisdictional relationships found in the United States'. In this view, the field is concerned with the study of the complexities of intergovernmental policy implementation, and has been increasingly concerned with problems of 'intergovernmental management' (Agranoff, 1986).

From a very different starting point, theories of intergovernmental competition based on economics have been influential for the study of federalism and subnational governments (Breton, 1996). In another set of parallel studies, theorists of 'polycentric government' have combined constitutional analysis, public choice theory and game theory in the study of problems of collective goods, with a strong preference for multiple, locally constituted systems of self-rule (McGinnis, 1999).

In Europe, the study of central–local relations was for long dominated by legal and institutional approaches, but in the 1980s in the United Kingdom and elsewhere it took on board ideas and concepts from intergovernmental relations and interorganizational analysis (Rhodes, 1988). Network analysis became a significant strand in the field (Kickert et al., 1997). In recent times, the complexities of relations across and between levels of government within the European Union have stimulated new conceptual and empirical analysis, drawing on interorganizational theory and network theory, as well as connecting strongly with the field of implementation studies in the public policy literature and with theories of inter-state cooperation and conflict in international relations. In an interesting terminological turn, political scientists in Europe have coined a new name for the field of study – 'multi-level governance' (Jordan, 2001).

That this term seemed to fit so aptly the complexities of political, financial and administrative relations within the multi-layered structures of the European Union is not surprising. Some who came to a 'governance' view of government did so from a background of studying intergovernmental relations (Rhodes, 2000: 60–2). It had long been taken for granted by students of intergovernmental relations that the presumptions of sovereignty, defined jurisdiction and unified authority conjured up by the term 'government' did not hold. Only in the abstract models of interjurisdictional competition of public choice theorists, and in some formalistic approaches to the study of central–local relations in unitary states, were these terms treated as unproblematic.

Similarly, the idea that the policy process was an orderly one focused on a set of identifiable, authoritative decision makers was for the most part not helpful. Stories of intergovernmental relations were about overlapping spheres of influence, power and resource sharing, collaboration and negotiation. In such

contexts, unofficial, 'informal' channels were often the most important, while there was a continuous blurring of the lines between 'government' and 'non-government' in the complex patterns of alliances and boundary-spanning political stratagems that emerged. Students of intergovernmental relations were long used to a world of partnerships, collaboration and networks. Thus, the usage of the term 'governance' to encompass a set of governing arrangements that brought together both state and non-state actors across traditional jurisdictional boundaries to work jointly on policy problems, in forms of interaction that were sometimes far removed from the conventional hierarchies of government, did not tread on strange ground for scholars of intergovernmental relations (Painter, 2001).

In this section of the Handbook, the three contributors reflect three of the major traditions or strands in a wide-ranging field of study. Hellmut Wollman draws on a predominantly European, historico-institutional tradition of the study of state structures. Cross-national comparisons using a systematic classificatory system illuminate the complexities of the institutional contexts of intergovernmental relations within different national-state traditions. Beryl Radin draws on and brings together the rich traditions of American scholarship in intergovernmental public policy implementation, connecting also with recent strands of thinking about intergovernmental management. This approach draws heavily on policy case study findings, building up a systematic depiction of the complex variety of the instruments of intergovernmental relations and the political stratagems they represent. Finally, Andy Smith critically surveys the emerging field of multi-level governance, drawing us into the heart of recent debates about the evolution of institutions and of new styles of political action within the EU, before he sets out an agenda for a new departure.

REFERENCES

Agranoff, Robert J. (1986) *Intergovernmental Management.* Albany, NY: State University of New York Press.

Breton, Albert (1996) *Competitive Governments: An Economic Theory of Politics and Public Finance.* Cambridge: Cambridge University Press.

Elazar, Daniel J. (1994) *The American Mosaic: the Impact of Space, Time, and Culture on American Politics*. Boulder, CO: Westview Press.

Elazar, Daniel J. (1998) *Constitutionalizing Globalization: The Postmodern Revival of Confederal Arrangements*. Lanham, MD: Rowman and Littlefield.

Jordan, Andrew (2001) 'The European Union: An Evolving System of Multi-level Governance ... Or Government', *Policy and Politics*, 29 (2): 193–208.

Kickert, W., Klijn, E.H. and Koppenjan, J.F.M. (1997) *Managing Complex Networks: Strategies for the Public Sector*. London: Sage.

McGinnis, Michael D. (1999) *Polycentric Governance and Development: Readings From the Workshop in Political Theory and Policy Analysis*. Ann Arbor, MI: University of Michigan Press.

Oates, Wallace E. (1972) *Fiscal Federalism*. London: Harcourt Brace Jovanovich.

Ostrom, Vincent (1987) *The Political Theory of a Compound Republic: Designing the American Experiment*, 2nd edn. Lincoln, NB: University of Nebraska Press.

Painter, Martin (2001) 'Multi-level Governance and the Emergence of Collaborative Federal Institutions in Australia', *Policy and Politics*, 29 (2): 137–50.

Rhodes, R.A.W. (1988) *Beyond Westminster and Whitehall: The Sub-central Governments of Britain*. London: Unwin–Hyman.

Rhodes, R.A.W. (2000) 'Governance and Public Administration', in John Pierre (ed.), *Debating Governance: Authority, Steering and Democracy*. Oxford: Oxford University Press.

Rosenau, James N. (2000) 'Change, Complexity and Governance in a Globalizing Space', in John Pierre (ed.), *Debating Governance: Authority, Steering and Democracy*. Oxford: Oxford University Press.

Wright, D.S. (1983) 'Managing the Intergovernmental Scene: The Changing Dramas of Federalism, Intergovernmental Relations and Intergovernmental Management', in W.B. Eddy (ed.), *The Handbook of Organization Management*. New York: Marcel Dekker.

47

Coordination in the Intergovernmental Setting

Hellmut Wollmann

DEFINITION, FOCUS AND STRUCTURE OF THE CHAPTER

Coordination (in its *process* dimension) can be understood (for a definition, see also Peters, 1998; Pollitt and Bouckaert, 2000: 79ff.) as the attempt to optimize the coherence and consistency of political decisions as well as policy implementation

- across policies (in order to overcome the sectoral fragmentation of policies and to achieve comprehensive and 'holistic' responses to complex problems);
- across actors and stakeholders (in order to accommodate the often-conflicting interests of political, socio-economic, administrative, professional etc. actors and actor 'communities'); and
- across levels (in order to overcome the vertical fragmentation of policies and actors – with coordination problems posed not least by the vertical actors communities, 'silos' and 'comradeships' sectorally entrenched and colluding across levels and resisting coordination across policies).

In the recent development of government and intergovernmental systems the challenges to coordination have increased enormously.

- The range and scope of public policies and public sector activities has been conspicuously enhanced through the expansion of the welfare state during the 1960s and 1970s.
- The array of political, administrative and socio-economic actors has concomitantly grown with an additional push in the wake

of New Public Management-induced 'agencification' and 'outsourcing' and its plethora of semi-public and private organizations, in what (in a recent almost inflationary debate) is called 'governance' (Rhodes, 1997).
- The number of levels has proliferated due to (downward) devolution (decentralization and deconcentration) of functions in the intra-national setting as well as to the addition of new levels because of inter- and supranationalization (such as the European Union).

While coordination problems loom large throughout the policy process – from policy *formation* through *implementation* to *termination,* with different arenas, actor constellations and strategies in each of these stages – this chapter will focus on implementation, that is, on the administrative side of the policy process and, hence, on (vertical and horizontal) co-ordination in the subnational space.

Furthermore, the chapter discusses the organizational and conceptual modalities of coordination from an analytical and empirical, rather than prescriptive standpoint. In doing so, it will pursue a hard-nosed, *institutionalist* approach (see Peters, 1995) by dwelling, for an empirical underpinning of the argumentation, on the coordination-related organizational settings and patterns in a number of particularly instructive countries.

LITERATURE

The debate on coordination has produced a vast literature (for overviews see Peters, 1998; Pollitt, 2001). The coordination of policy making and implementation has long been a prime object of reform-related and applied social science debate. In the early 1970s it was noted: 'No suggestion for reform is more common than "what we need is more coordination"' (Pressman and Wildavsky, 1974: 133). Recent examples of research on administrative modernization include the OECD report on 'Managing Across Levels of Government' (OECD, 1997b) and the recent spree of concern for 'joined up government' in the UK (Cabinet Office, 2000; Pollitt, 2001).

The academic debate has followed different tracks. A conceptual strand goes back to multi-disciplinary discourse in the mid- and late 1980s on the different modalities of coordination (Kaufmann et al., 1986; Thompson et al., 1991). Another important line of argument unfolded in studies on interorganizational (and intergovernmental) politics (and management), with early seminal work by Hanf and Scharpf (1978).

MODALITIES AND PATTERNS OF COORDINATION: CONCEPTUAL FRAMEWORK

Drawing on a widely accepted conceptualization (Kaufmann et al., 1986), essentially three (ideal-type) modalities and patterns of coordination will be distinguished: hierarchy, network and market.

Hierarchy

Hierarchy as a modality to ensure coordination (across policies, across actors and across levels) is characteristic of the state of the continental European *Rechtsstaat* tradition. The external comprehensive legal regulation of administrative activities as well as the internal hierarchical bureaucratic organization of public administration are crucial for the political control of parliamentary democracy over administration, and for holding government politically accountable for the operation of public administration (Schuppert, 2000: 57ff.). This nexus has found its classical formulation in Max Weber's concept of 'legal rule' (*legale Herrschaft*) and in his bureaucratic model as correlates (Weber, 1972: 124ff.). Under these political and organizational premises, the hierarchical relations hinging on command from superior to subordinate are instrumental for the politically accountable government to make sure that the lower levels of government carry out the policies in a coordinated manner. In an ideal-type abstraction, hierarchy, exerted in the interorganizational as well as intraorganizational setting, can be seen as endemic to the 'sovereign state' model (March and Olsen, 1989).

Network

The network is a configuration in which the actors find themselves basically in a parity or 'equal footing' situation. Ideally, networks are formed and maintained voluntarily and are based on shared values, trust, solidarity or consensus. Hence, networks and their ensuing interaction patterns can be typically related to a 'bargaining/negotiating' state (March and Olsen, 1989). In relying on trust and collaboration, networks are more likely to achieve coordination between conflicting interests than either hierarchies or markets (Lane and Bachmann, 1998) and to permit problem-solving and positive-sum solutions in potential conflicts between actors and policies (Scharpf, 1997).

Networks and negotiation have long been part and parcel of decision making and implementation in many countries, including countries of the *Rechtsstaat* tradition. This is clearest in countries with a consensus-oriented and corporatist political tradition, such as in Scandinavia, but also in Germany, whose federalism has generated pronouncedly 'cooperative' and 'negotiative' interaction patterns, due to its functional interlocking and intertwining (*Politikverflechtung*) (Benz, 2001). By expanding the spectrum of, and the interaction among public, semi-public and private actors and by thinning out the strict public sector/private sector divide traditionally characteristic of the 'sovereign' state, the latter has merged with features of the bargaining/negotiating state through evolving governance structures.

In the New Public Management (NPM) debate, which has been dominating the international discourse on public sector modernization since the 1980s, contracting and management by results have conceptually and strategically been given centre stage in directing (and coordinating) service delivery (Bogason, 1998: 337), leaving behind the hierarchical features of the sovereign state and consummating the bargaining state. Besides informal agreements, formal contracts setting performance targets between the actors – along the 'principal/agent' and the 'purchaser/provider' split – are a pivotal means of formalized interaction and exchange. Yet, if there is to be an effective 'principal' to monitor and check the performance of the 'agent' through performance measurement, report systems and possibly sanctions (without which 'policy coordination and coherence' can hardly be ensured – OECD, 1997a: 54), some re-hierarchization (reminiscent of the sovereign state) is bound to creep in.

Market

Finally, another key message in the recent NPM debate has been that market forms of coordination should wherever possible replace hierarchical coordination (Pollitt and Bouckaert, 2000: 80). The basic assumption is that coordination can be achieved through the 'invisible hand' working behind and through the self-interest of the participants in policy making and implementation, especially in the process of service delivery (Peters, 1998: 298). In its ideal-type abstraction, the market principle is geared to the 'supermarket state' model (March and Olsen, 1989). While it is essentially premised on the willingness of the participants to exchange resources in order to attain higher levels of collective welfare (Marin, 1990), it seems doubtful (as will be argued later in this chapter) whether this heroic assumption and expectation stand up to the test of reality.

ORGANIZATIONAL PRINCIPLES RELATING TO COORDINATION

For institutionalizing the political and administrative functions and tasks that need to be coordinated, the following organizational principles are of prime importance.

Devolution of functions to lower levels of government

Basically, two modalities are usually distinguished:

* *decentralization* as the devolution of political functions to elected authorities, and
* *deconcentration* as the transfer of administrative functions to subnational levels or units (Bennett, 1993: OECD, 1997b: 17; Pollitt and Bouckaert, 2000: 83).

On the regional or 'meso' level (Sharpe, 1993a), political decentralization finds its fullest expression in the federal system (with federal states, *Länder*, cantons etc., endowed with constitutionally entrenched powers exercised by regionally elected parliaments and governments), while a weaker form is in place in 'regionalized' countries where the regions (for instance, the *départements* in France) have elected regional parliaments and regional executives, yet lack the kind of constitutional status and legislative powers characteristic of federalism.

On the local level, political decentralization comes to bear in elected local government operating either under a constitutionally guaranteed local autonomy (general competence) formula (as in continental European countries) or under the (constitutionally precarious) 'ultra-vires' doctrine (as in the British tradition) (Wollmann, 2000b, 2000c: 34).

Territory-based multi-function versus single-function model

The multi-function model, typically going hand in hand with the organizational principle of territoriality (Wagener and Blümel, 2001: 98), hinges on the assumption that a territorially defined multi-purpose unit has the mandate (and the capability) to carry out and coordinate these functions. Dating back to seventeenth-century continental Europe's absolutist territorial state, the principle of territoriality-based multi-functionality has, in modern democratic decentralized government, been manifested in strong elected local self-government systems (which can currently be found in the Scandinavian countries and in Germany), which are called upon to carry out a wide scope of public tasks and services (Gustafsson, 1991: 245) and to act as 'essential integrator' (Hesse and Sharpe, 1991: 612).

In a similar vein the territorially defined administrative regional or meso level, such as the prefect-headed state component of France's *département* level, can have the multi-functional mandate to ensure coordination in the subregional space.

By contrast, the single-function (single-purpose) model of organization is directed at fulfilling solely one task and mission. In the traditional state organization, single-functionality characterizes a part of state administration (in some countries, a significant part) which, subordinated to sectoral central government ministries, is organized in vertical chains of deconcentrated single-purpose field offices. More recently, single-functionality has become a pivotal concept in the New Public Management, with the intent to have the delivery of public services guided – analogous to production in the private sector economy – by single-purpose-related efficiency, and competition-induced client responsiveness.

Spatial and demographic size of subnational levels and units of government

The spatial and demographic size of the subnational levels and units of government can also have a significant bearing on the coordination capacity of multi-function governmental levels and units, through the capacity of larger units to integrate a wide range of problems and interests, to 'minimize externalities' (Sharpe, 1993b: 15). The search for an optimal size of multi-functional government lay at the basis of the territorial reforms of elected local governments, particularly via amalgamation, in many countries during the 1960s and 1970s, with the idea of optimizing the territorial congruence of the problems to be solved, an idea that was a key concern in the then dominant planning debate. In what has been called a typical North European model of territorial reform of local government (Marcou and Verbelyi, 1993; Norton, 1994: 14), the average population size of the (lower level) local government units was raised to some 130,000 inhabitants in the United Kingdom districts, to some 30,000 in Sweden's *kommunen* and to about 9,000 in Germany's *Gemeinden* (in some *Länder*, up to 30,000). These far-reaching territorial reforms were typically accompanied by the conflict between an increase in administrative efficiency (including the coordination capacity) and the viability of local democracy and local political accountability. By contrast, the South European-type countries almost entirely refrained from territorial reforms of local government, with France, for instance, continuing to have her time-honoured myriad of communes of some 1,600 inhabitants on average (Wollmann, 2000c: 42).

Functional scope

Finally, an important organizational variance in the subregional intergovernmental setting comes from the functional scope of subregional and local field offices of deconcentrated state administration (sometimes called 'decos'), on the one hand, and of elected local governments, on the other. While the special purpose field offices of state administration are usually hierarchically controlled and coordinated by their respective sectoral central government ministry, the elected local governments operate within the principle of local autonomy and are subject to other, mostly less direct, forms of coordination from above. The more extended the functions of the subregional and local field offices of state administration, the more restricted the competences of elected local government, and vice versa.

THE INTERGOVERNMENTAL SETTING IN SELECTED COUNTRIES

In order to provide some more information for discussing the application and functioning of organizational principles and patterns of coordination, some brief accounts of the intergovernmental systems of a number of countries shall be given – with France, the United Kingdom, Sweden, Germany and the United States selected as cases in point.

France

Well into the 1970s, France was the epitome of a unitary, centrally governed country with the prefect (*préfet*) on the *département* level acting as the regional backbone of centralist government. Through decentralization and deconcentration, France since 1982 has seen an all but revolutionary (Mabileau, 1997: 364) transformation of her intergovernmental setting, even the 'end of the French unitary state' (Loughlin and Mazey, 1995).

- Since 1982 the scope of functions and of the autonomy of elected local self-government on the *département* and local *commune* levels has been significantly enlarged.
- At the same time, the formal powers of the departmental prefect to hierarchically control local government were greatly reduced and limited to legality review.
- The local government level continues to be marked by the myriad of 35,000 municipalities with some 1,600 inhabitants on the average.
- Following 1992, the vertical structures of special purpose state administration, which still play an important functional role beside and outside the local self-government authorities, have been internally deconcentrated.

The United Kingdom

Throughout the nineteenth century the UK was a unitary country, albeit a 'dual polity' with a politically and functionally strong local government level (Bulpitt, 1983; Jones, 1990: 208). With the advances of the welfare state throughout the twentieth century, the country saw a continuous political and administrative centralization in which, due to the traditional absence of a regional/meso level and reflecting the 'British anti-territorial bias' (Sharpe, 2000: 70), many crucial executive functions were carried out directly by central government units ('Whitehall'). Since the late 1970s, largely as a result of New Public Management-inspired reforms, the UK has experienced significant changes in its inter-governmental setting.

- After 1988 ('Next Steps'), important executive functions of central government have been transferred (deconcentrated) to some 140 single-purpose agencies, each operating on a nation-wide special-function jurisdiction.
- In 1994, for the first time in the UK's modern administrative history, a territorially defined regional administrative level was created with cross-sectoral Regional Offices for Government (ROGs).
- Since the early 1980s the strong local government system of the country has been significantly dismantled, while at the same time, pushed by NPM-guided policies, special-purpose agencies and quangos (quasi-autonomous government organiza-tions) have mushroomed (Wilson and Game, 2002: 133ff.).
- In the late 1990s, promoted by New Labour policies, the UK has seen asymmetrical political regionalization through the intro-duction of elected parliaments in Scotland and in Wales.

Sweden

Sweden is a unitary but, by tradition, a politically decentralized and administratively deconcen-trated country, with a remarkable degree of institutional continuity.

- Traditionally, central government largely restricts itself to policy making in a narrow sense.
- Dating back to the eighteenth century, impor-tant central level executive functions are car-ried out by some seventy largely independent special-purpose state agencies (*ämbetsverk*), each of which operates in a country-wide jurisdiction.
- Most public tasks and services have tradition-ally been carried out by strong elected local governments (at the county and the municipal levels). During the 1950s and 1970s the municipalities experienced massive territor-ial reforms, which brought their average

size up to some 30,000 inhabitants. The multi-functional profile of elected local government has recently been further enhanced: 'decentralization ... has been the dominant feature of public sector reform in Sweden during the last twenty years' (Premfors, 1998: 157).

- In recent years, Sweden's local level has seen a spree of NPM-inspired changes, such as outsourcing (Montin, 2000).

Germany

After 1945, the Federal Republic of Germany, in line with Germany's pre-Nazi constitutional history, was designed as a federal, strongly decentralized country, which, notwithstanding German Unification in 1990, has shown a remarkable degree of institutional continuity over fifty years (Benz, 1999).

- While the federal level constitutionally possesses most of the legislative powers, the executive and administrative functions (including the implementation of federal legislation and policies) lies almost entirely with the *Länder* which makes for 'functional interconnexion' and 'intertwining' (*Verflech-tung*) specific to Germany's federal system (Benz, 2001: 139).
- Within the *Länder*, the bulk of legislation (federal, *Länder* and increasingly the EU), public tasks and services are carried out by the county and municipal-level local authorities. Territorial reforms of local government, which were carried through by the *Länder* in the late 1960s and early 1970s, raised the average size of the municipalities to some 9,000 (in some *Länder* up to 30,000).
- Only to a limited degree, *Länder* ministries have special purpose administrative field offices ('decos') of their own.
- At the subregional (sub-meso) level in most *Länder,* territorially defined administrative districts, headed by a *Land* government appointed official (*Regierungspräsident*), coordinate the 'decos' and oversee the local authorities (Wollmann, 2000d).

The United States

- The United States is a federal system in which the federal level, as well as the individual States, exercise significant legislative and executive functions in their own right.

- The subnational intergovernmental setting of the United States has been described as a 'complex, jerry-built and varying structure' (Leach and O'Rourke, 1988: 18) constituting 'more a tangled web than a layered structure' (Norton, 1994: 393).
- The lower level of what, in most states, is a two-tier local government structure is made up of a multitude of elected local governments with elected councils, comparatively few functions and small populations (half of the some 20,000 localities having less than 1,000 inhabitants) and some 80,000 special districts (such as school districts) (Gunlicks, 1991: 82). Territorial reforms of local government were debated in the 1970s, but did not materialize.

PATTERNS AND EFFECTS OF COORDINATION IN THE SUBNATIONAL SPACE

The chapter now turns to analysing empirically observable patterns of coordination by focusing on the subnational space and by selecting three organizational constellations and their coordination functions:

- the territorially defined (multi-function) regional/meso level
- the territorially defined (multi-function) elected local government
- the single-purpose agency and organization.

Regional/meso level

The main function of the territorially defined administrative unit on the regional/meso level can be seen in

- coordinating the different central-government-level policies promoted by sectoral central-level ministries; and
- ensuring the coordination of such policies and programmes in the implementation process by single purpose/sectoral field offices of deconcentrated state administration or by multi-function elected local governments.

France

The classical examples of this constellation were the French *départements* and their *préfets* who,

institutionally dating back to nineteenth-century Napoleonic centralism, had the two-fold mandate of, first, carrying out a good deal of the sectoral policies through the *département* state administration and, second, to oversee local self-government in tight hierarchical fashion (*tutelle*) (Wollmann, 2000c: 40).

Since the 1982 reforms the prefect's organizational and power position has dramatically changed.

- The functions of the elected local governments have been expanded, while the prefect's direct executive functions have diminished.
- The prefect's oversight over the local authorities has been reduced to *a posteriori* legality review (OECD, 1997b: 56, Mabileau, 1997).
- At the same time, the prefect's supervision was extended to the deconcentrated special purpose units of state administration (*services extérieurs*) which, until the 1982 reform, had been overseen directly by central ministries.

Hence, the prefect's formal (vertical) control over the elected local governments has been curbed, while now the whole of subregional state administration falls within his coordinating reach (Pollitt and Bouckaert, 2000: 229). Although prefects have lost formal vertical control, particularly with regard to the municipalities, practice shows that they have remained key intergovernmental players, thanks to superior network capacities. They owe these capacities both to continuing intensive connections with central government ministries (and related *grands corps* networks) as well as to prime access to the distribution of crucial financial resources; this includes the infrastructural capital investment money (roads, bridges etc.) of those *services extérieurs* which come under their coordination. The informal power posture of the prefect has turned out to be considerable, particularly with regard to the myriad of small municipalities for which the prefect has become the crucial regional power broker and support. So, as was aptly put in an OECD international survey, France's prefect 'is well and alive' (OEDC, 1997b: 30).

Parallel to this organizational reform has run another approach since the 1980s, which, picking up on NPM, has introduced the concept of contracts, both between the central ministries and the elected local authorities in order to promote the implementation of cross-sectoral policies in the localities (Balme and Bonnet, 1995; Clark, 1998: 101) and between central ministries and administrative special purpose units, in specifying output objectives for 'centres of responsibility' formed within these administrative units (Postif, 1997: 218).

This parallel evolution of two distinct modernization logics has led to 'tensions between strengthening the regional prefect's coordinating capacity, in the name of the unity of the state, and empowering field service managers via service contracts with their parent ministries. This is part of the general tensions between the territorial and functional aspects of subsidiarity' (Clark, 1998: 109). Indeed, it was noted, the 'untidy system contradicts commonly advanced principles of clarity of functions and accountability. Nevertheless it ties interests together from top to bottom of the governmental ladder in networks of communication and influence' (Norton, 1994: 149).

Germany

In Germany's constitutional system the administrative and executive functions, including the implementation of federal legislation and programmes, formally lie with the *Länder*, while local authorities carry out most of the public tasks. Under the 'dual function' model characteristic of German-Austrian constitutional history, local authorities are traditionally in charge of administering functions delegated to them by the state, as well as carrying out their local self-government matters (Wollmann, 2001a: 156; 2000d: 918). Historically dating back to the adoption of the French system in the early nineteenth century, most *Länder* have territorially defined purely administrative, multi-function districts (*Regierungsbezirke*), headed by a *Land* government-appointed (prefect-type) official. Traditionally it is the main task of the *Regierungsbezirke* to fulfil a coordination function by supervising the special purpose field offices of *Land* administration, as well as overseeing local governments at the county and municipal levels. This second role consists in a legality review of local self-government matters and in a more comprehensive appropriateness control in delegated matters (Stöbe and Brandel, 1996). The *Regierungsbezirke* have long been criticized for producing 'over-hierarchization' and 'over-institutionalization', particularly in small *Länder*. Recently, some *Länder* have embarked upon significantly remoulding the organization of the *Regierungsbezirke* in order to improve their management, coordination and consultation function (Fürst, 1996: 129; Stöbe and Brandel, 1996: 79ff.).

Sweden

In Sweden, on the one hand, the county state administration (*landshövding*) was headed by the government-appointed governor, while on the other hand the county self-government (*landstingkommune*) was locally elected. The former exercised an oversight over the county state administration as well as over the local authorities at the county and municipal levels. Since the early 1970s this has changed. First, through what has been called 'hybridization' and power sharing between the county's state authority and the county's self-government (Norton, 1994: 293), the functions of the two have been largely merged. Second, the direction of the county state office by the governor has been practically abolished and replaced with a collegiate decision making body or board. Tellingly, the latter is made up, besides the governor, of fourteen members who are elected by the county council. The coordination of sectoral policies on that level has become a prime responsibility of elected local government, emphasizing the importance of local government in Sweden's intergovernmental system.

United Kingdom

Reflecting the UK's high degree of political and administrative centralization, a significant share of public tasks and executive functions was carried out by the central ministries, without a territorially defined regional or meso level (Sharpe, 1993c: 252; 2000: 70). Insofar as some sectoral central ministries did have offices of their own at the subnational level, the territorial jurisdictions of the latter differed in most cases for each ministry. Consequently, in the implementation of sectoral policies the coordination had to be done by the central ministries themselves.

In 1994, the UK finally moved to establish a territorially defined regional/meso level by creating ten Government Offices for the Regions (GORs) for integrating the offices of the sectoral ministries (Lynch, 1999: 73; Mawson and Spencer, 1997). One should bear in mind, though, that the coordination potential of the GORs will probably remain fairly limited, as a significant array of central government tasks has been transferred, following 1988, to 140 single-purpose agencies which are operating on a country-wide basis outside the regional jurisdictions of the GORs.

Territory-based multi-function elected local government

The coordination potential of the territory-based multi-function model of elected local government can be seen in the joint political and administrative local arena and joint institutional 'roof' of relevant actors, and in their political mandate and accountability to achieve coordination across policies, actors and levels and, thus, act as the 'essential integrator' (Hesse and Sharpe, 1991: 612). For instance, they may combine different infrastructural policies and resources to optimize the locational conditions for local economic development or they may put together sectoral policies and different services to bring comprehensive and holistic solutions to complex problems. Such politically and functionally strong local government systems can currently be found in the Scandinavian countries and in Germany.

At the same time, the very multi-functionality of local government and the ensuing existence of a multitude of actors and stakeholders with conflicting interests in one and the same political and administrative local arena may well increase coordination problems, since the interest positions and stakeholders with rival political, professional and socio-economic interests may be represented and entrenched in local committees, administrative departments and other decision making strongholds (Mabileau, 1997: 372; Stewart, 1995: 32, 2000 – 'departmentalisation'). Such constellations may also be found in vertical policy networks and 'silos', cooperating and interacting across levels in order to make their sectoral interests prevail, and accordingly impeding coordination.

Coordination in local government through local political leadership

An institutional avenue to coordination in the local political arena can be seen in the variant of political leadership. First, akin to the British 'government by commission' tradition, elected local government in Scandinavian countries has traditionally been directed by committees or boards, set up by the elected councils, as collegiate decision making bodies, with the executive committee being the most powerful one (Marcou and Verebelyi, 1993: 132). While exerting some form of political and executive local leadership, not least in the coordination of

policies, and while showing a tendency towards 'de-collectivization' of local decision-making, such as in the case of Norway (Larsen, 2002: 118), committees largely still pursue the collegiate type of leadership, which seems deeply rooted in the Scandinavian local government tradition as well as in the country's consensus culture (Norton, 1994: 314).

But elsewhere, there has been a movement from collegiate to executive styles of leadership. Although local government in the UK has been stripped of much of its historically rooted political and functional strength, changes in executive leadership in local government deserve to be taken up at this point of our argument. In the British local self-government tradition, the principle of 'government by committee' prevailed (Norton, 1994: 386ff.). Local councils appointed from among their members a range of sectoral committees that acted in a deliberative as well as executive function in directing local administration. In practice, sectoral committees showed the propensity to identify themselves with their respective sectoral departments and the professionals who run them, thus replicating and fostering the latter's sectoral fragmentation, and impeding coordination (Stewart, 2000: 54). Consequently, in a first reform move, in the early 1970s redress was sought in setting up a 'policy and resources committee' (Wilson and Game, 2002: 99) that was expected to 'give a "corporate" direction to the work of the council' (Hambleton, 2000: 937). Under the New Labour government, the 'confusion and inefficiency' (DETR, 1998: 8) of the traditional 'government by committee' system is being dealt with by a clearer 'separation of roles' (DETR, 1998: 26) between the policy and decision-making function of local government, assigned to executive leadership, and a scrutiny function reserved for the elected council (Stoker, 2002: 35). The three institutional options that have been introduced by the Local Government Act 2000 (with the elected mayor and cabinet, the leader and cabinet, and the elected mayor and council manager type) revolve around the idea of strengthening executive leadership and its coordinating capacity. (In the meantime, in most local authorities the 'leader and cabinet' model has been picked and adopted (Wilson and Game, 2002: 102ff.).) The institutional options that have been proposed have in common the concept of strengthening executive leadership and its coordinating capacity, particularly by having an executive mayor either elected directly or by the council.

Since the early 1990s in Germany, in a spectacular sequence of congruent legislation, all *Länder* have introduced the directly elected executive mayor, who chairs the local council and, at the same time, is the chief executive directing the local administration. A main argument for now generally adopting the directly elected 'strong mayor' model was that the governing and coordination capacity of local government would be greatly enhanced (Wollmann, 2003). The potentially dominant institutional position of the directly elected executive mayor, who combines political *and* administrative leadership, is held in check not least by the procedure of 'recalling' the mayor by local referendum (Wollmann, 2000b: 123; 2002: 80).

Coordination through local networks

On the local level coordination can be brought about by processes of 'democratization from below' (Bogason, 1998: 339ff.), in which, in part as a corrective to the effects of territorial reforms and amalgamation, participatory institutions of 'small democracy', such as neighbourhood councils, user boards and consumer councils, have emerged. This development can be presently observed in Scandinavian countries (Montin, 2000). As such groups are likely to combine and coordinate different sectoral policies and services to meet their more complex needs, the inherent tendency to focus on group-specific and selfish needs may be attenuated.

Single-purpose agencies and coordination

On a country-wide scale

Under the auspices of coordination, single-purpose agencies that operate in a country-wide jurisdiction can have the advantage of fostering cross-actor coordination in the respective policy field, but may consequently neglect policies and objectives outside the organization's single purpose.

Sweden
In Sweden, historically dating back to the eighteenth century, special purpose state agencies (at present some seventy) have been set up, each operating on a country-wide basis with significant independence from central government guidance. In fact, there has been recurring concern that ministries lack the capacity and

expertise to effectively supervise 'their' agencies (see OECD, 1998: 4). While coordination from above seems to be largely absent, a mechanism for achieving horizontal coordination (with other policy fields and related agencies) has evolved since 1945 when (layman) boards consisting of members of parliament and representatives of socio-economic organizations were established for the direction of the agencies (Marcou and Verebelyi, 1993: 61). Thus, the agencies have become tied into a political and socio-economic context which, in line with the solidarity values and the consensus-orientation of the country, appears to ensure a degree of coordination.

United Kingdom
In the attempt to significantly deconcentrate the hitherto highly centralized government operation and, at the same time, to draw on the managerialist and marketizing concepts of New Public Management, the Thatcher government in 1988 started to set up single-purpose executive agencies (Pollitt and Bouckaert, 2000: 273). While the Next Step agencies are meant to operate with 'managerialist' autonomy, with indicator-based performance targets laid down by the respective minister and fixed in contracts between the minister and the agency. Available empirical evidence suggests that 'agencification [has] exacerbated coordination problems' (Roberts, 1997: 106ff.). As each of the newly created single-purpose agencies tends to be primarily interested in meeting its own performance indicators, it is likely to ignore, if not counteract, the objectives of other agencies, to put up with externalities and hence to impede coordination (James, 2001, with a case study of the Social Security Benefits Agency set up in 1991). Besides, because of the build-up and use of institutions and instruments meant to monitor and check the performance targets, 'agencification' has so far had only a 'small effect on hierarchy' and may even re-produce hierarchical controls in new guise (Goldsmith and Page, 1996: 157).

Single-purpose organizations on the local level

In view of the high fragmentation of the local government structure (with some 20,000 municipalities and some 60,000 other special purpose districts – Gunlicks, 1991: 83), the influential US Advisory Commission on Intergovernmental Relations, ACIR, recommended in the 1970s that far-reaching territorial reforms of the local government level be carried out by amalgamation.

In 1987, however, ACIR, in adopting a public-choice-inspired New Public Management perspective, advocated retention of the existing local government structure and even further expansion of the special districts (Gunlicks, 1991: 86ff.). Hence, the multitude of local governments and special districts rely on voluntary negotiated cooperation and coordination (Norton, 1994: 393), resulting in a situation labelled by some international observers as 'organized chaos' (Norton, 1994: 44; Owen and Noregaard, 1991).

Local government in *France* is marked by a myriad of some 35,000 municipalities with an average population of some 1600 inhabitants (Norton, 1994: 142f.) and with boundaries mostly dating back to times prior to the French Revolution. No serious attempt has been made by any French government to carry out a territorial reform of the municipalities (Wollmann, 2000c: 42). While, following the decentralization reform of 1982, significant functions were transferred to municipalities, the many small localities lack the resources to cope with the new responsibilities. Hence, they are bound to cooperate (Norton, 1994: 146) with the neighbouring localities – through single-purpose organizations (*syndicats intercommunaux à vocation unique*, SIVU) as well as multi-purpose organizations (*syndicats intercommunaux à vocation multiple*, SIVOM). The emergence and existence of some 14,500 SIVU and 2,500 SIVOM (Mabileau, 1996: 50 ff.) has been criticized for further aggravating France's 'over-institutionalization' of the subnational space (Mabileau, 1996: 51).

Following 1979, the Thatcher government in *the UK* pursued the two-pronged policy of aggressively curtailing the competences of the elected (multi-function) local authorities, particularly with regard to the direct delivery of social services while, at the same time, pushing the NPM concepts of outsourcing, privatizing and marketizing these tasks to special-purpose organizations and agencies on the local level (Rhodes, 1988; Goldsmith and Page, 1996: 151). In this model, competition is expected also to provide the coordination mechanism. The subsequent mushrooming of 'quasi-autonomous non-governmental organizations' (quangos) (Painter et al., 1996; Skelcher et al., 2000) and of private and voluntary sector organizations has dramatically changed the organizational fabric and climate of service provision on the local level (Flinders and Smith, 1999).

As already pointed out, empirical evidence suggests that such single-purpose agencies increase coordination problems. Furthermore, there are indications that, in contradiction to the proclaimed policy intention to do away with hierarchical control allegedly endemic to the public sector, the outsourced and 'quangoized' organizations and agencies face an ever-denser web of ties and checks: they are often dependent on central government funding; central government appointees sit on their directing boards; and monitoring, inspecting and evaluating mechanisms have tightened (Clarke and Hoggett, 2000: 239). Consequently, hierarchical control persists, in the guise of the 'audit society' (Power, 1997).

SUMMARY

In the intergovernmental setting, in European countries in particular, a trend towards political decentralization and administrative deconcentration has gained momentum under the guidance of the 'subsidiarity principle' (Baldersheim, 2002; Höffe, 1996). Wider forces are also at work. The horizontal and vertical expansion and differentiation of levels and actors is being addressed in the debate on governance (Rhodes, 1997), which, as was said in an OECD report of 1997, 'reflects the pluralization of the important actors in governing and providing public services. The configuration of public institutions is changing: the roles of supra- and sub-national bodies are becoming more important and semi-public and private sector actors are becoming more widely and deeply involved. At the same time, interaction is becoming less authoritative and more cooperative' (OECD, 1997: 15).

Particularly in countries with a strong *Rechtsstaat* tradition, institutional and normative pressures retain significant hierarchical components, thus preserving constituent elements of the 'sovereign state' (March and Olsen, 1989). At the same time, actor networks, informal cooperation and negotiating have become increasingly important modalities of coordination. These modes have gained additional salience under the impulses of the recent NPM debate, through the contractualization of intergovernmental and interorganizational relations, thereby bringing to the fore elements of the bargaining/negotiating state. For coordination on the regional/meso level (between the central government and the local government levels), the organizational principle of having territorially defined, multi-function, meso-level units has been spreading (most recently in the United

Kingdom). In the cases of France and Germany, hierarchical oversight over the subregional space is being replaced with informal cooperation, networks, negotiation and persuasion. In view of conflicting interests between policies, actors and levels, the functioning of such de-hierarchized coordination patterns hinges not least on shared values. Such cultural underpinning of non-hierarchical coordination seems most advanced in Scandinavian countries where 'trust-bound' rather than 'rule-bound' approaches and 'managing by contacts rather than by contracts' have come to prevail (Jann and Reichard, 2003). This seems to be culturally rooted, in the case of Sweden, in the country's belief in *folkshem* ('people's home') solidarity.

In order to institutionalize the coordination function on the local level, the territoriality-based multi-function model of elected local self-government has recently been further strengthened (for instance in Sweden). In the UK, however, the local government system has been weakened since the early 1980s. Political leadership, with hierarchical connotations, has been accentuated as a coordinating method within local government, particularly in Germany's directly elected 'strong' executive mayor. But at the same time, institutions and procedures for 'bottom-up' participation have evolved, particularly in Scandinavian countries. While such consumer-oriented and clientele-related organizations may be inclined to develop and pursue group-specific interests and to eschew common-good-oriented coordination, they probably remain tied enough into the overarching spirit of the elected local government structure to keep group particularism in check.

By contrast, the creation of single-purpose agencies for the competitive delivery of public services (particularly in the UK under Next Steps and through 'marketization') primarily aims at optimizing economic efficiency and client responsiveness. There is empirical evidence that such functional and organizational differentiation and specialization have aggravated the coordination problems (Jann, 2001: 260). Inasmuch as these developments also pass the delivery of public services over to private sector operators, the private-regarding orientation is prone to take over. The envisaged reduction of hierarchical control tends to be offset by the build-up of new monitoring and supervising mechanisms (Clarke and Hoggett, 2000: 239). In sum, such drawbacks point at the kind of 'fatal remedy' (James, 2002; Seiber, 1981) in which one evil is driven out by calling in another, possibly more wicked one.

REFERENCES

Baldersheim, Harald (2002) 'Subsidiarity at work. Modes of multi-level governance in European countries', in Janice Caulfield and Helge Larsen (eds), *Local Government at the Millenium*. Opladen: Leske and Budrich. pp. 203–12.

Balme, Richard and Bonnet, Laurence (1995) 'From regional to sectoral policies: the contractual relations between the state and the regions in France', in John Loughlin and Sonia Mazey (eds), *The End of the French Unitary State?* London: Frank Cass.

Bennett, Robert J. (1993) 'European local government systems', in Robert J. Bennett (ed.), *Local Government in the New Europe*. London: Belhaven Press. pp. 28–50.

Benz, Arthur (1999) 'From unitary to asymmetric federalism in Germany: taking stock after 50 years', *Publius: the Journal of Federalism*, 29 (4): 55–78.

Benz, Arthur (2001) 'Interministerial relations in the federal system', in Klaus König and Heinrich Siedentopf (eds), *Public Administration in Germany*. Baden-Baden: Nomos. pp. 139–54.

Bogason, Peter (1998) 'Changes in the Scandinavian model, from bureaucratic command to interorganizational negotiation. *Public Administration*, 76: 335–54.

Bulpitt, James (1983) *Territory and Power in the United Kingdom*. New York: Dover.

Cabinet Office (2000) *Wiring It Up: Whitehall's Management of Cross-cutting Policies and Services*. London: Performance and Innovation Unit.

Clark, M.P. (1998) 'The modernization of the French civil service: crisis, change and continuity', *Public Administration*, 76 (1): 97–115.

Clarke, John and Hoggett, Paul (2000) 'Regressive modernisation? The changing patterns of social service delivery in the United Kingdom', in Hellmut Wollmann and Eckhard Schröter (eds), *Comparing Public Sector Reform in Britain and Germany*. Aldershot: Ashgate. pp. 198–224.

DETR (Department of the Environment, Transport and the Regions) (1998) White Paper: *Modern Local Government in Touch with the People*. London: DETR.

Flinders, M.V. and Smith, M.J. (1999) *Quangos, Accountability and Reform: The Politics of Quasi-government*. London: Macmillan.

Fürst, Dietrich (1996) 'The regional district in search of a new role', in Arthur Benz and Klaus H. Goetz (eds), *A New German Public Sector? Reform, Adaptation and Stability*. Aldershot: Dartmouth, pp. 119–36.

Goldsmith, Michael J. and Page, Edward C. (1996) 'Farewell to the British state?', in Jan-Erik Lane (ed.), *Public Sector Reform. Rationale, Trends and Problems*. London: Sage. pp. 147–67.

Gunlicks, Arthur B. (1991), 'Local government in the United States of America', in Joachim-Jens Hesse (ed.), *Local Government and Urban Affairs in International Perspective*. Baden-Baden: Nomos. pp. 80–96.

Gustafsson, Gunnel (1991) 'Swedish local government: reconsidering rationality and consensus', in Joachim, J. Hesse (ed.), *Local Government and Urban Affairs in*

International Perspective. Baden-Baden: Nomos. pp. 241–60.

Hanf, Kenneth and Scharpf, Fritz, W. (1978) *Interorganizational Policy-making: Limits to Coordination and Central Control*. Beverly Hills, CA: Sage.

Hesse, Joachim Jens and Sharpe, L.J. (1991) 'Local government in international perspective: some comparative observations', in Joachim-Jens Hesse (ed.), *Local Government and Urban Affairs in International Perspective*. Baden-Baden: Nomos. pp. 603–21.

Höffe, Otried (1996) 'Subsidiarity as a principle in the philosophy of government', *Regional and Federal Studies*, 6: 56–73.

James, Oliver (2001) 'Business-like government agencies – like what model of business', *Governance*, 14 (2).

James, Oliver (2002) 'New Public Management in the UK: enduring legacy or fatal remedy?', *International Review of Public Administration*, 6 (2): 15–26.

Jann, Werner (2001) 'Hierarchieabbau und Dezentralisierung', in Bernhard Blanke et al. (eds), *Handbuch zur Verwaltungsreform*, 2nd edn. Opladen: Leske and Budrich.

Jann, Werner and Reichard, Christoph (2003) 'Best Practice in central government modernization', in H. Wollmann (ed.), *Evaluating Public Sector Reforms*. Aldershot: Edward Elgar (forthcoming).

Jones, George (1990) 'Local government in Great Britain', in Jens Joachim Hesse (ed.), *Local Government and Urban Affairs in International Perspective*. Baden-Baden: Nomos. pp. 167–210.

Kaufmann, Franz-Xavier, Majone, Giacomendo and Ostrom, Vincent (eds) (1986) *Guidance, Control and Evaluation in the Public Sector*. Berlin: de Gruyter.

Lane, C. and Bachmann, R. (eds) (1998) *Trust Within and Between Organizations*. Oxford: Oxford University Press.

Larsen, Helge O. (2002) 'Directly Elected Mayors: Democratic Renewal or Constitutional Confusion?', in Janice Caulfield and Helge O. Larsen (eds), *Local Government at the Millennium*. Opladen: Leske & Budrich. pp. 111–34.

Leach, R.H. and O'Rourke, T.G. (1988) *State and Local Government: The Third Century of Federalism*. Englewood Cliffs, NJ: Prentice–Hall.

Loughlin, John and Mazey, Sonia (eds) (1995) *The End of the French Unitary State?* London: Frank Cass.

Lynch, Peter (1999) 'New Labour and the English regional development agencies: devolution as evaluation', *Regional Studies*, 33: 73–89.

Mabileau, Albert (1996) *Le Système local en France*, 2nd edn. Paris: Montchrestien.

Mabileau, Albert (1997) *Les génies invisible du local*, *Revue Francaise de Science Politique*, 47: 340–75.

March, James G. and Olsen, Johan P. (1989) *Rediscovering Institutions. The Organizational Basis of Politics*. New York: The Free Press.

Marcou, Gérard and Verebelyi, Imre (ed.) (1993) *New Trends in Local Government in Western and Eastern Europe*. Brussels: IISA.

Marin, Bernd (1990) 'Generalized political exchange: preliminary considerations', in B. Marin (ed.), *Generalized Political Exchange: Antagonistic Cooperation and Integrated Policy Circuits*. Frankfurt a.M.: Campus.

Mawson, J. and Spencer, K. (1997) 'Origins and operation of the Government Office for the English Regions', in J. Bradbury and J. Mawson (eds), *British Regionalism and Devolution*. London: Jessica Kingsley.

Mazey, Sonia (1993) 'Developments at the French *meso* level: modernizing the French state', in L.J. Sharpe, (eds), *The Rise of Meso Government in Europe*. London: Sage. pp. 61–90.

Montin, Stig (2000) 'Between fragmentation and coordination: The changing role of local government in Sweden', *Public Management*, 2 (1): 1–23.

Morgan, K., Rees, G. and Garmise, S. (1999) 'Networking for local economic development', in G. Stoker (ed.), *The New Management of British Governance*. London: Macmillan. pp. 181–96.

Norton, Allan (1994) *International Handbook of Local and Regional Government*. Aldershot: Edward Elgar.

OECD (1997a) *In Search for Results: Performance Management Practices*. Paris: PUMA/OECD.

OECD (1997b) *Managing Across Levels of Government*. Paris: OECD.

OECD (1998) *Budgeting in Sweden*. Paris: PUMA/OECD.

Owens, J. and Norregard, J. (1991) 'The Role of Lower Levels of Government: The Experience in Selected OECD Countries', in J. Owens and G. Panella (eds), *Local Government: An International Perspective*. Amsterdam: Elsevier.

Painter, C., Rouise, J., Isaac-Henry, K. and Munk, L. (1996) *Changing Local Governance: Local Authorities and Non-elected Agencies*. Luton: Local Government Management Board.

Peters, Guy B. (1998) 'Managing horizontal government: the politics of coordination', *Public Administration*, 76: 295–311.

Pollitt, Christopher (2001) 'Joined-up government: click or clunk?'. Unpublished manuscript (November 2001).

Pollitt, Christopher and Bouckaert, Geert (2000) *Public Management Reform*. Oxford: Oxford University Press.

Postif, Thierry (1997) 'Public sector reform in France', in Jan-Erik Lane (ed.), *Public Sector Reform*. London: Sage. pp. 208–24.

Power, M. (1997) *The Audit Society: Rituals of Verification*. Oxford: Oxford University Press.

Premfors, Rune (1998) 'Reshaping the democratic state. Swedish experiences in a comparative perspective', *Public Administration*, 76 (Spring): 141–59.

Pressman, J.L. and Wildavsky, A. (1974) *Implementation*. Berkeley, CA: University of California Press.

Rhodes, R.A.W. (1988) *Beyond Westminster and Whitehall*. London: Unwin–Hyman.

Rhodes, R.A.W. (1997) *Understanding Governance: Policy Networks, Governance, Reflexivity and Accountability*. Buckingham: Open University Press.

Roberts, S. (1997) 'The implementation of Dutch public management reforms 1980–1996', in *Ministry of*

Finance, Public Management Reform: Five Country Studies. Helsinki: Ministry of Finance. pp. 91–130.

Scharpf, Fritz W. (1997) *Games Real Actors Play: Actor-centered Institutionalism in Policy Research*. Boulder CO: Westview Press.

Schuppert, Gunnar Folke (2000) *Verwaltungswissenschaft*. Baden-Baden: Nomos.

Seiber, S. (1981) *Fatal Remedies. The Ironies of Social Intervention*. New York: Plenum Press.

Sharpe, L.J. (ed.) (1993a) *The Rise of Meso Government in Europe*, London: Sage.

Sharpe, L.J. (1993b) 'The European *meso*: an appraisal', in L.J. Sharpe (ed.), *The Rise of Meso Government in Europe*. London: Sage. pp. 1–39.

Sharpe, L.J. (1993c) 'The United Kingdom: the disjointed *meso*, in L.J. Sharpe (ed.), *The Rise of Meso Government in Europe*. London: Sage. pp. 247–95.

Sharpe, L.J. (2000) 'Regionalism in the United Kingdom: the role of social federalism', in Hellmut Wollmann and Eckhard Schröter (eds), *Comparing Public Sector Reform in Britain and Germany*. Aldershot: Ashgate. pp. 107–31.

Skelcher, C. et al. (2000) *Advance of the Quango State*. London: Local Government Information Unit.

Stewart, John (1995) *The Role of Local Government in the United Kingdom*. Institute of Local Government Studies: Birmingham.

Stewart, John (2000) *The Nature of British Local Government*. Basingstoke: Macmillan.

Stöbe, Sybille and Brandel, Rolf (1996) *Die Zukunft der Bezirksregierungen*. Berlin: Sigma.

Stoker, Gerry (2002) 'New Labour and Local Governance in Britain', in Janice Caulfield and Helge O. Larsen (eds), *Local Government at the Millennium*. Opladen: Leske & Budrich. pp. 27–46.

Thompson, G., Frances, J., Levacic, R. and Mitchel, J. (eds) (1991) *Markets, Hierarchies, Networks: The Coordination of Social Life*. London: Sage.

Wagener, Frido and Blümel, Willi (2001) 'State structure and administrative territories', in Klaus König and Heinrich Siedentopf (eds), *Public Administration in Germany*. Baden-Baden: Nomos. pp. 93–104.

Weber, Max (1972) *Wirtschaft und Gesellschaft*, 5th edn. Tübingen: Mohr (Paul Siebeck).

Wilson, D. and Game, C. (2002) *Local Government in the United Kingdom*, 3rd edn. Basingstoke: Palgrave.

Wollmann, Hellmut (1997) 'Institution building and decentralization in former socialist countries: the cases of Poland, Hungary, and East Germany', *Government and Policy*, 15: 463–80.

Wollmann, Hellmut (2000a) 'Comparing institutional development in Britain and Germany', in Hellmut Wollmann and Eckhard Schröter (eds), *Comparing Public Sector Reform in Britain and Germany*. Aldershot: Ashgate. pp. 1–26.

Wollmann, Helmut (2000b) 'The development and present state of local government in England and Germany – a comparison', in Hellmut Wollmann and Eckhard Schröter (eds), *Comparing Public Sector Reform in Britain and Germany*. Aldershot: Ashgate. pp. 107–31.

Wollmann, Hellmut (2000c) 'Local government systems: from divergence towards convergence? Great Britain, France and Germany as comparative cases in point', in *Environment and Planning C* (Government and Policy), 18: 33–55.

Wollmann, Hellmut (2000d) 'Local government modernization in Germany: between incrementalism and reform waves', *Public Administration*, 78 (4): 915–36.

Wollmann, Hellmut (2002) 'Local Government Reforms in Germany: A Trajectory of Change and Persistence', in Janice Caulfield and Helge O. Larsen (eds), *Local Government at the Millennium*. Opladen: Leske & Budrich. pp. 63–92.

Wollmann, Hellmut (2003) 'Strengthening Local Leadership through Directly Elected "Strong" (Executive) Mayors in German Local Government?', *International Journal of Urban and Regional Research* (forthcoming).

48

The Instruments of Intergovernmental Management

Beryl A. Radin

If this Handbook had been published two decades ago, the discussion of instruments of intergovernmental management would have been a very straightforward and relatively simple exposition. For at that point it would be assumed that intergovernmental management focused almost entirely on vertical relationships between levels of government and, occasionally, on horizontal relationships between levels of government. The metaphor that was developed in the US literature that captured this set of relationships was 'picket fence federalism' – alliances between program specialists or professionals that transcend the level of government in which they serve (Wright, 1988: 83).

The initial literatures that developed this frame of reference assumed that traditional approaches to institutional authority would remain. The first writings on intergovernmental management did not focus on changes in systems, structures, policies or programs. However, they did highlight management activities that effectively blended politics and administration by focusing on managers in the policy process. These managers include program and policy professionals as well as administrative generalists drawn from governmental entities. While much of this literature highlighted the role of national governments, it increasingly moved toward a flatter and less top-down approach to intergovernmental relationships. In fact, much of the literature accentuated a bottom-up, more collegial approach to these relationships.

It also became clear that many of the behaviors described in federal systems were also found in unitary political systems. In the United Kingdom, for example, researchers have described the distinctive interests in cities and the national state (Gurr and King, 1987). Many of the dynamics that stem from social, economic and political changes in unitary systems are very similar to the dynamics traditionally associated with federalism. But intergovernmental management can occur in both unitary and federal systems.

The framework that was established by those who pioneered the field of intergovernmental management remains as a basis for more contemporary analysis of the field. However, the changes that have occurred in the subsequent years have created a different set of constraints and demands on intergovernmental management that have set the context for a discussion of instruments that are relevant to the field. There are three sets of changes that have occurred within the past decade that are crucial to understanding this context:

1 an increase in boundary spanning activities;
2 the new management skills required as a result of the boundary spanning changes; and
3 the international expression of these changes.

An increase in boundary-spanning activities

The landscape of the public sector that is in place at the beginning of the twenty-first century appears to be quite different from that found several decades earlier. Several aspects of this changed landscape have contributed to the context for intergovernmental management.

Shifting policy boundaries

In the early period of intergovernmental management, relationships could be established that followed clear demarcations of policies and programs. Rural policy, for example, was defined as a part of agricultural policy and the relationships across levels of government were found within that policy sphere. By the end of the twentieth century, however, many countries found that rural policy was no longer defined solely within the agriculture sphere. Rather, it involved sectors including economic development, health, education, housing and infrastructure. Similar movement out of a single policy world has been found in other areas, such as drug policy, crime and welfare.

Shifting views about the role of government

The shifts that have taken place within the past decade have reflected quite dramatic changes in the way that both citizens and governments themselves think about the role of government in democratic societies. The traditional hierarchical bureaucratic structures with powers concentrated at the top of organizations have been subjected to criticism; criticism not only about the structure of government but also its span of powers has contributed to what has been called the 'hollowing' of government. This has led to a shrinking of the direct role of public agencies in actually delivering services to the public as well as a diminution of the span of responsibilities of the public sector. Privatization and contracting out of government roles have become increasingly common, utilizing public funds but relying on for-profit or nonprofit entities to deliver services. 'Hollowing out' involves a number of changes, including transfer of functions, loss of expertise and the breakdown of traditional relationships.

Interdependence between levels of government

The initial development of intergovernmental management represented an acknowledgement that many policies and programs required management activities that moved beyond a single level of government or a single jurisdiction, leading to alternative approaches to autonomous and separate governmental authority. In the years that have ensued, more and more policies have exhibited characteristics of interdependence between levels of government. This means that multiple levels of government are involved simultaneously in programs and policies and that a single level of government rarely has single power and influence over the way that programs are designed, funded, managed and delivered.

Public–private interdependence

The changes that have occurred in the reach and structure of government have made it obvious that the activities involving intergovernmental management do not end with players only from the public sector or government agencies. Rather, management of public sector programs involves a wide range of players from both the for-profit and nonprofit sectors. Each of these players now comes to the policy table with its own agenda and imperatives. In some cases, the representatives from the for-profit sector have had minimal experience with the limited authority and constraints placed on public sector officials. Reciprocally, the public sector officials have not had experience with these players.

A focus on performance

The concern about performance is closely linked to the reinvention movement popularized by Osborne and Gaebler (1992) and others who have emphasized reinvention of government at the state and local government levels. The reinvention movement accentuates the importance of measuring results. This rhetoric style employs a vocabulary that highlights outcomes rather than inputs, processes, or even outputs. It focuses on the benefits derived from the use of public sector funds and seeks to establish a framework that moves away from traditional incremental decision making in which budgets are created largely on the basis of past allocation patterns. It has been used as a way to counter the public's disillusion with government as well as the government-bashing that has been employed by political figures at all ends of the political spectrum. But while the concern about performance is pervasive, it is not expressed consistently; it takes many different forms and is attached to efforts at all levels of government.

Need for new management skills

Although the initial foray into intergovernmental management did highlight the importance of bargaining skills to facilitate relationships between levels of government, the changes that have been described above have placed new demands on intergovernmental managers. Managers have found that the traditional command and control paradigm, accentuating the authority of the individuals at the top of the hierarchy, did not provide an adequate framework to deal with the major issues found in the intergovernmental debate in the United States and in other countries. Neither did it capture the tension between national and local governmental units in unitary systems. This is the autonomy versus control debate – asking the question as to what extent should higher levels of government empower lower levels of government and then get out of the way so that they can get their jobs done? This involves the on-going question about the level of decentralization to be developed in countries around the world.

Over the past decade, an approach has developed around intergovernmental relations that emphasizes the importance of bargaining, compromise and networking as essential processes of decision making rather than traditional hierarchical command and control approaches on formal structures as venues for decision making. This highlights a movement away from a 'sorting-out' of intergovernmental roles to an interdependent approach. It focuses on the development of interorganizational networks that include both governmental and non-governmental actors and proceed along a path that includes the acceptance of the independent and separate character of the various members, avoidance of superior–subordinate relationships, interfacing of political and career actors, inclusion of appropriate specialists when needed to focus on technical issues, and agreement to abide by tasks and goals (Agranoff, 1986). It also includes a recognition of the use of informal relationships even when structural centralization appears to dominate (Gurr and King, 1987; Rhodes, 1988).

This approach includes both the process and substantive nature of contemporary issues. It suggests that different processes must be used to reach decisions. But it also draws on the policy notion of issue networks. This concept, developed by Hugh Heclo, is viewed as a 'web' of largely autonomous participants with variable degrees of mutual commitment or dependence on each other. Heclo (1979) focuses on the hybrid interests that provoke such alliances and comprise a large number of participants who move in and out of the network constantly. The issue network approach provides a way to include various interests in a process, cutting both horizontally (across multiple issues) as well as vertically (down the intergovernmental chain). It also establishes a framework that is responsive to the transient nature of policy coalitions, with various networks established for a particular situation but dissolved when that situation changes.

While this approach has intrigued intergovernmental scholars, it has not been used extensively in the world of practice. Intergovernmental dialogue continues to be characterized by a focus on separate programs, policies or organizations and a search for clarity and simplicity in the delineation of roles and responsibilities. This has been reinforced by a concern not only about efficiency in government but by a focus on the role of government in the broader economy (Painter, 1997).

The debate around intergovernmental issues has been waged at two often contradictory levels: a general, macro and sometimes symbolic approach and, sometimes at the same time, a specific policy approach. Both, however, reflect the high political stakes that are frequently involved in the determination of lines of authority as well as allocation of resources. As a result, the intergovernmental terrain has been subject to constant uprooting that reflects the ideology and political agenda of the party and officials in power. This creates a level of confusion for those managers who are caught in the middle of these debates.

New Public Management: the international expression of these changes

Many of the shifts that have been described above affecting intergovernmental management have coincided in time with the development of what has been called the New Public Management movement. This set of global developments has also been a response to developments across the world affecting economic problems and negative perceptions of bureaucracies. As Michael Barzelay has noted, these developments represent a 'substantial shift in governance and management of the 'state sector' in the United Kingdom, New Zealand, Australia, Scandinavia, and North America' (Barzelay, 2001: 3). While this movement is not composed of a well-defined set of principles and practices, a number of the behaviors that have been associated with it do have implications for intergovernmental management because they appear to shift the balance between central governments and state/provincial or local jurisdictions. Some of these developments support shifts in intergovernmental management, emphasizing decentralized systems and public–private relationships. Others, however, move to more centralized control systems and collide with developments in intergovernmental management.

The concern about performance is one aspect of the New Public Management movement. Yet another aspect of the movement highlights the importance of empowering those who actually deliver services. This has been a problem in the United States, where many of the national programs involve intricate intergovernmental relationships. Thus managers in national government agencies have struggled with ways to structure these relationships. National government agencies are balancing two competing imperatives. On one hand, they are attempting to hold third parties accountable for the use of the national government monies but, on the other hand, they are constrained by the political and legal realities that provide significant discretion and leeway to the third parties for the use of these national government dollars. In many ways, the performance movement at the national government level collides with strategies of devolution and a diminished national government role.

INSTRUMENTS OF INTERGOVERNMENTAL RELATIONS

The interdependence among levels of government in the US system and the persistence of the accountability/autonomy and collaboration/competition dilemmas means that it is increasingly necessary to focus attention on the instruments or tools of intergovernmental relations. These tools have emerged from many different sources and are best understood in the context of specific governmental structures and specific policy areas. Some of the tools have been primarily used as instruments of centralized control while others reflect a tendency to look to decentralized forms. Although one might argue that a situation that calls for a predictable, uniform approach would call for a top-down strategy, there are often extenuating circumstances (many of which emerge from the external environment of a policy or program), that might make use of such a tool difficult if not impossible.

Given the complexity of these linkages it is essential that an array of instruments be used to fashion the most effective working relationships among intergovernmental actors. Four broad categories of instruments are of particular interest:

1 structural;
2 programmatic;

3 research and capacity building; and
4 behavioral.

(See McDonnell and Elmore (1987) and Salamon and Lund (1989) for other approaches.)

Structural

Structural matters have to do with formal roles and relationships; patterns of authority and leadership; rules, policies and regulations; and mechanisms for differentiation and integration of formal roles, tasks and relationships. In some cases, the actual structure of the public service may actually provide the setting for intergovernmental management. This is the case in India where the design of the Indian Administrative Service is itself an instrument of federalism (Radin, 1999).

Reorganization

Formal roles and relationships are shaped and reshaped in the design and redesign of organizations. Patterns of authority and leadership are disrupted and reestablished. Redesign, or reorganization, is a tool frequently employed in government as a means of responding to changing needs and priorities. Reorganizations can bring together programs that seem to be related, thus affecting horizontal intergovernmental relationships. They can also sharpen the focus on the accountability/autonomy debate. However, reorganizations cannot settle these issues. Reorganization can be approached on a grand scale (as was the case in the United States with President Nixon's Ash Commission, charged with studying the organization of the national government) or on a more incremental base (as was the case with President Carter's Reorganization Project inside the Office of Management and Budget). Frequently, attempts are made to create mega-departments, assuming that these centralized bodies will improve efficiency of government operations and service delivery. In the United States, some state-level reorganizations have been spawned by national government incentives. In the 1970s, several states created departments of behavioral health or departments of substance abuse, believing that they would be in a better position to take advantage of national government grant funds targeted at comprehensive approaches to those issues. In the United Kingdom increasing centralization by the Thatcher government reduced local discretion over budgetary allocations and restructured local government (Gurr and King, 1987).

Commissions

Commissions are structural tools which can be used for any number of intergovernmental purposes. They are frequently a tool of horizontal integration but often appear to shift power to a centralized level. While some may view commissions as a coordination tool, they are likely to operate at a symbolic level that makes coordination difficult. This is particularly true in large federal systems where coordination across programs and across levels of government is difficult.

Coordination

Coordination and efficiency are the by-words of the structural approach. Coordinating mechanisms are tools for structural integration – the integration of units differentiated by function or level or geography. Implicit in attempts at reorganization is the assumption that increased coordination and efficiency will make it easier to manage both horizontal and vertical intergovernmental relationships. While it is disputed whether this actually occurs, proponents of this approach make such an argument.

In practice, coordination is often transparent. It is easy to say it is being done, but its tangible products are illusive. While inter-agency coordination has costs, it does not necessarily require new appropriations, or particular budgetary line-items. Unlike reorganization, coordination doesn't run the risk of alienating political constituencies, and it is difficult for one to argue that coordination is unnecessary or seriously detrimental to major interests. Applied properly as intergovernmental tools, formal mechanisms of interagency coordination can strengthen horizontal relationships. At the same time they can both strengthen a higher level of government's capacity to hold lower levels responsible for program performance and empower actors at those lower levels so that they can improve performance.

Premiers or governors meetings, bringing together the political leaders of states or provinces (as found in Australia and Canada), are sometimes used as a coordination device. Similarly, the Council of Australian Governments was created in 1992 to bring together state and central government officials to work on specific problems that required joint action (Painter, 2001). Scharpf has noted that coordination efforts can involve negative coordination (causing gridlock and lowest common denominator outcomes) (Scharpf, 1997: 112–14).

Deregulation

Rules, policies and regulations are instruments for controlling intergovernmental relationships; they are instruments for increasing accountability and decreasing autonomy. Consequently, deregulation swings the pendulum in the other direction. Mandates are impediments imposed on lower intergovernmental actors from above through regulatory mechanisms. Mandates are removed through deregulation and are relaxed or removed through ad hoc experiments such as waiver procedures or regulatory negotiation, or the creation of new coordinating mechanisms (Radin, 1998, 1999, 2001; Radin et al., 1996).

Devolution and decentralization

These are structural tools with which the national government may delegate power to the states or with which states may delegate power to local governments. When used, then, devolution and/or decentralization shift the pendulum toward autonomy. President Nixon's New Federalism in the United States was an attempt at devolution and a reaction to many of the centralizing tenets of Johnson's Creative Federalism. This effort provided decentralization within national government departments to field units and a general preference for relying on general purpose governments and elected officials rather than program specialists (Walker, 1995: 105.)

Devolution took the form of general and special revenue sharing and attempts by President Nixon to impound national government funds as a way to eliminate program resources. Proponents of devolution are quite willing to trade accountability to the national government for discretion on the part of state and local officials.

Decentralization has been employed in much the same manner by some states in an effort to manage intergovernmental relationships. Use of this tool involves passing authority (some would say 'passing the buck') to local units of government. In some instances, when states are given national government mandates without resources, they simply pass the mandates on to local government. This coping mechanism shifts the burden of the intergovernmental dilemma but it clearly does not solve it.

Regulation and oversight

Regulation is itself a structural intergovernmental tool even though the degree to which the national government exercises oversight with respect to its state and local grantees is, in part, a political/ideological matter. In the Nixon, Reagan and Bush administrations in the United States, for example, the operative ideology was minimal national government involvement and maximum state and local responsibility. Block grants and revenue sharing carry with them fewer strings than conditional grants.

Oversight can occur at the input, process or output side of programs. Input requirements generally specify the form and elements of the program design, leaving little discretion for the program implementers. Process requirements include elements such as citizen participation or planning requirements that are built in to insure accountability. Output and outcome requirements tend to rely on evaluation as an accountability tool.

Evaluation requirements are imposed by either legislative or administrative mandate. Depending on where one sits, evaluation can be looked at as a management tool which is necessary for intelligent decision making or as an unwarranted intrusion on management discretion. Evaluation requirements are often used to assure that grant recipients are able to justify the expenditure of funds. Not only are these requirements built into programs but recipients are often required to pay for them with grant funds. However, evaluation can also facilitate additional autonomy on the part of state and local grantees. If evaluation is related to performance rather than input or process (that is, focus on outcomes and program impacts), grantees may be given more discretion as to the way they produce those outcomes and impacts.

Process requirements can include citizen participation and planning approaches. Citizen participation requirements provide an opportunity for a form of accountability that is imposed early in the life of a program. While some may view them as a constraint, others view them as an opportunity to improve programs and avoid unnecessary conflict in their implementation. The idea of consulting with parties who will be affected by decisions is consistent with the general notion of empowerment; it empowers program clients as well as program operators.

Planning requirements can also be used as a form of process accountability. Like other requirements, they can be viewed as a set of constraints or as an effective instrument for intergovernmental management. Planning processes allow a jurisdiction to identify its current status, its goals and its strategy for change. This requirement might stipulate that the process will occur openly with ample opportunity for input from those affected by plan implementation. If plans are written to reflect the real status of the jurisdiction (rather than as compliance documents), they can both increase autonomy and ensure accountability.

Programmatic instruments

This second category of instrumentalities employed to deal with the intergovernmental dilemma involves the application of resources and redesign of programs and grant types. From the national government perspective, the intention has been to make it easier for states, provinces, localities or regions to attack social and economic problems by providing them with the resources to do so. In many instances, these resources have emerged as a result of lobbying by states and localities. While this approach was the most common response to newly identified problems, limited resources make it less commonly used. Various grant forms such as competitive project grants, formula grants, matching grants and block grants are still used as tools today.

The shift toward broader purpose grants

Highly specific categorical grants are the most restrictive but also the most targeted type of national government funding. These grant forms – particularly project grants – require potential eligible recipients to submit applications under guidelines specified by national government grantor agencies. Depending on the area, states continue to have discretion in this process. In some cases, applications from local units of government (or the private sector) must be reviewed and receive favorable recommendations from state agencies prior to submission to the national government grantor. As a general matter, however, categorical grants are heavily weighted toward the accountability side.

In the United States, block grants in law enforcement, employment and training, community development and social services were enacted which strengthened the hand of state and local officials in their dealing with national government grantors. While these approaches appear to be fairly radical approaches to intergovernmental management, they resulted in rather incremental changes in the system because the existing procedures were well entrenched and not easily modified.

Partnerships

As intergovernmental tools, partnerships generally involve setting priorities and providing incentives at higher levels of government and letting others take action to achieve them. It means less reliance on service delivery through public bureaucracies and more utilization of public–public or public–private partnerships. Partnerships involve national government, state and local governments and the private sector in a variety of activities. As Peters has noted, partnership involves two or more actors, at least one of which is public; each participant is a principal; there is an enduring relationship among the actors; each of the participants brings something to the partnership and a shared responsibility for outcomes of their activities (Peters, 1998: 12–13).

While states and localities have traditionally been partners in the intergovernmental arena, this approach focuses on the creation of specific partnership forms in response to the tensions inherent in the intergovernmental dilemma. Osborne and Gaebler (1992) point out that under partnership schemes governments share or trade services or contract with one another for specific services. Additionally, information, ideas and other resources may be shared in partnerships. Creating partnerships involves reframing the intergovernmental dilemma at the national government level. Rather than focusing on the trade-off between accountability and autonomy, this approach attempts to define accountability and, at the same time, do more to empower states and localities so that they can be full partners in the federal system.

Collaborations

Collaborations may involve the granting of national government funds to a set of state or local agencies conditioned upon their ability to work together and share resources. Often collaboration is based on a recognition that no single agency or system of services can effectively respond to the myriad of needs presented by those in or at risk for a particular service. Inter-agency collaboration envisions that partners will relinquish total control of resources in favor of the group process, pooling resources and jointly planning, implementing and evaluating new services. This programmatic approach overlaps with structural instruments in that it indicates a recognition by national government, state and local officials that old structures must give way to new ones if intergovernmental problems are to be solved.

Research and capacity-building instruments

The third category of intergovernmental instruments involves, in today's jargon, 'empowerment'. Implicit in this empowerment notion is the idea that steps may have to be taken to build increased management capacity at all levels if empowering is to have a chance of succeeding. So empowerment is an empty exercise if it does not also include the tools the newly empowered need to get the job done. Specific tools in this category include research, the collection, storage and dissemination of information and training, and other forms of capacity building.

Research

Research is an indirect tool of intergovernmental management aimed at helping people understand problems and issues, options and consequences. To the extent that public policy research is cross-cutting it can aid those promoting inter-agency coordination. To the extent that research produces useful knowledge which is in turn utilized below the national government level, it can increase the negotiating power, and thus the autonomy of state and local intergovernmental actors.

The provision of information

National and state governments often serve as clearinghouses for those seeking information on just about anything. This information is expected to improve inter-agency coordination and strengthen state and local discretion.

Capacity-building

This is one of the most widely used tools of intergovernmental management. Generally, it involves efforts by the national or state governments to strengthen the capabilities of state or local officials to manage programs on their own. Central governments often provide substantial technical assistance to officials at lower levels, and that they have been doing so for some time is often overlooked. This assistance can be in the form of grants or contracts which provide for training and skill-building in the areas of program design, planning and evaluation to name just three.

There are two ways in which capacity-building and the strengthening of state and local expertise in specific program areas is an intergovernmental management tool. First, it makes sense for the grantor to insure that grantees who are given additional discretion have the skills and abilities necessary to manage the grants. Second, it helps to insure accountability through development of management skills that facilitate compliance with national grant requirements.

Behavioral instruments of intergovernmental relations

The traditional view of the national official's dilemma is whether to allow more or less autonomy or to impose more or less accountability. Accountability can be framed in a narrow fashion, holding grantees accountable for inputs and processes. However, looking at the situation through a wider lens suggests that accountability should be for performance, and autonomy means that grantees are empowered and given the tools they need to accomplish that performance. This broader view of accountability requires attention to individual and group processes of communication and to processes of conflict management.

Conflict management

No matter what metaphor is used to describe the intergovernmental system, there is evidence of conflict. The issue, then, is not to attempt to avoid or suppress conflict but, rather, to prevent unnecessary conflict and to manage the conflict that does occur toward productive ends.

Conflict prevention in an intergovernmental context calls for attention to building consensus among actors in particular programmatic or policy areas. Actors are urged to identify and overcome barriers like the language and jargon of different program cultures and resistance to change among agency staff.

Conflict management might involve taking a negotiated approach to the promulgation of rules and regulations, as opposed to a 'decide, announce and defend' approach. For more than ten years, the US Environmental Protection Agency has engaged in a process of negotiated rule making referred to as 'reg-neg'. Regulatory negotiation involves affected parties and the agency in an orderly process of debate and discussion over proposed regulations. This consultative approach has produced environmental regulations which are acceptable to all. It has also enabled the EPA to move away from the decide, announce and defend approach which landed it in court more often than not.

Individual communication

Closely connected to the consensus building/conflict management notion is the idea of improving communications between levels of government as a way to manage the accountability/autonomy dilemma. Effective intergovernmental relationships in an environment of resource scarcity and political uncertainty demand openness in interactions across governments. They demand national officials who can listen, delegate, manage conflict and build consensus. The 'command and control' method of communicating from national to state and local levels is not viewed as an adequate way to manage intergovernmental relations.

Group communication

Hearings are among the time-honored and formal means of group communication in policy development. Hearings provide a forum for representatives of groups in and outside of government to take positions and express their views. They also provide a means for governmental actors to collect information and shape ideas that later become policy. Hearings can be traditional and formal or of the town meeting type. If one reframes the intergovernmental dilemma and looks at it as an opportunity rather than a problem, hearings can be another way to build consensus. If one looks at these issues in a narrow sense, hearings can be viewed as a way to exert national influence.

None of these four categories of intergovernmental tools or instruments is a panacea. Intergovernmental actors must look at issues from a number of different perspectives simultaneously. Structural, programmatic, educational and behavioral approaches are each appropriate under the right set of circumstances. While one might search for rules of thumb that make particular instruments more or less appropriate in particular situations, the determination to adopt one or several of these approaches appears to be highly idiosyncratic to particular countries and to specific situations.

A SPECIAL CASE: DEALING WITH PERFORMANCE

This discussion highlights six different approaches that have been taken recently within national agencies to deal with issues of performance and intergovernmental management. Because of the interest in the United States in this issue, this section of the chapter relies mainly on US experience. But other countries, particularly the United Kingdom, have also emphasized performance measurement. Some performance approaches have been devised as a result of legislation and others through administrative action. All are struggling with the tension between national agency accountability and devolution and discretion provided to state and local agencies. These include: performance partnerships, incentives, negotiated measures, building performance goals into legislation, establishment of standards and waivers.

Performance partnerships

Over the past ten years or so, a number of national agencies have adopted or at least explored the possibility of moving categorical programs into performance partnerships. These partnerships have become increasingly popular as agencies realize the limitations of their ability to achieve desired changes in complex settings. While partnerships between various agencies and government have been around in some form for some years, the performance orientation of the contemporary effort is new. The image of the partnership is one in which partners discuss how to combine resources from both players to achieve a pre-specified end-state. This end-state is expected to be measurable in order for a partnership to be successful.

The design of a performance partnership addresses what some have viewed as one of the most troubling problems faced by national managers: lack of control over outcomes. While the managers may have control over inputs, processes and outputs, they cannot specify end outcomes. Performance partnerships may involve agreements between national officials and state or local agencies; they may be ad hoc or permanent.

This process is not without problems. The General Accounting Office in the United States highlighted a number of what they called 'technical challenges':

- An absence of baseline data to use as the basis for measuring improvements
- The difficulty of quantifying certain results
- The difficulty of linking program activities to results
- The level of resources needed to develop a high-quality performance measurement system. (US GAO, 1999)

The experience of US EPA with performance partnerships illustrates some of the problems that are intrinsic to this performance strategy and agreement form. The individual negotiation between the national agency and (in this case) states, is likely to result in variability of agreements across the country. In fact, to some the individual tailoring of agreements is the strength of the mechanism. However, others are concerned that this variation results from differential treatment of jurisdictions.

The strategy is often attractive to national agencies charged with the implementation of programs that involve policy sectors that do not have well-established data systems or even data definitions. In such settings, it is difficult to establish and to garner data for the performance measures required to achieve the expectations of the approach.

Incentives

Over the past several decades, as the economics paradigm has increasingly influenced policy, some policy analysts have focused on the use of incentives as a way to change behavior. Incentives seek to induce behavior rather than command it. But bureaucrats and politicians tend to be attracted to direct regulation since they believe that incentives also require governmental intervention and therefore involve regulation.

To some degree, however, incentives have been at play in the past in a number of national programs through matching fund requirements. When the national government offers funds as an incentive to induce states or provinces to provide their own funds, the matching requirements do serve an incentive function. In many cases, however, performance expectations are not usually made explicit, particularly in programs carried over from the past.

There are a number of dilemmas involved in using an incentive strategy. It is difficult to ascertain the direct relationship between the behavior of the state or local government and specific outcomes. In addition, complex programs have an array of program goals and expectations and it is not easy to achieve agreement on performance standards. Some critics of the incentive strategy argue that state or local jurisdictions will attempt to game the system and develop policies that may meet the performance measures rather than achieve the basic expectations of the legislation. Others argue that this already occurs and so the situation is not much different than it has been in the past.

Negotiated performance measures

One of the most common complaints by state and local governments in the United States is that the national government imposes a set of requirements as to the use of its funds that do not meet the needs of the non-national jurisdiction. Indeed, this is one of the arguments that has been used to justify the transformation of categorical program grants into block grant efforts. Block grants have proved to be one of the most difficult grant forms on which to impose performance requirements. It has been problematic for national officials to balance the flexibility of the block grant (allowing states and localities to meet their own particular needs) with a desire for greater accountability for the use of those funds.

However, there are times when it is possible to achieve agreement on performance measures when certain conditions are met. Programs that are not politically volatile or do not have a widely disparate set of expert opinions are appropriate for this process. In addition, prior work and data systems can lay the foundation for consensus on many outcome and process objectives: measures can recognize and separate objectives over which grantees exercise influence and control from those that depend on external factors beyond their control. But even when these conditions are present, the negotiation process is time consuming and requires an investment of staff and resources by national agencies.

Building performance goals into legislation

Over the past few years various pieces of legislation in the United States have been crafted with attention to performance goals. In these cases, the legislation represented a move from an emphasis on input or process requirements to a focus on performance outcomes. Further refinements of these requirements were established by both national departments through the regulations development process. It is too early to know how effective the process will be and whether sanctions will be imposed for failure to comply with the requirements. In drafting both these pieces of legislation, Congress has assumed that the core indicators reflect common practices across the country and that data systems are available to report on achievement of the goals.

Establishment of standards

In some cases, the role of the national government has been to establish performance standards that are meant to guide the behavior of state, provincial or local governments. At least theoretically, these standards are to be voluntary and the ability of a state or locality to conform to them is not tied to eligibility for specific national dollars. The national role in this strategy may involve the development of the standards, provision of technical assistance, and at times could include payment for meeting these norms and guidelines.

The Clinton Administration's proposal for the development of a voluntary national test in reading and mathematics is an example of this approach. The response to this proposal, particularly by some governors and educational leaders, illustrates the types of problems that may emerge from this strategy. Although several governors were supporters of this administration proposal in 1997, others expressed concern about the initiative. A number of states already had test systems in place and did not want to replace their existing performance accountability systems with the national approach. Still others were uncomfortable with the content of the tests, particularly their accuracy and validity in measuring achievement and their substantive scope.

This proposal also uncovered another problem that is likely to be confronted whenever the standards strategy is employed: fear that the information gathered through these assessments has a life of its own and will be used inappropriately. This is particularly problematic because the information that is collected was meant to illustrate achievement at the individual level. Questions of privacy and information security have been raised and were not answered to the satisfaction of critics.

Waivers

Authority to grant waivers to state or local governments for specific programs has been in place for many years. While the waiver authority has been viewed as a way to meet the unique needs of individual states, it has also been closely tied to a research and development strategy, providing latitude to non-national jurisdictions to experiment with new innovations and new ways to deliver services. In the United States the waiver has been touted as a way to move beyond process or input requirements and, instead, to give states and localities the opportunity to devise their own approaches to achieve specific outcomes. The waiver authorization has usually been defined in the context of specific programs and the criteria for granting the waivers are established within the authorizing legislation or implementing regulations. Certain requirements (such as civil rights requirements or filing performance information) cannot be waived.

This authority has been employed extensively in the United States in several program areas, particularly involving welfare, Medicaid, and the Job Training Partnership Act. Waivers have been used to allow states to establish their own approach and to eliminate or modify input or process requirements. Many of the waivers require the proposed modification to be budget-neutral – that is, it does not incur new costs for either the waiving jurisdiction or the national government. For some, the waiver process is a mechanism that can be used to make a case for policy change. However, there are concerns that the rush to grant waivers does not really acknowledge safeguards and establish penalties because the waivers produce a situation where nobody will be watching, monitoring, holding those granted the waiver to account. Although some of the existing waiver authorities did highlight performance issues when they required evaluation as a condition of the waiver, the proposed legislation accentuated the streamlining of the process, not the results that emerged from the changes.

CONCLUSION

This discussion indicates that the instruments of intergovernmental management are closely attuned to other changes in the public management world. Both the macro changes that have taken place in this world as well as the interest in performance have put new demands on intergovernmental managers. This is true in both federal and unitary systems. These demands require managers to think about a repertoire of instruments that might be used in different situations.

Managers and management strategists must be sensitive to differences among policies and programs, differences among the players involved, the complexity of the worlds of both the national and non-national agencies involved, and the level of goal agreement or conflict. Focusing on a variety of approaches suggests that government-wide approaches are not particularly effective. The process of defining instruments should be devised in the context of specific programs, sensitive to the unique qualities surrounding those initiatives.

As this process unfolds, there are a number of elements that should be considered by those who seek to develop approaches that are sensitive to intergovernmental concerns. While there is not a template that can be used to determine the appropriate approach for a particular situation, the following checklist provides a framework for such a determination.

- Determining who is responsible for establishing the implementation effort
- Assessing whether the current system actually affords implementers the opportunity to redefine goals to meet their own needs
- Determining the type of policy involved. (It may be more difficult to deal with redistributive policies than with distributive or regulatory policies)
- Assessing the current policy instrument used to implement a program
- Determining whether the decision makers involved are general purpose government officials or program specialists
- Determining the extent of the national role or presence in the program area (for example, the level of funding involved)
- Determining the level of risk for non-compliance as perceived by both parties
- Determining whether sanctions are available for non-performance
- Assessing the history of past oversight relationships (collegial or conflictual)
- Determining the level of diversity of practices across the country.

While the information gleaned from this checklist will not always lead to a specific instrument, it will provide a rough outline for program and policy officials to use to think about the range of approaches that might make sense in a particular situation. The determination of a particular instrument calls on intergovernmental managers to exercise creativity and care as they confront the multiple pressures that are a part of the reality of the current intergovernmental landscape.

REFERENCES

Agranoff, Robert (1986) *Intergovernmental Management: Human Services Problem-Solving in Six Metropolitan Areas.* Albany, NY: State University of New York Press.

Barzelay, Michael (2001) *The New Public Management: Improving Research and Policy Dialogue.* Berkeley, CA: University of California Press.

Gurr, Ted Robert and King, Desmond (1987) *The State and the City.* Chicago: University of Chicago Press.

Heclo, Hugh (1979) 'Issue Networks and the Executive Establishment', in Anthony King (ed.), *The New American Political System.* Washington, DC: American Enterprise Institute for Public Policy Research. pp. 87–124.

McDonnell, Lorraine M. and Elmore, Richard F. (1987) *Alternative Policy Instruments.* Philadelphia: The Center for Policy Research in Education.

Osbourne, David and Gaebler, Ted (1992) *Reinventing Government.* Reading, MA: Addison–Wesley.

Painter, Martin (1997) 'Reshaping the Public Sector', in Brian Galligan, Ian McAllister and John Ravenhill (eds), *New Developments in Australian Politics.* Melbourne: Macmillan.

Painter, Martin (2001) 'Policy Capacity and the Effects of New Public Management', in T. Christenson and P. Lægreid (eds), *New Public Management: The Transformation of Ideas and Practice.* Aldershot: Ashgate.

Peters, B. Guy (1998) ' "With a Little Help From Our Friends": Public–Private Partnerships as Institutions and Instruments', in Jon Pierre (ed.), *Partnerships in Urban Governance: European and American Experience.* New York: St Martin's Press.

Radin, Beryl A., Agranoff, Robert, Bowman, Ann O'M., Buntz, C. Gregory, Ott, J. Steven, Romzek, Barbara, S. and Wilson, Robert H. (1996) *New Governance for Rural America: Creating Intergovernmental Partnerships.* Lawrence, KS: University Press of Kansas.

Radin, Beryl A. (1998) 'Bridging Multiple Worlds: Central, Regional and Local Partners in Rural Development', in Jon Pierre (ed.), *Partnerships in Urban Governance: European and American Experience.* New York: St Martin's Press.

Radin, Beryl A. (1999) 'Bureaucracies as Instruments of Federalism: Administrative Experience from India', in Ian Copland and John Rickard (eds), *Federalism: Comparative Perspectives from India and Australia.* New Delhi: Manohar Press.

Radin, Beryl A. (2001) 'Intergovernmental Relationships and the Federal Performance Movement', in Dall W. Forsythe (ed.), *Quicker, Better, Cheaper: Managing Performance in American Government.* Albany, NY: Rockefeller Institute Press.

Rhodes, R.A.W. (1988) *Beyond Westminster and Whitehall: The Sub-central Governments of Britain.* London: Unwin–Hyman.

Salamon, Lester M. and Lund, Michael S. (1989) 'The Tools Approach: Basic Analytics', in Lester Salamon (ed.), *Beyond Privatization: The Tools of Government Action.* Washington, DC: The Urban Institute Press.

Scharpf, Fritz (1997) *Games Real Actors Play: Actor-Centered Institutionalism in Policy Research.* Boulder, CO: Westview Press.

US General Accounting Office (1999) *Environmental Protection: Collaborative EPA-State Effort Needed to Improve New Performance Partnership System.* GAO/RCED-99-171, June 1999.

Walker, David B. (1995) *The Rebirth of Federalism: Slouching Toward Washington.* Chatham, NJ: Chatham House.

Wright, Deil S. (1988) *Understanding Intergovernmental Relations*, 3rd edn. Pacific Grove, CA: Brooks–Cole.

49

Multi-level Governance: What It Is and How It Can Be Studied

Andy Smith

In many parts of the world, and in Western Europe in particular, politics today is marked by growing uncertainties over boundaries and frontiers between levels and entities of government. This uncertainty is linked both to new 'public problems' associated with the regulation of increasingly interdependent economies but also to the institutional 'solutions' that have been set up, at least in part, to deal with them: the European Union, decentralization in France, devolution in the United Kingdom, 'autonomous communities in Spain', etc.

Within both political science and public administration, a considerable amount of research has now been devoted to discovering the origins and effects of this change in the nature of politics and government, a change that is seen as particularly novel in hitherto established and often centralized nation-states. A number of researchers have turned to the concept of 'governance' in order to theorize their findings. A sub-set of these researchers has gone a step further in coining the phrase 'multi-level governance' in order to stress the importance of political activity that now crosses traditional jurisdictional boundaries. Central to attempts to conceptualize this trend is an emphasis upon 'power-sharing' between levels of government with 'no centre of accumulated authority. Instead, variable combinations of governments on multiple layers of authority – European, national and subnational – form policy networks for collaboration. The relations are characterized by mutual interdependence on each others' resources, not by competition for scarce resources' (Hooghe, 1996: 18).

This chapter sets out to review the literature that has given rise to, and/or uses, the term multi-level governance, the objective of the exercise being to identify the central research questions defined and the conclusions reached. As the term multi-level governance itself indicates, the research it has inspired has clearly been influenced by more general publications which consider that trends in contemporary politics have brought about the need for political science to engage in a conceptual shift from 'government' to 'governance' (Campbell et al., 1991). Governance has been defined (Rhodes, 1999: xvii; 1997: ch. 3) as 'self-organizing intergovernmental networks with the following characteristics':

1 Interdependence between organizations. Governance is broader than government, covering non-state actors. Changing the boundaries of the state [means] the boundaries between public, private and voluntary sectors become shifting and opaque.
2 Continuing interactions between network members, caused by the need to exchange resources and negotiate shared purposes.
3 Game-like interactions, rooted in trust and regulated by rules of the game negotiated and agreed by network participants.
4 A significant degree of autonomy from the state. Networks are not accountable to the state; they are self-organizing. Although the state does not occupy a privileged, sovereign position, it can indirectly and imperfectly steer networks.

As will be shown below, this conception of governance has been challenged for minimizing the importance of political institutions (Pierre and Peters, 2000). Nevertheless, this is the definition used by most theorists of multi-level governance.

At least in chronological terms, the addition of the adjective 'multi-level' to the concept of governance has two related sources which provide a framework for the first two parts of this chapter: studies of 'local governance' and of 'the governance of the European Union'. Although many useful findings have been made by this strand of research, it will be suggested that the concept of 'multi-level governance' is both undertheorized and as such often leads researchers to set up research designs that almost inevitably lead to conclusions that are empirically fragile and excessively general. More precisely, in its current form 'multi-level governance' is essentially a useful term for synthesizing general trends in government practices but which does not encourage rigorous hypothesis-building and detailed analysis. The third part of this chapter sets out to take the concept of multi-level governance in a more analytical direction by identifying the 'black boxes' left behind by existing research and suggesting ways of shedding light in them. A call for a return to two fundamental concepts from political sociology – institutionalization and legitimation – summarizes my principal proposition for future research agendas.

LOCAL POLITICS AND MULTI-LEVEL GOVERNANCE

Beginning in the 1950s in North America and in the 1960s in Western Europe, studies of the way local politicians and officials make decisions or, more generally, create and exercise power, progressively became integral parts of mainstream political science. Two broad lines of questioning came to dominate this field: localized forms of power *per se* and their connections to their respective national political systems. In briefly summarizing these fields of study, it will be shown that the pertinence of treating different 'levels' of power separately has increasingly been challenged. Indeed, implicit in this critique is a wider challenge to analyses that take the national political system to be a 'natural' category of analysis.

From local government to local governance

Often brought together under the heading of 'local government', the first specialists in this field initially, and quite logically, concentrated their attention upon the politics of one or several

specific areas such as a city (Dahl, 1961), or a region (Sharpe, 1978). Codified by law and used in common speech, at this time most scholars saw no need to conceptualize, or often even define, the term 'local government'. For them, local government was quite simply what local authorities did. However, two notable exceptions to this trend took the term 'government' more seriously, sought to 'unpack' it and thereby devise sharper research questions and tools.

The first, and internationally most important, of these exceptions was a tradition that emerged early on in American political science which sought to highlight the inter-relations between local politicians and representatives of special interests within local society. Formalized around concepts such as 'community power' (Hunter, 1953), the key research question was no longer 'what does local government do?' but rather 'who governs'? (Dahl, 1961). In the 1970s and 1980s, analysis of this type flourished, producing in turn a plethora of new terms such as 'urban regimes' (Stone, 1989) and 'growth coalitions'. In the 1980s, this subject area continued to develop, in particular in order to follow an increasing tendency of local government to get actively involved in localized forms of economic development (Le Galès, 1995). Without wishing to downplay the debates that divided a very vibrant part of political science, gradually a consensus emerged that local government could no longer be studied in isolation. Instead, the authority and acts of representatives of local government had to be analysed using concepts such as policy networks (Rhodes, 1988, 1997). Given the emergence of this consensus on what has since been labelled 'networked polities' (Ansell, 2000), only a short step was required to convince many scholars that they were in fact studying local governance (power relations between actors of public, private and associative status) rather than local government (the activity of local authorities). Indeed, in 1992 this shift was formalized in Britain by the launch of a major research programme by the Economic and Social Research Council entitled 'Local governance' under the leadership of Gerry Stoker (1998). Although by no means all scholars in the field are convinced of the newness of governance or the usefulness of this new label (Stanyer, 1999), its relationship to the multi-level governance literature is nevertheless indisputable.

The second example of attempts to unpack the notion of government in order to revitalize the study of local politics occurred in France, a polity where one of the main planks of a centralizing constitution and political tradition was the idea that different territories within France did not govern themselves but were 'administered' by the state. Until the 1960s, French social science had done little to verify this thesis, let alone counter it. However, since that period the legalism of such approaches has been systematically challenged, first by a small group of organizational sociologists and then by a growing number of political scientists. Amongst many other findings, the sociologists emphasized the power that local notables continued to hold in France not only in spite of the power of French central government, but because of the way it was forced to make deals with 'the periphery' in order to create and perpetuate a semblance of order (Worms, 1966; Crozier and Thoenig, 1975). For this reason there was 'power at the periphery' in a polity that was 'falsely centralized' (Grémion, 1976). Inspired by their involvement in international comparative analysis, a group of political scientists took these ideas further in using the concept of government in order to study power relations in a series of medium-sized towns (Mabilieau and Sorbets, 1989). Bolstered by the effects of the 1982 decentralization laws, a whole generation of French political scientists have since used the concepts of government and governing in order to highlight the dynamics of local politics and why these differ so widely within the French polity. What is interesting in this case is that the notion of government is defined as an analytical concept which, to all intents and purposes, closely resembles what social scientists elsewhere label as governance.

Centre–periphery or intergovernmental relations

Although of relatively minor importance to the worldwide debate on how local politics should be studied, the French case is also of interest because of the early emphasis placed upon the relationship between representatives of local areas (the notables) and those of external power sources, in particular the state (ministers, prefects and other civil servants). Conceptualized in France as 'centre–periphery' and in North America as 'intergovernmental' relations, the question of external resources and constraints upon local governance has become the focus of an increasing number of single-country and comparative studies. In nearly every instance, the historical context of these relationships is stressed. Very obviously, for example, the French and American revolutions and their respective aftermaths have been the origins of

very different constitutions and interinstitutional arrangements. Scholars have, however, been more divided over the question of what provokes changes in the relationship between central, local and intermediary (for example, regional) levels of government. For some authors, political change is essentially a response to economic change such as the importance of socially networked industrial districts (Garfoli, 1992) or, more recently, reactions to the globalized deregulation of capital (Dunsford, 1997). Other authors focus more upon deep-seated cultural roots that help or hinder development and the fostering of ties with central government (Putnam, 1993). More multidimensional approaches focus upon the manner through which local elites develop, or fail to develop, a 'political capacity' to work within polities whose internal and external frontiers are no longer stable and where deals between local and national actors are constantly struck and restruck (Keating and Loughlin, 1997).

In short, this longstanding focus upon centre–periphery or intergovernmental relations has implicitly dealt for some time with the question of interaction between levels of government. Many of the authors involved have also turned to the concept of governance, or something akin to that term, in order to include non-public actors in their research. Many of the seeds for the term multi-level governance were thus sown by scholars working within a tradition of local government studies. From the mid-1980s onwards, the deepening of the European Union is the issue around which many of the lessons learnt from this tradition have given rise to the term multi-level governance.

THE EUROPEAN UNION AND MULTI-LEVEL GOVERNANCE

More precisely, the term multi-level governance has entered the lexicon of the social sciences as part of a debate about the driving forces of European integration in general and the nature of intergovernmental relations in the European Union in particular.

The causes of European integration

After about fifteen years of relatively low level change, from 1984 until the early 1990s the European Community (as it was known until 1991) experienced a revival in its fortunes that saw the deepening of its existing common policies (agriculture, competition, monetary cooperation etc.) and the emergence of genuine community-level policies in a number of other sectors (for example, research, regional development, the environment). This period was particularly marked by two major treaties. Ratified in 1987, the Single European Act (SEA) reaffirmed the commitment of national leaders not just to a goal of a customs union without tariffs on intra-Community trade, but to the completion by December 1992 of a 'single market' where other more hidden barriers to commerce would be eliminated. Significantly, the SEA prepared the ground for moving in this direction by extending a system of 'qualified majority' voting (QMV), as opposed to unanimity, as the basis for the making of Community law. Known often as 'the Maastricht Treaty', the Treaty on European Union (TEU) was signed by heads of state in 1991 and ratified, often with some difficulty, the following year. Amongst many other issues, the TEU set the guidelines for the introduction of European Monetary Union, gave more powers to the European Parliament, created a European Committee of the regions and introduced the notion of European Citizenship.

This brief but crowded episode of European integration history has been dwelt upon because, not surprisingly, it quickly attracted the attention of political scientists and, indirectly, gave rise to the term of multi-level governance. To cut a very long story extremely short, in the early 1990s the principal debate between scholars of the EU focused upon the following two questions: what had caused the relaunching of the EC in the mid-1980s and how should one characterize the EU as a whole?

Heavily influenced by their background in realist, American-based, International Relations theory, one group of scholars sought to downplay the changes that had taken place by attributing them to conscious and deliberate decisions taken by the governmental elites of Europe's largest member states, in particular France, Germany and the United Kingdom (Moravscik, 1993, 1998). According to this self-styled 'liberal intergovernmentalist' theory of European integration, national leaders had agreed to give up some of their sovereignty because business leaders within each of the above-cited countries had pressed their respective political counterparts to support the idea of a single market. Nevertheless, it was argued that national politicians were the key players working in and through the key intergovernmental arenas of the European Council of Ministers and the European Council. The EC's executive and bureaucracy, the European Commission, was very clearly not seen as a supranational source of change. It almost goes without saying that intergovernmentalists concluded that subnational forms of government had exercised no influence over the form of the SEA and TEU treaties, nor over their implementation and its effects upon the institutional shape of the EU as a whole. In summary, and to avoid confusion, this theory can usefully be labelled 'horizontal intergovernmentalism' because it is primarily concerned with diplomatic-style international government relations.

At least in the early 1990s, many publications on the EU were very much a response to intergovernmentalist hypotheses and conclusions. Essentially its opponents raised three objections and set out instead a more 'supranationalist' account of recent European history, an account in which multi-level governance makes a first appearance. The first objection to horizontal intergovernmentalist theory – its neglect of the role of the European Commission – is highly important but, for the purposes of this chapter, need not concern us greatly here. In summary, opponents of intergovernmentalism all point out the capacity of agents within the Commission to use their right to initiate EU law-making as a resource with which to engage in alliances with a variety of powerful actors and thereby shape the problems dealt with by the Council of Ministers and, consequently, the legislative 'solutions' it formally decides upon (Pierson, 1996).

Regions and the governance of Europe

The second and third objections to horizontal intergovernmentalist theory are more directly linked to our subject matter. The former concerns the conceptualization of linkages between economies and governments in Western Europe (Scharpf, 1994). Implicitly inspired by pluralist theories of state–society relations, horizontal intergovernmentalists posit that national politicians and officials consult national interest group leaders when formulating their preferences and strategies in EU level negotiations. The interests of corporate leaders therefore have an influence over the definition of 'the national interest' advanced by politicians, but ultimately this theory considers that the latter always prevail. Armed with a more 'neo-functionalist' and/or neo-corporatist vision of state–society relations, critics of intergovernmentalism have argued instead that economic, social and political elites are in fact more interdependent than horizontal intergovernmentalists realize and thus representatives of national governments in the Council most often hold more complex preferences and strategies. Indeed, given that interest groups are now increasingly organized at the level of the EU, they claim that one must also take into consideration relationships between economic, social and political actors which often cross-cut purely national lines of allegiance. In short, these authors consider that EU decision making is in reality multi-layered and that as such one can and should design research into the mechanisms through which, to quote the title of one of their edited books, there is now *Governance of the European Union* (Marks, Scharpf et al., 1996).

The third objection to horizontal intergovernmental theories of European integration is its almost total neglect of the role of subnational, that is, regional or local, actors (Marks, 1993; Marks et al., 1996; Hooghe and Marks, 2001). Whilst readily admitting that such actors have little or no direct access to the Council of Ministers and the European Council, and as such have relatively low influence over the preparation and negotiation of EU treaties, theorists of the EU as a space of interdependent, cross-cutting arenas of governance highlight the role played by regional representatives in other important respects. Gary Marks in particular was amongst the first scholars to study how the EU's policy in favour of disadvantaged areas – 'the structural funds' – has created opportunities for subnational actors to engage directly in EU policy-shaping and implementation. Indeed, in summarizing his findings, Marks was very probably the first to coin the phrase 'multi-level governance'.

Over and above the subsequent 'success' of this term, two related aspects of the approach developed by Marks and his colleagues to the question of EU subnational relations have attracted particular attention. The first is the extent to which the structural funds in particular, and the deepening of the EU in general, have caused or accompanied changes in vertical intergovernmental (that is, centre–periphery) relations within individual member states. As indicated in the previous section, in many West European countries, by the late 1980s these relations were already significantly different to what they had been twenty years earlier. The Marks approach to multi-level governance, however, had no hesitation in concluding that the structural funds were often a decisive influence in bringing about significant change in intergovernmental relations. More particularly, Marks stressed that often this change meant the bypassing of national government officials and more generally the sidelining of state influence over subnational politics. Without going into detail here, it should be underlined that a series of

empirical studies carried out in a variety of EU member states have shown Marks' conclusions on this point to be over-general and insufficiently researched (Jeffrey, 1996; Smith, 1997; Smyrl, 1997). In particular, the demise of the state as a level of government involved in regional development has clearly been overstated. This point is underlined more generally in Pierre and Peters' book *Governance, Politics and the State*, where they contend that in most countries in the world 'the state is restructuring in order to be able to remain a viable vehicle for the pursuit of collective interest in an era of economic globalization and increasing subnational institutional dynamics' (2000: 196).

The second hypothesis implicit in Marks' approach to multi-level governance claims that convergence in vertical intergovernmental relations has taken place, a trend frequently labelled as 'Europeanization'. Again, the conclusion of scholars who have put this hypothesis to the test of empirical study is mixed. Some argue that the EU changes little and that pre-existing balances of power are more important explanations of variation. This is particularly so in the case of Spain and the United Kingdom. In these countries, a number of scholars conclude that the influence of European funding and norms has not been to foster region-building, but rather to provide local actors with additional opportunities to seek out scarce, and often centrally controlled, resources (Bache and Jones, 2000; Martin and Pearce, 1999; Garmise, 1997). Other studies, however, suggest that the opportunities provided by European-level multi-level governance have been more significant for subnational government. This case is made more often for Germany, whose highly institutionalized intergovernmental structure provides fewer veto points to officials and politicians from the national (federal) government (Benz, 2000). Indeed, other research on Germany has led researchers to strongly conclude that the dichotomous reasoning at the heart of the 'strengthening versus the weakening of the state' argument is 'a dead end' (Börzel, 1997).

Behind this last criticism of some of the research on Europeanization inspired by the term multi-level governance lies the deeper problem of its conceptual definition and connection to appropriate and robust research designs. Indeed, as Claudio Radaelli rightly points out when reviewing the literature on 'Europeanization', after an 'early stage of research, when the analytic grid had to be broad enough to accommodate a wide range of empirical observations' (2001: 156), the time is now ripe for an end to what Sartori (1970) immortalized as 'conceptual stretching'. The future challenge for observers of the EU is to formulate more precise concepts capable of generating falsifiable hypotheses.

RESEARCHING MULTI-LEVEL *POLITICS*

Can multi-level governance become more than a term for describing the number of levels of government involved in European politics and synthesizing these findings in broadbrush and often impressionistic fashion? The answer, of course, depends upon what one sets out to study and to what end the concept of multi-level governance is put when building appropriate research designs. In terms of academic questions, moving from description to analysis in this subject area first means sharpening the focus upon change in the power relationships observed in and between subnational, national and supranational arenas. Before rushing out to undertake empirical investigation, however, considerable thought needs to be given to what one means by change and over what time-span this can reasonably be observed. A useful starting place from which to pin down the first question is to distinguish orders of change: the modification of policy instruments (for example, regional council aid to small business) probably is not of the same political magnitude as an altered tax-base for local government or a change in its electoral system. The question of time can best be tackled by engaging in longitudinal studies, a vantage point from which it is easier to distinguish superficial from genuine change (Stanyer, 1999: 237).

A second means of delimiting the question of change is to reconsider the relationship between policy and politics which is implicitly advanced in the current multi-level governance literature. Instead of limiting the question of change to the formulation and implementation of European Union policies, and then indirectly assessing the involvement of politicians in this process, it is more appropriate to adopt a more 'bottom-up' approach where political competition and power-wielding have more long-term impact than the making of individualizable policies (Jeffrey, 1996). More precisely, research designs need to be built from the premise that the dynamics of subnational politics are primarily structured by localized forces of political competition, executive–assembly relations and interest group representation, all of which contain an intergovernmental, or multi-level, dimension. From this perspective, the academic question of change is less about steering and public management

(multi-level governance) and more about the distribution of power: multi-level *politics*. A resolutely bottom-up approach to this question places emphasis not just upon policy networks but upon actors involved in negotiations within and between networks. Change at this level and over time is best studied using two fundamental concepts from political sociology: institutionalization and legitimation.

Institutionalization

Despite their differences, the 'historical' and 'sociological' branches of 'new institutionalism' concur that institutions are a range of 'state and societal' rules 'that shape how political actors define their interests and structure their relations of power to other groups' (Steinmo and Thelen, 1992: 2).

> In sum, institutions are not just another variable, and the institutionalist claim is more than just that 'institutions matter too'. By shaping not just actors' strategies (as in rational choice), but their goals as well, and by mediating their relations of cooperation and conflict, institutions structure political situations and leave their own imprint on political outcomes. (1992: 9)

It follows that institutionalization can be defined as the processes through which institutions are not only created, but are consolidated over time into being a structuring, and generally accepted, part of a regime.

In terms of the design of empirical study, the principal advantage of recourse to this approach and these definitions is that it obliges researchers to define what is meant by change at two distinct levels: the policy-specific and the regime.

Institutions at the policy-specific level are the laws, norms and informal practices which structure the regulation of an economic and/or administrative sector. In the case of the politics of wine production, for example, these institutions include limits on the planting of new vines, standardized evaluations of grape quality and controls on pesticide usage. Studying their institutionalization implies discovering the forces that have argued for and against them over time and the compromises that this process has entailed. Given that some laws and norms are EU-wide (pesticide control) whereas others are essentially set at national (vine planting) or local (grape quality) levels, the variable paths of institutionalization in this sector already highlight the patchiness of multi-level governance at the policy level (Smith, 2003b).

Institutions at the level of a regime are typically more centred upon the mechanisms that connect its component parts to one another in a configuration of actors and processes that is specific in a particular area. Channels of communication and interdependence institutionalize over time between and across executives and assemblies, political parties and sector-specific and more general interest groups. In the case of regional development in the French region of Brittany, for example, the institutionalized configuration had at its centre a relationship between local politicians and field officers of the central state whilst at its periphery it featured the unquestioning support of the business community and national MPs from the area. But this configuration is structured in such a way at a local level only because its dominant actors are simultaneously engaged (most often effectively) in negotiations at national, European and international levels. For example, the issue of grants for local economic development was structured and controlled at the local level by actors who made sure their preferences were taken into account from the outset in Brussels and Paris (Smith, 1997).

In summary, and contrary to first impressions, a focus upon institutions and institutionalization does not inevitably lead to the study of continuity or immobilism. Instead, it engages with the debate begun around the multi-level governance concept by rigorously defining what political change is and how it can be studied. This said, research into the processes of institutionalization alone does not provide sufficient criteria for identifying political change. This line of questioning needs to be completed by investigation into how new processes are rendered legitimate.

Legitimation

Although complex and contested, the question of the legitimacy of regimes can initially be addressed by opposing two ideal-types. On one end of the scale, certain regimes are based on consensus where their citizens, or their representatives, make constant cost–benefit analyses as to whether they accept its authority. On the other end, legitimate regimes are those whose citizens rarely question their authority and instead confer upon the regime a social value which encourages support or at least general obedience (Lagroye, 1985). This dichotomy is obviously schematic but it does provide the basis from which one can conduct empirical enquiry into how some regimes become generally considered as socially desirable, whereas others are so contested that their very existence is under constant threat. Labelled 'legitimation', the processes that merit study here involve politicians and other actors in the justification, but also the dramatization, of their preferences, decisions and other actions. In developing these two points successively, it will be strongly suggested that if elections are indeed an important dimension of the legitimacy of most politicians, the processes that go on between polling days – the daily interaction amongst the range of actors involved in a regime – are even more important aspects of legitimation which merit deeper study than is generally accorded in the existing multi-level governance literature.

Explicitly made justifications for decisions affecting public intervention are quite obviously one aspect of multi-level politics that any research on this subject has to encompass. Without being so naive as to unquestioningly believe that whatever an actor says in public is exactly what has actually motivated their behaviour, this is one means of beginning to map the preferences and strategies of the actors involved. In the context of French regionalization, the question of how regional councils should get involved in agricultural policy, a sector excluded from the decentralization laws, provides an example of the multi-level dimension of many such strategies. Whereas representatives from the Rhône-Alpes region devoted much of their energies to trying to assert their authority to make new, more rural policy in the name of a specifically regional form of government, their opposite numbers from Pays de la Loire simply rolled out central government set priorities in the name of a 'complementary' approach to a regionalized France (Le Pape and Smith, 1999).

However calculated and 'rational' such justifications may be, however, they are not likely to convince either other public decision makers or local citizens unless efforts are simultaneously made to engage in a second dimension of legitimation: dramatization. Although largely neglected by political scientists, anthropologists have quite rightly highlighted the importance of 'evocation' in politics (Abélès, 1989). Taking the form of discourse, symbols and gestures, the evocative dimension of legitimation appeals to the emotions rather than the intellect of those whom it targets. Ultimately any regime cannot survive only on the basis of constant rounds of cost–benefit analysis made by its constituents. Consequently much of politics is about constructing relationships of trust and socializing individuals through education and communication to, at least generally, respect the norms and practices linked to that trust.

A particularly strong vector of this relationship are the discursive and symbolic references so frequently made to territory by public actors, that is, to widely held social representations of space and of time. Defined sociologically, territories are categories of thought which largely determine the collective identity of social groups. From the point of view of political analysis, it is important to see how much of political representation appeals to these social representations of territory in order to legitimize itself (Faure, 1994). This is of particular interest in polities such as France where longstanding territorial categories (the nation, the *département*, the commune) are now challenged by newer categories (the European Union, the region, intercommunal groupings). In the wine sector, for instance, regional politicians in the Bordeaux area have been unable to construct their level of government as meaningful and legitimate. In Languedoc Roussillon, however, producer representatives and regional leaders have been much more successful in 'naturalizing' the region as a normal and unquestioned part of wine politics (Smith, 2003a).

Ultimately, establishing a firm link between institutionalization and legitimation is entirely logical and indeed almost tautological. Defined sociologically, norms and practices become institutions when they are taken for granted and accepted as a given, legitimate, part of a regime. This does not mean, however, that harmonious acceptance of authority is the rule and that change is always exceptional. Institutionalized practices are invariably in conflict and constantly produce contradictions which public actors paper over, publicize or alternatively fail to see. When contradictions become too great and conflicts too intense, regimes deinstitutionalize and, in most cases, then reinstitutionalize. At any one time, different parts of most regimes are undergoing a process of invention, atrophy or reinvention.

CONCLUSION

Although it does not use these terms, with hindsight one of the great merits of the local and multi-level governance literature dealt with earlier in this chapter has been to encourage political scientists to focus upon the relationship between policy-making and regime change. Whilst many studies of 'decentralization', 'regionalization' and even 'European integration' simply describe the processes and changes observed, if used astutely, the concept of multi-level governance can structure more analyticial and stimulating research into the causes and effects of these trends. The first advantage of such an approach is to recognize that this order of change does not come about without conflict and power-wielding. The second advantage is to push researchers to think more clearly about which actors or societal groups are actually benefiting from these changes. Indeed, one could even ask the question in some cases as to whether multi-level governance does not create its own agenda, thus causing politicians to lose sight of the more substantive goals they may have announced at the outset. More generally, the rise of multi-level governance gives rise to two sets of challenges for public administrators. The first concerns the respective role of politicians and civil servants in the 'steering' of public policies within multi-level regimes. If all policies end up being compromises between representatives of different levels of government, what role is left for democratically elected political leaders? Can these actors control and orientate the work of career bureaucrats as effectively as standard democratic theory would like? The second set of challenges concerns the management of interfaces between levels of government and the multitude of organizations involved in these mediations. How can decisions be implemented in reasonably uniform fashion in multi-level regimes where much leeway is left to subnational government and public–private partnerships? For example, how can EU environment policy not only be implemented in Brussels and in Bordeaux, but be linked up to sectorial policies such as agriculture and aid to industry? Finally, given the growing importance of world trade agreements, how can binding deals be negotiated between representatives of multi-level regimes?

To conclude, we have also seen that the concept of multi-level governance is no automatic ticket either to rigorous analysis, or to helping practitioners get a handle on the day-to-day problems linked to the practical realities of governing a multi-level world. All too often, multi-level governance is used as a descriptive rather than as an analytical tool. By reinforcing the academic questions inspired by this term with the well-defined concepts of institutionalization and legitimation, an emphasis on the causes and effects of the multi-level dimension of politics could and should be further sharpened.

REFERENCES

Abélès, Marc (1989) *Jours tranquilles en 89. Ethnologie politique d'un département français*. Paris: Odile Jacob.
Ansell, Chris (2000) 'The networked polity: regional development in Western Europe', *Governance*, 13 (3): 303–33.

Bache, Ian and Jones, R. (2000) 'Has EU regional policy empowered the regions? A study of Spain and the United Kingdom', *Regional and Federal Studies*, 10 (3): 1–20.

Benz, Arthur (2000) 'Two types of multi-level governance: intergovernmental relations in German and EU regional policy', *Regional and Federal Studies*, 10 (3): 21–44.

Benz, Arthur and Burkard, Eberlein (1999) 'The Europeanization of regional policies: patterns of multi-level governance', *Journal of European Public Policy*, 6 (2): 329–48.

Börzel, Tanya (1997) 'Does European integration really strengthen the state? The case of the Federal Republic of Germany', *Regional and Federal Studies*, 7 (3): 87–114.

Campbell, J., Hollingsworth, J. and Lindberg, Leon (eds) (1991) *Governance of the American Economy*. Cambridge: Cambridge University Press.

Christiansen, Thomas and Jorgenson, Knud Erik (2000) 'Transnational governance "above" and "below" the state: the changing nature of borders in Europe', *Regional and Federal Studies*, 10 (2): 62–77.

Crozier, Michel and Thoenig, Jean-Claude (1975) 'La régulation des systèmes organisés complexes. Le cas du système de décision politico-administratif local en France', *Revue française de sociologie*, 16 (1): 3–32.

Dahl, Robert (1961) *Who Governs? Democracy and Power in an American City*. New Haven, CT: Yale University Press.

Dunsford, Mick (1997) 'The economics of regionalism', in P. Le Galès and C. Lequesne (eds), *Regions in Europe*. London: Routledge.

Faure, Alain (1994) 'Les élus locaux à l'épreuve de la décentralisation', *Revue Française de Science Politique*, 44 (3): 462–79.

Garfoli, G. (1992) *Endogenous Development and Southern Europe*. Aldershot: Avebury.

Garmise, Sheri (1997) 'Region-building? The impact of European regional policy on the development of the regional tier in the UK', *Regional and Federal Studies*, 7 (3): 1–24.

Gremion, Pierre (1976) *Le Pouvoir périphérique*. Paris: Seuil.

Hooghe, Liesbet (1996) 'Introduction: Reconciling EU-wide policy and national diversity', in L. Hooghe (ed.), *Cohesion Policy and European Integration: Building Multi-level Governance*. Oxford: Oxford University Press. pp. 1–24.

Hooghe, Liesbet and Marks, Gary (2001) *Multi-level Governance*. New York: Rowan and Littlefield.

Hunter, Floyd (1953) *Community Power Structure: A Study of Decision-makers*. Chapel Hill, NC: University of North Carolina Press.

Jeffrey, Charlie (ed.) (1996) 'The regional dimension of the European Union. Towards a third level in Europe?', Special issue of *Regional and Federal Studies*, 6 (2).

Jobert, Bruno (ed.) (1994) *Le Tournant néo-libéral en Europe*. Paris: L'Harmattan.

Keating, Michael and Loughlin, John (eds) (1997) *The Political Economy of the Regionalism*. London: Frank Cass.

Lagroye, Jacques (1985) 'La légitimation', in M. Grawitz and J. Leca (eds), *Traité de science politique*, vol. 1. Paris: Presses Universitaires de France.

Le Galès, Patrick (1995) 'Du gouvernement des villes à la gouvernance urbaine', *Revue Française de Science Politique*, 45 (1): 57–95.

Le Pape, Yves and Smith, Andy (1999) 'Regionalizations and agricultures : Rhône-Alpes and Pays de la Loire compared', *Regional and Federal studies*, 9 (2): 16–32.

Mabileau, Albert and Sorbets, Claude (1989) *Gouverner les villes moyennes*. Paris: Pédone.

Marks, Gary (1993) 'Structural policy in the European Community', in A. Sbragia (ed.), *Euro-politics*. Washington, DC: Brookings Institution.

Marks, Gary, Hooghe, Liesbet and Blank, K. (1996) 'European integration from the 1980s: state-centric v. multi-level governance', *Journal of Common Market Studies*, 34 (3): 342–78.

Marks, Gary, Scharpf, Fritz, Schmitter, Philip and Streeck, Wolfgang (1996) *Governance in the European Union*. London: Sage.

Martin, Steve and Pearce, G. (1999) 'Differentiated multi-level governance? The response of British sub-national governments to European integration', *Regional and Federal Studies*, 9 (2): 32–52.

Moravscik, Andy (1993) 'Preferences and power in the European Community: a liberal intergovernmentalist perspective', *Journal of Common Market Studies*, 31: 473–524.

Moravscik, Andy (1998) *The Choice for Europe: Social Purpose and State Power from Messina to Maastricht*. Ithaca, NY: Cornell University Press.

Pierre, Jon and Peters, B. Guy (2000) *Governance, Politics and the State*. London: Macmillan.

Pierson, Paul (1996) 'The path to European integration. A historical institutionalist analysis', *Comparative Political Studies*, 29 (2): 123–63.

Putnam, Richard (1993) *Making Democracy Work. Civic Traditions in Modern Italy*. Princeton, NJ: Princeton University Press.

Radaelli, Claudio (2001) 'The domestic impact of European Union public policy: notes on concepts, methods and the challenge of empirical research', *Politique européenne, no. 5*: 150–87.

Rhodes, Rod (1988) *Beyond Westminster and Whitehall. The Sub-central Governments of Britain*. London: Unwin–Hyman.

Rhodes, Rod (1997) *Understanding Governance*. Milton Keynes: Open University Press.

Rhodes, Rod (1999) 'Foreward', in Gerry Stoker (ed.), *The New Management of British Local Government*. London: Macmillan.

Sartori, Giovanni (1970) 'Concept misformation in comparative politics', *American Political Science Review*, 64 (4): 1033–53.

Scharpf, Fritz (1994) 'Community and autonomy: multi-level policy-making in the European Union', *Journal of European Public Policy*, 1 (2): 219–42.

Sharpe, Jim (ed.) (1978) *Decentralist Trends in Western Democracies*. London: Sage.

Smith, Andy (1997) 'Studying multi-level governance: examples from French translations of the structural funds', *Public Administration*, 75 (4): 711–29.

Smith, Andy (2003a) 'Interest groups and territorial governance: the multi-level representation of agriculture in two French regions', in J. Bukowski, S. Piattoni and M. Smyrl (eds), *Territorial Governance*. New York: Rowan and Littlechild.

Smith, Andy (2003b) 'Interest group leadership and territory. The case of wine production in the Bordelais', in H. Baldersheim and J-P. Daloz (eds), *Political Leadership in a Global Age*.

Smyrl, Marc (1997) 'Does European Community regional policy empower the regions?', *Governance*, 10 (3): 287–309.

Stanyer, Jeffrey (1999) 'Something old, something new', in Gerry Stoker (ed.), *The New Management of British Local Government*. London: Macmillan.

Steinmo, Sven and Kathleen, Thelen (1992) 'Historical institutionalism in comparative politics', in Sven Steinmo, Kathleen Thelen and Frank Longstreth (eds), *Structuring Politics*. Cambridge: Cambridge University Press.

Stone, Clarence (1989) *Regime Politics: Governing Atlanta, 1946–1988*. Lawrence, KS: University of Kansas Press.

Stoker, Gerry (1998) 'Governance as theory: five propositions', *International Social Science Journal*, 15 (2): 17–28.

Worms, Jean-Pierre (1966) 'Le préfet et ses notables', *Sociologie du Travail*, July–Sept: 1–23.

Index